D1351655

ONE WEEK LOAN

THE OXFORD HANDBOOK OF

INTERNATIONAL TRADE LAW

THE OXFORD HANDBOOK OF

INTERNATIONAL TRADE LAW

Edited by

DANIEL BETHLEHEM

DONALD McRAE

RODNEY NEUFELD

ISABELLE VAN DAMME

OXFORD

UNIVERSITY PRESS

OXFORD
UNIVERSITY PRESS

Great Clarendon Street, Oxford OX2 6DP

Oxford University Press is a department of the University of Oxford.
It furthers the University's objective of excellence in research, scholarship,
and education by publishing worldwide in

Oxford New York

Auckland Cape Town Dar es Salaam Hong Kong Karachi
Kuala Lumpur Madrid Melbourne Mexico City Nairobi
New Delhi Shanghai Taipei Toronto

With offices in

Argentina Austria Brazil Chile Czech Republic France Greece
Guatemala Hungary Italy Japan Poland Portugal Singapore
South Korea Switzerland Thailand Turkey Ukraine Vietnam

Oxford is a registered trade mark of Oxford University Press
in the UK and in certain other countries

Published in the United States
by Oxford University Press Inc., New York

British Library Cataloguing in Publication Data

Data available

Library of Congress Cataloging in Publication Data

Data available

Typeset by Newgen Imaging Systems (P) Ltd., Chennai, India
Printed in Great Britain
on acid-free paper by
Antony Rowe, Chippenham, Wiltshire

ISBN 978–0–19–923192–8

1 3 5 7 9 10 8 6 4 2

FOREWORD

....

The process leading to the agreements establishing the WTO during the Uruguay Round between 1986 and 1994 involved the largest trade negotiation in history, and entailed the biggest reform of the world's trading system since the GATT was created after the end of World War II. Moreover, this promise has been largely borne out in practice, not least the practice of dispute settlement under the DSU – by far the most frequently used interstate dispute settlement system.

The scope of the WTO and its various agreements, its relative success at a turbulent and often dismal time in international relations, have given rise to a vast literature. This is usefully supplemented and synthesized here by the comprehensive treatment of 'The Economic and Institutional Context of the World Trading System' (Part I), 'Substantive Law' (Part II), and 'Settlement of Disputes' (Part III). But what sets this Handbook apart is its consideration of international trade law and the WTO regime against the broader background of general international law and its account of the relationship of WTO law with other international law 'regimes'. Of particular note is its exploration of 'Trade... The New Agenda and Linkage Issues' (Part IV) and 'The Wider Framework' (Part V).

Bodansky and Lawrence's essay on the legal interaction between trade and environment, for instance, canvasses the emergence of tensions between these two fields: its undeniable conclusion is that the task of reconciling the fundamental goals of free trade and environmental protection is still a work in progress. The authors note that conflicts between the two regimes might be addressed either on a case-by-case, *ad hoc* manner or legislatively through multilateral negotiations, concluding that despite many proposals for a legislative solution States have preferred the former approach. They conclude that 'case-by-case review... creates uncertainty and requires adjudicative bodies to make what are essentially policy choices... But... this is perhaps the best of an imperfect set of alternatives'.

Likewise Bartels' essay on trade and human rights affords a perceptive analysis of the interaction between these fields, advocating the adoption of policies 'to ensure that market access commitments do not impair the ability of countries to pursue human rights obligations by undertaking human rights impact assessments, to commit to the appropriate flanking policies to respond to any identified problems, and to ensure that trade rules permit countries to adopt measures in favour of human rights objectives'. By these means, trade liberalization can promote human rights objectives without replication of human rights instruments and institutions.

The varied contributions in Part V locate international trade law in its wider context. For example, Boisson de Chazournes and Boutruche note the increasing engagement of the UN with economic activities within the framework of its collective security mandate, resulting in 'a need to think about the overall international legal framework for these activities in a more coherent manner'.

The Handbook concludes with a contribution from JHH Weiler gazing into the ball of the WTO's far from crystalline future. According to Weiler 'one can appreciate changing conditions which might hearken a changing jurisprudence', whereby '[e]nlightened self-interest may begin to mobilize against protectionism and the WTO can be used increasingly as a tool to thwart domestic [s]pecial [i]nterests militating against the collective national interest'. That may be so – if by 'the collective national interest' is meant (as Weiler himself apparently means) an aggregate national interest going beyond the articulated interest of particular dominant nations or national groupings. In the meantime, the step-by-step approach envisaged by Bodansky and Lawrence and by Bartels may be the realistic way forward.

The Editors are to be commended on the production of a text that, while taking all necessary account of the form and content of the law, offers at the same time such a broad vision of international trade law within general international law and, for that matter, general public policy. It will be widely read and appreciated.

James R Crawford
Lauterpacht Centre for International Law
University of Cambridge
28 September 2008

ACKNOWLEDGEMENTS

Throughout the preparation of this Handbook the editors have received the cooperation and assistance of many people. At the outset John Jackson provided guidance to Daniel Bethlehem and Donald McRae in the planning of the project. An advisory committee of Steve Charnovitz, Valerie Hughes, Yuji Iwasawa, and Joost Pauwelyn assisted in ensuring that the range of topics was appropriate, and that contributors would be from across the world and at varying stages of their careers. John Louth of Oxford University Press was a prime motivator in the project and the assistance of Gwen Booth was critical to ensuring the smooth development of the ultimate appearance of this volume. The experience of Oxford University Press in the production of the Handbook series facilitated greatly the work of the editors. Finally, although this is a jointly edited project, the greatest part of that editing burden has fallen on Isabelle Van Damme, who with efficiency, acuity, organization, patience, and a sense of purpose has brought this project to fruition. The other three editors acknowledge their enormous debt of gratitude to Isabelle.

CONTENTS

....

PART I: THE ECONOMIC AND INSTITUTIONAL CONTEXT OF THE WORLD TRADING SYSTEM

PART II: SUBSTANTIVE LAW

PART III: SETTLEMENT OF DISPUTES

PART IV: TRADE AND . . . THE NEW AGENDA AND LINKAGE ISSUES

PART V: THE WIDER FRAMEWORK

CONCLUSION

LIST OF CONTRIBUTORS

Jeffery Atik, Professor of Law and Sayre Macneil Fellow, Loyola Law School, Los Angeles, USA.

Lorand Bartels, University Lecturer in International Law and Fellow of Trinity Hall, University of Cambridge.

Daniel Bethlehem, Legal Adviser to the United Kingdom Foreign and Commonwealth Office in succession to Sir Michael Wood. Prior to taking up this position, he was Director of the Lauterpacht Centre for International Law, Lecturer at the Faculty of Law, University of Cambridge, and Queens Counsel practising at 20 Essex Street Chambers, London. Mr Bethlehem has acted in a wide variety of matters across the full range of international law. He has appeared before the International Court of Justice, the International Tribunal for the Law of the Sea, the European Court of Justice, the World Trade Organization, the Iran-United States Claims Tribunal, the European Court of Human Rights, and the House of Lords. He was a panelist on the WTO indicative list of panelists and an Arbitrator of the Court of Arbitration for Sport. He is the author and editor of a number of books and articles.

Daniel Bodansky, Professor of Law and Emily and Ernest Woodruff Chair of International Law, University of Georgia School of Law, Athens, Georgia, USA. Professor Bodansky has written extensively on international environmental law generally, and climate change in particular. He served as the US Department of State's Climate Change Coordinator from 1999–2001, co-edited (with Jutta Brunnée and Ellen Hey) the *Oxford Handbook of International Environmental Law*, and is on the Editorial Board of the *American Journal of International Law*.

Jan Bohanes, Associate Sidley Austin LLP (Geneva), formerly Legal Counsellor Appellate Body Secretariat (2002–2006). Mr Bohanes' practice focuses on WTO law, in particular WTO dispute settlement.

Laurence Boisson de Chazournes, Professor of International Law and Head of the Department of Public International Law and International Organization at the Faculty of Law, University of Geneva, Switzerland. She is a member of the WTO indicative list of governmental and non-governmental panelists and a member of the Permanent Court of Arbitration. Between 1995 and 1999, she was Senior Counsel with the Legal Department of the World Bank.

Théo Boutruche, PhD in Laws, Graduate Institute of International Studies, Geneva. Associate Human Rights Officer, Office of the UN High Commissioner for Human Rights, Geneva.

William J Davey, Guy Raymond Jones Chair in Law, University of Illinois College of Law. Former Director of the WTO's Legal Affairs Division from 1995–1999.

Piet Eeckhout, Professor of European Law and Director, Centre of European Law, King's College London. Associate academic member, Matrix Chambers, London.

Craig Forcese, Associate Professor, University of Ottawa, Faculty of Law, Common Law Section.

David A Gantz, Samuel M. Fegtly Professor of Law and Director, International Trade and Business Law Program, University of Arizona, James E. Rogers College of Law.

Valerie Hughes, Department of Justice, Government of Canada, formerly Director WTO Appellate Body Secretariat.

John H Jackson, University Professor of Law, Director of the Institute of International Economic Law, Georgetown Law Center, Washington, D.C.; Editor-in-Chief of the Journal of International Economic Law. Professor Jackson also holds the title Hessel Yntema Zmeritus. Professor of Law at the University of Michigan and was recently awarded the Manley O. Hudson award (highest honour of the American Society of International Law). He has received an honorary doctorate award from Hamburg University and the European Institute.

Pieter-Jan Kuijper, Professor in the Law of International Organizations, University of Amsterdam. Former Director (1999–2002) of the Legal Affairs Division of the WTO Secretariat.

Andrew TF Lang, Lecturer in Law at the London School of Economics, teaching Public International Law with a specialty in International Economic Law, and formerly Gott Research Fellow in Law at Trinity Hall, University of Cambridge. He is a co-founder, with Colin Picker, of the Society of International Economic Law and sits on the Editorial Boards of the *Journal of International Economic Law* and the *Law and Development Review*. He has recently joined the faculty of the World Trade Institute's Masters of International Law and Economics.

Jessica Lawrence, J.D. 2007, University of Georgia School of Law.

Nicolas Lockhart, Partner, Sidley Austin LLP (Geneva), formerly Legal Counsellor Appellate Body Secretariat (1998–2003) and legal advisor to Judge David Edward at the European Court of Justice from 1995–1998. Mr Lockhart's practice focuses on WTO law, in particular WTO dispute settlement and negotiations, and he appears frequently before panels and the Appellate Body.

Gabrielle Marceau, Legal Counsellor, Cabinet WTO Director-General Pascal Lamy, WTO Secretariat since 2005 after 11 years as Counsellor in WTO Legal Affairs Division advising panelists in WTO disputes. Ms Marceau is also Associate Professor, Faculty of Law, University of Geneva.

Mitsuo Matsushita, Professor Emeritus of Tokyo University; Former WTO Appellate Body Member; Attorney-at-Law (Tokyo Bar).

Andrew D Mitchell, PhD (Cantab), LLM (Harv), Grad Dip Intl L (Melb), LLB (Hons) (Melb), BCom (Hons) (Melb). Associate Professor, Faculty of Law, University of Melbourne; Member, WTO indicative list of governmental and non-governmental panelists; Fellow, Tim Fischer Centre for Global Trade & Finance, Bond University; Barrister and Solicitor, Supreme Court of Victoria and High Court of Australia. Advisory Board Member, Melbourne Journal of International Law; Author of *Legal Principles in WTO Disputes* (Cambridge: Cambridge University Press, 2008).

Donald McRae, Hyman Soloway Professor of Business and Trade Law, University of Ottawa. LLB, LLM (University of Otago), Dip Int Law (Cantab). Professor McRae has written widely on international law generally, the law of the sea and international trade law. He has been counsel in WTO disputes and has sat on dispute settlement panels under the Canada–US Free Trade, Agreement, NAFTA, the WTO, and ICSID. He is a member of the International Law Commission.

Rodney Neufeld, LLB (Ottawa), LLM (LSE), Legal Officer Foreign Affairs and International Trade Canada. He worked as a legal associate to Daniel Bethlehem in Cambridge, UK, and as an officer in the Legal Affairs Division of the WTO, prior to returning to Canada. With the Department of Justice and now with the Department of Foreign Affairs, he has represented Canada in WTO committees, in international dispute settlement, including *UPS v Canada*, and has provided legal advice on Canada's boundary disputes and on matters related to Arctic sovereignty. He has taught international law, including international economic law, at the Universities of Ottawa and Carleton.

Hunter Nottage, Counsel at the Advisory Centre on WTO Law; formerly with the Trade Directorate of the Organisation for Economic Co-operation and Development (OECD).

Marcos A Orellana, Director, Trade and Sustainable Development Program at the Center for International Environmental Law (CIEL); Adjunct Professor at American University Washington College of Law. Prior to joining CIEL, Mr. Orellana was a Fellow at the Lauterpacht Research Centre for International Law, University of Cambridge, and Instructor Professor of Law at the Universidad de Talca, Chile.

Federico Ortino, Reader in International Economic Law, King's College, London.

Joel P Trachtman, Professor of International Law, Fletcher School of Law and Diplomacy, Tufts University.

Isabelle Van Damme, Turpin-Lipstein Fellow and College Lecturer, Clare College, University of Cambridge; Affiliated Lecturer, University of Cambridge.

Tania Voon, PhD (Cantab), LLM (Harv), Grad Dip Intl L (Melb), LLB (Hons) (Melb), BSc (Melb). Associate Professor, Melbourne Law School, University of Melbourne; Member, WTO indicative list of governmental and non-governmental panelists; Former Legal Officer, Appellate Body Secretariat, World Trade Organization; Fellow, Tim Fischer Centre for Global Trade & Finance, Bond University; Barrister and Solicitor, Supreme Court of Victoria and High Court of Australia. Advisory Board Member, Melbourne Journal of International Law; Editorial Board Member, Indian Journal of International Economic Law; Author of *Cultural Products and the World Trade Organization* (Cambridge: Cambridge University Press, 2007).

Gilbert R Winham, Professor Emeritus of Political Science and currently Adjunct Professor of Law at Dalhousie University, Halifax. He is a Fellow of the Royal Society of Canada. Dr Winham served on the staffs of the Macdonald Royal Commission on the Economy and on a Parliamentary Committee reviewing the Special Import Measures Act. He has served on federal trade advisory committees and as a panelist on numerous dispute settlement cases under NAFTA and Canada's Agreement on Internal Trade. Dr Winham regularly conducts training in trade negotiations at the WTO for government officials coming from developing countries.

Joseph HH Weiler Joseph Weiler is Director of the Jean Monnet Centre for International and Regional Economic Law and Justice at NYU School of Law.

Alan Yanovich, Legal Counsellor at the WTO Appellate Body Secretariat.

Werner Zdouc, Director of the WTO Appellate Body Secretariat.

LIST OF ABBREVIATIONS

1986 VCLT	1986 Vienna Convention on the Law of Treaties between States and International Organizations or between International Organizations, done at Vienna, 21 March 1986, Doc A/CONF.129/15; 25 ILM 543
AB	Appellate Body
ACC	United Nations Administrative Committee on Cooperation
ACP States	Asian, Caribbean and Pacific Group of States
Anti-Dumping Agreement	Agreement on Implementation of Article VI of the General Agreement on Tariffs and Trade 1994
AROO	Agreement on Rules of Origin
ARSIWA	Articles on Responsibility of States for Internationally Wrongful Acts
ATC	Agreement on Textiles and Clothing
Basel Convention	Basel Convention on the Control of the Transboundary Movement of Hazardous Wastes, done at Basel, 22 March 1989, 1673 UNTS 126; 28 ILM 657
Berne Convention 1971	Berne Convention for the Protection of Literary and Artistic Works, signed at Berne, 9 September 1886, completed at Paris, 4 May 1896, as revised at Paris, 24 July 1971, 1161 UNTS 30
BFA Committee	WTO Committee on Budget, Finance and Administration
BISD	Basic Instruments and Selected Documents
BOP Committee	WTO Committee on Balance-of-Payments Restrictions
BOP Understanding	Understanding on Balance-of-Payments Provisions of the General Agreement on Tariffs and Trade 1994
CARICOM	Caribbean Community

CBD	Convention on Biological Diversity, done at Rio de Janeiro, 5 June 1992, UNEP/Bio.Div./N7-INC5/4; 31 ILM 818
CEACR	Committee of Experts on the Application of Conventions and Recommendations
CESCR	United Nations Committee on Economic, Social and Cultural Rights
CFI	Court of First Instance
CITES	Convention on International Trade in Endangered Species, done at Washington, 3 March 1973, 993 UNTS 243; 12 ILM 1085
Codex	Codex Alimentarius Commission
COP	Conference of the Parties
covered agreements	The agreements listed in Appendix 1 to the Understanding on Rules and Procedures Governing the Settlement of Disputes
CPA	Coalition Provisional Authority
CPC	1991 UN Provisional Central Product Classification, Statistical Papers, Series M No 77, United Nations (1991), revised, version 1.1, Statistical Papers, Series M No 77, United Nations (2004)
CRTA	WTO Committee on Regional Trade Agreements
CSR	Corporate social responsibility
CTD	WTO Committee on Trade and Development
CTE	WTO Committee on Trade and Environment
CTG	Council for Trade in Goods
CTS	Council for Trade in Services
Customs Valuation Agreement	Agreement on Implementation of Article VII of the General Agreement on Tariffs and Trade 1994
DG	WTO Director-General
DSB	Dispute Settlement Body
DSU	Understanding on Rules and Procedures Governing the Settlement of Disputes (Dispute Settlement Understanding)
EC	European Communities
ECHR	European Court of Human Rights

ECJ	European Court of Justice
ECOSOC	United Nations Economic and Social Council
ECOWAS	Economic Community of West African States
ECT	Energy Charter Treaty, done at Lisbon, 17 December 1994, 34 ILM 360
EMIT Group	GATT Working Group on Environmental Measures and International Trade
Enabling Clause	Decision on Differential and More Favourable Treatment, Reciprocity, and Fuller Participation of Developing Countries, L/4903 (28 November 1979), BISD 26S/203
EPAs	Economic partnership agreements
EU	European Union
FDI	Foreign direct investment
FTAs	Free trade agreements
GATS	General Agreement on Trade in Services
GATS Council	Council for Trade in Services
GATT 1947	General Agreement on Tariffs and Trade 1947
GATT 1994	General Agreement on Tariffs and Trade 1994
GC	WTO General Council
GIs	Geographical indications
GPA	Agreement on Government Procurement
GPA Committee	WTO Committee on Government Procurement
GSP	Generalized System of Preferences
HS	International Convention on the Harmonized Description and Coding System
IACtHR	Inter-American Court of Human Rights
IAMB	International Advisory and Monitoring Board
ICC	International Criminal Court
ICCPR	International Covenant on Civil and Political Rights, adopted 16 December 1966, entered into force 23 March 1976, 999 UNTS 171; 6 ILM 368
ICESCR	International Covenant on Economic, Social and Cultural Rights, adopted 16 December 1966, entered into force 3 January 1976, 993 UNTS 3; 6 ILM 360

ICITO	Interim Commission for the International Trade Organization
ICJ	International Court of Justice
ICSID	International Centre for Settlement of Investment Disputes
IGOs	Inter-governmental organizations
ILC	International Law Commission
ILC Articles	Articles on Responsibility of States for Internationally Wrongful Acts
ILO	International Labour Organization
IMF	International Monetary Fund
IP	Intellectual property
IPPC	International Plant Protection Convention, done at Rome, 6 December 1951, 150 UNTS 67
IPU	Inter-Parliamentary Union
ISO	International Organization for Standardization
ITLOS	International Tribunal for the Law on the Sea
ITO	International Trade Organization
ITTC	Institute for Training and Technical Cooperation
ITU	International Telecommunications Union
LDC	Least-developed country
Licensing Agreement	Agreement on Import Licensing Procedures
MAI	Multilateral Agreement on Investment
MC	WTO Ministerial Conference
MEAs	Multilateral environmental agreements
MERCOSUR	Southern Cone Common Market, Treaty of Asuncion, done at Asuncion, 26 March 1991, 30 ILM 1041
MFA	Arrangement Regarding International Trade in Textiles
MFN	Most-favoured-nation
Montreal Protocol	Montreal Protocol on Substances that Deplete the Ozone Layer, done at Montreal, 16 September 1987, entered into force 1 January 1989, 26 ILM 1550
MRAs	Mutual recognition agreements
NAFTA	North American Free Trade Agreement, signed on 17 December 1992, 32 ILM 289, 605

NAMA	Non-agricultural market access
NGOs	Non-governmental organizations
NT	National treatment
NTBs	Non-tariff barriers
OECD	Organisation for Economic Co-operation and Development
OEEC	Organisation for European Economic Co-operation
OIE	International Office of Epizootics
OLA	UN Office of Legal Affairs
OTC	Organization for Trade Cooperation
Paris Convention 1967	Paris Convention for the Protection of Industrial Property, signed on 20 March 1883, revised at Stockholm, 14 July 1967, as amended on 28 September 1979, 8 UNTS 303
Plurilateral Trade Agreements	The agreements and associated legal instruments included in Annex 4 to the Agreement Establishing the World Trade Organization
PPA	Protocol of Provisional Application
PPMs	Process and production methods
PTAs	Preferential trade agreements
RTAs	Regional trade agreements
Rules of Conduct	Rules of conduct for the understanding on rules and procedures governing the settlement of disputes, WT/DSB/RC/1 (11 December 1996)
S&DT	Special and differential treatment
SACU	South African Customs Union
SCM Agreement	Agreement on Subsidies and Countervailing Measures
SCM Committee	WTO Committee on Subsidies and Countervailing Measures
Secretariat	Secretariat of the World Trade Organization
SPS Agreement	Agreement on the Application of Sanitary and Phytosanitary Measures
SPS Committee	WTO Committee on Sanitary and Phytosanitary Measures
SRSG	Special Representative of the Secretary-General
STEs	State trading enterprises

TBT Agreement	Agreement on Technical Barriers to Trade
TNC	Trade Negotiations Committee
TPR	Trade Policy Review
TPRB	Trade Policy Review Body
TPRD	Trade Policy Review Division of the WTO Secretariat
TPRM	Trade Policy Review Mechanism
TRIMS Agreement	Agreement on Trade-Related Investment Measures
TRIPS Agreement	Agreement on Trade-Related Aspects of Intellectual Property Rights
TRIPS Council	Council for Trade-Related Aspects of Intellectual Property Rights
TRTA	Trade-Related Technical Assistance
UDHR	Universal Declaration of Human Rights, UNGA Res 217A (III), A/810, adopted 10 December 1948
UK	United Kingdom
UNCITRAL	United Nations Commission on International Trade Law
UNCLOS	United Nations Convention on the Law of the Sea, done at Montego Bay, 10 December 1982, 1833 UNTS 3; 21 ILM 1261
UNCTAD	United Nations Conference on Trade and Development
UNECE	United Nations Economic Commission for Europe
UNESCO Convention on Cultural Diversity	UNESCO Convention on the Protection and Promotion of the Diversity of Cultural Expressions, done at Paris, 20 October 2005
UNIDO	United Nations Industrial Development Organization
US	United States
VCLT	1969 Vienna Convention on the Law of Treaties, done at Vienna, 23 May 1969, Doc A/Conf 39/27, 1155 UNTS 331
VER	Voluntary export restraints
WB	World Bank
WCO	World Customs Organization
WHO	World Health Organization
WIPO	World Intellectual Property Organization
Working Procedures	Working Procedures for Appellate Review

WPDR	Working Party on Domestic Regulation
WPGR	Working Party on GATS Rules
WPPS	Working Party on Professional Services
WTO	World Trade Organization
WTO Agreement	Marrakesh Agreement Establishing the World Trade Organization, done at Marrakesh, 15 April 1994, 1867 UNTS 154; 33 ILM 1144

List of Cited GATT Panel and Working Party Reports and their Common Abbreviations

....

Australia – Ammonium Sulphate	GATT Contracting Parties, *The Australian Subsidy on Ammonium Sulphate,* GATT/CP.4/39, adopted 3 April 1950, BISD II/188
Belgian Family Allowances	GATT Contracting Parties, *Belgian Family Allowances (Allocations Familiales),* G/32, adopted 7 November 1952, BISD 1S/59, 2S/18, 7S/68
Border Tax Adjustments	GATT Working Party Report, *Border Tax Adjustments,* L/3464, adopted 2 December 1970, BISD 18S/97
Canada – Alcohol	GATT Panel Report, *Canada – Import, Distribution and Sale of Certain Alcoholic Drinks by Provincial Marketing Agencies,* DS17/R, adopted 18 February 1992, BISD 39S/27
Canada – Foreign Investment Review Act (FIRA)	GATT Panel Report, *Canada – Administration of the Foreign Investment Review Act (FIRA),* L/5504, adopted 7 February 1984, BISD 30S/140
Canada – Herring and Salmon	GATT Panel Report, *Canada – Measures Affecting Exports of Unprocessed Herring and Salmon,* L/6268, adopted 22 March 1988, BISD 35S/98
Canada – Ice Cream and Yoghurt	GATT Panel Report, *Canada – Import Restrictions on Ice Cream and Yoghurt,* L/6568, adopted 5 December 1989, BISD 36S/68
EC – Citrus Products	GATT Panel Report, *European Community – Tariff Treatment on Imports of Citrus Products from Certain Countries in the Mediterranean Region,* L/5776, unadopted, circulated 7 February 1985
EEC – Audio Cassettes	GATT Panel Report, *Anti-Dumping Duties on Audio Tapes in Cassettes Originating in Japan,* ADP/136, unadopted, circulated 28 April 1995

EEC – Bananas II	GATT Panel Report, *European Economic Community – Import Regime for Bananas II*, DS38/R, unadopted, circulated 11 February 1994
EEC – Beef	GATT Panel Report, *European Economic Community – Imports of Beef from Canada*, L/5099, adopted 10 March 1981, BISD 28S/92
EEC – Newsprint	GATT Panel Report, *Panel on Newsprint*, L/5680, adopted 20 November 1984, BISD 31S/114
EEC – Oilseeds	GATT Panel Report, *European Economic Community – Payments and Subsidies Paid to Processors and Producers of Oilseeds and Related Animal Feed Proteins*, L/6627, adopted 25 January 1990, BISD 37S/86
EEC – Quantitative Restrictions	GATT Panel Report, *European Economic Community – Quantitative Restrictions against Imports of Certain Products from Hong Kong*, L/5511, adopted 12 July 1983, BISD 30S/129
French Assistance to Exports of Wheat and Wheat Flour	GATT Panel Report, *French Assistance to Exports of Wheat and Wheat Flour*, L/924, adopted 21 November 1958, BISD 7S/46
Germany – Imports of Sardines	GATT Contracting Parties, *Treatment by Germany of Imports of Sardines*, G/26, adopted 31 October 1952, BISD 1S/53
Japan – Agricultural Products	GATT Panel Report, *Japan – Restrictions on Imports of Certain Agricultural Products*, L/6253, adopted 2 February 1988, BISD 35S/163
Japanese Measures on Imports of Leather	GATT Panel Report, *Panel on Japanese Measures on Imports of Leather*, L/5623, adopted 15–16 May 1984, BISD 31S/94
Spain – Soyabean Oil	GATT Panel Report, *Spain – Measures Concerning Domestic Sale of Soyabean Oil – Recourse to Article XXIII:2 by the United States*, L/5142, unadopted, circulated 17 June 1981
Thailand – Cigarettes	GATT Panel Report, *Thailand – Restrictions on Importation of and Internal Taxes on Cigarettes*, DS10/R, adopted 7 November 1990, BISD 37S/200
The US Manufacturing Clause	GATT Panel Report, *The United States Manufacturing Clause*, L/5609, adopted 15–16 May 1984, BISD 31S/74

US – Tuna (Canada)	GATT Panel Report, *United States – Prohibition of Imports of Tuna and Tuna Products from Canada*, L/5198, adopted 22 February 1982, BISD 29S/91
US – Tuna (EEC)	GATT Panel Report, *United States – Restrictions on Imports of Tuna*, DS29/R, unadopted, circulated 16 June 1994
Uruguayan Recourse to Article XXIII	GATT Panel Report, *Report of the Panel on Uruguayan Recourse to Article XXIII*, L/1923, adopted 16 November 1962, BISD 11S/95

LIST OF CITED WTO PANEL AND APPELLATE BODY REPORTS, OTHER INITIATED WTO DISPUTES, AND THEIR COMMON ABBREVIATIONS

Argentina – Footwear (EC)	Appellate Body Report, *Argentina – Safeguard Measures on Imports of Footwear*, WT/DS121/AB/R, adopted 12 January 2000, DSR 2000:I, 515
Argentina – Footwear (EC)	Panel Report, *Argentina – Safeguard Measures on Imports of Footwear*, WT/DS121/R, adopted 12 January 2000, as modified by Appellate Body Report, WT/DS121/AB/R, DSR 2000:II, 575
Argentina – Poultry Anti-Dumping Duties	Panel Report, *Argentina – Definitive Anti-Dumping Duties on Poultry from Brazil*, WT/DS241/R, adopted 19 May 2003, DSR 2003:V, 1727
Argentina – Preserved Peaches	Panel Report, *Argentina – Definitive Safeguard Measure on Imports of Preserved Peaches*, WT/DS238/R, adopted 15 April 2003, DSR 2003:III, 1037
Argentina – Textiles and Apparel	Appellate Body Report, *Argentina – Measures Affecting Imports of Footwear, Textiles, Apparel and Other Items*, WT/DS56/AB/R and Corr.1, adopted 22 April 1998, DSR 1998:III, 1003
Australia – Automotive Leather II (Article 21.5 – US)	Panel Report, *Australia – Subsidies Provided to Producers and Exporters of Automotive Leather – Recourse by the United States to Article 21.5 of the DSU*, WT/DS126/RW, adopted 11 February 2000, DSR 2000:III, 1189
Australia – Salmon	Appellate Body Report, *Australia – Measures Affecting Importation of Salmon*, WT/DS18/AB/R, adopted 6 November 1998, DSR 1998:VIII, 3327
Australia – Salmon	Award of the Arbitrator, *Australia – Measures Affecting Importation of Salmon – Arbitration under Article 21.3(c) of the DSU*, WT/DS18/9, 23 February 1999, DSR 1999:I, 267

Australia – Salmon (Article 21.5 – Canada)	Panel Report, *Australia – Measures Affecting Importation of Salmon – Recourse by Canada to Article 21.5 of the DSU*, WT/DS18/RW, adopted 20 March 2000, DSR 2000:IV, 2031
Banana Tariff Arbitration	Award of the Arbitrator, *European Communities – The APC-EC Partnership Agreement – Recourse to Arbitration Pursuant to the Decision of 14 November 2001*, WT/L/616, circulated 1 August 2005
Banana Tariff Arbitration II	Award of the Arbitrator, *European Communities – The APC-EC Partnership Agreement – Second Recourse to Arbitration Pursuant to the Decision of 14 November 2001*, WT/L/625, circulated 27 October 2005
Brazil – Aircraft	Appellate Body Report, *Brazil – Export Financing Programme for Aircraft*, WT/DS46/AB/R, adopted 20 August 1999, DSR 1999:III, 1161
Brazil – Aircraft (Article 21.5 – Canada)	Appellate Body Report, *Brazil – Export Financing Programme for Aircraft – Recourse by Canada to Article 21.5 of the DSU*, WT/DS46/AB/RW, adopted 4 August 2000, DSR 2000:VIII, 4067
Brazil – Aircraft (Article 22.6 – Brazil)	Decision by the Arbitrators, *Brazil – Export Financing Programme for Aircraft – Recourse to Arbitration by Brazil under Article 22.6 of the DSU and Article 4.11 of the SCM Agreement*, WT/DS46/ARB, 28 August 2000, DSR 2002:I, 19
Brazil – Desiccated Coconut	Appellate Body Report, *Brazil – Measures Affecting Desiccated Coconut*, WT/DS22/AB/R, adopted 20 March 1997, DSR 1997:I, 167
Brazil – Retreaded Tyres	Appellate Body Report, *Brazil – Measures Affecting Imports of Retreaded Tyres*, WT/DS332/AB/R, adopted 17 December 2007
Canada – Aircraft	Appellate Body Report, *Canada – Measures Affecting the Export of Civilian Aircraft*, WT/DS70/AB/R, adopted 20 August 1999, DSR 1999:III, 1377
Canada – Aircraft	Panel Report, *Canada – Measures Affecting the Export of Civilian Aircraft*, WT/DS70/R, adopted 20 August 1999, upheld by Appellate Body Report, WT/DS70/AB/R, DSR 1999:IV, 1443
Canada – Aircraft (Article 21.5 – Brazil)	Appellate Body Report, *Canada – Measures Affecting the Export of Civilian Aircraft – Recourse by Brazil to Article 21.5 of the DSU*, WT/DS70/AB/RW, adopted 4 August 2000, DSR 2000:IX, 4299

Canada – Autos	Panel Report, *Canada – Certain Measures Affecting the Automotive Industry*, WT/DS139/R, WT/DS142/R, adopted 11 February 2000, as modified by Appellate Body Report, WT/DS139/AB/R, WT/DS142/AB/R, DSR 2000:VII, 3043
Canada – Autos	Appellate Body Report, *Canada – Certain Measures Affecting the Automotive Industry*, WT/DS139/AB/R, WT/DS142/AB/R, adopted 19 June 2000, DSR 2000:VI, 2985
Canada – Dairy	Appellate Body Report, *Canada – Measures Affecting the Importation of Milk and the Exportation of Dairy Products*, WT/DS103/AB/R, WT/DS113/AB/R and Corr.1, adopted 27 October 1999, DSR 1999:V, 2057
Canada – Dairy (Article 21.5 – New Zealand and US)	Appellate Body Report, *Canada – Measures Affecting the Importation of Milk and the Exportation of Dairy Products – Recourse to Article 21.5 of the DSU by New Zealand and the United States*, WT/DS103/AB/RW, WT/DS113/AB/RW, adopted 18 December 2001, DSR 2001:XIII, 6829
Canada – Dairy (Article 21.5 – New Zealand and US II)	Appellate Body Report, *Canada – Measures Affecting the Importation of Milk and the Exportation of Dairy Products – Second Recourse to Article 21.5 of the DSU by New Zealand and the United States*, WT/DS103/AB/RW2, WT/DS113/AB/RW2, adopted 17 January 2003, DSR 2003:I, 213
Canada – Film Distribution Services	*Canada – Measures Affecting Film Distribution Services*, WT/DS117, consultations requested 20 January 1998
Canada – Patent Term	Appellate Body Report, *Canada – Term of Patent Protection*, WT/DS170/AB/R, adopted 12 October 2000, DSR 2000:X, 5093
Canada – Patent Term	Panel Report, *Canada – Term of Patent Protection*, WT/DS170/R, adopted 12 October 2000, upheld by Appellate Body Report, WT/DS170/AB/R, DSR 2000:XI, 5121
Canada – Periodicals	Appellate Body Report, *Canada – Certain Measures Concerning Periodicals*, WT/DS31/AB/R, adopted 30 July 1997, DSR 1997:I, 449
Canada – Periodicals	Panel Report, *Canada – Certain Measures Concerning Periodicals*, WT/DS31/R and Corr.1, adopted 30 July 1997, as modified by Appellate Body Report, WT/DS31/AB/R, DSR 1997:I, 481
Canada – Pharmaceutical Patents	Panel Report, *Canada – Patent Protection of Pharmaceutical Products*, WT/DS114/R, adopted 7 April 2000, DSR 2000:V, 2289

EC – Bananas III	Appellate Body Report, *European Communities – Regime for the Importation, Sale and Distribution of Bananas*, WT/DS27/AB/R, adopted 25 September 1997, DSR 1997:II, 591
EC – Bananas III (Article 21.5 – EC)	Panel Report, *European Communities – Regime for the Importation, Sale and Distribution of Bananas – Recourse to Article 21.5 by the European Communities*, WT/DS27/RW/ECU, unadopted
EC – Bananas III (Ecuador)	Panel Report, *European Communities – Regime for the Importation, Sale and Distribution of Bananas, Complaint by Ecuador*, WT/DS27/R/ECU, adopted 25 September 1997, as modified by Appellate Body Report, WT/DS27/AB/R, DSR 1997:III, 1085
EC – Bananas III (Ecuador) (Article 22.6 – EC)	Decision by the Arbitrators, *European Communities – Regime for the Importation, Sale and Distribution of Bananas – Recourse to Arbitration by the European Communities under Article 22.6 of the DSU*, WT/DS27/ARB/ECU, circulated 24 March 2000, DSR 2000:V, 2237
EC – Bananas III (Guatemala and Honduras)	Panel Report, *European Communities – Regime for the Importation, Sale and Distribution of Bananas, Complaint by Guatemala and Honduras*, WT/DS27/R/GTM, WT/DS27/R/HND, adopted 25 September 1997, as modified by Appellate Body Report, WT/DS27/AB/R, DSR 1997:II, 695
EC – Bananas III (Mexico)	Panel Report, *European Communities – Regime for the Importation, Sale and Distribution of Bananas, Complaint by Mexico*, WT/DS27/R/MEX, adopted 25 September 1997, as modified by Appellate Body Report, WT/DS27/AB/R, DSR 1997:II, 803
EC – Bananas III (US)	Panel Report, *European Communities – Regime for the Importation, Sale and Distribution of Bananas, Complaint by the United States*, WT/DS27/R/USA, adopted 25 September 1997, as modified by Appellate Body Report, WT/DS27/AB/R, DSR 1997:II, 943
EC – Bed Linen	Appellate Body Report, *European Communities – Anti-Dumping Duties on Imports of Cotton-Type Bed Linen from India*, WT/DS141/AB/R, adopted 12 March 2001, DSR 2001:V, 2049
EC – Bed Linen (Article 21.5 – India)	Appellate Body Report, *European Communities – Anti-Dumping Duties on Imports of Cotton-Type Bed Linen from India – Recourse to Article 21.5 of the DSU by India*, WT/DS141/AB/RW, adopted 24 April 2003, DSR 2003:III, 965

EC – Tariff Preferences	Appellate Body Report, *European Communities – Conditions for the Granting of Tariff Preferences to Developing Countries*, WT/DS246/AB/R, adopted 20 April 2004, DSR 2004:III, 925
EC – Trademarks and Geographical Indications (Australia)	Panel Report, *European Communities – Protection of Trademarks and Geographical Indications for Agricultural Products and Foodstuffs, Complaint by Australia*, WT/DS290/R, adopted 20 April 2005, DSR 2005: X-XI, 4603
EC – Trademarks and Geographical Indications (US)	Panel Report, *European Communities – Protection of Trademarks and Geographical Indications for Agricultural Products and Foodstuffs, Complaint by the United States*, WT/DS174/R, adopted 20 April 2005, DSR 2005:VIII-IX, 3499
EC – Tube or Pipe Fittings	Panel Report, *European Communities – Anti-Dumping Duties on Malleable Cast Iron Tube or Pipe Fittings from Brazil*, WT/DS219/R, adopted 18 August 2003, as modified by Appellate Body Report, WT/DS219/AB/R, DSR 2003:VII, 2701
EC and Certain Member States – Large Civil Aircraft	*European Communities and Certain Member States – Measures Affecting Trade in Large Civil Aircraft*, WT/ DS316, Panel established 20 July 2005
Guatemala – Cement I	Appellate Body Report, *Guatemala – Anti-Dumping Investigation Regarding Portland Cement from Mexico*, WT/DS60/AB/R, adopted 25 November 1998, DSR 1998:IX, 3767
Guatemala – Cement II	Panel Report, *Guatemala – Definitive Anti-Dumping Measures on Grey Portland Cement from Mexico*, WT/ DS156/R, adopted 17 November 2000, DSR 2000:XI, 5295
India – Autos	Appellate Body Report, *India – Measures Affecting the Automotive Sector*, WT/DS146/AB/R, WT/DS175/AB/R, adopted 5 April 2002, DSR 2002:V, 1821
India – Autos	Panel Report, *India – Measures Affecting the Automotive Sector*, WT/DS146/R, WT/DS175/R and Corr.1, adopted 5 April 2002, DSR 2002:V, 1827
India – Patents (EC)	Panel Report, *India – Patent Protection for Pharmaceutical and Agricultural Chemical Products, Complaint by the European Communities*, WT/DS79/R, adopted 22 September 1998, DSR 1998:VI, 2661

US – 1916 Act	Appellate Body Report, *United States – Anti-Dumping Act of 1916*, WT/DS136/AB/R, WT/DS162/AB/R, adopted 26 September 2000, DSR 2000:X, 4793
US – 1916 Act (EC)	Panel Report, *United States – Anti-Dumping Act of 1916, Complaint by the European Communities*, WT/DS136/R and Corr.1, adopted 26 September 2000, upheld by Appellate Body Report, WT/DS136/AB/R, WT/DS162/AB/R, DSR 2000:X, 4593
US – Anti-Dumping Measures on Oil Country Tubular Goods (Mexico)	Appellate Body Report, *United States – Anti-Dumping Measures on Oil Country Tubular Goods (OCTG) from Mexico*, WT/DS282/AB/R, adopted 28 November 2005, DSR 2005:XX, 10127
US – Carbon Steel	Appellate Body Report, *United States – Countervailing Duties on Certain Corrosion-Resistant Carbon Steel Flat Products from Germany*, WT/DS213/AB/R and Corr.1, adopted 19 December 2002, DSR 2002:IX, 3779
US – Carbon Steel	Panel Report, *United States – Countervailing Duties on Certain Corrosion-Resistant Carbon Steel Flat Products from Germany*, WT/DS213/R and Corr.1, adopted 19 December 2002, as modified by Appellate Body Report, WT/DS213/AB/R and Corr.1, DSR 2002:IX, 3833
US – Certain EC Products	Appellate Body Report, *United States – Import Measures on Certain Products from the European Communities*, WT/DS165/AB/R, adopted 10 January 2001, DSR 2001:I, 373
US – Certain EC Products	Panel Report, *United States – Import Measures on Certain Products from the European Communities*, WT/DS165/R and Add. 1, adopted 10 January 2001, as modified by Appellate Body Report, WT/DS165/AB/R, DSR 2001:II, 413
US – Corn and Other Agricultural Products	*United States – Subsidies and Other Domestic Support for Corn and Other Agricultural Products*, WT/DS357, Panel established 17 December 2007
US – Corrosion-Resistant Steel Sunset Review	Appellate Body Report, *United States – Sunset Review of Anti-Dumping Duties on Corrosion-Resistant Carbon Steel Flat Products from Japan*, WT/DS244/AB/R, adopted 9 January 2004, DSR 2004:I, 3

US – Cotton Yarn	Appellate Body Report, *United States – Transitional Safeguard Measure on Combed Cotton Yarn from Pakistan*, WT/DS192/AB/R, adopted 5 November 2001, DSR 2001:XII, 6027
US – Countervailing Duty Investigation on DRAMS	Appellate Body Report, *United States – Countervailing Duty Investigation on Dynamic Random Access Memory Semiconductors (DRAMS) from Korea*, WT/DS296/AB/R, adopted 20 July 2005, DSR 2005:XVI, 8131
US – Countervailing Measures on Certain EC Products	Appellate Body Report, *United States – Countervailing Measures Concerning Certain Products from the European Communities*, WT/DS212/AB/R, adopted 8 January 2003, DSR 2003:I, 5
US – Countervailing Measures on Certain EC Products	Panel Report, *United States – Countervailing Measures Concerning Certain Products from the European Communities*, WT/DS212/R, adopted 8 January 2003, as modified by Appellate Body Report, WT/DS212/AB/R, DSR 2003:I, 73
US – DRAMS	Panel Report, *United States – Anti-Dumping Duty on Dynamic Random Access Memory Semiconductors (DRAMS) of One Megabit or Above from Korea*, WT/DS99/R, adopted 19 March 1999, DSR 1999:II, 521
US – Export Credit Guarantees	*United States – Domestic Support and Export Credit Guarantees for Agricultural Products*, WT/DS365, Panel established 17 December 2007
US – FSC	Appellate Body Report, *United States – Tax Treatment for "Foreign Sales Corporations"*, WT/DS108/AB/R, adopted 20 March 2000, DSR 2000:III, 1619
US – FSC (Article 21.5 – EC)	Appellate Body Report, *United States – Tax Treatment for "Foreign Sales Corporations" – Recourse to Article 21.5 of the DSU by the European Communities*, WT/DS108/AB/RW, adopted 29 January 2002, DSR 2002:I, 55
US – Gambling	Appellate Body Report, *United States – Measures Affecting the Cross-Border Supply of Gambling and Betting Services*, WT/DS285/AB/R and Corr.1, adopted 20 April 2005, DSR 2005:XII, 5663
US – Gambling	Panel Report, *United States – Measures Affecting the Cross-Border Supply of Gambling and Betting Services*, WT/DS285/R, adopted 20 April 2005, as modified by Appellate Body Report, WT/DS285/AB/R, DSR 2005:XII, 5797

US – Gambling (Article 21.5 – Antigua and Barbuda)	Panel Report, *United States – Measures Affecting the Cross-Border Supply of Gambling and Betting Services – Recourse to Article 21.5 of the DSU by Antigua and Barbuda*, WT/DS285/RW, adopted 22 May 2007
US – Gasoline	Appellate Body Report, *United States – Standards for Reformulated and Conventional Gasoline*, WT/DS2/AB/R, adopted 20 May 1996, DSR 1996:I, 3
US – Gasoline	Panel Report, *United States – Standards for Reformulated and Conventional Gasoline*, WT/DS2/R, adopted 20 May 1996, as modified by Appellate Body Report, WT/DS2/AB/R, DSR 1996:I, 29
US – Hot-Rolled Steel	Appellate Body Report, *United States – Anti-Dumping Measures on Certain Hot-Rolled Steel Products from Japan*, WT/DS184/AB/R, adopted 23 August 2001, DSR 2001:X, 4697
US – Hot-Rolled Steel	Panel Report, *United States – Anti-Dumping Measures on Certain Hot-Rolled Steel Products from Japan*, WT/DS184/R, adopted 23 August 2001, as modified by Appellate Body Report, WT/DS184/AB/R, DSR 2001:X, 4769
US – Lamb	Appellate Body Report, *United States – Safeguard Measures on Imports of Fresh, Chilled or Frozen Lamb Meat from New Zealand and Australia*, WT/DS177/AB/R, WT/DS178/AB/R, adopted 16 May 2001, DSR 2001:IX, 4051
US – Large Civil Aircraft	*United States – Measures Affecting Trade in Large Civil Aircraft*, WT/DS317, Panel established 20 July 2005
US – Lead and Bismuth II	Appellate Body Report, *United States – Imposition of Countervailing Duties on Certain Hot-Rolled Lead and Bismuth Carbon Steel Products Originating in the United Kingdom*, WT/DS138/AB/R, adopted 7 June 2000, DSR 2000:V, 2595
US – Line Pipe	Appellate Body Report, *United States – Definitive Safeguard Measures on Imports of Circular Welded Carbon Quality Line Pipe from Korea,* WT/DS202/AB/R, adopted 8 March 2002, DSR 2002:IV, 1403
US – Offset Act (Byrd Amendment)	Panel Report, *United States – Continued Dumping and Subsidy Offset Act of 2000*, WT/DS217/R, WT/DS234/R, adopted 27 January 2003, as modified by Appellate Body Report, WT/DS217/AB/R, WT/DS234/AB/R, DSR 2003:II, 489

US – Underwear	Appellate Body Report, *United States – Restrictions on Imports of Cotton and Man-made Fibre Underwear*, WT/DS24/AB/R, adopted 25 February 1997, DSR 1997:I, 11
US – Underwear	Panel Report, *United States – Restrictions on Imports of Cotton and Man-made Fibre Underwear*, WT/DS24/R, adopted 25 February 1997, as modified by Appellate Body Report, WT/DS24/AB/R, DSR 1997:I, 31
US – Upland Cotton	Appellate Body Report, *United States – Subsidies on Upland Cotton*, WT/DS267/AB/R, adopted 21 March 2005, DSR 2005:I, 3
US – Upland Cotton	Panel Report, *United States – Subsidies on Upland Cotton*, WT/DS267/R and Corr.1, adopted 21 March 2005, as modified by Appellate Body Report, WT/DS267/AB/R, DSR 2005:II-VI, 299
US – Upland Cotton (Article 21.5 – Brazil)	Appellate Body Report, *United States – Subsidies on Upland Cotton – Recourse to Article 21.5 of the DSU by Brazil*, WT/DS267/AB/RW, adopted 20 June 2008
US – Wheat Gluten	Appellate Body Report, *United States – Definitive Safeguard Measures on Imports of Wheat Gluten from the European Communities*, WT/DS166/AB/R, adopted 19 January 2001, DSR 2001:II, 717
US – Wool Shirts and Blouses	Appellate Body Report, *United States – Measures Affecting Imports of Woven Wool Shirts and Blouses from India*, WT/DS33/AB/R and Corr.1, adopted 23 May 1997, DSR 1997:I, 323
US – Zeroing (EC)	Appellate Body Report, *United States – Laws, Regulations and Methodology for Calculating Dumping Margins ("Zeroing")*, WT/DS294/AB/R and Corr.1, adopted 9 May 2006, DSR 2006:II, 417
US – Zeroing (Japan)	Appellate Body Report, *United States – Measures Relating to Zeroing and Sunset Reviews*, WT/DS322/AB/R, adopted 23 January 2007
US – Zeroing (Japan)	Panel Report, *United States – Measures Relating to Zeroing and Sunset Reviews*, WT/DS322/R, adopted 23 January 2007, as modified by Appellate Body Report, WT/DS322/AB/R

TABLE OF CASES

....

OTHER JURISDICTIONS

INTERNATIONAL COURTS/ARBITRAL BODIES

Permanent Court of International Justice

International Court of Justice

International Labour Organization Administrative Tribunal

International Centre for Settlement of Investment Disputes

UN Commission on International Trade Law

Other

REGIONAL COURTS: AMERICAS

Inter-American Court of Human Rights

MERCOSUR

CHAPTER 1

INTRODUCTION

DANIEL BETHLEHEM

DONALD MCRAE

RODNEY NEUFELD

ISABELLE VAN DAMME

ONE of the most important developments in international law over the past decade has been the growth in the content and application of international trade law. The Uruguay Round agreements establishing the World Trade Organization (WTO) expanded the range of trade disciplines in both traditional and new areas. The WTO created a new international institution and a binding dispute settlement system through which the rules of the agreements have been clarified and developed. Through that process international trade law has been expanded and enhanced and there has been a considerable development more broadly of the wider field of public international law.

The details of the new international trade regime have been dissected frequently by scholars, government officials, and trade law practitioners. Instead of replicating this body of work, the purpose of this Handbook is to put the international trade law regime in a broader context, to provide an overall perspective of the regime; how it fits with existing systems, how it affects and modifies them, and how it too is modified by them.

The contributors to the Handbook represent a wide variety of legal backgrounds and approaches to law and they have amongst them substantial and diverse experience in the field of international trade and in international economic relations generally. They were given the mandate to examine and critique existing approaches to their areas and to explore the implications of having a functioning system of international trade law for States, for other international regimes, for civil society, and for human welfare.

The topics dealt with in this Handbook range from the origins and structure of the international trading system, through the substantive obligations, or building blocks, of that system, the dispute settlement system and its consequences, the intersection of the international trading regime with other areas of international regulation, and then to the broader environment where the relevance of trade regulation has been more controversial and where the relationship to trade law has yet to be fully explored. In the final chapter, a look ahead to the future is provided.

The linkages between trade and other areas of international law are explored in Part IV. Some of the chapters contend with modern 'Trade and...' topics such as trade and the environment and trade and health. Others deal with topics, such as labour and investment, that were originally intended to be included in the work of the International Trade Organization had it come to fruition. Certain chapters address conflict, overlap, and interaction between trade law and other rules of international law. Some suggest room for improvement of existing rules or the adoption of new ones. Together, they show the reach of trade rules into other areas of domestic and international policy and they show how trade law has been influenced and affected by other rules and policies.

Some of the actors that have influenced the trading regime are considered in Part V, including the multinational corporation, civil society, and the United Nations. The three chapters in this Part look at the wider framework of international trade law. They analyse the respective roles played by multinational corporations and civil society in the development of trade law and its ongoing evolution. Another chapter considers the link between trade and international peace in security, arguing that the predominant 'exception oriented' approach of the WTO is overly limiting and the relationship between international trade law and UN law needs to be rethought. These chapters highlight the diverse interests of a number of actors in what has become an effective, global trade law regime. They point to the need for greater access, involvement, and coordination.

At one level, then, this is a book about international trade law as a vehicle for facilitating economic relationships, between economies of the original GATT order, and between those economies and the newly industrialized economies including the emerging major economies of China, India, and Brazil, and the least developed economies of the world. At another level, the book is concerned with the impact of the international trading regime on social values that States acting either individually or collectively through international fora seek to preserve and protect, including the more recent attention on issues of personal and national security.

This volume also takes stock of international trade law. The virtual explosion of the discipline since the advent of the WTO, the emergence of new scholarly publications and of associations of scholars, the development of international trade law and investment law bars, and the public debate about trade law and public policy, all make the broad perspective that this Handbook provides timely. It is, hopefully, also the start for new dialogues across many branches of the field as the scholarship and practice of international trade law continues to grow.

PART I

THE ECONOMIC AND INSTITUTIONAL CONTEXT OF THE WORLD TRADING SYSTEM

CHAPTER 2

....

THE EVOLUTION OF THE WORLD TRADING SYSTEM – THE ECONOMIC AND POLICY CONTEXT

....

GILBERT R WINHAM

I. Introduction

TRADE is the act of exchanging goods and services through barter or sale. International trade is the extension of commercial exchange outside a country's borders to the international arena; it is as old as the system of nation States, and by analogy extends back in history to collectivities such as tribes, city-states, or other political units. The term 'world trading system' refers to the various contemporary arrangements of trading relations between countries, and particularly the system of multilateral rules initiated at mid-twentieth century following two great wars and a worldwide economic depression.

Trade between collectivities encounters political impediments much greater than those that exist within collectivities. These impediments result from attempts by citizens to restrict the benefits of economic exchange to themselves and their fellow citizens. Thus, communalism and the trade restrictions imposed by the collectivity are important elements in any analysis of international or inter-societal trade. In the first half of the twentieth century, such restrictions were so onerous as to almost stop trade altogether, while in the second half of the century, they have been the subject of a lengthy and coordinated effort by trading countries to liberalize the flow of goods and services in the international economy. The result is that trade cannot be examined independent from trade policy.

II. The Basis for Trade

A. Trade: An Overview

The origins of trade are found in the beginnings of human history and social organization. Trade among our primitive ancestors was a means to acquire scarce commodities between groups with differing expertise or resources, but it also served as a means of communication. Early communities lived in ignorance and often fear of each other, and trade in tangible objects offered a useful glimpse into alternative forms of agriculture and material technology. Not least trade stimulated curiosity and encouraged exploration, and it played an important part in the furthering of social communication.[1] Despite its other functions, the basis for trade was economic. Trade lay at the centre of state revenue and state power for many of the ancient and medieval powers. This was certainly the case in ancient Greece. Athens, for example, was dependent on trade and developed in part through commercial activity with its neighbours. Athens exported silver and olive oil throughout the Mediterranean region and in turn imported the grain needed to feed its population. As for Corinth, the historian Thucydides noted that '[the Corinthians] provide trading facilities on both the land and sea routes [and] made their city powerful from the revenues which came to it by both these ways'.[2]

Trade played an important role in the transition from the ancient to the modern world. Historians have noted that international trade is intimately related to the course of human development. For example, there were trade routes from Asia and North Africa to Greece and then Rome, which broke down after the fall of the Roman Empire. From the sixth to the eighth centuries, social and physical communication between these areas and Europe and among the European communities themselves was severed, trade was disrupted, and the Medieval period settled in Europe. Trade recovered very slowly and from its resurgence the modern trading system has developed. As with the Ancient Greeks, the purpose of modern trading relationships has been to increase wealth.

B. Intellectual Argument for Trade

One cannot discuss the history of trade without also taking account of the regulation of trade. As John Condliffe has argued, trade may be ancient, but the regulation and taxation of trade are nearly as old.[3] As soon as trade routes were beaten out and traders began to profit from their endeavours, authorities intervened to control and tax the traders. The earliest expression of political interference with economic enterprise was tolls, which often were payments exacted by local leaders for permission to pass through territory. As trade itself became more sophisticated, so also did the methods of taxation and regulation, and tolls became replaced by tariffs and other non-tariff restrictions. Whereas tolls were often random or opportunistic, tariffs reflected organized government policy. Their main purpose was to raise revenue, and by the early 1700s the tariff had become the main source of government revenue

---

[1] K Deutsch, *Nationalism and Social Communication: An Inquiry into the Foundations of Nationality* (Cambridge, MA: MIT Press, 1953).

[2] Thucydides, *History of the Peloponnesian War*, trans Rex Warner, intro. MI Finley (Harmondsworth, UK: Penguin, 1954), at 43.

[3] J Condliffe, *The Commerce of Nations* (New York: WW Norton, 1950).

in Europe. Later, tariffs were intended to protect domestic producers from foreign competition. Both protection and revenue became essential elements of a policy known as mercantilism, in which countries sought to export more than import, and thereby to accumulate wealth and presumably power.

The regulation and management of trade has long been a subject of analysis and theory. The basic idea is specialization and exchange, or division of labour, which in its inception was applied to individuals and not nations. In establishing the rudiments of social organization, Plato argued in favour of specialization and exchange as follows: 'So the conclusion is that more things will be produced and the work be more easily and better done, when every man is set free from all other occupations to do, at the right time, the one thing for which he is naturally fitted.'[4] This idea, which is fundamental in economics, was not widely applied by pre-modern societies to trade between collectivities, even though trade itself was commonplace between early societies. The reason is that trade invoked the foreign and the suspicious, and it took time before theorists would allow themselves to apply to foreign trade the arguments that were used to explain economic behaviour between citizens.

The seminal argument in favour of free trade came from Adam Smith's 1776 treatise *Wealth of Nations*. Writing in response to popular mercantilist theories of the day, Smith first elaborated the notion that a self-interested individual was most fitted to allocate resources over which he had command, and that interference by authorities could only reduce the productivity of that individual. This analysis employed 'the key concept in assessing economic policy…of opportunity costs, or the trade-offs between alternative activities under resource constraints'.[5] Going further, Smith linked this concept to commercial policy by arguing, 'If a foreign country can supply us with a commodity cheaper than we ourselves can make it, better buy it off them with some part of the produce of our own industry, employed in a way in which we have some advantage…'[6] With this argument Smith focused attention on the fact that most government interference in commerce would carry costs that would be borne by the economy as a whole. Despite this argument, Smith was not a doctrinaire proponent of *laissez-faire*, but rather believed a role existed for government to support the market mechanism.

A half-century later, David Ricardo and James Mill extended Smith's argument with the theory of comparative advantage, which stated that in order to maximize their welfare countries should specialize and export their least-cost products (based ultimately on their relative endowment in the factors of production) and trade to receive their higher-cost products. This theory advanced the understanding of absolute advantage (which could be easily appreciated in the example of trade in cloth and wine between an industrialized country and an agricultural country) and applied

---

[4] Plato, *The Republic of Plato*, trans Francis MacDonald Cornford (New York: Oxford University Press, 1945) at 57.

[5] D Irwin, *Against the Tide: An Intellectual History of Free Trade* (Princeton: Princeton University Press, 1996), at 78.

[6] Ibid at 79.

the analysis to the situation where one country might have a cost advantage over another in both cloth and wine. In the latter case, trade still advantages the more highly endowed country (and likewise its trading partner) if it produces and exports the product in which it has the greatest advantage over its partner, and receives the other's product in imports. This elegant and parsimonious theory still stands as a point of departure in the economic analysis of international trade.

An alternative to the classical trade theory rooted in Ricardo and Mill was the contribution of Frederick List that focused on nationalism and national development. List attacked the notion that trade on the basis of comparative advantage maximized the economic welfare of nations. Instead he proposed a policy of national development that emphasized rapid industrialization for developing countries. Trade protectionism was a necessary policy to promote such industrialization. List's philosophy was not well received in England which was already industrialized, but the developing countries of his day, notably Germany and the US, incorporated List's thinking into their trade policies. Most modern developing countries also pursued policies consistent with List's ideas, for they used high tariffs and other measures to protect income-competing industries and to promote industrialization.

Despite its critics, the Classical Theory of Smith, Ricardo, and Mill remains the basis for the case for free trade. At the level of intellectual analysis it has neither been disproved nor discarded.[7] However, intellectual debate is one thing, while economic policy is another. Governments continue to interfere in international trade mainly because of the power of special interests to demand preferential treatment that advantages them even though posing costs for the wider community. Hence, the recommendations from theories of free trade are only one element that gets taken account of in the making of trade policy.

III. Trade in the Period 1860–1913

A. Significance of the Cobden-Chevalier Treaty

The history of international trade over the past two centuries has reflected contradictory trends towards either protectionism or free trade. In the late eighteenth century, protectionism was the norm in the countries of Europe. But after the Napoleonic Wars, British manufacturer Richard Cobden led a move towards free trade in that country. This movement had considerable success, in part because the Napoleonic Wars left Britain in an advantaged position compared to the European countries.

---

[7] Ibid at 230.

Britain became the world's creditor country and a dominant force in international economic relations. Trade with the US and the colonies was substantial, but trade with Europe was hampered with high tariffs on the Continent and the protectionist Corn Laws in Britain which restricted grain imports from Europe. British efforts to promote liberalism in Europe were met with demands that Britain should reduce or eliminate its duties on grain. These demands, combined with domestic pressure for political reform in Britain, led to the 1846 repeal of the Corn Laws, followed by administrative measures that put free trade into practice.

Trade liberalization spread to the European continent, in part due to a free trade movement in France led by Michel Chevalier. Chevalier attempted to convince the French government to follow the British example but had little success until the opportunity arose to incorporate a tariff negotiation into a commercial and political treaty with Great Britain. The result was the Cobden-Chevalier Treaty of 1860 which was instrumental in opening the French market to British manufacturers and demonstrated that trade agreements could be an effective means of trade liberalization.

B. Pattern of Bilateral Treaties and MFN

The Cobden-Chevalier Treaty stimulated a series of liberalizing trade agreements among the countries of Europe. These agreements were bilateral and arose without multilateral direction, though since most of these treaties contained provisions extending most-favoured-nation (MFN) treatment, they effectively created a rudimentary multilateral trading system. Under the MFN provisions, countries that negotiated a trade agreement with another country would agree to give to that country any concession that was subsequently extended to a third country.[8] As noted by Irwin, '...despite the lack of oversight mechanism or institutional basis, this regime...brought about relatively low tariffs'.[9] Since tariffs (and not non-tariff barriers) were the main instrument of protectionism, the result was a liberal and non-discriminatory trading system. By the third quarter of the nineteenth century in Europe, Adam Smith's concept of an international economy based on free exchange was as close to realization as it ever had been.

The period of free trade did not last long, however. Rapid technological improvements in the mid-1800s meant that increasingly the comparative advantage in grain cultivation was shifting towards the New World. At the same time, a slump occurred in European industrial production. International competition in manufactured goods as well as grains became severe. In 1870, Europe fell into a recession that was to be both serious and longstanding. In all countries there were pressures

---

[8] M Trebilcock and R Howse, *The Regulation of International Trade*, 2nd edn (London: Routledge, 1999), at 18.
[9] D Irwin, 'The GATT in Historical Perspective' 1995 *AEA Papers and Proceedings* 85(2) 323, at 323.

to take protectionist actions, and this had an effect on policy in country after country. Austria-Hungary raised tariffs in 1876, followed quickly by Italy and Germany. France responded to German protectionism with restrictions of its own. By the end of the century, Britain was the only major nation still practising free trade.

The leading 'developing country' of this period, the US, never joined the European movement toward free trade but rather remained firmly protectionist throughout the nineteenth century. The first tariff was introduced in 1789, having the intention and effect to generate government revenue. US tariff policy remained largely unchanged for the next twenty-five years, with alterations being made to correspond to the need (such as the War of 1812) for government revenue. After the war, the US introduced the Tariff of 1816, the first tariff created primarily to protect domestic industry and with revenue generation being only a secondary goal. Subsequent tariffs were also designed mainly for protection, consistent with the infant industry argument for tariff protection that had been vigorously promoted by Alexander Hamilton and others. US tariffs increased dramatically in the 1860s as a result of the Civil War, at a time when Europe was beginning its experiment with negotiations to lower duties. Tariffs remained high in the US for the remainder of the century, and indeed rose in the 1890s in response to hard times.

To sum up, the depression that began in the 1870s triggered a policy of protectionism that lasted more than half a century. Despite this development in the policy arena, the world at the end of the nineteenth century was relatively globalized in terms of behaviour. Compared to modern times, foreign investment flowed freely between countries, and there were substantial flows of people across national borders. Even trade flows grew at a healthy pace over the period 1870–1910. In the first decade of the twentieth century, the international trade system was balanced between a world economy that was relatively open in practice and trade policy in important countries that was protectionist in principle. Subsequent events tilted that balance strongly toward a closing of the world economy.

IV. Breakdown of the International Trade System

A. World War I and Its Aftermath

The four years of war after 1914 broke up the imperfect but workable equilibrium between internal economic policies and external trade and payments that had developed in the nineteenth century. Unmindful of treaty obligations, countries imposed higher tariffs and applied further constraints on foreign economic relations such as import quotas, licensing restrictions, and exchange controls. The result was a precipitous decline in world trade.

Economic production was returned shortly after the end of the war. Stocks of food and fuel that had been exhausted during the war were no longer in short supply by the end of the decade. However, industries lacked markets but not necessarily access to raw materials. As observed by Swiss economist William Rappard: 'What was missing was not equipment, nor produce, but confidence, credit, purchasing power and trade.'[10] It was the network of trading relations that had been built up prior to the war, in part through early inter-governmental cooperation, that was most absent in the war's aftermath.

Although they were overshadowed by the more visible conferences on disarmament and reparations, there were a number of attempts in the 1920s and 1930s to restore economic confidence and open up the trading system. These efforts included the International Finance Conference in 1920, the Genoa Conference of 1922, a conference on customs formalities in 1923, and the World Economic Conferences of 1927 and 1933. The early conferences sought to restore international trade to its pre-war levels, as it had fallen by almost half its volume after the war. Rather than the reduction of trade barriers *per se*, the initial emphasis was to re-establish a payments mechanism, for without some system of monetary exchange, trade was impossible.

The focus turned to trade in 1923 with the conclusion of an agreement between 35 countries to reform and harmonize border customs controls and procedures. This agreement did not deal with protectionist tariff levels themselves, but instead sought to reduce the arbitrary and often excessive formalities associated with national tariff practices. The most important of the early post-war economic conferences was the World Economic Conference of 1927 that produced the Geneva Convention on Import and Export Prohibitions and Restrictions. Until the GATT was negotiated in 1947, the Geneva Convention was the most ambitious attempt to promote international cooperation on trade. The Convention banned prohibitions on exports and imports, and created a common set of rules regarding the use of quantitative restrictions. The Convention did not deal specifically with tariffs, but it nevertheless represented an important effort to instill confidence in the multilateral trading system.

The drafting of the Convention was done carefully, in a manner to avoid the most sensitive commercial interests in the leading trading nations. The agreement was to come into force on the signature of 18 countries. It was signed quickly by the most important European trading countries but it failed by one country to get the necessary signatories, and support for the Convention quickly unravelled. The loss was regrettable, for an important opportunity was missed to build confidence in international trade management, and possibly to forestall the self-serving actions that nations took as they faced depression in the 1930s.

---

[10] W Rappard, *Post-War Efforts for Freer Trade*, Geneva Studies, Vol 9, No 2 (Geneva: Geneva Research Centre, 1938), at 17.

B. The US Smoot-Hawley Tariff

The US emerged from the First World War as the largest trading nation in the world. One result of this situation was that policies taken by that country would have major implications for the multilateral trading system. One particular action had a uniquely harmful effect. In 1930, the US passed the Smoot-Hawley Act that raised tariffs to historically high levels. This action did not represent a dramatic change in US trade protection, since tariffs were already at a high level, but it represented a visible and politically important step in the process of closing national boundaries to foreign imports.

The Smoot-Hawley tariff was the product of a number of factors in the US. First, there was a predominance of protectionist sentiment in the country, which formed the backdrop of any trade policies taken by the government. Then, too, the legislation was a product of increased nationalism produced by war and war-like diplomacy in Europe, together with a reaction or perhaps overreaction to the nationalist economic policies in other countries. Another factor in the passage of this legislation was the nature of the political process in the US federal government. The Act was written in congressional committees by legislators who often were unable to appreciate the complexity or the overall implications of the legislation. The process was especially vulnerable to pressure from well-organized and vocal special interest groups who were demanding protection. In the face of this pressure, Congress essentially granted protection to all those groups that demanded it.[11]

Governments in foreign countries closely observed the process that led to the Smoot-Hawley tariff in the US. With the passage of this Act, they moved quickly to retaliate. The 1930s became characterized by a series of moves and retaliatory moves in which tariffs were ratcheted upwards. Great Britain ended its historic policy of free trade in 1931, and in 1932 negotiated the Ottawa agreements that resulted in a tariff preference area in the British Commonwealth.

Competitive protectionism in especially the US, Britain, and the European countries completed the breakdown of the world trading regime by the mid-1930s. The impact of raising tariffs and implementing other protectionist measures was devastating, as world trade declined by approximately two-thirds from 1929 to 1934. Actions in the trading system helped to deepen the harmful effects of the world depression, which was underway in full force following the global stock market crash of 1929.[12] These economic circumstances, combined with the rise of fascism and nationalism in Europe, helped to make the Second World War a nearly inevitable occurrence. War completed the destruction of a cooperative international trade regime.

---

[11] E Schattschneider, *Politics, Pressures and the Tariff* (New York: Prentice Hall, 1935), at 283–4.
[12] C Kindleberger, *The World in Depression, 1929–39* (London: Allen Lane, Penguin Press, 1973).

V. The GATT Regime

A. GATT Creation and Objectives

During the war, officials in Washington and London commenced negotiations for a post-war economic system since it appeared unlikely that the informal arrangements of the nineteenth century would reappear on their own. These negotiations were based around a compromise between the American position, which promoted multilateralism along with a bias toward liberal economic policy, and the British position, which was more concerned with historical ties to the Commonwealth and the capacity of governments to intervene in and manage the domestic economy. This compromise led to the Bretton Woods Conference of 1944, which established the International Bank for Reconstruction and Development (World Bank) and the International Monetary Fund (IMF).[13] Additionally, the allies met in several conferences to establish the architecture of an international trading regime. Countries agreed to establish an International Trade Organization (ITO) in 1948, which would join the IBRD and IMF as a triad of international organizations in the economic area. The GATT, or General Agreement on Tariffs and Trade, was completed during a multilateral tariff negotiation in 1947, and was simply a body of trade rules intended to be part of the ITO.[14] In the event, the US Administration was unable to get Congressional approval for the ITO and the organization failed to come into existence, leaving the GATT 1947 as the principal legal instrument in multilateral commercial relations.

The main purpose of the GATT 1947 had been to establish a legal mechanism for tariff negotiations, and to provide rules that would deter countries from reinstating protectionism through non-tariff means that they might have bargained away in the context of tariff-reducing negotiations. The GATT 1947 was simply an agreement (a contract), its signatories were called 'Contracting Parties' and not 'Members', and it was not intended to function as an international organization. The fact that the GATT 1947 in time appeared to operate as an international organization was due largely to its unplanned and incremental accretion of political and legal powers. This amounted to institution-building through inadvertence.

The GATT 1947 mechanism for reducing high tariffs was contained in Article XXVIII*bis* (Tariff Negotiations), Article I (General MFN Treatment) and Article II (Schedules of Concessions). First, the GATT 1947 called upon Contracting Parties to take advantage of the history of tariff negotiations (and the more recent experience with the

---

[13] The seminal work on this subject is R Gardner, *Sterling-Dollar Diplomacy* (Oxford: Oxford University Press, 1956). The compromise between the American and British positions has been labeled 'embedded liberalism' in J Ruggie, 'International regimes, transactions, and change: embedded liberalism in the post-war economic order' 1982 *International Organization* 36(2) 379.

[14] See also chapter 3 of this Handbook.

Reciprocal Trade Agreements Act—RTAA—in the US),[15] stating that: '…negotiations on a reciprocal and mutually advantageous basis, directed to the substantial reduction of the general level of tariffs…are of great importance to the expansion of international trade'.[16] Such negotiations were to be conducted on a 'product-by-product basis' or by acceptable 'multilateral procedures', and were to be directed toward a reduction of duties, or the binding of duties or other undertakings related to tariffs.

Second, while it was understood such negotiations would be conducted on a bilateral basis with the principal supplier, it was mandated in Article I:1 GATT 1947 that 'any advantage' (for example, a lowered tariff) conferred by such negotiations would be 'accorded immediately and unconditionally to the like product' of all other GATT signatories. Thus the GATT 1947 incorporated the MFN procedure that had a prominent place in commercial history. Third, it provided in Article II that Contracting Parties would maintain transparent schedules of concessions that recorded the results of any tariff reductions, or bindings without reduction, resulting from negotiations. These tariff concessions amounted to contractual obligations, and they were said to be 'bound in GATT'.[17] Once bound in GATT, tariffs could not be raised without 'nullifying or impairing' a contractual obligation, which gave right of redress to other Contracting Party (ies) under GATT dispute settlement procedures. The measures sketched out above provided a means to ratchet downward over time the high tariffs produced by the first half of the twentieth century.

Other provisions in the GATT 1947 contributed to the movement towards lowered trade protectionism. A safeguards clause (Article XIX) envisaged a situation where negotiated tariff reductions may have created an especially difficult political problem in a Contracting Party, therefore it allowed for countries to backtrack on their commitments for a period of time to permit orderly adjustment of domestic markets. The purpose of this pragmatic measure was to ensure that problems in a single industry did not compromise the general movement toward liberalization. Other provisions were designed to ensure that protection given up through tariff reductions was not increased through different measures having a similar effect. For example, in Article VII (Valuation for Customs Purposes), the General Agreement provided that the valuation of imported merchandise (established by officials of the importing country) should be based on the 'actual value' of the merchandise, and not on 'arbitrary or fictitious values'. Similarly, Article XVI (Subsidies) attempted to place limits on the capacity to protect industries through the use of various benefits provided by governments to domestic industries. The GATT 1947 measures on customs valuation and subsidies did not create effective disciplines on the use of these practices by governments, and both measures have since been subject to further negotiation in GATT Rounds.

---

[15] The RTAA authorized the President to reduce tariffs from Smoot-Hawley levels in the context of trade negotiations with other countries. See G Winham, *The Evolution of International Trade Agreements* (Toronto: University of Toronto Press, 1992), at 19.

[16] Art XXVIII*bis*:1 GATT 1947.

[17] For a definition of a binding, see chapter 3 of this Handbook.

The approach of the GATT 1947 to liberalizing trade was to de-legitimize the use of protectionist measures other than tariffs, then to reduce tariffs gradually through negotiated concessions. Therefore, Article XI contained the stark obligation that 'no restrictions other than duties' shall be maintained on the importation of any product. Another important provision was Article III, which obliged countries to extend 'national treatment', that is, to treat foreign products—once they had been imported and all duties paid—no less favourably than domestically produced products with respect to taxes and other commercial requirements. Similar to Article I, which ensured countries could not discriminate externally between trade partners, Article III ensured that countries could not discriminate internally between products produced by foreigners and those produced by domestic producers. In terms of their effect on trade policy, both Articles III and XI removed a wide range of policy tools that governments had traditionally used to extend preferential treatment to domestic products. In the case of Article III, these tools were internal taxes, distribution requirements or other commercial guidelines, whereas for Article XI the tools were various forms of quantitative requirements or limitations. The continued importance of these old GATT 1947 provisions can be seen in the frequency with which these articles are invoked in current WTO dispute settlement proceedings.

B. GATT Negotiations: 1947–79

The GATT 1947 established the mechanism for reducing the prohibitively high tariffs that existed at the end of World War II, but the General Agreement left to trading countries themselves the task of initiating and carrying out negotiations to bring down the level of duties. This task was taken up vigorously. After 1947, there were some seven multilateral trade negotiations held under GATT auspices, concluding with the Uruguay Round that established the WTO. These negotiations were: Annecy, 1949; Torquay, 1951; Geneva, 1956; the Dillon Round, 1960–61; the Kennedy Round, 1963–67; the Tokyo Round, 1973–79; and the Uruguay Round, 1986–96.

The first four negotiations after 1947 did not make significant progress in reducing tariff levels on a multilateral basis. In contrast to the protectionist policies it had applied since the nineteenth century,[18] the US made some largely unreciprocated concessions in these negotiations. However, the European economies did not recover from the war as quickly as expected, and governments were therefore disinclined to increase the exposure to international competition through tariff liberalization. The first significant negotiation was the Kennedy Round of the 1960s. This was the first

---

[18] See H-J Chang, *Knocking Away the Ladder: Development Strategy in Historical Perspective* (London: Anthem Press, 2003), at 61, arguing that the US was the country '…which first systematized the logic of the infant industry promotion that Britain had used so effectively in order to engineer its industrial ascent'.

time that the six partners in the European Common Market participated as a single unit, which increased the stakes considerably for the US. The Kennedy Round produced a dramatic struggle between liberalizing and protectionist forces. The result is that the Kennedy Round took on importance as a symbol of the commitment to freer trade that was initiated in the immediate post-war period. In the end, the negotiation concluded successfully, and led to an average tariff reduction of about 35 per cent among the participants. This was in sharp contrast to an average reduction of less than 10 per cent in the Dillon Round that preceded the Kennedy Round, or even an average reduction of 20 per cent achieved in the initial tariff negotiation conducted in 1947.

Shortly after the Kennedy Round, the GATT Director-General (DG), Sir Eric Wyndham-White, encouraged the major trading nations to extend liberalization into the area of non-tariff barriers to trade. This process had already begun with the negotiation of an Anti-Dumping Code in the Kennedy Round. The idea of negotiating NTBs became more attractive in the early 1970s as countries resorted to creative forms of protection in response to the wave of exports from Japan and other newly industrializing economies. The task of dealing with NTBs produced new challenges for multilateral trade negotiations. Tariffs, which were the mainstay of GATT negotiations, were expressed in numbers, they were relatively transparent, and they could be negotiated on the basis of relatively straightforward trade-offs. NTBs, however, were often buried in domestic legislation that could have multiple purposes in addition to protectionism, with the result that gathering specific information about NTBs was an important but difficult preliminary step in the negotiation. Furthermore, NTBs were reduced (or 'disciplined') not through a negotiation over numbers, but rather through a complex verbal negotiation that created a code of conduct binding on all signatories.

The negotiation that followed the Kennedy Round, called the Tokyo Round, met the challenge of handling NTBs and produced six legal codes dealing with customs valuation procedures, import licensing practices, technical standards for products, subsidies and countervailing measures, government procurement, and anti-dumping practices. Altogether the Tokyo Round codes updated and reformed certain elements of GATT rules established in 1947. The main thrust of these codes was to improve marginally the openness, certainty, and non-arbitrariness of the rules governing international trade, and even more important, to commence the integration of the conflicting trade legislation of many countries into a coordinated set of international rules. The Tokyo Round codes established a firm precedent for the regulatory (or legislative) negotiations that were characteristic of the Uruguay Round of 1986–1993.

Although the major action of the Tokyo Round was not on tariffs, the negotiation nevertheless produced an average reduction of 35 per cent on industrial nations' duties. This result was comparable to the Kennedy Round that had focused mainly on tariffs. In other areas, the Tokyo Round achieved a series of revisions to the GATT 1947 known as the Framework Agreements that were designed to allow greater scope for trade rules to take account of the particular needs of developing countries. The Framework Agreements covered subjects such as deviations from

MFN requirements, export controls, and trade measures taken to correct payments deficits. These measures reflected the increasing influence of developing countries in trade negotiations, an influence that became much more pronounced in subsequent GATT and WTO negotiations.

A summary evaluation of GATT negotiations over the period 1947–79 would have to take account of many factors, but certainly two would stand out. First, there has been a substantial decline in tariff protection on industrial products in developed countries over this period. For example, as noted by Bhagwati, 'In the United States, the average tariff declined by nearly 92 per cent over the 33 years spanned by the Geneva Round of 1947 and the Tokyo Round'.[19] This decline produced a tariff of about 5.0 per cent in the US by the early 1980s, and was matched by near equivalent tariff levels in other actors such as Japan (5.4 per cent) and the European Economic Community (6.0 per cent). Although some tariff reductions might be the result of unilateral actions, it would be hard to discount the role of the GATT 1947 in producing this change, especially given its capacity to lock-in concessions that were extended in negotiations.

Second, over roughly the same period, the volume of trade grew by an annual average of 7 per cent, while the growth of world production averaged about 5 per cent.[20] It is possible to assume that decreasing protection has led to increased trade and output, but economic analysis tends not to support such easy answers. What can be said is that over three decades, a reduction in tariff protectionism has been apparently correlated with increases in world trade and output, and that this fact has been sufficient to encourage governments to continue to pursue trade negotiations as a means to economic growth in the future.

VI. The Uruguay Round Negotiation

A. International Trade in the Early 1980s

The GATT 1947, like the WTO after it, was established to promote international trade negotiations. When the stability of the trading seemed threatened, as in the 1960s with the formation of the European Common Market, or in the 1970s with the crisis in the international monetary system, the response of the GATT Contracting Parties had been to initiate a new negotiation to address the causes of the instability. A similar pattern repeated itself after 1980, with the result that GATT Contracting Parties initiated in September 1986, a new negotiation called the Uruguay Round.

---

[19] J Bhagwati, *Protectionism* (Cambridge, MA: MIT Press, 1989), at 4.
[20] *International Trade Statistics* (1970–1980) (Geneva: GATT), 1970–1980.

The Uruguay Round negotiation was the eighth multilateral trade negotiation conducted under GATT auspices. One might have assumed, as with the Tokyo Round, that the Uruguay Round would make incremental progress toward a more open and liberal international trading regime. The Uruguay Round did this, but it also did much more. By the time it was concluded, the agreements reached at the Round ensured that a profound transformation would occur in the trade regime and indeed throughout international economic relations more generally. Arguably, the Round amounted to system change in the world economy, a change that dramatically increased the profile of the world trading system in international relations.

The impetus for the Uruguay Round lay in the conditions of the world economy in the early 1980s. For much of the post-war period growth in trade and output had been buoyant, but growth rates fell as countries entered the 1970s, and then fell further under the impact of the shock of increasing oil prices after 1973, and again after the second shock in 1979. Inflation further compounded the situation, and the efforts to contain inflation helped bring on a recession in 1982. Throughout this period trade performance was equally dismal, which was made all the more worrisome given the increasing trade dependence (reflected in rising export/GDP ratios) in most developed countries.[21] By the early 1980s it was evident that the world economy was performing poorly for many developed countries, and even creating economic crisis through recession and debt in developing countries.

Further complicating the perspective on trade were problems in the agricultural sector, and the new issue of trade in services. By the 1980s, agriculture had declined to a very small portion of the economies and trade of developed countries and the increase in protectionism in major importers, particularly the EC, made a bad situation worse for agricultural exporters. Attempts had been made without success to liberalize agricultural trade in the Kennedy and Tokyo Rounds, with the result that for many countries (especially developing countries) agriculture had become a *sine qua non* for any real reform of the multilateral trading system. As for trade in services, the GATT 1947 had traditionally focused on merchandise trade and had relegated what would now be called services to a category called 'invisibles', with little attention being paid to their role in international trade. However, governments were well aware of the increasing importance of services in domestic economies, with the result that pressures mounted from developed countries to liberalize trade in service products. This pressure to include services in a new negotiation led to pitched opposition from developing countries on the grounds that further progress should be made on the goods side before the GATT 1947 turned to an issue that initially would benefit mainly developed countries. This proved to be the most painful issue faced by the Contracting Parties in the negotiations between 1981 and 1986 to initiate the Uruguay Round negotiation.

---

[21] A Maddison, *The World Economy in the 20th Century* (Paris: OECD, 1989), at 27.

To sum up, the situation in the world trading system was not good in the early 1980s, and there was widespread agreement that a new negotiation was needed to restore confidence in the GATT multilateral trading system. The GATT 1947 contract had been established to expand trade, but it was questionable whether this purpose was being served, given the slowdown of the international economy, or the inability of the GATT 1947 to reduce protectionism in agriculture and textiles, or to promote trade in services. Moreover, there were developments in world trade policies that ran completely contrary to the goals of the GATT 1947, such as the increasing use of 'voluntary' export restraint agreements or the use of unilateral trade sanctions by the US. It was clear that the rules of the GATT 1947 regime were no longer compatible with the international trading system as it was developing, and that trading countries faced a choice of either reforming the rules of the multilateral trading regime or risking their loss altogether.

B. The Accomplishments of the Uruguay Round Negotiation[22]

Negotiation of the Uruguay Round was a difficult if not tortured process that has been well described elsewhere.[23] The process took over seven years, and it was marred by lengthy periods of inaction due to the inability of the US and the EU to resolve bilateral differences on agriculture and other issues. On a positive note, however, the process was engaged much more by developing countries than was customary in past GATT negotiations, which lent credence to the notion that the GATT represented a multilateral trading regime that approached universality. On the other hand, however, the active engagement of developing countries increased the difficulties of resolving the issues in the negotiation, given that decision-making in the Uruguay Round was based on the GATT norm of consensus and that the issues in the Uruguay Round were settled on the basis of a single undertaking.[24]

The Uruguay Round negotiation was completed on 15 December, 1993. The results were a remarkable achievement in every sense. First, liberalizing agreements were struck in two old areas—agriculture and textiles—where previous GATT negotiations had been ineffective, or where countries had negotiated quantitative export restraints like the Multifibre Agreement on textiles that constituted an end run around GATT 1947 obligations. The agreements on agriculture and textiles effectively brought these areas back into the multilateral rules-based regime. Second, in the new areas of trade in services and intellectual property, the Uruguay Round

[22] See also chapter 3 of this Handbook.
[23] J. Croome, *Reshaping the World Trading System: A History of the Uruguay Round* (Geneva: World Trade Organization, 1995).
[24] Ibid at 34.

Agreements provided rules and procedures for the gradual liberalization of services over time, and they established multilateral rules that promised to reduce the conflicts that had developed over the infringement of intellectual property rights. In these areas, especially trade in services, the negotiation process demonstrated remarkable creativity by establishing rules in areas where the GATT had very little background or past administrative experience.

Third, the Uruguay Round Agreements made numerous improvements to existing GATT 1947 provisions or to those rules established in the Tokyo Round. One example was the SCM Agreement, where negotiators took on a subject that had been negotiated at the GATT 1947 and also the Tokyo Round without even achieving an operational definition of subsidies. The agreement at the Uruguay Round not only provided a legal definition of subsidies, but it also provided meaningful disciplines on a practice that was long a source of conflict between trading countries. The SCM Agreement was a prominent example of how far countries were prepared to go to reform the past practices of the trading regime.

Other examples of improvements to GATT rules included (i) the GATT 1947 SPS Agreement that elaborated importantly the provisions of Article XX GATT in regard to trade-related measures needed to protect human, animal, or plant life or health; (ii) the Safeguards Agreement that updated the provisions of Article XIX GATT 1947, and thereby succeeded in an area where the Tokyo Round negotiation had noticeably failed; and (iii) the Anti-Dumping Agreement that further reformed the permissible measures to be taken in this complicated area. In all these areas, and in others not mentioned, the thrust of the negotiation was to create rules that would be clear, actionable, and acceptable, and therefore capable of contributing to a workable rules-based regime for the regulation of international trade. The Uruguay Round Agreements confirmed the observation of the late Professor Raymond Vernon: 'The Agreements, if taken at their face value, show promise of reshaping trade relationships throughout the world.'[25]

C. Economic and Policy Context of the Uruguay Round

When countries reach negotiated agreements, it is usually assumed they have bargained hard and accepted the details of the package they have worked out. But negotiations do not occur in a vacuum, even less negotiations that occurred in the latter twentieth century when the world was undergoing sweeping changes. The late 1980s and 1990s were a time of increasing perceptions of change and even transformation in the world economy. As a noted writer expressed it, 'We are living through a transformation that will rearrange the politics and economics of the coming century...

---

[25] R Vernon, 'The World Trade Organization: A New Stage in International Trade and Development', 1995 *Haward International Law Journal* 36(2) 329.

[t]here will no longer be national economies, at least as we have come to understand the concept...'[26] As much as the details of the agreements that were reached at the Uruguay Round were important to ministers and negotiators, it is also likely that world events militated towards a successful conclusion of the negotiation.

First, the Uruguay Round was negotiated in a period that saw a startling shift in economic ideology towards the free market. The most prominent event of that shift was the breakup in 1989 of the Soviet Bloc and communist governments. In economic terms, the greatest impact of the fall of communism on the Uruguay Round was the loss of the model of a command economy, and the consequent discrediting of government intervention as a means to manage international trade relations. Conversely, the fall of communism promoted the rise of market principles in the world economy, which are the principles on which the GATT 1947 had been founded.

The enormity of the breakdown of the Soviet Bloc obscured the fact that market-based reform was already well underway independently in many countries. Economic reform began in the early 1980s, although it took on different guises depending on the circumstances of individual countries. In some countries it was Reagan or Thatcher-inspired deregulation, in other countries like Canada it was trade reform in the context of a bilateral free trade agreement. In many developing countries it was a flight from policies of import-substitution industrialization that had been the staple of economic policy in the previous two decades. The accumulative effects of these domestic changes improved the prospects for a negotiated settlement at the Uruguay Round.

All countries sought to achieve increased market access from their trading partners at the Uruguay Round, and the means to accomplish that was through the liberalization of trade. Economic reform in domestic economies ensured that the demands for change that arose from the Uruguay Round negotiation were consistent with the changes already underway in various countries. Taking the actions requested by trading partners was made less difficult where those actions were already consistent with domestic policy. To some extent the Uruguay Round Agreements were an international step in a direction that many countries were already moving in their domestic economies.

A second change that occurred concurrently with the Uruguay Round was a rising concern over globalization. The perception of globalization was created by many factors, including political, geographical, cultural, and economic, but the economic dimension was most important in regard to its impact upon trade or trade policy. Economic globalization has been described most straightforwardly as a 'simple extension of economic activities across national boundaries'.[27] Others have admitted more complexity by focusing on the increasing role of foreign trade in national economies, on the rapidly increasing scale of global financial

---

[26] R Reich, *The Work of Nations: Preparing Ourselves for 21st Century Capitalism* (New York: Vintage Books, 1991), at 3.

[27] P Dicken, *Global Shift: Transforming the World Economy*, 3rd ed (New York: Sage, 1998), at 5.

transactions, and on the growing role of foreign direct investment (FDI) in the GDP of many countries, both developed and developing. A definition of globalization that integrates these factors has been offered by Sylvia Ostry: 'The ever tightening and more complex linkages among nation-states, first by trade, then by financial flows, and more recently by a surge of foreign direct investment that have greatly enhanced the power and ubiquitousness of the multilateral enterprise in the international arena.'[28]

Any definition of economic globalization can have many aspects, but the basic mechanism of change is foreign investment.[29] This relationship was appreciated by the OECD in describing the globalization of industry as '...the transborder operations of firms undertaken to organize their development, production, sourcing, marketing and financial activities'.[30] This suggests that globalization is the integration of production across national boundaries, and it is important because of the effects it can have on other economic variables, and particularly international trade and trade policy. Again as noted by the OECD, '...international trade is being increasingly restructured by international investment and international collaboration between firms, as they expand and organize operations more broadly...'.[31]

The effect of this restructuring was to reorganize trade on a more regional basis, and then in the 1990s toward inter-regional or global markets.[32] As for the impact of this restructuring on trade policy, it is undeniable that globalization exerted pressure on governments for more liberal trade policies. This led some to suggest the State was in decline, but that seemed unlikely given the continued capacity of governments to tax, spend, or to direct transfers. However, governments did receive pressure from the business sector to liberalize trade policy, since protectionism is an impediment to firms that have already decided to orient their business activities to the international market. The lesson of the 1990s was that it had become necessary to think differently about international trade, namely, that trade that had always been the main economic link between national societies was now being integrated into a broader set of relationships that included foreign investment, corporate alliances, and other forms of collaboration. As one observer summarized it, '...the reality is that global companies competing in global markets ultimately require global rules...'.[33] In this way globalization created a perceived need for global rules, which in turn was a powerful incentive to complete the Uruguay Round.

---

[28] S Ostry, *The Post-Cold War Trading System: Who's on First?* (Chicago: University of Chicago Press, 1999), at xvi–xvii.

[29] See also chapter 22 of this Handbook.

[30] *Globalization of Industry: Overview and Sector Reports* (Paris: OECD, 1996), at 15.

[31] Ibid at 31.

[32] See also chapter 10 in this Handbook.

[33] G Feketekuty, *The New Trade Agenda* (Paris: OECD, 1992), at 29.

VII. THE WORLD TRADE ORGANIZATION

A. Operation of the WTO

The WTO came into being on 1 January 1995. It was created as part of the results of the Uruguay Round negotiation that were concluded on 15 December 1993 and adopted on 15 April 1994 at a meeting in Marrakesh, Morocco, by the ministers of 124 governments and the EC. Unlike the GATT 1947, the WTO was invested with a legal personality and organizational presence intended to be equivalent to the World Bank or the IMF.

The capacity of the WTO is augmented by the vigorous involvement of the Geneva delegations of WTO Members, which permits the WTO to get by with a much smaller Secretariat than other economic international organizations. The WTO is usually described as a 'member-driven' organization, meaning that Members and not the Secretariat are mainly responsible for carrying out the functions of the organization. In the important routine tasks of the organization, including substantive discussions of the relationship of trade with other issues (for example, environment, human rights, technical transfer), accession of new Members, initiation of complaints or disputes or interpretations of WTO rules, judgments on waivers of obligations, or working parties discussions on trade and technology transfer, action must be taken by officials from Members' governments. If a Member seeks to keep abreast of the issues coming before the organization, the workload on national delegations can be daunting.

An important task of the WTO is to promote trade negotiations. The WTO Agreement obliges the organization to 'provide a forum for negotiation' on matters arising under the Uruguay Round Agreements, and on further issues concerning the multilateral trade relations of the Members. The WTO lost no time in exercising its mandate to sponsor negotiations. In the Uruguay Round, the services negotiations concluded in 1993 without scheduled commitments being reached in financial or telecommunication services. These were negotiated after 1995, and by 1997 landmark agreements were concluded in both areas. Furthermore, in March 1997, 40 governments reached agreement on the WTO Ministerial Declaration on Trade in Information Technology Products that reduced tariffs on computer and telecommunications equipment. This agreement was significant because of the large amount of trade covered, and the fact that it represented the 'new economy' in terms of international commerce. Finally, there were further negotiations mandated in agriculture and services that were referred to as the 'built-in' agenda for work commencing in 2000. These negotiations got underway despite the failure of the Seattle Ministerial Conference (MC) of 1999 to establish a more complete agenda. The upshot is that negotiation has become a normal part of the business of multilateral trade policy making. The WTO is moving toward a regime of 'permanent negotiation', in which the organization begins to appear more like a typical national legislature and less like the occasional diplomatic encounters traditionally seen in international relations.

B. Developing Countries and the Doha Round

The WTO has 153 Members of which the great majority are developing countries. For much of the history of the GATT 1947, developing countries stood apart from much of the trade liberalization process that occurred in GATT negotiations. This changed dramatically in the Uruguay Round, when by 1991 developing countries had become some of the strongest proponents of a multilateral settlement in the negotiation.[34] Following the negotiation, it became clear that the organization would face a crucial test to integrate all its Members into WTO global trade rules. For example, in the TRIPS Agreement on intellectual property rights, all countries were expected to provide administrative procedures and remedies in their domestic legal regime to ensure that rights holders could effectively enforce their rights. For many developing countries, this required the creation of new laws and administrative procedures, which involved in turn the training of officials and the outlay of considerable administrative capital. As a result, implementation of the Uruguay Round Agreements became an important political issue for developing countries in the WTO, at the same time as some developed countries were considering a new negotiation to deal with yet unresolved problems such as investment or competition policy.

Issues came to a head in the Seattle MC in December 1999, which was the third such meeting since the commencement of the WTO. Some Members sought to use the MC to start a new comprehensive round of multilateral negotiations, others felt a negotiation should be confined to the 'built-in' issues of services, and still others felt issues of implementation should be addressed before new issues were taken up. In the months preceding the Seattle MC, it was clear that deep divisions existed between the Members, and particularly between the developed and developing countries. These divisions were carried into the MC, which in turn ended in a well-publicized failure.

Seattle was a serious defeat for the WTO, but the GATT regime had suffered from similar failures in the past—notably the Brussels Ministerial Meeting of 1990 that occurred during the Uruguay Round—and it had demonstrated its capacity to recover from such defeats. Following Seattle, painstaking efforts were made to reconcile the positions of developing and developed countries, which resulted in a successful MC in Doha, Qatar, two years later. At this meeting, Members produced a set of

---

[34] G Winham 'Explanations of Developing Country Behaviour in the GATT Uruguay Round' 1998 *World Competition: Law and Economic Review* 21(3) 109.

documents collectively known as the Doha Development Agenda.[35] The first was the Doha Declaration that established a new multilateral negotiation, the second was a Declaration on the TRIPS Agreement and Public Health that addressed the problem of access to affordable medicines, and the third was a Decision on Implementation-Related Issues and Concerns that addressed the implementation problems left over from the Uruguay Round. The Doha Declaration established a negotiation work programme of subjects, most of which were to be dealt with on the basis of a single undertaking. The Round was scheduled to conclude not later than 1 January 2005, and it was expected 'to place the needs of developing countries at the heart of the Doha Work Programme'.[36]

The Doha Round has had a difficult existence, and at this writing in March 2008 the negotiation has not concluded, nor do circumstances appear ripe for its conclusion. The Round was bitterly criticized by developing countries in the failed Cancún MC of September 2003, it was restarted in 2004, and later was kept alive by five grueling days of negotiation in the Hong Kong MC in December 2005. Since then negotiators have made indifferent progress. There have been both promising gestures and setbacks with neither being decisive, all the while leaving the impression of a suspension of believable progress.

Two general observations can be made about the progress of the Doha Round negotiation. First, depending on how one counted, there were at the outset about a dozen issues placed on the negotiating agenda by developed and developing countries. Several issues of interest to developed countries were dropped altogether and others were relegated to secondary status, until by 2006 and after there were but three major subjects on the table: agricultural subsidies, agricultural market access (mainly tariffs) and NAMA (non-agricultural market access, again, mainly industrial tariffs). In trade volumes the latter category simply dwarfs the former two. The two agricultural issues have the US and the EU deservedly on the defensive from demands especially from developing countries, while the third issue is somewhat more balanced between the demands of developed and developing countries. Much of the negotiation has come down to tariffs, which historically have been some of the most difficult issues to manage in multilateral negotiations. Many observers have commented that there is not much on the Doha Round agenda, but what is there is especially difficult to settle.

Second, negotiators at the Doha Round opted to tackle market access negotiations on the basis of a formula approach, in which agricultural tariffs would be arranged into four tiers from low to high, and NAMA tariffs would be handled according to a Swiss formula that would cut higher tariffs more deeply than lower tariffs (harmonization). Regarding agriculture, once the tiers were established, it was then necessary

---

[35] See chapter 3 of this Handbook.
[36] WTO, *Doha Ministerial Declaration*, WT/MIN(01)/DEC/1 (20 November 2001).

to insert numbers into the tiers to determine the amount by which tariffs on individual products or sectors would be cut. For example, tiers might be set at 0–5, 6–10, 11–15, and so forth, where tariffs in the lowest tier (for example, a 4 per cent tariff) might be cut by 20 per cent, tariffs in the next tier cut by 30 per cent, and so forth. Obviously countries negotiated over the definition of the tiers, the amount tariffs might be cut in each tier, and the differences that might be mandated for developed versus developing countries in applying this formula.

In NAMA, instead of tiers, negotiators used a Swiss formula of $Z=AX/(A+X)$, where X = initial tariff rate, A = coefficient, and Z = resulting lower tariff rate. In this formula, the lower the coefficient that is introduced, the greater the tariff reduction and the lower the final tariff. Again, countries negotiated over the coefficients to be used, and any differences in the coefficients to be used for developed versus developing countries. In pursuing this formula approach, it was assumed that once numbers were inserted into the tier structure or the Swiss formula, the resulting tariff reductions would be automatically derived for any product included in the calculation. In this way it was said that once the modalities (the numbers) were agreed—with allowance for exceptional treatment for some products—that about 80 per cent of the work of the negotiation would be completed.

The story of the Doha Round negotiation is that countries have simply been unable to set acceptable limits on agricultural subsidies, or to establish the modalities on agricultural market access and NAMA necessary to move to the next step in the negotiation. From mid-2005 onwards, negotiators have set deadlines for the tabling of modalities, only to have these deadlines pass without concrete action. The negotiation thus has focused more on process than substance, or alternatively, on setting dates for action rather than taking action. Most of the difficulties have been over the permissible differences in the modalities to be used by developed versus developing countries, although there have been other difficulties arising among developed countries themselves, and among developing countries as well. What is especially unfortunate is that at different times most of the major parties have said that although their current offers were fixed, they could be improved if there was first movement on the other side. This is an indication of failure at the negotiation table, not where the parties have insufficient instructions or leeway from government policy to reach a deal, but rather where they have sufficient negotiating authority to produce a contract zone but are still unable to reach an agreement because of the interaction in the negotiating process itself. Simply put, the negotiating environment of the Doha Round has not been conducive to an agreement, especially between developed and developing countries, and this is a problem that appears to go beyond the negotiating positions of individual countries.[37]

[37] For further discussion, see G Winham 'The Doha Round and its impact on the WTO' in D Lee and R Wilkinson (eds) *The WTO after Hong Kong* (London: Routledge, 2007).

VIII. The Future of the World Trading System

At the beginning of this chapter the term 'world trading system' was used to refer to a system of multilateral trade rules, which are mainly located in the WTO. The WTO is a unique phenomenon in international relations. It is an international organization, but more than that it is a regime; that is, it is a mode of management based on consensually derived rules and characterized especially by judicial and legislative powers. Judicial power resides in a robust and legally obligatory dispute settlement system, while legislative power resides in a negotiation process that has been over 50 years in the making. Negotiation is critical to the WTO, and as observed by a blue-ribbon committee, 'The World Trade Organization is in large measure a negotiating machine'.[38]

It is now clear in mid-2008 the negotiation in the WTO—the Doha Round—has lost control of its timetable, and it is unlikely that the Round will accomplish the ambitious goals it was intended to achieve. It will not enhance the WTO's reputation as a negotiating machine to have such grave difficulties in its first major multilateral trade negotiation. However, trade liberalization in GATT/WTO history has been a stop-start process, where success does not necessarily breed success, nor failure breed failure. Regardless of the outcome of the Doha Round, the WTO still offers its Members the broadest base of trade rules available in the international system, and these rules are backed up by impressive legislative and judicial functions. When the prospect of negotiating new rules is prevented by disagreement, it is probable that Members will pursue their interests by making greater use of judicial procedures under currently existing rules. Therefore, as many have said, one could expect to see greater use of WTO dispute settlement procedures in the wake of a failed Doha Round negotiation.

As for the issue of development, which has largely caused the negotiation process of the WTO to become stalled, it remains the most important issue on the WTO agenda and it will be negotiated again although not necessarily in the same manner as pursued in the Doha Round. Development is clearly a bigger issue than the machinery (trade negotiation) by which it has been addressed in the Doha Round. It will be necessary to rethink what the WTO can accomplish in economic development that is still consistent with the inherent capabilities and constraints of the trade negotiation process. Then, too, it may be necessary to rethink the hoary construct of 'developing country', and to question whether this construct as it is currently employed in

---

[38] WTO, *Future of the WTO: Addressing Institutional Challenges in the New Millenium Report by the Conservations Board to the Director-General Supachai Panitchpakdi* (Geneva: WTO, 2004), at 61.

WTO negotiations is conducive to dealing with the problems of underdevelopment and poverty in the international system. Developing countries are an economically diverse group in the WTO, and the most destabilizing dimension of this diversity is, in fact, economic development. It may be necessary to determine what about 'developing country' can be effectively addressed in a multilateral trade negotiation, and what about 'developing country' needs to be addressed by other policy tools.

The WTO's Doha Round negotiation has been a learning experience, but the problem it has sought to understand—development—may be one that cannot be mastered in a single sitting. This has occurred before in GATT history. In the 1970s the Tokyo Round negotiation tackled the conundrum of non-tariff barriers, and while the Round did not produce much in real trade liberalization, it did refine the methodology of negotiating regulatory agreements that laid the groundwork for the later successes of the Uruguay Round. In the same way the Doha Round may have laid the groundwork to address more effectively in the future the problem of development in the world trading system.

SELECTED BIBLIOGRAPHY

J Condliffe, *The Commerce of Nations*, (New York: WW Norton, 1950)

K Dam, *The GATT: Law and International Economic Organization* (Chicago: University of Chicago Press, 1970)

RE Hudec, *The GATT Legal System and World Trade Diplomacy* (New York: Praeger, 1975)

A Krueger (ed), *The WTO as an International Organization* (Chicago: University of Chicago Press, 2000)

P Macrory, A Appleton, and M Plummer (eds), *The World Trade Organization: Legal, Economic and Political Analysis* (New York: Springer, 2005)

E Preeg, *Traders in a Brave New World: The Uruguay Round and the Future of the International Trading System* (Chicago: University of Chicago Press, 1995)

M Trebilcock, and R Howse, *The Regulation of International Trade*, 3rd edn (London: Routledge, 2005)

G Winham, *International Trade and the Tokyo Round Negotiation* (Princeton: Princeton University Press, 1986)

CHAPTER 3

....

THE EVOLUTION
OF THE WORLD
TRADING
SYSTEM – THE
LEGAL AND
INSTITUTIONAL
CONTEXT

....

JOHN H JACKSON

I. Introduction and Overview[1]

THE history of the evolution of the GATT/WTO trading system demonstrates how a human institution can change over time, often in ways not expected by its creators. It also demonstrates how the political and geopolitical (strategic) context of the institutional activity and operation will deeply colour its direction, and in many cases stimulate innovation and change in the *de facto* (not always '*de jure*') legal structure. In the context of international law, based heavily on nation-state sovereignty and supremacy ideas, governments and societies consenting to become members of such institutions must do so with the realization that the institutional structures will not be frozen in time, and that such consent will inevitably bring surprises.

These lessons are more poignant with an institution such as the WTO and its predecessor the GATT 1947 because of its curious and somewhat defective origin, what some refer to as 'birth defects', as we shall see in later parts of this chapter.

An important and surprising aspect of this story was the strange position of the predecessor to the WTO, namely the GATT 1947. The GATT 1947 has often been described as the most important treaty for international trade relations, and the most important international organization for those relations. In a technical sense, neither of these descriptions was completely true. The GATT 1947 treaty as such never came fully into force, but was implemented in part by the 'Protocol of Provisional Application' (47 years of provisional application!). The GATT 1947 itself was also never intended to be an organization, as this chapter later describes, because the ill-fated ITO was supposed to be the institutional and organizational framework for trade rules, which would have included the GATT 1947. Yet when the 1948 draft ITO Charter failed to come into effect, the GATT 1947 had to fill the vacuum. This led to a strong pragmatic element in the GATT's institutional evolution and considerable confusion for international trade relations. This pragmatism influenced a trial and error or ad hoc approach, which promoted attitudes of realism and give and take that characterized the implementation of the trade rules. This undoubtedly had some causal relation to the spotty implementation for certain areas of economic endeavour such as agriculture and textiles. The fact that the GATT 1947 had very few textual clauses relating to its institutional structure lead to some makeshift arrangements, which, however, actually became quite powerful.

---

[1] See other works by this author for greater detail: JH Jackson, *Sovereignty, the WTO and the Changing Fundamentals of International Law* (New York: Cambridge University Press, 2006); JH Jackson, *The World Trading System: Law and Policy of International Economic Relations*, 2nd edn (Cambridge, Mass.: MIT Press, 2002); JH Jackson, WJ Davey, and AO Sykes, *Legal Problems of International Economic Relations: Cases, Materials and Text on the National and International Regulation of Transnational Economic Relations*, 4th edn (St. Paul, Minn.: West Group, 2002); JH Jackson, *World Trade and the Law of GATT* (Indianapolis, IN: The Bobbs-Merrill, 1969); and generally articles in the *Journal of International Economic Law*, at <http://www.jiel.oxfordjournals.org>.

This chapter is designed to give the reader a brief, condensed overview of the history of the most important international economic institution, including many unique historical developments. Readers interested in greater detail about this history may wish to explore other writings of this author, as well as other chapters in this Handbook.

II. GATT and Its History, Including Its 'Birth Defects'

Considerable thinking about post-World War II institutions occurred during the early 1940s, and an important part of this thinking (apart from the United Nations (UN) idea) focused on international economic institutions. There was a strong feeling that economic policy failures after World War I were a significant cause of the Second World War, and that the depression as well as other factors shared that responsibility. Economic actions such as the US high tariff of 1930, and numerous other national barriers as well as exchange rate manipulations were seriously damaging to the world economy. This led to important views that a total restructuring and creation of international institutions were necessary to help prevent yet another world war.

One product of this thinking was the 1944 Bretton Woods Conference in the US, which established charters for the World Bank and the International Monetary Fund, two of the three pillars which would constitute the 'Bretton Woods System'. It was recognized that a third pillar was also needed to address problems of trade, but the Bretton Woods Conference was directed and organized by financial ministries of governments concerned, and they felt that they did not have the appropriate authority to address trade concerns which tended to be under the jurisdiction of ministries of commerce or similar other departments of governments.

Prevention of another major war was clearly the most important strand of the institutional thinking of that period, but a second important strand of thinking was motivated by the views of important economists deeply involved in this institution-making, including ideas going back to Adam Smith in the prior century, and ideas and presence of persons such as John Maynard Keynes. This view believed that appropriate international economic institutions would assist in leading nation-state governments to adopt better economic policies such as liberalized trade and disciplines on exchange rate manipulation, which in turn would lead to better world economic development, which should increase the total economic welfare of the world population.

Soon after the Bretton Woods Conference (and the 1945 launch of the UN) diplomats began efforts to prepare an 'International Trade Organization' (ITO) to complete the 'Bretton Woods System'. Four preparatory conferences were held in 1946, 1947, and 1948 (Havana) with a total of more than twenty seven thousand pages in over one hundred volumes, all publicly available.[2] Many of the preparatory documents have been used in interpreting the GATT 1947, as the GATT Analytical Index demonstrates.[3] In the US, the Congress enacted the 1945 renewal of the reciprocal trade agreements legislation for a three-year period. Also in 1945, a negotiation for the reduction of tariffs began, with meetings part of the ITO draft preparations.

The history of the preparation of the GATT 1947 is thus intertwined with that of the preparation of the ITO Charter. The major 1947 Geneva meeting was actually an elaborate conference divided into several major parts, including preparation of a charter for a major international trade institution, the ITO, and negotiating the GATT 1947 as a multilateral agreement to reciprocally reduce tariffs. The basic idea was that the ITO would be the organization, and the GATT 1947 would be a specialized agreement as part of the ITO, and depend on the ITO for institutional support such as decisions, dispute settlement, membership obligations, etc. The general clauses of the draft GATT 1947 imposed obligations on nations to refrain from a variety of trade-impeding measures. These clauses had evolved in US bilateral trade agreements, and were seen as necessary to protect the value of any tariff-reducing obligations.[4]

At the end of the Geneva Conference in November 1947, a complete draft of the GATT 1947 (with its many schedules of 'tariff bindings')[5] was basically complete, but the charter for a new organization needed more work. This added work was scheduled for a conference in March 1948, and only at this Havana Conference was the ITO Charter draft completed. Much of the GATT 1947 text was drawn from the ITO Charter's chapter on trade. The GATT 1947 trade rules were designed to be changed later to conform to the comparable rules as they emerged in the final ITO Charter after Havana, once the ITO came into effect. Although the ITO Charter was submitted to governments for ratification, and by the US President to Congress, the

---

[2] The documents are mostly part of the UN document series labeled EPCT, Preparatory Committee of the UN Conference on Trade and Employment. See Jackson, *World Trade and the Law of GATT*, above fn 1, at app E, 901–12, for an explanation and list of the document series.

[3] For an article-by-article presentation of relevant interpretive documents, see A Porges, et al (eds), *Analytical Index: Guide to GATT Law and Practice, General Agreement on Tariffs and Trade*, 6th revised edn (Geneva: WTO, 1995).

[4] For example, if a tariff commitment for a maximum 10 per cent tariff charge were made, a country might nevertheless decide to use a quantitative restriction to prevent imports and thus would evade the trade-liberalizing effect of the tariff commitment.

[5] A 'binding' in a country's tariff schedule is an obligation under Article II GATT 1947 not to apply a tariff higher than the number stated in the binding, on imports of the product described in the binding. Large trading countries will have 10,000 or more bindings.

Congress would not act. Finally at the end of 1951, the President's office announced that the attempt to obtain approval of the ITO was abandoned.

Although other countries could have gone ahead, at this time the US was a preeminent economic power in the world, having emerged from the war largely unscathed. No country desired to enter an ITO that did not include the US. The irony was that it had been the US that had taken the principal initiative to develop the ITO Charter in the first place.

Since the GATT 1947, including its various tariff obligations, was completed by October 1947 as the Geneva Conference drew to a close, many negotiators believed that the GATT 1947 should be brought into force without waiting for the ITO. The solution agreed upon was the adoption of the Protocol of Provisional Application (PPA),[6] to apply the GATT 1947 treaty 'provisionally on and after 1 January 1948'. The Protocol contained two important clauses that altered the impact of the GATT 1947 itself. The first reduced the time required for withdrawal. This, however, was not particularly meaningful, given that withdrawal from the GATT 1947 was not a very viable option in practical terms, at least for any major participant.

The more important impact of the PPA, however, was its statement of the manner of implementing the GATT 1947. Parts I and III of the GATT 1947 are fully implemented without a PPA exception, but the PPA called for implementation of Part II 'to the fullest extent not inconsistent with existing legislation'. Part I contained the most-favoured-nation (MFN) provision and the tariff concession obligations, while Part III was mainly procedural. Part II (Articles III to XXIII) contained most of the principal substantive obligations including those relating to customs procedures, quotas, subsidies, antidumping duties, and national treatment. As to these important obligations, each GATT Contracting Party was entitled to 'grandfather rights' for any provision of its legislation that existed when it became a party, and that was otherwise inconsistent with a Part II obligation.

Many of these Part II obligations, especially those concerning national treatment, involved obligations that relate to domestic regulatory and other measures which reach deeply into national 'sovereignty'. These rules reflect the recognition by diplomatic negotiators that such internal measures could often be used to undermine the obligations relating to border measures (tariffs, quotas, customs procedures, etc), and therefore must be subjected to rule disciplines to prevent this. In later years of the GATT 1947, these internal 'non-tariff barriers' (NTBs) became an increasingly more significant danger to trade liberalization than border measures.

This provisional and grandfather exception allowed most governments, which would otherwise need to submit the GATT 1947 for legislative approval, to approve the PPA by executive or administrative authority without going to their legislatures. It was understood that after the ITO Charter had later been submitted to legislatures,

---

[6] *Protocol of Provisional Application of the General Agreement on Tariffs and Trade*, 55 UNTS 308 (1947).

the GATT 1947 would also be submitted for 'definitive' application. Although subsequent attempts were made to obtain 'definitive' application of the GATT 1947, none succeeded. Thus, even until nearly the end of the GATT 1947's existence, one could witness reliance on grandfather rights to justify certain national actions regarding international trade.[7] This legal context was an important part of the US bargaining position in the Tokyo Round (1973–1979) negotiations[8] and was also a central issue in some GATT panel proceedings.[9] Gradually many of the grandfather rights, however, became extinct. New legislation did not qualify for this PPA exception, and some of the old provisions passed out of existence, or for other reasons became nonoperative or were superseded. One of the features of the WTO is the elimination of any generalized idea of grandfather rights, although one or two are probably represented by some specific new obligations and exceptions.

III. GATT FILLS THE VACUUM: 47 YEARS OF PROVISIONAL APPLICATION

A major hole was left in the fabric intended for post-World War II international economic institutions because the ITO did not come into being. It was only natural that the GATT 1947 would find its role changing dramatically as nations turned to it as the forum in which an increasing number of problems of their trading relationships would be handled. More countries became Contracting Parties. Because of the fiction that the GATT 1947 was not an 'international organization', there was considerable reluctance at first to delegate any activity even to a committee. Gradually that reluctance faded, and soon there was even an 'intercessional committee' that met between sessions of the Contracting Parties.

No Secretariat existed for the GATT 1947. After Havana, however, an Interim Commission for the International Trade Organization (ICITO) was set up, in the typical pattern of preparing the way for a new international organization. A small staff was assembled to prepare the ground for the ITO, and this staff serviced the needs of the GATT 1947. As years passed and it became clear that the ITO was never to come into being, this staff found that all of its time was devoted to the GATT 1947, and as such it became *de facto* the GATT Secretariat (technically as a kind of a

---

[7] See E Vermulst and M Hansen, 'The GATT Protocol of Provisional Application: A Dying Grandfather?' 1987 *Columbia Journal of Transnational Law* 27(2) 263.

[8] See Jackson, *The World Trading System*, above fn 1, at Chapter 11, 279–303.

[9] GATT Panel Report, *The US Manufacturing Clause*.

'leased' group, whereby the GATT Contracting Parties 'reimbursed' the ICITO for the costs of the Secretariat).

By the mid 1950s, the GATT Contracting Parties began to prepare the GATT 1947 to play the role it was assuming as the central international institution for trade. They attempted (and only partly succeeded) to amend the GATT 1947, and also drafted a new organizational charter for an Organization for Trade Cooperation (OTC), which also failed to get approval. The GATT Contracting Parties then cautiously took a decision in 1960 to establish a 'Council' without any explicit treaty language and somewhat departing from the original political constraints against viewing the GATT 1947 as an international organization. The Council became the principal permanent institution for the GATT 1947, and increasingly shouldered the burden of directing it.

Thus, the GATT 1947 limped along for nearly fifty years with almost no basic constitution designed to regulate its organizational activities and procedures. Even so, the GATT 1947 by any fair definition must be deemed to have been a *de facto* international organization. Through trial and error, it evolved some fairly elaborate procedures for conducting its business. That it could do so, despite the flawed basic documents on which it had to build, is a tribute to the pragmatism and ingenuity of many of its leaders over the years.

In fact, the GATT 1947 can be praised for its considerable success, certainly beyond what could be predicted by its flawed origins. Within several decades, by 1970, the GATT 1947, with its series of seven major trade negotiations,[10] had succeeded in bringing about dramatic reductions in tariffs in the world, at least as to manufactured products imported into advanced industrial countries. By this time however, it was apparent that tariffs were no longer the major problem for trade liberalization. A plethora (some say thousands)[11] of NTBs were creating many problems for trade. The seventh trade negotiation, the Tokyo Round (1973–1979), was the first to focus on NTBs and resulted in a major expansion of the activity and competence of the GATT. This was not, however, done by amendment to the GATT 1947 treaty text because it was generally assumed that the treaty amendment requirements were too difficult to be practical. Instead the negotiators developed a series of separate instruments, sometimes called 'codes', each of which was technically a stand-alone treaty. These codes addressed a number of non-tariff measures that distort international trade

---

[10]   The dates and locations are as follows: 1947 at Geneva, 1949 at Annecy, 1951 at Torquay, 1956 at Geneva, 1960–1961 at Geneva (Dillon Round), 1964–1967 at Geneva (Kennedy Round), and 1973–1979 at Geneva (Tokyo Round).

[11]   See Jackson, *The World Trading System*, above fn 1, at 154, for a list of over 800. Some governments have been compiling annual lists, such as Japan, (Industrial Structure Council METI, *2005 Report on the WTO Inconsistency of Trade Policies by Major Trading Partners*, Tokyo 2005), the US (United States Trade Representative, *2005 National Trade Estimate Report on Foreign Trade Barriers*, at <http://www.ustr.gov/Document_Library/Reports_Publications/2005/2005_NTE_Report/Section_Index.html>) (last visited 12 May 2008), and the European Union (*Market Access Database*, at <http://www.mkaccdb.eu.int/mkaccdb2/indexPubli.htm> (last visited 12 May 2008).

flows, such as valuation methods, anti-dumping duties, government procurement regulations, the use of product standards to restrain imports, etc.[12]

During the Kennedy Round period (1962–1967), the GATT Contracting Parties adopted an amendment to the GATT 1947 general clauses, which was the last such 'true' GATT 1947 amendment. A protocol to add Part IV to the GATT 1947, dealing with problems of developing countries, was approved in 1965 and came into force in 1966.[13] Articles 36, 37, and 38 of this Part are primarily expressions of goals, and impose few if any concrete obligations. Nevertheless, this language has been relied on in legal and policy argumentation in the GATT 1947, and has had considerable influence. Many other institutional innovations that enabled the GATT 1947 to play its vacuum-filling role as the major international trade institution were also put in place without explicit treaty text authority.

IV. The Uruguay Round and the Birth of the WTO

The eighth and last of the major trade 'rounds' under the GATT 1947 umbrella was the Uruguay Round, launched at Punta del Este, Uruguay, in 1986, and finally concluded at a ministerial level final negotiating conference in Marrakesh, Morocco, in April 1994. This round was clearly the largest and most complex of all the GATT 1947 trade rounds, and probably the largest and most complex economic multilateral treaty negotiation in history. Its final text is approximately 26,000 pages long. Most of these pages are detailed schedules of concessions and obligations, but about 1,000 pages consist of reasonably dense and complex general treaty norms. The conclusion of the Uruguay Round was several times delayed, but surprisingly (to some at least) ended on a very high note with success for most of the subjects taken up. If half of the original aspirations for the Uruguay Round agenda were successful, that in itself would have been the largest conclusion of any of the GATT 1947 rounds. Many observers felt that the Uruguay Round was over 80 per cent successful.

A key measure of the round was the establishment of a new international organization, the WTO, which in fact had not been included in the original Punta Declaration of the negotiating agenda, but only rose to a high priority late in the negotiation. This

[12] JH Jackson, 'The Great 1994 Sovereignty Debate: United States Acceptance and Implementation of the Uruguay Round Results' 1998 *Columbia Journal of Transnational Law* 36(1–2) 157, at 165.

[13] *Protocol Amending the GATT to Introduce a Part IV on Trade and Development*, GATT, BISD 13 Supp 2 (1965).

turn of attention clearly was partly a result of the views of the negotiators who began to realize that the Uruguay Round results were so extensive and in some respects competence-extending, that a new institutional framework would be essential for the successful implementation of the substance. The Marrakesh text was submitted to governments for ratification, and sufficient acceptances occurred for the treaty to enter into force on 1 January 1995.

Apart from the new WTO organization, the Uruguay Round for the first time introduced intellectual property (IP) and services trade into the trade treaty system. Previously, the GATT 1947 only applied to goods ('products'), but in the early 1980s groups interested in intellectual property and services trade, respectively, advocated to their governments to include these subjects in the Uruguay Round agenda. To some extent, this represented not only a view that these subjects were becoming increasingly important (services representing for some countries a larger share of GDP than products)[14] but also that that these were beginning to be affected by various troublesome governmental measures to limit competition from foreign sources. There was a growing recognition that IP and services needed international treaty rules and that therefore a treaty application structure was essential for such rules to be worthwhile. The groups viewed the evolving dispute settlement rules of the GATT 1947 as admirable in their assistance to the effectiveness of the trade rules.

Certain other features of the Uruguay Round were also highly significant. For example, the Uruguay Round negotiators established a policy that the negotiations should result in a treaty that would be a 'single undertaking' or 'single package'. This meant that all participants in the negotiations who wished to become members of the new organization and participants in the Uruguay Round treaty norms, would be required to accept all the obligations of the massive treaty complex. This contrasted sharply with the approach of the Tokyo Round (1973–1979) that established a series of separate texts or 'codes' on various key subjects, which were in theory each 'stand alone' treaties allowing each government (GATT Contracting Parties) to decide which (if any) it would accept. This has been referred to as 'GATT *à la carte*'. The Uruguay Round result provided for a few exceptions to this single package approach, but mostly upheld the notion that all governments were required to accept almost all of the texts in the new treaty.

Like their predecessors in the Tokyo Round, the Uruguay Round negotiators felt that the GATT 1947 was too difficult to amend, so an interesting feature in the transition from the GATT 1947 to the WTO institutional structure was the technique of 'getting from here to there'. The WTO was constituted as an entirely new legal institution, this time a true 'international organization' with various treaty-based, institutional clauses including 'Members' rather than 'Contracting Parties'. The GATT 1947 was therefore ended as such, by the formal (or informal) withdrawal of

---

[14]   See Jackson, *The World Trading System,* above fn 1, at 306.

all GATT Contracting Parties.[15] However the 'GATT 1994' treaty text still exists, but now as Annex 1A to the WTO Agreement.

The subject of trade in agricultural products was particularly troublesome not only during the Uruguay Round negotiations, but also throughout the history of the GATT 1947. A variety of causes explain this difficulty, but among the most significant has been the long-run increase in productivity in the agricultural sector, so that a steady migration from rural to urban jobs and living circumstances has occurred. In the US, in 1880 approximately 44 per cent of the population lived and worked on farmland, but by 1995 this percentage was less than 2 per cent.[16] There has been a somewhat similar development in many other societies, particularly in Europe. Europeans also, in the immediate post-World War II period, had vivid memories of food shortages, and thus were determined to develop policies that ensured a sustainable supply of food.[17] These and other factors caused intense internal domestic support for protection against agricultural imports.

Largely unsuccessful attempts were made in the Tokyo Round to develop a trade rule discipline for agriculture.[18] In the Uruguay Round some headway was made with rules and negotiating principles including some phase-in provisions for norms that would discipline both barriers to 'market access' and subsidies (including those for export). These issues, however, are still quite central to plans for current (and later) negotiations.

Ever since the WTO came into force, Members have realized the necessity for new negotiations on a wide spectrum of WTO rules, in order to fill gaps left by the Uruguay Round but also to better tune the WTO system to cope with rapid economic and other changes in the world. Whether the new negotiation should be a 'round' or simply an 'agenda' for further work has been disputed, but in effect the world is using the term 'new round'. This would then become the first 'WTO round' or the ninth 'WTO-GATT' round. But the route to this destination has been extraordinarily laboured.

The highest-level body of the WTO is its Ministerial Conference (MC), which is mandated by the treaty to meet no less often than every two years. As of this writing (Fall 2007) there have been six MC meetings, the latest in December 2005 in Hong Kong. These conferences have become famous for troublesome protest activities in the streets, and also controversy about their policy directions.

The first WTO MC was at Singapore in December 1996. At this meeting, proposals were made to address some new issues (investment, labour, environment,

---

[15] The PPA only required a 60-day notice for withdrawal. It is not clear all took the necessary action, but in effect all GATT Contracting Parties became WTO Members.

[16] For 1880 data, see GT Kurian (ed), *Datapedia of the United States 1790–2000* (Lanham: Bernan Press, 2001). For 1995 data, see L Lobao and K Meyer, 'The Great Agricultural Transition: Crisis, Change, and Social Consequences of Twentieth Century US Farming' 2001 *Annual Review of Sociology* (27)103, at 108.

[17] See R Ackrill, *The Common Agricultural Policy* (Sheffield: Sheffield Academic Press, 2000), at 25.

[18] See TE Josling, *Agriculture in the GATT* (New York: St. Martin's Press, 1996), at 98–100.

competition policy) resulting mostly in measures to coordinate with other inter-national organizations (such as the International Labour Organization), or to study further. Likewise at the second MC in Geneva in 1998 similar issues were considered. It was at the third MC at Seattle in December 1999 when the WTO faced a heavy dose of street protest. Disagreement especially between the US and the EC prevented the negotiators from reaching an agreement on the future direction of the new organization. For some months thereafter the WTO embraced a work programme designed to redress some of the Seattle problems and to move forward.

The next MC was in Doha, Qatar, which turned out to occur only a month or so after the 9–11 disaster in New York City. Because of these circumstances, the Doha conference in November 2001 was heavily protected and consequently not as trou-bled by protest groups. Furthermore, the diplomatic leadership organized the Doha Conference with great attention to including key diplomats from all parts of the WTO membership, especially the developing world. This was partly a response to the criticisms at Seattle about the WTO's lack of transparency and inadequate par-ticipation by some Members' diplomats, who felt excluded. Prior GATT 1947 habits of often controlling 'Quad' meetings (US, EC, Japan, Canada) resulting in proposals that were then 'pushed' on the other GATT Contracting Parties were resented. The so-called 'Green Room' meetings (a small conference room at the WTO headquar-ters, which is adjacent to the Director-General's office) were also resented as allow-ing only selected Members to participate in some crucial decisions and negotiation preparations.

The Doha Ministerial Declarations seemed very progressive.[19] They established a work programme towards more negotiations, struggled about whether to entertain new subjects now called 'Singapore subjects' including investment and competition policy, and designated the ongoing activity to be a 'development round' to address many demands from developing countries. The Doha meeting contemplated a new set of negotiations that could be concluded in 2005, but which would be 'appraised' by an earlier MC held in Cancún, Mexico, in September 2004. This Cancún confer-ence, like Seattle, essentially failed. A tense confrontation developed with the newly organized 'G-20',[20] a group of 20 developing country Members making demands that challenged the richer WTO members, arguing against any Singapore issues, and demanding action to redress the harm that rich country agriculture policies were inflicting on many developing countries.

Shortly after Cancún, the principal EU diplomat termed the process and the WTO institution as 'medieval' and in urgent need of reform, while the US diplomat

---

[19] All Doha Ministerial Declarations and Decisions are available at <http://www.wto.org/english/thewto_e/minist_e/min01_e/min01_e.htm> (last visited 12 May 2008).

[20] The group included such countries as China, Brazil, and South Africa, and put pressure on the US, Europe, and Japan to reduce or eliminate their agriculture subsidies. The size of the group seemed to vary.

criticized the 'nay sayers' who prevented progress urged by the 'yay sayers'.[21] But tempers cooled, and considerable work went forward to develop positions that were considered at Hong Kong in December 2005. During 2006 and 2007, negotiations continued but by the summer of 2007 they were in deep trouble. As usual, agricultural issues were very troublesome and threatened to be a deal breaker. Other difficulties were also manifested, so that by Fall 2007 it was still unclear whether the Doha Round would totally fail, or result in minimal face-saving commitments only. As this is written, the world is still in a 'wait and see' mode regarding this negotiation. A failure of the round would very likely lead nations to turn to more dispute settlement cases, and to more regional preferential agreements.

V. WTO Legal and Institutional Structure

The WTO has a surprisingly complex institutional structure, no doubt influenced by the structure that was used for the negotiation of the Uruguay Round, but also responding to perceived problems of the GATT 1947, including its 'birth defects'. Here we will only briefly overview this complex structure and the reader is referred to other works for detail.[22] In addition, the all-important dispute settlement system is taken up in the next chapters, so it will not be detailed here.

A. The Uruguay Round Treaty Structure for the WTO

The Uruguay Round fundamentally overhauled the world trading institutional system. The GATT 1947 was terminated, and instead a new organization, the WTO, was established when the Uruguay Round treaty came into force on 1 January 1995. A beginning portion of that 26,000-page treaty is a brief 14-page text that establishes the WTO as a proper (no longer provisional) international organization. This portion of the long treaty is often called informally the 'WTO Charter' or 'WTO Agreement', but technically, the treaty is one entire unified document implementing the principle of a 'single undertaking'. The full text of the Uruguay Round agreement

---

[21] Comments of P Lamy, C Denny, et al, 'Brussels Urges Shakeup of "Medieval" WTO' *The Guardian* (16 September 2003); RB Zoellick, 'America Will Not Wait for the Won't-do Countries' *Financial Times* (22 September 2003).

[22] See citations, above fn 1; and other chapters in this Handbook.

is complex, and has many gaps as well as inconsistent provisions. This is partly the result of reluctance by the negotiators at late stages of the Uruguay Round negotiations, to permit the lawyers to do a 'legal scrub' to try to iron out such difficulties.

There are four annexes to the WTO Agreement. Three of the annexes and their contents are mandatory and all Members are bound by them. A fourth annex contains some optional treaty text. The outline of the annexes is as follows:

- Annex 1 contains most of the treaty pages. This annex is termed the 'Multilateral Agreements', which are mandatory substantive agreements. It is divided into three parts A, B and C.
  - Annex 1A consists of the GATT 1994 (distinguished from the GATT 1947) which includes the GATT 1947 treaty text (unchanged from when GATT 1947 existed) as amended towards the end of the GATT 1947. It also contains a number of newer texts, some derived from Tokyo Round side-agreements, and certain other 'understandings' and similar complementary documents. The most extensive part of Annex 1A is the elaborate tariff schedules (called 'bindings'), which mostly set maximum tariff commitments for each Member. Since the GATT 1947 text was not changed when incorporated into the WTO, there are provisions of GATT 1994 that are clearly superseded by other Uruguay Round treaty text. A brief text at the end of the WTO 'Charter' stipulates that if there is a conflict between the GATT 1994 and the various other texts (numbering dozens) in Annex 1A, the later shall prevail. This can present important interpretive problems, such as 'what is a conflict?'.
  - Annex 1B is the GATS and the schedules (much shorter than those for goods) for services commitments.
  - Annex 1C is the TRIPS Agreement.
- Annex 2 contains the DSU, a text of about twenty four pages which governs the dispute settlement procedures in some detail (compared to the dispute settlement provisions of the original GATT 1947, which consisted of about three paragraphs).
- Annex 3 contains the TRPM, a brief text designed to set up a structure of regularly scheduled institutional reviews of each Member's trade policies.
- Annex 4 contains agreements called 'Plurilateral' that are supposedly optional. This is the major explicit departure from the 'single undertaking' principle of the Uruguay Round. At the end of the Uruguay Round, there were four texts listed for Annex 4, but subsequently two relating to agriculture were terminated, so now there are two, namely a text on government procurement (which also has schedules of commitments), and a text on trade in civil aircraft. This annex could be a source of some dynamic flexibility for the WTO institution, but unfortunately the WTO Charter requires a 'consensus' of Members to add any new agreements to Annex 4,[23] a requirement that so far has been assumed not likely to be obtainable. On the other hand, in several accession negotiations, some existing Members

---

[23] Art X: 9 WTO Agreement.

have conditioned their support for the new Member on its willingness to accept a supposed 'optional' text in Annex 4. This has been the case particularly where accession protocols, like that of China, have stipulated that the government procurement text of Annex 4 be accepted by the new Member.[24]

Unlike the GATT 1947, the WTO Charter clearly establishes an international organization, endows it with legal personality, and supports it with the traditional treaty organizational clauses regarding 'privileges and immunities', Secretariat, Director-General (DG), budgetary measures, and explicit authority to develop relations with other inter-government organizations and, important to some interests, non-governmental organizations. The Charter prohibits staff of the Secretariat from seeking or accepting instructions from any government 'or any other authority external to the WTO'. The Secretariat 'rented' by the GATT 1947 became the WTO Secretariat.

There is strong indication in various parts of the WTO Charter of an intention to promote a sense of legal and practice continuity with the GATT 1947. For example, Article XVI:1 states that except as otherwise provided, the WTO and the Multilateral Trade Agreements shall 'be guided by the decisions, procedures and customary practices followed by [GATT 1947]'.

B. Institutional Structure

The governing structure of the WTO follows some of the GATT 1947 model, but also substantially departs from it. At the top there is a MC, which meets no less than every two years. Next there are not one, but four Councils. The General Council (GC) has overall supervisory authority, including responsibility for carrying out many of the functions of the MC between its sessions. In addition, however, there is a Council for each of the Annex 1 agreements, that is, for Goods, Services and Intellectual Property. Some Councils have established many committees for specific subjects. Overall there is some worry that the WTO structure is too ponderous, sometimes requiring draft documents or reports to work through various levels of attention before coming to a final decision.

A Dispute Settlement Body (DSB) is established to supervise and implement the dispute settlement rules in Annex 2. Likewise there is a TPRM Body for the Trade Policy Review Mechanism (Annex 3). The membership of each of these Councils and bodies is open to any WTO Member.[25] A number of the poorer countries of the

---

[24] See *Accession of the People's Republic of China: Decision of 10 November 2001*, WT/L/432 (23 November 2001); N. Lardy, *Integrating China into the Global Economy* (Washington, DC: Brookings Institution Press, 2002), at 101–02.

[25] A list of all 153 WTO Members is available at <http://www.wto.org/english/thewto_e/whatis_e/tif_e/org6_e.htm> (last visited 3 June 2008).

world feel they lack the resources to establish a 'mission' in Geneva for WTO representation. Also many WTO Members conduct their WTO representation from a general Geneva-based national mission for international organizations. With the enormous increase in WTO activity and meetings, such limited missions are clearly stretched, sometimes having only one or two persons who can devote attention to the WTO. The US mission has approximately sixteen officials and diplomats, and the mission of the EU Commission has about thirteen.

C. WTO Decision-Making

Since the GATT 1947 was not viewed as an organization, it is not surprising that it said little about decision-making. Article XXV GATT 1947 called for one-nation one-vote and decision by a majority of votes cast, unless otherwise provided. This GATT 1947 treaty language is remarkably broad. Although cautiously utilized (at least in the early years), it was the basis for much GATT activity. Most efforts in the GATT 1947 were accomplished through a process of negotiation and compromise, with varying degrees of formality and a tacit understanding that agreement was necessary among countries with important economic influence. In fact, a 'consensus' approach gradually began to be imperative for much of the activity, even though the word consensus does not occur in the GATT 1947 text—this, too, is changed in the WTO, with explicit reference to and definition of 'consensus'.

The GATT 1947 also had measures specifying the procedure and votes for amending the agreement and for adopting waivers. The WTO Agreement substantially changes all of this and contains an elaborate matrix of decision-making procedures, with important constraints around them. Basically there are five different techniques for making decisions or formulating new or amended rules of trade policy: decisions on various matters, 'interpretations', waivers, amendments to the agreements, and, finally, negotiation of new agreements. A variety of non-majority principles are applied, including consensus, but also super-majority requirements such as Article IX:2 WTO Agreement for the Members to make a definitive 'interpretation' of some Uruguay Round text. This requires a vote of three-fourths of the membership (not just those present). Treaty amendment requires—depending on the text— normally a two-thirds vote but will not bind those not voting to approve, unless the vote is three-fourths. Even in that case, there is provision for a hold-out Member to withdraw from the organization or negotiate a special dispensation. Since withdrawal by certain key Members would probably end the WTO's effectiveness, such key Members effectively have a veto regarding amendments.

In addition, it is important to understand the potential of the dispute settlement procedures, including panel and Appellate Body reports, for bringing about change or evolution in the trade rules, as can be seen in later chapters of this Handbook.

VI. The Trial and Error Pragmatic History of the GATT Dispute Settlement System and the Uruguay Round Makeover

Looking back over the 1946–1994 history of the GATT 1947 allows one to reflect on how surprising it was that this relatively feeble institution with many 'birth defects' managed to play such a significant role for almost five decades. It certainly was far more successful than could have been fairly predicted in the late 1940s.[26] This success must surely be a consequence of a strong perception about the need for an international trade institution widely recognized among nation-states. Other chapters in this Handbook provide excellent depth and detail about the WTO dispute settlement system, but here the focus is on the broad characteristics and general international relations implication of that system.

World economic developments pushed the GATT 1947 to a central role during the period from 1950 to 1990. The growing economic interdependence of the world was increasingly commented upon. Events that occur halfway around the world have a powerful influence on the other side of the globe. Armed conflict and social unrest in the Middle East affect the farmers in Iowa and France and the auto-workers in Michigan and Germany.

In this context, the GATT 1947 evolved and developed its dispute settlement mechanism. It is fair to say that this mechanism was quite successful. It was also flawed, due in part to the troubled beginnings of the GATT 1947. Yet these procedures worked better than expected, and arguably better than most other international dispute procedures. A number of interesting policy questions are raised by the experience of the procedure, not the least of which is the question about what should be the fundamental objective of the system: to solve the instant dispute (by conciliation, obfuscation, power-threats, or otherwise), or to promote certain longer-term systemic goals such as predictability and stability of interpretations of treaty text.

Even though some argued that the purpose of the GATT dispute settlement mechanism was merely to facilitate negotiations designed to reach a settlement, the original intention was for the GATT 1947 to be placed in the institutional setting of an ITO. Although the ITO Charter (which never came into force) would have established a rather elaborate dispute settlement procedure, the GATT 1947 had only a few paragraphs devoted to this subject.

---

[26] See JH Jackson, 'Dispute Settlement and the WTO: Emerging Problems' 1998 *Journal of International Economic Law* 1(3) 329.

Originally, the key to invoking the GATT dispute-settlement mechanism was almost always the Article XXIII GATT 1947 language 'nullification or impairment',[27] an unfortunately ambiguous phrase, and one that might connote either a 'power' or a 'negotiation'-oriented approach. It was neither sufficient nor necessary to find a breach of an obligation under this language, although later practice made doing so important. An early case in the GATT defined the nullification or impairment phrase as including actions by a Contracting Party that harmed the trade of another, and which 'could not reasonably have been anticipated...' by the other at the time it negotiated for a concession.[28] Thus the concept of 'reasonable expectations' was introduced, which is almost a contract-type concept.[29] But even this elaboration is ambiguous, and perhaps faulty.

At the beginning of GATT 1947's history, disputes were generally taken up by diplomatic procedures. At first they were dealt with at semi-annual meetings of the Contracting Parties. Later they would be brought to an 'intercessional committee' of the Contracting Parties, and even later were delegated to a working party set up to examine either all disputes, or only particular disputes brought to the GATT 1947.

However, around 1955 a major shift in the procedure occurred, largely because of the influence of the then DG Eric Wyndham-White. It was decided that rather than use a 'working party' composed of nations (so that each nation could designate the person who would represent it, subject to that government's instructions), a dispute would be referred to a 'panel' of experts. The three or five experts would be specifically named and were to act in their own capacities and not as representatives of any government. This development, it can be argued, represented a major shift from a 'negotiating' atmosphere of multilateral diplomacy, to an increasingly more juridical procedure designed to arrive impartially at the truth of the facts and the best interpretation of the law. Almost all subsequent dispute procedures in the GATT context (and the new WTO) have contemplated the use of a panel in this fashion.[30]

In 1962 an important case was brought by Uruguay, alleging that various practices of certain industrial countries violated their GATT 1947 obligations. The Panel grappled with the language of Article XXIII that called for 'nullification or impairment'

[27] An action may also be brought under Art XXIII GATT 1947 when the attainment of any objective of the agreement is being impeded.
[28] GATT Contracting Parties, *Australia - Ammonium Sulphate*. This case is sometimes called the *Marbury v Madison* of the GATT 1947; see RE Hudec, 'Retaliation Against Unreasonable Foreign Trade Practices' 1975 *Minnesota Law Review* 59(3) 461; RE Hudec, *The GATT Legal System and World Trade Diplomacy* (Salem, NH: Butterworth Legal Publishers, 1990), at 159; RE Hudec, 'GATT or GABB? The Future Design of the General Agreement on Tariffs and Trade' 1971 *Yale Law Journal* 80(7) 1299, at 1341.
[29] GATT Contracting Parties, *Australia - Ammonium Sulphate*; GATT Contracting Parties, *Germany - Imports of Sardines*. Both reports endorse the view that the GATT 1947 should be construed to protect 'reasonable expectations' of the Contracting Parties. See Hudec, *The GATT Legal System*, above fn 28, at 164, 167.
[30] *Understanding Regarding Notification, Consultation, Dispute Settlement and Surveillance* BISD 26S/210 (28 November 1979), especially at paras 10B21.

as the basis of a complaint, but it decided to push the jurisprudence beyond the language, and determined in its report that any 'violation' of the GATT 1947 would be considered a *prima facie* nullification or impairment',[31] which required a responding Contracting Party to carry the burden of proving that nullification or impairment did *not* exist. This case, followed by many subsequent GATT dispute panels, reinforced another shift in the focus of the cases towards the GATT 1947 treaty obligations, that is, in the direction of rule orientation. The panels still talked about the need to facilitate settlements and sometimes they acted like mediators. But in some cases occurring much later, panels that tried too much to 'mediate' were criticized for compromising issues without developing more precise and analytical 'legal' approaches.[32]

A Tokyo Round Understanding (1979) described the procedures of the GATT dispute settlement, noting the requirement of consultation as the first step, and providing explicit recognition of a conciliation role for the GATT DG (almost never utilized). If these steps did not result in a settlement, then there was provision for a panel process, established on decision of the Contracting Parties usually acting through their Council of Representatives. There was some ambiguity about whether the complaining party had a right to a panel process. If the process went forward, there was provision for oral and written advocacy from the disputants, and a written report by the panel. The Understanding reinforced the concept of the *prima facie* nullification or impairment and permitted the use of non-government persons for panels while stating a preference for government officials.

The procedure under the GATT was for a panel to make its report and deliver it to the Council. The practice then became firmly established that if the Council approved the report by consensus, it became binding. If the Council did not approve it, then the report would not have a binding status. The problem was consensus. It meant that the Contracting Party that lost before the panel and might otherwise be obligated to follow the panel's findings, could block the Council action by raising objections to the consensus. Thus, the losing party to the dispute could avoid the consequences of its loss. This 'blocking' was deemed to be the most significant defect in the GATT dispute settlement process.

In the 1980s, as the procedures became more legally precise and juridical in nature, there developed the idea that there were two types of cases: the violation cases (based on the *prima facie* concept), and certain 'non-violation' cases, which were cases not

---

[31] GATT Panel Report, *Uruguayan Recourse to Article XXIII*. The *prima facie* concept was also applied in situations involving quotas or domestic subsidies on products subject to agreed upon tariff limitations (tariffs bound under Article II). See generally Jackson, *World Trade and the Law of GATT*, above fn 1, at 182.

[32] See GATT Panel Report, *French Assistance to Exports of Wheat and Wheat Flour*; GATT Panel Report, *Spain – Soyabean Oil*; GATT Analytical Index, above fn 3, at 171 (explaining several Contracting Parties' criticism of the Spanish Oil Panel's conclusion that the term 'like products' meant 'more or less the same product').

involving a violation, but nevertheless alleging 'nullification or impairment'. In fact, the non-violation cases have been relatively few in the history of GATT 1947 and the WTO, only about four cases of this type out of a total of several hundred cases.[33] Nevertheless, some of these non-violation cases have been quite important.[34]

Many of the agreements resulting from the Tokyo Round negotiations (the 'side agreements') included special procedures devoted to the settlement of disputes relating to a particular agreement. Some of these closely followed the traditional GATT procedure, and unfortunately they utilized the language 'nullification or impairment'. In a few cases, special 'expert' groups have been called into the process to handle highly technical problems involving such things as scientific judgments.

A 1989 GATT panel (known as the *Oilseeds* case) pushed the *prima facie* concept a heroic step further, by deciding that the responding nation could not in that case rebut the presumption of 'nullification or impairment'. The *Oilseeds* case may perhaps be a high water mark of violation-based GATT dispute settlement, since it arguably reverses the treaty language by stating that a *prima facie* case cannot be rebutted. This makes the presumption of nullification or impairment derive *ipso facto* from a violation, thus almost discarding the nullification or impairment concept in favour of a focus on whether or not a violation or breach of obligation exists.

The GATT jurisprudence was thus brought almost full circle by the evolutionary case-by-case process of the procedure. However, before one accepts completely this conclusion, it must be said that it is not clear if the implications of the *Oilseeds* case— non-rebuttability—will be pursued in the future, since the language of the Article 3.8 DSU continues the phraseology of the 1979 Understanding, stating that measures found inconsistent with GATT obligations are *prima facie* findings of nullification and impairment and can be rebutted.

The GATT dispute settlement process still had a number of problems, mostly due to its flawed origins described in a prior section. These flaws included:

- Sparse language with little detail about goals or procedures.
- Imprecise power of the Contracting Parties concerning supervision of the dispute settlement process, leading to the practice of requiring consensus for many decisions which gave rise to 'blocking' defects.
- The first blocking potential could occur at the time of the request for a panel procedure by a complaining party; the defendant sometimes would block this decision, although by about the mid 1980s such a blocking vote became diplomatically very difficult to use.
- The second and more serious blocking problem would occur at the time the GATT Council (or a committee for one of the Tokyo Round side agreement procedures) would be asked to 'adopt' a panel report. As mentioned above, the losing party

---

[33]   See Jackson, Davey, and Sykes, above fn 1, at 287–88.
[34]   GATT Panel Report, *EEC – Oilseeds*.

could object, defeat the consensus, and thus block the adoption of the report. During the 1980s, various attempts to fix this problem were proposed, but none succeeded.

• Because there were separate dispute settlement procedures in various Tokyo Round side agreements, dispute settlement procedures were fragmented and disputes would occur over which procedure to use.

• There had been several unfortunate instances of a Contracting Party's government interfering with potential panel decisions by inappropriately pressuring a particular panelist.

When one reflects on the almost 50 years of pre-WTO history of the GATT dispute settlement process, some generalizations seem both apparent and quite remarkable. With very meager treaty language as a start, combined with diverging alternative views about the policy goals of the system, the GATT, like so many human institutions, took on a life of its own. Both as to the dispute procedures (a shift from 'working parties' to 'panels'), and as to the substantive focus of the system (a shift from general ambiguous ideas about 'nullification or impairment', to more analytical or 'legalistic' approaches to interpret treaty obligations), the GATT panel procedure evolved towards more rule orientation.

The Uruguay Round results, of course, apply the new DSU procedures to those subjects. Not all of the GATT problems have been solved, but the DSU measurably improves the dispute procedures:[35]

1. It establishes a unified dispute settlement system for all parts of the GATT/WTO system, including for the new subjects of services and IP. Thus, controversies over which procedure to use will likely not occur.

2. It clarifies that all parts of the Uruguay Round legal text relevant to the matter at issue and argued by the parties, can be considered in a particular case.

3. It reaffirms and clarifies the right of a complaining government to have a panel process initiated, preventing blocking at that stage.

4. It establishes a 'reverse consensus' rule for adopting panel reports, which results in almost automatic adoption with no chance for blocking.[36] However, an appeal can be made prior to adoption.

5. It establishes a unique new appellate procedure, which substitutes for some of the former procedures of Council approval of a panel report. If appealed, the dispute goes to an appellate 'division' of three members of the Appellate Body. After the Appellate Body division has ruled, its report goes to the DSB. The report will be deemed adopted unless there is a consensus against adoption; any major objector can defeat such negative consensus. The presumption is thus reversed, compared

---

[35] See also chapters 11–16 of this Handbook.

[36] Reverse consensus means that the matter is adopted unless there is consensus against adoption. Since such consensus against adoption is defeatable by any Member, the disputing Member who 'won' can prevent a blocking vote.

to the previous procedures. Ultimately, the appellate report will come into force as a matter of law in virtually every case. The opportunity for a losing party to block adoption of a panel report is no longer available.

The DSU is designed to provide a single unified dispute settlement procedure for almost all the Uruguay Round texts. However, some potential disparities remain. For example, parties to each of the plurilateral agreements (Annex 4) may make a decision regarding dispute settlement procedures and how the DSU shall apply (or not apply). In addition, another DSU appendix specifies exceptions for certain listed texts. The goal of uniformity of dispute settlement procedures may not be 100 per cent achieved. Actual practice will determine to what degree this may be a problem.

Despite the mentioned various difficulties about the WTO dispute settlement system, it is remarkably well received and supported by Members' diplomats, political leaders and business interests. Polling also shows considerable citizen approval. There are hundreds of ideas for changes but only a few have gained sufficient support to suggest action. Indeed, in at least one appraisal of the WTO dispute settlement system (part of an overall appraisal of the institutional aspect of the WTO) an expert group stated with regard to ideas for reform or improvement that the most important principle is to 'do no harm'.[37]

VII. Perceptions, Implications, and Conclusions

The evolution of the GATT and the WTO embodies a fascinating and possibly unique story of human institutional development to cope with serious international problems, currently focused in many ways on the risks, dangers, and opportunities associated with the ambiguous term 'globalization'.

The key to this story is the interplay of general diplomatic-political processes with the evolution of a remarkable juridical institution of dispute settlement. The conscious task of the diplomats creating the GATT and much later the WTO to severely limit the power of the new institution and its decision-making authority, coupled with the necessary development of a dispute settlement process to cope with the many interpretive problems of the lengthy and elaborate treaty text, has led to a certain tension between these two sides of the new organization.

---

[37] Consultative Board, *The Future of the WTO: Addressing Institutional Challenges in the New Millennium* (Geneva: WTO, 2004).

As we have seen, the decision-making and policy implementation procedures are very constrained, while the dispute settlement system became very powerful. It is probably the most powerful international tribunal type procedure with broad multilateral large world membership and broad subject-matter competence. With this 'policy tension' between different parts of the WTO, those participating diplomats and political leaders understandably look at the dispute settlement system as a means to achieve some success in implementing desired policy outcomes, especially in situations where the diplomatic/political side of the WTO seems unable to take action. This can lead to weighty matters being brought to the dispute settlement system for which it may be ill-prepared and ill-resourced.

Nevertheless, overall the WTO dispute settlement system is recognized as a great success, albeit somewhat defective (as are all human institutions). It is also the case, in the view of this observer, that juridical institutions are now more often seen by many official and unofficial participants in international affairs, as increasingly very necessary to the successful long-term evolution of many international institutions. The more than 60 years secular evolution of the GATT-WTO towards greater 'rule orientation' is a central feature of the history of this international economic activity.

The large measure of compliance with DSB reports is also significant in reinforcing the views of many officials and non-officials that the WTO dispute settlement system has been remarkably successful in the difficult tasks imposed upon it.[38] But, as other chapters of this Handbook excellently give witness, there are many other success stories to tell about various parts of the WTO (as well as some failures). The WTO as an institution must be understood also in the complex context of general institutional affairs, with the risks of wars and economic failures ever present.

Traditional subjects of international law have weaknesses in their fundamental or basic propositions that create problems in the challenging world of today. Treaty rigidity and the basic difficulties and defects of developing customary international law are examples. In addition, consent theory often does not adequately assist in the process of resolving differences about the extent of legitimacy for international norms. Treaty interpretation often becomes situated in the crossfire of tensions between objectives aimed at enhancing the efficiency and capability of necessary international action on the one hand, and the desire of national government officials or constituents to preserve prerogatives, privileges, economic or other benefits, or even meritorious 'policy space' to carry out measures designed to implement a society's chosen policy preferences, on the other hand. Many more complexities of the 'devilish detail' of the operation of international law norms could be noted.

Because of the broad extent and growing abundance of practice and jurisprudence in the areas of international economic activity, international economic law is a worthy subject of study in connection with the broader policy and theoretical

---

[38] Ibid.

tensions outlined in the previous paragraphs and in this chapter. With a remarkably extensive production of adopted DSB reports, the WTO is the most elaborate repository of international economic law, practice and jurisprudence in the world today, and many of the challenges and criticisms of international law are manifested in that practice and jurisprudence. From this experience, a series of lessons can be drawn from international economic law. It can easily be seen that a number of those lessons are relevant to particular logical conundrums of international law. To some extent these practices provide empirical evidence to support criticisms of some of the traditional foundations of international law, generally.

Consider, for example, the history of the GATT 1947 and the WTO described earlier. The evolution of the GATT 1947 after the ITO failure, and the change of the GATT 1947 into the WTO, manifested a belief of many nations that an institutional structure was needed for international trade discourse and disciplining constraints on national behavior. Pragmatic accommodation, good practical sense, and important leadership led a weak 'birth defected' GATT 1947 to become an important part of the world's international economic institutional landscape.

Equality of nations seemed mandated by the GATT 1947 treaty text, but in fact the practice veered away from voting and its dilemmas, to 'consensus approach' decision-making developed by practice. The practice itself was carried more formally into the WTO, although such an approach has a potential for impeding progress on important issues. Consensus has important values, in promoting full participation and greater transparency for all levels and types of participating nations in the institution, but consensus rules can also block 'constitutional' progress. Problems of treaty rigidity clearly diminished the ability of the GATT 1947 to evolve satisfactorily with the rapidly changing economic environment of the world.

With regard to rule orientation, the objectives of predictability and stability (reducing the risk premium of economic decisions of millions of entrepreneurs) are important, and lead to support for a rule-oriented system, with dispute settlement procedures in a 'juridical' system. Even without explicit treaty rules about this, the GATT dispute settlement system evolved and was accepted by the nation-state participants. Treaty interpretation becomes an important part of the system, and requires an important juridical approach. Questions are developing about whether the traditional customary international law approaches to treaty interpretation such as those articulated in the Vienna Convention of the Law of Treaties, are adequate for application to treaties that have large membership and long duration and thus are more like constitutions than a simpler paradigm of bilateral or mini-lateral treaties.[39]

In order for the world to cope with the challenges of instant communication, fast and cheap transportation, combined with weapons of vast and/or mass destruction, that world will have to develop something considerably better than either the

[39] See Jackson, *Sovereignty, the WTO, and Changing Fundamentals of International Law*, above fn 1.

historical and discredited Westphalian concept of sovereignty, or even the current, but highly criticized, versions of sovereignty still often articulated. That 'something' is not yet well defined, but it can be called 'sovereignty-modern', which is currently more an analytic and dynamic process of disaggregation and redefinition than a frozen-in-time concept or technique.

Finally, a general perspective suggests that a key lesson of the last one hundred years is that international institutions (including juridical institutions) are critical and are here to stay. They will increasingly play a larger role in world and local affairs. This lesson is even more strongly reinforced by the events of 11 September 2001 and the years closely following that event. Clearly a fragmented nation-state sovereignty emphasis will not be able to cope with the world reality that has been imposed on this globe, nor will myopic wishfulness for hegemonic supremacy be workable.

The only sensible solution thus appears to be international institutional development, in a context of norms of varying strength from soft law norms (and soft power) to hard law norms and juridical institutions to effectuate them. Hopefully, the WTO, with its background of GATT history and evolution as *acquis communautaire* will assist this process of international institutional development.

SELECTED BIBLIOGRAPHY

JH Jackson, *World Trade and the Law of GATT* (Indianapolis: Bobbs-Merrill Co., 1969)

JH Jackson, *The Jurisprudence of GATT and the WTO: Insights on Treaty Law and Economic Relations* (New York: Cambridge University Press, 2000)

JH Jackson, *The World Trading System: Law and Policy of International Economic Relations*, 2nd edn (Cambridge, Mass.: MIT Press, 2002).

JH Jackson, 'Sovereignty – Modern: A New Approach to an Outdated Concept' 2003 *American Journal of International Law* 97(4) 782.

JH Jackson, *Sovereignty, the WTO and the Changing Fundamentals of International Law* (New York: Cambridge University Press, 2006)

JH Jackson, 'The World Trade Organization After Ten Years: The Role of the WTO in a Globalized World' 2006 *Current Legal Problems (59) 427*

JH Jackson, WJ Davey, and AO Sykes, *Legal Problems of International Economic Relations: Cases, Materials and Text on the National and International Regulation of Transnational Economic Relations*, 4th edn (St Paul, Minn.: West Group, 2002)

AF Lowenfeld, *International Economic Law* (Oxford: Oxford University Press, 2003)

M Matsushita, TJ Schoenbaum, and PC Mavroidis, *The World Trade Organization – Law, Practice, and Policy*, 2nd edn (Oxford: Oxford University Press, 2006)

G Sacerdoti, A Yanovich, and J Bohanes (eds), *The WTO at Ten: The Contribution of the Dispute Settlement System* (Cambridge: Cambridge University Press, 2006)

P Van Den Bossche, *Law and Policy of the World Trade Organization*, 2nd edn (Cambridge: Cambridge University Press, 2008)

CHAPTER 4

....

THE PLACE OF
THE WTO IN THE
INTERNATIONAL
SYSTEM

....

DONALD McRAE

I. Introduction

THE WTO is a treaty, or a collection of treaties, and at the same time an international organization. As a treaty, the WTO consists of legally binding rights and obligations between the parties and mechanisms for clarifying those rights and determining compliance or non-compliance. As an international organization, the WTO operates through various organs and plays a role internationally, giving it an identity that goes beyond the regulation of reciprocal rights and obligations under the treaties.

To some extent, this distinction between treaty and international organization is blurred. The treaty provisions define the scope of the international organization. It consists of a framework for a reciprocal exchange of obligations—in that sense it is contractual in nature. As an international organization, the WTO provides a framework for the rules regulating the international trading regime, and in this sense may seem more normative than contractual, perhaps even something constitutional. As an intergovernmental organization, the WTO is an international actor that interacts with other actors in the international system, including other international organizations both governmental and non-governmental. As a creature of international law it is also a body that interprets and applies international law, in particular the provisions of the WTO agreements themselves. As a result, the WTO plays a role in the broader field of international law.

This chapter considers the WTO as an international organization within the international system. The starting point from a legal perspective is relatively simple. The WTO is a treaty—an agreement between States under which they establish certain rights and obligations. As a legally binding agreement, it is itself a creature of international law. All of this should be self-evident. Yet the origin of the WTO, the way in which the international trading regime has been viewed by international lawyers, and the attitude of some of the active participants in the GATT 1947 and in the WTO towards the regime they have created, have made what might seem to be obvious less clear.

The predecessor to the WTO, the GATT 1947, was viewed as a 'contract' by its Contracting Parties and by their representatives to various GATT bodies. Lawyers played a minimal role in the operation of the GATT 1947 and were often seen as unnecessary.[1] This was notwithstanding the fact that the development of a quintessentially legal institution—a dispute settlement mechanism—was in fact one of the most important achievements of the GATT 1947 and over time the dispute settlement process became a central part of that *de facto* international organization. Moreover, the various negotiating rounds held under the auspices of the GATT 1947 were treaty-making processes—the formulation of agreed commitments to be embodied

---

[1] See, generally, RE Hudec, *Enforcing International Trade Law* (Salem, NH: Butterworth, 1993).

in legally binding instruments.[2] So, while GATT participants might have viewed law as irrelevant, in fact they were engaged in creating and applying international law.

The scepticism on the part of the trade policy community with regard to the contribution of law to their field was generally reciprocated by the international legal community, which largely ignored the GATT 1947 and more broadly the field of international trade law.[3] And today, while international legal scholars are paying more attention to international trade law and to the WTO, there is still a debate about how to view the WTO—in constitutional or other terms—and about the extent to which international law is relevant to what appears to be a self-contained regime.

Against this background, I will consider, first, the character of the WTO as a legal institution. Second, I will consider the inter-relationship between the WTO and other international institutions including other trading regimes, such as customs unions and free trade areas, and non-governmental organizations (NGOs). Third, I will discuss the broader role of the WTO as a participant in the application and development of international law. Finally, I shall consider whether the WTO can be viewed as something more than an international organization, having some kind of particular constitutional status.

II. The WTO as a Legal Institution

A formal description of the WTO in legal terms starts with its treaty basis—the Agreement establishing the World Trade Organization (WTO Agreement). The WTO Agreement, however, is essentially an institutional arrangement, providing the legal framework for the variety of agreements (the 'Multilateral Trade Agreements', and where relevant the 'Plurilateral Trade Agreements') that make up what is commonly referred to as the WTO.[4] The complexity is largely one of form—the bundling of a variety of agreements under a common institutional framework—but it does have substantive implications when the question arises of the relationship between the obligations under the various agreements. In this regard, the WTO agreements resemble less the loose arrangement of interrelated agreements of the UN system

---

[2] DM McRae and JC Thomas, 'The GATT and Multilateral Treaty-Making: The Tokyo Round' 1983 *American Journal of International Law* 77(1) 51.

[3] DM McRae, 'The Contribution of International Trade Law to the Development of International Law' 1996 *Recueil des Cours* (260) 103.

[4] See chapter 3 of this Handbook.

and more the complex network of difficult and different relationships constituted by the treaties that make up the EU.

There are no generally accepted criteria for determining at what point a treaty between States establishes an organization possessing 'international legal personality'.[5] The existence of legal personality depends on a variety of factors including the intention of the members in creating the organization,[6] the existence of an organ or organs distinct from the organization's members and the existence of functions and responsibilities at the international level residing in the organization or its organs. While there may have been some doubt about the GATT 1947 in respect of these criteria,[7] the WTO undoubtedly meets them.

A. The Intention of the WTO Members

The intention of the WTO Members with respect to legal personality is found in Article VIII:1 WTO Agreement, which provides:

The WTO shall have legal personality, and shall be accorded by each of its Members such legal capacity as is necessary for the exercise of its functions.

This provision has two elements. It is a statement about the legal personality of the organization as well as a direction to Members to provide the necessary capacity to the WTO to carry out its functions. Thus, the first element can be understood as a statement about objective legal personality—a statement about international legal personality—and the second element can be seen as a statement about the way the organization is to be treated by its Members, presumably about what has to be done under their domestic law to enable the organization to carry out its functions.

B. The Organs of the WTO

The WTO is composed of a Ministerial Conference (MC) and a plenary General Council (GC), which also fulfills the functions of the Dispute Settlement Body (DSB) and of the Trade Policy Review Body, albeit each with a separate chair. There are also Councils on trade in goods, trade in services and TRIPS, as well as various

---

[5] P Sands and P Klein, *Bowett's Law of International Institutions*, 5th edn (London: Sweet and Maxwell, 2001), at 16; JE Alvarez, *International Organizations as Law-Makers* (New York: Oxford University Press, 2005), at 6–7.

[6] On international legal personality, see Alvarez, above footnote 5, at 129–39.

[7] I Brownlie, *Principles of Public International Law*, 3rd edn (Oxford: Clarendon Press, 1979), at 681.

committees, sub-committees, and working groups. Although generally operating through consensus, the intergovernmental organs of the WTO can take decisions by majority voting, which can vary, depending on the issue, from a simple majority to a two-thirds or three-fourths majority.

In this respect, the WTO operates as an entity that is distinct from its Members. But the WTO is also different from many other similar international organizations, because all of its organs are plenary. It does not have an executive organ with a limited membership. As Pieter-Jan Kuijper points out in Chapter 5 of this Handbook, this can be explained in terms of the history of the WTO but, as he argues, this places limitations on the ability of the WTO to function effectively. Nevertheless, it does not inhibit the WTO from acting as an international organization with international legal personality.

The WTO Secretariat, the continuation in many respects of the GATT Secretariat, is granted the independence of an international secretariat.[8] The responsibilities of the Secretariat and of its Director-General (DG) are to be 'exclusively international in character' and Secretariat officials are not to take instructions 'from any governments or any other authority external to the WTO'.[9] An independent Secretary-General and Secretariat are typical characteristics of international organizations that act with some degree of independence and autonomy in the international sphere. They are often seen as representing the organization.[10]

C. The Functions of the WTO as an Organization

The functions of the WTO are set out explicitly in the WTO Agreement. Article III WTO Agreement provides that these functions consist of facilitating the implementation, administration, and operation, and furthering the objectives, of the WTO Agreement and the other covered agreements; providing a forum for multilateral trade negotiations; administering the DSU annexed thereto, administering the trade policy review mechanism and cooperating with the World Bank and the IMF. In short, the WTO provides a legal framework of rights and obligations, a forum for discussing trade issues and facilitating trade negotiations, a mechanism for settling disputes between Members over their rights and obligations under the WTO agreements, and a mechanism for reviewing trade policies of WTO Members.

The power of the WTO to act as an entity that is distinct from its Members is, in formal terms, relatively limited. There are certain powers relating to the internal

---

[8] Art VI WTO Agreement. See also chapters 3 and 5 of this Handbook.
[9] Ibid at para 4.
[10] HG Schermers and NM Blokker, *International Institutional Law* (Leiden: Martinus Nijhoff, 2004), at 450.

operation of the WTO, such as the adoption of budgets, establishing committees and working groups, the organization of meetings, and the management of the Secretariat, which are clearly powers of the organization rather than powers of its Members. In respect of the external relations of the organization, it has the power to enter into a headquarters agreement[11] and agreements with certain other international organizations. The power to enter into other treaties with States and other international organizations is a corollary of its broad functions and powers.[12]

The powers of the WTO to change and amend the WTO agreements themselves are somewhat circumscribed. The MC has a role in respect of the amendment of the WTO agreements, although in most instances amendments have to be accepted by each WTO Member individually. Equally, the results of trade negotiations, although emanating from negotiating groups under the auspices of the WTO, still require acceptance by the Members. In this regard there is no power in the organization to impose new obligations on the Members. Thus, there is no general legislative role in the WTO organs or any real executive function.

In three areas, however, the WTO as an institution does have direct decision-making power in respect of its Members. The first is the area of the interpretation of the WTO covered agreements. Under Article IX WTO Agreement, the MC may by a three-fourths majority adopt authoritative interpretations of the WTO agreements. Such an interpretation is authoritative for panels and the Appellate Body in their interpretation of the WTO agreements,[13] and is binding on WTO Members, whether or not they voted in favour of the interpretation in the MC. Such an interpretive power has the potential for impinging on the power to amend, since there is no residual requirement for individual Member acceptance of an adopted interpretation as there is in the case of amendment. Furthermore, given the power of the Members to act through consensus, it may be possible to achieve interpretation and amendment in effect through the operation of consensus without going through the formal amendment or interpretive process.

The second area relates to waivers. The MC, again by a three-fourths majority, may grant a Member a waiver of an obligation under the WTO agreements for a specified period of time.[14] In effect, the organization has the power to rearrange, for the period of the waiver, the obligations between the parties under one of the agreements. This, too, is binding on WTO Members regardless of whether they voted for the waiver in the MC.

---

[11] Art VIII:5 WTO Agreement.
[12] In the *Reparations* Case, the ICJ considered that the UN had not only express powers but powers 'conferred on it by necessary implication as being essential to the performance of its duties'. ICJ, *Reparations for Injuries Suffered in the Service of the United Nations*, Advisory Opinion, 11 April 1949, ICJ Reports (1949) 174, at 182.
[13] Art 3.9 DSU.
[14] Art IX:3 WTO Agreement.

The third area relates to dispute settlement. The powers of the DSB are procedural in so far as its functions relate to the establishment of panels when a dispute is brought to the WTO,[15] but they are also substantive. The determination that a Member is not in compliance with its obligations under a WTO agreement, although resulting from a recommendation from a panel or the Appellate Body, is a ruling by the DSB.[16] Such a ruling is binding on the disputants and in respect of that particular dispute and a Member must bring its laws or other measures into compliance with the ruling. This represents a significant power in the organization to define and shape the obligations of Members.

D. The Implications of Legal Personality

The conclusion that an international organization possesses international legal personality does not say much about the organization. Most multilateral organizations are regarded as having international legal personality[17] but this tells us little about their particular powers and responsibilities. The express powers of an organization are set out in its constituent documents, but if the organization has international legal personality this carries with it the inference that certain further powers can be derived by implication from its functions. The law of international organizations generally upholds a functional concept of international legal personality. Hence, international legal personality extends as far as is necessary to enable the organization to carry out its functions.[18]

There are, however, two important consequences that flow from the conclusion that the WTO has international legal personality. The first is that in having international legal personality, the WTO represents an undoubted break from the GATT 1947, which institutionally moved only marginally beyond a treaty regime establishing reciprocal rights and obligations. The GATT dispute settlement system, while a significant international experiment, did little to endow the GATT with legal personality.

The more substantive implication of legal personality for the WTO is that it possibly engages the international responsibility of the organization—a responsibility that is distinct from the responsibility of its Members. Article 2 ILC Draft Articles on the Responsibility of International Organizations explains that the draft articles apply to 'an organization established by treaty or other instrument governed by

---

[15] See Art 6 DSU.

[16] Arts 16–17.14 and 21 DSU.

[17] In *Interpretation of the Agreement of 25 March 1951 between the WHO and Egypt*, Advisory Opinion, 20 December 1980, ICJ Reports (1980) 73, at para 37, the ICJ treated international organizations as *ipso facto* bound by international law.

[18] This is the clear implication of the *Reparations* Case, above fn 12.

international law and having its own international legal personality'. Clearly such a definition includes the WTO.

The implications of the responsibility of international organizations are still being discussed by the ILC and the draft articles have yet to be completed and finalized. Whether the obligations contained in the draft articles are to be regarded as part of customary international law is unclear. Nevertheless, the broad principle that international organizations are responsible for their wrongful acts appears to be widely accepted.[19]

At one level the practical consequences of the international legal responsibility of the WTO are well-recognized. The organization has had complaints made to the ILO Administrative Tribunal by employees complaining of a breach of obligations towards them.[20] More complicated is the question of the responsibility of the WTO in relation to States and other international organizations. Two potential questions arise. First, could the actions of the WTO entail international responsibility, that is to say, could the actions of the WTO be an internationally wrongful act? And, secondly, could a Member or a non-Member State, or another international organization, invoke the responsibility of the WTO for injury it has suffered as the result of the actions of the WTO.

In the case of WTO Members, their rights are no doubt governed by the WTO covered agreements. But could a non-Member State claiming to be harmed as a result, for example, of WTO-authorized retaliation against a WTO Member invoke the international responsibility of the WTO? Of course, any such claim would depend on showing that such injury results from a wrong committed by the organization, or that the suffering of harm itself entails responsibility. The point is that as the law of the responsibility of international organizations becomes more fully developed, the possibility of such questions arising will become greater.

III. The WTO and other Intergovernmental Institutions

The relationship of the WTO to other intergovernmental institutions falls into two categories. The first is the system of cooperation set up between the WTO and the

---

[19] See the 'First Report on the Responsibility of International Organizations' by the ILC Special Rapporteur Giorgio Gaja, A/CN.4/532 (26 March 2002), at para 35: 'It can certainly be said, as a general principle, that every internationally wrongful act on the part of an international organization entails the international responsibility of that organization'.

[20] See chapter 5 of this Handbook.

various specialized agencies and other bodies of the UN system. The second is the relationship between the WTO and regional economic arrangements.

A. The WTO and the UN System

The formal authority of the WTO to establish relations with other international institutions is set out in the WTO Agreement. It is first, to 'cooperate, as appropriate' with the IMF and the World Bank 'with a view to achieving greater coherence in global economic policy-making'[21] and, second, for the GC to 'make appropriate arrangements for effective cooperation with other international organizations that have responsibilities related to those of the WTO'.[22] On this basis, the WTO has concluded cooperation agreements with the IMF and the World Bank as well as agreements with UNCTAD and the United Nations Industrial Development Organization (UNIDO). These arrangements usually provide for exchange of information and general unspecified cooperation. In some cases the agreements provide for mutual observer status. In the case of both UNCTAD and UNIDO, the focus is on cooperation in technical assistance.

Like the GATT 1947 before it, the WTO is not a specialized agency of the UN, yet it does recognize the authority of the UN Charter and cooperates more broadly with the UN system. The primacy of the UN Charter as a matter of WTO law was recognized in Article XXI GATT 1994, which preserved the rights of Contracting Parties to take actions in pursuance of their obligations under the Charter relating to the maintenance of international peace and security.[23] The same exception has been continued in both the GATS and the TRIPS Agreement. These provisions ensure that the priority claimed in Article 103 UN Charter over all other international agreements is recognized in respect of international peace and security. It is unclear how a conflict between the UN Charter and the WTO agreements in other areas would be treated under the WTO agreements.

The WTO also participates in the work of the United Nations Administrative Committee on Cooperation (ACC), which is the coordinating forum for the UN and the Specialized Agencies. Although the WTO Agreement as such makes no provision for cooperation with the UN, Article XXVI GATS requires the GC to make 'appropriate arrangements' for cooperation with the UN and its specialized agencies in relation to trade in services.

The TRIPS Agreement provides for cooperation between the WTO and the World Intellectual Property Organization (WIPO). The agreement with WIPO includes substantive obligations in particular limiting the ability of the International Bureau

---

[21] Art III:5 WTO Agreement.
[22] Art V:1 WTO Agreement.
[23] See also chapter 25 of this Handbook.

of WIPO to re-communicate emblems under Article 6ter of the Paris Convention in respect of WTO Members after the date of their WTO membership.[24]

Finally, the WTO Agreement requires Members to provide the organization with privileges and immunities 'similar' to those set out in the UN Convention on Privileges and Immunities of the Specialized Agencies,[25] and the WTO utilizes the ILO Administrative Tribunal in respect of claims brought by Secretariat officials against the WTO. Moreover, least developed country status under the WTO is determined by reference to whether the country concerned has been recognized as such by the UN.[26] The WTO Agreement is also registered under Article 102 UN Charter.

B. The WTO and Regional Economic Arrangements

The relationship between the WTO and regional economic arrangements—customs unions and free trade areas—is more complex than that between the WTO and the UN. The WTO agreements do not explicitly address this relationship, but it comes up indirectly in two ways. First, accession to the GATT 1947 was open not just to States, but also to 'a goverment acting on behalf of a separate customs territory possessing full autonomy in the conduct of its external commercial relations'.[27] Although such a provision was designed to cover entities such as Hong Kong, on its face it would also have covered the EC. In fact, the EC was accorded a special status in the GATT 1947 and is mentioned specifically in the provisions relating to WTO membership.[28] However, the potential for membership by a customs union that was possible under the GATT 1947 still remains under the WTO.[29]

Second, Article XXIV GATT 1994 dealing with customs unions and free trade areas provides an exception for such arrangements that give preferences to their members inconsistent with the most-favoured-nation (MFN) obligation under the GATT 1994.[30] The objective of this provision is to excuse WTO Members that are parties to customs unions and free trade areas from the MFN obligation provided that those customs unions or free trade areas meet certain requirements. An equivalent provision is found in Article V GATS, which is titled 'Economic Integration'. No equivalent provision is found in the TRIPS Agreement, which simply sets minimum standards.

Neither the GATT 1994 nor the GATS provide for any form of institutional relationship between the WTO and other regional integration arrangements, though a substantive legal link obviously exists. Absent an exception to the MFN principle,

---

[24] Art 3(1)(b) WTO/WIPO Agreement. See also chapter 8 of this Handbook.
[25] Art VIII:5 WTO Agreement.
[26] Art XI:2 WTO Agreement.
[27] Art XXXIII GATT 1994.
[28] Art XI WTO Agreement.
[29] Art XII WTO Agreement.
[30] See also chapter 10 of this Handbook.

the provisions of the GATT 1994 or the GATS would apply to WTO Members that entered into any such arrangement. By expressly permitting such arrangements, the WTO agreements are at least implicitly asserting their priority over regional economic integration arrangements. WTO Members are permitted to enter into such agreements only to the extent that they are consistent with their WTO obligations.

The implications of the relationship between the WTO and customs unions or free trade areas have yet to be fully explored. In *Turkey – Textiles*, there was an opportunity for both the Panel and the Appellate Body to consider the relationship between the WTO and customs unions in broad terms. However, both avoided doing so. Turkey's claim that its quantitative restrictions were justified because it was action taken in accordance with its obligations under a customs union was treated as a question of interpretation of Article XXIV(8)(a)(i) GATT 1994 without any further consideration of the broader systemic implications of the relationship between the WTO and regional integration arrangements.

The more specific question of the relationship between the dispute settlement provisions of the WTO agreements and those of regional trade agreements has also arisen. In *Mexico – Taxes on Soft Drinks*,[31] the Appellate Body refused to take a position on whether a provision in the North American Free Trade Agreement (NAFTA) granting exclusive jurisdiction to a NAFTA tribunal over a matter that could be taken to a WTO dispute settlement panel would deprive that panel of jurisdiction. The Appellate Body also took that view that it was not the function of a WTO panel to make a determination on non-WTO disputes. In this respect, it made no distinction between disputes arising under customs unions or free trade areas and other types of non-WTO disputes that WTO Members may have.[32] In neither the Panel nor the Appellate Body report was the question of whether this was a matter of jurisdiction or admissibility fully clarified and their decisions raise doubts as to whether there is a doctrine of *forum conveniens* in WTO law.[33]

A further opportunity to address some of these issues arose in the more recent case of *Brazil – Retreaded Tyres*, where the EC had argued that MERCOSUR was not a customs union within the meaning of Article XXIV GATT 1994. The Panel decided that in view of its conclusion on other matters it could exercise judicial economy in respect of that claim. Although the Appellate Body itself exercised judicial economy on the EC appeal against the failure of the Panel to deal with this matter, it chided the Panel for failing to deal with the point.[34]

---

[31]   Appellate Body Report, *Mexico – Taxes on Soft Drinks*, at para 54.

[32]   In his discussion of the Panel report in *Mexico – Taxes on Soft Drinks*, Joost Pauwelyn treats the case as one of a conflict of jurisdictions, and does not suggest that Article XXIV GATT 1994 is relevant to resolving conflicts between the WTO and free trade areas or customs unions. See J Pauwelyn, 'Adding Sweeteners to Softwood Lumber – NAFTA "Spaghetti Bowl" is Cooking' 2006 *Journal of International Economic Law* 9(1) 197.

[33]   See also chapter 12 of this Handbook.

[34]   Appellate Body Report, *Brazil – Retreaded Tyres*, at para 257.

The Panel and the Appellate Body in *Brazil – Retreaded Tyres* did agree on one aspect of the relationship between the WTO and MERCOSUR, that is the way in which dispute settlement provisions of the regional arrangement might be viewed. Brazil had claimed that the exemption of MERCOSUR parties from its ban on the importation of retreaded tyres could not be considered as arbitrary discrimination because it was action taken as a result of a ruling by a MERCOSUR tribunal requiring it to open its borders to such imports. Both the Panel and the Appellate Body concluded that a measure taken in fulfilment of an obligation set out in a MERCOSUR ruling could not be regarded as arbitrary in the sense of being capricious or random.[35] In a sense, then, a degree of deference was accorded to the dispute settlement regime of the customs union.

Any conclusion by a panel or the Appellate Body that a customs union or a free trade area is incompatible with the conditions spelled out in Article XXIV GATT 1994 will be a clear assertion of the WTO's primacy over the regional agreement and is likely to have significant political ramifications. Implicitly primacy was in fact asserted in *Brazil – Retreaded Tyres*, at least in respect of dispute settlement regimes. The result of the decision was that Brazil, a WTO Member, could not comply with a ruling of a MERCOSUR tribunal without violating its WTO obligations. The Panel deferred the potential conflict by stating that Brazil would not be in violation of its WTO obligations until the volume of trade reached a certain level. But ultimately even under this approach the primacy of the WTO was being asserted.

The Appellate Body in *Brazil – Retreaded Tyres* appeared to want to avoid creating an irrevocable conflict between the WTO and a regional trade arrangement. It took the view that there was no conflict between MERCOSUR as such and the WTO because MERCOSUR also had an exception for health similar to Article XX(b) GATT 1994, which could have been raised by Brazil in the MERCOSUR arbitral proceedings.[36] Nevertheless, in practice a conflict has emerged because compliance by Brazil with its obligations under one of the institutions entails violation of its obligations under the other.

So far WTO panels and the Appellate Body have treated conflicts between the WTO and regional arrangements contemplated under Article XXIV GATT 1994 as no different than conflicts between the WTO and any other international arrangement or treaty obligations. Panels and the Appellate Body have treated the matter as an interpretation of the WTO agreements and have not differentiated between international or regional organizations more broadly and organizations that have status as free trade areas and customs unions under Article XXIV GATT 1994. Nor have they fully explored the relationship between the dispute settlement provisions of the

---

[35] Panel Report, *Brazil – Retreaded Tyres*, at para 7.272; Appellate Body Report, *Brazil – Retreaded Tyres*, at para 232. However, the Appellate Body did regard the measure as being applied in an arbitrary and unjustifiable manner in that the exemption for MERCOSUR countries could not be explained by reference to the objective of the measure to which it was an exemption.

[36] Appellate Body Report, *Brazil – Retreaded Tyres*, at para 234.

WTO and those of regional arrangements. The opportunity for the development of jurisprudence in this area remains.

IV. The WTO and Non-Governmental Organizations

The relationship between the WTO and NGOs has been the subject of frequent comment and analysis.[37] The drafters of the WTO covered agreements clearly contemplated that there would be some form of relationship with NGOs. That appears from the WTO Agreement itself, which provides that the GC will make 'appropriate arrangements for consultation and cooperation with non-governmental organizations, concerned with matters related to those of the WTO'.[38] Yet, the implementation of that provision has not met initial expectations.

To implement these obligations the GC adopted 'Guidelines for arrangements on relations with non-governmental organizations'.[39] However, rather than encouraging 'consultation and cooperation' these guidelines appear to distance the organization from NGOs. Under the guidelines, the role of NGOs was seen not in terms of influencing WTO activities, but rather in terms of increasing public awareness of WTO activities.[40] As far as having any input into WTO processes or decision-making was concerned, the guidelines closed the door, referring to 'a broadly held view that it would not be possible for NGOs to be directly involved in the work of the WTO or its meetings'. Instead, the guidelines advocated closer consultation and cooperation with NGOs 'through appropriate processes at the national level'.[41]

The perception that the WTO as an institution was not friendly to civil society manifested itself in demonstrations in Seattle and elsewhere,[42] and in a scholarly debate about how the WTO could be made more accessible to civil society input. The acceptance by the Appellate Body of a right of individuals and organizations, and even a WTO Member, to submit *amicus curiae* briefs to panels and the Appellate Body, was perceived as an attempt to make the WTO appear more open and transparent, although the apparent lack of influence of such briefs has led to scepticism

---

[37] See S Charnovitz, 'Opening the WTO to Nongovernmental Interests' 2000–2001 *Fordham International Law Journal* 24(1) 173. See also chapter 24 of this Handbook.

[38] Art V:2 WTO Agreement.

[39] GC, *Guidelines for arrangements on relations with non-governmental organizations*, WT/L/162 (18 July 1996).

[40] Ibid at para 2.

[41] Ibid at para 6.

[42] See also chapters 3 and 24 of this Handbook.

about this *amicus* process. Moreover, Members' reaction to the Appellate Body's attempt in *EC – Asbestos* to establish an orderly process for receiving *amicus* briefs[43] was in many respects a renewed manifestation of the view expressed in the 1996 guidelines that NGOs should exercise their influence at the national level, not at that of the WTO.

Nevertheless, a significant level of interaction between NGOs and the WTO exists. Not only can NGOs file *amicus* briefs during WTO dispute settlement, they can also submit position papers to the WTO, which are published on its web site. Public fora are held between NGOs and the WTO DG, and the Secretariat has initiated 'issue-specific dialogues' between WTO Members, the Secretariat, and NGOs.

Beyond this, there is also a degree of NGO involvement in the Doha Development Round of multilateral trade negotiations. A particularly striking example is in the negotiations on disciplines in respect of fisheries subsidies. In this area, much of the impetus for the negotiations arose out of a background paper prepared by the World Wildlife (WWF)[44] and the author of that paper has participated with WTO Members in the course of the negotiations. Although, there is no WWF or other NGO involvement in the formal negotiating sessions of this topic, undoubtedly the interaction between Members and NGOs on this issue has had a substantial impact on the course of the negotiations.

V. THE WTO AS A PARTICIPANT IN THE APPLICATION AND THE DEVELOPMENT OF INTERNATIONAL LAW

As an international organization, the WTO operates in an international arena as a subject of international law. But it is equally an institution active in applying and interpreting international law and contributing to its development. Building on the GATT 1947 model, the WTO dispute settlement system has taken on a prominent role in articulating, applying, and refining principles of international law. Some would take issue with this. Dispute settlement, from their perspective, is seen in more technical terms—as a mechanism for resolving disputes between Members

[43] Appellate Body, *EC – Asbestos – Communication from the Appellate Body*, WT/DS135/9 (8 November 2000).

[44] D Schorr, 'Healthy Fisheries, Sustainable Trade. Crafting New Rules on Fisheries Subsidies in the World Trade Organization' *WWF Position Paper* (June 2004), at <http://www.assets.panda.org/downloads/healthyfisheriessustainabletradefinal.pdf> (last visited 1 June 2008). See also chapter 24 of this Handbook.

over the interpretation and application of the WTO covered agreements, and not something that engages broader questions of international law.

On their face, the formal terms of WTO dispute settlement bear out this narrow perspective. The DSU largely addresses the dispute settlement process, including the preliminary phase of consultation, the constitution of panels and the Appellate Body, the procedures for hearing complaints, and the consequences of non-compliance. The language used in Article 11 DSU to describe the functions of panels, 'an objective assessment of the matter before it including an objective assessment of the facts of the case and the applicability of and conformity with the relevant covered agreements', is a formulation of a task that does not necessarily give the impression of identifying and applying legal rules.[45]

Other treaty language in the DSU counters this. Article 11 DSU itself indicates that the task of a WTO panel is to determine 'the applicability of and conformity with the relevant covered agreements'. This can be done in any particular situation only by reference to law and legal principles. Article 3.2 DSU provides that dispute settlement serves to 'preserve the rights and obligations of Members under the covered agreements, and to clarify the existing provisions of those agreements in accordance with the customary rules of interpretation of public international law'. If the provisions of the covered agreements are to be clarified through dispute settlement in accordance with the customary rules of interpretation of public international law, a panel as the initial clarifier of the agreements in dispute settlement must be required to apply those customary rules of interpretation in determining the applicability of and conformity with the covered agreements when a dispute comes before it.

A second indication that the task of a WTO panel is one of legal interpretation and the application of law is found in the provisions relating to the WTO Appellate Body. Article 17.6 DSU provides that an appeal to the Appellate Body 'shall be limited to issues of law covered in the panel report and legal interpretations developed by the panel'. The entire notion of an appeal under the DSU is predicated on the idea that a panel will have engaged in legal interpretation and the application of law.

In its report, the first WTO panel[46] treated the Article 3.2 DSU requirement of clarifying the covered agreements in accordance with customary international law as a reference to Article 31 Vienna Convention on the Law of Treaties (VCLT), an approach that was upheld by the Appellate Body. The requirement that the covered agreements are to be interpreted in accordance with the customary rules of interpretation of public international law was a clear recognition by the negotiators of the DSU that the WTO agreements were public international law instruments—they were treaties.

It is, thus, now no longer possible to argue that the GATT 1994 is just a 'contract' and not an institution with international law ramifications and consequences. This is reflected in the oft-quoted statement of the Appellate Body that 'the General

---

[45] See also chapter 14 of this Handbook.
[46] Panel Report, *US – Gasoline*, at para 6.7.

Agreement is not to be read in clinical isolation from public international law'.[47] What is less quoted is the first part of the Appellate Body's statement that Article 3.2 DSU 'reflects a measure of recognition' that the General Agreement was not to be read in clinical isolation from public international law. While it is not exactly clear what this qualification of 'a measure of recognition' means, it appears that the Appellate Body was not endorsing a wholesale adoption of public international law in interpreting the obligations of WTO Members under the covered agreements.

The question of the extent to which public international law is relevant to the interpretation and application of the WTO agreements has generated a substantial literature. In an early article, Palmeter and Mavroidis[48] argued that on the basis of Articles 3.2 and 7 DSU, which establish the standard terms of reference for panels, all of the sources of international law set out in Article 38(1)(c) ICJ Statute are sources of law for WTO panels and the Appellate Body, though they considered that resort to customary international law would be rare.[49]

The view that all of these sources are potentially applicable to WTO disputes is supported by Bartels,[50] even if he doubts that Article 7 DSU is a source for the incorporation of law. However, he qualifies his position by noting that there is a practical restriction on the incorporation of such law as a result of the limited jurisdiction of WTO panels, and the limitation in Article 3.2 DSU that recommendations or rulings of the DSB cannot add to the rights and obligations of Members under the WTO agreements.

The strongest advocate of the applicability of other principles of international law to WTO disputes is Pauwelyn. He takes the view that not only is all public international law potentially applicable to WTO disputes, but that a Member can rely on principles of public international law to justify non-compliance with its WTO obligations.[51] That view has been criticised, particularly by Trachtman, who argues that it is tantamount to rewriting what the negotiators agreed.[52] While Trachtman accepts that other rules of international law may be relevant to interpretation, he argues that there is no mandate in the WTO agreements for rules of international law, whether customary or treaty-based, to override what is provided for in the WTO agreements.

The whole question of the place of general international law in the interpretation and application of WTO agreements is dealt with thoroughly elsewhere in this Handbook.[53]

---

[47] Appellate Body Report, *US – Gasoline*, at 16.

[48] D Palmeter and PC Mavroidis, 'The WTO Legal System: Sources of Law' 1998 *American Journal of International Law* 92(3) 398, at 399.

[49] Ibid at 407.

[50] L Bartels, 'Applicable Law in WTO Dispute Settlement Proceedings' 2001 *Journal of World Trade* 35(3) 499, at 501.

[51] J Pauwelyn, *Conflict of Norms in Public International Law – How WTO Law Relates to Other Rules of International Law* (Cambridge: Cambridge University Press, 2003).

[52] JP Trachtman, 'Book Review' 2004 *American Journal of International Law* 98(4) 855.

[53] See chapter 12 of this Handbook.

VI. Constitutionalism and the WTO

The change from the GATT 1947 'contract' to the agreements establishing the WTO as an international organization has also led to speculation about whether the WTO can be understood in constitutional terms.[54] There are a variety of streams to this debate, often focusing on the relationship between the WTO and its Members, but there are also implications for the place of the WTO in the broader international system. The idea that the WTO is somehow unique finds its expression in the commentary to the ILC Draft Articles on State Responsibility, where the DSU provisions are treated as a form of *lex specialis* ousting the application of the normal rules on state responsibility in respect of certain remedies.[55]

In part, the debate about constitutionalism is founded in the work of John Jackson who titled his book describing the new international arrangements of the WTO as *The WTO: Constitution and Jurisprudence*.[56] Jackson was focusing on the new institutions of the WTO. The old GATT 1947 had provided a set of trade rules, but the WTO heralded not just a set of rules but rules and institutions—the beginning of an international trade law system. The new WTO provides for a constitution for the world trading system.[57]

For Ernst-Ulrich Petersmann, constitutionalism meant something different. A strong advocate of the European model of economic regulation with laws at the supranational level having direct effect within domestic legal systems, Petersmann saw the WTO as an opportunity to foster a notion of constitutionalism that sees international trade law as restraining the behaviour of governments and promoting the economic rights of individuals.[58] The international trade law regime as embodied in the new WTO could provide the constitutional framework for the protection of those rights. Petersmann's arguments have been avowedly prospective. He sees this as the direction that the WTO regime should develop; he is under no illusions that it is there yet.

The third strand of constitutionalism comes from the earlier work of Deborah Cass who has argued that a constitutional regime is developing through the interpretive work of the WTO Appellate Body.[59] Under the rubric of interpretation, Cass

[54] For a comprehensive discussion of the subject, see DZ Cass, *The Constitutionalization of the World Trade Organization; Legitimacy, Democracy and Community in the International Trading System* (Oxford: Oxford University Press, 2005).

[55] ILC, Draft Articles on the International Responsibility of States for Wrongful Acts, 2001 *Yearbook of the International Law Commission* II-2, at 140.

[56] JH Jackson, *The WTO: Constitution and Jurisprudence* (London: Royal Institute of International Affairs, 1998).

[57] Cass describes this form of constitutionalism as 'institutional managerialism'.

[58] See E-U Petersmann, *Constitutional Functions and Constitutional Problems of International Organizations* (Fribourg: University of Fribourg Press, 1991). Cass describes this as 'rights-based constitutionalism'.

[59] DZ Cass, 'The "Constitutionalization" of International Trade Law: Judicial Norm-Generation as the Engine of Constitutional Development in International Trade' 2001 *European Journal of International Law* 12(1) 39. Cass describes this as 'judicial norm-development'.

claimed, the Appellate Body has engaged in norm-creation and norm-development. This theory is based on a common law perception about the evolution of law through the interpretive role of courts. It is equally influenced by how the European Court of Justice has played a key role in the generation of an EC system and ethos. Cass argues that the interpretive work of the Appellate Body has resulted in the development of doctrine within the organization and the rearrangement of relationships between the organization and its Members. It also contributes to the legitimacy of the organization.

These attempts to view the WTO or the international economic order more broadly in constitutional terms are not without their critics. Howse and Nicolaides[60] argue that a comparison with the EU is not apposite. Constitutionalism developed in the EU as a response to expectations implicit in the EC treaties themselves; there is no such expectation in the WTO agreements. They warn that attempts to push a 'constitutionalism' agenda would be counter-productive and feed the fears of opponents of globalization and of the WTO.

Dunoff argues that there is no WTO constitution.[61] Rather, the constitutionalism debate surrounding the WTO is an attempt to give a greater status to the WTO than is justified and to surround it with the trappings of domestic constitutional systems. It is an attempt to bypass politics. Trachtman,[62] by contrast, points out the many different ways in which a WTO constitution can be perceived—an expansion, rather than a denial of the constitutionalism debate. Even Cass, in her later work, finds constitutionalist theories inadequate. She argues that the focus of the discussion on the future of international trade should be on legitimacy, democracy, and community.

There is no doubt, as Trachtman points out, that the WTO has a constitution in a technical sense.[63] It has a constituent instrument that establishes the framework of rules and institutions that regulate the world trading system. That, to some extent, was what Jackson was pointing out and it is not a new phenomenon in international law. The question that has engaged the scholarly debate is whether the WTO's constitution can be seen as a constitution in the same sense as the constitution of a State or even as the constitution of the EU.

The question relevant to this chapter is whether notions of constitutionalism have any implications for the WTO's position within the international system. This external aspect of the constitutionalism debate has not been given a great deal of attention. Dunoff notes that there is a broader conversation about the constitutionalization of international law. Trachtman, however, focuses more on the issue. He considers that

---

[60] R Howse and K Nicolaidis, 'Enhancing WTO Legitimacy: Constitutionalization of Global Subsidiarity?' 2003 *Governance: An International Journal of Policy, Administration, and Institutions* 16(1) 73–94.

[61] JL Dunoff, 'Constitutional Conceits: The WTO's "Constitution" and the Discipline of International Law' 2006 *European Journal of International Law* 17(3) 647.

[62] JP Trachtman, 'The Constitutions of the WTO' 2006 *European Journal of International Law* 17(3) 623.

[63] Ibid at 627.

an important part of any constitutionalism discussion is to see how the constitution of the WTO relates to the constitutions of other international organizations and to the wider field of international law. Cass argues that there are important differences between WTO law and other treaty arrangements in international law, though she considers that even if one were to view WTO simply as part of general international law, there would still be scope for considering a subset of constitutionalism in international trade law within the framework of international law.

The constitutionalism discourse in international law is longstanding. Wolfgang Friedmann claimed that the material for an 'international constitutional law' was immense.[64] For Friedmann, this international constitutional law consisted of an analysis of functions, competences, and divisions of powers of the UN and its Specialized Agencies. Although Friedmann admitted that there was no real adjudicative body that could play the role of domestic supreme courts in constitutional interpretation, he found the ICJ decisions interpreting the powers of the various UN organs as critical to this development of constitutional law. It is not clear, however, whether this notion of constitutional law has any particular content other than as a compendium term for the corpus of the law of international organizations.

For many who speak of constitutionalism in international law, the UN Charter is seen as a basic constitutional document. However, Fassbender argues that 'constitution' used in respect of the UN Charter is used as 'an autonomous concept' and not in the sense of the domestic constitutional law of a State.[65] In the same vein, Alvarez argues that domestic constitutional analogies for the UN Charter are misleading.[66] In this international law dialogue about constitutional law, the attribution of the term 'constitution' to the WTO seems unobjectionable. It is a way of talking about a framework of rules and institutions that make up the system (Jackson's sense) with the addition of a norm-interpretation and creation function through judicial interpretation (Cass' sense). Indeed, Friedmann might have seen the WTO as having what the UN Charter lacks as a constitutional document—a mechanism for resolving disputes, and developing basic principles through treaty interpretation. However, speaking of constitutions in this way potentially raises questions about the relationship of the WTO 'constitution' to the UN Charter 'constitution' and whether the Charter is a more basic constitutional document.

To the extent that a discussion of constitutionalism involves questions about the extent of the power of an international organization over its members – the issue of supranational power – the discussion is one of substance. And, that is at the heart of the constitutionalism debate about the WTO. Apart from this aspect, the constitutionalism debate may be more about definitions or typologies

---

[64] W Friedmann, *The Changing Structure of International Law* (London: Stevens & Sons, 1964), at 153.

[65] B Fassbender, 'The Meaning of International Constitutional Law' in R St. John Macdonald and DM Johnston (eds), *Towards World Constitutionalism: Issues in the Legal Ordering of the World Community* (Leiden: Martinus Nijhoff, 2005) 837, at 848.

[66] Alvarez, above fn5, at 67.

of systems of law. A constitutional structure may be a convenient way of describing an institutional arrangement. In this sense the idea of constitutionalism carries no particular connotations about the character of authority. It is this latter idea of constitution that seems to have pervaded the general international law discourse on constitutions.

Is there anything about the WTO that makes the international law discourse about constitutions inapposite? Cass argues that there are differences between WTO law and other treaty law.[67] She tentatively cites three distinctions, acknowledging that they all require further empirical research for substantiation. First, domestic law concepts are more deeply embedded in WTO law (proportionality and jurisdictional competence) while general international law is based on concepts such as jurisdiction and state responsibility that are inherently international. Second, international law is more diffuse; international trade law has its own defined interpretive community. Third, international trade law decisions are more widely accepted than decisions about other areas of international law.

Cass' views raise important questions about the relationship between WTO law and international law more generally. To argue that the WTO treaty has characteristics that are different from other multilateral treaties does not mean that WTO law is somehow different from general international law. Indeed, Cass argues that WTO constitutionalization can be seen as a form of sub-constitutionalization within the broader frame of international law. Even so, there is no doubt that in many respects the WTO constitution is more like the UN Charter than the 'constitutions' of many of the UN specialized agencies.

The WTO agreements do not merely provide a framework for cooperation. They set out the framework of an international economic regime relating to trade in goods, trade in services and the interrelationship of these regimes with the intellectual property regimes. Just as the UN Charter set out the basic obligations of States in respect of international peace and security, the WTO sets out the fundamental principles of the international trading regime in terms of basic legal obligations. And it goes further in making these obligations subject to binding dispute settlement with consequences attached to non-compliance.

By contrast, the UN specialized agencies are international organizations that provide frameworks for cooperation. Most do not impose basic legal obligations that must be observed by members, nor do they provide for dispute settlement or for organized consequences for non-compliance.[68] Instead they set out objectives and provide opportunities for States to meet those objectives including through the formulation of resolutions or binding treaty commitments. In many respects, the WTO resembles framework treaties like human rights treaties or the law of the

---

[67] Cass, above fn 54, at 53.
[68] Not all of the Specialized Agencies are the same. In fact, ICAO, which sets out certain obligations with respect to air navigation, resembles the WTO more than the FAO or UNESCO.

sea convention. But unlike those framework treaties, which have some institutional elements but no broad-based international organization, the WTO is also an international institution.

The conclusion that emerges from this constitutionalism dialogue is that viewed from the perspective of the international system, the WTO is something more than most of the multilateral, universalist, institutions established in the era of institution-making since 1945. The essence of that difference is that the WTO contains a regime of binding dispute settlement. That has the consequence that WTO Members frequently have to adapt their domestic law to comply with decisions resulting from the dispute settlement process. This distinguishes the WTO from other universal international institutions, and in this regard the only real parallel is with the EU. For this reason, analogies drawn from the EU are attractive, though they need to be viewed with caution.

VII. CONCLUSION

In many respects, the WTO is unremarkable as an international institution. By comparison with many international organizations the powers of its organs are relatively limited. It has neither an executive organ like the UN nor powers granted to organs to take decisions having a binding effect within the domestic systems of WTO Members. Plenary organs and consensus decision-making are the hallmark of the WTO.

Yet all of this changes when the dispute settlement process is considered. In this area, the power to take binding decisions affecting Members has in effect been delegated to the organs of the dispute settlement process. This significant transfer of power has in practice caused little controversy within the WTO, although outside of the organization it has been the focus of criticism both on the streets and in the literature. There have been proposals to place some limits on the power of the Appellate Body in the context of DSU reform and the reaction on the question of *amicus* briefs in *EC – Asbestos*, stand out in part because they stand in isolation. Moreover, for the most part, WTO Members routinely implement the results of dispute settlement even in the face of difficult domestic opposition. The dispute settlement process is seen as the 'jewel in the crown' of the WTO and not as a fundamental reorienting of power between States and international institutions.

Compulsory and binding dispute settlement between its Members sets the WTO apart as an international institution. This has resulted in criticisms of the WTO, particularly where WTO dispute settlement engages other areas, such as the environment, health, labour, and human rights. At the same time, it has led to suggestions that perhaps by bringing other areas of international regulation within the framework of the WTO agreements, those areas too could benefit from a robust dispute settlement process.

The idea that the WTO could become some type of super-agency revolving around a binding dispute settlement process seems remote and largely impractical. But it highlights that the particular significance of the WTO as an international institution is in its dispute settlement system. It has yet to prove itself as an institution that can engage in other forms of law-making. A successful Doha Round will indicate that the WTO negotiating processes are capable of delivering new binding agreements. Until that happens, the WTO will remain an organization whose institutional success rests on the development of a unique dispute settlement process incorporating appellate functions that previously have existed only domestically within States or amongst a more confined regional grouping.

SELECTED BIBLIOGRAPHY

JE Alvarez, *International Organizations as Law-Makers* (New York: Oxford University Press, 2005)

DZ Cass, *The Constitutionalization of the World Trade Organization; Legitimacy, Democracy and Community in the International Trading System* (Oxford: Oxford University Press, 2005)

S Charnovitz, 'Opening the WTO to Nongovernmental Interests' 2000–2001 *Fordham International Law Journal* 24(1) 173

JL Dunoff, 'Constitutional Conceits: The WTO's "Constitution" and the Discipline of International Law' 2006 *European Journal of International Law* 17(3) 647

R Howse and K Nicolaidis, 'Enhancing WTO Legitimacy: Constitutionalization of Global Subsidiarity?' 2003 *Governance: An International Journal of Policy, Administration, and Institutions* 16(1) 73

RE Hudec, *Enforcing International Trade Law* (Salem, NH: Butterworth, 1993)

JH Jackson, *Sovereignty, the WTO and the Changing Fundamentals of International Law* (New York: Cambridge University Press, 2006)

R St John Macdonald and DM Johnston (eds), *Towards World Constitutionalism: Issues in the Legal Ordering of the World Community* (Leiden: Martinus Nijhoff, 2005)

DM McRae, 'The Contribution of International Trade Law to the Development of International Law' 1996 *Recueil des Cours* (260) 103

JP Trachtman, 'The Constitutions of the WTO' 17 *European Journal of International Law* 17(3) 623

PART II

SUBSTANTIVE LAW

CHAPTER 5

···

WTO
INSTITUTIONAL
ASPECTS*

···

PIETER JAN KUIJPER

---

* This chapter in part develops my earlier article 'Some Institutional Issues Presently Before the WTO' in D Kennedy and J Southwick (eds), *The Political Economy of International Trade, Essays in Honor of Robert E Hudec* (Cambridge: Cambridge University Press, 2002) 81.

I. INTRODUCTION

INSTITUTIONAL studies of the WTO that are not policy-oriented or a reaction to the Sutherland Report of a few years ago are relatively rare.[1] Hence this contribution seeks to place the organization firmly within the framework of the European tradition of comparative institutional law of international organizations, while at the same time looking at a relatively limited number of topical issues that are considered of major importance. Other issues of reform or improvement can be suitably dealt with through a brief mention and reference to the most important literature on the point in question.

In order to understand the present structure of the WTO and why it is still close to the old GATT, it is indispensable to understand the constraints under which the organization was created, almost as an afterthought, during the Uruguay Round negotiations. This chapter starts with a brief historical discussion of these negotiations insofar as they bore on the creation of the WTO. Next, a brief overview will be given of the institutional structure of the WTO and of the allocation of powers between the different institutions. This will include a discussion of membership and observership.

If one really wants to understand how the WTO functions, it is necessary to take account of the large number of plenary organs and Committees of the organization, their interrelationship, and the division of powers between them. How matters

---

[1] See, eg, AH Qureshi, *The World Trade Organization: Implementing International Trade Norms* (Manchester: Manchester University Press, 1996); JH Jackson, *The World Trade Organization, Constitution and Jurisprudence* (London: Royal Institute of International Affairs, 1998); M Footer, *An Institutional and Normative Analysis of the World Trade Organization* (Leiden: Martinus Nijhoff, 2006); P Van den Bossche, *The Law and Policy of the World Trade Organization* (Cambridge: Cambridge University Press, 2005); WJ Davey, 'Institutional Framework' in PFJ Macrory, AE Appleton, and MG Plummer (eds), *The World Trade Organization, Legal, Economic and Political Analysis*, Vol 1 (Berlin: Springer, 2005) 51. See also Consultative Board, *The Future of the WTO: Addressing Institutional Challenges in the New Millennium* (Geneva: WTO, 2004).

are or are not moved up the decision-making ladder. Or are certain matters being delegated to lower plenary bodies for decision-making? Do such decision-making processes lead to true secondary law of the WTO, or not? And if so, how can the 'constitutionality' of this secondary law be guaranteed? In addition there is the problem of the organs specifically created for the Doha Round: the Trade Negotiations Committee (TNC) and the various negotiation groups. What is their status, how are they supposed to function in the WTO framework?

All these questions need to be considered against the background of the absence of a non-plenary organ, a unique feature for an organization that is worldwide and not regionally or functionally restricted in membership, like for instance the Council of Europe or ASEAN, and the OECD. A careful analysis of the reasons for, and the consequences of, this absence is called for.

In particular the consequence of this 'hole in the organization' for the position of the Director-General (DG) and the Secretariat, which in other world-wide international organizations usually live in a kind of symbiosis with the non-plenary organ, deserves to be analyzed at some length in the section devoted to the Secretariat and the DG. Finally, this chapter looks briefly at the great success story of the WTO, the dispute settlement system, but it will restrict itself to a few major institutional aspects that found expression in the political organs and are not discussed elsewhere in this Handbook. Its case law and enforcement aspects are also considered elsewhere in this Handbook.[2]

In conclusion, this chapter attempts to give a brief characteristic of the WTO and where as an institution it may be or should be heading, in the light of the material presented and in the light of the so-called constitutionalization debate.[3]

II. The WTO as an International Organization 'Lite'

It has been well documented how historically the proponents of the idea of creating a WTO as a kind of crown on the negotiations of the Uruguay Round were inspired by the historical accident that had prevented the founding of the International Trade Organization (ITO) as the third companion to the two Bretton Woods institutions, the IMF and the World Bank. While the ITO was being negotiated, first in Geneva (1947) and later in Havana (1948), negotiators agreed that they could sign a much

---

[2] See Part III of this Handbook.
[3] See, for an overview, DZ Cass, *The Constitutionalization of the World Trade Organization* (Oxford: Oxford University Press, 2005). See also chapter 4 of this Handbook.

less ambitious document that contained some core rules from the ITO and wide-ranging tariff cuts. This was the GATT 1947 that was provisionally applied through a special protocol to that effect and entered into force on 1 January 1948. The full ITO Charter was finalized during 1948 and the GATT 1947 would come to an end, while its tariff concessions would transit to the ITO once established. However, the composition and the mood of the US Congress changed and, in 1950, President Truman stopped his efforts to have it approved. Thus the GATT 1947 continued to be provisionally applied during all of its existence.[4] As will be shown below, this historical accident still influenced the US negotiators' mindset in the 1991–1993 negotiations on the institutional aspects of the Uruguay Round.

The GATT 1947 was an agreement, not an organization like the ITO, and hence initially it lacked any institutional framework, except for the Interim Commission for the International Trade Organization (ICITO). This was a small Committee of States that watched over the preparations for the ITO and supervised a small secretariat that was supposed to start building that organization as soon as its founding treaty was to enter into force. As the French say, 'il n'y a que le provisoire qui dure', and the ICITO, with such members as China and Iran that were not even Contracting Parties to the GATT 1947, was still serving as the body on which the GATT Secretariat legally depended on the eve of the creation of the WTO.[5]

Slowly in the first two decades of its existence the GATT 1947 developed into the kind of treaty organization that we now know so well in the field of the environment, a kind of multilateral environmental agreement (MEA) with a Conference of the Parties (COP) and a minimal secretariat. In short, a multilateral trade agreement. However, some modern MEAs have better structured decision-making powers for the COP and decisions from the COPs may be clearly legally binding and intended to create secondary law of the MEA.[6]

In this brief narrative, three well-known weak points of the GATT 1947 have already implicitly come to the fore. First of all, there was its provisional character, from a legal point of view expressed in the fact that all Contracting Parties adhered to the Protocol of Provisional Application. Second, the institutional weakness of the Secretariat stands out, dependent as it was on ICITO that included non-Contracting Parties to the GATT 1947. Third, there was its weak decision-making structure, exemplified by the Conference of the Contracting Parties, the Contracting Parties

---

[4] See JH Jackson, *The World Trading System, Law and Policy of International Economic Relations* (Cambridge, Mass.: MIT Press, 1997), at 36–37. See also Footer, above fn 1, at 12–18. See also chapters 2, 3, and 4 of this Handbook.

[5] The ICITO as such did not meet but once; it was actually its Executive Committee that acted for the ICITO, the last time when the assets of the GATT and its personnel were transferred to the WTO, see Davey, above fn 1, at 54. For other aspects of the transition from the ICITO to the WTO, see Footer, above fn 1, at 116–17 and 304–05.

[6] See RR Churchill and G Ulfstein, 'Autonomous Institutional Arrangements in Multilateral Environmental Agreements: A Little-Noticed Phenomenon in International Law' 2000 *American Journal of International Law* 94(4) 623.

writ large in GATT terminology, which at a certain stage created the General Council (GC) by decision and without any treaty basis. The consequence was that the GATT 1947 never had a non-plenary body as the ITO was supposed to have had and as all the other worldwide international organizations did have.

All decisions—another weakness—had to be taken in the plenary and on an extremely insecure basis, namely Article XXV GATT 1947 that provided for majority voting. In practice, this procedure was abandoned in favour of consensus, but never repealed. Moreover, Article XXV was extremely vague as to the binding character of the decisions taken.

Finally, the GATT 1947 had acquired a number of agreements attached to it, such as the agreements on Technical Barriers to Trade (TBT), on Anti-Dumping and on Subsidization. These so-called Codes, negotiated during the Tokyo Round (1979) did not have the same Contracting Parties as the GATT 1947, they had their own 'Conference of the Parties', and their relationship to the GATT 1947, of which they had further developed certain provisions, was never fully clarified.

These shortcomings of the GATT 1947 were well known and insofar as they were not, the respected GATT scholar John Jackson made sure that the Uruguay Round negotiators were made aware of them by his timely publication *Restructuring the GATT System*.[7] As Debra Steger has pointed out, Jackson was also active in discreetly but firmly lobbying for his ideas, especially with two participants in the group of leading negotiators during the Uruguay Round, the so-called 'Quad', that he believed would be the most receptive to his ideas, that is, Canada and the EC.

Steger also describes well how what was originally called the Multilateral Trade Organization (MTO) was fairly easily negotiated in Julio Lacarte's Institutional Group in the fall of 1991 on the basis of a Canada-EC draft.[8] The US later became much more circumspect about the result of that period of negotiations for internal political reasons, and even went so far as to put everything about the MTO into doubt towards the end of 1992, making a counter-proposal for a protocol that would tie all the results of the Uruguay Round together. If the US approach had been followed, the WTO would not have seen the light of day. Throughout the negotiations on what later became the WTO Agreement, the US emphasized that it was constrained by the so-called Fast-Track Authority granted by Congress to the US Trade Representative as negotiator.[9] This Fast-Track Authority did not foresee important institutional modifications of the GATT 1947, though it clearly laid down the requirement that the results of the negotiation should be a 'single undertaking'. Anything that went beyond this in the institutional field risked falling outside the Fast-Track authority

---

[7] JH Jackson, *Restructuring the GATT System* (New York: Council on Foreign Relations Press, 1990).

[8] D Steger, 'The World Trade Organization: A New Constitution for the Trading System' in D Steger, *Peace through Trade: Building the WTO* (London: Cameron May, 2004), at 25–45.

[9] On the US Fast-Track authority, see chapter 3 of this Handbook. The following is largely based on the author's participation in the MTO-WTO negotiations during the Uruguay Round.

and might even have to be submitted to the Senate as a regular treaty, losing its character of an executive-congressional agreement. At least, the US side so told its partners during this part of the negotiations.

Even with the benefit of hindsight it is difficult to fathom how much of this was US gamesmanship to provoke further concessions in other areas from its trading partners. However, most of the negotiators were lawyers with at least some knowledge of US constitutional law and especially of the intricacies of US public trade law and the Fast-Track procedure. They felt that there was a serious basis underlying the US caution with respect to the institutional side of the negotiations. Hence it came to be accepted that the institutional structure of the WTO could not become much more differentiated and sophisticated compared to that of the old GATT 1947, while one of its very visible functions (also to the US Congress) should be to secure the 'single undertaking'.

Wariness on the part of the US Congress did not decide entirely the fate of the WTO, as it had in 1947 sealed the fate of the ITO, but it is the basic reason why the institutional structure of the WTO remained rather primitive for a 'modern' international organization. The surfeit of plenary bodies, with the Ministerial Conference (MC) instead of Contracting Parties at the pinnacle, the absence of an 'Executive Board' as non-plenary body, as well as the very minimal provisions on the DG and the Secretariat can be explained in this way. It was to be an international organization 'lite'. It should be added that this approach suited many others as well. Especially developing countries were in large majority opposed to the creation of a non-plenary organ, because they feared it would reduce their influence and veto power.[10]

III. OVERVIEW OF THE STRUCTURE OF THE WTO

Before turning to the institutional structure as such, it is necessary to pay some attention to the preambular paragraphs of the WTO Agreement. They provide an outline of the 'object and purpose' of the WTO treaty system that should be an important element in interpreting of its individual provisions.[11] They are only five in number, of which the fourth clearly sets out the integrated nature of the treaty system; 'a more viable and durable multilateral trading system' that would include

[10] Given the enormous growth in membership of developing countries in the GATT 1947 prior to the creation of the WTO, it is unclear as to why many developing countries held this view. They were bound to have large numbers not only in the plenary organs, but also in any non-plenary organ that was likely to be based, at least in part, on the criterion of geographical representation.

[11] See also chapter 12 of this Handbook.

not only the GATT 1947, but also the results of past liberalization[12] and all the results of the Uruguay Round negotiations. Together with Article IV:2, this paragraph also forms the guarantee of the single undertaking.

The first two preambular paragraphs are of an astounding progressiveness for 1995 and articulate principles that continue to dominate the Doha Round: development and respect for the environment; an increase in growth of the share of world trade held by developing, and especially least-developed, countries, but also the need to achieve this on a sustainable basis. These principles remain of great importance 13 years after the WTO's founding and continue to inspire the reports of WTO panels and the Appellate Body.[13]

Returning to the institutional structure as such, Article II:1 WTO Agreement articulates the idea that the WTO would provide a 'common institutional framework for the conduct of trade relations among its Members in matters related to the agreements and associated legal instruments'. The MC, and its replacement organ, the GC, are the incarnation of this common institutional framework. They are both composed of representatives of all Members of the organization, respectively at the ministerial and ambassadorial level.

Especially the powers of the MC are extraordinarily broad. It shall carry out 'the functions of the organization',[14] which are listed in Article III WTO Agreement,[15] and shall take the actions necessary to this effect. Moreover, Article IV:1 also provides that the MC shall have power to 'take decisions on *all* matters under *any* of the Multilateral Trade Agreements'.[16] Such decisions shall be taken in accordance with the specific requirements for decision-making in the WTO Agreement and the relevant covered agreement. Although normally in the founding treaties of other international organizations, such broad powers do not normally denote the power to take binding decisions, here the specific reference to the decision-making provisions of the agreements demonstrates that such decisions may be binding, depending on the specific decision-making provision invoked.

There are also a number of powers that are specifically allocated to the MC, including the appointment of the DG (Article VI:2), the adoption of an authoritative interpretation of the WTO Agreement and the other covered agreements (Article IX:2), the granting of waivers (Article IX:3), the adoption (of the text) of amendments (Article X), and decisions on accession (Article XII).

---

[12] This was often called the 'acquis', a term that was originally mainly used in the framework of the EC, but which is increasingly also applied to the WTO.

[13] See, eg, Appellate Body Report, *US – Shrimp*, at paras 129–31.

[14] Art IV:1 WTO Agreement.

[15] Article III lists the following functions: (1) facilitating the implementation, administration and operation, and further the objectives, of the WTO Agreement and of the Multilateral Trade Agreements and providing a framework for the Plurilateral Trade Agreements; (2) providing a forum for negotiations among the Members concerning their multilateral trade relations; (3) administering the DSU and the TPRM; and (4) cooperating with the Bretton Woods institutions.

[16] Emphasis added.

The GC replaces the MC when the latter is not in session, that is to say always, except during the single week, every two years, when the MC effectively meets.[17] This is true even for the powers specifically allocated to the MC mentioned above. Thus the GC has appointed DGs,[18] granted waivers,[19] adopted an amendment (to the TRIPS Agreement),[20] and routinely makes decisions on accession.[21]

In addition the GC shall, according to Article IV:2, carry out the specific functions that the WTO Agreement assigns to it. These functions include establishing appropriate arrangements with other inter-governmental and non-governmental organizations (Article V), adopting Staff and Financial Regulations (Articles VI:3 and VII:3), and adopting the Budget (Article VII:3). As a result, the GC *de facto* exercises all its own and all the MC's powers, because even during its session, the latter hardly has time for the exercise of its own specific powers, unless they rise to the level of high politics, such as the accession of China and the granting of certain waivers at the Doha MC.

The GC has a somewhat special relationship to the two bodies that are, as it were, emanations of itself; the Dispute Settlement Body (DSB) and the Trade Policy Review Board (TPRB). According to the identical formulae used in paragraphs 3 and 4 of Article IV, 'the General Council shall convene as appropriate to discharge the responsibilities of the' DSB/TPRB 'as provided for in' the DSU/TPRM. This would seem to imply that the GC as DSB or TPRB can only exercise the specific powers as provided for in the DSU or TPRM. For the TPRB, which has very limited powers, this is not much of a problem, but for the DSB this is more of an issue, as is discussed below.

In addition, the GC has general oversight over the three specialized Councils: Council for Trade in Goods (CTG), the Council for Trade in Services (GATS Council), and the Council for Trade-Related Intellectual Property Rights (TRIPS Council). These specialized Councils are all of plenary composition. They shall receive 'guidance' from the GC, according to Article IV:5. There barely exist examples of such guidance, except in relation to the so-called implementation-related issues in the period after the Seattle MC, when the GC decided that it could

---

[17] Despite the two-year term, expiring at the end of 2007, the MC of that year has been put off, see GC, *Minutes of Meeting*, WT/GC/M/110 (15 November 2007), at 24.

[18] DG Lamy has been appointed by the GC by consensus on 26 May 2005 and assumed his functions on 1 September 2005. His predecessors (Renato Ruggiero, Mike Moore, and Supachai Panitchpakdi) were also appointed by the GC.

[19] The GC is normally the organ that grants or prolongs waivers, unless a waiver is brought to the MC for political reasons, as were the two Banana waivers concerning the special EC banana regime for ACP countries at the Doha MC, see MC, *European Communities – The ACP-EC Partnership Agreement*, WT/MIN(01)/15 (14 November 2001); MC, *European Communities – Transitional Regime for the EC Autonomous Tariff Rate Quotas on Imports of Bananas*, WT/MIN(01)/16 (14 November 2001).

[20] For the TRIPS amendment and the adoption of its text, see chapter 8 of this Handbook.

[21] A less routine accession was that of Saudi Arabia, for which a special GC meeting was reserved on 6 November 2006.

direct other WTO bodies 'to provide any appropriate inputs and to take any appropriate action'.[22] In the same period the GC also instructed the CTG 'to give positive consideration to individual requests presented in accordance with Article 5:3 (of the TRIMS Agreement) by developing countries for extension of the transition periods for implementation of the TRIMS Agreement'.[23]

Apart from 'general guidance', the GC can also 'assign functions' to the specialized Councils, according to Article IV:5. The GC thus seems to have a power of delegation to the specialized Councils. However, there are no known examples hitherto of such delegation.

Finally, the specialized Councils, just like the DSB and TPRB, have the powers (Article IV:5 once again speaks of 'carrying out the functions') given to them by the agreements they are supposed to 'oversee'. Such specific powers assigned to the specialized Councils are few and far between in the GATT 1994 and its connected agreements on trade in goods, the GATS, and the TRIPS Agreement. From the text of Article IV:5 it is not clear whether the 'overseeing' function is an independent basis for decision-making, in addition to the functions specifically assigned to the subordinate Councils in their respective agreements. As we have already seen with respect to higher organs of the WTO, in particular the MC (and hence also the GC), this is a general problem in the WTO, that is, a lack of clarity in the relationship between very broadly formulated general powers, such as general oversight, and rather more detailed powers specifically allocated to one organ.

The specialized Councils have the right, according to Article IV:6 WTO Agreement, to establish subsidiary bodies as required. However, in the area of trade in goods, in reality all agreements of Annex IA of the WTO Agreement, except the Pre-Shipment Inspection Agreement, set up their own Committees reporting to the CTG instead of the CTG establishing these Committees. The GATS Council, however, has amply used its power to set up subsidiary bodies and has created such entities as the Working Party on Professional Services[24] and the Working Party on Domestic Regulation.[25]

Article IV:7 WTO Agreement is in many ways comparable to Article IV:5. The Committee on Trade and Development (CTD), the Balance of Payments Committee (BOP Committee), and the Committee on Budget, Finance and Administration (BFA Committee) are charged with carrying out the functions assigned to them by the relevant agreements and by the GC. For the BFA Committee, this means that

---

[22] GC, *Minutes of Meeting Held on 3 and 8 May 2000*, WT/GC/M/55 (16 June 2000).

[23] As is implicit in the reference to minutes of a General Council meeting, see above fn 22, these decisions were taken in no specific form that could be recognized as a decision. This was a peculiar weakness of the WTO institutional structure, but it seems to have largely disappeared since the period around 2000.

[24] GATS Council, *Decision on Professional Services*, S/L/3 (4 April 1995).

[25] GATS Council, *Decision on Domestic Regulation*, S/L/70 (28 April 1999). See also chapter 7 of this Handbook.

it carries out the tasks laid down in the Financial Rules and Regulations. The CTD and the BOP Committee have been given so-called terms of reference by the GC in addition to their standard rules of procedure. They charge the BOP Committee with conducting the consultations (on balance of payments problems) under Articles XII:4 and XVIII:12 GATT 1994, Articles XII:5 GATS, and the provision of the BOP Understanding.[26] This is quite specific and operational compared to the terms of reference for the CTD which is charged with reviewing from time to time the application of the special provisions in favour of developing country Members and to consider any question that may arise with regard to the application of these special provisions and to report to the GC. Clearly, the CTD is primarily a discussion body.

It is interesting to note that the (standard) Rules of Procedure of the Councils, Committees, and other Subsidiary Bodies are based on the principle of consensus for all levels of the (plenary) decision-making machinery. If consensus cannot be reached the matter is referred to the next highest body, and in the last instance to the GC. This principle is laid down in Article 33 of the Rules of Procedure, which for the GC reads as follows:

The General Council shall take decisions in accordance with the decision-making provisions of the WTO Agreement, in particular Article IX thereof entitled 'Decision-Making'.[27]

In the case of the specialized Councils and most of their subsidiary bodies the provision reads as follows (the example is that of the Committee on Agriculture):

The Committee on Agriculture shall reach its decisions by consensus. Where a decision cannot be reached by consensus, the matter at issue should be referred to the Council for Trade in Goods if any delegation so requests.

Rule 33 of the Rules of Procedure of the CTG is identical, except that the referral is up to the GC.

The above short overview demonstrates how complex the interaction between these plenary organs is. However, the most striking aspect of the WTO institutional structure is that there is a complete absence of a non-plenary organ (an Executive Council) as exists in many world-wide international organizations. The allocations of tasks in such organizations as the WHO, the FAO, etc. is that the General Assembly which normally meets every two years, just as the WTO MC, is charged with setting out the broad outlines of the work of the organization, whilst the non-plenary Executive Council controls the day-to-day activities in close consultation with the DG, who in many ways actually runs the organization with the Secretariat. In the WTO it is a plenary organ, the GC, that in many ways fulfils (or ought to fulfil) the

---

[26] GC, *WTO Committee on Balance-of-Payments Restrictions*, WT/L/45 (23 February 1995).

[27] In practice this is a reference to consensus, see Article IX:1 WTO Agreement: 'The WTO shall continue the practice of decision-making by consensus followed under GATT 1947'.

role of sounding board for the DG to guide him in his day-to-day stewardship of the organization, but that is a role that, because of its size alone, it cannot easily fulfil.

Moreover, the Secretariat and the DG could only be mentioned very briefly in the WTO Agreement, laying down essentially what had developed under the GATT 1947. Otherwise the US Congress might baulk, regarding a more elaborate mention as going beyond the Fast-Track Authority it had granted Congress. Article VI WTO Agreement is an extremely spare provision, just laying down the appointment of the DG by the MC, the appointment of the staff of the Secretariat by the DG, and minimal rules to safeguard the international character of the Secretariat, complemented by the provisions on privileges and immunities of the staff laid down in Article VIII:3 WTO Agreement.

Another remarkable absence among WTO organs is a parliamentary organ. Normally world-wide organizations of the UN-type do not have parliamentary organs. If one looks at international organizations that do have parliamentary assemblies, they are normally regional organizations in parts of the globe where there is a reasonably homogeneous tradition of parliamentarianism; and often at the same time organizations of which the legal instruments may have far-reaching influence on domestic economic and regulatory policies. The EU is an example of both and the European Parliament acts as co-legislator, together with the Council, in the large majority of cases where the organization adopts legislation that applies directly or after transformation in the legal systems of the Member States.

The WTO could be said to fall in the second category; its agreements, its 'secondary law', and the interpretation of these by the dispute settlement bodies can considerably influence domestic policies. Viewed from this perspective, the WTO should certainly have a parliamentary assembly, especially now that the rather undemocratic tradition of European States with respect to trade policy is slowly overcome.[28] Former DG Moore, in his time, made valiant efforts to use the Inter-Parliamentary Union (IPU), a type of international organization of parliaments, as the conduit through which parliamentary interest in, and parliamentary legitimacy of, the WTO could be stimulated. The IPU reacted positively and under its auspices a first parliamentary meeting on international trade was organized in Geneva on 8 and 9 June 2001. At a later stage, the European Parliament also became involved in this initiative and in mid-February 2003 the first meeting was held of what became later known as the Parliamentary Conference on the WTO.[29] Since then, there have

---

[28] Under the EC Treaty the provisions concerning trade policy (Article 113 and later 133) did not foresee any powers for the European Parliament, not even a power of advice. It is only with the recently signed Treaty of Lisbon that the Parliament exercises normal co-legislators' powers together with the Council over autonomous trade policy measures and has a right of approval for trade agreements. See Article 207 and 218 Lisbon Treaty (consolidated version).

[29] See Final Declaration of 18 February 2003, at <http://www.ipu.org/splz-e/trade/dcl.htm> (last visited 4 June 2008).

been yearly meetings of this Parliamentary Conference, which has also organized meetings in parallel with the WTO MCs in Cancún in 2003 and in Hong Kong in 2005. At present, this is the only way to secure a minimum of parliamentary supervision of the WTO, given that the WTO itself lacks the legal authority and the funds to create a parliamentary organ.

It is remarkable that the WTO Agreement itself does not devote a word to one of the most important aspects of the organization, namely its (quasi-)judicial system, except for the provision which states that the GC as the DSB shall govern the dispute settlement system (Article IV:3). The panel system and the Appellate Body can only be found in the DSU. The WTO Agreement differs from constituent treaties of other international organizations like the UN Charter, the EC Treaty, and the Law of the Sea Convention, which contain at least some basic references to their principal judicial organ in their main treaty, while details of dispute settlement and the functioning of their courts are laid down in a separate annex or Statute of the Court that is an integral part of the founding treaty. In the WTO, everything with respect to the dispute settlement is laid down in such a separate agreement.

The dispute settlement system is intended strictly for settling disputes between the Members, usually about the alleged breach of the treaty obligations by another Member. The DSU does not cover the review of the legality of acts of organs or officers of the WTO in the light of the WTO Agreement and its annexes. It is only incidentally, in the framework of a complaint between Members, that a panel or the Appellate Body may need to judge the legality of acts of an organ or an officer of the organization. In practice this happens only very rarely, a well-known example being the *US – FSC* case, in which the legal value of a certain Chairman's statements and so-called decisions that were adduced by the US in its defence was heavily discounted.[30]

Finally it is necessary in this overview of the institutional structure to devote a few words to membership and observers. It has already been remarked in passing that all organs mentioned in Article IV WTO Agreement, as well as all their subsidiary organs, are plenary organs. Membership in the WTO, like in most other organizations, is subject to certain conditions and acceptance by (a qualified majority of) the other Members in the plenary organ.[31] Some international organizations—and notably those that have developed a certain 'acquis' in the form of secondary law and of mutual liberalization—require even negotiations with the candidate country before it can be accepted. In this respect, the WTO is like the Bretton Woods institutions

---

[30] Appellate Body Rep, *US – FSC*, at paras 104–14.
[31] See Art II(2) FAO Constitution (two-thirds majority in the Assembly provided that more than half of the membership is present); Art 1(4) ILO Constitution (admission by two-thirds of the delegates present and voting, including two-thirds of the government delegates); Arts 2(2)(b) and II(2) Agreement of the World Bank and the IMF respectively (new Members may accede at such times and in accordance with such terms as agreed by the Bank or the Board of Governors respectively).

and the EU, requiring considerable negotiations before a new Member can be officially accepted.[32] The WTO, though like the EU, requires acceding Members to buy themselves into the considerable trade concessions that the 'old' Members have already granted to each other, and does not make the Members the final judge of the accession by requiring national ratification of an accession agreement. The Protocol of Accession, that is the sum of the concessions that the new Member has made in negotiations with other Members that are its major trade partners, is concluded with the organization and is adopted by the MC (or GC), through the decision on accession by a two-thirds majority of the Membership.[33]

In connection with membership it is necessary to discuss briefly the way in which the WTO has organized itself for the negotiations of the Doha Development Agenda. During the Uruguay Round, a TNC had been instituted by the Declaration of Punta del Este and attached to it were a number of negotiation groups.[34] Since the GATT 1947 itself had so little of an institutional structure and non-Contracting Parties—in particular the observers in the process of acceding—also wished to participate in the Round, the TNC is best seen as a self-standing inter-governmental Committee with a number of sub-committees charged with different sectors of the negotiations. The overall results of these negotiations, as approved by the TNC, were then offered to an Inter-governmental Conference at Marrakesh, organized under the auspices of the GATT, which proceeded to the collective signing ceremony of the edifice of treaties that had come out of the negotiations and created a new organization, the WTO. The WTO was at the same time the successor and continuation of the GATT 1947, while remaining legally distinct from it insofar as it included identical legal rules as the GATT 1947 (in particular the GATT instrument itself).[35]

Under the Doha Ministerial Declaration,[36] the temporary structure for the future negotiations was firmly placed within the WTO. A TNC was once again created and was this time firmly placed under the authority of the GC.[37] The TNC was given the power to create 'appropriate' negotiation mechanisms as required and to supervise the process of negotiations.

The new institutional situation in the WTO has interesting legal consequences for the adoption of the results of the Doha Development Agenda. The results of the negotiations will consist in part of amendments to Members' schedules of tariff concessions, including agricultural tariffs and other agricultural commitments relating to the Aggregate Measurement of Support, and to their schedules of services

[32] WTO Membership is open to States and autonomous customs territories. See Art XXVI:4(c) GATT 1947 and Art XII:1 WTO Agreement.

[33] Art XII:2 WTO Agreement.

[34] See Declaration of Punta del Este, 20 September 1986, Chapeau.

[35] This was to safeguard the 'single undertaking' and avoid the problem of free riders.

[36] Legally speaking, the Doha Declaration is a decision of the MC under Articles III and IX WTO Agreement.

[37] MC, *Ministerial Declaration Adopted on 14 November 2001*, WT/MIN(01)/DEC/1 (20 November 2001), at para 46.

commitments, and also of amendments to the various WTO covered agreements that need to be adopted each according to the procedures laid down in Article X WTO Agreement. These procedures are highly complicated and may take some time, but if the result of the negotiations can be reached by consensus in the TNC, there should be no reason to assume that subsequently the procedural requirements of Article X, including the requisite majorities, could not be fulfilled and a period of acceptance within which Members have to finalize their constitutional procedures could not be respected.

With respect to observers, the WTO follows a completely split policy with respect to governments, inter-governmental organizations (IGOs) and non-governmental organizations (NGOs). In addition, different rules for observer status apply in different organs. In principle each organ is autonomous in its decision to accept governments or IGOs as observers. The case of NGOs is entirely separate.

All three groups can be an observer to the MC. Governments and IGOs can be observers to the GC and other subordinate bodies. For governments, this is in principle their first step on the way to membership in the organization.[38] IGOs can seek observer status because they have responsibilities related to those of the WTO.[39] In the latter case there will often be arrangements between the WTO and the IGOs concerned, pursuant to Article V:1 WTO Agreement. IGOs need to make their request to the specific organs of the agreement. For example, the Codex Alimentarius Commission, the International Office of Epizootics (OIE) and the International Plant Protection Convention (IPPC) are represented only in the Committee on Sanitary and Phytosanitary Measures (SPS Committee) in which they obviously have great interest because the observance of their guidelines, standards, or recommendations by a WTO Member leads to a presumption of conformity with the WTO SPS Agreement (Article 3(2) SPS Agreement).

Some IGOs have permanent observer status in one WTO body and an ad hoc observer status, decided meeting by meeting, in others. In spite of the rather complicated rules, there is a clear list established of all IGOs that in some way or another profit from observer status.[40]

This is not the case for NGOs. They suffer from the basic principle that WTO meetings 'shall ordinarily be held in private', though it can be decided that a particular meeting or meetings shall be public. It has become normal practice that NGOs can be invited to the meetings of the MC, but they still do not have observer

---

[38] See GC, *Request by the Former Yugoslav Republic of Macedonia for Observer Status in WTO Bodies*, WT/L/16 (20 January 1995), Annex 2.

[39] Ibid. Annex 3.

[40] WTO, *International intergovernmental organizations granted observer status to WTO bodies*, at <http://www.wto.org/english/thewto_e/igo_obs_e.htm> (last visited 4 June 2008). See also chapter 24 of this Handbook.

status to the extent that they can speak or put documents before the MC. They are in attendance, can be present at the meetings, and elaborate arrangements have been created for an NGO Centre at these Conferences.[41] In such centres space is made available for all accredited NGOs, computer and copying facilities are put at NGOs disposal, and meeting rooms for lobbying activities are available. In the experience of the author, the NGO centre has the atmosphere of a big and bustling market, where everybody can and does put forward his or her cause or take on the ongoing Conference, both to the press and to the delegates with whom the NGOs interact throughout the MC. The process of accreditation is again completely ad hoc for each MC. In respect of admitting NGOs as observers, the WTO probably has most to learn from the UN ECOSOC, which has operated for a long time a three-tiered system of observership pursuant to Article 71 UN Charter: general consultative status, special consultative status, and 'the roster'. Broadly these categories correspond to organizations with a demonstrable general interest in the work of the organization (they get the most extensive rights, including the right to speak at the level of the highest organs); organizations with a more narrow interest (they only have the right to speak in the subsidiary organ of their expertise); and organizations whose contribution to the work of the organization may be useful, but only occasionally and on very specific topics (they have no right to intervene in any forum, but enjoy a limited number of privileges with respect to being notified of and being invited to specific meetings).[42]

Article V:2 WTO Agreement certainly gives sufficient leeway to introduce such a multi-tiered system that would apply to the organization as a whole and all its organs and do away with the need for frantic accreditation activity before every MC. However, in the present circumstances there seems to be little likelihood of movement. This is confirmed by the fact that the personal initiative of the then DG Dr Supachai Panitchpakdi to establish an Informal NGO Advisory Body had relatively limited resonance with NGOs. Although this group continues to meet about once a year, mainly to discuss progress (or not) in the Doha Development Agenda, not all major NGOs decided to participate. They preferred to keep their hands free and since it was a personal initiative of the DG, not supported by any decision of the GC, it could not be a high-profile event.

[41] See P Van den Bossche, 'NGO Involvement in the WTO, A lawyer's perspective on a glass half-full or half-empty' *Maastricht Working Papers* 2006–10, at <http://www.unimaas.nl/bestand. asp?id=6981> (last visited 4 June 2008); W Benedek, 'Relations of the WTO with other International Organizations and NGOs' in F Weiss, E Denters, and P de Waart (eds), *International Economic Law with a Human Face* (The Hague: Kluwer, 1998) 479. See also chapter 24 of this Handbook.

[42] See P Van den Bossche, 'Rules on NGO Accreditation, Do Existing Legal Arrangements Facilitate the Legitimization of the Role of NGOs in International Organisations' *Maastricht Working Papers* 2005–10, at <http://www.unimaas.nl/default.asp?template=werkveld.htm&id=F60BL5P00MJO466V 63M6&taal=nl> (last visited 4 June 2008).

IV. Questions Raised by the Overview of the WTO Institutional Structure

The above overview of the institutional structure shows that the central axis around which the whole WTO decision-making machinery turns is the GC, since in normal times it exercises:

- the general decision-making power of the MC, covering the whole sphere of competence of the organization;
- the specific powers attributed by the WTO Agreement to the MC;
- the specific functions assigned to the GC itself;
- the general power of guidance over the specialized Councils.

In addition, the TNC functions under its authority and hence it also keeps track of and broadly supervises the progress of the Doha Development Agenda.

In other international organizations one often finds a certain 'balance of powers'[43] between different institutions, but there is hardly any room for this in the WTO, for the simple reason that there is no other organ that has been given at least a minimum of countervailing weight to the GC by the WTO Agreement.[44] On the one hand, there is the total absence of a non-plenary 'executive' organ. Anything that is temporarily called into life to fill that gap, normally some type of 'Green Room' phenomenon, is only tolerated and lacks any legitimacy in the eyes of many Members, and therefore is never really capable of filling that gap. On the other hand, the DG has only very limited powers under the WTO Agreement as leader of the Secretariat and proposer of the budget, and in spite of some very remarkable and strong-willed personalities that have occupied the post, the DG cannot create enough counterweight to the GC. One step forward is the fact that the DG has been made chair of the TNC.

The main institutional problems in the field of decision-making, therefore, relate to the allocation of competences between organs of the same composition: the plenary organs. As we have seen in the institutional overview above, these problems have

---

[43] Not a real separation of powers, as in national constitutional systems, but a type of balance between the institutions and the powers they have been allocated by the constitutive treaty. Already at a very early stage, when the European Parliament did not yet have 'co-legislative' powers, the ECJ nevertheless considered this balance between the institutions as important: see ECJ, Case 138/79, *Roquette Frères v Council*, [1980] ECR 3333; ECJ, Case 139/79, *Maizena v Council*, [1980] ECR 3393; S Prechal, 'Institutional Balance: A Fragile Principle with Uncertain Contents' in T Heukels, N Blokker, and M Brus (eds), *The European Union after Amsterdam: A Legal Analysis* (The Hague: Kluwer, 1998) 273.

[44] The Appellate Body has let it clearly be known that it does not believe in the balance of powers where the WTO is concerned, see Appellate Body Report, *India – Quantitative Restrictions*, at paras 102–05.

to do with the hierarchy between the plenary organs ('guidance', straight-forward delegation, and the other side of the coin, pushing matters up for decision at the next highest level). They also have to do with the tension between very general powers of decision-making and the implied powers that may flow from such general powers, on the one hand, and what seem to be very specifically attributed powers allocated to specific organs, on the other hand.

In the following sections the specific powers of such organs as the TPRB, the DSB, the specialized Councils, and other subsidiary bodies will be analyzed in greater detail. How do the general decision-making power and the specific decision-making competence of the GC (exercised either on behalf of the MC or on its own account) relate to the specific powers allocated by the agreements to specialized Councils and lower bodies? Is the WTO an organization where attributed powers are dominant or rather general powers from which implied powers may be derived? Is it even useful, in spite of the fact that the treaty language clearly indicates that certain powers are specifically attributed to certain organs, to speak of attributed powers in an institutional system in which the hierarchy between organs of the same composition is an important if not dominant feature? Are the sub-ordinated Councils and subsidiary bodies jealous of their allocated powers or do they not hesitate to pass a final decision upward, respecting hierarchy rather than exercising their attributed powers?

Moreover, the strange mix of 'pouvoirs d'attribution', broad powers of a general nature suitable to an implied powers interpretation, and hierarchy between organs of the same composition raises questions in respect of Rule 33 of the Rules of Procedure mentioned earlier, which states that, if no decision on the basis of consensus can be reached in the lower organ, it can be moved to the higher organ. Can this rule be squared with the institutional structure of the WTO? It could lead to a delegation upwards to a higher level, if consensus cannot be reached at the lower level, even in cases where the power in question has been specifically allocated to the specialized or lower organ. However, it could also lead to a situation where consensus is reached at the lower level and as a consequence there is no need to push the decision upwards to the higher or more general level, while the power to take the decision in question has been specifically reserved to the higher level.

In addition, the question may be raised whether the different 'functions' and decision-making powers bestowed by the WTO Agreements on the different WTO organs lead to the creation of a true system of 'secondary law' of the WTO that is derived from a legal basis laid down in the agreements; or whether most WTO decisions have a *sui generis* character or are even of a primary law type, that is, have the same rank as the WTO agreements themselves.

The questions raised above can only be clarified through an analysis of the general and specific powers of the MC, the GC, the 'emanations' of the GC (in particular the DSB), the specialized Councils, such as the GATS Council and the TRIPS Council, and the other subsidiary bodies, in particular those dependent on the CTG.

V. POWERS AND PRACTICE OF DIFFERENT WTO ORGANS

A. Methods of Decision-Making

Article IX WTO Agreement is formal; the WTO shall continue the GATT 1947 practice of consensus, which is defined as the situation in which no Member, present at the meeting when the decision is taken, formally objects to the proposed decision.[45] Nevertheless, if no consensus can be reached, 'the matter at issue shall be decided by voting', defined as a majority of the votes cast, unless otherwise provided in the WTO Agreement or in the relevant covered agreements (the special majorities of two-thirds and three-quarters of the Members mentioned *inter alia* in Article IX:2 and 3, and Article X:1, 3, 4, and 5). In spite of the binding 'shall' in this provision, there is no example so far of a successful application of majority voting by any chair in the WTO's history. In reality, therefore, the WTO is governed entirely by consensus, even where Articles IX:2 and 3 and XII are involved. Due to the difficulty, if not impossibility, to have two-thirds or three-quarters of the WTO Members represented and present at meetings of the GC, it was felt and expressed in a Chairman's statement of 15 November 1995[46] that consensus would be sufficient and in conformity with the spirit of the WTO on such occasions. This is a clear example of (re)-interpreting or *de facto* modifying the WTO provisions without having to resort to the constitutional techniques of the authoritative interpretation under Article IX:2 and of amendment under Article X.

B. The General and Specific Powers of the MC, Also When Exercised by the GC

The MC has the authority to take decisions on all matters under any of the WTO covered agreements and can take any action necessary to the carrying out of the functions of the WTO. A good example of the exercise of this power is the decision adopted by the MC at Doha on 'Implementation-Related Issues and Concerns' (that is, all the issues and worries, of in particular the developing countries, relating to matters of implementation of the Uruguay Round results, where there were problems of meeting deadlines or lack of capacity to implement, etc). In this decision,

[45] See fn 1 to Art IX WTO Agreement. Note that in the Doha Declaration, above fn 37, there is a reference to so-called 'explicit consensus'.

[46] Statement of the Chairman, *Decision-Making Procedures under Articles IX and XII of the WTO Agreement*, WT/L/93 (24 November 1995).

the MC 'reaffirms' certain views, 'takes note' of certain reports, 'urges' Members, 'requests' that the CTG examines certain proposals, 'instructs' the SPS Committee, and 'directs' the SCM Committee and the TRIPS Council to do certain things.[47] Especially the directions and instructions are notable, since they mostly concern powers that have been specifically granted to the organs in question and they direct the organ in question to exercise that power in a specific way; thus the SCM Committee is enjoined to exercise its power to prolong the transition period for the elimination of prohibited export subsidies by developing countries according to certain prescribed criteria.

As to the specific powers of the MC, it is important to note that its power to grant waivers under Article IX:3 is exercised on a regular basis by the GC and only exceptionally by the MC itself. Such an exception occurred when the MC itself had to grant the waivers for the EC-ACP Partnership Agreement and the EC Banana Regime[48] in respect of the ACP-countries at Doha, primarily because of the political profile that this issue had obtained in the period leading up to the Doha MC.

That the GC normally also grants very important waivers in lieu of the MC is exemplified by the waiver relating to the TRIPS Agreement granted by the GC pursuant to the Doha Declaration on the TRIPS Agreement and Public Health.[49] This waiver should enable WTO Members that have insufficient or no pharmaceutical manufacturing capacities to make effective use of compulsory licensing by having recourse to supplies from other Members especially to ensure that in this way they can confront major plagues, like HIV/AIDS, malaria, dengue, etc in a comprehensive way.[50] As will be discussed below, this waiver was only a stopgap measure on the road to a more permanent solution through an amendment of the TRIPS Agreement, in particular Article 31.[51]

Accession is another specific power of the MC that is normally handled by the GC. But it can rise to the level of the MC itself in the event of highly political accessions, such as the example of China's accession that was approved by the Doha MC.

Authoritative interpretation pursuant to Article IX:2 WTO Agreement thus far is an untested specific power of the MC. Neither the MC itself nor the GC has ever formally exercised this power. Notably, however, the Decision on Implementation-Related Issues and Concerns adopted by the Doha MC contains a number of paragraphs that could be seen as authoritative interpretations of several WTO agreements, including the GATT 1994, the SPS Agreement, the TBT Agreement,

---

[47] MC, *Implementation-Related Issues and Concerns*, WT/MIN(01)/17 (20 November 2001).

[48] See above fn 19.

[49] MC, *Declaration on the TRIPS Agreement and Public Health*, WT/MIN(01)/DEC/2 (20 November 2001). See also chapter 8 of this Handbook.

[50] GC, *Implementation of Paragraph 6 of the Doha Declaration on the TRIPS Agreement and Public Health*, WT/L/540 (2 September 2003).

[51] The Analytical Index in its commentary on Article IX WTO Agreement mentions 20 waivers relating to RTAs and 16 other substantial waivers, next to some 85 Combined Nomenclature waivers.

and the Anti-Dumping Agreement.[52] The terms 'reaffirm' relative to a specific interpretation and 'shall be understood' in respect of specific words or phrases clearly point in that direction. The decision of the MC is not explicitly based on Article IX:2, but refers to Article IX in general. Given the broad scope of the Decision on Implementation-Related Issues and Concerns, the best interpretation may be that the drafters sought by the general reference to Article IX to be as inclusive as possible of the different powers contained in that provision, including the power of authoritative decision.[53]

So far, there exists only one example of the exercise of the power of amendment by the GC on behalf of the MC, namely the approval of the Decision on the Amendment of the TRIPS Agreement, and in particular Article 31, in order to make the TRIPS waiver in this respect superfluous.[54] This first application of the normal amendment procedure is also a test whether the normal use of the amendment procedure can operate within a reasonable time-span and be used for the eventual amendments resulting from the Doha Round. The result so far is not entirely encouraging. Although the requisite consensus could be found in the GC in early December 2005, the Protocol of Amendment of the TRIPS Agreement was opened for two years, until 1 December 2007, but at that date only between ten and twenty Members had deposited their act of acceptance or ratification and a renewal of the period for another two years had to be decided.[55] In the case of results after the conclusion of the Doha Round, a ratification period of four years could be totally unacceptable; a period of one year would be the absolute maximum.[56]

C. The General and Specific Powers of the GC and Its Emanations

The general powers of the GC have already briefly been discussed and it has been shown that there are no known examples of the GC assigning (new) functions to the specialized Councils—it has been rather the MC that has instructed and prescribed specific steps to the specialized Councils or even their subordinate bodies. However, the GC has used these general powers, namely in the decisions on

---

[52] See MC, above fn 47, at paras 1.1, 3.1, 3.2, 5.2, and 7.2.

[53] Note that this power may be used by the MC and the GC to correct 'wrong' interpretations of WTO provisions by panels or the Appellate Body, see Section VII of this chapter.

[54] That a waiver was considered a shaky foundation is demonstrated by the decision to go ahead with the amendment.

[55] TRIPS Council, *Amendment of the TRIPS Agreement – Proposal for a Decision on an Extension of the Period for the Acceptance by Members of the Protocol Amending the TRIPS Agreement*, IP/C/45 (29 October 2007); TRIPS Council, *Annual Review of the Decision on the Implementation of Paragraph 6 of the Doha Declaration on the TRIPS Agreement and Public Health*, IP/C/46 (1 November 2007).

[56] At the end of the Uruguay Round there was a period for ratification of 8 months.

Implementation-Related Issues and Concerns adopted by the GC in the year after Seattle (in May and December 2000) and that constituted the first step towards the MC decision on the same issue adopted at Doha. The May decisions, which touched in particular on the method of work of the GC itself on Implementation-Related Issues and on the TRIMS Agreement, were not in an explicit decision format. However, the decision of 15 December was clearly presented as such and referred to its legal bases in the WTO Agreement, while setting out specific instructions from the GC to *inter alia* the Committee on Agriculture, the SCM Committee, etc.[57]

As to the specific powers of the GC, the making of 'appropriate arrangements' (Article V:1) for effective cooperation with other international organizations supposes that the WTO has treaty-making powers and that it is for the GC to exercise that power. However, on this point there is somewhat of a clash with provisions of the GATS (Article XXVI) and the TRIPS Agreement (Article 68), which purport to charge respectively the GATS Council and the TRIPS Council with discussions with the UN and other organizations active in the field of services and with WIPO. The GATS Council, for example, approved the text of a cooperation agreement with the International Telecommunications Union (ITU) in March 1999.[58] Similarly the TRIPS Council approved the text of the arrangement with WIPO. Ultimately, in both instances the conflict rule of Article XVI:3 prevailed and Article V:1 was applied: the GC gave the final approval and concluded the agreement.[59]

Another specific power is the approval of the Financial Regulations and the (annual) budget. The exercise of this power has led to a legally interesting dilemma. When it was considered necessary to move to a biennial budget cycle, the question arose whether that should be considered contrary to the terms of Article VIII WTO Agreement, which spoke of the annual budget estimate in several places. GC considered several methods;[60] an amendment or an (interpretive) decision of Article VII under Article IX:2 WTO Agreement was probably the most adapted to the purposes, but the ultimate solution deviated from the letter of the pertinent provisions. Ultimately, it was decided that the DG would henceforth present 'two estimated budgets covering a biennial period with effect from the time of the estimates for 2004 and 2005'. This is, if one may say so, a typical GATT 1947 decision. The GC does what it wants to do; a vague cloak of legality is cast over its decision by finding a formula that is not openly at odds with the wording of paragraphs 1 and 3 of Article VIII, though it is quite clearly at loggerheads with its intention. In GATT 1947 days such solutions worked because the GATT Council operated in certain circumstances as a meeting of the Contracting Parties outside the GATT 1947, a kind of *rex*

[57] GC, *Implementation-Related Issues and Concerns*, WT/L/384 (19 December 2000).

[58] WTO, *WTO Annual Report 1999* (Geneva: WTO, 1999), at 68.

[59] It is not necessary to dwell on the GC's specific power in respect of the relationship of the WTO with NGOs (Article V:2 WTO Agreement), which has been discussed in an earlier section of this chapter.

[60] See Footer, above fn 1, at 220–21.

legibus solutus that by consensus could create new GATT 1947 rules at will. These times are over. In the WTO, there now exist secondary rules for norm-creation. Understandably in this particular situation, even if an amendment would nearly have been of the character of Article X:4—one not altering the rights and obligations of Members and thus requiring acceptance only by two-thirds of the Members—this was considered too time-consuming (for reasons of better planning one wanted to start the new budgeting procedure quickly). However, it is difficult to fathom why a serious effort to ensure the presence of at least the three-quarters majority of the Members required for an authoritative interpretation at a GC was not considered worthwhile, especially because ultimately such decisions may be adopted by consensus.[61] Was it fear of the assertion that such an authoritative interpretation was in reality a circumvention of an amendment procedure against which Article IX:2 *in fine* warns? The result now is the suspicion that there may be a double circumvention; namely, the procedure of Article IX:2 is circumvented in order to avoid the suspicion that the GC wanted to circumvent Article X:4. The least one can say is that the legitimacy of the change is not enhanced by this way of proceeding.

The TPRB and the DSB are the 'emanations' of the GC. The TPRB does not raise any major institutional issues. This is not to belittle the importance of the work of the TPRB. Its review procedures are of the utmost importance and are based on the solid foundation of similar 'reviews', also called 'examinations', in the OEEC—where they served principally to check whether Marshall aid was properly used—and its successor organization, the OECD, where they were turned into full-fledged critical appraisals of the macro-economic policy of its Member States. The techniques used are also highly similar: a report by the Member State, a report by the Secretariat, and critical questioning in the meeting by the representative of one or more other Members that have specifically studied the reports.[62]

The TPRM and the huge effort of the Secretariat that is behind the reports has been generally beneficial in most observers' views to Members' proper implementation of their WTO obligations, even though the reports are not supposed to serve specific enforcement purposes or as a basis for dispute settlement procedures.[63] The effect of the obligation to report on one's own trade policy and to respond to a critical report by the Secretariat has often been described as salutary by several policymakers in the field of trade policy.[64]

The DSB, in contrast to the TPRB, has grappled with some problems related to its general and specific powers. Article 2.1 DSU is drafted (especially the word 'accordingly') so as to create the impression that the DSB's general power of administering

---

[61] See Statement of the Chairman, above fn 46.

[62] On the OEEC and OECD 'examination technique', nowadays called 'peer review', see OECD Policy Brief, 'Peer review: a tool for co-operation and change', at <http://www.oecd.org/dataoecd/5/59/22350184.pdf> (last visited 4 June 2008).

[63] TPRM, Annex 3, point (ii).

[64] Personal statements to the author.

the DSU consists of a number of specific powers, such as establishing panels, adopting reports of panels and of the Appellate Body, engaging in surveillance of the implementation of such reports, authorizing the suspension of concessions, etc.[65]

Nevertheless, the DSB adopts decisions of a different type from these specific powers that, according to a strict interpretation of Article 2.1, would limitatively constitute the administration of the rules and procedures of the DSU. For example, disputants occasionally conclude *inter se* agreements on the procedural aspects of cases in which they are involved. Many of these agreements relate to the well-known problem of sequencing, arising from the fact that there is a right to request an implementation panel under Article 21.5 DSU and a simultaneous (and seemingly irreconcilable) duty to demand authorization to suspend concessions within the 6-month deadline mentioned in Article 22.6 DSU. Other agreements relate to the extension of time periods, the composition of compliance panels or of panels for the establishment of the proper level of the authorized suspension of concessions, etc.

Many of these agreements are simply notified to the DSB, which does not need to take a position on them or to adopt them—especially for such a controversial subject as sequencing this is only too logical. Hence they exist in a legal grey area. In some instances, particularly concerning extensions of the reasonable period of time fixed by arbitration under Article 21.3 DSU or the period given by the panel for the withdrawal 'without delay' of a prohibited subsidy under Article 4.7 SCM Agreement, the defendant wants to be well-protected and sometimes asks for an extension of the period by the DSB. An example is the US request, without objection of the complainant (the EC), for the extension of the period of one month for withdrawal of a prohibited subsidy in the *US – FSC* case;[66] the DSB granted the extension.

It may be argued that such permission by the DSB is necessary and desirable, since third Members' interests and rights are at issue. On the other hand, such prolongation by a political body of implementation periods laid down in the report of a (quasi-)judicial body or authority leads to awkward questions about the relationship between the DSB and the panels and arbitrators, whose reports are not supposed to be altered by that body.

Another DSB decision that *prima facie* does not fall under any of the specific powers of the DSB granted by the DSU is the one establishing the 'Rules of Conduct', which also covers problems of conflict of interest for members of dispute settlement panels and members of the Secretariat servicing them.[67] It is probably realistic to assume that the latter decision comes under the general power of 'administering the rules and procedures' of the DSU and that the former, though it might come under the same general power, can better be seen as an exponent of the specific power of

[65] See the specific powers in Arts 6, 16, 21, and 22 DSU.
[66] DSB, *Minutes of Meeting held on 12 October 2000*, WT/DSB/M/90 (31 October 2000).
[67] DSB, *Rules of Conduct for the Understanding on Rules and Procedures Governing the Settlement of Disputes*, WT/DSB/RC/1 (11 December 1996) without written version of the Decision (no legal basis is known therefore).

'surveillance of the implementation of reports' of panels and the DSB—which might help make it palatable that the DSB *de facto* modifies details of a panel or arbiter's report.

It is thus fair to assume that the DSB experiences similar problems concerning the relation between general powers and specific powers, as we already discovered to exist for the MC and the GC. In most cases, and also here, the general powers and their broad interpretation win out; in practice the specific powers are hardly ever seen as an obstacle to an expansive approach to the general powers.

D. The Powers and Practice of the GATS Council and Its Subordinate Bodies

It bears recalling that, according to Article IV:5 WTO Agreement, the GATS Council shall oversee the functioning of the GATS and carry out the functions assigned to it to facilitate the operation of this agreement, and further its objectives. Among the GATS provisions granting powers to the GATS Council, there are first of all provisions on the power to receive information and notifications,[68] secondly the power to establish subsidiary bodies as laid down in Article XXIV GATS, for which specific guidelines were laid down in the Ministerial Decision, adopted at Marrakesh, on Institutional Arrangements for the General Agreement on Trade in Services.

A special characteristic of the GATS is formed by the numerous negotiation provisions it contains in protocols attached to it (for example, the Protocols on Financial and Telecommunication Services), and in the GATS itself, such as the negotiation provisions on safeguards (Article X:1), government procurement (Article XIII), and subsidies (Article XV). A Working Party on GATS Rules has been established to discharge these mandates, which more generally could be said to fall within the forum function as mentioned in Article III:2 WTO Agreement.

In sum, the GATS Council has not received many specific powers beyond the broad functions and powers as laid down in Articles III and IV WTO Agreement. Exceptions include the power to develop disciplines on domestic regulation under Article VI:4 GATS and the power to establish rules and procedures for rectification and modification of schedules under Article XXI:5. Looking at the practice of the GATS Council, the last mentioned power has been exercised in two steps: a Decision on Procedures for the Implementation of Article XXI GATS (Modification of Schedules) of 19 July 1999[69] and a Decision on Procedures for the Certification of

---

[68] Arts III:3 and 5, V*bis* (a), VIII:3 and 4, X:2, and XIV*bis*:2 GATS. In addition, Article XXI:5 grants the power to establish procedures for rectification and modification of schedules of specific commitments.

[69] GATS Council, *Decision on Procedures for the Implementation of Article XXI of the General Agreement on Trade in Services (GATS)*, S/L/7 (20 October 1999); GATS Council, *Procedures for*

Rectifications or Improvements of Schedules of Specific Commitments of 14 April 2000.[70] Whilst the latter decision relates to purely technical modifications to schedules of commitments, the former can be seen as the GATS-equivalent to the procedures of Article XXVIII GATT 1994.[71] An example of the 'overseeing function' laid down in Article IV:5 WTO Agreement are the 'Guidelines on Notifications' adopted by the GATS Council on 1 March 1995, with a standard notification format attached.

It has been explained in some detail elsewhere[72] how the GATS Council coped with the complicated technical issues surrounding the implementation of the Second Annex on Financial Services and the entry into force (or not) of the Second Protocol (on Financial Services). This operation entailed opening the possibility, in the event that the Second Protocol would not enter into force, for Members to withdraw commitments and (re-)inscribe Article II exemptions—actions that formally were contrary to Articles II and XXI GATS. This was done by decisions of the GATS Council that, though formally illegal, were foreseen or authorized in the Ministerial Decision on Financial Services adopted in Marrakesh. This Ministerial Decision has to be seen as an agreement between the parties to the WTO agreements on the (temporary) modification or the interpretation of Articles II and XXI GATS within the meaning of Article 31 Vienna Convention on the Law of Treaties (VCLT).

It is helpful to draw a parallel here to the so-called 'Decision of the Representatives of the Member States meeting within the Council' practised within the framework of the EC and ECSC ('décision cadre' in French). These serve as intergovernmental decisions (or 'traités en forme simplifiée'), not requiring ratification or approval by national parliaments, that are used for small treaty modifications that serve the global purpose of the Community, the classical example being the acceleration of the transitional periods laid down in the old EEC Treaty.[73]

It has been argued that it would be more appropriate to adopt similar decisions in the WTO also within a clearly intergovernmental framework of the collectivity of the Members and not within an organ of the organization, which would thus

the Implementation of Article XXXI of the General Agreement on Trade in Services (GATS), S/L/80 (29 October 1999).

[70] GATS Council, Decision on Procedures for the Certification or Rectification or Improvements to Schedules of Specific Commitments, S/L/83 (18 April 2000); GATS Council, Procedures for the Certification or Rectifications or Improvements to Schedules of Specific Commitments, S/L/84 (18 April 2000).

[71] This power of the GATS Council has been exercised for the first time, when the EC reconsolidated its GATS schedule in 2006, see GATS Council, Communication from the European Communities and Its Member States Certification, S/C/W/273 (9 October 2006).

[72] See PJ Kuijper, 'Some Institutional Issues Presently Before the WTO' in D Kennedy and J Southwick (eds), The Political Economy of International Trade, Essays in Honor of Robert E Hudec (Cambridge: Cambridge University Press, 2002) 81, at 90–92.

[73] See B De Witte in PJG Kapteyn and P VerLoren van Themaat (eds), Het Recht van de Europese Unie en de Europese Gemeenschappen (The Law of the European Union and the European Communities), 6th edn (Deventer: Kluwer, 2003), at 255.

formally act contrary to the treaty.[74] An example where this could have been applied is the repeated deferral of the date of the start of the negotiations on safeguards in the services sector, which had originally been put off by successive decisions of the GATS Council before they finally started in the course of 2000.[75] Having such a decision changing a date laid down in the treaty taken by the collectivity of Members rather than by a WTO organ might give its validity greater weight before panels or the Appellate Body, in case that issue in an indirect way were to come before them.

Finally it has been pointed out that the GATS Council's power, laid down in Article VI:4 GATS, to establish disciplines in the field of domestic regulation 'through appropriate bodies' has resulted in the Disciplines on Domestic Regulation in the Accountancy Sector.[76] These disciplines are only to become legally binding in the course of services negotiations in the Doha Round. They do contain a stand-still provision or a promise not to introduce new measures contrary to the account-ancy disciplines, which is considered to be immediately legally binding. The binding character of this standstill provision, which also appeared in the decisions adopting the Protocols on Financial Services, is best explained as an application of the gen-eral principle of good faith in treaty negotiation, especially during the period of the finalization of the text and its entry into force, as laid down in Article 18 VCLT, but here applied within the WTO-GATS context.

E. The Powers and Practice of the TRIPS Council

The overseeing and monitoring powers of the TRIPS Council do not differ sub-stantially from similar powers of the GC and the GATS Council, but these powers do have peculiar features because of the character of the TRIPS Agreement. The TRIPS Council oversees an enormous notification program of all Members' laws and regulations in the field of intellectual property, which is particularly onerous for the Members.[77] In particular circumstances, once there is a common register of national laws and regulations on intellectual property together with WIPO, the TRIPS Council may decide to waive the obligation. From the text of Article 63.2 TRIPS Agreement it is not clear what procedure should be followed, but it is unlikely that the general provision on waivers of Article IX:3 WTO Agreement applies.[78]

It is important to note that Article 68, which establishes the TRIPS Council and attributes it with a general 'overseeing power' contains an interesting slip of the pen

---

[74] See Kuijper, above fn 72, at 90–92.
[75] See GATS Council, *Decision on Negotiations on Emergency Safeguard Measures*, S/L/43 (2 December 1997); GATS Council, *Second Decision on Negotiations on Emergency Safeguard Measures*, S/L/73 (5 July 1999); GATS Council, *Third Decision on Negotiations on Emergency Safeguard Measures*, S/L/90 (8 December 2000).
[76] See Kuijper, above fn 72, at 94.
[77] Art 63 TRIPS Agreement.   [78] See Kuijper, above fn 72, at 95–96.

when it states 'it shall carry out such other responsibilities as assigned to it by the Members'. It has just been argued above that in certain situations, where one wants to make minor adjustments to the WTO agreements, such as a change in dates, it may be important to emphasize that it is not an organ of the WTO that is trying to modify treaty language without observing the applicable rules for amendment, but rather the Members collectively who are doing so by agreement *inter se*. Here, however, we are not in that situation. It was clearly the intention to delegate certain matters to the TRIPS Council, which should not be decided by the Members outside of the WTO framework, but by one of the highest organs within the organization, the MC, or the GC, as an expression of their general power of 'guidance'. It is in this way that the provision should be read.[79]

Two other oversight functions for the TRIPS Council are laid down in Articles 24 and 71 TRIPS Agreement. The first states that the TRIPS Council shall supervise any negotiations with a view to increasing the protection of geographical determinations. The second provides for a biannual review of the implementation of the agreement, once the transitional period for implementation of the agreement by the developing countries has expired; the result of the review may be an amendment under Article X:6 WTO Agreement.

Finally, the TRIPS Council enjoys two very specific TRIPS powers. One may result in a mini-amendment to be adopted by consensus; namely a modification or prolongation of the five-year period of the non-application of the so-called non-violation and situation complaints to the TRIPS Agreement. This modification or prolongation of Article 64(3) needed to be applied as from 31 December 1999 but initially it wasn't. The second grants a power of 'mini-waiver' to the TRIPS Council, meaning that it can decide to allow a prolongation of the special ten-year transitional period in favour of the least developed countries, as laid down in Article 66(1) TRIPS Agreement, upon a duly motivated request from a least-developed country. The further prolongation of that special ten-year transitional period was one of the points of the Declaration on the TRIPS Agreement and Public Health adopted by the MC at Doha.[80] The TRIPS Council duly obliged and applied the mini-waiver of Article 66(1) for another 14 years (until 1 January 2016) to all least-developed countries.[81] The legal text of that provision needed to be tortured for that purpose, because it originally foresaw only an individual prolongation for a least-developed country that duly had made a request for a prolongation.[82] As a consequence of this mini-waiver, a real waiver from Article 70.9 TRIPS Agreement became necessary because that

[79] For a detailed explanation of the origin of this provision, see Kuijper, above fn 72, at 96, 100–01.

[80] See MC, above fn 49, at para 7.

[81] TRIPS Council, *Extension of the Transition Period under Article 66.1 of the TRIPS Agreement for Least-Developed Country Members for Certain Obligations with Respect to Pharmaceutical Productions*, IP/C/25 (1 July 2002).

[82] Paragraph 7 of MC, above fn 49, was considered to be this duly motivated request for the prolongation, see TRIPS Council, above fn 81, third preambular para.

provision could oblige least-developed countries to grant exclusive marketing rights to pharmaceutical products in specific circumstances.

The prolongation of the mini-amendment to continue the suspension of non-violation and situation complaints in respect of TRIPS questions has been amply discussed in the TRIPS Council. It is a highly controversial question. After the passing of the deadline of 31 December 1999 it became part of the so-called implementation discussion in the WTO but it has not been possible to agree on an ad hoc extension of the deadline, as in the continuing discussion on safeguards in services. Thus non-violation and situation complaints can be brought again in de domain of TRIPS. However no such complaints have been brought *de facto* subsequently to an unopposed statement from the Chair of the GC made at the meeting of 16–17 December 1999, just before the expiry of the deadline to the effect that Members would show self-restraint in those areas of dispute settlement where discussions were ongoing.[83] Notably, this rather shaky legal situation was improved in the later prolongations. The Doha Ministerial Decision on Implementation-related Issues and Concerns stated that, while discussions on this issue continued, 'in the meantime Members will not initiate such complaints'.[84] This formula was called a 'moratorium' in the GC decision of 2 August 2004, the so-called post-Cancún 'July package' and would be extended until the sixth MC in Hong-Kong,[85] where the MC repeated the formula of Doha.[86] Whatever one may say about these attempts at 'upgrading' the legal certainty of this 'moratorium', at least the technique of the Chairman's statement has been abandoned and replaced by a Ministerial Decision twice repeated. This considerably increases the chances of any Member that would, nevertheless, be exposed to a non-violation complaint in the TRIPS area to invoke successfully these decisions as a defense.[87]

Earlier sections of this chapter have discussed how the potential clash between Article 68 TRIPS Agreement (*in fine*) on the powers of the TRIPS Council to 'establish appropriate arrangements' with WIPO and the general powers of the GC to do so with all IGOs that have responsibilities related to those of the WTO (Article V:1 WTO Agreement). The TRIPS Council agreed the text of the agreement with WIPO,[88] but final approval and conclusion were left to the GC. The agreement with WIPO was linked to a decision of the TRIPS Council under Article 63(2) *in fine* TRIPS Agreement on the notifications pursuant to the obligations under the TRIPS Agreement stemming from the provisions of Article 6*ter* Paris Convention. The

[83] GC, *Annual Report (2000)*, WT/GC/44 (12 February 2001), at 4.
[84] See MC, above fn 47, at para 11.1. Although the language is not fully binding, the wording has become much more positive and was included in a formal decision of the MC.
[85] GC, *Doha Work Programme*, WT/L/579 (2 August 2004), at para 1(h).
[86] MC, *Doha Work Programme – Ministerial Declaration*, WT/MIN(05)/DEC (22 December 2005), at para 45.
[87] See above fn 66 and accompanying text.
[88] TRIPS Council, *Minutes of Meeting held on 11 December 1995*, IP/C/M/5 (5 January 1996), at 2.

more general obligation of the Members to notify implementing legislation under Article 63(2) has also been subject to a decision setting out procedures to this effect.

F. The Powers and Practice of the CTG and Its Subsidiary Bodies

The CTG rules over a very varied landscape of subsidiary bodies, but 'ruling' may not be the proper expression for the relationship between the CTG and what are notionally subordinate bodies. Some of the Committees were created not so much by the CTG. They resulted from the decentralized negotiation during the Uruguay Round and were established by the agreements and understandings or continued their existence dating from the Tokyo Round. Especially the latter, such as *inter alia* the Anti-Dumping Committee, always had a different composition than that of the GATT Council and worked largely autonomously from it. They and the Committees created under the new Uruguay Round agreements and understandings were, at the end of the negotiation, forced into the WTO framework and placed under the authority of the CTG. It is clear that these Committees could be expected to be quite independent from the CTG, in part because of the great variety and sometimes technicality of the domains they covered.

Apart from the powers granted to it in Articles IV:5 and 6 WTO Agreement, the CTG carries out directly the powers of the Contracting Parties in the GATT 1994, except those that fall under the remit of the BOP Committee and the CTD, both established by Article IV:7 and placed under the direct authority of the GC. Although the general idea of Article IV:5 is that the CTG in addition carries out the functions assigned to it by the agreements contained in Annex I A to the WTO Agreement, in reality only few of these agreements confer any powers on the CTG. Rather, they give these powers to their own Committees, thus once more emphasizing the fragmentation and relative autonomy of the various sectors within the area of trade in goods. This is even further accentuated by the fact that these Committees are also exercising the tasks of the Contracting Parties in respect of those GATT 1994 provisions (Article VI—Anti-Dumping, Article VII—Customs Valuation, Article XVI—Subsidies, and Article XIX—Safeguards), which have been further developed in the relevant Annex I A Agreements.[89]

If one attempts to look in a somewhat analytical fashion at the powers of the different Committees in the trade in goods area and their relationship to the CTG, it is best to leave out of consideration the Pre-shipment Inspection Agreement, the Agreement on Agriculture, and the Agreement on Textiles and Clothing (ATC). The last one is too specific and no longer of actual interest; the other two have no or

---

[89] The other GATT functions exercised directly by the CTG are those of Arts II, VIII, X, XIII, and XV.

virtually no institutional provisions. There is a near-uniformity in the institutional provisions of the Anti-Dumping Agreement, the SCM Agreement, the Customs Valuation Agreement, and the TBT Agreement. If we take the Anti-Dumping Agreement as an example, the relevant article reads as follows:

There is hereby established a Committee on Anti-Dumping Practices (referred to in this Agreement as the 'Committee') composed of representatives from each of the Members. The Committee shall elect its own Chairman and shall meet not less than twice a year and otherwise as envisaged by relevant provisions of this Agreement at the request of any Member. The Committee shall carry out responsibilities as assigned to it under this Agreement or by the Members and it shall afford Members the opportunity of consulting on any matters relating to the operation of the Agreement or the furtherance of its objectives. The WTO Secretariat shall act as the secretariat to the Committee.

All these agreements were originally negotiated as Tokyo Round Codes and obviously used the same model without giving great thought to it. Especially the reference to 'the Members' instead of 'The Parties' from the Tokyo Round Codes is not in conformity with the new structure of the WTO. In this respect the Agreement on Rules of Origin (AROO), not derived from a Tokyo Round Code, but borrowing the same language, was better attuned to the new times by referring to the 'Council for Trade in Goods' instead of 'the Members'. Since the TRIMS and Safeguards Agreements also use the 'Council for Trade in Goods' in a comparable context, it is safe to conclude that these words should be read everywhere instead of 'the Members' in these provisions.[90]

The Agreements on Import Licensing and on the Rules of Origin have comparable institutional provisions, with the former having no possibilities of the CTG assigning new tasks to it. Both these Committees, as many others, have the explicit duty to report to the CTG. The old Tokyo Round Code Committees, mentioned above, did not have such an obligation—a heritage of their former semi-independent status from the GATT 1947.

The TRIMS Agreement is the only one of the Annex I A Agreements that is closely linked to the CTG and actually charges the CTG with making the most important decisions under the Agreement. After all, the TRIMS Agreement was merely a codification of the most important GATT case law under Articles III:4 and XI GATT 1947. Article 7.2 TRIMS Agreement is in substance rather close to the provision quoted above from the Anti-Dumping Agreements, but also imposes on the TRIMS Committee a duty to report annually to the CTG, in line with similar provisions in the Licensing and Rules of Origin Agreements. The most important decision-making power, namely that of prolonging the transition period for developing countries, has been reserved to the CTG.[91]

The Committees of the SPS Agreement, the TBT Agreement, the Anti-Dumping and SCM Agreements, and to a lesser extent of the Safeguards Agreement, stand out for their specific features in respect of institutional finesse or decision-making power.

---

[90] See also Art 68 TRIPS Agreement.   [91] Art 5.3 TRIMS Agreement.

In respect of the SPS Agreement, the text provides explicitly that the Committee can decide only by consensus (Article 12.1). It may well be argued that there is nothing new here, since all the lower WTO bodies, according to Article 33 Rules of Procedure, are supposed to decide by consensus. Nevertheless, this explicit rule makes sense in connection with the footnote to this provision, introduced at the level of the GC, which states that the consensus rule should also be followed at the higher level, when the agreement concerned prescribes consensus. This excludes that, even at the level of the GC, it should ever be contemplated to have recourse to the theoretical possibility of majority voting under Article IX:1 WTO Agreement. Thus it is guaranteed that decision-making at all levels on sanitary and phytosanitary matters must always take place by consensus—presumably because of the particularly sensitive character of the subject-matter.

The TBT, Anti-Dumping, and SCM Agreements have granted a power to establish subsidiary bodies,[92] and this power has been used. This is the third level removed from the GC and the fourth level from the MC. As a result, this possibly creates some complications, especially as such subsidiary bodies in principle will again be of a plenary character. The SCM Committee had a power somewhat comparable to that of the TRIPS Council under Article 64.3 TRIPS Agreement, namely the power to prolong the period of five years during which certain specific subsidies could be regarded as non-actionable notwithstanding their specificity; this concerned research, regional, and environmental subsidies (Articles 8 and 9 SCM Agreement). Ultimately, the SCM Committee could not agree on the extension of this period. The deadline of 31 December 1999 passed and the Committee never attempted to lift the matter to a higher level.

The Safeguards Committee is even equipped with a quasi-judicial power. According to Article 13.1(e) Agreement on Safeguards, it should determine whether a Member that proposes to take a safeguard measure and plans to pay for it under Article 8.1, as it cannot manage to satisfy the conditions of Article 8.3 for being allowed to safeguard measures for three years without compensation, has been subjected to compensatory suspension of concessions that are 'substantially equivalent' to the safeguard measures taken. So far, the Safeguards Committee has not yet exercised this power.

G. The Question of Attributed Powers v. Implied Powers: Examples in the Field of Trade in Goods

There are a number of rather important powers in the field of trade in goods specifically attributed to the Committees established under certain Article IA agreements. The way these powers have been exercised by these Committees or by the CTG or

---

[92] Art 16.2 Anti-Dumping Agreement; Art 24.2 SCM Agreement; Art 13.2 TBT Agreement.

rather the way the exercise of these powers has been 'delegated up' to the GC gives an impression of how (un)important the system of specifically attributed powers is considered to be in the WTO.

The TBT Committee has been given the power pursuant to Article 12.8 TBT Agreement to grant 'specified time-limited exceptions in whole or in part from obligations under this Agreement' in favour of developing country Members that face special difficulties in fully implementing the TBT Agreement. This amounts to a type of 'mini-waiver'. Similarly, under Article 27.4 SCM Agreement, the SCM Committee has been given the power to determine whether a request to extend the special transitional period for the maintenance of export subsidies by developing countries is justified. The Committee under Article 29.4 SCM Agreement may also grant departures from the notified programmes and transitional measures from a centrally planned economy and their time frames for Members with an economy in transition, if such departures are deemed necessary for the process of transformation.

As noted above, the TRIMS Agreement also contains a very important power to modify Members' rights and duties under the agreement, which however has not been granted to the Committee, but has been reserved to the CTG. Under Article 5.1 TRIMS Agreement, Members can notify illegal TRIMS measures that are still on their statute books and obtain a special transitional period for putting such measures into conformity with the agreement; for developing countries the transitional period is five years and thus ended on 31 December 1999. The CTG may extend this transition period pursuant to Article 5.3 TRIMS Agreement at the request of a developing country Member that demonstrates particular difficulties in implementing the provisions of that agreement.

If one looks at the practice with respect to these attributed powers, it is quite striking to note that they are not always fully defined as powers of the Committees in question (or in the case of the TRIMS Agreement, the CTG) but sometimes referred to higher authority, possibly under Rule 33 that enjoins lower bodies where no consensus can be reached to refer the decision to the higher body—thus giving preference to that procedural rule over the strict attribution of the particular power to the specialized, but lower body.

For example, decisions taken with respect to the application of Articles 5.1 and 5.3 TRIMS Agreement were finally taken at the level of the GC, rather than that of the CTG. Among various decisions concerning procedures for extensions under Article 27.4 for certain developing-country Members, one was taken post-Doha by the SCM Committee itself,[93] another one—even though the SCM Committee had agreed on the text—was pushed up to the level of the GC.[94] Politically this may be understandable as an expression of high-level political interest in issues relating to

---

[93] SCM Committee, *Procedures for Extensions under Article 27.4 for Certain Developing Country Members*, G/SCM/39 (20 November 2001).

[94] Decision of 27 July 2005 based on SCM Committee, *Article 27.4 of the Agreement on Subsidies and Countervailing Measures*, G/SCM/120 (17 July 2005).

the so-called Implementation Related Issues and Concerns—action on this topic forms a type of underlying condition for the continued progress of the Doha Round. Legally it remains significant that specifically allocated powers cede before such political interest of the higher bodies.

On the other hand, there is the rather remarkable record of the SPS Committee. As we saw, this is one of the few Committees subordinated to the CTG, which has been given a broad decision-making power and a specific voting rule, namely consensus.[95] Given the controversial character of most SPS issues it is quite impressive that this Committee has produced a fairly steady stream of useful decisions, and revisions of decisions. These decisions were sometimes taken under guidance from the MC or the GC and sometimes in the framework of the Decision on Implementation Related Issues and Concerns. Nonetheless, the decisions were always worked out in the Committee and never referred 'upstairs' to the CTG or the GC.

The SPS Committee has produced in the course of the years a Decision on the Implementation of Article 4 SPS Agreement (on the question of equivalence) and its revision.[96] In more or less close connection to that decision, the Committee adopted Guidelines to Further the Practical Implementation of Article 5.5 SPS Agreement (on achieving consistency in the application of the concept of appropriate level of protection);[97] in addition to Recommended Procedures for Implementing the Transparency Obligations of the SPS Agreement (Article 7) and its revision.[98] Moreover, the 1997 Procedure to Monitor the Process of International Harmonization was revised in 2004.[99] Not all of these decisions may be of particular great importance or strictly speaking legally binding. Nevertheless, their adoption points to a capacity to agree and a considerable consistency in approach—and might well be emulated by other Committees under Annex IA agreements.

H. Concluding Remarks about the Plenary Organs, Their Inter-relationship, and Decision-making

The powers of all the discussed different plenary organs often overlap, and there is a certain hierarchy that permits the higher organs to give 'guidance' to the lower ones.

---

[95] Art 12.1 SPS Agreement.

[96] SPS Committee, *Decision on the Implementation of Article 4 of the Agreement on the Application of Sanitary and Phytosanitary Measures*, G/SPS/19/Rev.2 (23 July 2004), the earlier decision dates back to 26 October 2001.

[97] SPS Committee, *Guidelines to Further the Practical Implementation of Article 5.5*, G/SPS/15 (18 July 2000).

[98] SPS Committee, *Recommended Procedures for Implementing the Transparency Obligations of the SPS Agreement (Article 7)*, G/SPS/7/Rev.2 (2 April 2002).

[99] SPS Committee, *Revision of the Procedure to Monitor the Process of International Harmonization*, G/SPS/11/Rev.1 (15 November 2004).

Equally, the strict attribution of powers to some of these organs does not mean very much, because hierarchy and consensus-seeking at a higher level impose themselves and thus set aside the strict attribution of powers. Such strict attribution of powers seems to have positive value only in the case of highly specialized Committees that take highly technical decisions that are of importance and have an impact only on the application of the specific agreement covered by the Committee. The way in which the SPS Committee succeeds in regularly taking useful decisions is an example. The application of consensus decision-making at all levels, except in cases where it was clearly desired by the drafters, such as in respect of all SPS decisions, does not generally have a positive effect. It is enormously time-consuming and often leads to very minimal or no result. Moving up a draft decision to higher levels only makes sense, if some change can be expected from that move because either the composition or the decision-making modus of the organs changes. Actually the present text of Article X:1 WTO Agreement permits the MC and the GC (and only these two organs) to take decisions by majority of the votes cast. If that text were given some real life, moving up decisions through organs with the same composition could be given some meaning again. If necessary it could be combined with the approach recently taken in the OECD—another organization that functions in principle by consensus—where the Council has taken a decision (by consensus) to expand the list of subjects that can be decided by majority vote.[100]

VI. THE ABSENCE OF NON-PLENARY ORGANS

The absence of an organ of restricted composition in the WTO is a unique feature for a world-wide organization. It has been briefly indicated in the introduction how this was a consequence of the institutionally truncated nature of the GATT and the limitations the Uruguay Round negotiators imposed on themselves in the light of the limitations of the US negotiating mandate.

On this issue, and in so many other respects, the WTO is a perfect continuation of the GATT 1947 in a slightly more institutionalized guise. The GATT 1947 had already been struggling with the absence of a Board or Council for quite some time once its membership began to grow to a number above forty, several attempts were made to

---

[100] OECD Council, *Resolution of the Council on a New Governance Structure for the Organisation*, C(2006)78/Final (24 May 2006), Report of the Working Party in the Annex to the Resolution, at para 44.

bring about such a body of restricted membership. During the Tokyo Round, the so-called Group of 18 functioned more or less on an official basis. Later the so-called 'Green Room' phenomenon arose, so named after the green decoration of a meeting room across the hall from the DG's office.[101]

Given the realities of the 'explosion' of GATT 1947 and WTO membership during the Uruguay Round and just after the creation of the WTO,[102] there was no alternative for the WTO but to continue with the 'Green Room' approach after its creation. 'Within the Green Room', there was always also a particularly powerful group of Members, whose agreement was considered absolutely necessary for any successful result of a round. During the Uruguay Round, this group was called the 'Quad' and consisted of the US, the EC, Japan, and Canada, with India as a type of equally indispensable outsider. During the Doha Round, a new group of this type has emerged, consisting this time of the US, the EC, India, and Brazil, possibly with China as the indispensable outsider.

Another technique that has been used in order to smooth decision-making at MCs and to create at least *ad hoc* some mechanisms of representativeness, was to select some time in advance of the MC a number of Trade Ministers of countries that can be considered representative for a group of Members and who personally have a good reputation, as Vice-Presidents of the Conference. Through early and intensive contacts with the Secretariat and the main negotiators, they were supposed to support the Trade Minister of the Host State, who normally presides the MC and to serve as go-betweens for 'their group' with the Chairman of the MC and the DG and *vice versa*. Sometimes, this approach has certainly helped (for instance Doha); other times, it has not been able to prevent chaos and 'rebellion' by a number of Ministers (at Seattle).

The Seattle MC of 1999 did a lot to delegitimize the 'Green Room phenomenon'. The criteria for inviting Members into the Green Room on a consistent or *ad hoc* basis (for instance only for agriculture, or only for issues of trade and development), for inviting certain Trade Ministers to be Vice-Presidents of the Conference repeatedly, and others only once, are highly non-transparent. Using the Vice-Presidents to smooth decision-making on the basis of them being 'representative' or 'responsible' for a certain group of Members, may work, but by its nature requires extensive telephone contacts or small confidential preparatory meetings that do not exactly enhance transparency for the other Members. All these elements contributed to the climate of lack of understanding and mistrust that led to the 'rebellion' of a large number of Ministers from developing countries at Seattle and contributed to the breakdown at Cancún.

What is clear from the various *de facto* techniques used in the WTO to continue the 'Green Room' technique without confessing to it, is that there are a number of

---

[101] The name 'Green Room' continued after the colour of the decoration changed.
[102] Presently the WTO has 153 Members.

requirements that must be satisfied by a non-plenary body in the WTO. It must be representative of the membership at large, it must give special representation to Members without whose participation a negotiation cannot succeed (see the Quad phenomenon), and it must be adaptable (see the change in the composition of what once was 'the Quad') in order to reflect changing economic realities in the world.

Keeping this in mind and looking at the various models provided by the existing Boards and Councils of specialized UN agencies, the conclusion is well-neigh inevitable that the model of the appointment of the government representatives in the ILO Governing Body is the best example to be followed by the WTO. Slightly over one third of government representatives are appointed by the Members of 'chief industrial importance' and the rest shall be appointed by the Members selected for that purpose by the government delegates to the Labour Conference, excluding the Members of chief industrial importance. The criterion of 'chief industrial importance', which has been based in the ILO on the basis of varying criteria over the years,[103] has permitted the composition of the Governing Body to be automatically adapted from time to time in the light of shifts in economic realities, while at the same time assuring the presence and the influence on the ongoing negotiations in the organization of these countries that are indispensable. The remaining members of the Governing Body are truly representative of the overall membership. It has certainly helped the Governing Body to maintain its effectiveness and legitimacy with the membership over the years.[104]

It is to be regretted that the Sutherland Report has not dared to break fully the taboo and simply to propose the creation of a non-plenary Board or Council.[105] There can be no doubt that the WTO is in need of such an organ. The long history of both the GATT 1947 and the WTO groping for informal ways to heal this GATT birth defect, which has been transmitted to the WTO, is testimony to that need. All these attempts have lacked legitimacy and transparency. And here is the rub: one sometimes suspects that a large number of Members want to keep the WTO in this position where *de facto* Green Room mechanisms continue to be used, because it is accepted that a non-plenary body is necessary just as in all other world-wide organizations, but are happy to keep matters in a quasi-illegitimate

---

[103] See Art 7 ILO Constitution, especially Article 7.3 that charges an impartial Committee with looking into all questions relating to the selection of members of chief industrial importance before they are decided by the Governing Body. See ILO Committee on Legal Issues and International Labour Standards, *Fourth Item on the Agenda: Composition of the Governing Body – Criteria for Geographical and Country Representation within the Governing Body*, GB.300/LILS/4 (November 2007). This document sketches the evolution of the notion 'Members of chief industrial importance'.

[104] Personal discussion with Member of the ILO Legal Office.

[105] It got stuck in proposing halfway solutions, such as regular special meetings of capital-based high trade officials.

situation so that the outcomes of these non-plenary mechanisms may be discarded or 'unmasked' as the results of an illegitimate process, when that seems politically advantageous.

However, a clear alternative that satisfies all the requirements that are presently taken into account, when trying to achieve efficient decision-making in the organization and in the preparation of the MCs, is readily at hand and should be openly embraced. Otherwise the organization will remain mired in informal solutions that lack sufficient legitimacy to carry consistently the weight of important and controversial decisions. The crucial question, when following the ILO example, will be selecting the criterion or criteria governing the selection of the Members of 'chief trade importance', which should be the core of a new Board or Council. Perhaps pure trade weight is too simple and some attention should also be given to general industrial weight in the world. On the other hand, if the rest of the Members of the Board or Council are selected on the ground of pure representativeness, there is sufficient counterweight inside the body to make a simple trade-weighted selection feasible.[106] To this end, it is also necessary to carefully balance the number of Members of each group with the decision-making rules in the Board or Council to prevent any veto. In short, the absence of a non-plenary organ in the WTO has clearly become a major handicap in WTO governance and a solution to that gap should be found to avoid any doubt about the legality of the decisions of that body or about the legitimacy and representativeness of its very existence.

A crucial question is, of course, how to envisage the relationship between the Board or Council and the GC. The most radical solution would be to follow in the well-established footsteps of the UN specialized agencies and create a system in which the MC continues to meet every two years and in the interim all powers (except a number of very clearly circumscribed major powers) are devolved to the non-plenary body. In spite of the fact that this is a well-tested model, it is perhaps too radical for the WTO. A good middle way might be to continue to allow the GC to meet once or twice a year, mainly concentrating on the exercise of important powers that the WTO treaties presently delegate downward from the MC in the interim between two sessions (such as waivers, accessions, etc.), whilst the non-plenary body would exercise all GC powers that belong to the Council as such (with the exception of the power to adopt authoritative interpretations).

---

[106] Note that trade weight would not determine the number of votes, only the selection. The rule should remain one state one vote. In the literature, Thomas Cottier has consistently made highly elaborate, but also realistic proposals for weighted voting in the WTO that would also considerably improve the situation with respect to decision-making. At the present stage this author believes that priority should be given to the creation of a legitimate non-plenary organ because that will have very beneficial secondary effects for WTO governance, notably for the DG and the Secretariat who will have a very valuable and legitimizing sounding board or counterpart. More generally, such an organ will contribute to the balance between the organs of the WTO.

VII. THE DG AND THE SECRETARIAT

A. The DG

The function of DG gets a minimum treatment in the WTO Agreement for reasons that are basically identical to those of the absence of a non-plenary organ—the need not to deviate too obviously from the GATT 1947 model to avoid putting the US delegation on a collision course with Congress. Apart from a few specific powers related to the preparation of the Budget[107] and the appointment and the direction of the personnel of the organization,[108] Article VI:2 WTO Agreement refers to a future decision of the MC containing regulations that set out the powers, duties, conditions of service, and term of office of the DG. After the disastrous election process that ended in Michael Moore and Supachai Panitchpakdi sharing a term of office of six years (1999–2005), the GC managed to come up with a decision on the election process to be followed for DGs.[109]

This is quite a remarkable document in the field of the law of international organizations in that it sets out the whole process in detail and *inter alia* involves a meeting with the whole WTO membership in a formal GC meeting. It is also quite interesting from the point of view of WTO law, since it formally opens the possibility that, if consensus turns out not to be possible before the deadline for the appointment ends, 'Members should consider the possibility of recourse to a vote as a last resort'.[110] However, this should 'be understood to be an exceptional departure from the customary practice of decision-making by consensus, and shall not establish any precedent for such recourse in respect of any future decisions in the WTO'.[111] The decision lays down a term of office of four years and allows reappointment for another term of four years. It also makes clear that the DG's remuneration package shall be determined by the Committee on Budget, Finance and Administration, subject to approval by the GC. The text states explicitly that the remuneration package shall not be negotiable with the DG-designate.[112] This decision, therefore, does not set out the powers and the duties of the DG beyond the two powers that have been bestowed on him or her directly by the WTO Agreement, the direction of the Secretariat and the presentation of the budget. The DG, therefore, has a fairly weak

---

[107] Art VII:1 WTO Agreement.   [108] Art VI:3 WTO Agreement.

[109] The actual GC decision of the meeting of 10 and 11 December 2002 has proved elusive; the draft (that probably was not changed) is GC, *Procedures for the Appointment of Directors-General*, WT/GC/W/482/Rev.1 (6 December 2002).

[110] See GC, *Procedures for the Appointment of Directors-General*, WT/GC/W/482/Rev.1 (6 December 2002), at para 21.

[111] Ibid.

[112] Ibid., at paras 22 and 25. To what extent the non-negotiable character of the package will be sustainable in reality is questionable.

position in relation to the other organs of the WTO and to the Members. This is also true in comparison to other international organizations of the same type and responsibility. In UNESCO, for instance, the DG has a recognized right of initiative (Article XI UNESCO Constitution). In the WHO, the DG is *ex officio* secretary of the Health Assembly and of the Board (Article 31 WHO Constitution). In the FAO, the DG, subject to the general supervision of the Conference and the Council, shall have full power and authority to direct the work of the organization (Article VII:4 FAO Constitution). In the IMO, there is also a provision implying that it is the DG who is in charge of the work of the organization, namely where the DG is charged with keeping the Members informed of the activities of the organization (Article 46 IMO Convention). In the ILO, the DG has a direct link with the Governing Body that appoints him and he shall be responsible for the efficient conduct of the activities of the organization (Article 8 ILO Constitution). In the IMF, the Managing Director is even President of the Executive Board (Article XII:4 IMF Articles of Agreement).

It is obvious that, in the WTO, the DG *de facto* takes greater responsibilities than merely directing the Secretariat and proposing the budget. This has been recognized by granting him or her the presidency of the TNC and thus giving him or her, also formally, a certain responsibility for the conduct of the negotiations in the Doha Development Agenda (DDA). It is well known that previous DGs have also played a central role in trade negotiations, even to the point of producing draft texts under their own responsibility, as Arthur Dunkel did during the Uruguay Round.[113] On the other hand, as long as there is no decision of the GC spelling out the duties and powers of the office, every WTO DG will need to fight for his or her place and to assert himself or herself, more so than colleagues in other international organizations who benefit from clearer provisions as to their powers and functions. The current mantra of the WTO as a supposedly Member-driven organization[114] prevents the DG being recognized as having full powers to direct the activities of the organization, similar to his or her colleague in the FAO. However, it would seem worthwhile if Members in the GC were to invest some time in producing a decision setting out the powers and duties of the DG, just as they did for the election, term of office, and remuneration of the DG.[115]

The lack of a non-plenary organ is also to the detriment of the position of the DG, since in other international organizations, even if he or she is not the chairman of the Executive Body, it still is his or her sounding board for all matters of some importance in the life of the organization. Discussing matters with the Executive Body is a way of gaining legitimacy for his or her day-to-day leadership of the organization. This need is demonstrated by the durability of the 'Green Room phenomenon' in the WTO. However, as has been signalled earlier, the 'Green Room' has been heavily

[113] The so-called Dunkel draft, TNC, *Draft Final Act Embodying the Results of the Uruguay Round of Multilateral Trade Negotiations*, MTN.TNA/W/FA (20 December 1991).

[114] JH Jackson, 'The WTO "Constitution" and Proposed Reforms: Seven "Mantras" Revisited' 2001 *Journal of International Economic Law* 4(1) 67.

[115] This is also one of the points supported by the Consultative Board, above fn 1, at 73–74.

discredited after the Seattle MC and at any moment can be discredited again, if it suits the interests of a few (non)-participants. Hence, a clear formalization of an Executive Board remains very important for the proper functioning of the DG and the WTO as a whole.

B. The Secretariat

The Secretariat of the GATT 1947 had always been very small compared to other international organizations—a few hundred persons at most. Officially it was the Secretariat of what was called ICITO-GATT. Upon the creation of the WTO, a transition from ICITO-GATT to the new organization was necessary. This raised the issue of what model the Secretariat should follow. Should it stay with the UN system of salaries and benefits to which the ICITO-GATT had always been linked, even though the GATT was not officially a UN specialized agency?[116] Or should it attempt to follow the Bretton Woods organizations? The latter in the end was not in the cards, since the Members were not ready to follow the level of remuneration prevailing in the IMF and the World Bank,[117] but the UN system was not exactly loved by the personnel that had suffered from considerable variations in purchasing power of their salaries and pensions with the many vicissitudes of the dollar in international markets during the eighties.

Ultimately, it was possible to create an autonomous system of insurance and pensions with the help of a large insurance company specialized in international organizations. In the end, this was the option chosen, including a WTO system of remunerations with a self-standing salary scale. The technical side of this transition and the consultation of personnel took a considerable time. After adoption of the Staff Regulations and Staff Rules in conformity with Article VI:2 WTO Agreement[118] the formal transition from the ICITO-GATT to the WTO Secretariat could take place only on 1 January 1999.

There is nothing surprising about how the international character and independence of the Secretariat and its leader, the DG, are safeguarded by the WTO Agreement. Article VI:4 WTO Agreement contains the usual formulae about the exclusive international character of the responsibilities of the DG and the Secretariat and how, on the one hand, the Secretariat shall not seek or accept instructions from anyone outside the WTO, whereas, on the other hand, the Members shall respect the international character of the Secretariat and not influence it in the discharge of

---

[116] However, the ITO was supposed to become a UN specialized agency and hence the ICITO operated under UN auspices and under its system of salaries and benefits.

[117] The IMF and IBRD are largely autonomous in setting their salary scales, as they earn their own income, whilst the WTO remains dependent on Members' contributions.

[118] WTO, *Staff Regulations – Proposed WTO Text (Revised Draft) – Purpose and Scope*, WT/BFA/9, L/7636 (25 September 1995).

its duties. Similarly, the officials of the organization (as well as the representatives of the Members to the organization) shall have the necessary functional privileges and immunities as are usual for other international organizations. This is expressed by referring in Article VIII:4 to the Convention on the Privileges and Immunities of the Specialized Agencies. On this point, the WTO followed the UN model. The organization itself, of course, has also the necessary privileges and immunities *vis-à-vis* its Members.

Another important aspect of the creation of the WTO and its own Secretariat has been the conclusion of a headquarters agreement with Switzerland.[119]

There can be some doubt about the extent to which the staff has at all times been happy by the choice that has been made to leave the UN mould and to create Staff Regulations and Rules and a system of salaries and benefits that stands on its own. However, it is unrealistic to think of a way back, especially as the WTO has never considered becoming a UN specialized agency, not even in the rather independent way in which the IMF and the World Bank have managed to maintain that status.[120]

In the period of the Uruguay Round negotiations and the first years of the WTO, the Secretariat grew compared to the GATT Secretariat, but still remained very modest in size; presently some 635 staff compared to over 5,000 for the FAO and well over 6,000 for the World Bank.[121] With this number the WTO is among the smallest of Secretariats of world-wide organizations. Nevertheless, the staff became less 'family' and whereas during the GATT period staff conflicts were usually kept inside and were settled by some compromise, after the turn of the century staff members started to find their way to the ILO Administrative Tribunal. So far, the Tribunal decided seven WTO-related cases, the last three decisions all found their origin in the same operation of reassessing a number of old, so-called local recruitments to see whether they had in reality been international recruitments, and were all dismissed.[122] Two cases concerned staff members that were dissatisfied with amicable settlements offered to them by the administration in reaction to a complaint.[123]

---

[119] GC, *Headquarters Agreement – Decision by the General Council on 31 May 1995*, WT/L/69 (1 June 1995).

[120] See W Meng, 'Commentary to Article 63' in B Simma et al (eds), *The Charter of the United Nations, A Commentary*, 2nd edn (Oxford: Oxford University Press, 2002), at 18–19.

[121] See H Nordstrom, 'The WTO Secretariat in a World of Change' 2005 *Journal of World Trade* 39(5) 819, at 847. Nordstrom could only dispose of comparative figures for 1996, when WTO regular staff was at 510. The figure of about 635 in the text is based on information available on the WTO website.

[122] The difference between a local and an international recruitment is important, since benefits such as 'home leave', expatriation allowance, etc. are linked to international recruitment. See ILO Administrative Tribunal, *Judgment No. 2637*, 103rd Session (11 July 2007); ILO Administrative Tribunal, *Judgment No. 2638*, 103rd Session (11 July 2007); ILO Administrative Tribunal, *Judgment No. 2639*, 103rd Session (11 July 2007).

[123] See ILO Administrative Tribunal, *Judgment No. 2186*, 94th Session (3 February 2003); ILO Administrative Tribunal, *Judgment No. 2531*, 101st Session (12 July 2006). The first one granted damages 50 per cent higher than the offer for moral injury as well as costs; the second one imposed exactly the settlement offer of the administration.

Therefore, only two cases remain that represent a serious conflict where the administration was wrong.[124] The overall working climate in the organization would seem, therefore, to remain quite good. There have been collective actions for higher salaries and benefits, but these are more or less normal occurrences in most international organizations. As one observer has remarked, it would seem to be, after all, the policy of many Members to keep international organizations on the brink of bankruptcy.[125] The impression that this is also true for the WTO cannot be entirely suppressed. It has been convincingly pointed out that since its inception the tasks of the WTO have enormously expanded and the number of regular staff has not grown commensurately.[126] It is not just that the number of meetings held and the number of documents issued have increased dramatically, but that also the number of trade policy reviews has grown with the number of Members, the need for public relations activities must have increased dramatically with the initially rather negative press that the new WTO was getting (including maintaining one of the best websites of all international organizations), the steady growth in not only the number but also the sheer volume of individual cases of dispute settlement,[127] and the huge increase in technical cooperation activities and training courses that became an important element of the post-Doha climate.

Members have reacted to these developments with not much willingness to meet the staffing and other resource needs of the Secretariat. Developed countries, however, have been willing to improve the climate after the Doha MC with generous voluntary contributions earmarked for capacity-building in developing countries and other technical assistance issues—for which a special trust fund has been set up. Undoubtedly, such help is welcome, but it is very narrowly focused and does not do justice to the general overburdening of the Secretariat, both on the logistical side (infrastructure, meetings, and language services) and on the conceptual and policy side (less than half the personnel is working in these sectors).

A former insider of the Secretariat notes that the Secretariat under this pressure is actually moving in the direction of outsourcing certain of its activities to other

[124] ILO Administrative Tribunal, *Judgment No. 2226* (16 July 2003); ILO Administrative Tribunal, *Judgment No. 2254*, 95th Session (16 July 2003). The first one concerned a director abruptly laterally removed by the DG without any serious procedure, who received damages for moral injury. The second one is legally the most interesting one, since it posited the principle that the administration cannot accept, without any serious reflection and further discussion with the person concerned, the latter's waiver of a disciplinary procedure.

[125] J Klabbers, *An Introduction to International Institutional Law* (Cambridge: Cambridge University Press, 2002) chapter 6.

[126] Nordstrom, above fn 121 at 847–48. He mentions *inter alia* a near doubling of the number of meetings between 1996 and 2001 to some 4,500 meetings per year and an increase in the number of documents and pages published per year with some 50 per cent and over 30 per cent respectively in the years 1996–2000. Regular staff grew 25 per cent in the years 1996–2008.

[127] Cases such as those involving GMOs and alleged subsidies to Airbus and Boeing have reached gargantuan proportions with bookcases full of document binders and very complicated arrangements of safe-keeping for documents that are highly business confidential.

international organizations.[128] This would seem to be corroborated by what one can read on the WTO website. The WTO is implementing its trade-related technical assistance (TRTA) largely in cooperation with UNCTAD, the International Trade Center (a joint venture of UNCTAD and WTO), and the OECD. The academic world is also encouraged to bid for WTO TRTA activities. Similar tendencies can be seen for economic research and analysis. Here, the OECD and UNCTAD are also left much of the work that the WTO Secretariat should do, especially as the OECD has a developed country perspective on trade and UNCTAD is supposed to have a vision that is more congenial to developing countries.

However, outsourcing seems to be a solution that is *de facto* forced upon the Secretariat and not the consequence of a clear choice of the DG and the Secretariat. The option has been considered that the Secretariat should maintain its 'lean' image, but add a little bit more of the 'mean' to it, especially by being more activist in advancing possible options or even 'the solution' in the trade negotiations and by being more emphatic, when it would seem that Members are not fulfilling their obligations under the WTO agreements.[129]

Moreover, the Secretariat can only be stronger and 'meaner' when its leader, the DG, will have a stronger position. This becomes only possible if the GC will finally provide him or her with a proper description of his or her powers and duties and with a proper and legitimate sounding board in the form of an Executive Council with official status.

VIII. Some Institutional Aspects of WTO Dispute Settlement

A. The DSB

The DSB is not a judicial organ. It is an atavism that had to be maintained in the WTO institutional system, once again to placate the US Congress—and it is suspected also other Members—by pretending that very little had changed and that

---

[128] Nordstrom, above fn 121, at 849.

[129] Ibid.; Consultative Board, above fn 1, at 73. The Consultative Board even goes so far as to borrow the term 'guardian of the treaties' from European law, where it has been used to describe the Commission's powers in the so-called infringement procedure laid down in Articles 227 and 228 EC Treaty. This parallel would seem to drive matters too far, given that the Secretariat has no comparable powers in the WTO Agreement and that the TPRM, the typical procedure during which the Secretariat is capable of signaling unsatisfactory implementation of the rules of the various WTO agreements, may not be used for dispute settlement purposes.

acceptance of panel reports and even Appellate Body reports by a political organ—the GC in its dispute settlement disguise—was still indispensable. However, the fact that (positive) consensus, that is, the need to have consensus on the adoption of a panel report—which often was lacking since the losing party often broke the consensus—was replaced by so-called 'negative consensus', that is, the need to have consensus on not adopting a panel or Appellate Body report[130]—which would never be reached, since it required the 'winning party' to act against its own interest by breaking consensus—implied that the DSB inevitably became a rubber stamp for adopting these reports. Its action on reports was therefore purely symbolic and the idea that the WTO, because adoption by a political organ remains necessary, is only a quasi-judicial system is largely a useful fiction.[131]

The DSB's real function lies in the debate that follows after the adoption of a panel report and in its surveillance function during the months—and sometimes years—that follow after the meeting where the report was adopted. The debate gives the opportunity to the losing party to let off steam and voice its disappointment, and sometimes even vent its frustration at having lost or having made arguments that could find no favour with the panel or the Appellate Body.[132] Sometimes, it even serves as a forum where the winning party can caution the judicial organs that some aspects of the report should not be carried too far or too easily be extrapolated to other areas of WTO law. The debate becomes particularly valuable, when not only the winning party crows victory and the losing party protests more or less vehemently, but when other Members join the debate and go beyond some perfunctory remarks to support or to express doubts about the report that has just inevitably been adopted. There is a well known saying in the US that 'The Supreme Court knows who won the last elections'. It serves to demonstrate that the highest judicial authority in a country may decide on strictly legal terms, but is not entirely politically naïve and understands the general climate in society at a certain time and thus will take care that its judgment, especially in its reasoning, takes account of that climate. In the same way the discussions in the DSB on the occasion of the adoption of panel reports, especially if they are generalized among the Members, offer precious indications to the Appellate Body what the prevailing mood is among the membership and thus can help it in improving its reasoning in future cases.

---

[130] Only Art 17.14 DSU on the adoption of Appellate Body reports speaks explicitly of 'negative consensus'. Art 16.4 DSU on the adoption of panel reports simply states that a panel report shall be adopted at a DSB meeting within 60 days after its circulation to the parties, unless it is appealed.

[131] The same is true for the establishment of panels and the authorization of suspension of concessions and other obligations.

[132] Sometimes, some losing parties have gone too far in criticizing the Appellate Body. Even though this usually happens under strong internal political pressure and in cases were internal legislation is at issue that will be very difficult to reform, it does not excuse the loss of the minimum level of respect and deference that is due to the judicial arm of the WTO. Discussion in strong terms of important judicial decisions, including Appellate Body reports, in society at large is only to be welcomed, but it should not be stoked up by governments.

However, even more important is the surveillance of cases that have not yet been implemented by the losing party both during the 'reasonable period of time' that a party has obtained for implementation and thereafter, even when suspension of concessions and other obligations has already been authorized and been used. This is the period when the DSB serves as the forum for 'the mobilization of shame'. If a Member is reminded month after month in the DSB that it has not yet followed the rulings and recommendations of the panel or Appellate Body report it inevitably undermines its authority and prestige within the WTO as a law-abiding Member.

There is no doubt that in the cases that require a modification of legislation, especially in the large Members and when such legislation is based on a long tradition or is strongly supported by important and vocal segments of the public,[133] it may prove extremely difficult or even impossible to implement the particular reports. This goes against the spirit and perhaps the letter of the DSU,[134] but nevertheless a price is being paid both in the continued suspension of concessions and other obligations (normally higher import duties) and in the loss of authority and prestige that is reaffirmed regularly in the DSB meetings. No emperor likes to be told regularly that he has no clothes on.[135]

A final remark on the DSB and its functioning in the WTO institutional framework relates to the fact that the DSB should be extremely circumspect in handling panel and Appellate Body reports. The DSU grants the DSB the authority only to adopt (and in the unlikeliest of cases, not to adopt) panel and Appellate Body reports. It should never interfere with the content of the reports, at least not with the substantive content and reasoning of the report. It has been mentioned earlier that in one particular case, the DSB took a decision at the request of the losing party and the acceptance of the winning party to change a time limit for implementation, in that case the withdrawal of a prohibited subsidy, laid down in the report. That is acceptable as being within the surveillance powers of the DSB and did not fundamentally undermine the authority of the report, especially since the change remained limited. It is suggested, however, that the DSB should not go further than such procedural issues.

[133] One can think of the hormones and GMO legislation in the EC and the anti-dumping legislation in the US.

[134] See the debate between Hippler Bello and Jackson in the *American Journal of International Law* in 1996 and 1997, and later summarized and revisited in JH Jackson, 'International Law Status of WTO Dispute Settlement Reports: Obligation to Comply or Option to "Buy Out"' 2004 *American Journal of International Law* 98(1) 109.

[135] It is important that the possibility of monetary compensation be considered. This would make it feasible for small economies to retaliate against big economies without hurting themselves and it would ensure that the national legislature is confronted every year in the budget it has to approve with the monetary cost of its own unwillingness to implement a panel or Appellate Body report. This might provide the extra stimulus needed. Finally, monetary compensation in general international law is the recognized alternative for specific performance. See M Bronckers and N van den Broek, 'Financial Compensation in the WTO: Improving Remedies in WTO Dispute Settlement' 2005 *Journal of International Economic Law* 8(1) 101.

B. The GC

Matters became much more serious and dangerous for the dispute settlement system when the GC interfered with the power of self-organization of the Appellate Body under Article 17(9) DSU. The issue was undoubtedly contentious, namely the unorganized practice that developed of sending panels, and later also the Appellate Body, so-called *amicus curiae* briefs. Many of these briefs came from industry associations, from public interest NGOs, etc.[136] Most developing countries were opposed at the time to such *amicus* briefs, since they believed that they would be coming essentially from organizations from developed countries and thus lead to a developed country bias in these procedures. The Appellate Body decided that in principle panels could accept or not accept *amicus* briefs, given the broad wording of Article 12 and 13 DSU on panel procedures and the right of panels to seek information, especially in the light of a panel's duty to make an objective assessment of the facts.[137] When the Appellate Body in a later case[138] decided to lay down a somewhat organized procedure to grant leave to file *amicus* briefs, if the organization in question could demonstrate that it could make a contribution to the debate that was not likely to be repetitive of the contributions already made by the parties and the interveners in the dispute, all hell broke loose. The Appellate Body based this action explicitly on its powers of self-organization. A large group of developing country Members demanded a special meeting of the GC,[139] at which they proceeded to level harsh criticisms at the Appellate Body for its action; only the US supported the Appellate Body.

With the benefit of hindsight it is easy to see that this was a typical example of the ethos of diplomats, combined with the mantra of the Member-driven character of the organization, coming into head-on collision with the rule of lawyers.[140] The Members' representatives in the GC were simply unable to see the necessity for a judicial body anticipating a stream of *amicus* briefs and to provide a mechanism to receive such briefs, even though it was aware of the controversial character of the issue. Justice should not only be done, but should also be seen to be done and that was only possible through an established procedure for leave to file an *amicus* brief.

The diplomats, on the other hand, simply did not want the *amicus* briefs and denied their existence and the ensuing problems related to this refusal. Invoking

---

[136]   See also chapters 13 and 24 of this Handbook.

[137]   Appellate Body Report, *US – Shrimp*, at paras 104–06.

[138]   Appellate Body Report, *EC – Asbestos*, at paras 51–52. Note that the Appellate Body had already decided that in principle it could, just like panels, accept *amicus* briefs, but had not found it useful to take them into account in that particular case, see Appellate Body, *US – Lead and Bismuth II*, at para 39.

[139]   GC, *Minutes of Meeting Held on 22 November 2000*, WT/GC/M/60 (23 January 2001).

[140]   See JHH Weiler, 'The Rule of Lawyers and the Ethos of Diplomats: Reflections on the Internal and External Legitimacy of WTO Dispute Settlement' *Harvard Jean Monnet Working Paper* 9/00, at <http://www.jeanmonnetprogram.org/papers/00/000901.htm> (last visited 4 June 2008).

the Member-driven mantra, they seemed to resent that the Appellate Body had exercised its right to interpret the DSU in *US – Shrimp*—a right that they seemed to claim for themselves without acknowledging that Members had given that right to the Appellate Body in the highest instance when they ratified the DSU. The Chairman of the GC more or less saved the day by reading a statement ending with a warning that the Appellate Body—in the absence of express rules on the matter—should exercise extreme caution in future cases concerning *amicus* briefs, 'until Members had considered what rules were needed'. This was a considerable intimidating statement that basically pretended that Members could reclaim the authority to interpret the WTO agreements. However, given what was said that day, matters could have been worse. The Chairman was right, since the negotiators had foreseen that, as in any democratic system, decisions of the highest judicial organ must be open to parliamentary override, the Parliament in this case being the MC or the GC. Article IX:2 WTO Agreement reserves the right to adopt authoritative interpretations of the WTO Agreement and the other covered agreements, including the DSU, to these organs by a three-fourths majority of the Members.[141] However, it is characteristic for the prevailing situation in the WTO that the GC at no moment considered the possibility to follow up on what seemed to be the strong convictions of a very large majority and actually use the procedure of Article IX:2 WTO Agreement.

The result left the Appellate Body damaged but no remedial 'legislative action' was taken.[142] This diagnosis is unfortunately confirmed by another such episode, where the Appellate Body tried to use its powers of self-organization again, this time to put order into such a simple question as judicial holiday of which the Appellate Body and its personnel are in constant danger of having none, depending on the vicissitudes of whether and when panel reports are distributed and appealed. A brief grumble of some big users sufficed to make the Appellate Body renounce these plans of self-regulation once again and one must conclude that the Appellate Body's powers of '*autogestion*' in Article 17.9 have basically been frittered away by the Members or, in any case, lost by the Appellate Body.

---

[141] Given the numbers in the special GC meeting, it would certainly not have seemed impossible to mobilize the requisite numbers in the GC at a later meeting to adopt an authoritative interpretation of Arts 12 and 13 DSU, namely that the absence of clear rules meant that the filing of *amicus* briefs was prohibited.

[142] This is a situation that has been deplored often in a somewhat different form, namely that the political organs are not capable of taking decisions and that therefore the burden is on the dispute settlement system and its organs. See CD Ehlermann, 'Six Years on the Bench of the "World Trade Court": Some Personal Experiences as Member of the Appellate Body of the WTO' in M Bronckers and G Horlick (eds), *WTO Jurisprudence and Policy: Practitioners' Perspectives* (London: Cameron May, 2004) 13. My diagnosis on the basis of the above-related episode unfortunately seems to arrive at an even worse conclusion, namely that the WTO's political organs are strong and/or thoughtless enough to damage the judicial organs without being sufficiently interested in following up and using the proper procedures to remedy their grievances, leaving both sides of the organization enfeebled.

One might ask whether the above diagnosis of the Appellate Body's position is too pessimistic, given that very many in and around the WTO continue to tout the dispute settlement system as the success story of the organization. In the legal academic community there is occasionally robust and healthy criticism of the decisions of panels and the Appellate Body, but nothing of a nature to warrant the conclusion that the WTO judicial organs deserve severe sanction or that their performance is much worse than that of the supreme or constitutional courts of most countries.[143] It is all the more worrying that Members who lose cases are increasingly willing to go over the top in their statements of criticism of the Appellate Body in the DSB; and that collectively the Members in the GC have been demonstrating an insouciance of the health and prestige of the Appellate Body that could put at risk the very survival of the dispute settlement system that they claim to be such a success.

IX. Conclusion

In her fascinating study of the constitutionalization of the WTO, Deborah Cass mentions as one of the defining elements of the elusive process of constitutionalization that there should be 'a constitutional moment', when a new '*Grundnorm*' is being defined.[144] On the basis of the above analysis of the WTO's institutional aspects, one arrives inevitably at the conclusion that the MC at Marrakesh may have been such a constitutional moment insofar as the new dispute settlement system was concerned. With its binding procedures for the institution of panels and the virtual impossibility to block panel and Appellate Body reports, as well as the automatically available appellate jurisdiction, the DSU indeed constituted a sea change from the earlier system. For the rest, however, on the purely institutional aspects of the WTO 'Constitution' such a 'constitutional moment' was lacking. The continuity with the GATT 1947 was simply too great; no quantum leap was made. The most likely way to bring about such a constitutional revolution would consist of the formal creation of a non-plenary board and a clear definition of the powers of the DG and the Secretariat in conformity with Article VI:2 WTO Agreement. The creation of a non-plenary organ, in which a limited number of Members would be of special trade importance, would have a multitude of secondary beneficial effects

---

[143] See WJ Davey, 'Has the WTO Dispute Settlement System Exceeded its Authority?: A Consideration of Deference Shown by the System to Member Governments and its Use of Issue-Avoidance Techniques' 2001 *Journal of International Economic Law* 4(1) 79; see also chapter 16 of this Handbook.

[144] See Cass, above fn 3.

on the functioning of the DG and the Secretariat. It would also introduce in the WTO the type of balance between organs of different composition and responsibilities that has been an organizing principle with legal overtones in other international organizations. Without this step the WTO might easily remain stuck in a rather sterile back and forth between different plenary organs without serious collaboration. In this way it will never function as the international organization that Members intended to create. It will continue to be largely incapable of taking incremental decisions and changes in the rules of international trade, and continue to suffer from what one may call 'Round sickness', that is to say that decisions to make progress can only be taken at cataclysmic multi-annual events called 'Rounds'. And it will continue to constrain DGs to function below their potential without the legitimate sounding board of an Executive Board. This is all the more regrettable because there are indications in the system that progress can be made in a more rational and incremental way, witness the relatively good record of the SPS Committee. This chapter is also a plea for more research into the reasons why in the WTO certain things work and others don't.

SELECTED BIBLIOGRAPHY

I Alexovicová and P Van den Bossche, 'Effective Global Economic Governance by the World Trade Organization' 2005 *Journal of International Economic Law* 8(3) 667

Consultative Board, *The Future of the WTO: Addressing Institutional Challenges in the New Millennium* (Geneva: WTO, 2004)

T Cottier, 'Preparing for Structural Reform in the WTO' 2007 *Journal of International Economic Law* 10 (3) 497

WJ Davey, 'Institutional Framework' in PFJ Macrory, AE Appleton, and MG Plummer (eds), *The World Trade Organization, Legal, Economic and Political Analysis*, Vol 1 (Berlin: Springer, 2005)

M Footer, *An Institutional and Normative Analysis of the World Trade Organization* (Leiden: Martinus Nijhoff, 2006)

JH Jackson, *The World Trade Organization, Constitution and Jurisprudence* (London: Royal Institute of International Affairs, 1998)

H Nordström, 'The World Trade Organization Secretariat in a Changing World' 2005 *Journal of World Trade* 39(5) 819

E-U Petersmann, 'Addressing Institutional Challenges to the WTO in the New Millennium: a Longer-Term Perspective' 2005 *Journal of International Economic Law* 8(3) 647

AH Qureshi, *The World Trade Organization: Implementing Trade Norms* (Manchester: Manchester University Press, 1996)

DP Steger, 'The Culture of the WTO: Why it Needs to Change' 2007 *Journal of International Economic Law* 10(3) 483

P Van den Bossche, 'Radical Overhaul or Pragmatic Change? The Need and Scope for Reform of Decision-Making in the World Trade Organization' *Maastricht Faculty of Law Working Papers* 2006–1

P Van den Bossche, *The Law and Policy of the World Trade Organization* 2nd ed. (Cambridge: Cambridge University Press, 2008)

CHAPTER 6

....

GATT

....

FEDERICO ORTINO

'Chi siete?
Cosa portate?
Si, ma quanti siete?
Un fiorino!'
Ie doganiere in *Non ci resta che piangere* (1984)

I. Introduction

THE importance of the General Agreement on Tariffs and Trade (GATT), concluded in Geneva on 30 October 1947, applied on a provisional basis from January 1948 until December 1994 and reincarnated since the establishment of the WTO in 1995 in the GATT 1994, cannot be overstated. As it functioned as the major international 'agreement' and 'institution' at the heart of the multilateral trading system, the GATT accomplished much of its original mandate: the substantial reduction of tariffs and other barriers to trade and the elimination of discriminatory treatment in international commerce.[1]

Scholars have described the GATT 1994 as an 'incomplete contract' for at least three sets of reasons. First, the GATT 1994 directly binds only certain trade policies, leaving WTO Members significant discretion over domestic regulatory and fiscal policies with a potentially high trade impact. Second, the GATT 1994 employs vaguely worded provisions, leaving the determination of the actual meaning of the agreement subject to adjudication or to further treaty negotiations. Third, the GATT 1994 includes more or less explicitly an ambitious built-in agenda with regard to the liberalization of Members' trade policies, conditioning the success of this agenda to Members' ability to reach a consensus in future negotiating rounds.[2] In this sense, the GATT 1994 is no different from most other international treaties, which suffer from similar 'birth defects'.

The present chapter addresses a few selected key issues stemming out of the 'incomplete' character of the GATT 1994, and which remain controversial. The chapter is structured in three parts, along the lines of Mavroidis' subdivision of GATT 1994 disciplines: (i) disciplines on 'trade instruments' (measures affecting importation or exportation), (ii) disciplines on 'domestic instruments' (measures affecting production or consumption), and (iii) disciplines on 'state contingencies' (specific emergencies dealing, for example, with balance of payments, currency exchange, and dumping).[3] The chapter advances that while the GATT 1994 has, so far, accomplished a lot in terms of establishing the key principles and approaches to the regulation of trade in goods, it has still further challenges to meet in its not-too-distant future.

---

[1] See further chapters 2, 3, and 4 of this Handbook.

[2] PC Mavroidis, *The General Agreement on Tariff and Trade: A Commentary* (Oxford: Oxford University Press, 2005); H Horn, G Maggi, and R Staiger, 'Trade Agreements as Endogenously Incomplete Contracts' *2006 NBER Working Paper* No W12745, at <www.papers.nber.org/papers/w12745> (last visited 27 March 2008).

[3] PC Mavroidis, *Trade in Goods – An Analysis of International Trade Agreements* (Oxford: Oxford University Press, 2007).

II. Disciplines on Trade Instruments

This section focuses on two specific contentious issues surrounding GATT 1994 disciplines dealing with trade instruments: (a) the scope of the *per se* prohibition on import restrictions pursuant to Article XI GATT 1994 particularly as it concerns 'process and production standards' or standards that regulate the manner or method in which products are produced or manufactured, and (b) the reduction of tariffs as part of the GATT 1994 built-in agenda and the Doha Round negotiations on non-agricultural market access.

A. The Scope of Article XI GATT 1994 *Per Se* Prohibitions on Restrictions on Importation and Process Standards

Despite the clear prohibition in Article XI, for several years GATT Contracting Parties maintained, and at times increased, quantitative restrictions on the importation of products.[4] During the Uruguay Round, the need to devise mechanisms to phase-out quantitative restrictions in sectors such as agriculture and textiles and clothing was expressly recognized and reflected in several WTO Agreements, including the GATT 1994 BOP Understanding (Articles 2 and 3), the Safeguards Agreement (Articles 6 and 11), the Agreement on Agriculture (Article 4), as well as the ATC.[5]

The most problematic feature of Article XI GATT 1994 relates to the scope of application or the 'objective element' of the prohibition of quantitative restrictions. In other words, how far should a WTO panel interpret the notion of 'restriction on the importation of products'? The difficulty in ascertaining the precise scope of application of Article XI stems initially from an apparent contrast between its heading 'General Elimination of *Quantitative Restrictions*' and the actual wording of its basic obligation in paragraph 1 prohibiting, more broadly, import restrictions made effective through quotas, import or export licences, or *other measures*. Secondly, the existence of Article III GATT 1994 dealing with internal regulation raises the issue of the dividing line between the far-sweeping *per se* prohibition of Article XI and the potentially more lenient non-discrimination principle of Article III.

---

[4] Article XI also prohibits restrictions on exportation. However, this section will only focus on import restrictions.

[5] See Panel Report, *Turkey – Textiles*, at paras 9.63–9.65.

Looking at GATT panel practice and WTO case-law dealing with the concept of 'restriction on the importation', the term 'restriction' has generally been given a *broad* interpretation taking into account the potential trade effects of the measure under review.[6] This is most obvious with regard to quotas,[7] and in particular with regard to import or export bans or zero-quotas,[8] which are usually deemed to constitute *per se* restrictions or prohibitions on importation (or exportation) in violation of Article XI:1.

On the other hand, the term 'on importation' has generally been interpreted in a *strict* manner limiting the scope of Article XI to measures (i) *directly regulating* the importation of products (*Canada – Foreign Investment Review Act (FIRA)*) and (ii) *applying exclusively* to imported products (*Canada – Alcohol II*).[9] This reading is based on the Note Ad Article III envisaging the possibility of a conflict in the application of Article III:4 and Article XI. The Note provides as follows:

> any law, regulation or requirement of the kind referred in paragraph 1 which applies to an imported product and the like domestic product and is [...] enforced in the case of the imported product at the time or point of importation, is nevertheless to be regarded as [...] a law, regulation or requirement of the kind referred to in paragraph 1, and is accordingly subject to the provisions of Article III.[10]

Although the Note appears to refer only to the case of a *single* measure that is applied or enforced in different 'places' depending on whether the products are imported or domestic, its rationale is sufficiently clear to include the case of *two apparently*

---

[6] See Panel Report, *India – Quantitative Restrictions*, at para 5.128, where the Panel found that the import licensing system maintained by India, being a discretionary import licensing system because licences were not granted in all cases but rather on unspecified 'merits', operated as a restriction on imports within the meaning of Article XI.1.

[7] See GATT Panel Report, *EEC – Quantitative Restrictions*; GATT Panel Report, *Japanese Measures on Imports of Leather*; GATT Panel Report, *Japan – Agricultural Products*; Panel Report, *Turkey – Textiles*, at para 9.66.

[8] See GATT Panel Report, *Canada – Herring and Salmon*, at para 4.1; Panel Report, *Canada – Periodicals*, at para 5.5.

[9] See GATT Panel Report, *Canada – Foreign Investment Review Act (FIRA)*; GATT Panel Report, *Canada – Alcohol II*. For WTO decisions see Panel Report, *India – Quantitative Restrictions*, at para 5.142, fn 338; Panel Report, *Korea – Various Measures on Beef*, at paras 114 and 702–05; Panel Report, *Dominican Republic – Import and Sale of Cigarettes*, at paras 7.261–7.262. A further confirmation of the meaning and purpose of Article XI may be gained by looking at the historical antecedent to the GATT 1947: International Convention for the Abolition of Import and Export Prohibitions and Restrictions, done at Geneva, 8 November 1927, League of Nations Doc C.559, M.201 1927.IIB (1927), reproduced in 46 US Statute at Large 2461. See also F Ortino, *Basic Legal Instruments for the Liberalisation of Trade: A Comparative Analysis of EC and WTO Law* (Oxford: Hart, 2004), at 83–85.

[10] See GATT Panel Report, *Canada – Foreign Investment Review Act (FIRA)*, at para 5.14. For a different view on the scope of application of Article XI GATT 1994, see JHH Weiler, 'The Constitution of the Common Marketplace: Text and Context in the Evolution of the Free Movement of Goods' in P Craig and G de Búrca (eds), *The Evolution of EU Law* (Oxford: Oxford University Press, 1999), at 355–8.

distinct measures applying a similar standard respectively to domestic products and imported products.[11]

Despite the general approach described above, GATT/WTO practice has taken a contrasting approach with regard to import prohibitions based on 'process and production standards'. The issue was first raised in the two famous (albeit una-dopted) GATT Panel Reports on *US – Tuna*.[12] These cases concerned a US measure prohibiting both the taking of dolphins incidental to harvesting yellowfin tuna in the Eastern Tropical Pacific Ocean (ETP) and the importation of yellowfin tuna and tuna products harvested in the ETP not using fishing techniques designed to reduce the incidental taking of dolphins. While the complainants had argued that the US import prohibition constituted a quantitative restriction on importation within the meaning of Article XI GATT 1947, the US had counter-argued that the US import prohibition of tuna and tuna products merely constituted the 'border arm' of the US laws regulating the harvesting of (domestic) tuna and thus were internal regulations under the Note Ad Article III. Both Panels rejected the applicability of Article III:4 on the basis that 'Article III covers only measure affecting products as such'.[13] They found that the US measures constituted import prohibitions for purposes of Article XI:1.[14]

The *Tuna* Panels' approach was followed, though only implicitly, by the WTO Panel in *US – Shrimp*,[15] another dispute regarding a US process standard. In that case, the US measure at issue prohibited imports of shrimp from any country not meeting certain policy conditions protecting sea turtles imposed in the US. The Panel found that the measure under review imposed a 'prohibition or restriction' within the meaning of Article XI:1.[16]

The implication of this reading is that process standards (although in principle applied to both domestic and imported products/manufacturers alike) are caught by the *per se* prohibition of Article XI. It appears that this interpretation is premised on an incorrect reading of Article III. In particular, both *Tuna* Panels confused the language employed to define the 'scope of application' of Article III with the language describing the 'normative content' of Article III. With regard to the former, internal regulations are caught by Article III if they *affect* the internal sale, purchase, distribution, etc. of products. For purposes of this determination, the scope of application of Article III is quite broad. It practically covers any type of national regulation that has an effect, even if indirect, on the competitive conditions of products. With regard to the 'normative content', Article III provides that

[11] See Panel Report, *EC – Asbestos*.
[12] GATT Panel Report, *US – Tuna I*; GATT Panel Report, *US – Tuna (EEC)*.
[13] GATT Panel Report, *US – Tuna I*, at paras 5.10–16.
[14] Ibid at paras 5.17–18; GATT Panel Report, *US – Tuna (EEC)*, at para 5.10.
[15] Panel Report, *US – Shrimp*.
[16] Ibid at para 7.17. The US Government had not argued that the measure imposed on imports of shrimp and shrimp products fell under Article III.

internal regulations should not be *applied* to imported or domestic products so as to afford protection to domestic production. This should simply be read as imposing on WTO Members an obligation to regulate their markets without discriminating between *products* on the basis of their origin or nationality. In this context, the reference to 'products' as such should be viewed as a specification of the subject matter of the GATT 1994, not as limiting the scope of application of Article III.[17]

Applying this view to the measure at issue in *US – Shrimp*, if the US import ban is seen as the border arm of an equivalent internal regulation prohibiting the use of turtles-unfriendly nets for catching shrimp and thus affecting the internal sale of shrimp products, the import ban should not be caught by the *per se* prohibition of Article XI. It should be reviewable under the non-discrimination principle of Article III.[18]

Since *US – Shrimp*, no further decisions have been rendered on the applicability of Articles III and XI to 'process standards'. Nevertheless, the Panel Report in *EC – Asbestos*[19] seems to support the argument advanced in this section. Although the case related to an import restriction based on 'product standards', the Panel confirmed that the dividing line between Articles III and XI GATT 1994 is drawn on the basis of whether or not the measure under review is simply part of a broader regulatory framework applicable to both imported and domestic products, even if not in an identical manner.[20]

In conclusion, for purposes of deciding the applicability of Article XI (and Article III), it should not matter whether the measure at hand is a process-standard or a product-standard. Both types of regulation may be considered as falling either under Article XI or Article III. For example, an import ban on shrimps caught without using turtles friendly devices (a process-standard) or an import ban on asbestos (a product-standard) may be caught *either* by Article XI if they are applied *only* to imported products *or* by Article III if similar requirements are also imposed on domestic products.

B. Tariff Reduction Under the GATT 1994 and the Doha Round Negotiations on Non-Agricultural Market Access

One of the major accomplishments of the GATT 1994 has been the reduction of customs duties on international trade in goods. In its original text, the only express

---

[17] R Howse and D Regan, 'The Product/Process Distinction: An Illusory Basis for Disciplining "Unilateralism" in Trade Policy' 2000 *European Journal of International Law* 11(2) 249, at 253–57; J Wiers, *Trade and Environment in the EC and the WTO: A Legal Analysis* (Amsterdam: Europa Law Publishing, 2002), at 277–78. For a different view see JH Jackson, 'Comments on *Shrimp/Turtle* and the Product/Process Distinction' 2000 *European Journal of International Law* 11(2) 303.

[18] See also Mavroidis, above fn 3, at 76–80.   [19] Panel Report, *EC – Asbestos*.

[20] The Panel drew particular attention to the Note Ad Article III, which specifically covers a situation in which a law, regulation, or requirement applies both to an imported product and the like domestic product and is enforced in the case of the imported product at the time or point of importation. See also Wiers, above fn 17, at 176–77.

reference to tariff reduction was in one of the recitals of the Preamble to the GATT 1994. However, with the adoption of Article XXVIII*bis* GATT 1947 on *Tariff Negotiations* during the Review Session of 1954–55,[21] GATT Contracting Parties recognised that 'customs duties often constitute serious obstacles to trade'. Therefore, they may sponsor from time to time negotiations on a reciprocal and mutually advantageous basis, directed towards the substantial reduction of the general level of tariffs.

In this respect, the central obligation has been the 'tariff concession', which is a commitment to levy no more than an agreed duty on a particular item.[22] Tariff concessions are inserted in each WTO Member's Schedule of concessions. The Schedules annexed to the GATT 1994 become an integral part of the agreement.[23] Article II, under the heading 'Schedules of Concessions', contains a general prohibition against less favourable treatment to imports compared with that provided for in a Member's Schedule.[24]

Since 1947, eight 'rounds' of multilateral tariff and trade negotiations have been completed. As a result, tariffs are now set on average at single-digit levels: full implementation of the Uruguay Round resulted in the bound simple average tariff of 7 per cent across all merchandise trade and all WTO Members. However, the picture is more complex as there are differences in the current level of customs duties between products such as manufactured (industrial and textiles) and agricultural products, between developed and developing countries as well as between different developed countries and between different developing countries.

For example, the post-Uruguay Round bound average tariff of all WTO Members is for manufactured goods 6 per cent, for textiles and clothing 12 per cent, and for agriculture 32 per cent. The bound average tariff rate across all commodities for developed countries is 4 per cent, and for developing countries 25 per cent. Developed countries' number of imports whose tariff rates are 'bound' is 99 per cent of product lines, while for developing countries the number is 73 per cent.[25]

The average tariff rate on manufactured products in developed countries is 3.8 per cent (US 3.9 per cent, EU 4.1 per cent, Japan 3.5 per cent), while developing countries' average tariff rate on manufactured products is 21 per cent (Korea 11.7 per cent,

[21] GATT, *Analytical Index: Guide to GATT Law and Practice*, 6th edn (Geneva: GATT, 1994), at 912.

[22] JH Jackson, WJ Davey, and AO Sykes, *Legal Problems of International Economic Relations: Cases and Materials* (St. Paul: West Publishing Co., 1995), at 384; JH Jackson, *World Trade and the Law of GATT* (Indianapolis: Bobbs-Merrill, 1969), at 201.

[23] Art II:7 GATT 1994.

[24] Following the Uruguay Round, the Understanding on the Interpretation of Article II:1(b) was included in the GATT 1994 as a clarification of the rule in Article II:1 relating to 'other duties or charges'.

[25] WB, 'Market Access for Developing Countries' Exports' (27 April 2001), at <http://www.siteresources.worldbank.org/BRAZILINPOREXTN/Resources/3817166-1185895645304/4044168-1186409169154/21Market.pdf> (last visited 27 March 2008), at 16.

Malaysia 17.2 per cent, Brazil 30 per cent, India 58.7 per cent; in Latin American countries it ranges between 25 per cent and 50 per cent).[26]

The average tariff rate on agricultural products in developed countries is 27 per cent (EU 18 per cent, US 12 per cent), while in developing countries it is 52 per cent. Commodities with the highest average tariff include dairy products (116 per cent in OECD countries and 74 per cent in non-OECD countries), frozen beef, pork or poultry (106 per cent in OECD countries and 75 per cent in non-OECD countries), sugar beet (104 per cent OECD countries and 64 per cent in non-OECD countries), and fresh beef, pork or poultry (96 per cent in OECD countries and 73 per cent in non-OECD countries).[27]

Relevant differences exist between bound and applied rates, the latter being on average half of the former. In 1996, for example, the applied simple average tariff across all merchandise trade was 3 per cent for developed countries and 13 per cent for developing countries (compared to bound rates of, respectively, 4 per cent and 25 per cent). For both industrial products and textiles and clothing, developed countries' applied tariff rates usually remain lower than those of developing countries. With regard to agricultural products, on the other hand, developed countries' applied rates are on average greater than those applied by developing countries (in 1996, it was 27 per cent and 18 per cent respectively) because there is usually no difference between the bound and applied rates for agricultural products in developed countries, including the EU and US.[28]

Further tariff reduction is one of the core objectives of the ninth trade round, the Doha Round, which was launched in 2001 and at the time of writing has yet to be concluded. From a political perspective, negotiations for liberalizing trade in agricultural and manufactured products are unavoidably linked. From a legal and structural perspective, however, they proceed separately. Negotiations on the reduction of tariffs (and other trade-restrictive instruments) on agricultural products are carried out by the Special Session of the Committee on Agriculture and within the framework of the Agreement on Agriculture. Negotiations on the reduction of tariffs on manufactured products (including textiles and clothing) are carried out by the Negotiating Group on Market Access and within the framework of the GATT 1994. The latter negotiations, which in WTO parlance are also referred to as the non-agricultural market access (NAMA) negotiations, are the focus of the remainder of this section.

On the basis of the latest draft 'modalities' of July 2007, reflecting WTO Members' most recent positions in the NAMA negotiations and the Chairman's introduction to the draft modalities, two issues require emphasis.

[26] M Bacchetta and B Bora, *Industrial Tariff Liberalization and the Doha Development Agenda* (Geneva: WTO, 2003).
[27] USDA Economic Research Service, 'Profiles of Tariffs in Global Agricultural Markets' *2001 Agricultural Economic Report* No 796, at <http://www.ers.usda.gov/publications/aer796/AER796.PDF> (last visited 27 March 2008), at 18–9.
[28] WB, above fn 25, at 18.

First, the NAMA negotiating group is operating on the basis of the principle that all WTO Members should contribute to the reduction of tariffs on manufactured products, though special attention should be given to the needs of developing country Members. In other words, NAMA negotiations rest neither on the principle of 'full reciprocity' nor on the overarching principle that the Doha 'Development' Round is principally aimed at ensuring that developing country Members 'benefit from the increased opportunities and welfare gains that the multilateral trading system generates'; rather, what is required is 'less than full reciprocity in reduction commitments'.[29] This is to some extent a clarification but it certainly does not provide for a mechanism capable of quantifying the 'less than full' parameter. The difficulty stems also from the diversity and complexity of the interests at play. As correctly noted by the Chairman of the negotiating group, the NAMA negotiations are not simply a confrontation between the interests of developed and developing countries: 'developing countries' interests and positions are diverse and they are as often opposed as are the positions of developed and developing countries'.[30]

Second, in terms of the architecture of the modalities, besides the simple Swiss formula (cutting higher tariffs faster than lower tariffs) with two coefficients (for developed and developing countries), the July 2007 draft modalities envisage a set of further flexibilities for developing and least-developed country Members. These include: (1) exemptions or reduced reductions for some sensitive tariff lines for those developing countries subject to the tariff reduction formula (30 developing countries, including most of the larger emerging markets)[31] and (2) differentiated contributions from small, vulnerable economies, developing countries with low levels of tariff binding coverage and least developed countries.[32] While the draft modalities are structurally capable of providing the necessary flexibility, the difficult task for WTO Members is to agree on the details of such flexibility. Once again, the difficulty stems from the WTO Members' different levels of development, diverse commercial interests, and highly varied NAMA tariff schedules. The Chairman has correctly emphasized in this respect that Members should not try to modify the general framework in order to satisfy specific requests from individual Members.[33]

[29] WTO, *Ministerial Declaration*, WT/MIN(01)/DEC/1 (20 November 2001), at paras 2 and 16.

[30] WTO, Negotiating Group on Market Access, *Chairman's Introduction to the Draft NAMA Modalities* (17 July 2007), at <http://www.wto.org/english/tratop_e/markacc_e/namachairtxt_17july07_e.pdf> (last visited 27 March 2008), at para 13.

[31] For example, developing country Members would be able to apply less than formula cuts for up to 10 per cent of non-agricultural tariff lines provided that the cuts are no less than half of the formula cuts and that these tariff lines do not exceed 10 per cent of the total value of a Member's non-agricultural imports (para 7).

[32] For example, these developing Members would be able to avoid the formula cuts as long as they bind 90 per cent of non-agricultural tariff lines at an average level that does not exceed 28.5 per cent (para 8).

[33] WTO Negotiating Group on Market Access, above fn 30, at para 11.

At the start of 2008, it is highly uncertain whether or when the Doha Round will ever come to a conclusion. In the WTO of the 21st century, consensus is much harder to achieve, partly because the level of engagement of WTO Members (outside the Quad)[34] is much higher than during the Uruguay Round negotiations. This may, nevertheless, represent an opportunity for the multilateral trading system. The present impasse may constitute a stimulus for a broader debate on the underlying character and *modus operandi* of the entire organization: will the WTO be able to move away from a system based on *quid pro quo*, mercantilistic bargains towards a system that favours the search for sound disciplines truly beneficial to, and sustainable for, the entire membership?

III. Disciplines on Domestic Instruments

This section focuses on the notion of 'nationality discrimination' under Article III GATT 1994 in the light of the developing dispute settlement jurisprudence and the type of legal test applied to screen the validity of the public policy justifications under Article XX GATT 1994.

A. Language, Effect, Inherence, and Intent: Different or Concurrent Ways of Understanding Article III National Treatment Obligation?

Notwithstanding the several new and 'advanced' disciplines introduced following the Uruguay Round (in particular in the SPS, TBT, and TRIPS Agreements), the GATT 1994 national treatment (NT) obligation under Article III remains the provision most commonly invoked in WTO dispute settlement.[35]

Despite being one of the cornerstones of the multilateral trading system, the content of the NT principle remains subject to much debate. At a general level, the NT principle is an application of the better known prohibition of discrimination based

---

[34] Members of the Quadrilaterals or 'Quad' are the US, the EU, Japan, and Canada.

[35] H Horn and PC Mavroidis, 'The WTO Dispute Settlement System 1995–2004: Some Descriptive Statistics' (31 January 2006), at <http://www.siteresources.worldbank.org/INTRES/Resources/469232-1107449512766/HornMavroidisWTODSUDatabaseOverview.pdf> (last visited 27 March 2008), at 13–5.

on nationality (or more simply the prohibition of 'nationality discrimination'). But what does 'granting NT' mean? How far does the concept of nationality discrimination extend (and thus the provision prohibiting it)? This section attempts to highlight the debate surrounding these questions and sketches the evolution of the interpretation of Article III GATT 1994 by the WTO adjudicative bodies.

There are several ways in which the NT principle can be understood. Most of them, however, can be captured by focusing on four possible key features of an allegedly discriminatory measure: language, effect, inherence, and intent.

The first reading of the NT principle is based on the discriminatory *language* of the national measure under review, more commonly known as formal or *de jure* discrimination.[36] Formal discrimination on grounds of nationality may occur when a measure *explicitly* employs the prohibited factor (nationality) as *the* differentiating criterion (for example, a domestic fiscal regime which requires foreign companies to pay 20 per cent corporate tax, while domestic companies need only pay 10 per cent tax).

The prohibition of nationality discrimination may also be extended to cover notions of substantial or material discrimination.[37] In other words, formally *different* treatment between domestic and imported products may not in itself constitute unequal treatment and formally *identical* treatment may not guarantee by itself equal treatment. The focus here is on the adverse *effect* or detrimental impact on foreign products compared to the effect on domestic products. The thorny questions surrounding the concept of material or *de facto* discrimination relate to the *determination* of the products whose treatment should be compared, as well as the *type* and *amount*[38] of detrimental effect that is necessary to establish *de facto* discrimination.

A third way in which the prohibition on nationality discrimination may be understood is based on the *inherent* discriminatory character of the national measure under review. For example, regulatory measures based on geographical differences (for example, only wine above 15 per cent in alcohol content may be sold in Malta as wine).[39] Obviously, defining when a national measure is inherently discriminatory may constitute a rather difficult task.[40] Depending on how rigorous or loose such principle is defined, its scope may change dramatically.

---

[36] Hudec has hinted, quite correctly, that the NT principle appears to have been developed in international economic law with formal discrimination in mind. RE Hudec, 'GATT/WTO constraints on national regulation: requiem for an "aim and effects" test' 1998 *International Lawyer* (32) 619, at 622.

[37] See G Davies, *Nationality Discrimination in the European Internal Market* (The Hague: Kluwer, 2003), at 10–1.

[38] This is where a broad interpretation of what constitutes material discrimination on grounds of nationality may equate in practical terms to the principle of equality.

[39] Eeckhout calls this type of discrimination 'indirect' discrimination to distinguish it from a purely factual or effects-based discrimination. P Eeckhout, 'Constitutional concepts for free trade in services' in G de Búrca and J Scott (eds), *The EU and the WTO: Legal and Constitutional Aspects* (Oxford: Hart Publishing, 2001), at 233–4.

[40] G de Búrca, 'Unpacking the Concept of Discrimination in EC and International Trade Law' in C Barnard and J Scott (eds), *The Law of the Single European Market: Unpacking the Premises* (Oxford: Hart Publishing, 2004), at 189.

A further possible understanding of nationality discrimination is based on the discriminatory *intent* of the national legislator. This view seems to be premised essentially on the objective of eradicating protectionism. Although discriminatory or protectionist intent may be said to be more or less objectively identified, it seems that the fundamental feature of this strand rests on attributing relevance to the policy purposes of the national measure under review. In other words, an inquiry over the policy reasons underlying the national measure is necessary to detect discriminatory or protectionist intent.[41] If a valid argument can be made that the measure under question has been adopted to pursue a legitimate public policy goal, this can be used as evidence disproving the existence of protectionist intent.[42]

Looking at past WTO case-law interpreting Article III GATT 1994, it appears that all four dimensions mentioned above play a role in defining the NT principle.

There is no controversy about reading the NT principle in Article III GATT 1994 to include a prohibition on formally discriminatory measures (origin-based measures). Equally, it is safe to say that in establishing whether an origin-neutral measure affords protection to domestic products (or 'less favourable treatment' to foreign products) in violation of Article III GATT 1994, the principal focus has been so far on the incriminated measure's 'disproportionate adverse impact' on foreign products compared with the treatment afforded to 'like' domestic products.[43] In other words, after determining what products are 'like' on the basis of their *competitive relationship*, the enquiry is one of examining the measure's *aggregate* impact on *all* domestic and imported like products.[44] This was the position evidenced in the several disputes over origin-neutral regulations, such as *Japan – Film*,[45] *EC – Asbestos*,[46]

[41] On the relevance of protectionist intent, see Hudec, above fn 36, at 625–6; D Regan, 'Regulatory Purpose and "Like Products" in Article III:4 of the GATT' 2002 *Journal of World Trade* 36(3) 443, at 443–4.

[42] See H Horn and P Mavroidis, 'Still Hazy after All These Years: The Interpretation of National Treatment in the GATT/WTO Case-law on Tax Discrimination' 2004 *European Journal of International Law* 15(1) 39–69.

[43] This is what Horn and Weiler call the 'objective approach' to the interpretation of Article III GATT 1994. H Horn and JHH Weiler, 'European Communities – Measures Affecting Asbestos and Asbestos-Containing Products' in H Horn and PC Mavroidis (eds), *The WTO Case Law of 2001* (Cambridge: Cambridge University Press, 2004), at 21–22. See F Ortino, 'From "Non-discrimination" to "Reasonableness": A Paradigm Shift in International Economic Law?' 2005 *Jean Monnet Working Paper* No 1/05, at <http://www.jeanmonnetprogram.org/papers/05/050101.pdf> (last visited 27 March 2008), at 19.

[44] L Ehring, '*De Facto* Discrimination in WTO Law: National and Most-Favored-Nation Treatment – or Equal Treatment?' *2001 Jean Monnet Working Paper* No 12/01, at <http://www.jeanmonnetprogram.org/papers/01/013201.html> (last visited 27 March 2008).

[45] Emphasizing the consistent focus of GATT/WTO jurisprudence on ensuring effective equality of competitive opportunities between imported and domestic products, the Panel in *Japan – Film* stated that the complaining party is called upon to make a detailed showing of any claimed *disproportionate impact* on imports resulting from the origin-neutral measure. Panel Report, *Japan – Film*, at para 10.85.

[46] Albeit in an *obiter dictum*, the Appellate Body noted that after a determination of likeness, 'a complaining Member must still establish that the measure accords to the group of "like" *imported*

Dominican Republic – Import and Sale of Cigarettes,[47] and *EC – Biotech Products,*[48] as well as over origin-neutral taxation, such as *Chile – Alcoholic Beverages.*[49]

Besides discriminatory 'language' and 'effect', discriminatory 'intent' and 'inherence' also appear to play a role in defining the NT principle under Article III GATT 1994.

In *Chile – Alcoholic Beverages*, the Appellate Body apparently allowed consideration of a measure's *purpose* only to rebut a finding of 'disproportionate adverse impact' of an internal tax.[50] In *EC – Asbestos*, the Appellate Body (and in particular a 'dissenting' Appellate Body Member) emphasized the serious health risks of chrysotile asbestos fibres to reverse the Panel's finding that products containing chrysotile asbestos fibres were 'like' products containing certain substitute fibres.[51] More recently, in *Dominican Republic – Import and Sale of Cigarettes*, the Appellate Body seemed to attribute weight to whether the disputed measure is *inherently discriminatory*, even if it eventually confirmed the Panel's findings based on the lack of adverse effect on imported cigarettes. The Appellate Body noted that 'the existence of a detrimental effect on a given imported product resulting from a measure does not necessarily imply that this measure accords less favourable treatment to imports if the detrimental effect is explained by factors or circumstances unrelated to the foreign origin of the product, such as the market share of the importer in this case.'[52]

The outcome of this evolution is that, while the prohibition of origin-based measures remains undisputed, using Article III GATT 1994 as a tool to regulate origin-neutral measures is more limited compared to the first generation of Appellate Body reports (*EC – Bananas III* and *Japan – Alcoholic Beverages II*). The starting point to determine 'less favourable treatment' remains the disproportionate adverse impact based on 'aggregate comparison' of imported and domestic like products (*EC – Asbestos* and *EC – Biotech Products*). However, it may now be possible to rely on

products "less favourable treatment" than it accords to the group of "like" *domestic* products'. Appellate Body Report, *EC – Asbestos*, at para 100 (original emphasis).

[47] Panel Report, *Dominican Republic – Import and Sale of Cigarettes*, at paras 7.282–300, where the Panel concluded that no 'less favourable treatment' for imported products was shown because the bond requirement did not create a disincentive against importing cigarettes, and the difference in per-unit costs between domestic and imported cigarettes was so minimal that it did not alter the conditions of competition in the relevant market to the detriment of imported products.

[48] Panel Report, *EC – Biotech Products*, at para 7.2402. According to the Panel, in order to establish whether a national measure is discriminating on the basis of the origin of the product, albeit in an indirect manner, it is necessary to take into consideration all imported like products that receive a more favourable treatment as well as all domestic like products that receive a less favourable treatment. In the Panel's view, it was not clear that the EC measure was predominately disadvantaging products of non-EC origin.

[49] Appellate Body Report, *Chile – Alcoholic Beverages*, at paras 63–66.

[50] Ibid at para 71. See G Verhoosel, *National Treatment and WTO Dispute Settlement* (Oxford: Hart, 2002).

[51] Appellate Body Report, *EC – Asbestos*, at paras 101–18.

[52] Appellate Body Report, *Dominican Republic – Import and Sale of Cigarettes*, at para 96.

other explanations to justify a finding of disproportionate adverse impact (*Chile – Alcoholic Beverages* and *Dominican Republic – Import and Sale of Cigarettes*).[53]

The exact content of the NT principle is unavoidably a 'moving target' and further decisions will clarify whether this 'conservative' trend will consolidate or retreat. Certainly, one reason for a stricter reading of the NT obligation may be the growing realization within the system that the so-called 'new generation agreements' based on 'reasonableness' rather than 'non-discrimination', such as the TBT and SPS Agreements, respond to the needs to 'combat' protectionist measures that were previously addressed by a broad reading of the NT obligation.

B. 'Cost-Effectiveness Test' versus 'Cost-Benefit Balancing' under Article XX?

Since the Appellate Body in *Korea – Various Measures on Beef* interpreted for the first time the word 'necessary' in Article XX GATT 1994, the 'necessity' test has generally been referred to as a process of *weighing and balancing* a series of factors that prominently include the contribution made by the measure under review to the achievement of a specified goal, the importance of the common interests or values protected by that measure, and the accompanying impact of the measure on imports or exports.[54]

The reference to the term 'weighing and balancing' by the Appellate Body (as well as the reference to the 'importance of the protected values' as a factor included in process of weighing and balancing) has spurred a debate on the nature of the necessity test in Article XX GATT 1994 (and Article XIV GATS). Is this test really about balancing different societal values such as trade, the protection of public morals or public health, or is it merely a mechanism to determine whether the measure under review is the least-trade-restrictive alternative reasonably available to the Member to achieve its public policy goal?[55]

The former approach would clearly be more intrusive in WTO Members' regulatory autonomy as it would equate to what in EC law terminology is the test of 'proportionality *stricto sensu*'. According to this test, the European Court of Justice (ECJ) may balance the national interest in pursuing a legitimate public policy against the Community interest in ensuring the free movement of goods. On the basis of this test, for example, it would be possible to strike down a national measure even if it is found to be 'necessary' to pursue a legitimate aim like environmental protection on the basis that, on balance, the measure's negative effects on trade are

---

[53] See also chapter 9 of this Handbook.
[54] Appellate Body Report, *Korea – Various Measures on Beef*, at para 164.
[55] D Regan, 'The Meaning of "Necessary" from *Korea – Beef* to *Dominican Republic – Cigarettes*: The Myth of Cost-Benefit Balancing' 2007 *World Trade Review* 6(3) 347.

disproportionate to its benefits on the environment.[56] This test is also referred to as 'cost-benefit balancing'.[57]

The approach based on the 'least-trade-restrictive' test, and enunciated in the famous GATT Panel report in *US – Section 337*,[58] excludes, at least in theory, any cost-benefit balancing. This test involves an inquiry into whether, among the several regulatory instruments capable of achieving the public policy objective pursued by the Member, the chosen regulatory instrument (under review) is the least-trade-restrictive in order to fulfil the specified policy objective. Within this calculation, the policy objective pursued by the Member and the level of protection determined by the Member itself is not called into question. In other words, under a rigorous least-trade-restrictive test (or 'necessity' test *stricto sensu*) the measure's high (even disproportionately high) adverse effects on trade should not matter as long as that measure is the least-trade-restrictive alternative reasonably available to the Member in order to achieve the specified level of public policy protection.[59] This test is also referred to as the 'cost-effectiveness test'.

As starkly noted by one author in the field of military intervention, the crucial difference between 'necessity' and 'proportionality' is one between tactical and strategic proportionality, namely 'tactical proportionality asks that a commander minimize civilian casualties, given the military objective. Strategic proportionality asks that civilian casualties be weighed against the justification for using force in the first place'.[60] In other words, tactical proportionality (or cost-effectiveness test) involves a review of the instruments chosen to achieve the given objective, while strategic proportionality (or cost-benefit balancing) implies a review of the given objective itself.

As noted by Regan,[61] the debate over the proper character of the 'necessity' test revolves around some apparently contradictory language used by the Appellate Body in its interpretation of the term 'necessary' in *Korea – Various Measures on Beef*. The Appellate Body appeared to put forward a full-blown balancing test when it stated that:

determination of whether a measure, which is not 'indispensable', may nevertheless be 'necessary' within the contemplation of Article XX(d), involves in every case a process of

---

[56] See also E Ellis (ed), *The Principle of Proportionality in the Laws of Europe* (Oxford: Oxford University Press, 1999).

[57] For an example of the full proportionality test applied by the ECJ see ECJ, Case 302/86, *Commission v Denmark*, [1988] ECR 4607.

[58] GATT Panel Report, *US – Section 337*.

[59] See A Mattoo and PC Mavroidis, 'Trade, Environment and the WTO: The Dispute Settlement Practice Relating to Article XX of GATT' in E-U Petersmann (ed), *International Trade Law and the GATT/WTO Dispute Settlement System* (London: Kluwer, 1997) 338; D Osiro, 'GATT/WTO Necessity Analysis: Evolutionary Interpretation and its Impact on the Autonomy of Domestic Regulation' 2002 *Legal Issues of Economic Integration* 29(2) 123, at 137; Ortino, above fn 9.

[60] R Wedgwood, 'Proportionality and Necessity in American National Security Decision Making' 1992 *American Society of International Law Proceedings* (86) 58, at 59.

[61] Regan, above fn 55.

weighing and balancing a series of factors which prominently include (a) the contribution made by the compliance measure to the enforcement of the law or regulation at issue, (b) the importance of the common interests or values protected by that law or regulation, and (c) the accompanying impact of the law or regulation on imports or exports.[62]

Quoting from the GATT Panel report in *US – Section 337*, the Appellate Body went back to the previous least-trade-restrictive test noting that:

a contracting party cannot justify a measure inconsistent with another GATT provision as necessary in terms of Article XX(d) if an alternative measure which it could reasonably be expected to employ and which is not inconsistent with other GATT provisions is available to it.[63]

In line with a least-trade-restrictive test, the Appellate Body also clarified that WTO Members get to choose their own level of (consumer) protection by stating that 'it is not open to doubt that Members of the WTO have the right to determine for themselves the level of enforcement of their WTO-consistent laws and regulations'.[64]

Unfortunately, this contradictory language may be found in all the subsequent reports addressing Article XX GATT 1994 (or Article XIV GATS). For example, in *US – Gambling*, the Appellate Body stressed, on the one hand, that the determination of whether a measure is 'necessary' should be determined through a process of weighing and balancing and, on the other hand, that the necessity test in Article XIV GATS requires that there be no 'reasonably available' WTO-consistent alternative. It added that a 'reasonably available' alternative measure must be a measure that would preserve for the responding Member its right to achieve its desired level of protection with respect to the objective pursued.[65] The Appellate Body's attempt in *US – Gambling* to somehow reconcile the two tests should also be emphasized:

A comparison between the challenged measure and possible alternatives should then be undertaken, and the results of such comparison should be considered in the light of the importance of the interests at issue. It is on the basis of this 'weighing and balancing' and comparison of measures, taking into account the interests or values at stake, that a panel determines whether a measure is 'necessary' or, alternatively, whether another, WTO-consistent measure is 'reasonably available'.[66]

It must be recognized that the Appellate Body's original intent in *Korea – Various Measures on Beef* was perhaps to respond to the two diverging needs of 'flexible application' and 'legal certainty'. If the Appellate Body recognizes the inescapable and indispensable flexibility in applying concepts such as the 'necessity' requirement, it also tries to provide the elements upon which to base a 'necessity' determination. However, the uncertainty caused by these remarks needs to be properly

---

[62] Appellate Body Report, *Korea – Various Measures on Beef*, at para 164 (original emphasis).
[63] Ibid at para 165.   [64] Ibid at para 176.
[65] Appellate Body Report, *US – Gambling*, at paras 305–08.
[66] Ibid at para 307.

addressed by the Appellate Body by confirming that there is no real weighing and balancing at play in applying the necessity test in Article XX GATT 1994. On the contrary, the factors listed in *Korea – Various Measures on Beef* are more simply the elements that invariably need to be taken into account to determine whether there exists an alternative measure that is less restrictive than that found to violate one of the obligations of the GATT 1994, and may equally achieve the relevant policy objective at issue set by the Member.[67]

Three further clarifications regarding the necessity test should be made here. First, even the cost-effectiveness test understood as a least-trade-restrictive test may involve some form of 'balancing'. For example, determining what is the 'appropriate level of protection' (pursued by the regulating Member) is not a scientific exercise. It grants judicial organs a certain margin of appreciation (determining Korea's relevant level of consumer protection in *Korea – Various Measures on Beef* was a key, and somewhat controversial, issue).[68] Similarly, deciding whether a least-trade-restrictive alternative achieves the same level of protection (as well as deciding whether an alternative is less restrictive) involves a certain margin of appreciation. Clearly this would not be 'balancing' of the same type as that characterizing cost-benefit balancing. It is, rather, a form of balancing that cannot be avoided even in applying 'necessity' and 'least-trade-restrictive' tests. This is arguably what the Appellate Body was trying to grapple with in *Korea – Various Measures on Beef*; this could explain the reference to 'a range of degrees of necessity', the so-called 'continuum', as well as the reference to the 'trade costs' and 'contribution to the realization of the end pursued'. Also, the reference to the importance of the values protected by the regulating Member (the first criterion mentioned by the Appellate Body in *Korea – Various Measures on Beef*) may be simply an attempt by the Appellate Body to come to face with an unavoidable factor at play in applying the 'necessity test' (rather than as part of a cost-benefit balancing). The importance of the public policy goal will be one of the criteria guiding a WTO panel in its appreciation of the measure's 'necessity'.

Second, even the cost-effectiveness test may be quite demanding on WTO Members as it may require an inquiry into whether the regulatory protections of the country of origin are *functionally equivalent* to those of the host country. For example, the requirement that imported products comply strictly and exactly with the provisions or technical requirements laid down for products manufactured in the State of importation when those imported products (conforming with similar

---

[67] See also Appellate Body Report, *Korea – Various Measures on Beef*, at para 166, cited by Appellate Body Report, *US – Gambling*, at para 305.

[68] Despite its statement of principle in favour of respecting Members' level of protection, the Appellate Body in *Korea – Various Measures on Beef* appears to improperly assess Korea's intended level of protection. While it recognized that, in establishing the dual retail system, Korea could well have intended to secure a *higher* level of consumer protection, the Appellate Body determined that this could not have been Korea's intention and that Korea's desired level of protection was indeed the 'significant reduction' of fraud rather than its 'total elimination'. Appellate Body Report, *Korea – Various Measures on Beef*, at paras 178–80. See Ortino, above fn 9, at 207–10.

standards required in the State of manufacture) afford users the *same level of protection* would be contrary to the necessity test because those measures are not indispensable to pursue the public policy goal at hand.[69]

Third, in a cost-effectiveness analysis it is crucial how 'costs' are defined. In the light of their principal function, the main relevant cost is usually determined by taking into account the level of trade-restrictiveness of the measure at hand. While the adverse effects on trade flows may be the main relevant cost at issue under a cost-effectiveness test, it is evident that other costs, incurred by both public and private parties, may be brought into the equation. Other costs may include administrative costs incurred by the public authority in implementing the alternative measure, compliance costs of private business, or even costs imposed on other public policies. Thus, the scope of the costs considered in a cost-effectiveness analysis will influence the outcome of the analysis itself. WTO case-law on this point is not very developed. In *US – Gambling*, the Appellate Body recognized that a purely 'theoretical alternative' is not enough for purposes of the least-trade-restrictive test if, for example, 'the responding Member is not capable of taking it or where the measures imposes prohibitive costs or substantial technical difficulties'.[70] Leaving the issue of the definition of the relevant costs open, this statement simply allows WTO panels flexibility in applying the necessity test.

In conclusion, the character of the test under Article XX GATT 1994 needs to be clarified by emphasizing that necessity does not envisage cost-benefit balancing, and by spelling out the key factors underlying the cost-effectiveness test. Such clarification will also have important ramifications outside the context of the GATT 1994, and in particular with regard to the TBT and SPS Agreements. Being fundamentally a detailed articulation of the principles set out in Article XX GATT 1994, the TBT and SPS disciplines are equally premised on the delicate balance between liberalization rules and Members' regulatory prerogatives. An adequate understanding of the cardinal principle in Article XX GATT 1994 (the necessity test) will offer an indispensable key to interpret several of the main rules found in the TBT and SPS Agreements.

IV. DISCIPLINES ON STATE CONTINGENCIES

This section addresses some aspects of two disciplines on state contingencies that have broader implications for the multilateral trading system. First, it focuses on the role of the International Monetary Fund (IMF) in the administration of the balance

---

[69]   Weiler, above fn 10, at 365.
[70]   Appellate Body Report, *US – Gambling*, at para 308.

of payments exceptions under Articles XII and XVIII GATT 1994 and the exchange restrictions under Article XV GATT 1994. Second, it deals with the emergency safeguards exception under Article XIX GATT focusing on the apparent 'conflict' between Article XIX(a) GATT 1994 and Article 2.1 Safeguards Agreement.

A. Balance of Payments (Articles XII and XVIII GATT 1994) and Exchange Restrictions (Article XV GATT 1994): What Role for the IMF?

The threat to the financial stability of Members is one of the contingencies justifying WTO Members' recourse to trade measures (such as tariffs and quotas) in violation of GATT 1994 obligations. Several GATT 1994 provisions stipulate substantive and procedural disciplines regulating WTO Members' ability to adopt trade measures incompatible with other GATT 1994 obligations to safeguard their financial stability. Focusing on the specific role of the IMF in administering these GATT 1994 exceptions, the present section seeks to highlight the extent to which the WTO is cooperating with other international organizations in global economic policy-making.

Two central obligations setting out 'exceptions' to other GATT 1994 obligations deal with 'exchange measures' and 'balance-of-payment (BOP) restrictions'. Article XV:9 GATT 1994 allows Members to use 'exchange controls or exchange restrictions in accordance with the Articles of Agreement of the International Monetary Fund'. Article XVIII:9 GATT 1994 allows a developing country Member to impose 'import restrictions' to safeguard its balance of payments as long as these are 'necessary to forestall the threat of, or to stop, a serious decline in its monetary reserves, or in the case of a contracting party with inadequate monetary reserves, to achieve a reasonable rate of increase in its reserve'.[71]

While there are several WTO agreements envisaging cooperation with other international organizations,[72] formal recognition of the role played by the IMF within the multilateral trading system is found expressly in the GATT 1994. Principally, this agreement regulates the relationship between GATT 1994 obligations on trade matters and IMF obligations on exchange matters to avoid conflicting rights and obligations for members of the Fund and the WTO (jurisdictional relationship) and the extent and effect of consultation between the WTO and the IMF (consultation).

With regard to the jurisdictional relationship, Article XV:9 permits WTO Members to use *exchange measures* ('exchange controls or exchange restrictions') even if in violation of any other GATT 1994 obligations, as long as these measures

---

[71] Article XII GATT 1994 provides a similar opportunity for developed country Members.

[72] See, for example, the reference in the TBT and SPS Agreements to international standard-setting bodies.

are in accordance with the Fund's Articles of Agreement. Crucial to the application of the Article XV:9 exception is the definition of 'exchange measures'. For example, in order to determine whether an exchange measure is an 'exchange restriction' for purposes of Article XV:9, the relevant criterion is to be found in a Fund's Decision of 1960 specifying that an exchange restriction involves a 'direct governmental limitation on the availability or use of exchange as such'.[73]

With regard to consultation, Article XV:2 GATT 1994 disciplines the scope of the requirement as well as the effect of the consultation. Article XV:2 provides that Contracting Parties[74] 'shall consult fully' with the IMF any time they are called upon to consider or deal with problems concerning *monetary reserves, balances of payments,* or *foreign exchange arrangements.* In such consultation, moreover, Contracting Parties 'shall accept' all findings of statistical and other facts presented by the Fund, the Fund's determination of whether action by a Contracting Party in exchange matters is in accordance with the IMF Articles of Agreement, and the Fund's determination on the existence of some of the criteria set forth in Article XVIII:9 for BOP measures.[75] While the first determinations are 'findings of fact', the other two are 'findings of law'. Article XV:2 has been supplemented by the 1996 IMF/WTO Cooperation Agreement which includes the Fund's obligation to respond to a request from the WTO to consult (even if coming from dispute settlement panels).[76]

Despite the apparently mandatory language of Article XV:2, WTO adjudicating bodies have been reluctant to expressly recognize a duty to consult with the IMF on both issues of BOP and exchange measures. In *India – Quantitative Restrictions,* India relied *inter alia* on the BOP exception in Article XVIII GATT 1994 to justify a series of import restrictions on agricultural, textile, and industrial products. While India argued that the duty to consult under Article XV:2 only applies to the WTO General Council (GC) or BOP Committee (given the

---

[73] Panel Report, *Dominican Republic – Import and Sale of Cigarettes,* at para 7.132: 'The Panel considers that the ordinary meaning of the "direct limitation on availability or use of exchange . . . as such" means a limitation directly on the use of exchange itself, which means the use of exchange *for all purposes.* It cannot be interpreted in a way so as to permit the restriction on the use of exchanges that only affects importation. To conclude otherwise would logically lead to the situation whereby any WTO Member could easily circumvent obligations under Article II:1(b) by imposing a foreign currency fee or charge on imports at the customs and then conveniently characterize it as an "exchange restriction"'. Ibid at para 7.137 (original emphasis).

[74] When acting jointly, GATT Contracting Parties are referred to in GATT documents as 'CONTRACTING PARTIES'. The term will be simply capitalized in the text below.

[75] Several provisions in Articles XII, XV, and XVIII set out notification requirements (such as XII:4(a) and XVIII:12(a)) as well as consultation mechanisms for the Contracting Parties (the WTO General Council) to review, monitor, and regulate Members' trade measures adopted on the basis of these Articles, such as Articles XII:4(b)–(f) and 5, XVIII:12(b)–(f).

[76] *Agreement Between the International Monetary Fund and the World Trade Organization,* 9 December 1996, at <http://www.imf.org/external/pubs/ft/sd/index.asp?decision=DN26> (last visited 28 March 2008), at para 8.

reference therein to 'Contracting Parties'), the US argued that the Panel was required under Article XV:2 GATT 1994 to consult with the IMF. The Panel did not resolve this issue but, nevertheless, requested a statement from the Fund on India's BOP situation on the basis of its general authority under Article 13 DSU to 'seek information and technical advice from any individual or body which it deems appropriate'.[77]

WTO adjudicating bodies have equally been reluctant to recognize the effect of IMF determinations following a request for consultation. In *Dominican Republic – Import and Sale of Cigarettes*, the Panel did 'seek more information' from the IMF on the precise legal nature and status of the foreign exchange fee, which had been found to violate Article II GATT 1994 and which the Dominican Republic argued had been approved by the Fund. The Panel treated the information provided by the IMF as simply confirming its previous findings on the matter.[78] Moreover, although the Panel (as well as the IMF) had concluded that the Dominican Republic's foreign exchange fee was not an exchange restriction or control for purposes of Article XV:9, the Panel still considered whether the measure complied with the Fund's Articles.[79] More than going against a principle of judicial economy, such analysis undermines the role that has been attributed to the IMF by Article XV:2 with regard to whether an exchange measure has been taken in accordance with the Fund's Articles.

A similar approach was followed by the Appellate Body in *India – Quantitative Restrictions*. In that case, the Appellate Body considered India's appeal based on the claim that the Panel had delegated to the IMF its duty to make an objective assessment of the matter, that is, whether India's BOP situation justified recourse to the Article XVIII:9 exception, as required by Article 11 DSU. The Appellate Body rejected India's claim and found that:

nothing in the Panel Report supports India's argument that the Panel delegated to the IMF its judicial function to make an objective assessment of the matter. A careful reading of the Panel Report makes clear that the Panel did not simply accept the views of the IMF. The Panel critically assessed these views and also considered other data and opinions in reaching its conclusions.[80]

Such reluctance is not justified on either legal or policy arguments. In legal terms, the extent and effect of the consultation with the IMF under Article XV:2 are relatively clear. The language used—'shall consult' and 'shall accept'—appears mandatory rather than discretionary. Equally, the fact that Article XV:2 only refers to 'Contracting Parties' does not justify the argument that Article XV:2 does not apply

---

[77] Panel Report, *India – Quantitative Restrictions*, at paras 5.12–13. See also Panel Report, *Dominican Republic – Import and Sale of Cigarettes*, at paras 7.139–141. Contra Appellate Body Report, *Argentina – Textiles and Apparel*, at para 84 (dicta).

[78] Panel Report, *Dominican Republic – Import and Sale of Cigarettes*, at paras 7.137 and 7.145.

[79] Ibid at para 7.150.

[80] Appellate Body Report, *India – Quantitative Restrictions*, at para 149.

to WTO adjudicating bodies. On the contrary, if the highest political organ of the WTO is required to consult and to accept the IMF's determinations, dispute settlement panels *a fortiori* should comply with such requirements. Moreover, the policy rationale of Article XV:2 GATT 1994 is to delineate the division of labour between different international economic organizations (clearly expressed on a jurisdictional level by Article XV:9 GATT 1994) as well as to make the expertise of such other organizations available to any WTO body, whether the GC or a dispute settlement panel.[81]

There are indeed limits to the effect of the Fund's factual findings and legal determinations, which are identified in Article XV:2. However, within those limits, a dispute settlement panel should treat those findings and determinations as dispositive.

The collaboration between the WTO and the IMF clearly goes beyond that envisaged by Article XV GATT 1994. Article V WTO Agreement expressly envisages the GC making 'appropriate arrangements for effective cooperation with other intergovernmental organizations that have responsibilities related to those of the WTO'. To this effect, WTO Members added, in 1994, a Ministerial Declaration on Achieving Greater Coherence in Global Economic Policy Making calling on the WTO to cooperate with the IMF and the World Bank. Although implementation of this mandate has included cooperation on rule-making, technical assistance and capacity-building, economic research and surveillance, adjustment lending, and staff and high-level contacts, it is difficult to assess the actual extent and success of such cooperation.[82] From the limited experience in the application of Article XV GATT 1994 in WTO dispute settlement, it appears that the cooperation between the WTO and the IMF could be strengthened.[83] The apparent lack of confidence among international organizations—particularly when operating in closely related fields (such as the WTO and the IMF)—is not beneficial to the development of coherent global policies. If the WTO fails to strengthen cooperation with other 'sister' economic organizations, one can imagine what the record may be in building links with other organizations operating in non-economic areas such as health, labour, and environment.

---

[81] It may be argued that the reason for deferral to the IMF also relates to the fact that the IMF operates on the basis of weighted voting rather than consensus. For a detailed analysis and critique of these issues, see generally D Siegel, 'Legal Aspects of the IMF/WTO Relationship: The Fund's Articles of Agreement and the WTO Agreements' 2002 *American Journal of International Law* 96(3) 561, at 581–84.

[82] See M Aubon, 'Fulfilling the Marrakesh Mandate on Coherence: Ten Years of Cooperation between the WTO, IMF and World Bank' *2007 WTO Discussion Paper* No 13, at <http://www.wto.org/english/res_e/booksp_e/discussion_papers13_e.pdf> (last visited 28 March 2008).

[83] As part of the Doha Round's discussion on 'implementation-related issues and concerns', it has been proposed to take the review of BOP measures outside the scope of the dispute settlement system.

B. Emergency Safeguards and the 'Unforeseen Development' Requirement in Article XIX GATT 1994: the Relationship between Article XIX GATT 1994 and the Safeguards Agreement

Article XIX GATT 1994 allows a WTO Member to take 'emergency action' against an unforeseen increase of imports from other Members, which threatens to cause serious injury to its domestic industry. More specifically, Article XIX conditions the availability of emergency safeguards measures to the following requirements: (a) an increase of imports of the product in question, (b) the increase of imports must be caused by developments that were not foreseen and must result from any GATT 1994 obligation of the Member applying the safeguard measure, and (c) the increase of imports must cause or threaten to cause 'serious injury' to a domestic industry producing a 'directly competitive' product.[84]

Following the conclusion of the Safeguards Agreement, which was aimed at 'clarifying and reinforcing' Article XIX GATT 1994,[85] controversy over the relationship between the Safeguards Agreement and Article XIX GATT 1994 arose in the context of the 'unforeseen developments' requirement. While this is one of the requirements specified in Article XIX GATT 1994, it finds no reference in Article 2.1 Safeguards Agreement setting out the required 'conditions' for a safeguard measure. Is there a conflict between the two disciplines? And if so, how does one solve the conflict?

The Panel in *Argentina – Footwear (EC)* was confronted with this issue and attributed meaning to the 'express omission' of the 'unforeseen developments' criterion in the Safeguards Agreement. It concluded that such criterion is no longer required.[86] The Appellate Body reversed the Panel's finding and concluded that safeguard measures must comply with the provisions of both the Safeguards Agreement and Article XIX GATT 1994. In particular, the Appellate Body noted the language in Articles 1 and 11.1 Safeguards Agreement excluding an intention by the Uruguay Round negotiators to 'subsume' the requirements of Article XIX within the Agreement on Safeguards. The Appellate Body found that:

Article 1 states that the purpose of the *Agreement on Safeguards* is to establish 'rules for the application of safeguard measures which shall be understood to mean *those measures provided for* in Article XIX of GATT 1994'. (emphasis added) This suggests that Article XIX continues in full force and effect, and, in fact, establishes certain prerequisites for the imposition of safeguard measures. Furthermore, in Article 11.1(a), the ordinary meaning of the language 'unless such action *conforms with the provisions of that Article applied in accordance with this Agreement*' (emphasis added) clearly is that any safeguard action must *conform*

---

[84] M Matsushita, TJ Schoenbaum, and PC Mavroidis, *The World Trade Organization: Law, Practice and Policy*, 2nd edn (Oxford: Oxford University Press, 2006), at 440.

[85] Preamble to the Safeguards Agreement, para 2.

[86] Panel Report, *Argentina – Footwear (EC)*, at paras 8.58–69.

with the provisions of Article XIX of the GATT 1994 *as well as* with the provisions of the *Agreement on Safeguards*. Neither of these provisions states that any safeguard action taken after the entry into force of the *WTO Agreement* need only conform with the provisions of the *Agreement on Safeguards*.[87]

Accordingly, expressly excluding, for purposes of the General Interpretative Note to Annex 1A of the WTO Agreement,[88] the existence of a 'conflict' between Article XIX(a) GATT 1994 and Article 2.1 Safeguards Agreement, the Appellate Body applied the two provisions cumulatively.

Two interrelated observations may be put forward in this context. First, many of the disciplines originally included in the GATT 1947 have been supplemented by rules (or agreements) following the Uruguay Round and the entry into force of the WTO Agreement. WTO Members felt they needed to 'reform',[89] elaborate,[90] or clarify[91] several of the GATT disciplines on trade measures, domestic regulation, and state contingencies alike.

Second, the relationship between GATT 1994 disciplines and these additional agreements may at times become problematic, raising the highly debated and controversial issue of 'treaty conflicts' or 'conflict of norms' within the WTO. For purposes of this chapter, it suffices to highlight some of the problematic elements of the Appellate Body's stance on the apparent conflict between Article XIX GATT 1994 and the Safeguards Agreement as evidenced in its decision in *Argentina – Footwear (EC)*.

The Appellate Body's interpretation of the relationship between Article XIX(a) GATT 1994 and Article 2.1 Safeguards Agreement has been criticized because it is a *narrow* interpretation of the term 'conflict' for purposes of the General Interpretative Note to Annex 1A and it overlooks WTO Members' conscious departure from Article XIX's 'unforeseen developments' requirement.[92]

In general, I share the view of those that advocate a *broad* definition of the notion of conflict of norms in WTO law according to which '[t]here is a conflict between norms [...] if in obeying or applying one norm, the other is necessarily or potentially violated'.[93] Only by first acknowledging the existence of contradictions or conflicts among norms, it becomes possible to resolve such contradictions in an appropriate and fair manner. As noted by Pauwelyn, 'by refusing to recognise certain situations as conflicts [...] strict definition indirectly resolves a number of contradictions

---

[87] Appellate Body Report, *Argentina – Footwear (EC)*, at para 83.

[88] 'In the event of conflict between a provision of the General Agreement on Tariffs and Trade 1994 and a provision of another agreement in Annex 1A to the Agreement Establishing the World Trade Organization (referred to in the agreements in Annex 1A as the 'WTO Agreement'), the provision of the other agreement shall prevail to the extent of the conflict.'

[89] Preamble to Agreement on Agriculture, para 1.

[90] Preamble to the SPS Agreement, last para.

[91] Preamble to the Safeguards Agreement, para 2.

[92] Mavroidis, above fn 3, at 476.

[93] E Vranes, 'The Definition of "Norm Conflict" in International Law and Legal Theory' 2006 *European Journal of International Law* 17(2) 395, at 418.

in favour of the strictest norm'.[94] For example, as WTO agreements contain both 'rights' and 'obligations', a strict definition would tend to favour the latter vis-à-vis the former.[95]

Accordingly, the starting point in analysing the relationship between Article XIX(a) GATT 1994 and Article 2.1 Safeguards Agreement is to acknowledge the existence of a contradiction or conflict in the broad sense between the two norms: applying Article 2.1 would necessarily violate Article XIX(a) as only the latter provision conditions the availability of safeguard measures to 'unforeseen developments'.

The second step in the analysis consists of searching for any relevant rule that would resolve the conflict, a 'conflict of norms rule'. Before relying on the general rule contained in the Interpretative Note to Annex 1A of the WTO Agreement (Annex 1A Agreements prevail over the GATT 1994 in the case of a conflict), a WTO panel would first look at whether a more specific conflict of norms rule can be found in either of the respective conflicting provisions or agreements. Admittedly, the Safeguards Agreement does not include an 'express' or clear conflict rule compared with other Annex 1A Agreements.[96] Nevertheless, do Articles 1 and 11.1(a) Safeguards Agreement provide for such conflict of norms rule? Possibly, but certainly not as explicitly as the Appellate Body has suggested. For example, reference in Article 1 to 'measures provided for in Article XIX of GATT' may be interpreted as simply an identification of the types of measures covered by the Safeguards Agreement ('emergency action on imports of particular products') rather than an 'implicit' conflict of norms rule. Equally, the apparent *subordination* in Article 11.1(a) of the requirement that emergency action conform with the provisions of Article XIX, to the provisions of the Safeguards Agreement[97] may be interpreted to exclude Article 11.1(a) as an 'implicit' conflict of norms rule. The absence of either an express or an implicit conflict of norms rule in the specific agreements at issue would simply require applying the express general conflict of norms rule in the Interpretative Note to Annex 1A.

The main criticism advanced here vis-à-vis the Appellate Body's approach with regard to the relationship between Article XIX(a) and Article 2.1 does not really concern the specific reading of Articles 1 and 11.1(a) Safeguards Agreement found

---

[94] J Pauwelyn, *Conflict of Norms in Public International Law: How WTO Relates to Other Rules of International Law* (Cambridge: Cambridge University Press, 2003), at 170.

[95] L Bartels, 'Treaty Conflicts in WTO Law' in S Griller (ed), *At the Crossroads: The World Trading System and the Doha Round* (Vienna: Springer, 2008) 135.

[96] For example, Article 10 SCM Agreement provides that 'Members shall take all necessary steps to ensure that the imposition of a countervailing duty [. . .] is in accordance with the provisions of Article VI of GATT 1994 and the terms of this Agreement. [. . .]'. See also Art 2.4 SPS Agreement.

[97] Article 11.1(a) states as follows: 'A Member shall not take or seek any emergency action on imports of particular products as set forth in Article XIX of GATT 1994 unless such action conforms with the provisions of that Article *applied in accordance with this Agreement*' (emphasis added).' It would have been a conflict of norms rule if the phrase 'applied in accordance with this Agreement' were preceded by the term 'and', excluding such apparent subordination. See also Article 10 SCM Agreement.

in *Argentina – Footwear (EC)*. It rather deals with the lack of clarity in the Appellate Body's overall stance on the issue of conflict of norms within the WTO and in particular the refusal to acknowledge the existence of a conflict and the need to identify a conflict of norms rule. The lack of clarity on the issue of conflict of norms is reflected throughout the WTO legal system in both adjudication and law-making, with even more controversial consequences in the debate over potential conflicts between norms of international law.[98]

V. Conclusion

Despite its long and intense life, there are several issues surrounding the GATT 1994 that remain unresolved or controversial. This chapter has focused on a few of these outstanding issues dealing with GATT 1994 disciplines on trade instruments, domestic instruments, and state contingencies. Two major strands can be highlighted.

First, several of the core principles in the GATT 1994 are still in search of a certain level of clarity. For example, the exact scope of the *per se* prohibition on import restrictions in Article XI GATT 1994 remains an open question, particularly with regard to the politically sensitive 'process and production standards'. As global competition increasingly depends on the costs related to standards regulating the manner or method in which products are manufactured (in order to protect, for example, labour and the environment), this issue will soon have to be confronted by the WTO dispute settlement.

Equally, the exact content of the NT principle under Article III GATT 1994 is still a 'moving target'. While the prohibition of origin-based measures under Article III remains undisputedly strong, using Article III as a tool to regulate origin-neutral measures appears more limited compared to the first generation of Appellate Body reports. While disproportionate adverse impact based on an 'aggregate comparison' of imported and domestic like products remains the starting point to determine 'less favourable treatment', it may now be possible to rely on other explanations (lack of protectionist intent or inherent discrimination) to justify a preliminary finding of disproportionate adverse impact. This stricter reading of the NT obligation may be due to the growing realization within the system that the so-called 'new generation agreements' based on 'reasonableness' rather than 'non-discrimination', such as the TBT and SPS Agreements, are responding to the

---

[98] See Pauwelyn, above fn 94.

need to 'combat' protectionist measures that were previously addressed by a broad reading of the NT obligation.

Furthermore, despite several decisions interpreting and applying Article XX GATT 1994, uncertainty also exists about the character of the necessity test employed to limit the availability of public policy exceptions. Is the necessity test about cost-benefit balancing or is it more simply the equivalent of a cost-effectiveness test? The uncertainty may be due to the political sensitivity in expressly allowing the former, on the one hand, and the perceived ineffectiveness of the latter in sorting out truly legitimate policy justifications, on the other hand. Nevertheless, clarification is desirable, especially in the light of important ramifications outside the context of the GATT 1994. An adequate understanding of the cardinal principle in Article XX GATT 1994 will offer an indispensable key to interpret several of the main rules found in the increasingly important TBT and SPS Agreements.

A second strand stemming from the above analysis deals with certain major institutional aspects that have yet to be fully explored by WTO Members and the various WTO institutional bodies. For example, the experience of applying the balance of payments exceptions under Articles XII and XVIII GATT 1994 and the exchange restrictions under Article XV GATT 1994 shows the need to strengthen cooperation between the WTO and the IMF. The apparent lack of confidence among international organizations—particularly when operating in closely related fields (such as the WTO and the IMF)—is not beneficial to the development of coherent global policies. A stronger cooperation between the WTO and other 'sister' economic organizations will only encourage the WTO to build stronger links with other organizations operating in non-economic areas such as health, labour, and the environment. It is paramount that multilateral institutions keep apace and conform to the realities of a more complex, dynamic, and interrelated world.

Equally, the fundamental concern about the Appellate Body's approach to the relationship between Article XIX(a) GATT 1994 and Article 2.1 Safeguards Agreement relates to the lack of clarity in its overall stance on the issue of conflict of norms within the WTO, and its refusal to acknowledge the existence of a conflict. The lack of clarity on the issue of conflict of norms is reflected throughout the WTO legal system in both adjudication and law-making, with even more controversial consequences in the debate over potential conflicts between international norms.

Finally, the present impasse in the Doha Round negotiations, including those aimed at reducing tariffs on non-agricultural products under the GATT 1994, highlights the need to open a broader discussion over the underlying character and *modus operandi* of the WTO. It might be time to move away from a system based on *quid pro quo*, mercantilistic bargains towards a system that favours the search for sound disciplines truly beneficial to, and sustainable for, the entire membership.

In conclusion, there is no doubt that the GATT 1994 still represents the core agreement within the multilateral trading system. Although it has been supplemented by a plethora of additional disciplines, the GATT 1994 still embodies many of the key principles and approaches that characterize the WTO today. The GATT 1994 has accomplished a lot so far but it still has many challenges to meet in its not-too-distant future.

Selected Bibliography

Consultative Board, *The Future of the WTO: Addressing Institutional Challenges in the New Millennium* (Geneva: WTO, 2004)

L Ehring, '*De Facto* Discrimination in WTO Law: National and Most-Favored-Nation Treatment – or Equal Treatment?' *2001 Jean Monnet Working Paper* 12/01

GATT, *Analytical Index: Guide to GATT Law and Practice*, 6th ed. (Geneva: GATT, 1994)

R Howse and D Regan, 'The Product/Process Distinction: An Illusory Basis for Disciplining "Unilateralism" in Trade Policy' 2000 *European Journal of International Law* 11(2) 249

JH Jackson, *World Trade and the Law of GATT* (Indianapolis: Bobbs-Merrill, 1969)

PC Mavroidis, *Trade in Goods – An Analysis of International Trade Agreements* (Oxford: Oxford University Press, 2007)

F Ortino, *Basic Legal Instruments for the Liberalisation of Trade: A Comparative Analysis of EC and WTO Law* (Oxford: Hart Publishing, 2004)

J Pauwelyn, *Conflict of Norms in Public International Law: How WTO Relates to Other Rules of International Law* (Cambridge: Cambridge University Press, 2003)

D Regan, 'The Meaning of "Necessary" from *Korea – Beef* to *Dominican Republic – Cigarettes*: The Myth of Cost-Benefit Balancing' 2007 *World Trade Review* 6(3) 347

D Siegel, 'Legal Aspects of the IMF/WTO Relationship: The Fund's Articles of Agreement and the WTO Agreements' 2002 *American Journal of International Law* 96(3) 561

CHAPTER 7

···

GATS

···

ANDREW TF LANG

I. INTRODUCTION

SINCE the middle of the 1990s, the world has seen the rapid development of a large network of treaties governing international trade in services. Although NAFTA was the first international agreement directly relating to trade in services to enter into force,[1] the initial impetus for extending international trade rules to services came at the multilateral level, with the commencement of the Uruguay Round of GATT negotiations in 1986.[2] These multilateral negotiations concluded eight years later, and in 1995 the General Agreement on Trade in Services (GATS) came into force. From then on, services rules quickly spread through a growing network of regional trade agreements (RTAs). For the first five years or so, from 1995 to 1999, this was almost exclusively an American phenomenon: Mexico concluded six new services RTAs with Central and South American partners during this period, MERCOSUR expanded its remit to include a services Protocol at much the same time, and the Andean Community and CARICOM followed suit soon after.[3] But since the turn of the millennium, services RTAs have become a truly global phenomenon. An average of just under five RTAs covering services have been concluded each year since then, and the nations actively negotiating such agreements now prominently include countries from South, Southeast, and East Asia.[4] By now, there are almost 50 services RTAs in existence, accounting for almost 20 per cent of all RTAs worldwide.[5]

There have been numerous attempts to explain the origins of this phenomenon. Among the most interesting and compelling of these is the detailed story told by

[1] It is true that the EEC Treaty governed trade in services from the outset, but, as Eeckhout has noted, the 'freedom to provide services [is] subsidiary to the other basic freedoms of the internal market', perhaps in part because when the treaty was drafted 'trade in services' had not been conceptualized: P Eeckhout, 'Constitutional Concepts for Free Trade in Services' in G de Búrca and J Scott (eds), *The EU and the WTO: Legal and Constitutional Issues* (Oxford: Hart, 2001), at 212. In addition, the Canada-US Free Trade Agreement, concluded in 1989, has been described as a 'precursor' to the current services RTAs: M Roy, J Marchetti, and H Lim, 'Services Liberalization in the New Generation of Preferential Trade Agreements: How Much Further than the GATS?' *WTO Staff Working Paper* ERSD-2006–07 (September 2006), at <http://www.wto.org/english/res_e/reser_e/ersd200607_e.pdf> (last visited 10 March 2008).

[2] WJ Drake and K Nicolaïdis, 'Ideas, Interests and Institutionalization: "trade in services" and the Uruguay Round' 1992 *International Organisation* 46(1) 37.

[3] For an interesting account of this period, see SM Stephenson (ed), *Services Trade in the Western Hemisphere: Liberalization, Integration and Reform* (Washington, DC: Brookings, 2000) especially the introductory chapter by Stephenson, and chapters 6–10.

[4] Key protagonists in this area include India, China, Hong Kong, Thailand, Malaysia, Korea, and Singapore. See 'Regional Trade Agreements Notified to the GATT/WTO and in Force by Type of Agreement', at <http://www.wto.org/english/tratop_e/region_e/type_e.xls> (last visited 4 March 2008); Roy, Marchetti, and Lim, above fn 1, at 7.

[5] These figures reflect only those RTAs that have been notified to the WTO under Article V GATS, see above fn 4. Given that these figures are certainly incomplete, the actual number of services RTAs in existence is almost certainly well above 50.

Drake and Nicolaïdis of two decades of effort and activity, starting in the early 1970s, and leading almost up to the conclusion of the GATS in 1994.[6] It is a story of the creation, consolidation, and growth of an 'epistemic community' of scholars, officials, think tanks, and others, who came to share the view that transnational services activities could be understood in a new way as 'trade in services', and who began to explore the idea that standard trade theory could and should be applied to these activities. The authors chart the processes by which this epistemic community came to fix on the idea that not only trade in goods but also 'trade in services' ought to be liberalized, and that the new round of GATT negotiations ought to include an effort to create a legal framework for the liberalization of trade in services. They show how members of this epistemic community managed to convince key countries in the GATT of their view, so that services were added to the Uruguay Round agenda. They tell the story of the progress of the negotiations, and in particular demonstrate the ways in which concepts, data, and analysis developed by this growing community of experts both enabled and deeply shaped those negotiations—even if the ultimate GATS text departed from these ideas in some ways.

The story told by Drake and Nicolaïdis is important because it highlights the fact that the present period we live in—in which a vast international legal infrastructure covering trade in services is in the process of construction—was built on the back of a prior conceptual revolution. What this epistemic community did in the years before and during the Uruguay Round, was to 'define and socially construct a new reality'[7]—that is, to re-characterize certain kinds of economic activity as 'trade in services', to re-characterize certain types of government measures as 'barriers to trade in services', and then to build new models and theories on the basis of these new categories. The Uruguay Round therefore began as a learning process for services negotiators, through which they came to accept the fundamental premises of an emerging body of knowledge about global services liberalization.[8] And it was this learning process that enabled—that is, provided the common basis for—the more familiar processes of strategic bargaining that occurred in the final stages of the Round. What Drake and Nicolaïdis make clear then, is the simple but important point that the negotiation of an international legal framework covering trade in services depended on the prior construction and dissemination of a shared body of knowledge among the participants to those negotiations.

---

[6] Drake and Nicolaïdis, above fn 2. I say 'almost' since their account ends in 1992, about 18 months or so prior to the conclusion of the Uruguay Round.

[7] Ibid at 45.

[8] For interesting accounts of negotiations as processes of learning, see JP Singh, 'The evolution of national interests: new issues and North-South negotiations during the Uruguay Round' in J Odell (ed), *Negotiating Trade: Developing Countries in the WTO and NAFTA* (Cambridge: Cambridge University Press, 2006) 41; K Nicolaïdis (eds), 'Learning While Negotiating: How Services Got on the Uruguay Round Agenda' in A Bressand and K Nicolaïdis, *Strategic Trends in Services – An Inquiry into the Global Services Economy* (New York: Harper and Row, 1989) 161.

This chapter is not intended to be another summary of the GATS legal frame-work to add to the many existing ones. Instead, I want to use Drake and Nicolaïdis' story as a departure point for reflection on the current services negotiations, and more generally on services-related activity at the WTO since the Uruguay Round. Part 2 sets out an overview of that activity, covering the sectoral negotiations in the immediate aftermath of the Uruguay Round, the four-pronged rule-making nego-tiations conducted under the auspices of the Working Parties on GATS Rules and Domestic Regulation, the GATS 2000 negotiations, as well as dispute settlement activity related to the GATS. The basic picture that emerges from this overview is one of a legal framework that is hampered by serious difficulties and not fully deliv-ering on expectations. Part 3 suggests—following but also modifying Drake and Nicolaïdis' argument—that these difficulties exist partially because the existing body of knowledge about the global services economy is insufficiently mature and developed. The GATS is thus a classic illustration of the truth that legal systems rest on—are intimately connected to—systems for the social production of knowledge. I offer three simple illustrations to substantiate and extend this argument. Part 4 then briefly offers one tentative view of the implications of this argument, both for WTO scholars, as well as for government officials directly and indirectly involved in the WTO itself.

II. THE GATS IN THE POST-URUGUAY ROUND PERIOD

A. The Outcomes of the Uruguay Round

It is worth beginning by briefly recapitulating a few of the basic features of the GATS as it emerged from the Uruguay Round negotiations. At the most general level, the GATS sets out certain limits on measures imposed by WTO Members, which affect 'trade in services'. Its conceptual cornerstone, then—and probably its most import-ant conceptual innovation—is its definition of trade in services. For the purposes of the GATS, trade in services is defined in Article I:2 by reference to four different ways in which such trade can occur: services may be supplied cross-border ('Mode 1'); a consumer from one country may travel to another country to receive the service ('Mode 2'); a service supplier from one country may set up a commercial presence in another country ('Mode 3'); or a service supplier from one country may send person-nel to another country to supply services in that country ('Mode 4').[9] Although this

---

[9] Art I: 2 GATS.

definition has become canonical, it is worth noting that it was the subject of considerable disagreement and negotiation during the Uruguay Round—particularly in relation to the blurry line between trade in services and activities more commonly thought of as immigration and portfolio investment.[10]

It is one thing to agree on a definition of trade in services, it is another to determine what substantive disciplines ought to be applied to measures affecting such trade.[11] It was decided early on that the key GATT disciplines of most-favoured-nation (MFN) treatment, national treatment (NT), and transparency should be imported directly into the GATS framework. They ultimately appeared in Articles II, XVII, and III of the text, respectively.[12] It proved to be more difficult, however, to transplant market access obligations from the GATT. In the services area there were no easy analogues to the types of measures to which these commitments typically applied, such as tariffs, quantitative restrictions, and other border measures. In the end, a list of measures that were thought to be roughly analogous to these measures was drawn up, and subject to the prohibition under Article XVI GATS.

However, it soon became apparent to GATS negotiators that the wholesale application of these four disciplines, immediately and across all service sectors, was a practical impossibility. This was for at least two reasons. First, given the huge variety of service sectors covered by the GATS, from telecommunications to distribution services, and from business process services to haircutting, there would often be a need to modify or add to these general obligations in specific sectoral contexts. It was originally thought, in fact, that the GATS would comprise a general framework accompanied by multiple sectoral 'annexes' for precisely this reason, but in the end the process of drafting full sectoral annexes proved to be more problematic than expected.[13] Second, because barriers to trade in services were most often in the form of domestic regulation (not border barriers), imposing a national treatment requirement would be the equivalent of granting full, unconditional, and immediate market access in services—something never achieved or even contemplated in the goods context.[14] Ultimately, the answer to both of these problems lay in the creation of two different categories of obligation: 'general obligations' applying across all sectors immediately upon entry into force of the GATS; and 'specific commitments' applying only to those services which a Member inscribes in its so-called Schedule of Commitments, and subject to any qualifications inscribed in those Schedules. MFN and transparency were classed as general obligations, NT and market access as specific commitments.

---

[10] Drake and Nicolaïdis, above fn 2, at 72ff.

[11] This 'narrative' is of course a stylized one, told to help reveal the basic structure and shape of the GATS, rather than a historical chronology.

[12] Drake and Nicolaïdis, above fn 2, at 70.

[13] Ibid at 79–83. Of course, the GATS was ultimately accompanied by a handful of sectoral annexes, but these annexes did not turn out to be the kind of documents originally envisaged.

[14] Ibid at 71.

The designation of the potentially most intrusive disciplines as 'specific commitments' turned out to be crucial in giving GATS negotiators the flexibility and comfort to agree to the overall GATS framework, without being fully aware of the consequences that full liberalization would potentially have in specific sectors. Negotiators, in other words, reduced the level of commitments they offered to reflect their uncertainty over the potential consequences of such commitments. In fact, as it turned out, WTO Members ultimately inscribed relatively few liberalization commitments in their GATS Schedules at the conclusion the Uruguay Round—indeed, the vast majority that were made were at, or more often below, existing levels of liberalization.[15] In Sauvé's words, the overall result was 'clearly biased at every turn towards regulatory precaution'.[16]

There are, of course, numerous other obligations and exceptions contained in the GATS, but it is not the purpose of this chapter to catalogue them. What is more relevant to the present argument is that even at the conclusion of the Uruguay Round, the GATS was in many respects an incomplete project. It was incomplete in the normal sense that liberalization was conceived—just like in the case of goods—as a progressive project. It was envisaged, in other words, that WTO Members agree to progressively greater and greater liberalization commitments through periodic negotiating rounds. But it was also incomplete in the sense that negotiations on a number of outstanding issues had yet to be concluded, and that continuing discussions on these issues were mandated in the text of the treaty itself.

B. Sectoral Negotiations in the Immediate Aftermath of the Uruguay Round

In the tight final months of the Uruguay Round negotiations, it proved impossible to reach agreement on the exchange of concessions in a number of crucial service sectors, including financial services and telecommunications.[17] As a result, negotiators continued to work on these issues even after the formal completion of the Round,

[15] B Hoekman, 'Assessing the General Agreement on Trade in Services' in W Martin and LA Winters (eds), *The Uruguay Round and Developing Countries* (Cambridge: Cambridge University Press, 1996) 88; R Adlung, 'Services Negotiations in the Doha Round: Lost in Flexibility?' 2006 *Journal of International Economic Law* 9(4) 865, at 874.

[16] P Sauvé, 'Developing Countries and the GATS 2000 Round' 2000 *Journal of World Trade* 34(2) 85, at 86.

[17] In addition, negotiations continued on the movement of Natural Persons (see *Marrakesh Decision on Negotiations on the Movement of Natural Persons*, at <http://www.wto.org/english/docs_e/legal_e/47-dsnat_e.htm> (last visited 11 March 2008), as well as GATS Council, *Draft Decision on Movement of Natural Persons Commitments*, S/C/W/8 (21 July 1995); GATS Council, *Report of the Meeting Held on 21 July 1995 – Note by the Secretariat*, S/C/M/5 (29 August 1995); WTO, *Third Protocol to the General Agreement on Trade in Services*, S/L/12 (24 July 1995)); as well as on Maritime Transport Services (see *Marrakesh Decision on Negotiations on Maritime Transport Services*, at <http://www.wto.org/english/

intending initially to complete negotiations within approximately six months. But this timetable proved to be optimistic. In the financial services negotiations, an 'interim' agreement was concluded in July 1995. This interim agreement did not include the US, which had withdrawn its offer at a late stage due to its dissatisfaction with the liberalization commitments offered by others.[18] Negotiations therefore recommenced in April 1997 and by the end of that year resulted in the Fifth Protocol to the GATS, signed by 70 Members.[19] This Protocol essentially had the effect of updating the GATS Schedules of all the signatories to the Protocol to reflect the more extensive specific commitments in the financial services sector that these Members had agreed to during the course of negotiations.

In the telecommunications negotiations, a similar process resulted in the Fourth Protocol to the GATS, signed by 69 Members, finalized in February 1997 (after an abortive first attempt in April 1996), and entering into force a year later.[20] Importantly, these negotiations generated not only the Fourth Protocol, but also the so-called 'Reference Paper'. This document contained significant further obligations in the telecommunications sector, above and beyond the general disciplines contained in the GATS, which required the establishment of pro-competitive regulation, set out conditions for network interconnection, and established disciplines on the transparency and independence of regulators, among other matters. Though the Reference Paper itself has no binding force, some of the obligations contained in it were incorporated into the schedules of 63 of the 69 negotiating Members as part of their specific commitments—most with no or only minor modifications.[21]

C. Negotiations on 'Rules'

In addition to these and other 'spillover' sectoral negotiations, the GATS mandated ongoing negotiations to produce new general rules relating to four distinct issue areas: safeguards, subsidies, government procurement, and so-called 'domestic regulation'. The Working Party on GATS Rules (WPGR) was established in March 1995 in part to facilitate and host negotiations on the first three of these issues. Its

docs_e/legal_e/49-dsmar_e.htm> (last visited 11 March 2008); GATS Council, *Report of the Meeting Held on 28 June 1996 – Note by the Secretariat*, S/C/M/11 (8 August 1996).

[18] EH Leroux, 'Trade in Financial Services under the World Trade Organization' 2002 *Journal of World Trade* 36(3) 413, at 426.

[19] Of those 70 Members, all but three had accepted the Protocol by the time of the most recent WTO, *Annual Report of the Committee on Trade in Financial Services to the Council for Trade in Services (2006)*, S/FIN/16 (28 November 2006), at para 2.

[20] WTO, *Fourth Protocol to the General Agreement on Trade in Services*, S/L/20 (30 April 1996).

[21] See WTO, *History of Telecommunications Negotiations*, at <http://www.wto.org/english/tratop_e/serv_e/telecom_e/telecom_history_e.htm> (last visited 4 March 2008).

negotiating mandate in respect of safeguards is contained in Article X:1 GATS (along with what was in retrospect an unrealistic deadline for their conclusion):

There shall be multilateral negotiations on the question of emergency safeguard measures based on the principle of non-discrimination. The results of such negotiations shall enter into effect on a date not later than three years from the date of entry into force of the WTO Agreement.

The initial discussions, from as early as March 1995 to around the second half of 1998, represented an attempt to develop shared ideas about what safeguard measures in different contexts might look like—what their purpose might be, what contexts they could be used in, what mechanism of protection they could feasibly use, and so on—as well as the more general topic of the feasibility and desirability of deploying such measures in the services context. Despite a reasonable degree of effort and engagement on the part of many delegations, it proved impossible to reach broad agreement on these basic issues.[22]

From late 1998, therefore, and in the face of what seemed to be faltering negotiations on these basic issues, delegates in the WPGR changed tack somewhat, and began to develop a template for safeguards rules 'from the top down', as it were, using existing GATT terminology and jurisprudence to identify a list of technical and textual issues that would need resolution if rules on safeguards were to be agreed.[23] The records of WPGR meetings display a relatively intense degree of effort and discussion on these issues. They have been discussed in over 40 papers by delegations, complemented by almost twice that number of notes from the Secretariat and Chairperson of the Working Party, over the course of well over 70 formal and informal meetings of the WPGR.[24] However, as the Chairperson noted in a 2003 report (which remains as apropos now as it was then), this level of activity...

is far from indicating that substantial progress has been achieved towards convergence on the various issues at stake...my assessment is that the Working Party has not moved very far in respect of its tasks to identify, elaborate and consolidate common elements for an ESM [emergency safeguard measures] and to address the question of feasibility and desirability of ESM.[25]

---

[22] WPGR, *Negotiations on Emergency Safeguard Measures*, S/WPGR/9 (14 March 2003), provides an overview of the first eight years of these negotiations. Further detail can be found in the documents listed in the Annex to S/WPGR/9, as well as in the Annual Reports of the WPGR to the Council for Trade in Services.

[23] See, eg, WPGR, *Communication from Hong Kong, China*, S/WPGR/W/26 (10 February 1998); WPGR, *Communication from ASEAN*, S/WPGR/W/30 (14 March 2000); WPGR, *Communication from the European Communities and their Member States*, S/WPGR/W/38 (21 January 2002), among numerous others listed in the Annex to WPGR, *Negotiations on Emergency Safeguard Measures*, S/WPGR/9 (14 March 2003).

[24] WPGR, above fn 22.

[25] Ibid at para 17.

Indeed, the documentary record of these meetings portrays a picture of discussions, which are largely ungrounded and rudderless, disclosing 'no common basis'[26] on which to draft rules.

Negotiations on subsidies in the WPGR have fared little better. The mandate, contained in Article XV:1 GATS, is in a similar form to the safeguards mandate:

Members recognize that, in certain circumstances, subsidies may have distortive effects on trade in services. Members shall enter into negotiations with a view to developing the necessary multilateral disciplines to avoid such trade-distortive effects. The negotiations shall also address the appropriateness of countervailing procedures. Such negotiations shall recognize the role of subsidies in relation to the development programmes of developing countries and take into account the needs of Members, particularly developing country Members, for flexibility in this area.

Negotiations began in May 1996, but have been characterized by less intense activity than the safeguards negotiations. While a large number of issues have been identified, few have progressed beyond that stage, and the agenda of the WPGR in respect of these negotiations has looked much the same over the course of the entire decade since their inception.[27] One major part of the work carried out by the WPGR so far has been the collection (with the assistance of the Secretariat) of data on the nature and extent of subsidies currently imposed by WTO Members affecting services trade.[28] But this project has been hampered by the lack of a clear definition of what constitutes a subsidy in the services field, and in particular how to identify and distinguish those subsidies which are 'trade distortive' and those which are not. Defining trade-distortive subsidies has proved difficult for at least two reasons. The first is simply the lack of empirical data on the economic effects of measures that could be considered subsidies, and thus the degree of trade 'distortion' caused by them.[29] The second, at least as important, is the lack of a common normative framework to distinguish between legitimate and illegitimate forms of subsidies. It is clear to negotiators that identifying particular governmental measures as trade 'distortive' subsidies is not solely an empirical question, but also involves a degree of political choice. As a result, a number of papers and proposals have been advanced, attempting to develop a language and conceptual framework for distinguishing between 'trade distortive' and other kinds of subsidies, using concepts such as 'specificity' taken from the goods context, as well as more general

---

[26] Ibid at para 18.

[27] A useful summary of the negotiations up to March 2003 can be found in WPGR, *Negotiations on Subsidies – Report by the Chairperson of the Working Party on GATS Rules*, S/WPGR/10, (30 June 2003).

[28] This is in accordance with the mandate set out Article XV:1 GATS, which requires Members to 'exchange information concerning all subsidies related to trade in services that they provide to their domestic service suppliers'.

[29] A Jara and M del Carmen Domínguez, 'Liberalization of Trade in Services and Trade Negotiations' 2006 *Journal of World Trade* 40(1) 113, at 118.

terms such as 'public policy' and 'social objectives' drawn from trade discourse more generally.[30] But this framework remains under construction, and the negotiations themselves have effectively stalled.[31]

The third set of negotiations within the WPGR relate to rules on government procurement. They are mandated by Article XIII:2 GATS:

There shall be multilateral negotiations on government procurement in services under this Agreement within two years from the date of entry into force of the WTO Agreement.

Although in principle this issue was first added to the agenda of the WPGR in December 1995, discussions were relatively relaxed for the first six or so years.[32] Since late 2001, however, in the lead-up to the Doha Ministerial Conference (MC), negotiations on government procurement became subject to a different dynamic, relating to the conduct of the broader Round. The question of the inclusion of negotiations on government procurement in the broader work programme of the WTO has been a highly contentious one, pitting (in broad terms) a large coalition of developing countries on the one hand against the EC as the primary champion of government procurement negotiations on the other. Paragraph 26 of the Doha Work Programme included a reference to negotiations on government procurement, 'on the basis of a decision to be taken, by explicit consensus, at [Cancún] on modalities', but limited such negotiations to 'transparency aspects'.[33] Three years later, after the collapse of the Cancún talks, the General Council (GC) adopted a decision suspending all work on government procurement in the Doha Round. One result of the tension over this issue has been, in the words of Jara and del Carmen Domínguez, that government procurement has become 'a politically incorrect issue' in all venues within the WTO.[34] The relationship between the GC's decision and the WPGR's mandate remains somewhat ambiguous; the EC has continued to make submissions on government procurement, but developing country Members continue to resist the discussion of most issues relating to government procurement in the WPGR.[35]

The fourth and final element of the inbuilt rule-making agenda of the GATS is contained in Article VI:4, on 'domestic regulation':

---

[30] Discussions on a provisional definition of trade-distortive subsidies have been ongoing since 2005.

[31] Although not part of these negotiations, it is worth noting that the WTO's *World Trade Report 2006* was largely devoted to the issue of subsidies, including in world services trade. WTO, *World Trade Report 2006* (WTO: Geneva, 2006)

[32] See generally WPGR, *Negotiations on Government Procurement – Report by the Chairperson of the Working Party on GATS Rules*, S/WPGR/11 (30 June 2003).

[33] WTO, *Ministerial Declaration*, WT/MIN(01)/DEC/1 (20 November 2001).

[34] Jara and del Carmen Domínguez, above fn 29, at 118.

[35] See, eg, WPGR, *Annual Report of the Working Party on GATS Rules to the Council for Trade in Services (2005)*, S/WPGR/15 (22 September 2005), at para 6; WPGR, *Annual Report of the Working Party on GATS Rules to the Council for Trade in Services (2006)*, S/WPGR/16 (23 November 2006), at para 6.

With a view to ensuring that measures relating to qualification requirements and procedures, technical standards and licensing requirements do not constitute unnecessary barriers to trade in services, the Council for Trade in Services shall, through appropriate bodies
it may establish, develop any necessary disciplines...

After the Uruguay Round, it was decided to pursue this broad mandate initially on
a sector-specific basis, starting with the accountancy sector. The Working Party on
Professional Services (WPPS) duly achieved this initial goal; the text of these disciplines was adopted in December 1998, and was expected to become binding at the
completion of the Doha Round.[36] In April 1999, the newly created Working Party
on Domestic Regulation (WPDR)[37] took over the work of the WPPS, with the mandate to develop horizontal disciplines for domestic regulation (as defined in Article
VI:4) generally, and to develop disciplines applicable to all professional services.
Despite regular meetings, and a good level of participation and engagement by delegations, the achievements of the WPDR (at least in terms of producing agreed texts)
are generally considered modest over the first six years of its life. From the second
half of 2005, in the lead-up to the Hong Kong Ministerial Conference, and continuing through the first half of 2006, activity intensified considerably, essentially as a
result of the intensification of the Doha Round negotiations more generally. During
this brief period, countries submitted numerous new papers on the various issues
relating to rules on domestic regulation, meeting rates increased, and, on 12 July,
a preliminary and tentative draft consolidated text of Article VI:4 disciplines was
circulated.[38] Ultimately, there was time for only a few preliminary consultations on
this draft before the Doha Round negotiations were suspended at the end of July that
year, and little of substance has happened since.[39]

D. The GATS 2000 Negotiations and the Doha Round

As alluded to earlier, in addition to these four strands of ongoing rule-making negotiations, the GATS envisions a process of periodic trade rounds, through which
WTO Members commit to greater and greater levels of liberalization in services:

In pursuance of the objectives of this Agreement, Members shall enter into successive
rounds of negotiations, beginning not later than five years from the date of entry into force
of the WTO Agreement and periodically thereafter, with a view to achieving a progressively

---

[36] GATS Council, *Disciplines on Domestic Regulation in the Accountancy Sector*, S/L/64 (17
December 1998); GATS Council, *Decision on Disciplines Relating to the Accountancy Sector*, S/L/63
(15 December 1998).

[37] GATS Council, *Decision on Domestic Regulation*, S/L/70 (28 April 1999).

[38] WPDR, *Disciplines on Domestic Regulation Pursuant to GATS Article VI:4 Consolidated Working
Paper – Note by the Chairman*, JOB(06)/225 (12 July 2006).

[39] WPDR, *Annual Report of the Working Party on Domestic Regulation*, S/WPDR/9 (20 November
2006), at para 6.

higher level of liberalization. Such negotiations shall be directed to the reduction or elimination of the adverse effects on trade in services of measures as a means of providing effective market access. This process shall take place with a view to promoting the interests of all participants on a mutually advantageous basis and to securing an overall balance of rights and obligations.[40]

The first of these new rounds of services negotiations commenced as required in 2000—before the launch of the Doha Round, and in principle independent of it—and a set of Revised Negotiating Guidelines were agreed in March 2001.[41] According to these guidelines, negotiations were to proceed on a bilateral 'request-offer' basis; each Member was to submit requests to its trading partners setting out the liberalization commitments it was seeking from them, and then respond to requests made of it with an offer of liberalization commitments. This process of exchanges of requests and offers only really began in earnest after the commencement of the Doha Round in late 2001.[42] While the requests themselves were and remain confidential, indications are that numerous requests were made by the deadline of the end of June 2002.[43] But the initial offers made in response—and, as negotiations progressed, revised offers—were significantly delayed, and only a small number of Members made the initial deadline.[44] New deadlines for revised and outstanding initial offers were extended by the GC, but by the end of September 2005, only 69 of nearly 150 Members had submitted initial offers, and only 28 had gone so far as revising their offers during the course of negotiations.[45]

The delay and the small number of these offers were matched by their relatively insignificant content.[46] In a report by the Chairman of the Special Session of the GATS Council to the Trade Negotiations Committee (TNC) in mid-2005, the position was summarized in this way:

For most sector categories, a majority of the offers do not propose any improvement. If the current offers were to enter into force, the average number of sub-sectors committed by Members would increase only from 51 to 57. Likewise, less than half of the schedules would contain commitments of any kind in sectors such as distribution, postal-courier, or road transport. There is thus no significant change to the pre-existing patterns of sectoral bindings. As well, less than half of the offers envisage improvements to horizontal commitments

---

[40] Art XIX GATS.

[41] GATS Council, *Guidelines and Procedures for the Negotiations on Trade in Services*, S/L/93 (29 March 2001).

[42] Jara and del Carmen Domínguez, above fn 29, at 115.

[43] Ibid at 116.

[44] R Adlung and M Roy, 'Turning Hills into Mountains? Current Commitments Under the General Agreement on Trade in Services and Prospects for Change' 2005 *Journal of World Trade* 39(6) 1161, at 1183. For some reasons that Members have offered for the delay, see Jara and del Carmen Domínguez, above fn 29.

[45] Ibid at 1183. See also GATS Council, *Special Session of the Council for Trade in Services – Report by the Chairman of the Trade Negotiations Committee*, TN/S/20 (11 July 2005).

[46] See GATS Council, above fn 45; Adlung and Roy, above fn 44.

on Mode 4. With respect to MFN exemptions, only 15 offers propose improvements; some 400 exemptions would remain...[47]

As one commentator has noted, the services negotiations seemed for a long time to be stuck 'in a low-level equilibrium trap where little is expected and little is offered'.[48] The focus for many delegations seemed to be on accommodating defensive rather than offensive interests,[49] and what new liberalization commitments were offered tended to be narrowly focused on particular modes and sectors.

To some extent, the Hong Kong MC injected some momentum into these negotiations. The Ministerial Declaration introduced a modified plurilateral request-offer approach to negotiations, which a number of observers had suggested may facilitate more productive negotiations, and there was a flurry of new activity around March and April 2006.[50] Again, though, it is difficult to assess whether this period actually constituted a substantial turning point in the negotiations, as shortly after they were of course affected by the overall collapse of the Round in July. The temporary revival of negotiations in July/August of 2008 saw further movement, but again the ultimate fate of the services negotiations remains tied to that of the Doha Round generally.

E. GATS-related Dispute Settlement

Finally, it is necessary to take stock of that other very important area of WTO activity related to services, namely dispute settlement. At the time of writing, there have been 13 disputes alleging violations of GATS provisions (counting disputes with multiple complainants as a single dispute). Four have resulted in panel reports,[51] of which three have been appealed.[52] Two complaints are pending,[53] and the remainder have been settled, whether amicably or otherwise. These disputes have been spread relatively evenly over time, at a rate of about one per year. There was a moderate concentration early on, with half of all GATS disputes so far having been initiated in the first four years of its existence, and only two in the four years from 2005 to 2008. Developing countries have been complainants in four disputes, and respondents

---

[47] GATS Council, above fn 45, at para 3.

[48] A Mattoo, 'Services in a Development Round: Three Goals and Three Proposals' 2005 *Journal of World Trade* 39(6) 1223, at 1223.

[49] Adlung, above fn 15, at 871.

[50] See, eg, GATS Council, *Report of the Meeting Held on 2 March 2007 – Note by the Secretariat*, TN/S/M/23 (5 April 2007); GATS Council, *Report of the Meeting Held on 27 April 2007 – Note by the Secretariat*, TN/S/M/24 (30 May 2007); GATS Council, *Report of the Meeting Held on 8 June 2007*, TN/S/M/25 (28 June 2007).

[51] Panel Reports in *EC – Bananas III (Ecuador)*, *Canada – Autos*, *Mexico – Telecoms*, and *US – Gambling*.

[52] Appellate Body Reports in *EC – Bananas III*, *Canada – Autos*, and *US – Gambling*. Note that both the *EC – Bananas III* and *US – Gambling* disputes also have associated Article 21.5 arbitrations.

[53] *China – Trading Rights and Distribution Services*.

in five, while developed countries have been complainants in nine disputes, and respondents in seven.

By any measure this is a low level of dispute settlement activity. These disputes represent only about 4.4 per cent of total disputes brought since the creation of the WTO, and only 3.2 per cent since 2002. Even given the relatively low level of liberalization commitments contained in Members' schedules during the Uruguay Round, one might have expected more activity, particularly given that recent estimates put services trade at around 20 per cent of total world trade.[54]

One important point about the substance of these disputes is that the bulk of them involve fact patterns in which goods and services issues are closely interconnected. Two of the thirteen disputes were relatively unusual in that they related to the imposition of broad-based trade sanctions against a particular country for reasons of 'high politics'.[55] But of the remaining eleven, only four involved what might be called 'pure' services issues. The more typical case involves a complaint against barriers to imports of goods of a relatively traditional kind, which is accompanied by additional claims under the GATS. The classic example is *EC – Bananas III* which primarily concerned the EC's import regime for bananas (goods), but which for reasons specific to the design of the regime also affected those who were engaged in the distribution and wholesale trade of bananas (services). Another example is *Canada – Autos*, which concerned different tariff treatment for autos and auto parts, but which incidentally also related to the supply of distribution services for those cars. Indeed, distribution services have been at issue in a remarkable five disputes, all of which also involved barriers to trade in the goods being distributed.[56] A further example is *China – Integrated Circuits*, which related to China's favourable tax treatment of local integrated circuits, but again also had spillover effects on suppliers of design services to manufacturers of such circuits. I will return to this observation below.

III. Explaining Post-Uruguay Round GATS Practice

The broad picture that emerges from this overview, then, is relatively clear. Commentators agree that GATS-related activity in the WTO is proceeding slower than anticipated, producing fewer results (in terms of agreed texts and new

[54] WTO Secretariat, *World Trade Report 2006* (Geneva: WTO, 2006).

[55] See also *US – The Cuban Liberty and Democratic Solidarity Act*; *Nicaragua – Measures Affecting Imports from Honduras and Colombia*.

[56] See also *Japan – Distribution Services*; *Canada – Film Distribution Services*; *China – Trading Rights and Distribution Services*.

commitments) than expected, and attracting less energy and enthusiasm than originally desired. A number of reasons for this have been advanced. At the most immediate level, some have pointed to the attitude with which the delegations themselves have approached the negotiations—prioritizing defensive interests, lacking in ambition, and divided over the core objectives of the negotiations.[57] Others focus on the organisational and procedural context within which the negotiations have taken place.[58] Perhaps, for example, the request-offer approach set out above was not the right one.[59] More generally, the GATS negotiations are often seen as the victim of the failures of the broader Doha Round—as merely one 'part of a stagnant whole'.[60] Still others concentrate attention at the domestic level. If it is true that 'national positions in trade negotiations tend to reflect the participating countries' internal balance of protection-seeking and liberalizing interests',[61] then perhaps the underlying cause of the problems is the lack of mobilization of pro-liberalization domestic constituencies. It is certainly true that many service sectors in many countries lack relevant business associations, and those that exist are often hardly engaged in the Doha negotiating process.[62] In addition, other analysts have pointed to deficiencies in the GATS text itself as a reason for the reticence on the part of negotiators—deficiencies relating generally to the ambiguity of the text itself,[63] or more specifically to the lack of an agreed safeguards mechanisms, leading governments to be cautious about making irreversible commitments.[64]

All these explanations no doubt form part of the story. But I want to put forward a different explanation, which draws inspiration from the story told by Drake and Nicolaïdis with which I began.[65] Recall their claims about the central role of the ideas of a small epistemic community in generating, shaping, and facilitating the services negotiations during the Uruguay Round. From this story we learn that the project of creating an international legal infrastructure governing trade in services depends on a prior project of re-description—that is to say, a prior project of re-describing certain phenomena as 'trade in services', or as 'barriers' to trade in services, and of building an entire conceptual framework for interpreting the world in these terms. Put another way, the creation of the GATS depended on the prior creation of a shared body of knowledge about the nature and dynamics of the global services economy,

[57] Jara and del Carmen Domínguez, above fn 29, at 127.
[58] Mattoo, above fn 48, at 1229.
[59] Jara and del Carmen Domínguez, above fn 29, at 122.
[60] Mattoo, above fn 48, at 1223.
[61] Adlung and Roy, above fn 44, at 1166.
[62] Jara and del Carmen Domínguez, above fn 29, at 120; Adlung and Roy, above fn 44, at 1167. For an account of the need to educate domestic actors on 'GATS-speak' in order to mobilize them for trade negotiations, see generally SM Cone III, 'Legal Services in the Doha Round' 2003 *Journal of World Trade* 37(1) 29.
[63] Mattoo, above fn 48, at 1231.
[64] R Adlung, 'Negotiations on Safeguards and Subsidies in Services: A Never-ending Story?' 2007 *Journal of International Economic Law* 10(2) 235, at 243.
[65] Drake and Nicolaïdis, above fn 2, and accompanying text.

including authoritative theories about the possible meaning and consequences of liberalization.

The claim I wish to make, then, is that the difficulties that have beset the GATS-related activity of the WTO in the post-Uruguay Round period result in part from the fact that this body of knowledge remains seriously incomplete and underspecified. Those involved in elaborating and applying the GATS framework are still in a period of generating shared understandings of how the concepts, categories, tools, norms, and conclusions of trade discourse can and ought to be applied in that arena of economic activity we now understand as the global services economy. In this part, I substantiate this claim using three very straightforward illustrations, which elaborate in a little more detail some of the matters dealt with in Part 2 above.

A. Lack of Basic Data to Guide Negotiators

Successful negotiations in the services context depend on participants having access to a broad information base: information about the nature and extent of trade in services (who is trading what services with whom, in what quantities, and by what method); the nature and extent of existing and potential barriers to trade; the relative size and importance of these barriers, as well as of their socio-economic impacts; and the likely consequences of the removal or modification of these barriers. This type of information allows governments to determine their interests, to define clear strategies for negotiations, to help mobilize domestic constituencies, and to compare and commensurate their concessions with those of their negotiating partners.[66]

The lack of such information was a serious impediment during the Uruguay Round negotiations. Indeed, one seasoned observer has noted that many sectors remained unbound at the end of those negotiations 'because countries were unsure, for lack of information, of the real implications of making commitments'.[67] And although the body of relevant knowledge available to negotiators has significantly increased since that time, insufficient information remains a serious and well-recognized problem for GATS negotiations.[68] For example, the dearth of information on the extent of subsidies in services sectors—as well as on the nature of alternative policy instruments, which may be used to achieve the same purposes as subsidies but with less trade distortion—has made it difficult for the subsidies negotiations to go far beyond the stage of issue

[66] Ibid at 54; Jara and del Carmen Domínguez, above fn 29, at 121. See also M Robert, 'Negotiating Services Agreements: Challenges Ahead' in Stephenson, above fn 3, at 250.

[67] Robert, above fn 66, at 251 citing G Feketekuty. See also Drake and Nicolaïdis, above fn 2, at 41; GATS Council, *Report of the Meeting Held on 30 July 1996*, S/C/M/12 (19 September 2006), at para 17, for similar views.

[68] See, eg, GATS Council, *Report of the Meeting Held on 1 March 1995*, S/C/M/1 (22 March 1995), at paras 32–39.

identification.[69] As Jara and del Carmen Domínguez note, without such knowledge it is impossible for governments to determine whether disciplines are required, and what kind.[70] In the safeguards negotiations, lack of basic data has played a different role. As a number of countries have noted, the lack of extant statistics on flows of traded services may make it impossible to implement any agreed emergency safeguard measure, by making it impossible for countries wishing to do so to objectively demonstrate an increase in imports, the extent of 'injury' to domestic producers, the causation of such injury, among other factors central to the safeguards process.

But the problem of lack of data is much broader than these specific issue areas. More fundamentally, there is also a continuing lack of minimally comprehensive, reliable data on the nature and extent of global flows of services trade, and the nature and incidence of trade barriers in services. This has been recognized as a serious problem from the very earliest days of the GATS. At the Singapore MC in 1996, for example, the Ministers ordered the GATS Council to develop an information exchange programme to facilitate the generation and dissemination of precisely this type of information.[71] As part of this programme, a series of discussions were held on specific services sectors, 'aimed at enabling Members to identify negotiating issues and priorities'.[72] To stimulate and guide discussion, the Secretariat produced background papers over the course of 1998 and 1999 on various sectors containing some information on 'the economic importance of the service, issues of definition, the main ways in which the service was trade and regulated, [and] existing regulatory barriers to trade'.[73] But these papers remained at a very broad level of generality, and in the lead-up to the GATS 2000 negotiations, delegates in the GATS Council began to note more pointedly that 'trade in services suffered from a serious lack of statistical information'[74] on which to base negotiating positions. This view was echoed by many observers and experts in the field.[75]

Existing sources of statistics on international trade flows in services—primarily the IMF's Balance of Payments Manual, the System of National Accounts 1993, and Foreign Affiliates Trade Statistics—had been surveyed earlier, and found to be incomplete or inadequate for the purposes of negotiations in a variety of significant ways. The Secretariat summarized these inadequacies:

The sectoral and modal structure of commitments under the GATS does not coincide with the existing structure of trade statistics. The scope of the Agreement is far wider than what

[69] See text accompanying above fn 29.
[70] Jara and del Carmen Domínguez, above fn 29, at 125.
[71] The MC endorsed a recommendation of the GATS Council, *Report to the General Council*, S/C/3 (6 November 1996), at para 47.
[72] GATS Council, *Report to the General Council on Activities during 1998*, S/C/6 (7 December 1998), at para 5.
[73] Ibid at para 6; see also Adlung and Roy, above fn 44, at 1191.
[74] GATS Council, *Report (1999) of the Council for Trade in Services to the General Council*, S/C/10 (26 October 1999), at para 13.
[75] See, eg, Robert, above fn 66, at 250–51.

statistics conventionally measure (ie, trade between residents and non-residents in balance of payments (BOP) statistics). The activities of foreign-owned companies in their host economy markets—covered by commitments on commercial presence (Mode 3)—are not reflected in these conventional statistics. Moreover, the IMF Balance of Payments Manual services classification, on which the majority of global trade statistics in services are based, is far less detailed than the UN Central Product Classification (CPC) which, in turn, has served as a building stone for the Services Sectoral Classification list widely used by Members for scheduling purposes (MTN.GNS/W/120).[76]

In addition, as other commentators have noted, existing data sources are problematic in that they do not disaggregate trade in services by origin, and exhibit serious flaws relating to coverage, consistency, concordance, and comparability.[77]

The WTO, it should be acknowledged, has been involved in a major project to address these problems since as early as 1995, namely the Interagency Task Force on Statistics of International Trade in Services, which is a collaboration between the OECD, the WTO, the IMF, UNCTAD, Eurostat, and the UN Statistics Division. In 2002, this body produced the *Manual on Statistics of International Trade in Services*, which sets out an agreed framework within which national and international statistics agencies will collect data, including guidelines to improve coverage and comparability.[78] The GATS was, to a great extent, at the forefront of participants' minds as this framework was created. The Manual notes that:

a particular impetus for the preparation of a separate manual on statistics of international trade in services has arisen from the recent tendency for trade agreements to cover services as well as goods, and the need for statistics both to guide the negotiations and to support implementation of these agreements. The most well-known and wide-reaching agreement involving services is the *General Agreement on Trade in Services*...[79]

The authors go on to note that the 'special requirements' of the GATS 'have informed several of the Manual's recommendations for extensions to existing statistical frameworks'.[80] The GATS negotiations—and the conceptual framework contained within the GATS text itself—have therefore acted to guide and shape the efforts of institutions involved in the production of knowledge about the global services economy.

Work has also intensified on the task of generating more detailed maps of extant barriers to trade in services on a sector-by-sector basis. This work has so far been

---

[76] GATS Council, *Note by the Secretariat – Second Review of the Air Transport Annex*, S/C/W/27/Add.2 (28 September 2007), at para 2.

[77] JS Kang, 'The services sector in output and international trade' in C Findlay and T Warren (eds), *Impediments to Trade in Services: Measurement and Policy Implications* (London: Routledge, 2000) 18, at 19; P Chang, G Karsenty, A Mattoo, and J Richtering, 'GATS, the Modes of Supply and Statistics on Trade in Services' 1999 *Journal of World Trade* 33(3) 93.

[78] *Manual on Statistics of International Trade in Services* (Geneva: UN, 2002), at <http://www.unstats.un.org/unsd/tradeserv/TFSITS/manual.htm> (last visited 10 March 2008).

[79] Ibid at 3.   [80] Ibid.

carried out largely by the academic research community,[81] but, interestingly, has drawn heavily on information collected by the WTO. Seminal early work by Hoekman, for example, used the information contained in GATS Schedules to obtain rough measures of liberalization across countries and sectors.[82] This has since been updated by information gleaned from WTO Trade Policy Reviews, from notifications collected by relevant WTO Committees, as well as from the work of other regional and international organizations.[83] Research has also begun on measuring such barriers quantitatively (using comparisons either between local and international prices, or between expected and actual trade flows), as well as on modelling the economic impact of liberalization.[84]

As important as this work is, however, it still suffers from significant problems. Collection of raw data is highly resource-intensive, and sector-and country-coverage of existing data remains seriously incomplete. The theoretical models used to predict the likely impacts of liberalization are highly speculative, and have been described as 'unlikely ever to be sufficiently accurate to be used directly in the actual conduct of GATS negotiations.'[85] A more fundamental problem, and one which a number of researchers have pointed out,[86] is that even the determination of a list of 'trade barriers' for measurement is inevitably, in part, a subjective judgement. There are at present few generally shared ideas that can guide researchers in selecting from among the rather huge vista of regulatory measures with which a service supplier must comply when entering a foreign market. The problem, therefore, is not just a lack of data, but the lack of an agreed basis on which to collect it.

B. Lack of Shared 'Scripts' to Give Comfort to Regulators

Due to the nature of impediments to services trade, it is often said that opening services tends to look more like a process of regulatory reform than liberalization as

[81] The bulk of the relevant research is extensively reviewed in Z Chen and L Schembri, 'Measuring the Barriers to Trade in Services: Literature and Methodologies' in JM Curtis and D Ciuriac (eds), *Trade Policy Research 2002* (Ottawa: Department of Foreign Affairs and International Trade, 2002), at 219–85. In addition to this academic research, UNCTAD has established its MAST database, which is intended ultimately to provide a comprehensive database of measures affecting trade in services. At present, however, it is largely based on GATS Schedules and suffers from the same deficiencies.

[82] Hoekman, above fn 15; B Hoekman and CA Primo Braga, 'Protection and Trade in Services: A Survey' *World Bank Policy Research Working Paper* 1747 (March 1997).

[83] See, eg, C Findlay and T Warren, 'Introduction' in Findlay and Warren, above fn 77, at 7.

[84] See, eg, DK Brown and RM Stern, 'Measurement and Modelling of the Economic Effects of Trade and Investment Barriers in Services' *2001 Review of International Economics* 9(2) 262; OECD, *Quantification of Costs to National Welfare from Barriers to Services Trade: A Literature Review*, TD/TC/WP(2000)24 (2000).

[85] Chen and Schembri, above 82, at 248; see also OECD, above fn 84, at 13.

[86] Ibid at 251.

traditionally understood. It is not surprising, then, that one of the two primary reasons for the continued difficulties facing the WTO in the area of services, identified by Mattoo, is 'the failure to win the consent and support of regulators'.[87] Adlung and Roy, too, point to the difficulties of coordination between negotiators and ministries and agencies that are 'neither experienced with trade negotiations nor necessarily supportive of the underlying objectives'.[88] Jara and del Carmen Domínguez, also, refer to the 'daunting' task facing trade ministries in 'mobilising and coordinating numerous agencies' at the national level, and convincing them to devote time and attention to WTO negotiations.[89]

If trade negotiations in services depend on regulatory 'buy-in', then regulatory buy-in in turn depends on the existence of a set of shared regulatory 'scripts', or 'models', which provide regulators with a picture (at some level of generality) of what a liberalized market in a particular services sector might look like, precisely what role regulators should play in it, and how to go about transitioning to it. One of the difficulties is that such models do not always exist in many of the most significant sectors under negotiation (and where they do, they are highly controversial). Given the fact that many services sectors have historically not been internationalized, and given the relatively recent provenance of even the idea of liberalizing many service sectors, regulators are understandably uncertain of the consequences of liberalization, and even of what the process of liberalization actually means in the sector for which they are responsible.[90] Regulators rarely have clear and settled ideas about the new challenges that the process of internationalization will throw up, let alone clear guidance on the tools that may be used to address such challenges. In addition, there is evidence that regulators are concerned that the elaboration of international legal rules governing the liberalization of their sector may reduce the variety of regulatory tools available to them to achieve their current objectives. This caution is no doubt born in significant part out of the inevitable degree of scepticism and mutual distrust that exists whenever different normative communities confront one another: domestic regulators are concerned that trade negotiators do not fully understand the particularities of the sector they regulate, that distant international organizations may not fully appreciate their local concerns and conditions, and that their particular normative priorities and responsibilities may be inadequately grasped in the press to liberalize markets.

The generation and dissemination of shared 'scripts' of the type I am talking about can overcome these problems in a number of ways. They can give comfort to regulators by providing them with a framework to understand the liberalization process,

---

[87] Mattoo, above fn 48, at 1229.
[88] Adlung and Roy, above fn 44, at 1163.
[89] Jara and del Carmen Domínguez, above fn 29, at 119.
[90] Committee on Trade in Financial Services, *Report of the Meeting Held on 7 June 1995*, S/FIN/M/4 (19 June 1995), at para 15, contains a reference acknowledging the hesitate of many negotiators to lock-in 'new and untested' regulatory arrangements.

and to comprehend its costs and benefits. They can help to mediate between the norms of the trade policy community and those of sectoral regulatory communities, providing a basis for dialogue and mutual learning. They can also help give regulators a sense of ownership of trade policy norms and prescriptions, by giving them a basis on which to determine for themselves how those norms and principles might be applied and adapted in local contexts. And they can help to reduce the specific legal concerns of regulators, by providing some basic parameters for the interpretation and application of basic principles of WTO law in particular sectors.[91]

It has not traditionally been the role of the WTO to give advice to Members about how they ought to carry out liberalization programmes—though that is arguably changing. Nevertheless, there are some interesting examples of the GATT/WTO system itself playing a part in the generation and dissemination of policy templates in the services area. During the Uruguay Round, for example, financial services regulators were invited to take a direct role in the negotiations, particularly during the early 'conceptual' phases. Although there is some evidence that the initial lack of enthusiasm on the part of such regulators made negotiations more difficult to start with,[92] over time the negotiations themselves acted as a learning environment, as a venue for the exchange of information and for dialogue across jurisdictions as well as across trade and finance ministries, and helped to create a shared sense of how trade principles 'fit' with pre-existing normative commitments among financial service regulators. Since then, the Committee on Financial Services has established a mechanism for continuing information exchange of a similar sort, through which regulators and experts from a different country each meeting address delegates on their recent experience with financial liberalization, and share ideas and lessons learnt.[93] In a similar vein, perhaps, is Mattoo's more general proposal to establish a 'credible' and institutionalized link between WTO liberalization commitments on the one hand, and the delivery of 'policy advice and technical assistance' by other international organizations on the other.[94] The two should be integrated, he argues, in order to 'reassure regulators', and to ensure that liberalization is accompanied by appropriate 'regulatory reform'.[95] While I do not wish to prejudge the normative desirability of this proposal, what is interesting about it in the present context is the way that it, too, is based on a recognition of the intimate connection between

---

[91] I am not making any claim about the desirability of such scripts—I am merely noting that at some level they seem to be a precondition for the continued generation of a legal framework for services in the WTO.

[92] Drake and Nicolaïdis, above fn 2, at 83.

[93] Brief reference to this programme can be found in the Annual Reports of the Committee on Trade in Financial Services to the GATS Council (eg, S/FIN/16 (28 November 2006), at para 4; S/FIN/14 (20 September 2005), at para 4; S/FIN/12 (26 November 2004), at para 4; S/FIN/10 (2 December 2003), at para 4; S/FIN/8 (4 December 2002), at para 4).

[94] Mattoo, above fn 48, at 1232.

[95] Ibid.

the creation of legal rules and the generation and dissemination of 'background knowledge' in the form of regulatory templates.[96]

C. Uncertainty in the Application of GATS Law

Negotiations and dispute settlement related to the GATS have also faltered because of governments' concerns about unexpected and unpredictable legal consequences. Again, this is a well recognized problem, and is reasonably often referred to in the literature on the GATS.[97] Most commentators locate this problem in the text itself: specific ambiguities in certain provisions; the confusing overlapping structure of GATS obligations;[98] or the vague and general wording of its most important disciplines.[99] But ambiguities of this type are not unusual in international legal texts generally. What is more unusual about the services context is that there is as yet only a rudimentary body of shared knowledge and norms to mediate this ambiguity, to ground the application of the law, and define the boundaries of reasonable interpretation. In many cases, there is not even a single obvious way to describe the economic activity in question in terms of the language and concepts of trade in services, let alone to apply substantive GATS norms themselves.

Some examples help make the point clearer. Many forms of modern economic activity, particularly in the context of complex, geographically dispersed production networks, can be characterized in multiple or unpredictable ways, each triggering a different application of WTO legal disciplines. The production and export of clothing, for example, has traditionally been characterized as an instance of trade in goods. But this characterization is complicated by the geographic dispersion of production facilities in contemporary transnational production networks. The government of Honduras, for example, classifies its *maquila* industry as exporters of manufacturing services to foreign clothing brands, rather than solely as goods exporters—even though the economic activity in question is indistinguishable in practice from that which is traditionally characterized as goods production. This ambiguity in characterization may have significant legal consequences: does it mean that not just the GATT 1994 but also the GATS can apply to measures affecting trade in the garments produced by that industry (since such measures also affect trade in manufacturing

---

[96] See also Committee on Trade in Financial Services, *Report of the Meetings Held on 12 and 14 November 1997*, S/FIN/M/18 (21 November 1997), at paras 12, 18.

[97] Jara and del Carmen Domínguez, above fn 29, at 117; Mattoo, above fn 48, at 1231.

[98] A Mattoo, 'National Treatment in the GATS: Corner-stone or Pandora's Box?' 1997 *Journal of World Trade* 31(1) 107; J Pauwelyn, *'Rien ne Va Plus?* Distinguishing domestic regulation from market access in GATT and GATS' 2005 *World Trade Review* 4(2) 131; P Delimatsis, 'Don't Gamble with GATS – The Interaction between Articles VI, XVI, XVII and XVIII GATS in the Light of the *US – Gambling* Case' 2006 *Journal of World Trade* 40(6) 1059.

[99] See, eg, Committee on Trade in Financial Services, *Report of the Meeting Held on 10 April 1997 – Note by the Secretariat*, S/FIN/M/13 (29 April 1997), under Item D.

services)?[100] A second example can be taken from *China – Integrated Circuits*, which concerned the differential tax treatment of imported and domestically produced integrated circuits. The production and sale of integrated circuits is, of course, typically characterized as goods production, and subject to the GATT 1994. However, in some cases, domestic Chinese producers of integrated circuits were outsourcing the manufacture of circuits that they designed—thus enabling the recharacterization of their activities as the 'supply of design services', and triggering the application of the GATS. *Canada – Periodicals* provides a third example, albeit in a different context. As is well known, that case concerned Canadian measures restricting the imports of split-run periodicals. The production and sale of periodicals was again understood by all parties as an example of trade in goods and the provisions of the GATT 1994 applied. But—as some arguments in the case made clear[101]—the production of periodicals can also be perfectly legitimately recharacterized as the supply of advertising services (to those who pay to advertise in the periodicals), or in some cases even the supply of publishing services (to content providers). Such recharacterization could, in principle, trigger the application of the GATS to forms of economic activity traditionally and commonly understood as solely goods-related.[102] A fourth and final hypothetical example might concern a large oil company charged with extracting, storing, transporting, and selling oil on the world market under the terms of a concession contract with a developing country government. Depending on the precise terms of the concession contract, the activities of the company may be characterized as the provision of services to the government (oilfield services, oil exploration services, management and operation of oilfield infrastructure, and so on), or as the production of a good—that is, oil. Does this raise the possibility that the GATS may apply to an oil embargo by one country against another?[103]

Regardless of the specifics of these examples, the broad point is that one type of economic activity can very often be characterized in multiple ways, as trade in goods, trade in services, or both. Economic activities do not classify themselves; over time communities come to agree on shared classifications for them. Precisely

---

[100] The potential application of the GATS to the provision of 'manufacturing services' has been discussed in the Committee on Specific Commitments. After some discussion, delegates to the Committee drew a distinction between 'services provided to manufacturers', 'services incidental to manufacturing', and 'manufacturing services'. They came to a preliminary view that the latter category ought not to be covered by GATS provisions, see Committee on Specific Commitments, *Report of the Meeting Held on 11 July 2000 – Note by the Secretariat*, S/CSC/M/16 (11 September 2000); Committee on Specific Commitments, *Report of the Meeting Held on 4 October 2000 – Note by the Secretariat*, S/CSC/M/17 (24 November 2000).

[101] Appellate Body Report, *Canada – Periodicals*, at 3–4, 18–20.

[102] This has again been raised in discussions within the GATS Council, see GATS Council. *Report of the Meeting Held on 14 and 15 December 1998 – Note by the Secretariat*, S/C/M/32 (14 January 1999), under heading 'Classification Issues'.

[103] See generally Committee on Specific Commitments, *Report of the Meeting Held on 25 November 2004 – Note by the Secretariat*, S/CSC/M/35 (27 January 2005), at para 14 and surrounding.

because the conceptual framework of international trade in services remains so new and underdeveloped, such commonly agreed classifications do not yet exist in many areas. As a result, the application of the GATS to various sectors is inherently unpredictable, and likely to produce surprises.

In the same way that the same economic activity can be characterized as the production of either a good or service, a governmental measure can often be characterized either as a measure affecting goods or a measure affecting trade in services, or both. The GATS dispute settlement experience referred to earlier illustrates this well. In *Canada – Autos,* for example, the measure at issue was preferential tariff treatment of imports of certain makes of cars and car parts—a classic example of a barrier affecting trade in goods. The complainants argued, however, that this also could be understood as a measure affecting trade in services: since wholesale distributors of cars and car parts in practice only imported one make of car and car part (each), then, it was argued, discriminatory treatment as between makes of car also discriminated in practice between suppliers of wholesale distribution services in respect of those cars. The Panel agreed with that reasoning, and this part of its analysis was not overturned on appeal.[104] The implications of this decision are potentially very broad. At its limit, it might imply that any measure affecting trade in goods can be recharacterized as a measure affecting the supply of services relating to that good, at least where there is some degree of vertical integration between the supplier of the service and the producer of the good. There is no reason why, in principle, this could not apply to 'upstream' as well as 'downstream' services. Can, for example, preferential tariff treatment granted to X-brand widgets be characterized as a measure giving preferential treatment to the service supplier who designed X-brand widgets (and thus subject to the GATS)? Would it make any difference if the designer and exporter of these widgets were vertically integrated?

The decision in *EC – Bananas III* takes this difficulty one step further. This case concerned the EC's discriminatory import regime for bananas, part of which involved a discriminatory mechanism for allocating import licenses between different importers. The complainants characterized this mechanism as a measure affecting services—since importers of bananas could be understood as suppliers of 'wholesale trade services' or 'distribution services' for bananas. As a matter of fact, many of the banana importers were not suppliers of such services, at least not in any traditional sense: they were vertically integrated, they handled the bananas at all stages through wholesale distribution, warehousing, ripening, all the way through to onward sale to retailers. Nevertheless, the Panel found that:

where operators form part of vertically integrated companies, they have the capability and opportunity to enter the wholesale service market. They could at any time decide to re-sell

---

[104] Panel Report, *Canada – Autos*, at paras 10.238–246, and Appellate Body Report in the same case, at paras 158–67 (overturning the approach of the Panel, but not addressing this reasoning, and explicitly leaving open the possibility that this reasoning is correct.)

bananas which they have imported or acquired from EC producers, or cleared in customs, or ripened instead of further transferring or processing bananas within an integrated company. Since Article XVII of GATS is concerned with conditions of competition, it is appropriate for us to consider these vertically integrated companies as service suppliers for the purposes of analysing the claims made in this case.[105]

This finding was explicitly upheld on appeal.[106] Again, the implications of this are potentially wide-ranging. Taken to its logical conclusion, it seems that any measure that applies directly to an entity can be characterized as a measure affecting the supply of any of the services which that entity currently performs in-house, but which could in principle be outsourced or externalized, or for which an externalized market is in principle imaginable.

It is my argument that the uncertainties illustrated by these cases are in part the result of the immaturity of the conceptual framework on which the GATS rests. The text of the GATS is ambiguous and broad, to be sure, but its potential for surprising and unforeseen results would normally be reduced by collective shared understandings among the trade community about what does and does not constitute a measure affecting trade in services—that is, about the kinds of measures that the GATS was and was not designed to address. It is in part the absence or underdevelopment of such shared understandings that results in the present pervasive legal uncertainty.

IV. Implications and Conclusion

The core argument of this chapter has been that current WTO services negotiations are hampered by the lack of a body of authoritative and generally shared knowledge about how trade concepts can and ought to be applied to the services economy, and about the meaning and likely consequences of liberalization (or regulatory reform) in different services sectors. Of course, this knowledge exists to some extent, even if in a relatively immature form—otherwise the GATS likely would not exist at all. But without further development of this knowledge, negotiators will be reluctant to make further commitments, rule-making negotiations will lack the buy-in of regulators, and the application of GATS norms will remain radically uncertain. Where might these observations lead?

One apparent and obvious implication is that more resources and energy ought to be devoted to building up and disseminating this body of knowledge among

---

[105]   Panel Report, *EC – Bananas III*, at para 7.320 (fns omitted).
[106]   Appellate Body Report, *EC – Bananas III*, at para 227.

the relevant communities. But there is a danger in moving too quickly to that conclusion: after all, 'progress' in GATS negotiations is not an end in itself, nor should we assume that all possible processes of knowledge production are equally desirable. If it is true that legal systems and systems for the social production of knowledge are deeply interconnected, then the first task—for scholars at least—must be to explore and map the nature of those connections. The WTO, as we have seen, is already deeply involved in processes of knowledge production, in a number of different ways. Actors within the WTO are at times directly involved in the task of collecting and interpreting data—in other words, in the actual elaboration of the underlying interpretive frameworks and knowledge deployed in the services context. More often, however, the WTO is involved in the dissemination of such knowledge, to negotiators, domestic regulators, as well as other constituencies. In addition, the WTO plays an important role in the institutionalization of knowledge created about the global services economy—through its legal texts imbuing certain types of knowledge with authority and apparent objectivity, and guiding the activity of those institutions tasked with producing authoritative knowledge.

For scholars, then, three sets of research questions present themselves. First, there is a set of research questions relating to the character and operation of the ideational system that enables international trade relations, and in particular on the ways that this ideational system influences the operation of the WTO's legal system. How exactly does the 'shared reality' on which legal practice depends influence formal legal processes? Does it simply 'give meaning' to legal texts, and aid in their interpretation? Or does it perhaps operate more subtly to help disputants define and narrow their disputes in a way that is amenable to legal resolution? A second set of questions relates, conversely, to the role of the WTO's legal system in constructing, disseminating, and sustaining this ideational system. How, exactly, we might ask, is the law involved in the process by which meaning is made in the trade community, and a shared social reality is constructed within it? How, for example, is the process of legal interpretation related to the collective application of economic concepts to economic reality? Does the inscription of new concepts (such as the definition of 'trade in services') in legal texts help to institutionalize them? In what ways does the law guide the social production of knowledge? And a third research task is not empirical but normative—namely a critical appraisal of the WTO's work at the ideational level. Although I have argued that the construction of a shared social reality is in some sense a fundamental precondition to an effective WTO legal system, it does not follow that all ways of doing this are equal. The normative dimension of these processes is at present very unclear: who should be involved in these processes? How ought they to be organized? Can we distinguish between different ways in which they are carried out within the WTO and on what basis are we to evaluate one against the other?

That said, there is also clearly room for creative thought about the different ways to overcome some of the obstacles to the current services negotiations identified in this chapter. How might the WTO assist in the task of facilitating the creation and dissemination of the relevant 'knowledge' in more effective, sustainable, and legitimate ways? At least three possibilities spring immediately to mind, which may provide avenues for further thought. First, echoing the comments made by a number of others,[107] there may be greater room for the direct involvement of domestic regulators and other directly affected constituencies in GATS negotiations, so as to provide greater opportunities for dialogue, learning, and the generation of collective interpretive and normative frameworks among different communities with an interest in trade in services. For greatest effectiveness, this could be combined with a greater emphasis on separate sectoral and even sub-sectoral negotiating bodies.[108] Second, there may also be scope for harnessing the trend towards regionalism to help in this process. As others have noted, preferential trade agreements (PTAs) of all kinds can provide a context in which government officials can experience with the norms and principles of services, and develop local meanings for these concepts, as well as a degree of comfort with them. Indeed, through the incorporation of services disciplines in PTAs, trade negotiators and domestic authorities have already started to become more familiar with trade concepts and norms. Moreover, regional arrangements can provide opportunities for sense-making on a smaller scale, and can even facilitate conceptual experimentation—a possibility already in evidence in the rule-making negotiations on subsidies, safeguards, and government procurement, as negotiators have explicitly surveyed the text of extant PTAs for inspiration and useful innovations.[109] Third, and perhaps most obviously, greater resources and attention might be devoted to the long-term project of building and coordinating

---

[107] Mattoo, above fn 48, at 1233; Jara and del Carmen Domínguez, above fn 29, at 119; P Sauvé, 'Making Progress on Trade and Investment: Multilateral versus Regional Perspectives' in Stephenson, above fn 3, 72, at 81.

[108] The need for sectoral committees has been raised regularly during negotiations (see, eg, Committee on Trade in Financial Services, *Report of the Meeting Held on 23 June 2005 – Note by the Secretariat*, S/FIN/M/49 (24 August 2005), at para 61), though the discussions around the creation of a Committee on telecommunications in 1997 illustrate the sensitivities and complications around the issue (See, eg, GATS Council, *Report of the Meeting Held on 25 July 1997 – Note by the Secretariat*, S/C/M/20 (25 August 1997)).

[109] See, eg, WPGR, *Update to the Annual Report of 2002 of the Working Part on GATS Rules to the Council for Trade in Services (2003)*, S/WPGR/W/12 (3 Jul 2003); WPGR, *Safeguard Provisions in Regional Trade Agreements – Note by the Secretariat*, S/WPGR/W/2 (5 October 1995); WPGR, *Safeguards Procedures in Regional Trade Agreements – Note by the Secretariat*, S/WPGR/W/4 (24 November 2005); WPGR, *Overview of Government Procurement-Related Provisions in Economic Integration Agreements – Note by the Secretariat*, S/WPGR/W/44 (24 June 2003); WPGR, *Overview of Subsidy Disciplines Relating to Trade in Services in Economic Integration Agreements*, S/WPGR/W/46 (12 November 2003). See also Mattoo, above fn 48, at 1234; Stephenson, 'Overview: Services Issues for the Western Hemisphere' in SM Stephenson, above fn 3. On PTAs as venues for experimentation and learning, see A Sen, ' "New Regionalism" in Asia: A Comparative Analysis of Emerging Regional and Bilateral Trading Agreements involving ASEAN, China and India' 2006 *Journal of World Trade* 40(4) 553; World Bank, *Global Economic Prospects: Trade, Regionalism, and Development* (Washington, DC: World Bank, 2005).

the institutional infrastructure needed to generate detailed maps of the global services economy, tailored to GATS negotiations, as well as usable databases of existing barriers to trade.

International trade relations are shaped by the political, economic, and institutional contexts in which they occur. It is less well understood that they also have an interpretive dimension—the dimension of ideas, knowledge, and sense-making—that help to set the basic terrain over which more visible political and economic forces operate. The post-Uruguay Round experience of the WTO in the area of services offers us a narrow window onto the importance of the processes by which this terrain is constructed and changed.

SELECTED BIBLIOGRAPHY

R Adlung, 'Services Negotiations in the Doha Round: Lost in Flexibility?' 2006 *Journal of International Economic Law* 9(4) 865

R Adlung and M Roy, 'Turning Hills into Mountains? Current Commitments under the GATS and Prospects for Change' 2005 *Journal of World Trade* 39(6) 1161

A Ahnlid, 'Comparing GATT and GATS: Regime Creation under and after Hegemony' 1996 *Review of International Political Economy* 3(1) 65

WJ Drake and K Nicolaïdis, 'Ideas, Interests and Institutionalization: "Trade in Services" and the Uruguay Round' 1992 *International Organization* 46(1) 37

A Jara and M del Carmen Domínguez, 'Liberalization of Trade in Services and Trade Negotiations' 2006 *Journal of World Trade* 40(1) 113

M Krajewski, 'Public Services and Trade Liberalization: Mapping the Legal Framework' 2003 *Journal of International Economic Law* 6(2) 341

EH Leroux, 'What is a "Service Supplied in the Exercise of Governmental Authority" under Article I:3(b) and (c) of the GATS?' 2006 *Journal of World Trade* 40(3) 345

EH Leroux, 'Eleven Years of GATS Case Law: What Have WE Learned?' 2007 *Journal of International Economic Law* 10(4) 749

A Mattoo, 'National Treatment in the GATS – Corner-Stone or Pandora's Box?' 1997 *Journal of World Trade* 31(1) 107

A Mattoo and P Sauvé (eds), *Domestic Regulation and Service Trade Liberalization* (Washington, DC: World Bank and Oxford University Press, 2003)

PC Mavroïdis, T Cottier, and P Blatter (eds), *Regulatory Barriers and the Principle of Non-discrimination in World Trade Law* (Ann Arbor: University of Michigan Press, 2000)

J Nielsen and P Sauvé, *Trade in Services: Negotiating Issues and Approaches* (Paris: OECD, 2001)

F Ortino, 'Treaty Interpretation and the WTO Appellate Body Report in *US – Gambling*: A Critique' 2006 *Journal of International Economic Law* 9(1) 117

J Pauwelyn, '*Rien ne va plus?* Distinguishing Domestic Regulation from Market Access in GATT and GATS' 2005 *World Trade Review* 4(2) 131

P Sauvé and RM Stern (eds), *GATS 2000: New Directions in Services Trade Liberalisation* (Washington, DC: Brookings, 2000)

SM Stephenson (ed.), *Services Trade in the Western Hemisphere: Liberalization, Integration and Reform* (Washington, DC: Brookings, 2000)

WTO Secretariat, *Guide to the GATS: An Overview of Issues For Further Liberalization of Trade in Services* (London: Kluwer, 2001)

CHAPTER 8

TRIPS

ANDREW D MITCHELL
TANIA VOON

I. The Nature of the TRIPS Agreement

During the Uruguay Round of negotiations that finally created the WTO in 1995, the TRIPS Agreement was one of the most controversial new agreements added by the GATT 1947 Contracting Parties.[1] The TRIPS Agreement defines 'intellectual property' (IP) as copyright and related rights, trademarks, geographical indications, industrial designs, patents, layout-designs (topographies) of integrated circuits, and undisclosed information (Article 1.2). Thus, this agreement on 'trade-related aspects' of IP bears on subjects as wide-ranging as books, computer programs, inventions, and trade secrets. Not surprisingly, given this subject matter, its 'strongest proponents' have been the US, the EC, and Japan, along with their IP industries.[2]

The TRIPS Agreement establishes minimum standards for the protection of IP rights in each of the seven defined areas of IP, meaning that WTO Members are generally entitled to provide higher but not lower levels of IP protection. The most important way in which the TRIPS Agreement establishes these standards is by incorporating several existing multilateral treaties on IP. In particular, Members must comply with Articles 1 to 12 and 19 of the Paris Convention 1967 (Article 2.1) and with Articles 1 to 21 of the Berne Convention 1971 (excluding Article 6*bis*) (Article 9.1). The TRIPS Agreement builds on these existing treaties by imposing additional substantive obligations while recognizing certain exceptions, such as those regarding security and anti-competitive practices (Articles 73, 40.2).

Like several other WTO agreements, the TRIPS Agreement also creates general obligations of 'national treatment' and 'MFN treatment'. With regard to IP protection, subject to permitted exceptions (again defined in part by reference to existing IP treaties), Members agree to accord to the nationals of other Members 'treatment no less favourable' than they accord to their own nationals (Article 3) and to accord immediately and unconditionally to the nationals of all Members 'any advantage, favour, privilege or immunity' granted to the nationals of any other country (Article 4).

The TRIPS Agreement also incorporates rigorous requirements concerning the enforcement of IP rights through judicial and administrative proceedings and appropriate remedies (Part IV) and a sophisticated system for resolving disputes between Members pursuant to the DSU (Part V). The TRIPS Council monitors the operation of the TRIPS Agreement and Members' compliance with it (Article 68).

A frequent criticism of the TRIPS Agreement is that it has no place in the WTO because it entails harmonizing laws (positive integration) rather than removing or prohibiting barriers to international trade (negative integration). Moreover, the grant

---

[1] See, generally, chapters 2 and 3 of this Handbook.
[2] L Helfer, 'Regime Shifting: The TRIPs Agreement and New Dynamics of International Intellectual Property Lawmaking' 2004 *Yale Journal of International Law* 29(1) 1, at 2.

of exclusive or monopoly rights pursuant to the TRIPS Agreement may itself constitute a trade barrier.[3] Cottier responds that other aspects of the WTO agreements are
'equally harmonizing' and that the recognition of IP rights does not of itself conflict
with the goals of trade liberalization; rather, the impact on trade and global welfare
depends on the balance struck between providing incentives to innovate and protecting investment, on the one hand, and safeguarding competitive opportunities,
on the other.[4] The TRIPS Agreement does recognize (under the explicit heading
'Objectives') the relevance of IP rights to 'social and economic welfare' and the need
to achieve 'a balance of rights and obligations' (Article 7).[5]

Another, perhaps more serious, challenge to the TRIPS Agreement arises from
'the strong and widespread perception that [it] is against the interests of developing
countries'.[6] Notwithstanding the variation in interests among developing country
Members, their eventual acceptance during the Uruguay Round of WTO obligations concerning IP is generally regarded as having been a necessary sacrifice in
order to achieve broader liberalization objectives,[7] though they arguably received a
poor bargain given the relatively limited disciplines agreed in sectors such as agriculture and textiles.[8] The TRIPS Agreement does allow developing country and
LDC Members longer transition periods to implement their obligations and also
provides for developed country Members to assist them with technical and financial
cooperation in this regard (Articles 65–67). However, like many special and differential treatment provisions, these were insufficient to address the difficulties faced by
many developing countries in implementing the TRIPS Agreement,[9] and they did

---

[3] See, eg, A Deardorff, 'What Might Globalization's Critics Believe?' 2003 *World Economy* 26(5)
639, at 653–54; E-U Petersmann, 'From Negative to Positive Integration in the WTO: The TRIPs
Agreement and the WTO Constitution' in T Cottier and P Mavroidis (eds), *Intellectual Property:
Trade, Competition, and Sustainable Development* (Ann Arbor: University of Michigan Press, 2003)
21, at 22–23; cf W Davey and W Zdouc, 'The Triangle of TRIPS, GATT and GATS' in Cottier and
Mavroidis, ibid, 53, at 54. See also Preamble and Arts 7 and 8.2 TRIPS Agreement.

[4] T Cottier, 'The Agreement on Trade-Related Aspects of Intellectual Property Rights' in
P Macrory, A Appleton, and M Plummer (eds), *The World Trade Organization: Legal, Economic and
Political Analysis*, Vol I (New York: Springer, 2005) 1041, at 1054. Cottier refers to 'safeguards, dump-
ing, subsidies, and agriculture'. Consider also, eg, the SPS Agreement.

[5] See also Art 8 TRIPS Agreement; C Correa, *Trade-Related Aspects of Intellectual Property
Rights: A Commentary on the TRIPS Agreement* (Oxford: Oxford University Press, 2006), at 91–114.

[6] J Watal, *Intellectual Property Rights in the WTO and Developing Countries* (Boston: Kluwer, 2001)
363; cf F Abbott, 'Intellectual property rights in world trade' in A Guzman and A Sykes (eds), *Research
Handbook in International Economic Law* (London: Edward Elgar, 2007) 444, at 453.

[7] A Pacón, 'What Will TRIPs Do For Developing Countries' in FK Beier and G Schricker (eds), *From
GATT to TRIPs: The Agreement on Trade-Related Aspects of Intellectual Property Rights* (Munich: Max
Planck Institute, 1996) 329, at 332–33; F Abbott, 'Commentary: The International Intellectual Property
Order Enters the 21st Century' 1996 *Vanderbilt Journal of Transnational Law* 29(3) 471, at 472–73, 476;
Petersmann, above fn 3, at 32–33.

[8] AD Mitchell, 'A legal principle of special and differential treatment for WTO disputes' 2006
World Trade Review 5(3) 445, at 449–50.

[9] See, eg, TRIPS Council, *Special and Differential Treatment Proposals Referred to the TRIPs
Council: Report to the General Council by the Chair*, IP/C/36 (20 July 2005); TRIPS Council, *Annual
Report (2006)*, IP/C/44 (4 December 2006), at para 9.

little to change the fact that the main beneficiaries of stronger IP rights were (at least initially) industrialized countries.[10]

In the second part of this chapter, we outline certain significant developments under the TRIPS Agreement since its entry into force in 1995, namely in the course of dispute settlement and in relation to public health. The third part explores some of the issues under the TRIPS Agreement that are yet to be resolved: exhaustion, anti-competitive practices, and geographical indications. In the final part, we address a number of areas in which TRIPS-related issues expand beyond the boundaries of the WTO. In particular, we consider the role of the World Intellectual Property Organization (WIPO), the increasing frequency of 'TRIPS-plus' provisions in preferential trade agreements, and the call for greater acknowledgement of human rights concerns in interpreting and applying the TRIPS Agreement. Due to space constraints, we do not address the many other important subjects arising under the TRIPS Agreement, such as traditional knowledge and biodiversity. The following overview nevertheless exemplifies the wide range of dilemmas arising under the TRIPS Agreement, which is sure to continue as one of the chief battlegrounds in the development of WTO law, even as bilateral trade agreements and other areas of public international law, such as human rights, intervene.

II. Developments to Date

In this section, we examine two areas in which the TRIPS Agreement has undergone major developments: disputes arising under the TRIPS Agreement that have proceeded to formal adjudication in the WTO, and negotiation among WTO Members regarding access to medicines and public health under the TRIPS Agreement.

A. Dispute Settlement

As at the end of 2006, 25 formal complaints had been brought in connection with the TRIPS Agreement: a reasonable number, though not as many as under several other WTO agreements[11] such as the GATT 1994, the SCM Agreement, or the Agreement

---

[10] F Abbott, 'Toward a New Era of Objective Assessment in the Field of TRIPS *and* Variable Geometry for the Preservation of Multilateralism' 2005 *Journal of International Economic Law* 8(1) 77, at 80–83.

[11] K Leitner and S Lester, 'WTO Dispute Settlement 1995–2006—A Statistical Analysis' 2007 *Journal of International Economic Law* 10(1) 165, at 171.

on Agriculture. In addition, on 10 April 2007, the US requested consultations with China alleging violations of the TRIPS Agreement in relation to the availability of criminal procedures and penalties for IP infringement, the disposal of goods that infringe IP rights, and the denial of copyright protection for works that have not been authorized for publication or distribution within China.[12] To date, nine Panel reports (some related) and three Appellate Body reports in relation to the TRIPS Agreement have been circulated and adopted.

The most recent TRIPS dispute to reach the stage of a final Panel report concerned geographical indications (GIs), which are also the subject of continued negotiations in the Doha Round as discussed below. Indeed, Australia and the US may have decided to challenge the EC's GIs scheme in part to buttress their position in negotiations on this issue.[13] In this case, which was not appealed, the Panel found that several aspects of the EC's scheme violated the national treatment (NT) obligations in the TRIPS Agreement and the GATT 1994. For example, the Panel found that such violations stemmed from the *prima facie* case made by Australia and the US (not successfully rebutted by the EC) that a GI located in another WTO Member could be registered under the relevant EC regulation only if the Member had adopted an equivalent system for GIs protection and provided reciprocal protection to EC products.[14]

The US and EC have also played prominent roles in several other TRIPS disputes. In two cases, the EC challenged the US, once regarding its protection of trademarks used in connection with a business or assets that were confiscated by the Cuban government,[15] and once regarding its limitations on performers' copyright for certain broadcasts.[16] The US has not yet implemented the adverse rulings in either of these cases,[17] much to the annoyance of other Members, particularly given the US role in championing the TRIPS Agreement.[18] Other TRIPS disputes have explored matters such as the term of patent protection required under Article 33,[19] the limited exceptions to patent protection allowed under Article 30,[20] the transition period for

---

[12] WTO, *China – Intellectual Property Rights: Request for Consultations by the United States*, WT/DS362/1, IP/D/26, G/L/819 (16 April 2007).

[13] M Handler, 'The WTO Geographical Indications Dispute' 2006 *Modern Law Review* 69(1) 70, at 79.

[14] Panel Report, *EC – Trademarks and Geographical Indications (Australia)*, at paras 7.89, 7.152, 7.249, 7.272, 8.1(e), 8.1(f)(i), 8.1(i)(i); Panel Report, *EC – Trademarks and Geographical Indications (US)*, at paras 7.38, 7.102, 7.213, 7.238, 8.1(c), 8.1(d)(i), 8.1(h)(i).

[15] *US – Section 211 Appropriations Act.*   [16] *US – Section 110(5) Copyright Act.*

[17] WTO, *United States – Section 211 Omnibus Appropriations Act of 1998: Status Report by the United States – Addendum*, WT/DS176/11/Add.53 (13 April 2007); WTO, *United States – Section 110(5) of the US Copyright Act: Status Report by the United States – Addendum*, WT/DS160/24/Add.28 (13 April 2007).

[18] DSB, *Minutes of Meeting Held on 20 February 2007*, WT/DSB/M/226 (26 March 2007), at paras 4–13, 22.

[19] *Canada – Patent Term.*   [20] *Canada – Pharmaceutical Patents.*

developing country Members,[21] and the provision of a 'mailbox' filing system for patent applications pending the availability of a patent protection system.[22]

The TRIPS Agreement has given rise to two other developments in WTO dispute settlement. First, developing countries have often considered the TRIPS Agreement a useful instrument in responding to another Member's failure to implement an adverse ruling by the DSB, even when the original violation was in respect of goods or services rather than IP rights. This generally requires the retaliating developing country Member to establish that 'it is not practicable or effective to suspend concessions or other obligations with respect to the same' sector or agreement and that 'the circumstances are serious enough' to warrant suspension under the TRIPS Agreement instead.[23] For example, Brazil proposed suspending concessions under the TRIPS Agreement rather than increasing tariffs on imports in response to US violations of the SCM Agreement because, '[g]iven the asymmetries between the two economies, additional import duties would have a much greater negative impact on Brazil than on the [US]'.[24]

Whether 'cross-retaliation' of this kind is allowed in the WTO depends on the circumstances of the case. If the implementing Member does not object to the proposed suspension, the DSB authorizes it by reverse consensus. If the implementing Member does object, arbitrators (usually the original panel) determine whether it accords with the relevant dispute settlement provisions.[25] One such arbitration approved Ecuador's request to suspend concessions to the EC under the TRIPS Agreement following EC violations regarding banana imports, noting that 'the considerable economic differences between a developing WTO Member and the world's largest trader ... confirm ... that it may not be practicable or effective for Ecuador to suspend concessions or other obligations under the [GATS] or with respect to all product categories under the GATT'.[26] The utility of this approach for a developing country Member may nevertheless be limited by constraints under its domestic law or other IP conventions to which the Member is a party, as well as economic considerations.[27]

A second noteworthy feature of the TRIPS Agreement in connection with WTO dispute settlement is that 'non-violation' and 'situation' complaints as described respectively in Article XXIII:1(b) and (c) of the GATT 1994 were precluded under Article 64.2 TRIPS Agreement until 1 January 2000 and since that date have

---

[21] *Indonesia – Autos.*

[22] *India – Patents (EC); India – Patents (US).*   [23] Art 22.3 DSU.

[24] WTO, *United States – Subsidies on Upland Cotton: Recourse to Article 7.9 of the SCM Agreement and Article 22.2 of the DSU by Brazil*, WT/DS267/26 (7 October 2005), at 2.

[25] Art 22.6 DSU.

[26] Decision by the Arbitrators, *EC – Bananas III (Ecuador) (Article 22.6 – EC)*, at paras 126, 138, 173(d).

[27] E Vranes, 'Cross Retaliation under GATS and TRIPS – An Optimal Enforcement Device for Developing Countries?' in F Breuss, S Griller, and E Vranes (eds), *The Banana Dispute: An Economic and Legal Analysis* (Vienna: Springer, 2003) 113, at 124–28.

remained inapplicable by agreement between the Members.[28] In the GATT 1994 context, violation complaints are much more common (under Article XXIII:1(a)), but a Member may also bring a WTO dispute where it considers that, as a result of a Member's measure that does not necessarily violate WTO law or some other situation, its WTO benefits are being nullified or impaired, or the attainment of any objective of the agreement is being impeded. Special dispute settlement provisions apply to these complaints under Article 26 DSU. The Council for TRIPS continues to work on the scope and modalities for complaints of this type under the TRIPS Agreement,[29] which could cover, for example, a patent regime imposing 'an excessively high level of inventive step' for pharmaceutical products that effectively preclude patent protection for these products without banning it outright.[30] Some regard non-violation complaints as unnecessary in the TRIPS context, given that the agreement is less concerned with market access and tariff concessions than the GATT 1994; others regard it as crucial in preventing Members from circumventing their TRIPS obligations. The impact of such complaints on security and predictability of trade is debated.[31]

B. Access to Medicines and Public Health

The TRIPS Agreement recognizes the relationship between IP rights and public health,[32] allowing Members to 'adopt measures necessary to protect public health and nutrition... provided that such measures are consistent with the provisions of this Agreement' (Article 8.1). Patent protection for pharmaceutical products as mandated in the TRIPS Agreement represents one possible obstacle to public health measures and provides the setting for some of the most crucial advances made under the TRIPS Agreement and, indeed, the WTO agreements as a whole, since their enactment.

Subject to certain limited exceptions,[33] Members must make patents available for pharmaceuticals, and owners of these patents have exclusive rights to prevent others

---

[28] MC, *Doha Work Programme: Ministerial Declaration Adopted on 18 December 2005*, WT/MIN(05)/DEC (22 December 2005) (Hong Kong Declaration), at para 45.

[29] TRIPS Council, *Minutes of Meeting Held on 13 February 2007*, IP/C/M/53 (22 March 2007), at paras 62–64.

[30] K Lee and S von Lewinski, 'The Settlement of International Disputes in the Field of Intellectual Property' in Beier and Schricker, above fn 7, 278, at 313.

[31] TRIPS Council, *Non-Violation and Situation Complaints: Summary Note by the Secretariat – Revision*, IP/C/W/349/Rev.1 (24 November 2004), at paras 10–12.

[32] See also chapter 21 of this Handbook.

[33] These include excluding inventions from patentability where 'necessary to protect *ordre public* or morality, including to protect human, animal or plant life or health', but 'provided that such exclusion is not made merely because the [commercial exploitation of the invention] is prohibited by their law': Art 27.2 TRIPS Agreement.

from making, selling, or importing the relevant products (Articles 27–28). These rights tend to elevate the prices of patented medicines (as compared to 'generic' or 'off-patent' medicines),[34] creating a potential difficulty particularly for developing countries seeking to manufacture or import them to deal with serious public health concerns, such as HIV/AIDS crises. Without further discussion, this difficulty would have crystallized when the transition period for pharmaceutical patents ended on 1 January 2005 for many developing countries such as India, and on 1 January 2006 for LDCs (Articles 65.1, 65.2, 65.4, 66.1).

Exceptions in Articles 30 and 31 might have assisted, in particular, by allowing the grant of compulsory licences to manufacture patented pharmaceuticals subject to conditions such as the payment of adequate remuneration and prior attempts to negotiate a voluntary licence on reasonable commercial terms and conditions (which condition could be waived 'in the case of a national emergency or other circumstances of extreme urgency or in cases of public non-commercial use') (Article 31(b)). However, under Article 31(f), this kind of 'use of the subject matter of a patent without the authorization of the right holder' is to be 'authorized predominantly for the supply of the domestic market of the Member authorizing such use', meaning that a Member without sufficient capacity to manufacture the requisite pharmaceuticals could not take advantage of a compulsory licence to import these products from another Member. These Members might have been able to rely on the principle of international exhaustion (as discussed further below) to import products made under compulsory licence, but on one view parallel imports invariably violate the patent owner's rights unless they are imports of products made under voluntary licence.[35]

In recognition of this predicament, the WTO Members at the Fourth Ministerial Conference (MC) in Doha in 2001 issued a declaration 'affirm[ing] that the Agreement can and should be interpreted and implemented in a manner supportive of WTO members' right to protect public health and, in particular, to promote access to medicines for all'.[36] Among other things, this Ministerial *Declaration on the TRIPS Agreement and Public Health* noted Members' freedom to determine the grounds for granting compulsory licences and acknowledged that 'public health crises, including those relating to HIV/AIDS, tuberculosis, malaria and other epidemics, can represent a national emergency or other circumstances of extreme urgency'.[37] It also provided the setting for several more substantive changes. First, LDC Members were granted an additional transition period until 1 January 2016 in relation to

[34] F Abbott, 'The Doha Declaration on the TRIPS Agreement and Public Health: Lighting a Dark Corner at the WTO' 2002 *Journal of International Economic Law* 5(2) 469, at 472.

[35] Ibid at 495–97.

[36] MC, *Declaration on the TRIPS Agreement and Public Health Adopted on 14 November 2001*, WT/MIN(01)/DEC/2 (20 November 2001), at para 4.

[37] Ibid at para 5.

certain obligations regarding pharmaceutical patents.[38] Second, Members agreed on a waiver of Article 31(f) so that LDC Members and other Members lacking sufficient manufacturing capacity may import pharmaceutical products created under compulsory licence, subject to certain conditions.[39] This waiver will become permanent through an amendment to the TRIPS Agreement after two-thirds of the Members accept it; this would be the first ever formal amendment to the WTO agreements, introducing a new Article 31bis into the TRIPS Agreement.[40]

Although these steps are very welcome, their practical implications have been limited to date. At the time of writing, only 18 of the 153 WTO Members[41] have accepted the amendment,[42] and a handful of Members have implemented legislation to enable them to issue compulsory licences in accordance with the waiver.[43] At the end of 2007, the GC noted that acceptance of the amending protocol by two-thirds of the Members was 'taking longer than initially foreseen' and therefore decided, on the recommendation of the TRIPS Council, to extend the deadline for acceptance from 1 December 2007 to 31 December 2009 'or such later date as may be decided by the Ministerial Conference'.[44]

[38]   TRIPS Council, *Extension of the Transition Period under Article 66.1 of the TRIPS Agreement for Least-Developed Country Members for Certain Obligations with Respect to Pharmaceutical Products: Decision of 27 June 2002*, IP/C/25 (1 July 2002), at para 1; GC, *Least-Developed Country Members – Obligations Under Article 70.9 of the TRIPS Agreement with Respect to Pharmaceutical Products: Decision of 8 July 2002*, WT/L/478 (12 July 2002), at para 1.

[39]   GC, *Implementation of Paragraph 6 of the Doha Declaration on the TRIPS Agreement and Public Health: Decision of 30 August 2003*, WT/L/540 (1 September 2003). A waiver of Article 31(h) is also included so that an importing Member need not pay adequate remuneration where it has already been paid in the exporting Member.

[40]   GC, *Amendment of the TRIPS Agreement: Decision of 6 December 2005*, WT/L/641 (8 December 2005), at para 4.

[41]   <http://www.wto.org/english/thewto_e/whatis_e/tif_e/org6_e.htm> (last visited 24 August 2008).

[42]   <http://www.wto.org/english/tratop_e/trips_e/amendment_e.htm> (last visited 24 August 2008). See also latest revisions of TRIPS Council, *Protocol Amending the TRIPS Agreement – Status of acceptances: Note from the Secretariat (Revision)*, IP/C/W/490/Rev.1 (19 October 2007).

[43]   Council for TRIPS, *Annual Review of the Decision on the Implementation of Paragraph 6 of the Doha Declaration on the TRIPS Agreement and Public Health: Report to the General Council*, IP/C/46 (1 November 2007), at para 19 (Switzerland); TRIPS Council, *Annual Review of the Decision on the Implementation of Paragraph 6 of the Doha Declaration on the TRIPS Agreement and Public Health: Report to the General Council*, IP/C/42 (2 November 2006), at para 5 (European Communities); TRIPS Council, *Annual Review of the Decision on the Implementation of Paragraph 6 of the Doha Declaration on the TRIPS Agreement and Public Health: Report to the General Council*, IP/C/37 (3 November 2005), at para 5 (Canada), at para 6 (India), at para 7 (Korea); TRIPS Council, *Annual Review of the Decision on the Implementation of Paragraph 6 of the Doha Declaration on the TRIPS Agreement and Public Health: Report to the General Council*, IP/C/33 (8 December 2004), at para 4 (Norway).

[44]   GC, *Amendment of the TRIPS Agreement – Extension of the Period for the Acceptance by Members of the Protocol Amending the TRIPS Agreement: Decision of 18 December 2007*, WT/L/711 (21 December 2007). See also TRIPS Council, *Amendment of the TRIPS Agreement: Proposal for a Decision on an Extension of the Period for the Acceptance By Members of the Protocol Amending the TRIPS Agreement*, IP/C/45 (29 October 2007).

One positive development stands out. On 17 July 2007, Rwanda (an LDC) became the first Member to notify the TRIPS Council of its intention to use the waiver of Article 31(f) as an importing Member. The notification concerned the HIV/AIDS drug TriAvir, manufactured in Canada by generic pharmaceutical company Apotex, Inc.[45] In turn, Canada notified the TRIPS Council in early October 2007 of its grant of a compulsory licence as an eligible exporting Member to enable the manufacture and export of TriAvir to Rwanda.[46] The successful outcome of this arrangement may encourage further use of the flexibilities on which the Members have agreed.

III. Outstanding Issues

We now consider three areas under the TRIPS Agreement raising questions that the Members are yet to resolve: the exhaustion of IP rights associated with a product through the sale of that product with the right holder's authority, the relationship between IP rights and anti-competitive conduct, and the category of GIs. Of these, only GIs are currently subject to negotiation under the Doha Round.

A. Exhaustion and Parallel Imports

In his seminal work, Warwick Rothnie describes parallel imports as follows:

They are lawfully put on the market in the place of *export*, the foreign country. But, an owner of the [IP] rights in the place of *importation*, the domestic country, opposes their importation... [S]ome enterprising middleman buys stock in the cheaper, foreign country and imports them into the dearer, domestic country. Hence, the imports may be described as being imported in 'parallel' to the authorised distribution network.[47]

Under a rule or system of 'national exhaustion', by authorizing the first sale of a product in a given country, the owner of IP rights in that product exhausts those rights in that country only, such that a parallel import of the product into another

---

[45] TRIPS Council, *Rwanda – Notification under Paragraph 2(A) of the Decision of 30 August 2003 on the Implementation of Paragraph 6 of the Doha Declaration on the TRIPS Agreement and Public Health*, IP/N/9/RWA/1 (19 July 2007).

[46] TRIPS Council, *Canada – Notification under Paragraph 2(C) of the Decision of 30 August 2003 on the Implementation of Paragraph 6 of the Doha Declaration on the TRIPS Agreement and Public Health*, IP/N/10/CAN/1 (8 October 2007).

[47] W Rothnie, *Parallel Imports* (London: Sweet & Maxwell, 1993), at 1 (original emphasis).

country may infringe the IP owner's rights in the second country. Under a system of 'international exhaustion', the first sale exhausts the IP rights associated with the product worldwide, allowing parallel imports of the product after that sale. A country's choice of which system to adopt in relation to any given category of IP (as the considerations may differ for each)[48] raises the same balancing questions as determining the extent of protection of IP rights more generally. International exhaustion may encourage lower-priced parallel imports and promote competition, benefiting consumers and industrial users of the relevant products, while national exhaustion may advance the interests of IP owners and creators.[49] Jayashree Watal cautions against assuming that developing countries would necessarily benefit from international exhaustion.[50]

Article 6 TRIPS Agreement provides that, '[f]or the purposes of dispute settlement under this Agreement, subject to the provisions of Articles 3 and 4 nothing in this Agreement shall be used to address the issue of exhaustion of [IP] rights'. This provision reflects a failure to agree on the treatment of exhaustion and parallel imports and, consequently, a degree of discretion for WTO Members. Nevertheless, whatever approach a Member chooses, it must apply this on a non-discriminatory basis, that is, in accordance with the principles of NT and MFN treatment as set out in Articles 3 and 4. The choice for patents may affect the Member's ability to respond to public health crises as discussed above.[51] Accordingly, the 'Doha Declaration on TRIPS and Public Health' confirms that '[t]he effect of the provisions in the TRIPS Agreement that are relevant to the exhaustion of [IP] rights is to leave each member free to establish its own regime for such exhaustion without challenge, subject to the MFN and national treatment provisions'.[52] This makes clear that Article 6 is not to be interpreted as being limited to dispute settlement such that, for example, the substantive TRIPS Agreement provisions on patents could be read as mandating international exhaustion.[53]

Although Members are not examining exhaustion in the Doha Round, given the absence of agreement to date as to a uniform approach on this issue, it may resurface to be resolved in future.

---

[48] F Abbott, 'First Report (Final) to the Committee on International Trade Law of the International Law Association on the Subject of Parallel Importation' 1998 *Journal of International Economic Law* 1(4) 607, at 614.

[49] V Chiappetta, 'The Desirability of Agreeing to Disagree: The WTO, TRIPS, International Exhaustion and a Few Other Things' 2000 *Michigan Journal of International Law* 21(3) 333, at 336, 341, 350–53; Rothnie, above fn 47, at 3. See also above section I.

[50] Watal, above fn 6, at 303.

[51] See above section II.B.

[52] MC, *Declaration on the TRIPS Agreement and Public Health Adopted on 14 November 2001*, WT/MIN(01)/DEC/2 (20 November 2001), at para 5(d).

[53] Watal, above fn 6, at 296–97.

B. Anti-competitive Practices

Article 8.2 TRIPS Agreement allows Members to take '[a]ppropriate measures, pro-vided that they are consistent with the provisions of this Agreement, ... to prevent the abuse of [IP] rights by right holders or the resort to practices which unreasonably restrain trade or adversely affect the international transfer of technology'. The scope of this allowance therefore depends on how other TRIPS Agreement provisions are interpreted in relation to anti-competitive practices. In addition, Article 40.1 TRIPS Agreement recognizes that 'some licensing practices or conditions pertaining to [IP] rights which restrain competition may have adverse effects on trade and may impede the transfer and dissemination of technology'. Accordingly, Members are entitled to 'specif[y] in their legislation licensing practices or conditions that may in particular cases constitute an abuse of [IP] rights having an adverse effect on com-petition in the relevant market' (Article 40.2).[54] Article 40.2 provides examples of the kinds of practices that may be anti-competitive ('exclusive grantback conditions, conditions preventing challenges to validity and coercive package licensing') but not an exhaustive or binding list. Indeed, apart from an obligation to enter consultations on request in relation to these matters (Article 40.3), the provisions regarding anti-competitive conduct are 'permissive rather than mandatory'.[55]

The question whether WTO Members should adopt additional, mandatory rules aimed at harmonizing competition laws or producing an overarching international competition law goes beyond the TRIPS Agreement,[56] and, potentially, the WTO itself.[57] It concerns numerous aspects of the WTO agreements, including goods, services, and dispute settlement. The WTO's Working Group on the Interaction between Trade and Competition Policy was previously discussing the 'interaction between trade and competition policy, including anti-competitive practices, in order to identify any areas that may merit further consideration in the WTO framework'.[58]

---

[54] See also Arts 17, 22–4, 30, 39 TRIPS Agreement; A Heinemann, 'Antitrust Law of Intellectual Property in the TRIPs Agreement of the World Trade Organization' in Beier and Schricker, above fn 7, 239, at 240, 244.

[55] R Anderson, 'Intellectual Property Rights, Competition Policy and International Trade: Reflections on the Work of the WTO Working Group on the Interaction between Trade and Competition Policy (1996–1999)' in Cottier and Mavroidis, above fn 3, 235, at 240.

[56] See generally M Taylor, *International Competition Law: A New Dimension for the WTO?* (Cambridge: Cambridge University Press, 2006). See also chapter 23 of this Handbook.

[57] W Fikentscher, 'Historical Origins and Opportunities for Development of an International Competition Law in the TRIPs Agreement of the World Trade Organization (WTO) and Beyond' in Beier and Schricker, above fn 7, 226; 'OECD Committee Lacks Enthusiasm for Draft International Antitrust Code' (1993) 65 ATRR 771; M Desta and N Barnes, 'Competition Law and Regional Trade Agreements: An Overview' in L Bartels and F Ortino (eds), *Regional Trade Agreements and the WTO Legal System* (Oxford: Oxford University Press, 2006) 239, at 243.

[58] MC, *Ministerial Declaration adopted on 13 December 1996*, WT/MIN(96)/DEC (18 December 1996), at para 20. See also MC, *Ministerial Declaration adopted on 14 November 2001*, WT/MIN(01)/DEC/1 (20 November 2001) (Doha Declaration), at paras 23–25.

However, this so-called 'Singapore issue' has now been excised from the Doha Work Programme and is no longer under negotiation.[59] Nevertheless, the absence of a multilateral competition framework is problematic and will need to be addressed at some point. 'Although competition law has traditionally dealt with private action within the border, while trade law has traditionally dealt with public action at the border',[60] this dichotomy is weakening. In relation to IP rights as in other areas, the effects of domestic competition laws and anti-competitive practices frequently extend across national borders, increasing the risk of conflict and unnecessary costs on consumers and firms.[61]

C. Geographical Indications

The TRIPS Agreement defines GIs as indications that 'identify a good as originating in the territory of a Member, or a region or locality in that territory, where a given quality, reputation or other characteristic of the good is essentially attributable to its geographical origin' (Article 22.1). The WTO website offers the examples of Champagne, Tequila, and Roquefort.[62] Members have a general obligation to provide the legal means for interested parties to prevent the use of GIs for goods (for example in a trademark) in such a way as to mislead the public about the origin of the good or to constitute unfair competition (Articles 22.2–22.4). Members must provide greater protection in relation to GIs for wines and spirits—that is, preventing their use in relation to wines or spirits not originating in the relevant place 'even where the true origin is indicated or the [GI] is used in translation or accompanied by expressions such as "kind", "type", "style", "imitation" or the like' (Article 23.1). Some exceptions apply, such as for GIs that are generic terms, or where a GI was used continuously in good faith before 15 April 1994 (when the WTO agreements were signed) or was included in a trademark registered in good faith (Articles 24.4–24.6).

GIs provide one issue that remains under negotiation in the Doha Round. At Doha in 2001, Members agreed, in accordance with Article 23.4 TRIPS Agreement, 'to negotiate the establishment of a multilateral system of notification and registration of [GIs] for wines and spirits'.[63] Members have since 'agree[d] to intensify these negotiations'.[64] Members are currently negotiating on the basis of three main

---

[59] GC, *Decision Adopted by the General Council on 1 August 2004*, WT/L/579 (2 August 2004), at para 3.

[60] AD Mitchell, 'Broadening the Vision of Trade Liberalisation: International Competition Law and the WTO' 2001 *World Competition* 24(3) 343, at 346.

[61] Ibid at 347–51; A Guzman, 'International competition law' in Guzman and Sykes, above fn 6, 418, at 428–32.

[62] <http://www.wto.org/english/tratop_e/trips_e/gi_e.htm> (last visited 14 January 2008).

[63] Doha Declaration, at para 18.   [64] Hong Kong Declaration, at para 29.

proposals in this regard.[65] In addition, although Members disagree as to the link with the wines and spirits negotiations and the Doha Round more generally, they are discussing the extension of the higher level of GI protection to products other than wines and spirits, as arguably envisaged in Article 24.1 TRIPS Agreement.[66]

The alignment of Members on both sides of the GI debate is illustrated by existing proposals regarding the register for wines and spirits. The EC, long an advocate for GIs, calls for the higher levels of protection for wines and spirits to be simply extended to all products, along with a multilateral register for all products whereby registration of a particular GI would create, for participating Members not having lodged a reservation in respect of that GI, 'a rebuttable presumption of the eligibility for protection of that [GI]'.[67] Hong Kong, China has submitted a proposal under which registration of an indication would provide *prima facie* evidence of ownership and that the indication is a GI protected in the country of origin.[68] In contrast, under a third proposal, participating Members would have much greater flexibility: they would merely have to ensure that they provide for consultation of the register when making domestic decisions regarding trademarks and GIs for wines and spirits. This proposal is endorsed by Argentina, Australia, Canada, Chile, Costa Rica, Dominican Republic, Ecuador, El Salvador, Guatemala, Honduras, Japan, Mexico, New Zealand, Nicaragua, Paraguay, Chinese Taipei, and the US.[69] In many of these 'New World' countries, terms that the EC regards as GIs are already considered generic.[70]

This is an extremely sensitive area of negotiations, made more complex by the uncertain effects that GI protection may have on different Members. For instance, Evans and Blakeney suggest that, whereas 'large, commodity-dependent developing countries, such as India, Egypt, or Kenya, are well placed to take advantage of an extension of additional protection for agricultural products, foodstuffs,

---

[65] See TRIPS Council, *Side-by-Side Presentation of Proposals: Prepared by the Secretariat*, TN/IP/W/12 (14 September 2005), TN/IP/W/12/Add.1 (4 May 2007), TN/IP/W/12/Add.1/Corr.1 (10 May 2007).

[66] See TNC, *Issues Related to the Extension of the Protection of Geographical Indications Provided for in Article 23 of the TRIPS Agreement to Products Other Than Wines and Spirits: Compilation of Issues Raised and Views Expressed – Note by the Secretariat*, WT/GC/W/546, TN/C/W/25 (18 May 2005). See also Doha Declaration, at paras 12, 18; Hong Kong Declaration, at para 39.

[67] TRIPS Council, Special Session, *Geographical Indications: Communication from the European Communities*, WT/GC/W/547, TN/C/W/26, TN/IP/W/11 (14 June 2005), at paras 2–3, 16.

[68] TRIPS Council, Special Session, *Multilateral System of Notification and Registration of Geographical Indications under Article 23.4 of the TRIPS Agreement: Communication from Hong Kong, China*, TN/IP/W/8 (23 April 2003), at para 4(iv).

[69] TRIPS Council, Special Session, *Proposed Draft TRIPS Council Decision on the Establishment of a Multilateral System of Notification and Registration of Geographical Indications for Wines and Spirits*, TN/IP/W/10 (1 April 2005), at para 4, TN/IP/W/10/Add.1 (18 November 2005), TN/IP/W/10/Add.2 (7 April 2006), TN/IP/W/10/Add.3 (20 April 2006).

[70] J Martín, 'The WTO TRIPS Agreement: The Battle between the Old and the New World over the Protection of Geographical Indications' 2004 *Journal of World Intellectual Property* 7(3) 287, at 288.

and traditional handicrafts', other developing countries may lack 'the financial resources, the technical expertise and the institutional capacity' necessary to commercialize goods that could benefit from GI protection and to provide that protection.[71] Ultimately, a link exists between negotiations on the extension of GIs beyond wines and spirits, the multilateral register, and agriculture more generally. Failure in any one of these areas may necessitate failure in the other two.[72]

IV. Beyond the WTO

In this final section, we identify three ways in which the TRIPS Agreement is influenced by outside forces and consider how these forces are changing international IP law. We first consider WIPO before turning to IP provisions in preferential, regional, or free trade agreements (FTAs)[73] and then the growing drive for a human rights approach to the TRIPS Agreement.

A. WIPO

WIPO is a specialized agency of the United Nations (UN) established by a treaty signed in 1967 'to promote the protection of [IP] throughout the world through cooperation among States and, where appropriate, in collaboration with any other international organization'.[74] It has 184 contracting parties,[75] as compared with the WTO's 153 Members.[76] The preamble to the TRIPS Agreement records the Members' desire 'to establish a mutually supportive relationship between the WTO and [WIPO] as well as other relevant international organizations'. Certain other TRIPS Agreement provisions also refer to WIPO, including Article 68, which directs the

---

[71] G Evans and M Blakeney, 'The Protection of Geographical Indications After Doha: Quo Vadis?' 2006 *Journal of International Economic Law* 9(3) 575, at 607–08.

[72] Ibid at 575, 606–07.

[73] We use the term 'free trade agreements' to refer to bilateral and regional agreements between States or customs territories that focus at least in part on liberalizing trade between the parties, as distinct from the multilateral system established under the WTO. 'FTAs' therefore include free-trade areas and customs unions within the meaning of Art XXIV GATT 1994.

[74] *Convention Establishing the World Intellectual Property Organization*, done at Stockholm, 14 July 1967, 828 UNTS 3, Art 3(i).

[75] See <http://www.wipo.int/treaties/en/ShowResults.jsp?lang=en&treaty_id=1> (last visited 14 January 2008).

[76] See above fn 41.

TRIPS Council to 'seek to establish...appropriate arrangements for cooperation with bodies of that Organization'. The two organizations entered a cooperation agreement in 1995, pursuant to which, among other things, they provide access to each other's collection of countries' IP laws and regulations and cooperate in technical assistance activities.[77] WIPO has observer status in meetings of the GC,[78] the TRIPS Council and certain other WTO bodies.[79]

The locus for multilateral IP negotiations shifted from WIPO to the GATT 1947 with the Uruguay Round of negotiations leading to the WTO, largely on the initiative of the US and the EC, though WIPO 'continues to function as a critically important venue for [IP] lawmaking by all of its member states in a post-TRIPs environment'.[80] Since the WTO was established, WIPO has concluded several treaties expanding international IP coordination.[81] These newer treaties are not incorporated into the TRIPS Agreement leading some WTO Members to suggest their inclusion either in the TRIPS Agreement[82] or through the alternative route of FTAs, as discussed in the following section.

B. TRIPS-plus in FTAs

A common feature in the proliferation of FTAs[83] in recent years[84] (and particularly those of the US) has been the insertion of so-called 'TRIPS-plus' provisions, requiring FTA partners to impose higher standards of IP protection than those set in the TRIPS Agreement.[85] This tends to increase IP protection not only between the FTA partners but more broadly across the WTO Membership, because the

---

[77] *Agreement Between the World Intellectual Property Organization and the World Trade Organization,* signed 22 December 1995, entered into force 1 January 1996, Arts 2, 4.

[78] See Art V:1 WTO Agreement.

[79] See <http://www.wto.org/english/thewto_e/igo_obs_e.htm#trips> (last visited 18 May 2007); WTO, *Rules of Procedure for Sessions of the Ministerial Conference and Meetings of the General Council,* WT/L/161 (25 July 1996) Annex 3.

[80] Helfer, above fn 2, at 20–23, 26; see also Watal, above fn 6, at 400–02.

[81] See, eg, *WIPO Copyright Treaty,* done at Geneva, 20 December 1996, 36 ILM 65; *WIPO Performances and Phonograms Treaty,* done at Geneva, 20 December 1996, 36 ILM 76; *Patent Law Treaty,* done at Geneva, 1 June 2000, 39 ILM 1047; *Singapore Treaty on the Law of Trademarks,* done at Singapore, 27 March 2006 (not yet in force at time of writing).

[82] See, eg, TRIPS Council, *Work Programme on Electronic Commerce: Communication from Australia,* IP/C/W/144 (6 July 1999), at para 21; TRIPS Council, *Work Programme on Electronic Commerce: Communication by the European Communities and their Member States,* IP/C/W/140 (7 May 1999), at para 12.

[83] See, generally, chapter 10 of this Handbook.

[84] See, eg, Consultative Board, *The Future of the WTO: Addressing Institutional Challenges in the New Millennium* (Geneva: WTO, 2004), at para 76; World Bank, *Global Economic Prospects: Trade, Regionalism, and Development* (Washington DC: World Bank, 2005), at 28–30.

[85] See, generally, C Fink and P Reichenmiller, 'Tightening TRIPS: The Intellectual Property Provisions of Recent US Free Trade Agreements', World Bank Trade Note 20 (7 February 2005), at

TRIPS Agreement does not include a general exemption from the MFN rule for FTAs. Because of the US push to align others' IP laws with its own, it also continues the process of international harmonization of IP laws supported by the TRIPS Agreement.[86] Here, too, the TRIPS Agreement may be seen as having failed developing countries in particular, who remain prey to bilateral pressures to accept and impose higher standards because the TRIPS Agreement imposes minimum but not maximum thresholds of protection.[87]

As foreshadowed above, in some instances, TRIPS-plus is achieved by requiring FTA partners to become party to certain WIPO treaties not incorporated in the TRIPS Agreement. For example, Article 17.1.4 *Australia – United States Free Trade Agreement*[88] provides that '[e]ach Party shall ratify or accede to the *WIPO Copyright Treaty* (1996) and the *WIPO Performances and Phonograms Treaty* (1996) by the date of entry into force of this Agreement, subject to the fulfilment of their necessary internal requirements'.

Other FTA provisions remove the flexibility maintained under the TRIPS Agreement. Thus, the *Agreement between the United States of America and the Hashemite Kingdom of Jordan on the Establishment of a Free Trade Area*[89] restricts the circumstances in which a party may permit the use of the subject matter of a patent without the patent owner's authority. Whereas the TRIPS Agreement does not prescribe the circumstances in which a WTO Member may grant a compulsory licence, for example to address a public health concern (provided that certain conditions are met such as payment of adequate remuneration) (Article 31(h)), the FTA between the US and Jordan precludes such licences except to remedy anti-competitive practices, where the patent owner has not sufficiently worked the patent, or 'in cases of public non-commercial use or in the case of a national emergency or other circumstances of extreme urgency, provided that such use is limited to use by government entities or legal entities acting under the authority of a government'.[90] Several commentators regard these and other common TRIPS-plus provisions put forward by the US as reducing access to medicines in developing countries and

<http://www.siteresources.worldbank.org/INTRANETTRADE/Resources/Pubs/TradeNote20.pdf> (last visited 27 March 2008).

[86] B Mercurio, 'TRIPS-Plus Provisions in FTAs: Recent Trends' in Bartels and Ortino, above fn 57, 215, at 220–23.

[87] S Picciotto, 'Is the International Trade Regime Fair to Developing States?: Private Rights v Public Interests in the TRIPS Agreement' 2003 *American Society of International Law Proceedings* (97) 167, at 168; see also A Endeshaw, 'Free Trade Agreements as Surrogates for TRIPs-Plus' 2006 *European Intellectual Property Review* (28) 374, at 379–80; Art 1.1 TRIPS Agreement.

[88] Signed 18 May 2004, entered into force 1 January 2005.

[89] Signed 24 October 2000, entered into force 17 December 2001.

[90] Art 4.19. In contrast, Article 31(b) TRIPS Agreement provides that in cases of public non-commercial use, national emergency, or other circumstances of extreme urgency, the Member may waive the requirement to 'ma[k]e efforts to obtain authorization from the right holder on reasonable commercial terms and conditions'. These circumstances are not a prerequisite to compulsory licensing *per se*.

'negat[ing] the letter and spirit of the Doha Declaration'.[91] Some even query whether they may violate WTO law.[92]

TRIPS-plus approaches in FTAs, as highlighted above, are closely linked to US trade policies and negotiating strategies and are therefore subject to change. For instance, in May 2007, the Bush Administration reached a conceptual agreement with Congress regarding IP protections in pending FTAs that would (particularly for developing countries) increase flexibility in relation to pharmaceuticals and public health.[93] Nevertheless, the general trend towards strengthening TRIPS through FTAs remains apparent.[94]

C. A Human Rights Approach to TRIPS

Since the creation of the WTO, various UN bodies have commented on the relationship between human rights and WTO law.[95] The resulting work includes several statements regarding the relationship between human rights and the TRIPS Agreement in particular. The UN Sub-Commission on the Promotion and Protection of Human Rights has warned that an 'actual or potential conflict exists between the implementation of the TRIPS Agreement and the realization of economic, social and cultural rights, in particular the rights to self-determination, food, housing, work, health and education, and in relation to transfers of technology to developing countries'.[96]

In 2001, the UN High Commissioner for Human Rights expressed support for the notion of a 'human rights approach' to the TRIPS Agreement, which 'would explicitly place the promotion and protection of human rights... at the heart of the objectives of intellectual property protection, rather than only as permitted

[91]   C Correa, 'Implications of Bilateral Free Trade Agreements on Access to Medicines' 2006 *Bulletin of the World Health Organization* 84(5) 399, at 402; see also J Kuanpoth, 'TRIPS-Plus Intellectual Property Rules: Impact on Thailand's Public Health' 2006 *Journal of World Intellectual Property* 9(5) 573, at 584–89; above section II.B.

[92]   F Abbott, 'Intellectual Property Provisions of Bilateral and Regional Trade Agreements in Light of U.S. Federal Law', UNCTAD-ICTSD Capacity Building Project on Intellectual Property Rights and Sustainable Development, Issue Paper No 12 (2006) 18–19.

[93]   See, eg, Office of the United States Trade Representative, *Bipartisan Agreement on Trade Policy: Intellectual Property Provisions* (May 2007); 'Peru IPR Text Reflects FTA Template, Shows Reduced PhRMA Sway' *Inside US Trade* (6 July 2007) 27.

[94]   See, eg, 'U.S. Seeks New Anti-Counterfeiting Treaty With Key Trading Partners' *Inside US Trade* (26 October 2007) 42; 'Baucus Calls for Stronger TRIPS Deal As Part of New Trade Policy' *Inside US Trade* (12 October 2007) 40.

[95]   See also chapter 20 of this Handbook.

[96]   United Nations High Commissioner for Human Rights, Sub-Commission on the Promotion and Protection of Human Rights, *Intellectual Property and Human Rights: Sub-Commission on Human Rights Resolution 2001/21*, Preamble.

exceptions that are subordinated to the other provisions of the Agreement'.[97] The High Commissioner referred specifically to Article 15 *International Covenant on Economic, Social and Cultural Rights* (ICESCR)[98] as requiring States, in protecting IP rights, to balance the public interest in accessing new knowledge with the interests of knowledge creators.[99] On one view, Members already have sufficient discretion to take a human rights approach to the TRIPS Agreement, for example, by using domestic competition rules to avert practices that infringe the right to health.[100]

More recently, the Committee on Economic, Social and Cultural Rights, which monitors the implementation of the ICESCR, issued a general comment on Article 15(1)(c), distinguishing IP rights from the right recognized under that provision ('to benefit from the protection of the moral and material interests resulting from any scientific, literary or artistic production of which he or she is the author').[101] Among other things, the Committee called on States parties to the ICESCR to 'exclud[e] inventions from patentability whenever their commercialization would jeopardize the full realization of … human rights and dignity, including the rights to life, health and privacy', in some contrast to the TRIPS Agreement's exception for excluding inventions from patentability.[102]

Concerns relating to the impact of the TRIPS Agreement on the right to health have been partially addressed by the WTO's work in relation to compulsory licensing as discussed above.[103] One might even argue that paragraph 4 of the *Declaration on the TRIPS Agreement and Public Health* embodies a limited human rights approach to the TRIPS Agreement in affirming that 'the Agreement can and should be interpreted and implemented in a manner supportive of WTO Members' right to protect public health'. However, as already mentioned,[104] some FTAs threaten to undermine this progress.[105]

---

[97] ECOSOC, Commission on Human Rights, Sub-Commission on the Promotion and Protection of Human Rights, *The impact of the Agreement on Trade-Related Aspects of Intellectual Property Rights on human rights: Report of the High Commissioner*, E/CN.4/Sub.2/2001/13 (27 June 2001), at para 22.

[98] Done at New York, 16 December 1966, 993 UNTS 3.

[99] ECOSOC, above fn 97, at para 10.

[100] F Abbott, 'The "Rule of Reason" and the Right to Health: Integrating Human Rights and Competition Principles in the Context of TRIPS' in T Cottier, J Pauwelyn, and E Bürgi (eds), *Human Rights and International Trade* (Oxford: Oxford University Press, 2005) 279, at 291, 297, 300.

[101] ECOSOC, Committee on Economic, Social and Cultural Rights, *General Comment No 17 (2005): The right of everyone to benefit from the protection of the moral and material interests resulting from any scientific, literary or artistic production of which he or she is the author (article 15, paragraph 1(c), of the Covenant)*, E/C.12/GC/17 (12 January 2006), at paras 2–3.

[102] See above fn 33 and corresponding text.

[103] See above section II.B.   [104] See above fn 87 and corresponding text.

[105] ECOSOC, Commission on Human Rights, Sub-Commission on the Promotion and Protection of Human Rights, *Economic, Social and Cultural Rights: Globalization and its impact on the full enjoyment of human rights*, E/CN.4/Sub.2/2001/10 (2 August 2001), at paras 21, 25.

V. CONCLUSION

The TRIPS Agreement raises an array of complex questions and its implications for development, trade, and competition are difficult to identify in the abstract. On the one hand, it risks favouring IP owners, traditionally residing in developed countries, at the expense of vigorous competition and open trade. On the other hand, as the scope of IP expands (for example in the context of GIs), it offers potential benefits to at least some developing countries. In addition, it provides developing country Members with the possibility of cross-retaliation as an effective means of inducing compliance of other Members with their WTO obligations following adverse rulings in WTO dispute settlement. The Members' ultimate response to the public health problems of developing countries (especially those with limited pharmaceutical manufacturing capacity) is also a significant achievement, although this would be best consolidated through the passing of a formal amendment to the TRIPS Agreement and the use of the available flexibilities in practice.

Moving beyond the first decade of the TRIPS Agreement, and even beyond Doha, WTO Members may need to reinvigorate discussions on areas of disagreement such as non-violation complaints, exhaustion, and anti-competitive practices. At the same time, they must recognize that the TRIPS Agreement is not operating in a vacuum. Especially in the absence of progress under the TRIPS Agreement from the perspective of all Members, IP laws including those relevant to international trade will continue to advance outside of the WTO. This is already evident in the work of WIPO and several FTAs, most often in the direction of strengthening IP rights, which may upset the balance achieved in the TRIPS Agreement (if indeed it is regarded as having struck an appropriate balance to begin with). On the opposite side, UN calls for greater appreciation of human rights in the TRIPS Agreement and its application should remind Members of the need to consider the wider ramifications of stronger IP protection in the longer term. While many debated the propriety of including the TRIPS Agreement in the WTO to begin with, it need not be a one-sided document in future.

SELECTED BIBLIOGRAPHY

F Abbott, 'Commentary: The International Intellectual Property Order Enters the 21st Century' 1996 *Vanderbilt Journal of Transnational Law* 29(3) 471

F Abbott, 'First Report (Final) to the Committee on International Trade Law of the International Law Association on the Subject of Parallel Importation' 1998 *Journal of International Economic Law* 1(4) 607

F Abbott, 'The Doha Declaration on the TRIPS Agreement and Public Health: Lighting a Dark Corner at the WTO' 2002 *Journal of International Economic Law* 5(2) 469

F Abbott, 'The "Rule of Reason" and the Right to Health: Integrating Human Rights and Competition Principles in the Context of TRIPS' in T Cottier, J Pauwelyn, and E Bürgi (eds), *Human Rights and International Trade* (Oxford: Oxford University Press, 2005) 279

F Abbott, 'The WTO Medicines Decision: World Pharmaceutical Trade and the Protection of Public Health' 2005 *American Journal of International Law* 99(2) 317

F Abbott, 'Toward a New Era of Objective Assessment in the Field of TRIPS *and* Variable Geometry for the Preservation of Multilateralism' 2005 *Journal of International Economic Law* 8(1) 77

F Abbott, 'Intellectual Property Provisions of Bilateral and Regional Trade Agreements in Light of U.S. Federal Law', *UNCTAD-ICTSD Capacity Building Project on Intellectual Property Rights and Sustainable Development Issue Paper* No 12 2006

F Abbott, 'Intellectual Property Rights in World Trade' in A Guzman and A Sykes (eds), *Research Handbook in International Economic Law* (London: Edward Elgar, 2007) 444

R Anderson, 'Intellectual Property Rights, Competition Policy and International Trade: Reflections on the Work of the WTO Working Group on the Interaction between Trade and Competition Policy (1996–1999)' in T Cottier and P Mavroidis (eds), *Intellectual Property: Trade, Competition, and Sustainable Development* (Ann Arbor: University of Michigan Press, 2003) 235

J Atik and HH Lidgard, 'Embracing Price Discrimination – TRIPS and Parallel Trade in Pharmaceuticals' 2007 *University of Pennsylvania Journal of International Economic Law* (28) 1043

L Bartels and F Ortino (eds), *Regional Trade Agreements and the WTO Legal System* (Oxford: Oxford University Press, 2006)

FK Beier and G Schricker (eds), *From GATT to TRIPs: The Agreement on Trade-Related Aspects of Intellectual Property Rights* (Munich: Max Planck Institute, 1996)

V Chiappetta, 'The Desirability of Agreeing to Disagree: The WTO, TRIPS, International Exhaustion and a Few Other Things' 2000 *Michigan Journal of International Law* 21(3) 333

Consultative Board, *The Future of the WTO: Addressing Institutional Challenges in the New Millennium* (Geneva: WTO, 2004)

C Correa, 'Implications of Bilateral Free Trade Agreements on Access to Medicines' 2006 *Bulletin of the World Health Organization* 84(5) 399

C Correa, *Trade-Related Aspects of Intellectual Property Rights: A Commentary on the TRIPS Agreement* (Oxford: Oxford University Press, 2006)

T Cottier, 'The Agreement on Trade-Related Aspects of Intellectual Property Rights' in P Macrory, A Appleton, and M Plummer (eds), *The World Trade Organization: Legal, Economic and Political Analysis*, Vol. I (New York: Springer, 2005) 1041

T Cottier and P Mavroidis (eds), *Intellectual Property: Trade, Competition, and Sustainable Development* (Ann Arbor: University of Michigan Press, 2003)

W Davey and W Zdouc, 'The Triangle of TRIPS, GATT and GATS' in T Cottier and P Mavroidis (eds), *Intellectual Property: Trade, Competition, and Sustainable Development* (Ann Arbor: University of Michigan Press, 2003) 53

A Deardorff, 'What Might Globalization's Critics Believe?' 2003 *World Economy* 26(5) 639

M Desta and N Barnes, 'Competition Law and Regional Trade Agreements: An Overview' in L Bartels and F Ortino (eds), *Regional Trade Agreements and the WTO Legal System* (Oxford: Oxford University Press, 2006) 239

A Endeshaw, 'Free Trade Agreements as Surrogates for TRIPs-Plus' 2006 *European Intellectual Property Review* (28) 374

G Evans, 'A Preliminary Excursion into TRIPS and Non-Violation Complaints' 2000 *Journal of World Intellectual Property* 3(6) 867

G Evans and M Blakeney, 'The Protection of Geographical Indications After Doha: Quo Vadis?' 2006 *Journal of International Economic Law* 9(3) 575

W Fikentscher, 'Historical Origins and Opportunities for Development of an International Competition Law in the TRIPs Agreement of the World Trade Organization (WTO) and Beyond' in FK Beier and G Schricker (eds), *From GATT to TRIPs: The Agreement on Trade-Related Aspects of Intellectual Property Rights* (Munich: Max Planck Institute, 1996) 226

E Fox, 'Trade, Competition, and Intellectual Property – TRIPS and its Antitrust Counterparts' 1996 *Vanderbilt Journal of Transnational Law* 29(3) 481

S Frankel, 'WTO Application of "the Customary Rules of Interpretation of Public International Law" to Intellectual Property' 2005 *Virginia Journal of International Law* 46(2) 365

J Gathii, 'The Legal Status of the Doha Declaration on TRIPS and Public Health Under the Vienna Convention on the Law of Treaties' 2002 *Harvard Journal of Law and Technology* 15(2) 291

J Gathii, 'How Necessity May Preclude State Responsibility for Compulsory Licensing Under the TRIPS Agreement' 2006 *North Carolina Journal of International Law and Commercial Regulation* 31(4) 943

D Gervais, *The TRIPS Agreement: Drafting History and Analysis*, 2nd edn (London: Sweet & Maxwell, 2003)

M Geuze and H Wager, 'WTO Dispute Settlement Practice Relating to the TRIPS Agreement' 1999 *Journal of International Economic Law* 2(2) 347

A Guzman, 'International Competition Law' in A Guzman and A Sykes (eds), *Research Handbook in International Economic Law* (London: Edward Elgar, 2007) 418

A Guzman and A Sykes (eds), *Research Handbook in International Economic Law* (London: Edward Elgar, 2007)

M Handler, 'The WTO Geographical Indications Dispute' 2006 *Modern Law Review* 69(1) 70

A Heinemann, 'Antitrust Law of Intellectual Property in the TRIPs Agreement of the World Trade Organization' in FK Beier and G Schricker (eds), *From GATT to TRIPs: The Agreement on Trade-Related Aspects of Intellectual Property Rights* (Munich: Max Planck Institute, 1996) 239

L Helfer, 'Regime Shifting: The TRIPs Agreement and New Dynamics of International Intellectual Property Lawmaking' 2004 *Yale Journal of International Law* 29(1) 1

J Kuanpoth, 'TRIPS-Plus Intellectual Property Rules: Impact on Thailand's Public Health' 2006 *Journal of World Intellectual Property* 9(5) 573

J Martin, 'The WTO TRIPS Agreement: The Battle between the Old and the New World over the Protection of Geographical Indications' 2004 *Journal of World Intellectual Property* 7(3) 287

K Maskus and J Reichman (eds), *International Public Goods and Transfer of Technology Under A Globalized Intellectual Property Regime* (Cambridge: Cambridge University Press, 2005)

D Matthews, 'WTO Decision on Implementation of Paragraph 6 of the Doha Declaration on the TRIPS Agreement and Public Health: A Solution to the Access to Essential Medicines Problem?' 2004 *Journal of International Economic Law* 7(1) 73

AD Mitchell, 'Broadening the Vision of Trade Liberalisation: International Competition Law and the WTO' 2001 *World Competition* 24(3) 343

AD Mitchell, 'A Legal Principle of Special and Differential Treatment for WTO Disputes' 2006 *World Trade Review* 5(3) 445

K Nowak, 'Staying Within the Negotiated Framework: Abiding by the Non-Discrimination Clause in TRIPs Article 27' 2005 *Michigan Journal of International Law* 26(3) 899

A Pacón, 'What Will TRIPs Do For Developing Countries' in FK Beier and G Schricker (eds), *From GATT to TRIPs: The Agreement on Trade-Related Aspects of Intellectual Property Rights* (Munich: Max Planck Institute, 1996) 329

S Picciotto, 'Is the International Trade Regime Fair to Developing States?: Private Rights v Public Interests in the TRIPS Agreement' 2003 *American Society of International Law Proceedings* (97) 167

D Rangnekar, 'Geographical Indications: A Review of Proposals at the TRIPs Council' *UNCTAD/ICTSD Capacity Building Project on Intellectual Property Rights and Sustainable Development Paper* (2002)

M Rimmer, 'The Jean Chrétien Pledge to Africa Act: Patent Law and Humanitarian Aid' 2005 *Expert Opinion on Therapeutic Patents* 15(7) 889

W Rothnie, *Parallel Imports* (London: Sweet & Maxwell, 1993)

FM Scherer and J Watal, 'Post-TRIPS Options for Access to Patented Medicines in Developing Nations' 2002 *Journal of International Economic Law* 5(4) 913

D Shanker, 'The Vienna Convention on the Law of Treaties, the Dispute Settlement System of the WTO and the Doha Declaration on the TRIPs Agreement' 2002 *Journal of World Trade* 36(4) 721

H Sun, 'The Road to Doha and Beyond: Some Reflections on the TRIPS Agreement and Public Health' 2004 *European Journal of International Law* 15(1) 123

M Taylor, *International Competition Law: A New Dimension for the WTO?* (Cambridge: Cambridge University Press, 2006)

M Vincent, 'Extending Protection at the WTO to Products Other Than Wines and Spirits: Who Will Benefit?' 2007 *Estey Centre Journal of International Trade Law and Policy* 8(1) 57

E Vranes, 'Cross Retaliation under GATS and TRIPS – An Optimal Enforcement Device for Developing Countries?' in F Breuss, S Griller, and E Vranes (eds), *The Banana Dispute: An Economic and Legal Analysis* (Vienna: Springer, 2003) 113

J Watal, *Intellectual Property Rights in the WTO and Developing Countries* (Boston: Kluwer Academic Publishers, 2001)

World Bank, *Global Economic Prospects: Trade, Regionalism, and Development* (Washington DC: World Bank, 2005)

CHAPTER 9

....

RESPONDING
TO NATIONAL
CONCERNS

....

GABRIELLE MARCEAU
JOEL P TRACHTMAN*

  * The views expressed in this chapter are personal to the authors and do not bind the WTO
Secretariat or its Members. This entry is based upon the authors' 'The Technical Barriers to Trade
Agreement, the Sanitary and Phytosanitary Measures Agreement, and the General Agreement on
Tariffs and Trade: A Map of the World Trade Organization Law of Domestic Regulation of Goods'
2002 *Journal of World Trade* 36(5) 811.

I. Introduction

FREE trade and regulatory autonomy are often at odds with one another. National measures of an importing State may impose costs on international trade, for example, by regulating goods in ways that vary from home market regulation. National measures may restrict market access of imported goods but may or may not be intended to act as protectionist measures favouring domestic industry to the detriment of imports. At the same time, domestic regulation may protect important values. The distinction between a protectionist measure—condemned for imposing discriminatory or unjustifiable costs—and a non-protectionist measure restricting trade incidentally (and thus imposing some costs) is difficult to make.

The search for the right balance between disciplining protectionist measures and allowing Members to maintain regulatory autonomy has characterized the evolution of the GATT rules—namely Articles I, III, XI, and XX GATT 1994, the TBT Agrement, and the SPS Agreement. This chapter compares the disciplines on domestic regulation contained in each of these agreements, and provides an analysis of the conditions for application of each agreement.

While the WTO Agreement and its annexes is today a single treaty, its provisions were originally negotiated through 15 different working groups, which may not have been sufficiently coordinated with one another. In grouping under a framework agreement various negotiated texts, without any extensive discussion of the internal organization and hierarchy of WTO norms, negotiators may have hoped that the flexibility inherent in some of the WTO treaty provisions would suffice to reconcile all tensions among its various provisions. The wording of some WTO provisions does not always support such hope. It thus becomes very difficult to define clearly and precisely the legal parameters of the relationships among the provisions of different WTO agreements.

This chapter focuses mainly on a comparison among (i) Articles III, XI, and XX GATT 1994, (ii) the TBT Agreement, and (iii) the SPS Agreement, all of which impose different regulatory constraints on government actions relating to standards, technical and sanitary regulations, etc. The text identifies disciplines inherent and common to each set of provisions, it compares them, discusses their interaction, and suggests some understandings.

II. Comparing the Disciplines of the SPS Agreement, the TBT Agreement, and the GATT 1994

The SPS and the TBT Agreements and the GATT 1994 each contain a number of different disciplines on national regulation. This section discusses selected disciplines under the following categories:

(1) Non-discrimination: national treatment and most-favoured-nation
(2) Necessity tests
(3) Appropriate level/scientific basis
(4) Harmonization; conformity with international standards
(5) (Mutual) recognition and equivalence
(6) Internal consistency
(7) Permission for precautionary action
(8) Balancing
(9) Product/process issues and the territorial-extraterritorial divide

To some extent these disciplines relate to each other. Often they are specifically addressed in those WTO Agreements and the jurisprudence has had to deal with them. They represent different aspects of the WTO disciplines on the domestic normative autonomy of Members. These disciplines work in varying combinations within each of these three sources of WTO law. They also work together from the broader perspective of general WTO law. To a great extent, the TBT and SPS Agreements can be seen as an evolution of GATT provisions.

A. Non-Discrimination: National Treatment and Most-Favoured-Nation

Obligations of non-discrimination in internal regulation, including the application of internal regulation at the border, occupy a primary position in the GATT 1994, and in the SPS and TBT Agreements. Discrimination between products and between situations is condemned. In this section the obligation of non-discrimination is examined as between domestic and imported products: national treatment (NT).

1. *GATT*

(a) *Article III GATT – National Treatment Obligation*
Article III GATT 1994 has been interpreted in several GATT and WTO cases. In its first report, *Japan—Alcoholic Beverages*, the WTO Appellate Body declared that

the broad purpose of Article III is to prohibit 'protectionism',[1] a concept that it did not define. It also rejected the 'aims-and-effects' approach to the obligation of NT, at least as a search for subjective intent. It refused to see any issue of the subjective intent of the Member in Article III determinations:

It does not matter that there may not have been any desire to engage in protectionism in the minds of the legislators or the regulators who imposed the measure. It is irrelevant that protectionism was not an intended objective if the particular tax measure in question is nevertheless, to echo Article III:1, applied to imported or domestic products so as to afford protection to domestic production. *This is an issue of how the measure in question is applied.*[2]

The Appellate Body stated that 'it is possible to examine objectively the underlying criteria used in a particular tax measure, its structure, and its overall application, to ascertain whether it is applied in a way that affords protection to domestic products'.[3] For a violation of Article III:4 to be established, the complaining Member must prove that the measure at issue is a 'law, regulation, or requirement affecting their internal sale, offering for sale, purchase, transportation, distribution, or use'; that the imported and domestic products at issue are 'like products'; and that the imported products are accorded 'less favourable' treatment than that accorded to like domestic products.[4]

The prohibition against discrimination in the NT obligation can apply only when imported and domestic products are 'like', interpreted to be as broad a concept as products 'directly competitive' in Article III: 2 (FNT) Appellate Body report, *EC-Asbestos*, at para. XX. The majority of the Appellate Body in *EC – Asbestos* found that 'likeness' under Article III:4 is, 'fundamentally, a determination about the nature and extent of a competitive relationship between and among products'.[5] To perform such an assessment, the Appellate Body recalled that the four classic, and basic, criteria, derived from the *Border Tax Adjustment* report— (i) the physical properties of the products in question; (ii) their end uses; (iii) consumer tastes and habits *vis-à-vis* those products; and (iv) tariff classification[6]— are to be used as tools in the determination of this competitive relationship between products. These criteria do not exhaust inquiry.

The less favourable treatment criterion involves an 'effects test'. In *Korea – Various Measures on Beef*, the Appellate Body reversed the Panel, which had concluded that a regulatory distinction based exclusively on the origin of the product necessarily violated Article III GATT 1994. The Appellate Body emphasized the fact that 'differential treatment' may be acceptable, so long as it is 'no less favourable'. Article III

---

[1] Appellate Body Report, *Japan – Alcoholic Beverages II*, at 16.
[2] Ibid at 28 (emphasis added).   [3] Ibid at 29.
[4] Appellate Body Report, *Korea – Various Measures on Beef*, at para 133.
[5] Appellate Body Report, *EC – Asbestos*, at para 99. Note the different opinion with regard to the very specific aspects mentioned in para 154.
[6] GATT Working Party Report, *Border Tax Adjustments*.

only prohibits discriminatory treatment, which 'modifies the conditions of competition in the relevant market to the detriment of imported products'.[7]

In *EC – Asbestos*, the Appellate Body made the following statement:

A complaining Member must still establish that the measure accords to the group of 'like' imported products 'less favourable treatment' than it accords to the group of 'like' domestic products. The term 'less favourable treatment' expresses the general principle, in Article III:1, that internal regulations 'should not be applied ... so as to afford protection to domestic production.[8]

And as it had stated in *Korea – Various Measures on Beef,* 'a formal difference in treatment between imported and like domestic products is thus neither necessary, nor sufficient, to show a violation of Article III:4'. Whether or not imported products are treated less favourably than like domestic products should be assessed, instead, by examining whether a measure modifies the conditions of competition in the relevant market to the detriment of imported products. Thus, it is not enough to find a single foreign like product that is treated differently from a domestic like product. The class of foreign like products must be treated less favourably than the class of domestic like products. In order for this to occur, it would seem necessary that the differential regulatory treatment be predicated, either intentionally or unintentionally, on the foreign character of the product.

Indeed, the Appellate Body Report in *EC – Asbestos* first stated that ' ... a member may draw distinctions between products which have been found to be "like", without, for this reason alone, according to the group of "like" imported products "less favourable treatment" than that accorded to the group of "like" domestic products.'[9] In *Dominican Republic – Cigarettes*, the Appellate Body clarified that "the existence of a detrimental effect on a given imported product resulting from a measure does not necessarily imply that this measure accords less favourable treatment to imports *if the detrimental effect is explained by factors or circumstances unrelated to the foreign origin of the product,* such as the market share of the importer in this case".[10] The *EC – Approval and Marketing of Biotech Products* Panel reports also suggested that discrimination would not create less favourable treatment when the difference is justified by non-protectionist policies based on government/consumers' perceptions. The Panel concluded that there was no need to determine whether biotech and non-biotech were like products since '[i]t is not self-evident that the alleged less favourable treatment of imported biotech products is explained by the foreign origin rather than, for instance, a perceived difference between biotech and non-biotech

---

[7] Appellate Body Report, *Korea – Various Measures on Beef,* at para 137.
[8] Appellate Body Report *EC – Asbestos*, at para 100.
[9] WTO Appellate Body Report, *EC – Asbestos*, WT/DS135/AB/R, adopted 5 April 2001, at para. 100.
[10] WTO Appellate Body Report, *Dominician Republic – Cigarettes*, WT/DS302/AB/R, adopted 19 May 2005, para. 96 (emphasis added). For a detailed analysis of this question see the chapter of Lorand Bartels, Trade and Human Rights, in this publication.

products in terms of their safety....'.[11] The Panel rejected the claim of violation of national treatment.

(b) Most-Favoured-Nation Principle

Article I GATT 1994 provides that for all matters referred to in paragraphs 2 or 4 of Article III GATT 1994, any advantage, favour, privilege, or immunity granted by any Member to any product originating in or destined for any other country shall be accorded immediately and unconditionally to the like product originating in or destined for the territories of all other Members.

Article 2.3 SPS Agreement and Article 2.1 TBT Agreement provide similar MFN obligations. Interestingly, both Article 4 SPS Agreement and Article 6.3 TBT Agreement encourage 'mutual recognition' agreements. Mutual recognition agreements (MRAs), of course, reduce barriers to imports of goods from beneficiary States, but they may provide inferior treatment to imports of goods from non-beneficiary States. This could arguably violate the MFN obligation[12] depending on the 'architecture' and functioning of the specific MRA. These MRAs are part of the positive integration exercise, along with harmonization discussed below.

2. TBT Agreement

Article 2.1 TBT Agreement, following closely Articles III and I GATT 1994, requires that 'treatment no less favourable than that accorded to like products of national origin and to like products originating in any other country'. However, it is worth noting that the TBT Agreement has no equivalent of Article XX GATT 1994, providing an exemption under certain circumstances.

Problems may occur if the scope of the term 'like products' is the same as that under Article III:4, while justifications under Article XX are not available to violations of Article 2.1 TBT Agreement. It is conceivable that the 'accordion' of like products[13] may allow a distinction between 'like' products of Article III (or I) GATT 1994 and that of 2.1 TBT Agreement. The emphasis of the Appellate Body on the 'no less favourable' language may serve as a defence for non-protectionist domestic regulation and therefore reduce the need to invoke Article XX to justify measures based on listed non-protectionist policy goals. Otherwise, an incongruous situation could appear where for instance many environment-based technical regulations could be inconsistent with Article 2.1 while the same regulations would be authorized by Article XX (after a prior determination that it was *prima facie* inconsistent with Article III:4 GATT 1994).

---

[11] Panel Report, *European Communities – Measures affecting the approval and marketing of biotech products*, WT/DS291/36, adopted 23 November 2007, paras 7.2509, 2516.

[12] See WJ Davey and J Pauwelyn, 'MFN Unconditionality: A Legal Analysis of the Concept in View of its Evolution in the GATT/WTO Jurisprudence with Particular Reference to the Issue of "Like Product"' in T Cottier, PC Mavroidis, and P Blatter (eds), *Regulatory Barriers and the Principle of Non-Discrimination in World Trade Law* (Ann Arbor, MI: University of Michigan Press, 2000), at 23–24.

[13] Appellate Body Report, *Japan – Alcoholic Beverages II*, at 23.

3. *SPS Agreement*

Two provisions of the SPS Agreement concern discrimination directly: Articles 2.3 and 5.5. The SPS Agreement should be understood, to some extent, as an expansion of Article XX GATT 1994, and its drafters were concerned with the need to (1) expand the scientific and procedural requirements for a Member to impose an SPS measure, and (2) encourage reliance on and participation in international standard-setting bodies. Although both these provisions seem to have adapted their operative language from the chapeau of Article XX GATT 1994, the Panel in *Australia – Salmon (Article 21.5 – Canada)*, was of the view that Article 2.3 SPS Agreement prohibits discrimination between both similar and different products.[14] The scope of Article 2.3 would thus be much broader than that of Article 5.5 which was said to be 'but a complex and indirect route'[15] to proving the discrimination prohibited by Article 2.3. Article 5.5, which imposes a form of internal consistency requirement, and the Guidelines on Article 5.5 adopted by the SPS Committee, are further discussed below.

The test under the SPS Agreement is different from that under Articles III, XI, and XX GATT 1994; there is no like products analysis or product-process distinction *per se* (as with Article III GATT 1994) in the SPS Agreement. The focus of the analysis is the justification for discrimination between situations under the SPS prohibition itself.

B. Necessity Tests

One important general discipline on domestic regulation in WTO law is the necessity test, which, until the reports in *EC – Asbestos* and *Korea – Various Measures on Beef*, was generally interpreted as requiring that the domestic regulation be the least trade restrictive method of achieving the desired goal. The TBT and SPS Agreements have made it a 'positive requirement' for all relevant regulations while the GATT 1994 keeps it, under Article XX, as a 'justification' for restrictions found to violate other provisions, including basic market access rights.

1. *The Necessity Test in the GATT 1994*

Since its inception, the GATT 1994 has always recognized that legitimate government policies may justify measures contrary to its basic market access rules. Traditionally under the GATT 1994, the exceptional provisions of Article XX(b) and (d) are available to justify measures—otherwise incompatible with other GATT provisions—if they are 'necessary'. This has been interpreted to require that the country invoking

---

[14] Panel Report, *Australia – Salmon (Article 21.5–Canada)*, at para 7.112.
[15] On the relationship between Articles 2.3 and 5.5 SPS Agreement, see Appellate Body Report, *Australia – Salmon*, at para 252.

these exceptions demonstrate that no other WTO-compatible or less restrictive alternative was reasonably available to pursue the desired policy goal.[16]

The WTO jurisprudence has changed the traditional reading of Article XX GATT 1994, including the parameters of the so-called 'necessity test'. First, in *US – Gasoline*, the Appellate Body determined that compliance with Article XX is now to be demonstrated in a two-prong test: first, whether the challenged measure is covered by one of the sub-paragraphs of Article XX and, second, whether or not the measure is 'applied' in a manner that constitutes arbitrary or unjustifiable discrimination or a disguised restriction on trade. While Members have a right to invoke the exceptions, the exceptions should not be applied so as to unjustifiably frustrate the legal obligations owed to other Members under the GATT 1994.[17]

The Article XX necessity test was addressed in *Korea – Various Measures on Beef*, where Korea attempted to justify its dual retail system for beef by arguing the need for compliance with a domestic regulation against fraud. The Appellate Body interpreted the necessity test of Article XX(d) to imply a requirement for balancing among at least three variables:

> In sum, determination of whether a measure, which is not 'indispensable', may nevertheless be 'necessary' within the contemplation of Article XX(d), involves in every case a process of weighing and balancing a series of factors which prominently include the contribution made by the compliance measure to the enforcement of the law or regulation at issue, the importance of the common interests or values protected by that law or regulation, and the accompanying impact of the law or regulation on imports or exports.[18]

After reiterating that WTO Members have the right to determine for themselves the level of enforcement of their domestic laws[19] (a concept close to the 'appropriate level of protection' referred to in the SPS Agreement), the Appellate Body called for an authentic balancing and weighing of (at least) these variables: '[t]he more vital or important those common interests or values are, the easier it would be to accept as 'necessary' a measure designed as an enforcement instrument';[20] '[t]he greater the contribution [to the realization of the end pursued], the more easily a measure might be considered to be "necessary" ';[21] or 'a measure with a relatively slight impact upon imported products might more easily be considered as 'necessary' than a measure with intense or broader restrictive effects'.[22]

In *EC – Asbestos*, the Appellate Body tried to reconcile its new balancing test with the traditional least trade restrictive alternative test. For the Appellate Body, the balancing referred to in *Korea – Various Measures on Beef* is part of the determination

---

[16]   GATT Panel Report, *US – Section 337*, at para 5.26; GATT Panel Report, *US – Malt Beverages*, at para 5.52; GATT Panel Report, *Thailand – Cigarettes*, at paras 73–75.

[17]   Appellate Body Report, *US – Gasoline*, at 22.

[18]   Appellate Body Report. *Korea – Various Measures on Beef*, at para 164. See also chapter 6 of this Handbook.

[19]   Ibid at para 177.   [20]   Ibid at para 162.
[21]   Ibid at para 163.   [22]   Ibid.

of whether a WTO-compatible or less trade restrictive alternative exists to obtain the end pursued (as called for by the traditional necessity test of Article XX(b)).[23] The Appellate Body noted that the protection of human life is vital and important to the highest degree.[24] It is not yet clear what the impact of such a policy of the highest importance has had on the rest of the determination. But it seems that Panels and the Appellate Body are asked to assess the reasonableness and importance of the values at the basis of the challenged measure.[25] In *EC – Asbestos*, Appellate Body concluded that 'the remaining question, then, is whether there is an alternative measure that would achieve the same end and that is less restrictive of trade than a prohibition'.[26] Once the respondent has made a *prima facie* case that the challenged measure is 'necessary' with this new test, it is for the complainant to raise a WTO-consistent alternative measure that, in its view, the responding party should have taken.[27] In *Brazil – Retreaded Tyres*, the Appellate Body clarified that in order to be necessary a measure needs to bring about a 'material contribution' to the achievement of its objective and that a contribution exists when there is a genuine relationship of ends and means between the objective and the measure.[28] Importantly, it also confirmed that while the responding party must demonstrate that a measure is necessary – in contributing materially to its legitimate goal – its does not have to show, in first instance, that there are no reasonably available alternative measures to achieve its objective. Rather it is for the complaining party to submit WTO-consistent alternative measures that would allow the respondent to reach the desired level of protection and achieve the same objectives.[29]

It is important at this stage to note the similarity between the wording of the necessity tests under Article XX GATT 1994, that of Article 2.2 TBT Agreement, and that of Article 5.6 SPS Agreement and its footnote, although of course Article XX GATT 1994 operates as a defence. The possibility for common interpretation is discussed below.

(a) The Test Under Article XX(g) GATT 1994

In its *US – Gasoline* report, although the parties had both relied on the GATT 'primarily aimed at' test, the Appellate Body noted that the threshold of Article XX(g) did not contain a requirement that the measure be 'primarily aimed at', but only a requirement that the measure be 'related to'.[30] The Appellate Body examined whether 'the means (the challenged regulations) are, in principle, reasonably related to the ends' and whether 'such measures are made effective in conjunction with restrictions

---

[23] Appellate Body Report, *EC – Asbestos*, at para 172.   [24] Ibid.
[25] Appellate Body Report, *Korea – Various Measures on Beef*, at para 162.
[26] Ibid at para 172.
[27] Appellate Body Report, *US – Gambling*, at paras 308–11.
[28] Appellate Body Report, *Brazil – Retreaded Tyres*, at para 210.
[29] FNT *Brazil – Retreaded Tyres*, at para. 156.
[30] Appellate Body Report, *US – Gasoline*, at 17–22.

on domestic production or consumption' ('...a requirement of even-handedness in the imposition of restrictions').[31] In *US – Shrimp*, the Appellate Body focused on the means-ends relationship between the measure and the goal pursued.[32]

(b) The Chapeau of Article XX GATT 1994

In *US – Shrimp*, the Appellate Body stressed the fact that the chapeau of Article XX is a recognition of the need to maintain a balance between the right of a Member to invoke one of the exceptions in Article XX GATT 1994 and the substantive rights of other Members under the GATT 1994. It noted that the task of applying the chapeau is a delicate one of finding and marking out a 'line of equilibrium'[33] between these two sets of rights in such a way that neither will cancel out the other.

The chapeau of Article XX GATT 1994 establishes three standards regarding the application of measures for which justification under Article XX may be sought: first, there must be no 'arbitrary' discrimination between countries where the same conditions prevail; second, there must be no 'unjustifiable' discrimination between countries where the same conditions prevail; and, third, there must be no 'disguised restriction on international trade'.[34]

2. TBT Agreement

The exceptional provisions of Article XX GATT 1994 only become relevant after a violation of another provision of the GATT 1994 is found. This is a significant distinction from both the SPS Agreement and the TBT Agreement, which apply requirements of least trade restrictiveness independently. Thus, whether a specific measure is an SPS measure or technical regulation under the TBT Agreement, or rather another type of measure under Article XX GATT 1994 (say a measure adopted for environmental purposes) will determine which Member bears the burden of proof in case of a challenge. An important distinction between Article 2.2 TBT Agreement and Article XX GATT 1994 is that the former does not contain a closed list of policies. Rather, any 'legitimate' policy may be the basis for a TBT regulation.

3. SPS Agreement

The SPS Agreement also contains in Article 5.6 a necessity test, subject to a 'reasonable availability' qualification, requiring that SPS measures be 'not more trade restrictive than required to achieve their appropriate level of protection, taking into account technical and economic feasibility'.[35] In *Australia – Salmon*, the Appellate

---

[31] Ibid at 20–22.
[32] Appellate Body Report, *US – Shrimp*, at paras 156–60.   [33] Ibid.
[34] See Appellate Body Report *US – Gasoline*, at 21–22; Appellate Body Report, *US – Shrimp (Article 21.5 – Malaysia)*, at para 118; Appellate Body Report, *US – Shrimp*, at para 150.
[35] Art 5.6, fn 3 SPS Agreement: 'For purposes of paragraph 6 of Article 5, a measure is not more trade-restrictive than required unless there is another measure, reasonably available taking into

Body stated that Article 5.6 clearly provides a three-pronged test to establish a violation. The complaining party must prove that there is a measure that: (1) is reasonably available taking into account technical and economic feasibility; (2) achieves the Member's appropriate level of sanitary or phytosanitary protection; and (3) is significantly less restrictive to trade than the SPS measure contested.

Article 5.4 SPS Agreement exhorts (but does not require) WTO Members, 'when determining the appropriate level of sanitary or phytosanitary protection, [to] take into account the objective of minimizing negative trade effects'. Arguably this is similar to (or even less stringent than) the third variable (impact on trade) of the balancing test developed in *Korea – Various Measures on Beef*. A Member must ensure that its appropriate level of protection is consistently applied to the extent required by Article 5.5 SPS Agreement. The jurisprudence has confirmed that 'the level of protection deemed appropriate by the Member establishing a sanitary . . . measure, is a prerogative of the Member concerned'.[36]

C. Appropriate Level/Scientific Basis

1. *SPS Agreement*

Article 2.2 SPS Agreement provides that SPS measures must be based on scientific principles and may not be maintained without sufficient scientific evidence, except as permitted under Article 5.7. It requires Members to ensure that any measure is applied only to the extent necessary to protect human, animal or plant life or health. The interpretive question here relates to the significance of the term 'applied'. This term appears here, and also in the chapeau of Article XX GATT 1994. In *US – Shrimp* and *US – Gasoline*,[37] the Appellate Body suggested that the chapeau's requirements relate not to the substance of the measure itself but to the way in which it is applied, for example, whether it is applied in a way that constitutes arbitrary or unjustifiable discrimination. Article 5.6, also imposing a 'least trade restrictive alternative' requirement, does not limit itself to the manner in which the measure is applied, but addresses measures themselves.

Article 3.3 SPS Agreement permits Members to introduce measures that result in a higher level of protection than international standards, if (a) there is scientific justification, or (b) as a consequence of the Member's appropriate level of

account technical and economic feasibility, that achieves the appropriate level of sanitary or phytosanitary protection and is significantly less restrictive to trade'. This is necessity testing subject to a 'reasonably available' qualification. See also Art 2.2: 'Members shall ensure that any sanitary or phytosanitary measure is applied only to the extent necessary to protect human, animal or plant life or health . . .'.

[36] Appellate Body Report, *Australia – Salmon*, at para 199.
[37] Appellate Body Report, *US – Shrimp*, at para 115; Appellate Body Report, *US – Gasoline*, at 22.

protection.[38] Under Article 3.3, a Member may decide to set for itself a level of protection different from that implicit in the international standard, and to implement or embody that level of protection in a measure not 'based on' the international standard. The Member's appropriate level of protection may be higher than that implied in the international standard. The right of a Member to determine its own appropriate level of sanitary protection is an important right.[39]

In all cases where a standard other than an international standard is used, the Member imposing an SPS measure must be able to rely on a relevant risk assessment pursuant to Articles 5.1 to 5.4 SPS Agreement. In *Australia – Salmon*, the Appellate Body stated:

On the basis of [the] definition [prescribed in the first part of paragraph 4 of Annex A], we consider that, in this case, a risk assessment within the meaning of Article 5.1 must: (1) identify the diseases whose entry, establishment, or spread a Member wants to prevent within its territory, as well as the potential biological and economic consequences associated with the entry, establishment, or spread of these diseases; (2) evaluate the likelihood of entry, establishment, or spread of these diseases, as well as the associated potential biological and economic consequences; and (3) evaluate the likelihood of entry, establishment, or spread of these diseases according to the SPS measures which might be applied.[40]

These requirements were interpreted in each of the three cases under the SPS Agreement: *EC – Hormones*, *Australia – Salmon*, and *Japan – Agricultural Products II*.

2. *TBT Agreement*

The Preamble of the TBT Agreement also makes clear that each Member may determine the level of protection it considers appropriate. This 'appropriate' level will be reflected in the choice of a specific measure that itself is subject to Article 2.2 TBT Agreement, concerned with less trade restrictive measures reasonably available to attain the end pursued. The TBT Agreement does not explicitly regulate risk assessments or require scientific bases for regulation.

3. *The GATT 1994*

In *EC – Asbestos*, the Appellate Body noted 'that it is undisputed that WTO Members have the right to determine the level of protection of health that they consider appropriate in a given situation'.[41] It equally noted that 'a Member is not obliged, in setting health policy, automatically to follow what, at a given time, may constitute a majority

---

[38] Note 2 to Article 3.3 explains that a scientific justification exists if, on the basis of scientific evidence, the regulating State determines that international standards are insufficient to achieve appropriate level of protection.

[39] Appellate Body Report, *EC – Hormones*, at para 172.

[40] Appellate Body Report, *Australia – Salmon*, at para 121.

[41] Appellate Body Report, *EC – Hormones*, at para 186.

scientific opinion'.[42] Relevant to this regulatory autonomy is the Appellate Body's conclusion in *US – Shrimp,* which affirms that a Member may unilaterally determine its policy within the parameters of Article XX:

It appears to us…that conditioning access to a Member's domestic market on whether exporting Members comply with, or adopt, a policy or policies unilaterally prescribed by the importing Member may, to some degree, be a common aspect of measures falling within the scope of one or another of the exceptions (a) to (j) of Article XX.[43]

While this right to determine an (appropriate) level of protection is absolute, pursuant to Article XX, the measure chosen to implement the end pursued and the appropriate level of protection can be challenged and set aside by WTO adjudicating bodies.[44] Moreover, since the specific level of protection is not always clearly stated by a Member, the Appellate Body seems to reserve to the Panel or itself the right to identify the 'authentic' level of protection desired by the concerned Member.

D. Harmonization, Conformity with International Standards

One of the core problems facing the WTO is the imbalance between its new (since 1994) dispute settlement authority, on the one hand, and its extremely limited legislative capacity, on the other hand. While this chapter describes certain negative integration powers (the power of the WTO to strike down domestic regulations) available in WTO dispute settlement, to be exercised through the application of general standards, the WTO has much more limited powers of positive integration (the power of the WTO to 're-regulate' at a multilateral level) available to be exercised through the legislation of specific rules. Positive integration has two main potential components: harmonization (international legislation or standardization) and recognition. While these agreements contain no requirements of harmonization, they provide some incentives for States to formulate and conform to international standards developed in other fora.

1. *SPS Agreement*

In the Uruguay Round, in the area of SPS measures, certain quasi-legislative authority was referred to certain other functional organizations. That is, the definition of 'international standards' contained in Annex A to the SPS Agreement appoints the Codex Alimentarius Commission (Codex), the International Office of Epizootics (OIE), and the International Plant Protection Convention (IPPC) as 'quasi-legislators' of these standards in relevant areas. What is the meaning of 'quasi-legislators'?

---

[42] Appellate Body Report, *Korea – Various Measures on Beef,* at para 178.
[43] Ibid at para 121.   [44] Ibid at paras 161–64.

First, the standards developed by Codex, OIE, and IPPC for human, animal, and plant health, respectively, are, under the terms of their own constitutive documents, non-binding. However, Article 3.1 SPS Agreement provides that 'Members shall base their sanitary or phytosanitary measures on international standards, guidelines or recommendations, where they exist, except as otherwise provided for in this Agreement, and in particular in paragraph 3'. Moreover, Article 3.2 states that SPS measures of WTO Members that are in conformity with international standards, guidelines, or recommendations shall be 'presumed to be consistent with the relevant provisions of this Agreement'. In *EC – Hormones*, the Appellate Body found that the terms 'based on' in Article 3.1 and 'in conformity with' in Article 3.2 have different meanings. 'Based on' means simply derived from, and provides greater flexibility to Members.[45] However, reversing the Panel, the Appellate Body found that while Article 3.2 was a safe harbour, it did not establish the converse presumption; the Panel erred in presuming that measures that did not conform to international standards were inconsistent with the SPS Agreement. Members can always adopt norms above international standards as long as they comply with the SPS Agreement, including Article 5 on risk assessments.[46] This is true also for Article 2.5 TBT Agreement.

2. *TBT Agreement*

Article 2.4 TBT Agreement requires Members to use international standards as a basis for their technical regulations, unless the international standards are an inappropriate or ineffective means to achieve legitimate objectives, so deviation from international standards is discouraged.

This provision was interpreted in *EC – Sardines*. The Appellate Body determined that a Codex Alimentarius standard was a 'relevant international standard' within the meaning of Article 2.4, despite the fact that it was not adopted by consensus. Thus, Members may find that standards that they did not accept—that they in fact rejected—need to be taken into account and have other legal significance under Article 2.4 TBT Agreement. Article 2.4 requires that Members use 'relevant international standards' as a basis for their technical regulations. The Appellate Body found that for a standard to be used 'as a basis for' a technical regulation, it must be 'used as the principal constituent or fundamental principle for the purpose of enacting the technical regulation'.[47] Furthermore, one thing cannot be the basis for another if the two are contradictory.[48] The Appellate Body found no general rule-exception

---

[45] In *EC – Hormones*, at para 165, the Appellate Body rejected the Panel's finding that 'based on' and 'conform to' have the same meaning.

[46] Therefore, Article 3.3 permits Members to introduce measures, which result in a higher level of protection than international standards, if (a) there is scientific justification, or (b) as a consequence of Member's appropriate level of protection. Members can always adopt norms above international standards as long as they comply with the SPS Agreement including Article 5 on risk assessment.

[47] Appellate Body Report, *EC – Sardines*, at para 243.   [48] Ibid at para 248.

relationship between the first and second parts of Article 2.4. Therefore, it was for Peru to bear the burden of proving a violation of Article 2.4 *as a whole*.

3. *The GATT 1994*

The GATT 1994 does not specifically require the use of international standards, though the least trade restrictive alternative requirements under Article XX and/or the good faith requirement under the chapeau of Article XX may include a requirement to attempt to create an international or regional standard before applying a unilateral one.

Clearly, and 'as far as possible', a multilateral approach is strongly preferred. Yet it is one thing to *prefer* a multilateral approach in the application of a measure that is provisionally justified under one of the subparagraphs of Article XX of the GATT 1994; it is another to require the *conclusion* of a multilateral agreement as a condition of avoiding 'arbitrary or unjustifiable discrimination' under the chapeau of Article XX. There is, in this case, no such requirement.[49]

Reliance on international or even regional standards may provide a *de facto* presumption of good faith as required by Article XX.[50]

E. (Mutual) Recognition and Equivalence

1. *SPS Agreement*

Article 4.1 SPS Agreement requires recognition of other Members' regulations. In 2001, the SPS Committee adopted a decision on the implementation of Article 4 on equivalence to 'make operational the provisions of Article 4 of the Agreement on the Application of Sanitary and Phytosanitary Measures'.[51] It imposes an obligation on an importing Member, upon the request of the exporting Member, to explain the objective and rationale of the SPS measure, to identify clearly the risks that the relevant measure is intended to address, and to indicate the appropriate level of protection, which its SPS measure is designed to achieve. In addition, the exporting Member must provide reasonable access, upon request, to the importing Member for inspection, testing, and other relevant procedures for the recognition of equivalence. Such requests should proceed rapidly, especially with traditional imports, and should not in themselves disrupt or suspend ongoing imports.

---

[49] See Appellate Body Report, *US – Shrimp (Article 21.5 – Malaysia)*, at para 124 (emphasis added).

[50] Ibid at paras 130–31. See also G Marceau, 'A Call for Coherence in International Law – Praises for the Prohibition Against "Clinical Isolation" in WTO Dispute Settlement' 1999 *Journal of World Trade* 33(5) 87.

[51] SPS Committee, *Decision on the Implementation of Article 4 of the Agreement on the Application of Sanitary and Phytosanitary Measures*, G/SPS/19 (26 October 2001).

2. *TBT Agreement*

The requirement of the SPS Agreement is stronger than the more hortatory obligation of Article 2.7 TBT Agreement, which simply requires Members to give positive consideration to accepting foreign regulation as equivalent, if the foreign regulation fulfils the importing Member's objectives. Since Article XX GATT 1994 requires that Members maintain an appropriate level of flexibility in the administration of their regulatory distinctions,[52] it is probable that Article 2.7 (or Article 2.2 in a manner parallel to Article XX) will be interpreted as requiring sufficient flexibility in normative determinations and good faith consideration of the alternative and equivalent standards suggested by the exporting country.

3. *The GATT 1994*

The GATT 1994 contains no explicit equivalency requirement or facility of recognition. However, it is possible that necessity requirements under Article XX (b) or (d) could require recognition. In addition, the Appellate Body in *US – Shrimp (Article 21.5 – Malaysia)* seems to have identified such an embryonic requirement in the chapeau of Article XX, when writing that 'an approach based on whether a measure requires essentially the same regulatory programme . . . as that adopted by the importing Member . . . [does] not meet the requirements of the chapeau of Article XX'. A measure requiring US and foreign regulatory programmes to be 'comparable in effectiveness', as opposed to being 'essentially the same' would comply with the prohibition against a disguised restriction on trade.[53] This appears to function as a 'soft' equivalency requirement.

F. Internal Consistency

1. *SPS Agreement*

Article 5.5 SPS Agreement requires a regulating Member to 'avoid arbitrary or unjustifiable distinctions in the levels it considers to be appropriate in different

---

[52] Appellate Body Report, *US – Shrimp*, at para 165; Appellate Body Report, *US – Shrimp (Article 21.5 – Malaysia)*, at paras 135–52.

[53] Ibid at para 144: 'In our view, there is an important difference between conditioning market access on the adoption of essentially the same programme, and conditioning market access on the adoption of a programme comparable in effectiveness. Authorizing an importing Member to condition market access on exporting Members putting in place regulatory programmes comparable in effectiveness to that of the importing Member gives sufficient latitude to the exporting Member with respect to the programme it may adopt to achieve the level of effectiveness required. It allows the exporting Member to adopt a regulatory programme that is suitable to the specific conditions prevailing in its territory. The Panel correctly reasoned and concluded that conditioning market access on the adoption of a programme comparable in effectiveness, allows for sufficient flexibility in the application of the measure so as to avoid 'arbitrary or unjustifiable discrimination'.

situations, if such distinctions result in discrimination or a disguised restriction on international trade'. This provision adds a specific route to be followed to demonstrate discrimination generally prohibited by Article 2.3 SPS Agreement. In *EC – Hormones*, the Appellate Body identified three elements that cumulatively must be demonstrated for a violation of Article 5.5 and pointed to 'warning signals':

The first element is that the Member imposing the measure complained of has adopted its own appropriate levels of sanitary protection against risks to human life or health in several different situations. The second element to be shown is that those levels of protection exhibit arbitrary or unjustifiable differences ('distinctions' in the language of Article 5.5) in their treatment of different situations. The last element requires that the arbitrary or unjustifiable differences result in discrimination or a disguised restriction of international trade. We understand the last element to be referring to the measure embodying or implementing a particular level of protection as resulting, in its application, in discrimination or a disguised restriction on international trade...[54]

The Appellate Body in *Australia – Salmon* found that an unexplained distinction in the levels of protection imposed by Australia ('internal inconsistency') resulted in a disguised restriction on international trade, in violation of Article 5.5 SPS Agreement, and by implication, Article 2.3.[55] The test under Article 5.5 is definitely more sophisticated than that under the chapeau of Article XX. Members have a right to take SPS measures, but it is a conditional right and the conditions are stringent. Under Article XX GATT 1994, Members have an exceptional right to take measures based on policies therein listed. The conditions attached are less stringent but this right has to be balanced against the market access rights of other WTO Members.

2. *TBT Agreement*
The TBT Agreement does not contain any explicit consistency requirement but, as discussed hereafter, the Article XX GATT 1994 necessity test appears to contain a soft consistency requirement. A similar requirement could thus exist in the operationalization of the Article 2.2 necessity test.

3. *The GATT*
Although there is no formal consistency requirement in Article XX(d) GATT 1994, the Appellate Body in *Korea – Various Measures on Beef* seems to have read some soft consistency requirement into it, or at least considered that the absence of consistency may be evidence of the lack of objective necessity of the measure.[56]

[54] Ibid paras 214–15.
[55] Appellate Body Report, *Australia – Salmon*, at para 240. See also J Pauwelyn, 'The WTO Agreement on Sanitary and Phytosanitary Measures (SPS) as Applied in the First Three SPS Disputes' 1999 *Journal of International Economic Law* 2(4) 641.
[56] Appellate Body Report, *Korea—Various Measures on Beef*, at para 170.

G. Permission for Precautionary Action

1. *SPS Agreement*

The precautionary principle has been the subject of extensive debate, which cannot be replicated here. However, it is worth pointing out that the precautionary principle is stated in a very specific, and limited, form in Article 5.7 SPS Agreement.[57] It is available to allow provisional measures where scientific evidence is insufficient, where the Member acts on the basis of available information, and where the Member seeks to obtain the additional information needed for a more objective assessment of risk within a reasonable period of time. In *EC – Hormones,* the Appellate Body did not reach any conclusion whether the 'precautionary principle' had indeed crystallized to become a general principle of law.[58] For the Appellate Body, various elements, including the right of Members to determine the level of protection they want, confirmed that aspects of the precautionary principle were already reflected in different provisions of the SPS Agreement.

In *Japan – Agricultural Products II,* the Appellate Body found that Article 5.7 is available subject to the satisfaction of four cumulative requirements: (i) relevant scientific evidence is insufficient, (ii) the measure is adopted on the basis of available pertinent information, (iii) the Member seeks to obtain the additional information necessary for a more objective assessment of risk, and (iv) the Member reviews the measure accordingly within a reasonable period of time.[59] In the instant case, the Panel made a finding only as to the insufficiency of relevant scientific evidence, determining that there was indeed sufficient scientific evidence on the issues at hand.

2. *TBT Agreement*

The preamble of the TBT Agreement also confirms the right of Members to determine the level of risk and protection they want to follow. Under the TBT Agreement, there is no requirement of any form of specific evidence and no provision for situations where scientific evidence would be insufficient to justify a norm. Yet Article 2.2, in requiring that measures be no more restrictive than necessary, will call for some demonstration that some objective necessity exists. Scientific evidence may be called for.

---

[57] It is reported that Article 5.7 SPS Agreement was initially drafted to be used in emergency situations where, for example, the spread of a disease had to be stopped urgently before it may be feasible to complete a risk assessment. Discussion with Gretchen Stanton, Secretary of the SPS Committee.

[58] The Appellate Body in *EC – Hormones,* at para 123, stated that 'the status of the precautionary principle in international law continues to be the subject of debate among academics, law practitioners, regulators, and judges. [...] We consider, however, that it is unnecessary, and probably imprudent, for the Appellate Body in this appeal to take a position on this important, but abstract, question'.

[59] Appellate Body Report, *Japan – Agricultural Products II,* at para 89.

3. The GATT 1994

If Members' rights to determine their own level of protection, to be prudent and to rely on minority opinion, are expressions or indications of the precautionary principle—as the Appellate Body seems to have established—one may argue that the interpretation of Article XX GATT 1994 has already taken into account aspects of a precautionary principle. As with the SPS Agreement, the crystallization of the precautionary principle would not reduce the requirements contained in Article XX nor could it be enforced autonomously before a WTO adjudicating body. However, it could be used in the interpretation of WTO provisions. For the Appellate Body, Article XX GATT 1994 and Article 11 DSU have to be interpreted in light of this right of democratic government to be responsible and prudent:

> In the context of the SPS Agreement, we have said previously, in *European Communities—Hormones*, that responsible and representative governments may act in good faith on the basis of what, at a given time, may be a divergent opinion coming from qualified and respected sources. In justifying a measure under Article XX(b) of the GATT 1994, a Member may also rely, in good faith, on scientific sources which, at that time, may represent a divergent, but qualified and respected, opinion. A Member is not obliged, in setting health policy, automatically to follow what, at a given time, may constitute a majority scientific opinion.[60]

In *EC – Asbestos*, the Panel had also stated that 'to make the adoption of health measures concerning a definite risk depend upon establishing *with certainty* a risk…would have the effect of preventing any possibility of legislating in the field of public health'.[61]

H. Balancing

To many commentators, the idea of balancing tests in contexts where domestic regulation is subject to international scrutiny has been anathema to judicial restraint and national sovereignty. The GATT 1994 has no specific language authorizing a balancing test. The SPS and TBT Agreements, while providing for least trade restrictive alternative analysis, also avoid specific reference to balancing tests. And yet, dispute settlement has often turned to balancing.

1. The GATT 1994

As noted above, the classic 'least trade restrictive alternative' test has been challenged by the Appellate Body's decisions in *Korea – Various Measures on Beef* and *EC – Asbestos*. In *Korea – Various Measures on Beef*, the Appellate Body first examined the definition of 'necessity' under Article XX(d) GATT 1994, finding that it could

---

[60] Appellate Body Report, *Korea – Various Measures on Beef*, at para 178 (fn omitted).
[61] Panel Report, *EC – Asbestos*, at para 8.221 (emphasis added).

comprise something less than absolute indispensability. Indeed, the Appellate Body set up, rather explicitly, a balancing test. It considered the degree to which the measure contributes to the realization of the end pursued: 'the greater the contribution, the more easily a measure might be considered to be "necessary"'.[62] It also considered the 'extent to which the compliance measure produces restrictive effects on international commerce'.[63] The Appellate Body's statement will be breathtaking to some:

In sum, determination of whether a measure, which is not 'indispensable', may nevertheless be 'necessary' within the contemplation of Article XX(d), involves in every case a process of weighing and balancing a series of factors which prominently include the contribution made by the compliance measure to the enforcement of the law or regulation at issue, the importance of the common interests or values protected by that law or regulation, and the accompanying impact of the law or regulation on imports or exports.[64]

This statement constitutes a significant shift towards a greater role of the WTO adjudicating bodies in weighing regulatory values against trade values. Interestingly, in its decision regarding *EC – Asbestos*, the Appellate Body referred to its decision in *Korea – Various Measures on Beef* to the effect that in determining whether another alternative method is reasonably available, it is appropriate to consider the extent to which the alternative measure 'contributes to the realization of the end pursued'.[65] Although the Appellate Body in *US – Gambling* referred extensively to such balancing and weighing exercise under the necessity test, it seems to have deliberately avoided the use of such a concept in the latest *Brazil – Retreaded Tyres* and concluded that a measure is necessary if it 'contributes materially' to the achievement of the objective policy invoked (FNT Appellate Body Report, *Brazil – Retreaded Tyres*, at para. 210). It nonetheless stated that '[t]he weighing and balancing is a holistic operation that involves putting all the variables of the equation together and evaluating them in relation to each other after having examined them individually, in order to reach an overall judgement' (FNT Appellate Body Report, *Brazil – Retreaded Tyres*, at para. 182).

Even after possible balancing under the 'necessity' provisions of Article XX, there is also a broader balancing of rights and obligations called for by the chapeau of Article XX.[66] In *US – Shrimp*, the Appellate Body stated that the chapeau of Article XX 'embodies the recognition of the...need to maintain a balance of rights and obligations' between the right of a Member to invoke the exceptions of Article XX, on the one hand, and the rights of the other Members under the GATT 1994, on the other hand. This interpretation and application of Article XX requires 'locating and marking out a line of equilibrium between the right of a Member to invoke

---

[62] Appellate Body Report, *Korea – Various Measures on Beef*, at para 163.
[63] Ibid (citation omitted).   [64] Ibid at para 164.
[65] See Appellate Body Report, *EC – Asbestos*, at para 172, citing Appellate Body Report, *Korea – Various Measures on Beef*, at paras 161–164.
[66] The chapeau requires that measures exempted under Article XX must not be applied in a manner that would constitute 'a means of arbitrary or unjustifiable discrimination between countries where the same conditions prevail, or a disguised restriction on international trade...'.

an exception under Article XX and the rights of the other Members under varying substantive provisions' and 'the location of the line of equilibrium is not fixed and unchanging; the line moves as the kind and the shape of the measures at stake vary and as the facts making up specific cases differ'.[67]

2. *TBT Agreement*

It seems reasonable to expect that the interpretation of the positive requirements of Article 2.2 TBT Agreement for a measure not more trade restrictive than necessary will be parallel to that developed under the necessity test of Article XX GATT 1994.

3. *SPS Agreement*

The criteria identified by the SPS jurisprudence seem to call for a necessity/ balancing test under Article 5.6 SPS Agreement fairly similar to that developed in *Korea – Various Measures on Beef* and *EC – Asbestos*, discussed above. Yet, contrary to Article XX, the test under Article 5.6 SPS Agreement does not appear to call for an assessment of the degree of the measure's contribution to the end. As with the classic least trade restrictive alternative 'reasonably available', the degree of contribution to the end seemed before to be inviolable: Members were entitled to complete accomplishment of the end reflected in their regulation.

I. Product/Process Issues and the Territorial–Extraterritoriality Divide

Finally, an area of great importance is the territorial scope of application of the national measures, that is, to what extent can a Member take action under its domestic law to protect health or other domestic regulatory values outside its own territory? This issue has arisen explicitly in connection with the application of Article XX(b) and (g) GATT 1994, but has also arisen implicitly, in the form of the product-process distinction.[68]

1. *The GATT 1994*

The legal issue is whether GATT/WTO law authorizes Members to maintain regulatory distinctions based on process and production methods (PPMs) of imported

---

[67] Appellate Body Report, *US – Shrimp*, at para 158.

[68] For discussions of the product/process distinction, see RE Hudec, 'The Product-Process Doctrine in GATT/WTO Jurisprudence' in M Bronckers and R Quick (eds), *New Directions in International Economic Law: Essays in Honour of John H Jackson* (The Hague: Kluwer Law International, 2000) 187; R Howse and D Regan, 'The Product/Process Distinction-An Illusory Basis for Disciplining "Unilateralism" in Trade Policy' 2000 *European Journal of International Law* 11(2) 249, and the cogent response from JH Jackson, 'Comments on *Shrimp/Turtle* and the Product/Process Distinction' 2003 *European Journal of International Economic Law* 11(2) 303.

products. In particular the debate has focused on whether products that comply with specified PPM criteria and those that do not are 'like' for the purpose of the NT obligations of Article III GATT 1994.

Various elements support the view that Article III does not apply to regulatory distinctions based on extraterritorial policy considerations not affecting the products. Article III refers to measures affecting 'internal sales'; its concern is the internal market of the importing Member. The wording of Articles I, II, III, and XI GATT 1994 only refer to 'products'. Annex 1A covers rules applicable to trade in goods. Moreover, the Appellate Body has recognized that when determining whether two products are directly competitive or substitutable for the purpose of Article III GATT 1994, Article 4 Agreement on Safeguards, or Article 6.1 ATC, it is looking at the 'product characteristics'.

The determination of likeness requires consideration of any evidence that indicates whether the products are in a competitive relationship in the marketplace.[69] For the Appellate Body, evidence relating to health risks[70] (carcinogenicity, or toxicity) associated with the product can be examined under the existing *Border Tax Adjustment* report categories of physical properties, consumer tastes and habits and products' end-use.[71] This fuelled the argument that consumer preferences could legitimate the examination of PPM distinctions under the like product test in Article III.

To summarize, the WTO jurisprudence has not yet clarified whether Article III applies to or covers PPM-type regulatory distinctions. If Article III does not cover PPM-type regulations, then, under *Ad* Article III, PPM regulations will be viewed as border import restrictions (a ban on products not respecting the PPM prescriptions) controlled by Article XI. If Article III covers PPM-type regulations, the Appellate Body's application of a competition-based test in *EC – Asbestos* suggests that in most cases, different PPMs would be insufficient to make products 'un-like'. The test under Article III would then prohibit treating like products differently on the basis of PPM considerations. In this sense the product/process distinction may often serve as a proxy to control the extraterritorial application of national measures, which is perhaps exceptionally permitted under the circumstances set forth in Article XX.

2. *TBT Agreement*

Annex 1 of the TBT Agreement defines 'technical regulation' as a 'document which lays down product characteristics or their related processes and production methods, including the applicable administrative provisions with which compliance is mandatory'. Many developing countries have argued that the TBT Agreement does

---

[69] Appellate Body Report, *EC – Asbestos*, at paras 97–99.

[70] Note the inconsistency between this perspective and the economic theory of regulation, which assumes that the reason for regulatory intervention is because the health risks are not sufficiently reflected in the market place.

[71] Appellate Body Report, *EC – Asbestos*, at para 117.

not 'cover' PPM regulations and have politically challenged notifications of labeling requirements based on social considerations[72] and timber process[73] that have no physical impact on the product traded. It is important to note that the non-application of the TBT Agreement to PPM-type regulations would not make such PPM regulations incompatible with WTO law. If the TBT Agreement does not cover or apply to PPM regulations, such regulations will be examined under Articles III/XI GATT 1994 and may find justification under Article XX. To remove PPM-type regulations from the coverage of the TBT Agreement would exempt them from the other requirements of the same TBT Agreement, including those on notification, harmonization, and mutual recognition. Furthermore, unlike the case of the SPS Agreement, the TBT Agreement contains no presumption of compliance with GATT 1994.

3. *SPS Agreement*

Annex A to the SPS Agreement contains a definition of 'sanitary and phytosanitary measures' that includes only measures that protect health within the territory of the regulating Member. It therefore excludes from its coverage measures addressing health outside the regulating Member's territory. This leaves importing state regulation seeking to regulate PPMs in the exporting Member, with the goal of protecting health outside the territory of the importing Member, outside the coverage of the SPS Agreement, but potentially subject to the GATT 1994 or the TBT Agreement. Importantly, it includes measures of importing Members regulating PPMs outside of their territory, where the goal is to protect health within the territory; for example, regulation of foreign slaughterhouse practices may be considered to be SPS measures.

III. Application of the Agreements

The purpose of this Chapter has been to outline certain critical rules applicable under the GATT 1994 and the SPS and TBT Agreements. Due to lack of space, a full analysis of the scope of application of these various provisions cannot be provided, but several relevant issues have already been raised. In the following paragraphs, the scope of application of each of the agreements is summarized.

---

[72] See TBT Committeee, *Notification by Belgium*, G/TBT/N/BEL/2 (16 January 2001); TBT Committee, *Minutes of the Meeting Held on 30 March 2001*, G/TBT/M/23 (8 May 2001); TBT Committee, *Minutes of the Meeting Held on 29 June 2001*, G/TBT/M/24 (14 August 2001).

[73] See TBT Committee, *Notification by The Netherlands*, G/TBT/Notif.98.448 (2 September 1998); TBT Committee, *Minutes of the Meeting Held on 15 September 1998*, G/TBT/M/13 (18 September 1998); TBT Committee, *Minutes of the Meeting Held on 20 November 1998*, G/TBT/M/14 (10 February 1999); TBT Committee, *Minutes of the Meeting Held on 30 March 2001*, G/TBT/M/23 (8 May 2001); TBT Committee, *Minutes of the Meeting Held on 29 June 2001*, G/TBT/M/24 (14 August 2001).

A. The GATT 1994 Versus the SPS Agreement

Article 2.4 SPS Agreement provides that:

Sanitary or phytosanitary measures which conform to the relevant provisions of this Agreement shall be presumed to be in accordance with the obligations of the Members under the provisions of GATT 1994, which relate to the use of sanitary or phytosanitary measures, in particular the provisions of Article XX(b).

This provision has two conditions: first, it addresses sanitary or phytosanitary measures, and second, those measures must not violate the SPS Agreement. If these conditions are met, this provision establishes a presumption that the relevant measures comply with the GATT 1994.

This presumption is probably best understood as rebuttable.[74] As a presumption, it would operate in the same way as Article 3.2 SPS Agreement, as interpreted by the Appellate Body in *EC – Hormones*, shifting the burden of proof to the complaining party, but not providing any substantive support to the defending party. It is possible to imagine circumstances where a difficult question arises. For example, the SPS Agreement would apply to PPM regulations that are intended to safeguard health in the importing Member. If a panel or the Appellate Body were to hold that such measures conform to the SPS Agreement, this provision would raise a presumption that they also conform to the GATT 1994. If the analysis is continued under Article XX GATT 1994, the challenged Member would carry the benefits of this presumption in its Article XX analysis (as a factual matter) and its measure would be presumed to be justified under Article XX. It would be for the challenging Member to reverse this presumption and demonstrate that less trade-restrictive alternatives were reasonably available to the importing Member to ensure the same reasonable level of protection. It is doubtful that a Member that did not succeed in demonstrating the existence of such less trade restrictive alternatives in its SPS claim would manage to do so to rebut the application of Article XX GATT 1994.

So long as the necessity tests in Article 5.6 SPS Agreement and Article XX GATT 1994 are similar (or at least so long as Article XX is not more stringent), and the two disputing parties have exactly the same evidence for both legal analyses, a Member who managed to avoid a violation under the SPS Agreement should not be caught under Article XX. It may, however, be concluded that the new test under Article XX calls for an actual balancing of the degree to which the challenged measure

---

[74] If the intent were to deem such measures to comply with the GATT 1994, the treaty could have said so, or could have stated that the presumption is irrebuttable. In any event, the plain language of 'presumption' will likely be taken to mean nothing more. See Appellate Body Report, *EC – Hormones*, at para 170 (terming the unqualified presumption in Article 3.2 SPS Agreement 'rebuttable'). However, see Article 3.8 DSU, clearly stating that the presumption there is rebuttable. On the parallel application of the TBT Agreement and the GATT 1994, see R Howse and E Tuerk, 'The WTO Impact on Internal Regulations – A Case Study of the Canada – EC Asbestos dispute' in G de Búrca and J Scott (eds), *The EU and the WTO: Legal and Constitutional Aspects* (London: Hart Publishing, 2001) 283.

contributes to the end pursued, while Article 5.6 SPS Agreement does not. If this were the case, it would be possible that an SPS measure that passes Article 5.6 could be found inconsistent with Article XX. Of course, a measure would only be required to comply with Article XX if it violates another provision of the GATT 1994.

B. The GATT 1994 Versus the TBT Agreement

The TBT Agreement lacks an explicit provision relating it to the GATT 1994. As with the SPS Agreement, it would be best if compliance with the TBT Agreement gave rise to a presumption of compliance with the GATT 1994. In addition, compliance with an international standard (Articles 2.4 and 2.5 TBT Agreement) should lead to a presumption of compliance with Article 2.2 TBT Agreement, and not simply the presumption of necessity provided for by Article 2.5. The use of such international standards should also *de facto* lead to the conclusion that the domestic TBT measure is necessary for the purpose of Article XX. The same should generally be true for any measure that complies with Article 2.2 TBT Agreement. Since the TBT Agreement adds different obligations to those of the GATT 1994, does it mean that a single measure may be in violation of the TBT Agreement while compatible with the GATT 1994? Possibly.

Another interesting issue is the coverage of Article 2.1 TBT Agreement and its relationship with Articles I, III, and XX GATT 1994. If the scope and meaning of Article 2.1 is similar to that of Articles III and I, a single technical regulation could be a *prima facie* violation of Article III but be justified under Article XX GATT 1994, while also in violation of Article 2.1 TBT Agreement without any possibility of justification—even if the same regulation were found not to be in violation of Article 2.2 TBT Agreement. One may argue that Article XX GATT 1994 could be invoked as a defence to a violation of Article 2.1 and this seems to have been accepted by the Appellate Body in *EC – Asbestos* when it concluded that the TBT Agreement was applicable to the measure at issue but decided not to complete the analysis under that agreement (for various reasons including judicial economy). Its findings were that the measure could in any case be justified under Article XX GATT 1994. But Canada had made a claim under Article 2.1 TBT Agreement. If there was a possibility that the French measure violated Article 2.1 without any acceptable defence—in the TBT Ageement or in the GATT 1994—the Appellate Body would have committed a denial of justice against Canada in refusing to address its claim under Article 2.1 TBT Agreement.

Another interesting issue is the fact that the TBT Agreement allows Members to base their TBT regulations on 'any legitimate governmental policies' while Article XX contains a closed list of policies. Therefore it is conceivable that a measure based on a policy not listed in Article XX (say the protection of the French language) could be considered not more restrictive than necessary pursuant to Article 2.2 TBT

Agreement, while not being able to find any provisional justification under any of the sub-paragraphs of Article XX GATT 1994. Unless the TBT Agreement is understood as *lex specialis* to the exclusion of the GATT 1994, the GATT 1994 provisions continue to apply while the TBT Agreement may also be applicable.

C. The SPS Agreement Versus the TBT Agreement

Article 1.5 TBT Agreement provides that the TBT Agreement does not apply to SPS measures, as defined in the SPS Agreement. Thus it covers all technical regulations, other than those that are SPS measures as defined in the SPS Agreement. This means that the purpose of a measure—whether or not it is applied to protect against pests and diseases, as well as food-borne dangers[75]—is central to the division of jurisdiction between the TBT Agreement and the SPS Agreement.

However, there are measures, such as some extraterritorial ones, that would not be included as SPS measures by virtue of their extraterritorial protective purpose, but which are intended to protect health. If the TBT Agreement covers PPMs or extraterritorial considerations, some of these measures may be covered by the TBT Agreement even if the SPS Agreement does not apply to them. The possibility depends on whether 'technical regulations' include measures intended to protect extraterritorial human, animal or plant life that specify 'product characteristics or their related processes and production methods'. This of course depends on how these words are interpreted.

Article 1.4 provides that nothing in the SPS Agreement affects rights under the TBT Agreement, with respect to measures not covered by SPS Agreement. Article 1.5 TBT Agreement provides that the TBT Agreement does not apply to SPS measures. Thus, where the SPS Agreement applies by its terms, the TBT Agreement would be inapplicable and *vice versa*. It is however possible that aspects or components of a specific measure could be covered by the SPS Agreement while others would be covered by the TBT Agreement or the GATT 1994, depending on how one defines the measure.

IV. CONCLUSION

Each of the bases for evaluation of domestic regulation considered above, and some of them as applied together, has the same purpose—to distinguish between national product regulation that is permissible, and national product regulation that is impermissible. Members agreed on these tests not because they are opposed to

---

[75] See the definition of 'sanitary or phytosanitary measure' in Annex A to the SPS Agreement.

their own domestic regulation, but because they wished reciprocally to agree not to impose excessive costs on one another through their domestic regulation. The bases for evaluation discussed in this chapter must be understood in this context.

With greater international economic integration—greater trade—it becomes easier and in some ways more attractive for States to formulate their regulation in ways that impose costs on foreign producers. These are costs of adjustment or costs of lost profits due to barriers to market access. Yet Members recognize that there are good purposes to be served and do not wish to establish legal rules that will hamper the achievement of these purposes. The tests we have reviewed—complex and sometimes indeterminate as they are—are those that have been developed over time to minimize costs imposed on foreigners while minimizing also the loss of local autonomy to regulate. Thus, the right to trade and the right to regulate—both important for individual and national welfare, are reconciled. Will these evaluations sometimes seem wrong, and indeed be wrong? Of course. It may be possible over time and with careful analysis to improve on these bases for evaluation. It may be that Members decide, through harmonizing measures or recognition measures, to remove certain measures from the scope of these evaluations. This has already happened in some areas, and may be expected to continue happening. As these bases for evaluation are revised over time, and as Members engage in harmonization and mutual recognition agreements, they constantly revise the scope of national autonomy—of sovereignty. It is important to recognize that it is not the WTO that decides to do these things, but the Members of the WTO, in the exercise of their sovereignty.

SELECTED BIBLIOGRAPHY

J Bhagwati, 'The Demands to Reduce Domestic Diversity among Trading Nations' in J Bhagwati and R Hudec (eds), *Fair Trade and Harmonization: Prerequisites for Free Trade? Vol. I : Economic Analysis* (Cambridge, MA: MIT Press, 1996) 9

T Christoforou, 'Settlement of Science-Based Trade Disputes in the WTO: A Critical Review of the Developing Case Law in the Face of Scientific Uncertainty' 2000 *New York University Environmental Law Journal* 8(3) 622

R Howse, 'Democracy, Science and Free Trade: Risk Regulation on Trial at the World Trade Organisation' 2000 *Michigan Law Review* 98(7) 2329.

R Howse, 'From Politics to Technocracy – and Back Again: The Fate of the Multilateral Trading Regime' 2002 *American Journal of International Law* 96(1) 94

R Howse, 'A New Device for Creating International Legal Normativity: The WTO Technical Barriers to Trade Agreement and "International Standards"' in C Joerges and E-U Petersmann (eds), *Constitutionalism, Multilevel Trade Governance and Social Regulation* (Portland, Oreg.: Hart Publishing, 2006) 383

R Howse and E Tuerk, 'The WTO Impact on Internal Regulations – A Case Study of the Canada – EC Asbestos dispute' in G de Búrca and J Scott (eds), *The EU and the WTO: Legal and Constitutional Aspects* (London: Hart Publishing, 2001) 283

RE Hudec, 'The Product–Process Doctrine in GATT/WTO Jurisprudence' in M Bronckers and R Quick (eds), *New Directions in International Economic Law: Essays in Honour of John H Jackson* (The Hague: Kluwer Law International, 2000) 187

D Leebron, 'Lying Down with Procrustes: An Analysis of Harmonization Claims' in J Bhagwati and R Hudec (eds), *Fair Trade and Harmonization: Prerequisites for Free Trade? Vol. I : Economic Analysis* (Cambridge, MA: MIT Press, 1996) 41

G Marceau and J Trachtman, 'The Technical Barriers to Trade Agreement, the Sanitary and Phytosanitary Measures Agreement, and the General Agreement on Tariffs and Trade: A Map of the World Trade Organization Law of Domestic Regulation of Goods' 2002 *Journal of World Trade* 36(5) 811

PC Mavroidis, 'A New Device for Creating International Legal Normativity: The WTO Technical Barriers to Trade Agreement and "International Standards"' in C Joerges and E-U Petersmann (eds), *Constitutionalism, Multilevel Trade Governance and Social Regulation* (Portland, Oreg.: Hart Publishing, 2006) 283

PC Murray, 'The International Environmental Management Standard, ISO 14000: A Non-Tariff Barrier or a Step to an Emerging Global Environmental Policy?' 1997 *University of Pennsylvania Journal of International Economic Law* 18(2) 557

J Neumann and E Teurk, 'Necessity Revisited: Proportionality in World Trade Organization Law After *Korea – Beef*, *EC – Asbestos*, and *EC – Sardines*' 2003 *Journal of World Trade* 37(1) 199

J Pauwelyn, 'The WTO Agreement on Sanitary and Phytosanitary Measures (SPS) as Applied in the First Three SPS Disputes' 1999 *Journal of International Economic Law* 2(4) 641

A Porges and J Trachtman, 'Robert Hudec and Domestic Regulation: The Resurrection of Aim and Effects' 2003 *Journal of World Trade* 37(4) 783

T Stewart and D Johansen, 'The SPS Agreement of the World Trade Organization and International Organizations: The Roles of the Codex Alimentarius Commission, the International Plant Protection Convention, and the International Office of Epizootics' 1998 *Syracuse Journal of International Law and Commerce* 26(1) 27

J Trachtman, 'Trade and . . . Problems, Cost-Benefit Analysis and Subsidiarity' 1998 *European Journal of International Law* 9(1) 32

J Trachtman, 'Lessons for the GATS from Existing WTO Rules on Domestic Regulation' in A Mattoo and P Sauve (eds), *Domestic Regulation and Service Trade Liberalization* (Washington, DC: World Bank/Oxford University Press, 2003) 57

DG Victor, 'The Sanitary and Phytosanitary Agreement of the World Trade Organinzation: An Assessment after Five Years' 2000 *NYU Journal of International Law and Policy* 32(4) 865

WTO CTE, *Secretariat Note for the Committee on Trade and Environment, Negotiating History of the Coverage of the Agreement on Technical Barriers to Trade with Regard to Labelling Requirements, Voluntary Standards, and Processes and Production Methods Unrelated to Product Characteristics*, WT/CTE/W/10 (29 August 1995)

WTO TBT Committee, *Decision on Principles for the Development of the International Standards, Guides and Recommendations with Relation to Articles 2, 5 and Annex 3 of the Agreement*, G/TBT/9 Annex 4 (13 November 2000)

CHAPTER 10

REGIONAL TRADE AGREEMENTS

DAVID A GANTZ

I. INTRODUCTION

VARIOUS regional trading arrangements have existed for many years. However, regional trade agreements (RTAs), including but not limited to free trade agreements and customs unions as defined in Article XXIV GATT 1994, have only recently become the darlings of international trade negotiators. WTO Members are not abandoning the WTO, which with its GATT predecessor has served the world economy well for more than sixty years. Rather, in addition to frustration with the stalled 'Doha Development Agenda' negotiations in Geneva, some WTO Members increasingly believe that it may be possible to accomplish a degree of trade liberalization on a sub-global level that is impossible or at least more difficult to achieve globally. Others remain staunchly committed to a global approach, criticizing the RTA movement as a beggar-thy-neighbour policy that primarily diverts resources and personnel from the multilateral negotiation, liberalization, and law making process, and isolates the less significant trading nations. Given the number of nations now negotiating RTAs, their formation will likely continue at a significant rate even if (as seems unlikely) the Doha negotiations are ultimately successful.[1]

In this chapter, the term 'RTAs' primarily covers comprehensive free trade agreements (FTAs), such as NAFTA, and customs unions such as the EU or MERCOSUR, which arguably meet the requirements of Article XXIV GATT 1994. The term also encompasses agreements that are more limited in scope (whether or not Article XXIV-compliant) such as those permitted under the GATT 'Enabling Clause'. About 84 per cent of RTAs are FTAs; the rest are either customs unions or 'partial scope' arrangements.[2] Further, the term 'regional' is a misnomer, as 'non-global' provides a more accurate description. Even the term 'free trade agreement' is suspect, given that most such arrangements are in reality 'preferential trade agreements' when comparing the benefits accorded to members and the hurdles imposed on non-members.[3]

The RTA is an increasingly common phenomenon. Whereas 12–15 years ago only a few dozen functioning agreements existed, there are now hundreds. According to

[1] As of this writing (February 2008) new texts had been circulated on market access but the negotiations have effectively been stalled since mid-2006, and there seems little likelihood of a breakthrough in 2008. See WTO, 'Doha Development Agenda: Negotiations, Implementation and Development', at <http://www.wto.org/english/tratop_e/dda_e/dda_e.htm> (last visited 21 January 2008); D Pruzin, 'Economics and Politics in 2008 Dampen Hopes for Conclusion to Doha Round' 2008 *International Trade Reporter (BNA)* (25) 90.
[2] R Fiorentino, L Verdeja, and C Toqueboeuf, *The Changing Landscape of Regional Trade Agreements: 2006 Update* (Geneva: WTO Secretariat, 2007), at 5.
[3] J Bhagwati, *Free Trade Today* (Princeton: Princeton University Press, 2002), at 106–07.

the WTO Secretariat, as of mid-2005, only one WTO Member (Mongolia) was not a party to at least one RTA. More than 330 RTAs have been notified to the WTO or its GATT predecessor, over 200 since January 1995; at least 180 are actually in force.[4] For the EU, only nine WTO Members are subject to MFN duties;[5] all of the rest enjoy various preferential tariff regimes under RTAs or unilateral systems such as Generalized Systems of Preferences (GSP) or the economic partnership agreements (EPAs) that are replacing the Cotonou Agreements for the 'Asian, Caribbean and Pacific' (ACP) States.

Given this chapter's focus on Article XXIV GATT 1994, it is useful to set out the pertinent paragraphs at the outset:

4. The contracting parties recognize the desirability of increasing freedom of trade by the development, through voluntary agreements, of closer integration between the economies of the countries parties to such agreements. They also recognize that the purpose of a customs union or of a free-trade area should be to facilitate trade between the constituent territories and not to raise barriers to the trade of other contracting parties with such territories.

5. Accordingly, the provisions of this Agreement shall not prevent, as between the territories of contracting parties, the formation of a customs union or of a free-trade area or the adoption of an interim agreement necessary for the formation of a customs union or of a free-trade area; *Provided* that:

    (a) with respect to a customs union, or an interim agreement leading to a formation of a customs union, the duties and other regulations of commerce imposed at the institution of any such union or interim agreement in respect of trade with contracting parties not parties to such union or agreement shall not on the whole be higher or more restrictive than the general incidence of the duties and regulations of commerce applicable in the constituent territories prior to the formation of such union or the adoption of such interim agreement, as the case may be;

    (b) [essentially identical to (a) but for free trade agreements]; and

    (c) any interim agreement referred to in subparagraphs (a) and (b) shall include a plan and schedule for the formation of such a customs union or of such a free-trade area within a reasonable length of time.

6. If, in fulfilling the requirements of subparagraph 5(a), a contracting party proposes to increase any rate of duty inconsistently with the provisions of Article II, the procedure set forth in Article XXVIII [modification of schedules] shall apply. In providing for compensatory adjustment, due account shall be taken of the compensation already afforded by the reduction brought about in the corresponding duty of the other constituents of the union.

7. (a) Any contracting party deciding to enter into a customs union or free-trade area, or an interim agreement leading to the formation of such a union or area, shall promptly notify the Members and shall make available to them such information

[4] WTO, 'Understanding the WTO: Regionalism: Friends or Rivals?', at <http://www.wto.org/english/thewto_e/whatis_e/tif_e/bey1_e.htm> (last visited 1 May 2008).
[5] WTO, *Trade Policy Review – European Communities – Report by the Secretariat*, WT/TPR/S/177/Rev.1 (15 May 2007), at vii.

regarding the proposed union or area as will enable them to make such reports and recommendations to contracting parties as they may deem appropriate.

(b) If, after having studied the plan and schedule included in an interim agreement referred to in paragraph 5 in consultation with the parties to that agreement and taking due account of the information made available in accordance with the provisions of subparagraph (a), the Members find that such agreement is not likely to result in the formation of a customs union or of a free-trade area within the period contemplated by the parties to the agreement or that such period is not a reasonable one, the Members shall make recommendations to the parties to the agreement. The parties shall not maintain or put into force, as the case may be, such agreement if they are not prepared to modify it in accordance with these recommendations.

* * *

8. For the purposes of this Agreement:

(a) A customs union shall be understood to mean the substitution of a single customs territory for two or more customs territories, so that

(i) duties and other restrictive regulations of commerce (except, where necessary, those permitted under Articles XI, XII, XIII, XIV, XV and XX) are eliminated with respect to substantially all the trade between the constituent territories of the union or at least with respect to substantially all the trade in products originating in such territories, and,

(ii) subject to the provisions of paragraph 9, substantially the same duties and other regulations of commerce are applied by each of the members of the union to the trade of territories not included in the union;

(b) A free-trade area shall be understood to mean a group of two or more customs territories in which the duties and other restrictive regulations of commerce (except, where necessary, those permitted under Articles XI, XII, XIII, XIV, XV and XX) are eliminated on substantially all the trade between the constituent territories in products originating in such territories.

* * *

10. The Members may by a two-thirds majority approve proposals which do not fully comply with the requirements of paragraphs 5 to 9 inclusive, provided that such proposals lead to the formation of a customs union or a free-trade area in the sense of this Article.

* * *

Part II of this chapter considers the debate over RTAs versus the global (GATT/WTO) system as well as key legal, policy, and economic issues raised by RTAs. Part III focuses on the legal relationships of RTAs to the WTO system. Part IV considers possible conflicts and scope issues arising between WTO and RTA obligations and among dispute resolution fora. Part V provides some concluding remarks.

II. The Benefits and Costs of Regionalism

The current debate about regionalism raises a broad range of issues, including economic, political, strategic, security, and international and national legal process considerations. All have importance, especially to certain players on the world stage, but no single issue is likely to determine whether particular agreements will be concluded.

A. Likely Benefits

Jeffrey Schott suggests that RTAs may provide a 'depth' of incremental trade reform going beyond what has occurred to date in Geneva, in part because of the requirement that parties eliminate tariffs and other restrictions on 'substantially all trade' instead of simply reducing them. He cites the 'bicycle' theory of trade negotiations: if one fails to continue moving forward, even when global negotiations are stalled, the loss of momentum can prove counterproductive.[6] Agreements among smaller groups of 'like-minded' States (such as NAFTA) are easier to negotiate than agreements among 153 WTO Members in Geneva.

Certain issues, such as investment protection[7] and competition law, have been included in RTAs but are only tangentially covered by WTO agreements. Similarly, there is virtually no substantive coverage of labour and human rights and environmental protection in the WTO agreements, except for a few long-standing but narrowly interpreted exceptions to WTO rules for protecting human, animal, or plant life or health, or exhaustible natural resources.[8] NAFTA, in contrast, incorporates distinct 'side agreements' applicable—imperfectly—to both areas[9] and all subsequent US RTAs contain labour and environmental provisions, again imperfectly, in the texts of the agreements themselves. In the EU, the Treaty of Lisbon, as with its predecessors, gives human rights the highest priority: 'The Union is founded on the

[6] JJ Schott, 'Free Trade Agreements: Boon or Bane of the World Trading System?' in JJ Schott (ed), *Free Trade Agreements: US Strategies and Priorities* (Washington, DC: IIE, 2004) 3, at 10–13.
[7] See NAFTA Chapter 11 (providing protection for foreign investment and mandatory investor-state international arbitration of disputes); WTO GC, *Decision Adopted by the General Council on 1 August 2004*, WT/L/579 (2 August 2004), at para (g)bis. See also chapters 19, 20, 22, and 23 of this Handbook.
[8] Arts XX(b) and XX(g) GATT 1994.
[9] *North American Agreement on Environmental Cooperation*, done at Washington 9, 13 and Ottawa 12, 14 September 1993, 32 ILM 1480 (1993); *North American Agreement on Labour Cooperation,* done at Washington 9, 13 and Ottawa 12, 14 September 1993 (1993), 32 ILM 1499.

values of respect for human dignity, freedom, democracy, equality, the rule of law, and respect for human rights, including the rights of persons belonging to minorities'.[10] EU EPAs with the ACP States also incorporate reaffirmation of the parties' human rights commitments.[11]

The content of RTAs thus varies widely. Some deal only with trade in manufactured goods and perhaps a few agricultural products and services, while others contemplate full coverage of manufactured and agricultural goods, services, investment, intellectual property, etc. It is not really clear whether 'more is better' in terms of breadth of coverage, though the trend, at least for major RTAs concluded by the EU and the US, points in that direction.

The argument persists that a State required to make internal reforms to comply with an RTA is less likely to adopt protectionist policies, even with regime change. Protectionist policies would probably violate the agreement and trigger either retaliatory acts or requests for dispute settlement by other parties. Some may criticize this loss of sovereignty,[12] in part because RTAs do restrict the flexibility of its signatories to take unilateral action, as do the WTO covered agreements. The early experience of NAFTA showed how a party to an RTA could be dissuaded from protectionism. In December 1994, Mexico drastically devalued its currency and raised tariffs for virtually all of its trading partners except those with which it had concluded RTAs.[13]

Notably, proponents of the 'learn by doing' argument contend that the experience of a State in negotiating an RTA can be a helpful preparation for global trade negotiations. Many also believe that the successful conclusion of RTAs, such as NAFTA and APEC in the early 1990s, may act as a stimulus for the completion or launch of global trade negotiations, as with the Uruguay Round in 1994, and the Doha Round in 2001.[14] Others disagree.[15] It has also been suggested that the often-criticized and less than ideal 'spaghetti bowl' approach to freer trade, discussed below, may have the potential of serving as building blocs rather than stumbling blocs for a global system of free trade.[16]

---

[10] *Treaty of Lisbon amending the Treaty on European Union and the Treaty establishing the European Community*, signed at Lisbon, 13 December 2007, Article 1a ff, at <http://www.eur-lex.europa.eu/JOHtml.do?uri=OJ:C:2007:306:SOM:EN:HTML> (last visited 18 December 2007).

[11] *Economic Partnership Agreement Between the Cariforum States, of the One Part, and the European Community and its Member States, of the other Part*, done (initialled) at Bridgetown, 16 December 2007, Preamble, at <http://www.bilaterals.org/article.php3?id_article=10956> (last visited 21 January 2008).

[12] See R Nader and L Wallach, 'GATT, NAFTA and the Subversion of the Democratic Process' in J Mander and E Goldsmith (eds), *The Case Against the Global Economy* (San Francisco: Sierra Club Books, 1996), at 93–94 (trade agreements threaten democracy by shifting decision-making power from local and national governments to international regimes).

[13] See GL Springer and JL Molina, 'The Mexican Financial Crisis: Genesis, Impact and Implications' 1995 *Journal of Interamerican Studies and World Affairs* 37(2) 57.

[14] Schott, above fn 6, at 13.   [15] See G de Jonquieres, 'Comment' in Schott, above fn 6, at 31.

[16] RE Baldwin, 'Multilaterialising Regionalism: Spaghetti Bowls as Building Blocs on the Path to Global Free Trade' 2006 *The World Economy* 29(11) 1451, at 1452.

B. Likely Costs

1. *Inherent Discrimination*

First and foremost, RTAs are by their nature discriminatory. They conflict (even if legally) with the non-discrimination principle under Article I GATT 1994 (MFN treatment).[17] Trade diversion is usually one of the objectives of an RTA even if it acknowledges trade creation as an overall goal. For more than half a century economists have been studying RTAs in an effort to determine whether they are beneficial or harmful to world trade. Jacob Viner suggested in 1950 that the answer would depend on whether trade-creating or trade-diverting forces were predominant as the result of the creation of a customs union (to use his terminology).[18] A more recent analysis by Richard Pomfret also embraces the 'trade-diversion, trade-creation dichotomy' and views discriminatory trade policies as 'second-best' to non-discriminatory global freer trade. Pomfret suggests that '[i]n a world of trade barriers and imperfections, there are costs and benefits of discriminatory trade policies, but actual GDAs [geographically discriminatory arrangements] have tended to be designed in such ways as to increase sectional rather than global economic welfare'.[19] Professors Bhagwati and Panagariya have concluded that RTAs, which they also term somewhat derisively 'preferential trade agreements', often have minimal economic benefits and actually may cause more economic harm than benefit. They argue that FTAs among States whose parties consist of both high tariff and low tariff countries (such as NAFTA) may result in a significant redistribution of income away from and a net welfare loss to the high tariff country.[20]

2. *Rules of Origin*

Virtually all FTAs have distinct (and often very complex) rules of origin, a necessary evil to prevent the denial of preferential tariff treatment to goods that did not 'originate' in the region.[21] These rules are designed to prevent 'trade deflection' in a free trade area where external trade barriers such as tariff levels differ. This ensures that imports of the product will not always enter the region through the low-tariff country, depriving the others of revenue and any protection the tariff may provide to the higher tariff party's enterprises.[22] Rules of origin also discourage third country

---

[17] See discussion *infra*, at 247.

[18] J Viner, *The Customs Union Issue* (New York: Carnegie, 1950), at 44.

[19] R Pomfret, *The Economics of Regional Trading Arrangements* (Oxford: Clarendon Press, 1997), at 384–85.

[20] J Bhagwati and A Panagariya, 'Preferential Trading Areas and Multilateralism – Strangers, Friends, or Foes?' in J Bhagwati and A Panagariya (eds), *The Economics of Preferential Trade Agreements* (Washington, DC: AEI Press, 1996), at 7, 8–27.

[21] See, eg,, Article 401 and Annex 401 NAFTA.

[22] Pomfret, above fn 19, at 185–86.

producers from using simple final assembly or 'screwdriver' operations drawing on non-regional parts and components from benefiting from duty free regional trade. For example, under NAFTA, a colour television assembly enterprise located in Mexico may export large screen televisions to the US and Canada as duty-free 'originating goods' only if the colour picture tube, about 50 per cent of the value of the television and in the past imported from Korea or Japan, was itself a product of North America.

No two RTAs have identical rules of origin, even those multiple FTAs negotiated by a single State or customs union, such as the US, Mexico, Chile, or the EU. Rules of origin constitute significant non-tariff barriers for exporters and importers, and are likely difficult or impossible to enforce by developing country customs authorities.[23]

3. The 'Spaghetti Bowl' Problem

The WTO Secretariat, among others, has suggested that RTAs may weaken the global system by setting up competing regulatory frameworks, creating 'a global patchwork of differing trade regulations'.[24] This overlapping 'spaghetti bowl'[25] or 'hub and spoke' system of RTAs leads to complex and multiple layers of regulation, causing difficulties for traders and customs officials alike. In the US, as of 2008, there were twenty different 'special' tariff rates for different FTA partners and nations subject to unilateral preferential tariffs.[26] The South African Customs Union (SACU) Members are all to be parties to an economic partnership agreement with the EU, and South Africa alone is a party to a free trade agreement with the EU, which the other four SACU Members have not accepted.[27] These situations result in a series of overlapping tariff rates and other obligations.

4. Negotiating Imbalances, Administrative Costs, and Geography

For some States, institutional and administrative costs of negotiating RTAs may well outweigh the benefits of training negotiators. Major WTO Members such as the US, the EU, Brazil, Mexico, Canada, and Japan, have sufficiently large and well-qualified trade bureaucracies to conduct negotiations simultaneously at both the

---

[23] See D Gantz, 'Implementing the NAFTA Rules of Origin: Are the Parties Helping or Hurting Free Trade?' 1995 *Arizona Journal of International and Comparative Law* 12(2) 367.

[24] WTO TPRB, *Overview of Developments in the International Trading Environment – Annual Report by the Director-General*, WT/TPR/OV/9 (20 February 2004), Part 10.

[25] See Bhagwati and Panagariya, above fn 20, at 53.

[26] Harmonized Tariff, Schedules of the United States, Products Eligible for Special Tariff Treatment, General Notes, (2008), at 7, at <http://www.hotdocs.usitc.gov/docs/tata/hts/bychapter/0801gn.pdf#page=3> (last visited 5 May 2008).

[27] R Kirk and M Stern, 'The New South African Customs Union Agreement' 2005 *The World Economy* 28(2) 169, at 186.

WTO and the RTA levels. Smaller countries, particularly developing countries such as the ACP States, often do not. Under such circumstances, RTA negotiations may be unbalanced, especially if large economic powers such as the US, the EU, and China are negotiating with smaller developing countries.[28] This may produce unfortunate precedents for global negotiations. Since the Seattle WTO Ministerial Conference (MC) in 1999, the 'Quad' countries (the US, the EU, Japan, and Canada) no longer dominate negotiations. Major developing Members such as Brazil, China, and India are increasingly involved in the process.[29]

The availability of the RTA option in a context that provides significant new market access or other benefits may be more apparent than real for many WTO Members. The economic power of the US and the EU, as well as the importance of access to their lucrative markets, reduces the bargaining power (and perhaps the sovereignty) of potential FTA partners. This lack of balance may also result in charges that the large economic powers are taking advantage of their negotiating partners, as has occurred in the course of the EU EPA negotiations.

Even if innovations are possible among small groups of like-minded nations, negotiations among large and diverse regional groupings, such as the stalled Free Trade Area of the Americas negotiations, may be no less complicated than similar negotiations on a global level. The internal political complications can also notable. In the US, at least, it may take almost as much political capital to obtain the passage of a series of bilateral FTAs by the Congress as to obtain Congressional approval of the results of a new WTO negotiating round. Many of the same protectionist groups oppose both. However, business and some agricultural interests are likely to be far more supportive in lobbying Congress for a global trade liberalization package than for one involving relatively minor trade volumes. From their perspective, the new trade opportunities inevitably apply to a broader group of potential export destinations.

Economic arguments against RTAs may be weaker for RTAs among adjacent groupings (for example, Canada, US, and Mexico; Brazil, Argentina, Uruguay, and Paraguay; or the EU Member States) than for distant pairings (for example, US—Singapore, Japan—Mexico) due to the more 'naturally' high levels of trade resulting from geographical proximity. RTAs among nations with complementary economies and exports may be more effective than those among competing economies. Views differ on the viability of RTAs comprised of members that are all developing countries, and those comprising both developed and developing economies. UNCTAD officials have recently suggested that developing countries in 'North-South' RTA negotiations suffer not only from unequal bargaining power, limited supply capacities, and competitiveness and difficulties in complying with rules of

[28] See Schott, above fn 6, at 16.
[29] See D Gantz, 'Failed Efforts to Initiate the "Millennium Round" in Seattle: Lessons for Future World Trade Negotiations' 2000 *Arizona Journal of International and Comparative Law* 17(2) 349.

origin, but also from unwelcome constraints on the use of industrial and agricultural policy.[30]

5. *An Inconclusive Debate?*

The interplay of various political, policy, economic, and legal factors complicates an observer's ability to reach firm conclusions as to the advantages and disadvantages of RTAs. This is particularly true if the determination depends on the extent to which the RTA creates new trade flows (including trade from outside the region into the region that is subject to MFN tariffs) rather than simply diverting existing trade from extra-regional to intra-regional. Other relevant factors include the extent to which regional trade displaces local industries that cannot compete (affecting jobs and tax revenues among others), the extent and source of government tax revenues replacing lost tariff revenues from intra-regional trade, and the extent to which tariff-free entry of previously taxed capital goods from developed countries' FTA partners stimulates the economy. In the final analysis, 'the assessment [of the pros and cons] depends importantly on how the FTAs are crafted and the volume of trade covered, who participates, and whether significant progress on multilateral reforms proceeds in tandem with the WTO'.[31]

III. REGIONAL TRADE REGIMES AND THE WTO SYSTEM

A. History of Article XXIV GATT 1994

If the GATT 1947 had lacked an exception for customs unions, this would have been inconsistent with broadly accepted post-World War II foreign policy in Europe. In addition to the Marshall Plan and the efforts of the World Bank, the US strongly supported the economic unification of Western Europe as an antidote to a possible World War III. Marshall Plan aid was channelled through a common European programme, rather than on a country-by-country basis. Further, the US opposed French efforts to prevent Germany from becoming again an industrial power.[32]

---

[30] UNCTAD, *Trade and Development Report* 2007 (Overview), UNCTAD/TDR/2007, at <http://www.unctad.org/en/docs/tdr2007overview_en.pdf> (last visited 15 January 2008), at ix–x.

[31] Schott, above fn 6, at 4–5.

[32] See D Chalmers, *European Union Law: Law and EU Government* (Hanover: Dartmouth, 1998), at 8–9.

Churchill among others suggested in 1946 that a (customs) union of France and Germany could be the initial step in a broader union of European nations.

John Jackson observes that some countries treated various regional agreements as exceptions to MFN treatment well before the GATT 1947 was drafted. Others, such as the US, sought a 'dismantling' of trade preferences in the GATT 1947 and the ill-fated International Trade Organization (ITO) Charter, where particular concerns had arisen with respect to the preferences extended to members of the British Commonwealth.[33] However, according to Jackson, even the US was willing to permit such arrangements 'without opening the door to the introduction of all preferential systems under guise of a customs union.'[34] Although the US pressed for immediate adoption of such arrangements, other delegations called for a transition or interim period: this latter view ultimately prevailed in Article XXIV GATT 1947. It was at the Havana Conference, where the ill-fated ITO Charter was drafted, that a free trade area was added to the exceptions for customs unions.

Some of the shortcomings of the spread of RTAs, perceived since the Havana Conference, can be blamed on the limitations of Article XXIV GATT 1947 and the manner in which it has been applied (or not applied) by the GATT Contracting Parties and more recently WTO Members.[35] However, one wonders how realistic it is to suggest that somehow the GATT 1947 and now the WTO, with their limited resources and limited dispute resolution powers until 1995, could have implemented a careful monitoring of Article XXIV compliance. This section examines the challenges faced by the WTO in assessing the GATT 1994 consistency of RTAs.

B. Requirements of Article XXIV and GATT/WTO Review

The dichotomy of Article XXIV GATT 1994 is reflected in the text itself, particularly paragraphs 4 and 5, reproduced earlier. This language likely reflects the desire of the drafters to strike a balance between preserving MFN treatment, and recognizing the need for an FTA/customs union exception, but only where Members meet strict conditions for such exceptions. Under Article XXIV, despite the reporting requirements, neither the GATT nor the WTO has effectively applied the approval or disapproval criteria. The creation of the European Economic Communities (EEC) in the 1950s contemplated from the outset a single internal market without restrictions on goods and eliminating restrictions on movement of persons, services, and capital.[36]

---

[33] JH Jackson, *World Trade and the Law of the GATT* (New York: Bobbs-Merrill, 1969), at 576–80.

[34] Ibid at 577.

[35] See Consultative Board, *The Future of the WTO: Addressing Institutional Challenges in the New Millennium* (Geneva: WTO, 2004), at 20–21.

[36] EC Commission, *Completing the Internal Market, White Paper from the Commission to the European Council (Milan, 28–29 June 1985)*, COM(85) 310 final, at <http://www.ec.europa.eu/comm/off/pdf/1985_0310_f_en.pdf> (last visited 1 May 2008), at Introduction, para 4.

In retrospect this would have been an ideal test case. However, GATT Contracting Parties' scrutiny was not extensive, apparently because the EEC Members (then Belgium, France, Germany, Italy, Luxembourg, and The Netherlands) threatened to leave the GATT 1947 if the Treaty of Rome were held to be inconsistent with Article XXIV.[37] At least since 1980, review of RTAs by the GATT Contracting Parties and WTO Members has been primarily after the fact, at times because notification has occurred only after approval of the RTAs by national legislatures, or due to the short time period between signature and ratification. Concerns raised in the Working Party report often arrived too late to be considered by the Members.[38]

Despite some efforts as part of the Uruguay Round to improve Members' discipline, there is little indication that the process significantly changed in the 1995–2005 period. It was only in mid-2006 that 'procedures to enhance transparency' of the RTA review process were agreed upon.[39] It is too early to determine efficacy of these procedures. Given the lack of careful oversight, WTO Members contemplating RTAs are unlikely to be concerned that the review of their proposed agreement by other WTO Members will have any adverse consequences, or prevent the agreement from becoming effective.

1. *Definitional Issues*

The GATT does not use the term 'regional trade agreements'. Rather, those agreements which may qualify for the Article XXIV exception are either FTAs or customs unions (or interim agreements leading to one or the other), as defined in Article XXIV:8. Thus, a free trade area requires the elimination of most, if not all 'duties and other restrictive regulations of commerce' for 'substantially all' trade among signatories of a given FTA. A customs union goes a step further and requires that the members of the customs union apply 'substantially the same duties and other regulations of commerce' to non-members, that is, what is normally termed a 'common external tariff'.[40]

2. *Substantive Requirements*

The essential requirements for a free trade area or customs union relate to breadth of coverage ('substantially all trade') and to the time permitted from the date of

---

[37] B Hoekman and M Kostecki, *The Political Economy of the World Trading System: The WTO and Beyond* (Oxford: Oxford University Press, 2001), at 353.

[38] See R Bhala, *International Trade Law: Interdisciplinary Theory and Practice*, 3rd edn (New York: Lexis/Nexis, 2007), at 714.

[39] WTO, *Negotiating Group on Rules – Report by the Chairman to the Trade Negotiations Committee, Annex: Transparency Mechanism for Regional Trade Agreements – Draft Decision*, TN/RL/18 (13 July 2006).

[40] According to the WTO Appellate Body, the use of the term 'substantially the same' offers the Members a limited degree of 'flexibility' in establishing the common external tariff, but nevertheless a high degree of 'sameness'. Appellate Body Report, *Turkey – Textiles* at para 50.

inception to the formation of the RTA (the so-called 'interim period'). Article XXIV GATT 1994 also imposes certain limitations on the permitted adverse effects on non-parties, and establishes notification requirements for those WTO Members contemplating RTAs. John Jackson observed nearly forty years ago that Article XXIV incorporates 'criteria for permissible regional arrangements under GATT [that] are ambiguous and difficult to apply'.[41] His observation remains largely true today despite periodic attempts at clarifying and improving WTO review procedures.

The phrase 'recognize the desirability' in Article XXIV:4 appears to be essentially hortatory, a statement of principle. Hence, once an RTA has met the substantive requirements of Articles XXIV:5–8, it need not satisfy a test of its purpose to be consistent with the GATT 1994.[42] The Appellate Body in *Turkey – Textiles* confirmed this interpretation.[43]

No definitive indication exists to determine whether the 'substantially all' trade requirement in Article XXIV:8 refers to the volume of trade among the parties to the RTA or to the full coverage of all relevant sectors. For example, is an RTA that covers substantially all intra-regional trade but excludes agriculture (even if the non-agricultural trade constitutes 90 per cent or more of total trade) legal under this provision? Further, it is not evident whether 'substantially all' refers to pre or post-agreement trade. For example, what if no agricultural trade among the parties occurred pre-agreement, but with full coverage (elimination of duties and other regulations of commerce), trade in agriculture could reasonably be expected to amount to 15 per cent, 20 per cent, or more of the aggregate?

The Appellate Body in *Turkey – Textiles* made the following observation about the meaning of 'substantially all':

Neither the GATT Contracting Parties nor the WTO Members have ever reached an agreement on the interpretation of the term 'substantially' in this provision. It is clear, though, that 'substantially all the trade' is not the same as *all* the trade, and also that 'substantially all the trade' is something considerably more than merely *some* of the trade.[44]

GATT Contracting Parties' concerns with FTAs that did not cover substantially all trade are reflected in the 1994 Understanding, which states that the '[C]ontribution [of FTAs or customs unions to the expansion of world trade] is increased if the elimination between the constituent territories of duties and other restrictive regulations of commerce extends to *all* trade and diminished *if any major sector of trade is excluded*'.[45] In any event, the uncertainty will remain until the Appellate Body

[41] Jackson, above fn 33, at 621.

[42] See Z Hafez, 'Weak Discipline: GATT Art XXIV and the Emerging WTO Jurisprudence on RTAs' 2003 *North Dakota Law Review* 79(4) 879, at 890–92 (discussing in detail the arguments for and against a purpose test).

[43] Appellate Body Report, *Turkey – Textiles*, at para 57.

[44] Ibid at para 48 (original emphasis).

[45] Preamble Uruguay Round Understanding on the Interpretation of Article XXIV of the General Agreement on Tariff and Trade 1994 (emphasis added).

further narrows the differences between 'some' and 'all'. Alternatively, the WTO Ministerial Conference (MC) or General Council (GC) could provide an authoritative interpretation of 'substantially all'.[46]

Article XXIV coverage of 'trade' other than trade in goods was not an issue in 1947 because the GATT 1947 did not cover services and intellectual property. Consequently, there is no requirement under Article XXIV, or related documents, that the coverage of an RTA extend to these additional areas. To the extent that there is coverage in RTAs of services the GATS applies, as discussed below.

The vast majority of RTAs are 'interim agreements'. All trade restrictions are *not* removed immediately upon the entry into force of the agreement, but over a specified period of time. While Article XXIV:5 (c) explicitly contemplates this situation, it provides that '[A]ny interim agreement... shall include a plan and schedule for the formation of such customs union or of such a free trade area within a reasonable period of time'.

The objective of specifying a reasonable period of time is to avoid open-ended arrangements under which the parties would enjoy the Article XXIV exemption without actually moving to establish freer trade. However, for decades there was no agreement among the GATT Contracting Parties as to what constituted a 'reasonable period of time' so there could be no effective enforcement against agreements that contemplated periods of 15, 20, or more years. That issue was to a considerable degree resolved by the Understanding, which provides in pertinent part:

The 'reasonable length of time' referred to in paragraph 5(c) of Article XXIV should exceed 10 years only in exceptional cases. In cases where Members parties to an interim agreement believe that 10 years would be insufficient they shall provide a full explanation to the Council for Trade in Goods of the need for a longer period.[47]

Members desiring a longer interim agreement can use a procedure to provide an explanation to the Council for Trade in Goods. In the absence of a strict review process, one may reasonably question whether the requirement can be fully effective. However, it likely exerts some restraint on parties to RTAs and may discourage flagrant violations.

Concerns about the adverse effects of RTAs on non-parties have frequently been at the forefront of the Article XXIV dichotomy. Thus, Article XXIV:5 essentially provides that FTAs and customs unions (or interim agreements leading to either) should not become more trade restrictive for non-members than was the situation before the formation of the RTA, and that the interests of non-members should otherwise not be harmed. When WTO Members avail themselves of the opportunity to form free trade areas or customs unions, they may not use that situation to raise trade barriers to imports from non-members of the FTA or customs union.

---

[46] Art IX:2 WTO Agreement.
[47] Paragraph 3 of Uruguay Round Understanding on the Interpretation of Article XXIV of the General Agreement on Tariff and Trade 1994.

Determination of whether the parties to the agreement are complying with the requirement has proven problematic. Prior to the Uruguay Round, the GATT Contracting Parties disagreed on whether the determination of whether the duties are higher or more restrictive is to be based on a trade weighted average or on a simple arithmetical calculation; whether the foregoing determination is to be based on the 'bound' tariff rates agreed to by the Contracting Parties in their negotiated annexes to the GATT 1947, or on the lower 'applied' rates; and on the scope of the term 'other regulations of commerce'. The differences between customs unions and free trade areas, or interim agreements aimed at either, are significant here. By definition, a customs union will have a common external tariff, which likely means the higher tariff and lower tariff members will need to compromise in negotiating and achieving a common tariff rate structure.

Much of the confusion over these issues was resolved with the adoption of the Understanding, which specifies:

> The evaluation under paragraph 5(a) of Article XXIV of the general incidence of the duties and other regulations of commerce applicable before and after the formation of a customs union shall in respect of duties and charges be based upon an *overall assessment of weighted average tariff rates and of customs duties* collected ... For this purpose, *the duties and charges to be taken into consideration shall be the applied rates of duty*. It is recognized that for the purpose of the overall assessment of the incidence of other regulations of commerce for which quantification and aggregation are difficult, the examination of individual measures, regulations, products covered, and trade flows affected may be required.[48]

This language confirms that an overall assessment is required; it also provides guidance for the methodology and affirms that the applied (effective) rates of duty should be used for the calculations. However, it leaves some ambiguity as to the meaning of 'other regulations of commerce'. The Understanding indicates that individual measures and regulations (such as quotas and licensing rules) are to be covered and assessed on a case-by-case basis.   .

3. *Procedural Requirements*

The various procedural requirements and their implementation (or lack thereof) have also proven problematic. Further improvements, including those of 2006, may lead to better compliance with Article XXIV procedural requirements. This section assesses this possibility by looking at the legal notification and consultation requirements, and then discusses the review process by the Committee on Regional Trade Agreements (CRTA) of the GC.[49]

The Article XXIV exception to GATT disciplines is sufficiently important to require a series of notification and transparency requirements, as specified in

[48] Paragraph 2 of Uruguay Round Understanding on the Interpretation of Article XXIV of the General Agreement on Tariff and Trade 1994 (emphasis added).
[49] GC, *Committee on Regional Trade Agreements*, WT/L/127 (7 February 2006), at para 1.

Article XXIV:7. WTO Members may after study and consultations follow up with recommendations to the Members contemplating the RTA, if they find 'that such agreement is not likely to result in the formation of a customs union or of a free-trade area within the period contemplated by the parties to the agreement or that such period is not a reasonable one'.[50] Furthermore, 'the parties shall not maintain or put into force, as the case may be, such agreement if they are not prepared to modify it in accordance with these recommendations'.[51]

The review procedures were formally tightened in 1994. The Understanding noted that 'the need to reinforce the effectiveness of the role of the Council for Trade in Goods in reviewing agreements notified under Article XXIV, by clarifying the criteria and procedures for the assessment of new or enlarged agreements, and improving the transparency of all Article XXIV agreements'.[52] All notifications are to be examined by the CRTA. The CRTA is to report its findings to the Council for Trade in Goods, which then makes any appropriate recommendations to the Members contemplating the RTA. With interim agreements, the CRTA may include recommendations on the proposed time frame within the report and include a plan and schedule if none is provided. 'Substantial changes' in the interim agreement must be notified to the CRTA.

A further effort to establish more effective WTO oversight over RTAs took place in 2006, resulting in the enactment of a new 'transparency mechanism'. This mechanism calls for early announcement of new RTA negotiations, accompanied by the provision of basic information such as the identification of affected WTO provisions along with the full text including annexes and protocols. The necessary data is to be submitted by the parties within 10 weeks of notification (20 weeks for developing countries). The WTO Secretariat is to make a factual presentation (which cannot be used as a basis for dispute settlement), followed by a meeting of the Members in the CRTA (if issues arise under GATT and GATS)[53] or the Committee on Trade and Development (if issues arise under the Enabling Clause, paragraph 2(c)).

The impact of the transparency mechanism on the formulation of RTAs remains uncertain, despite the explicit requirement of a report and recommendations. The problem remains that the Article XXIV:7 requirements are honoured more in their breach than in their observance. The proliferation of RTAs effectively means that if the CRTA functions effectively, some WTO Members' delegations and the Secretariat could become overwhelmed, despite the benefit in having all RTAs being reviewed in a single committee, which can then deal with systemic issues that cut

---

[50] Art XXIV:7 (b) GATT 1994.   [51] Ibid.

[52] Paragraphs 7–10 of Uruguay Round Understanding on the Interpretation of Article XXIV of the General Agreement on Tariff and Trade 1994.

[53] While the Understanding referred only to Art XXIV GATT 1994, the Transparency Mechanism explicitly also covers Article V GATS.

across individual RTAs.[54] Since almost all WTO Members are now parties to at least one RTA, they necessarily must feel also some uneasiness in being overly critical of other Members' proposed customs unions or FTAs, lest similar criticisms be lodged against them.

Members who are affected by increases in bound rates of duty may seek also direct negotiations with the parties to the RTA, as specified under Article XXIV:6 GATT 1994. The Understanding provides only limited guidance on how to assess the existence and magnitude of an increase in duties. The Understanding does confirm that the Article XXIV:6 procedures 'must be commenced before tariff concessions are modified or withdrawn upon the formation of a customs union or an interim agreement leading to the formation of a customs union'.[55] The potential complexity of such negotiations is reflected in the fact that the EU and other WTO Members were still engaged in compensation discussions three years after the May 2004 EU expansion.[56]

C. Special Standards for Developing Countries: The 'Enabling Clause'

The GATT and now the WTO have afforded 'special and differential treatment' to developing country Members.[57] This treatment includes the 1979 Enabling Clause, which serves as the basis for developed countries to extend tariff preferences and non-tariff measures on a non-reciprocal basis to developing countries.[58] It also permits Members to 'accord differential and more favourable treatment to developing countries' through:

(c) Regional or global arrangements entered into amongst less-developed contracting parties for the mutual reduction or elimination of tariffs and, in accordance with criteria or conditions which may be prescribed by the [Members], for the mutual reduction or elimination of non-tariff measures, on products imported from one another.[59]

The Enabling Clause allows developing countries to conclude RTAs among themselves without having to be pre-occupied, for example, about covering 'substantially

---

[54] One scholar has suggested that a CRTA executive committee with rotating membership would facilitate the WTO review process. CB Picker, 'Regional Trade Agreements v the WTO: A Proposal for Reform of Article XXIV to Counter this Institutional Threat' 2005 *University of Pennsylvania Journal of International Economic Law* 26(2) 267, at 269.

[55] Paragraph 4 of Uruguay Round Understanding on the Interpretation of Article XXIV of the General Agreement on Tariff and Trade 1994.

[56] D Pruzin, 'EU Extends Deadline for WTO Talks on Enlargement-Related Compensation' 2007 *International Trade Reporter (BNA)* (24) 14.

[57] This includes Part IV GATT 1994, entitled 'Trade and Development'.

[58] Paras 1, 2(a), 2(b) Enabling Clause.   [59] Para 2(c) Enabling Clause.

all trade' or implementing an interim agreement within a reasonable period of time. However, the special and differential treatment is subject to certain limitations:

Any differential and more favourable treatment provided under this clause: a) shall be designed to facilitate and promote the trade of developing countries and not to raise barriers to or create undue difficulties for the trade of any other contracting parties; b) shall not constitute an impediment to the reduction or elimination of tariffs and other restrictions to trade on a most-favoured-nation basis.[60]

Sub-paragraph (a) reflects in substance the idea of Article XXIV:5 while sub-paragraph (b) states a vague objective that is probably impossible to monitor. Moreover, WTO Members have never formally prescribed 'criteria and conditions' for implementing this exception, either in the Understanding or elsewhere.

Review procedures for RTAs covered by paragraph 2(c) of the Enabling Clause are generally similar to those relating to Article XXIV GATT 1994 (and GATS) but are entrusted to the Committee on Trade and Development rather than the CRTA.

D. RTAs and the GATS

Uruguay Round negotiators realized that GATS would also have to deal with the issue of a potential conflict between principles such as MFN treatment in Article II GATS and the likelihood that services provisions exceeding the obligations of WTO Members' services annexes would be included in many post-Uruguay Round RTAs. The result was Article V GATS:

1. This Agreement shall not prevent any of its Members from being a party to or entering into an agreement liberalizing trade in services between or among the parties to such an agreement, provided that such an agreement:
    (a) has substantial sectoral coverage, and
    (b) provides for the absence or elimination of substantially all discrimination, in the sense of Article XVII, between or among the parties, in the sectors covered under subparagraph (a), through:
        (i)   elimination of existing discriminatory measures, and/or
        (ii) prohibition of new or more discriminatory measures,
    either at the entry into force of that agreement or on the basis of a reasonable time-frame, except for measures permitted under Articles XI, XII, XIV and XIV bis.
2. In evaluating whether the conditions under paragraph 1(b) are met, consideration may be given to the relationship of the agreement to a wider process of economic integration or trade liberalization among the countries concerned.

---

[60] Para 3 Enabling Clause.

4. Any agreement referred to in paragraph 1 shall be designed to facilitate trade between the parties to the agreement and shall not in respect of any Member outside the agreement raise the overall level of barriers to trade in services within the respective sectors or subsectors compared to the level applicable prior to such an agreement.

As is evident from the language, there are again three major requirements: 1) 'substantial sectoral coverage' (a weaker requirement than the parallel 'substantially all trade' in Article XXIV GATT 1994); 2) non-discrimination (national treatment) in those sectors covered by the agreement; and 3) no increase in services trade barriers for non-members.

However, Article V:3(a) states that 'flexibility shall be provided' where developing countries are parties to agreements under paragraph 1, 'in accordance with the level of development of the countries concerned, both overall and in individual sectors and subsectors'. If only developing countries are party, 'more favourable treatment may be given to juridical persons owned or controlled by natural persons of the parties'.[61] This means that some discrimination in favour of domestic interests is provided beyond the normal national treatment requirement. RTAs covering services are also subject to periodic reporting requirements.[62]

Application of Article V GATS potentially raises even more questions than Article XXIV GATT 1994. For example, determining when an RTA covering services has resulted in 'substantial sectoral coverage' is likely to be problematic. Similarly, unless there is actually a withdrawal of concessions granted to non-parties under GATS, it may be difficult to determine whether the services provisions in individual RTAs have effectively raised barriers to non-parties in contravention of Article V:4, thereby requiring compensation. This appears most likely to occur if a common services regime adopted by the RTA is more restrictive toward non-parties than the GATS services commitments of one or more of the RTA participants.

IV. CONFLICTS BETWEEN THE WTO AND RTAS

So far, relatively few conflicts between WTO agreements and RTAs have been adjudicated in the WTO. More will likely arise as the number of RTAs in force increases. Most of the disputes have concerned the scope of Article XXIV GATT 1994 and have raised questions of overlapping jurisdictions of the DSB and dispute settlement

---

[61] Arts V:3(a) and V:6 GATS.   [62] Art V:7 GATS.

systems created under RTAs. Since Article XXIV GATT 1994 and Article V GATS are exceptions to the MFN principle, one might reasonably expect the Appellate Body to interpret the exceptions narrowly when a Member invokes them in defence of actions that would otherwise be inconsistent with its MFN obligations.

A. Scope of Article XXIV GATT 1994

Neither the GATT dispute settlement system nor that of the WTO has fully articulated the precise limits of Article XXIV GATT 1994, though several reports have offered some clarification. In a 1985 unadopted panel report, a GATT Panel concluded that it lacked jurisdiction over challenges based on Article XXIV.[63] This report likely had a chilling effect on the willingness of subsequent panels to scrutinize closely issues relating to Article XXIV. This problem was cured in the Understanding, which provides that:

> The provisions of Articles XXII and XXIII of GATT 1994 as elaborated and applied by the Dispute Settlement Understanding may be invoked with respect to any matters arising from the application of those provisions of Article XXIV relating to customs unions, free-trade areas, or interim agreements leading to the formation of a customs union or free-trade area.[64]

Since 1994, the Appellate Body has addressed Article XXIV concerns directly in *Turkey – Textiles* and indirectly in several safeguards cases including *Argentina – Footwear (EC)* and *US – Steel Safeguards*. In *Brazil – Retreated Tyres*, it has also invited panels to scrutinize the use of Article XXIV as a defence to actions that would otherwise be inconsistent with related GATT 1994 obligations.

1. Turkey – Textiles

After the customs union between Turkey and the EU became effective in 1996, Turkey harmonized its customs duties with those of the EU. Turkey also adopted quotas on imports of textiles and clothing similar to those being applied by the EU.[65] India argued that the quantitative restrictions applied by Turkey were inconsistent with the ATC and not justified by Article XXIV GATT 1994. The Panel agreed with India and, consequently, Turkey appealed the report.

The Appellate Body held that Article XXIV GATT 1194 could be invoked as a 'defence' to what would otherwise be a violation of other GATT/WTO provisions, but only under very limited circumstances. It interpreted the phrase 'shall not

---

[63] GATT Panel Report, *EC – Citrus Products*, at para 4.15.

[64] Paragraph 12 Uruguay Round Understanding on the Interpretation of Article XXIV of the General Agreement on Tariff and Trade 1994.

[65] Panel Report, *Turkey – Textiles*, at paras 2.10–16.

prevent' in the chapeau of Article XXIV:5: as meaning 'shall not make impossible.' According to the Appellate Body:

Article XXIV may justify a measure which is inconsistent with certain other GATT provisions. However, in a case involving the formation of a customs union, this 'defence' is available only when two conditions are fulfilled. First, the party claiming the benefit of this defence must demonstrate that the measure at issue is introduced upon the formation of a customs union that fully meets the requirements of sub-paragraphs 8(a) and 5(a) of Article XXIV. And, second, that party must demonstrate that the formation of that customs union would be prevented if it were not allowed to introduce the measure at issue. Again, *both* these conditions must be met to have the benefit of the defence under Article XXIV.[66]

The Appellate Body did not consider the first prong of the test, since the Panel had assumed that the customs union was valid, and that issue was not before it.[67] The Appellate Body decided that Turkey could have met its needs through rules of origin that would have allowed the EU to distinguish between Turkish and non-Turkish goods in its own imports. Thus, Article XXIV did not justify the quantitative restrictions adopted by Turkey.[68] The Appellate Body also reiterated that the purpose of a customs union is to 'facilitate' trade among its members rather than 'to raise barriers to the trade' with third countries.[69]

   Turkey – Textiles set a high bar for the use of Article XXIV GATT 1994 as a defence to measures which would otherwise be inconsistent with Article I or other GATT 1994 obligations. The Member invoking the exception must demonstrate that the RTA is legal under Articles XXIV:8(a) and XXIV:5(a) and that the measure was necessary to the formation of the RTA. The latter, as in any 'necessity' defence under the GATT/WTO system, is problematic as in the instant case. It is also unclear as to whether the first prong of the test would bar the Article XXIV defence for measures taken after the 'formation' of the customs union, rather than at the time of formation, and how that language would apply to an interim customs union (such as MERCOSUR at the present time) still in the process of formation.

2. Brazil – Retreaded Tyres

The EC argued that Brazil's import ban on retreaded tyres, along with fines and other restrictions on the importation and marketing of retreaded tyres, were discriminatory under Articles III and XI GATT 1994. It also contended that Article XX(b) was not available to Brazil because the measure was not 'necessary'. Equally, the requirements of the chapeau were not met. Brazil's import ban on retreaded tyres exempted its MERCOSUR partners and, the EC claimed, was an 'arbitrary' and 'unjustifiable' discrimination. The EC further argued, conditionally, that the exemption Brazil provided to other MERCOSUR Members was inconsistent with

---

[66] Appellate Body Report, *Turkey – Textiles*, at para 58.
[67] Ibid at para 60.   [68] Ibid at paras 61–63.
[69] Ibid at para 57.

258 DAVID A GANTZ

Articles I and XIII GATT 1994. Finally, and also conditionally, the EC relied on *Turkey – Textiles* to argue that Article XXIV was not available to Brazil because MERCOSUR was not a valid customs union. It did not cover 'substantially all trade' under Article XXIV:8 (a). The EC submitted that Brazil had failed to demonstrate that duties and other restrictive regulations of commerce under MERCOSUR were not less restrictive after the formation of MERCOSUR than before.

Brazil did not contest that the import ban on retreaded tyres and related measures were inconsistent with Articles I, III, XI, and XIII GATT 1994. It contended that such measures were justified under Articles XX(b), XX(d), and XXIV GATT 1994. Furthermore, it submitted that its obligations under MERCOSUR required it to exempt other MERCOSUR Members from the import ban and related restrictions.

The Appellate Body determined that the import ban and other restrictions applying to non-parties but not to MERCOSUR Members resulted in arbitrary and unjustifiable discrimination under the chapeau of Article XX.[70] It did not rule on the conditional appeals based on Articles I, XIII, and XXIV GATT 1994 because the Panel had not done so. The Appellate Body did emphasize that a 'panel's discretion to decline to rule on different claims of inconsistency . . . is limited by its duty to make findings that will allow the DSB to make sufficiently precise recommendations and rulings "in order to ensure effective resolution of disputes to the benefit of all Members" '.[71]

The Appellate Body did not make any determinations under Article XXIV; it focused squarely on the discriminatory character of Brazil's import ban. As in *Turkey – Textiles*, a review of the WTO-consistency of an RTA was avoided. One can easily imagine the political repercussions if the Appellate Body were to determine, directly or indirectly, that an RTA is *per se* inconsistent with the requirements of Article XXIV. Despite the Appellate Body's instructions to panels, one can reasonably expect panels and the Appellate Body to avoid Article XXIV if possible, in favour of other non-discrimination provisions of the GATT 1994.

3. Argentina – Footwear (EC) *and* US – Steel Safeguards

Free trade areas and customs unions often incorporate provisions under which the parties to the RTA provide special treatment to the other parties in the event that one party decides to avail itself of the benefits of Article XIX GATT or the Safeguards Agreement. Other RTA parties may thus be excluded from any global safeguards measures otherwise imposed. The issue is complicated by the fact that the Safeguards Agreement contains, in Article 2.1, a non-discrimination provision dictating that 'Safeguard measures shall be applied to a product being imported irrespective of its source'.

---

[70] Appellate Body Report, *Brazil – Retreaded Tyres*, at para 258(b).
[71] Ibid at para 257, quoting Appellate Body Report, *Australia – Salmon*, at para 223.

In *Argentina – Footwear (EC)* and *US – Steel Safeguards*, the Appellate Body avoided determining whether the Article XXIV exception would permit discrimination in any or all circumstances concerning safeguards measures.[72] Instead, it embraced 'parallelism' and avoided a more direct examination of the scope of Article XXIV GATT 1994.

In *Argentina – Footwear (EC)*, Argentina contended that it could consider all imports of footwear in determining that serious injury had occurred, but impose global safeguards only on footwear imports from non-MERCOSUR Members, excluding those from Brazil. It relied on a footnote to Article 2.1 Safeguards Agreement that gives customs unions a certain leeway in how they impose safeguards when safeguards are imposed on behalf of the customs union or of a single Member.[73]

The Panel assumed that footnote 1 to Article 2 Safeguards Agreement was applicable, even though the measure was applied by Argentina rather than by MERCOSUR. The Appellate Body disagreed and decided that Argentina could not rely on its status as a Member of MERCOSUR for safeguards measures that discriminated against other sources of imported footwear imports in violation of Article 2.2 Safeguards Agreement.[74]

The Appellate Body also decided that it was inappropriate for the Argentine authorities to consider intra-MERCOSUR footwear imports in determining the existence of serious injury, but impose safeguard measures that excluded footwear imports from other MERCOSUR Members. Under Article 2.2 Safeguards Agreement, if Argentina relied on imports from all sources as the basis for its serious injury finding, it was obliged to apply the safeguards measures to imports from all sources.

The Appellate Body took a similar 'parallelism' approach in *US-Steel Safeguards*.[75] The US International Trade Commission (USITC) excluded from its steel safeguards NAFTA Parties Mexico and Canada, and its FTA partners Israel and Jordan.[76] The Panel had found that 'the increase of these [excluded] imports cannot be used to support a conclusion that the product in question "is being imported in such increased quantities so as to cause serious injury". *This makes it necessary… to account for the fact that excluded imports may have some injurious impact on the domestic industry'.*[77] The USITC's exclusion of imports from Mexico, Canada, Israel, and Jordan from the safeguard measures, after relying on them for the injury determination, created in the view of the Appellate Body a 'gap between the imports that were taken into account in the investigation performed by the USITC and the imports falling within

---

[72] The Appellate Body Report in *US – Wheat Gluten* follows a similar reasoning.

[73] See also R Bhala and D Gantz, 'WTO Case Review 2000' 2001 *Arizona Journal of International and Comparative Law* 18(1) 1, at 76.

[74] Appellate Body Report, *Argentina – Footwear (EC)*, at paras 99–114. The footnote would have applied only if MERCOSUR, rather than Argentina individually, had applied the safeguards.

[75] See also R Bhala and D Gantz, 'WTO Case Review 2003' 2004 *Arizona Journal of International and Comparative Law* 21(2) 317, at 393.

[76] NAFTA, unlike MERCOSUR, provides no mechanism for regional application of safeguards.

[77] Appellate Body Report, *US – Steel Safeguards*, at para 434 (quoting the Panel Report).

the scope of the measures as applied'.[78] It was the USITC's responsibility 'to justify this gap by establishing explicitly, in its report, that imports from sources covered by the measures—that is imports from sources *other than* the excluded countries of Canada, Israel, Jordan, and Mexico—satisfy, *alone*, and in and of themselves, the conditions for the application of a safeguard measure...'[79]

The principle emerging from these Appellate Body reports is that if imports from RTA partners are used in the determination of serious injury, they cannot be excluded from the safeguard measures. The safest approach for the investigating authority is to exclude RTA partner imports at the outset from the imports used as the basis of determining serious injury.[80] While the reasoning does not depend on Article XXIX, the implications for RTAs are significant. The rationale makes it much more difficult for the RTA Members to protect other Members from safeguards measures, potentially creating significant political and economic issues within the RTA, and acting as yet another factor discouraging WTO Member usage of global safeguards.

B. Conflicts Between WTO and RTA Dispute Settlement Mechanisms

The paucity of conflicts to date between the WTO DSB and parallel mechanisms in RTAs may result in part from the fact that many of the RTAs concluded by WTO Members other than the EU and the US have traditionally avoided rules-based dispute settlement mechanisms, preferring 'soft,' diplomatically oriented systems. However, this is changing as it becomes more evident that the lack of a rules-based system makes it difficult to move the RTAs towards deeper and more effective integration.

Several of the decisions discussed in this section turn on unusual factors or RTA provisions that make repetition in other contexts unlikely, even though conflicts between WTO and RTA obligations themselves are likely to increase. Under many RTA dispute settlement provisions a complaining Party must make an election between the RTA mechanism and the DSB.[81] As these examples suggest, the election requirement is not always effective.

1. Mexico – Tax Measures on Soft Drinks

The dispute arose between the US and Mexico regarding Mexican taxes on soft drinks using corn syrup (HFCS) instead of cane sugar. Mexico saw the case as a

---

[78] Ibid at para 443.   [79] Ibid at para 444.

[80] Under Article 802 NAFTA, Parties are required to exclude imports from other Parties unless 'imports from a Party, considered individually, account for a substantial share of total imports' and such imports 'contribute importantly to the serious injury, or threat thereof, caused by imports'.

[81] See, eg, Art 2005(1) NAFTA.

dispute between the two countries over Mexican sugar exports to the US; the US did not. Mexico sought adjudication of the sugar issues under Chapter 20 NAFTA, but the US refused to cooperate in the appointment of a panel.[82] Mexico retaliated by imposing certain taxes on HFCS, which became the basis of the US' WTO complaint. That complaint did not request the DSB to consider the NAFTA-related (sugar) aspects of the broader controversy.

Mexico asked the WTO Panel to refrain from exercising jurisdiction over the tax dispute, but the Panel and later the Appellate Body demurred. Both reasoned that the Panel had an obligation, under Article 11 DSU, to decide the case and that it lacked the authority to decline to exercise its jurisdiction and thus fail to make the required 'objective assessment'. The Panel and the Appellate Body also agreed, citing Articles 3.2 and 19.2 DSU, that should a panel decide not to exercise jurisdiction in a case properly before it, the report would diminish the rights of a complainant under the DSU and relevant WTO texts seeking redress for an alleged violation of obligations owed to it.[83]

The Appellate Body also concurred with the Panel's finding that 'neither the subject matter nor the respective positions of the parties are identical in the dispute under the NAFTA ... and the dispute before us'. This conclusion was based in part on Mexico's admission that it 'could not identify a legal basis that would allow it to raise, in a WTO dispute settlement proceeding, the market access claims it is pursuing under the NAFTA' and that no NAFTA panel had actually decided the broader dispute.[84] While the Appellate Body did not foreclose the possibility that there might be 'other circumstances in which legal impediments could exist that would preclude a panel from ruling on the merits of the claims that are before it', it emphasized that it saw 'no basis in the DSU for panels and the Appellate Body to adjudicate non-WTO disputes'.[85]

Whether the Appellate Body would have treated the issues differently had there been a NAFTA Chapter 20 Panel decision or had such panel proceedings been underway at the time of the WTO complaint cannot be determined. The report strongly suggests, however, that the Appellate Body is not prepared to adjudicate complaints based on substantive provisions of RTAs that are not also contained in the GATT 1994 or other WTO agreements. Similar conflicts have arisen within MERCOSUR.[86]

---

[82] The NAFTA Chapter 20 system is flawed in the sense that panel selection is automatic only if the Parties have designated standing panel rosters, as required by Art 2009(1). Since the NAFTA Parties have never done so, panel section must be made on an *ad hoc* basis, and either disputing party can prevent the dispute from moving forward simply by refusing to cooperate in appointment of the panel.

[83] Appellate Body Report, *Mexico – Taxes on Soft Drinks*, at paras 51–53.

[84] Ibid at para 54.

[85] Ibid at paras 54–56. See also chapter 12 of this Handbook.

[86] See Panel Report, *Argentina – Poultry Anti-Dumping Duties,* at paras 7.17–42, where the Panel declined Argentina's request either to refrain from ruling or to consider the earlier MERCOSUR arbitral tribunal ruling.

2. *NAFTA*, US Safeguards – Brooms[87]

After a domestic industry petition was filed under both Article 801 NAFTA and the WTO Safeguards Agreement, and the investigating authority completed the required investigations, the US sought to apply safeguard measures to protect its broomcorn broom industry.[88] However, the US applied the safeguards only under the GATT/WTO provisions, not under the parallel provisions of Chapter 8 NAFTA.[89] The dispute was addressed only by a NAFTA Chapter 20 Panel; it never reached the DSB.

Mexico requested the establishment of a Chapter 20 Panel to examine the legality of the safeguards 'in light of the relevant provisions of the North American Free Trade Agreement' which deal explicitly with global as well as regional safeguards.[90] The Panel, at least initially, viewed Mexico's contention as a 'single overarching legal claim' incorporating the GATT/WTO rules that control basic safeguards measures under NAFTA.

The US argued that the Panel had no jurisdiction to adjudicate the conformity of US actions with 'global safeguard measures' but only with those under NAFTA. Article 802 NAFTA, unlike some other NAFTA provisions, does not incorporate GATT/WTO law by reference, and the US asserted that it was the intent of the NAFTA Parties that any issues related to global safeguards be pursued through the DSB. Mexico argued that the present dispute arose under both NAFTA and the WTO, and that the Panel necessarily had jurisdiction to dispose of all overlapping GATT 1994 issues involved in the dispute.

The Panel avoided what could have become a bitter intra-NAFTA dispute by disposing of the issues under NAFTA alone. The Panel decided, moreover, that both NAFTA and the Safeguards Agreement contained the same rules requiring the investigating authority to publish a report detailing its findings and reasoned conclusions on all pertinent issues; the result was the same whether it applied NAFTA law or WTO law. In either instance, the USITC had failed to meet the applicable standard. This approach by the Panel was at least partly a result of the US and Mexico coming to the conclusion that it was probably best to avoid NAFTA panel rulings based on interpretations of the WTO covered agreements.

Brooms illustrates the risk of RTAs either incorporating GATT/WTO principles directly into RTAs or cross-referencing without formal incorporation. Given the broad jurisdiction of many RTA dispute settlement systems, it seems likely that from time to time it will be difficult for panels to resolve the RTA issues without addressing, at least indirectly as in *Brooms*, the validity of the measure under WTO law.

[87] NAFTA Chapter 20 Panel, *US Safeguard Action Taken on Broomcorn Brooms from Mexico*, Case No USA-97-2008-01, decided 30 January 1998, at <http://www.nafta-sec-alena.org/DefaultSite/index_e.aspx?DetailID=76> (last visited 22 June 2007).
[88] Brooms made of natural fibre rather than plastic.
[89] NAFTA Chapter 20 Panel, above fn 87, at paras 12–13.
[90] Arts 802 and 803 NAFTA.

The possibility of divergent interpretations of WTO law, as both the US and Mexico ultimately feared, cannot be excluded. Nor is a provision in the RTA barring panels from adjudicating WTO issues likely to be effective, since in some instances it may be impossible for a panel to rule without resolving questions under the global legal system, at least implicitly.

3. *The* Softwood Lumber *Dispute*

A detailed analysis of the softwood lumber actions taking place on parallel tracks in the DSB and under Chapter 19 NAFTA is well beyond the scope of this Chapter.[91] Generally, antidumping (AD) and countervailing duty (CVD) determinations such as those involving Canadian softwood lumber exports to the US may not be challenged under Chapter 20 NAFTA.[92] However, NAFTA has no provision for dealing directly with potential conflicts between the DSU and Chapter 19. In such circumstances, no choice of forum is required, and it is therefore possible for the DSB and NAFTA to exercise concurrent jurisdiction. Chapter 19, a dispute settlement system that is unique among RTAs,[93] provides a means for private 'interested parties' to challenge national administrative AD/CVD determinations made under national law before the matter is brought before bi-national panels, which sit essentially as surrogates for the respective federal courts of the Parties. Numerous challenges relating to antidumping, countervailing duty, injury, and administrative review decisions relating to lumber have been lodged under Chapter 19.[94]

Simultaneously, Canada initiated a series of WTO actions against the US.[95] They involved the same administrative decisions but engaged a different body of law. NAFTA bi-national panels and WTO panels and the Appellate Body reached different conclusions on the same administrative determinations. With some exceptions, Canadian views prevailed before the NAFTA bi-national panels, and US views prevailed before the DSB. Still, neither process was effectively final when the parties reached a settlement agreement in October 2006. It is telling that both the WTO and NAFTA dispute settlement procedures are displaced by a settlement agreement. The agreement provides that disputes under it are to be settled exclusively through

---

[91] See JL Dunoff, 'The Many Dimensions of *Softwood Lumber*' 2007 *Alberta Law Review* 45(2) 319.

[92] Art 2004 NAFTA.

[93] Chapter 19 NAFTA has not been replicated in any of the many subsequent FTAs concluded by the NAFTA Parties with other States.

[94] Art 1904 NAFTA. See *Softwood Lumber Products from Canada (Injury)*, USA-CDA-2002-1904-07 (19 April 2004, 31 August 2004); *Softwood Lumber Products from Canada (CVD)*, USA-CDA-2002-1904-03 (7 June 2004, 1 December 2004); *Softwood Lumber Products from Canada (Dumping)*, USA-CDA-2002-1904-02 (9 June 2005), at <http://www.nafta-sec-alena.org/DefaultSite/index_e.aspx?DetailID=76> (last visited 13 June 2007).

[95] See, eg, Appellate Body reports in *US – Softwood Lumber IV* and *US – Softwood Lumber V* and Panel report in *US – Softwood Lumber VI*.

arbitration at the London Court of International Arbitration (LCIA).[96] As of early 2008, the US had initiated two arbitrations before the LCIA.[97]

It is possible that parties will make special arrangements in NAFTA or other RTAs to exclude in certain matters and on an *ad hoc* basis the jurisdiction of the DSB or the RTA dispute settlement system in certain matters on an ad hoc basis. However, the uniqueness of the Chapter 19 NAFTA mechanism needs to be empha-sized. Ultimately, lawyers will likely find ways of framing disputes in such a manner as to permit parallel actions both in the WTO and within the RTA mechanism, thereby evading choice of forum requirements in the RTA provisions and giving those States two bites of the apple, as in softwood lumber.

V. Conclusions

Despite the proliferation of RTAs in recent years, there is no consensus on whether the effect of RTAs on the multilateral trading system is harmful or beneficial as a whole, or whether that analysis can only be addressed on a case-by-case basis. Nor is it clear, even with the adoption of the 2006 Transparency Mechanism, that the WTO is capable of monitoring effectively the consistency of new RTAs with Article XXIV GATT 1994 and Article V GATS through the CRTA or in the DSB. Recent reports suggest that the Appellate Body is now prepared to rule on key issues related to RTAs, such as discrimination between RTA members and non-members. However, its willingness to determine that a particular RTA is fundamentally inconsistent with Article XXIV GATT 1994 is as yet untested. The proliferation of RTAs will almost certainly continue, even if the Doha Round is eventually successfully con-cluded. This factor, along with a tendency towards more rules-based dispute settle-ment in existing RTAs, such as in MERCOSUR and the ASEAN FTA, also make it likely that conflicts between RTAs and the WTO covered agreements and among dispute settlement systems will increase over time.

Selected Bibliography

J Bhagwati, *Free Trade Today* (Princeton: Princeton University Press, 2002)

J Bhagwati and A Panagariya (eds), *Economics of Preferential Trade Agreements* (Washington, DC: American Enterprise Institute, 1996)

[96] Article XIV:2 Softwood Lumber Agreement between the Government of Canada and the Government of the US of America, done at Ottawa, 12 September 2006, at <http://www.dfait-maeci.gc.ca/eicb/softwood/pdfs/SLA-en.pdf> (last visited 25 January 2008).

[97] R Brevetti, 'US Files Second Arbitration under Canada Lumber Pact' 2008 *International Trade Reporter (BNA)* (25) 132.

R Bhala, *Modern GATT Law* (London: Thomson/Sweet & Maxwell, 2005)

V Bulmer-Thomas, *The Economic History of Latin America Since Independence* (Cambridge: Cambridge University Press, 2003)

O Cadot, A Estavaderoral, AS Eisenmann, and T Verdier (eds), *The Origin of Goods* (Oxford: Oxford University Press, 2006)

Consultative Board, *The Future of the WTO: Addressing Institutional Challenges in the New Millennium* (Geneva: WTO, 2004)

JL Dunoff, 'The Many Dimensions of *Softwood Lumber*' 2007 *Alberta Law Review* 45(2) 319

J Frankel, *Regional Trading Blocs in the World Economic System* (Washington: Institute for International Economics, 1997)

D Gantz, *Regional Trade Agreements: Law, Policy & Practice* (Durham: Carolina Academic Press, forthcoming 2009)

Z Hafez, *The Dimensions of Regional Trade Integration in Southeast Asia* (New York: Transnational, 2004)

T Hartley, *The Foundations of European Community Law*, 6th edn (Oxford: Oxford University Press, 2007)

B Hoekman and M Kostecki, *The Political Economy of the World Trading System: The WTO and Beyond* (Oxford: Oxford University Press, 2001)

K Kennedy (ed.), *The First Decade of NAFTA: The Future of Free Trade in North America* (New York: Transnational, 2004)

J Mander and E Goldsmith (eds), *The Case Against the Global Economy* (San Francisco: Sierra Club Books, 1996)

T O'Keefe, *Latin American Trade Agreements* (Boston: Brill/Martinius Nijhoff, 2007)

R Pomfret, *The Economics of Regional Trading Arrangements* (Oxford: Clarendon Press, 1997)

R Porrata-Doria, Jr, *MERCOSUR: the Common Market of the Southern Cone* (Durham: Carolina Academic Press, 2005)

HS Shapiro, *Fast Track: A Legal, Historical, and Political Analysis* (New York: Transnational, 2006)

J Viner, *The Customs Union Issue* (New York: Carnegie, 1950)

JHH Weiler, *The Constitution of Europe* (Cambridge: Cambridge University Press, 1999)

WTO, *Overview of Developments in the International Trading Environment, A Global View of RTAs* (Geneva: WTO, 2004)

PART III

SETTLEMENT OF DISPUTES

CHAPTER 11

THE INSTITUTIONAL DIMENSION

VALERIE HUGHES

I. INTRODUCTION

A. Origins

THE WTO dispute settlement system has its origins in Articles XXII and XXIII GATT 1947. These two articles provide that complaints about matters affecting the operation of the GATT 1947, or failure to carry out GATT obligations, are to be discussed by the parties concerned with a view to finding a solution. If none is found, the GATT membership as a whole must investigate the complaint and make a recommendation or give a ruling and, in some circumstances, authorize retaliation. Other than these very general directives, Articles XXII and XXIII are silent on applicable rules and procedures. The mechanism for resolving disputes under the GATT 1947 essentially left the details to those that found themselves in disagreement about GATT obligations, with the result that the dispute resolution procedure evolved over time as needs arose and experience suggested.

In the very early days, trade disputes were dealt with at plenary meetings of the GATT membership on a semi-annual basis; subsequently, they were addressed by intercessional committees of the membership. Later, Working Parties composed of a number of GATT 1947 Contracting Parties (five to twenty, depending upon how many were interested in a particular dispute) were tasked with resolving differences. Eventually, by the early 1950s, disputes were commonly adjudicated by panels of three or five persons. Procedural conventions developed over time, which were formalized in 1979 during the Tokyo Round negotiations. The GATT Contracting Parties adopted the Understanding Regarding Notification, Consultation, Dispute Settlement and Surveillance,[1] which included an Annex entitled 'Agreed Description of the Customary Practice of the GATT in the Field of Dispute Settlement (Article XXIII:2)'. The Annex recorded the 'customary practice of the GATT in the field of dispute settlement' and concluded that it should be continued along with a few 'improvements' set out in the Understanding.[2]

By the 1980s, the GATT dispute settlement system had evolved considerably, but it was far from ideal. It remained essentially a diplomatic rather than legal exercise, and emphasis was placed on diplomacy and agreement rather than legal rules and procedures. This approach had its strengths, but it was also plagued by weaknesses. No legal process could be pursued unless there was positive consensus by all Contracting Parties to do so. A defending party was able to block or significantly delay—even by years—the establishment of a dispute settlement panel, and a party could block the adoption of a panel report that went against it. Moreover, the system

---

[1] GATT, *Understanding Regarding Notification, Consultation, Dispute Settlement and Surveillance*, L/4907 (28 November 1979), BISD 26 Supp 210 (1980).

[2] Ibid at 2.

produced highly uneven results in terms of legal quality of decisions. GATT dispute settlement was also described as 'more responsive to the interests of the strong than the interests of the weak'.[3]

B. Underlying Principles

Against this background, Uruguay Round negotiators determined to develop a rules-based dispute settlement system and they set out to craft a system that would eliminate the weaknesses perceived to exist under the GATT 1947. At the conclusion of the Uruguay Round, in the Marrakesh Declaration of 15 April 1994, Ministers 'welcomed' the new dispute settlement system and underlined 'the stronger and clearer legal framework they [had] adopted for the conduct of international trade, including a more effective and reliable dispute settlement mechanism'.

The current dispute settlement process, adopted in 1995 when the WTO was established, is governed by the Understanding on Rules and Procedures Governing the Settlement of Disputes (DSU). The DSU contains procedural rules set out in 27 articles and four appendices, and is complemented by the Working Procedures for Appellate Review, which govern the appellate process.

WTO dispute settlement is founded on certain underlying principles set out in the opening paragraphs of the DSU. Article 3.2 DSU describes the WTO dispute settlement system as 'a *central* element in providing *security and predictability* to the multilateral trading system'.[4] It also stipulates that 'the *aim* of the dispute settlement mechanism is to secure a *positive solution* to a dispute'.[5] And finally, it says that 'the *first* objective of the dispute settlement mechanism is usually *to secure the withdrawal of the measures* concerned if these are found to be inconsistent with the provisions of any of the covered agreements'.[6] These principles inform the rules set out in the DSU and govern dispute settlement generally: dispute settlement is a central component of the WTO, not a sideline. It is intended to provide security and predictability to the trading system, not *ad hoc* solutions to specific disputes; its goal is securing resolution of a problem, not creating regulatory uncertainty; and the primary objective is withdrawal of the offending measure, not retaliation and punitive damages.

The WTO dispute settlement system has been widely praised and was considered a success from the beginning.[7] One reason is the significant improvements

---

[3] RE Hudec, *Enforcing International Trade Law: The Evolution of the Modern GATT Legal System* (Salem, N.H.: Butterworths, 1993), at 353.

[4] Emphasis added.

[5] Emphasis added.

[6] Emphasis added.

[7] See Consultative Board, *The Future of the WTO: Addressing Institutional Challenges in the New Millennium* (Geneva: WTO, 2004).

it provides over the GATT system. For example, the current system is regarded as rules-based rather than power-based, avoiding the criticism levelled at the GATT process of favouring the 'strong' over the 'weak'.[8] Another important enhancement is the virtual 'automaticity' of certain steps in the regime. As noted above, under the GATT system, it was necessary to have a positive consensus of all GATT Contracting Parties to establish a dispute settlement panel and to adopt panel reports. This was difficult to achieve given that the challenged or losing GATT Contracting Party could block these procedures. Under the WTO rules, panels are established and reports are adopted unless there is consensus of WTO Members *not* to do so, which is unlikely to occur. In fact, no panel or Appellate Body report has ever failed to be adopted by the Dispute Settlement Body (DSB).[9]

Perhaps the most significant change brought about by the new dispute settlement system is the right to appellate review of panel reports. The establishment of the WTO Appellate Body has led to the development of a rich body of international trade law, now found in close to 90 Appellate Body reports, that serves to guide WTO Members and panels in applying and enforcing WTO rights and obligations.

Despite its undoubted and oft-cited success, the WTO dispute settlement system does have its critics and there are flaws in its design. Some criticize its confidentiality, as much of the dispute settlement activity goes on behind closed doors. Others complain that the system is too slow, as it can take two or three years to obtain a ruling and remedies are not retroactive. The lack of enforcement tools is also considered to be a weakness. None of these alleged weaknesses, however, has posed significant problems thus far. Developed and developing WTO Members continue to demonstrate confidence in the system by resorting to it regularly; dispute settlement activity has not abated over time. Indeed, the WTO dispute settlement system remains the busiest international law adjudicative system in the world.[10] Moreover, the compliance rate with WTO reports remains very high (only

---

[8] The fact that the very first decision rendered by the WTO Appellate Body was in favour of two developing countries (Venezuela and Brazil) that had challenged a US measure made it difficult to allege otherwise. Appellate Body Report, *US – Gasoline*.

[9] One WTO panel report (*EC – Bananas III (Article 21.5 – EC)*) was circulated in 1999 but has never been adopted. However, this was not because there was a positive consensus not to adopt the report; rather, the report was never put forward for adoption. The case, however, was somewhat unusual. The EC had requested the establishment of a panel to determine that certain measures taken with a view to implementing a WTO ruling must be presumed to conform to WTO rules because they had not been challenged under the DSU. WTO Members who had launched the original complaint against the EC (the US, Honduras, and Guatemala) leading to the compliance action in question declined to participate in the Panel. The Panel found against the EC, with the result that the EC never requested adoption of the report. Nor did the original complainants.

[10] At the end of 2007, 132 panel reports had been adopted (110 regular panel reports and 22 compliance panel reports) and the Appellate Body had issued 84 reports. In addition, 43 arbitrations

a handful of adopted reports have not been implemented) and non-compliance is generally confined to especially contentious matters, often with a history dating back to pre-WTO times.[11]

C. Discussions on Reforming Dispute Settlement Procedures

Discussions are ongoing on possible 'improvements and clarifications' to the DSU. These discussions have been underway since 1999, pursuant to a decision taken by WTO Members in 1994.[12] It was assumed, before the DSU was put in place, that it would be necessary to examine the dispute settlement rules once they had been operating for a few years to see whether they were working properly and to adjust them in the light of experience as necessary. A limited number of proposals for reform were to be considered at the Ministerial Conference (MC) held in Seattle in 1999, but the meeting ended in failure before there was an opportunity to discuss them. Discussions have continued over the years, both in formal WTO negotiating sessions in a Special Session of the DSB and in informal groups composed of six or seven WTO Members.[13] Several WTO Members, both developed and developing, have put forward numerous proposals. Some suggestions call for changes of a technical character, while others call for significant amendments to the DSU that would alter the nature of the system as originally crafted.[14] Some of these proposals are discussed below.

The DSU discussions are not formally part of the Doha Development Agenda negotiations. Strictly speaking, therefore, DSU reform need not await progress in other subject areas. Nevertheless, it is widely accepted that the DSU negotiations will figure in the broader package of WTO reform. Given the glacial pace of the Doha negotiations, DSU reform is not likely to take place very soon.

(under Articles 21.3, 22.6, and 25 DSU) and 1 mediation were completed. Compare with the ICJ: in its first 50 years it issued 61 judgments plus 23 advisory reports.

[11] See B Wilson, 'Compliance By WTO Members With Adverse WTO Dispute Settlement Rulings' in ME Janow, V Donaldson, and A Yanovich (eds), *The WTO: Governance, Dispute Settlement & Developing Countries* (Huntington, New York: Juris Publishing, Inc., 2008) 777.

[12] MC, *Decision on the Application and Review of the Understanding of Rules and Procedures Governing the Settlement of Disputes*, LT/UR/D-1/6 (15 April 1994).

[13] One group was referred to informally as the 'Magnificent Seven'. The original members were Argentina, Brazil, Canada, India, Mexico, New Zealand, and Norway.

[14] For an in-depth review of proposals for amendment, see V Hughes, 'The WTO dispute settlement system – from initiating proceedings to ensuring implementation: what needs improvement?' in G Sacerdoti, A Yanovich, and J Bohanes (eds), *The WTO at Ten: The Contribution of the Dispute Settlement System* (Cambridge: Cambridge University Press, 2006) 193.

II. The Institutions

A. Director-General of the WTO

The Director-General (DG), the head of the WTO chosen by the Members, can participate in dispute settlement in different ways. Article 5.6 DSU states that the DG may act in an *ex officio* capacity and 'offer good offices, conciliation, or mediation with a view to assisting Members to settle a dispute'.[15] Although it is difficult to know exactly how often good offices or conciliation services have been provided given their confidential character, not many Members are thought to have taken advantage of these options. Indeed, in a statement issued in July 2001, the DG indicated that Article 5 facilities had never been used since the inception of the WTO.[16] He encouraged resort to good offices, conciliation, and mediation as means of reaching mutually agreed solutions (as opposed to legal conclusions, which he considered best left to formal dispute settlement) and set out nine procedures to be followed for action pursuant to Article 5. The procedures require that consultations pursuant to Article 4 DSU precede a request to the DG for the provision of good offices, conciliation, or mediation. They permit *ex parte* communications and stipulate that all communications during the process 'shall remain confidential and shall not be revealed at any time, including during any other procedures undertaken pursuant to the DSU'.[17] Moreover, third parties may participate only with the concurrence of the disputants.

We know that at least one mediation has taken place. In 2002, the Philippines, Thailand, and the EC requested the DG 'to examine the extent to which the legitimate interests of the Philippines and Thailand are being unduly impaired as a result of the implementation by the European Communities of the preferential tariff treatment for canned tuna originating in ACP states'.[18] With the consent of the parties, the DG appointed Deputy DG Rufus Yerxa as mediator. The results of the mediation remain confidential pursuant to the request of the WTO Members involved. Interestingly, the parties did not consider the matter to be a 'dispute' falling under the DSU, but agreed that the mediation process could be guided by the procedures set out by the DG for Article 5 processes. Communications about the mediation, limited in detail though they were, were made to the General Council (GC) and not to the DSB.[19]

---

[15] Art 5.6 DSU.

[16] WTO, *Article 5 of the Dispute Settlement Understanding – Communication from the Director General*, WT/DSB/25 (17 July 2001).

[17] Ibid, at Appendix B, point 7.

[18] GC, *Request for Mediation by The Philippines, Thailand and the European Communities – Communication from the Director-General, Addendum*, WT/GC/66/Add.1 (23 December 2002).

[19] GC, *Request for Mediation by the Philippines, Thailand and the European Communities – Communication from the Director-General*, WT/GC/66 (16 October 2002).

The DG can also play a role in selecting panelists when disputing Members are unable to agree on panel composition. If there is no agreement on panelists within 20 days after the establishment of a panel, either party to the dispute may request the DG to appoint one or more panelists. The DG must make the appointment(s) within 10 days of receiving the request.[20] This option has been used regularly almost from the beginning, though resort to DG composition has been used in a higher percentage of cases in recent years.[21] One can only speculate as to why this is so. Perhaps it is because it is difficult to reach agreement among parties on someone perceived as neutral when numerous WTO Members are involved in a dispute in one capacity or another. It may also be explained, at least in part, by the fact that some WTO Members have developed opposing preferences over time in terms of panelists' qualities, such as academics versus diplomats, or lawyers versus technical specialists (for example, in SPS matters). In addition, most disputing parties require panel experience, but with that quality may come a reputation for one approach or another, with the result that a party will not agree to appoint certain people given a previous performance on a panel. It must also be acknowledged that some Members seek to delay the start of the panel process by holding back agreement on panelists, with the result that the other party turns to the DG to get the process back on track. Whatever the reason, it is more likely now than in the first few years of WTO dispute settlement that the DG will be called upon to compose a panel in a particular dispute.

B. DSB

The DSB was established pursuant to Article 2.1 DSU to administer the dispute settlement process. It generally meets monthly[22] and membership is open to all WTO Members. Its Chair is selected from among the WTO ambassadors in Geneva to serve for one year. It is a prestigious appointment, and is often the stepping stone to the chairmanship of the GC, the WTO's most influential decision-making body. The DSB Chair is assisted by the WTO Secretariat, which prepares the agenda for the meetings based on matters submitted by WTO Members, drafts the minutes of the meetings and provides advice to the Chair on rules and procedures.

---

[20] Art 8.7 DSU.

[21] According to statistics compiled by the WTO Legal Affairs Division, in 1995, the DG was not involved in composing any of the four panels composed that year; in 2005, the DG was involved in composing all seven panels composed that year. In the first few years of the WTO (1995–2000), DG involvement in panel composition occurred on average in 42 per cent of panels composed each year. In more recent years (2001–2007), the DG has been involved on average in 75 per cent of panels composed each year. See also DSB (Special Session), *The European Communities' Replies to India's Questions – Communication from the European Communities*, TN/DS/W/7 (30 May 2002), at 2.

[22] Art 2.3 DSU provides that the DSB shall meet as often as necessary to carry out its functions. Special DSB meetings are scheduled from time to time to deal with time-sensitive matters.

The DSB establishes panels, adopts panel and Appellate Body reports, and authorizes suspension of concessions and other WTO obligations when Members are not in compliance with their WTO obligations. Decisions are taken by consensus. The DSB also maintains surveillance of implementation of panel and Appellate Body reports, requiring progress reports by Members at the meetings. In addition, the DSB administers the process for appointing Appellate Body Members.

During DSB meetings, WTO Members often deliver important position papers or politically charged statements either agreeing or disagreeing with interpretations of WTO obligations in panel or Appellate Body reports, or decrying the failure by a losing party to implement a dispute settlement report. There are a few cases that have been on the DSB's surveillance list for years because implementation remains outstanding.[23] The DSB does not respond to such statements and merely takes note of them in the minutes. Although DSB meetings are not open to the public, minutes of DSB meetings are made available on the WTO website 45 days after they are circulated to WTO Members.

Negotiations on dispute settlement reform take place in a 'special session' of the DSB, presided over by a different chairperson. The frequency of these sessions has varied considerably over the years.

C. Panels

If disputes between WTO Members cannot be resolved through formal consultations as provided for in Article 4 DSU, WTO Members have recourse to the panel process. Panels are established by the DSB at the request of a complaining party Member.[24] They are composed on an *ad hoc* basis of three individuals selected by the parties.[25] Panel selection is carried out with the assistance of the WTO Secretariat, which puts forward a list of names to the parties at a meeting at the WTO.[26] Although parties 'shall not oppose nominations except for compelling reasons',[27] rejection of proposed individuals occurs regularly and compelling reasons are not always provided. If the first list of names does not meet with the parties' agreement in whole or in part, a further list or lists of names are presented until there is agreement on three

---

[23] Examples include *US – Hot-Rolled Steel* and *US – Offset Act (Byrd Amendment)*.

[24] Art 6 DSU.

[25] Art 8.5 DSU permits five-member panels though none has ever been established.

[26] Art 8.6 DSU. The Secretariat maintains a list of qualified individuals from which panelists may be drawn. From time to time, WTO Members propose governmental and non-governmental individuals to be included on the indicative list pursuant to Article 8.4 DSU. Although the indicative list includes a number of individuals that have served as panelists, it is not relied upon exclusively for panel selection purposes because proposals for addition are not vetted and placement on the list is not necessarily indicative of ideal qualifications to serve as panelists.

[27] Art 8.6 DSU.

individuals. This process can take several weeks or even months unless, as indicated above, one of the parties moves to request the DG to compose the panel. The DG does not negotiate panel composition; he or she simply provides the names of the individuals to the parties and the panel is composed.

Panelists serve in their individual capacities and not as representatives of their governments. The necessary qualifications are set out in the DSU: well-qualified governmental or non-governmental individuals, including persons who have served on a panel, presented a case to a panel, served as a government representative on a GATT or WTO Committee, served as a senior trade policy official of a government, worked in the WTO Secretariat and taught or published on international trade law or policy.[28] Panelists need not be lawyers, though a panel composed of three non-lawyers is rare. Members usually insist on having persons with panel experience. Panelists cannot be citizens of disputing parties or of third party participants, unless there is agreement otherwise.[29] For this reason, citizens of heavy users of the system like the US and the EC do not often sit on panels. Most panel members are current or former government officials and their nationality varies considerably, though citizens from New Zealand, Australia, and Switzerland top the list (in that order).[30] Panel members must adhere to rules of conduct 'designed to maintain the integrity, impartiality, and confidentiality of proceedings conducted under the DSU'[31] and are required to be independent and impartial, avoid direct or indirect conflicts of interest, and respect the confidentiality of proceedings. Although assisted by Secretariat staff, serving as a panellist is time-consuming, especially in fact-intensive cases, and remuneration is minimal.[32] Nevertheless, it remains a prestigious and sought-after appointment.

At the end of 2007, a total of 158 panels had been established by the DSB, an average of twelve per year.[33] The peak was in 1999, when twenty panels were established; 1995 was the low point with only five panels established. The number of panels established in 2004 and 2005 was on the low side at seven and eight, respectively. However, the downturn was short-lived, as there were twelve panels established in 2006 and eleven in 2007.

WTO panels (and the WTO Appellate Body) are sometimes referred to as 'quasi-judicial' institutions. Technically, panels are not 'courts' and those who sit in judgment are not 'judges'. Panels do not make 'decisions'; rather, they issue reports

---

[28] Art 8.1 DSU.   [29] Art 8.3 DSU.

[30] See K Leitner and S Lester, 'WTO Dispute Settlement 1995–2007 – A Statistical Analysis' 2008 *Journal of International and Economic Law* 11(1) 179.

[31] See WTO, *Appellate Body – Working Procedures*, WT/AB/WP/5 (4 January 2005), Annex II.

[32] Panelists are paid a fee of 600 Swiss francs per day. Air fare (plus 200 francs for airport transfers) and an allowance (between 360 and 421 Swiss francs per day) for accommodation and meals when attending panel meetings in Geneva are also provided. Government employees who serve as panelists are not entitled to the 600 francs fee.

[33] This includes panels established to hear compliance cases under Article 21.5 DSU. The total number of panels composed as of that date is 135.

that contain findings and conclusions about the matters in dispute. When a panel concludes that a Member's measure is inconsistent with one or more WTO provisions, the panel makes a 'recommendation' that the DSB request the Member to bring its measure(s) into conformity with WTO obligations.[34] Although the DSU permits panels also to 'suggest ways in which the Member concerned could implement the recommendations',[35] this does not occur frequently. A panel report must be adopted by the DSB within 60 days of its circulation to WTO Members, unless it is appealed.

The objective in designing a quasi-judicial system was to preserve Member control and not to surrender final decision-making to a third party. This was a hold-over from early GATT days when dispute settlement was conducted first by the membership at large and later by panels of diplomats that included representatives of disputing parties. This approach also provided a measure of comfort to several WTO Members who had little or no experience with international dispute settlement and who feared entrusting too much power to a separate entity. It has become clear, after twelve years of WTO dispute settlement experience, that the quasi-judicial character of these institutions is more form than substance. The reality is that panel rulings invariably are leaked before they are circulated and are treated as decisions rather than recommendations to the WTO membership. In any event, the likelihood of non-adoption of a report is virtually nil, largely due to the negative consensus rule by which adoption will occur unless there is consensus not to adopt.

The panel process is widely considered to be working well. Panels generally have been regarded as fair and competent. They have addressed complex and sensitive issues covering more than a dozen WTO agreements.[36] One recurring criticism relates to delays in the panel process. The 'general rule' in the DSU calls on panels to issue the final report to the parties within six months of panel composition;[37] the DSU recognizes that it may not always be possible to meet this deadline but it stipulates that 'in no case should the period from the establishment of the panel to the circulation of the report to the members exceed nine months'.[38] In fact, the six-month deadline is met rarely and the nine-month deadline is usually missed as well.[39] Delays are due mainly to protracted panel composition discussions, complexity of cases including those involving the need for scientific expert advice, and translation

[34] Art 19.1 DSU.   [35] Ibid.

[36] The DSU, the GATT 1994, the SCM Agreement, the Anti-Dumping Agreement, and the Agreement on Agriculture are the most frequently raised WTO agreements in dispute settlement.

[37] In case of urgency, including in disputes related to perishable goods, panels are to aim to issue reports within three months (Art 12.8 DSU). Shorter time frames are also imposed for certain challenges under the SCM Agreement (see Arts 4 and 7) and the Agreement on Government Procurement (see Art XXII.6).

[38] Art 12.9 DSU. Note that the nine-month timeline refers to the time from panel establishment, whereas the six-month deadline refers to time from panel composition.

[39] See W Davey, 'Expediting the Panel Process in WTO Dispute Settlement' in Janow, Donaldson, and Yanovich, above fn 11, at Table 1, 441–54, 460–62.

requirements.[40] If one measures from the time the panel is composed (as opposed to established), however, and excludes the time required for translation, the panel process usually takes less than a year. Thus despite some complaints about delays, the panel process compares quite favourably to most domestic court proceedings as well as to most international adjudicative processes.

The reform proposals concerning panels have focused on the need to move from a purely *ad hoc* system of panel selection to one where panelists are selected from a permanent roster of experts.[41] The impetus behind such proposals is the perception that panel selection more often than not takes too long. One proposal calls for establishing a roster of twenty-five persons or more who would stand ready to serve anytime during a fixed term of six years. The DG would choose panelists from that roster within five days of establishment of a panel.[42] Another approach would have a permanent roster coupled with the possibility of choosing some panelists who do not appear on the roster. A third idea calls for a permanent roster of panel chairpersons.[43]

There is a good deal of support among WTO Members and commentators for a roster approach.[44] However, some Members oppose permanent rosters, preferring to retain control over panellist selection. In their view, their domestic constituencies would better accept a process where Members have full control over who is to decide the outcome of important cases with significant financial implications. The irony is that in recent years, most panels have been composed by the DG, which involves no consultation with disputing parties. Concern has also been expressed that a system of selection from a set list will not provide sufficient flexibility to choose a panellist with a specialization that may arise in a particular dispute. Opposition has also come from developing country and least-developed country Members concerned about having an insufficient number of developing country panelists on any set list. This

[40] Panel reports must be circulated to Members in English, French, and Spanish, the three official WTO languages.

[41] This would be different from the current indicative list, which includes individuals with no specialized WTO expertise.

[42] DSB, *Contribution of the European Communities and Its Member States to the Improvement and Clarification of the WTO Dispute Settlement Understanding*, TN/DS/W/38 (23 January 2003). The proposal refers, at para 14.3, to '*persons of recognized authority, with demonstrated expertise in international trade law, economy or policy and the subject matter of the covered agreements generally, and/or past experience as a GATT/WTO panellist*' (original emphasis).

[43] DSB, *Contribution to Clarify and Improve the Dispute Settlement Understanding: Panel System, Communication from Thailand*, TN/DS/W/31 (22 January 2003), at 1–2.

[44] The Consultative Board Report suggests that 'a combination of roster and ad hoc appointments might serve the institution very well and ease somewhat the particular problems that have been witnessed in a few of the panel selection procedures'. Consultative Board Report, above fn 7, at 57. See also C-D Ehlermann, 'Six Years on the Bench of the "World Trade Court" – Some Personal Experiences as a Member of the Appellate Body of the World Trade Organization' 2002 *Journal of World Trade* 36(4) 605, at 628, writing in favour of a standing panel body stating that modifying the panel system would 'guarantee structurally the stability of panels and, thus, the independence of their members'; Davey, above fn 39, at 430.

concern could be allayed somewhat should there be acceptance of proposals requiring a minimum number of developing country or least-developed country Members on a panel where developing and/or least-developed countries are the main parties to the dispute.[45] In any event, prospects for a permanent roster of panelists seem far off at best. Even if a roster model were eventually agreed upon, which does not appear feasible given significant opposition from some important Members, consensus on roster membership among 153 WTO Members would be very difficult to achieve. A more likely future scenario would have panels composed exclusively by the DG due to failure by the parties to agree, with the DG turning regularly to experienced panelists with whom he (or she) is familiar. As a practical matter, this would not be much different from establishing a permanent panel roster.

D. Appellate Body

Although the panel process existed during the GATT 1947, the appellate phase only came into being with the establishment of the WTO. Appeals are as of right; there is no need to obtain leave to appeal a panel report. Only parties to the dispute may appeal a panel report, but Members that participated as third parties before the panel may also participate in the appeal process.[46] Appeals are limited to 'issues of law covered in the panel report and legal interpretations developed by the panel'.[47] The appellate procedure is governed by the Working Procedures for Appellate Review (Working Procedures), discussed in more detail below.

During the Uruguay Round negotiations, those involved in drafting the DSU assumed that the appellate phase would be invoked only rarely, such as to overturn a decision of a rogue panel. In fact, the opposite has occurred. During the first two years of the WTO, every panel report was appealed. The rate of appeal has fluctuated considerably over the years, going as low as 50 per cent of panel reports in 2002 and 2007; on average, however, about 66 per cent of panel reports are appealed each year.[48]

The standing Appellate Body is composed of seven permanent members who are appointed to serve a four-year term. They may be reappointed once. The terms are staggered so that not all seven posts are vacated at the same time, which means that there is always a mix of experienced and newer members. Appellate Body

---

[45] DSB, *Text for LDC Proposal on Dispute Settlement Understanding Negotiations, Communication from Haiti (on behalf of the LDC Group)*, TN/DS/W/37 (22 January 2003), at 1–2; DSB, *Jordan's Contribution Towards the Improvement and Clarification of the WTO Dispute Settlement Understanding*, TN/DS/W/43 (28 January 2003), at 3.

[46] Art 17.4 DSU.

[47] Art 17.6 DSU.

[48] Appellate Body, *Appellate Body Annual Report for 2007*, WT/AB/9 (30 January 2008), Annex 4, at 31.

members are 'persons of recognized authority, with demonstrated expertise in law, international trade, and the subject matter of the covered agreements generally'.[49] They must not be affiliated with any government and membership of the Appellate Body is to be broadly representative of membership in the WTO. Unlike panelists, Appellate Body members are not disqualified from sitting on cases because they are nationals of a disputing party. Like panelists, Appellate Body members are subject to rules of conduct and conflict of interest rules.[50]

The selection process for Appellate Body members is administered by the DSB. When there is a vacancy as a result of completion of a four-year term or otherwise,[51] WTO Members are invited to nominate individuals for consideration. Although Members usually nominate their own nationals, this is not required.[52] A selection committee composed of the DG and the chairpersons of several WTO Committees interviews each nominee individually and makes a recommendation to the WTO Membership.[53] In addition, a practice has developed whereby candidates call on various diplomatic missions in Geneva with a view to securing support in the selection process. Final selection is made during a DSB meeting, with Members usually agreeing on consensus with the recommendation of the selection committee as put forward by the DSB Chair. There is a good deal of informal discussion among Members prior to the DSB meeting with a view to avoiding a vote or open rejection of a particular candidate or candidates.[54]

Officially, there are no 'secure' seats on the Appellate Body. However, in the twelve years since its establishment, the Appellate Body has always included a European and an American member. This is to be expected and is probably good for the system given the significant trade flows and high dispute settlement activity of those two Members. The Appellate Body has almost always had an Egyptian and a Japanese member as well. Other Appellate Body members have come from Australia, Brazil, China, India, New Zealand, the Philippines, South Africa, and Uruguay. Overall membership has always included representation from the major trading regions of the world, namely Africa, Asia Pacific, Europe, and the Americas.

The Appellate Body generally has not been criticized for political bias for or against one group or another. Although there have been accusations from time to time in the US of anti-US sentiment on the part of the Appellate Body, a study conducted by

---

[49] Art 17.3 DSU.

[50] Rules 8–11 Working Procedures and Rules of Conduct, above fn 31.

[51] Two Appellate Body members have died while serving: Christopher Beeby (New Zealand) and John Lockhart (Australia).

[52] See, eg, Canada nominated Julio Lacarte Muró of Uruguay for the Appellate Body in 1995.

[53] The Chairpersons of the General Council, the DSB, the Council for Trade in Goods, the Council for Trade in Services, and the TRIPS Council. These persons are usually resident Ambassadors of WTO Members; they are not on the staff of the WTO Secretariat.

[54] Consensus was achieved in the November 2007 selection process only after Chinese Taipei withdrew is objections related to the Chinese nominee, Professor Yuejiao Zhang.

the US Government Accounting Office found that the WTO ruled for and against the US and other Members in roughly the same ratios.[55]

Sitting and former Appellate Body members have had varied careers, including as diplomats, civil servants, trade negotiators, university professors, judges, and private legal practitioners. Appellate Body members are appointed to serve on a part-time basis and most have other employment (such as in academia or arbitration work) while serving. As noted above, the Uruguay Round negotiators thought that resort to the Appellate Body would be the exception rather than the rule, and hence requiring only part-time service on the Appellate Body was a sensible approach. Contrary to those expectations, however, serving on the Appellate Body requires considerable devotion of time. This is due to several factors. First, panel reports are appealed more often than not. Moreover, the character of dispute settlement has changed dramatically from GATT 1947 days when written submissions usually were short and panel decisions even shorter. WTO disputes, by contrast, often concern complex issues and may involve multiple parties whose submissions run to hundreds of pages. Some cases involve extensive and technically-complex evidence. Panel reports are commensurately long and multi-faceted, as are Appellate Body reports.[56] The workload of Appellate Body members is thus of a completely different order than that surmised during the Uruguay Round negotiations.

The unpredictability of timing of appeals also contributes to making the commitment more time-consuming than one might suppose. The DSU does not provide for an Appellate Body recess, with the result that there is no period during the year when appeals may not be filed. The DSU also requires Appellate Body members to 'be available at all times and on short notice'.[57] The Appellate Body has no control over the number of appeals or their timing; an appeal may be filed anytime during a period of 60 days following the issuance of a panel report. Add to this the fact that the date of circulation of panel reports is often unknown, especially given that panel reports are rarely circulated within DSU timelines, and that translation requirements have an impact on scheduling. Together with the very short appeal period of 90 days, all of this means that Appellate Body members must always be available to devote time to an appeal at a moment's notice at any time of year, while other professional endeavours must be set aside. Under these circumstances, the engagement is anything but part-time. This situation has led to calls for an official change of status to full-time, an idea that has considerable merit. Although there have been slow

---

[55] GAO, *World Trade Organization – Standard of Review and Impact of Trade Remedy Rulings, Report to the Ranking Minority Member, Committee on Finance, U.S. Senate* (July 2003), at <http://www.gao.gov/new.items/do3824.pdf> (last visited 22 April 2008).

[56] Panel reports generally include lengthy summaries of parties' arguments plus reasoning and often run to hundreds of pages, plus exhibits. Appellate Body reports generally run from 100 to 300 pages.

[57] Art 17.3 DSU.

appeal periods from time to time,[58] full-time Appellate Body members would have more time to discuss and work through legal issues and trends in general, outside of the context of a particular appeal. Current Appellate Body members do engage in this type of reflection and study at an annual retreat, but full-time membership would provide more opportunities to do so. In addition, more time could be devoted to preparing for especially complex anticipated appeals before they are filed, rather than having to address them within the 90-day timeline. Again, advance preparation does occur under the current system. For example, Appellate Body members devoted study to the fact-heavy GMOs (*EC – Biotech Products*) case in anticipation of an appeal being filed because they wanted to understand the substantial factual aspects of the case before addressing legal issues on appeal. As it turned out, the case did not end up before the Appellate Body but, if it had, the pre-study would have facilitated consideration of the more than 1000-page Panel report.

If the engagement were to be changed to full-time, this would imply adjustments to the compensation package provided to Appellate Body members. The anticipated light workload and infrequency of appeals led the WTO membership to design a compensation package that is not reflective of the demands of a full-time post. Currently, the maximum fee for Appellate Body work is approximately $700 (US) per day, plus an allowance for accommodation and meals when working in Geneva.[59] Appellate Body members also receive a monthly retainer of about $8000 (US), which is intended to compensate Appellate Body members who must refrain from engaging in consultative or arbitration work in order to devote time to WTO duties at a moment's notice. Given their part-time status, benefits (such as health insurance) are minimal, and there is no pension plan. This compensation package would have to be significantly enhanced to attract high-quality, experienced people to accept the post on a full-time basis.

In the course of the ongoing negotiations to reform the dispute settlement rules, some WTO Members have suggested that the system might benefit from modifying the term of service of Appellate Body members. As mentioned above, under the current rules, a member is appointed for a term of four years, renewable once. The proposal is to have only one term of a longer duration—perhaps six to eight years—to avoid any suggestion that an Appellate Body member may act in such a way as to seek to secure nomination for a second term.[60] These proposals have always been accompanied by assurances that no such behaviour has ever been suspected of anyone who is serving or has served on the Appellate Body. Thus far, however, the proposal has not taken on any momentum.

---

[58] In 2004 and 2006, only five appeals were filed; in 2007, only four appeals were filed.

[59] Compare the rates charged by other international adjudicators: NAFTA Chapter 19 and 20 panelists: about $800/day; NAFTA Chapter 11 arbitrators: $350–$450 (US)/hour; ICSID arbitrators: $2500 (US)/day.

[60] See Hughes, above fn 14, at 217.

The size of the Appellate Body has also been the subject of reform proposals. At seven, it is a small bench in international adjudication circles[61] and it has been suggested that the Appellate Body should be enlarged by two or three more members.[62] Those promoting a larger bench argue that heavy workloads have forced the Appellate Body to delay circulation of reports beyond the 90-day deadline set out in the DSU and that an additional two or three members would allow the Appellate Body to hear and decide more cases at the same time.[63] Experience suggests that enlarging the Appellate Body for workload purposes may not be necessary. Although the caseload rose fairly steadily until it hit a peak of 13 appeals filed in 2000, since then the number of appeals has fluctuated; in fact, in 2007 only four appeals were filed, the lowest volume since 1996. In any event, the Appellate Body has an extremely good record of meeting the 90-day timeline, missing it only seven times in 84 appeals,[64] and only twice because of a heavy work-load.[65]

The small size of the Appellate Body is also considered by some commentators as one of the institution's abiding strengths, for it ensures that the members know each other well and have an opportunity to meet regularly in small and informal settings, which in turn facilitates free and frank exchanges and sharing of experiences.[66] This is especially important for a body that is composed of part-time members with various backgrounds who live in seven different regions of the world. A large bench would involve a more cumbersome decision-making process and deliberations necessarily would be highly structured and formalized. The Working Procedures require Appellate Body members to meet on a regular basis to discuss matters of policy, practice, and procedure '[t]o ensure consistency and coherence in decision-making, and to draw on the individual and collective expertise of the members'.[67]

[61] The International Court of Justice sits as a bench of 15 plus *ad hoc* judges if one of the parties is not represented on the Court. The Law of the Sea Tribunal has 21 judges plus *ad hoc* members from time to time. Although it is possible for the International Court of Justice and the Law of the Sea Tribunal to sit in smaller chambers, this is exceptional.

[62] See Hughes, above fn 14, at 216–17.

[63] Some suggest that the impetus for additional members on the Appellate Body is related more to politics than practicalities, as more spaces mean more opportunities for WTO Members to have a national on the Appellate Body.

[64] As of December 2007. The seven appeals where Appellate Body reports were issued more than 90 days after the Notice of Appeal was filed are *EC – Hormones*; *US – Lead and Bismuth II*; *EC – Asbestos*; *Thailand – H-Beams*; *US – Upland Cotton*; *EC – Export Subsidies on Sugar*; *Mexico – Anti-Dumping Measures on Rice*.

[65] An unusually heavy docket explains the delays in *EC – Asbestos* and *Thailand – H-Beams*. In other cases, there were different reasons for the delays: death of a Member of the Division assigned to the appeal (Christopher Beeby passed away in March 2000, after the hearing had taken place in *US – Lead and Bismuth II*, with the result that a second hearing was scheduled where Julio Lacarte, Beeby's replacement on the Division, participated), the need for extra time to permit translation of submissions from Spanish to English and English to Spanish (*Mexico – Anti-Dumping Measures on Rice*), and especially complex and extensive appeals with numerous participants (*US – Upland Cotton* and *EC – Export Subsidies on Sugar*).

[66] See Ehlermann, above fn 44, at 610.

[67] Rule 4(1) Working Procedures for Appellate Review.

THE INSTITUTIONAL DIMENSION   285

This practice, referred to as 'collegiality', is highly valued by the Appellate Body. In the words of former Appellate Body member Claus-Dieter Ehlermann, the small size of the Appellate Body is a 'precious good' having 'extremely positive effects on the intimacy and collegiality of the deliberations'.[68]

A small bench may also assist in avoiding a proliferation of separate and dissenting opinions, in keeping with the requirement that the 'Appellate Body and its divisions shall make every effort to take their decisions by consensus'.[69] Only one of the 84 reports issued by the Appellate Body in its first twelve years contains a dissenting opinion, and it is only a partial one relating to a single finding in an appeal covering numerous issues.[70] Another report included a 'concurring statement', wherein the Appellate Body member indicated that he agreed with the Appellate Body division's conclusions but would have gone even further, though this would not have affected the overall result.[71] The experience of the Appellate Body in this regard stands in marked contrast to that of the 15-member International Court of Justice, where lengthy separate and dissenting opinions are the norm.

Views differ as to whether dissenting opinions are problematic or not. On the one hand, it is important not to allow the search for consensus to dilute important findings; on the other hand, a record of solid decisions, especially in the nascent years of an institution like the WTO, serves to contribute to clarity in the law and the establishment of a well-respected and authoritative institution. Frequent dissents in the early years would have eroded any authority the Appellate Body might have achieved. Moreover, in the early years, it was especially important that delegations not speculate about or seek to exploit opposing doctrinal views of individual Appellate Body members. Former Appellate Body members maintain that regularly achieving consensus was more coincidence than design, and was always the result of frank and thorough discussions. Most would agree that this has served the Appellate Body well and that dissents are likely to continue to be the exception rather than the rule.

The DSU requires the Appellate Body to draw up its own working procedures 'in consultation with the Chairman of the DSB and the Director-General, and communicated to the members for their information'.[72] The Working Procedures were developed by the Appellate Body and adopted in 1996, following consultation with the DG and the chair of the DSB, as well as discussions at two informal meetings of WTO Members. The Working Procedures are more detailed than the procedures

---

[68] See Ehlermann, above fn 44, at 610.

[69] Rule 3(2) Working Procedures for Appellate Review.

[70] Appellate Body Report, *US – Upland Cotton*.

[71] The identity of the concurring member is not a matter of public record but the masculine 'he' is appropriate because the three members of the Division who signed the report are male. The 'concurring Member' concluded that the products in question were not like, whereas the majority said only that likeness had not been proved.

[72] Art 17.9 DSU.

governing the panel process found in the DSU: they include 33 rules[73] and annexes covering duties and responsibilities of Appellate Body members as well as rules governing appellate procedures, including commencement of an appeal, submissions, hearings, and working schedules. The Working Procedures have been amended a few times to make improvements and address lacunae that came to light over the years.[74] Changes have dealt with the contents of and procedures for amending notices of appeal, procedures for third participants who attend hearings without filing written submissions, timelines for filing submissions, procedures for correcting clerical errors in submissions, and the length of term of Appellate Body Chairperson.[75]

Unlike DSU amendments, it is not necessary to achieve WTO Member consensus on amendments to the Working Procedures. The Appellate Body develops its own rules but is required to consult with the DG and DSB chair, who communicates this to WTO Members 'for their information'. Member approval, however, is not required. In 2002, in response to dissatisfaction on the part of some WTO Members with the level of consultation provided for by the DSB Chair for amendments then under consideration, the DSB adopted procedures requiring the DSB Chair to discuss proposed amendments during DSB meetings, afford an opportunity for WTO Members to set out comments in writing, and request the Appellate Body to take Members' views into account.[76] Although not bound to follow Members' views, thus far the Appellate Body has not strayed far from them and it is doubtful that the Appellate Body would adopt procedures wholly at odds with the membership's wishes.[77] Indeed, it made a number of adjustments to a series of amendments proposed in 2004 after taking into account Members' views and even abandoned a proposal relating to the possibility of suspending the 90-day appeal period during periods in August and December each year to allow for a recess.[78]

Article 17 DSU establishes that three of the seven Appellate Body members shall decide an appeal and that members shall serve on cases in rotation. The Working Procedures provide that a division of three shall be selected 'on the basis of rotation,

---

[73] They are numbered 1 to 32, but include rule 23*bis*. The current version is found in WT/AB/WP/5 (4 January 2005).

[74] See Appellate Body, *Proposed Amendments to the Working Procedures for Appellate Review – Communication from the Appellate Body*, WT/AB/WP/W/8 (8 April 2004), which includes an explanation about the more significant modifications.

[75] For a thorough discussion of the Working Procedures and the amendments that have been adopted over the years see V Donaldson and A Yanovich, 'The Appellate Body's working procedures for appellate review' in Sacerdoti, Yanovich, and Bohanes, above fn 14, 386.

[76] DSB, *Additional Procedures for Consultations between the Chairperson of the DSB and WTO Members in Relation to Amendments to the Working Procedures for Appellate Review*, WT/DSB/31 (20 December 2002).

[77] There was considerable controversy when the Appellate Body adopted procedures for filing *amicus curiae* briefs in *EC–Asbestos*, but that was not in connection with proposed amendments to the Working Procedures. Rather, the procedures were adopted for the purposes of that appeal only. See also chapters 13 and 24 of this Handbook.

[78] See Donaldson and Yanovich, fn 75, at 398–99.

while taking into account the principles of random selection, unpredictability and opportunity for all Members to serve regardless of their national origin'.[79] Thus unlike the panel process, nationality is not relevant in determining who sits on a division for a particular appeal. This underscores the (quasi-)judicial character of the process and the importance of independence of the members. In any event, had the rules been otherwise, it would have posed significant difficulties because the US and the EC appear so often before the Appellate Body with the result that two of the seven members of the Appellate Body would almost always have to recuse themselves.

The system of rotation is secret and known only to the Appellate Body members. Shortly after a notice of appeal is filed, parties are informed who is on the division as well as the appeal timetable.[80] Each division elects a Presiding member for the appeal, whose responsibilities include coordinating the conduct of the appeal, chairing hearings, and coordinating the drafting of the decision. Unlike some domestic courts, the Presiding member is not chosen on the basis of seniority; rather, Appellate Body members generally take turns in this role.

Although only the three members of the division participate in the hearing and sign the Appellate Body report, all seven members participate in the development of the decision. For each appeal, the seven Appellate Body members meet over two or more days for what is called an Exchange of Views, during which all members share their views on the appropriate result. This is provided for in Rule 4(1) Working Procedures. The Appellate Body members who do not hear the appeal review all the written submissions as well as a transcript of the hearing. Although this 'collegial' approach was not set out in the DSU, it has not led to objections on the part of WTO Members. Indeed, it seems a wise approach, functioning as a means of quality control to test the division's theory and approach. The benefits of the Exchange of Views have been described by former Appellate Body Chairman Claus-Dieter Ehlermann in the following words:

The system of 'exchange of views' among all members has proved to be of enormous benefit to the work of the Appellate Body. As intended, the exchanges have permitted divisions to draw on the individual and collective expertise of all members. In addition, they have contributed greatly to consistency and coherence of decision making. The exchanges of views have thus contributed to 'providing security and predictability to the multilateral trading system', which is, according to DSU Article 3.2, the fundamental aim of the dispute settlement system of the WTO.... The system of exchange of views combines the benefits of deliberations of all seven Appellate Body members with the advantages of decision-making by divisions composed of only three members.[81]

---

[79] Rule 6(2) Working Procedures.
[80] The timetable for appeals is found in Working Procedures, Annex I.
[81] Ehlermann, above fn 44, at 612–13. In the same article, Ehlermann opines that the introduction of decision-making by the Appellate Body *en banc* would be 'neither necessary nor desirable'.

The 'collegial' approach likely contributes to the consistency of jurisprudence and the irregularity of dissents as the reasoning from one appeal to the next reflects the views of all seven members. Indeed, decisions are adopted as reports of the Appellate Body, and not of a particular division.

Appellate Body hearings generally are quite different from panel hearings. Before panels, disputing parties usually are given an opportunity to deliver lengthy statements at the opening of the hearings, ranging from 30 minutes to an hour or even longer. This is usually followed by questions posed by the panel, and the parties may also pose questions to each other. Questions may also be sent to parties following the hearings, for which written responses must be provided within a set timeframe. Some panels are relatively quiet during hearings; some are very active in posing questions. Parties' answers before panels are of a preliminary type, as they are permitted to file written responses a week or two later. An Appellate Body hearing is generally more demanding of counsel. Parties usually are permitted between five and thirty minutes for their opening statements, depending on the issues and number of participants; if one exceeds the time limit, one is usually cut off. Questioning is intense; division members take turns asking anywhere from fifty to eighty (or more) probing and difficult questions about the issues presented on appeal. It becomes very clear to the parties at this stage that even though only 35 to 40 days have passed since the notice of appeal was filed, division members have read the panel report and parties' submissions with great care and are thoroughly familiar with the arguments. Many questions are prepared in advance; others flow from responses provided. Contrary to the procedure before panels, parties' answers are not considered preliminary; there is no opportunity to send written responses later.[82] Parties (including third participants) can comment on each other's responses but they may not pose questions of each other. Hearings take from one to three days depending on the number and complexity of issues as well as the number of participants.[83] At the end of the hearing, parties are given an opportunity to make concise closing statements.

Although some counsel who have appeared before the Appellate Body are experienced litigators, most are not. Well-honed advocacy skills are no doubt useful in this forum, especially to avoid being led into a line of questioning that exposes weaknesses in one's arguments, but court experience is not essential. Counsel who fare better are those with a solid foundation in international trade law, as well as a deep appreciation of public international law, especially as it relates to treaty interpretation. In addition, although the Appellate Body is not mandated to make findings of fact and must accept the facts as determined by the panel, the Appellate Body often delves into the facts of a particular case in order to better understand the potential implications of deciding one way or another. Some counsel who have

---

[82] On rare occasions, the Appellate Body has requested additional memoranda to be filed after the hearing, but these were not opportunities when parties could supplement responses provided during the hearing. See Appellate Body Report, *US – FSC (Article 21.5 – EC)*, at para 11.

[83] One hearing day runs seven to eight hours, excluding the lunch break.

appeared before the Appellate Body have been surprised when asked detailed questions about factual matters. Experience suggests that counsel should always be prepared to do so when appearing before the Appellate Body. Finally, there is no substitute for experience. Familiarity with the members and the style of hearing will enhance any appearance before the Appellate Body.

The DSU authorizes the Appellate Body to 'uphold, modify or reverse the legal findings and conclusions of the panel'.[84] Strictly speaking, Appellate Body reports, once adopted by the DSB, are binding only on the parties to the dispute in question. Nevertheless, the rulings of the Appellate Body generally have been treated—albeit not explicitly—as establishing legal precedent; they are regularly cited by WTO Members in submissions, by panels in their decisions, and by the Appellate Body itself in its reasoning.

Examples where panels have not followed the Appellate Body are extremely rare. The first time a panel explicitly disagreed with the Appellate Body was in 2003 in *Argentina – Preserved Peaches*, where the Panel disagreed with the Appellate Body's interpretation of 'unforeseen developments' as it appears in Article XIX GATT 1994.[85] The Panel report was not appealed so the Appellate Body never had the chance to deal with the panel's approach. It was not until 2006 that a panel once again explicitly disagreed with the Appellate Body, this time on the permissibility under the Anti-Dumping Agreement of using a particular methodology known as zeroing to calculate a dumping margin. The Panel stated that 'while we recognize the important systemic considerations in favour of following adopted panel and Appellate Body reports, we have decided not to adopt that approach...' and also observed that '[i]t is well established that panel and Appellate Body reports are not binding, except with respect to resolving the particular dispute between the parties to the dispute'.[86] On appeal in that case, the Appellate Body reversed the Panel and confirmed its interpretation that zeroing is not permissible.[87] A few months' later, another panel decided not to follow the Appellate Body's rulings on zeroing, even though it recognized that its reasoning was 'very similar to' that in two previous cases that were reversed by the Appellate Body. The Panel explained that '[i]n light of our obligation under Article 11 of the DSU to carry out an objective examination of the matter referred to us... we have felt compelled to depart from the Appellate Body's approach...'.[88] On appeal in that case, the Appellate Body dealt head on with the obligations of a panel in the face of legal interpretations and *ratio decidendi* contained in adopted Appellate Body reports. The Appellate Body stated that it was 'deeply concerned about the Panel's decision to depart from well-established Appellate Body jurisprudence clarifying

---

[84] Art 17.13 DSU.

[85] Panel Report, *Argentina – Preserved Peaches*, at para 7.24, disagreeing with Appellate Body Report, *Argentina – Footwear (EC)*, at para 131.

[86] Panel Report, *US – Zeroing (Japan)*, at para 7.99 and fn 733.

[87] Appellate Body Report, *US – Zeroing (Japan)*.

[88] Panel Report, *US – Stainless Steel*, at para 7.106.

the interpretation of the same legal issue'[89] and considered that the Panel's approach had 'serious implications for the proper functioning of the WTO dispute settlement system'.[90] The Appellate Body recalled that it had determined in *US – Shrimp (Article 21.5 – Malaysia)* that adopted Appellate Body reports create legitimate expectations among WTO Members and therefore 'should be taken into account'.[91] It noted that in *US – Oil Country Tubular Goods Reviews (Argentina)*, it had held that following conclusions in earlier reports 'is not only appropriate, but is what would be expected from panels, especially when the issues are the same'.[92] The Appellate Body also observed that 'dispute settlement practice demonstrates that WTO Members attach significance to reasoning provided in previous panel and Appellate Body reports'[93] by relying on them in subsequent proceedings. It also pointed to the 'hierarchical structure contemplated in the DSU' and to the intention of Uruguay Round negotiators of 'strengthening' dispute settlement by establishing an Appellate Body to review legal interpretations developed by panels.[94] Finally, the Appellate Body underlined the importance of promoting security and predictability in the dispute settlement system and concluded that the Panel's failure to follow adopted Appellate Body reports addressing the same issues 'undermines the development of a coherent and predictable body of jurisprudence clarifying members' rights and obligations' under the WTO agreements.[95]

It remains to be seen whether the Appellate Body's admonition will have an impact on how panels rule on the zeroing issue in the future. If panels continue to depart from Appellate Body rulings on this issue, no matter how respectfully, this could undermine the integrity of the dispute settlement system that has served the membership so well. Adopted Appellate Body reports do not simply reflect the view of the Appellate Body; they are adopted by the Members of the WTO sitting as the DSB. Accordingly, it is for WTO Members, not panels, to seek to effect a change in the law as determined by the Appellate Body. This could be done in the context of the Doha negotiations. It is also possible to move more quickly, as the membership could adopt an authoritative interpretation under Article IX WTO Agreement[96] respecting the permissibility of zeroing under the Anti-Dumping

---

[89]   Appellate Body Report, *US – Stainless Steel*, at para 162.   [90]   Ibid.

[91]   Ibid at para 159, quoting from Appellate Body Report, *US – Shrimp (Article 21.5 – Malaysia)*, at para 109.

[92]   Ibid, quoting from Appellate Body Report, *US – Oil Country Tubular Goods Reviews (Argentina)*, at para 188.

[93]   Ibid at para 160.

[94]   Ibid at para 161.

[95]   Ibid. Several WTO Members participating as third participants in the appeal weighed in on the issue, including the EC, Japan, Thailand, and Chile. The first three considered that previous Appellate Body reports should be followed, while Chile argued that there was no obligation to do so. Ibid at paras 149–52.

[96]   Article IX:2 states that the GC has authority to adopt interpretations of the WTO agreements on the basis of a three-fourths majority. This provision has never been used.

Agreement. Another option would be to dedicate a session of the GC to a discussion on the relevance of prior Appellate Body rulings on zeroing and the desirability or otherwise of panels' following them in future. The discussion would give the broader membership an opportunity to discuss the issue from a systemic perspective rather than in the context of a specific dispute and could prove instructive for future panels.[97]

It must be borne in mind, however, that the zeroing 'row' is unique and, as noted above, the general tendency on the part of panels and the membership is to follow and apply previous Appellate Body rulings. This has led to the development of a considerable body of settled trade law, both in terms of substantive trade rights and obligations, as well as procedural matters.

In just twelve years, the Appellate Body has issued rulings covering a wide spectrum of trade rights and obligations. The Appellate Body has been called upon most often to address questions relating to the interpretation of the DSU and the GATT 1994, followed by trade remedies matters under the SCM Agreement and the Anti-Dumping Agreement. A distant third in terms of frequency addressed by the Appellate Body is the Agreement on Agriculture. In all, the Appellate Body has ruled on provisions in thirteen of the WTO agreements.

Equally important are the Appellate Body's decisions on procedural matters, which have profoundly influenced the shape of the WTO dispute settlement process. The DSU does not refer to matters such as due process, burden of proof, standard of review, representation by counsel, or *amicus curiae* briefs. Nor does it speak to the distinction between a factual matter and an issue of law, despite explicitly reserving appeals to the latter.[98] It fell to the Appellate Body to decide, as cases arose, how to apply such concepts in WTO dispute settlement.

Of particular significance is the Appellate Body jurisprudence on treaty interpretation. In its first report,[99] the Appellate Body established its signature approach, founding its analysis on the treaty interpretation rules codified in Article 31(1) Vienna Convention on the Law of Treaties (VCLT).[100] The Appellate Body has applied this rule of interpretation in every decision to date. Article 31(1) VCLT requires that a treaty be interpreted 'in good faith in accordance with the ordinary meaning to be given to the terms of the treaty in their context and in the light of its object and

---

[97] The GC held a special session to discuss the admissibility of *amicus curiae* briefs in November 2000 after the Appellate Body adopted a procedure to deal with a number of such briefs filed in *EC – Asbestos*. The GC suggested to the Appellate Body that it exercise extreme caution in this regard. See GC, *Minutes of meeting held on 22 November 2000*, WT/GC/M/60 (23 January 2001), at 28.

[98] Art 17.6 DSU; see also chapter 14 of this Handbook.

[99] Appellate Body Report, *US – Gasoline*, at 17. See also chapter 12 of this Handbook.

[100] Article 3.2 DSU requires that the WTO agreements be clarified in accordance with the 'customary rules of interpretation of public international law'. The Appellate Body has determined that Articles 31 and 32 VCLT have attained the status of customary rules of interpretation of public international law. See Appellate Body Report, *US – Gasoline*, at 17; Appellate Body Report, *Japan – Alcoholic Beverages II*, at 10.

purpose'. Applying this rule, the Appellate Body has focused on treaty terms, that is, the text of provisions at issue in an appeal, explaining that 'Article 31 [...] provides that the words of the treaty form the foundation for the interpretive process'[101] and observing that 'interpretation must be based above all upon the text of the treaty'.[102] The Appellate Body has made clear that the 'duty of a treaty interpreter is to examine the words of the treaty to determine the intentions of the parties'.[103] The Appellate Body's systematic approach to interpretation has proved highly valuable, providing guidance for evaluating strengths and weaknesses of positions and in formulating arguments and submissions in dispute settlement. It has also informed trade negotiations, as Members seek to revise provisions to reflect a desired approach that the Appellate Body has, or has not, supported in its rulings.[104]

The Appellate Body has been widely praised, but it has not escaped criticism. Some have argued that it is too literalist in its interpretive approach. Others claim the Appellate Body engages in gap-filling or judicial activism, adding obligations that are not found in the treaty provisions. Overall, however, the assessment of the Appellate Body has been positive and there is every indication that WTO Members will continue to rely regularly on the Appellate Body to resolve trade disputes in the future.

Finally, although it was probably not contemplated by those who designed the WTO dispute settlement system, Appellate Body members have played a significant role in the compliance stage of the dispute settlement system. This is because WTO Members have consistently chosen sitting or former Appellate Body members to serve as arbitrator under Article 21.3(c) DSU, which deals with binding arbitration to determine the reasonable period of time to comply with DSB rulings. When Members could not agree on whom to appoint as the arbitrator, the DG has always appointed an Appellate Body member or former member. It is not clear why the practice developed to have Appellate Body members fulfil this role. One possible reason is that WTO Members thought it prudent to choose someone familiar with the case or the WTO agreements generally; another reason might have been that Appellate Body members are known to the WTO Members.

---

[101] Appellate Body Report, *Japan – Alcoholic Beverages II*, at 11.

[102] Ibid. The Appellate Body was quoting from ICJ, *Territorial Dispute (Libyan Arab Jamahiriya/ Chad)*, 3 February 1994, ICJ Reports (1994) 6, at 20; ICJ, *Maritime Delimitation and Territorial Questions between Qatar and Bahrain, Jurisdiction and Admissibility*, 15 February 1995, ICJ Reports (1995) 6, at 18.

[103] Appellate Body Report, *India – Patents (US)*, at para 45.

[104] This has occurred in negotiating sessions on the Anti-Dumping Agreement and the SCM Agreement. John Weekes, former WTO negotiator and Canadian Ambassador to the WTO, has observed that the impact of dispute settlement on trade negotiations is 'substantial'. J Weekes, The External Dynamics of the Dispute Settlement Understanding: An Initial Analysis of its Impact on Trade Relations and Trade Negotiations' in J Lacarte and J Granados (eds), *Inter-Governmental Trade Dispute Settlement: Multilateral and Regional Approaches* (London: Cameron May, 2004), at 81.

By the end of 2007, a total of twenty five Article 21.3(c) awards had been issued. Common approaches have developed over time and, as with arguments before panels and the Appellate Body, parties refer to previous awards in support of their positions and arbitrators refer to previous awards in their reasoning.

E. WTO Secretariat

Although there was no legal officer position during much of the GATT 1947 history, the WTO Secretariat has a number of legal divisions, all of which have a role in the dispute settlement system. The DSU provides that the Secretariat 'shall have the responsibility of assisting panels, especially on the legal, historical, and procedural aspects of matters dealt with, and of providing secretarial and technical support'.[105] There are two divisions in the WTO Secretariat that primarily provide assistance to panels, though other divisions contribute specialized expertise from time to time. The Rules Division assists with dumping and subsidy/countervailing duties cases, while the Legal Affairs Division assists panels dealing with all other disputes. The divisions each comprise about a dozen staff, most of them lawyers, from various countries.[106] Other divisions, such as the Trade in Services Division, assist in cases where specialized expertise is required.[107] Staff of the Secretariat are subject to a code of conduct similar to that which applies to panelists.

The legal divisions receive legal submissions and exhibits and assist with panel selection, scheduling, and logistical matters. They also attend panel hearings and, when requested to do so by panelists, conduct legal research on procedural and substantive issues raised in disputes.

The DSU also requires the WTO Secretariat to 'make available a qualified legal expert . . . to any developing country Member which so requests . . . to assist the developing country Member in a manner ensuring the continued impartiality of the Secretariat'.[108] Although many developing countries would benefit from such assistance given the highly complex and specialized dispute settlement regime, it is not often sought, nor is it generally considered very useful given the impartiality limitation. There is, however, an alternative. The Advisory Centre on WTO Law (ACWL), a Geneva-based intergovernmental organization established in 2001, has to a large degree alleviated the need for such assistance to be provided by the WTO itself. The ACWL provides legal advice and assistance to developing and least developed

---

[105] Art 27.1 DSU. The Secretariat is also tasked with conducting training courses for WTO Members concerning dispute settlement procedures and practices (Art 27.3 DSU).

[106] Although it varies, these Divisions usually have about 12 lawyers on staff at any particular time, plus a few student interns.

[107] For example, the Trade in Services Division provided assistance to the Panel in *Mexico – Telecoms*.

[108] Art 27.2 DSU.

countries in WTO dispute settlement proceedings.[109] Although the Centre is not part of the WTO, many WTO Members are also members of the Centre.

F. Appellate Body Secretariat

The DSU provides that the Appellate Body 'shall be provided with appropriate administrative and legal support as it requires'.[110] The Appellate Body is assisted by a Secretariat of lawyers and administrative assistants with expertise in WTO law and procedure. The Appellate Body Secretariat staff members are WTO employees, but the Secretariat operates independently from the rest of the WTO Secretariat to ensure the independence and confidentiality of the appellate process. In addition, staff members are subject to a code of conduct.

Originally, the Appellate Body Secretariat was very small, consistent with the assumption that appeals would be rare. The size of the staff more than doubled after a few years once it became clear that appeals were to be the rule rather than the exception. There are between ten and twelve lawyers from several countries on staff plus students who are hired for three-month internships. The Secretariat receives submissions and assists with scheduling and logistics. Staff members attend appellate hearings and may assist Appellate Body members with appeals by conducting legal research. Staff members also assist Appellate Body members when they are acting as arbitrators under Article 21.3(c) DSU.

III. Some Future Challenges

WTO dispute settlement institutions have proved to be *the* success story of the WTO. While the diplomatic institutions have struggled, the dispute settlement institutions have achieved remarkable results. To be sure, there is room for improvement and WTO Members continue to work towards this end. In the meantime, however, the system continues to evolve and improve on an informal basis. For example, WTO Members have found a way to deal with what is known as the 'sequencing' problem, which refers to the failure of the DSU to define the relationship between Articles 21 (surveillance and implementation) and 22 (compensation and suspension of concessions). Members have addressed this issue through *ad hoc* agreements as the

---

[109] See chapter 17 of this Handbook for additional information about the Centre.
[110] Art 17.7 DSU.

need has arisen. Another issue is *amicus curiae* briefs. These used to give rise to very strong protests when they were admitted by panels or the Appellate Body. Although there is still strong opposition in principle to the admissibility of such briefs on the part of some WTO Members, specific objections to them appear to be less severe in recent times.

Another area that seems to be evolving is transparency. The panel process currently is conducted largely on a confidential basis; parties' written submissions are confidential unless the parties choose to make them public[111] and hearings are almost always held behind closed doors. Although some Members and commentators have long promoted open hearings, others remain firmly opposed to the idea, arguing that the *in camera* government-to-government nature of WTO dispute settlement must be preserved.[112] In 2005, however, after ten years of WTO dispute settlement practice, a panel hearing was open in part to members of the public via closed circuit television at WTO headquarters in Geneva.[113] Since then, two other panels have opened their sessions, at least in part, to the public.[114] In each case, the panels did so at the request of the disputing parties. All of the 'open' hearings have involved the US and the EC as disputing parties, and one has involved Canada.

Open hearings are still very rare, however. Although over 150 panels have been established since the beginning of the WTO in 1995, only three panels have held

---

[111] Art 18.2 and Appendix 3, para 3 DSU. The DSU permits Members to make their own submissions public. Few Members do so, however.

[112] See DSB, *Contribution of the United States to the Improvement of the Dispute Settlement Understanding of the WTO Related to Transparency*, TN/DS/W/13 (22 August 2002), at 1–2; DSB, *Further Contribution of the United States to the Improvement of the Dispute Settlement Understanding of the WTO Related to Transparency*, TN/DS/W/46 (11 February 2003), at 1–3; DSB, *Contribution of the European Communities and Its Member States to the Improvement of the WTO Dispute Settlement Understanding*, TN/DS/W/1 (13 March 2002), at 6–7; DSB, *Contribution of Canada to the Improvement of the WTO Dispute Settlement Understanding*, TN/DS/W/41 (24 January 2003), at 5–6. Former Appellate Body Chairman James Bacchus has argued in favour of opening the hearings to the public. In his view, '[i]f the doors were opened to dispute settlement proceedings in the WTO, then the world would see that those who have been entrusted by the Members of the WTO with the responsibility of helping resolve trade disputes are fulfilling that responsibility correctly and conscientiously. WTO jurists are independent, impartial, fair, objective, and utterly exhaustive in examining virtually every nuance of every legal issue that is raised in every dispute. It is only because the doors are closed that anyone is able to suggest otherwise'. See J Bacchus, 'Let the Sunshine In: One View of Dispute Settlement Understanding Review' in Lacarte and Granados, above fn 104, at 144.

[113] In *US – Continued Suspension* and *Canada – Continued Suspension*, pursuant to a request of the disputing parties, the Panel agreed to a partially open process. Arrangements were made to permit two hundred members of the public to observe a portion of the panel hearings through closed-circuit television on the premises of the WTO. Access was not permitted for the portion of the hearing when third parties were making submissions due to objections by some third parties.

[114] Panels agreed to parties' requests for open hearings in *EC – Bananas III (Article 21.5 – US)* (the hearings were held on 6–7 November 2007) and in *US – Continued Zeroing*, (the hearings were held on 29–30 January 2008 and 22–23 April 2008).

open hearings. Transparency is an especially sensitive subject that is rooted in legal traditions and perceptions about the character of the WTO dispute settlement procedure itself. Under the circumstances, broad-based reform in this area may be very hard to achieve. Nevertheless, the fact that some panel hearings have been opened up to some degree and the fact that those Members in favour of transparency (Canada, the EC, and the US) are among the most frequent players in the system, suggest that closed panel sessions could eventually be the exception rather than the rule.

To date, no appellate proceeding has been open to the public and some argue that, contrary to the flexibility in the procedures governing panels, the DSU explicitly requires appellate hearings to be confidential.[115] It is expected that the Appellate Body will soon be requested to hold an open hearing.[116] Even if the Appellate Body feels compelled to deny the request given the prohibitive language in the DSU, it could nevertheless express in *obiter dicta* a preference to conduct open hearings if it could. Such a pronouncement could influence attitudes in the future.

There are other areas that could be improved and WTO Members continue to explore solutions in the context of the negotiations on improvements and clarifications to the DSU. These include a permanent solution to the sequencing issue mentioned above, as well as the possibility of introducing a remand procedure, enhanced third party rights, and post-retaliation issues. Progress in these areas, however, likely will come only with the conclusion of the Doha negotiations.

SELECTED BIBLIOGRAPHY

Consultative Board, *The Future of the WTO: Addressing Institutional Challenges in the New Millennium* (Geneva: WTO, 2004)

C-D Ehlermann, 'Six Years on the Bench of the "World Trade Court" – Some Personal Experiences as a Member of the Appellate Body of the World Trade Organization' 2002 *Journal of World Trade* 36(4) 605

ME Janow, V Donaldson, and A Yanovich (eds), *The WTO: Governance, Dispute Settlement & Developing Countries* (Huntington, New York: Juris Publishing, Inc., 2008)

J Lacarte and J Granadas (eds), *Inter-Governmental Trade Dispute Settlement: Multilateral and Regional Approaches* (London: Cameron May, 2004)

K Leitner and S Lester, 'WTO Dispute Settlement 1995–2007 – A Statistical Analysis' 2008 *Journal of International and Economic Law* 11(1) 179

A Mitchell (ed.), *Challenges and Prospects for the WTO* (London: Cameron May, 2004)

G Sacerdoti, A Yanovich, and J Bohanes (eds), *The WTO at Ten: The Contribution of the Dispute Settlement System* (Cambridge: Cambridge University Press, 2006)

---

[115] Article 17.10 DSU states that the 'proceedings of the Appellate Body shall be confidential'.
[116] In the appeal from *Canada – Continued Suspension* and *US – Continued Suspension*.

Y Taniguchi, A Yanovich, and J Bohanes (eds), *The WTO in the Twenty-First Century* (Cambridge: Cambridge University Press, 2007)

R Yerxa and B Wilson (eds), *Key Issues in WTO Dispute Settlement* (Cambridge: Cambridge University Press, 2005)

WTO, *A Handbook on the WTO Dispute Settlement System* (Cambridge: Cambridge University Press, 2004)

WTO, *Appellate Body Annual Report for 2007* (Geneva: WTO, 2008)

CHAPTER 12

....

JURISDICTION, APPLICABLE LAW, AND INTERPRETATION

....

ISABELLE VAN DAMME

I. INTRODUCTION

THE jurisdiction, applicable law, and interpretive practices of the WTO dispute settlement system define its power within the WTO institutional structure and its influence on other international courts and tribunals. The question of the applicable law only arises once jurisdiction has been established; the question of interpretation only arises once the applicable law is identified. Identifying the applicable law, however, might also necessitate some interpretation. The distinction between finding the applicable law and interpreting that law is less clearly defined than the distinction between establishing jurisdiction and finding the applicable law, because identifying the applicable law already entails a considerable amount of interpretation.

The WTO Dispute Settlement Understanding (DSU) states that panels and the Appellate Body have jurisdiction over violation and non-violation claims arising under the WTO covered agreements. The DSU is mostly silent on the applicable law but uniquely explains that the WTO covered agreements need to be interpreted in accordance with the customary principles of treaty interpretation. The DSU established a compulsory and binding dispute settlement system, consisting of a panel and appellate level, with the capacity to authorize the enforcement of findings and recommendations in adopted panel and Appellate Body reports. The DSU, special provisions in particular agreements, and the Working Procedures for panels and the Appellate Body govern the proceedings in WTO dispute settlement. They also offer the possibility of alternative dispute resolution such as good offices, conciliation, arbitration, and meditation. The latter co-exist with the adversarial proceedings, 'are undertaken voluntarily if the parties to the dispute so agree' and 'may be requested at any time by any party to a dispute'.[1]

II. THE JURISDICTION OF WTO PANELS AND THE APPELLATE BODY

A. Compulsory, Exclusive, Not General

The jurisdiction of WTO panels and the Appellate Body is compulsory, exclusive, but not general. WTO panels and the Appellate Body have jurisdiction over disputes

---

[1] Arts 5.1–5.3 DSU. See, eg, Award of the Arbitrator, *Banana Tariff Arbitration*; Decision by the Arbitrators, *Banana Tariff Arbitration II*.

between WTO Members 'brought pursuant to the consultation and dispute settlement provisions' in the covered agreements.[2] Only claims to enforce benefits under the WTO covered agreements can be brought to WTO dispute settlement. Claims do not necessarily need to refer to obligations, as situation complaints and non-violations complaints are allowed.[3] WTO Members can settle disputes about the interpretation and the application of the WTO covered agreements by agreement or by third-party decision. If they want a third party to settle their dispute, recourse to dispute settlement under the DSU is the only option. If WTO Members cannot settle their dispute by agreement, Article 23 DSU leaves no doubt that 'the WTO dispute settlement mechanism is the only means available to WTO Members to obtain relief, and only the remedial actions envisaged in the WTO system can be used by WTO Members'.[4] Article 23 DSU states, though not explicitly establishing an exclusive jurisdiction, that WTO Members '*shall* have recourse to, and abide by, the rules and procedures under this Understanding'.[5] Panels and the Appellate Body have the power to determine their own jurisdiction.[6] This may require the interpretation of the jurisdiction of other WTO organs. Panels and the Appellate Body cannot 'adjudicate non-WTO disputes', that is, address direct claims to 'determine rights and obligations outside the covered agreements', though the extent to which this might be done indirectly remains unsettled and speculative.[7] Their jurisdiction is compulsory because WTO Members by acceding to the WTO automatically consent to the jurisdiction of the WTO dispute settlement system.

All limits to all powers of international courts and tribunals ultimately derive from the principle of consensual jurisdiction, irrespective of how this consent is expressed. An exhaustive list of such limits is aspirational and irreconcilable with the judicial function as such. But a few core principles can, nevertheless, be identified and discussed with application to the WTO dispute settlement system. One

---

[2] Art 1.1 DSU. A court or tribunal has jurisdiction 'whenever it has been regularly seised and whenever it has not been shown, on some other ground, that it lacks jurisdiction or that the claim is inadmissible'. ICJ, *Nottebohm Case (Liechtenstein v Guatemala) (Preliminary Objection)*, 18 November 1953, ICJ Reports (1953) 111, at 122. The competence of a court or tribunal is broader and 'includes both jurisdiction and the element of the propriety of the Court's exercising its jurisdiction in the circumstances of the concrete case'. S Rosenne, *The Law and Practice of the International Court 1920–1996*, Vol I, 3rd edn (The Hague: Martinus Nijhoff, 1997), at 536.

[3] Art XXIII:1 GATT 1994 (see also Art 19 Agreement on Agriculture, Art 11 SPS Agreement, Art 14(1) TBT Agreement, Art 8 TRIMS Agreement, Art 8 Preshipment Inspection Agreement, Art 8 Rules of Origin Agreement, Art 6 Licensing Agreement, Art 30 SCM Agreement, Art 14 Safeguards Agreement, Art 64 TRIPS Agreement, Art XXIII:3 GATS, Art 26 DSU, (Art 17(1)(3) Anti-Dumping Agreement, Article 19(1)–(2) Customs Valuation Agreement). Art 8(10) ATC refers to the DSU, but only to Art XXIII:2 GATT 1994.

[4] Panel Report, *US – Certain EC Products*, at para 6.23.

[5] Emphasis added.

[6] Appellate Body Report, *US – 1916 Act*, at para 54, fn 30.

[7] Appellate Body Report, *Mexico – Taxes on Soft Drinks*, at paras 56, 78.

limitation is the principle of *non ultra petita*.[8] Panels and the Appellate Body should not decide more than they have jurisdiction. In other words, the Appellate Body 'shall address each of the issues raised in accordance with paragraph 6 during the appellate proceeding'[9] and no more.[10] The exception to this principle in appellate review is that the Appellate Body may review the exercise of inherent powers by panels, even in the absence of a claim to that effect.[11] Another example is the principle that judges cannot legislate,[12] though this is not to be taken too literally, and they need to interpret treaties 'as they stand'.[13] Another limitation is the principle that it is for the State to decide how to implement and give effect to its international obligations, including obligations resulting from decisions of international courts and tribunals with judicial finality.[14] Article 19.1 DSU confirms that 'the panel or the Appellate Body may suggest ways in which the Member concerned could implement the recommendations'. This merely reflects the general principle, they can suggest but not impose.[15]

Understanding the judicial function requires a study of the type of powers of judges, as well as their sources. It implies a comparative survey of practices of various courts and tribunals to detect emerging principles of international procedural law and inherent powers associated with the status of the international judge. Simply put, the function of the international judge in contentious cases is to decide in concrete cases on the determination of particular rights, obligations, powers by reference to established rules of international law. The international judge can only exist because of the consent of States to the creation of his function. His or her function is not to create law, though this power is not entirely excluded from the function.

The powers of any international judge can only be determined by reference to the constitutive document establishing the court or tribunal of which he or she is part,

---

[8] ICJ, *Request for the Interpretation of the Judgment of November 20th, 1950, in the Asylum Case (Colombia/Peru)*, Judgment, ICJ Reports (1950) 395, at 402.

[9] Art 17.12 DSU, referring to Art 17.6 DSU ('An appeal shall be limited to issues of law covered in the panel report and legal interpretations developed by the panel').

[10] See, eg, Appellate Body Report, *Canada – Aircraft*, at para 21. See also chapter 14 of this Handbook.

[11] See, eg, Appellate Body Report, *US – Offset Act (Byrd Amendment)*, at para 208.

[12] ICJ, *Legality of Threat or Use of Nuclear Weapons*, Advisory Opinion, ICJ Reports (1996) 226, at 267, para 18; Appellate Body Report, *US – Wool Shirts and Blouses*, at 340; Appellate Body Report, *US – Upland Cotton*, at para 509; Appellate Body Report, *India – Patents (US)*, at para 45.

[13] PCIJ, *Question Concerning the Acquisition of Polish Nationality*, PCIJ Reports (1923) Ser. B, No 7, at 20; ICJ, *Competence of the General Assembly for the Admission of a State to the United Nations*, Advisory Opinion, ICJ Reports (1950) 4, at 8; ICJ, *Arbitral Award of 31 July 1989 (Guinea-Bissau v Senegal)*, ICJ Reports (1991) 53, at para 48; ICJ, *Case Concerning the Territorial Dispute (Libyan Arab Jamahiriya/Chad)*, ICJ Reports (1994) 6, at 25, para 51; ICJ, *LaGrand Case (Germany v United States of America)*, ICJ Reports (2001) 466, at 494, para 77.

[14] See, eg, ICJ, *LaGrand Case*, ICJ Reports (2001) 466, at 513–14, para 125. More intrusive approaches to national implementation are visible, however, in EC law and international criminal law.

[15] Panels are under no obligation to make such suggestions, see, eg, Panel Report, *US – Stainless Steel (Mexico)*, at paras 8.4–5; Panel Report, *EC – Salmon*, at paras 6.31–32.

as well as supplementary procedural decisions and rules. In the WTO, for example, the DSU establishes the jurisdiction of panels and the Appellate Body, defines their standard terms of reference, informs the goals of the system, and sets out the procedural framework within which disputes between WTO Members will be resolved by third party dispute settlement. This treaty is an integral part of the WTO covered agreements, and is supplemented by a range of other procedural rules. These other rules are not all treaty language.

B. Jurisdiction Over Facts and Law

Panels have jurisdiction to decide factual and legal issues. Panels' terms of reference are 'to examine, in the light of the relevant provisions [...] the matter referred to the DSB [...] and to make such findings as will assist the DSB [Dispute Settlement Body] in making the recommendations or in giving the rulings provided for in that/those agreement(s)'.[16] These terms of reference imply a due process objective. They also establish the jurisdiction of a Panel in a particular dispute.[17] The Appellate Body has found that Article 11 DSU defines the standard of review for panels:

...a panel should make an objective assessment of the matter before it, including an objective assessment of the facts of the case and the applicability of and conformity with the relevant covered agreements, and make such other findings as will assist the DSB in making the recommendations or in giving the rulings provided for in the covered agreements.[18]

In contrast, the Appellate Body can only be seized of legal issues and '[a]n appeal shall be limited to issues of law covered in the panel report and legal interpretations developed by the panel'. Article 17.6 DSU makes the Appellate Body prone to the description of 'more or less [a] court of cassation', which 'confirms the essentially legal nature of the system'.[19] But on appeal, the Appellate Body 'may uphold, modify or reverse the legal findings and conclusions of the panel'.[20] The Appellate Body can do more than merely annul panel reports but it has no remand authority, though it occasionally completes the legal analysis of panels if certain conditions are met. This suggests that the role of the Appellate Body is broader than that of a court of cassation.

---

[16]   Art 7.1 DSU.

[17]   Appellate Body Report, *Brazil – Desiccated Coconut*, at 186; also Appellate Body Report, *India – Patents (US)*, at paras 92–93.

[18]   See Appellate Body Report, *EC – Hormones*, at para 119. Special standards of review may apply to particular agreements. Article 17.6 Anti-Dumping Agreement sets out a special standard of review, though complementary to Art 11 DSU. Appellate Body Report *US – Hot-Rolled Steel*, at paras 50–62.

[19]   P Lamy, 'The Place of the WTO and its Law in the International Legal Order' 2006 *European Journal of International Law* 17(5) 969, at 976.

[20]   Art 17.13 DSU.

C. Conflicts of Jurisdiction

Conflicts of jurisdiction arise when another treaty provides jurisdiction over similar or identical claims as those arising under the WTO covered agreements. The treaty language may be identical; but the source of law will always be different, thus also the context in which to appreciate and interpret the applicable law. If another court or tribunal has jurisdiction to decide claims arising under the WTO covered agreements, this grant of jurisdiction is in violation of the commitment in the DSU to bring WTO disputes *only* to the WTO dispute settlement system.

The specialization of international law has created potentially competing jurisdictions between different international courts or tribunals. Disputes such as *Softwood Lumber* and *Mox Plant* are examples of how different courts have dealt with the specialization of international law. This is not a new phenomenon. A conflict of jurisdiction may exist:

'(1) when two fora claim to have exclusive jurisdiction over the matter or similar or parallel matter; (2) when one forum claims to have exclusive jurisdiction and the other offers jurisdiction, on a permissive basis, for dealing with the same matter or a related one; or (3) when two jurisdictions offer—on a non-mandatory basis—their respective dispute settlement mechanisms to examine the same or similar matters'.[21]

The controversy relates to what law panels and the Appellate Body should apply in the exercise of their jurisdiction and how this jurisdiction co-exists with that of other international dispute settlement systems. In theory, all depends on whether one agrees with the general proposition that:

...all international law exists in systemic relationship with other law, no such application can take place without situating the relevant jurisdiction-endowing instrument in its normative environment [...] although a tribunal may only have jurisdiction in regard to a particular instrument, it must always *interpret* and *apply* that instrument in its relationship to its normative environment—that is to say 'other' international law.[22]

In the context of the specificity of the DSU, this general proposition fails to capture the subtleties in the text of the DSU. The DSU does not address the relationship between the WTO dispute settlement system and other international courts and tribunals;[23] it merely establishes compulsory jurisdiction. An exception is the right

[21] G Marceau, 'Conflict of Norms and Conflicts of Jurisdiction – The Relationship between the WTO Agreement and MEAs and other Treaties' 2001 *Journal of World Trade* 35(6) 1081, at 1109.

[22] *Report of the ILC Study Group, Fragmentation of International Law: Difficulties Arising from the Diversification and Expansion of International Law – Finalized by Martti Koskenniemi and Draft conclusions of the work of the Study Group (Fragmentation Report (2006)),* A/CN.4/L.682 and Add. 1 and Corr. 1, 2 May 2006 (and taken note of by the UNGA Sixth Committee, A/61/454, at para III.4), at para 423 (original emphasis).

[23] Compare with Art 151.8 UNCLOS, Art XIII:6 International Plant Protection Convention, and Art 2005 NAFTA.

in Article 11.3 SPS Agreement to resort to the good offices and dispute settlement systems of other international organizations or established under any other treaty. Exclusive jurisdiction cannot be ceded. Panels and the Appellate Body have, so far, not declined to exercise their jurisdiction or suspended proceedings in deference to another court or tribunal. In part, this is due to the 'quasi-automaticity of the compulsory and binding WTO dispute settlement mechanism'.[24] The emerging confidence and self-awareness of the Appellate Body about its effect on international law also helps to explain why panels and the Appellate Body are not likely to cede jurisdiction, in the event of parallel proceedings before different courts and tribunals. This has contributed to negative perceptions of the specialization or diversification of international law.

D. Inherent Powers

The WTO dispute settlement system is often described as formally a quasi-judicial or juridical system, though the Appellate Body operates and exercises its jurisdiction as if it were a court. This observation is not novel, nor is it surprising after more than a decade of Appellate Body jurisprudence—even if this development of the dispute settlement system was not entirely inevitable. It raises, however, questions of international procedural law that have yet to be explained and understood, at least by the audience of its decisions. In particular, the scope of inherent powers of the Appellate Body remains, perhaps necessarily, unclear.

The analogy of the WTO dispute settlement system with other courts and tribunals applies to the Appellate Body, but less so to panels. The Appellate Body is a permanently constituted body that has interpreted the same, large, and complex treaty language numerous times. It has decided to function as if it were a court, even if finality of its decisions requires political approval by reverse consensus. Appellate Body members perceive themselves as members of a judicial body exercising the international judicial function, not very different in principle from, for example, the International Court of Justice (ICJ).[25] The seven Appellate Body members are

---

[24] Lamy, above fn 19, at 983.

[25] See, eg, G Abi-Saab, 'The Appellate Body and treaty interpretation' in G Sacerdoti, A Yanovich, and J Bohanes (eds), *The WTO at Ten – The Contribution of the Dispute Settlement System* (Cambridge: Cambridge University Press, 2006) 453, at 455–56; G Sacerdoti, 'WTO Law and the "Fragmentation" of International Law: Specificity, Integration, Conflicts' in ME Janow, V Donaldson, and A Yanovich (eds), *WTO at Ten: Governance, Dispute Settlement and Developing Countries* (Huntington: Juris Publishing Inc, 2008) Chapter 34 ; FP Feliciano, 'WTO Case Law in an International Context' in ME Janow, V Donaldson, and A Yanovich (eds), *WTO at Ten: Governance, Dispute Settlement and Developing Countries* (Huntington: Juris Publishing Inc, 2008) Chapter 39; also JHH Weiler, 'The Rule of Lawyers and the Ethos of Diplomats – Reflections on the International and External Legitimacy of WTO Dispute Settlement' 2001 *Journal of World Trade* 35(2) 191, at 200–01.

appointed for four years with the possibility of reappointment.[26] They have diverse backgrounds and do not need to be lawyers, though most are.[27]

The DSU is the starting point for defining the function of WTO panels and the Appellate Body. It is their first and primary source of powers. But other powers may exist and be sourced elsewhere. General international law is not merely limited to customary international law applicable to all States. Fundamental principles rooted in principles of due process and the rule of law are also part of general international law governing international adjudication.

Inherent powers are powers that the judge enjoys by mere fact of his or her status as a judge. In the words of the ICJ in the *Nuclear Tests Case*:

... an inherent jurisdiction enabling it to take such as may be required, on the one hand to ensure that the exercise of its jurisdiction over the merits, if and when established, shall not be frustrated, and, on the other, to provide for the orderly settlement of all matter in dispute, to ensure the observance of the 'inherent limitations on the exercise of the judicial function' of the Court, and to 'maintain its judicial character' .... Such inherent jurisdiction ... derives from the mere existence of the Court as a judicial organ established by the consent of States, and is conferred upon it in order that its basic judicial functions may be safeguard.[28]

Judge Higgins in her Separate Opinion in *Legality of Use of Force* observed that:

The Court's inherent jurisdiction derives from its judicial character and the need for powers to regulate matters connected with the administration of justice, not every aspect of which may have been foreseen in the Rules.[29]

The very occasional need to exercise inherent powers may arise as a matter *in limine litis*, or as a decision by the Court not to exercise a jurisdiction it has, or in connection with the conduct or the merits of a case.[30]

In principle, the judge will enjoy inherent powers absent contradictory language in the constitutive document. It can exercise these powers on its own initiative, irrespective of the claims and arguments made by the disputants or third parties/participants. Even so, it is desirable for any court of tribunal to invite the views of the disputants on its exercise of a particular inherent power in a specific proceeding.[31]

---

[26] Art 17.2 DSU. See also Chapter 12 of this Handbook.

[27] Art 17.3 DSU.

[28] ICJ, *Nuclear Tests Case (Australia v France)*, Merits, ICJ Reports (1974) 253, at 259–60 (citing ICJ, *Northern Cameroons*, ICJ Reports (1963) 15, at 29).

[29] ICJ, *Legality of Use of Force (Serbia and Montenegro v Spain)*, Preliminary Objections, Separate Opinion Judge Higgins, ICJ Reports (2004) 1214, at 1216–17, para 10, relying on the PCIJ's reasoning for admitting the filing preliminary objections to jurisdiction in PCIJ, *The Mavrommatis Palestine Concessions*, PCIJ Reports (1924) of Ser. A, No 2, 16.

[30] Ibid at 1217, para 11.

[31] Eg , the Appellate Body in *Canada – Autos* found that 'for purposes of transparency and fairness to the parties, a panel should, however, in all cases, address expressly those claims which it declines to examine and rule upon for reasons of judicial economy'. Appellate Body Report, *Canada – Autos*, at para 117. More generally, see E Lauterpacht, ' "Partial" judgments and the inherent jurisdiction of

In the event of contradictory language, either the entity created is not a court and tribunal and hence should not enjoy inherent powers (or at least not inherent judicial powers), either the inherent power will prevail over language that is contradictory to fundamental principles of due process of justice, or the more particular language will trump the inherent powers.

It follows from its choice to function as a court or tribunal that the Appellate Body can exercise (certain) inherent powers associated with this status. Its most basic inherent power is to determine its own jurisdiction. But other inherent powers have been exercised or at least claimed, including the power to complete the analysis in respect of a claim over which a panel exercised judicial economy. Other inherent powers may be available to the Appellate Body, but have not yet been claimed or exercised, mostly because there was no need to.

All panel and Appellate Body reports are ultimately subject to the control of WTO Members. Every report needs to be adopted by reverse consensus.[32] It has become practically impossible for a panel or Appellate Body report to be blocked as occurred in GATT dispute settlement. Despite this formalistic and political imprimatur, panels and Appellate Body reports are approached as decisions of 'judicial tribunals in the international law sense', without necessarily implying the full scope of inherent powers of international courts and tribunals.[33]

When establishing jurisdiction, panels and the Appellate Body exercise their inherent power to determine their own jurisdiction. The Appellate Body in *US – 1916 Act* confirmed the existence of the 'widely accepted rule that an international tribunal is entitled to consider the issue of its own jurisdiction on its own initiative, and to satisfy itself that it has jurisdiction in any case that comes before it'.[34] This requires

---

the International Court of Justice' in V Lowe and M Fitzmaurice (eds), *Fifty Years of the International Court of Justice – Essays in Honour of Sir Robert Jennings* (Cambridge: Cambridge University Press, 1996) 465, at 482–83; ICJ, *Legality of Use of Force*, Separate Opinion Judge Higgins, ICJ Reports (2004) 1214, at 1217.

[32]   Arts 16.4 and 17.14 DSU.

[33]   J Pauwelyn, 'The Role of Public International Law in the WTO: How Far Can We Go?' 2001 *American Journal of International Law* 95(3) 535, at 553. Not all WTO Members share this view. See, eg, DSB, *Negotiations on Improvements and Clarifications of the Dispute Settlement Understanding, Further Contribution of the United States on Improving Flexibility and Member Control in WTO Dispute Settlement, Communication from the United States*, TN/DS/W/82 (24 October 2005); DSB, *Flexibility and Member Control, Revised Textual Proposal by Chile and the United States, Communication from Chile and the United States*, TN/DS/W/89 (31 May 2007).

[34]   Appellate Body Report, *US – 1916 Act*, at para 54, footnote 30; also Appellate Body Report, *US – Offset Act (Byrd Amendment)*, at para 208: '...the issue of a panel's jurisdiction is so fundamental that it is appropriate to consider claims that a panel has exceeded its jurisdiction even if such claims were not raised in the Notice of Appeal'. The Appellate Body found support in PCIJ, *Case Concerning the Administration of the Prince von Pless (Preliminary Objection)*, PCIJ Reports (1933) Ser. A/B, No 52, at 15; ICJ, *Anglo-Iranian Oil Co. Case (United Kingdom v Iran) (Preliminary Objection)*, Individual Opinion Judge McNair, ICJ Report (1952) 116; ICJ, *Case of Certain Norwegian Loans (France v Norway)*, Separate Opinion Judge Lauterpacht, ICJ Reports (1957) 34, at 43; ICJ, *Interhandel*, Dissenting Opinion Judge Lauterpacht, ICJ Reports (1959) 95, at 104; Iran – US Claims Tribunal, *Marks & Umann v Iran*,

also the power of panels and the Appellate Body to objectively identify the dispute at issue. This power, sometimes called the principle of *Kompetenz-Kompetenz* or the principle of jurisdiction over jurisdiction, is not exclusive to the judicial function. Its exercise can involve interpreting the jurisdiction of other WTO organs.[35] In principle, a court or tribunal can only determine the scope of its own jurisdiction, it cannot decide that of another court or tribunal. Appellate review of such a decision is not an exception to this principle so long as the review is procedurally provided, as in the WTO. In that event, the appellate court or tribunal may review the decision of the lower court or tribunal to determine its own jurisdiction, though the applicable standard of review will be contextual. One Appellate Body member has described the principle, writing in an extra-judicial context, as meaning that:

'. . . a court is the master of its own proceedings, that it determines the limits of its own jurisdiction, and it decides on challenges to it'.[36]

The Appellate Body in *Mexico – Corn Syrup (Article 21.5 – US)* elaborated on the inherent power of panels and the Appellate Body to determine their own jurisdiction and their duty to address jurisdictional issues. It found that:

First, as a matter of due process, and the proper exercise of the judicial function, panels are required to address issues that are put before them by the parties to a dispute. Second, panels have to address and dispose of certain issues of a fundamental nature, even if the parties to the dispute remain silent on those issues. In this regards, we have previously observed that '[t]he vesting of jurisdiction in a panel is a fundamental prerequisite for lawful panel

Case No 458, 8 IRAN-US CTR 290, at 296–97; and doctrine (including Hudson, Fitzmaurice, Rosenne, Podesta Costa, Ruda, Diez de Velasco Vallejo, van Hof). The principle was authoritatively established by the ICJ in the earlier cases (not referred to by the Appellate Body) of ICJ, *Interpretation of Peace Treaties with Bulgaria, Hungary and Romania* (First Phase), ICJ Reports (1950) 65, at 75 ; ICJ, *The Corfu Channel Case (Merits)*, Judgment, ICJ Reports (1949) 4, at 25–26. In *Fisheries Jurisdiction*, the Court added that 'there is no burden of proof to be discharged in the matter of jurisdiction'. ICJ, *Fisheries Jurisdiction Case (Spain v Canada) (Jurisdiction)*, ICJ Reports (2002) 432, at 450. The clearest affirmation of the principle was offered in ICJ, *Nottebohm Case (Liechtenstein v. Guatemala) (Preliminary Objection)*, ICJ Reports (1953) 111, at 119:

> Since the *Alabama* case, it has been generally recognized, following the earlier precedents, that, in the absence of any agreement to the contrary, an international tribunal has the right to decide as to its own jurisdiction and has the power to interpret for this purpose the instruments which govern that jurisdiction.

The irony is, of course, that by declaring this power to apply to all international courts and tribunals, the ICJ is in fact trespassing on the inherent power of those other courts and tribunals, and thus the essence of the principle it is declaring to apply.

[35] The Panel in *Turkey – Textiles* refused to determine the scope of its own jurisdiction and exercised judicial economy, mostly on the ground that the resolution of the dispute did not require a finding on the WTO-compatibility of a customs union – a matter it found more appropriate for the WTO Committee on Regional Trade Agreements to determine. Panel Report, *Turkey – Textiles*, at paras 9.52–54. This part of the report was not appealed, though others were.

[36] G Abi-Saab, 'Whither the Judicial Function? Concluding Remarks' in L Boisson de Chazournes, CPR Romano, and R Mackenzie (eds), *International Organizations and International Dispute Settlement: Trends and Prospects* (New York: Transnational Publishers, 2002) 241, at 246.

proceedings'. For this reason, panels cannot simply ignore issues which go to the root of their jurisdiction – that is, to their authority to deal with and dispose of matters. Rather, panels must deal with such issues – if necessary, on their own motion – in order to classify themselves that they have authority to proceed.[37]

The Appellate Body thus found that a panel is obliged 'to address issues' in at least two instances. The first obligation exists when objections are raised by the parties. It is merely an obligation to address the issue. The second obligation means that a panel must respond to certain objections 'of a fundamental nature' even if they are not raised by the parties. This is an obligation to address and dispose of the issue. Such a fundamental issue is a panel's jurisdiction. In this case, Mexico complained about the lack of consultations before referring an issue to the Panel and other irregularities in the consultation procedure. But it did not raise these objections in its two written submissions to the Panel, nor at the DSB meeting, nor in a request for a preliminary ruling. It only put these issues before the Panel at the occasion of first oral meeting. Even then, Mexico merely noted the issue and agreed with a third party's more formal request at the oral meeting that the Panel consider the matter. The Appellate Body considered this to be insufficient to qualify as a explicit objection. The Appellate Body found the situation to fall under the first obligation on panels to address issues relating to their authority to hear and dispose of the claims. As Mexico did not explicitly raise the objection, the Panel had the power to decline to address objections to its seisin if these are not explicitly stated:

The requirements of good faith, due process and orderly procedure dictate that objections [to the authority of the Panel], especially those of such potential significance, should be explicitly raised. Only in this way will the panel, the other party to the dispute, and the third parties, understand that a specific objection has been raised, and have an adequate opportunity to address and respond to it.[38]

If Mexico had formally raised the matter, preferably in its written submissions to the Panel, the Appellate Body observed that 'the Panel may well have been required to "address" those objections, whether by virtue of Article 7.2 and 12.7 of the DSU, or the requirements of due process'.[39] But the duty to address a matter does not entail a duty to decide the matter:

In such circumstances, however, the Panel could have satisfied that duty simply by stating in its Report that it declined to examine or rule on Mexico's "objections" due to the *untimely* manner in which they were raised.[40]

The first duty thus applies if the objection is raised explicitly and timely. If these conditions are not met, a panel still has the power to address and dispose of the

[37] Appellate Body Report, *Mexico – Corn Syrup (Article 21.5 – US)*, at para 36 (referring also to Appellate Body Report, *US – 1916 Act*, at para 54, footnote 32).
[38] Ibid. at para 47.
[39] Ibid. at para 49; see also Appellate Body Report, *EC – Hormones*, at para 152.
[40] Ibid. (original emphasis).

matter but is under no obligation to do so. The Appellate Body still considered whether the issues raised by Mexico were, nevertheless, of such a fundamental character to trigger the second obligation. If this were the case, the Panel should have addressed and disposed of the issues on its own initiative, irrespective of the lack of an explicit and timely objection. The test was whether the issues 'are of such a nature that they could have deprived the Panel of its authority to deal with and dispute of the matter'.[41] The lack of consultations was not such an issue, the Appellate Body found.[42] Despite their 'undoubted practical importance',[43] consultations are a right of the respondent party. If that party does not respond or declines to give effect to the request, it is presumed to have waived that right and the complaining party may request the establishment of a panel. An effective interpretation of Articles 4.7 and 6.2 DSU further confirmed that the lack of consultations was not a procedural deficiency that could affect a panel's jurisdiction.[44] The Appellate Body concluded that the second obligation did not apply because 'the lack of prior consultations is not a defect that, by its very nature, deprives a panel of its authority to deal with and dispose of a matter, and that, accordingly, such a defect is not one which a panel must examine even if both parties to the dispute remain silent thereon'.[45] Similarly, the failure to comply with the obligation in Article 6.2 DSU to indicate whether consultations were held was also not such a defect.[46] The same conclusion applied to the alleged failure of the complaining party to 'exercise its judgement as to whether action ... would be fruitful', as stated in Article 3.7 DSU.[47] As a result, the second obligation of a panel to address and dispose of issues on its own initiative applies, at least, to issues of jurisdiction but not to issues of seisin and other informative and good faith obligations on disputants. The Appellate Body did not in this case decide whether that obligation applies to questions of admissibility.

The jurisdiction of a court or tribunal is built on the consent of States, *ante hoc* or *ad hoc* to submit all or certain disputes to that court for third party resolution.[48] Once jurisdiction is validly established, most courts and tribunals have seized the power to declare a case inadmissible, or at least to examine whether certain reasons compel the court not to exercise its jurisdiction. Such admissibility phase is procedurally not foreseen in the DSU. The jurisdictional stage is about whether a court or tribunal *can* hear a case and involves appreciating jurisdictional objections. If it can, the admissibility stage is about whether a court or tribunal *should* hear the case. It is

---

[41] Ibid. at para 53.   [42] Ibid.

[43] Ibid. at para 56, also footnote 48.

[44] Ibid. at paras 62–63.   [45] Ibid. at para 64.

[46] Ibid. at para 70.   [47] Ibid. at para 74.

[48] See, eg, ICJ, *Corfu Channel*, Competence, Joint Separate Opinion Judges Basdevant, Alvarez, Winiarski, Zoričič, de Visscher, Badawi Pasha, and Krylov, ICJ Reports (1948) 31; ICJ, *Peace Treaties (First Phase)*, ICJ Reports (1950) 71.

a question to be answered 'on some other ground than [the] ultimate merits'[49] but for 'reasons why the Court should not proceed to an examination of the merits'.[50]

If a court or tribunal determines that it can and should hear a case, it is competent to hear that dispute.[51] This understanding of competence was the basis for Mexico's argument before the Panel in *Mexico – Taxes on Soft Drinks* that:

> ... the mere conclusion that the Panel has substantive jurisdiction to hear the case [...] does not exhaust all issues relevant to the Panel's competence in this dispute.[52]
>
> ...
>
> The reason is that even though the substantive jurisdiction of any international court or tribunal may be granted explicitly by treaty, once such a forum has been seized of a specific matter, it has certain implied jurisdictional powers that derive from its nature as an adjudicative body.[53]

The distinction made by Mexico between jurisdiction and admissibility is common knowledge in most contexts of dispute settlement, but it was a novel argument in the WTO context. Mexico characterized the power to decide on the admissibility as an 'implied jurisdictional power', though arguably it intended to label it an inherent power. The circumstances in which a court or tribunal can raise admissibility on its own initiative are less general than with respect to jurisdiction, though the possibility should not be excluded.

It is normally assumed that the occasion for declining jurisdiction cannot occur in the WTO, and so far panels and the Appellate Body have not declined to exercise their jurisdiction. As mentioned earlier, the jurisdiction of WTO panels and the Appellate Body is compulsory, contentious, exclusive, but not general. WTO panels and the Appellate Body do not enjoy advisory jurisdiction. They have jurisdiction over disputes between WTO Members 'brought pursuant to the consultation and dispute settlement provisions' in the covered agreements.[54]

---

[49] G Fitzmaurice, *The Law and Procedure of the International Court of Justice*, Vol 2 (Cambridge: Grotius Publications, 1986), at 438. Fitzmaurice defined the 'merits of a dispute' as consisting of 'all those propositions of fact and of law which must be established by a party in order to enable it to obtain a judgment in its favour, on the assumption that the tribunal has jurisdiction to entertain these propositions, and that there is no objection to the substantive admissibility of the claim'. Ibid. at 448. This definition was a refinement of the definition offered by Judge Read in ICJ, *Anglo-Iranian Oil Co. Case (United Kingdom v Iran) (Preliminary Objection)*, Dissenting Opinion Judge Read, ICJ Reports (1952) 142, at 148.

[50] ICJ, *Case Concerning Oil Platforms (Islamic Republic of Iran v United States) (Merits)*, ICJ Reports (2003) 161, at 177, para 29.

[51] See S Rosenne, *The Law and Practice of the International Court 1920–2005*, Vol II, 4th edn (The Hague: Martinus Nijhoff, 2006) at 524. Fitzmaurice notes the terminological confusion between jurisdiction and competence, but still upholds the distinction between 'the question of the general class of cases in respect of which a given tribunal has jurisdiction ...; and ... the question of its competence to hear and determine a particular individual case'. G Fitzmaurice, above fn 49, at 434.

[52] Panel Report, *Mexico – Taxes on Soft Drinks*, at para 4.184 (representing Mexico's argument as part of its request for a preliminary ruling).

[53] Ibid at para 4.185.   [54] Art 1.1 DSU.

Once the jurisdiction of a panel or the Appellate Body is established, the DSU does not contemplate the case being declared inadmissible. On first glance, it would appear that the decision on the merits of the case cannot be preceded by an admissibility phase, only a jurisdictional phase. The absence of an admissibility phase in the DSU does not mean that this core stage in the judicial process is precluded from the life of a WTO dispute. The Appellate Body is seen to assert that it could have the power to declare a case inadmissible, even in the absence of exercising it. Such power would not find any basis in the DSU, not even in a broad construction of it. The Appellate Body would have this power as inherent to its judicial function—a power with limitations.

Inherent powers and admissibility were central in the *Mexico – Taxes on Soft Drinks* dispute. A dispute arose between the US and Mexico about the enforcement of particular sugar quota rights under NAFTA. Mexico responded to the US' refusal to cooperate in establishing a NAFTA Chapter 20 Panel by imposing discriminatory taxes on US imports of soft drinks. The discriminatory tax was the measure at issue in the WTO dispute.[55] On appeal, Mexico did not dispute that the Panel had jurisdiction, but disagreed with the conclusion that a WTO panel does not enjoy the discretion to decline to exercise its jurisdiction. In Mexico's view, the Panel should have deferred to the jurisdiction of the NAFTA Chapter 20 Panel that Mexico sought to establish but the US had blocked.[56]

Before the Panel, Mexico had already argued that the Panel enjoyed 'the power to decide whether it should refrain from exercising its validly established substantive jurisdiction'.[57] It cautioned, however, that this power was only available 'in the extraordinary circumstances of this case since there is an available forum for both parties to solve the dispute in a comprehensive manner'.[58] During the first substantive meeting, the Panel questioned Mexico and the other parties on this matter. In particular, it was interested to hear whether the DSU explicitly sets out the inherent

[55] There were no conflicting jurisdictions in this dispute: two separate measures were taken by two different WTO Members/NAFTA Contracting Parties in respect of which each State made different claims before different courts or tribunals with different jurisdictions. See Panel Report, *Mexico – Taxes on Soft Drinks*, at para 7.14.

[56] Mexico's request for establishing a NAFTA Chapter 20 Panel remained pending during the WTO proceedings. The US refused to appoint NAFTA panelists.

[57] Panel Report, *Mexico – Taxes on Soft Drinks*, at para 4.185 (representing Mexico's argument as part of its request for a preliminary ruling).

[58] Ibid. at para 4.190 (representing Mexico's argument as part of its request for a preliminary ruling). The extraordinary circumstance in this case was the fact that 'a broader dispute exists, as recognized by both parties, the United States and Mexico, but the United States has frustrated the Mexican right to have recourse to the appropriate dispute settlement mechanism in order to resolve its grievance'. Ibid. at para 4.192 (representing Mexico's argument as part of its request for a preliminary ruling). In fact, the two disputes were inter-related, but not identical: different claims with respect to different measures were raised in different fora.

power invoked by Mexico.[59] In a sense, this question misses the point. Although the DSU or any procedural agreement may confirm inherent powers, no explicit treaty basis is required for their exercise. The more relevant question, also asked by the Panel, was whether the DSU prevents panels from declining to exercise their jurisdiction. In other words, whether the DSU excluded admissibility.[60] Mexico's response was that:

>...there is no provision in the WTO agreements that explicitly rules out or excludes such powers. By implicit consent, the Panel may have recourse to and apply the principles of public international law. As international adjudicative bodies, WTO panels too have such incidental jurisdiction.[61]

The Panel refused to decline exercising its jurisdiction in favour of the jurisdiction of a NAFTA Chapter 20 Panel. Its finding is somewhat open-ended (similar to that of the Appellate Body on appeal). It found that the DSU offered it 'no discretion to decide whether or not to exercise its jurisdiction in a case properly before it'.[62] 'Even if it had such discretion', it added, the facts of this case did not warrant using this discretion and declining to exercise jurisdiction.[63] Furthermore, the Panel clarified that 'it makes no findings about whether there may be other cases where a panel's jurisdiction might be legally constrained, notwithstanding its approved terms of reference'.[64] Overall, the Panel signalled that inadmissibility would conflict with its mandate under Article 11 DSU, while confusing admissibility and jurisdiction.[65]

On appeal, the Appellate Body confirmed that panels have inherent jurisdictional powers, including the power to establish their own jurisdiction and the scope of this jurisdiction. This is the principle of *Kompetenz-Kompetenz*. The Appellate Body was correct in characterizing this as an inherent jurisdictional power, but what about admissibility? Inherent powers could not stretch so far that 'once jurisdiction has been validly established, WTO panels would have the authority to decline to rule on the entirety of the claims that are before them in a dispute'.[66] To conclude otherwise, it reasoned, would imply a modification of the rights and obligations in the DSU,[67] and would also prevent a panel from fulfilling its obligation under Article 11 DSU. Here, the Appellate Body excluded the possibility that, once jurisdiction is validly established, a panel declines to exercise its jurisdiction with respect of the entire set of claims defining the terms of reference of panels. At this stage in its reasoning,

---

[59] Panel Report, *Mexico – Taxes on Soft Drinks*, Annex C-1, Response by Mexico to Questions Posed by the Panel after the First Substantive Meeting (20 December 2004), Question 2, see also Question 35 ('... what would be the legal basis for this specific jurisdictional powers and for the discretion that Panels may have under those powers to abstain from exercising its jurisdiction').

[60] Ibid.   [61] Ibid.   [62] Ibid. at para 7.1.

[63] Ibid.   [64] Ibid. at para 7.10.

[65] Ibid. at para 7.8.

[66] Appellate Body Report, *Mexico – Taxes on Soft Drinks*, at para 46.

[67] Ibid (relying on Appellate Body Report, *India – Patents (US)*, at para 46). The Appellate Body still continued with the interpretation of the silences in Articles 3.2, 7.1, 7.2, 11, 19.2, and 23 DSU.

it did not rule out the possibility of declaring part of a claim inadmissible. Quite understandably so, as panels have repeatedly exercised judicial economy, whether right or false,[68] with respect to particular claims or parts thereof. Exercising judicial economy implies declining to exercise jurisdiction over one or more particular claims, once jurisdiction has been established and exercised and when deemed necessary in the light of findings on other claims. This has not been disputed, and the Appellate Body has confirmed that panels have this inherent power though it has also attempted to discipline them in using this power.

Ultimately, the Appellate Body in *Mexico – Taxes on Soft Drinks* left its report open-ended and internally contradictory. Despite its assumption that a decision of inadmissibility over the entire claim would diminish the rights of the complaining party under Articles 3.2 and 19.2 DSU,[69] the Appellate Body did hint to the inherent power of panels to declare an entire claim inadmissible. It cautioned that '[m]indful of the precise scope of Mexico's appeal, [it] express[es] no view as to whether there may be other circumstances in which legal impediments could exist that would preclude a panel from ruling on the merits of the claim that are before it'.[70] This cannot be considered as an affirmation of inherent powers to declare the entire claim inadmissible because, after all, the Appellate Body expressed no view on the matter. Nevertheless, the statement has two effects. First, it has the effect of calling into question the strength of its earlier statement that inadmissibility could only be an option for part of a claim, not the entire claim. Second, it signals that the Appellate Body reserves the freedom to assert and establish in the future the power to declare the entire claim inadmissible. At least for the moment, the power is neither excluded, nor included.

Once jurisdiction is established and the admissibility hurdle is overcome, inherent and implied powers continue to be relevant for panels and the Appellate Body in applying and interpreting the covered agreements, and especially (though not exclusively) the DSU. These powers might be greater with respect to procedural than substantive rules. It is inherent to the judicial function of panels and the Appellate Body that they ensure due process and uphold the rule of law in the context in which they operate. If the DSU and other existing procedural rules are incomplete in providing them with the tools to perform this task, panels and the Appellate Body cannot sacrifice their inherent function as a court or tribunal. In *Chile – Price Band*

---

[68] False judicial economy is the exercise of judicial economy in defiance of panels' duty, under Article 7.1 DSU, 'to make such findings as will assist the DSB in making the recommendations or in giving the rulings provided for in that/those agreement(s)' or in defiance of certain particular other obligations of panels (such as Article 4.7 SCM Agreement). See, eg, Appellate Body Report, *Australia – Salmon*, at para 224; Appellate Body Report, *EC – Export Subsidies on Sugar*, at para 335.

[69] Appellate Body Report, *Mexico – Taxes on Soft Drinks*, at para 53.

[70] Ibid at para 54. The Panel, during its first substantive meeting, had also questioned the parties on whether there might be any NAFTA provision preventing the US from have recourse to WTO dispute settlement. Panel Report, *Mexico – Taxes on Soft Drinks*, Annex C-1, Response by Mexico to Questions Posed by the Panel after the First Substantive Meeting (20 December 2004), Question 4.

314 ISABELLE VAN DAMME

System, the Appellate Body confirmed that due process 'is an obligation inherent in the dispute settlement system'.[71] As one Appellate Body member put it:

... the DSU provides a bare outline of the dispute settlement system. But, for the Appellate Body to exercise its judicial activity, it needs detailed rules of procedure and evidence, which are hardly provided therein. The Appellate Body had to formulate these rules, particularly the rules of evidence, from scratch, by reference to the general principles of law and of international law. And nobody protested against that.[72]

Procedural rules are defined as rules governing the dispute settlement system. They govern not only the behaviour of WTO Members, but equally that of panels and the Appellate Body. Such rules are functional, they exist only in function of and for the purpose of enforcing the substantive rules. They may be equally incomplete and imperfect as the substantive rules, but a greater responsibility is reserved for panels and the Appellate Body in administering them. These rules enable them to exercise their judicial function. As long as they do not act contrary to the DSU or the consent of the disputants in a particular case, panels and the Appellate Body are the masters of their procedure. This power offers them flexibility in changing procedural rules with the consent of the disputants and when found appropriate and necessary. Part of this flexibility is described in the DSU. Article 17.9 DSU authorizes the Appellate Body to draft its own working procedures without defining the scope of such procedural rules. In *US – Lead and Bismuth II*, the Appellate Body interpreted Article 17.9 to mean that it 'has broad authority to adopt procedural rules which do not conflict with any rules and procedures in the DSU or the covered agreements'.[73]

In *Brazil – Aircraft*, the Appellate Body also relied on this authority to establish that it could adopt additional procedural rules on business confidential information, though ultimately it found no need to.[74] According to Article 12.2 DSU, 'panel procedures should provide sufficient flexibility so as to ensure high-quality panel reports, while not unduly delaying the panel process'. Similarly, the Appellate Body in *EC – Hormones* acknowledged that 'the DSU, and in particular its Appendix 3, leave panels a margin of discretion to deal, always in accordance with due process, with specific situations that may arise in a particular case and that are not explicitly regulated'.[75] In *EC – Bananas III*, for example, the Appellate Body decided that private counsel could represent disputants at hearings.[76] Other examples include

---

[71] Appellate Body Report, *Chile – Price Band System*, at para 175.

[72] G Abi-Saab, 'The Appellate Body and Treaty Interpretation' in G Sacerdoti, A Yanovich, and J Bohanes (eds), *The WTO at Ten – The Contribution of the Dispute Settlement System* (Cambridge: Cambridge University Press, 2006) 453, at 463

[73] Appellate Body Report, *US – Lead and Bismuth II*, at para 39.

[74] Appellate Body Report, *Brazil – Aircraft*, at paras 120–25; also Appellate Body Report, *Canada – Aircraft*, at para 141. The decision in *Brazil – Aircraft* was the subject of a preliminary ruling.

[75] Appellate Body Report, *EC – Hormones*, at para 152, fn 138; also Appellate Body Report, *US – FSC (Article 21.5 – EC)*, at paras 247–49.

[76] Appellate Body Report, *EC – Bananas III*, paras. 10–12 [noting that 'nothing [...] in customary international law or the prevailing practice of international tribunals, [...] prevents a WTO Member

the applicable standard of review,[77] the required interest to bring a claim,[78] or the effect of the late filing of a submission or other organizational issues relating to the proceedings.

III. Applicable Law in WTO Dispute Settlement

The applicable law in WTO dispute settlement is touched upon in several provisions, but the DSU lacks a separate provision on the scope of the applicable law. The DSU does not define the applicable law in a similar way to Article 38(1) ICJ Statute, Article 37 of the 1907 Convention on the Permanent Court of Arbitration, Article 42(1) ICSID Convention, Article 21(1) ICC Statute, or Article 293(1) UNCLOS. Interpreted narrowly, Article 3.2 DSU is not silent. It simply does not deal with the question of the applicable law. Of course, only claims arising under the WTO covered agreements can be brought before panels and the Appellate Body.[79] But once the jurisdiction of a panel or the Appellate Body is properly established, it is less clear what law panels and the Appellate Body may apply. In other words:

A limited jurisdiction does not, however, imply a limitation of the scope of the law applicable in the interpretation and application of those treaties. [...] While the [DSU] limits the jurisdiction to claims which arise under the WTO covered agreements only, there is no explicit provision identifying the scope of applicable law.[80]

Naturally, the WTO covered agreements apply.[81] The crux of the issue is whether the applicable law extends to other rules of general international law, other than the customary principles of treaty interpretation, and of sub-systems of international law. This question, in turn, depends to a large extent on the interpretation of Article 3.2 DSU, but equally on the extent to which the WTO treaty language itself encapsulates general international law. Much of the debate traces back to the fear that a broad definition of the applicable law might evolve towards a general jurisdiction of the WTO dispute settlement system. The WTO covered agreements can be interpreted against

from determining the composition of its delegation in Appellate Body proceedings']; also Panel Report, *Indonesia – Autos*, at para 14.1; Panel Report, *Korea – Alcoholic Beverages*, at paras 10.31–33. Note that the three decisions were the subject of a preliminary ruling.

[77] See Appellate Body Report, *EC – Hormones*, at paras 114–17.
[78] See Appellate Body Report, *EC – Bananas III*, at paras 15–17, 133–38.
[79] Art 1.1 DSU.
[80] Fragmentation Report (2006), above fn 22, at para 45.
[81] See Art 3.4 DSU.

the background of other rules of international law. One Appellate Body member, at least, has interpreted 'any relevant rules of international law' in Article 31(3)(c) Vienna Convention on the Law of Treaties (VCLT) to mean that:

These *a fortiori* include the rules of general international law, which are applicable to all members of the international community. But this provision does not provide the criteria (or the circumstances) warranting such reference.[82]

The narrow interpretation of Article 3.2 DSU proposes that only the customary principles of interpretation of public international law apply in WTO dispute settlement. This interpretation might find support in general international law and in an *a contrario* reading of the ICJ's observation that:

It can therefore be assumed that the reference expressly made, in this provision, to the 'rules and principles of international law', if it is to be meaningful, signifies something else. In fact, the Court observes that the expression in question is very general and, if interpreted in its normal sense, could not refer solely to the rules and principles of treaty interpretation. [...] This wording shows that the Parties had no intention of confining the rules and principles of law applicable in this case solely to the rules and principles of international law relating to treaty interpretation.[83]

Article 7.2 DSU provides a basis for this interpretation, as do other DSU provisions that only mention the 'covered agreements'.[84] Only this understanding, some claim, guarantees that DSB reports do not 'add to or diminish the rights and obligations provided in the covered agreements'.[85]

Some DSU negotiators also assert that they only intended to make the customary principles of treaty interpretation applicable in WTO dispute settlement, and no other customary international law or general principles of international law. Other negotiators have acknowledged that many participants did not realize the substantive implications of the language of Article 3.2 DSU and failed to foresee that 'it is a natural phenomenon that negotiators are surprised when neutral "judges" who were not involved in the negotiations start interpreting a text outside of the context of negotiations'.[86] The DSU negotiators intended to give panels and the Appellate Body guidance on their expectations. These expectations might have been less aligned than originally perceived. While some Members appeared to read Article 3.2 as merely referring to the principles of treaty interpretation in the VCLT, others perhaps had a broader understanding of the variety of such principles—supported

---

[82] Abi-Saab, above fn 25, at 463.

[83] ICJ, *Case Concerning Kasikili/Sedudu Island (Botswana/Namibia)*, ICJ Reports (1999) 1045, at 1102, para 93.

[84] See, eg, Arts 1.1, 3.4, 3.5, 3.7, 3.8, 4, 7.1, 11, 19.1, 22.2, and 22.9 DSU.

[85] DP Steger, 'The Jurisdiction of the World Trade Organization' 2004 *ASIL Proceedings* (98) 142, at 144.

[86] PJ Kuijper, 'A Legal Drafting Group for the Doha Round: A Modest Proposal' 2003 *Journal of World Trade* 37(6) 1031, at 1032.

by interpretive practices of other courts and tribunals such as the ECJ, the ECHR, or the ICJ.

In reaction to panels' and the Appellate Body's interpretation and application of Article 3.2 DSU, Chile and the US submitted in 2002 a paper to the DSB. They drew attention to occasions where 'the relevant WTO text does not address an issue, leading to concerns over whether an adjudicative body might "fill the gap" and consequently add to or diminish rights and obligations under the relevant agreement instead of clarifying those rights and obligations'; and to situations in which 'legal concepts outside the WTO texts have been applied in a WTO dispute settlement proceeding, including asserted principles of international law other than customary international law rules of interpretation'.[87] They proposed 'providing some form of additional guidance to WTO adjudicative bodies concerning (i) the nature and scope of the task presented to them [...] and (ii) rules of interpretation of the WTO agreements'.[88] The proposal appeared to have been abandoned but is now again being discussed in the DSB.[89] However, many WTO Members continue to rely on other rules of international law in their submissions and pleadings before panels and the Appellate Body. This can be viewed either as an implied acknowledgement of the relationship between WTO law and other rules and principles of international law, or as a litigation strategy. The latter is understandable in the light of the Appellate Body's acknowledgement that it has 'difficulty in envisaging circumstances in which a panel could add to the rights and obligations of a Member of the WTO if its conclusions reflected a correct interpretation and application of provisions of the covered agreements'.[90]

A more far-reaching view is that, in the absence of an explicit clause on the applicable law, the WTO dispute settlement system should follow, as a default position, the example of other international courts and tribunals to which such a clause applies.[91] On this view, the practice in general international law and other subsystems of international law fills the gap in the DSU.[92] The proposition is that the

---

[87] DSB, *Contribution by Chile and the United States*, TN/DS/W/74 (15 March 2005), at para 4.

[88] Ibid at para 6(f).

[89] DSB, *Negotiations on Improvements and Clarifications of the Dispute Settlement Understanding, Further Contribution of the United States on Improving Flexibility and Member Control in WTO Dispute Settlement, Communication from the United States and Addendum*, TN/DS/W/82/Add. 1 and Add. 2 (25 October 2005/17 March 2006).

[90] Appellate Body Report, *Chile – Alcoholic Beverages*, at para 79.

[91] J Pauwelyn, 'The Jurisdiction of the World Trade Organization' 2004 *ASIL Proceedings* (98) 135, at 138. Contra J Trachtman, 'Jurisdiction in WTO dispute settlement' in R Yerxa and B Wilson (eds), *Key Issues in WTO Dispute Settlement – The First Ten Years* (Cambridge: Cambridge University Press, 2006) 132, at 136.

[92] See D Palmeter and PC Mavroidis, *Dispute Settlement in the World Trade Organization – Practice and Procedure*, 2nd edn (Cambridge: Cambridge University Press, 2004), at 399. Bartels agrees, but cannot concur with Palmeter and Mavroidis that the basis for this proposition is Article 7 DSU. L Bartels, 'Applicable Law in WTO Dispute Settlement Proceedings' 2001 *Journal of World Trade* 35(3) 499, at 499.

limited jurisdiction of the WTO dispute settlement system does not necessarily affect the scope of the applicable law.[93] On the other hand, it could be argued that had the negotiators resolved to define the applicable law in general terms they would have included a separate clause similar to those provisions in the statutes of other international courts and tribunals. Instead, Article 3.2 DSU only refers to 'rules of interpretation' and, thus, 'the drafters demonstrated an intent to exclude other international law by virtue of their decision not to mention it'.[94]

Pauwelyn has suggested two avenues to apply non-WTO law in WTO disputes. He proposes that panels and the Appellate Body can apply international law either 'as a fallback when [...] faced with certain questions not regulated in the WTO treaty itself' or 'in defense of a claim of a WTO violation', except if WTO Members contracted out of international law.[95] The Appellate Body often complements the WTO covered agreements, and particularly the DSU and other procedural provisions, with rules and principles of international law. This common practice in the Appellate Body's jurisprudence is gradually becoming accepted as ensuring the effectiveness of the DSU and the other covered agreements.[96] It is in this line of thought that the Panel in *Korea – Government Procurement* found that:

> Customary international law applies generally to the economic relations between WTO Members. Such international law applies to the extent that the WTO treaty agreements do not 'contract out' from it.[97]

The Panel defined 'contracting out' as 'conflict or inconsistency, or an expression in a covered WTO agreement that implies differently'.[98] It was the first to decide that other general international law besides the customary principles of interpretation may apply in WTO disputes. *Korea – Government Procurement* also illustrates how panels and the Appellate Body often recognize established principles of general international law in the text they interpret. The Panel recognized the principle of *pacta sunt servanda* in Article XXIII:1(b) GATT 1994.[99]

---

[93] Bartels, above fn 92, at 502. Bartels has clarified his understanding of Article 3.2 DSU as a conflicts clause and now proposes to read Article 3.2 DSU as 'add to or diminish applicable rights and obligations in the covered agreements'. L Bartels, 'Comments' in M Andenas and F Ortino (eds), *WTO Law and Process* (London: BIICL, 2005) 514, at 517.

[94] J Trachtman, 'The Jurisdiction of the World Trade Organization' 2004 *ASIL Proceedings* (98) 139, at 139–41; J Trachtman, 'The Domain of WTO Dispute Resolution' 1999 *Harvard International Law Journal* 40(2) 333, at 338, 342. Trachtman relies on the principle of *expressio unius est exclusio alterius*.

[95] Pauwelyn, above fn 91, at 136; also J Pauwelyn, *Conflict of Norms in Public International Law – How WTO Law Relates to Other Rules of International Law* (Cambridge: Cambridge University Press, 2003), at 478–86.

[96] Trachtman, 'Jurisdiction', above fn 94, at 139.

[97] Panel Report, *Korea – Government Procurement*, at para 7.96.

[98] Ibid.

[99] Ibid at para 7.93; also Appellate Body Report, *US – FSC*, at para 166.

The second avenue, in contrast, is less firmly supported by the jurisprudence.[100] Pauwelyn accepts the possibility that, in the event of a conflict between a WTO rule and another principle or rule of international law, non-WTO law 'may disapply WTO rules in particular respects'.[101] Others would remedy such situations of conflict by 'interpreting the conflict away'.[102] Many commentators aim to integrate WTO law with the broader corpus of international law, but define the relationship through different modes.[103] An illustration is provided in the Report of the ILC Fragmentation Study Group:

> There seems, thus, little reason of principle to depart from the view that general international law supplements WTO law unless it has been specifically excluded and that so do other treaties, which should, preferably, be read in harmony with the WTO covered treaties.[104]

Much of the disagreement between these different views on the applicable law finds its origin in the distinction between general international law and different sub-systems of international law. General international law includes, for example, general principles of law such as good faith; due process; customary principles and rules on treaty formation, interpretation, and application; and the principles on state responsibility and the responsibility of international organizations. All these rules and principles share the characteristic that they are not intended to regulate a particular type of behaviour. They are about how international law, including WTO law, should be created, applied, interpreted, and enforced.[105] In other words, 'it is in the nature of "general law to apply generally"—namely inasmuch as it has not been specifically excluded'.[106] To argue that general international law does not apply in WTO dispute settlement is to doubt the treaty basis of the WTO. But to argue that general international law applies in WTO dispute settlement does not answer the question of *when* it applies.

The application of general international law transcends the debate on whether a presumption of application of international law exists in WTO dispute settlement

---

[100] Pauwelyn's argument is mostly based on ICJ decisions (for example, *Lockerbie*) and the prohibition of interpretations *contra legem*.

[101] Pauwelyn, above fn 91, at 137.

[102] Marceau, above fn 21, at 1083, 1096–97, 1107. In the event that non-WTO law is invoked as a defence under Article XX GATT 1994, Marceau recommends that 'the interpretation and the application of Article XX, drafted in permissive terms, should be undertaken in such a manner as to ensure (1) avoidance of conflict with; and (2) the effectiveness of the relevant MEA'. This recommendation does not, however, necessarily clarify the available judicial techniques to resolve such conflicts.

[103] Much also depends on the type of conflict, the character of the conflicting provisions and the identity of the signatories to the different conflicting rules. See, eg, Marceau, above fn 21, at 1097–1100.

[104] Fragmentation Report (2006), above fn 22, at para 169.

[105] See, eg, Panel Report, *Turkey – Textiles*, at paras 9.33–43; Appellate Body Report, *EC – Hormones*, at para 128; Appellate Body Report, *Canada – Patent Term*, at paras 71–79.

[106] Fragmentation Report (2006), above fn 22, at para 185.

or whether this requires an explicit confirmation in the WTO covered agreements. Whether general international law applies depends on the extent to which the WTO covered agreements, on the one hand, carve out a *lex specialis* in relation to general international law, and, on the other hand, confirm general international law. One Appellate Body member has said in more general terms that:

General international law, not economic or political expediency, drives the resolution of disputes within which the new organization and its rules operate.[107]

The DSU and the other WTO agreements are also silent on the general application of different sub-systems of international law as a defence for a violation of the covered agreements. WTO Members enter the WTO legal regime with a commitment to abide by *all* their international legal obligations. This does not automatically bring with it the power to enforce all these rights and obligations. Absent a clause like Article 38(1) ICJ Statute, it is understandable that panels and the Appellate Body try to avoid this question. On a political and institutional issue as the application of other sub-systems of international law the silence may be properly interpreted as exclusion by omission. If this leaves certain disputes unresolved, then this is due to the design of the WTO and not the stamina of panels and the Appellate Body.

The debate about the scope of Article 3.2 DSU is distinct from the application of other principles or rules of international law in the event of explicit and possibly implicit references in the WTO covered agreements to such principles or rules,[108] or as matters of fact.[109]

On this point there does not appear to be any disagreement. An outsider has described the Appellate Body's affirmation of general international law as a 'painful process'.[110] But the position that only the WTO covered agreements apply in WTO dispute settlement has always been untenable. It is not a question of whether general international law applies, but of when and how much general international law applies and of whether secondary and/or primary rules apply. There is no single test to determine this.

---

[107] G Sacerdoti, 'The Dispute Settlement System of the WTO: Structure and Function in the Perspective of the First 10 Years', Bocconi University Institute of Comparative Law 'Anglo Sraffa' (IDC) Legal Research Paper Series, Research Paper No 07–03, at <http://www.papers.ssrn.com/sol3/papers.cfm?abstract_id=981029> (last visited 13 December 2007).

[108] J Trachtman, 'Jurisdiction', above fn 94, at 139; Palmeter and Mavroidis, above fn 92, at 69–73. For example, the 1967 Paris Convention, the 1971 Berne Convention, an 'international undertaking on official export credits' (Annex I(k) SCM Agreement) and 'international standards, guidelines or recommendations' (Art 3.1 SPS Agreement).

[109] See, eg, Appellate Body Report, *US – Shrimp*, at para 167.

[110] T Treves, 'The International Tribunal for the Law of the Sea: applicable law and interpretation' in Sacerdoti, Yanovich, and Bohanes, above fn 25, 490, at 490–95. ITLOS Judge Treves also contrasts the Appellate Body's excessive reliance on the VCLT with the practice of ITLOS.

IV. Treaty Interpretation in WTO Dispute Settlement

A. Principles of Treaty Interpretation

Treaties are perhaps no longer 'the only and sadly overworked instrument[s]'[111] of international law, but treaties remain the basic instrument for establishing rights and obligations under international law. Since 1945, the body of international treaties has grown exponentially, governed by a relatively stable law of treaties of which the VCLT is part. The multiplication of various types of treaties has raised doubts about the effectiveness of certain VCLT provisions to deal with the expansion and diversification of international law.[112] Some question whether the VCLT principles on interpretation are still adequate to interpret new forms or categories of treaties. Such concerns should not bring the law of treaties itself into question.

Every legal system has developed principles to guide and justify the reasoning process of the adjudicator in interpreting and applying the law. Similarly, international law has produced principles of treaty interpretation. The Commentary on the ILC Draft Articles on the Law of Treaties emphasized that 'statements can be found in the decisions of international tribunals to support the use of almost every principle or maxim of which use is made in national systems of law in the interpretation of statutes and contracts'.[113] Interpretation as a 'holistic' process means:

> ...one integrated operation which uses several tools simultaneously to shed light from different angles on the interpreted text; these tools should not be seen as watertight compartments or as a series of separate sub-operations but, rather, as connected (even overlapping) and mutually reinforcing parts of a whole, of a continuum or a continuous and multifaceted process that cannot be reduced to a mechanical operation and which partakes as much of art (the art of judgement) as of science (the science of law).[114]

---

[111] AD McNair, 'The Functions and Differing Legal Character of Treaties' 1930 *British Yearbook of International Law* (11) 100, at 101. The different classes of treaties McNair envisaged included transitory or dispositive treaties, treaties akin to charters of incorporation, contractual and law-making treaties, the latter including treaties creating constitutional international law and pure law-making treaties, or treaties creating or declaring ordinary international law.

[112] JH Jackson, *Sovereignty, the WTO and Changing Fundamentals of International Law* (Cambridge: Cambridge University Press, 2006), at 182–92. Already in 1930, McNair questioned whether all types of treaties 'can be effectively governed by the same system of rules'. McNair, above fn 111, at 101.

[113] *Draft Articles on the Law of Treaties with commentaries 1966*, ILC Yb. 1966, II, 177 as part of *Report of the International Law Commission on the work of its eighteenth session (4 May–19 July 1966) (ILC Draft Articles (1966))*, Doc A/6309/Rev.1, ILC Yb. 1966, II, at 218, para 3 citing Waldock Third Report (1964), below fn 119, at 54, para 5.

[114] Abi-Saab, above fn 25, at 459.

Principles of treaty interpretation are neither rules, nor principles in the classical sense of 'something [...] which underlies a rule, and explains or provides the reason for it'.[115] They underlie the interpretation of the rule, not the rule itself. They help answer why a rule is to be given one meaning and not another. They are 'principles of logic and good sense' that guide the interpreter in finding and justifying the meaning of the treaty language.[116] Discrepancies exist in the manner in which courts and tribunals explain and justify how they interpret the treaty language. But even if they articulate in clear terms their interpretive practice, it is less common for adjudicators to specify the reasons for preferring certain principles of interpretation to others. An analysis of any court's interpretive practices relies on a degree of pragmatism shown in its decisions. There is no guarantee that a judgment discloses all the principles applied, all the elements of interpretation taken into account, and the weight given to the latter by the adjudicator. In most cases, interpretation is also a 'matter of judicial instinct'.[117]

Since 1969, a distinction can be made between codified and non-codified principles of treaty interpretation. The ILC codified the 'comparatively few general principles which appear to constitute general rules' for the interpretation of treaties.[118] Special Rapporteur Waldock did not think it advisable to codify 'principles whose appropriateness in any given case depends so much on the particular context and on a subjective appreciation of varying circumstances'.[119] Such principles of treaty interpretation have developed over time and through practice; they reflect the interpretive memory of past adjudicators.

B. The DSU and Treaty Interpretation

The interpretation of the WTO covered agreements is governed by the same principles as those that apply to the interpretation of other treaties. Article 3.2 DSU provides that panels and the Appellate Body are 'to clarify the existing provisions of those agreements in accordance with customary rules of interpretation of public international law'. In part, Article 3.2 merely confirms the principle of *jura novit curia*; panels and the Appellate Body can decide themselves how to interpret the

---

[115] G Fitzmaurice, 'The General Principles of International Law Considered from the Standpoint of the Rule of Law' 1957 *Receuil des Cours* 92(II) 5.

[116] ILC Draft Articles (1966), above fn 113, at 218, para 4.

[117] L Neville Brown and T Kennedy, *The Court of Justice of the European Communities*, 5th edn (London: Sweet & Maxwell, 2000), at 323.

[118] ILC Draft Articles (1966), above fn 113, at 218, para 5. Contra R Wolfrum, 'Article IX WTO Agreement' in R Wolfrum, P-T Stoll, and K Kaiser (eds), *WTO – Institutions and Dispute Settlement* (Leiden: Martinus Nijhoff, 2006) 106, at 113, para 16.

[119] *Third Report of the Special Rapporteur, Sir Humphrey Waldock* (Waldock Third Report (1964)) (16th Session of the ILC (1964)) UN Doc A/CN.4/167 and Add. 1–3, ILC Yb. 1964, II, 5, at 54, para 8.

WTO covered agreements.[120] Since not all WTO Members have signed and ratified the VCLT, the DSU negotiators decided to refer to the customary rules on interpretation; the alternative being to mention Articles 31 to 33 VCLT.[121] It may be presumed that Article 3.2 refers to customary international law on treaty interpretation as it existed on and evolved after 1 January 1995. The Appellate Body confirmed in its first reports that Articles 31 and 32 VCLT have attained the status of 'customary rules of interpretation of public international law'.[122] It later made the same point about Article 33 VCLT.[123] Article 3.2 seems self-evident.[124] Perhaps the essence of the Appellate Body's interpretive practice lies in the fact that Articles 31 to 33 also require that panels and the Appellate Body interpret the VCLT[125] and determine what those customary principles of interpretation of public international law are.[126]

The Appellate Body has tried to justify its interpretations on the basis of the VCLT without treating the VCLT as a rigid, binding structure of rules, though exceptions exist. This understanding of Articles 31 to 33 VCLT as principles, not rules, is not sufficiently appreciated by WTO law and its audience. These principles do not need to be revised or reformulated, but they should be better understood. As with any treaty, the VCLT could not be complete. The VCLT might be imperfect and incomplete in many ways, but Articles 31 to 33 continue to reflect the basic principles on which a broader catalogue of principles of interpretation is built. Articles 31 to 33 are formally treaty rules, but materially principles of logic and order. They need to be interpreted and applied together with non-codified principles of treaty interpretation.

The understanding in general international law that the category of customary principles of treaty interpretation is broader than the principles codified in the VCLT has not been sufficiently appreciated by some WTO Members. In *EC – Computer Equipment*, the Appellate Body found that 'the *only* rules which may be applied in interpreting the meaning of a concession are the general rules of treaty

---

[120] The principle of *jura novit curia* was recognized in Appellate Body Report, *EC – Tariff Preferences*, at para 105.

[121] Some WTO Members cannot become a party to the VCLT because they are not a State or are not recognized as a State.

[122] Appellate Body Report, *US – Gasoline*, at 16–17; Appellate Body Report, *Japan – Alcoholic Beverages II*, at 104. See also, eg, Appellate Body Report, *EC – Computer Equipment*, at para 84; Appellate Body Report, *US – Shrimp*, at para 114; Appellate Body Report, *Korea – Dairy*, at para 81; Appellate Body Report, *US – India (US)*, at para 46.

[123] Appellate Body Report, *US – Softwood Lumber IV*, at para 59; Appellate Body Report, *Chile – Price Band System*, at para 271; Appellate Body Report, *EC – Bed-Linen (Article 21.5 – India)*, at para 123, fn 153.

[124] C-D Ehlermann, 'Six Years on the Bench of the "World Trade Court"—Some Personal Experiences as a Member of the Appellate Body of the World Trade Organization' 2002 *Journal of World Trade* 36(4) 605, at 618; A Mitchell, *Legal Principles in WTO Disputes* (Cambridge: Cambridge University Press, 2008); also ICJ, *Kasikili/Sedudu Island*, above fn 83, at 1102, para 93.

[125] See, eg, Panel Report, *Korea – Government Procurement*, at para 7.94 (interpreting the principle of good faith in the VCLT with the help of the preparatory work of the VCLT).

[126] See ICJ, *Case Concerning Military and Paramilitary Activities in and against Nicarágua (Nicarágua v United States of América) (Merits)* ICJ Reports (1986) 14, at 97, para 184.

interpretation set out in the Vienna Convention'.[127] But the Appellate Body has equally applied principles of interpretation that are not codified in the VCLT. Abi-Saab comments on the common interpretation that Article 3.2 DSU refers to Articles 31 to 33 VCLT that:

…the representation may not be completely faithful, nor reflect certain aspects of the customary rules that may also continue to evolve beyond the moment the snapshot was taken.[128]

The Consultative Board has expressed doubts on whether the customary principles of interpretation are entirely adequate for interpreting the WTO agreements. It remarked that '[t]he customary international rules of interpretation are, themselves, sometimes questionable when applied in the context of very detailed and intricate economic obligations of the WTO'.[129] Despite the reference to the customary principles of interpretation, the Consultative Board's doubts focus particularly on Articles 31 and 32 VCLT.[130]

The Appellate Body has applied codified and non-codified principles of treaty interpretation, but it appears less open in acknowledging its use of non-codified principles. In *EC – Poultry*, Brazil claimed that 'customary international law cautions against the application of one legal maxim for the interpretation of treaties to the exclusion of others', but the Appellate Body remained silent on the matter.[131] The Appellate Body appears to struggle with the functions of guidance and justification of principles of interpretation, to the point that one Appellate Body member questions whether 'if the reasoning is there, is it not better to shed the camouflage?'[132] Another former Appellate Body Chairman contemplates that 'security and predictability would be better served by broad statements of principle that allow WTO Members to orient their activities in the future'.[133] Both statements share a concern about excessive formalism in interpreting treaties and drafting reports. DG Lamy, on the other hand, interprets this attachment to the VCLT 'as a clear confirmation that the WTO wants to see itself as being as fully integrated into the international legal order as possible'.[134] This might well be the case but there exist limits to this function of Articles 31 to 33. The jurisdiction of and the applicable law in WTO dispute settlement prevent the type of integration that DG Lamy describes.

Overall, the Appellate Body has succeeded in producing a relatively consistent body of interpretations of WTO law. In the absence of a strict notion of *stare decisis*,

---

[127] Appellate Body Report, *EC – Computer Equipment*, at para 84 (emphasis added).

[128] Abi-Saab, above fn 25, at 458.

[129] Consultative Board, *The Future of the WTO: Addressing Institutional Challenges in the New Millennium* (Geneva: WTO, 2004), at 53, para 235.

[130] When the Consultative Board calls into question the customary principles of interpretation, it also puts into doubt the treaty language in Article 3.2 DSU. It is unfortunate that the Consultative Board implicitly chose to identify the customary principles of interpretation as a systemic problem underlying the WTO dispute settlement system.

[131] Appellate Body Report, *EC – Poultry*, at para 57.

[132] Abi-Saab, above fn 25, at 462.

[133] Ehlermann, above fn 124, at 638.   [134] Lamy, above fn 19, at 979.

the interpretations of panels and the Appellate Body are case-specific. Nevertheless, a tempered type of 'jurisprudence constante' operates in WTO dispute settlement, and many interpretations on substance and procedure have survived in subsequent DSB reports.[135] At different times and in relation to various parts of the WTO covered agreements, panels and the Appellate Body have occasionally produced different, even contradictory interpretations. The resulting interpretive uncertainty can be resolved by the WTO Members through the adoption of an authoritative interpretation of the provision in question. Usually uncertainty can only be clarified if a new dispute about the same interpretive question is brought before a panel or the Appellate Body. The Appellate Body has found that Article 3.2 DSU encapsulated the principle that 'absent cogent reasons, an adjudicatory body will resolve the same legal question in the same way in a subsequent case'.[136] So far, the DSU does not provide for the possibility to request a clarification or revision by the DSB, a panel or the Appellate Body of a particular finding, recommendation, or reasoning.[137] The Appellate Body occasionally clarifies or corrects misunderstandings about its original reasoning and recommendations in subsequent compliance proceedings,[138] or in subsequent appeals in other disputes.[139]

The need to provide security and predictability to the WTO Members also requires law to be distinguished from politics. Panels and the Appellate Body are called upon to uphold the covered agreements. They should not be preoccupied with political debates between Members, especially those arising in the context of ongoing trade negotiations. Nevertheless, they cannot deny their institutional and political context. Synergies between trade negotiations and dispute settlement have become more influential and apparent under the WTO than under the GATT. A few panel and Appellate Body reports, such as *US – Cotton Subsidies*, have helped to shape the debate during the Doha Development Round, and they have defined and influenced the Doha agenda. For example, the Panel report in *EC – Biotech Products* may have an impact on the ongoing agriculture negotiations on food safety. Some contentious matters on the negotiating agenda are also being litigated during the negotiations.[140] WTO Members bargain in the shadow of the GATT *acquis*,[141] WTO

---

[135] Jackson, above fn 112, at 173–77.

[136] Appellate Body Report, *US – Stainless Steel*, at para 160.

[137] Compare with Art 60 ICJ Statute: 'The judgment is final and without appeal. In the event of dispute as to the meaning or scope of the judgment, the Court shall construe it upon the request of any party'.

[138] See, eg, Appellate Body Report, *Chile – Price Band System (Article 21.5 – Argentina)*, at paras 229–41.

[139] See, eg, Appellate Body Report, *EC – Customs Matters*, at para 200 (interpreting its previous reports in EC – *Bananas III* and *EC – Poultry* on the scope of Art X:3(a) GATT 1994).

[140] See, eg, DSB, *United States – Domestic Support and Export Credit Guarantees for Agricultural Products*, Request for Consultations by Brazil; DSB, *United States – Subsidies and Other Domestic Support for Corn and Other Agricultural Products*, Request for Consultations by Canada.

[141] Art XVI:1 WTO Agreement: 'Except as otherwise provided under this Agreement or the Multilateral Trade Agreements, the WTO shall be guided by the decisions, procedures and customary practices followed by the CONTRACTING PARTIES to GATT 1947 and the bodies established in the framework of GATT 1947'.

dispute settlement, and international law, while panels and the Appellate Body adjudicate in the shadow of the GATT *acquis*, ongoing trade negotiations, and international law. The WTO covered agreements are continually interpreted and applied outside the WTO institution by exporters, importers, national customs authorities, legislators, national courts, and regulators. These informal interpretations can be non-transparent, implicit, and are as such not binding. But they may internalize past jurisprudence of GATT panels, as well as of WTO panels and the Appellate Body. As such they can influence judicial interpretation.

C. Contextual and Effective Interpretation

The interpretation of the ordinary meaning of the treaty language in the light of its object and purpose is part of a broader appreciation of contextualism in treaty interpretation, which obviously embraces Article 31(2). The Appellate Body has adopted a broader understanding of context than the ILC perhaps initially intended.[142] Either context in the VCLT is read broadly or, if read narrowly, the Appellate Body might not apply the VCLT correctly. However, other nuances in the definition of context are possible. The Appellate Body applies a broader idea of contextualism, which reconciles the language of Articles 31(1) and 31(2) VCLT with the other codified and non-codified principles of interpretation.

The ILC did not explain what 'ordinary meaning' entails. The Appellate Body's jurisprudence suggests that the 'ordinary' meaning already implies a considerable amount of contextualization of the treaty language as part of what is perceived as literal interpretation. Even if the VCLT drafters realized that context has a broader meaning and impact in treaty interpretation, the language in Article 31(2) mirrors the ultimate consensus that could be reached. Also, at the time of the VCLT negotiations there was little practice of courts and tribunals, such as WTO panels and the Appellate Body, who continuously revisit the same treaties. This might point to a certain disjuncture between the treaty language in Articles 31 to 33 VCLT and the interpretive practice of international courts and tribunals.

The Appellate Body has associated the means of interpretation in Articles 31(3) and 32 VCLT with the notion of context. The Appellate Body often attempts to justify its interpretation under the most specific and detailed category of means of interpretation in the VCLT. If this is not possible, the Appellate Body resorts to non-codified principles of treaty interpretation or relies on contextualism. Contextualism can correspond to the definition of context in the VCLT, but may also reach beyond the language of Article 31(2) VCLT and be used as a general label to justify the interpretation. A case in point is *EC – Biotech Products*, where despite initial appearances

---

[142] A similar analysis may apply to the interpretation of context by some panels. See Panel Report, *US – Shrimp (Article 21.5 – Malaysia)*, at para 5.124, fn 240.

the Panel eventually departed from a formalistic approach towards Articles 31 to 33 VCLT. Its narrow interpretation of Article 31(3)(c) did not preclude that 'other rules of international law may in some cases aid a treaty interpreter in establishing, or confirming, the ordinary meaning of treaty terms in the specific context in which they are used'.[143] It is not entirely clear to what extent the Panel intended to say that rules of international law may be part of the context. This conclusion on the value of rules of international law for treaty interpretation is a welcome contribution. It illustrates how interpretation is not a process of qualifying means of interpretation, but transcends the categories established by Articles 31 to 33 VCLT.

No doctrine of 'plain meaning' exists in WTO jurisprudence. This doctrine has been criticized in international law because its rationale is, in part, 'the desire to make the decision appear more convincing and to give the embellishment of plausibility and apparent soundness to a result reached in other ways'.[144] Depending on how broadly or narrowly the doctrine of 'plain meaning' is perceived, the Appellate Body's practice of contextualizing the ordinary meaning defeats assumptions about strict adherence to the plain meaning. On the one hand, the Appellate Body has rarely concluded that the text of the treaty was clear without need to consider context or other means of interpretation. On the other hand, the Appellate Body appears to accept the relevance of contextual elements if they support the ordinary meaning but not if they modify the meaning.

Despite appearances and criticisms, dictionaries do not necessarily command the Appellate Body's interpretation of the WTO covered agreements. If there is a preference to justify interpretations with reference to dictionary definitions this can be explained partly on the ground that dictionaries introduce an element of predictability and counteract the impression of arbitrariness. Cases such as *US – Upland Cotton*,[145] where the Appellate Body built its interpretation only to a limited extent on dictionary definitions, raise the question of why the Appellate Body did so. It may be that, even if not explained by the Appellate Body, dictionaries are not necessary because the plain meaning of a term is sufficient. Or the Appellate Body might find the available dictionary definitions of little use. In all cases, the Appellate Body's justification of its interpretations may be criticized but this is in the eye of the beholder. Interpretive flexibility entails the freedom how and to what extent to justify the choices made; this may depend on considerations of (institutional) legitimacy and judicial integrity.

The Appellate Body appears to always start from the assumption that the drafters had a particular effect and purpose in mind when negotiating and concluding the entire treaty regime, a particular treaty, and individual treaty provisions. The

---

[143] Panel Report, *EC – Biotech Products*, at para 7.92.

[144] H Lauterpacht, *The Development of International Law by the International Court*, revised edn (London: Stevens & Sons Ltd, 1958), at 54.

[145] Appellate Body Report, *US – Upland Cotton*, at para 363 (citing the Panel Report, at para 7.494(i)); also Appellate Body Report, *Turkey – Textiles*, at paras 45–46.

ordinary meaning, context, and object and purpose in Article 31(1) VCLT are closely intertwined. Consequently, assumptions about the effect and purpose are borne in mind when contextualizing the ordinary meaning. These are merely assumptions because the actual effect and purpose may only be established after interpreting the treaty language. Nevertheless, general perceptions, extrinsic instruments, and a *prima facie* consideration of the treaty language may allow the Appellate Body to construe certain assumptions. Here, the institutional context of the Appellate Body should not be ignored. *Mexico – Corn Syrup (Article 21.5 – US)* is an example of how the assumed intent and effect come into play in contextualizing dictionary meanings. In determining the scope of panels' duties under Article 12.7 DSU, the Appellate Body interpreted 'basic rationale' in that provision by examining separately the dictionary definitions of 'basic' and 'rationale'.[146] These dictionary definitions had to be read together with 'findings and recommendations' in Article 12.7, which 'establishes a minimum standard for the reasoning that panels must provide in support of their findings and recommendations', and includes providing 'explanations and reasons sufficient to disclose the essential, or fundamental, justification for those findings and recommendations'.[147] This interpretation reflected the principles of fundamental fairness and due process that underlie the WTO dispute settlement system and the objectives set forth in Article 3.2 DSU.[148]

There are limits to the justificatory value of the principles of interpretation in the VCLT and there comes a point when reliance on these principles will actually diminish the credibility of the interpretation. The Appellate Body appears increasingly torn between its formal attachment to Articles 31 to 33 VCLT and the recognition that the VCLT ultimately offers only limited means of interpretation. The Appellate Body's notion of contextualism represents this tension well. Contextualism occasionally pushes the edges of voluntarism in the VCLT.

The Appellate Body has recognized and emphasized the value of the principle of effectiveness as the underlying structure and justification of its interpretations. In *US – Gasoline*, the Appellate Body explained that '[a]n interpreter is not free to adopt a reading that would result in reducing whole clauses or paragraphs of a treaty to redundancy or inutility'.[149] In *US – Offset Act (Byrd Amendment)*, it stressed that the principle of effectiveness was an 'internationally recognized interpretative principle'.[150]

---

[146]   Appellate Body Report, *Mexico – Corn Syrup (Article 21.5 – US)*, at para 106 (consulting The New Shorter Oxford English Dictionary).

[147]   Ibid (original emphasis).   [148]   Ibid at para 107.

[149]   Appellate Body Report, *US – Gasoline*, at 21.

[150]   Appellate Body Report, *US – Offset Act (Byrd Amendment)*, at para 271; also Appellate Body Report, *US – Gasoline*, at 21; Appellate Body Report, *Japan – Alcoholic Beverages II*, at 106, 111; Appellate Body Report, *Korea – Dairy*, at para 80; Appellate Body Report, *Canada – Dairy*, at para 133; Appellate Body Report, *Argentina – Footwear (EC)*, at para 81; Appellate Body Report, *US – Underwear*, at 24; Appellate Body Report, *US – Section 211 Appropriations Act*, at paras 161, 338; Appellate Body Report, *US – Upland Cotton*, at para 549; Appellate Body Report, *EC – Chicken Cuts*, at para 214.

The principle of effectiveness can perform different functions. Effectiveness can be an independent ground on which the interpreter relies to construe the meaning of the treaty language, but it may equally serve a mere confirming or corrective function. It is often relied upon as a benchmark to review a particular interpretation. In this context, the function of the principle is negative. When consulting dictionary definitions, the Appellate Body has also appreciated the principle of effectiveness. It has looked at the effectiveness of the treaty language in terms of the treaty's application and enforcement. Equally, it has considered the functioning of the WTO as an institution under the header of effectiveness. How the Appellate Body applies the principle may depend, to some extent, on whether the treaty language concerns substantive rights and obligations of WTO Members or rather procedural or operational provisions.

The functions of the principle of effectiveness in interpreting the WTO covered agreements are still not sufficiently appreciated or accurately assessed.[151] For example, the principle has been contrasted to the 'principal hermeneutic approach' of the Appellate Body.[152] To the extent that the role of the principle in the Appellate Body's jurisprudence has been recognized, the discussion is often not devoid of a certain distrust or scepticism towards it.[153] The practice of the Appellate Body demonstrates how the principle accompanies each phase in the interpretation process, starting from the consideration of the contextualized dictionary or plain meaning of the treaty language.

The Appellate Body systematically interprets the same corpus of treaties within an institutional structure. This reality necessarily influences the weight given to the values, the object and purpose of the treaty, the institutional network of which the Appellate Body forms part, and the wider and deeper system of WTO law.[154] Effectiveness is a relative concept. What the Appellate Body finds an effective interpretation is determined by its institutional, judicial, and political context and function, and will not necessarily conjure with what the disputants, other WTO Members, stakeholders, and observers perceive as an effective interpretation. Its relative character also helps to explain why the principle ultimately was not codified in the VCLT, the concept was not imaginable to define.[155] The preoccupation of the

[151] Compare Marceau, above fn 21, at 1089, fn 70 with G Marceau, 'Balance and coherence by the WTO Appellate Body: who could do better?' in Sacerdoti, Yanovich, and Bohanes, above fn 25, 326, at 330.

[152] Trachtman, 'Jurisdiction', above fn 94, at 140.

[153] See, eg, D McRae, 'The legal ordering of international trade: from GATT to the WTO' in R MacDonald and D Johnston (eds), *Towards World Constitutionalism: Issues in the Legal Ordering of the World Community* (Leiden: Martinus Nijhoff, 2005) 543, at 564.

[154] 'Deeper' denotes how the WTO legal system is not only reflected in the written words of the WTO covered agreements, but equally in the silences of those agreements and the practice and law resulting from the WTO institutional bodies. 'Wider' refers to the relationship between the WTO covered agreements and general international law and other sub-systems of international law.

[155] Therefore, caution is advised when evaluating that a certain interpretation would 'disregard the *effet utile*' of a covered agreement.

Appellate Body with giving effect to the rights and obligations of WTO Members, and by extension the values and objectives underlying the WTO legal system, has been translated in different types of application of the principle and has been met by certain limitations to the principle.[156]

The function and meaning of the principle of effectiveness in the Appellate Body's interpretation of the WTO covered agreements illustrate why the ILC ultimately and wisely decided not to codify the principle. The principle is rarely the sole guidance and explanation for a particular interpretation. In most cases, it accompanies the application of other principles of interpretation and functions as a touchstone to review the possible meanings of the treaty language. The principle can also be a vehicle to emphasize certain values in the treaty. This is mostly the case when an adjudicator continuously revisits the same treaty language. Values in treaty interpretation are unavoidable, and do not make the principle of effectiveness an instrument to realize certain political objectives through dispute settlement.

D. Harmonious Interpretation of the WTO Covered Agreements

The interpretation of the WTO covered agreements against the background of international law can contribute to the development of international law itself. In its first decision, the Appellate Body made the general observation that the WTO covered agreements are 'not to be read in clinical isolation from public international law'[157] and it has consistently followed this line. Nowadays, it may equally be accurate to say that general international law and other sub-systems of international law can no longer be read in clinical isolation from WTO law and its growing body of jurisprudence.[158]

The principle of harmonization means that a treaty should be read in harmony and consistent with the broader context of international customary and conventional law.[159] In the words of the ICJ in *Namibia*:

'...an international instrument has to be interpreted and applied within the framework of the entire legal system prevailing at the time of the interpretation'.[160]

---

[156] See Lauterpacht, above fn 144, at 229.

[157] Appellate Body Report, *US – Gasoline*, at 16.

[158] See, eg, Arbitral Award, *SGS Société Générale de Surveillance SA v Islamic Republic of Pakistan (Jurisdiction)*, 6 August 2003, 8 ICSID Reports (2005) 406, 42 ILM (2003) 1290, at para 171, fn 178.

[159] The ILC Fragmentation Study Group accepts that the principle of harmonization is 'a widely accepted principle of interpretation', Fragmentation Report (2006), above fn 22, at para 38. It equally recognizes the principle's function to resolve conflicts of norms (Conclusions Nos 4, 42).

[160] ICJ, *Legal Consequences for States of the Continued Presence of South Africa in Namibia (South West Africa) notwithstanding Security Council Resolution 276 (1970)*, Advisory Opinion, ICJ Reports

The principle of harmonization also means that a treaty should be interpreted on the assumption that the treaty does not intend to violate existing international law, except when States explicitly contract out of international law.[161] Its role was recently emphasized by the ILC Fragmentation Study Group and by WTO DG Lamy,[162] and its scope of application is not limited to treaties.

The Appellate Body has relied on other rules and principles of international law as context, to ensure the effectiveness of the treaty regime, or as a fallback if the treaty is unclear or incomplete. It relies on other international law, as interpreted by other courts where relevant and applicable.[163] This is especially the case when the language in the covered agreements refers to other rules of international law, such as in Articles 1.1 TBT Agreement and in the preamble of the SPS Agreement. These references can be to treaties, customary international law, general principles of law, and even non-binding instruments. Other international law then becomes part of the context.

Another basis for interpreting treaties in the light of other rules and principles of international law is Article 31(3)(c) VCLT:

3. There shall be taken into account, along with the context:
...
(c) any relevant rules of international law applicable in the relations between the parties.

Article 31(3)(c) VCLT is the only codified principle of interpretation that explicitly refers to other international law. The provision expresses the idea that treaties need

---

(1971) 16, at 31; also ICJ, *Case Concerning Right of Passage over Indian Territory (Portugal v India) (Preliminary Objections)*, ICJ Reports (1957) 125, at 142.

[161] In this sense, the principle of harmonization resembles the Charming Betsy doctrine in US statutory interpretation. *Murray v The Schooner Charming Betsy*, 6 US (2 Cranch) 64 (1984) [see for criticism and controversy over the doctrine: *United States v Palestine Liberation Organization*, 695 F Supp 1456 (SDNY 1988)]. See also treaty-consistent interpretation: ECJ, C-61/94, *Commission v. Germany (Failure by a Member State to fulfil its obligations – International Dairy Arrangement)*, 10 September 1996, [1996] ECR I(8–9)-3989, at para 52; ECJ, Case–53/96, *Hermès International (a partnership limited by shares) v FHT Marketing Choice BV*, 16 June 1998, [1998] ECR I–3603, at para 32. A NAFTA Chapter 19 Panel has relied on the Charming Betsey doctrine to contend that US statutes should, to the extent possible, be read in a way that avoids violation of the US international legal commitments, in casu its obligations under the WTO covered agreements. As a result, the US was told to comply with the DSB report in *US – Softwood Lumber v* NAFTA Chapter 19 Panel, *In the Matter of Certain Softwood Lumber Products from Canada: Final Affirmative Antidumping Determination*, 9 June 2005, at <http://www.nafta-secalena.org/app/DocRepository/1/Dispute/english/NAFTA_Chapter_19/USA/uao2022e.pdf>, at 43–44 (last visited 10 March 2008).

[162] ICJ, *Fisheries Jurisdiction Case (Spain v Canada) (Jurisdiction)*, 4 December 1998, ICJ Reports (1998) 432, at 460; AD McNair, *The Law of Treaties*, 2nd edn (Oxford: Clarendon Press, 1961), at 466; RY Jennings and A Watts (eds), *Oppenheim's International Law*, 9th edn (London: Longmans, 1992), at 1275; Fragmentation Report (2006), above fn 22, at paras 169–70, 413–23, 465 (and references therein), Conclusions Nos 17–23; Lamy, above fn 19, at 972, 977–84.

[163] Terris, Romano, and Swigart quoting also an Appellate Body member admitting that 'I think we would never take on the ICJ. Whenever there is a reference, it is a reference as an authority'; D Terris, CPR Romano, and L Swigart (eds), *The International Judge: An Introduction to the Men and Women who Decide the World's Cases* (Oxford: Oxford University Press, 2007), at 121.

to be interpreted against the background of international law. The principle has been subject to criticism. It can be instrumental in achieving a certain degree of synchronization between sub-systems of international law. Its application can help to stabilize and structure the specialization of international law, but this characteristic is not unique to this principle and hardly guides the interpreter in a concrete dispute.

It is not the purpose here to revisit the debate on the fragmentation of international law or to recapitulate the different interpretations of Article 31(3)(c) VCLT.[164] The interpretive difficulties of Article 31(3)(c) relate to whether the rules of international law need to be applicable between all disputants, all parties to the treaty under interpretation or reflect the common intention of the parties to the treaty under interpretation; what 'relevant' means; the question of inter-temporality; and how broad 'rules of international law' should be defined. It suffices to refer to the relatively broad and pragmatic interpretation of the ILC Fragmentation Study Group and to contemplate the narrower interpretation:

Article 31(3)(c) also requires the interpreter to consider other treaty-based rules so as to arrive at a consistent meaning. Such other rules are of particular relevance where parties to the treaty under interpretation are also parties to the other treaty, where the treaty rule has passed into or expresses customary international law or where they provide evidence of the common understanding of the parties as to the object and purpose of the treaty under interpretation or as to the meaning of a particular term.

A better solution is to permit reference to another treaty provided that the *parties in dispute* are also parties to that other treaty. Although this creates the possibility of eventually divergent interpretations (depending on which States parties are also parties to the dispute), that would simply reflect the need to respect (inherently divergent) party will as elucidated by reference to those other treaties as well as the bilateralist character of most treaties underpinned by the practices regarding reservations, *inter se* modification and successive treaties, for example.[165]

The commotion about Article 31(3)(c) VCLT in the wider discussion about fragmentation of international law gives the false impression that its meaning is obscure.

---

[164] See I Van Damme, '"Systemic Integration" of International Law: Views from the ILC, the WTO CTE, and UNESCO' in CCIL (eds), *Fragmentation: Diversification and Expansion of International Law – CCIL 34th Annual Conference 2005* (Ottawa: CCIL, 2006) 59; I Van Damme, 'What Role is there for Regional International Law in the Interpretation of the WTO Agreements?' in L Bartels and F Ortino (eds), *Regional Trade Agreements and the WTO Legal System* (Oxford: Oxford University Press, 2006) 553; J Klabbers, 'Reluctant Grundnormen: Articles 31(3)(c) and 42 of the Vienna Convention on the Law of Treaties and the Fragmentation of International Law' in M Craven, M Fitzmaurice, and M Vogiatzi (eds), *Time, History and International Law* (Leiden: Martinus Nijhoff, 2007) 141; C McLachlan, 'The Principle of Systemic Integration and Article 31(3)(c) of the Vienna Convention' 2005 *International and Comparative Law Quarterly* 54(2) 279. On the negotiating history of Article 31(3)(c) VCLT, see P Merkouris, 'Debating the Ouroboros of International Law: The Drafting History of Article 31(3)(c)' 2007 *International Community Law Review* 9(1) 1.

[165] Fragmentation Report (2006), above fn 22 Conclusion No 21, at para 472 (original emphasis).

The application of the provision can be relatively straightforward.[166] Once a court or tribunal has decided what 'the parties', 'relevant', 'rules', or the inter-temporal question mean,[167] the meaning of Article 31(3)(c) can be more clearly defined than, for example, that of context in Article 31. This raises the question of why courts and tribunals have not applied Article 31(3)(c) more often or more explicitly. Several reasons help to explain why the appeal of Article 31(3)(c) is larger in theory than in practice. In most cases, the adjudicator does not need other international law to understand the meaning of the treaty language. The general principle in Article 31 and principles derived from Article 31 often suffice. The focus on fragmentation of international law and Article 31(3)(c) causes many to overestimate the use of especially other treaties in interpretation. As ICJ President Higgins observes 'we should not exaggerate the phenomenon of fragmentation'.[168] The ILC Fragmentation Study Group seems to agree with this caution.[169] A broad interpretation of Article 31(3)(c) can justify reliance on many other rules or principles of international law, but this does not make it necessary in a particular dispute. The lack of hierarchy does not convey to each principle in Article 31 the same practical use.

The drafters of the VCLT insisted that the text, which was presumed to reflect the intentions of the parties, should be the main focus in applying principles of interpretation. The starting point remains, of course, the text but the ILC has now clarified how the text relates to its context. The earlier assumption was perhaps too simplistic to reflect the practice of courts and tribunals in interpreting treaties and caused some misunderstanding about the intentions of the drafters of the VCLT. The character of the treaty may not only refer to whether the treaty covers, for example, international economic law, but may also depend on the object and purpose of the treaty. The objects and purposes of a treaty are often multiple and broadly described, such as the objective of 'sustainable development' in the preamble of the WTO Agreement. The object and purpose of a treaty can inform the Appellate Body that it might be useful to consult other rules of international law, including principles and rules of other sub-systems. But this is not necessarily the case. Also, it is not because the preamble mentions 'sustainable development' or 'climate change' that environmental treaties automatically become relevant.

---

[166] In support, Judge Buergenthal wrote in his Separate Opinion in *Oil Platforms* that the principle of Article 31(3)(c) VCLT 'is sound and undisputed in principle as far as treaty interpretation is concerned'. ICJ, *Case Concerning Oil Platforms (Islamic Republic of Iran v United States of America)*, Separate Opinion Judge Buergenthal, ICJ Reports (2003) 270, at para 22.

[167] This is the lack of clarity to which Judge Weeramantry referred in ICJ, *Case Concerning Gabcíkovo-Nagymaros Project (Hungary v Slovakia)*, Separate Opinion Judge Weeramantry, ICJ Reports (1997) 88, at 114.

[168] R Higgins, 'A Babel of Judicial Voices? Ruminations from the Bench' 2006 *International and Comparative Law Quarterly* 55(4) 791, at 796; also M Lennard, 'Navigating by the Stars: Interpreting the WTO Agreements' 2002 *Journal of International Economic Law* 5(1) 17, at 38. Sacerdoti also points out that a broad understanding of context can make reliance on 'external sources' unnecessary. Sacerdoti, above fn 25, Chapter 34.

[169] Fragmentation Report (2006), above fn 22, at para 20.

In *US – Shrimp*, the Appellate Body found that the objective of sustainable development informs the meaning of the generic term 'natural resources' in Article XX(g) GATT 1994. 'Natural resources' was a term 'not "static" in its content or reference but [...] rather "by definition, evolutionary"'.[170] A 'generic term' has been defined as 'a known legal term, whose content the Parties expected would change through time'[171] or a term whose 'meaning was intended to follow the evolution of the law'.[172] It is difficult to predict which terms are 'generic'. Did the Appellate Body find that 'natural resources' is a generic term as such or was this conclusion the result of interpretation in the light of the objective of sustainable development in the preamble and the context of Article XX(g)? If certain terms are generic *per se*, this raises the question of when a particular term is generic and was intended to be generic in *all* of the WTO covered agreements, including schedules. The Appellate Body concluded that 'measures to conserve exhaustible natural resources, whether *living* or *non-living*, may fall within Article XX(g)'.[173] This interpretation was justified on the basis of the principle of effectiveness, not Article 31(3)(c) VCLT.[174] Negotiating history was briefly acknowledged in a footnote when the Appellate Body observed that the 'drafting history does not demonstrate an intent on the part of the framers of the GATT 1947 *to exclude* "living" natural resources from the scope of application of Article XX(g)'.[175]

The limited application of Article 31(3)(c) VCLT has created uncertainty among WTO Members on how the WTO covered agreements relate to other rules of international law. In response to this uncertainty, disputants are increasingly justifying interpretations on the basis of Article 31(3)(c). It is difficult to appreciate whether this is part of a litigation strategy to force the Appellate Body to address Article 31(3)(c) or simply a function of the type of treaty language under interpretation in a particular dispute. So far, the Appellate Body has not been impressed by such arguments. The Panel in *EC – Biotech Products* was more willing to engage in debate on the principle, partly because of the subject matter of the dispute.

In *EC – Biotech Products*, the Panel adopted a narrow interpretation of Article 31(3)(c) VCLT. The EC argued that the 1992 Convention on Biological Diversity[176]

---

[170]   Compare Appellate Body Report, *US – Shrimp*, at para 130 with ICJ, *Namibia*, above fn 160, at 31.

[171]   ICJ, *Kasikili/Sedudu Island*, above fn 83, Declaration Judge Higgins, 1113, at paras 2–3.

[172]   ICJ, *Aegean Sea Continental Shelf Case (Greece v Turkey) (Jurisdiction)*, ICJ Reports (1978) 3, at 32; also Fragmentation Report (2006), above fn 22, Conclusion No 23.

[173]   Appellate Body Report, *US – Shrimp*, at para 131 (original emphasis).

[174]   Ibid.

[175]   Ibid at para 131, fn 114 (original emphasis). See similarly Arbitral Award, *In the Arbitration Regarding the Iron Rhine ('Ijzeren Rijn') Railway (Belgium v Netherlands)*, 24 May 2005, at <http://www.pca-cpa.org/upload/files/BE-NL%20Award%20corrected%20200905.pdf> (last visited 10 March 2008), at para 80. This observation was made not in relation to the interpretation of a generic term, but in the context of new technological developments in the operation and capacity of the Iron Rhine railway.

[176]   The Convention on Biological Diversity is binding on the EC, Argentina, and Canada; and signed by the US.

and the 2000 Biosafety Protocol[177] informed the scope of Article 5.7 SPS Agreement, and whether this provision established the precautionary principle as part of WTO law.[178] Article 31(3)(c) was seen as a guarantee against the degression of the rights and obligations protected under international law. The standard in international law, if established, should be upheld. Such an argument reflects a move away from formalism in interpreting treaties. The Panel recognized that treaties and customary international law, but equally general principles of law, qualify as 'rules of international law'.[179] The interpretation of the phrase 'the parties' was less straightforward. The Panel rejected an evolutionary and effective interpretation of 'the parties' because this would defeat the actual text of the treaty as well as Article 2.1(g) VCLT. The Panel wanted to be consistent in interpreting the VCLT as a whole. It explained the difference in wording between Article 31(3)(c) and Article 31(2)(a) by reference to the logic between paragraphs (a) and (b) of Article 31(2).[180] As a result, 'the parties' meant 'the States which have consented to be bound by the treaty which is being interpreted, and for which that treaty is in force'.[181] But perhaps an effective interpretation of 'the parties' in the WTO context cannot mean 'all the parties', not least because of Taiwan and the EC.

The Panel assumed that Article 31(3)(c) does not give the interpreter discretion to apply the principle or not. If the conditions are met, the interpreter has no other option than to take account of international law.[182] The Panel concluded that the function of Article 31(3)(c) was to 'ensure[. . .] or enhance[. . .] the consistency of the rules of international law applicable to these States and thus [to] contribute[. . .] to avoiding conflicts between the relevant rules'.[183] It explained that interpretation in good faith requires choosing the interpretation 'more in accord with other applicable rules of international law'.[184] This is a reference to the principle of harmonious interpretation.

[177] The Biosafety Protocol is binding on the EC; and signed by Argentina and Canada. The US has not signed the Protocol, and the EC argued that the US had not persistently objected to the Protocol.

[178] For the discussion of the status of the precautionary principle as a general principle of law, see Panel Report, *EC – Biotech Products*, at paras 7.87–89. A similar approach was adopted to decide whether the 'polluter pays' principle is a general principle of international law in Arbitral Award, *Case Concerning the Auditing of Account between the Kingdom of the Netherlands and the French Republic pursuant to the Additional Protocol of 25 September 1991 to the Convention of 3 December 1976 on the Protection of the Rhine against Pollution by Chlorides*, 12 March 2004, at <http://www.pca-cpa.org/ENGLISH/RPC/#Netherlands/France> (last visited 10 March 2008), at para 103.

[179] Panel Report, *EC – Biotech Products*, at para 7.67. See similarly ICJ, *Reparation for Injuries*, Advisory Opinion, ICJ Reports (1993) 111, at 182; ECHR, *Case of Al-Adsani v United Kingdom*, 21 November 2001, ECHR (2001) XI, at para 55; ECHR, *Golder Case*, 21 February 1975, ECHR (1975) Ser A, No 18, at para 35; ECHR, *Case of Loizidou v Turkey (Preliminary Objections)*, 23 March 1995, ECHR (1995) Ser A, No 310, at para 44.

[180] Ibid at para 7.68, fn 191.

[181] Ibid.   [182] Ibid at para 7.69.

[183] Ibid at para 7.70. But the Panel was less convincing in its application of this principle (for example, at paras 7.241–42, 7.277–78).

[184] Ibid at para 7.69.

Ultimately, the narrow interpretation of Article 31(3)(c) VCLT did not preclude that 'other rules of international law may in some cases aid a treaty interpreter in establishing, or confirming, the ordinary meaning of treaty terms in the specific context in which they are used'.[185] Thus, other rules of international law can be context. The Panel in *Mexico – Telecoms* had already taken a similar approach and had interpreted 'anti-competitive practices' in Section 1 of Mexico's Reference Paper in the context of international competition instruments but without a discussion of Article 31(3)(c).[186] The Panel's conclusion in *EC – Biotech Products* on the relation between context and Article 31(3)(c) VCLT is a contribution to the interpretation of the VCLT. It illustrates how Articles 31 to 33 VCLT are not mutually exclusive categories. In contrast with Article 31(3)(c), the Panel assumed it had discretion to consider other rules of international law as context to inform the ordinary meaning under Article 31(1).[187]

The significance of Article 31(3)(c) VCLT should not be exaggerated. The theoretical interpretations of this principle have been extensively discussed, but it is up to courts and tribunals to decide how to apply the provision in individual cases. This decision will depend on how a court or tribunal applies and interprets other principles of treaty interpretation. Article 31(3)(c) is by no means the only principle that can justify treaty interpretation in the light of international law. Other principles of treaty interpretation have, so far, more often justified the use of international law. The case law of WTO panels and the Appellate Body illustrates the subsidiary value of Article 31(3)(c). The discussion about fragmentation of international law and treaty interpretation needs to move beyond Article 31(3)(c) and take note of the broader framework in which different principles of treaty interpretation allow and justify the consideration of other rules of international law. Tensions on questions of interpretation between different levels and fora of dispute settlement are a sign of international law's maturity, provided that levels of competition do not become an impediment for sound judgments, awards, and reports.

E. Special Principles of Treaty Interpretation

Vague calls for special principles of treaty interpretation in WTO law have been made. It has been questioned whether 'there was a special rule of treaty interpretation law that had developed in GATT which might prevail over a more general international law proposition' but then failed to articulate any such principle. In the same vein, it has been argued that 'there is room for rethinking the application and adequacy of the VCLT regarding treaty interpretation'. The idea that the VCLT

---

[185] Ibid at para 7.92. See also Feliciano, above fn -25.
[186] Panel Report, *Mexico – Telecoms*, at para 7.236.
[187] Panel Report, *EC – Biotech Products*, at paras 7.90–7.94.

might be outdated has been voiced by others.[188] The Consultative Board did not engage in a more comprehensive discussion of treaty interpretation and the interpretive practices of WTO panels and the Appellate Body. One Appellate Body member has responded that the WTO jurisprudence 'does not reveal any mention of, or reference to, one or more rules of interpretation specific to this particular field that would come to complement or substitute for the [...] general rules'.[189]

It is one thing to say that the VCLT principles of interpretation are unsatisfactory; it is something else to construct new and more acceptable principles. Critiques of the VCLT commonly fail to appreciate how non-codified principles have been interpreted and applied and they neglect to actually formulate new principles. If the interpretation of, for example, an MEA differs from the interpretation of similar language in one of the WTO covered agreements, this is presumably due to the character of the provision(s) under interpretation, the respective treaties as a whole, the context of the dispute, and the broader institutional context of the interpretation. Specialized principles of treaty interpretation will not cure these differing interpretations.[190] Interpretation necessarily implies that each interpretive exercise will have particular features in different areas of law, institutional settings, and dispute settlement systems.[191] Abi-Saab has admitted this:

... each of [these treaty regimes] constitutes a legal universe quite different from the others. The difference can be explained not only by the disparity in the structure, mandate, and composition, but also, and perhaps mainly, by the 'judicial policy' of each forum, which is also a function of its environment.[192]

Panels and the Appellate Body have not endorsed and applied WTO-specific principles of interpretation. In *EC – Chicken Cuts*, the Appellate Body refused to accept and apply an 'interpretative principle directing Panels to bias towards the reduction of tariff commitments'.[193] The Appellate Body found it more appropriate to define the object and purpose of the WTO Agreement and the GATT 1994 in terms of achieving 'security and predictability of the "reciprocal and mutually advantageous

---

[188] J Pauwelyn, 'Chapter 6. Relationship with International Law, Comments' in Andenas and Ortino, above fn 93, at 494–95. Klabbers agrees that the VCLT needs rethinking on the doctrines of *rebus sic stantibus* and interim obligations, but it is less clear if he would come to a similar conclusion on Articles 31 to 33 VCLT. J Klabbers, 'Re-inventing the Law of Treaties: The Contribution of the EC Courts' 1999 *Netherlands Yearbook of International Law* (30) 45, at 46, 73–74.

[189] Abi-Saab, above fn 25, at 460.

[190] Contra G Ress, 'The Interpretation of the Charter' in B Simma, H Mosler, A Randelzhofer, C Tomuschat, and R Wolfrum (eds), *The Charter of the United Nations – A Commentary*, 2nd edn, Vol 1 (Oxford: Oxford University Press, 2002) 13, at 23–24.

[191] Under this understanding, the idea that WTO panels' and the Appellate Body's interpretation of the TRIPS Agreement would be identical to that of the GATT 1994 cannot be entertained. Contra S Frankel, 'WTO Application of "the Customary Rules of Interpretation of Public International Law" to Intellectual Property' 2006 *Virginia Journal International Law* 46(2) 365, at 365–66.

[192] Abi-Saab, above fn25, at 460.

[193] Appellate Body Report, *EC – Chicken Cuts*, at para 243 (citing the EC's appellant's submission, at para 189).

arrangements directed to the substantial reduction of tariffs and other barriers to trade"'.[194] This reasoning shows that whatever the motivation for new or special principles, the same result can likely be realized on the ground of an existing principle of treaty interpretation.

F. Authentic Interpretation Versus Judicial Interpretation

The interpretations of the WTO covered agreements by panels and the Appellate Body are formally authoritative for the dispute being decided, not for others. Even if the reverse consensus rule has made political control of panel and Appellate Body reports rather a formality, Article IX:2 WTO Agreement reserves the ultimate interpretive authority to WTO Members:

The Ministerial Conference and the General Council shall have the exclusive authority to adopt interpretations of this Agreement and of the Multilateral Trade Agreements. In the case of an interpretation of a Multilateral Trade Agreement in Annex 1, they shall exercise their authority on the basis of a recommendation by the Council overseeing the functioning of that Agreement. The decision to adopt an interpretation shall be taken by a three-fourths majority of the Members. This paragraph shall not be used in a manner that would undermine the amendment provisions in Article X.[195]

Generally, authoritative interpretations are 'binding on the parties and any organ which decides on their rights and duties on a basis of delegated authority'.[196] In practice, WTO Members have been incapable of adopting such authoritative interpretations.[197] The responsibility for clarifying the provisions of the WTO covered agreements lies mainly, if not exclusively, with panels and the Appellate Body. Their

[194] Ibid [citing the Panel Report, at para 7.318, quoting Appellate Body Report, *EC – Computer Equipment*, at para 82].

[195] On the formal character of different types of interpretation in GATT practice, see C-D Ehlermann and L Ehring, 'The Authoritative Interpretation Under Article IX:2 of the Agreement Establishing the World Trade Organization: Current Law, Practice and Possible Improvements' 2005 *Journal International Economic Law* 8(4) 803, at 804–05.

[196] G Schwarzenberger, *International Law and Order* (London: Stevens & Sons Ltd, 1971), at 119; also, generally, I Voïcu, *De l'interprétation authentique des traités internationaux* (Paris: A Pédone, 1968); A Papaux, 'Article 33' in O Corten and P Klein (eds), *Les Conventions de Vienne sur le Droit des Traités – Commentaire article par article*, II (Bruylant: Brussels, 2006), at 1373–400.

[197] So far, only one request for an authoritative interpretation has been submitted: GC, *Request for an Authoritative Interpretation Pursuant to Article IX:2 of the Marrakesh Agreement Establishing the World Trade Organization, Communication from the European Communities.* See Ehlermann and Ehring, above fn 195, at 814–15. However, Members can give interpretive guidance to panels and the Appellate Body. For example, WTO Members agreed in the Doha Ministerial Declaration that the TRIPS Agreement 'can and should be interpreted and implemented in a manner supportive of WTO Members' right to protect public health and, in particular, to promote access to medicines for all'. MC, *Declaration on the TRIPS Agreement and Public Health Adopted on 14 November 2001*, WT/MIN(01)/DEC/2 (20 November 2001), at para 5(d). See also chapter 8 of this Handbook.

interpretations are only binding on the disputants and applicable to the specific subject-matter of the dispute; whereas authoritative interpretations by the MC and the GC are binding on all WTO Members.[198] Article 3.9 DSU specifies that judicial interpretations do not prejudice the right of WTO Members to exercise their competence under Article IX:2 WTO Agreement. The ultimate interpretive authority lies with WTO Members but in practice panels and the Appellate Body exercise interpretive autonomy.

It is likely that if the required majority can be reached, Members might prefer to strengthen that majority and opt to amend the treaty language in question.[199] But amendment requires ratification. An authoritative interpretation requires a three-fourths majority, though there is a preference for consensus, and a simple majority of WTO Members should be present.[200] An amendment needs the support of all WTO Members or, if no consensus can be reached, a three-quarters majority.[201] An amendment may be adopted by a two-thirds majority but will only bind those Members that approve the amendment in accordance with their constitutional processes. In the event of an amendment, Members effectively refer the interpretation of the modified treaty language to the dispute settlement system. The practice under Article IX:2 has meant that 'decisions [of the Appellate Body] are likely to have a kind of *de facto* finality as interpretations of law, even if they lack *de jure* finality'.[202]

Authoritative interpretations cannot add to or diminish the rights and obligations of WTO Members, only an amendment or waiver can.[203] Rights and obligations of WTO Members can only be changed with their consent and amendments only bind consenting Members.[204] The alternative conclusion would make the provisions on the amendment of the treaty ineffective.[205] Article IX:2 as such does not prohibit adding or diminishing the rights and obligations in the covered agreements, compared with

[198] Appellate Body Report, *Japan – Alcoholic Beverages II*, at 107; Appellate Body Report, *US – FSC*, at paras 112–13, fn 217.

[199] See also Ehlermann and Ehring, above fn 195, at 806.

[200] Arte IX:2 WTO Agreement and Rule 16 of the Rules of Procedure for Sessions of the Ministerial Conference and of the Rules of Procedure for Meetings of the General Council.

[201] Article X WTO Agreement, which also contains more detailed rules on different avenues for amendment.

[202] R Howse, 'The Most Dangerous Branch? WTO Appellate Body Jurisprudence on the Nature and Limits of the Judicial Power' in T Cottier and PC Mavroidis (eds), *The Role of the Judge in International Trade Regulation – Experience and Lessons for the WTO*, World Trade Forum, Vol 4 (Ann Arbour: University of Michigan Press, 2003) 11, at 15.

[203] Contra Ehlermann and Ehring, above fn 195, at 808–11; Sacerdoti, above fn 107 (arguing that an authentic interpretation 'might even entail a modification to any existing provision').

[204] Art X:3, first sentence WTO Agreement: 'Amendments to provisions [...] of the nature that would alter the rights and obligations of the Members, shall take effect for the Members that have accepted them upon acceptance by two thirds of the Members and thereafter for each other Member upon acceptance by it.' Eg, GC, *Amendment of the TRIPS Agreement*, WT/L/641 (8 December 2005).

[205] See also H Nottage and T Sebastian, 'Giving Legal Effect to the Results of WTO Trade Negotiations: An Analysis of the Methods of Changing WTO Law' 2006 *Journal of International Economic Law* 9(4) 989, at 1003.

Article 3.2 DSU. Authoritative interpretations cannot add to or diminish the rights and obligations of WTO Members, or at least no more than panels and the Appellate Body can. The phrase 'add[ing] or diminish[ing] [. . .] rights and obligations' is relative; an understanding that has so far been insufficiently acknowledged.

The Appellate Body's approach to authoritative interpretations is not yet settled. In *US – FSC*, the Appellate Body refused to recognize a 1981 Council Action as an authoritative interpretation, partly because the Chairman of the GATT 1947 Council had declared that 'the adoption of these reports together with understanding *does not affect the rights and obligations of contracting parties under the General Agreement*'.[206] The Appellate Body assumed that if the 1981 Council action was intended as an authoritative interpretation 'all contracting parties [. . .] would have said so in reasonably recognizable terms'.[207] The action was also not sufficiently formulated in general terms to be generally binding and applicable.[208] The Appellate Body appears to expect that WTO Members will explain clearly that their decision is based on Article IX:2 WTO Agreement.

The Appellate Body has suggested that authoritative interpretations would 'in all probability, have been perceived by the contracting parties as affecting their rights and obligations, and would not, therefore, have been accompanied by such a statement'.[209] The observation that an authoritative interpretation should 'affect' the rights and obligations of WTO Members does not imply that the Appellate Body accepts that such interpretation can 'add to or diminish' these rights and obligations. In fact, any interpretation necessarily 'affects' the rights and obligations of WTO Members, and how they are applied and enforced. As a result, a declaration that a decision does not affect the rights and obligations of WTO Members precludes that the decision can be an authoritative interpretation, which always affects their rights and obligations.

If an authoritative interpretation were adopted, the Appellate Body will likely read the WTO treaty language and its authoritative interpretation as one inseparable subject of interpretation—similar to how it has read treaty provisions together with *Ad* Articles. The authoritative interpretation merges with the covered agreements, which are then interpreted in the light of the customary principles of treaty interpretation.

The question whether authoritative interpretations should be interpreted as treaty language or be qualified as means of interpretation is distinct from whether the GC and the MC are bound to apply the customary principles of treaty interpretation. Article IX:2 WTO Agreement does not refer to the 'customary rules of interpretation of public international law'.[210] The function of principles of treaty

---

[206] Appellate Body Report, *US – FSC*, at para 112 (original emphasis).
[207] Ibid.   [208] Ibid at para 109.
[209] Ibid at para 112.
[210] See also Ehlermann and Ehring, above fn 195, at 810–11. They come to similar conclusions but on different grounds.

interpretation becomes visible and concrete in dispute settlement. In other contexts, such as diplomacy, interpretations of treaties are often not documented but are implicitly assumed. This does not mean that States will not start with the text of the treaty and, depending on their political agenda, opt for a contextual interpretation or prioritize a certain objective. In essence, such interpretations are often merely bolder applications of the principles on which panels and the Appellate Body rely.

Partly in response to the paralysis of Article IX:2 WTO Agreement and the lack of progress in trade negotiations, the Consultative Board has proposed to add an intermediate level of control over panel and Appellate Body reports. The objective of this 'reasonably impartial, special expert group of the DSB' would be to produce constructive criticism on certain systemic interpretive issues flowing from the jurisprudence.[211] It is doubtful whether any such 'reasonably impartial' group would add anything more to the present system than superfluous and not necessarily well-qualified statements. The debates in the DSB and outside the meeting rooms in Geneva, independent criticism of DSB decisions in the literature, and finally the quality of Appellate Body reports themselves are reasons against such a proposal. Although Article IX:2 has yet to be tested, an authoritative interpretation would appear to be the only acceptable 'necessary instrument of checks and balances *vis-à-vis* the WTO's quasi-judiciary' before amending the treaty.[212] The value of authoritative interpretations in relation to judicial interpretations lies especially in the ability of the former to react against the latter. One Appellate Body member regrets that 'one of the major weaknesses ... [is] that the politics is not able to correct what the judiciary has gotten wrong'.[213] This does not preclude that a uniform interpretation by all or a majority of Members be taken into account as subsequent practice—though this is not an authoritative interpretation in the sense of Article IX:2.

V. Conclusion

The uniqueness of the WTO dispute settlement system needs to be emphasized but not overestimated. The system was created by a treaty to apply and interpret a treaty. For the purpose of this chapter, three characteristics need to be borne in mind. First, the political control exercised by the DSB over panel and Appellate Body reports may not be able to block the adoption of reports. Nevertheless, it matters

---

[211] Consultative Board, above fn 129, at 56, paras 251–52; also M Matsushita, 'WTO Appellate Body Roundtable' 2005 *ASIL Proceedings* (99) 175, at 181.

[212] Ehlermann and Ehring, above fn 195, at 812 (original emphasis).

[213] Terris, Romano, and Swigart, above fn 163, at 128.

in terms of the context in which panels and the Appellate Body operate and justify their interpretations. Second, Article 3.2 DSU might seem self-evident but the provision emphasizes that WTO Members expect that they will be able to understand panel and Appellate Body reports in the light of the customary principles of treaty interpretation. The jurisprudence reflects an increasing tension between the Appellate Body's, sometimes excessive, formalism towards Articles 31 to 33 VCLT and its, sometimes unsatisfactory, informality towards non-codified principles of treaty interpretation. Third, the lack of an explicit clause on the applicable law is of conceptual and institutional importance. There is no single test to answer the question of how much other international law is part of the applicable law, besides the WTO covered agreements. It is a matter to be decided by WTO Members and, in the absence of such decision, it is a test to be designed by panels and the Appellate Body. The WTO covered agreements are obviously part of the applicable law in WTO dispute settlement. But the WTO covered agreements are incomplete, and sometimes applying other international law becomes necessary. This question of necessity has mostly been approached by the Appellate Body through treaty interpretation.

Selected Bibliography

G Abi-Saab, 'The WTO Dispute Settlement and General International Law' in R Yerxa and B Wilson (eds), *Key Issues in WTO Dispute Settlement – The First Ten Years* (Cambridge: Cambridge University Press, 2005) 7

L Bartels, 'Applicable Law in WTO Dispute Settlement Proceedings' 2001 *Journal of World Trade* 35(3) 499

C Brown, *A Common of International Adjudication* (Oxford: Oxford University Press, 2007)

JI Charney, 'Is International Law Threatened by Multiple International Tribunals?' 1998 *Recueil des Cours* (271) 101

C-D Ehlermann and L Ehring, 'The Authoritative Interpretation Under Article IX:2 of the Agreement Establishing the World Trade Organization: Current Law, Practice and Possible Improvements' 2004 *Journal of International Economic Law* 8(4) 803

R Gardiner, *Treaty Interpretation* (Oxford: Oxford University Press, 2008)

R Howse, 'The Most Dangerous Branch? WTO Appellate Body Jurisprudence on the Nature and Limits of the Judicial Power' in T Cottier and PC Mavroidis (eds), *The Role of the Judge in International Trade Regulation – Experience and Lessons for the WTO, World Trade Forum*, Vol 4 (Ann Arbour: University of Michigan Press, 2003) 11

J Klabbers, 'On Rationalism in Politics: Interpretation of Treaties and the World Trade Organization' 2005 *Nordic Journal of International Law* 74(3) 40

P Lamy, 'The Place of the WTO and its Law in the International Legal Order' 2006 *European Journal of International Law* 17(5) 969

H Lauterpacht, 'Restrictive Interpretation and the Principle of Effectiveness in the Interpretation of Treaties' 1949 *British Yearbook International Law* (26) 48

H Lauterpacht, *The Development of International Law by the International Court*, revised edn (London: Stevens & Sons Limited, 1958)

M Lennard, 'Navigating by the Stars: Interpreting the WTO Agreements' 2002 *Journal of International Economic Law* 5(1) 17

U Linderfalk, *On the Interpretation of Treaties – The Modern International Law as Expressed in the 1969 Vienna Convention on the Law of Treaties* (Dordrecht: Springer, 2007)

G Marceau, 'A Call for Coherence in International Law' 1999 *Journal of World Trade* 33(5) 87

G Marceau, 'Conflicts of Norms and Conflicts of Jurisdictions – The Relationship between the WTO Agreement and MEAS and other Treaties' 2001 *Journal of World Trade* 35(6) 1131

C McLachlan, 'The Principle of Systemic Integration and Article 31(3)(c) of the Vienna Convention' 2005 *International and Comparative Law Quarterly* 54(2) 279

AD McNair, *The Law of Treaties*, reissued 1961 edn (Oxford: Clarendon Press, 1986)

A Mitchell, *Legal Principles in WTO Disputes* (Cambridge: Cambridge University Press, 2008)

F Ortino, 'Treaty Interpretation and the WTO Appellate Body Report in *US – Gambling*: A Critique' 2006 *Journal of International Economic Law* 9(1) 117

D Palmeter and PC Mavroidis, 'The WTO Legal System: Sources of Law' 1998 *American Journal of International Law* 92(3) 398

J Pauwelyn, *Conflict of Norms in Public International Law* (Cambridge: Cambridge University Press, 2003)

J Pauwelyn, 'How to Win a WTO Dispute Based on Non-WTO Law' 2003 *Journal of World Trade* 37(6) 997

C Ryngaert, *Jurisdiction in International Law* (Oxford: Oxford University Press, 2008)

Y Shany, *The Competing Jurisdictions of International Courts and Tribunals* (Oxford: Oxford University Press, 2003)

J Trachtman, 'Jurisdiction in WTO Dispute Settlement' R Yerxa and B Wilson (eds), *Key Issues in WTO Dispute Settlement – The First Ten Years* (Cambridge: Cambridge University Press, 2005) 132

JHH Weiler, 'The Rule of Lawyers and the Ethos of Diplomats – Reflections on the International and External Legitimacy of WTO Dispute Settlement' 2001 *Journal of World Trade* 35(2) 191

CHAPTER 13

....

PROCEDURAL
AND
EVIDENTIARY
ISSUES

....

ALAN YANOVICH
WERNER ZDOUC*

* Any views expressed in this chapter are those of the authors and should not be attributed to the Appellate Body, its Secretariat, or the WTO Secretariat. We include several references to other chapters in this Handbook that provide more exhaustive explanations of some of the issues discussed in this chapter. These cross-references do not necessarily imply that we endorse the views expressed in those chapters.

I. Introduction

An effective procedural framework is of crucial importance in any dispute settlement system. It ensures that a claim is adjudicated efficiently and that the complaining party obtains relief without undue delay. Procedural rules also ensure that the due process rights of the respondent party are respected and that the outcome is the result of a fair and impartial process.

The WTO dispute settlement system has become one of the most prominent international dispute resolution systems. It is widely considered to operate efficiently and effectively. Since the establishment of the WTO in 1995, 369 disputes have been initiated, 158 panels have been established, and 84 Appellate Body reports have been adopted.[1] The efficiency with which the system has operated is a positive reflection of the procedural framework provided in the Understanding on Rules and Procedures Governing the Settlement of Disputes (DSU). At the same time, it reflects a degree of procedural flexibility that has allowed it to evolve and to find procedural solutions to difficult issues that have arisen over the years.[2] This ability to evolve derives, in large part, from the flexibility that the DSU leaves to WTO adjudicative bodies—panels and the Appellate Body—to adopt their own working procedures.[3]

Any examination of the procedural rules applicable to WTO dispute settlement should proceed from the following basic considerations. First, the principle of due process applies to all stages of the dispute settlement process. Procedural decisions must always conform to the basic dictates of due process. Second, Article 3.2 DSU emphasizes that 'Members will engage in these procedures in good faith in an effort to resolve the dispute'. Third, as the Appellate Body has stressed, '[t]he procedural rules of WTO dispute settlement are designed to promote, not the development of litigation techniques, but simply the fair, *prompt and effective resolution* of trade disputes'.[4]

This chapter focuses on the procedures used in WTO dispute settlement and some of the procedural and evidentiary issues that have been raised since the new system began operating. It begins by briefly recalling the legacy of the General Agreement on Tariffs and Trade (GATT) and describing the most significant

---

[1] As of 31 December 2007. The number of Appellate Body reports includes reports issued in compliance proceedings under Article 21.5 DSU.

[2] A Yanovich, 'The evolving WTO dispute settlement system' in Y Taniguchi, A Yanovich, and J Bohanes (eds), *The WTO in the Twenty-first Century: Dispute Settlement, Negotiations, and Regionalism in Asia* (Cambridge: Cambridge University Press, 2007) 248.

[3] Article 12.1 DSU provides that panels shall follow the working procedures set out in Appendix 3 to the DSU unless a panel decides otherwise after consultation with the parties to the dispute. Article 17.9 DSU authorizes the Appellate Body to draw up its working procedures in consultation with the Chairman of the DSB and the Director-General. See *Working Procedures for Appellate Review*, WT/AB/WP/5 (4 January 2005).

[4] Appellate Body Report, *US – FSC*, at para 166 (emphasis added).

changes made to GATT dispute settlement practice in the Uruguay Round. Next, it describes the procedures used in WTO dispute settlement and explains some of the main procedural and evidentiary issues that have been raised. Some thoughts about the future of WTO dispute settlement are offered in the concluding section.

II. The GATT 1947 and the Uruguay Round DSU

Much has been written about how GATT dispute settlement developed from what was essentially a conciliation mechanism to a more adjudicatory model. Articles XXII and XXIII GATT 1947 said very little, if anything, about the procedures that applied to dispute settlement. The procedures had to be adopted on a case-by-case basis and evolved over time. Practice was codified on several occasions.[5] The first codification took place at the end of the Tokyo Round,[6] followed by the Decision taken in connection with the 1982 GATT Ministerial Conference.[7] Additional improvements were adopted following the Uruguay Round's midterm Montreal session.[8] Procedural rules thus gradually emerged in the GATT. Although these rules remained rather elementary, the GATT dispute settlement system worked well for many years.[9]

As part of the WTO agreements concluded during the Uruguay Round, WTO Members negotiated a new agreement that would govern dispute settlement, commonly referred to as the DSU. This new agreement codified some of the procedures that were developed under the GATT. However, the DSU also included significant improvements. The DSU is often described as a further step in the process of 'judicialization' of the GATT/WTO dispute settlement system.

Some of the most important improvements sought to eliminate the possibility that the procedures could be blocked by the respondent. These improvements

---

[5] In addition, on 5 April 1966, the GATT Contracting Parties adopted a Decision on Procedures under Article XXIII (1996 Decision), which were applicable in disputes between a less-developed Contracting Party and a developed Contracting Party.

[6] *Understanding Regarding Notification, Consultation, Dispute Settlement and Surveillance*, L/4907 (28 November 1979), BISD 26S/210.

[7] *Thirty-eighth Session at Ministerial Level, Ministerial Declaration*, L/5424 (29 November 1982), BISD 29S/9, section entitled 'Dispute Settlement Procedures', at 13.

[8] *Improvements to the GATT Dispute Settlement Rules and Procedures*, L/6489 (12 April 1989), BISD 36S/61.

[9] See R E Hudec, *Enforcing International Trade Law: The Evolution of the Modern GATT Legal System* (Salem: Butterworth, 1993).

brought an important degree of 'automaticity' to the procedures. The most important change involved the rule applicable to some of the decisions taken during the
process: the establishment of a panel; the adoption of the reports of the adjudicative
bodies; and the authorization to adopt countermeasures. Under GATT procedures,
the respondent could prevent the establishment of a panel, because the decision to
establish one was made on the basis of positive consensus; in other words, the party
whose measure would be examined by the panel had to consent to the panel's establishment. By contrast, under the DSU, the decision to establish a panel is taken on
the basis of reverse consensus. This means that a panel will be established unless
all WTO Members object, including the Member requesting it. Therefore, once the
consultations phase has been exhausted, the respondent party cannot prevent the
complaining party from proceeding to the adjudicatory phase. The reverse consensus rule applies also to the decision to adopt panel and Appellate Body reports.
Although these reports must be adopted by WTO Members before they are binding
upon the parties to the dispute (as was the case with panel reports under the GATT
1947), adoption will result unless the winning party objects. The reverse consensus
rule applies as well to the decision to authorize the complaining party to take countermeasures when the respondent party is found not to have brought its measures
into compliance with WTO law after a reasonable time period for implementation
has expired.

The DSU also introduced appellate review of panel reports. This is a significant
innovation compared to both the dispute settlement system under the GATT 1947
and other international dispute settlement mechanisms. An appellate stage is not
a common feature of international adjudication and dispute resolution systems.
Commentators have suggested that the introduction of the appellate stage in WTO
dispute settlement was related to the change from the positive to the reverse consensus rule applicable to the adoption of panel reports.[10] Given that panel reports would
be adopted almost automatically under the reverse consensus rule, it was thought
prudent to provide a possibility for Members to seek review of a panel's findings and
conclusions before they became binding. The expectation was that parties would
appeal panel reports infrequently. This has not been the case in practice. In the
early years, almost every panel report was appealed. More recently the frequency
of appeals has decreased; around two thirds of panel reports have been appealed in
recent years.[11]

The other significant change made in the DSU with respect to the GATT dispute
settlement procedures is the development of new and more detailed rules on implementation and enforcement. These rules set out detailed procedures to be followed

[10] P Van den Bossche, 'From afterthought to centrepiece: the WTO Appellate Body and its rise to
prominence in the world trading system' in G Sacerdoti, A Yanovich, and J Bohanes (eds), *The WTO
at Ten: The Contribution of the Dispute Settlement System* (Cambridge: Cambridge University Press,
2006) 289, at 292–4.

[11] See WTO, *Appellate Body Annual Report for 2007*, WT/AB/9 (30 January 2008).

after a panel or Appellate Body report containing a finding of WTO-inconsistency is adopted by the Dispute Settlement Body (DSB). They include rules on the reasonable period of time for implementation, procedures for the review of whether implementation measures bring about full compliance, and rules on the authorization of countermeasures if there is no compliance.

The procedures applicable in WTO dispute settlement are described in more detail in the next section.

III. WTO Dispute Settlement Procedures

A. General Characteristics

1. *Objectives*

The objectives of the WTO dispute settlement system are outlined in Article 3.2 DSU. The system is intended to 'provid[e] security and predictability to the multilateral trading system'. It does this by helping 'to preserve the rights and obligations of Members under the covered agreements' and by 'clarify[ing] the existing provisions in those agreements in accordance with customary rules of interpretation of public international law'.

The DSU recognizes that dispute settlement panels and the Appellate Body are called upon in particular disputes to clarify WTO provisions in accordance with customary rules of interpretation. The adoption of authoritative interpretations of those provisions applicable to all WTO Members is reserved exclusively to the Members acting through the Ministerial Conference (MC) or the General Council (GC) under Article IX:2 WTO Agreement.[12] This limitation is reinforced by the express requirement that the recommendations and rulings of the DSB not add to or diminish the obligations in the covered agreements.[13]

Even though the DSU brings the WTO dispute settlement closer to a judicial system, it retains some elements that more closely resemble the model of arbitral proceedings. One such element is the emphasis on resolving a specific dispute through a settlement that is mutually acceptable to the parties. Article 3.7 DSU states that '[a] solution mutually acceptable to the parties to a dispute and consistent with the

---

[12] Article IX:2, however, must not be used in a manner that would undermine the amendment provisions in Article X WTO Agreement.

[13] Arts 3.2 and 19.2 DSU.

covered agreements is clearly to be preferred'. However, the comparison with the arbitration model cannot be taken too far; although a mutual settlement is preferred, the DSU makes clear that the settlement must be 'consistent with the covered agreements'. Bilateral settlements could be challenged in WTO dispute settlement, though other WTO Members would arguably be reluctant to file a complaint unless the settlement directly affects them.

2. *Automatic and Exclusive Jurisdiction*

One of the most salient features of the WTO dispute settlement system is its automatic jurisdiction over any dispute between WTO Members involving an infringement of a provision in the WTO agreements or nullification or impairment of benefits arising from them. By ratifying the WTO agreements, which include the DSU, a WTO Member accepts *ex ante* to submit itself to the WTO dispute settlement system. Jurisdiction is not only automatic, it is also exclusive. WTO Members agree not to submit any dispute arising under the WTO agreements to another forum. Nor are they allowed to make a unilateral determination of whether the WTO agreements have been infringed.[14]

The DSU procedures apply to disputes arising under any of the 'covered agreements'. These are listed in Appendix I of the DSU and include the WTO Agreement; all the multilateral agreements annexed to it relating to trade in goods, trade in services, and the protection of intellectual property rights; and the DSU itself. The application of the DSU to disputes under the plurilateral agreements annexed to the WTO Agreement is subject to the terms of these agreements, or decisions by the parties to these agreements setting out the terms for the application to the individual agreement.[15]

3. *Uniformity of Procedures, but with the Option of Using Alternative Means of Dispute Resolution*

The procedures in the DSU apply uniformly to disputes arising under the various agreements, with some limited exceptions that are specifically or additionally provided for in particular agreements. The special or additional rules are listed in Appendix II to the DSU and include, for example, a specific standard of review applicable to disputes brought under the Anti-Dumping Agreement,[16] shorter timeframes for prohibited export subsidy disputes under the SCM Agreement, and the possibility of panels establishing technical expert groups in disputes under the TBT and SPS Agreements.

---

[14] Art 23 DSU. See also chapter 12 of this Handbook.
[15] The Agreement on Government Procurement and the Agreement on Trade in Civil Aircraft.
[16] See also chapter 14 of this Handbook.

Parties may have recourse to alternative means of dispute resolution, which are also set out in the DSU. At any time, parties may voluntarily request good offices, conciliation, or mediation. This option has not been used,[17] despite the fact that WTO Director-General (DG) Supachai Panitchpakdi made a declaration in 2001 emphasizing his readiness to assist WTO Members in settling disputes and describing the procedures that could apply when a WTO Member requests good offices, conciliation, or mediation.[18] Alternatively, parties may seek to have the matter resolved in a special arbitration procedure under Article 25 DSU. Resort to arbitration is subject to mutual agreement of the parties, who also have to agree on the procedures that would be followed in the arbitration. There has been only one recourse to Article 25 although it was not used in lieu of panel or Appellate Body proceedings, but rather in the implementation stage of a dispute after it had been adjudicated by a panel. The purpose of that arbitration was to set an amount of compensation pending full compliance.[19] Finally, the DSU allows a developing country Member bringing a complaint against a developed country Member to invoke the procedures set out in a GATT Decision of 1966, which provides for expedited proceedings. Because the alternative mechanisms provided in the DSU seldom have been used, this chapter will focus on the regular procedures involving consultations, an adjudicative phase before a panel, the possibility of appellate review, and an implementation stage.

4. *Decentralized Enforcement under Collective Supervision*

WTO Members acting through the DSB collectively supervise the WTO dispute settlement system. Although parties and the adjudicative bodies are given a margin of discretion over the procedures to follow in a particular case, ultimate control is exercised by the DSB. Thus, it is the DSB that establishes a panel. In addition, the DSB must adopt panel and Appellate Body reports before these reports become

---

[17] Recently, Colombia and Panama each requested the WTO DG's good offices in relation to their requests for consultations concerning the EC's regime for the importation of bananas (*EC – Bananas III – Request for Consultations by Colombia*, WT/DS361/1, G/L/818 (26 march 2007); and *EC – Bananas III – Request for Consultation by Panama*, WT/DS364/1 (27 June 2007)). However, their requests were made pursuant to the 1966 Decision, which developing country Members have the right to invoke in disputes against developed Members pursuant to Article 3.12 DSU. In 2002, the Philippines, Thailand, and the EC requested mediation by the WTO DG to examine the extent to which the legitimate interests of the Philippines and Thailand were being unduly impaired as a result of the implementation by the EC of preferential tariff treatment for canned tuna from certain third countries. The requesting Members, however, did not formally invoke Article 5 DSU because they did not consider the matter at issue to be a 'dispute' within the terms of the DSU. Nevertheless, they agreed that the mediator could be guided by procedures similar to those envisaged for mediation under Article 5 DSU. See GC, *Request for Meditation by the Philippines, Thailand and the European Communities*, WT/GC/66 (16 October 2002) and WTO Secretariat, *A Handbook on the Dispute Settlement System* (Geneva: WTO, 2004), at 95.

[18] GC, *Article 5 of the Dispute Settlement Understanding – Communication from the Director-General*, WT/DSB/25 (17 July 2001). See also chapter 16 of this Handbook.

[19] Award of the Arbitrators, *US – Section 110(5) Copyright Act (Article 25.3)*.

legally binding on the disputants. Through adoption, panel and Appellate Body findings become recommendations and rulings of the DSB.

After a panel or the Appellate Body finds a WTO Member's measure to be WTO-inconsistent, the matter is placed on the agenda of the DSB and remains on it until the matter is resolved. This requires the respondent WTO Member to report to the DSB its progress toward full implementation at every regular meeting of the DSB.

The DSB also plays an important role in securing compliance with panel and Appellate Body reports. The DSB does not itself enforce or execute the rulings of a panel or the Appellate Body but, rather, permits the successful complaining party to 'self-enforce' the DSB recommendations by authorizing recourse to proportionate countermeasures as a last resort. However, important limitations are imposed on the right to take countermeasures. The most important limitation is that the complaining party must obtain prior authorization from WTO Members acting collectively through the DSB. There are also limitations as regards the level of the countermeasures and the trade sectors in which they can be applied.

Although the decision to authorize countermeasures is taken by the DSB by reverse consensus, the role of the DSB should not be underestimated. Appellate Body member Giorgio Sacerdoti has written that '[p]utting the weight of the entire membership behind any decision resolving a dispute induces implementation by making the political consequences of non-implementation harder to bear for any party that has to face the whole constituency, and not just its opponent in the dispute'.[20]

B. Consultations

A dispute is formally initiated by filing a request for consultations in accordance with Article 4 DSU. The main purpose of consultations is to afford the WTO Members involved an opportunity to arrive at a mutually agreeable settlement. As the Appellate Body described it, '[t]hrough consultations, parties exchange information, assess the strengths and weaknesses of their respective cases, narrow the scope of the differences between them and, in many cases, reach a mutually agreeable solution'.[21] Often parties have discussed the issue previously in other contexts. Nevertheless, the DSU requires that consultations be initiated within the WTO framework before it is possible to proceed to the adjudicative phase of dispute settlement.

The request for consultations must conform to several formal requirements set out in Article 4.4 DSU. First, the request must be made in writing. In practice, the request usually takes the form of a letter from one WTO Member to another. Second, besides being sent to the WTO Member to which the request is directed, the request for consultations must be notified to the DSB and to the relevant Councils

---

[20] G Sacerdoti, 'The Dispute Settlement System of the WTO in Action: A perspective on the first ten years' in Sacerdoti, Yanovich, and Bohanes, above fn 10, 35, at 38.

[21] Appellate Body Report, *Mexico – Corn Syrup (Article 21.5 – US)*, at para 54.

and Committees. Notification to the DSB results in the circulation of the request to all WTO Members. Third, it must provide 'reasons for the request, including identification of the measures at issue and an indication of the legal basis for the complaint'. There is an additional requirement that applies in cases involving a prohibited export subsidy. Article 4.2 SCM Agreement requires that, in the case of a prohibited subsidy, the request for consultations 'include a statement of available evidence with regard to the existence and nature of the subsidy in question'.[22]

The WTO Member to which the request for consultations is directed must respond to the request within 10 days after its receipt. Consultations must be entered into within 30 days of receipt of the request. If there is no response within 10 days, or consultations are not held within 30 days, the Member requesting the consultations need not wait any longer, but may proceed directly to request the establishment of a panel. In almost all cases, however, Members accept to hold consultations within the 60-day period foreseen for that purpose. The Member initiating consultations may request the establishment of a panel only after that 60-day period has expired, unless both parties agree prior to the expiration that the consultations have failed to settle the dispute.

Consultations are confidential. Article 4.11 DSU provides that, in certain circumstances, other WTO Members may request to join the consultations. This is possible when the Member requesting the consultations has invoked Article XXII GATT 1994; the requesting Member may prevent other Members from joining the consultations by invoking Article XXIII instead. In addition, WTO Members wishing to join the consultations must claim to have a substantial trade interest. The determination of whether the claim of substantial trade interest is well-founded is made by the Member to which the request for consultations was directed. In other words, the WTO Member responding to the request for consultations has some control on whether other Members can join the consultations. Some have expressed concern that the absence of clear guidelines about what constitutes a 'substantial trade interest' could allow the Member to whom the request for consultations was made, to refuse without good cause a third party request to join in the consultations. They have suggested that WTO Members adopt guidelines for making such a determination.[23] A WTO Member that has not been able to join consultations requested by another Member has the right to request its own consultations.

Although consultations are held before the adjudicative stage, the wording of the request for consultations may have consequences for the scope of the adjudicative stage. In particular, there must be some identity between the scope of the dispute at

---

[22] The Appellate Body has emphasized the importance of 'bear[ing] in mind that the requirement to submit a statement of available evidence applies in the earliest stages of WTO dispute settlement, and that the requirement is to provide a "statement" of the evidence and not the evidence itself'. Appellate Body Report, *US – Upland Cotton*, at para 308.

[23] See DSB, *Contribution by Jamaica to the Doha Mandated Review of the Dispute Settlement Understanding (DSU) – Communication from Jamaica*, TN/DS/W/21 (10 October 2002).

the consultations stage and the scope of the dispute that is submitted to a dispute settlement panel for adjudication. Respondent parties have sometimes requested that panels exclude from their consideration certain issues that they claim were not properly raised in the consultations. The Appellate Body has indicated that there need not be a 'precise and exact identity'[24] between the request for consultations and the request for the establishment of a panel and that, '[a]s long as the complaining party does not expand the scope of the dispute, [the Appellate Body would] hesitate to impose too rigid a standard for the "precise...identity" between the scope of consultations and the request for the establishment of a panel'.[25] Although the Appellate Body has not directly ruled on the issue, it has expressed a preference for determining the scope of the consultations on the basis of what is stated in the request for consultations as opposed to what actually took place in the consultations. This is because the request for consultations is in writing and notified to the DSB; by contrast, 'there is no public record of what actually transpires during consultations and parties will often disagree about what, precisely, was discussed'.[26]

Even though consultations are a 'prerequisite to panel proceedings',[27] there may be circumstances in which the Member to which the request is directed could be seen as having waived its right to prior consultations. The Appellate Body held that 'where the responding party does not object, explicitly and in a timely manner, to the failure of the complaining party to request or engage in consultations, the responding party may be deemed to have consented to the lack of consultations and, thereby, to have relinquished whatever right to consult it may have had'.[28] Thus, the Appellate Body found that the lack of consultations in that case did not deprive the Panel of the authority to rule on the matter submitted to it.[29] Approximately half of the requests for consultations do not advance to the panel stage.[30]

C. Panel Proceedings

1. *Overview*

If consultations are unsuccessful, the party requesting the consultations may seek to proceed to the adjudicative phase by requesting the establishment of a panel. There is no requirement under the DSU for the WTO Member requesting the establishment

---

[24] Appellate Body Report, *Brazil – Aircraft*, at para 132.

[25] Appellate Body Report, *US – Upland Cotton*, at para 293 (footnote omitted).

[26] Ibid at para 287.

[27] Appellate Body Report, *Mexico – Corn Syrup (Article 21.5 – US)*, at para. 58.

[28] Ibid at para 63.   [29] Ibid at para 64.

[30] For an evaluation of the results achieved through consultations, see W Davey, 'Evaluating WTO dispute settlement: what results have been achieved through consultations and implementation of panel reports?' in Y Taniguchi, A Yanovich, and J Bohanes (eds), *The WTO in the Twenty-first Century: Dispute Settlement, Negotiations, and Regionalism in Asia* (Cambridge: Cambridge University Press, 2007) 98, at 102–7.

of a panel to demonstrate a legal interest; instead, 'a Member has broad discretion whether to bring a case against another Member'.[31] Article 3.7 does require that the complaining Member 'exercise its judgement as to whether action under [the DSU] would be fruitful'. The Appellate Body has explained that this reflects 'a basic principle that Members should have recourse to WTO dispute settlement in good faith'.[32] This requirement, however, is 'largely self-regulating' and panels are not authorized 'to look behind a Member's decision to bring a case'.[33]

The formal requirements that apply to a request for the establishment of a panel are set out in Article 6.2 DSU. The request must be made in writing and must (i) indicate whether consultations were held; (ii) identify the specific measures at issue; and (iii) provide a brief summary of the legal basis of the complaint sufficient to present the problem clearly. In order 'to present the problem clearly', the request for the establishment of a panel 'must plainly connect the challenged measure(s) with the provision(s) of the covered agreements claimed to have been infringed, so that the respondent party is aware of the basis for the alleged nullification or impairment of the complaining party's benefits'.[34] If the complaining Member requests that the panel be established with other than standard terms of reference, it must include the proposed text of the terms of reference in the request for the establishment of a panel.

The request for the establishment of a panel is submitted to the DSB and circulated to all WTO Members. It will be included on the agenda of the next regular meeting of the DSB, but the WTO Member making the request can ask that a special meeting of the DSB be held within 15 days of the request, provided that at least 10-days' advance notice of the meeting is given. The respondent Member can object to the establishment of a panel at the first DSB meeting in which the issue is considered. The request will then be considered for a second time at the next meeting of the DSB. This time, however, the reverse consensus rule applies and the panel will be established unless all WTO Members object to its establishment, including the WTO Member making the request.

The panel will be established with standard terms of reference unless the parties agree otherwise within 20 days from the establishment of the panel. The standard terms of reference are provided in Article 7.1 DSU and require the panel to examine, in the light of the provisions of the WTO agreements cited by the parties to the dispute, the matter referred to the DSB by the complaining party in the request for the establishment of a panel, and to make such findings as will assist the DSB in making the recommendations or in giving the rulings provided for in that/those agreement(s). The Appellate Body has explained that the 'matter' to be examined by the panel 'consists of two elements: the specific measures at issue and the legal basis

---

[31]   Appellate Body Report, *EC – Bananas III*, at para 135.
[32]   Appellate Body Report, *Mexico – Corn Syrup (Article 21.5 – US)*, at para 73.
[33]   Ibid at para 74; Appellate Body Report, *EC – Bananas III*, at para 135.
[34]   Appellate Body Report, *US – Oil Country Tubular Goods Reviews*, at para 162.

of the complaint (or the claims)',[35] both of which are supposed to be indicated in the request for the establishment of the panel.

Accordingly, the request for the establishment of a panel plays a crucial role in determining the scope of the panel's examination. It forms the basis for the panel's terms of reference[36] and, consequently, establishes the panel's jurisdiction.[37] As a result, 'where a panel request fails to identify adequately particular measures or fails to specify a particular claim, then such measures or claims will not form part of the matter covered by the panel's terms of reference'.[38] The request for the establishment of a panel also has another important purpose: it serves 'the due process objective of notifying the parties and third parties of the nature of a complainant's case'.[39]

The next step in the process is the composition of the panel. The WTO Secretariat will propose the names of panelists to the parties, which are not supposed to object 'except for compelling reasons'. If the parties cannot agree on the panelists within 20 days after the establishment of the panel, either party may request that the panelists be appointed by the WTO DG in consultation with the Chairman of the DSB and the Chairman of the relevant Council or Committee. Where such a request is made, the composition of the panel will be communicated to WTO Members by the DSB Chairman within 10 days of the request. In just over half of the panels composed between 1995 and 2006, at least one panellist was appointed by the DG. The trend indicates a growing reliance by parties on the DG for the appointment of panelists. Unless the parties agree otherwise, panelists may not be nationals of the WTO Members that are parties or third parties in the dispute. Pursuant to Article 8.10, in cases between a developing country Member and a developed country Member, the developing country Member has the right to request that at least one of panellist be from a developing country Member.

Panelists and others assisting the panels (such as experts and WTO Secretariat staff) are subject to the Rules of Conduct for the Understanding on Rules and Procedures Governing the Settlement of Disputes (Rules of Conduct), which were adopted by the DSB.[40] The Rules of Conduct seek to maintain the integrity, impartiality, and confidentiality of proceedings. In order to avoid conflicts of interests, they require panelists and those who assist them to disclose 'any information...which...is likely to affect or give rise to justifiable doubts as to their independence or impartiality',[41] including information regarding financial and

---

[35] Appellate Body Report, *Guatemala – Cement I*, at para 72 (emphasis omitted).
[36] Appellate Body Report, *EC – Bananas III*, at para 142.
[37] Appellate Body Report, *Brazil – Desiccated Coconut*, at 186.
[38] Appellate Body Report, *Dominican Republic – Import and Sale of Cigarettes*, at para 120.
[39] Appellate Body Report, *US – Carbon Steel*, at para 126 (emphasis omitted).
[40] *Rules of Conduct for the Understanding on Rules and Procedures Governing the Settlement of Disputes, as adopted by the DSB on 3 December 1996*, WT/DSB/RC/1 (11 December 1996).
[41] Rule VI.2 Rules of Conduct.

professional interests, statements of personal opinion, and employment or family interests.

Article 9 DSU foresees the possibility that several WTO Members challenge the same measure applied by another WTO Member. If feasible, a single panel should be established in such a situation. The panel, however, must organize its examination and present its findings to the DSB in a manner that does not impair the rights that the parties to the dispute would have enjoyed had separate panels examined the complaints. Moreover, a party may request that the panel submit separate reports on the dispute concerned. The written submissions by each of the complainants must be made available to the other complainants, and each complainant has the right to be present when any one of the other complainants presents its views to the panel. Article 9 goes on to provide that, if it is not possible to establish a single panel, separate panels should be composed, to the extent possible, by the same panelists and the timetables should be harmonized.

After a panel is established and composed, it must adopt working procedures. The DSU does not provide uniform panel procedures. Instead, pursuant to Article 12 DSU, each panel may adopt its own working procedures after consulting with the parties to the dispute. Model working procedures are provided in Annex 3 to the DSU. More detailed working procedures have developed in dispute settlement practice. A typical panel process begins with an initial organizational meeting in which the panel, in consultation with the parties to the dispute, sets the timetable for the process. For this purpose, the organizational meeting is usually held with the parties within one week of the panel's composition. The panel will adopt its working schedule at that meeting or shortly thereafter.

Next, parties and third parties file a first set of written submissions. The complaining party files its written submission first, followed a few weeks later by the respondent party and the third parties. A first meeting with the panel is held a few weeks later. After the first meeting, the complaining and respondent parties file rebuttal submissions simultaneously, which are followed by a second meeting with the panel. At the meetings with the panel, the parties and third parties (in the first meeting) make an oral statement and respond to questions from the panel. Parties may also ask questions of each other. Although parties respond orally to questions from the panel and the other party, they are also allowed to file written responses to the questions within a few days after the meetings.

Following the second meeting with the parties, the panel deliberates and drafts its report, which is issued in four stages. First, in accordance with Article 15, the panel provides the parties with a draft of the descriptive section of its report, containing a summary of the facts and the arguments presented by the parties and third parties. The descriptive part is reviewed by the parties who may then offer comments to the panel. Next, the panel issues an interim report to the parties containing both the descriptive section and the panel's findings and conclusions. Parties are again offered an opportunity to submit comments to the panel. In addition, parties may request a further meeting with the panel. In some cases, parties have asked for an opportunity to file written responses to the other side's interim review comments rather than requesting an additional meeting with the panel. Following this interim review stage, the panel issues its final report to the parties. A few weeks later, once translation has been completed, the report is circulated to all WTO Members in the three official languages of the WTO. The 60-day deadline provided in Article 16 DSU for adoption of the panel report by the DSB, or for appealing it, starts only upon circulation to all WTO Members.

In cases where the challenged measures is found to be WTO-inconsistent, panels usually include a recommendation that the respondent Member bring its measure into conformity with the corresponding WTO agreement. Panels may also suggest ways in which the respondent Member could implement the recommendations pursuant to the second sentence of Article 19.1. This is a discretionary right, and panels are not required to make a suggestion.[42] Although some panels have exercised the right to make a suggestion,[43] most panels decline to do so.

According to Article 12 DSU, the time period in which the panel conducts its examination, that is, the time period that elapses between when the panel is composed and its terms of reference are agreed to until the panel report is circulated to the parties, should not exceed six months. If a panel anticipates that it will not be able to meet this deadline, it must inform the DSB in writing of the reasons for the delay and provide an estimate of when it intends to issue its report. Article 12 goes on to provide that, in no case, should the period from the panel's establishment to the circulation of the report to WTO Members exceed nine months. In practice, panels have difficulty meeting these deadlines for various reasons, including the complexity and number of issues litigated or the need to procure opinions of experts.[44]

2. *Significant Procedural Issues*

Several procedural issues have been raised before panels in the course of the 13 years since the WTO dispute settlement system began to operate. The most significant of these issues are described below.

Preliminary Rulings
The DSU does not contain specific provisions regarding preliminary rulings. Nevertheless, parties have sometimes requested that panels make rulings in the

---

[42] Appellate Body Report, *US – Anti-Dumping Measures on Oil Country Tubular Goods*, at para 189.
[43] See eg, Panel Report, *Mexico – Steel Pipe*, at paras 8.9–8.13.
[44] In reviewing panel reports issued by September 2006, Davey notes that the median time between panel establishment and circulation of the report was close to 12.5 months. He proposes several changes to expedite the process, including: applying the reverse consensus rule at the DSB meeting in which the panel request is first considered; selecting panelists from a Permanent Panel Body, reducing the time given to the complaining Member to present its first written submission, and eliminating the interim review. See WJ Davey, 'Expediting the Panel Process in WTO Dispute Settlement' in ME Janow, V. Donaldson, and A Yanovich (eds), *The WTO: Governance, Dispute Settlement and Developing Countries* (New York: Juris Publishing, 2008) 409.

early stages of the proceedings.[45] For instance, parties have requested panels to rule that certain claims are outside the panel's terms of reference because the request for the establishment of the panel did not comply with the requirements of Article 6.2 DSU. In a few instances, panels have acceded to such requests and ruled on issues before circulation of their report. These rulings are notified to the parties by letter and the ruling is reflected in the panel report. In other instances, panels have declined to make preliminary rulings and instead deferred their decision until the time that the panel report is issued. Some panels now include specific provisions about the timing of requests for preliminary rulings in their working procedures.

As regards the timing of any procedural objections, the Appellate Body has emphasized that 'the principle of good faith requires that responding Members seasonably and promptly bring claimed procedural deficiencies to the attention of the complaining Member, and to the DSB or the panel'.[46] If a Member fails to raise an objection in a timely manner, despite having an opportunity to do so, it runs the risk of being deemed to have waived its right to have a panel consider the objection.[47] Determination of the timeliness of an objection falls within 'the discretion given to panels, under the DSU, to deal with specific situations that may arise in a particular case and that are not explicitly regulated'.[48] As the Appellate Body has explained, 'it is the panel that sets the timetable for panel proceedings and, therefore, it is the panel that is in the best position to determine whether, under the particular circumstances of each case, an objection is raised in a timely manner'.[49]

Burden of Proof

Rules on the burden of proof are not expressly provided in the DSU. When the question of burden of proof arose in an early case, the Appellate Body articulated the following rules on the allocation of the burden of proof in WTO dispute settlement:

We find it difficult, indeed, to see how any system of judicial settlement could work if it incorporated the proposition that the mere assertion of a claim might amount to proof. It is, thus, hardly surprising that various international tribunals, including the International Court of Justice, have generally and consistently accepted and applied the rule that the party who asserts a fact, whether the claimant or the respondent, is responsible for providing proof thereof. Also, it is a generally-accepted canon of evidence in civil law, common law and, in

---

[45] The need to deal with requests for preliminary rulings and other procedural issues has been cited as one of the reasons that would justify moving from *ad hoc* panels to a roster of permanent panelists. See DSB, *Contribution of the European Communities and its Member States to the Improvement of the WTO Dispute Settlement Understanding – Communication from the European Communities*, TN/DS/W/1 (13 March 2002) and WJ Davey, 'The Case for a WTO Permanent Panel Body' (2003) *Journal of International Economic Law* 6(1) 177.

[46] Appellate Body Report, *US – FSC*, at para 166.

[47] Appellate Body Repoort, *Mexico – Corn Syrup (Article 21.5 – US)*, at para 50.

[48] Appellate Body Report, *Canada – Wheat Exports and Grain Imports*, at para 206.

[49] Ibid.

fact, most jurisdictions, that the burden of proof rests upon the party, whether complaining or defending, who asserts the affirmative of a particular claim or defence. If that party adduces evidence sufficient to raise a presumption that what is claimed is true, the burden then shifts to the other party, who will fail unless it adduces sufficient evidence to rebut the presumption.[50]

The Appellate Body has further explained that '[t]he nature and extent of the evidence required to satisfy the burden of proof will vary from case to case'.[51]

As the above excerpt indicates, a party that invokes an affirmative defence has the burden of proving the elements of such a defence. Provisions of the WTO covered agreements considered to be affirmative defences include Article XI:2(c)(i), Article XX,[52] and Article XXIV[53] GATT 1994, the fifth sentence of footnote 59 SCM Agreement, and Article XIV GATS.[54] A specific rule applies to the GATT 1979 Decision on Differential and More Favourable Treatment, Reciprocity, and Fuller Participation of Developing Countries (Enabling Clause).[55] Although the burden of proving that the challenged measure meets the requirements of the Enabling Clause rests on the party invoking it (presumably the respondent), the complaining party must indicate which obligations of the Enabling Clause are not met by the respondent in its request for the establishment of a panel. This obligation does not, however, mean that the complaining party must prove an inconsistency with the Enabling Clause.[56] Finally, in a few instances, a provision of a WTO agreement may modify the generally applicable rules on the allocation of the burden of proof. One example of such a provision is Article 10.3 Agreement on Agriculture, which places under certain conditions the burden of proof on the respondent.[57]

Evidentiary Issues

The DSU does not expressly set out rules on evidence. However, as would be expected in any dispute settlement system, many evidentiary issues have arisen in WTO dispute settlement proceedings.

There are no formal discovery procedures provided for in the DSU. As explained earlier, consultations can be used by one party to a dispute to seek information from the other party to the dispute. Pursuant to Article 13 DSU, panels have the authority to seek information from any source. This authority includes the ability to consult individual experts and the right to request advisory reports on scientific or technical issues from expert review groups. Procedures on the establishment of expert

---

[50] Appellate Body Report, *US – Wool Shirts and Blouses*, at 335 (fns omitted).
[51] Appellate Body Report, *US – Carbon Steel*, at para 157.
[52] Appellate Body Report, *US – Wool Shirts and Blouses*, at 337.
[53] Appellate Body Report, *Turkey – Textiles*, at para 58.
[54] Appellate Body Report, *US – Gambling*, at para 309.
[55] *Differential and More Favourable Treatment, Reciprocity and Fuller Participation of Developing Countries*, L/4903 (28 November 1979), BISD 26S/203.
[56] Appellate Body Report, *EC – Tariff Preferences*, at paras 104, 105, and 118.
[57] See Appellate Body Report, *Canada – Dairy (Article 21.5 – New Zealand and US)*, at para 71.

review groups are set out in Appendix 4 to the DSU. The Appellate Body has clarified, however, that a panel's authority to seek information from external sources is discretionary, and 'a panel is not duty-bound to seek information in each and every case or to consult particular experts'.[58] At the same time, in view of the rules on the allocation of burden of proof, the Appellate Body has cautioned that a panel may not use its authority to seek information 'to make the case for a complaining party'.[59]

A related issue involves situations where a party refuses to provide the information requested by the panel. According to the Appellate Body, WTO Members are 'under a duty and an obligation to "respond promptly and fully" to requests made by panels for information'.[60] Panels have the authority to draw adverse inferences where a WTO Member refuses to provide the requested information.[61] Like the authority to seek information, a panel's authority to draw adverse inferences is discretionary.[62]

Issues concerning the admissibility of evidence have been raised in a few disputes. The Appellate Body has explained that the DSU 'does not establish time limits for the submission of evidence'.[63] Panels may regulate the submission of evidence in their working procedures, and they have a margin of discretion in determining whether evidence is seasonably submitted.[64] The Appellate Body, however, has cautioned that the submission of new facts at a late stage in the panel proceedings can raise due process concerns.[65] It has noted that the model working procedures set out in Appendix 3 to the DSU 'contemplate two distinguishable stages in a proceeding before a panel': 'the complaining party should set out its case in chief, including a full presentation of the facts on the basis of submission of supporting evidence, during the first stage', whereas '[t]he second stage is generally designed to permit "rebuttals" by each party of the arguments and evidence submitted by the other parties'.[66] The respondent is also expected to submit the evidence in support of its defence in its first written submission to the panel.[67] Moreover, the Appellate Body has held that '[t]he interim review stage is not an appropriate time to introduce new evidence' and has upheld panels that have refused to accept new evidence at this stage.[68] The Appellate Body has pointed out that the purpose of the interim review, according to Article 15 DSU, is the verification of 'precise aspects' of the panel report and, therefore, it 'cannot properly include an assessment of new and unanswered evidence'.[69]

[58] Appellate Body Report, *Argentina – Textiles and Apparel*, at para 84.
[59] Appellate Body Report, *Japan – Agricultural Products II*, at para 129.
[60] Appellate Body Report, *Canada – Aircraft*, at para 87.
[61] Ibid at para 203.   [62] Appellate Body Report, *US – Wheat Gluten*, at para 173.
[63] Appellate Body Report, *Argentina – Textiles and Apparel*, at para 79.
[64] Ibid at paras 80–81.   [65] Appellate Body Report, *US – Gambling*, at para 271.
[66] Appellate Body Report, *Argentina – Textiles and Apparel*, at para 79.
[67] Appellate Body Report, *US – Gambling*, at para 271.
[68] Appellate Body Report, *EC – Sardines*, at para 301.
[69] Ibid. As regards the submission, at the appellate stage, of evidence not in the panel record, the Appellate Body has been reticent to accept such evidence given that Article 17.6 DSU limits the scope of appeals to legal issues. Appellate Body Report, *US – Softwood Lumber V*, at para 9.

With respect to the appreciation of the evidence, the Appellate Body has repeatedly emphasized that panels enjoy a margin of discretion as the triers of fact.[70] This margin of discretion includes determining what credibility and weight to give to a particular piece of evidence.[71] A panel need not 'accord to factual evidence of the parties the same meaning and weight as do the parties'.[72] Moreover, a panel may 'decide which evidence it chooses to utilize in making findings'.[73] However, it is a panel's 'duty to examine and consider all evidence before it, not just the evidence submitted by one or the other party'.[74] A panel may not disregard, refuse to consider, distort, or misrepresent the evidence.[75] Nor can a panel 'make affirmative findings that lack a basis in the evidence contained in the panel record'.[76]

Standard of Review

The standard of review that panels must apply when reviewing a domestic measure is set out in Article 11 DSU, which states that 'a panel should make an objective assessment of the matter before it, including an objective assessment of the facts of the case and the applicability of and conformity with the relevant covered agreements, and make such other findings as will assist the DSB in making the recommendations or in giving the rulings provided for in the covered agreements'.[77] The standard of review in Article 11 applies to all the covered agreements. A specific standard applies under the Anti-Dumping Agreement,[78] as set out in Article 17.6 of that Agreement.

As regards a determination by a domestic authority, the Appellate Body has clarified that, 'although panels are not entitled to conduct a *de novo* review of the evidence, nor to *substitute* their own conclusions for those of the competent authorities, this does *not* mean that panels must simply *accept* the conclusions of the competent authorities'.[79] This means that a panel can assess:

. . . whether the competent authorities' explanation for its determination is reasoned and adequate *only* if the panel critically examines that explanation, in depth, and in the light of the facts before the panel. Panels must, therefore, review whether the competent authorities' explanation fully addresses the nature, and, especially, the complexities, of the data, and responds to other plausible interpretations of that data. A panel must find, in particular, that an explanation is not reasoned, or is not adequate, if some alternative *explanation* of the

---

[70] Appellate Body Report, *Japan – Apples*, at para 221.
[71] Appellate Body Report, *EC – Hormones*, at para 132.
[72] Appellate Body Report, *Australia – Salmon*, at para 267.
[73] Appellate Body Rep, *EC – Hormones*, at para 135.
[74] Appellate Body Report, *Korea – Dairy*, at para 137.
[75] Appellate Body Report, *EC – Hormones*, at para 132.
[76] Appellate Body Report, *US – Carbon Steel*, at para 142.
[77] See also chapter 14 of this Handbook.
[78] The EC argued that a more deferential standard (similar to Article 17.6 Anti-Dumping Agreement) applied to disputes brought under the SPS Agreement, but this argument was rejected by the Appellate Body. Appellate Body Report, *EC – Hormones*, at para 114. The US was also unsuccessful when it argued that the standard in Article 17.6 Anti-Dumping Agreement applies to disputes under the SCM Agreement. Appellate Body Report, *US – Lead and Bismuth II*, at para 49.
[79] Appellate Body Report, *US – Lamb*, at para 106 (original emphasis).

facts is plausible, and if the competent authorities' explanation does not seem adequate in the light of that alternative explanation.[80]

When reviewing a determination made by a domestic investigating authority, a panel may not base its conclusions on evidence not contained in the record of the domestic investigation.[81] Neither may a panel rely on evidence not in existence at the time the domestic authority conducted the investigation and made its determination.[82] Furthermore, in two cases, the Appellate Body found that the panels had not made a 'qualitative analysis' of the evidence.[83] Finally, the Appellate Body faulted a panel for examining circumstantial evidence 'piecemeal' rather than in its totality (contrary to the approach followed by the domestic investigating authority) and for refusing to admit certain evidence.[84] In so doing, the panel had made a *de novo* review of the domestic determination which it was not entitled to do.

Article 17.6 Anti-Dumping Agreement sets forth a special standard of review that applies solely to disputes regarding anti-dumping investigations and determinations. Paragraph (i) of Article 17.6 applies to a panel's assessment of the facts and requires that the panel 'determine whether the authorities' establishment of the facts was proper and whether their evaluation of those facts was unbiased and objective'. The panel must confirm the domestic authorities' evaluation if it determines that 'the establishment of the facts was proper and the evaluation was unbiased and objective, even though the panel might have reached a different conclusion'. Paragraph (ii) of Article 17.6 relates to the interpretation of the provisions of the Anti-Dumping Agreement, which are to be interpreted in accordance with the customary rules of interpretation of public international law. The provision adds that, '[w]here the panel finds that a relevant provision of the [Anti-Dumping] Agreement admits of more than one permissible interpretation, the panel shall find the authorities' measure to be in conformity with the Agreement if it rests upon one of those permissible interpretations'.[85] The Appellate Body has held that there is no conflict between Article 17.6(i) Anti-Dumping Agreement, which deals with a panel's assessment of the facts, and Article 11 DSU. According to the Appellate Body, 'it is inconceivable that Article 17.6(i) should require anything other than that panels make an *objective* "assessment of the facts of the matter"'.[86]

Rights of Third Parties

WTO Members other than the complaining and responding parties are allowed to participate in a dispute. WTO Members wishing to participate in the dispute

---

[80] Ibid.   [81] Appellate Body Report, *US – Wheat Gluten*, at paras 160–63.

[82] Appellate Body Report, *US – Cotton Yarn*, at paras 65–81.

[83] Appellate Body Report, *US – Oil Country Tubular Goods Reviews*, at para 215; Appellate Body Report, *US – Anti-Dumping Measures on Oil Country Tubular Goods*, at paras 209–10.

[84] Appellate Body Report, *US – Countervailing Duty Investigation on DRAMS*, at paras 188–90 and 192.

[85] Appellate Body Report, *EC – Bed Linen (Article 21.5 – India)*, at para 108. See also chapter 12 of this Handbook.

[86] Appellate Body Report, *US – Hot-Rolled Steel*, at para 55 (original emphasis).

must notify their interest within 10 days of the establishment of the panel. However, the rights of such interventions are more limited in the WTO than in other international fora. Third parties may submit written submissions to the panel and have the right to obtain copies of the parties' first written submissions. In addition, third parties may participate in the first meeting of the panel with the parties in a special session reserved for this purpose. However, third parties are generally not allowed to participate in the remainder of the first meeting with the panel, nor in the second meeting of the panel with the parties. Nor do third parties have a right to receive the rebuttal submissions filed by the parties, and they are also excluded from the interim review stage.

In certain disputes, WTO Members have requested that they be given additional rights of participation as third parties. These WTO Members have sought permission to observe the entirety of the first meeting between the panel and the parties, observe also the second meeting, and obtain the parties' rebuttal submissions.[87] This practice, which has come to be known as 'enhanced third party rights', has been adopted by several panels in disputes that substantially affect the trade interests of third parties.[88]

Transparency

One of the issues that has received a lot of attention in relation to panel proceedings is external transparency. According to the DSU, only governments can have recourse to WTO dispute settlement as parties, and only governments may participate as third parties. Article 14.1 DSU provides that panel deliberations shall be confidential. According to Article 18.2 DSU, written submissions filed with the panel shall be treated as confidential unless a party decides to disclose statements of its own positions to the public. A number of WTO Members make their written submissions available to the public by posting them on the internet. Parties that do not make their written submission public are supposed to provide a non-confidential summary upon request of a Member.

Panel meetings with the parties are not open to the public or to WTO Members that are not parties or third parties to the dispute. Recently, upon the request of the parties, some panels have opened their hearing to public viewing. Some panels have done so through closed-circuit television. In one of these disputes, the panel meeting with the third parties was not open to public viewing because of opposition from some of the third parties.[89] In *EC – Bananas III (21.5 – US)*, the public was allowed into the meeting room to observe the hearing.[90]

---

[87] See, eg, Panel Report, *EC – Tariff Preferences*, Annex A.
[88] See, eg, the Panel Report in *EC – Bananas III*.
[89] Panel proceedings in *US – Continued Suspension* and *Canada – Continued Suspension*.
[90] See 'WTO hearing on banana dispute opened to the public', *WTO News Item* (29 October 2007) at <http://www.wto.org/english/news_e/news07_e/dispu_banana_7nov07_e.htm> (last visited 8 March 2008).

A related issue involves the protection of business confidential information. Several panels have adopted special procedures, at the request of the parties, to ensure the confidentiality of certain business confidential information. Both the issues of transparency and of the protection of business confidential information arose in the panel hearing in the Boeing-Airbus disputes.[91] The panels agreed to open their hearings to public viewing using closed-circuit television, but the transmission was deferred in order to ensure that business confidential information was not accidentally disclosed.

Although only WTO Members may participate in WTO dispute settlement, panels have the authority to receive unsolicited submissions from non-governmental organizations (NGOs) or private persons. These unsolicited written submissions are known as *amicus curiae* submissions. Although panels have the authority to receive briefs from *amici*, they are under no obligation to take them into account in the disposition of the issues.[92]

Representation by Private Counsel

Another issue, not addressed by the DSU, that arose is whether WTO Members could be represented at panel hearings by private counsel. The Panel in *EC – Bananas III* ruled that private counsel retained by some of the third parties could not attend the panel meeting because they were not government officials. In the appeal, the Appellate Body noted that 'representation by counsel of a government's own choice may well be a matter of particular significance—especially for developing country Members—to enable them to participate fully in dispute settlement proceedings'.[93] The Appellate Body held that private counsel could participate in its oral hearings.[94] Following the Appellate Body's decision to allow private counsel in its oral hearings, panels now routinely allow parties to be represented by private counsel at panel meetings.

Judicial Economy

Panels have the discretion to exercise judicial economy by not making a finding on each and every claim raised by the complaining party.[95] However, as the Appellate Body has indicated, '[a] panel has to address those claims on which a finding is necessary in order to enable sufficiently precise recommendations and rulings so as to allow for prompt compliance by a Member'; a panel that provides 'only a partial resolution of the matter at issue would [exercise] false judicial economy'.[96]

---

[91] Panel proceedings in *US – Large Civil Aircraft* and *EC and Certain Member States – Large Civil Aircraft*.

[92] Appellate Body Report, *US – Shrimp*, at para 109.

[93] Appellate Body Report, *EC – Bananas III*, at para 12.

[94] Ibid.

[95] Appellate Body Report, *US – Wool Shirts and Blouses*, at 339–40.

[96] Appellate Body Report, *Australia – Salmon*, at para 223.

D. Appellate Review

1. *Overview of Appeal Procedures*

Article 17.9 DSU provides that the Appellate Body shall draw up its working procedures in consultation with the Chairman of the DSB and the WTO DG. Pursuant to this authority, the Appellate Body drew up its Working Procedures for Appellate Review (Working Procedures), which apply uniformly to every appeal. The Working Procedures were originally adopted in 1996 and have been amended on five occasions, most recently on 4 January 2005.[97] The current version of the Working Procedures is contained in WTO document WT/AB/WP/5. The Rules of Conduct are attached to the Working Procedures and apply to Appellate Body Members and the staff of the Appellate Body Secretariat.

An appeal may be initiated by the complaining party or the respondent. An appeal is initiated by the filing of a Notice of Appeal. The requirements for the Notice of Appeal are set out in Rule 20 of the Working Procedures. In addition to certain information about the party filing it, the Notice of Appeal must contain:

> ...brief statement of the nature of the appeal, including: (i) identification of the alleged errors in the issues of law covered in the panel report and legal interpretations developed by the panel; (ii) a list of the legal provision(s) of the covered agreements that the panel is alleged to have erred in interpreting or applying; and (iii) without prejudice to the ability of the appellant to refer to other paragraphs of the panel report in the context of its appeal, an indicative list of the paragraphs of the panel report containing the alleged errors.

The Notice of Appeal not only serves to 'trigger' the appeal, but also has an important due process justification as it ensures 'that the appellee also receives notice, albeit brief, of the "nature of the appeal" and the "allegations of errors" by the panel'.[98] The appellant is not expected to develop its argumentation in the Notice of Appeal; rather, legal arguments are to be developed in written submissions filed afterwards, namely, the appellant's submission and subsequently the submission of the other party, which is known as the appellee.

Following the filing of the Notice of Appeal, the parties are informed of the names of the three Members of the Appellate Body that will hear the appeal, which are known as the 'Division'. Parties also receive the working schedule for the appeal. Standard deadlines apply in all appeals, with the exception of appeals involving prohibited export subsidies which have more expedited procedures. The appeals timetable is reproduced below.

After one party has initiated the appeal, the other party may also appeal the panel report on the basis of other legal errors by the panel. In this case that party is known

---

[97] See V Donaldson and A Yanovich, 'The Appellate Body's Working Procedures for Appellate Review' in Sacerdoti, Yanovich, and Bohanes, above fn 10, 386.

[98] Appellate Body Report, *US – Countervailing Measures on Certain EC Products*, at para 62.

as the 'other appellant'. Under the original Working Procedures,[99] the other appeal was initiated by filing a written submission known as the 'other appellant's submission' without the need to have previously filed a Notice of Appeal. However, the Working Procedures were amended to require the filing of a Notice of Other Appeal, similar to the Notice of Appeal, which is then followed by the other appellant's submission containing the full argumentation. Where there is another appeal, both parties file an appellee's submission.

Third parties before the panel may also participate in the appeal as third participants; however, it is not possible for WTO Members to become third participants at the appellate stage if they had not been third parties before the panel.[100] Third participants have the right to file a written submission and they may attend and make a statement at the oral hearing. Under the original Working Procedures, third parties were required to have filed a written submission in order to participate in the oral hearing. In some cases, upon request and with the consent of the other parties, third parties who did not file a written submission were allowed to attend the oral hearing as passive observers. In January 2005, the Working Procedures were amended to facilitate third party participation. According to the amended Working Procedures, third parties who do not wish to file a written submission may notify their interest in participating in the oral hearing.[101]

The oral hearing takes place around 35–45 days after the initiation of the appeal. At the oral hearing, the appellant(s), appellee(s), and third participant(s) make oral statements followed by questioning by the Division hearing the appeal. There is only one oral hearing and it usually lasts from one to three days. The oral hearing is closed to the public and to those WTO Members not participating in the appeal as an appellant, an appellee, or a third participant. Unlike panel proceedings, there is no separate session for third parties. Instead, third parties are allowed to participate in the entirety of the oral proceedings.

Pursuant to Rule 18 of the Working Procedures, the Division hearing an appeal may, at any time during the appellate proceedings, request additional memoranda from any participant or third participant. The additional memoranda must be made available to the other participant(s) and the third participant(s) and they must be given an opportunity to respond. Divisions have availed themselves of the authority to request additional memoranda on only a few occasions.[102]

The period that follows the oral hearing is used for the deliberations of the Division hearing the appeal and for the drafting of the report. During this period,

---

[99] Appellate Body, *Working Procedures for Appellate Review*, WT/AB/WP/1 (15 February 1996).

[100] Costa Rica has proposed allowing a WTO Member to reserve their right as third parties at the appellate stage, irrespective of whether that Member had reserved its right as third party during the panel stage. *DSB, Proposal by Costa Rica – Third Party Rights – Communication from Costa Rica, Revision*, TN/DS/W/12/Rev.1 (6 March 2003).

[101] Rule 24(2) of the Working Procedures.

[102] See, eg, Appellate Body Report, *US – FSC (Article 21.5 – EC)*, at para 11; Appellate Body Report, *US – Section 211 Appropriations Act*, at para 13; and Appellate Body Report, *Canada – Patent Term*, at para 8.

the Division holds an 'exchange of views' with the other four Appellate Body members who are not part of the Division. The four Appellate Body members who are not on the Division receive all the documents relating to the appeal. The 'exchange of views' is foreseen in Rule 4(3) of the Working Procedures and is intended to promote consistency and coherence in decision-making, and also seeks to draw on the individual and collective expertise of the Appellate Body members. The decision on the issues appealed, however, rests solely on the three members of the Division responsible for the appeal. Although the Working Procedures foresee the possibility that an appeal may be decided through majority voting, appeals have been decided by consensus with only two exceptions: there was a concurrent opinion in *EC – Asbestos* and a separate opinion on one issue in *US – Upland Cotton*.[103]

It should be noted that the Working Procedures include a mechanism to deal with procedural questions not otherwise covered by the Working Procedures. Rule 16(1) allows the Division hearing an appeal, 'in the interests of fairness and orderly procedure', to adopt an *ad hoc* procedure, for purposes of that appeal only, 'provided that it is not inconsistent with the DSU, the other covered agreements and these Rules'. When a Division adopts a special procedure pursuant to Rule 16(1), it must immediately notify the participants to the appeal as well as the other members of the Appellate Body.

An Appellate Body report must be circulated within 60 days after the appeal is initiated, but this time period can be extended to 90 days. In practice, the majority of Appellate Body reports are circulated on Day 90. Shorter time periods apply in cases involving prohibited export subsidies, in which the Appellate Body report must be circulated no later than 60 days after the appeal is initiated. Appellate Body reports are circulated simultaneously to all WTO Members in the three official WTO languages. They are also made publicly available immediately on the WTO website. Unlike in panel proceedings, Appellate Body reports are not issued in stages (descriptive part followed by the full report) and there is no interim review.

The timetable for the various stages of a typical appeal is set out in Table 1 overleaf: The DSU provides that a DSB meeting shall be scheduled within 30 days of circulation of an Appellate Body report to consider its adoption. As indicated earlier, the reverse consensus rule applies to the decision to adopt the reports. The Appellate Body report and the panel report are adopted together. Because panel findings may be upheld, and often only a small number of panel findings are appealed, it is important to look at both the Appellate Body report and the panel report in order to grasp fully the disposition of a case.

---

[103] Appellate Body Report, *EC – Asbestos*, at para 139; Appellate Body Report, *US – Upland Cotton*, at para 631.

Table 1 Timetable for appeals

	General Appeals Day	Prohibited Subsidies Appeals Day
Notice of Appeal	0	0
Appellant's submission	7	4
Notice(s) of Other Appeal	12	6
Other appellant's submission(s)	15	7
Appellee's submission(s)	25	12
Third participant's submission(s)	25	12
Third participant's notification(s)	25	12
Oral hearing	35–45	17–23
Circulation of Appellate Body report	60–90	30–60
DSB meeting for adoption	90–120	50–80

2. *Some Significant Procedural Issues*

Preliminary Rulings

Requests for preliminary rulings have also been made at the appellate stage. As indicated earlier, the DSU does not provide for specific procedures in relation to preliminary rulings. Neither do the Working Procedures set out a particular mechanism for preliminary rulings. Requests for preliminary rulings at the appellate stage have concerned, among other issues, the sufficiency of the Notice of Appeal, the participation of third parties (prior to the amendment of Rule 24), and the protection of business confidential information. The practice of the Appellate Body has been to invite the other participants to comment on the request for the preliminary ruling before deciding the issue.

Scope of Appellate Review

The scope of appellate review in WTO dispute settlement is circumscribed, in general, by Article 17.6 DSU, which provides that '[a]n appeal shall be limited to issues of law covered in the panel report and legal interpretations developed by the panel'. The Appellate Body has read this to mean that findings of fact are in principle not subject to appellate review. Two qualifications are necessary, however. First, the Appellate Body has said that '[t]he consistency or inconsistency of a given fact or set of facts with the requirements of a given treaty provision is . . . a legal characterization issue' and, therefore, is 'a legal issue' subject to review.[104] Second, the Appellate Body will review a factual finding of a panel where an appellant claims that the panel did not

[104] Ibid.

properly discharge its duties, under Article 11 DSU, 'to make an objective assessment of the matter, including an objective assessment of the facts'.[105] Nevertheless, in examining a claim under Article 11 DSU, the Appellate Body has repeatedly emphasized that panels enjoy a margin of discretion as triers of facts.[106]

In addition to the general limitation in Article 17.6, the scope of a specific appeal will be determined by the claims listed by an appellant or other appellant in the Notice of Appeal. Failure to include a claim in the Notice of Appeal may lead to a ruling that the claim is outside the scope of the appeal.[107] Moreover, where an appellant intends to argue that the panel did not fulfil its duties to make an objective assessment of the matter under Article 11 DSU, the claim must be specifically included in the Notice of Appeal; such a claim 'cannot be "assumed" merely because there is a challenge to a panel's analysis of a substantive provision'.[108]

Transparency

Like in panel proceedings, written submissions filed in an appeal are confidential, unless a participant decides to make its submission public. Appellate Body hearings are open only to the participants and third participants. Unlike panels, as of this writing, there has not been a request from participants to open an Appellate Body hearing to the public.[109] Like panels, the Appellate Body has the authority to and has accepted *amicus curiae* submissions from NGOs and private persons, but it is not obliged to take them into account.[110] The Appellate Body has also accepted an *amicus curiae* brief from a WTO Member that did not participate as a party or third party in the underlying panel proceedings.[111]

In *EC – Asbestos*, the Appellate Body adopted additional procedures under Rule 16(1) of the Working Procedures regarding the submission of *amicus curiae* briefs.[112] Those procedures applied only to that appeal. Some have advocated that WTO Members adopt generally applicable procedures to regulate the submission of *amicus curiae* briefs in order to ensure efficiency and transparency. The EC, for instance, proposed a two-stage approach similar to that adopted by the Appellate Body in *EC – Asbestos*, where persons must first apply for leave to file an *amicus curiae* brief and, only upon receiving authorization, could the brief be filed.[113] Stoler has argued that in the absence of specific rules on *amicus curiae* briefs, 'we are in a totally

---

[105] See above section on 'Standard of Review'.

[106] See, eg, Appellate Body Report, *Japan – Apples*, at paras 221–22.

[107] Appellate Body Report, *EC – Bananas III*, at para 152.

[108] Appellate Body Report, *Japan Apples*, at para 127.

[109] By contrast, panels have received such requests. See above section on 'Transparency' under 'Panel proceedings'.

[110] Appellate Body Report, *US – Lead and Bismuth II*, at para 39.

[111] Appellate Body Report, *EC – Sardines*, at paras 164–67.

[112] Appellate Body, *EC – Asbestos – Communication from the Appellate Body*, WT/DS135/9 (8 November 2000).

[113] DSB, *Contribution of the European Communities and its Member States to the Improvement of the WTO Dispute Settlement Understanding*, TN/DS/W/1 (13 March 2002).

non-transparent situation where WTO Members—by their own selection—seem to want to be kept in the dark about when *amicus curiae* briefs are submitted'.[114] Some WTO Members, however, consider that *amicus curiae* briefs should not be accepted by WTO adjudicatory bodies.[115]

In two cases, the Appellate Body was asked to adopt additional procedures to protect business confidential information. The Appellate Body declined to adopt additional procedures emphasizing that WTO Members were already bound to protect the confidentiality of the proceedings under Articles 17.10 and 18.2 DSU and the Appellate Body and its staff were subject to the Rules of Conduct.[116]

Lack of Remand Power and Completion of the Analysis

It is generally understood that the Appellate Body does not have the power to remand a case to the panel. The lack of remand authority has led to certain difficulties in two situations: (i) when the Appellate Body is asked to rule on a claim which the panel had not decided because the panel exercised judicial economy; and (ii) when the Appellate Body reverses or modifies a panel's legal interpretation and must then apply the new interpretation to the facts of the case in order to determine whether the challenged measure is WTO-consistent. In these situations, the Appellate Body has adopted a practice of 'completing the legal analysis'. The Appellate Body will resolve the claim not addressed by the panel or apply the new interpretation to the facts if the panel has made sufficient findings of fact or if there are sufficient undisputed facts in the record to enable it to do so.[117] By completing the analysis in these situations, the Appellate Body has sought to facilitate the prompt settlement of the dispute in accordance with the objective set out in Article 3.3 DSU. In several cases, however, there have been insufficient factual findings or undisputed facts in the panel record and the Appellate Body was unable to determine whether the measure was WTO-consistent. In such a situation, under the DSU as it stands, the complaining party would have to re-initiate panel proceedings if it wants its claim to be resolved.

Proposals have been made to establish a remand procedure. Hughes has suggested that '[t]here appears to be considerable support for adding a remand procedure of some kind'.[118] She notes, however, several technical issues that would need to be

[114] A Stoler, 'Enhancing the Operation of the WTO Panel Process and Appellate Review: Lesson from Experience and a Focus on Transparency' in Janow, Donaldson, and Yanovich, above fn 44, at 539.

[115] See DSB, *Text for the African Group Proposals on Dispute Settlement Understanding Negotiations – Communication from Kenya*, TN/DS/W/42 (24 January 2003); DSB, *Dispute Settlement Understanding Proposals: Legal Text – Communication from India on Behalf of Cuba, Dominican Republic, Egypt, Honduras, Jamaica and Malaysia*, TN/DS/W/47 (11 February 2003).

[116] Appellate Body Report, *Brazil – Aircraft*, at paras 119 and 123–25; Appellate Body Report, *Canada – Aircraft*, at paras 141 and 145–7.

[117] A Yanovich and T Voon, 'Completing the Analysis in WTO Appeals: The Practice and its Limitations' 2006 *Journal of International Economic Law* 9(4) 933.

[118] V Hughes, 'The WTO dispute settlement system—from initiating proceedings to ensuring implementation what needs improvement?' in Janow, Donaldson, and Yanovich, above fn 44, 193, at 224.

resolved as part of any modification, including determining whether the remand procedure would be initiated by one of the parties to the dispute or by the Appellate Body itself. An additional issue concerns the status of findings that are not subject to the remand procedure: would these findings be adopted by the DSB or would adoption have to wait until the remand procedure is completed?

E. Implementation

The implementation stage begins after the DSB has adopted the panel report and, where applicable, the Appellate Body report. Obviously, it is only relevant where there is a finding of WTO-inconsistency. For purposes of the discussion that follows, the reference to the respondent Member relates to a respondent Member that has been found by a panel or the Appellate Body to be acting inconsistently with its WTO obligations.

Prompt Compliance and Reasonable Period of Time for Implementation

The first step that the respondent Member has to take is to inform the DSB whether and how it intends to comply. No WTO Member has ever formally announced in the DSB that it would not comply. However, a few disputes remain on the agenda of the DSB for years despite the fact that Article 21.1 DSU emphasizes that 'prompt compliance . . . is essential in order to ensure effective resolution of disputes to the benefit of all Members'. According to Article 21.3 DSU, compliance should in principle be immediate. If this is impracticable, the next step is for the complaining and respondent Members to agree on a reasonable period of time for the respondent Member to come into compliance. The reasonable period of time may be: (a) a period of time proposed by the respondent Member and agreed by the DSB; (b) a period of time mutually agreed between the complaining and respondent Members; or (c) a period of time determined through binding arbitration.

In the event of an arbitration, the arbitrator should be selected by agreement between the parties. When this is not possible, either party may request the WTO DG to appoint an arbitrator. To date, all arbitrations on the reasonable period of time for implementation have been conducted by serving or former Appellate Body members. There have been 25 arbitrations undertaken pursuant to Article 21.3(c).[119] In four of them, the arbitrator did not have to make a determination on the reasonable period of time because the parties reached an agreement before the proceedings concluded.[120] The arbitrator was selected by agreement between the parties in 17 arbitrations and appointed by the WTO DG in 8 arbitrations.

[119] As of 31 December 2007.
[120] See the Awards of the Arbitrators in *Dominican Republic – Import and Sale of Cigarettes*; *US – Softwood Lumber V*; *US – Line Pipe*; and *US – Zeroing (Japan)*.

Article 21.3(c) provides that the arbitration must be completed within 90 days after the date of adoption by the DSB of its recommendations and rulings. In practice, requests for arbitration have often been made close to the end of that 90-day period and sometimes even after its expiration. Thus, this deadline has proven to be insufficient considering that, prior to resorting to arbitration, parties take some time trying to negotiate a reasonable period of time. In practice, therefore, parties to Article 21.3(c) arbitration proceedings have often agreed to extend the time period beyond 90 days after the adoption of the DSB recommendations and rulings.

The DSU does not specify the procedures to be followed in an arbitration. The procedures and the working schedule for the arbitration are drawn up by the arbitrator in consultation with the parties. Arbitrators have usually asked parties for one set of written submissions and have held one oral hearing. In earlier arbitrations, the written submissions were filed simultaneously by the parties. In recent arbitrations, the respondent Member has been asked to file its written submission first, explaining what steps it intends to take towards implementation and how much time would be needed; the complaining Member has filed its written submission subsequently, reacting to the arguments on intended regulatory or legislative steps and the time needed to take them.[121]

Arbitrators have carefully circumscribed their mandate. They have emphasized that their task is limited to determining how much time the respondent Member should take to implement and they have refused to suggest ways and means of implementation. Arbitrators have made clear that '[c]hoosing the means of implementation is, and should be, the prerogative of the implementing Member'.[122]

Article 21.3(c) states that a 'guideline' for the arbitrator is that the reasonable period of time should not exceed 15 months from the date of adoption of the panel report or the panel and Appellate Body reports. Nevertheless, according to that provision, the reasonable period of time 'may be shorter or longer, depending upon the particular circumstances'. To date, the reasonable periods of time determined through arbitration have always been within the range of 6 months to 15 months plus 1 week; but the majority of arbitrators have determined a reasonable period of time of between 10 and 12 months. Arbitrators have generally awarded longer time periods when implementation requires legislative action and shorter time periods when implementation involves only administrative action.

The preferred outcome is that the respondent Member terminates or modifies the WTO-inconsistent measure before the reasonable period of time expires. If this is not possible, the respondent Member may offer compensation to the complaining Member. In the WTO context, compensation is usually understood to involve tariff reductions on a different product, rather than monetary compensation.

---

[121] See Award of the Arbitrator, *EC – Chicken Cuts*, at para 4.
[122] Award of the Arbitrator, *Australia – Salmon*, at para 35.

Compensation is voluntary; the complaining Member is under no obligation to accept the compensation offered. Furthermore, compensation is usually understood to be temporary pending full compliance. Withdrawal or modification of the WTO-inconsistent measure is the ultimate objective.

Compliance Proceedings

Parties sometimes disagree on whether measures taken to comply (by the end of the reasonable period of time for implementation) bring about full or only partial compliance. When such disagreements occur, the complaining Member may request that a panel be established to examine the matter under Article 21.5 DSU. To the extent possible, the same panelists who served in the original proceedings should be appointed in the compliance proceedings. Their task is to examine what measures the respondent Member has taken to comply and to determine whether these measures are consistent, not only with the DSB recommendations and rulings in the original proceedings, but also with the covered agreements. Recent years have seen an increase in compliance proceedings under Article 21.5. This has been accompanied by disagreements between the parties on the proper scope of Article 21.5 proceedings and, more particularly, on what measures may be challenged and what claims may be raised in those proceedings, as opposed to in new panel proceedings.

In principle, the general DSU provisions apply in Article 21.5 proceedings although compliance proceedings are more expedited than the original panel proceedings. For example, Article 21.5 proceedings usually involve only one meeting between the panel and the parties. No interim review stage is required, but some Article 21.5 panels have chosen to issue an interim report. Although the DSU states that Article 21.5 proceedings should be completed within 90 days, they usually take longer. In a few disputes, there has been more than one round of Article 21.5 proceedings.[123]

Countermeasures and Arbitration on their Level and Nature

When the respondent Member has not taken actions sufficient to comply fully with the DSB recommendations and rulings in the original proceedings, and if there is no agreement on compensation, then the complaining Member may request authorization from the DSB to impose countermeasures, known in WTO parlance as 'suspension of concessions or other obligations'. It must be emphasized that countermeasures may be applied only after obtaining authorization from the DSB. Article 23 DSU prohibits unilateral action. The reverse consensus rule applies to the DSB's decision to authorize countermeasures, which means that the complaining Member requesting authorization would have to vote against its own request in order for it not to be approved.

---

[123] There were two rounds of Article 21.5 proceedings in *US – FSC*, *Brazil – Aircraft*, and *Canada – Dairy*. Only in *US – FSC* was the second Article 21.5 panel report appealed.

The right to apply countermeasures is not unfettered. Article 22.4 DSU requires that '[t]he level of suspension of concessions or other obligations authorized by the DSB shall be equivalent to the level of nullification or impairment'. In addition, Article 22.3 requires that, in principle, countermeasures be applied in the same trade sector or under the same WTO agreement under which the violation occurred. Countermeasures may be applied in another trade sector and under another WTO agreement only if applying them in the same sector or under the same WTO agreement is not practicable or effective.[124] Where the respondent Member disagrees with the level of the countermeasures proposed by the complaining Member, or with the proposed alternative sector or agreement in which the countermeasures would be imposed, it may request an arbitration pursuant to Article 22.6. Usually, this arbitration is carried out by the members of the original panel, unless they are unavailable.

Controversies have arisen regarding the sequencing between the request for authorization to apply countermeasures under Article 22 DSU and the examination of the WTO-consistency of a measure taken to comply with the recommendations and rulings of the DSB pursuant to Article 21.5 DSU.[125] Articles 21.5 and 22 do not clearly address the sequencing question. WTO Members have been able to resolve the issue in practice by mutual agreement whereby the requests for suspension of concessions and referral to an Article 21.5 panel are made simultaneously, but the retaliation procedures are suspended until the Article 21.5 proceedings have been concluded.[126] Alternatively, the parties have agreed to preserve a complaining Member's right to request authorization to suspend concessions until after the Article 21.5 compliance proceedings are completed, even if this is after the expiry of the deadline foreseen in Article 22 DSU.[127]

Another issue that has come up relates to the termination of the suspension of concessions or other obligations. The DSU contains no express rules on this issue, but provides that the suspension of concessions and other obligations shall be temporary and only be applied until such time as the WTO-inconsistent measure has been removed. In *EC – Hormones*, the EC submitted that it had complied with the DSB recommendations and rulings. The US and Canada disagreed and refused to terminate the suspension of concessions against the EC, which the DSB had authorized to apply. Some considered that in this scenario the EC should have sought an Article 21.5 panel. Instead, the EC opted to request that a new panel examine the WTO-consistency of the suspension of concessions by Canada and the US.[128]

[124] See also chapter 8 of this Handbook.

[125] See WTO Secretariat, *A Handbook on WTO Dispute Settlement* (Cambridge: Cambridge University Press, 2004), at 85.

[126] See ibid at 85–86. For an example of such an arrangement, see *Japan – Measures Affecting the Importation of Apples – Confirmed Procedures between Japan and the United States under Articles 21 and 22 of the DSU*, WT/DS245/10 (2 July 2004).

[127] Ibid at 86.

[128] See *Canada – Continued Suspension Of Obligations in the EC – Hormones Dispute, Request for the Establishment of a Panel by the European Communities*, WT/DS321/6 (14 January 2005); and

DSB Surveillance

As indicated earlier, the DSB plays an important surveillance role in relation to implementation of its recommendations and rulings. Every dispute in which implementation is required is placed on the agenda of the DSB meeting six months after the date of establishment of the reasonable period of time and remains on the agenda until the issue is resolved.[129] Prior to each DSB meeting, the respondent Member must submit a status report of its progress in the implementation of the recommendations or rulings. Moreover, Article 3.6 DSU requires that all mutually agreed solutions to matters formally raised under the consultation and dispute settlement provisions of the covered agreements be notified to the DSB and the relevant WTO Councils and Committees.

VI. CONCLUSION

Most observers consider dispute settlement to be one of the activities that the WTO has performed with most success. Indeed, the dispute settlement system set out in the DSU has proven to be remarkably effective in the first 13 years of the WTO. The procedural framework provided by the DSU has efficiently handled a larger number of disputes than most other international mechanisms. It has also been sufficiently flexible to allow parties, panels, and the Appellate Body to efficiently and successfully deal with a number of procedural and evidentiary issues that have arisen in dispute settlement practice and are not expressly dealt with in the DSU. These issues include the allocation of the burden of proof, the standard of review, requests for preliminary rulings, the admissibility of evidence, participation by private counsel, unsolicited submissions, and many other issues.

Pursuant to a Ministerial Decision that was adopted in 1994 and forms part of the Uruguay Round results, a review of the WTO dispute settlement procedures started in 1997. The review should have been completed by 1 January 1999. The deadline was extended, but agreement on revisions to the DSU was not reached in the context of this review.

At the MC held in Doha in November 2001, WTO Members launched negotiations to improve and clarify the DSU. These negotiations were not part of the 'single package' of negotiations known as the Doha Development Agenda. Instead, the DSU negotiations were to be completed in May 2003. The GC extended this

---

United States – Continued Suspension of Obligations in the EC – Hormones Dispute, Request for the Establishment of a Panel by the European Communities, WT/DS320/6 (14 January 2005).

[129] Art 21.6 DSU.

deadline to May 2004 and, after it had expired, extended the negotiating mandate without setting a new deadline.

DSU negotiations take place in special sessions of the DSB. WTO Members have tabled a wide variety of proposals relating to the different stages of the dispute settlement procedures. Some of these proposals were briefly described in the preceding discussion. Many of proposals could be described as technical adjustments and none seek to change the nature of the current procedures. At this time, the negotiations are ongoing and it is difficult to predict when the negotiations will conclude and which proposals will be adopted by WTO Members.

SELECTED BIBLIOGRAPHY

G Abi-Saab, 'The WTO Dispute Settlement and General International Law' in R Yerxa and B Wilson (eds), *Key Issues in WTO Dispute Settlement: The First Ten Years* (Cambridge: Cambridge University Press, 2005) 7

S Andersen, 'Administration of Evidence in WTO Dispute Settlement Proceedings' in R Yerxa and B Wilson (eds), *Key Issues in WTO Dispute Settlement: The First Ten Years* (Cambridge: Cambridge University Press, 2005) 29

Consultative Board, *The Future of the WTO: Addressing Institutional Challenges in the New Millennium* (Geneva: WTO, 2004)

W Davey, 'Evaluating WTO Dispute Settlement: What Results Have Been Achieved Through Consultations and Implementation of Panel Reports?' in Y Taniguchi, A Yanovich, and J Bohanes (eds), *The WTO in the Twenty-first Century: Dispute Settlement, Negotiations, and Regionalism in Asia* (Cambridge: Cambridge University Press, 2007) 98

V Donaldson and A Yanovich, 'The Appellate Body's Working Procedures for Appellate Review' in G Sacerdoti, A Yanovich, and J Bohanes (eds), *The WTO at Ten: The Contribution of the Dispute Settlement System* (Cambridge: Cambridge University Press, 2006) 386

JH Jackson, *The World Trading System: Law and Policy of International Economic Relations*, 2nd edn (Cambridge: MIT Press, 1997)

G Marceau, 'Consultations and the Panel Process in the WTO Dispute Settlement System' in R Yerxa and B Wilson (eds), *Key Issues in WTO Dispute Settlement: The First Ten Years* (Cambridge: Cambridge University Press, 2005) 29

D Palmeter and P Mavroidis, *Dispute Settlement in the World Trade Organization: Practice and Procedure*, 2nd edn (Cambridge: Cambridge University Press, 2004)

J Pauwelyn, 'Appeal Without Remand – A Design Flaw in WTO Dispute Settlement and How to Fix it', *ICTSD Issue Paper No 1* (Geneva, 2007)

G Sacerdoti, 'The Dispute Settlement System of the WTO in Action: A Perspective on the First Ten Years' in G Sacerdoti, A Yanovich, and J Bohanes (eds), *The WTO at Ten: The Contribution of the Dispute Settlement System* (Cambridge: Cambridge University Press, 2006) 35

Y Taniguchi, 'Understanding the Concept of Prima Facie Proof in WTO Dispute Settlement' in ME Janow, V Donaldson, and A Yanovich (eds), *The WTO: Governance, Dispute Settlement and Developing Countries* (New York: Juris Publishing, 2008) 553

D Unterhalter, 'The Burden of Proof in WTO Dispute Settlement' in ME Janow, V Donaldson, and A Yanovich (eds), *The WTO: Governance, Dispute Settlement and Developing Countries* (New York: Juris Publishing, 2008) 543

P Van den Bossche, 'From Afterthought to Centrepiece: the WTO Appellate Body and its Rise to Prominence in the World Trading System' in G Sacerdoti, A Yanovich, and J Bohanes (eds), *The WTO at Ten: The Contribution of the Dispute Settlement System* (Cambridge: Cambridge University Press, 2006) 289

T Voon and A Yanovich, 'The Facts Aside: The Limitation of World Trade Organization Appeals to Issues of Law' 2006 *Journal of World Trade* 40(2) 239

WTO Appellate Body Secretariat, *WTO Appellate Body Repertory of Reports and Awards: 1995–2006* (Cambridge: Cambridge University Press, 2007)

WTO Secretariat, *A Handbook on the Dispute Settlement System* (Geneva: WTO, 2004)

A Yanovich and T Voon, 'Completing the Analysis in WTO Appeals: The Practice and its Limitations' 2006 *Journal of International Economic Law* 9(4) 933

W Zdouc, 'The Panel Process' in P Macrory, A Appleton, and M Plummer (eds), *The World Trade Organization: Legal, Economic and Political Analysis*, Vol I (New York: Springer, 2005) 1233

CHAPTER 14

....

STANDARD OF REVIEW IN WTO LAW

....

JAN BOHANES

NICOLAS LOCKHART[*]

* We would like to thank Claus-Dieter Ehlermann, Todd Friedbacher, and Niall Meagher for their excellent comments on the draft. We owe a particular debt of gratitude to Claus-Dieter Ehlermann, with whom Nicolas had the pleasure and honour to collaborate on an earlier article on standard of review (2004 *Journal of International Economic Law* 7(3) 491). Errors remain our own.

I. Introduction

Typically, the standard of review relates to the nature and intensity of review by a court or tribunal of decisions taken by another governmental authority or, sometimes, by a lower court or tribunal. In the law of the WTO, the standard of review reflects the extent to which WTO adjudicating bodies can declare measures taken by WTO Members to be WTO-inconsistent. The standard of review is therefore a touchstone of the WTO dispute settlement system, reflecting the balance of power between the 'judicial branch' of the WTO and decision-making responsibilities of the WTO Members, as well as the balance of power between the two levels of the WTO's judicial branch.

This chapter examines the different standards of review that apply in WTO dispute settlement. Section II describes the concept of standard of review in general terms. Section III sets out the general principles of standard of review as it operates in WTO law. Section IV then discusses the different standards of review that apply to the different tasks performed by panels in WTO disputes, most critically legal interpretation and factual determinations. For factual determinations, the Chapter identifies three different standards of review that apply to three different categories of WTO dispute/agreement—trade remedy agreements, the TBT Agreement and the SPS Agreement, and the 'classical disputes' under GATT 1994. Section IV concludes with a discussion of the standard of review that WTO panels apply to domestic law. Section V discusses the standard of review that applies between the WTO adjudicating bodies, namely, the standard of review that the Appellate Body applies when reviewing panel decisions. Section VI provides a conclusion.

II. What Is Standard of Review?

The term 'standard of review' is used in many domestic legal systems to describe the role of a court or tribunal in reviewing decisions taken by another authority, for example, the legislative or (more frequently) executive branches of government. The 'standard of review' is a shorthand way of describing the degree of deference or discretion that the court accords to legislators and regulators; or, looked at from the other perspective, the degree of intrusiveness or invasiveness into the legislator's or regulator's decision-making process.

An example may help to illustrate: when a government's decision to authorize the construction of a new highway is challenged, just how closely should the court

380 JAN BOHANES AND NICOLAS LOCKHART

inquire into the decision? Should the court gather new facts and decide for itself whether a new highway is needed? Is the court entitled to consider the detailed aspects of the highway project, for instance, the precise route of the new highway? Should it accept to some extent the authority's own assessment of the facts? Should it defer to the government's interpretation of the law?

The concept of 'standard of review' provides the answers to all of these questions. Essentially, the standard of review defines the parameters within which judges work and, correspondingly, within which legislators and regulators work. It establishes areas in which judges must respect the choices made by legislators or regulators, provided that these choices remain within some basic general parameters defined by law, such as the notion of 'reasonableness'. The standard of review defines the circumstances in which the first decision-maker has discretion to make choices that the judge cannot reconsider as long as basic general parameters of legality are respected.

Sometimes, the term standard of review is also used in a broader sense to describe 'no go' areas in which judges do not have the authority to review an executive authority's decision *at all*. For instance, as we shall see below, WTO Members may autonomously set their desired level of health protection, and this decision must be accepted by WTO adjudicating bodies.[1] In this case, the appropriateness of the level of health protection is completely removed from the ambit of review by a WTO panel and is, in other words, unreviewable. In these circumstances, the concept of standard of review describes the *absence* of any power to review and highlights the exclusive, non-reviewable competence of a governmental authority to take certain decisions.[2]

In general terms, the standard of review is, therefore, an important part of the system of checks and balances in government, helping to ensure the accountability of the different governmental actors. By establishing limits on the role of the judiciary, on the one hand, and the outer bounds of the discretion of the legislature and executive, on the other hand, the standard of review also functions to separate the decision-making powers of the three different branches of government.

Because there is no 'correct' division of powers between the three branches of government, there is also no 'correct' standard of review. Each legal system develops a standard that suits its own particular needs. In some systems, the judiciary is expected to scrutinize the work of the legislature and executive more closely than in other systems. Further, even within a single system, there may be different standards of review depending upon the decision under review. For example, a legislative act may be entitled to more (or less) respect—deference—than a decision

---

[1] The same holds for technical regulations under the TBT Agreement. The Panel in *EC – Sardines* stated that 'it is up to WTO Members to decide which policy objectives they wish to pursue and the levels at which they wish to pursue them'. Panel Report, *EC – Sardines*, at para 7.120.

[2] See M Oesch, *Standards of Review WTO Dispute Resolution* (Oxford: Oxford University Press, 2003), at 14–15.

by an executive agency. Moreover, the standard of review may also evolve because of changing perceptions about the respective roles of the legislature, executive, and judiciary.

In WTO dispute settlement, the standard of review functions in a similar way. Panels are typically called upon to examine the WTO consistency of legislative, regulatory, and administrative acts adopted by WTO Members. In almost every case, therefore, panels review a decision taken by a first decision-maker at national level, perhaps the legislator or an executive agency. The question that immediately arises is what level of discretion a panel should afford to the first decision taken at national level. Should a panel second-guess the authority's assessment of the facts and law surrounding the disputed measure? For instance, how should a panel assess whether, in the particular circumstances at hand, a measure is indeed required to protect human health? Should a panel start afresh in its examination of the issues or should it accept to some extent the authority's own assessment? As they do at the national level, the answers to these questions differentiate the respective roles and powers of WTO panels, on the one hand, and national legislators and regulators, on the other hand.

However, because WTO panels review the acts of sovereign States, the standard of review takes on additional significance and sensitivity. By establishing the intensity of a panel's review of acts adopted by the legislature and the executive of sovereign States, the standard of review influences the decision-making autonomy of WTO Members, and the extent to which they can decide for themselves—through their legislature and executive—whether and how to comply with WTO law. Although a panel's scrutiny of national acts may sometimes be perceived as unwarranted interference with national sovereignty, it is nevertheless crucial to the rules-based trading system on which the WTO is built. In short, if each WTO Member could decide for itself whether it complied with its WTO obligations, the uniformity, effectiveness, and ultimately the viability of the WTO would be jeopardized.

Under the WTO agreements, the standard of review is one of the mechanisms attempting to strike an appropriate balance between the autonomy of WTO Members and the need for uniform and effective enforcement of WTO law.

However, the particular balance defined by the WTO standard of review is not only that between WTO Members and the WTO adjudicating bodies. The standard of review applied by the Appellate Body vis-à-vis panel decisions also serves to allocate the responsibilities between the two adjudicative tiers of the WTO dispute settlement system, namely, the panel stage and appellate review.[3]

---

[3] The standard of review also defines the relationship between panels and other bodies within the WTO system that, at least theoretically, also exercise a sort of 'quasi-judicial' function. These other bodies are, for instance, the Committee on Regional Trade Agreements and the Committee on Balance of Payments Restrictions (and formerly also the now defunct Textiles Monitoring Body). This particular issue, however, remains outside the scope of this chapter. On this topic, see for instance, Oesch, above fn 2, at 33–40.

III. THE GENERAL STANDARD OF REVIEW IN WTO LAW

Article 3.2 DSU sets forth objectives for the WTO dispute settlement system. It states that this system 'is a central element in providing security and predictability to the multilateral trading system'. The same provision also stipulates that the dispute settlement system serves to 'preserve' the balance of WTO Members' rights and obligations. The pursuit of these goals shows that the WTO membership attaches a great deal of importance to a cohesive and stable trading regime where WTO rules are applied in the same way by different Members. Although panels and the Appellate Body do not routinely refer to Article 3.2 when defining the applicable standard of review, the core goals of Article 3.2 influence the standard of review applied to the scrutiny of national measures in WTO dispute settlement. Of course, although the level and intensity of that scrutiny promotes the 'security and predictability' of the trading system, it must also respect the prerogatives that the WTO agreements leave to individual WTO Members.

When the Appellate Body addressed standard of review for the first time, in *EC – Hormones*, it explicitly referred to the link between standard of review and the balance of powers between WTO Members and the WTO. The Appellate Body acknowledged that:

The standard of review ... must *reflect the balance* established in [the particular WTO agreement] between the jurisdictional competences conceded by the Members to the WTO and the jurisdictional competences retained by the Members for themselves ... [4]

In striking this 'finely drawn balance', the Appellate Body turned to Article 11 DSU, as it has done consistently since.[5] This provision states that 'a panel should make an *objective assessment* of the matter before it, including an objective assessment of the facts ...' (emphasis added). In *EC – Hormones*, the Appellate Body said that Article 11 articulates a standard of review that is generally applicable to all WTO disputes.[6]

---

[4] Appellate Body Report, *EC – Hormones*, at para 115 (emphasis added). The Appellate Body has also said that standard of review 'goes to the very core of the integrity of the WTO dispute settlement process itself'. Appellate Body Report, *EC – Poultry*, at para 133.

[5] Appellate Body Report, *EC – Hormones*, at para 115.

[6] Art 17.6 Anti-Dumping Agreement provides special standards of review for disputes concerning anti-dumping measures that apply in conjunction with Art 11 DSU. These special standards were introduced into the Anti-Dumping Agreement after prolonged negotiations that proved to be among the most contentious issues in the Uruguay Round. Some negotiators sought to have the standards of review in Art 17.6 applied to all WTO agreements. In the end, a Ministerial Decision was adopted that requires WTO Members to review the standards of review in Art 17.6, after three years, 'with a view to considering the question of whether it is capable of general application' (Decision on the Review

Even if Article 11 is generally applicable, however, the standard of an 'objective assessment' is couched in rather broad terms that do very little to provide substantive guidance on the nature and intensity of the scrutiny that panels should apply in reviewing national measures.[7] The term 'objective assessment' speaks more obviously to the fairness, impartiality, and even-handedness of panels' examination than to the discretion that they must afford to domestic decision-makers.

To illustrate, take two different possible standards of review. One requires a panel to conduct a detailed factual enquiry and decide whether it would have reached the same decision as the national authority; the second requires the panel to review a national measure merely to determine whether a national authority's decision is reasonable, without at the same time conducting a detailed review of the facts. In both cases, a panel could perform an 'objective assessment of the matter', whilst respecting the rather different standards of review. However, because a very different level of deference is afforded to the national decision-maker in the two situations, it is perfectly possible that the outcome of an 'objective assessment' could be different. In other words, requiring panels to make an 'objective assessment' does not provide any meaningful indication of the intensity of review that panels are expected to apply.[8] Any assessment, whether highly deferential, marginally deferential, or not deferential at all, can be an 'objective assessment'.

In addition to giving little indication of the appropriate level of scrutiny, reliance upon Article 11 as a universal standard also creates the impression that every question relating to standard of review can be answered by resort to the notion of 'objective assessment'. However, in practice, this impression has not proved to be accurate. In WTO law, the concept of standard of review has raised a number of questions that have not received a uniform response. Certainly, panels perform an 'objective

---

of Art 17.6 of the Agreement on Implementation of Article VI of the General Agreement on Tariffs and Trade 1994). To date, WTO Members have not conducted the review envisaged in the Decision. Thus, the standards of review in Art 17.6 Anti-Dumping Agreement continue to apply only to disputes concerning anti-dumping measures. See Appellate Body Report, *US – Lead and Bismuth II*, at para 50. For a detailed history of the negotiations on Art 17.6 Anti-Dumping Agreement, see SP Croley and JH Jackson, 'WTO Dispute Procedures, Standard of Review, and Deference to National Governments' 1996 *American Journal of International Law* 90(2) 193, at 199.

[7] See also C-D Ehlermann and N Lockhart, 'Standard of Review in WTO Law' 2004 *Journal of International Economic Law* 7(3) 491, at 495; Oesch, above fn 2, at 9.

[8] The possibility of applying the standard of an 'objective assessment' in conjunction with another, more detailed, standard of review is confirmed in WTO case law. The Appellate Body has indicated that the requirement for panels to conduct an 'objective assessment' can apply in conjunction with different underlying standards of review. In examining the special standards of review in Art 17.6(i) Anti-Dumping Agreement, the Appellate Body has said that 'it is inconceivable that Article 17.6(i) should require anything other than that panels make an *objective* "assessment of the facts of the matter"'. Appellate Body Report, *US – Hot-Rolled Steel*, at para 55 (original emphasis).

assessment'; but the scope and intensity of a panel's assessment is not the same for every issue.

In the remainder of this chapter, we explore how the standard of review has been applied in practice, and attempt to add flesh to the bare bones of an 'objective assessment'. In exploring the particulars of the standard(s) of review that panels apply in practice, three considerations should be borne in mind. First, the work of a panel, like other tribunals, comprises three basic activities. Panels make findings that: (a) are purely legal in nature; (b) are purely factual; and (c) involve the application of the facts to the law. This last activity is the most complex and difficult to categorize. It involves weighing and appreciating the facts, and then characterizing them, in terms of the relevant legal rules.

In principle, the same standard of review in Article 11 applies to each of these tasks, without variation. This is because Article 11 provides that a panel's duty to conduct an 'objective assessment' relates to its overall consideration of the *matter*, which includes both the factual and legal issues that arise in examining a contested national measure.[9] Thus, irrespective of the basic task that a panel is performing, panels apply the same standard: they must make an 'objective assessment'. However, despite the apparent generality of Article 11 as a universal standard of review, the nature and intensity of a panel's scrutiny differs considerably depending on which of these three activities it is performing.

Second, the nature of a panel's review may change with the WTO agreement that forms the subject-matter of a dispute. For instance, a public health measure examined under the SPS Agreement is subject to a different level of review from that applied to a measure taken under the Safeguards Agreement. Although panels make an 'objective assessment' in all disputes, the intensity of the review that is applied is not always the same, and the differences depend in part on the particular WTO agreement at issue.

Third, and related to the second point, the decision-making process by which a national measure was adopted at the national level also influences the intensity of the review applied by a WTO panel. In particular, if a measure results from a treaty mandated investigative procedure, conducted at national level, that dictates a more lenient level of review than applies to a measure where no similar national procedure is required under WTO law.[10] Again, therefore, although an 'objective assessment' applies in all situations, it does not require the same intensity of review in all situations.

---

[9] The term 'matter' has been defined as a reference to the case-specific set of facts including the contested national measure and the legal basis of a complaining party's complaint regarding that measure. Appellate Body Report, *Guatemala – Cement I*, at para 72. Art 11 DSU states explicitly that the objective assessment of the 'matter' includes the facts as well as 'the applicability of and conformity with the relevant covered agreements'.

[10] See below section IV.B.2.

IV. The Standard of Review For The Different Tasks Performed By Panels

A. Legal Determinations

1. *A Panel's Review of Legal Determinations in General*

Panels perform three basic tasks: legal interpretation, fact-finding, and the application of the facts to the law. Although Article 11 DSU applies to all three of a panel's basic tasks, the precise character and intensity of its review is not the same in each case. In *EC – Hormones*, the Appellate Body was careful to distinguish between the review applicable to 'the determination and assessment of the *facts*' and the review applicable to *legal* determinations.[11] In particular, the Appellate Body prefaced its oft-quoted statement—that 'the applicable standard is neither *de novo* review as such, nor "total deference"'—with the words '[s]o far as fact-finding is concerned'.[12]

In the next paragraph of that report, the Appellate Body addressed 'legal questions' separately, stating that panels have a 'duty to apply the customary rules of interpretation of public international law', as required by Article 3.2 DSU. Thus, although a panel must 'objectively assess' interpretive questions, it does so according to a different standard.

Legal questions arise in every dispute and, each time, panels and the Appellate Body approach the questions from first principles, as if they were the first decision-maker to address the legal issue. In other words, they perform a *de novo* review of the law. In many cases, panels and the Appellate Body are actually the first to interpret the applicable *WTO law* because national authorities generally apply *national law*, albeit often law implementing WTO rules. For example, when a national legislator adopts a tax measure that is allegedly discriminatory, it does so in application of national law and not WTO law. The legislator usually does not engage in an interpretation of WTO law and there is no interpretation of WTO law to which panels could defer, even if they wanted to. The same applies to a national court that reviews the tax measure under national law. However, even in cases where national authorities have applied rules that are the same as, or similar to, WTO rules, panels and the Appellate Body reach their own entirely independent conclusions with respect to interpretive questions.

As the Appellate Body said in *EC – Hormones*, this approach is dictated by the text of the DSU, which requires panels and the Appellate Body to follow the customary rules of interpretation of public international law. The Appellate Body has

---

[11] Appellate Body Report, *EC – Hormones*, at para 116, see also paras 112, 114, and 117. The EC's appeal on standard of review related solely to the Panel's treatment of the facts.
[12] Ibid at para 117.

stated that the relevant customary rules are codified in the Vienna Convention on the Law of Treaties (VCLT).[13] In terms of Articles 31 and 32 VCLT, the treaty interpreter must seek out the ordinary meaning of the text. The treaty interpreter cannot set aside what it considers is the ordinary meaning of the text even in the event that, for example, the national authorities' decision is based on, or reflects, an alternative reasonable reading of the text.[14] Members have not instructed panels and the Appellate Body to afford this type of discretion to WTO Members and their authorities.

For purely legal questions there is, therefore, *de novo* review of a national authority's legal determination, regardless of whether that authority has given a 'first' interpretation of WTO law. This absence of discretion in the case of legal interpretation is explained by the distinct roles of the national authorities that adopted a contested measure and WTO panels.

The WTO dispute settlement system has exclusive jurisdiction to hear disputes between WTO Members relating to the WTO agreements.[15] In that system, the membership has given panels and the Appellate Body a unique responsibility for interpreting, or as the DSU says 'clarifying', the WTO agreements.[16] Moreover, under Article 3.2 DSU, the dispute settlement system seeks to guarantee 'security and predictability' to the trading system, and to 'preserve' the WTO Members' balance of rights and obligations.

Panels and the Appellate Body play a crucial part in achieving these goals by providing for a uniform interpretation of WTO law. If individual WTO Members were afforded discretion to interpret WTO law, the uniform interpretation would be lost. It would lead to what Palmeter and Spak have described as a 'Tower of Legal Babel'.[17] The obligations assumed by WTO Members, and the rights acquired, would differ from Member to Member, undermining the core objectives of the rules-based system. There is, therefore, considerable justification for requiring panels and the Appellate Body to conduct an original *de novo* review of a national authority's legal determinations, without granting deference to any interpretation of WTO law given by a national authority.

---

[13] Appellate Body Report, *US – Gasoline*, at 17; Appellate Body Report, *Japan – Alcoholic Beverages II*, at 104.

[14] This may be contrasted with the special standard of review in Art 17.6(ii) Anti-Dumping Agreement. Under this provision, panels and the Appellate Body will accept a national authority's decision if it rests upon a 'permissible' interpretation of the Anti-Dumping Agreement.

[15] See Art 23.1 DSU.

[16] Under Art IX:2 WTO Agreement, the MC and the GC have 'the exclusive authority to adopt interpretations' of the WTO agreements. These interpretations must be adopted by three-fourths majority of the WTO membership. The interpretations are thereafter binding upon all WTO Members in a uniform manner.

[17] D Palmeter and GJ Spak, 'Resolving Anti-Dumping and Countervailing Duty Disputes: Defining GATT's Role in an Era of Increasing Conflict' 1993 *Law and Policy in International Business* 24(4) 1145, at 1158.

2. A Panel's Review of Legal Interpretations under the Anti-Dumping Agreement

The only context in which panels are called upon to apply a different standard of review with respect to legal interpretations of WTO law arises under Article 17.6(ii) Anti-Dumping Agreement. It is worth quoting this provision in full:

> [T]he panel shall interpret the relevant provisions of the Agreement in accordance with customary rules of interpretation of public international law. Where the panel finds that a relevant provision of the Agreement admits of more than one permissible interpretation, the panel shall find the authorities' measure to be in conformity with the Agreement if it rests upon one of those permissible interpretations.[18]

Under this provision, a panel's primary interpretive responsibility is the same as it is under the other WTO agreements. In the first sentence of Article 17.6(ii), Members have reiterated the requirement in Article 3.2 DSU for panels to rely upon the customary rules of interpretation. This means that, under both Article 3.2 DSU and Article 17.6(ii) Anti-Dumping Agreement, panels must interpret treaty text according to Articles 31 and 32 VCLT.[19] In so doing, panels must interpret the relevant legal provisions in the same way that they do in disputes under other covered agreements, consistent also with the duty to make an objective assessment under Article 11 DSU.[20]

The added twist in Article 17.6(ii) comes in the second sentence of the provision. It states that where a national authority's anti-dumping measure rests upon a '*permissible*' interpretation of a WTO norm, panels and the Appellate Body must accept the measure as WTO-consistent. This standard of review 'presupposes' that provisions of the Anti-Dumping Agreement 'admit [...] of more than one permissible interpretation'.[21] In the light of the requirement to interpret WTO law according to the VCLT, the Appellate Body has emphasized that the multiple permissible

---

[18] At the time of the conclusion of the Uruguay Round, this provision continued to provoke disagreement. Some negotiating parties sought to have the phrase 'reasonable interpretation' included instead of the word 'permissible interpretation'. This standard of 'reasonableness' would appear to be drawn from the *Chevron* doctrine in United States administrative law, see *Chevron USA, Inc. v Natural Resources Defense Council, Inc*, 467 US 837 (1984). The word 'reasonable' was opposed by others, with agreement finally being reached on the word 'permissible' in the closing days of the Round. For a detailed history of the negotiations on this point see Croley and Jackson, above fn 6, at 199; Oesch, above fn 2, at 72–79. In the *USGAO Report* to the Senate Finance Committee, GAO notes that '[a] majority of the experts [GAO consulted] maintained that the United States was not successful in getting the standard of review it wanted in the Anti-Dumping Agreement...' GAO, *World Trade Organization – Standard of Review and Impact of Trade Remedy Rulings, Report to the Ranking Minority Member, Committee on Finance, U.S. Senate* (July 2003), at <http://www.gao.gov/new.items/d03824.pdf> (last visited 22 April 2008), at 30.

[19] Appellate Body Report, *US – Hot-Rolled Steel*, at para 57.

[20] Ibid at para 62. The Appellate Body stated that the special standard of review in Art 17.6(ii) does not replace the requirement to make an 'objective assessment' but supplements it. There is, therefore, no conflict between Arts 11 DSU and 17.6(ii) Anti-Dumping Agreement.

[21] Ibid at para 59.

interpretations of a provision must each result from the application of the rules embedded in the VCLT.[22]

Some commentators have suggested that reconciling the two sentences of Article 17.6(ii) creates certain difficulties for the treaty interpreter. Article 31 VCLT is intended to elicit what the VCLT describes as '*the* ordinary meaning' of the treaty. Article 32 VCLT also refers, three times, to '*the* meaning' of the treaty. Article 32, in fact, provides rules to enable the interpreter to arrive at 'the meaning' of a treaty even where the text is 'ambiguous or obscure'. In other words, the rules of the VCLT are arguably designed to produce a single meaning for a text, and not the multiple 'permissible' meanings envisaged in the second sentence of Article 17.6(ii). This has led commentators to question when there might be multiple permissible interpretations of a provision of the Anti-Dumping Agreement. In particular, Croley and Jackson have said that 'it is not clear in light of [the VCLT] whether or how a WTO panel could ever reach the conclusion that provisions of an agreement admit of more than one interpretation'.[23]

There is, therefore, a perception that the first and second sentences of Article 17.6(ii) are in tension. Under the first sentence, panels must follow Articles 31 and 32 VCLT instructing the treaty interpreter to find a single meaning of the treaty. Yet, Article 17.6(ii) 'presupposes' that there are provisions of the Anti-Dumping Agreement, which admit of more than one permissible interpretation under the rules of the VCLT.[24]

The text of the Anti-Dumping Agreement does little to assist the treaty interpreter in resolving this perceived tension. There is no guidance as to which provisions admit of multiple permissible interpretations nor is there any guidance on how to read the first and second sentences of Article 17.6(ii) so as to give proper meaning to both. In particular, there is nothing in the Anti-Dumping Agreement to suggest that parts of the VCLT do not apply to interpretation under Article 17.6(ii).[25]

B. Factual Determinations

1. *A Panel's Review of Factual Determinations in General*

The second and third tasks undertaken by a panel—fact-finding and application of the facts to the law—both involve an assessment of facts. According to the Appellate

---

[22] Ibid at para 60; see also Panel Report, *US – DRAMS*, at para 6.53, fn 499. See also chapter 12 of this Handbook.

[23] Croley and Jackson, above fn 6, at 200. Davey has also said 'The provisions [of Art 17.6] are worded in such general terms, however, that it remains to be seen whether they will have much impact on the results of panel decisions'. WJ Davey, 'The WTO /GATT World Trading System: An Overview' in P Pescatore, WJ Davey, and AF Lowenfeld (eds), *Handbook of WTO/GATT Dispute Settlement* (The Hague: Kluwer, 1995), at 7.

[24] Appellate Body Report, *US – Hot-Rolled Steel*, at para 60.

[25] See Croley and Jackson, above fn 6, at 201.

Body, for factual matters, the standard of review requires that panels make an 'object-ive assessment'.[26] Yet, once again, this broad formulation does not assist in defining an operable standard of review because any assessment of the facts, whether highly deferential, marginally deferential, or not deferential at all, can be 'objective'. Article 11 DSU is, therefore, not the end of the road in the search for a standard of review for the facts.

Beyond an 'objective assessment', the search for the appropriate standard of review must take into account a crucial aspect of each dispute. When we speak of the standard of a panel's *review* of the facts underlying a contested measure, we make an assumption. That assumption is that the measure results from some kind of national process in which a first decision-maker has examined, and reached conclusions, on the facts. In that situation, the panel becomes the 'second-tier' decision-maker, and the issue is what degree of deference the panel should afford to the determinations made by the national authority.

If there is no prior formal national process in which factual determinations are made, the panel cannot grant deference to a national authority for its factual find-ings. In that event, the only possibility is for the panel to conduct an original or *de novo* assessment as the *trier of first impression* of the facts.

When we speak of a 'national process', we mean some *formal* administrative, or (quasi-) judicial procedure involving substantive and procedural elements. Clearly, any decision taken by any government authority will involve some form of an internal decision-making process. However, the national process that is relevant from the perspective of the WTO standard of review is one in which an authority conducts a formal factual inquiry that precedes, and publicly provides the basis for, the authority's decision.

In WTO law, a variety of national processes are foreseen. Some agreements mandate that a measure must result from a national investigation, which includes participatory rights for foreign parties. In the trade remedy area, in particular, anti-dumping, countervailing, and safeguard measures are all imposed by national authorities following a formal investigation mandated by WTO law. Under these agreements, a national authority, therefore, makes factual determinations as the trier of first impression. The question, therefore, arises as to the standard of review that a panel should apply as the second-tier reviewer of the national authority's findings.

Other WTO agreements do not mandate a formal investigation, yet it is *possible* that a measure could result from a national factual inquiry. For example, import restrictions imposed for public health reasons may result from a factual enquiry carried out by an executive agency;[27] similarly, customs valuation decisions are also

---

[26] Appellate Body Report, *EC – Hormones*, at para 117.

[27] For instance, in *Australia – Salmon*, an Australian agency had conducted an investigation and prepared a report entitled the 'Australian Salmon Import Risk Analysis of December 1996'. During WTO proceedings, Australia put forward this report as its risk assessment within the meaning of Article 5.1 SPS Agreement. Panel Report, *Australia – Salmon*, at paras 2.1 and 8.70.

based on a more impromptu assessment of the facts regarding an import transaction. In these situations, questions also arise as to the deference that panels should afford to a domestic inquiry that is not required by WTO law.

Finally, there are yet other agreements that do not require, or otherwise envisage, that a national measure should result from an investigation or a factual inquiry. For example, a national authority may adopt an internal market rule regulating advertising without assessing the potential discriminatory impact of the measure.

Although panels always conduct an 'objective assessment', the underlying nature and intensity of a panel's review cannot be, and is not, the same in these quite different situations. A panel's review of factual issues must, therefore, be analysed from the perspective of the different types of WTO agreement, taking into account the structure and specific obligations of each agreement.

2. *Trade Remedy Agreements*

a. *Anti-Dumping Agreement*

The Standard for Reviewing Purely Factual Questions

Under the Anti-Dumping Agreement, an anti-dumping measure may only be adopted following an investigation that is to be conducted at national level by a specially designated investigating authority.[28] For anti-dumping measures, which are adopted pursuant to this national investigation, Article 17.6(i) Anti-Dumping Agreement provides a special standard of review for factual matters. Like the special standard of review in Article 17.6(ii) for interpretive matters, the standard in Article 17.6(i) does not appear in other WTO agreements.[29]

Article 17.6(i) explicitly confers broad discretion upon the national authority for its 'assessment' of the facts. The provision provides two separate standards, the first applying to the national authority's 'establishment' of the facts and the second to its 'evaluation' of the facts. One commentator has described the process of 'establishing' facts as creating a record of 'raw' evidence, and the 'evaluation' of the facts as the process of drawing of 'factual conclusions' or inferences from raw evidence.[30]

Article 17.6(i) states that a panel must respect the authority's *'establishment'* of the facts if it is 'proper'. This standard seeks to prevent a panel from rejecting factual findings made at the national level just because it prefers an alternative finding. Indeed, under this provision, the focus of a panel's review should not be on the facts themselves, but rather on whether the process of establishing those facts was 'proper'. If that process was 'proper', the facts found as a result of the process should be accepted, 'even though the panel might have reached a different conclusion'.[31]

---

[28] On the extensive role of the national authorities in an anti-dumping determination, see, for instance, Articles 3, 5, 6, and 9–12 Anti-Dumping Agreement.

[29] See above fn 6 concerning the Ministerial Decision on Art 17.6 Anti-Dumping Agreement.

[30] See Oesch, above fn 2, at 117ff and 133ff.

[31] Art 17.6(i) Anti-Dumping Agreement.

There is, therefore, no *de novo* review and panels cannot substitute their own appreciation of the facts for that of the national authority. Only in cases where there is a manifest or egregious impropriety will a panel find that a national authority's establishment of the facts was not 'proper'. In short, the word 'proper' carries with it a considerable margin of discretion.

Article 17.6(i) also requires that the *evaluation* of the facts be 'unbiased and objective'. Again, this provision is designed to prevent panels from making their own independent assessment of the facts. Instead, panels should consider whether the national authority conducted the factual evaluation in an appropriate way— are the authority's factual conclusions based on an 'unbiased and objective' evaluation of the record? This equates to something akin to whether the authority was balanced, impartial, and open-minded in its evaluation of the facts. This standard also implies a considerable degree of discretion for the authority, as long as the authority's evaluation remains within the bounds of balance, impartiality and open-mindedness.

Although Article 17.6(i) establishes a special standard of review for anti-dumping disputes, it does not displace the ubiquitous standard of an 'objective assessment' in Article 11 DSU. The Appellate Body has said that the language in Article 17.6(i) 'reflects closely the obligation imposed on panels under Article 11'.[32] The Appellate Body added that, although Article 17.6(i) 'does not expressly state that panels are obliged to make an assessment of the facts which is "*objective*"', 'it is inconceivable that Article 17.6(i) should require anything' else.[33] As a result, in anti-dumping disputes, Article 17.6(i) applies in conjunction with Article 11 DSU.

We examine below the tools that panels have used to assess whether investigating authorities have complied with the standard of review in Article 17.6(i), in particular the examination of the authority's explanation.

The Standard for Reviewing Mixed Questions of Fact and Law

Article 17.6 Anti-Dumping Agreement seeks to draw a bright line between a panel's review of the national authority's assessment of the facts and its review of the authority's legal determination. In Articles 17.6(i) and 17.6(ii), the Agreement has two separate 'boxes', one with a standard of review for factual questions and the other with a standard for legal questions.

In practice, this division between legal and factual issues is not so clear. Many of the most difficult questions that confront a panel are mixed questions of fact and law. In particular, where a panel is characterising the facts in terms of the legal rules, it is engaged simultaneously in an assessment of the facts and an interpretation of the rules.

Take, for example, a panel's review of an injury determination under Article 3 Anti-Dumping Agreement. First, a panel must determine the factual basis for its

---

[32] Appellate Body Report, *US – Hot-Rolled Steel*, at para 55.
[33] Ibid (original emphasis).

review, namely the relevant economic data. Second, it must interpret the treaty provisions relating to injury. The first task clearly involves factual review, the second legal interpretation. However, finally, a panel must review the national authority's determination that the particular set of facts constitutes a situation of injury. That is not just a question of evaluating all the economic data. Simply reviewing the data, in isolation, does not indicate whether the data establishes injury. Nor is it simply a question of interpretation of the injury provisions in the abstract. Rather, a panel must make a judgment that combines, inseparably, an appreciation of the facts with an interpretation of legal norms. It is, perhaps, the interpretation of legal rules *in concreto* rather than *in abstracto*. As this characterization process is very much a mixed question of fact and law, it is difficult to decide which of the two 'boxes' in Article 17.6 applies because, in a sense, both do.[34]

If WTO Members had a broad discretion as regards the legal characterization of a given set of facts, there would be a considerable risk that the goal of security and predictability in Article 3.2 DSU would not be achieved because the uniform application of WTO law could fragment. In very similar fact situations, one Member may determine that it has the right to apply an anti-dumping measure, while another may determine that it does not. To avoid this, panels would have to apply a more intensive review of these mixed characterization questions that would ensure the predictability and balance that stems from uniformity. In practice, panels and the Appellate Body appear to adopt a pragmatic 'sliding scale' of review that defies easy formulation: the more purely factual a question, the more deference is afforded; in contrast, the more legal a question is, the more a panel and the Appellate Body are inclined to intervene to ensure that the legal characterization meets the requirements of WTO law.

The Temporal Constraints on the Panel's Review of the Facts

Another feature of a panel's review relates to the temporal scope of its factual inquiry. Article 17.5(ii) Anti-Dumping Agreement states that a panel's examination is to be 'based upon...the facts made available' to the national authority during its investigation. Thus, Article 17.5(ii) imposes a temporal constraint on the scope of the panel's factual review that stems from the exclusion of a *de novo* review. Because a panel must assess whether the authority's assessment of the facts satisfied Article 17.6(i) at the time the authority made its determination, a panel must respect the timeframe of that investigation. The reason is that, if a panel's review extends beyond that timeframe, the panel becomes the investigator for the extended period—and this would amount to a form of *de novo* review.

Panels have not taken a consistent approach to interpreting Article 17.5(ii). The Panel in *Guatemala – Cement II* found that, under Article 17.5(ii), 'we are not to examine *any new evidence* that was not part of the [authority's] record of the

---

[34] The situation is all the more complex because the process of making a final determination does not just involve an injury determination. National authorities will typically make a large number of sub-determinations on the way to making a final determination.

investigation'.[35] This reading appears to prevent a panel from reviewing 'any new evidence'. However, other panels have been much more generous in admitting evidence under Article 17.5(ii). Generally, panels have been willing to allow respondents to 'organize' the evidence in the record in a different 'format' from that in which it appeared in the record.[36] In *EC – Bed Linen*, the Panel allowed the respondent to present an entirely new document that was not in the record because it contained data that formed part of the record.[37] Thus, on this view, so long as the *data* presented to a panel was before the authority, the format in which the data is organized and presented may be new.

The evolution of the case law to allow evidence to be presented in a new format may undermine the rule against *de novo* review as well as the due process rights of interested parties. During the investigation, Articles 6.4 and 6.9 Anti-Dumping Agreement allow interested parties to review and comment upon the factual material that an authority will use to make its determinations. If a Member is permitted to reformat evidence from the record in a different way, selecting and adjusting the data as it does so, it is essentially changing the record on which interested parties were allowed to comment and on the basis of which the authority reached its decisions. In short, the more the evidence and information in the record is altered, the more the due process rights of the interested parties are eroded, and the more the responding Member is entitled to reinvent the facts that were before the authority. Furthermore, in permitting new evidence, panels stray into the territory of *de novo* review by reviewing determinations in the light of a different factual constellation from that which the authority considered.

For example, in *EC – Salmon (Norway)*, during the investigation, the authority informed interested parties that sales data relating to the UK could not be 'isolated' from sales data for the EC as a whole.[38] Yet, before the Panel, the EC was able to 'isolate' this data and present it separately from the data pertaining to the rest of the EC. Thus, the EC had thereby selected among the record data in ways that the authority had claimed were impossible, and had produced a data sub-set that the authority claimed it had not examined on its own. Nonetheless, the Panel held that the EC was entitled to present this new evidence because the data relating to the UK had been before the authority as part of the EC-wide data.[39] This finding undermines the due process rights of the interested parties, which were denied access to the information. The Panel also allowed the respondent to alter the factual record that the authority had used in making its determinations, and it thereby undertook a *de novo* review of factual information—sales information relating solely to the UK—that the authority itself did not review in that way.

[35] Panel Report, *Guatemala – Cement II*, at para 8.19 (emphasis added).
[36] Panel Report, *EC – Salmon (Norway)*, at para 7.838.
[37] Panel Report, *EC – Bed Linen*, at para 6.43.
[38] Panel Report, *EC – Salmon (Norway)*, at para 7.853.
[39] Ibid at para 7.854.

The Appellate Body has not yet examined the meaning of Article 17.5(ii), but it has addressed a different question relating to new evidence in reviewing a trade remedy measure under another WTO agreement. The Appellate Body drew a distinction between new evidence that is based on 'old' data and new evidence that is based on 'new' data. Thus, in *US – Cotton Yarn*, a safeguard case brought under the now-defunct ATC, the Appellate Body held that the Panel erred by considering US census data that was not yet published when the national authority reached its decision.[40] In other words, the Panel could not review the decision of the national authority in the light of 'new' data that did not exist at the time of the national authority's decision. That leaves open whether a panel may be entitled to review a measure in the light of 'old' data that did exist when the investigation was conducted.

Although a panel is entitled to examine only the evidence that was before the investigating authority, it is, in general, not limited to examining only the arguments that were put to the authority. In other words, new arguments can be advanced in WTO proceedings that were not considered in the domestic proceedings.[41] Without recourse to new arguments, a panel would be restricted largely to determining whether the national authority's decision is internally coherent—which could allow deficiencies in the original decision to escape review. Moreover, there are good institutional reasons for allowing a panel to look beyond the original arguments put to the national authority. Most importantly, in domestic proceedings, the national authority applies the domestic rules implementing WTO rules, and not the WTO rules themselves. Further, WTO Members participating in a WTO dispute as complainant or third parties may not have participated in the national investigation. Accordingly, WTO Members are not limited to repeating arguments that have been previously made to the national authorities.

The Rationale for Making the Authority the Trier of First Impression for Facts and the Panel the Reviewer of Fact

The rationale for the discretion granted to national authorities through Articles 15.5(ii) and 17.6(i) lies in the structure of the Anti-Dumping Agreement itself. An anti-dumping measure may only be adopted following an investigation conducted at national level by a specially designated investigating authority. The Agreement sets out in great detail when the national authority may initiate an investigation; when it must terminate an investigation; how the investigation is to be conducted by the authority, including publication and notification requirements; specific issues to be examined; a duty to seek out and examine information; and opportunities for interested parties to be heard. It also provides a series of procedural guarantees

---

[40] Appellate Body Report, *US – Cotton Yarn*, at para 78. The holding in *US – Cotton Yarn* was made under the now defunct ATC, which does not include a provision similar to Article 17.5(ii) Anti-Dumping Agreement. The holding was based on the principles underlying the exclusion of *de novo* review. We will consider this further below.

[41] Appellate Body Report, *Thailand – H-Beams*, at para 94; Appellate Body Report, *US – Wheat Gluten*, at paras 55–59.

to protect the interests of parties likely to be affected by an anti-dumping measure. Further, although an anti-dumping measure can be maintained only if it is still necessary, the Agreement stipulates that the determination of ongoing necessity is to be made by the national authority in a second investigation.[42]

The Anti-Dumping Agreement has, therefore, established very clearly that, in the first instance, the determination of the need for anti-dumping measures is to be carried out at national level. It is for the national authority to gather and analyse the evidence, to make factual findings, and to determine whether the conditions permitting the application of an anti-dumping measure are, and continue to be, present. The Agreement, therefore, gives a pre-eminent position to the national investigation.

The character of a panel's review, as directed by the provisions of Articles 17.5 and 17.6, takes into account that the Anti-Dumping Agreement gives national authorities the responsibility for investigating the facts and making an initial determination. The role of panels is, therefore, confined to reviewing the investigation and determinations made at national level. To respect the structure of the Agreement, the Agreement requires panels to show deference to the national investigative process.

Yet, even without Articles 17.5(ii) and 17.6(i), the structure of the Anti-Dumping Agreement suggests that national authorities should be accorded a considerable degree of deference in fact-finding. Any other standard would disregard the division of responsibility between national authorities and panels, and would undermine the treaty-mandated role of the national authority.[43] In short, in terms of the treaty-mandated separation and balance of powers, a panel would usurp the treaty-mandated role of the national authority if it conducted a fresh inquiry or otherwise imposed its own assessment of the facts. Moreover, in practical terms, it would be almost impossible for a panel to conduct a wholly new inquiry as it does not have the resources or technical expertise to do so. A panel is also likely to be operating in a different country, or even continent, and to be working in a different language from that of the national authority.[44]

In our view, this reasoning has led panels and the Appellate Body to apply the same standard of review to countervailing and safeguard measures, even though the SCM

---

[42] See Arts 11.1 and 11.2 Anti-Dumping Agreement.

[43] We note with interest that several commentators have suggested that Art 17.6(i) Anti-Dumping Agreement was not novel but simply codified the existing practice of GATT panels. In other words, according to these commentators, even in the absence of Art 17.6(i), panels accorded a very similar level of deference to national authorities for fact-finding, in anti-dumping disputes, under the earlier Tokyo Round Anti-Dumping Code. See GN Horlick and PA Clarke, 'Standards for Panels Reviewing Anti-dumping Determinations under the GATT and WTO' in E-U Petersmann (ed), *International Trade Law and the GATT/WTO Dispute Settlement System* (The Hague: Kluwer, 1997), at 6, 11, and 13; J. Bourgeois, 'GATT/WTO Dispute Settlement Practice in the Field of Anti-Dumping Law' in E-U Petersmann (ed), *International Trade Law and the GATT/WTO Dispute Settlement System* (The Hague: Kluwer, 1997), at 52–53.

[44] The WTO has, at 1 January 2008, 153 Members, and three official and working languages: English, French, and Spanish.

Agreement and the Safeguards Agreement do not contain provisions equivalent to Articles 17.5(ii) and 17.6(i).

b. Safeguards Agreement and SCM Agreement

The Anti-Dumping Agreement is not the only WTO agreement that envisages national measures based on a treaty-mandated investigation conducted at national level. The Safeguards Agreement and the SCM Agreement also require a national authority to conduct a comprehensive investigation, with WTO-mandated procedural guarantees, before a WTO Member can adopt either a safeguard or countervailing measure.[45] Similarly, under these agreements, national authorities also have responsibility for determining, in a new investigation, whether there is ongoing need for such measures.[46] The structure of these two agreements, therefore, replicates the structure of the Anti-Dumping Agreement. In all three agreements, a national investigating authority is given a pre-eminent position in the decision-making process.[47]

As with the Anti-Dumping Agreement, this structure influences the respective roles of the panel and national authorities. In disputes under these agreements, a panel must recognize that responsibility for the investigation and initial determinations lies, in the first place, with the national authority. The role of a panel is to review, not redo on a *de novo* basis, what has been done at national level.

Formally, the standard of review under the Safeguards Agreement and the SCM Agreement is the general 'objective assessment' standard under Article 11 DSU. Pursuant to Article 11 DSU, the well-established rule excluding *de novo* review has been held to apply to the review of measures adopted under these agreements.[48] However, the special standard of review in Article 17.6 Anti-Dumping Agreement does not apply.

By definition, even though Article 17.6(i) does not apply, the exclusion of *de novo* review means that panels afford a considerable measure of discretion to national authorities for fact-finding. Thus, as in anti-dumping disputes, panels do not have

---

[45] See Arts 2–4 Safeguards Agreement and Arts 11–20 SCM Agreement.

[46] See Art 7 Safeguards Agreement and Art 21 SCM Agreement.

[47] Art 6 ATC provides for rules on safeguard measures concerning these products. The Agreement does not, however, specify either the organ or the procedure through which a Member makes a safeguard determination. The Appellate Body has ruled that the principles of standard of review under Art 11 DSU that are applicable to the Safeguards Agreement apply equally to a review of a safeguard determination under the ATC. Appellate Body Report, *US – Cotton Yarn*, at para 76.

[48] For the Safeguards Agreement, see Appellate Body Report, *US – Lamb*, at paras 106–7. For the ATC, see Appellate Body Report, *US – Cotton Yarn*, at para 74. For countervailing measures under Part V of the SCM Agreement, see Appellate Body Report, *US – Lead and Bismuth II*, at para 51. Although the Appellate Body held that the standard of review in Art 11 DSU applies to disputes concerning countervailing measures, it did not refer explicitly to the exclusion of *de novo* review. Nonetheless, it cited approvingly *EC – Hormones*, where the exclusion of *de novo* was mentioned by the Appellate Body (at para 46).

the freedom to conduct a fresh inquiry nor to substitute their own judgment for that of a national authority. It is not open to panels to reach their preferred factual conclusion. This also reflects that, as with anti-dumping disputes, panels are not the appropriate bodies to conduct factual investigations because they do not have the necessary resources or expertise. As a result, panels are very likely to be disposed to accept the national authority's establishment of the facts, unless there is some manifest flaw in those findings.

As with anti-dumping disputes, the most difficult issues for a panel relate to the characterization of the facts in terms of legal rules—for instance, does a particular set of facts constitute 'injury'? Again, this process of characterization involves mixed questions of fact and law. In general, panels have sought to leave national authorities a margin of discretion, whilst at the same time attempting to preserve the uniform application of WTO law. This balance is, however, delicate and not easy for panels and the Appellate Body to strike.

Another feature of panels' deferential approach to national investigations relates to the scope of the factual inquiry. Article 17.5(ii) Anti-Dumping Agreement requires panels to 'base' their examination on facts made available to the national authority. This has been read by one panel to exclude any new evidence from the panel process.[49] For the other trade remedy agreements, the position appears to be similar. In *US – Cotton Yarn*, under the ATC, the Appellate Body held that panels could not examine data that did not exist at the time of the national investigation. This ruling constrains the factual scope of a panel's review and guarantees that panels respect the temporal limits of a national investigation. However, as with review under the Anti-Dumping Agreement, complainants in WTO proceedings are 'not confined merely to rehearsing arguments that were made' to the national authorities, but may make new arguments.[50]

In sum, therefore, the approach taken to the review of factual matters for safeguard and countervailing measures is very close to the deferential approach that flows from Articles 17.5(ii) and 17.6(i) Anti-Dumping Agreement.[51] This view is confirmed by case law regarding the mechanisms that panels use to conduct their review of trade remedy measures.

---

[49] Panel Report, *Guatemala – Cement II*, at para 8.19.

[50] Appellate Body Report, *US – Lamb*, at para 113.

[51] This conclusion, perhaps, bears out the suggestion of some commentators that the standard of review applied in anti-dumping disputes, prior to the adoption of Article 17.6(i) Anti-Dumping Agreement, was rather similar to the standard that now applies under that provision. It seems that panels apply a similarly deferential standard of review to factual matters in all trade remedy disputes and this standard has been codified in Article 17.6(i) for anti-dumping disputes. Our conclusion that, in practice, there appears to be a similar standard of review for factual matters in all trade remedy disputes is also consonant with the Uruguay Round Ministerial Declaration on Dispute Settlement Pursuant to the Agreement on Implementation of Article VI of the General Agreement on Tariffs and Trade 1994 or Part V of the SCM Agreement that recognizes 'the need for consistent resolution of disputes arising from anti-dumping and countervailing duty measures'.

c. The Standard for Reviewing Factual Determinations under the Trade Remedy Agreements Must Respect the Division of Responsibilities between Investigating Authorities and Panels

There Is No De Novo Review of an Authority's Determination

The general standard of review for the trade remedy agreements, including the Anti-Dumping Agreement,[52] is that panels must make an 'objective assessment' of the facts. However, these words do not provide much assistance in understanding the nature and intensity of a panel's review of trade remedy measures.

However, beyond generic references to an 'objective assessment', there are few statements in which panels and the Appellate Body positively describe what constitutes the nature and intensity of the review that panels apply to the facts. Domestic law will often spell out standards such as 'clearly erroneous', 'clear error of judgment', 'abuse of discretion', 'reasonable' decision-making, and similar concepts. Some panels have suggested that panels decide whether the contested determination is one that an *unbiased and objective* national authority could have reached.[53] In *US – Softwood Lumber VI (Article 21.5 – Canada)*, the Appellate Body quoted directly from the Panel when it held that it would be acceptable to consider whether the determination is one that '*could* have been reached by an <u>unbiased and objective</u> decision maker based on the facts'.[54] While certainly helpful, the 'unbiased and objective' language does not impart a great deal of clarity because it merely traces the language of Article 17.6(i).

Perhaps more helpful is the standard of 'reasonableness'. Traces of this standard are discernible in both GATT and WTO decisions. Thus, the GATT Panel in *US – Softwood Lumber II* examined whether a '*reasonable, unprejudiced person*' could have arrived at the conclusion reached by the authority on the basis of the evidence.[55] In a later iteration of the lumber saga, the Appellate Body said, in *US – Softwood Lumber VI (Article 21.5 – Canada)*, that a panel may examine whether could the authority '*reasonably*' find that the evidence supports a particular factual finding.[56]

Instead of defining the standard of review in positive terms, panels and the Appellate Body have often expressed what is *not* the WTO standard of review in a formulation characterized by a remarkable degree of consistency dating back to GATT decisions. In *EC – Hormones*, in a classic statement of the law that built upon

---

[52] Appellate Body Report, *US – Hot-Rolled Steel*, at para 55.

[53] See, eg, Panel Report, *US – Hot-Rolled Steel*, at para 7.232; Panel Report, *US – Countervailing Measures on Certain EC Products*, at para 7.100; Panel Report, *EC – DRAMS*, at para 7.373; Panel Report, *Mexico – Rice*, at para 7.86; Panel Report, *EC – Tube or Pipe Fittings*, at para 7.178 (emphasis added).

[54] Appellate Body Report, *US – Softwood Lumber VI (21.5 – Canada)*, at para 112, quoting the Panel Report, *US – Softwood Lumber VI (21.5 – Canada)*, at para 7.19 (original emphasis, underlining added).

[55] GATT Panel Report, *US – Softwood Lumber II*, at paras 335, 366, 386, 393, and 403 (emphasis added).

[56] Appellate Body Report, *US – Softwood Lumber VI (Article 21.5 – Canada)*, at para 112.

GATT panels decisions,[57] the Appellate Body rejected two possible standards: 'the applicable standard is neither *de novo* review as such, nor "total deference" '.[58] In this vein, panels and the Appellate Body have expressed what is not permitted under the WTO standard of review, in particular by adding meaning to the exclusion of '*de novo*' review.

Given the importance of the principle that there is no *de novo* review, it is worth reflecting on what this rule means. According to the Appellate Body, *de novo* review arises where a panel redoes an investigation into the facts that has already been done by a national authority, with a panel assuming for itself the 'complete freedom' to substitute its own analysis and judgment for that of the national authority.[59] In other words, a *de novo* review would occur if a panel conducted a new inquiry without affording any deference to the national investigation, and established its own set of facts. A *de novo* review would also occur where a panel conducted its own independent assessment of some or all of the facts before the authority, reaching its own conclusion on the determinations that those facts support.

In short, panels do not act as the trier of fact in the way that they usually do; instead, the national authority is the trier of first impression for factual matters. Rather than weighing and appreciating the evidence as the trier of fact, with a view to deciding what determinations are supported by the facts, a panel must decide whether the authority's decision is one (possibly among many) that is warranted in the light of the facts on which the authority relied.

It is implicit in this description of a panel's function that it should accord a considerable degree of discretion to national authorities in the determination and assessment of facts. A panel must 'put itself in the place of [the national authority] at the time it made its determination' and review the authority's decision 'on its own terms'.[60] It should not seek to displace the national authority by doing its own factual investigation; nor should it reject factual findings by the national authority because it prefers other findings. Also, a panel's task is not to decide whether the authority's decision is supported by different facts from those relied upon by the authority because, in that event, a panel substitutes its own assessment of the facts for that of the authority.

As discussed above, the exclusion of *de novo* review makes sense under the trade remedy agreements. Under the treaty, the Members have decided that the initial decisions in the matters must be taken by a national authority that conducts a formal investigation governed by WTO law. The respective roles of the authorities and panels must respect that division of powers.

---

[57] GATT Panel Report, *US – Softwood Lumber II*, at para 335; GATT Panel Report, *US – Stainless Steel Plate*, at para 284; GATT Panel Report, *US – Lead and Bismuth Carbon Steel*, at para 369; and GATT Panel Report, *EEC – Audio Cassettes*, at para 450.

[58] Appellate Body Report, *EC – Hormones*, at para 117.

[59] Ibid at para 111.

[60] Appellate Body Report, *US – Cotton Yarn*, at para 78; Appellate Body Report, *Japan – DRAMS (Korea)*, at para 131.

An Example of De Novo Review: Japan – DRAMS (Korea)?

Although GATT and WTO panels, and the Appellate Body, have very successfully avoided undertaking *de novo* reviews, the Appellate Body's ruling in *Japan – DRAMS (Korea)* appears, to us, to cross the line into the territory of *de novo* review. In that case, the national authority had decided that the totality of the facts in the record supported the conclusion that a financial contribution had been made through 'entrustment' or 'direction', under Article 1.1(1)(a)(iv) SCM Agreement, by the government to certain creditors that had agreed to a 'December 2002 Restructuring' for the indebted company, Hynix.[61] In making this finding, the authority relied on, among others, factual conclusions drawn from the following factors: (1) evidence that the creditors' decision in relation to this restructuring was not 'commercially reasonable'; (2) evidence that the government was in a position to influence the creditors' decision; and (3) evidence that the government had the 'political intent' to see the debtor survive and had been following the restructuring discussions.[62]

The Panel found that the investigating authority did not have a proper basis for finding that the private creditors were 'entrusted' or 'directed' to participate in the 2002 December Restructuring. The Panel's reasoning was that the investigating authority had relied on 'the totality of numerous items of evidence obtained'.[63] However, with respect to one of those 'items'—namely, category (1) above—the Panel found that the authority was not permitted to rely on that evidence in making its determination that the participation of the creditors was not 'commercially reasonable'.[64] The Panel found that the investigating authority had not considered whether the remaining evidence viewed in isolation—that is, categories (2) and (3), to the exclusion of category (1)—supported a conclusion of 'entrustment' and 'direction'. Therefore, the Panel found that:

> there is no basis for us to conclude whether or not the JIA could properly have relied on such evidence (absent consideration that the restructuring was not commercially reasonable) to make a determination of government entrustment or direction. It is not our role to conduct a *de novo* examination of that issue by asking whether such a finding could have been made by the JIA.[65]

On appeal, the Appellate Body did not object to the Panel's finding that the investigating authority had no basis for its conclusion drawn from evidence in category (1)

---

[61] Appellate Body Report, *Japan – DRAMS (Korea)*, at para 132.

[62] Panel Report, *Japan – DRAMS (Korea)*, at para 7.253; Appellate Body Report, *Japan – DRAMS (Korea)*, at paras 132–33. The Panel noted that, according to Japan, the defending party, the investigating authority had relied on elements additional to the three elements mentioned. The Panel then found that, although the parties disagreed on whether or not Korea, the complainant, had properly identified all of the elements considered and the intermediate factual conclusions drawn by the investigating authority, it was not necessary for the panel to resolve this issue in order to dispose of Korea's claims. Panel Report, *Japan – DRAMS (Korea)*, at fn 304.

[63] Ibid. at para 7.253.

[64] Ibid. at para 7.247.

[65] Ibid. at para 7.253 (fns omitted).

and that this conclusion should not have been relied upon by the authority, as this finding had not been appealed.[66] The Appellate Body also accepted that this evidence, to the effect that the creditors' decision was not 'commercially reasonable', may have been an 'important' factor in the authority's decision.[67]

Nevertheless, the Appellate Body reversed the Panel's finding, holding that the Panel should have decided whether, absent the 'important' evidence in category (1), the remaining evidence in categories (2) and (3) was sufficient to support a finding on entrustment. Naturally, to decide upon the sufficiency of the remaining evidence, the appropriate decision-maker must weigh and appreciate the evidence, exercising judgment on the relative strength and credibility of the evidence in the three different categories. However, the investigating authority had not undertaken this examination because it had incorrectly relied on the 'totality' of all three categories of evidence in combination. Thus, the examination of the remaining evidence necessarily involved a *first* or *new* assessment of that evidence, a task that had never previously been performed.

The Panel therefore correctly held that it could not make a judgment on the probative value of the remaining evidence because, under the Anti-Dumping Agreement, the investigating authority is charged with the responsibility for conducting the first assessment of the evidence; as the Panel said, if it undertook the analysis, it would be a *de novo* review of first impression.[68]

The Appellate Body, however, found that the Panel should have conducted precisely such a review. Thus, in cases where an authority relies on several evidentiary factors, and one or more is found by a panel to be flawed, the Appellate Body appears to believe that a panel should conduct its own an assessment of the remaining evidence, and decide for itself whether that evidence is sufficient to support a determination. As an alternative to examining the remaining evidence, the Appellate Body also said that a panel may examine whether the flawed evidence (category 1) was '*so central*' and '*indispensable*' to the overall finding that the overall finding must be flawed, if supported only by the 'remaining evidence'.[69]

Accordingly, on the Appellate Body's view, the Panel was compelled itself to weigh and appreciate the 'remaining evidence' and the flawed evidence, and reach its own conclusion on the relative merits of the different evidentiary factors. However, the authority never examined the importance of the 'remaining evidence' in isolation from the flawed evidence; nor did it conclude that the flawed evidence was 'central' or 'indispensable' to its conclusions. As a result, in performing the examination of the facts envisaged by the Appellate Body, the Panel would, *by definition*, be undertaking a '*first*' or a '*new*' assessment of the 'remaining evidence' because the authority *never* performed an analysis of this *particular constellation of facts*. This is the very

---

[66] Appellate Body Report, *Japan – DRAMS (Korea)*, at para 127.
[67] Ibid at para 133.
[68] Panel Report, *Japan – DRAMS (Korea)*, at para 7.253.
[69] Appellate Body Report, *Japan – CVDs on DRAMS*, at paras 135 and 137 (emphasis added).

essence of a *de novo* review, which panels cannot perform. A panel would be acting as the trier of 'first impression' in investigating facts where the SCM Agreement has decided that investigating authorities are the trier of first impression.

The Appellate Body appeared to believe that the Panel should undertake an examination of the totality of the remaining evidence, because the authority's decision was based on the 'totality' of the evidence.[70] However, as the Appellate Body noted, a panel must review an authority's determination 'on [the authority's] own terms'.[71] Thus, the Panel must assess whether the authority's decision was warranted in light of the *particular constellation of facts that the authority had found constituted the totality of the facts*. If a panel assesses whether a determination of say 'entrustment' is warranted by a *different constellation of facts*, it ceases to review the authority's determination 'on its own terms', and conducts an examination of first impression – a *de novo* review – that the authority did not conduct.

In *Japan – DRAMS (Korea)*, the Panel and the Appellate Body both found that the flawed evidence on 'commercial reasonableness' played an 'important' part in the authority's decision. The outcome of the inquiry into the significance to be attached to the remaining evidence is, therefore, not a foregone conclusion. No doubt, the Panel and the Appellate Body had an opinion on whether the remaining evidence was sufficient to support a finding of entrustment. However, if they impose *their opinion* on whether the facts support a particular determination, they would be encroaching upon the responsibility of the investigating authority and, effectively, substituting their opinion for an opinion that should be given by the authority. It is not for a panel or the Appellate Body to 'second-guess' (farless 'first-guess') what the authority might have done had it considered a different constellation of facts.

The approach suggested by the Appellate Body also invites panels to make decisions on the facts that will inevitably prove to be controversial. A cornerstone of the trade remedy agreements is that the responsibility for making the initial decision of first impression, particularly with respect to the facts, lies with national authorities. In these disputes, panels are not the trier of first impression. Instead of finding facts themselves, their role is limited to establishing whether the national authority has *exceeded the bounds of its discretion*—in much the same way that the Appellate Body's role in an appeal of the facts is limited to examining whether panels have exceeded the bounds of their discretion.

The decisions made by investigating authorities are usually politically sensitive for domestic constituencies in both the exporting and the importing country. Asking panels to make factual findings of first impression in such disputes is unlikely to enhance the perceived legitimacy of the WTO. Indeed, this is likely one reason why panels and the Appellate Body have studiously avoided *de novo* factual reviews over the years.

Instead of asking a panel to review the remaining evidence, a better course is for the investigating authority to reassess the evidence during the reasonable period for

---

[70] Ibid at para 131.   [71] Ibid.

implementation. Consistent with the division of tasks in the trade remedy agreements, the authority is given a chance to decide upon the appropriate weight to accord to the remaining evidence; it can also decide to seek out additional evidence, if it considers that appropriate (which panels cannot do). Throughout the implementation period, the respondent can continue to apply the WTO-inconsistent measure. Thus, the fact that panels cannot undertake a *de novo* review does not prevent the respondent from maintaining a measure in the short-term.

d. *The Standard of Review of Trade Remedy Measures Is Influenced by the Particular Obligation at Issue*

Although panels are generally deferential in reviewing an investigating authority's assessment of the facts, the precise character and intensity of a panel's review depends on the specific obligations that are at issue.[72] Under the trade remedy agreements, national authorities are generally subject to obligations of two different types. The first are what might be called procedural obligations governing the particular steps and methodologies to be taken in an investigation, while the second are what could be termed 'substantive' obligations relating to the content of their determinations. In reviewing trade remedy measures, the Appellate Body has drawn a distinction between these procedural and substantive aspects of the decision-making process at the national level.[73]

Review of Procedural Obligations – A 'Check List' Approach
In many situations, the trade remedy agreements specify that an investigating authority must act in a particular way in completing aspects of the investigation. These procedural obligations include notification obligations, such as on initiation; duties to consult, for example in selecting a sample; duties to request information; duties of disclosure; and duties to provide notices and explanations. In addition, in the course of making certain substantive determinations, some provisions require an authority, almost as a procedural obligation, to examine certain issues, irrespective of the substantive outcome of the enquiry. For example, under Articles 3.2 Anti-Dumping Agreement and 15.2 SCM Agreement, an authority must review the price effects of dumped/subsidized imports. Or, under Articles 3.4 and 15.4, they must examine a list of specified injury factors.

In cases where claims are made regarding these procedural type obligations, panels often resolve the matter, without inquiring into the facts before the authority, by ruling that the particular procedural step has not been taken. This may be characterized as a 'check list' or 'yes/no' review approach whereby a panel verifies as a formal matter whether or not a particular step in the process has been taken. A review of this type implies no judgment by a panel on the substance of the decision, and a panel thereby avoids an often more controversial assessment of the national authority's judgment on the merits of the decision. By reviewing compliance with

---

[72] Appellate Body Report, *US – Lamb*, at para 105.
[73] Ibid at para 103.

procedural obligations, panels do not interfere with the division of responsibilities that Members have established between national authorities and panels.

One example of such a 'check list' review is *Argentina – Footwear (EC)*, where it was held that Argentina had not examined one of the economic factors listed in the Safeguards Agreement.[74] This did not imply that there was, or could be, no substantive justification to impose a safeguard measure. Rather, the ruling meant that the WTO Member in question had not satisfied the procedural requirements for the conduct of the investigation to examine a specified substantive issue.

A rigorous procedural review along these lines is important because a failure to respect the required steps in the process may affect the content of the final determination. For example, if interested parties are denied process rights, they may be denied an opportunity to provide relevant information that could influence the outcome; or, if an authority does not examine a particular injury factor, that could affect the injury determination.

Review of Substantive Obligations – The Reasoned and Adequate Explanation

The review of the legality of trade remedy measures is not confined to a formal analysis of whether an authority completed certain steps in the investigation. The trade remedy agreements impose a number of substantive conditions that govern whether, and when, a trade remedy measure can be imposed. Even if the national authority has fully respected the procedural obligations in an agreement, and has completed all the formal steps in the analysis, it might determine that a measure can be applied even though the facts do not support that conclusion.

A 'check list' approach to review, which examines only whether or not all the formal steps have been taken, would not test compliance with the substantive conditions required by the WTO agreements. Such an approach would obviously not be satisfactory in a rules-based system because formal compliance may mask serious shortcomings in substantive aspects of the decision-making process. An authority may, for example, formally examine each of the injury factors, yet conclude that there is injury even though the domestic industry is in a perfectly healthy state.

In *EC – Tube and Pipe Fittings*, the Panel rejected a 'checklist' approach to review, holding that the provision of the Anti-Dumping Agreement at issue 'require[d] substantive, rather than purely formal, compliance'.[75] More recently, the Appellate Body reversed the Panel's findings in *US – Softwood Lumber VI (Article 21.5 – Canada)* because the Panel had failed to 'look[. . .] behind the [authority's] reasoning to test its adequacy in the light of the evidence on the record'.[76]

---

[74] Appellate Body Report, *Argentina – Footwear (EC)*, at para 137. Argentina failed to examine capacity utilisation and productivity (at para 134). In *EC – Tube or Pipe Fittings*, the Appellate Body held that, in some circumstances, it is permissible to discern from the record of an anti-dumping investigation that a particular factor has been evaluated, even if there is no separate record of that evaluation (at para 161).

[75] Panel Report, *EC – Tube and Pipe Fittings*, at para 7.310.

[76] Appellate Body Report, *US – Softwood Lumber VI (Article 21.5 – Canada)*, at para 124.

In substantive reviews, panels must tread very carefully to avoid perceptions that they are encroaching upon the responsibilities of the national authorities, and engaging in controversial fact-finding. Because no *de novo* review is permissible, a panel cannot, for example, decide for itself whether, in the particular circumstances, there is (or is not) injury to the domestic industry; in reviewing a dumping determination, a panel cannot decide whether or not a company's accounts reasonably reflect the costs associated with the production of the product under consideration; in reviewing a subsidy determination, it cannot conclude that a benefit was (or was not) conferred. The responsibility for making these decisions rests with the investigating authority alone.

To avoid the need for reaching conclusions that imply a judgment on the substantive content of decisions, panels and the Appellate Body have transformed a procedural obligation into a universal tool for reviewing the adequacy of the substance of a decision. Each of the trade remedy agreements obliges the investigating authority to provide an explanation of the material issues of fact and law underpinning the decision.[77] This explanation must, therefore, address the substantive conditions for imposing a trade remedy measure, with the precise explanation required depending upon the specific substantive obligations at issue. As the Appellate Body said in *US – Lamb*, the character of a panel's review 'is mandated by the specific obligations' imposed.[78] For example, a dumping determination calls for an explanation of one set of issues, whereas an injury determination calls for another.

To be sure, the duty to explain is a procedural obligation that promotes the transparency of decision-making. Yet, given that the explanation must address all *material issues of fact and law*, it is a procedural obligation that transcends the formality of mere procedures, and touches upon every substantive determination of any importance. In short, the duty to explain provides panels with a window into the substance of an authority's decision, without requiring panels to exercise their own judgment regarding the substance of that decision. For example, instead of finding that there is no injury in a particular set of facts, a panel can find that the authority has failed to explain how the facts support the conclusion that there is injury. Panels can, therefore, fully respect the division of responsibilities in the trade remedy agreements, without ever making a decision on the substantive merits of the facts for themselves. This is the very essence of deferential review.

The Appellate Body progressively developed the duty to explain as a tool for conducting substantive review over the first decade of its existence. In *US – Lamb*, a dispute involving safeguard measures, the Appellate Body expressly linked a panel's substantive review of a challenged measure with the duty to explain:

The *substantive aspect* [of the review] *is* whether the competent authorities have given a *reasoned and adequate explanation for their determination*...[79]

---

[77] See Art 12.2 Anti-Dumping Agreement; Art 22.3 SCM Agreement; Art 3.1 Safeguards Agreement.
[78] Appellate Body Report, *US – Lamb*, at para 104.
[79] Ibid at paras 100 and 106 (emphasis added).

The Appellate Body's findings in *US – Softwood Lumber VI (Article 21.5 – Canada)* provide the most comprehensive statement of the duty to explain as a standard of review. In that appeal, the Appellate Body agreed with Canada that the Panel had failed to undertake a critical review of the substance of the authority's decision. At the outset, the Appellate Body articulated the standard of review in a lengthy passage:

It is well established that a panel must neither conduct a *de novo* review nor simply defer to the conclusions of the national authority. A panel's examination of those conclusions must be <u>critical and searching, and be based on the information contained in the record and the explanations given by the authority in its published report</u>. A panel must examine whether, in the light of the evidence on the record, <u>the conclusions reached by the investigating authority are reasoned and adequate</u>... The panel's scrutiny should test whether the reasoning of the authority is <u>coherent and internally consistent</u>. The panel must undertake an in-depth examination of <u>whether the explanations given disclose how the investigating authority treated the facts and evidence in the record and whether there was positive evidence before it to support the inferences made and conclusions reached by it</u>. The panel must examine whether the explanations provided demonstrate that the investigating authority took proper account of the complexities of the data before it, and that it explained why it rejected or discounted alternative explanations and interpretations of the record evidence. A panel must be open to the possibility that the explanations given by the authority are not reasoned or adequate in the light of other plausible alternative explanations, and must take care not to assume itself the role of initial trier of facts, nor to be passive by 'simply *accept[ing]* the conclusions of the competent authorities'.[80]

... it will often be appropriate, or necessary, for a panel 'to examine the sufficiency of the evidence supporting an investigating authority's conclusion ... by looking at each individual piece of evidence' ... [A] panel must also, with due regard to the approach taken by that authority, examine how the totality of the evidence supports the overall conclusion reached.[81]

Finally, we observe that it is in the nature of anti-dumping and countervailing duty investigations that an investigating authority will gather a variety of information and data from different sources, and that these may suggest different trends and outcomes. The investigating authority will inevitably be called upon to reconcile this divergent information and data. However, the evidentiary path that led to the inferences and overall conclusions of the investigating authority must be clearly discernible in the reasoning and explanations found in its report.[82]

In the same report, the Appellate Body summarized the standard of review in the following terms. Although these statements pertain specifically to the threat of material injury, they nevertheless set out universally applicable principles for a panel's factual standard of review:

In sum, a panel charged with reviewing the factual basis for a threat of injury determination must determine whether the investigating authority has provided 'a reasoned and adequate explanation' of:

---

[80] Appellate Body Report, *US – Softwood Lumber VI (Article 21.5 – Canada)*, at para 93, citing Appellate Body Report, *US – Lamb*, at para 106 (original italics, underlining added).

[81] Ibid at para 94, citing Appellate Body Report, *US – Countervailing Duty Investigation on DRAMS*, at para 145.

[82] Ibid at para 97.

(a) how individual pieces of evidence can be reasonably relied on in support of particular inferences, and how the evidence in the record supports its factual findings;

(b) how the facts in the record, rather than allegation, conjecture, or remote possibility, support and provide a basis for the overall threat of injury determination;

(c) how its projections and assumptions show a high degree of likelihood that the anticipated injury will materialize in the near future; and

(d) how it examined alternative explanations and interpretations of the evidence and why it chose to reject or discount such alternatives in coming to its conclusions.[83]

In sum, the duty to explain encompasses the authority's establishment and evaluation of the facts, as well as its characterization of the facts in legal terms. For instance, an authority must explain how the evidence in the record supports its factual conclusions, just as they must explain how those facts support a conclusion that there is, for example, injury.

The Appellate Body has also addressed the quality of the explanation that is required, stating that a reasoned and adequate explanation:

…must be *clear and unambiguous*. It must *not merely imply or suggest* an explanation. It must be a *straightforward explanation* in express terms.[84]

Furthermore, 'a "reasoned conclusion" is not one *where the conclusion does not even refer to the facts that may support that conclusion*'.[85]

The Appellate Body has, therefore, placed the quality and content of an investigating authority's explanation at the very heart of a panel's review of whether the authority has complied with the substantive conditions governing the imposition of trade remedy measures. By scrutinizing the explanation, a panel can review whether the national authority's determination complies with the substantive obligations of an agreement, without making its own decision on the substance.

A good example is *US – Lamb*, where the Appellate Body held that the national authority's explanation of the facts was insufficient to support a finding of threat of injury.[86] The Appellate Body accepted the factual record of the investigation, but ruled that the national authority had not properly explained how these facts could fall within the meaning of the term 'threat of serious injury'. Although it ruled that the explanation did not support the determination, it did not rule that the facts did not, or could not, amount to a threat of injury. Its conclusion was 'simply that the [national authority] has *not* adequately explained how the facts relating to prices support its determination'.[87]

The standard of an 'adequate and reasoned' explanation for the substantive findings falls far short of requiring panels to decide whether the national authority's

---

[83] Ibid at para 99.
[84] Appellate Body Report, *US – Line Pipe*, at para 217 (emphasis added).
[85] Appellate Body Report, *US – Steel Safeguards*, at para 326 (emphasis added).
[86] Appellate Body Report, *US – Lamb*, at paras 140–41 and 153–61.
[87] Ibid at para 160.

determination is 'right' or 'wrong'. Instead, the notion of an adequate explanation carries with it a margin of discretion for the national authority. Even if a panel would have preferred a different determination, it should treat the substantive explanation as adequate if the authority provides a coherent and logical set of reasons that address the key features in the data. In *US – Lamb*, the explanation was inadequate because it did not deal, among other things, with an apparent contradiction in the data on prices that suggested that the domestic industry could have been in the process of recovery, rather than on the verge of serious injury.

Another example is *EC – Salmon (Norway)*, where the national authority made certain findings that imports of salmon from Canada and the US consisted mostly of wild salmon, which it found did not compete with farmed salmon.[88] Although the authority stated its factual conclusions in bald terms, it did not provide any explanation of how the facts in the record supported that conclusion. The Panel found that the EC's determination, therefore, violated Article 3.5 Anti-Dumping Agreement. It opined that:

> in the absence of any indication as to what information was considered and any explanation of how the investigating authority assessed the relevant information, it is not possible for us to determine that the facts were properly established.[89]

The Panel was careful to insist, though, that it 'cannot itself determine whether the investigating authority's factual findings are correct'.[90]

Although panels and the Appellate Body have used the duty to explain as an effective, and largely uncontroversial, tool for engaging in substantive review, there is one line of cases that undermines this approach. In *US – Countervailing Duty Investigation on DRAMS*, the Appellate Body held that, in certain circumstances, a Member is entitled to defend an authority's determination on the basis of information contained in the record, even if that information is not contained in the explanation.[91]

This approach should be used with caution. Although an authority need not address in its explanation every fact in the record, if the explanation is to serve as the basis for review, it must provide a self-contained justification for the authority's determination. It is the authority's only opportunity to explain how it exercised the responsibilities conferred upon it under the Anti-Dumping Agreement. If panels accept the argument that information not addressed in the explanation constitutes the basis for a determination, they are inevitably straying into controversial territory where they will be forced to exercise their own judgment in deciding whether the unexplained facts, which are not even referenced in the explanation, support the authority's determination. Under the trade remedy agreements, the authorities are given that responsibility and, in return, they must explain how they have exercised

---

[88] Panel Report, *EC – Salmon (Norway)*, at para 7.664.
[89] Ibid at para 7.668.
[90] Ibid at para 7.664.
[91] Appellate Body Report, *US – Countervailing Duty Investigation on DRAMS*, at paras 161–65.

it. Moreover, in the long run, insisting on a self-contained explanation promotes the goal of transparency that underlies the duty to explain, and encourages high quality decision-making in connection with measures that impose duties in excess of bound tariffs.

3. *TBT and SPS Agreements*

a. *TBT Agreement*

Trade remedy measures are adopted following a national investigation; the same is not true for national measures covered by all other WTO agreements. In other words, under many WTO agreements, Members adopt measures that do not result from a formal national investigation. In these cases, the notion and institutional impropriety of *de novo* review does not arise in the same way because there is no treaty-mandated, first investigation that panels can reprise.

The TBT Agreement contains largely substantive obligations regulating technical regulations and standards that constitute barriers to trade. It creates few procedural rules on the process that a Member should follow in developing such regulations.[92] The TBT Agreement certainly does not require a national authority to carry out a formal investigation, with fact-finding. Nor does the justification for a TBT measure need to be explained in a detailed report.[93] Although TBT measures can only be applied so long as justified, the TBT Agreement does not require that the determination of this ongoing justification be made, in the first place, by a national authority in a national investigation. The structure of the TBT Agreement is, therefore, very different from the trade remedy agreements.[94]

In our view, this difference influences the nature of the review that a panel should conduct under Article 11 DSU. The TBT Agreement does not establish a marked division of responsibility between a national authority and a panel. A panel can review the consistency of a TBT measure without having to defer to, or wait for, any formal national investigation—because none is foreseen in the Agreement. In such a situation, the exclusion of *de novo* review has no meaning because a panel is, under the WTO agreements, the first body formally to engage in fact-finding.

Although the TBT Agreement does not prescribe a formal process for adopting TBT measures, a Member may elect to adopt TBT measures on the basis of a formal process. It is not clear what degree of deference panels and the Appellate

---

[92] See Arts 2.1–2.8 TBT Agreement. Under Articles 2.9–2.12, a WTO Member is, *inter alia*, obliged to notify proposed technical regulations to other Members and take account of their comments. Members must also publish proposed technical regulations.

[93] Under Art 2.9.2 TBT Agreement, a Member must provide a 'brief indication of the objective and rationale' for a proposed technical regulation. This falls far short of the 'detailed', 'adequate', 'reasoned' explanation that is expected of national authorities in trade remedy investigations. Moreover, this obligation applies only in particular factual circumstances, set out in Article 2.9, and applies only vis-à-vis other WTO Members, rather than the general public, as in the case of trade remedies.

[94] See also Ehlermann and Lockhart, above fn 7, at 513.

Body would accord to formal fact-finding in such an elective process. If the national process incorporated the range of procedural guarantees provided in trade remedy investigations, national authorities might be accorded deference similar to the trade remedy context. This would be consistent with a strict application of the rule against *de novo* review. However, the rationale for the deference accorded in the trade remedy setting lies in the balance that the WTO Members have struck, in the agreements, between the respective 'jurisidictional competences' of the Members and of the WTO.[95] The trade remedy agreements prescribe that national authorities are to make the initial determination, and subsequent re-determinations, and the agreements prescribe, in detail, how that is to be done. The TBT Agreement does not prescribe any formal national process and panels are not, therefore, subjected to the same constraints by the structure of the agreements. Moreover, as the WTO agreements do not prescribe a formal process for national authorities to apply, it is doubtful whether panels should apply a lower level of scrutiny to a Member choosing to apply a formal process.

As regards the scope of a panel's review of a TBT measure, there is no reason in the TBT Agreement to exclude any data or other evidence from the inquiry. The justification for the exclusion of new data in trade remedy cases seems to be that panels are obliged to respect the temporal limitations of the national investigation and the procedural rights of interested parties to see and comment on evidence. Panels cannot examine, for the first time, new data that the national authority has not yet examined. Under the TBT Agreement, there is no formal investigation that must precede the panel's examination of the WTO-consistency of a TBT measure. Article 2.3 TBT Agreement precludes Members from 'maintain[ing]' TBT measures if 'changed circumstances' mean that the measure is no longer justified in its present form. Unlike the trade remedy agreements, the TBT Agreement imposes this ongoing obligation without prescribing that a national authority should assess the 'changed circumstances' before a panel does.[96] Instead, there do not appear to be any qualifications on the factual scope of a panel's assessment of the WTO-consistency of TBT measures. Accordingly, a panel's examination may include any evidence of 'changed circumstances'.

Panels and the Appellate Body have taken a *de novo* approach to standard of review under the TBT Agreement. In *EC – Sardines*, the Panel conducted a detailed inquiry into whether the EC was entitled to disregard an international standard on the use of the term 'sardines', on the grounds that this standard was 'ineffective or inappropriate' to fulfil the legitimate objectives pursued by an EC Regulation. The EC argued,

---

[95] See Appellate Body Report, *EC – Hormones*, at para 115.

[96] In examining whether Article 2.4 TBT Agreement applies to measures that existed before the adoption of the TBT Agreement, the Appellate Body observed that 'the use of the present tense [in Article 2.4] suggests a continuing obligation for existing measures...' Appellate Body Report, *EC – Sardines*, at para 205. In our view, the grammatical structure of Article 2.3 ('Technical regulations shall not be maintained...') is equally indicative of an ongoing or continuing obligation.

inter alia, that EC consumers had grown to expect that the term 'sardines' applied to a narrower product range than envisaged under the international standard. The EC argued that this expectation had to be protected in the interest of consumer protection, market transparency, and fair competition. The Panel critically examined the facts and then rejected the EC's arguments. For instance, the Panel found that, contrary to the EC's assertion, 'it has not been established that consumers in most [EC] member States... have always associated the common name "sardines" exclusively with [the narrow product range]'.[97] The Panel eventually concluded that the EC Regulation was inconsistent with Article 2.4.[98]

b. SPS Agreement

The SPS Agreement allows WTO Members to adopt measures to protect human, animal or plant life or health. In many respects, the SPS and TBT Agreements have a similar structure, though the SPS Agreement has an additional wrinkle that the TBT Agreement does not have. Article 5.1 SPS Agreement requires that an SPS measure be 'based on an assessment... of the risks to human, animal or plant life or health'.

The significance of this requirement was examined in *EC – Hormones*, where the Panel found that:

> ...there is a <u>minimum procedural requirement</u> contained in Article 5.1. In our view, the Member imposing a sanitary measure needs to submit evidence that at least it actually *took into account* a risk assessment when it enacted or maintained its sanitary measure in order for that measure to be considered as *based on* a risk assessment.[99]

The existence of minimum procedural requirements could suggest that a Member has to conduct a formal national process before adopting an SPS measure. However, the Appellate Body reversed the Panel's finding and rejected the existence of 'minimum procedural requirements' for a risk assessment.[100] In reaching this finding, the Appellate Body emphasized the 'substantive requirements' that regulate the adoption of SPS measures, essentially that an SPS measure must be justified by science.[101] The Appellate Body also drew on Article 2.2 SPS Agreement, which requires that there be 'sufficient' scientific evidence to justify an SPS measure. The Appellate Body also held that, absent national procedural requirements, a Member may rely on a risk assessment conducted by another Member or by an international organization.[102]

---

[97] Panel Report, *EC – Sardines*, at para 7.137.

[98] Although the Appellate Body subsequently reversed this finding on the grounds that the Panel incorrectly allocated the burden of proof, it confirmed the Panel's finding that Peru had demonstrated that the international standard was not 'ineffective' or 'inappropriate'. Appellate Body Report, *EC – Sardines*, at para 290.

[99] Panel Report, *EC – Hormones (US)*, at para 8.113 (original italics, underlining added).

[100] Appellate Body Report, *EC – Hormones*, at para 189.

[101] Ibid at para 193.

[102] Ibid at para 190. In *Australia – Salmon*, the Appellate Body set out the substantive requirements for a risk assessment. Appellate Body Report, *Australia – Salmon*, at para 121.

Thus, although the Agreement identifies the substantive issues to be addressed in the assessment, it does not lay down any procedures for how the risk assessment is to be conducted. There is no requirement to conduct an investigation, to engage in formal fact-finding, or to publish a report explaining how the SPS measure is justified. The structure of the SPS Agreement, therefore, differs markedly from the trade remedy agreements and is much closer to the TBT Agreement.

The standard of review that applies under the SPS Agreement reflects this. The standard is an 'objective assessment' under Article 11 DSU. In practice, however, the 'objective assessment' applied under the SPS Agreement is clearly not the same as the assessment applied under the trade remedy agreements.

Similar to the TBT Agreement, a panel will often be the first body to engage in formal fact-finding, for instance, concerning scientific justification. It will be unable to defer to a national authority's fact-finding because, absent 'procedural requirements', there may be none. Again similar to the TBT Agreement, this might be different only where a Member elected to conduct a formal process, with adequate procedural guarantees, for determining the need for an SPS measure. However, it is questionable whether the scope, nature, and intensity of a panel's review should change simply because a Member opts to apply a formal process that is not required or regulated by the WTO agreements.

The case law again confirms that panels apply a *de novo* review under the SPS Agreement. For instance, in *Japan – Apples*, the Panel engaged in extensive fact-finding and evaluated scientific evidence submitted by both parties. In addition, the Panel consulted scientific experts. It found that there was insufficient scientific evidence that certain apples would harbour populations of bacteria;[103] these apples were unlikely to harbour populations of bacteria capable of transmitting fire blight,[104] and it was 'unlikely' that these apples would be infected by fire blight if they did not show any symptoms.[105] On the basis of these, and other, factual findings, the Panel concluded that Japan was maintaining its import restrictions on apples without sufficient scientific evidence, contrary to Article 2.2 SPS Agreement. The Panel also concluded that, contrary to Japan's allegations, available relevant scientific evidence was not insufficient, and that Japan could therefore not rely on Article 5.7 SPS Agreement.[106] In the subsequent compliance dispute, it found again against Japan under several provisions of the SPS Agreement, on the basis of a detailed *de novo* review and evaluation of the scientific evidence.[107]

Also similar to the TBT Agreement, the SPS Agreement does not prevent a panel from examining any data or other new evidence in reviewing SPS measures. Under Article 2.2, Members must have sufficient scientific evidence to 'maintain' an SPS measure. Similarly, under Article 5.6, in 'maintaining' an SPS measure, a Member

[103] Panel Report, *Japan – Apples*, at paras 8.123–128.
[104] Ibid at paras 8.129–36.
[105] Ibid at paras 8.137–9.
[106] Ibid at paras 8.221–222.
[107] Panel Report, *Japan – Apples (21.5 – US)*.

must ensure that the measure is no more trade-restrictive than necessary. Both these obligations are ongoing and require Members with SPS measures to keep abreast of the latest scientific developments. Consistent with the absence of 'minimum procedural requirements', the SPS Agreement does not qualify the obligations in Article 2.2 and 5.6 by indicating that the determination of ongoing justification must first be made at national level in a new risk assessment.[108] It seems, therefore, that panels can review, at any time, whether an SPS measure is justified by the latest scientific information. Thus, in *Japan – Apples*, the Panel examined a claim under Article 2.2 SPS Agreement in the light of very recent scientific evidence that had not yet been taken into account in a national risk assessment.[109]

Although panels may be unable to defer to national *fact-finding*, they do accord deference in reviewing *policy choices* made by Members in adopting SPS measures. First, Members have absolute freedom to determine their own individual 'level of protection' (the level of health risk they are willing to take).[110] Second, although Article 2.2 requires that an SPS measure be justified by 'sufficient scientific evidence', Members are entitled to rely on a divergent or minority scientific opinion.[111] Sufficiency, therefore, need not refer to the quantity of the evidence but equally may refer to its quality. Third, in *EC – Hormones*, the Appellate Body appeared to endorse an approach of examining whether the scientific evidence is '*reasonably* sufficient' to justify the SPS measure.[112] There is, therefore, considerable scope for Members to adopt SPS measures tailored to their own needs, provided that they can point to some sound scientific evidence to support the measures.[113]

In sum, the obligations and structure of the TBT and SPS Agreements indicate that panels are less constrained in their fact-finding than they are under the trade remedy agreements.[114] Neither of these agreements provides for a formal national procedure

---

[108] This may be contrasted with Article 5.7 SPS Agreement which indicates that, for provisional SPS measures adopted without sufficient scientific evidence, a Member should 'review the [SPS] measure... within a reasonable period of time', in light of the latest information. In the case of provisional measures, the Agreement apparently envisages a periodic national review and allows a reasonable period for that review.

[109] Panel Report, *Japan – Apples*, at para 8.124. The contested SPS measure dates from 1994 and Japan carried out risk assessments in 1996 and 1999. The Panel considered evidence from a 2003 scientific study.

[110] Appellate Body Report, *Australia – Salmon*, at para 199. The sole constraint on this freedom is found in Art 5.5 SPS Agreement, which provides that a Member 'shall avoid arbitrary or unjustifiable distinctions in the levels [of protection] it considers to be appropriate in different situations, if such distinctions result in discrimination or a disguised restriction on international trade'.

[111] Appellate Body Report, *EC – Hormones*, at para 194.

[112] Ibid at para 198 (emphasis added).

[113] Art 5.7 SPS Agreement provides a temporary exception to the need for SPS measures to be justified by scientific evidence. Although these issues have not been addressed in dispute settlement cases under the TBT Agreement, it would seem likely that the TBT Agreement will be found to give similar discretion to Members in pursuing 'legitimate objectives' under that agreement.

[114] For legal determinations, we have already noted that panels engage in an interpretation of the relevant WTO rules, using the VCLT, on a *de novo* basis.

prior to the adoption of a measure. The exclusion of *de novo* review is unlikely, therefore, to arise because there has been no formal fact-finding at the national level. Moreover, in the light of the specific obligations in these agreements, the review of a TBT or SPS measure appears to be open-ended and contemporaneous, with panels entitled to examine whatever relevant scientific and technological evidence. This may be contrasted with the trade remedy agreements, where the review is limited and historical, as it respects the parameters of the national investigative process. The nature and intensity of review under the TBT and SPS Agreements seems to differ from review under the trade remedy agreements.

4. *The GATT 1994*

Articles III and XX GATT 1994 provide yet another perspective on standard of review. Broadly, Article III GATT 1994 imposes a non-discrimination rule that requires imported goods to be treated no less favourably than domestic goods. Article XX creates a series of 'general exceptions' from general WTO rules, such as Article III, for interests such as public policy and health.

Members have complete freedom in the way in which they adopt rules covered by these provisions of the GATT 1994, as no national procedures whatsoever are prescribed. In other words, Articles III and XX govern solely the substantive aspects of relevant national rules. This feature of the WTO obligations influences, again, the nature of a panel's review.

Certainly, the general requirement for an 'objective assessment' applies; but, in a context where there is unlikely to have been much, if any, national fact-finding, the standard of review cannot be the same as in the trade remedy context.[115] By definition, absent a national fact-finding process, a panel is engaged in an original or *de novo* review of the facts. As such, the usual rule that panels cannot conduct a *de novo* review does not apply. Moreover, there is no basis to exclude any evidence from their review. This is essentially the same standard of review that is applicable to TBT and SPS measures.

A good example is *Chile – Alcoholic Beverages*, where the Panel had to determine whether a Chilean beverage, 'pisco', was 'like' certain other beverages, such as whisky, gin, and tequila.[116] In addressing this issue, the Panel made a series of factual findings on the competitive relationship between the different beverages. Its inquiry was entirely *de novo* as there was no prior national investigation of this question. Furthermore, there were no limitations on the data, or other evidence, which the Panel could examine. Its inquiry was, therefore, *de novo*, open-ended, and contemporaneous. In essence, the Panel examined, in absolute terms, whether Chile's tax afforded protection to pisco, under Article III:2 GATT 1994.

---

[115] As with TBT and SPS measures, it is possible that a Member elects to adopt a measure after engaging in a formal process that includes fact-finding. In this situation, it may also be questioned whether panels and the Appellate Body should accord considerable deference to a national process that is neither required nor regulated by the WTO agreements.

[116] Panel Report, *Chile – Alcoholic Beverages*.

The position is similar under Article XX GATT 1994. As mentioned, this provision allows Members to adopt measures that derogate from WTO rules, provided certain conditions are respected. In reviewing whether a measure complies with these conditions, a panel must inquire into facts that are unlikely to have been formally examined before. Again, in this situation, a panel conducts a *de novo* review of those facts because no one else has examined them before. Moreover, there is no reason for a panel to exclude any relevant evidence from its review.

In *EC – Asbestos*, the Panel reviewed whether a ban on the use of chrysotile asbestos was justified by the need to protect health, under Article XX(b). The Panel examined the evidence submitted on this point to determine whether the ban was justified under Article XX. The Panel did not need to defer to any national authority's factual findings because it was the first to conduct a, therefore, *de novo* review of the issues.

Similar to the SPS Agreement, although there is very limited scope for deference to national *fact-finding*, panels show deference in assessing *policy choices* made by Members under Article XX. Each Member decides for itself whether, and to what extent, it will protect the interests identified in Article XX. For instance, in examining Article XX(b), the Appellate Body has stated that 'WTO Members have the right to determine the level of protection of health that they consider appropriate in a given situation'.[117] Further, in making policy choices under Article XX, a Member need not rely on the 'majority scientific opinion' but may rely on a divergent opinion.[118] Accordingly, panels leave Members a considerable margin for making policy choices in pursuing the interests covered by Article XX.

Disputes under other provisions of the GATT 1994 also require a panel to make a *de novo* review of the facts before it. For instance, in *EC – Customs Matters*, the US argued that a range of customs administration practices of different EC Member States—for instance, customs classification, treatment of advance tariff classification rulings, and requirements of prior approval for certain customs valuation methods—amounted to non-uniform administration of customs laws and regulations within the meaning of Article X:3(a). No previous factual enquiry on this issue had been conducted by an EC authority. The Panel examined in detail the evidence submitted by the US and made a number of factual findings on the basis of this evidence, accepting some of the US' claims, but rejecting others.[119]

Similarly, in *Canada – Wheat Exports and Grain Imports*, the Panel conducted a *de novo* factual analysis under Article XVII. For example, it examined whether the Canadian Wheat Board was giving Western Canadian wheat producers an incentive to over-produce high quality wheat by paying price premiums for such

---

[117] Appellate Body Report, *EC – Asbestos*, at para 168.   [118] Ibid at para 178.

[119] See Panel Report, *EC – Customs Matters*, at paras 7.205, 7.216, 7.249–7.265, 7.306–7.329, and 7.380–7.385. The Panel found, for example, that allegedly divergent tariff classification practices in different EC Member States did not amount to non-'uniform' administration of customs regulations, because the products classified by the different customs authorities were different products and therefore there was an 'objectively justifiable basis' for the differential treatment. Panel Report, *EC – Customs Matters*, at paras 7.264–265.

wheat.[120] The Panel similarly examined whether the Canadian Wheat Board over-sold the overproduction at discounted prices in certain markets to meet price competition from lower quality wheat.[121]

5. The Standard of Review Applicable to Domestic Law

a. Domestic Law Is an Issue of Fact

The treatment of domestic law by panels and the Appellate Body raises certain specific questions relating to the standard of review that warrant separate consideration. Domestic law is, from the perspective of international law in general, and WTO law in particular, an issue of fact.

The Appellate Body has referred approvingly to the decision in *Certain German Interests in Polish Upper Silesia*, according to which '[f]rom the standpoint of International Law and of the Court which is its organ, *municipal laws are merely facts* which express the will and constitute the activities of States'.[122] The Appellate Body further emphasized that panels consider domestic law as part of their task as triers of fact, and that they do not interpret domestic law 'as such'.[123]

Because domestic law is an issue of fact, panels should approach it in the same manner as they approach fact-finding in cases involving SPS, TBT, and GATT measures; that is, they should conduct a *de novo* inquiry into the facts to establish the meaning of domestic law. In principle, panels should not merely accept a defending Member's representations about the meaning of its domestic law and show deference, but rather they should develop their own, original analysis of the meaning of domestic law based on the totality of the evidence. Indeed, the Panel in *US – Section 301 Trade Act* stated that panels 'are not bound to accept' the views offered by the respondent of its own laws.[124] The evidence that panels examine in considering the meaning of domestic law includes the text of the relevant domestic legal instruments, pronouncements of domestic courts, opinions of legal experts, and the writings of recognized legal scholars.[125]

At the same time, it cannot be denied that WTO panellists are not experts in the municipal law of individual WTO Members. Moreover, the authorities of the defending WTO Member, including the officials of that Member appearing before a WTO panel, typically have unique expertise and experience in interpreting their own municipal law. As a result, in assessing the evidence regarding the meaning of domestic law, panels inevitably grant a degree of deference towards the defending WTO Member's representations, within the limits of what is shown in the remainder

---

[120] Panel Report, *Canada – Wheat Exports and Grain Imports*, at paras 136–37.

[121] Ibid at paras 138–41.

[122] PCIJ, *Certain German Interests in Polish Upper Silesia*, PCIJ Reports (1926) Ser. A, No 7, at 19 (emphasis added), quoted in Appellate Body Report, *India – Patents (US)*, at para 65.

[123] Appellate Body Report, *India – Patents (US)*, at para 66.

[124] Panel Report, *US – Section 301 Trade Act*, at para 7.19.

[125] Appellate Body Report, *Dominican Republic – Import and Sales of Cigarettes*, at para 111, quoting Appellate Body Report, *US – Carbon Steel*, at para 157.

of the evidence. As the Panel in *US – Section 301 Trade Act* stated, 'any Member can reasonably expect *considerable deference* be given to its views on the meaning of its own law'.[126] The term 'considerable deference' suggests a high degree of discretion, and implies that the assessment of domestic law falls short of the type of *de novo* assessment that a panel conducts with respect to other evidence.

As a result, in comparison with other factual evidence assessed by a panel, domestic law occupies a somewhat unique position. In particular, panels can be expected to show *some* deference to the defending WTO Member's representations, despite the fact that they are conducting a *de novo* review of the totality of the evidence. This expectation is borne out by existing case law.

b. Do Panels and the Appellate Body Apply a Deferential Standard of Review in Determining the Meaning of Domestic Law?

Overall, the approach of panels and the Appellate Body to questions of domestic law is difficult to characterize in a uniform fashion. Some findings appear to be more deferential to WTO Members than others, and scholarly writing has argued that the case law is inconsistent.[127] However, it must also be borne in mind that it is very difficult to compare the findings in different disputes because of the varied factual circumstances particular to each case.

The Panel in *US – Section 301 Trade Act* is generally perceived to have been deferential to the US' understanding of its own law.[128] As noted above, it stated expressly that 'any Member can reasonably expect *considerable deference* be given to its views on the meaning of its own law'.[129] The Panel justified its reliance on the US' representations by stating:

The representations and statements by the representatives of the US appearing before us were solemnly made, in a deliberative manner, for the record, repeated in writing and confirmed in the Panel's second hearing. There was nothing casual about these statements nor were they made in the heat of argument. There was ample opportunity to retract. Rather than retract, the US even sought to deepen its legal commitment in this respect.

We are satisfied that the representatives appearing before us had full powers to make such legal representations and that they were acting within the authority bestowed on them. Panel proceedings are part of the DSB dispute resolution process. It is inconceivable except in extreme circumstances that a panel would reject the power of the legal representatives of a Member to state before a panel, and through the panel to the DSB, the legal position of a Member as regards its domestic law read in the light of its WTO obligations. The panel system would not function if such a power could not be presumed.[130]

In contrast, less deference appears to have been given by the Panel and the Appellate Body in *India – Patents (US)*. In this case, the Panel found that, despite argument and

---

[126] Panel Report, *US – Section 301 Trade Act*, at para 7.19 (emphasis added).
[127] See, eg, Oesch, above fn 2, at 196.   [128] Ibid.
[129] Panel Report, *US – Section 301 Trade Act*, at para 7.19 (emphasis added).
[130] Ibid. at paras 7.122–123.

evidence submitted by India, there was insufficient evidence of the existence and legal validity of administrative practice that would override Indian patent legislation that was, on its face, WTO-inconsistent.[131] On appeal, the Appellate Body agreed with the Panel's approach and stated that the Panel had correctly conducted a 'detailed examination of domestic law'.[132] Likewise, the Appellate Body was not persuaded by representations by India that the administrative instructions at issue could override express contrary provisions in Indian law.[133] Some commentators have argued that the approach of the Panel and the Appellate Body in *India – Patents (US)* 'did not reveal particular deference towards India's view on the meaning of its own legal system' and contrasts with that of the Panel in *US – Section 301 Trade Act*.[134]

However, it is difficult to compare these two cases directly because the nature and the wording of the legal provisions at issue were different. For instance, the Indian law at issue was 'mandatory';[135] in contrast, the US' law was not mandatory, and the WTO-(in)consistent application of the US' law depended on the exercise of the executive's discretion. Moreover, the credibility of the rebuttal evidence supplied by the defendants in the two cases cannot easily be judged from afar.

In *US – Hot-Rolled Steel*, the Appellate Body found the defending Member's representations about its own laws more persuasive than in *India – Patents (US)*. In that case, Japan made an 'as such' claim regarding a legislative provision of US law containing the words 'shall focus primarily on . . .'. The Appellate Body noted that the words at issue had not acquired a definitive meaning in municipal law.[136] Thus, the domestic law did not, on its face, mandate WTO-inconsistent conduct but left room for a WTO-consistent interpretation. During the proceedings, the US 'explained the meaning of the words . . . in a variety of ways'.[137] The Appellate Body narrated the 'variety' of explanations provided by the US.[138] In its reasoning, the Appellate Body relied explicitly on responses given by the US to questions posed by the Panel and also on statements made by the US at the oral hearing before the Appellate Body.[139] Partly on the basis of these representations, the Appellate Body held that the legislation was not 'as such' WTO-inconsistent.[140]

Canada – Pharmaceutical Products is another example of deference to a Member's representations about its own law. In that case, the Panel relied on 'Canada's

---

[131] Panel Report, *India – Patents (US)*, at paras 7.35–41.

[132] Appellate Body Report, *India – Patents (US)*, at para 67.

[133] Ibid at paras 69–70.

[134] Oesch, above fn 2, at 192 and 196, with further references.

[135] Appellate Body Report, *India – Patents (US)*, at para 69.

[136] Appellate Body Report, *US – Hot-Rolled Steel*, at para 200.

[137] Ibid at para 201.

[138] Ibid at paras 201–03.

[139] Ibid at para 203, citing responses given to the Panel, and at para 207, citing a statement made at the oral hearing referred to in para 201.

[140] Ibid at para 208.

representations as to the meaning of [its] law'[141] and stated that the finding of conformity 'would no longer be warranted if, and to the extent that, Canada's representations as to the meaning of that law were to prove wrong'.[142] Davey has argued that this case demonstrates 'deference to governmental decisions in the social field, since the measure was designed to lower prescription drug prices'.[143] However, another commentator has argued that a direct comparison with the *India – Patents (US)* case is not easily made, because the Canadian measure contained elements of discretion.

In contrast, a dispute in which a WTO Member's interpretation of its own law was not accepted is *EC – Trademarks and Geographical Indications (Australia)*. The EC's measure provided that geographical indications (GIs) for products originating in a third country could be registered in the EC only if that third country had adopted a system for GI protection equivalent to that in the EC. The EC argued that products originating in WTO Members were not covered by the reciprocity requirement of the EC Regulation. The Panel conducted a detailed examination of the text of the EC's measure, of EC statements in the TRIPS Council,[144] and before the Panel,[145] and agreed with the interpretation of EC law advanced by the complainants.[146] The Panel even went as far as stating explicitly that the obligation to make an objective assessment of the facts, pursuant to Article 11 DSU, 'prohibit[ed] [it] from accepting the interpretation . . . presented by the European Communities'.[147] Thus, although a panel defers to the interpretation offered by the respondent of its own law, it cannot accept that interpretation uncritically, without making an objective assessment.

It is difficult to make a generalized comment on the extent to which panels (and the Appellate Body) should grant deference to WTO Members' representations regarding the meaning of domestic law. It is true, as is sometimes argued, that the national authorities of the defending WTO Members enjoy 'intimate familiarity with domestic law', whereas panels and Appellate Body have no or at best limited legal expertise in a particular municipal legal order.[148] It would certainly be incorrect to dismiss a WTO Member's representations about the meaning of its domestic law, or to exclude it from the totality of evidence that a panel must weigh to arrive at its conclusion. And it is also true that deference to a WTO Member's interpretation of its municipal law does not conjure up the same risk of a 'tower of legal Babel' as would deference to WTO Members' interpretation of WTO law.

---

[141]   Panel Report, *Canada – Pharmaceutical Products*, at para 7.99.

[142]   Ibid.

[143]   WJ Davey, 'Has the WTO Dispute Settlement System Exceeded its Authority? A Consideration of Deference Shown by the System to Member Government Decisions and its Uses of Issue-Avoidance Techniques' 2001 *Journal of International Economic Law* 4(1) 79, at 92.

[144]   Panel Report, *EC – Trademarks and Geographical Indications (Australia)*, at paras 7.77–81.

[145]   Ibid at paras 7.84–95.   [146]   Ibid at paras 7.52–74.

[147]   Ibid at para 7.101.   [148]   Oesch, above fn 2, at 206.

On the other hand, these considerations do not compel considerable deference simply because a WTO Member is making a statement about its own legal order. The fact that panels are no experts in a municipal legal system should not be treated differently than the fact that panels are no experts in, for instance, matters of health and science. Panels should carefully consider all of the evidence regarding the meaning of municipal law, including the text of the law; evidence of its application; pronouncements by domestic courts; expert statements; and scholarly writings on the meaning of municipal law.[149] In considering this evidence, there is no reason why representations made by one litigating party should *a priori* enjoy greater credibility than other sources of evidence. As the Panel in *US – Section 301 Trade Act* recognized, for reasons of litigation strategy and tactics, and in the 'heat' of litigation,[150] respondents may not always provide a WTO panel with a full picture of domestic law. It is therefore important that panels conduct a rigorous and objective analysis in ascertaining the meaning of domestic law.

Viewed in this light, the question of how a panel should treat a WTO Member's statements about its own municipal law is perhaps better characterized not as one of deference versus non-deference, but rather as one of weighing and balancing the reliability and credibility of the evidence of the meaning of municipal law.

c. Domestic Law as 'Evidence of Compliance'

Yet another wrinkle attaches to the treatment of domestic law. In *India – Patents (US)* and in *US – Section 211 Appropriations Act*, the Appellate Body stated that a panel's findings on the meaning of municipal law fall within the scope of appellate review.[151] The reason given by the Appellate Body is that 'the municipal law of WTO Members may serve not only as evidence of facts, but also as evidence of compliance or non-compliance with international obligations';[152] and because 'a panel . . . examine[s] the municipal law of a WTO Member for the purpose of determining whether that Member has complied with its [WTO] obligations . . . a panel's assessment of municipal law as to its consistency with WTO obligations is subject to appellate review'.[153] In other words, the Appellate Body found that, because the ultimate purpose of determining the precise meaning of municipal law is to decide whether that municipal law is consistent with WTO law, a panel's finding on the precise meaning of municipal law is automatically a finding of law. Therefore, according to the Appellate Body, the finding on the precise meaning of municipal law is subject to appellate review.

---

[149]   Appellate Body Report, *US – Carbon Steel*, at para 157.

[150]   Panel Report, *US – Section 301 Trade Act*, at paras 7.122–123.

[151]   Appellate Body Report, *US – Section 211 Appropriations Act*, at para 105; Appellate Body Report, *India – Patents (US)*, at para 65.

[152]   Ibid at para 105.

[153]   Ibid.

The Appellate Body's finding thus results in the unique situation that a panel's conclusions on the meaning of municipal law are simultaneously findings of fact and findings of law. As a result, such panel findings can be challenged before the Appellate Body without even invoking Article 11 DSU. However, the logic of the Appellate Body's finding is difficult to understand. Just because a panel assesses whether a domestic legal act—which represents a fact from the perspective of WTO law—is consistent or inconsistent with WTO law does not suddenly turn the meaning of the domestic legal act into a question of WTO law. Put differently, a factual finding by a panel—for instance, that a WTO Member levied a 10 per cent tariff on a particular product—does not suddenly metamorphose into a legal finding simply because a panel goes on to determine whether that fact (levying a 10 per cent tariff) was legally consistent with that WTO Member's obligations under the GATT 1994 and its tariff schedule. Even if one accepts that, as might be argued, there is close nexus between the factual findings on the meaning of domestic law and the legal issues before a panel or the Appellate Body, there must still be a discernable line between issues of fact and issues of law. After all, the Appellate Body's jurisdiction is circumscribed precisely by this distinction.

A possible explanation for this finding is that the Appellate Body would like to retain the ability to review a panel's finding on municipal law even in the absence of errors that rise to the level of an Article 11 DSU violation. Although formally a *factual* matter, municipal law nevertheless remains *law*, and judges intuitively want to assess the meaning of law, whether it is municipal or international. The strangely hybrid status of domestic law in the Appellate Body's case law thus mirrors, at the appellate level, the unusual position that domestic law has in a panel's factual inquiry—although panels should conduct a *de novo* review of municipal law, it affords a measure of deference to the defendant.

V. THE APPELLATE BODY'S STANDARD FOR REVIEWING DECISIONS BY PANELS

A. General Considerations

So far, this chapter has focused primarily on the standard of review applied by WTO panels to national measures enacted by WTO Members. The following section now brings the Appellate Body into the discussion.

The function of the Appellate Body is to review 'issues of law covered in the panel report and legal interpretations developed by the panel'. Hence, unlike panels, the

Appellate Body's principal role is not to review WTO Members' measures for their WTO consistency, but rather to review a panel's findings and conclusions about those measures.[154] The question therefore arises as to the standard of review that the Appellate Body will apply to a *panel's legal and factual conclusions* challenged in appellate review.

The work of panels, like other tribunals, comprises three basic activities. Panels make findings that: (a) are purely legal in nature; (b) are purely factual; and (c) involve the application of the facts to the law.[155] This trichotomy is very helpful in discerning the standard of review applied by the Appellate Body when reviewing panel findings. There are certain parallels between how the Appellate Body approaches the different types of panel findings, and how WTO panels approach findings of national authorities in trade remedy disputes.

B. The Appellate Body's Review of a Panel's Purely Legal Findings

With respect to panels' *purely legal findings*, the Appellate Body performs a *de novo* review. The Appellate Body examines afresh the legal significance of a given provision of WTO law and does not give any deference to panels. The Appellate Body will reverse panel findings where it disagrees with the panel's approach to a particular provision[156] or with a more generic legal-interpretive approach applied by a panel.[157]

As with the *de novo* standard of review applied by panels vis-à-vis the national authorities' interpretations of WTO law, there are several fundamental reasons why the Appellate Body does not grant discretion or deference to WTO panels in their legal interpretations.

First, under Article 17.6 DSU, one of the core functions of the Appellate Body is the examination of a panel's legal interpretations. Article 17.6 does not provide for any discretion or deference to be granted to a panel's interpretations of WTO legal provisions. Quite to the contrary, Article 17.12 stipulates that the Appellate Body

---

[154] The Appellate Body will, however, directly review a WTO Member's measures for their WTO-consistency when it completes the panel's legal analysis. When it does so, the Appellate Body applies the same standard of review as a panel. However, given its jurisdictional limitations, the Appellate Body can only complete the analysis if there are sufficient factual findings by the panel or uncontested facts on the record. See, eg, Appellate Body Report, *US – Hot-Rolled Steel*, at para 235; Appellate Body Report, *Canada – Dairy (Article 21.5 – New Zealand and US)*, at para 98; Appellate Body Report, *US – Section 211 Appropriations Act*, at para 343.

[155] See Appellate Body Report, *US – Upland Cotton (Article 21.5 – Brazil)*, at para 385, on the difficulty of distinguishing between issues of fact and mixed issues of fact and law.

[156] See, eg, Appellate Body Report, *US – Softwood Lumber V*, at para 139, with respect to Article 2.2.1.1 Anti-Dumping Agreement.

[157] Appellate Body Report, *India – Patents (US)*, at para 48, reversing the Panel's reliance on WTO Members' 'legitimate expectations' in interpreting the TRIPS Agreement.

shall 'address each of the issues' raised in accordance with Article 17.6, without any qualifications and any deference to be granted to a panel. Furthermore, Article 17.13 states that the Appellate Body may uphold, modify, or reverse the legal findings and conclusions of a panel. There is nothing in these provisions that could serve as a basis for adopting a deferential approach to a panel's legal interpretation. Nothing in Article 17 DSU picks up the language of Article 17.6(ii) Anti-Dumping Agreement, referring to different permissible interpretations of WTO law.

Second, the very reason why the Appellate Body was established during the Uruguay Round was to create an institution that would control the uniformity and internal cohesiveness of the WTO dispute settlement system, as well as to provide a check against erroneous panel decisions.[158] This is again a reflection of the goal to prevent a 'tower of legal Babel', here a situation in which various panels adopt different interpretations of WTO law. The Appellate Body sits at the apex of the dispute settlement system and functions as the final 'judicial' arbiter, subject to the powers of the MC and the GC under Article IX:2. The notion of giving deference to a panel's interpretation of WTO law runs directly counter to the Appellate Body's function within the architecture of the dispute settlement system.

Third, and related to the second reason, WTO Members agreed to the idea of giving up their 'veto' power to block the adoption of panel reports, and they established the negative consensus rule precisely because they created an appellate review process that could correct legally flawed panel decisions. The creation of the Appellate Body was the 'quid pro quo' of Members giving up their veto power over the adoption of panel reports.[159] Again, any idea of giving deference to a panel's legal interpretation of WTO law runs directly counter to this intention.

C. The Appellate Body's Review of a Panel's Purely Factual Findings

1. *Substantive Review of a Panel's Assessment of the Facts*

With respect to panels' *factual findings*, issues of fact, in principle, fall outside the scope of appellate review and outside the Appellate Body's jurisdiction.[160]

However, findings of fact are not entirely excluded from the Appellate Body's examination. The Appellate Body has consistently held that, whether or not a panel has made an objective assessment of the facts before it, as required by Article 11 DSU, is also a *legal* question that, if properly raised on appeal, would fall within the scope

---

[158] P Van den Bossche, 'The WTO Appellate Body and its rise to prominence' in G Sacerdoti, A Yanovich, and J Bohanes (eds), *The WTO at Ten. The Contribution of the Dispute Settlement System* (Cambridge: Cambridge University Press, 2006) 289, at 292–93.

[159] Ibid. at 292–94.

[160] Appellate Body Report, *EC – Hormones*, at para 132.

of appellate review.[161] At the same time, the Appellate Body is entitled to review a panel's factual findings *only to the extent necessary* to determine whether it has performed an 'objective assessment' of the facts before it.

This suggests a deferential standard of review, and deference is indeed reflected in the Appellate Body's approach to panels' factual findings. The Appellate Body has consistently refused to reverse a panel finding where an appellant alleged simple disagreement with a panel's factual finding. It has held that a panel is the 'trier of facts',[162] and it will not interfere lightly with a Panel's assessment of the facts.[163]

This discretion afforded to panels covers not only the establishment of (raw) facts, but also their evaluation. The Appellate Body has stated that:

Determination of the credibility and weight properly to be ascribed to (that is, the appreciation of) a given piece of evidence is part and parcel of the fact-finding process and is, in principle, left to the discretion of a panel as the trier of facts.[164]

The Appellate Body has not stipulated a positive, affirmative standard for when a panel will violate the obligation to provide an 'objective assessment' of the facts. The reason for this is probably that the establishment and evaluation of facts will vary on a case-by-case basis, and the Appellate Body does not wish to set out a generic standard that might limit its flexibility to consider each case on its merits.

Examples of a violation of Article 11 DSU with respect to factual findings can be found in *US – Oil Country Tubular Goods Reviews (Argentina)* and *US – Anti-Dumping Measures on Oil Country Tubular Goods (Mexico)*. In both cases, the Panel found, as a matter of fact, that the US Department of Commerce considered three scenarios set out in that Department's so-called Sunset Policy Bulletin, as determinative or conclusive of the likelihood of continuation or recurrence of dumping. In both cases, the

---

[161] Ibid.

[162] Appellate Body Report, *US – Upland Cotton (Article 21.5 – Brazil)*, at para 293; Appellate Body Report, *US – Softwood Lumber V*, at para 174; Appellate Body Report, *EC – Asbestos*, at para 161. See also, eg, Appellate Body Report, *EC – Tube or Pipe Fittings*, at para 125; Appellate Body Report, *EC – Bed Linen (Article 21.5 – India)*, at paras 170, 177, and 181; Appellate Body Report, *EC – Sardines*, at para 299; Appellate Body Report, *Korea – Alcoholic Beverages*, at paras 161–62; Appellate Body Report, *Japan – Agricultural Products II*, at paras 141–42; Appellate Body Report, *US – Wheat Gluten*, at para 151; Appellate Body Report, *Australia – Salmon*, at para 266; Appellate Body Report, *Korea – Dairy*, at para 138.

[163] Appellate Body Report, *US – Wheat Gluten*, at para 151; see also Appellate Report, *EC – Hormones*, at para 132; Appellate Body Report, *Chile – Price Band System*, at para 224; Appellate Body Report, *Dominican Republic – Import and Sale of Cigarettes*, at para 111. Appellate Body Report, *US – Softwood Lumber V*, at para 174. Despite a widely held perception to the contrary, the Appellate Body in *EC – Hormones* never stated that it would reverse a panel's factual finding only where it found that the panel had made an 'egregious error that calls into question the good faith of a panel' (at para 133). Based on the arguments of the EC in that appeal, the Appellate Body stated that such an error would be a reason to find that the Panel violated Article 11 DSU, but did not state that such an error exhausted the basis on which a violation of Art 11 could be found. Subsequent decisions, including reversals of Panel's factual findings under Art 11, have borne out that the Appellate Body will reverse a panel's factual finding even in the absence of an 'egregious error'.

[164] Appellate Body Report, *EC – Hormones*, at para 132.

Appellate Body reversed these findings. In *US – Oil Country Tubular Goods Reviews (Argentina)*, it did so because the Panel report 'reveal[ed] no qualitative analysis of even some of the cases in Exhibit ARG-63, and…contain[ed] only a single sentence justifying its conclusion based on the overall statistics'.[165] In *US – Anti-Dumping Measures on Oil Country Tubular Goods (Mexico)*, the Appellate Body's reason was that:

> the Panel's analysis does not reveal that the affirmative determinations, in the 21 specific cases reviewed by it, were based *exclusively on the scenarios to the disregard of other factors*. Nor does the Panel's review of these cases reveal that the USDOC's affirmative determinations were based solely on the [Sunset Policy Bulletin] scenarios, when the probative value of other factors might have outweighed that of the identified scenarios. Accordingly, we conclude that the Panel did not conduct a 'qualitative assessment' of the USDOC's determination such that the Panel could properly conclude that the [Sunset Policy Bulletin] requires the USDOC to treat the factual scenarios of Section II.A.3 of the [Sunset Policy Bulletin] as determinative or conclusive.[166]

The Appellate Body's approach in reviewing purely factual findings by panels is not only appropriate in view of the jurisdictional limitations placed upon appellate review by Article 17.6 DSU, but also stems from certain practical considerations. The Appellate Body has been set up, *inter alia*, to provide for uniform interpretations of WTO law. In contrast, the structure and duration of the appellate process does not enable the Appellate Body to conduct an extensive examination of a panel's factual record (let alone collect additional facts). The maximum duration of the appellate review process is only 90 days, a time limit that stands in sharp contrast to the 9 months granted to panels (and often exceeded in practice). Nor is the Appellate Body in the position of a trier of *first impression* and, consequently, it cannot fully appreciate how the fact-gathering process at the panel stage shapes a panel's perception of the persuasiveness and credibility of the evidence. Finally, the institutional resources of the Appellate Body are more limited than those of panels, because the Appellate Body is precluded from relying on substantive support from individuals other than staff members of the Appellate Body Secretariat.

Thus, there is a certain analogy in the relationship between the Appellate Body and panels and the relationship between panels and a national investigating authority with respect to the ability to conduct a factual inquiry. This relationship strongly argues in favour of a deferential approach by the Appellate Body to panels' factual findings.

2. *Procedural Review of a Panel's Assessment of the Facts – Reasoned and Adequate Explanation*

In its recent *US – Upland Cotton (Article 21.5 – Brazil)* report, the Appellate Body appears to have added a new element to the standard for reviewing a panel's objective

---

[165] Appellate Body Report, *US – Oil Country Tubular Goods Reviews (Argentina)*, at para 215.

[166] Appellate Body Report, *US – Oil Country Tubular Goods Reviews (Argentina)*, at para 209 (emphasis original, fns omitted).

assessment under Article 11 DSU. In the course of examining an appeal under Article 11 against the compliance panel's treatment of the evidence, the Appellate Body noted:

> In cases concerning a panel's examination of determinations by domestic investigating authorities, the Appellate Body has also held that a panel must assess 'whether the explanations provided by the authority are "reasoned and adequate"…and [assess] the coherence of its reasoning'…In cases where a panel operates as the initial trier of facts, such as this one, it would *similarly be expected to provide reasoned and adequate explanations and coherent reasoning*.[167]

The Appellate Body thus drew an explicit parallel between the standard of review applied by a panel in reviewing findings of domestic investigating authorities, and the standard of review applied by the Appellate Body in reviewing a panel's findings.[168] In the remainder of the report, the Appellate Body used language that echoes closely the standard previously applied by panels to the findings of investigating authorities. Thus, the Appellate Body found, for instance:

> For the same reasons, we also do not believe that the Panel failed to provide a 'reasoned and adequate explanation' for its conclusions in the light of 'possible alternative explanations',[169] as alleged by the United States.[170]

> For this reason, we do not consider that the Panel wilfully distorted and misrepresented the studies submitted by the United States on counter-cyclical payments, nor that it failed to provide a reasoned and adequate explanation for its conclusions in the light of plausible alternative explanations.[171]

On the basis of this standard, the Appellate Body held that the compliance panel had failed to make an objective assessment under Article 11 DSU because its reasoning regarding certain evidence was 'internally incoherent'.[172]

Under a long-standing interpretation of Article 11 DSU, the Appellate Body has held that panels are not obliged to examine each and every piece of evidence in their reasoning; nor are they required to address all of the arguments made by the parties.[173] However, it seems that a panel can now be found to violate Article 11 if it fails to address certain evidence and arguments.

In previous appeals, the Appellate Body typically accepted that the evidence had all been examined (even if it was not the subject of express explanation), and

---

[167] Appellate Body Report, *US – Upland Cotton (Article 21.5 – Brazil)*, at fn 618 (emphasis added).

[168] This would appear to apply to a panel's findings of fact, as well as on mixed issues of law and fact.

[169] See Appellate Body Report, *US – Lamb*, at para 106 (original fn).

[170] Appellate Body Report, *US – Upland Cotton (Article 21.5 – Brazil)*, at para 381 (underlining added, fn omitted).

[171] Ibid at para 404 (underlining added), also para 415.

[172] Ibid at para 294.

[173] Appellate Body Report, *US – Upland Cotton*, at para 446; Appellate Body Report, *Dominican Republic – Import and Sales of Cigarettes*, at para 125; Appellate Body Report, *EC – Poultry*, at paras 135 and 143; Appellate Body Report, *Brazil – Retreaded Tyres*, at para 202; Appellate Body Report, *Chile – Price Band System (Article 21.5 – Argentina)*, at para 240; Appellate Body Report, *Japan – Agricultural Products II*, at para 91, fn 39.

it reviewed whether the panel's conclusions rested on a 'plausible view of the facts' and whether its conclusions 'seem to be supported' by the facts.[174] In this appeal, the Appellate Body held that Article 11 DSU required that certain evidence and argument be explicitly addressed in the reasoning because the evidence provided the basis for a 'plausible *alternative* explanation' of the facts.

Thus, it may no longer be sufficient for the panel's findings to represent a plausible view of the facts if the evidence supports an *alternative plausible* view. This standard, on its face, intrudes into a panel's discretion as the trier of fact more than the Appellate Body has been willing to do in the past.

On the basis of one appeal, it is not yet clear, though, to what extent panels must now provide more elaborate reasoning regarding an alternative 'plausible' view of the facts. In particular, although the Appellate Body was rather strict in establishing a duty to explain with regard to certain of the evidence in the record, it was less strict in considering other evidence in the same dispute. For example, the Appellate Body noted that, '[a]lthough [the panel's] analysis of China's role [in the market for upland cotton] was succinct', it was nonetheless acceptable.[175] The Appellate Body also accepted the Panel's explanation of certain econometric modeling, even though 'the Panel could have gone further in its evaluation'.[176] Similarly, the Appellate Body approved certain conclusions that 'we understand the Panel's findings to *imply*', even though these conclusions were not the subject of any express explanation by the Panel.[177]

It may be that the Appellate Body considers that more explanation is required in connection with evidence that plays a more important role in a panel's determination. For example, in *US – Upland Cotton (Article 21.5 – Brazil)*, the Appellate Body found that the Panel's explanation of the evidence was deficient in circumstances where the evidence was 'critical' to the Panel's findings.[178] In practice, though, it will be rather difficult for panels to predict what pieces of evidence must be better explained on the grounds that the Appellate Body might subsequently consider that they support a 'plausible alternative' explanation.

Although encouraging comprehensive explanations by panels is certainly a good policy, the Appellate Body's approach raises other questions besides the scope of a panel's duty to explain pursuant to Article 11 DSU. First, as the Appellate Body has always said,[179] an investigating authority's duty to provide a 'reasoned and adequate explanation' derives from the specific text of the trade remedy agreements.

---

[174] Appellate Body Report, *US – Upland Cotton*, at paras 449, 450, and 445, citing Appellate Body Report, *Australia – Salmon*, at para 267.

[175] Appellate Body Report, *US – Cotton (Article 21.5 – Brazil)*, at para 381.

[176] Ibid at para 358.

[177] Appellate Body Report, *US – Upland Cotton (Article 21.5 – Brazil)*, at para 364 (emphasis added).

[178] Ibid at para 321.

[179] See, eg, Appellate Body Report, *US – Countervailing Duty Investigation on DRAMS*, at para 186.

For example, Article 12.2.1 Anti-Dumping Agreement requires 'sufficiently detailed explanations', including the reasons that interested parties' arguments were 'accepted or rejected'.[180] In contrast, no such textual basis exists in the DSU (or any other agreement) for applying this standard to panels.

The only provision that spells out a duty for panels to explain their decisions is Article 12.7 DSU, requiring panels to provide a 'basic rationale' for their findings. However, as the Appellate Body has said of Article 12.7:

> ... [It] 'establishes a *minimum standard* for the reasoning that panels must provide in support of their findings and recommendations', namely, that the explanations and reasons provided must suffice 'to disclose the essential, or fundamental, justification for those findings and recommendations'. Panels need not 'expound at length on the reasons for their findings and recommendations' in order to satisfy their obligations under Article 12.7.[181]

Interestingly, however, the Appellate Body in *US – Upland Cotton (Article 21.5 – Brazil)* offered no insights into the relationship between a panel's different duties to explain in Articles 11 and 12.7 DSU. It is, therefore, not clear whether Article 11 adds an additional duty to explain that is more demanding than the 'basic rationale' set forth in Article 12.7 and, if so, how the text of the covered agreements supports this interpretation, particularly in light of the distinction between the text of the trade remedy agreements and the text of Articles 11 and 12.7 DSU.

Second, panels and investigating authorities should arguably be subject to different standards of review because of their different institutional roles and fact-finding authority. Investigating authorities apply unilateral trade-restrictive measures that undermine a Member's negotiated market access commitments. A more demanding explanation, therefore, serves an important role because it obliges an investigating authority to justify the immediate use of this far-reaching power.

Further, investigating authorities have at their disposal wide-ranging fact-finding powers that are set forth in the WTO agreements, and that are backed by the authority of domestic legal enforcement. Also, even though investigating authorities have extensive fact-finding powers, they can, and do, make frequent use of 'facts available' to justify their decisions. In contrast, WTO panels have only rudimentary fact-gathering authority, very limited ability to sanction a WTO Member that fails to provide requested evidence, and they make very sparing use of 'facts available' against sovereign States to complete the factual picture.

The scope and significance of a panel's duty to explain under Article 11 DSU will no doubt be clarified further, as will its relation to a panel's duty to explain under Article 12.7 DSU.

---

[180] See generally Art 12.2 Anti-Dumping Agreement; Art 22.3 SCM Agreement; Art 3.1 Safeguards Agreement.

[181] Appellate Body Report, *Chile – Price Band System (Article 21.5 – Argentina)*, at para 243 (emphasis added); also Appellate Body Report, *Mexico – Corn Syrup (Article 21.5 – US)*, at paras 108–09.

D. The Appellate Body's Review of a Panel's Application of Law to the Facts

The nature of the Appellate Body's review of mixed issues of law and fact, that is, the application of law to the facts, is difficult to describe in the abstract. Indeed, as discussed at the end of this section, it is often difficult to pin down exactly when a panel is applying the law to the facts and when it is making a purely factual determination. The process of applying the law to the facts involves weighing and appreciating the facts, and then characterizing them, in terms of the relevant legal rules. Any given finding may be predominantly factual or predominantly legal, or somewhere in between, depending on the issue and the circumstances of the specific case.

The Appellate Body has clearly stated that mixed findings of law and fact are properly regarded as legal findings and therefore fall within the scope of appellate review.[182] At the same time, this should not be, and has not been, taken to suggest that the Appellate Body will conduct a de novo review of the factual components of such mixed findings of law and fact. To the contrary, as discussed below, a number of Appellate Body decisions reveal the Appellate Body's awareness that factual and legal issues are intertwined in findings involving the application of the law to the facts.

It appears fair to say that, like panels with respect to national authorities' decisions, the Appellate Body has adopted something of a sliding scale in reviewing the application of the law to the facts. The greater the factual component of a particular finding, and the more an appellant's challenge is focused on this factual component, the more deference the Appellate Body will show to a panel's analysis and the less likely it will reverse the finding. Conversely, where the Appellate Body perceives that a panel committed an error with respect to the legal aspect of a finding, it will grant less discretion or even no discretion at all, and will conduct a probing and critical review.

An example for the more deferential approach is the Appellate Body's finding in *Japan – Apples*, in which the Appellate Body was requested to reverse the Panel's finding that a Japanese SPS measure at issue was being maintained 'without sufficient scientific evidence', within the meaning of Article 2.2 SPS Agreement. The Appellate Body stated:

whether a given approach or methodology is appropriate in order to assess whether a measure is maintained 'without sufficient scientific evidence', within the meaning of Article 2.2, depends on the 'particular circumstances of the case', and must be 'determined on a case-by-case basis'. Thus, the approach followed by the Panel in this case—disassembling the sequence of events to identify the risk and comparing it with the measure—does not exhaust the range of methodologies available to determine whether a measure is maintained 'without sufficient scientific evidence' within the meaning of Article 2.2. *Approaches different from that followed by the Panel in this case could also prove appropriate to evaluate whether a measure is maintained without sufficient scientific evidence within the meaning of Article 2.2.* Whether or not a

---

[182] Appellate Body Report, *EC – Hormones*, at para 132.

particular approach is appropriate will depend on the 'particular circumstances of the case'. *The methodology adopted by the Panel was appropriate to the particular circumstances of the case before it and, therefore, we see no error in the Panel's reliance on it.*[183]

Japan's appeal pertained to the methodology adopted by the Panel to identify the health risk allegedly addressed by the Japanese measure. Although the Panel's finding was ultimately *legal* —namely, that the measure was being maintained without sufficient scientific evidence within the meaning of Article 2.2 SPS Agreement— Japan's appeal focused heavily, if not exclusively, on a factual aspect of the Panel's analysis. The Appellate Body's approach was, accordingly, a deferential one: the Appellate Body acknowledged that the Panel could have followed a different analytical approach in assessing the scientific evidence, but accepted that the Panel enjoyed a margin of discretion in its choice of the appropriate methodology.

Another example of a deferential approach is the appeal in *US – Softwood Lumber V*. In that case, Canada challenged the Panel's finding that the US had not acted inconsistently with Article 2.2.1.1 in assessing costs of production, and argued that, contrary to the Panel's finding, the national investigating authority had failed to exercise its discretion in an even-handed manner. Canada's argument was that the national authority had treated differently two investigated companies that were similarly situated.

The Appellate Body expressly characterized the overall Panel's finding challenged by Canada as a *legal* finding and therefore as falling within the Appellate Body's jurisdiction.[184] However, the Appellate Body then went on to find that the particular element of the Panel's finding challenged by Canada—namely, the Panel's findings on the allegedly inconsistent treatment of two investigated companies—was a question of *fact*.[185] Accordingly, the Appellate Body again adopted a deferential standard of review, stating that it saw no 'error that warrant[ed] disturbing the Panel's factual finding' and rejecting Canada's appeal.[186]

In contrast, *EC – Asbestos* provides an example of a panel's application of the law to the facts to which the Appellate Body adopted a rather non-deferential approach to a more predominantly legal question. In that dispute, the Appellate Body reversed the Panel's finding that certain types of fibres were 'like products'. Although the Panel had correctly articulated, in the abstract, the legal standard under Article III:4 and had identified the correct criteria for assessing 'likeness' of products, the Appellate Body found that the Panel had failed to apply this legal standard correctly to the facts before it. The Appellate Body found that:

the Panel disregarded the quite different 'properties, nature and quality' of chrysotile asbestos and PCG fibres, as well as the different tariff classification of these fibres; it *considered no*

---

[183] Appellate Body Report, *Japan – Apples*, at para 164 (emphasis added, fns omitted).
[184] Appellate Body Report, *US – Softwood Lumber V*, at para 163.
[185] Ibid at para 174.
[186] Ibid.

STANDARD OF REVIEW IN WTO LAW   431

evidence on consumers' tastes and habits; and it found that, for a 'small number' of the many applications of these fibres, they are substitutable, but it *did not consider the many other end-uses for the fibres that are different*. Thus, *the only evidence supporting the Panel's finding of 'likeness' is the 'small number' of shared end-uses of the fibres.*[187]

In contrast to the finding in *Japan – Apples* and *US – Softwood Lumber V*, the Appellate Body in *EC – Asbestos* focused on a predominantly *legal* aspect of the Panel's finding under Article III:4. The Appellate Body disagreed with its application of the relevant legal standard, granting no discretion to the Panel in this respect, and reversed the panel's finding.

The Appellate Body report in *US – Upland Cotton* illustrates well, as we noted at the outset of this section, that it is not always easy to decide whether a particular question involves a review of fact-finding or a review of the application of the law to the facts. This distinction is important because an appeal of fact-finding must be made under Article 11 DSU, whereas an appeal of the application of the law to the facts may be made under substantive provisions.[188] In *US – Upland Cotton*, the US argued that the Panel had erred under Article 6.3(c) SCM Agreement. In response to an objection by Brazil, the Appellate Body ruled that the appeal was properly brought under this substantive provision and was not an appeal against fact-finding that should have been brought under Article 11.[189] The Appellate Body said that the appreciation and weighing of the evidence under Article 11 is different from the application of the law to the facts.[190] One would also expect that a different standard of review applies to the two activities.

Although the Appellate Body accepted that the appeal involved a legal question regarding the application of the law to the facts, it—confusingly—resolved the appeal using reasoning that was explicitly drawn from its decisions under Article 11 regarding the appreciation and weighing of the facts. For example, the US challenged the Panel's assessment of how market prices influenced US producers' decision to plant cotton or other crops. After reviewing the evidence, the Appellate Body found that:

the Panel adopted a *plausible view of the facts* in connection with expected prices and planting decisions, even though it attributed to these factors a *different weight* or meaning than did the United States. As the Appellate Body has said, *it is not necessary for panels to 'accord to factual evidence of the parties the same meaning and weight as do the parties'*.[191]

The Appellate Body's reasoning is explicitly based on a review of the Panel's appreciation and weighing of the evidence. The Appellate Body's formulation is not only

---

[187] Appellate Body Report, *EC – Asbestos*, at para 125 (emphasis added).

[188] The Appellate Body has ruled that appeals made pursuant to Art 11 DSU must be identified as such in the notice of appeal. See Appellate Body Report, *Canada – Wheat Exports and Grain Imports*, at para 177; Appellate Body Report, *US – Offset Act (Byrd Amendment)*, at para 190.

[189] Appellate Body Report, *US – Upland Cotton*, at para 399.

[190] Ibid.

[191] Ibid at para 445 (emphasis added).

reminiscent of its rulings in appeals under Article 11 DSU, but it actually quotes directly from a decision in *Australia – Salmon* that was made pursuant to Article 11.

This ruling suggests that, in some cases, questions surrounding the application of the law to the facts may have such a heavy factual component that they are virtually indistinguishable from purely factual questions. In that event, as held in *US – Upland Cotton*, the Appellate Body's standard of review for a legal question is identical to its standard for review of a panel's fact-finding.

Hopefully, these cases remain very much the exception, and the Appellate Body will succeed in maintaining a relatively bright line between legal and factual questions that does not entirely collapse the different standards of review that apply to each. Maintaining this distinction is important to respect the different institutional roles that panels and the Appellate Body play within the WTO dispute settlement system.[192]

The recent *US – Upland Cotton (Article 21.5 – Brazil)* report suggests that the Appellate Body will, in fact, seek to draw a line between issues of pure fact and mixed issues of fact and law. In this appeal, the US again argued that the Panel had erred under Article 6.3(c) SCM Agreement, focusing extensively on the compliance Panel's weighing and appreciation of the evidence. Unlike the original proceedings, the Appellate Body stated that it would distinguish between those of the appellant's arguments that addressed the application of the law to the facts, and those that addressed the weighing and appreciation of the evidence.[193] With respect to issues of fact, the Appellate Body said it would consider them under Article 11 DSU, rather than under Article 6.3(c) SCM Agreement.[194] In other words, the Appellate Body indicated that issues of fact and mixed issues of fact and law can, and should be, distinguished, and subjected to different standards of review.

The Appellate Body recognized that 'the boundary between an issue that is purely factual and one that involves mixed issues of law and fact is often difficult to draw', and made an initial attempt to distinguish between them.[195] The US had appealed the methodology applied by the Panel to calculate US cotton producers' costs of production in order to assess whether US subsidies covered a gap between costs and revenues.[196] The Appellate Body ruled that this was 'not an issue of legal interpretation or application under Article 6.3(c) of the SCM Agreement'. It noted that examination of a revenue gap is 'not a legally required benchmark under Article 6.3(c)' and added that 'there is no legal consequence under Article 6.3(c) that necessarily flows' from the existence of a shortfall in revenues.[197] Thus, the Appellate Body concluded that a particular finding was factual in nature on the basis of the 'legal consequences' flowing (or not) from that finding.

---

[192] See also chapter 13 of this Handbook.
[193] Appellate Body Report, *US – Upland Cotton (Article 21.5 – Brazil)*, at para 385.
[194] Ibid.   [195] Ibid.
[196] Ibid. at para 424.   [197] Ibid.

It is a welcome development that the Appellate Body is seeking to distinguish between issues of fact and mixed issues of fact and law on the basis of objective criteria. However, the 'legal consequences' criterion relied on in this appeal may not always provide clear answers. The choice of a methodology or benchmark —including its detailed components[198]—often has an important interpretive element because a benchmark must be apt to meet the relevant legal standard. In other words, choices made regarding benchmarks and methodologies have an inherent legal quality and are intimately linked to interpretations of the relevant legal standard. The benchmark of a gap between revenues and costs under Article 6.3(c) is a good example. If one accepts the benchmark of a gap between revenues and costs as a legally valid methodology under Article 6.3(c), then methodological questions surrounding the costs elements that may or must be taken into account are linked to the interpretation of Article 6.3(c). Similar questions can arise, for instance, in selecting a benchmark under Article 1.1(b) SCM Agreement to identify a 'benefit'; under that provision, no particular benchmark is 'legally required' and yet the specific choice of a benchmark has 'legal consequences' and must be apt to identify a 'benefit' as that term is defined in the treaty text.

VI. Conclusion

Panels are always obliged to conduct an 'objective assessment of the matter' under Article 11 DSU, but there is no generally applicable approach to review for all WTO disputes. The phrase 'objective assessment' is essentially a non-descript label applied to a range of quite different analytical situations. It does not indicate the degree of deference, if any, to be accorded to any formal fact-finding at the national level nor does it shed light on the scope of a panel's factual and legal inquiry. Instead, it dictates that, whatever the specific nature and degree of review, a panel should approach its task in an 'objective' fashion. Thus, the term begs the question that it purportedly answers.

To identify the applicable standard of review in a particular WTO dispute, it is necessary to look beyond the phrase 'objective assessment'. If a panel is reviewing a purely legal issue, it conducts an original or *de novo* interpretation of WTO law, using the rules of interpretation of the VCLT. This task must, of course, be done 'objectively'. If Article 17.6(ii) Anti-Dumping Agreement applies, a panel must also

---

[198] For instance, in *US – Upland Cotton (Article 21.5 – Brazil)*, the US appealed issues such as whether 'opportunity costs' are properly included in determining whether there is a gap between producers' revenues and costs or whether variable costs should be used instead of total costs. Ibid at para 419.

determine whether an anti-dumping measure is based on a 'permissible' interpretation of the Anti-Dumping Agreement.

Where a panel addresses the establishment or evaluation of facts, the decisive factor in identifying the standard of review is the particular WTO agreement, and the specific provisions of that agreement, at issue. Under the trade remedy agreements, panels review measures resulting from a national investigation that is prescribed by those agreements. A panel provides a 'second-tier' review of the national measure that is constrained by the earlier 'first-tier' examination by the national authority, which has a privileged place in the process. The limitations on panels relate both to the degree of deference accorded to the national authority's establishment and evaluation of the facts, and also to the temporal scope of their factual inquiry.

At the other end of the spectrum are disputes where a panel reviews measures that did not result from any formal investigative process at the national level. A panel provides the 'first-tier' of review and its examination is original, open-ended, and contemporaneous. There is no formal fact-finding at the national level to which a panel can defer. Disputes under various provisions of the GATT 1994, including Articles III, XXVII, and XX, fall into this category.

There are also WTO agreements that do not fit neatly into either one of these two categories, such as the TBT and SPS Agreements. Under these agreements, there is no treaty-mandated investigation of the type required by the trade remedy agreements. Nonetheless, both agreements call for some evaluation—usually scientific—at national level, prior to the adoption of a measure. However, the WTO requirements of the national process are limited, with very few formal procedural requirements, and the agreements place fewer constraints on a panel's review. Unlike in trade remedy cases, panels can assess the ongoing justification for TBT and SPS measures on the basis of the latest information, without any need to await a new national process. The review is, therefore, more akin to review under the GATT 1994 in that it is both open-ended and contemporaneous, and typically original.

We have also seen that municipal law constitutes a particular category of fact in WTO dispute settlement that influences the standard of review. Municipal law is, from the perspective of WTO law, an issue of fact that is subject to an original, *de novo* review by a panel. Although panels have said that a degree of deference must be shown to the views of the defending WTO Member on the meaning of its own law, panels should conduct a critical analysis of the meaning of the municipal law, as they do with other forms of evidence advanced by the respondent.

Perhaps the most striking feature of the WTO rules on standard of review is that, beneath the overarching requirement for an 'objective assessment', there are several different approaches to the standard of review that apply in different treaty contexts. This suggests that panels and the Appellate Body have attempted to give practical effect to the divergent approaches set forth in the various WTO agreements regarding the role and prerogatives of Members vis-à-vis the WTO.

In essence, the different approaches to standard of review trace a different line with respect to those roles and prerogatives. It is clear, though, that there is a tension between granting discretion to Members and ensuring 'security and predictability' through the uniform application of WTO law. It is a tension between the interests of one Member in pursuing its own sovereignty and the collective interests of all WTO Members— including the one Member—in preserving the multilateral rules-based system.

For the long-term success of the system, both these interests are important. As the WTO dispute settlement system is still relatively new, and as the WTO agreements are being re-negotiated, it is likely that the rules on standard of review will evolve over time. It is also to be hoped that, over time, panels and the Appellate Body will, in general, continue to strike the 'right' balance between affording discretion to WTO Members and preserving the uniformity of WTO law.

Finally, the question of the appropriate standard of review arises also in the relationship between the Appellate Body and panels. The Appellate Body applies a standard of review to panel findings that, in some respects, is akin to the standard applied by panels in trade remedy disputes: on purely factual findings, the Appellate Body affords panels considerable discretion, whereas on mixed questions of law and fact, it applies a sliding scale in which the degree of discretion varies according to the factual content of the challenged finding. On purely legal issues, the Appellate Body applies a *de novo* standard. These standards of review also reflect the institutional balance between the two adjudicative tiers of the WTO dispute settlement system, as well as the jurisdictional limits and practical realities facing the Appellate Body.

SELECTED BIBLIOGRAPHY

J Bourgeois, 'GATT/WTO Dispute Settlement Practice in the Field of Anti-Dumping Law' in E-U Petersmann (ed), *International Trade Law and the GATT/WTO Dispute Settlement System* (The Hague: Kluwer, 1997)

SP Croley and JH Jackson, 'WTO Dispute Procedures, Standard of Review, and Deference to National Governments' 1996 *American Journal of International Law* 90 (2) 193

WJ Davey, 'The WTO /GATT World Trading System: An Overview' in P Pescatore, WJ Davey, and AF Lowenfeld (eds), *Handbook of WTO/GATT Dispute Settlement* (The Hague: Kluwer, 1995)

WJ Davey, 'Has the WTO Dispute Settlement System Exceeded its Authority? A Consideration of Deference Shown by the System to Member Government Decisions and its Uses of Issue-Avoidance Techniques' 2001 *Journal of International Economic Law* 4(1) 79

C-D Ehlermann and N Lockhart, 'Standard of Review in WTO Law' 2004 *Journal of International Economic Law* 7(3) 491

GAO, *World Trade Organization – Standard of Review and Impact of Trade Remedy Rulings, Report to the Ranking Minority Member, Committee on Finance, U.S. Senate* (July 2003)

GN Horlick and PA Clarke, 'Standards for Panels Reviewing Anti-dumping Determinations under the GATT and WTO' in E.-U. Petersmann (ed), *International Trade Law and the GATT/WTO Dispute Settlement System* (The Hague: Kluwer, 1997) 6

M Oesch, *Standards of Review in WTO Dispute Resolution* (Oxford: Oxford University Press, 2003)

P Van den Bossche, 'The WTO Appellate Body and Its Rise to Prominence' in G Sacerdoti, A Yanovich, and J Bohanes (eds), *The WTO at Ten. The Contribution of the Dispute Settlement System* (Cambridge: Cambridge University Press, 2006) 289

CHAPTER 15

REMEDIES AND COMPLIANCE

PIET EECKHOUT

I. INTRODUCTION

THE WTO dispute settlement system is a sophisticated and dedicated regime for resolving trade disputes between WTO Members. With the growth of WTO membership, it is inexorably moving towards a wholly universal regime. In its short life it has already produced thousands of pages of case law, in which many aspects of the WTO legal regime have been clarified, or at least analysed and debated, in a judicial style. Much of this Handbook is devoted to discussions of that case law. Indeed, the fact that an Oxford Handbook is produced in this area of law constitutes one of the clearest indications of at least academic recognition of the importance of WTO law. The case law is in large measure responsible for that.

This chapter looks at the settlement of WTO disputes as such; it looks inside the very engine of WTO law and investigates one of the most critical features of that engine. Does it actually work? Does the dispute settlement system contribute to better compliance with WTO law? The WTO Members clearly have certain rights under the WTO Agreement, but is there also an *effective* system of remedies and are remedies equally available to all WTO Members? Are dispute rulings properly implemented and complied with?

These questions can be studied from a number of different perspectives. This chapter does not record an empirical study of the WTO compliance record. The (limited) efforts undertaken in that direction confirm that rulings are generally respected and implemented.[1] In this respect, the WTO builds on the GATT tradition and *acquis*. GATT panel reports were remarkably successful in compliance terms, notwithstanding the near total lack of formal legal enforcement mechanisms ('retaliation' was used only once, early on). Explanations therefore had to be found outside the realm of positive law. There is indeed a burgeoning literature in political science and international relations theory on the reasons why regimes such as those of the GATT and the WTO display a successful compliance record.[2] This chapter, however, is focused on questions of positive law. In contrast with the GATT, the WTO takes a more formal, law-oriented direction, including at the level of implementation and compliance. Already at the surface, the WTO case law belies the diminutive description of a system of norms that 'is not to be read in clinical isolation from public international law'.[3] The case law is steeped in sophisticated legal analysis, and replete with references to all kinds of norms of public international law. It has thus been said that the Vienna Convention on the Law of Treaties (VCLT)

---

[1] See, eg, B Wilson, 'Compliance by WTO Members with Adverse Dispute Settlement Rulings: The Record to Date' 2007 *Journal of International Economic Law* 10(2) 397.

[2] For an overview of the literature, see N van den Broek, 'Power Paradoxes in Enforcement and Implementation of World Trade Organization Dispute Settlement Reports – Interdisciplinary Approaches and New Proposals' 2003 *Journal of World Trade* 37(1) 127.

[3] Appellate Body Report, *US – Gasoline*, at 16.

has become one of the 'covered agreements'. This constitutes a seismic shift from the GATT era, when the regime's norms were almost wholly self-referential.

This interaction with public international law as a whole is also at play at the level of implementation and compliance. Indeed, some of the thorniest theoretical questions to which this interaction gives rise gravitate around concepts concerned with implementation and compliance. International law terminology distinguishes between primary and secondary rules, the latter being understood as rules on the legal consequences of breach of the primary (substantive) rules. Since the *Tehran Hostages* decision of the ICJ, scholarly debate on whether particular treaty systems are self-contained focuses on the specific question of the 'completeness' of a system's secondary rules.[4] Thus, an analysis of the interaction between the WTO's secondary rules and the international law of state responsibility may illuminate the extent to which the WTO system is self-contained. Such an analysis may also help to clarify the legal nature and features of the remedies that WTO law offers, and locate them in the broader public international law setting.

A wide range of fundamental legal issues arises when scrutinizing WTO law on implementation and compliance. What precisely are the legal effects of WTO dispute settlement decisions? Are they 'binding'? If so, on whom, and what does binding mean? A WTO Member who has been found in breach must bring the relevant measure 'into conformity'. Is this legal instruction prospective, or can it equally be retrospective? Answers to these questions are necessarily coloured by conceptions of the basic functions of dispute settlement and the remedies it offers. What are these functions? Is the emphasis on inducing compliance, or on restoring the 'balance of concessions' (as it is called) between the disputants?

The specific remedies that WTO law offers in case of continued non-compliance—compensation and suspension of concessions (retaliation)—also require further scrutiny. What are their characteristics, and how are they applied? Are these remedies satisfactory, or is it necessary to reflect about alternatives?

These questions are essentially questions of international law, and the answers will be affected by the relationship between WTO law and general international law. However, the implementation of WTO dispute reports necessarily involves national (domestic, municipal) law as well. Where a WTO Member is found to be in breach, compliance measures will need to be adopted at a national level. What then is the relationship between WTO dispute settlement decisions and national law? Does WTO law itself have anything further to say about domestic implementation? Could it reach into national law?

This chapter attempts to explore these and other questions. As they are formulated here, they may seem abstract, divorced from the daily grind in the coalpit of trade disputes. The media language used to narrate such disputes, some of which seeps

---

[4] B Simma and D Pulkowski, 'Of Planets and the Universe: Self-contained Regimes in International Law' 2006 *European Journal of International Law* 17(3) 483, at 493–94.

into academic writing, is much more colourful. There is talk of fights, even wars (bananas!), winners and losers, retaliation, and shooting oneself in the foot. WTO disputes become stories of a modern day Wild West. Indeed an observer may easily conclude that the rule of law plays but a limited role in WTO dispute settlement, and that all depends on the politics of power. As this chapter attempts to show, however, there is definitely scope for a greater role for the law than is often considered.

II. State Responsibility and Self-Contained Legal Systems

The ILC's Articles on Responsibility of States for Internationally Wrongful Acts (ILC Articles) contain a number of principles and rules that are worth highlighting before looking any further at WTO implementation and compliance issues.[5] Every internationally wrongful act of a State entails the international responsibility of that State (Article 1). There is such an act when conduct is (a) attributable to the State under international law, and (b) constitutes a breach of an international obligation of the State (Article 2). Breaches of WTO law clearly come within those provisions (subject to what will be said below about contracting-out). The ILC Articles set out the legal consequences that such international responsibility entails (Article 28). First, those consequences do not affect the continued duty of the responsible State to perform the obligation breached (Article 29). Second, the State responsible for the internationally wrongful act is under an obligation to cease that act, if it is continuing, and to offer appropriate assurances and guarantees of non-repetition (duties of cessation and non-repetition, Article 30). Third, the responsible State is under an obligation to make full reparation for the injury caused (duty of reparation, Article 31). The ILC Articles provide for three forms of reparation: restitution, compensation, and satisfaction. They may be applied either singly or in combination (Article 34). Restitution amounts to re-establishing the situation which existed before the wrongful act was committed, provided that it is not materially impossible and does not involve a burden out of all proportion (Article 35). Compensation for the damage caused by the wrongful act is required insofar as such damage is not made good by restitution (Article 36). A further part of the ILC Articles addresses the implementation of State responsibility. One form of implementation is for the injured State to

---

[5] *Articles on Responsibility of States for Internationally Wrongful Acts*, adopted by the ILC at its 53rd Session, Official Record of the General Assembly, 56th Session, Supplement No. 10 (A/56/10). See also JR Crawford, *The International Law Commission's Articles on State Responsibility* (Cambridge: Cambridge University Press, 2002).

take countermeasures against the State responsible for an internationally wrongful act in order to induce that State to comply with the obligations listed above. Such countermeasures are limited to the non-performance for the time being of international obligations of the State taking the measures towards the responsible State. They shall, as far as possible, be taken in such a way as to permit the resumption of performance of the obligations in question (Article 49). Countermeasures must be commensurate with the injury suffered, taking into account the gravity of the internationally wrongful act and the rights in question (proportionality, Article 51). Finally, the ILC Articles do not apply where and to the extent that the conditions for the existence of an internationally wrongful act or the content or implementation of the international responsibility of a State are governed by special rules of international law (*lex specialis*, Article 55).

The latter provision doubtless applies to the case of the WTO.[6] Article 23(1) Dispute Settlement Understanding (DSU) provides that Members seeking redress of a violation shall have recourse to, and abide by, the DSU rules and procedures. The WTO appears to have set up a complete system of remedies, with panels and the Appellate Body hearing and deciding cases; and with the Dispute Settlement Body (DSB) confirming their reports, as well as monitoring the implementation of rulings. In case of continued non-compliance, it is possible for the winning party to employ the remedies of compensation or suspension of concessions. As adumbrated above, since *Tehran Hostages* a 'self-contained regime' designates a particular international legal subsystem that embraces a full, exhaustive, and definitive set of secondary rules. The principal characteristic of such a regime is its intention to totally exclude the application of the general legal consequences of wrongful acts as codified by the ILC, and in particular countermeasures.[7] Simma and Pulkowski argue that the WTO is such a regime; that it has declared its independence. Suspension of concessions, in particular, is said to be equivalent to countermeasures. In their view the object and purpose of the DSU do not permit a state to have parallel recourse to claims for compensation or countermeasures under the general law of state responsibility.[8]

This may well be the case. It is in any event clear from the case law (*US – Section 301 Trade Act*) that a WTO Member cannot resort to unilaterally adopted countermeasures as a response to an alleged breach by another Member.[9] However, this narrow construction of the concept of a self-contained regime does not amount to a total exclusion of the general law on state responsibility. The *lex specialis* principle of Article 55 ILC Articles seems purely functional: the Articles do not apply *where and to the extent* that there are special rules. The WTO legal texts, rich as they may

---

[6] Simma and Pulkowski, above fn 4, at 520, with reference to the ILC Commentaries.

[7] Ibid at 492–93.

[8] Ibid at 523; see also PJ Kuyper, 'The Law of GATT as a Special Field of International Law' 1994 *Netherlands Yearbook of International Law* (XXV) 227, at 252.

[9] Panel Report, *US – Sections 301 Trade Act*, at paras 7.38–39.

be, do not cover all aspects of international responsibility, and the gaps can easily be filled with the ILC Articles. For example, there is an internationally wrongful act when conduct is attributable to the State and constitutes a breach of an international obligation. On the question of breach, WTO law itself is of course determinative. But as regards attribution of conduct the legal texts offer very little guidance. The case law implicitly recognizes this and has endorsed the attribution rules of the ILC Articles.[10] There are surely many other aspects of the ILC Articles that could be relevant in a WTO dispute. Panels and the Appellate Body constantly refer to wider international law rules and principles to fill the gaps in the WTO legal system. Its self-contained character is therefore rightly recognized as being limited, also at the level of remedies.

A further question then arises concerning the interplay between the ILC Articles and WTO law on remedies. Could the law on state responsibility also guide the *interpretation* of the remedies (legal consequences of breach) for which WTO law *does* provide? That is an important question, which is further explored in other sections of this chapter.[11] Briefly, here, the DSU is very short in its definition of the consequences of breach: panels and the Appellate Body 'recommend that the Member concerned bring the measure into conformity' (Article 19(1)). Little else is stated, and the precise meaning of 'bringing into conformity' is unclear and contested. In the language of the ILC Articles, the losing party appears at least subject to the duty of cessation. But does Article 19(1) also encompass elements of reparation, such as restitution: an obligation to re-establish the situation as it existed before the wrongful act was committed? There is at least scope for the argument that 'bringing into conformity' may include a restitution element.

III. Binding or Non-Binding?

WTO panels and the Appellate Body routinely establish in their reports that certain measures of a WTO Member are inconsistent with certain WTO obligations. They then recommend, pursuant to Article 19(1) DSU, that the Member concerned bring the measures into conformity with its obligations. The reports are adopted by the DSB, a WTO organ representing the membership, as a matter of course. Members routinely treat that process as establishing an obligation to follow the

---

[10] For an overview, see SM Villalpando, 'Attribution of Conduct to the State: How the Rules of State Responsibility May Be Applied Within the WTO Dispute Settlement System' 2002 *Journal of International Economic Law* 5(2) 393.

[11] See sections V and VI of this chapter.

recommendation and to comply. And yet there is a debate whether DSB reports give rise to an obligation to comply; whether, in other words, they are 'binding'.[12] For an external observer this must be puzzling indeed. What would be the use of having such an elaborate dispute settlement process, if the rulings do not need to be respected; another Wild West story?

A closer look at the system reveals that there is some basis for the debate. There are two sources of confusion. The first is the language and terminology used in the DSU. The text carefully avoids employing judicial-type terms and concepts.[13] There are no courts or judges, merely 'panels' and an 'Appellate Body'. They do not issue judgments or rulings, but 'reports'. The conclusion in those reports is a 'recommendation' to bring the measure into conformity. Compensation or suspension of concessions are temporary measures, but neither is 'preferred' to full implementation. The impression conveyed is one of a system in which dispute rulings are fundamentally ambivalent, leaving room for manoeuvre and, ultimately, non-compliance.[14]

The second source of confusion revolves around the remedy of suspension of concessions. If a Member perseveres in not complying, the complaining Member may re-establish the balance between them by suspending other concessions, at a level equivalent to the 'nullification and impairment', in other words the trade and economic damage caused by the breach. No further remedies are available in case of continued non-compliance. In practice, therefore, the Member concerned appears to have the option to buy itself out of its obligations.

From a broader international law perspective, however, there seems little doubt that DSB reports are 'binding'. One should first of all bear in mind that the fundamental purpose of any system of secondary rules is to enforce the primary, substantive rules. Such systems serve to strengthen the most fundamental principle of treaty law, *pacta sunt servanda*. As Simma and Pulkowski observe, the fact that States decide to go through the cumbersome process of multilateral treaty-making suggests that the rules elaborated in this process are of particular importance. In their view, even though, hypothetically, States are free to negotiate special norms of international law with a view to softening their obligations, we should not presume lightly that States would be less willing to live up to special obligations than to duties under general international law. They rightly argue that, absent a clear indication,

---

[12] See in particular the debate between JH Bello, 'The WTO Dispute Settlement Understanding: Less is More' 1996 *American Journal of International Law* 90(3) 416–18 and JH Jackson, 'International Law Status of WTO Dispute Settlement Reports: Obligation to Comply or Option to "Buy Out"?' 2004 *American Journal of International Law* 98(1) 109.

[13] JHH Weiler, 'The Rule of Lawyers and the Ethos of Diplomats: Reflections on the Internal and External Legitimacy of WTO Dispute Settlement', *Jean Monnet Working Paper* 9/00, at <http://www.jeanmonnetprogram.org/papers/00/000901.html> (last visited 18 April 2008).

[14] Griller argues that the European Court of Justice in its case law on the lack of direct effect of WTO law is a victim of that impression, see S Griller, 'Judicial Enforceability of WTO Law in the European Union' 2000 *Journal of International Economic Law* 3(3) 441.

special rules must be deemed to embody a particular commitment.[15] The fact that the WTO Members decided to set up a dispute settlement system with automatic, compulsory jurisdiction indicates the importance attached to their compliance with WTO obligations. It is a system that is in many ways much stronger than most other dispute settlement systems established by multilateral agreements.

The ILC Articles on State responsibility further show that a breach of treaty norms produces a range of legal consequences, and brings different remedies into the picture. The DSU does something very similar. It is important to distinguish between what triggers responsibility and dispute settlement in the first place—breach of a primary obligation—and the various legal consequences of such a breach. The ILC Articles confirm that the legal consequences of an internationally wrongful act do not affect the continued duty of the responsible State to perform the obligation breached (Article 29). One would likewise assume that the legal consequences of a breach of WTO law do not affect the continued duty of the WTO Member concerned to perform the relevant WTO obligation. It would be very strange indeed if one of the consequences of going to WTO dispute settlement would be that the respondent party would be under some kind of lesser, weaker obligation to comply with WTO law than prior to this legal process. Clearly, that cannot be the case.

A textual analysis of the DSU also leads to the conclusion that there is an international law obligation to comply with panel and Appellate Body reports, as Jackson has convincingly shown.[16] The reader may be referred to that analysis.

However, most significant, in this author's view, is the consistent practice of the Members, together with the case law that has developed as part of that practice. Pursuant to Article 21.5 DSU, disagreements 'as to the existence or consistency with a covered agreement of measures taken to comply with the recommendations and rulings ... shall be decided through recourse to these dispute settlement procedures, including wherever possible resort to the original panel'. Such a compliance panel will look at the measures adopted to comply with an earlier ruling. A substantial number of WTO Members have used this opportunity. A mere cursory examination of panel reports adopted in such compliance cases shows that, routinely, (a) complainants claim that the defending party has failed to comply with the rulings and recommendations of the DSB, and (b) panels confirm or deny such claims, depending on the outcome of their substantive examination. Compliance panels may be appealed. The Appellate Body has not as yet squarely been asked whether rulings and recommendations of the DSB are 'binding'; WTO Members simply accept that they are bound to comply. Nevertheless, the Appellate Body has been faced with several tangential issues and arguments, and its response to those arguments is straightforward and telling. In *EC – Bed Linen*, for example, the issue was whether it was possible, in a compliance case, to re-examine an unappealed finding by the

---

[15] Simma and Pulkowski, above fn 4, at 507.
[16] Jackson, above fn 12.

original panel; a finding, therefore, adopted by the DSB. The Appellate Body's reply is worth quoting in full:

in our view, an *unappealed* finding included in a panel report that is *adopted* by the DSB must be treated as a *final resolution* to a dispute between the parties in respect of the *particular* claim and the *specific* component of a measure that is the subject of that claim. This conclusion is supported by Articles 16.4 and 19.1, paragraphs 1 and 3 of Article 21, and Article 22.1 of the DSU. Where a panel concludes that a measure is inconsistent with a covered agreement, that panel shall *recommend*, according to Article 19.1, that the Member concerned bring that measure into conformity with that agreement. A panel report, including the *recommendations* contained therein, shall be *adopted* by the DSB within the time period specified in Article 16.4—unless appealed. Members are to *comply* with recommendations and rulings *adopted* by the DSB promptly, or within a reasonable period of time, in accordance with paragraphs 1 and 3 of Article 21 of the DSU. A Member that does not comply with the recommendations and rulings adopted by the DSB within these time periods must face the consequences set out in Article 22.1, relating to compensation and suspension of concessions. Thus, a reading of Articles 16.4 and 19.1, paragraphs 1 and 3 of Article 21, and Article 22.1, taken together, makes it abundantly clear that a panel finding which is not appealed, and which is included in a panel report *adopted* by the DSB, must be accepted by the parties as a *final* resolution to the dispute between them, in the same way and with the same finality as a finding included in an Appellate Body Report adopted by the DSB—with respect to the particular claim and the specific component of the measure that is the subject of the claim. Indeed, the European Communities and India agreed at the oral hearing that both panel reports and Appellate Body Reports would have the same effect, in this respect, once adopted by the DSB.[17]

Even more straightforward is the position of the arbitrator in *EC – Chicken Cuts*. The arbitration award concerned the reasonable period of time for implementing the ruling in that case, which concerned the customs classification of chicken cuts. The EC argued that, in order to comply, it first needed to obtain a new decision by the World Customs Organization on the classification issue. The arbitrator was concerned that this could mean that implementation would become conditional on such a decision. In response, he stated:

It is axiomatic that alleged violations of the covered agreements must be redressed exclusively through the procedures set out in the DSU, providing for examination of such allegations by a panel and possibly the Appellate Body, and that, if violations are found and the relevant reports are adopted by the DSB, the respondent Member is obliged to implement promptly the recommendations and rulings of the DSB. These recommendations and rulings are *binding* on implementing Members, and give rise to an *obligation* to bring their WTO-inconsistent measures into conformity with their obligations under the covered agreements.[18]

The conclusions to be drawn from the above analysis are obvious. Adopted panel and Appellate Body reports thus create a clear, unconditional obligation to comply

---

[17] Appellate Body Report, *EC – Bed Linen (Article 21.5 – India)*, at paras 92–93 (original emphasis).
[18] Award of the Arbitrator, *EC – Chicken Cuts*, at para 55 (emphasis added). The arbitrator was James Bacchus, former member and Chairman of the Appellate Body.

with the recommendations they contain (namely, for the responding party to bring its measures into conformity) within a reasonable period of time. If correct implementation is lacking, it is possible to agree on compensation, or to suspend concessions. These remedies, however, are not an alternative to compliance. Rather, they seek to induce compliance.[19] The fact that these remedies exist should not be seen as in any way diminishing the obligation to comply, but as enhancing it. They show the importance that WTO Members attach to an effective and efficient system of dispute settlement. The WTO is not a Wild West.

IV. THE BASIC FUNCTION OF DISPUTE SETTLEMENT

In the light of the discussion in the preceding section, what is the basic, primary function of WTO dispute settlement and the remedies it offers? If DSB reports are binding on Members in the way described above, the fundamental purpose of the system appears to be to induce compliance. That is indeed how the system is described in WTO rulings.[20]

There exist, however, competing theories. Palmeter and Alexandrov challenge the proposition that suspension of concessions is intended to induce compliance. In their view, such suspension amounts to a mere re-balancing of reciprocal obligations. They are concerned that the emphasis on inducing compliance may lead to suspension of concessions being used as a punitive instrument. They advance various policy arguments against punitive measures, including concerns over sovereignty and equity.[21] They are further worried that there is too much emphasis on *pacta sunt servanda*: that the system cannot sustain this, and that it is not what Members signed up to.

Such concepts, focusing on the re-balancing character of suspension of concessions, rather than on an obligation to comply, are widely defended. Perhaps the strongest theoretical argument in support of such an approach is the one developed by Schwartz and Sykes, which is based on the economic theory of contracts.[22] That

---

[19] See also section IV of this chapter.

[20] See D Palmeter and SA Alexandrov, 'Inducing Compliance in WTO Dispute Settlement' in DLM Kennedy and JD Southwick (eds), *The Political Economy of International Trade Law: Essays in Honor of Robert E Hudec* (Cambridge: Cambridge University Press, 2002) 646.

[21] Ibid at 660–62.

[22] WF Schwartz and AO Sykes, 'The Economic Structure of Renegotiation and Dispute Resolution in the World Trade Organization' 2002 *Journal of Legal Studies* 31(1–part 2) 179.

theory distinguishes between efficient and inefficient breaches of contractual obligations. A breach is efficient if the economic gains for the party committing the breach are greater than the losses for the party to whom the obligation is owed. Schwartz and Sykes apply this theory to the WTO. The gains and losses that they focus on are those of the domestic political actors who decide to conclude trade agreements. They thus take a public choice perspective. If a breach of WTO law amounts to greater political gain for relevant political actors in the country committing the breach, compared to the political losses in the affected WTO Members, the breach is efficient. The Member in breach is unlikely to prefer compliance, nor would such compliance be economically efficient. Suspension of concessions is therefore an efficient tool, which permits efficient breaches.

Attractive and theoretically astute though it may seem at first blush, this extension of the theory of efficient breach to WTO dispute settlement is ultimately unconvincing.[23] It advocates a peculiar type of economic efficiency that is not the 'real' economic efficiency resulting from free trade in world markets. Rather, it is a concept of efficiency applied to political actors, a calculus of the respective political capital of decision-makers in various WTO Members. The usefulness of public choice theory for understanding some of the reasons why countries conclude trade agreements cannot be denied. It does not follow however that public choice should also become a normative standard. It may well be possible to *explain* the conclusion of trade agreements by means of economic concepts applied to the political process, but that does not mean that the agreements thus concluded *ought* to be *interpreted* using the same efficiency arguments. The economic efficiency which the WTO seeks to promote is that of free trade and free markets, not that of political actors. From that perspective, suspension of concessions (or retaliation) as a reaction to a breach of WTO law is of course recognized as being wholly inefficient. The trade restrictions operated by the Member in breach of its obligations are aggravated by further restrictions in the complaining country. Indeed, most economists comment that retaliation makes no economic sense, and that the Member imposing trade sanctions 'shoots itself in the foot' and damages its own economy. In fact, if one accepts standard economic theories on the benefits of free trade, it is difficult to see what role there could be for the theory of efficient breach. The default position is that trade restrictions are not economically efficient for the Member imposing them. How then could the economic gains in the Member restricting trade surpass the losses in the country of exportation?

It becomes increasingly necessary to focus on companies and markets, and not trade between countries. Trade between countries is a conceptual construct, a construct that is quickly losing its explanatory force. As eloquently discussed in *US – Section 301 Trade Act*, trade takes place between private operators.[24] From the perspective

---

[23] See also Jackson, above fn 12.

[24] Panel Report, *US – Section 301 Trade Act*, at paras 7.76–77.

of those operators, economic efficiency is not just enhanced by the absence of trade restrictions. It is further enhanced by what the DSU calls, with great accuracy and insight, the security and predictability of the multilateral trading system. Article 3.2 DSU recognizes that the dispute settlement system of the WTO is a central element in providing such security and predictability. Suspension of concessions is, in itself, wholly antithetical to such security and predictability, as the practice shows: exports of French mustard to the US are restricted in retaliation for the EU's refusal to admit beef treated with hormones. What is the connection, and how could one argue that this is predictable and enhances the security of trade? Suspension of concessions can therefore only be understood and defended in the broader framework of the dispute settlement system, as a remedy that serves to induce compliance. If the WTO agreements make economic sense, which should be assumed and should guide their interpretation, the basic function of dispute settlement must be inducing compliance.

Of course, re-balancing of concessions as an ultimate instrument in certain cases of non-compliance is not excluded. A provision of WTO law that has been violated can be amended, and WTO Schedules can be modified.[25]

V. 'BRING INTO CONFORMITY' – PROSPECTIVE OR RETROSPECTIVE?

Panel and Appellate Body reports, duly adopted by the DSB, are binding on the Member found to be in breach. There is an obligation to comply with the relevant rulings, and the basic function of the dispute settlement system and of the remedies it offers is to induce compliance. But what does 'compliance' precisely mean?

Article 19.1 DSU provides:

Where a panel or the Appellate Body concludes that a measure is inconsistent with a covered agreement, it shall recommend that the Member concerned bring the measure into conformity with that agreement. In addition to its recommendations, the panel or Appellate Body may suggest ways in which the Member concerned could implement the recommendation.

Panels and the Appellate Body duly make these recommendations to establish conformity. Exceptionally, by contrast, they apply the second sentence by making more specific suggestions on implementation.[26] There is thus very little case law on what

---

[25] As was the US response in *US – Gambling*; see DSB, *Minutes of Meeting Held on 22 May 2007*, WT/DSB/M/232 (25 June 2007), at 9 ff.

[26] For an account, see PC Mavroidis, 'Remedies in the WTO Legal System: Between a Rock and a Hard Place' 2000 *European Journal of International Law* 11(4) 763, at 784–88.

'bringing into conformity' may mean. Nevertheless, it is something of a WTO mantra to assume that these recommendations are to be purely prospective, *ex nunc*, and do not concern themselves with past consequences of the breach of WTO law.[27] WTO dispute settlement is pragmatic, so the reasoning goes. The basic function of dispute settlement is to induce compliance, to bring the sinner back to orthodoxy, not to repair past wrongs. This is claimed to continue the pre-WTO GATT practice. It must be noted though, that in the field of anti-dumping and countervailing duties there were GATT panel reports recommending repayment of the duties that had been levied in breach of the relevant GATT provisions.[28] This was obviously a retrospective remedy.

The DSU does not merely describe compliance in terms of a recommendation to 'bring the measure into conformity'. Article 3.7 DSU speaks of 'the first objective of the dispute settlement mechanism' usually being 'the withdrawal of the measures concerned if these are found to be inconsistent with the provisions of any of the covered agreements'. The term withdrawal is twice repeated in the same provision. That same term is used in Article 4.7 SCM Agreement, a provision that can be considered *lex specialis* as regards remedies:

If the measure in question is found to be a prohibited subsidy, the panel shall recommend that the subsidizing Member withdraw the subsidy without delay....

A particular interpretation of this provision was developed by the compliance panel in *Australia – Leather II (Article 21.5 – US)*.[29] The Panel squarely opted for reading the term 'withdraw' as encompassing repayment of an illegal subsidy. It accepted that Article 19.1 DSU is generally understood to require a Member to 'withdraw the measure' in a prospective sense.[30] However, Article 19.1 DSU, even in conjunction with Article 3.7 DSU, did not require the limitation of the specific remedy in Article 4.7 SCM Agreement to purely prospective action—Article 4.7 would otherwise become indistinguishable from the general DSU provisions.[31] The Panel considered that repayment was consistent with the object and purpose of the SCM Agreement. Furthermore, a different reading 'would give rise to serious questions regarding the efficacy of the remedy in prohibited subsidy cases involving one-time subsidies paid in the past'.[32] It may be noted that similar issues may arise in the context of other agreements. A safeguard measure contrary to WTO law may well be withdrawn as a result of dispute settlement, but may by then have served its purpose of temporary protection. Other examples are not difficult to find, indeed one of the recurring critiques of WTO dispute settlement is that its operation is too slow for private parties affected by trade barriers, notwithstanding the strict time limits for panels and the Appellate Body.

This report was not appealed (because Australia had previously relinquished its right to appeal), but was nevertheless heavily criticized in the DSB meeting in which

---

[27] Ibid at 789–90.   [28] Ibid at 775–76.
[29] Panel Report, *Australia – Automotive Leather II (Article 21.5 – US)*, at paras 6.18–6.49.
[30] Ibid at para 6.30.   [31] Ibid at para 6.31.
[32] Ibid at para 6.35.

it was scheduled for adoption. Several Members insisted that WTO remedies can only be prospective, and do not encompass repayment of the type advocated by the Panel.[33] The reverse consensus rule regarding the adoption of panel reports nevertheless produced its usual effects, showing the automaticity of dispute settlement, even in the case of 'adventurous' rulings.

The report in *Australia – Leather II (Article 21.5 – US)* had the virtue of opening a debate on the mantra of prospective remedies. It is submitted that the terms prospective/retrospective, or *ex nunc/ex tunc* are deceptive and do not withstand deeper analysis. Even the law cannot travel back in time. Retrospective remedies are a fiction in the sense that they aim to restore the legal position to what it was before the breach was committed. The act of restoration however necessarily takes place in the present or future, not in the past. The DSU language instructing the losing Member to 'bring the measure into conformity', or to 'withdraw' that measure, does not in itself exclude retroactive effects in the sense of attempts to restore the legal position to what it was before the breach. In the language of the ILC Articles on State Responsibility such attempts amount to restitution, one of the three forms of reparation. Article 35 ILC Articles expresses the limitations of restitution well: a State is under an obligation to make restitution, that is, to re-establish the situation that existed before the wrongful act was committed, provided and to the extent that restitution is not materially impossible, and does not involve a burden out of all proportion to the benefit deriving from restitution instead of compensation. The provision recognizes that time-travel is impossible and adds a sensible rule that the legal simulation of time-travel is not required to take unreasonable proportions.

The *Australia – Leather II (Article 21.5 – US)* case nicely illustrates the limitations of 'retroactive' remedies. The prohibition of export subsidies serves to avoid trade distortions due to such subsidies. The Panel's instruction that Australia seek repayment of the illegal subsidies does not wholly restore the legal position to what it was before the subsidy was granted: the companies concerned have for some time been able to export, benefiting from the subsidies, and thereby distorting trade. The injury to competing producers is not wholly removed by withdrawing the subsidy. On the other hand, the 'retroactive' remedy of repayment is clearly more effective than a mere 'prospective' one. In the case of a one-time subsidy, an interpretation of 'bringing into conformity' that does not encompass any repayment whatsoever will mean that the dispute ruling is merely declaratory. It does not even appear to include a duty of non-repetition (Article 30 ILC Articles). In such cases, a purely prospective remedy is clearly wholly ineffective.

The case of one-time subsidies further illustrates that an exclusion of all retroactive effects would create grave imbalances in the remedies that WTO law offers. Compare *Australia – Leather II (Article 21.5 – US)* with, for example, *US – FSC*. If no repayment had been ordered in the former case, Australia would effectively have had

---

[33] DSB, *Minutes of Meeting*, WT/DSB/M/75 (7 March 2000).

to do nothing to implement the WTO ruling. In the *US-FSC* case, by contrast, the US has had to rescind its entire company tax regime to secure compliance. It is doubtful that such inequality in remedies is a defensible interpretation of the DSU provisions on implementation and compliance.

The Panel in *Australia – Leather II (Article 21.5 – US)* advocated an intermediate solution to the problem of restoring past wrongs by limiting its interpretation to Article 4.7 SCM Agreement, thereby accepting that the general DSU provisions are merely prospective. Its construction of the relationship between the SCM Agreement and the DSU is not wholly persuasive. Both Articles 4.7 SCM Agreement and 3.7 DSU use the term withdrawal. Article 4.7 SCM Agreement could be interpreted as *lex specialis* as regards the time element: a panel shall recommend withdrawal 'without delay', and it 'shall specify in its recommendation the time period within which the measure must be withdrawn'. There is, however, no obvious need for a different interpretation of the term 'withdrawal' itself.

There are other types of breaches of WTO law that would merit considering forms of repayment as an appropriate remedy. Wherever a government imposes illegal taxes—be they customs duties, anti-dumping duties, or even general taxes— there is an argument for requiring the repayment of those taxes. It may be noted that, in contrast with *Australia – Leather II (Article 21.5 – US)*, such repayment does not interfere with private rights, since it would be the government that would be required to repay, not private companies. It may further be noted that in EU law such 'retroactive' remedies are self-evident. Companies that have received illegal state aid (subsidies) are required to repay them. Companies or individuals who have paid taxes or charges contrary to EU law can obtain full restitution from the national authorities concerned. This may go back many years, and the only exception is that the European Court of Justice may consider that the correct interpretation of EU law was not obvious. It may therefore decide that, in view of the dimensions of the financial or other consequences, the correct interpretation and application of the EU law norm applies for the future only.[34] The differences between the EU and the WTO are obvious, and it is not clear that the WTO at its current stage could sustain a complete system of remedies like in the EU. However, if WTO dispute settlement is to be successful and effective, the remedies must also be to some degree effective, and they must be balanced across all areas of WTO law. The DSU language of 'bringing into conformity' and 'withdrawal' leaves a lot of discretion. That seems appropriate at the current stage of WTO law. This discretion must be sensibly employed, but it is doubtful whether the mantra of purely prospective remedies is apposite in all cases. Also in this regard the ILC Articles on State Responsibility may be a useful point of reference. The remedy of restitution, in particular, may be a source of inspiration.

---

[34] See eg, ECJ, Case C-209/03, *Bidar*, [2005] ECR I-2199, at paras 64–71.

VI. REMEDIES IN CASE OF CONTINUED NON-COMPLIANCE

As is well known, Article 22.2 DSU outlines two remedies in case of non-compliance with a dispute settlement ruling at the end of the reasonable period of time for implementation: compensation and suspension of concessions. These remedies are usually presented as alternatives, but it must be noted that Article 22.2 sequences them. The preference is for mutually acceptable compensation, and it is only where no such compensation can be agreed that the party having invoked the dispute settlement procedures may request authorization to suspend concessions. In practice, cases of agreed compensation are very rare.[35] Where compliance is not forthcoming, the aggrieved Member is left with the choice of either suspending concessions, with all the problems that entails,[36] or leaving the case on the agenda of the DSB and exercising further diplomatic pressure.

As discussed earlier, the objective of suspension of concessions is to induce compliance with the dispute settlement ruling, and with the primary WTO obligations. Such suspension is therefore a form of countermeasure, in the meaning of the ILC Articles.[37] It involves 'the non-performance for the time being of international obligations of the State taking the measures towards the responsible State' (Art 49(2) ILC Articles). The DSU tightly regulates suspension of concessions in Articles 22.3 to 22.8. The conditions and procedures imposed by those provisions can also be read in the light of the ILC Articles. Article 22.4, for example, requires that the level of the suspension of concessions or other obligations authorized by the DSB be equivalent to the level of nullification or impairment. This should be interpreted in accordance with Article 51 ILC Articles on the proportionality of countermeasures: they 'must be commensurate with the injury suffered, taking into account the gravity of the internationally wrongful act and the rights in question'.

The inadequacies and deficiencies of suspension of concessions have been extensively analysed and debated.[38] The Member employing trade sanctions shoots itself in the foot when it responds to trade barriers by imposing restrictions of its own, and free trade is simply further limited. As Pauwelyn put it, such sanctions

---

[35] An instance is the *US – Section 110(5) Copyright Act* dispute, see B O'Connor and M Djordjevic, 'Practical Aspects of Monetary Compensation' 2005 *Journal of International Economic Law* 8(1) 127.

[36] See further below.

[37] Simma and Pulkowski, above fn 4, at 521; J Pauwelyn, 'Enforcement and Countermeasures in the WTO: Rules are Rules – Toward a More Collective Approach' 2000 *American Journal of International Law* 94(2) 335.

[38] See in particular M Bronckers and N van den Broek, 'Financial Compensation in the WTO – Improving the Remedies of WTO Dispute Settlement' 2005 *Journal of International Economic Law* 8(1) 101, at 104–06.

are the epitome of mercantilism.[39] Another defect is that the sanctions remedy is in practice not equally available to all WTO Members. Developing countries with smaller markets cannot wield those sanctions in an effective way.[40] Furthermore, the *EC – Hormones* litigation has revealed the difficulties associated with identifying at which point in time the suspension of concessions needs to be terminated. The DSU does not, as it stands, provide for a procedure for this.[41]

There is in any event a question mark over the effectiveness of these WTO countermeasures. The pre-WTO GATT virtually never employed them and nevertheless appeared to have a compliance record comparable to that of the WTO. The essential problem may well consist in the fact that the victims of sanctions and the perpetrators of breaches of WTO law are not the same. It is not the Member of the WTO (State or regional organization) committing the breach that is penalized as such. The victims are companies exporting from that Member. The effectiveness of the countermeasures therefore depends on the extent to which those companies are able to exercise pressure on their government to comply. In this sphere we again see the dichotomy between governments and market operators.

The only real defence for suspension of concessions is the basic rationale of dispute settlement: to induce compliance. In the light of its downsides, however, it is unsurprising that there is extensive debate about possible alternatives. Most of that debate concentrates on developing forms of compensation.[42]

This chapter does not attempt to offer a full analysis of proposals to improve implementation. One critical issue is nevertheless worth highlighting. When considering systems of compensation a strict distinction is needed between forms of compensation that focus on the WTO Member found in breach, and those that focus on the traders affected by the illegal measures in issue. It would be relatively straightforward to introduce new DSU provisions imposing an obligation on the Member that was found in breach to offer compensation in other trade sectors. What is currently a voluntary remedy could be turned into a compulsory one. A number of questions would of course arise concerning the calculation of such compensation; whether it may be discriminatory; whether it is time-limited or permanent; etc. Leaving those questions aside, it must be noted that such a remedy would not be primarily aimed at inducing ultimate compliance. The WTO Member concerned could in fact conceive of such compensation as a method for buying itself out of the obligation that triggered dispute settlement. Such a remedy would fit with the theory of efficient breach, discussed earlier. It would not fit so well with the rationale of inducing compliance. Nor would it fit with the overall aim of dispute settlement to strengthen the security and predictability of the world trading system. Companies and consumers benefiting from the enhanced market access that constitutes compensation will be

---

[39] Pauwelyn, above fn 37, at 343.
[40] See also chapter 17 of this Handbook.
[41] See Panel Report, *US – Continued Suspension*.
[42] But see also Pauwelyn's proposal for collective enforcement, above fn 37.

different from those suffering from the illegal trade restriction. In fact the introduction of such a remedy may increase insecurity to the extent that WTO Members would endorse and seek to employ the theory of efficient breach. Members may well be tempted to start looking at WTO dispute settlement merely as a mechanism for re-balancing concessions. The negative effects of an established breach of WTO law would simply consist of an obligation to further liberalize, in a trade sector that is less politically sensitive.

By contrast, systems of compensation that focus on affected traders would be more orthodox in the light of some of the basic principles that this chapter has aimed to identify. Such systems would come closer to the concept of reparation in the ILC Articles: it is the actual damage caused by the WTO-illegal measure that is compensated. Security and predictability of the multilateral trading system would be enhanced in the sense that traders could develop some confidence that compensation for violations of WTO law is available, and that they will not be left in the cold. If the compensation is paid from the coffers of the government responsible for the breach, such a remedy is also likely to improve compliance. Government expenditure invariably sharpens the attention of politicians. The EU experience with financial sanctions imposed on Member States for continued non-compliance with their EU obligations (see Article 228 EC Treaty) is a case in point: there are very few cases where this remedy needs to be employed, because governments comply as soon as they are threatened with such sanctions.

It is of course another matter whether the international trade system is sufficiently mature to contemplate the introduction of compensation systems for traders affected by WTO violations. There are undoubtedly many participants and commentators who would reply in the negative. This is a matter for further reflection and debate. It may nevertheless be noted that in another important area of international economic law, international investment law, compensation of private companies is an ordinary remedy.

VII. Compliance and Municipal Law

Finally it may be useful to say a few words about compliance and municipal law. The standard doctrine in international law is that, in the absence of specific provisions setting out in what manner municipal law needs to implement certain international obligations, it is for domestic legal systems to determine how implementation will be shaped. International law does not as a rule determine its effect in municipal law. The WTO Agreement appears to be no exception. Article XVI:4 WTO Agreement merely provides, in general terms: 'Each Member shall ensure the conformity of its laws, regulations and administrative procedures with its obligations as provided in the annexed Agreements'. Whether WTO law has 'direct' or 'self-executing' effect seems a matter for municipal law. It must be added that there appear to be very few WTO Members, if any, whose legal system recognizes full direct or self-executing effect of WTO law.

It is beyond the scope of this chapter to offer a broader analysis of the direct effect question.[43] One should nevertheless note the connection with implementation and compliance. It is obvious that a legal system which is monist, and which recognizes that WTO law forms part of domestic law, will make its own, strong contribution to compliance. That is in particular so where that system also recognizes that internal legislation needs to comply with the international norm (primacy), and empowers courts to uphold that norm.

As an example, the above discussion on compensation may be connected with claims brought by traders in the EU affected by the EU's legislation on respectively bananas and beef treated with hormones; and by the retaliatory sanctions imposed by the US. Those traders brought actions for compensation of damage (so-called non-contractual liability) against the EC before the Court of First Instance. If those actions had been successful (which they were not),[44] their effect would have been to secure the compensation of private traders, referred to above. Municipal law would have in effect provided for the sort of compensation that further strengthens the security and predictability of the multilateral trading system. If such an approach were generalized, WTO law itself would be in lesser need of providing for an effective remedy. This goes to show the interaction between international and municipal law in matters of compliance.

Moreover, it is not so obvious that the WTO Agreement says very little about municipal implementation. Next to the general provision of Article XVI:4 WTO Agreement, there are specific provisions in various agreements which may have a particular relevance for municipal implementation. An example is the TRIPS

---

[43] As regards the EU, see P Eeckhout, *External Relations of the European Union – Legal and Constitutional Foundations* (Oxford: Oxford University Press, 2004) Chapter 9. For a recent discussion of the policy issues involved, see JH Jackson, 'Direct Effect of Treaties in the U.S. and the EU, the Case of the WTO: Some Perceptions and Proposals' in A Arnull, P Eeckhout, and T Tridimas (eds), *Continuity and Change – Essays in Honour of Sir Francis Jacobs* (Oxford: Oxford University Press, 2008) 361.

[44] CFI, Case T-19/01, *Chiquita and Others v Commission*, [2005] ECR II-315; CFI, Case T-69/00 *FIAMM v Council and Commission*, [2005] ECR II-5393; CFI, Case T-383/00, *Beamglow v EP, Council and Commission*, [2005] ECR II-5459; CFI, Case T-320/00, *Cartondruck v Commission and Council*, [2005] ECR II-27; CFI, Case T-301/00, *Groupe Fremaux v Council and Commission*, [2005] ECR II-25; CFI, Case T-151/00, *Laboratoire du Bain v Council and Commission*, [2005] ECR II-23; CFI, Case T-135/01, *Giorgio Fedon & Figli v Council and Commission*, [2005] ECR II-29. See further A Thies, 'Case-Note: Cases T-69/00, *FIAMM and FIAMM Technologies*, T-151/00, *Le Laboratoire du Bain*, T-301/00, *Fremaux*, T-320/00, *CD Cartondruck AG*, T-383/00, *Beamglow Ltd* and T-135/01, *Giorgio Fedon & Figli S.p.A., Fedon S.r.l. and Fedon America USA Inc.*, Judgments of 14 December 2005, Grand Chamber of the Court of First Instance' 2006 *Common Market Law Review* 43(4) 1145.

Agreement and its provisions on enforcement of intellectual property rights (Part III of the TRIPS Agreement). Those provisions address the range of remedies and procedures (including judicial procedures) for violation of such rights that WTO Members must make available. Case law may soon develop on the meaning and scope of those provisions.[45] Panels and the Appellate Body may thus be called upon to examine municipal legal systems in greater depth than in the case of claims about non-compliance with substantive WTO provisions. The experience of the European Court of Justice shows that it is often through cases on domestic issues of remedies and procedures that the international norms become more intrusive.[46]

A further point concerns interjudicial dialogue. The fact that in most legal systems WTO law does not have direct or self-executing effect does not preclude that municipal courts are confronted with issues of WTO law, in one way or other. Often, for example, the lack of direct effect is distinguished from principles of consistent, conform, or harmonious interpretation. Many legal systems recognize that domestic legislation needs to be interpreted in the light of binding international norms. Municipal courts may thus start looking at the WTO case law itself. In particular, questions may arise as to the legal effect of WTO dispute rulings—panel and Appellate Body reports. In the EU such questions have in fact already arisen. Whilst the EU Courts appear reluctant to recognize any particular, separate legal effect of WTO dispute rulings,[47] recent international legal history does show that interjudicial dialogues may quickly develop across legal boundaries. It is not excluded that, at some point, municipal courts start forming some type of coalition with the WTO adjudicators, in particular the Appellate Body.

Finally, in a 21st century approach to international law, there may be scope for arguing that WTO law directly confers certain rights on private parties. In the *LaGrand* case, the ICJ accepted Germany's argument that a provision of the Vienna Convention on Consular Relations 'creates individual rights'. The provision at issue concerned communication between a foreign detained person and the consular post of that person's home State. The Court noted that the article expressly spoke of the detained person's 'rights'. The clarity of those provisions admitted of no doubt. It followed that the Court had to apply them as they stood, and thus as recognizing individual rights.[48] Such reasoning can easily be extended to parts of WTO law, in particular the TRIPS Agreement, which frequently speaks of the rights of intellectual property holders. In the *LaGrand* case, the ICJ did not indicate that such individual rights can be directly relied upon in a municipal context; it was for Germany, through the proceedings before the ICJ, to seek to uphold the rights

---

[45] See, eg, the ongoing *China- Intellectual Property Rights* dispute.

[46] See P Craig and G de Búrca, *EU Law – Text, Cases and Materials*, 4th edn (Oxford: Oxford University Press, 2007), at 305–43 (discussing cases like *Simmenthal, Factortame,* and *Francovich*).

[47] For further discussion see P Eeckhout, 'A Panorama of Two Decades of EU External Relations Law' in Arnull, Eeckhout, and Tridimas, above fn 43, 323, at 334–36.

[48] ICJ, *LaGrand (Germany v United States)*, Judgment, ICJ Reports (2001) 466, at para 77.

of the LaGrand brothers. But even if the individual rights in question can only be protected at the international level, adjudicative rulings recognizing such rights do expose municipal systems that are impervious to the international norm being directly applied in judicial proceedings. If the Appellate Body were ever to accept that provisions of the TRIPS Agreement, for example, create individual rights, there would be strong pressure on municipal legal systems to provide for adequate protection of such rights.

VIII. Conclusions

The WTO dispute settlement system is self-contained, in that it does not permit any parallel application of the general law of State responsibility. That does not mean that the ILC Articles are wholly irrelevant. Norms of general international law may fill the gaps in the WTO dispute settlement system. They may also form an aid to interpreting and developing the specific remedies that WTO law offers.

Dispute rulings are binding on the parties, notwithstanding the ambivalent DSU language and the scope for suspension of concessions. Both a textual analysis of the DSU and the consistent practice of WTO Members and organs confirm this. The remedies of compensation and suspension of concessions are not alternatives to compliance. Their function is to induce compliance, not to re-balance. There is no room for theories of efficient breach, simply because continued non-compliance combined with retaliation are not, as a rule, economically efficient. The efficiency that the dispute settlement system seeks to promote is that of a global market place where traders can be confident that WTO norms are protected: the security and predictability of the multilateral trading system.

The mantra that the recommendation by panels and the Appellate Body to 'bring into conformity' is purely prospective needs to be revisited. The Panel in *Australia – Leather II (Article 21.5 – US)* was correct to consider that 'withdrawal' may be retrospective as well as prospective. The provisions in the ILC Articles on reparation (in particular restitution) are a good aid to further develop the content of what 'bring into conformity' and 'withdrawal' may mean in specific cases.

Suspension of concessions is a remedy with many defects. It is definitely useful to reflect about alternative remedies, in particular those focusing on compensation for the trade damage that a breach has inflicted. Such reflection should be geared towards systems offering compensation for companies and traders. Compensation consisting of liberalizing trade in other sectors, by contrast, is unlikely to induce compliance and strengthen security and predictability. It risks becoming an easy method for buying-out of one's obligations.

Lastly, the link between the international and municipal levels should not be ignored. Panels and the Appellate Body are likely to develop further principles on municipal implementation issues. The WTO adjudicators and municipal courts and tribunals may also develop a dialogue across legal boundaries. WTO adjudicators may even, dare one say it, at one point accept that certain provisions of WTO law create individual rights.

The author is aware that the above reflections are virtually all oriented towards strengthening compliance with WTO norms and with dispute settlement rulings. But in fact many observers question whether the trading system should be oriented towards better compliance. It is beyond the scope of this chapter to address such fundamental questioning. It is obvious that WTO norms need to be sensibly interpreted and applied, and that there needs to be room for domestic political manoeuvre, in particular where non-economic concerns are at stake. However, that does not preclude better compliance. Experience teaches that international rulings that, when adopted, were regarded as intolerable challenges to national sovereignty may quickly become part of general legal heritage and culture.

SELECTED BIBLIOGRAPHY

JH Bello, 'The WTO Dispute Settlement Understanding: Less is More' 1996 *American Journal of International Law* 90(3) 416

M Bronckers and N van den Broek, 'Financial Compensation in the WTO – Improving the Remedies of WTO Dispute Settlement' 2005 *Journal of International Economic Law* 8(1) 101

JH Jackson, 'International Law Status of WTO Dispute Settlement Reports: Obligation to Comply or Option to "Buy Out"?' 2004 *American Journal of International Law* 98(1) 109

JH Jackson, 'Direct Effect of Treaties in the U.S. and the EU, the Case of the WTO: Some Perceptions and Proposals' in A Arnull, P Eeckhout, and T Tridimas (eds), *Continuity and Change – Essays in Honour of Sir Francis Jacobs* (Oxford: Oxford University Press, 2008) 361

RZ Lawrence, *Crimes and Punishments? Retaliation under the WTO* (Washington, DC: Institute for International Economics, 2003)

PC Mavroidis, 'Remedies in the WTO Legal System: Between a Rock and a Hard Place' 2000 *European Journal of International Law* 11(4) 763

D Palmeter and SA Alexandrov, 'Inducing Compliance in WTO Dispute Settlement' in DLM Kennedy and JD Southwick (eds), *The Political Economy of International Trade Law* (Cambridge: Cambridge University Press, 2002) 646

J Pauwelyn, 'Enforcement and Countermeasures in the WTO: Rules are Rules – Toward a More Collective Approach' 2000 *American Journal of International Law* 94(2) 335

WF Schwartz and AO Sykes, 'The Economic Structure of Renegotiation and Dispute Resolution in the World Trade Organization' 2002 *Journal of Legal Studies* 31(1-2) 179

B Simma and D Pulkowski, 'Of Planets and the Universe: Self-contained Regimes in International Law' 2006 *European Journal of International Law* 17(3) 483

N van den Broek, 'Power Paradoxes in Enforcement and Implementation of World Trade Organization Dispute Settlement Reports – Interdisciplinary Approaches and New Proposals' 2003 *Journal of World Trade* 37(1) 127

SM Villalpando, 'Attribution of Conduct to the State: How the Rules of State Responsibility May Be Applied Within the WTO Dispute Settlement System' 2002 *Journal of International Economic Law* 5(2) 393

JHH Weiler, 'The Rule of Lawyers and the Ethos of Diplomats: Reflections on the Internal and External Legitimacy of WTO Dispute Settlement', *Harvard Jean Monnet Working Paper* 9/00

B Wilson, 'Compliance by WTO Members with Adverse Dispute Settlement Rulings: The Record to Date' 2007 *Journal of International Economic Law* 10(2) 397

CHAPTER 16

THE LIMITS
OF JUDICIAL
PROCESSES

WILLIAM J DAVEY

I. INTRODUCTION

THE WTO dispute settlement system has generally been viewed as a success.[1] It has been heavily used by developed countries and advanced developing countries,[2] and the overall settlement and compliance rates are impressive for international state-to-state dispute settlement.[3] The system is far from perfect, of course. While many advanced developing countries make extensive use of it, most developing countries and almost all least developed countries do not use it at all.[4] While compliance is usually achieved, the system often takes much longer than intended to produce results.[5] Prolonged non-compliance has occurred in several high-profile cases, which means that the overall effectiveness of the system has sometimes been put into question.[6] Moreover, there have been extensive criticisms of the jurisprudence produced by the system—by activists,[7] academics,[8] and WTO Members.[9] Any overall assessment of the system and consideration of the limits on judicial processes in the WTO must bear these problems in mind and must also consider the context in which the system operates. This last consideration is of great importance given that the success of the dispute settlement system has not been

---

[1] WJ Davey, 'The WTO Dispute Settlement System: The First Decade' 2005 *Journal of International Economic Law* 8(1) 17.

[2] The use of the system in terms of consultation requests has fallen since its early years, but it remains quite active and there is no reason to expect further declines. WJ Davey, 'The WTO: Looking Forwards' 2006 *Journal of International Economic Law* 9(1) 3, at 9–20.

[3] Davey, above fn 1, at 45–49; WJ Davey, 'Evaluating WTO Dispute Settlement: What Results Have Been Achieved Through Consultations and Implementation of Panel Reports?' in Y Taniguchi, A Yanovich, and J Bohanes (eds), *The WTO in the Twenty-First Century: Dispute Settlement, Negotiations and Regionalism in Asia* (Cambridge: Cambridge University Press, 2007) 98, at 102–07.

[4] WJ Davey, 'The WTO Dispute Settlement System: How Have Developing Countries Fared?' (30 November, 2005), at <http://www.ssrn.com/abstract=862804> (last visited 31 July 2007).

[5] WJ Davey, 'Expediting the Panel Process in WTO Dispute Settlement' in M Janow, V Donaldson, and A Yanovich (eds), *The WTO: Governance, Dispute Settlement & Developing Countries* (Huntington, New York: Juris Publishing, Inc., 2008) 409, at 415–21.

[6] Examples include compliance with Appellate Body Report, *EC-Bananas III*; Appellate Body Report, *EC-Hormones*; Appellate Body Report, *US-FSC*; Appellate Body Report, *US-Offset (Byrd Amendment)*. As of Summer 2007, these cases were the only ones in which retaliatory action for non-compliance had been taken.

[7] L Wallach and P Woodhall, *Whose Trade Organization? A Comprehensive Guide to the WTO*, 2nd edn (New York: New Press, 2004) Chapter 5.

[8] The American Law Institute Project on Principles of Trade Law: The World Trade Organization has a series of thoughtful criticism of many panel and Appellate Body reports, at <http://www.ali.org/index.cfm?fuseaction=projects.proj_ip&projectid=10> (last visited 31 July 2007). For a general description of various criticisms, see C Barfield, *Free Trade, Sovereignty, Democracy: The Future of the World Trade Organization* (Washington, DC: The AEI Press, 2001), at 70–96.

[9] Eg, most WTO Members heavily criticized the Appellate Body decisions permitting *amicus curiae* briefs. GC, *Minutes of Meeting held on 22 November 2000*, WT/GC/M/60 (23 January 2001). See also chapter 13 of this Handbook.

matched by other WTO organs, as the breakdown in the Doha negotiations so vividly demonstrates.[10] Indeed, one consequence of the dispute settlement system's
general success, on the one hand, and the glacial pace of negotiations and decision-
making generally in the WTO, on the other, is that the dispute settlement system
is being presented with cases where WTO Members try to achieve in a judicial
process what they have not been able to achieve through negotiations.[11] It is in the
light of all of these factors that the essential issue treated in this chapter must be
evaluated: what are or should be the limits of judicial processes in the WTO?

In considering the limits of judicial processes, it is useful to first determine the
role of judicial processes in international dispute settlement and what it is expected
to achieve. Generally speaking, judicial processes occur where other forms of
dispute settlement have not resolved a dispute. On the international level, those
other forms of dispute settlement are typically considered to be consultation and
negotiation, mediation, inquiry (also referred to as fact-finding), conciliation, and
arbitration.[12]

The provisions of the WTO Dispute Settlement Understanding (DSU) essentially
reflect these general approaches to international dispute settlement. The first step
in the formal process of WTO dispute settlement is consultations, which are a prerequisite for commencing the judicial process.[13] At anytime there is a possibility, if
the parties agree, of using good offices, conciliation, or mediation, and the WTO
Director-General (DG) is authorized to provides such services.[14] If the parties wish
to have a different (perhaps less formal) arbitral process than that provided in the
DSU, specific provision is made for it.[15] More generally, on its 'philosophy' of dispute
settlement, the DSU provides:

The aim of the dispute settlement mechanism is to secure a positive solution to a dispute.
A solution mutually acceptable to the parties to the dispute and consistent with the [WTO]
agreements is clearly to be preferred. In the absence of a mutually agreed solution, the first
objective...is...the withdrawal of [any inconsistent] measures... [C]ompensation should
be resorted to only if the immediate withdrawal of the measure is impracticable... The last
resort...is the possibility of [retaliatory action].[16]

---

[10]   Some of the problems of WTO decision-making have been explored in the so-called Sutherland
Report, which was prepared by a group of leading international trade experts appointed by the WTO
DG. Consultative Board, *The Future of the WTO: Addressing Institutional Challenges in the New
Millennium* (Geneva: WTO, 2004), at 61–72.

[11]   Eg, in 2002, Brazil initiated dispute settlement proceedings against the EC in respect of sugar
subsidies (with Australia and Thailand), and against the US in respect of cotton subsidies. It won both
cases. Appellate Body Report, *EC – Export Subsidies on Sugar*; Appellate Body Report, *US – Upland
Cotton*. More recently, Canada and Brazil have separately challenged US agricultural subsidies in
cases now pending: *US – Corn and Other Agricultural Products*; *US – Export Credit Guarantees*.

[12]   JG Merrills, *International Dispute Settlement*, 3rd edition (Cambridge: Cambridge University
Press, 1998), at 1–120; J Collier and V Lowe, *The Settlement of Disputes in International Law: Institutions
and Procedures* (Oxford: Oxford University Press, 1999), at 19–44.

[13]   Art 4 DSU. See also chapter 13 of this Handbook.

[14]   Art 5 DSU.   [15]   Art 25 DSU.   [16]   Art 3.7 DSU.

Although mutually agreed solutions are preferred, they must conform to the rules; and the DSU explicitly provides that recommendations and rulings of the Dispute Settlement Body (DSB) 'cannot add to or diminish the rights and obligations provided in the [WTO] agreements'.[17] In setting out these goals, the DSU opts for a more rules-based system than a power-based system—concepts that we return to below—since it emphasizes compliance with the agreed norms so as to provide predictability for the multilateral trading system.[18]

In considering these provisions, there is obviously a tension between the desire to promote mutually agreed solutions and the desire to enforce the agreed-upon norms. Indeed, one can ask if the character of a judicial process that declares one side to be a winner and the other a loser, is capable of achieving mutually acceptable outcomes. Thus, one question to be explored in an analysis of the limits of judicial processes in the WTO system is whether the system can achieve these two goals simultaneously (or in the event that the two goals are fundamentally not compatible, the extent to which the system could best partially achieve them). The fact that the system is a state-to-state one also raises a more general question of whether judicial processes can resolve difficult disputes among sovereign States. The question of limits of judicial processes also arises in a systemic way. If the system is charged with enforcing the rules—how does it achieve that end? General notions of governance usually assign a limited role to judicial organs because they tend to be less transparent in their internal decision-making and less accountable than the other organs. Particularly in systems like the WTO where the process of norm-setting is slow and ponderous, there are inevitably concerns about the extent to which the judicial organ may impose obligations not agreed to by the Members—either through judicial activism, resolution of intended ambiguities, or otherwise.

As the foregoing makes clear, the question of the limits of judicial processes may be approached from various perspectives. This chapter will examine four of those perspectives in the context of the WTO's dispute settlement mechanism. Initially, there is the issue of whether disputes are best solved through an adversarial judicial process or whether other alternative approaches should be used, such as mediation or conciliation. This issue arises in all systems of dispute settlement—national and international alike. The remaining three issues are of particular salience in an international organization like the WTO. First, there is a question of whether judicial processes are able to resolve certain types of disputes likely to arise in the international arena when negotiated agreements are at issue. In particular, there is the question of whether treaty texts, which are inevitably the result of compromises and use ambiguous language to paper over differences such that parties can plausibly claim that the text means radically different things, should be subject to a dispute settlement mechanism that attempts to give one, and only one, meaning to the text. Second, there is the question of whether judicial processes can ever be effective

---

[17] Art 3.2 DSU.   [18] Ibid.

in resolving disputes between sovereign States since the decisions produced by the processes are not strictly enforceable. Finally, there is the question of whether judicial processes are appropriate in a system where the applicable rules can be changed only with great difficulty over considerable time.

II. Judicial Processes versus Consultation, Mediation, and Conciliation: Compatible Alternatives?

In most national judicial systems, there has been a trend over the years to recognize alternative dispute settlement mechanisms—ranging from private arbitration to mediation to conciliation.[19] Even within judicial systems themselves, case management techniques have been adopted that require contending parties (or their lawyers) to meet to narrow issues and consider possible settlements.[20] This raises the obvious question of whether the WTO dispute settlement system makes adequate use of these other mechanisms for resolving disputes. This is a particular issue for the WTO system because one can legitimately ask whether, in its rush to become more court-like, it abandoned some useful aspects of the GATT system, which by its nature was arguably a more conciliation/mediation system.[21] Indeed, it has been argued that the very character of the obligations and the fact that the parties to GATT 1947 (and now the WTO) were governments meant that there were significant limitations on the use of law and legal processes—a theory espoused prominently by former GATT DG Olivier Long.[22]

In fact, the WTO system embodies an admirable combination of judicial and non-judicial processes. Indeed, while this chapter focuses on the WTO's formal

[19] RJ Niemic, D Stienstra, and RE Ravitz, *Guide to Judicial Management of Cases in ADR* (Washington, DC: Federal Judicial Center, 2001).

[20] WW Schwarzer and A Hirsch, *The Elements of Case Management: A Pocket Guide for Judges*, 2nd edn (Washington, DC: Federal Judicial Center, 2006). The Federal Judicial Center has an extensive series of publications on ADR and case management.

[21] On the GATT system generally, see RE Hudec, *Enforcing International Trade Law: The Evolution of the Modern GATT Legal System* (Salem, NH: Butterworth Legal Publishers, 1993); RE Hudec, 'GATT Dispute Settlement After the Tokyo Round: An Unfinished Business' 1980 *Cornell International Law Journal* 13(1) 145; WJ Davey, 'Dispute Settlement in GATT' 1987 *Fordham International Law Journal* 11(1) 51.

[22] O Long, *Law and Its Limitations in the GATT Multilateral Trade System* (Dordrecht: Kluwer, 1985); see also G Malinverni, *Le reglement des différends dans les organizations internationals économiques* (Leiden: AW Sijthoff, 1974).

dispute settlement procedures, it is important to note that there are additional, more informal mechanisms in the WTO system that work to resolve disagreements so that formal dispute settlement proceedings are not needed at all. For example, a separate committee typically oversees the operation of each WTO agreement and in doing so may assist in resolving potential disputes. For example, a study of the SPS Committee found that over one-third of some 235 specific trade concerns raised in the Committee were wholly or partially resolved.[23]

If informal mechanisms do not lead to the resolution of a dispute, there is the requirement of consultations between the disputing Members, which is a prerequisite for moving to the 'judicial' stage of dispute settlement. While the usefulness of the consultation process has been questioned in the DSU reform discussions, in many cases the process works as intended and it leads to mutually accepted resolution of the dispute—the goal of the DSU as stated in Article 3.7. In that regard, a 2005 study[24] found that of the 89 disputes[25] where consultation requests were made between 1 January 1995 and 1 July 2002 and no panel was established, 26 disputes were settled and a notice to that effect was filed with the DSB, and another 20 disputes were settled, but without the required notification to the DSB. In addition, a number of cases were not pursued because the measure at issue was either removed or never imposed. This was true in 17 of the cases. Moreover, there were additional cases where the consultations seem to have led the complaining Member to conclude that the case was not worth pursuing.

Overall, it would seem that the consultation phase was quite useful. It is, of course, true that some cases are too contentious to expect consultations to resolve them. In those cases the consultation requirement can be viewed as a waste of time, though 60 days is not a long period of time—especially given the actual length of most contentious proceedings under the DSU.[26] Thus, the consultation requirement in the DSU is a fine example of melding non-judicial and judicial processes in a way that resolves many disputes. While DSU negotiators might not have been particularly aware of trends in alternative dispute settlement mechanisms—the consultation requirement came from the GATT in any event—they seem to have achieved a system that does embody modern case-management ideas.[27]

[23] J Scott, *The WTO Agreement on Sanitary and Phytosanitary Measures* (Oxford: Oxford University Press, 2007), at 57. See also chapter 5 of this Handbook.

[24] Davey, above fn 1, at 45–49.

[25] Related consultation requests were counted as involving one dispute.

[26] Davey in Janow, Donaldson, and Yanovich, above fn 5, at 409, 415–21.

[27] As the consultation process has been relatively successful, it would be unwise to tinker with it. Some who have viewed it as a waste of time have suggested that consultations should be formalized so as to allow the use of what might be characterized as pre-trial discovery techniques—mandatory responses to written questions, etc. Such formalization would reduce and possibly destroy the proven valuable function that the consultation requirement now serves. W J Davey, 'WTO Dispute Settlement: Segregating the Useful Political Aspects and Avoiding "Over-Legalization"' in M Bronckers and R Quick (eds), *New Directions in International Economic Law: Essays in Honor of John J. Jackson* (The Hague: Kluwer, 2000) 291, at 293–96.

In addition to the consultation requirement, the DSU also contains a provision under which the DG is to offer conciliation and mediation services to those Members that wish to make use of them. While there has been an attempt made to promote the use of these services,[28] they have in fact been used only once in twelve and one-half years[29] suggesting that they are largely a dead letter. Since such techniques have been used in national systems to beneficial effect and in some international contexts as well, one can ask why should they not be used in the WTO? The answer probably is that many of the diplomats representing WTO Members in Geneva and elsewhere by and large view themselves as professional negotiators and believe that they can effectively use the consultation process to the extent feasible to resolve disputes, and that outsiders as conciliators and mediators would not be particularly helpful. This may not completely explain the disuse of these opportunities. While major-country diplomats may have this view, it is probably less pervasive among many developing country diplomats and particularly amongst the poorest Members. Given that many of those Members lack any real capability of participating in dispute settlement proceedings, their failure to use the possibilities of mediation and conciliation may be more due to lack of resources and skills than of interest. Moreover, one can imagine how the usefulness of these procedures may be limited if the participants vary in economic strength. In such circumstances, the setting would seem to be rife for unbalanced results favouring the stronger Member. Of course, mediators have to deal regularly with the problems of unbalanced proceedings. Nevertheless, it may be doubtful whether the standard solution—the mediator indirectly or informally favouring the weaker party[30]—would be accepted in the WTO or trade context.[31]

Mediation/conciliation procedures might be useful to resolve trade disputes among smaller countries and developing countries, where power imbalances would not be a significant factor. In that context, how can the WTO procedures be improved to make them more attractive? Concerns over Secretariat neutrality in general are likely such that any effort to make the procedures more attractive would have to involve the creation of an Appellate Body-like organization within the WTO Secretariat, which would imply a group with its own and separate budget and hiring process and which would not be involved in Secretariat activities. The office would have to be quite small, at least initially because there would be little work and there would be criticisms as to whether the resources devoted to such a function represented the best use of limited resources. Still, the cost of several professionals,

---

[28] DSB, *Article 5 of the Dispute Settlement Understanding: Communication from the Director-General*, WT/DSB/25 (17 July 2001). See also chapter 13 of this Handbook.

[29] DSB, *Request for mediation by the Philippines, Thailand and the European Communities*, WT/GC/66 (16 October 2002).

[30] NR Page, 'Dealing with power imbalance: Another stab', at <http://www.mediate.com/articles/pageN2.cfm> (last visited 12 July 2007) (with bibliography).

[31] WTO Members have expressed concerns about bias and the need to maintain Secretariat impartiality in dispute settlement. GATT Contracting Parties, *Improvements to the GATT Dispute Settlement Rules and Procedures*, BISD 36S/61 (12 April 1989), at 66, para H.1.

with appropriate support staff, would be small enough that it could be tried, if only as an experiment. Even without cases, there would be some work to be done by this group. In particular, it could establish—in consultation with WTO Members—more detailed procedures for mediation and conciliation. Another reason for the non-use of Article 5 is probably uncertainty over applicable procedures.

There has been some experience with formal conciliation/mediation procedures in the context of international environmental agreements, where such procedures have worked in the absence of a more formal legalistic dispute settlement system.[32] But close analysis of the issues and procedures at play suggests that the procedures may work in these contexts because they help solve a major underlying cause of non-compliance—lack of resources, which is not typically the reason for non-compliance in the WTO context. Moreover, one careful study of the procedures concluded that they were not frequently used in so-called difficult cases.[33] Nonetheless, it might be useful to consider such procedures. Since they rely on discussions by committees of Members with the non-complying party, one could argue that the WTO trade policy review process is closer to these procedures than anything in the WTO dispute settlement process. There has, of course, been hesitation in the WTO to have the trade policy review process take on elements of an adversarial or dispute settlement character.[34]

In conclusion, the WTO dispute settlement system seems to combine effectively both judicial and non-judicial processes to promote the effective resolution of disputes. To the extent that improvements are necessary, it would appear that the focus should be on strengthening the non-judicial processes and promoting their use amongst smaller and developing country Members, drawing perhaps in part on techniques used in international environmental agreements.

III. WTO Dispute Settlement and Ambiguous Texts

It is commonplace that international agreements are full of ambiguous language crafted by negotiators eager to make a deal by papering over real disagreements so

---

[32] See generally DG Victor, K Raustiala, and EB Skolnikoff (eds), *The Implementation and Effectiveness of International Environmental Commitments: Theory and Practice* (Cambridge, MA: MIT Press, 1998).

[33] DG Victor, 'The Operation and Effectiveness of the Montreal Protocol's Non-Compliance Procedure' in Victor, Raustiala, and Skolnikoff, above fn 32, at 137, 165–67.

[34] Paragraph A(i) of the TPRM provides that the trade policy review mechanism 'is not, however, intended to serve as a basis for the enforcement of specific obligation under the Agreements or for dispute settlement procedures'.

that all parties can claim that their position prevailed. In a system with no real dispute settlement mechanism, the ambiguities are simply left to be resolved another day in another negotiation. In the WTO context, the situation is more complex. The ambiguous text can be given meaning by the dispute settlement process and Members that do not comply can suffer serious consequences. Whether the WTO system is resolving intended ambiguities and consequently imposing 'additional' obligations on Members to which they never agreed in violation of Article 3.2 DSU is hotly contested in the WTO. To what extent should the dispute settlement system recognize this problem and choose not to resolve ambiguities? The problem is a difficult one because for the dispute settlement system to attempt to avoid resolving ambiguities requires that it first identifies such ambiguities, which is not that easy. It will always be in the interest of the party accused of violating a WTO provision to argue that the provision is ambiguous and that consequently it is innocent. There are various decision-making tools that national and international tribunals use to avoid making decisions.[35] While avoiding decisions on the grounds of *non-liquet per se* is questionable,[36] tribunals can avoid resolving real ambiguities through interpretation and conclusions that the complaining party has failed to establish a case—something that courts do all the time. In the WTO context, there is support for such an approach by panels and the Appellate Body in their reliance on the maxim *in dubio mitius*, which was recognized by the Appellate Body in *EC – Hormones*.[37] That maxim essentially stands for the proposition that where it is doubtful that a State has undertaken an obligation, one should conclude that it has not. In addition, one WTO agreement—the Anti-Dumping Agreement—has an explicit provision along those lines by providing in Article 17.6(ii) that 'where the panel finds that a relevant provision of the Agreement admits of more than one permissible interpretation, the Panel shall find the... measure to be in conformity with the Agreement if it rests upon one of those permissible interpretations'. To date, the Appellate Body has arguably given effect to the *in dubio mitius* maxim in cases involving environmental and health measures,[38] but, as discussed further below, it has largely ignored Article 17.6.

Against that background, one can ask to what extent the WTO dispute settlement system has experienced difficulties in dealing with ambiguity, and whether panels and the Appellate Body have been too quick in according discretion to governments or too miserly in doing so? A review of the first five years of WTO decisions found only one area of decisions where WTO negotiators would have been surprised at dispute settlement decisions and that was in the case of safeguards,[39]

---

[35] WJ Davey, 'Has the WTO Dispute Settlement System Exceeded Its Authority?' 2001 *Journal of International Economic Law* 4(1) 79, at 96–110.

[36] A *non liquet* occurs when a judicial body decides not to rule on an issue because the law is unclear or there is a gap in the law. The device is not generally favoured. Ibid at 106.

[37] Appellate Body Report, *EC – Hormones*, at para 165 and fn 154.

[38] Eg, Appellate Body reports in *US – Gasoline*, *EC – Hormones*, *US – Shrimp*, and *EC – Asbestos*.

[39] Davey, above fn 35, at 95.

and particularly the decision to make the elements of Article XIX GATT 1994 pre-requisites for imposing safeguards under the WTO Safeguards Agreement, not-withstanding the fact that it is a 'comprehensive agreement', which 'establishes rules for the application of safeguards measures which shall be understood to mean those measures provided for in [Article XIX GATT]'.[40] In the ensuing years, two other ambiguities have been resolved by the Appellate Body. In *US – Upland Cotton*, an Appellate Body member dissented from the Appellate Body's conclusion that the US had violated Article 10.1 Agreement on Agriculture, which prohibits the use of export subsidies not listed in Article 9 to circumvent the agreement's export subsidy commitments.[41] The US argued that its export credit programme—the measure at issue, which admittedly involved an export subsidy—should not be viewed as a circumvention of its commitments because Article 10.2 committed the WTO Members to develop and abide by an international agreement on export credits. Did the commitment to negotiate on export credits mean that they were not covered by Article 10.1? The matter could go either way, but the majority was probably correct. Article 10.2 did not say that there would be no control of export credits until such an agreement would be reached and export credit practices could certainly be used to circumvent the export subsidy commitments. In respect of the somewhat analogous GATS provision requiring negotiations on the possibility of safeguards, it seems unlikely to successfully argue that safeguards were permitted until such negotiations were completed.[42]

The second example would be the zeroing controversy. Zeroing is the term used to describe a method of calculating dumping margins through the comparison of export and home-market prices.[43] It has long been bitterly contested among GATT/WTO Members as to whether this practice is appropriate. While zeroing was the subject of Uruguay Round negotiations, the Anti-Dumping Agreement does not use the term. It does, however, require the use of either average-to-average comparisons or transaction-to-transaction comparisons in the investigative phase of an antidumping proceeding, with a limited exception.[44] More generally, the Anti-Dumping Agreement requires that a fair comparison must be made between export and home-market prices.[45] Ultimately, the Appellate Body ruled that zero-ing violates the fair comparison requirement of the Anti-Dumping Agreement, as

[40] Preamble and Art 1 Safeguards Agreement.

[41] Appellate Body Report, *US – Upland Cotton*, at paras 632–39.

[42] Art X GATS. The argument is harder to make since the GATS provision explicitly allows for the use of safeguards for a short transitional period, suggesting that they would not be available after its expiration.

[43] Whenever a comparison is made that produces a negative dumping margin (there is no dumping because the export price exceeds the home-market price), that comparison is recorded as 'o' for purposes of being aggregated with other price comparisons so as to produce an overall dumping margin. As a practical matter, the practice produces higher dumping margins than would be the case if such negative dumping margins were used to offset positive margins found in other transactions.

[44] Art 2.4.2 Anti-Dumping Agreement.

[45] Art 2.4 Anti-Dumping Agreement.

well as the provision on average-to-average or transaction-to-transaction comparisons.[46] While the arguments are too complex to go into here, the evolution of the Appellate Body's jurisprudence is uneven at best,[47] even if its ultimate decision was more or less comprehensive. It seems clear that the agreement was ambiguous on the matter. After all, the term 'zeroing' was not mentioned in the agreement and the ultimate reasoning of the Appellate Body suggests that zeroing has always been inconsistent with the rules, although the long, hard negotiations on the subject over the years would suggest otherwise. In any event, the Appellate Body found no ambiguity and virtually gave no consideration to the Anti-Dumping Agreement's provision on permissible interpretations.

While there may be other examples, it seems clear that at a minimum the Appellate Body has made rulings in some cases where the relevant language in the agreement at issue is ambiguous. But the question remains whether these instances present, overall, a significant problem for the WTO dispute settlement system. Of course, one effect may be that Members will be less willing in the future to agree on ambiguous language as a way to paper over important real differences for fear of later losing a case before the Appellate Body. That may have an adverse affect on negotiations, but it is difficult to estimate how much because the results of negotiations are typically evaluated on an overall basis and not on the basis of a negotiated ambiguity in one agreement. More important for this discussion is the question of whether Appellate Body activity in this regard is a serious problem. Although there have been few reports that can be categorized as resolving *intended* ambiguities, it is necessary to appreciate the consequences of such decisions.

One can argue that the consequences have not been that dramatic. In respect of zeroing, it is only a margin calculation issue. While the prohibition of zeroing will mean that some cases that formerly would have had margins now will not, it is not clear how often this will occur. Based on cases from the early 1980s, it was estimated that perhaps one-third of the cases would have found no dumping had zeroing been abolished.[48] However, antidumping authorities have very broad discretion with respect to many calculation issues and may well be able to reduce the impact of the zeroing decisions through other techniques. Indeed, the Appellate Body's ban on zeroing is subject to an exception in the Anti-Dumping Agreement in any event.[49] While the exception was never used by authorities who thought they could zero more generally, they will likely start relying on the exception. The

---

[46] Appellate Body reports in *US – Zeroing (Japan)*, *US – Zeroing (EC)*, and *US – Softwood Lumber V (Article 21.5 – Canada)*.

[47] For an admittedly one-sided view critiquing the Appellate Body's reasoning, see DSB, *United States – Measures Relating to Zeroing and Sunset Reviews, Communication from the United States*, WT/DS322/16 (26 February 2007).

[48] WJ Davey, 'Anti-dumping Laws: A Time for Restriction' in B. Hawk (ed), *1988 Fordham Corporate Law Institute* (New York: Matthew Bender, 1989) 8–1, at 8–25 to 8–29, reprinted in WJ Davey, *Enforcing World Trade Rules* (London: Cameron May, 2006) 265, at 284–87.

[49] Art 2.4.2, last sentence Anti-Dumping Agreement.

scope of the exception might be broad enough to significantly reduce the impact of the Appellate Body's decisions. In the case of safeguards, however, the effect of the Appellate Body's jurisprudence has generally been very limiting on the possibilities of using the Safeguards Agreement. Nevertheless, the impact of its resolution of ambiguities in the agreement (particularly the question of the continued relevance of the prerequisites of Article XIX GATT 1994) has not played a particularly important role in that regard. Rather, the restriction on the ability of Members to use the Safeguards Agreement has arisen from the Appellate Body's decisions interpreting the requirements for increased imports and causation and its generally intrusive approach to reviewing the decisions of national authorities.[50]

To conclude, it would seem that ambiguities in international agreements are probably inevitable. Nonetheless, it would be difficult to formulate a rule that would prevent a dispute settlement system from considering issues that may involve some degree of ambiguity. There is, of course, the possibility that the WTO dispute settlement system could go too far in resolving ambiguities (in the sense that Members' dissatisfaction would undermine their support for the system as a whole), but to date this has not been the case. This situation is likely to continue in the future. If there is a future problem, it is likely to arise from an excess of judicial activism, an issue considered more generally below.

IV. WTO Dispute Settlement in the Setting of Sovereign States

One often mentioned limitation on judicial processes in the international setting arises out of the fact that the parties are sovereign States and there is ultimately no way for an international tribunal—like the WTO dispute settlement system—to enforce its writ. This idea has been expressed in a number of related, but distinct ways. For example, concerns have been raised that a system like that of the GATT or the WTO will inevitably founder because of 'wrong' cases[51]—cases that cannot be resolved by the dispute settlement system because the interests of the States involved are too great and they will refrain from implementing the decisions if they lose. A second aspect of this is that sovereign States, fearing that they may lose in such future situations, will never take international dispute settlement of the type found

---

[50] See, eg, Appellate Body Report, *US – Lamb*, at paras 103–06, 162–88; JH Jackson, WJ Davey, and AO Sykes, *Legal Problems of International Economic Relations*, 4th edition (St. Paul, MN: West Group, 2002), at 289–94, 650–51.

[51] Hudec, above fn 21, at 159–66.

in the WTO seriously and ultimately will not use it.[52] Others argue more generally that the sovereign character of States suggests that any dispute settlement system should follow more the GATT principles than the WTO model and they emphasize the resolution of disputes through negotiations as opposed to rulings by independent tribunals.[53]

In response, one can ask whether the WTO dispute settlement system is truly threatened by wrong cases. In fact, the history of the system suggests that it can resolve most disputes and that those few unresolved cases do not threaten the viability of the system as a whole. In the first five years of WTO dispute settlement, several highly controversial disputes were brought to the WTO dispute settlement system, but all were ultimately resolved with the exception of the *Hormones* case and the Canada-Brazil aircraft cases.[54] It is unlikely that ongoing cases like the aircraft subsidies cases and those relating to GMOs and US agricultural subsidies will lead to a collapse of the system. More likely, the disputants will reach some sort of agreement on aircraft subsidies in the next few years. While it may not truly resolve the dispute, it will defuse it for the time being. As to the GMO/food safety cases, WTO Members will likely agree to disagree on their approach to these matters, as the disputants did in the *Hormones* case. While some level of retaliatory action may sometimes be taken, it will probably not be significant, especially in light of the flexibilities inherent in the SPS Agreement.[55] As long as the system works satisfactory in general, the occasional difficult (wrong) case does not threaten the system or represent a true limitation on the effectiveness of judicial processes. To the extent that difficult cases do not undermine the system, the concern that States will ultimately abandon the system because of sovereignty concerns seems insignificant.[56] As to the more general issue of whether a judicial-like system is preferable to a more negotiation-based system—a distinction that Jackson has characterized as rules-based versus power-based[57]—this matter has been dealt with at length elsewhere.[58] As noted there, it would make no sense to spend years and years in arduous negotiations on detailed rules for international trade if there is no serious dispute settlement system to resolve disputes over the meaning of those rules and to ensure their enforcement. A negotiation- or power-based system will ultimately undermine the agreed-upon rules and

---

[52] See generally EA Posner and JC Yoo, 'Judicial Independence in International Tribunals' 2005 *California Law Review* 93(1) 1.

[53] See generally Barfield, above fn 8.

[54] Davey, above fn 1, at 18–21.

[55] The flexibilities of the SPS Agreement are discussed in WJ Davey, 'Reflections on the Appellate Body Decision in the *Hormones* Case and the Meaning of the SPS Agreement' in GA Bermann and PC Mavroidis (eds), *Trade and Human Health and Safety* (Cambridge: Cambridge University Press, 2006) 118.

[56] Davey, above fn 2, at 18–21.

[57] JH Jackson, 'The Crumbling Institutions of the Liberal Trade System' 1978 *Journal of World Trade Law* 12(4) 93.

[58] Davey, above fn 21, at 68–81.

favor the strong. While it is true that the sovereign character of States places some limits on the effectiveness of a strict rules-based system, the history of GATT and WTO dispute settlement demonstrates that Members almost always comply with the results of the system,[59] mostly because of their collective perception of the system as being in their overall interest to preserve.

V. WTO DISPUTE SETTLEMENT AND JUDICIAL OVERREACHING

The final topic to be considered in this chapter on the limits of judicial processes in the WTO concerns the problem of judicial activism. The severity of this problem depends on the ease by which other organs of the basic entity can modify judicial pronouncements. If that can be done easily by a legislative or executive organ, the problem of judicial activism may arise, but any negative impacts are easily corrected. Where the legislative and executive organs are unable to take corrective action when the judicial organ goes astray, serious problems could arise.

In the WTO, it is generally accepted that the legislative organ is not capable of responding quickly to decisions of panels and the Appellate Body. That is to say, that even if there is widespread dissatisfaction within the WTO membership with a decision of the Appellate Body, there is arguably little that the membership can do. The classic example of this problem is presented by the Appellate Body's decisions on the submission of *amicus curiae* briefs. It initially decided that Article 13 DSU, which authorizes panels 'to seek' information from any source, authorizes a panel to accept unsolicited information that is submitted to it.[60] As a result, a panel receiving a written submission from a non-governmental organization (NGO) or an individual can decide to accept and consider the submission, even if it had not requested it. WTO Members expressed considerable criticism of this decision.[61] Notwithstanding the criticism, the Appellate Body subsequently decided that it also had the power to accept *amicus* briefs, despite the absence of any language on the issue in the DSU or in the Appellate Body's own rules.[62] Many WTO Members also criticized this decision.[63] The criticism became particularly virulent when the Appellate Body in

[59] Davey, above fn 1, at 45, 49; Davey in Taniguchi, Yanovich, and Bohanes, above fn 3, at 102–07.
[60] Appellate Body Report, *US – Shrimp*, at paras 79–91.
[61] DSB, *Minutes of Meeting held on 6 November 1998*, WT/DSB/M/50 (14 December 1998), at 1–18.
[62] Appellate Body Report, *US – Lead and Bismuth II*, at paras 36–42. See also chapters 13 and 24 of this Handbook.
[63] DSB, *Minutes of Meeting held on 7 June 2000*, WT/DSB/M/83 (7 July 2000).

EC – Asbestos established procedures to guide its decisions as to the acceptance of *amicus* submissions in that case.[64] A special meeting of the WTO General Council (GC) was held for the sole purpose of criticizing this decision.[65]

The *amicus* brief dispute epitomizes the problem of judicial activism in the WTO setting. Despite the very widespread criticism of the appropriateness of accepting *amicus* briefs at all and of the issue being decided by the Appellate Body instead of the WTO membership, one WTO Member—the US—was happy with the result. As a result, the consensus rule in WTO decision-making prevented WTO Members from overturning the Appellate Body decision, despite broad objections on substantive and/or procedural grounds. The *amicus* matter is also instructive, however, because it may demonstrate informal means to control judicial activism in the WTO through actions by Members, such as the meetings held to criticize the Appellate Body's *amicus* decisions. Subsequent to the GC meeting, the Appellate Body determined not to accept any of the proposed *amicus* filings in the *Asbestos* case.[66] Indeed, the Appellate Body has never explicitly relied on *amicus* filings—it normally accepts a filing and notes that it did not find it useful.[67] Thus, the WTO legislative organ may have some ability to restrain judicial activism. It is not clear whether this derives from its ultimate power to select the Appellate Body members or simply from the judicial organ's desire not to get too far out of step with the membership for institutional reasons.

Against the background of the *amicus* issue, one can ask whether the Appellate Body has engaged in judicial activism, which can be defined for purposes of this chapter as occurring when a judicial body interprets a rule in a way that most of those who adopted the rule never intended.[68] If so, is this a problem necessitating a response from Members? If it does present such a problem, how might the system address it?

A preliminary question relates to how judicial activism can be recognized. Besides the examples of *amicus curiae* briefs and zeroing, three examples of judicial activism can be cited: (i) the decision in *Canada – Periodicals* that the Appellate Body could 'complete the analysis' in the event that it rejects a panel's rationale for finding a violation;[69] (ii) the *US – Shrimp* report in general;[70] and (iii) the various cases interpreting the substantive provisions of the Safeguards Agreement.[71] Other reports have been inappropriately cited as examples of judicial activism, such as the report

---

[64] Communication from the Appellate Body, *EC – Asbestos*, WT/DS135/9 (8 November 2000).

[65] GC, *Minutes of Meeting held on 22 November 2000*, WT/GC/M/60 (23 January 2001).

[66] Appellate Body Report, *EC – Asbestos*, at paras 55–57.

[67] See, eg, Appellate Body Report, *US – Lead and Bismuth II*, at para. 42.

[68] Obviously, there are difficulties in determining the intent of the parties and whether a provision is truly ambiguous.

[69] Appellate Body Report, *Canada – Periodicals*. See also chapter 13 of this Handbook.

[70] Appellate Body Report, *US – Shrimp*.

[71] In particular, the Appellate Body reports in *Argentina – Footwear (EC)* and *US – Lamb*.

in *India – Quantitative Restrictions*.[72] However, this is simply a case in which the Panel and the Appellate Body followed past decisions in a manner that ensured that WTO obligations would be enforceable.[73] Another example is the report in *US – FSC*,[74] where there is reason to believe that the US was not surprised at the result but overall it is difficult to consider this report as a case of judicial activism. There may be many cases where one can disagree with the reasoning of the Appellate Body, but that is insufficient to conclude that a case involves judicial activism.

As to the genuine examples of judicial activism, the Appellate Body in *Canada – Periodicals* ruled that the law violated Article III:2, second sentence GATT 1994 (dissimilar taxation of competitive products), after rejecting the conclusion of the Panel that the challenged Canadian law violated Article III:2, first sentence GATT 1994 (differential taxation of like products). The Appellate Body argued that it could do so without engaging in fact-finding (clearly not an appellate function) because there were sufficient uncontested facts in the record to enable it to make the necessary finding of a violation of Article III:2, second sentence.[75] This reasoning arguably implied an expansion of the notion of appellate jurisdiction. There have probably been few, if any, adverse consequences of this judicial activism. It has the very positive practical effect of avoiding the situation where the complaining party would have to initiate a new dispute simply because a panel had erred and the Appellate Body had no remand authority. Since the Appellate Body has generally exercised caution in completing the analysis, there would seem to have been no significant adverse consequences of this ruling.

The report in *US – Shrimp* is another example of judicial activism. The activism in this case was more a matter of interpretive approaches than of actual results. The interpretive issues arose in the Appellate Body's consideration of the meaning of 'exhaustible' natural resources in Article XX(g) GATT 1994. The Appellate Body's approach was somewhat unusual since the issue—could turtles, as living organisms, be an exhaustible natural resource, or was the term limited to natural resources of the geological sort—had been resolved in prior GATT and WTO cases. Adopted GATT panel reports had held that tuna, salmon, and herring were covered by Article XX(g),[76] and a WTO panel previously had reached that conclusion for clean air.[77] The Appellate Body essentially ignored those cases and relied on the notion of evolving meanings as evidenced by various conventions on environmental

[72] Appellate Body Report, *India – Quantitative Restrictions*; Barfield, above fn 8, at 54–6.

[73] WJ Davey, 'A Comment on Are the Judicial Organs of the World Trade Organization Overburdened?' in RB Porter, P Sauvé, A Subramanian, and A Beviglia Zampetti (eds), *Efficiency, Equity and Legitimacy: The Multilateral Trading System at the Millennium* (Washington, DC: Brookings Institution Press, 2001) 329.

[74] Appellate Body Report, *US – FSC*.

[75] Appellate Body Report, *Canada – Periodicals*, at 20–28.

[76] GATT Panel Report, *Canada – Herring and Salmon*, at 113; GATT Panel Report, *US – Tuna (Canada)*, at 108.

[77] Panel Report, *US – Gasoline*, at para 6.37.

issues to which some of the disputing parties were not party.[78] The notion that the meaning of the WTO agreements was not fixed upset Members, but the result of the Appellate Body's interpretive efforts was completely consistent with past precedent, and the use of outside sources in defining terms is commonly accepted—witness the use by the Appellate Body of dictionaries that Members had no input into. Moreover, although *US – Shrimp* was hailed by environmentalists as evidencing a new sensitivity on the part of the WTO dispute settlement system to environmental concerns,[79] the ultimate result was consistent with past GATT precedents, as interpreted by the Panel in the case.[80] Thus, once again, actual judicial activism did not seem particularly worrisome.

The third example of judicial activism is in the area of the Safeguards Agreement. Arguably, the Safeguards Agreement was aimed at regulating the use of safeguards in a way that would promote their use in a transparent manner (as compared to the common use of largely secret voluntary export restraints in the 1980s) for defined periods of time (three years without the need to provide compensation). The underlying rationale was that using safeguards under such circumstances was a positive measure and provided a useful safety valve when domestic industries were seriously injured by imports. If this was the actual intention, it is debatable whether the Appellate Body has largely undermined the usefulness of the agreement in a series of decisions that make it difficult to establish increased imports, serious injury, and causation. For example, despite the absence of any suggestive language, the Appellate Body has ruled that the increase in imports must have been sudden, sharp, and recent.[81] Its decisions on causation are difficult to understand and leave little or no discretion to national authorities in evaluating injury and causation.[82] It is arguable that national authorities—knowing how the Appellate Body expects the agreement to be interpreted—will be able to adjust their practices to meet the Appellate Body's expectations. An alternative view suggests that the decisions have made the use of safeguards under the agreement so difficult that WTO Members are simply ignoring the agreement altogether by imposing informal safeguards. It remains to be seen which view is correct. In the area of safeguards, the Appellate Body seems to have been most judicially active in a way that probably limits WTO Members' discretion beyond what they thought they had agreed upon.

If the forgoing is a fair summary of major examples of judicial activism by the WTO dispute settlement system, it is difficult to argue that these examples have impacted WTO Members and agreements in a substantial manner. Nonetheless,

---

[78] Appellate Body Report, *US – Shrimp*, at paras 127–34. See also chapter 12 of this Handbook.

[79] See, eg, L de la Fayette, 'United States – Import Prohibition of Certain Shrimp and Shrimp Products – Recourse to Article 21.5 of the DSU by Malaysia' 2002 *American Journal of International Law* 96(3) 685.

[80] Appellate Body Report, *US – Shrimp*, at para 161.

[81] Appellate Body Report, *Argentina – Footwear (EC)*, at paras 125–31.

[82] Appellate Body Report, *US – Lamb*, at paras 103–06, 162–88.

it is worth considering how WTO Members can control such activism—such as it now exists or as it may develop in the future. One possible approach is some form of outside review. Indeed, this was proposed in the US, when the Uruguay Round agreements were approved by Congress, as a way of ensuring that the system did not inappropriately deprive the US of its rights or impose upon it additional obligations. The so-called Dole Commission would have provided for a review by a panel of US judges of WTO decisions against the US.[83] The proposal never came into being, but the idea of a small group reviewing WTO panel and Appellate Body decisions has been raised in other contexts. For example, the Consultative Board proposed that a group of WTO Members meet regularly for a similar purpose.[84] Although the critiques of such a group would have some influence on future Appellate Body decisions, such a procedure would seem undesirable as it could undermine the authority of the Appellate Body because this review group would somehow have to be viewed as having some sort of superior authority. Indeed, it is interesting that the idea of the Dole Commission was severely criticized as representing an interference in the independence of the WTO dispute settlement system. It would seem that any review group—whether multinational or not—still impinges unnecessarily and undesirably on the independence of the system. For the moment, the problem of judicial activism has simply not been sufficiently serious as to necessitate any reforms.

VI. Conclusion

The WTO dispute settlement system has generally been viewed as a success. There are, however, critics that question whether the system is appropriately constrained given the context in which it operates. This chapter has examined four issues: first, does the WTO system contain the right mix of judicial and non-judicial approaches to dispute settlement? Second, does the system adequately resolve disputes over ambiguous treaty language? Third, can the system handle controversial cases involving issues of great importance to sovereign States? Finally, can the WTO function properly with an activist dispute settlement system and a weak norm-setting mechanism? The chapter concludes that the WTO dispute settlement system has an effective mix of judicial and non-judicial approaches to dispute settlement and is able to handle controversial cases. While there have been some problems with

---

[83] 'Dole Calls for Passage of Bill To Set Up WTO Review Commission' 1996 *BNA International Trade Reporter* 13(19) (8 May 1996).

[84] Consultative Board, *The Future of the WTO: Addressing Institutional Challenges in the New Millennium* (Geneva: WTO, 2004), at paras 251–52.

unexpected treaty interpretations and judicial activism, to date those problems have not been significant.

SELECTED BIBLIOGRAPHY

J Collier and V Lowe, *The Settlement of Disputes in International Law: Institutions and Procedures* (Oxford: Oxford University Press, 1999)

WJ Davey, 'Dispute Settlement in GATT' 1987 *Fordham International Law Journal* 11(1) 51

WJ Davey, 'The WTO Dispute Settlement System: The First Decade' 2005 *Journal of International Economic Law* 8(1) 17

WJ Davey, 'The WTO: Looking Forwards' 2006 *Journal of International Economic Law* 9(1) 3

WJ Davey, 'Evaluating WTO Dispute Settlement: What Results Have Been Achieved Through Consultations and Implementation of Panel Reports?' in Y Taniguchi, A Yanovich, and J Bohanes (eds), *The WTO in the Twenty-First Century: Dispute Settlement, Negotiations and Regionalism in Asia* (Cambridge: Cambridge University Press, 2007) 98

D Georgiev and K Van der Borght (eds), *Reform and Development of the WTO Dispute Settlement System* (London: Cameron May, 2006)

RE Hudec, 'GATT Dispute Settlement After the Tokyo Round: An Unfinished Business' 1980 *Cornell International Law Journal* 13(1) 145

RE Hudec, *Enforcing International Trade Law: The Evolution of the Modern GATT Legal System* (Salem, NH: Butterworth Legal Publishers, 1993)

JG Merrills, *International Dispute Settlement*, 3rd edn (Cambridge: Cambridge University Press, 1998)

D Palmeter and P Mavroidis, *Dispute Settlement in the World Trade Organization: Practice and Procedure*, 2nd edn (Cambridge: Cambridge University Press, 2004)

DG Victor, K Raustiala, and EB Skolnikoff (eds), *The Implementation and Effectiveness of International Environmental Commitments: Theory and Practice* (Cambridge, MA: MIT Press, 1998)

J Waincymer, *WTO Litigation: Procedural Aspects of Formal Dispute Settlement* (London: Cameron May, 2002)

PART IV

TRADE AND . . . THE NEW AGENDA AND LINKAGE ISSUES

CHAPTER 17

....

TRADE AND DEVELOPMENT

....

HUNTER NOTTAGE*

* Many thanks to Petina Gappah, Niall Meagher, Frieder Roessler, Lorand Bartels, Hamish Smith,
and Constantine Michalopoulos for helpful comments and discussions. The views expressed reflect
those of the author.

I. INTRODUCTION

A paramount challenge for the WTO this millennium will be the extent to which it assists the economic development of the world's poor. Over two thirds of WTO Members are developing or least-developed countries (LDCs). The legitimacy of the multilateral trading system will be undermined unless WTO rules further these Members' development objectives. The launch of the current trade round as the Doha 'Development' Agenda reflects the immediacy of the challenge, yet development has been an issue of central importance since the inception of the GATT in 1947.

This chapter evaluates the integration of developing countries in the WTO legal regime. The relationship between trade and development has been typically the domain of economic analysis. As Jackson notes, the subject 'generally involves the expertise of economists rather than lawyers' and this is an area where 'the economics literature is extensive'.[1] This chapter aims to complement that analysis with a legal assessment of the rules that have attempted to accommodate the special position of developing countries in world trade.

A legal analysis is warranted in light of the increasingly legalistic nature of the WTO. When the Uruguay Round was concluded in 1994, one of its most noteworthy successes was the introduction of binding dispute settlement procedures pursuant to the DSU. Building upon GATT dispute settlement practice, the DSU contains innovations that resulted in a paradigm shift from a system based on economic power and politics to one based on the rule of law. The resulting increased legality of the WTO has been hailed as a considerable benefit to smaller countries, of which many are developing countries and LDCs. As Steger and Hainsworth comment, the shift 'is particularly beneficial for smaller countries, as without the rules and procedures of the DSU ... they would not have the necessary bargaining power vis-à-vis the larger powers'.[2] Similarly, Weiler notes the advantages of the legalised WTO model, 'especially for the meek economically and politically unequal'.[3]

Despite these perceived benefits, the vast majority of developing countries have not participated actively in the WTO dispute settlement system. This raises concerns that they are not benefiting fully from the WTO legal regime. As Bown and Hoekman observe, 'a systemic pattern of missing dispute settlement activity calls into question whether the full public good and positive externality benefits of the

---

[1] JH Jackson, *The World Trading System: Law and Policy of International Economic Relations*, 2nd edn (Cambridge: MIT Press, 1999), at 319.

[2] DP Steger and S Hainsworth, 'World Trade Organization Dispute Settlement: The First Three Years' 1998 *Journal of International Economic Law* 1(2) 199, at 225.

[3] JHH Weiler, 'The Rule of Lawyers and the Ethos of Diplomats: Reflections on the Internal and External Legitimacy of WTO Dispute Settlement' 2001 *Journal of World Trade* 35(2) 191, at 192.

trading system are sufficiently exploited'.[4] Davey also has commented that '[o]nly an effective dispute settlement system can ensure rule enforcement, which in turn provides predictability and stability in trade relations'.[5]

In the light of these concerns, this chapter evaluates developing-country integration in the WTO legal regime. To that end, Part II provides a historical overview of the GATT 1947 and WTO rules that have attempted to accommodate the concerns of developing countries. Part III then reviews developing-country participation in WTO dispute settlement, observing the lack of engagement by the vast majority of developing countries. It outlines the four constraints commonly identified as explaining that lack of participation: (i) a relative lack of legal expertise or resources to fund external lawyers, (ii) a lack of domestic mechanisms to identify and act against trade barriers faced, (iii) low levels of world trade and small domestic markets, and (iv) the fear of political and economic retaliation. The focus of Part III, however, is on a fifth factor that has yet to receive much attention, namely, that a high proportion of developing-country trade falls under preferential rules that are not enforceable in WTO dispute settlement proceedings. Consequently, when developing countries trade under those rules they do not benefit from the increased legality of the WTO system. For this reason, for many developing countries, the much-lauded benefits of the shift to a rules-based system remain largely illusory. The chapter concludes that in this legal sense, many developing countries remain *outside* the WTO legal regime.

This chapter does not attempt to resolve the economic debate on the development benefits of non-reciprocal preferential rules for developing countries. Rather, it is intended to raise an awareness of the opportunity costs of those rules as a matter of enforceable WTO law. In this regard, it adopts an analytical distinction between the *economic* and *legal* evaluation of the approach of the multilateral trading system to developing countries, as first developed by Hudec.[6] In his analysis, Hudec commented that the multilateral trading system's relationship with developing countries points to 'one major question throughout': whether a policy of non-reciprocal preferential treatment is of greater benefit than one based on reciprocity and non-discrimination? In analysing this question, Hudec noted that the economic argumentation has been developed rather extensively and he focuses on the 'legal criticisms of the current policy'.[7] His conclusions were that if developing countries trade under non-reciprocal preferential rules they will often lose: (i) the 'internal impact' of multilateral disciplines that assist developing countries in making internal reform, and (ii) the 'external impact' as developed countries are more reluctant

[4] C Bown and B Hoekman, 'WTO Dispute Settlement and the Missing Developing Country Cases: Engaging the Private Sector' 2005 *Journal of International Economic Law* 8(4) 861, at 863.
[5] WJ Davey, 'The WTO Dispute Settlement System' 2000 *Journal of International Economic Law* 3(1) 15, at 15.
[6] RE Hudec, *Developing Countries in the GATT Legal System* (London: Gower, 1987).
[7] Ibid at 128.

to provide real and binding market access benefits in a one-sided system.[8] Despite the continued pertinence of Hudec's analysis, it was written prior to the introduction of the DSU. This chapter updates Hudec's work by analysing the loss of 'enforcement impact' when developing countries trade under preferential rules that are not enforceable in the WTO's binding dispute settlement system.

II. OVERVIEW OF GATT 1947 AND WTO LAW ADDRESSING DEVELOPING COUNTRIES

Historically, the concept of special and differential treatment (S&DT) has been at the forefront of efforts of the GATT and the WTO to facilitate the integration of developing countries into the multilateral trading system. This concept champions different legal rights and obligations for developing countries to accommodate for their special development needs. In 2004, a group of eminent trade experts conducted an evaluation of the WTO concluding that S&DT is now so pervasive that it is 'part of the WTO's legal "*acquis*"'.[9] It has been characterized as 'the most basic principle of the international law of development'.[10]

Nonetheless, at its inception in 1947, the GATT did not promote S&DT. Although eleven of the original twenty-three GATT Contracting Parties were developing countries,[11] there was no formal recognition of such a group nor any special provisions or exceptions that covered their rights and obligations.[12] Consequently, developing countries were subject to the universal application of the principle of non-discrimination, participating in GATT activities as equal partners subject to the same legal rules as their developed counterparts.

Soon thereafter, developing countries began to call for S&DT, emphasising the uniqueness of their development challenges and the need to be treated differently and more favourably in the GATT 1947.

---

[8] Ibid, Chapters 9 and 10.

[9] Consultative Board, *The Future of the WTO: Addressing Institutional Challenges in the New Millennium* (Geneva: WTO, 2004), at para 89 (emphasis added).

[10] Appellate Body Report, *EC – Tariff Preferences*, at para 14 (referring to European Communities Appellant's Submission).

[11] Brazil, Burma (Myanmar), Ceylon (Sri Lanka), Chile, China, Cuba, India, Lebanon, Pakistan, Southern Rhodesia (Zimbabwe), and Syria.

[12] The only exception was for pre-existing preferences to developing countries under colonial regimes pursuant to Article I:2 GATT 1947.

Developing countries pressed initially for measures that would enable them to protect their domestic industries. These demands culminated in the redrafting of Article XVIII GATT 1947 ('Government Assistance to Economic Development') at the 1954–55 GATT Review Session. It was the first time that provisions were adopted to address the needs of developing countries as a group and permitted them exclusively, under certain conditions, to derogate from their scheduled tariff commitments in order to promote the establishment of a particular industry, use quantitative restrictions for balance-of-payments purposes, and a spectrum of other measures to promote certain industries.[13] At the same time, special treatment was extended to developing countries under Article XVI: GATT 1947, allowing the use of export subsidies for manufactured goods, and Article XXVIII*bis* GATT 1947, permitting more flexible tariff protection.

Article XVIII described developing countries as those 'economies... which can only support low standards of living and are in the early stages of development'.[14] Despite this provision being the first of extensive references in the GATT 1947 to special rights and obligations accorded to developing countries, it is noteworthy that what constitutes a 'developing country' remains largely undefined in WTO law. In essence, WTO Members self-select their designation.[15]

Developing countries sustained the push for S&DT during the Kennedy Round, culminating in the adoption in 1965 of Part IV of the GATT 1947, which specifically addressed 'Trade and Development'. Part IV contained three new articles, Article XXXVI ('Principles and Objectives') recognizing the need for 'positive efforts' to improve market access for products of interest to developing countries, Article XXXVII ('Commitments') requiring developed countries to accord high priority to the reduction of barriers to products of export interest to developing countries, and Article XXXVIII ('Joint Action') calling for 'joint action' to permit developing countries to secure a share in international trade 'commensurate with the needs of their economic development'.

These calls for 'joint action' coincided with agreement in 1968 under the auspices of the United Nations Conference on Trade and Development (UNCTAD) on the benefits of granting preferential market access to developing-country exports through a Generalized System of Preferences (GSP).[16] As preferential tariff treatment is inconsistent with the most-favoured-nation (MFN) obligation contained in Article I:1

---

[13] Art XVIII, sections A, B, and C GATT 1947.

[14] Art XVIII:1 and *Ad* Art XVIII GATT 1947.

[15] For countries that have acceded to the WTO after 1995, their status has sometimes been taken up during accession negotiations. Unlike developing countries, the WTO designates LDCs in accordance with the United Nations' official list of LDCs, which currently totals forty-nine countries of which twenty-nine are WTO Members. See also G Verdirame, 'Definition of Developing Countries under the GATT and other International Law' 1996 *German Yearbook of International Law* (39) 164.

[16] See Resolution 21(II) of the Second UNCTAD Conference. UNCTAD, *Proceedings of the Conference of 1968*, TD/97, Report and Annexes.

GATT 1947, it required a GATT waiver.[17] That waiver was granted in 1971[18] and made a permanent feature of GATT 1947 through the adoption of the *Decision on Differential and More Favourable Treatment, Reciprocity and Fuller Participation of Developing Countries* (the Enabling Clause) in 1979.[19] The Enabling Clause placed S&DT at the heart of the GATT legal regime and is arguably the central pillar of S&DT in WTO law. The Appellate Body has acknowledged its 'critical role' and it has been characterized as the 'most concrete, comprehensive and important application of the principle' of S&DT.[20]

The other core pillar of S&DT prior to the Uruguay Round was the concept of non-reciprocity. Non-reciprocity was formalized in 1965 through Part IV of the GATT 1947. Article XXXVI:8 affirmed that '[t]he developed contracting parties do not expect reciprocity for commitments made by them in trade negotiations to reduce or remove tariffs and other barriers to trade of less-developed contracting parties'. An interpretive note clarified the phrase 'do not expect reciprocity' to mean that there will be 'no balancing of concessions granted on products of interest to developing countries by developed participants' leaving the contribution that developing countries made to trade liberalization to their own discretion in light of their 'development, financial and trade needs'.[21]

While not addressing directly S&DT, the Tokyo Round in 1979 was nevertheless significant as its results were included in plurilateral agreements that did not need to be accepted by all GATT Contracting Parties. Deviating from the multilateral paradigm, this approach permitted many developing countries not to undertake the same commitments as their developed counterparts.[22]

By the 1980s, however, it was becoming apparent that the introduction of these various S&DT provisions and approaches had not reversed developing countries' marginalization within the international trading system. Consequently, a number of countries and observers began to query the overall effectiveness and value of S&DT. These concerns were linked to a critical reassessment of development policy and how trade should be regulated to support the developmental process.

---

[17] The MFN obligation has been described as the 'central organising rule of the GATT' and requires that the best tariff and non-tariff conditions extended to one GATT Contracting Party must be automatically and unconditionally extended to all other Contracting Parties. See Consultative Board, above fn 9, at para 58. See also chapter 6 of this Handbook.

[18] GATT Document L/3545 (25 June 1971), BISD 18S/24.

[19] GATT Document L/4903 (28 November 1979), BISD 26S/203, at para 1: 'Notwithstanding the provisions of Article I of the General Agreement, contracting parties may accord differential and more favourable treatment to developing countries, without according such treatment to other contracting parties'.

[20] Appellate Body Report, *EC – Tariff Preferences*, at para 14.

[21] See GATT, COM.TD/W/37 (6 January 1967), at 9.

[22] In particular, many developing countries did not accept the obligations under the various non-tariff barrier 'codes' of the Round (covering technical barriers to trade, customs valuation, import licensing, subsidies and countervailing measures, anti-dumping measures, and government procurement).

Notably, the protection of domestic industries via import substitution policies and infant industry protection was increasingly challenged as evidence mounted that industries developed behind punitive tariffs were not internationally competitive, suggesting that these policies did not in fact promote development.[23] At the same time, a number of market access concerns were revived. In particular, increasing use of contingency protection measures by developed countries, such as anti-dumping duties, countervailing measures, and 'grey-area measures' ('voluntary' export restraints and orderly marketing arrangements), appeared to be affecting developing countries' export interests negatively.[24] Furthermore, market access preferences began to be questioned, especially as GSP preferences became less effective as margins of preference were eroded with periodic reductions of MFN tariffs and the proliferation of regional trade arrangements (RTAs).[25] Perhaps most significantly, products from key sectors of interest for developing countries were either essentially excluded from the GATT 1947, such as agriculture, or subject to GATT-sanctioned derogations allowing for discriminatory restrictions, as was the case for textiles and clothing until the expiry of the ATC in 2005.[26] The dearth of significant concessions by developed countries in these sectors was attributed, in part, to the lack of reciprocal concessions by developing countries. As two respected observers put it, '[i]f you want a free lunch, you can hardly expect a banquet'.[27]

As a consequence, by the 1980s, a significant shift in developing countries' attitudes towards S&DT was taking shape. There was increased questioning of the extent to which trade policies ought to differ along development lines.[28] Developing

[23] See M Pangetsu, 'Special and Differential Treatment in the Millennium: Special for Whom and How Different?' 2000 *The World Economy* 23(9) 1289.

[24] WTO Secretariat, *Developing Countries and the Multilateral Trading System: Past and Present – Background Note by the Secretariat* (17–19 March 1999), at <http://www.wto.org/english/tratop_e/devel_e/publ_e.htm> (last visited 5 April 2008), at 17.

[25] In addition to preference erosion, other economic concerns relating to preferences included the exclusion of sectors of competitive advantage, non-trade conditions attached to receiving preferences, and restrictive rules of origin. See generally, Consultative Board, above fn 9, at paras 93–102.

[26] WTO Secretariat, above fn 24, at 17.

[27] See K Bhagwati and A Panagariya, 'The Truth About Protectionism' *Financial Times* (30 March 2001) where they call for developing countries not to shy away from reducing trade barriers on the basis that historically and '[u]nsurprisingly, giving few concessions of their own, poor countries got little in return'.

[28] See generally C Michalopoulos, 'The Role of Special and Differential Treatment for Developing Countries in the GATT and the WTO' *World Bank Working Paper Series* No. 2388 (31 July 2000), at <http://www-wds.worldbank.org/external/default/main?pagePK=64193027&piPK=64187937&theSitePK=523679&menuPK=64187510&searchMenuPK=64187283&theSitePK=523679&entityID=000094946_00081505321046&searchMenuPK=64187283&theSitePK=523679> (last visited 5 April 2008), at 30; T Srinivasan, 'Developing Countries in the World Trading System: From GATT, 1947 to the third Ministerial Meeting of the WTO, 1999' 1999 *The World Economy* 22(8), at 1047–64; J Finger, L Winters, and A Hirsch, 'What Can the WTO Do for Developing Countries?' in A Krueger (ed), *The WTO as an International Organisation* (Chicago and London: University of Chicago Press, 1998) 365.

countries entered the Uruguay Round negotiations advocating less emphasis on non-reciprocity with the negotiating objective of accepting a dilution of S&DT in exchange for better market access and strengthened rules.[29] Notably, they did not seek exemption from the multilateral trade agreements accepting the 'single undertaking' approach of the Round.

Despite the 'single undertaking' approach, the Uruguay Round did not put an end to S&DT. In fact, the WTO agreements feature no less than 145 S&DT provisions. The WTO has classified these under five main headings, with a sixth heading referring to additional provisions relating specifically to LDCs.[30] These headings distinguish between provisions: (1) aimed at increasing trade opportunities through market access, (2) requiring WTO Members to safeguard the interests of developing countries, (3) providing greater flexibility of commitments, (4) allowing for longer transitional time periods, (5) providing for technical assistance, and (6) relating to LDCs. While a number of these provisions were carried forward from earlier instruments, it is important to note the fundamental shift in focus of S&DT that occurred under the WTO agreements. In particular, new provisions on transitional periods and technical assistance were adopted to allow developing countries to accept the same commitments as their developed counterparts, but under more flexible terms, in recognition of their unique implementation and adjustment difficulties.[31]

Today, S&DT continues to be discussed and negotiated in the WTO. The concept has assumed renewed pertinence following the Doha Ministerial Conference (MC), with Ministers mandating that the WTO's future work 'shall take fully into account the principle of special and differential treatment'[32] including consideration of 'how special and differential treatment may be incorporated into the architecture of WTO rules'.[33]

---

[29] Although this is not to say that they were critical of all aspects of S&DT and certainly continued to advocate for preferential access to developed country markets, see E Kessie, 'Enforceability of the Legal Provisions Relating to Special and Differential Treatment under the WTO Agreements' 2000 *Journal of World Intellectual Property* 3(6) 962.

[30] WTO Secretariat, *Implementation of Special and Differential Treatment Provisions in WTO Agreements and Decisions – Note by the Secretariat*, WT/COMTD/W77 (25 October 2000), at 3; WTO Secretariat, above fn 24, at 18.

[31] As Whalley summarized, '[s]pecial and differential treatment changed from a focus on preferential [market] access and special rights to protect, to one of responding to special adjustment difficulties in developing countries stemming from the implementation of WTO decisions'. J Whalley, 'Special and Differential Treatment in the Millennium Round' 1999 *The World Economy* 22(8) 1073.

[32] MC, *Ministerial Conference – Fourth Session – Doha, 9–14 November 2001 – Implementation-Related Issues and Concerns – Decision of 14 November 2001*, WT/MIN(01)/17 (14 November 2001), at para 50.

[33] Ibid at para 12.

III. Legal Evaluation of the Integration of Developing Countries in the WTO Legal Regime

The perception that developing countries benefit from the increased legality of the WTO stems from the view that a rules-based system where legal rights and obligations are enforceable through the DSU's binding dispute settlement process is preferable for the economically weak than a power-based system. The DSU itself proclaims to provide 'security and predictability to the multilateral trading system' and to ensure a 'proper balance between the rights and obligations of Members'.[34]

This part provides a critical evaluation of that perception. It demonstrates that the vast majority of developing countries do not enforce their rights through dispute settlement. It then outlines the constraints explaining that lack of participation, with a special focus on the reality that a large proportion of developing-country trade occurs under rules that are not enforceable through WTO dispute settlement.

A. The Participation of Developing Countries in WTO Dispute Settlement

Measuring the extent of developing-country participation in WTO dispute settlement activity depends on how one interprets the available data and statistics. A cursory analysis of the WTO Secretariat data for the first ten years of dispute settlement activity provides a relatively positive picture. 127 of the 335 consultations requests made during that period were from developing countries,[35] 40 of the 96 panel proceedings completed involved developing-country complainants,[36] and 24 of the 53 appearances before the Appellate Body in 2006 were from developing countries.[37] A further positive development is the increasing use of the system over time. Davey notes that, by increasing their share of initiated consultations requests from 25 per cent in the first five years of the system's existence to over 60 per cent in the following

---

[34] Arts 3.2 and 3.3 DSU.

[35] WTO Secretariat, *Update of WTO Dispute Settlement Cases, New Developments since Last Update (Until 1 December 2005)*, WT/DS/OV/25 (12 December 2005), at iii–iv.

[36] R Abbott, 'Are Developing Countries Deterred from Using the WTO Dispute Settlement System? Participation of Developing Countries in the DSM in the years 1995–2005' *ECIPE Working Paper* No. 01/2007, at <http://www.ecipe.org/publications/ecipe-working-papers/are-developing-countries-deterred-from-using-the-wto-dispute-settlement-system/PDF> (last visited 5 April 2008), at 4.

[37] WTO, *Appellate Body – Annual Report for 2006*, WT/AB/7 (23 January 2007), at 12. Developing country Members made 3 appearances as appellants, 8 as other appellants, 10 as appellees, and 41 as third participants.

five years, 'developing countries have become more frequent users of WTO dispute settlement, both in absolute and relative terms'.[38] The Consultative Board is equally positive, commenting on the 'much greater participation of developing countries than was the case in the GATT dispute settlement system' and that 'developing countries—even some of the poorest...—are increasingly taking on the most powerful'.[39]

These figures and statements do not portray, however, the full picture. Statistical analysis illustrates that the dispute settlement activity of developing countries is highly concentrated with a few main users. Only five developing countries account for 60 per cent of activity.[40] Together with another eight developing countries, 90 per cent of activity is covered.[41] While this practice demonstrates that some developing countries, notably Brazil and India, are using the system effectively, the strong concentration of activity in a few developing countries highlights that the vast majority of developing countries are largely absent from the process. This is particularly the case for LDCs, with Bangladesh the only LDC to have initiated consultations in a dispute to date.[42]

When the data is examined from this perspective, a more critical assessment of developing-country participation in WTO dispute settlement activity seems warranted. Certainly, it has been commented that '[t]he poorest countries in the WTO system are almost completely disengaged from the enforcement of market access rights through formal dispute settlement litigation'.[43] Elsewhere, concerns regarding 'the absence from the game' of a large number of developing countries,[44] and the 'miniscule' participation of countries from Africa,[45] have been raised.

B. Commonly Identified Constraints Limiting Developing-Country Participation in WTO Dispute Settlement

There have been a number of analyses of the constraints limiting developing-country participation in WTO dispute settlement proceedings. This section evaluates

[38] WJ Davey, 'The WTO Dispute Settlement System: The First Ten Years' 2005 *Journal of International Economic Law* 8(1) 17, at 24; see also Abbott, above fn 36, at 8 ('the higher ratio for the most recent period 2001–2005 suggests that developing members, after a slow start within a new system, are beginning to find it more familiar and learning it can be used to best advantage').

[39] Consultative Board, above fn 9, at 50.

[40] See Abbott, above fn 36, at 9–11. The main developing-country users are Brazil, India, Thailand, Chile, and Argentina.

[41] Ibid.

[42] Request for Consultations by Bangladesh, *India – Anti-Dumping Measure on Batteries from Bangladesh*, WT/DS306/1, G/L/669, G/ADP/D52/1 (2 February 2004).

[43] See Bown and Hoekman, above fn 4, at 862.

[44] See Abbott, above fn 36, at 11.

[45] V Mosoti, 'Africa in the First Decade of WTO Dispute Settlement' 2006 *Journal of International Economic Law* 9(2) 427, at 435.

critically the commonly identified constraints,[46] noting that some have been largely addressed while others remain.

1. *Lack of Legal Expertise and Financial Resources*

Some WTO Members and commentators hold the perception that the WTO dispute settlement system is 'overly complicated and expensive' resulting in insurmountable 'human resource as well as financial implications' for developing countries.[47]

It is undeniable that the costs of litigating disputes in the WTO have increased exponentially in recent years. Commentators have estimated that 'a "litigation only" bill of US$500,000 to an exporter for a market access case is likely to be fairly typical'.[48] Legal fees can of course be much greater, with reports of fees for parties in panel proceedings in excess of US$10 million.[49]

These increased costs can be attributed, in part, to the multiple stages of WTO dispute settlement under the DSU whereby challenged measures may be subject to reviews by a panel, the Appellate Body, an arbitrator determining the reasonable period of time to comply, further reviews to determine compliance, as well as arbitration on the level of suspension of concessions.[50]

The costs of participation in these multiple stages of WTO dispute settlement are compounded by a trend towards increasingly complex and technical submissions. The WTO agreements that came into effect in 1995 include legal standards that hinge on detailed scientific or economic determinations that were not as central under the GATT 1947. For example, with the introduction of the SPS Agreement, scientific evidence of human, animal, and plant risks has been heavily litigated.[51] Similarly, provisions requiring detailed economic analysis have been the subject of a number of recent disputes under the SCM Agreement and the Agreement on Agriculture.[52]

---

[46] See, eg, G Shaffer, 'The Challenges of WTO law, Strategies for Developing Country Adaptation' 2006 *World Trade Review* 5(2) 177, at 177.

[47] This view has been espoused by the African Group in the context of negotiations on DSU review. Proposal by the African Group, *Negotiations on the Dispute Settlement Mechanism Understanding*, TN/DS/W/15 (25 September 2002), at 2; see also Bown and Hoekman, above fn 4, at 889.

[48] Bown and Hoekman, above fn 4, at 870. Nordström and Shaffer come to a similar conclusion for a dispute of medium complexity through to the Appellate Body stage. See H Nordström and G Shaffer, 'Access to Justice in the World Trade Organization: A Case for a Small Claims Procedure', *ICTSD Dispute Settlement and Legal Aspects of International Trade Issue Paper* No. 2 (June 2007), at <http://www.ictsd.org/issarea/dsu/resources/Nordstrom%20&%20Shaffer_Small_Claims.pdf> (last visited 5 April 2008), at 9–10.

[49] Nordström and Shaffer, above fn 48, at 9. Referring to the legal fees in the context of the Panel Report, *Japan – Film*. Presumably that figure will have been exceeded in subsequent complex disputes.

[50] These stages are set out in, respectively, Articles 11, 17, 21.3(c), 21.5, and 22.6 DSU. See chapters 11–16 of this Handbook.

[51] The fourth, and latest, report being the Panel Report, *EC – Biotech Products*.

[52] See, eg, Panel Report, *US – Upland Cotton*; Panel Report, *EC – Export Subsidies on Sugar*; and the ongoing disputes based on the Request for the Establishment of a Panel by the United States, *European Communities and Certain Member States – Measures Affecting Trade in Large Civil Aircraft*, (*Second Complaint*), WT/DS347/3, WT/DS316/6 (11 April 2006); and Request for the Establishment of

The binding nature of WTO dispute settlement also means that governments (and the companies behind them) are taking each dispute far more seriously, which seems to lead to longer and more detailed submissions. It also has been observed that the lack of retrospective remedies for businesses affected by illegal protectionist measures gives respondents an incentive to further complicate, hence delay, the dispute settlement process.[53]

The cost problems faced by developing countries in the WTO are accentuated by their small trade shares and government budgets. If low levels of trade are affected, the *relative* costs of litigation are higher,[54] especially in light of the high opportunity costs of investing in WTO litigation as opposed to other pressing social needs.[55] They also may lack support from well-financed private industries able to contribute resources to assist the government. These factors have resulted in developing countries being at an undeniable resource and cost disadvantage in WTO dispute settlement proceedings.

The DSU contains certain provisions designed to address these resource constraints. The utility of these provisions to date is debatable. For example, Article 27.2 DSU provides that the WTO Secretariat shall make available experts to provide 'additional legal advice and assistance' to developing countries. However, these experts may only assist 'in respect of dispute settlement' and cannot provide legal advice before a dispute is initiated. Furthermore, they may only assist the developing country Member 'in a manner ensuring the continued impartiality of the Secretariat', making it impossible to act as an advocate in a legal proceeding.

The DSU also attempts to address resource constraints indirectly by providing for simplified and expedited procedures. For example, Article 3.12 DSU allows a developing-country Member to invoke the provisions contained in the 1966 Procedures[56] that envisage, following the 'good offices' of the WTO Director-General (DG), an expedited panel process of only two months in contrast to the nine-month general rule in Article 20 DSU. Similarly, Article 24.2 of the DSU contemplates LDCs requesting the alternative procedures of 'good offices, conciliation and mediation' by the DG. In addition, Articles 5 ('Good Offices, Conciliation, and Mediation') and 25 ('Arbitration') DSU provide for alternative approaches available to all Members. Since the establishment of the WTO, however, developing countries have rarely utilized

a Panel by the European Communities, *United States – Measures Affecting Trade in Large Civil Aircraft (Second Complaint)*, WT/DS317/5, WT/DS353/2 (23 January 2006).

[53] ML Busch and E Reinhardt, *Testing International Trade Law: Empirical Studies of GATT/WTO Dispute Settlement*, Paper presented at the University of Minnesota Law School Conference on the Political Economy of International Trade Law (15–16 September 2000), at <http://www.userwww.service.emory.edu/~erein/research/titl.pdf> (last visited 5 April 2008).

[54] See Bown and Hoekman, above fn 4, at 867. Providing a simple economic model reflecting that 'a country will file a complaint if the legal fees are lower than the discounted gain in profits the complainant would receive from increased market access due to the removal of the WTO-inconsistent measure'.

[55] See Shaffer, above fn 46, at 185.

[56] GATT, *Decision of 5 April 1966 on Procedures Under Article XXIII*, BISD 14S/18.

these alternative procedures. Notable exceptions are resort to the 1966 Procedures in a dispute between Colombia and the EC in 2007[57] and a request for mediation by the Philippines, Thailand and the EC in 2002.[58] Roessler attributes the relative lack of use of these procedures to a 'fear that the application of procedural provisions biased in [developing countries'] favour may detract from the legitimacy of the result... hence reduce the normative force of the rulings'.[59] Elsewhere, doubts have been raised whether these provisions truly address resource and capacity constraints.[60] An alternative explanation may simply be that more time is needed before developing countries feel comfortable using these less conventional approaches.

While the effectiveness of these special provisions in the DSU at addressing developing countries' capacity constraints may be questioned, certain initiatives independent of the DSU appear to have been more successful. The most far-reaching initiative came in 2001, when a group of WTO Members established the Advisory Centre on WTO Law (ACWL) as an independent inter-governmental organization with the mandate to provide developing countries with support in WTO dispute settlement proceedings, as well as legal advice and training on WTO law.[61] The ACWL provides its legal services to developing countries for free or at heavily subsidized rates.[62] These services are financed largely by an endowment fund of developed-country and developing-country contributions. The ACWL has been identified as being the first 'international legal aid' centre in international law.[63] Ehlermann, former Chairman of the Appellate Body, stated at the inauguration of the ACWL that the organization 'will strengthen the notion that the dispute

---

[57] Request for Consultations by Colombia, *European Communities – Regime for the Importation of Bananas*, WT/DS361/1 (26 March 2007). The 'good offices' process commenced in December 2007 and continued into 2008. The provisions of the 1966 Decision were resorted to on six occasions between 1978 and 1993 by developing countries. *Analytical Index: Guide to GATT Law and Practice*, Vol 2 (Geneva: WTO, 1995) at 765–66.

[58] Communication from the DG, *Request for Mediation by the Philippines, Thailand and the European Communities*, WT/GC/66 (16 October 2002). This mediation was not requested pursuant to Article 5 DSU but followed the procedures in that provision.

[59] See F Roessler, 'Special and Differential Treatment of Developing Countries under the WTO Dispute Settlement System' in F Ortino and E-U Petersmann (eds), *The WTO Dispute Settlement System 1995–2003* (The Hague: Kluwer, 2004) 89.

[60] The African Group of countries in the WTO has commented that these provisions of the DSU have 'not fully and coherently addressed the core difficulties developing country Memebers face in seeking to use the WTO dispute settlement system'. See Proposal by the African Group, *Negotiations on the Dispute Settlement Mechanism Understanding*, TN/DS/W/15 (25 September 2002).

[61] As of January 2008, the services of the ACWL were available to 27 developing countries that had become Members of the ACWL and the 42 LDCs that were WTO Members or were in the process of acceding to the WTO. See ACWL webpage at <http://www.acwl.ch> (last visited 25 January 2008).

[62] Legal advice and training is provided for free to all ACWL developing-country Members and all LDCs. Support in dispute settlement proceedings is charged according to hourly rates that vary between CHF 40 and CHF 324 according to each country's share of world trade and income per capita. These rates are applied in conjunction with a time budget established by the Management Board.

[63] Speech delivered by DG Moore at the Inauguration of the ACWL (5 October 2001), at <http://www.acwl.ch/e/tools/news_detailsphoto_e.aspx?id=a6e9c8a0-ce05–417c-8f56-d2eabb3d11f7> (last visited 5 April 2008).

settlement system of the WTO is available to the economically weak as much as it is available to the economically strong'.[64]

It has been commented that, since its establishment, the ACWL 'has largely addressed many of the capacity constraints' faced by developing countries in WTO dispute settlement procedures.[65] At the time of writing, the ACWL has provided support in 25 dispute settlement proceedings, which represents over 20 per cent of all proceedings initiated since 2001. The ACWL has provided hundreds of legal opinions on issues of WTO law, including the merits of potential dispute settlement proceedings. It also provides detailed training activities for Geneva-based delegates of developing countries and LDCs.[66]

While the ACWL does not address all constraints faced by developing countries in accessing the WTO dispute settlement system, the extent to which a lack of legal expertise limits their participation is now considerably mitigated.

2. Lack of Domestic Mechanisms to Identify and Act against Trade Barriers

Despite initiatives such as the ACWL, access to lawyers is of little use if WTO Members lack domestic mechanisms to identify and to act against trade barriers in the first place. In this regard, Abbott notes that developing countries may still be at a disadvantage when initial steps are taken to 'identify the trade barrier' which 'clearly has to precede any help with legal evaluation'.[67]

It is true that a WTO Member's participation in dispute settlement activities will be a function of its ability to identify trade barriers faced by the private sector. As Shaffer comments, pre-requisites for effective use of the WTO system are mechanisms to 'perceive injuries to its trading prospects, identify who is responsible, and mobilize resources to bring a legal claim or negotiate a favourable settlement'.[68]

This 'naming, blaming, and claiming' process is dependent upon effective procedures for gathering and processing information on trade barriers. It is an area where many developing countries lack capacity. This can be contrasted with the procedures in most developed WTO Members such as the EC, the US, and Japan.[69] It has been

---

[64] Speech delivered by the Appellate Body Chairman Claus-Dieter Ehlermann at the Inauguration of the ACWL (5 October 2001), at <http://www.acwl.ch/e/tools/news_detailsphoto_e.aspx?id=fe20e0da-ad83–479f-9dc8-c8908b40f63d> (last visited 5 April 2008).

[65] Abbott, above fn 36, at 12; see also Bown and Hoekman, above fn 4, at 875.

[66] ACWL, 'How to Use the Services of the ACWL: A Guide for Developing Countries and LDCs' (October 2007), at <http://www.acwl.ch/e/tools/news_detailsphoto_e.aspx?id=8abfec8d-a635-4753-bca3-a7a38bdde9ae> (last visited 5 April 2008).

[67] See Abbott, above fn 36, at 12–3.

[68] See Shaffer, above fn 46, at 179.

[69] Resulting in the (i) the European Commission Market Access Database, (ii) the USTR Annual National Trade Estimate Reports on Foreign Trade Barriers and 'Special 301' Reports on intellectual property, and (iii) Japan's Ministry of Economy, Trade and Industry (METI) Annual Reports on the WTO Inconsistency of Trade Policies by Major Trading Partners.

suggested that developing countries should request the assistance of development agencies and foundations to assist them in identifying trade barriers faced by their private sectors.[70] A more radical suggestion has been for 'an independent Special Prosecutor or Advocate' mandated 'to identify potential WTO violations on behalf of developing countries'.[71] A market-oriented solution would be the development of public-private networks for trade litigation to assist export sectors to communicate trade barriers to the government. The majority of developed-country governments have fostered such coordination with the private sector and certain of the more active developing country litigants, notably Brazil, have taken significant steps in this direction.[72] Nonetheless, for the majority of developing countries, the lack of effective mechanisms to identify trade barriers remains a severe limitation curtailing their use of the WTO dispute settlement system.

3. *Low Levels of World Trade and Small Domestic Markets*

A further explanation for the lack of developing-country participation in WTO dispute settlement might be the relatively low volumes in which many developing countries trade. Statistical analysis has found that developing countries tend to have smaller aggregate and disaggregate trading stakes.[73] Bown and Hoekman consider that these low volumes, often in competitive markets with low profit margins, 'make it difficult to charge mark-ups to cover any non-economic (that is, litigation) costs associated with maintaining or enforcing market access rights'.[74] The rationale being that claims involving smaller trade stakes are not offset by smaller litigation costs. Examination of the data confirms that a WTO Member's level of participation in dispute settlement activity reflects fairly closely its stake in world trade.[75]

This consideration may explain the relative dearth of dispute settlement cases *brought by* the smaller developing countries. Similarly, the small size of their domestic markets may explain why those same countries have not been regularly *targeted as* defendants. One proposed solution for developing-country complainants has been the introduction of 'lighter' and less costly dispute settlement mechanisms into the WTO, such as a 'small claims procedure' for disputes that involve low monetary values of trade.[76] As noted above, however, options already exist under the DSU for expedited and less costly dispute resolution.

---

[70] See Shaffer, above fn 46, at 184.

[71] B Hoekman, 'Strengthening the Global Trade Architecture for Development' 2002 *World Trade Review* 1(1) 23, at 26.

[72] See G Shaffer, *Defending Interests: Public–Private Partnerships in WTO Litigation* (Washington, DC: Brookings Institution, 2003).

[73] See Nordström and Shaffer, above fn 48, at 1–8.

[74] See Bown and Hoekman, above fn 4, at 863.

[75] See Abbott, above fn 36, at 13.

[76] See, eg, the small claims procedure proposed by Nordström and Shaffer, above fn 48.

An associated constraining factor might be the inability of many developing countries to enforce positive rulings due to their lack of domestic market power. Without domestic market power, the WTO's enforcement measures have been characterized as 'virtually meaningless'.[77] The argument is that Article 22 DSU envisages a right of retaliation through the suspension of trade concessions, but developing countries with small domestic markets are not able to impose sufficient economic or political losses within the respondent Member to generate the requisite pressure to induce compliance. In fact, the suspension of concessions may be *more* detrimental to the developing country. For example, Ecuador never used its right to retaliation in *EC – Bananas III*, citing 'the enormous imbalance in trade relations between Ecuador and the European Communities, the difference in degree of economic development and the serious economic situation it was facing'.[78] Studies of the data give the somewhat alarming picture that a developing country has *never* imposed retaliation measures to induce compliance.[79]

These constraints ought not to be overstated. While some developing countries may trade in relatively low volumes, initiatives such as the ACWL permit litigation at heavily discounted rates. Furthermore, while a lack of enforcement power is a reality for many developing countries, in practice the ability to retaliate may not be a significant determinant of implementation. In this regard, Davey's analysis of the first ten years of the WTO dispute settlement system indicates a successful implementation rate of adopted panel and Appellate Body reports of 83 per cent.[80] Only 10 of the 181 initiated disputes examined resulted in no implementation or disagreement over implementation.[81] That said, the constraint of a lack of effective retaliation ability should not be discounted entirely.[82] Numerous suggestions have been made over the years to address the problem.[83] One proposal that has gained

---

[77] M Footer, 'Developing Country Practice in the Matter of WTO Dispute Settlement' 2001 *Journal of World Trade* 35(1) 55, at 94. See also chapter 15 of this Handbook.

[78] DSB, *Minutes of the Meeting of the Dispute Settlement Body Held on 19 November 1999*, WT/DSB/M/71 (11 January 2000), at 5.

[79] K Bagwell, PC Mavroidis, and RW Staiger, 'The Case for Tradable Remedies in WTO Dispute Settlement', *World Bank Policy Research Paper* No. 3314 (2004), at <http://www-wds.worldbank.org/external/default/main?pagePK=64193027&piPK=64187937&theSitePK=523679&menuPK=64187510&searchMenuPK=64187283&theSitePK=523679&entityID=000112742_20040727165316&searchMenuPK=64187283&theSitePK=523679> (last visited 5 April 2008), at 14–15.

[80] Davey, above fn 38, at 46–8.

[81] Ibid. at 47.

[82] WJ Davey, 'The WTO: Looking Forwards' 2006 *Journal of International Economic Law* 9(1) 3, at 12. Noting that the US Congress has tended to implement in cases where 'failure to do so results in sanctions on US exports being applied (or threatened)'.

[83] For an overview, see RE Hudec, 'The Adequacy of WTO Dispute Settlement Remedies for Developing Country Complainants' in B Hoekman, A Mattoo, and P English (eds), *Development, Trade and the WTO: A Handbook* (Washington, DC: The World Bank, 2002).

considerable support in the DSU review negotiations has been the possibility of tradable retaliation rights.[84]

4. *Fears of Political and Economic Pressures*

Commentators have noted that developing and least-developed countries may be unwilling to initiate WTO dispute settlement proceedings against trade barriers of developed countries due to their particular vulnerability to retaliation in other areas such as development assistance or preferential market access.[85] It has been observed that 'there may be little that a small developing country can do to counter threats to withdraw preferential tariff benefits or foreign aid...were the country to challenge a trade measure'.[86] It is difficult to determine whether these pressures are applied in practice.[87] Nevertheless, it is apparent that many developing countries *perceive* that such consequences might flow from the initiation of a WTO dispute. This in turn may have a chilling effect on their participation. Romano has written that of all the factors affecting the decision to litigate 'perhaps the most fundamental one is...the willingness to utilise international judicial bodies'.[88] That said, the lack of participation of certain developing countries in dispute settlement activity may be a rational decision not to dedicate resources to a dispute that is already being litigated by another WTO Member. Where restrictive measures are applied to imports of all origins, or relate to subsidies that affect the trade a number of WTO Members, there is a degree of logic behind smaller WTO Members not actively participating in disputes initiated by other WTO Members and merely free-riding on the implementation of positive rulings through the operation of the various MFN clauses of the WTO agreements.

The above analysis of the commonly identified constraints limiting developing-country participation in WTO dispute settlement illustrates that while certain limitations have been largely addressed, a priority area remains creating effective *domestic* mechanisms for governments to identify and act against trade barriers faced by their private sectors.

---

[84] See Proposal by Mexico, *Negotiations on Improvements and Clarifications of the Dispute Settlement Understanding*, TN/DS/W/23 (4 November 2002), at 5–6.

[85] See Bown and Hoekman, above fn 4, at 863.

[86] See Shaffer, above fn 46, at 193.

[87] Shaffer states that threats of this nature have been 'confirmed in a number of interviews, including with a former member of USTR'. See Shaffer, above fn 46, at 193, fn 66. In contrast, Abbott notes that 'there is not much empirical evidence that this has actually happened'. See Abbott, above fn 36, at 14. Bown and Hoekman, reflect on the lack of certainty, noting that the 'evidence as to whether such political arrangements affect the willingness of countries to engage in WTO dispute settlement activity relating to their trading interests is inconclusive'. See Bown and Hoekman, above fn 4, at 863, fn 9.

[88] CPR Romano, 'International Justice and Developing Countries (Continued): A Qualitative Analysis' 2002 *The Law and Practice of International Courts and Tribunals* 1(3) 539, at 551–52.

C. The Reality that a Significant Portion of Developing-Country Trade Occurs Under Rules that Are Not Part of Enforceable WTO Law

Even if all the commonly-identified constraints were addressed fully, it would not ensure a surge in developing-country participation in WTO disputes. This is due to the reality, largely ignored by commentators to date, that a significant portion of developing-country trade falls under rules that are not enforceable through WTO dispute settlement.

1. *The Limited Scope of Enforceable WTO Law*

A WTO Member may enforce the rules under which it trades in the WTO dispute settlement system only if those rules are contained in a relevant WTO agreement. Article 1 DSU limits the scope of enforceable rights and obligations to those in the WTO Agreement, the multilateral trade agreements annexed to it, as well as the two remaining plurilateral trade agreements (collectively the 'covered agreements'). In this respect, enforceable WTO law has a limited scope. As the Appellate Body confirmed, the WTO dispute settlement system cannot be used 'to determine rights and obligations *outside the covered agreements*'.[89]

2. *Many Rules Governing Developing-Country Trade Are Not Part of Enforceable WTO Law*

Analysis of developing-country trade illustrates that a significant portion is regulated by rules that are not part of enforceable WTO law. In particular, many developing countries and LDCs access markets in developed countries through preferential schemes that do not create rights enforceable in WTO dispute settlement proceedings.

When developed countries provide preferential market access to developing countries, they have tended to not bind that treatment in their WTO schedules. Unless bound in a WTO schedule, this preferential treatment is not part of enforceable WTO law. This situation can be contrasted with treatment bound in WTO schedules. As WTO schedules are an integral part of the GATT 1994 and the GATS, the treatment bound in a schedule is part of the 'covered agreements' and failure to

---

[89] Appellate Body Report, *Mexico – Taxes on Soft Drinks*, at para 56 (emphasis added). See Articles 1.3, 2, 7.1, 11, 19.2, and 23 DSU. Noting that while panels and the Appellate Body cannot *enforce* rules in instruments outside the covered agreements, they may examine those instruments as part of a legal justification for measures otherwise inconsistent with WTO law (for example a regional trade agreement consistent with Article XXIV GATT 1994 or preferential agreement consistent with the Enabling Clause may be examined as justification for measures otherwise inconsistent with Article 1:1 GATT 1994). See also chapter 10 of this Handbook.

accord that treatment can be raised as a claim in DSU proceedings. For example, a failure to 'accord to the commerce of [another Member]' the treatment specified in a goods schedule is a breach of Article II GATT 1994. Similarly, a failure to 'accord services and service suppliers of any other Member' the treatment specified in a services schedule is a breach of Articles XVI:1 and XVII:1 GATS. This has led to unbound preferential treatment being described as a 'strategy that is fundamentally unstable' with 'scope for ad hoc decisions' whereby preferences are 'withdrawn at the discretion of the preference-provider'.[90]

Nonetheless, a significant portion of developing-country trade into developed-country markets is regulated by preferential rules. As noted, since the early 1960s, most developed countries have provided non-reciprocal preferential access through GSP schemes for which the Enabling Clause was obtained.[91] Other preferential schemes, limited to a subset of WTO Members, include the preferential treatment granted to the EC market for goods of African, Caribbean and Pacific (ACP) origin as required by the Cotonou Agreement and its predecessor the Lomé Convention, and preferential treatment granted to the US market for goods of African, Andean Community, and Caribbean origin as required by the African Growth and Opportunity Act, the Andean Trade Preferences Act, and the Caribbean Basin Economic Recovery Act. A number of WTO Members also provide duty-free and quota-free access to LDCs under 'Everything But Arms' schemes justified by the Enabling Clause.

A comprehensive OECD study finds that approximately half of all imports from eligible developing countries into the EC and Australian markets and approximately one third of all such imports into the US, Canadian, and Japanese markets enter under preferential rules.[92] For many developing countries the value of trade under preferences is considerable.[93] While a proportion of imports from larger developing countries also enter these markets under MFN tariffs, LDCs and small developing-country suppliers have the highest shares of trade falling under preferential rules.[94]

The lack of legal security and predictability when trading under preferential rules has led to a number of calls by beneficiary countries for tariff preferences to be bound

[90] A Keck and P Low, 'Special and Differential Treatment in the WTO: Why, When and How', *WTO Staff Working Paper* ERSD 2004–03 (January 2007), at <http://www.wto.org/english/res_e/reser_e/ersd200403_e.htm >(last visited 5 April 2008), at 12.

[91] Currently, the WTO Members that grant preferences under the Enabling Clause include: Australia, Belarus, Canada, the EC, Japan, New Zealand, Norway, Poland, Russia, Switzerland, and the US. See WT/COMTD/W/93.

[92] D Lippoldt and P Kowalski, 'Trade Preference Erosion: Potential Economic Impacts', *OECD Trade Policy Working Paper* No. 17, TD/TC/WP(2004)30/FINAL (26 April 2005), at <http://www.olis.oecd.org/olis/2004doc.nsf/LinkTo/NT000096AE/$FILE/JT00183004.PDF> (last visited 5 April 2008), at para 48.

[93] A number of developing countries exported over USD 100 million in trade to each of the five destination markets studied. Ibid at para 51. See also Jackson, above fn 1, at 325. At its peak in 1994, the US GSP system reportedly covered upwards of USD 19 billion worth of imports.

[94] Ibid. at para 7.

in Members' WTO schedules.[95] The binding of preferences remains, however, controversial. Developed countries would lose the flexibility to alter the programmes in response to competing policy considerations. Currently, the only area where there seems to be a political will to bind tariff preferences relates to the granting of duty-free and quota-free market access to products from LDCs. The Hong Kong Ministerial Declaration states that by 2008, or the start of the Doha Round implementation period, 'developed-country Members shall' provide duty-free and quota-free market access 'on a lasting basis...in a manner that ensures stability, security and predictability'.[96] There is some controversy whether this declaration creates a legal obligation or would need to be re-stated in a separate instrument before being enforceable.[97]

While developing-country beneficiaries cannot enforce unbound preferential treatment through WTO dispute settlement, the nature of preferential market access makes it vulnerable to DSU challenge by developing countries excluded from those schemes. Developing countries excluded from preferential schemes often have a commercial motivation to challenge such schemes as their market access opportunities in lucrative developed-country markets is curtailed through the margin of preference granted to beneficiaries.

All preferential schemes require a legal justification for preferences that are otherwise inconsistent with the MFN obligation in Article I:1 GATT 1994. That legal justification can take the form of the Enabling Clause, discrete waivers granted under Article IX WTO Agreement, or RTAs consistent with Article XXIV GATT 1994. Where a developing country excluded from a scheme feels that the conditions in these justifications are not fulfilled, it may challenge the scheme in DSU proceedings.

For example, the Enabling Clause requires that preferential tariff treatment under GSP schemes be 'generalized, non-reciprocal and non-discriminatory'.[98] In *EC – Tariff Preferences*, India claimed successfully that certain aspects of the EC GSP scheme, from which it was excluded, were not applied in accordance with those conditions.[99] It is noteworthy that disputes brought against GSP schemes are

---

[95] These calls are not limited to binding concessions in goods schedules. In 2006, the LDC Group put forward a proposal whereby developed countries 'shall' provide 'non-reciprocal special priority' in services sectors and modes of supply of interest to LDCs 'on a permanent basis and in a manner that ensures security, stability and predictability'. Communication from the Republic of Zambia on behalf of the LDC Group, *A Mechanism to Operationalize Article IV:3 of the GATS*, TN/S/W/59 (28 March 2006).

[96] WTO MC, *Hong Kong Ministerial Declaration Adopted on 18 December 2005*, WT/MIN(05)/DEC (22 December 2005), at paras 36–37, read with proposal 36 in Annex F.

[97] H Nottage and T Sebastian, 'Giving Legal Effect to the Results of WTO Negotiations: An Analysis of the Methods of Changing WTO Law' 2006 *Journal of International Economic Law* 9(4) 989, at 1003–10.

[98] Enabling Clause, fn 3 read in conjunction with para 2(a).

[99] Appellate Body Report, *EC – Tariff Preferences*, at para 145.

rare.[100] Roessler has observed that 'if a developing country challenges a condition that it must fulfill to obtain preferences, it runs the risk of no longer being able to obtain the preferences under any conditions'.[101] Thus, the 'fear factor' identified above as one of the constraints facing developing countries may deter a developing country from challenging a GSP scheme.

Where preferential tariff schemes do not meet the conditions of the Enabling Clause, notably where preferences are limited to a subset of WTO Members, they have often been justified through discrete waivers to the MFN obligation. The EC's preferential tariff treatment to products of ACP origin has been justified, at times, in this manner.[102] This preferential treatment has been challenged, however, in WTO dispute settlement on a number of occasions by non-beneficiaries. Most recently, in 2007, five Latin American banana-producing countries challenged preferences granted to ACP bananas on the basis that the conditions in the relevant waiver had not been fulfilled.

A further possible legal justification for preferential tariff treatment otherwise inconsistent with Article I:1 GATT 1994 is an RTA falling within the meaning of Article XXIV GATT 1994. Traditionally, this mechanism has not been associated with classical preferential market access granted to developing countries as Article XXIV requires *reciprocal* liberalization by the developing country.[103] Nonetheless, the EC has been active in promoting RTAs as legal justification for continuing preferential tariff treatment, most recently in the Economic Partnership Agreements it has negotiated with ACP countries.[104] In *Turkey – Textiles*, the Appellate Body effectively confirmed that panels and the Appellate Body have the jurisdiction to examine whether an RTA fulfils Article XXIV conditions.[105]

The key message remains that developing-country beneficiaries are not able to enforce unbound preferential treatment through WTO dispute settlement. Thus, when developing countries trade under preferential rules they are effectively

---

[100]   The only other example, since the Enabling Clause was enacted in 1971, related to the Request for Consultations by Brazil, *European Communities – Measures Affecting Soluble Coffee*, WT/DS209/1 (19 October 2000).

[101]   F Roessler, 'The Scope of WTO Law Enforced through the WTO Dispute Settlement Procedures' in M Janow, V Donaldson, and A Janovich (eds), *The WTO: Governance, Dispute Settlement & Developing Countries* (New York: Juris Publishing, 2008) Chapter 23.

[102]   For example, in 2001 a waiver was granted to the extent necessary to permit the EC to provide preferential tariff treatment for imports of products originating in ACP States as required by Article 36.3, Annex V and its Protocols of the Cotonou Agreement. MC Decision, *European Communities – The ACP-EC Partnership Agreement*, WT.MIN(01)/15 (15 November 2001).

[103]   GATT Panel Report, *EEC – Bananas*, at para 162.

[104]   See, generally, L Bartels, 'The Trade and Development Policy of the European Union' 2007 *European Journal of International Law* 18(4) 715.

[105]   Appellate Body Report, *Turkey - Textiles*, at paras 59–60. However, as noted, developing countries that are part of an RTA cannot use the WTO dispute settlement system to enforce preferential treatment granted in those arrangements. Appellate Body Report, *Mexico – Taxes on Soft Drinks*, at paras 56 and 78.

excluded from the benefits of the 'security and predictability' provided by WTO legal regime and the DSU.

This conclusion applies equally with respect to those S&DT provisions in the WTO agreements that are vague, permissive, or aspirational. As one commentator concluded, 'much of the WTO provisions dealing with special and differential treatment could be said to be unenforceable, as they are expressed in imprecise and hortatory language'.[106]

IV. Conclusion

The introduction of binding WTO dispute settlement is perceived to be of considerable benefit for developing countries. The shift from a power- to a rules-based system is seen to permit even the smallest and weakest economic powers to enforce the rules under which they trade and consequently to provide unprecedented security and predictability in their trading relations. This benefit could be characterized as the 'enforcement impact' of the DSU.

This chapter has evaluated that perception, with a focus on the reality that a significant proportion of developing-country trade occurs under preferential rules that are not part of enforceable WTO law.

This reality leads to certain important conclusions. First, it should come as no surprise that those developing countries that trade most under preferential rules, especially the LDCs, are not particularly active in WTO dispute settlement activity. Second, this will remain the case as long as the multilateral trading system continues to segregate the rules under which the poorest trade from those enforceable in WTO dispute settlement. Third, the perception that the WTO's shift to a rules-based system benefits the small and the weak, while correct in legal theory, is misplaced when developing countries trade under unbound preferences. Thus, the integration of developing countries in the WTO legal regime is stunted relative to their developed counterparts.

This chapter does not attempt to provide an economic evaluation of the benefits of non-reciprocal preferential rules for development. Some believe that 'special and differential treatment has had only a marginal effect on country economic performance, especially through GSP'[107] and that 'empirical studies of the impact of GSP schemes conclude that little benefit has in fact accrued to developing countries'.[108]

[106]   See Kessie, above fn 29, at 975.
[107]   J Whalley, 'Non-discriminatory Discrimination: Special and Differential Treatment under the GATT for Developing Countries' 1990 *The Economic Journal* (100) 1318.
[108]   See Consultative Board, above fn 9, at para 99.

These criticisms warrant further analysis. At the same time, it is widely recognized that other aspects of S&DT, such as transition periods and technical assistance, are essential. Furthermore, few would challenge the proposition that, on occasion, some differentiation of substantive obligations is required to accommodate the special position of developing countries in world trade. The economic evaluation at this juncture is, therefore, not whether to have S&DT, but where and in what form it is most effective.[109] In this regard, it has been noted that S&DT should not be pursued as a mantra to the detriment of multilateral commitments that would benefit developing countries.[110]

Regardless of the economic situation, a legal evaluation of the rules that attempt to integrate developing countries in world trade demonstrates that many developing countries are still to benefit fully from the enforcement impact provided by the DSU. It is hoped that this chapter will trigger further analysis of the relationship between trade and development from not only an economic perspective but also a legal perspective and thus respond to the call for a 'deeper and more focused engagement ... to ensure that the trading system contributes to development and growth'.[111]

SELECTED BIBLIOGRAPHY

R Abbott, 'Are Developing Countries Deterred from Using the WTO Dispute Settlement System? Participation of Developing Countries in the DSM in the years 1995–2005'

L Bartels, 'The Trade and Development Policy of the European Union' 2007 *European Journal of International Law* 18(4) 715

C Bown and B Hoekman, 'WTO Dispute Settlement and the Missing Developing Country Cases: Engaging the Private Sector' 2005 *Journal of International Economic Law* 8(4) 861

Consultative Board, *The Future of the WTO: Addressing Institutional Challenges in the New Millennium* (Geneva: WTO, 2004)

J Finger, L Winters, and A Hirsch, 'What can the WTO do for Developing Countries?' in A Krueger (ed), *The WTO as an International Organisation* (Chicago and London: University of Chicago Press, 1998) 365

B Hoekman, 'Strengthening the Global Trade Architecture for Development' 2002 *World Trade Review* 1(1) 23

RE Hudec, *Developing Countries in the GATT Legal System* (London: Gower, 1987)

RE Hudec, 'The Adequacy of WTO Dispute Settlement Remedies for Developing Country Complainants' in B Hoekman, A Mattoo, and P English (eds), *Development, Trade and the WTO: A Handbook* (Washington, DC: World Bank, 2002) 81

---

[109] See Pangetsu, above fn 23, at 1295.

[110] Keck and Low, above fn 90, at 8–10. H Nottage, 'Trade and Competition in the WTO: Pondering the Applicability of Special and Differential Treatment' 2003 *Journal of International of Economic Law* 6(1) 23, at 47.

[111] WTO, *Annual Report 2007 – Forward to the World Trade Report 2007 by Pascal Lamy* (Geneva: WTO, 2007), at iii–iv.

JH Jackson, *The World Trading System: Law and Policy of International Economic Relations*, 2nd edn (Cambridge: MIT Press, 1999)

M Janow, V Donaldson, and A Janovich (eds), *The WTO: Governance, Dispute Settlement & Developing Countries* (New York: Juris Publishing, 2008)

A Keck and P Low, 'Special and Differential Treatment in the WTO: Why, When and How', *WTO Staff Working Paper* ERSD 2004–03 (January 2007)

D Lippoldt and P Kowalski, 'Trade Preference Erosion: Potential Economic Impacts' *OECD Trade Policy Working Paper* No. 17, TD/TC/WP(2004)30/FINAL (26 April 2005)

C Michalopoulos, 'The Role of Special and Differential Treatment for Developing Countries in the GATT and the WTO', *World Bank Working Paper Series* No. 2388 (2000)

C Michalopoulos, 'Special and Differential Treatment: The Need for a New Approach' in GP Sampson and WB Chambers (eds), *Developing Countries and the WTO: Policy Approaches* (New York: UNU Press, 2008)

R Newfarmer (ed), *Trade, Doha, and Development: A Window into the Issues* (Washington, DC: World Bank, 2005)

M Pangetsu, 'Special and Differential Treatment in the Millennium: Special for Whom and How Different?' 2000 *The World Economy* 23(9) 1285

F Roessler, 'Special and Differential Treatment of Developing Countries under the WTO Dispute Settlement System' in F Ortino and E-U Petersmann (eds), *The WTO Dispute Settlement System 1995–2003* (The Hague: Kluwer Law International, 2004) 87

G Shaffer, 'The Challenges of WTO Law, Strategies for Developing Country Adaptation' 2006 *World Trade Review* 5(2) 117

J Whalley, 'Special and Differential Treatment in the Millennium Round' 1999 *The World Economy* 22(8) 1065

WTO Secretariat, *Developing Countries and the Multilateral Trading System: Past and Present – Background Note by the Secretariat* (17–19 March 1999)

WTO Secretariat, *Implementation of Special and Differential Treatment Provisions in WTO Agreements and Decisions – Note by the Secretariat*, WT/COMTD/W77 (25 October 2000)

CHAPTER 18

....

TRADE AND ENVIRONMENT

....

DANIEL BODANSKY
JESSICA C LAWRENCE*

* The authors would like to thank David Balton, Lorand Bartels, Steve Charnovitz, Theodore Lawrence, and Gregory Shaffer for their valuable comments.

I. INTRODUCTION

THE relationship between the trade and environmental regimes has been a turbulent one, raising fundamental questions of policy and practice. Are the two regimes mutually supportive or in tension with one another? To the extent that conflicts arise, how should they be addressed? Can the objectives of free trade and environmental protection be reconciled, or are conflicts inevitable? And if the latter, what is the appropriate balance between the two?

To some degree, these questions have been present since the birth of the international trade regime in the 1940s,[1] and they began to receive significant attention in the early 1970s,[2] when international environmental issues first came to prominence. But the linkages and potential conflicts between international trade liberalization and environmental protection have truly come to the fore only in the last two decades.

The emergence of tensions between the two regimes is unsurprising. As the scope of each has expanded, they have inevitably come into greater contact with one another, increasing the potential for conflict. On the one hand, the success of the WTO and other agreements in reducing tariffs has caused an increased focus on the threat posed by non-tariff trade barriers (NTBs), including environmental regulations, which have themselves grown dramatically in number and scope over the past several decades. On the other hand, the expansion of international trade has led to heightened concern about the potentially negative impacts of deregulated international commerce on the environment.

These tensions have been exacerbated by a 'two cultures' problem.[3] As Daniel Esty notes, trade and environmental experts tend to have different styles and perspectives. The trade community generally takes a more anthropocentric, outcome-oriented approach, emphasizing efficiency. Environmentalists take a more absolutist, moralistic approach, encompassing non-human values. Trade lawyers tend to see regulations as barriers to trade; environmentalists as a means of preventing destructive types of behaviour. Indeed, even the word 'protection' carries a very different

---

[1] The Charter of the never-formed International Trade Organization (ITO) included an exception for measures 'taken in pursuance of any inter-governmental agreement which relates solely to the conservation of fisheries resources, migratory birds, or wild animals...'. *Havana Charter for an International Trade Organization*, done at Havana, 24 March 1948, UN Doc. E/Conf. 2/78 (not in force), Arts 45(1)(a)(x) and 70(1)(d).

[2] See, eg, CS Pearson, 'The Trade and Environment Nexus: What is New Since '72' in D Zaelke et al (eds), *Trade and the Environment: Law, Economics, and Policy* (Washington, DC: Island Press, 1993), 23.

[3] DC Esty, *Greening the GATT: Trade, Environment, and the Future* (Washington, DC: Institute for International Economics, 1994); CP Snow, *Two Cultures and the Scientific Revolution* (Cambridge: Cambridge University Press, 1959).

meaning in the two communities. For environmentalists it 'warms the heart' while for trade lawyers it 'sends chills down the spine'.[4]

To add further complication, an undercurrent of conflict between developed and developing countries pervades the discussion of trade-environment linkages. The global South has been sceptical of what are sometimes seen as attempts by well-funded Western NGOs to link trade and the environment to the detriment of developing States. This suspicion grows out of a sense that developed countries are unfairly seeking to hold the developing world to standards that the wealthier nations did not observe during their own economic development. Southern States frequently construct environmentalism differently than their Northern trading partners, and they see the developed world's prioritization of certain environmental issues and exclusion of others as closely linked to the needs of international traders.[5] As a result, many in the South perceive developed country environmental regulations as veiled attempts to deny them market access and protect Northern industries, rather than as legitimate measures to achieve environmental aims. Although UNCTAD and other development organizations have worked to highlight the needs and perspectives of developing States,[6] their efforts have had limited success.

As the linkages between trade and environment have moved to the centre of the scholarly map, a number of debates have crystallized regarding the scope and purpose of the international trade regime and its relationship to domestic and international environmental protection. Should trade agreements be self-contained, or should they incorporate environmental principles or consider other (environmental) agreements—for example, in the context of dispute settlement? Conversely, should national governments be free to impose trade restrictions in furtherance of their environmental goals, either individually or through multilateral environmental agreements? More generally, should the international community privilege free trade or environmental protection when conflicts between the two arise?

In recent years, the trade and environmental communities have had a partial rapprochement, as each has become more sensitive to the other. However, a significant number of questions about the compatibility of environmental measures with trade rules remain unanswered. The task of reconciling the fundamental goals of free trade and environmental protection remains very much a work in progress.

---

[4] Esty, above fn 3, at 36.

[5] G Shaffer, 'The World Trade Organization under Challenge: Democracy and the Law and Politics of the WTO's Treatment of Trade and Environment Matters' 2001 *Harvard Environmental Law Review* 25(1) 1, at 32–35.

[6] UNCTAD's Trade & Sustainable Development Section has held several high-level meetings and published numerous reports on the subject, see UNCTAD, *Trade and Development*, at <http://www.unctad.org/trade_env/index.asp> (last visited September 2008).

II. Relationships Between Free Trade and Environmental Protection

It is useful to distinguish two different sorts of trade-and-environment relationships. First, there are the physical and economic effects of trade on the environment. For example, free trade tends to increase income levels, which can allow for better environmental protection, but trade in certain products such as endangered species or hazardous wastes can also contribute to environmental harms. Second, there is the relationship between the trade and environmental regimes. Here, the focus is on the rules and policies of the two regulatory systems: to what degree are they compatible or conflicting? These two types of relationships can themselves be related—in some cases, a negative effect, real or perceived, of free trade on the environment provides the impetus for environmental regulations limiting trade, thereby creating conflicts between the two regimes. But, often, the two types of relationships have little to do with each other. Many environmental regulations that affect trade do not respond to trade-related harms. They are adopted for other reasons and serve other functions—for example, to pressure or provide an incentive to another country to change its environmental policies. This chapter briefly considers the first type of relationship, because empirical questions about the actual effects of free trade on the environment form an important part of the backdrop for the trade-and-environment debate. The bulk of the chapter, however, will focus on the second type of relationship, that is, the legal interactions between the two regimes.

A. The Physical and Economic Effects of Free Trade on the Environment

To what extent and in what ways does trade help or hurt the environment? This issue has spawned a large literature, reflecting very different perspectives. At one extreme, ecological economists believe that the environment imposes limits to growth. According to this neo-Malthusian view, free trade is fundamentally incompatible with environmental protection, since it aims to promote economic growth, while environmental protection requires limits to growth.[7] At the other end of the spectrum, neo-liberal economists argue that free trade and environmental protection are fundamentally compatible, since they both seek the same goal: the efficient use

---

[7] EF Schumacher, *Small Is Beautiful* (New York: Harper & Row, 1975); HE Daly and KN Townsend (eds), *Valuing the Earth: Economics, Ecology, Ethics* (Cambridge, MA: MIT Press, 1993).

of resources, through comparative advantage in the case of trade law, and by internalizing environmental externalities in the case of environmental law.[8] Conflicts between the two regimes are therefore not intractable, but simply reflect a failure by one regime or the other to adopt efficient policies.

As usual, the truth lies somewhere in between these contrasting perspectives. Trade can have many different effects on the environment, some positive and others negative. Which type of effect dominates at a given place and time depends to a great extent on individual circumstances.

1. *Positive Effects*

In many respects, trade liberalization and environmental regulation can complement one another. To begin with, enhancing competition by lowering trade barriers leads to more efficient use of resources.[9] When resources are used more efficiently, fewer are wasted and the environment benefits.

Second, free trade can lead to the dissemination of good environmental practices and the transfer of cleaner technology from countries with high environmental standards (particularly those with large import markets) to their trade partners. This upward harmonization, sometimes known as the 'California Effect', occurs when exporters find it more efficient to manufacture one environmentally friendly version of their product than to create multiple product lines to take advantage of weaker standards in some countries.[10]

Third, the higher standards of living that come with increased income can lead to higher levels of environmental protection. In countries with very low incomes, poverty causes economic pressure to exploit environmental resources in an unsustainable manner. Conversely, in countries with higher levels of income, more resources are available for environmental protection. The link between poverty and environmental degradation has long been recognized in the 1987 Brundtland Report,[11] Principle 5 of the Rio Declaration,[12] and Chapter 2 of Agenda 21;[13] all view poverty alleviation as a necessary component of sustainable development, and note the role of trade in raising income levels.

---

[8] Esty, above fn 3, at 61–62.

[9] WTO CTE, *Environmental Benefits of Removing Trade Restrictions and Distortions*, WT/CTE/W/67 (7 November 1997); WTO Secretariat, *Trade and Environment at the WTO* (Geneva: WTO, 2004), at <http://www.wto.int/english/tratop_e/envir_e/envir_wto2004_e.pdf> (last visited September 2008), at 23.

[10] D Vogel, *Trading Up: Consumer and Environmental Regulation in a Global Economy* (Cambridge, MA: Harvard University Press, 1995), at 248–70.

[11] World Commission on Environment and Development, *Our Common Future* (Oxford: Oxford University Press, 1987), at 84.

[12] The UN Conference on Environment and Development, *Annex I, Rio Declaration on Environment and Development*, A/CONF.151/26 (12 August 1992), at Principle 5.

[13] Report of the United Nations Conference on Environment and Development, UN GAOR, 46th Sess, *Annex II, Agenda Item 21*, A/CONF.151/26 (12 August 1992), at Chapter 2.

In certain cases, this relationship reflects what is known as an 'Environmental Kuznets Curve' (EKC), an inverted U-shaped curve used to describe the relationship between development and environmental degradation.[14] The EKC postulates that as a country begins to develop economically little weight is given to environmental concerns, and pollution levels rise due to industrialization and the exploitation of resources to meet basic human needs. But at a critical point in the development process, when these needs are being met and more resources are available for investing in environmental protection, pollution levels begin to decline. This 'technique effect' has been demonstrated for a number of pollutants, particularly those (like sulphur dioxide and nitrogen dioxide) associated with industrial production, for which pollution-reduction technologies exist and can be deployed as a country becomes wealthier.[15] However, emissions of other pollutants like carbon dioxide and some persistent organic pollutants, as well as environmental harms such as loss of biodiversity, do not seem to follow this pattern, and are dominated by 'scale effects', increasing as wealth and consumption levels rise. Furthermore, even for those pollutants most associated with industrial production, the environmental benefits of increased wealth frequently accrue only locally, as polluting facilities do not simply disappear, but rather move to new, typically less-developed, locations. Invocation of the EKC to support the complementarity of economic growth and environmental protection can thus be problematic,[16] but the EKC does suggest that, for at least some forms of environmental degradation, increased income levels are correlated with greater environmental protection.

2. *Negative Effects*

More widely discussed—and far more controversial—are the ways in which free trade and environmental protection can conflict. Increased international trade can have a negative impact on the environment directly and indirectly. Trade in products derived from endangered species, for example, directly causes environmental harm by encouraging poaching, and for that reason is controlled by the Convention on International Trade in Endangered Species (CITES). Trade in hazardous products, likewise, can lead to environmental damage both during transportation and at the source and destination sites and is therefore regulated under the Basel Convention on the Control of the Transboundary Movement of Hazardous Wastes

[14] DI Stern et al., 'Economic Growth and Environmental Degradation: The Environmental Kuznets Curve and Sustainable Development' 1996 *World Development* 24(7) 1151, at 1152; S Kuznets, 'Economic Growth and Income Inequality' 1955 *American Economic Review* 45(1) 1. Kuznets did not link economic development to environmental degradation, but rather to reduced inequalities in income distribution.

[15] MA Cole et al, 'Trade Liberalisation and the Environment: The Case of the Uruguay Round' 1998 *The World Economy* 21(3) 337–47.

[16] See, eg, MR Poirier, 'It Was the Best of Times, It Was the Worst of Times...: Science, Rhetoric and Distribution in a Risky World' 2002 *Case Western Reserve Law Review* 53(2) 409, at 417–19.

(Basel Convention). Additionally, the movement of transport vehicles can encourage the spread of invasive alien species and contribute to air and water pollution through the release of exhaust, waste, and fuel.

Trade can also cause environmental harm indirectly. One primary vector through which free trade arguably harms the environment is through the migration of polluting industries from countries with stringent environmental standards to those where levels of protection are lower. According to this 'pollution haven hypothesis', if conforming to environmental standards were costly, then in a world where it is easy to relocate a production facility to a country with lower standards, a rational profit-maximizing company would find it cost-efficient to make the move.[17]

Despite the fears of environmentalists, empirical studies have tended to conclude that few companies actually move to countries with lower environmental standards in order to take advantage of lower costs of production.[18] Yet, so long as regulators continue to fear that an industry might leave, a regulatory chill may inhibit them from passing stronger environmental laws or enforcing those already on the books. Or even worse, it can lead to a race to the bottom, in which countries compete with one another to attract business by lowering their regulatory standards.[19]

Scholars continue to debate the actual effects of freer international trade on environmental degradation, and both environmental and trade groups continue to release new studies at a rapid pace.[20] But the evidence, to date, suggests that while downward harmonization has occurred in some cases, upward harmonization of environmental standards has been, if anything, more common.[21] It is likely that the continued development of international environmental law will help accelerate this process.

[17] The economic rationale for this type of behaviour was infamously articulated by Lawrence Summers, former chief economist of the World Bank, who began a leaked 1991 memorandum with the words: 'Just between you and me, shouldn't the World Bank be encouraging more migration of the dirty industries to the LDCs?'. L Summers, 'Let Them Eat Pollution' *The Economist* (8 February 1992), at 66.

[18] J Bhagwati, 'Trade Liberalisation and "Fair Trade" Demands: Addressing the Environmental and Labour Standards Issues' in J Bhagwati (ed), *A Stream of Windows: Unsettling Reflections on Trade, Immigration, and Democracy* (Cambridge, MA: MIT Press, 1998) 247, at 252–53; MA Cole et al, 'Why the Grass is Not Always Greener: The Competing Effects of Environmental Regulations and Factor Intensities on US Specialization', University of Nottingham Research Paper No. 21 (2004).

[19] As with fears of relocation, however, there is little empirical support for the fear that countries will engage in a race to the bottom. See, eg, JM Dean, 'Trade and the Environment: A Survey of Literature' in Low, above fn 18, at 15; G Eskeland and A Harrison, 'Moving to Greener Pastures? Multinationals and the Pollution-Haven Hypothesis' *World Bank Policy Research Working Paper* No 1744 (1997). Despite the lack of evidence, however, '[t]he political influence of the "race to the bottom" imagery has been considerable'. D Vogel and RA Kagan (eds), *Dynamics of Regulatory Change: How Globalization Affects National Regulatory Policies* (California: University of California Press, 2004), at 3.

[20] See, eg, JA Frankel and AK Rose, 'Is Trade Good or Bad for the Environment? Sorting out the Causality' 2005 *Review of Economics & Statistics* 87(1) 85; P Thompson and LA Strohm, 'Trade and Environmental Quality: A Review of the Evidence' 1996 *Journal of Environment & Development* 5(4) 363.

[21] Vogel, above fn 10, at 5.

B. Conflicts Between the Trade and Environmental Regimes

While the physical and economic effects of free trade on the environment are mixed, the legal relationship between the two regimes has been more one-sidedly conflictual. To be sure, in particular contexts, the two regimes can reinforce one another. Energy, agricultural, and fisheries subsidies provide a good illustration. Not only do these subsidies distort trade flows, they also encourage overuse of resources. Thus, reducing them produces a win-win outcome that is good for both trade and the environment. More commonly, however, when trade rules and environmental rules come into contact, they collide. And as both regimes have become wider and deeper, encompassing a broader array of issues through more stringent rules, the potential for conflict has increased.

The bias towards conflict between the trade and environmental regimes should not be surprising, since at their core, they work in opposite ways. Environmental regulation typically involves 'public' governmental intervention in the 'private' marketplace to correct perceived market failures, while trade policy represents an attempt to limit government intervention and allow the unimpeded flow of goods and services. Like the silhouette/vase illusion, in which the same picture can be seen in alternative ways, as either a vase or two faces, conflicts between environmental and trade rules tend to be perceived quite differently, depending on one's starting premises. Environmentalists start from the premise that States have authority to address environmental harms, and view trade rules that limit the permissible forms of environmental regulation as suspect. Trade experts, by contrast, start from the premise that States should refrain from interfering in private transactions and attribute conflicts between the two regimes to environmental rules that hinder trade, which require special justification. Since the WTO dispute settlement system has been the main forum to address trade-and-environment disputes, the trade perspective has predominated in framing the debate.

In what ways might environmental measures hinder trade and come into conflict with the WTO regime? Some environmental measures do so directly and intentionally—for example, by prohibiting commercial trade in endangered species, forbidding exports of hazardous wastes to countries that lack adequate disposal facilities, or prohibiting imports of tuna from countries whose fishing fleets use nets that entrap and kill dolphins. These trade-related environmental measures (TREMs)[22] raise obvious concerns for the trade regime—in particular, the aim of prohibiting all restrictions on trade other than tariffs, reflected in Article XI GATT 1994.

Even when an environmental measure does not directly target trade, it may affect trade indirectly and thereby create potential conflicts. First, different national

---

[22] P Demaret, 'TREMs, Multilateralism, Unilateralism and the GATT' in J Cameron, P Demaret, and D Geradin (eds), *Trade and the Environment: The Search for Balance* (London: Cameron & May, 1994) 52.

product standards make it more difficult for producers to sell a single homogeneous product globally. When environmental regulations differ from one country to another, producers must get information about each country's environmental standards and then tailor the products they sell to meet those standards. This can be expensive, and companies may be unwilling to invest the necessary time and money, particularly in smaller markets. In addition, facially neutral environmental measures may, *de facto*, have different impacts, favouring domestic over imported goods or goods from one country over another. For example, a carbon tax on electricity, while seemingly non-discriminatory, actually favours imports of electricity from countries with clean energy sources, such as hydroelectricity, over those with dirtier sources, such as coal. Measures such as these, although ostensibly adopted for environmental reasons, raise the spectre of protectionism on account of their disparate impacts.

The trade-impeding aspects of environmental standard-setting tend to have particularly adverse impacts on developing countries, whose exporters and governments are less able to bear the costs of adjusting to environmental measures. Developing country governments have therefore often viewed developed-world environmental regulations with suspicion—particularly because developed countries seem selective in their environmental concerns, ignoring the negative environmental impacts of their own agricultural subsidies and of the TRIPS Agreement. Reflecting this developing country perspective, both the Marrakesh Ministerial Decision on Trade and Environment and the Doha Declaration note with concern the effect that environmental measures can have on market access for developing Members.[23]

III. History of Trade and Environment Issues

A. Early History in the GATT 1947

The use of trade measures for environmental purposes is not new. Trade restrictions have been an important part of the regulatory toolkit since the advent of the environmental movement in the late nineteenth century. As early as 1890, a convention to preserve African wildlife recognized the need for export restrictions, and in the early twentieth century, trade bans on illegally hunted wildlife were included in treaties to protect fur seals and migratory birds. As a result, even though the

---

[23] MC, *Marrakesh Ministerial Decision on Trade and Environment*, MTN.TNC/45(MIN) (14 April 1994); MC, *Doha Ministerial Declaration*, WT/MIN(01)/DEC/W/1 (14 November 2001), at para 32(i).

environmental movement was still in its infancy when the GATT 1947 was adopted (and the word 'environment' did not even appear in the agreement), States were familiar with environmental measures to restrict trade, and attempted to address them through Article XX GATT 1947.[24]

In the 1970s, trade-and-environment issues began to gain greater salience within both the environmental and trade communities. The growth of environmental consciousness led to increased concern about the effects of free trade on the environment. At the same time, the proliferation of environmental laws prompted concern among trade experts about the effects of environmental regulation on free trade. In response, the GATT Contracting Parties created a Working Group on Environmental Measures and International Trade (EMIT Group) in 1971, during the run-up to the 1972 Stockholm Conference on the Human Environment.

Even after the trade-and-environment issue had emerged onto the GATT 1947 agenda, progress was slow and there was little serious discussion of the connections between trade rules and environmental protection. It is telling that after its formation in 1971, the EMIT Group did not meet for more than two decades, until just before the next big UN environmental conference, the 1992 Rio Summit.

To the extent that trade-and-environment issues did receive attention during this period, the focus was on the effects of trade on the environment. In 1982, for example, concern about exports of domestically-prohibited products prompted the GATT Ministerial Meeting to examine how to bring such exports under control, a decision that resulted in the establishment in 1989 of a Working Group on the Export of Domestically Prohibited Goods and Other Hazardous Substances. In contrast, environmental measures restricting trade—such as those imposed by CITES—were generally seen by trade experts as justified under Article XX GATT 1947 and therefore unproblematic.[25] Indeed, in the 1970s, even the threat of unilateral trade sanctions by the US against countries that failed to support a proposed moratorium on commercial whaling did not occasion any protest under the GATT 1947. As late as 1987, an expert opinion by the GATT Secretariat concluded that the trade provisions in the newly adopted Montreal Protocol on Substances that Deplete the Ozone Layer—which for the first time required parties to use trade measures to discourage non-parties from free-riding[26]—fell within the Article XX exceptions.[27]

---

[24] S Charnovitz, 'Exploring the Environmental Exceptions in GATT Article XX' 1991 *Journal of World Trade* 25(1) 37.

[25] R Housman, D Goldberg, B van Dyke, and D Zaelke, *The Use of Trade Measures in Selected Multilateral Environmental Agreements* (Geneva: UNEP, 1995), at 165.

[26] The Montreal Protocol's trade measures: (1) require parties to prohibit trade with non-parties in ozone-depleting ('controlled') substances, (2) envisage limitations on the import from non-parties of products containing or produced using controlled substances, and (3) urge parties to discourage 'to the fullest practicable extent' the export to non-parties of technologies for producing or using controlled substances. Article 4 Montreal Protocol.

[27] UNEP, *Report of the Ad Hoc Working Group on the Work of Its Third Session*, UNEP/WG.172/2 (8 May 1987), at 18.

B.   Emergence of Conflict: The *Tuna/Dolphin* Cases

The first real confrontation between the trade and environmental regimes came in 1991, when the *US – Tuna I* case thrust the issue to the forefront of public consciousness. The *Tuna/Dolphin* cases involved a challenge to the US Marine Mammal Protection Act (MMPA),[28] which sought to protect dolphins in the Eastern Tropical Pacific Ocean by prohibiting imports of certain tuna from countries whose tuna fishing vessels use nets that endanger dolphins. Reflecting the growing confidence of the trade regime, the GATT panels in both *US – Tuna I* and *US – Tuna (EEC)* concluded that the MMPA was not justifiable under Article XX and hence violated the GATT 1947. In *US – Tuna I*, the MMPA was found to impose an impermissible quantitative restriction that distinguished between tuna based on production processes (whether they were caught in a dolphin-safe manner) and also because the law operated outside of US territory.[29] In *US – Tuna (EEC)*, the Article XX(b) and (g) exceptions were unsuccessfully invoked to justify coercive measures.[30] Though the reports were never adopted by the GATT Council,[31] they nonetheless became a lightning rod in the debate between free trade proponents and environmentalists.

C.   Developments in the WTO

With consciousness of the potential conflicts between trade and environmental rules thrown into relief by the *Tuna/Dolphin* decisions, both sides began efforts at compromise. On the one hand, environmental agreements since the *Tuna/Dolphin* disputes have not followed the Montreal Protocol's example of using trade measures to promote participation and compliance. On the other hand, the 1994 Uruguay Round agreements that established the WTO included several important environmental provisions.[32] Most notably, the Preamble to the WTO Agreement recognizes the 'objective of sustainable development' and the importance of protecting and preserving the environment. In an effort to forestall future conflicts, the Marrakesh meeting

---

[28]   Marine Mammal Protection Act of 1972, 16 USCA 1361 (West 1985 & Supp 1994).

[29]   GATT Panel Report, *US – Tuna I*, at paras 5.15, 5.32.

[30]   GATT Panel Report, *US – Tuna (EEC)*, at paras 5.27, 5.39, 6.1.

[31]   Under the GATT 1947, consensus among GATT Contracting Parties was required for adopting a panel report. In this case, no vote was taken because Mexico and the US entered into bilateral consultations that eventually resulted in the 1995 Panama Declaration, in which the US, Mexico, and eight other tuna-fishing countries established dolphin mortality conservation limits.

[32]   These included modification of the Standards Code, and the insertion of environmental clauses into the WTO Agreement, the GATS, the Agreement on Agriculture, the SPS Agreement, the SCM Agreement, and the TRIPS Agreement. See S Charnovitz, 'The WTO's Environmental Progress' 2007 *Journal of International Economic Law* 10(3) 685.

also adopted a Ministerial Declaration on Trade and Environment, establishing a new Committee on Trade and Environment (CTE) to replace the EMIT Group, with a broad mandate to examine the relationship between trade and environmental measures and to issue recommendations on how to make 'international trade and environmental policies mutually supportive'.[33] Since the advent of the WTO, perhaps the most significant effort to reconcile the trade and environmental regimes has come from the newly created Appellate Body. In both *US – Gasoline*, which involved a US law mandating different methods for calculating emissions from foreign and domestic gasoline, and *US – Shrimp*, which involved a US prohibition on the importation of shrimp caught in ways that harm endangered sea turtles, the Appellate Body interpreted Article XX(g) GATT 1994 less restrictively, showing greater sensitivity to environmental values. In both cases, the Appellate Body found that the US measures 'related to the conservation of an exhaustible natural resource'—in *US – Gasoline*, air quality,[34] and in *US – Shrimp,* endangered sea turtles.[35] Although in *US – Gasoline* (and initially in *US – Shrimp*) the Appellate Body found the US measures arbitrary and unjustified and therefore contrary to the chapeau of Article XX, the Appellate Body in *US – Shrimp (Article 21.5 – Malaysia)* ultimately upheld the US import ban after the US pursued good faith negotiations with other countries to reach agreement on broad-based measures to conserve sea turtles, relying, in part, on the new language in the Preamble to the WTO Agreement regarding sustainable development.[36] Moreover, the Appellate Body responded to concerns by environmentalists that the WTO dispute settlement process was closed and secretive by allowing an environmental group to file an *amicus* brief, thereby displaying an openness to broader participation by civil society. As a result, although the initial decision in *US-Shrimp* against the US turtle-conservation measure inspired a great deal of controversy and negative press, many environmentalists welcomed the ultimate approach of the Appellate Body, believing that it signalled an openness to environmental trade measures so long as a country had first made an effort to act multilaterally.[37]

The Appellate Body has also relaxed its interpretation of the 'necessity' requirement in Article XX(b) GATT 1994, replacing the 'least-restrictive-means' standard

---

[33]   Marrakesh Ministerial Decision on Trade and Environment, above fn 23.

[34]   Appellate Body Report, *US – Gasoline*, at 19.

[35]   In finding that sea turtles are an 'exhaustible natural resource', the Appellate Body held that the meaning of exhaustible natural resource is not fixed, but must be interpreted in the light of the evolving rules of international law, including the principle of sustainable development, which the Preamble to the WTO Agreement explicitly recognizes. Appellate Body Report, *US – Shrimp*, at paras 130–31. See also chapter 12 of this Handbook.

[36]   Appellate Body Report, *US – Shrimp (Article 21.5 – Malaysia)*, at paras 134, 152–153.

[37]   See SL Sakmar, 'Free Trade and Sea Turtles: The International and Domestic Implications of the Shrimp-Turtles Case' 1999 *Colorado Journal of International Environmental Law & Policy* 10(2) 345.

adopted by earlier GATT panels with a multi-factored balancing test.[38] Most recently, in *Brazil – Retreaded Tyres*, the Appellate Body found that a Brazilian regulation banning the import of retreaded tyres was necessary for the 'reduction of the risks of waste tyre accumulation'.[39] Although the Brazilian measure was ultimately struck down as arbitrary and unjustified because it contained an exception for imports from other MERCOSUR Member States,[40] it is significant from an environmental perspective that the Appellate Body essentially faulted the law for not being trade-restrictive *enough*.

Nevertheless, while recent decisions reflect a greater deference to environmental measures restricting trade, other aspects of the WTO system have created the potential for new types of conflicts, in particular, the WTO's expansion into new subject areas and its increased willingness to police general governmental measures that impinge on trade.

Prior to the Uruguay Round, the trade regime addressed only trade in goods, pursuant to the GATT 1947. The WTO agreements expanded the scope of the regime to include trade in services and trade-related aspects of intellectual property rights. In doing so, these agreements create the potential for new sources of conflict with environmental measures, despite the inclusion of environmental provisions that seek to mitigate such conflicts. For example, although the GATS contains an exception for health measures similar to Article XX(b) GATT 1994, it does not contain an exception for conservation measures that parallels Article XX(g) GATT 1994.[41] As a result, conservation measures that limit trade in, say, transportation or tourism, could raise GATS problems. Similarly, because the TRIPS Agreement requires that patents or some form of *sui generis* protection be provided for most genetic materials, it could conflict with the Convention on Biological Diversity (CBD), which recognizes national sovereignty over genetic resources.

The agreement that creates perhaps the greatest source of conflict with environmental regulation is the SPS Agreement, which applies to certain product standards that protect human, animal, or plant life or health.[42] The SPS Agreement seeks to ensure that health regulations restrict market access as little as possible and are not used as disguised barriers to trade. Although it recognizes the sovereign right of WTO Members to adopt non-discriminatory environmental measures, it encourages them to use international standards where possible, by (a) creating a form of

---

[38] The development of the balancing test has a long history, and was significantly developed, *inter alia*, by the Appellate Body's reports in *Korea – Various Measures on Beef* and *US – Gambling*. In *Brazil – Retreaded Tyres*, the Appellate Body interpreted 'necessary' as that which 'brings about a material contribution to the objective' when viewed in light of its regulatory context and balanced against the importance of the interests at stake, the trade-restrictiveness of the measure, and possible alternatives. Appellate Body Report, *Brazil – Retreaded Tyres*, at paras 150–5.

[39] Ibid. at para 134.   [40] Ibid. at para 233.   [41] Art XIV GATS.
[42] See also chapters 9, 20, and 21 of this Handbook.

immunity from challenge for regulations that conform to international standards,[43] and (b) requiring that States have a scientific basis for going beyond the applicable international standards.[44] In all of the SPS disputes that have been decided so far,[45] the Appellate Body interpreted the latter requirement quite strictly, striking down national health measures on the grounds that they were not based on adequate information or risk assessment procedures, as required by the SPS Agreement. In doing so, the Appellate Body has displayed considerable scepticism of SPS measures that address environmental and health issues about which significant scientific uncertainty exists, a problem discussed below.

IV. Factors in Assessing Environmental Measures

In assessing the compatibility of environmental measures with the trade regime, scholars and tribunals have suggested a wide array of criteria:

- whether an environmental measure is directed at trade in particular, or affects trade only incidentally;
- whether it serves a function deemed legitimate or illegitimate;
- whether it is adopted by a country unilaterally or through multilateral negotiations;
- whether it is intended to protect resources outside or within a country's territory;
- whether it relates to the processes by which a product is produced or characteristics of the product itself; and
- whether it is supported by scientific evidence.

The use of these various yardsticks to determine the validity of environmental measures from a trade perspective is the topic of this section.

---

[43] Art. 3.2 SPS Agreement.

[44] Arts 2.2, 2.3, 3.2, 5.1, 5.6, and 5.7 SPS Agreement. The TBT Agreement, which applies to environmentally-based product standards other than SPS measures, also creates a preference for international standards, but provides that national product specifications can go beyond an international standard where the international standard would be 'an ineffective or inappropriate means for the fulfillment of the legitimate objectives pursued' and explicitly identifies environmental protection as a legitimate objective. Art 2.4 TBT Agreement.

[45] Appellate Body Report, *EC – Hormones* at 208; Appellate Body Report, *Australia – Salmon* at 136; Appellate Body Report, *Japan – Agricultural Products II* at 113–14; Appellate Body Report, *Japan – Apples* at 216; and Panel Report, *EC – Biotech Products* 7.3008–3214.

A. Is an Environmental Measure Specifically Directed at Trade?

Traditionally, an important threshold question in considering the compatibility of an environmental measure with the trade regime was whether the measure limited trade directly or indirectly. The GATT 1994 focuses primarily on direct restrictions on trade. Article XI prohibits all restrictions on trade other than tariffs; GATT schedules (together with Article II) set limits on permissible tariff rates on a country-by-country, product-by-product basis; and Article I prohibits WTO Members from discriminating between imports from different countries (the most-favoured-nation principle).[46] In contrast, the GATT 1994 does little to limit the authority of WTO Members to adopt governmental measures of a more general character, not directed at trade, except to prohibit them from doing indirectly what they cannot do directly, namely to inhibit trade by preferring domestic over foreign goods.

Within this analytical framework, whether an environmental measure is specifically directed at trade structures the rest of the analysis. TREMs, such as the restrictions on trade in endangered species and hazardous wastes in CITES and the Basel Convention, are *prima facie* prohibited and are inconsistent with the GATT 1994 unless they can be justified under one of the Article XX exceptions. In contrast, more general environmental measures are permissible under Article III GATT 1994 and *Ad* Article III unless they afford 'less favourable treatment' to 'like' foreign products.[47] Analysis of TREMs focuses on the scope of the Article XX exceptions; analysis of general environmental measures focuses on the concepts of 'likeness' and 'less favourable treatment'.

As the trade regime has evolved, however, this distinction between trade-related environmental measures and other measures has lost much of its significance. On the one hand, the Appellate Body's more relaxed interpretation of the Article XX exceptions in *US – Shrimp* means that future panels are more likely to uphold TREMs as long as they do not constitute an 'arbitrary and unjustified restriction on trade'—in essence, a non-discrimination norm that is similar to, although more relaxed than, the one found in Article III. On the other hand, as the trade regime proved successful in addressing direct restrictions on trade, it has imposed increasingly stringent disciplines on more general governmental measures – in particular through the TBT and SPS Agreements, which seek to ensure that technical and health standards do not serve as non-tariff barriers to trade. As the *EC – Hormones* and *EC – Biotech Products* reports illustrate, this has led to the paradoxical result that the trade regime may subject general environmental measures to more, not

---

[46] See also chapter 6 of this Handbook.
[47] Appellate Body Report, *Dominican Republic – Import and Sale of Cigarettes*, at paras 92–99.

less, stringent disciplines than trade-restrictive measures.[48] SPS measures must meet the SPS Agreement's requirements regarding risk assessment and scientific evidence, whereas trade-restrictive conservation measures must satisfy only Article XX, which requires simply that conservation measures not constitute an 'arbitrary or unjustified' restriction on trade.

B. What Is the Function of an Environmental Measure?

Environmental measures may serve a variety of functions, which may be relevant in assessing their compatibility with the WTO regime. These functions include:

- *Prevention.* Environmental measures are often used to limit the harmful effects of trade. For example, to the extent that trade in endangered species or in hazardous wastes causes environmental harms, limitations on such trade can help prevent these harms from occurring.
- *Coercion.* Environmental measures may limit trade to induce other countries to change their environmental policies, as the Montreal Protocol and the US Pelly Amendment illustrate.[49] Coercive measures differ from preventive measures in two related ways. They do not protect the environment directly. In order to be effective, they require a change in behaviour by the target State or by private traders within that State. However, this means that they do not need to target a particular product to be effective. They can limit trade in any product that is important to the country at which the measure is directed.
- *Defence.* Environmental measures limiting trade can serve to defend a country against 'unfair' competition from countries with lower environmental standards. When a country imposes a strict environmental regulation, the additional costs of compliance may place domestic producers at a competitive disadvantage. The environmental standard forces them to internalize their environmental externalities, while their foreign competitors do not. Arguably, countries with lower environmental standards are in effect providing their businesses with a kind of subsidy. In response, some environmentalists argue that countries should be allowed to 'level the playing field' by imposing an 'eco-duty' or 'border tax

---

[48] S Charnovitz, 'The World Trade Organization and Environmental Supervision' 1994 *International Environment Reporter* 17, at 89, 92 (discussing the irony of WTO's rigid rules on health and environment in the context of its soft stance on protectionism).

[49] The Pelly Amendment allows the US President to restrict the import of fishery or wildlife products from countries that diminish the effectiveness of international fishery or endangered species programmes. 22 USCA § 1978 (West 1990 & Supp 1994); see also S Charnovitz, 'Environmental Trade Sanctions and the GATT: An Analysis of the Pelly Amendment on Foreign Environmental Practices' 1994 *American University Journal of International Law & Policy* 9(3) 751.

adjustment,' particularly in cases involving transboundary or global harms.[50] Such defensive measures would force foreign companies to internalize the environmental costs of their production processes, and pressure environmentally weak States to implement more stringent protection measures.[51]

- *Expression*. Even when a TREM holds little promise of preventing environmental harm, a country may wish to disassociate itself from the offending behaviour. For example, a country might wish to ban imports of furs caught with leg-hold traps, if its citizens find this practice offensive, even if there is no realistic prospect that the ban will prevent such traps from being used.
- *Punishment*. TREMs can be used after the fact, to punish countries for violations of an international environmental standard.
- *Protectionism*. Finally, measures that are ostensibly environmental may serve a purely protectionist function, to benefit domestic over foreign producers.

The first and last of these functions present relatively easy cases. On the one hand, when a measure directly prevents an environmental harm, it clearly serves a legitimate environmental function. Conversely, when an ostensibly environmental measure is adopted for protectionist purposes, it is clearly unjustified, and striking down the measure raises no conflict between the trade and environmental regimes. But how about the other functions that governmental measures can serve in encouraging, defending, expressing, and enforcing environmental values? Significantly, the trade regime has not confined itself to rooting out pure protectionism. Instead, it has questioned the use of trade-affecting environmental measures for these other purposes as well.

The attempt to exclude environmental measures from serving functions other than direct prevention raises two difficulties. First, in many cases, environmental measures serve a variety of functions, both permitted and forbidden.[52] Second, since the trade regime itself uses trade restrictions for defensive and coercive purposes,

---

[50] But, as critics note, once the lack of environmental standards is recognized as a subsidy or grounds for dumping charges, it is a 'slippery slope' to recognizing other government expenditures (or the lack thereof) as subsidies. GATT Secretariat, *Trade and the Environment*, GATT/1529 (3 February 1992), at 20.

[51] Former French Prime Minister Dominique de Villepin, for example, proposed imposing a border tax adjustment on energy-intensive imports from countries (such as the US) that failed to ratify the Kyoto Protocol. 'Mandelson wants free trade in "green" goods' *Euractiv* (29 June 2007), at <http://www.euractiv.com/en/climate-change/mandelson-wants-free-trade-green-goods/article-161632> (last visited September 2008).

[52] Eg, the US import ban on tuna from countries that lack conservation measures comparable to those of the US was seen by the GATT Panel in *US – Tuna (EEC)* as coercive in nature. But it also served a preventive function, by limiting demand for tuna caught in a manner that harms dolphins. MJ Trebilcock and R Howse, *The Regulation of International Trade*, 3rd edn (London: Routledge, 2005), at 522–23. The measure could also be seen as serving an expressive function (reflecting Americans' love of marine mammals) or a defensive function (to protect any US fisherman who continued to fish in waters with high tuna-dolphin interaction and thus were required by US law to use expensive, dolphin-safe fishing methods).

excluding such uses to promote environmental protection seems parochial and biased. Granted, there is considerable question about the effectiveness of trade measures in inducing other States to change their behaviour.[53] But if countries can impose trade measures in response to violations of the trade regime, why shouldn't they be able to do the same in the environmental realm? Particularly given the lack of other enforcement tools, taking trade measures off the table leaves the environmental regime with few means at its disposal to address the twin problems of participation and compliance.[54]

C. Is a Measure Multilateral or Unilateral?

Both TREMs and more general environmental measures can be adopted either unilaterally or multilaterally. Given the difficulties of international standard-setting, most environmental standards are still developed at the national level. However, trade measures like those in the Montreal Protocol, the Basel Convention, and CITES have become a common feature of multilateral environmental agreements (MEAs), and are included in some 20 of the more than 200 MEAs currently in force.[55] In addition, international standard-setting bodies such as the Codex Alimentarius Commission and the International Organization for Standardization (ISO) have developed a growing number of product standards relating to health and the environment.

In general, multilateral environmental measures pose less of a danger to trade than unilateral national measures, and are hence favoured by the trade regime. National measures raise three types of concerns. First, they prompt fears of protectionism. The law at issue in *US – Gasoline* was struck down because it calculated different permissible emission levels for foreign and domestic gasoline, and thereby privileged US producers. Second, even when national measures are not adopted for protectionist reasons, they inhibit trade indirectly, by making it more difficult for producers to sell a single homogeneous product globally. Finally, unilateral national measures can raise sovereignty issues when they are used to pressure other countries to change their environmental policies. Developing countries, in particular, have expressed this concern, criticizing the imposition of Western environmental standards on countries of the global South as 'Eco-Imperialism', which values environmental protection over the lives of the world's poor and ignores problematic aspects of the North's own policies, such as agricultural subsidies.[56]

---

[53] Ibid. at 510.

[54] S Barrett, *Environment and Statecraft: The Strategy of Environmental Treaty-Making* (Oxford: Oxford University Press, 2003).

[55] WTO Secretariat, above fn 9, at 36.

[56] See, eg, P Driessen, *Eco-Imperialism: Green Power, Black Death* (Bellevue, WA: Merril Press, 2003).

Multilateral measures are less susceptible to all three of these problems. The fact that a measure has been accepted by a large number of States reduces the potential for protectionism.[57] Moreover, uniform international standards do not present additional impediments to trade (beyond those set forth in the standards themselves), since producers need to learn about only a single standard and can produce a single, uniform product. Finally, although multilateral trade measures can be used coercively—as UN Security Council sanctions illustrate—they typically are seen as more legitimate and less susceptible to abuse than unilateral measures, because they result from a more broadly participatory process.[58]

For these reasons, trade law displays a marked preference for multilateral measures. Article 104(1) NAFTA goes so far as to create an explicit exemption for measures adopted pursuant to enumerated MEAs. Although the WTO agreements, by contrast, do not specifically exempt MEAs from their strictures, the decision in *US – Shrimp*, with its emphasis on multilateral negotiations, suggests a similar result. The preference for international standards is even clearer in the SPS and TBT Agreements, which provide a safe harbour for health and technical standards that conform to international standards.[59]

Although the trade regime encourages WTO Members to act multilaterally when possible, it does not exclude the use of unilateral measures.[60] In some cases, international standards do not exist, and agreement is not possible, so the choice is not between unilateral and multilateral action, but between action and inaction.[61] Moreover, as both the SPS and TBT Agreements recognize, WTO Members have different values, traditions, and regulatory cultures, so uniform standards may not be appropriate.[62]

---

[57] Even multilateral measures may raise questions of fairness, particularly in the context of multilateral trade measures adopted by parties to an MEA against non-Parties.

[58] Multilateral agreement does not fully eliminate the problem of coercion, since it may simply reflect powerful States' success in forcing their will on other States. For a discussion of the legitimacy of Security Council sanctions, see DD Caron, 'The Legitimacy of the Collective Authority of the Security Council' 1993 *American Journal of International Law* 87(4) 552. See also chapter 25 of this Handbook.

[59] Art 3.2 SPS Agreement; Art 2.4 TBT Agreement. To qualify as an 'international' standard, a standard need not be adopted by consensus, see Appellate Body Report, *EC – Sardines*, at para 227.

[60] As mentioned above, the SPS and TBT Agreements allow WTO Members to go beyond international standards in pursuing legitimate objectives such as environmental protection. Art 3.3 SPS Agreement; Art 2.4 TBT Agreement. Similarly, Agenda 21 of the Rio Conference provides only that environmental measures should be based on international consensus 'as far as possible'. UN, *Earth Summit, Agenda 21: The United Nations Programme of Action from Rio* (New York: United Nations, 1992), at <http://www.un.org/esa/sustdev/agenda21text.htm> (last visited 20 February 2008), at para 2.22(i).

[61] D Bodansky, 'What's So Bad about Unilateral Action to Protect the Environment?' 2000 *European Journal of International Law* 11(2) 339.

[62] As the Appellate Body has noted, 'it is undisputed that WTO Members have the right to determine the level of protection of health that they consider appropriate in a given situation'. Appellate Body Report, *EC – Asbestos*, at para 168.

The ultimate acceptance of a unilateral measure in *US – Shrimp*, after the US made a good faith effort to negotiate multilateral turtle conservation measures, was taken as good news by many environmental activists, particularly those who see unilateral action as a frequent prerequisite of multilateral cooperation and upward harmonization.[63] But it should be noted that developing countries have questioned the fairness of the decision. To say, as *US – Shrimp* implied, that a developed country like the US can unilaterally adopt trade-restrictive environmental measures so long as it makes an attempt to negotiate, ignores the fact that the negotiating playing field is far from level. Because of the enormous differentials between the global North and South in both market and 'discursive' power, Northern States can essentially decide on a rule, go through a formal negotiating process, and then adopt a trade-restrictive environmental regulation unilaterally, regardless of any objection by Southern trading partners.[64]

D.   Is an Environmental Measure Extraterritorial?

Whether an environmental measure is extraterritorial is also sometimes seen as relevant to its acceptability under the GATT 1994. Environmental measures can be extraterritorial in two respects. First, they may seek to influence extraterritorial conduct (for example, fishing on the high seas or in waters under the jurisdiction of another State). Second, they may seek to protect extraterritorial resources (for example, African elephants). The two types of extraterritoriality raise different types of concerns. Regulating extraterritorial conduct creates the potential for conflict with exercises of jurisdiction by other States. Seeking to protect extraterritorial resources raises questions about whether a State has a sufficient interest in regulation.[65]

In assessing the permissibility of unilateral environmental measures, GATT jurisprudence has focused on the second type of extraterritoriality. In *US – Tuna I*, the GATT Panel concluded that a US import ban was not justified under Article XX because it was aimed at protecting dolphins outside the US.[66] Conversely, the

[63] See, eg, RB Bilder, 'The Role of Unilateral State Action in Preventing International Environmental Injury' 1981 *Vanderbilt Journal of Transnational Law* 14(1) 51; S Charnovitz, 'Free Trade, Fair Trade, Green Trade: Defogging the Debate' 1994 *Cornell International Law Journal* 27(3) 459, at 493–98.

[64] G Shaffer, 'Power, Governance, and the WTO: A Comparative Institutional Approach' in M Barnett and R Duvall (eds), *Power in Global Governance* (Cambridge: Cambridge University Press, 2005) 130; D McRae, 'Trade and the Environment: Competition, Cooperation or Confusion?' 2003 *Alberta Law Review* 41(3) 745, at 757.

[65] See L Bartels, 'Article XX of GATT and the Problem of Extraterritorial Jurisdiction' 2002 *Journal of World Trade* 36(2) 353.

[66] Although the US import ban involved both types of extraterritoriality, the Panel focused on the second type in concluding that the US measure did not satisfy Art XX GATT 1947.

WTO Appellate Body in *US – Shrimp* upheld a US import ban aimed at protecting sea turtles, because the sea turtles migrated through US waters and therefore had a 'sufficient [territorial] nexus' with the US.[67]

A territorial limit on environmental measures, however, does not appear justified either on textual or policy grounds. As Charnovitz points out, 'the phrase "human, animal or plant life or health" in a treaty would not ordinarily be limited to the humans, animals, or plants in one party' and if the drafters had intended to create an 'inward-looking exception' they could have included the term 'national' in Article XX(b), as they did in Article XX(f), which provides an exception for measures 'imposed for the protection of *national* treasures of artistic, historic or archaeological value'.[68]

Requiring a territorial nexus for environmental measures assumes that States have a legitimate interest in protecting only their own resources, not those found outside their territory. But this assumption ignores developments in international environmental law over the last half century. Certainly, a State's interest is greatest when it seeks to protect its own resources. But this does not mean that a State lacks a legitimate interest in protecting resources found within another State, not to mention the global commons. Many international environmental regimes—like CITES and the World Heritage Convention—are predicated on the idea that all States have an interest in global commons resources, and even some resources found within the territory of other States. Although a State's interest in these extraterritorial resources does not mean that anything goes, it does imply that a governmental measure is not *per se* invalid because it relates to a resource outside the State's territory.

E. Is an Environmental Measure a Product Standard or a PPM Standard?

Environmental standards can apply to characteristics of a product (for example, whether it contains ozone-depleting substances) or to the process by which the product was produced (for example, whether it was produced using ozone-depleting substances). An important question is whether environmental measures can justifiably distinguish between products based on their 'process and production methods', or PPMs.[69] Can countries, for example, adopt regulations that treat unrecycled paper less favourably than recycled paper, to the detriment of imported products? Or are recycled and unrecycled paper 'like' products, which must be treated equally favourably under the MFN and national treatment principles?

---

[67] Appellate Body Report, *US – Shrimp*, at para 133.

[68] S Charnovitz, 'A Critical Guide to the WTO's Report on Trade and Environment' 1997 *Arizona Journal of International & Comparative Law* 14(2) 341, at 354–55.

[69] See also chapters 9 and 19 of this Handbook.

The legal test for determining whether two products are 'like' for the purposes of the GATT 1994 has changed over time. In *US – Tuna I*, the GATT Panel rejected a US PPM standard, finding that tuna was alike regardless of whether it had been caught using dolphin-safe nets. According to the Panel, likeness can be determined only by examining the physical characteristics of the product itself, not by considering PPMs, unless they leave some physical trace in the final product. The WTO's Appellate Body, however, has followed the more nuanced approach first articulated by the 1970 Working Party on *Border Tax Adjustments*,[70] and has considered a number of different factors in determining 'likeness', including '(i) the properties, nature, and quality of the products; (ii) the end-uses of the products; (iii) consumers' tastes and habits...; and (iv) the tariff classification of the products', together with other 'pertinent evidence'.[71] This test may leave some space for the consideration of PPMs as part of the analysis of 'consumers' tastes and habits' and other non-trade concerns. Moreover, even if products with different PPMs are considered 'like' products, the Appellate Body has stressed that a PPM standard would violate Article III GATT 1994 only if it affords 'less favourable treatment' to imported products[72]—that is, if it is protectionist.

Even if a PPM measure is deemed to violate the non-discrimination principles in the GATT 1994, WTO Members may still be able to justify such measures under one of the Article XX exceptions. In *US – Shrimp*, the Appellate Body upheld a US import ban that focused on the process by which shrimp are caught on the basis of Article XX GATT 1994. However, as the decision illustrates, meeting the requirement of Article XX's chapeau has not proven easy, and debate over whether WTO Members should be allowed to discriminate using PPM-based environmental rules without needing to rely on an Article XX exception continues full-steam.

Many trade experts argue that environmental impact should not be a legitimate criterion for finding products unlike, and governments should not be able to discriminate between products based on their production methods. Several developing country WTO Members have also opposed including PPMs in the likeness analysis. Fearing loss of market access and competitive advantage, they have accused northern NGOs and governments of using production methods as thinly veiled pretexts for protectionism.[73] Environmentalists, by contrast, argue that it is essential for environmental regulations to target unsound production methods, for example, through taxes or regulations that favour 'clean' energy sources over 'dirty' ones. In their view, the trade regime's focus on whether environmental friendly and environmental unfriendly products are 'alike,' in order to determine whether governments can

---

[70] GATT Working Party Report, *Border Tax Adjustments*, at para 18.
[71] Appellate Body Report, *EC – Asbestos*, at paras 101–03.
[72] Appellate Body Report, *Dominican Republic – Import and Sale of Cigarettes*, at para 96.
[73] cf J Bhagwati, 'The Question of Linkage' 2002 *American Journal of International Law* 96(1) 126, at 133 (arguing that Unilateral PPMs carry out the 'white man's burden' through 'gunboat diplomacy').

permissibly distinguish between them, gets the analysis backward. The substantive question is whether regulations focusing on the production process are reasonable. The answer to that question should drive what products are considered alike, not the other way around.[74]

F.   Does an Environmental Measure Have a Scientific Basis?

The question of scientific justification is relevant to several regulatory provisions under the WTO, as well as a number of MEAs. In the GATT 1994, this issue features in the application of the Article XX exceptions as a component of the 'necessary' or 'related to' determination.[75] It also arises in the context of its non-discrimination provisions, as scientific justification helps demonstrate a measure's non-trade-related intent.

The scientific justification provisions of the SPS Agreement have been most controversial. Article 3.3 SPS Agreement provides that countries are free to implement SPS standards that are more stringent than those agreed upon internationally, but only with the backing of 'sufficient scientific evidence'. However, exactly how much scientific evidence is required to justify safety standards that restrict trade in a potentially hazardous product is unclear. Additionally, the 'sufficient scientific evidence' requirement is in tension with an emerging principle of international environmental law—the precautionary principle—that allows States to regulate environmental risks even in the absence of scientific certainty.[76]

The question of how much scientific evidence is required to justify a trade restriction has come before WTO dispute settlement panels and the Appellate Body on several occasions. In 1998, the EU attempted to justify a ban on imports of beef from cattle that had been treated with growth-inducing hormones, invoking the precautionary principle in support of its zero-risk policy. The Appellate Body found that the ban was inconsistent with the SPS Agreement because it was not based on a proper risk assessment as required by Article 5.1.[77] Although it rejected the Panel's finding that the measure was discriminatory, it held that the absence of risk assessment violated the SPS Agreement irrespective of whether there was actual discrimination against foreign goods.[78] As Hudec commented, this decision pushed the

---

[74] RL Howse and DH Regan, 'The Process/Product Distinction – An Illusory Basis for Disciplining "Unilateralism" in Trade Policy' 2000 *European Journal International Law* 11(2) 249, at 260.

[75] See, eg, Appellate Body Report, *EC – Asbestos*, at paras 164–75.

[76] Principle 15 Rio Declaration on Environment and Development. The precautionary principle 'finds reflection' in Article 5.7 SPS Agreement, which allows WTO Members to adopt provisional SPS measures based on the available information, even where the relevant scientific information is insufficient. Appellate Body Report, *EC – Hormones*, at para 124.

[77] Ibid. at paras 125–208.

[78] Ibid. at paras 208, 246.

SPS's scientific requirements into the realm of the 'post-discriminatory', calling on the DSB not merely to police the WTO's non-discrimination provisions, but rather to second-guess the justifications behind regulatory provisions as a matter of principle.[79] Similarly, in 2006, the Panel in *EC – Biotech Products* found that several EU Member States' safeguard measures on imports of genetically modified organisms were not based on adequate risk assessments and therefore were presumed to be maintained without sufficient scientific evidence.[80]

As these decisions indicate, the debate over whether and how much scientific evidence should be required before trade restrictions can be imposed is far from settled. Some have questioned whether scientific data can adequately answer the questions these provisions are asking,[81] and whether this type of 'post-discriminatory' prevention of 'unnecessary' unscientific regulation should be a part of the WTO's mandate at all.[82] Environmentalists frequently argue, citing the precautionary principle, that countries should be allowed to prevent imports or exports of potentially hazardous goods any time there is a question regarding their safety. Furthermore, they generally oppose the suggestion that all States should be required to conform to a standard practice of risk assessment. On the other side of the debate, trade experts voice concern about the potential for abuse, noting that a product might be banned on 'precautionary' grounds in order to disguise purely protectionist motives. Developing countries share this concern, despite wide acceptance of the precautionary principle as a feature of MEAs and of domestic lawmaking.

V. Ways of Addressing Trade and Environment Issues

The 1994 Ministerial Decision on Trade and Environment states that 'there should not be, nor need be, any policy contradiction between upholding and safeguarding an open, non-discriminatory and equitable multilateral trading system on the one hand, and acting for the protection of the environment, and the promotion of sustainable development on the other'. But allowing sufficient space within the trade

---

[79] RE Hudec, 'Science and "Post-Discriminatory" WTO Law' 2003 *Boston College International & Comparative Law Review* 26(2) 185, at 187-188; see also DM Driesen, 'What is Free Trade: the Real Issue Lurking Behind the Trade and Environment Debate' 2001 *Virginia Journal International Law* 41(2) 279.

[80] Panel Report, *EC – Biotech Products,* at para 8.14(d).

[81] See, eg, VR Walker, 'The Myth of Science as a "Neutral Arbiter" for Triggering Precautions' 2003 *Boston College International & Comparative Law Review* 26(2) 197.

[82] Hudec, above fn 79, at 188.

regime for the enforcement of legitimate environmental regulation, while at the same time continuing to pursue the goals of lowering barriers to trade and preventing discrimination, has proven difficult.

Conflicts between the trade and environmental regimes, both actual and potential, could be addressed in two general ways, either on an *ad hoc*, case-by-case basis by tribunals, or in a prospective, 'legislative' manner through multilateral negotiations among States. Overarching both of these alternatives is the question of whether trade-and-environment issues should be addressed within or outside of the WTO.

Many feel that the WTO should look no further than its own four corners, and that any environmental problems posed by the deregulation of international trade should be dealt with separately through environmental law and policy.[83] *The Economist*, for example, favours keeping the trade and environment regimes separate, arguing that 'the best remedy [for environmental ills] is good environmental policy, not trade sanctions, which merely keep poor countries poor'.[84] The WTO Secretariat has similarly stated that 'the WTO in not an environmental protection agency and does not aspire to become one'; adding that the organization's 'competence in the field of trade and environment is limited to trade policies and to the trade-related aspects of environmental policies which have a significant effect on trade'.[85] Some environmentalists agree, arguing that the WTO lacks the expertise to address environmental issues, and is 'incapable of providing a balanced response to the competing interests at stake in [trade-and-environment] conflicts'.[86]

Others argue that because of the strong connections between trade and environmental issues, the WTO—irrespective of its desires or intentions—cannot help but play a role in environmental governance. As Petersmann notes, 'since 1980, the GATT dispute settlement procedures seem to have been used for the settlement of international disputes over national environmental measures more frequently than the dispute settlement procedures of any other worldwide organization'.[87] Moreover, many argue that, as a major international actor, the WTO has an affirmative obligation to promote environmental protection, and cannot abdicate this responsibility merely by claiming that it is 'not an environmental protection agency'.[88]

The Appellate Body has given some indication that it leans toward the latter position, and it looked to general principles of international law in *US – Shrimp* when

---

[83] See, eg, JP Trachtman, 'The Domain of WTO Dispute Resolution' 1999 *Harvard International Law Journal* 40(2) 333, at 342.

[84] 'Environmental Imperialism: GATT and Greenery' *The Economist* (15 February 1992), at 78.

[85] WTO Secretariat, above fn 9, at 6.

[86] JL Dunoff, 'Institutional Misfits: The GATT, the ICJ & Trade-Environment Disputes' 1994 *Michigan Journal of International Law* 15(4) 1043, at 1128.

[87] E-U Petersmann, 'International Trade Law and International Environmental Law: Prevention and Settlement of International Environmental Disputes in GATT' 1993 *Journal of World Trade* 27(1) 43, at 53.

[88] WTO Secretariat, above fn 9, at 6.

determining that sea turtles were an exhaustible natural resource. Likewise, a 2006 study argued that there is 'little reason of principle to depart from the view that general international law supplements WTO law unless it has been specifically excluded and that so do other treaties, which should, preferably, be read in harmony with the WTO covered treaties'.[89]

A.   Adjudicative Approaches

1.   *Interpretation of Existing Trade Rules through WTO Dispute Settlement*

Since its creation in 1995, the WTO Appellate Body has helped quell the antagonism between the trade and environmental regimes. Its approach in *US – Shrimp*, in particular, showed greater respect for environmental values and helped reassure environmentalists that the WTO was not necessarily a hostile forum. Given the lack of political will among States to negotiate solutions to the many questions that remain unanswered about the compatibility of the trade and environmental regimes, it is likely that these issues will continue to be resolved on an *ad hoc*, case-by-case basis as they arise, through interpretation and application of the existing WTO rules within the WTO dispute settlement system.[90]

One way to address trade-and-environment disputes would be for the WTO dispute settlement process to interpret the Article XX GATT 1994 exceptions to allow more environmental rules to meet the tests of XX(b), XX(g), and the chapeau—including by taking greater account of emerging principles of international environmental law such as the precautionary principle and the polluter-pays principle.[91] To some degree, the Appellate Body has already started down this road, through its reference to the developing corpus of international environmental law in interpreting the phrase 'exhaustible natural resources' in Article XX(g);[92] its statement

---

[89]   *Report of the ILC Study Group, Fragmentation of International Law: Difficulties Arising from the Diversification and Expansion of International Law – Finalized by Martti Koskenniemi*, A/CN.4/L.682 at para 169.

[90]   See also chapter 12 of this Handbook.

[91]   Barral has suggested that the DSU should be amended to mandate interpretation of WTO commitments with the corpus of international public law in mind. This would allow the dispute settlement body to accept international public policy principles—like sustainable development—as 'valid hermeneutical tools'. W Barral, 'Reforming the DSU' in A Najam et al (eds), *Trade and Environment: A Resource Book* (Geneva: International Institute for Sustainable Development, 2007), at <http://www.trade-environment.org/page/southernagenda/RB_fulltext.pdf> (last visited 20 February 2008), at 70.

[92]   Appellate Body Report, *US – Shrimp*, at paras 129–31.

that general principles of international law can provide 'interpretive guidance' with respect to the Article XX chapeau,[93] and its more relaxed reading of 'necessity' in Article XX(b) and 'related to' in Article XX(g).[94] Additional steps might include the following:

- Article XX(g) could be read to allow countries to adopt unilateral measures to protect the environment outside of their national borders (possibly even within the national territories of other States).
- The chapeau's requirement that trade restrictions must not arbitrarily or unjustifiably discriminate between like products and must not constitute disguised restrictions on trade could be reinterpreted to be more protective of environmental values.[95] For example, the Appellate Body could adopt a more permissive test that presumes environmental measures to be in compliance with the chapeau 'provided that they are not *operated* in a discriminatory manner'.[96]
- The status of MEAs could be clarified, through a *per se* rule that multilateral environmental measures satisfy the requirements of the Article XX chapeau (though this would raise further issues about the number of parties necessary to qualify an agreement as 'multilateral').
- Article XX(a), which allows measures 'necessary to protect public morals',[97] could be interpreted to allow morality-based environmental regulations—for example, measures meant to protect animal welfare, such as the EU's ban on the importation of furs from countries that allow the use of leg-hold traps,[98] or the recent Belgian and Dutch bans on the import of seal products in response to the continued use of hakapik clubs.[99]

Other provisions of the WTO agreements could also be interpreted in more environmentally oriented ways. For example, Article III GATT 1994 could be interpreted

[93] Ibid at paras 152–55.

[94] Appellate Body Report, *Brazil – Retreaded Tyres*, at para 156; Appellate Body Report, *US – Shrimp*, at paras 136–42.

[95] The Appellate Body found that a US law failed to qualify under the Art XIV GATS exception because it failed to demonstrate the 'consistency' of its measure. Appellate Body Report, *US – Gambling*, at paras 349–72. More recently, the Appellate Body noted that the 'arbitrary or unjustifiable discrimination' requirement of Art XX GATT 1994 should take account of the objective of the measure. The Brazilian law at issue did not meet the test because it permitted an exception that was contrary to its own objective. Appellate Body Report, *Brazil – Retreaded Tyres*, at para 228.

[96] See, eg, R Howse, 'The World Trade Organization and the Protection of Workers' Rights' 1999 *Journal of Small & Emerging Business Law* 3(1) 131, at 169.

[97] For a detailed discussion of the possible uses of Art XX(a) GATT 1994, see S Charnovitz, 'The Moral Exception in Trade Policy' 1998 *Virginia Journal of International Law* 38(4) 689.

[98] Council Decision 97/602, 1997 OJ L/242; Art 3 Commission Regulation 3254/91, 1991 OJ L/308).

[99] T Argitis, 'Canada Files Complaint at WTO Against Belgium Over Seal Ban' *Bloomberg* (31 July 2007). The GATS also contains an exception for measures 'necessary to protect public morals or to maintain public order', which could be used in a similar way to prohibit, for example, the trade in cross-border animal transportation services that failed to comply with animal welfare standards. Art XIV(a) GATS.

to allow discrimination between products based on their production processes—for example, through eco-labels, taxes, or marketing restrictions. Similarly, border tax adjustments on imports from Members with weaker environmental standards could be recognized as permissible.

Finally, panels and the Appellate Body could apply the principles of general international law regarding treaties to clarify the relationship between the WTO covered agreements and MEAs. Some scholars have argued that the public international law principles of *lex specialis* (that a more specialized agreement prevails over a more general one) and *lex posterior* (that an agreement signed later in time prevails over an earlier one) should govern dispute settlement procedures in MEA cases. The application of these rules may prove confusing, however, because while many environmental rules may be considered *lex specialis*, WTO rules— which generally date from 1994—will frequently be *lex posterior*, and the highly specialized harmonized system of tariffs could itself be considered *lex specialis*. Others have suggested that an MEA requiring trade sanctions should prevail over any contrary WTO rule as an *inter se* agreement.[100] However, obvious problems would arise if such sanctions were applied against non-parties to the MEA. Alternatively, some have suggested that MEA rules addressing transboundary externalities should prevail because, as the ICJ stated in the *Nuclear Weapons* decision, 'the general obligation of States to ensure that activities within their jurisdiction and control respect the environment of other States or of areas beyond national control is now part of the corpus of international law relating to the environment'.[101]

Clearly there are limits to what could be accomplished through interpreting and applying existing rules. For example, proposals that low environmental standards should be considered actionable subsidies under the SCM Agreement, which would justify the imposition of eco-duties by other Members in response,[102] could not be achieved simply through 'interpretation' of the SCM Agreement, since the agreement defines a subsidy as involving a government outlay or revenue foregone.[103] But significant progress could be made in addressing conflicts between the trade and environmental regimes through creative interpretation. And, given the almost complete inability to reach negotiated solutions over the past twenty years, adjudication remains the most likely place where trade-and-environment issues will be addressed.

---

[100] E-U Petersmann, *International and European Trade and Environmental Law after the Uruguay Round* (London: Kluwer Law International, 1995), at 41; see also J Pauwelyn, *Conflict of Norms in Public International Law: How WTO Law Relates to Other Rules of International Law* (Cambridge: Cambridge University Press, 2003).

[101] ICJ, *Legality of the Threat or Use of Nuclear Weapons*, Advisory Opinion, 8 July 1996, ICJ Reports (1996) at para 29.

[102] TK Plofchan, Jr, 'Recognizing and Countervailing Environmental Subsidies' 1987 *International Law Journal* (26) 85; Dunoff, above fn 86, at 1061.

[103] Art 1.1 SCM Agreement; see also Dunoff, above fn 86, at 1060.

2. *Creating a More Neutral Forum for Dispute Resolution*

The Appellate Body's willingness in *US – Shrimp* to accept an *amicus* brief filed by an environmental NGO, and its ultimate decision upholding the US import ban, have helped reduce the perception that the WTO dispute settlement system does not provide a fair forum for addressing trade-and-environment disputes.[104] But many still argue that the WTO dispute settlement system is tilted toward the trade perspective (after all, it can strike down an environmental measure as inconsistent with the GATT 1994, but not *vice versa*), and that a more neutral forum is needed. As critics of the current system note, the DSU does not contain a requirement that panels hearing environmental disputes include members with environmental expertise, in contrast to the provisions regarding financial services disputes, which include expertise requirements. Panelists and Appellate Body Members are generally drawn from the trade community and, in the view of critics, give too little weight to environmental issues when making decisions.[105] Moreover, while panels have the ability to accept *amicus curiae* briefs and solicit technical assistance when deciding environmental cases,[106] they are not required—and have several times declined—to do so. This lack of environmental expertise is compounded by the fact that the hearings are closed to the public—and therefore NGOs and public interest groups—unless otherwise agreed by the parties involved.[107]

There are several alternative fora that could hear trade/environmental disputes. The ICJ, for example, has an as yet unused Chamber for Environmental Matters, and the Permanent Court of Arbitration (PCA) has established a set of rules for the arbitration of environmental disputes.[108] But these may be inadequate, given their lack of expertise in dealing with environmental issues, the lack of clarity in international environmental law, and strict standing rules that do not grant access to individuals or NGOs and limit the ability of States not directly injured by the acts at issue to bring suit, for example, on the basis of injuries to the global commons, future generations, or non-human species.[109]

---

[104] Expert committees of the kind established by the SPS Agreement provide a less formal venue that could potentially be used to address disputes. See J Scott, *The WTO Agreement on Sanitary and Phytosanitary Standards: A Commentary* (Oxford: Oxford University Press, 2007)

[105] See, eg, W Lang, 'WTO Dispute Settlement: What the Future Holds' in SSC Tay and DC Esty (eds), *Asian Dragons and Green Trade: Environment, Economics and International Law* (Singapore: Times Academic Press, 1996) 145.

[106] Art 13 DSU. See also chapters 13 and 16 of this Handbook.

[107] As Charnovitz has pointed out, the rules could have been drafted to allow NGO participation; the draft ITO Charter, for example, provided for 'suitable arrangements for consultation and cooperation with nongovernmental organizations concerned with matters within the scope of this Charter'. S Charnovitz, '*The Environment vs Trade Rules: Defogging the Debate*' 1992 Environmental Law 23(2) 475 at 511, fn 164 (quoting the Art 87.2 ITO Charter).

[108] Other international tribunals with the capacity to resolve environmental disputes include, *inter alia*, the International Tribunal for the Law of the Sea, arbitral tribunals created under the provisions of various environmental treaties, the European Court of Human Rights, the Inter-American Court of Human Rights, and the Court of Justice of the European Communities.

[109] See, eg, Dunoff, above fn 86, at 1093–106.

As a result, what is needed, some argue, is a dedicated international environmental court that could adjudicate environment and trade issues. Potential benefits of a new environmental court include a more balanced composition (including more experts in international environmental law), greater openness and transparency, recognition of standing for individuals and NGOs in cases where national remedies have been exhausted, and recognition of the common interest of human kind in protecting the global environment.[110] On the other hand, some argue that the creation of a new tribunal would only further fragment international environmental dispute settlement,[111] and that it would therefore be better to concentrate on improving the ability of existing tribunals to handle environmental disputes. Moreover, adjudicating trade-environment disputes before an international environmental court would to some extent only recreate the current system's myopia.

Thus, although the WTO dispute settlement system has its problems, there does not appear to be a perfect institutional alternative. The choice of a forum for resolving trade–environment disputes will ultimately have to be decided on the grounds of strategic and policy considerations relating to ethos and expertise, and rules regarding access and participation.[112]

B. Negotiated Approaches

Typically, States prefer to address international issues through negotiation rather than adjudication, since this allows them to keep greater control over the ultimate outcomes. When the WTO was initially created, its Members appeared ready to address trade-and-environment issues through a negotiated, political process, and they have continued to include environmental issues in the mandate of the current Doha Round of negotiations.[113]

In practice, however, WTO Members have shown little appetite to address trade-and-environment issues through these political and diplomatic channels. Although the CTE meets on a regular basis and has served as a forum for discussion, leading to increased transparency, it has made little progress in resolving specific

---

[110] For further discussion of the benefits of an International Environmental Court, see KF McCallion and HR Sharma, 'Environmental Justice Without Borders: The Need for an International Court of the Environment to Protect Fundamental Environmental Rights' 2000 *George Washington Journal of International Law & Economics* 32(3) 351, at 359–65.

[111] E Hey, *Reflections on an International Environment Court* (The Hague: Kluwer, 2000), at 9–14.

[112] Shaffer, above fn 64, at 158.

[113] The Doha Declaration specifically identifies in para 31 as priorities 'enhancing the mutual supportiveness of trade and environment', clarifying the relationships between the WTO and MEAs and the reduction or elimination of tariff and non-tariff barriers to environmental goods and services.

issues. If anything, it continues to reflect the lack of agreement among Members on how to proceed.[114]

But although political solutions are unlikely anytime soon, in the long run they may be essential to prevent conflicts between the two regimes. Given the polycentric nature of environmental disputes, which are not easily susceptible to judicial resolution, as well as the bounded quality of judicial interpretation, there are limits to what can be accomplished in resolving trade-and-environment issues through adjudication.[115] In many cases, these issues involve important policy questions about the appropriate trade-offs between trade and environmental values, which may be better addressed through political channels.

1. *Amendment of the Trade Regime*

Rather than rely on WTO dispute settlement, WTO Members could undertake negotiations within the WTO to resolve the outstanding issues regarding the compatibility of environmental measures with free trade. For example, negotiations could address the status of MEAs. As noted above, NAFTA includes a provision that explicitly creates a carve-out for an enumerated list of MEAs, including CITES and the Montreal Protocol. The GATT 1994 could be amended to create a similar exemption.[116] Another possibility would be to use Annex IV of the WTO Agreement to bring MEAs into the WTO as plurilateral agreements.[117] During the Doha MC, WTO Members agreed to spell out the relationship between WTO rules and MEAs that contain 'specific trade obligations',[118] though this mandate is limited to conflicts between WTO Members who are also parties to an MEA, not conflicts between MEA parties and non-parties.[119] Nevertheless, it remains to be seen where WTO Members will take the principle of 'mutual supportiveness' in the future.

---

[114] More progress has been possible in addressing trade-and-environment issues in bilateral or regional trade agreements, due to the smaller number of States involved. For example, recent free trade agreements between China and Chile, Japan and Mexico, and the US and Peru all contain environmental provisions.

[115] As Dunoff argues, 'international environmental issues often do not present the sort of "bilateral" dispute that is well-suited for adjudication. The "polluters" in the case of climate change or ozone depletion for example, include all the nations of the earth. All nations would likewise be potential plaintiffs, because all are affected... Traditional litigation simply does not lend itself to the resolution of this type of dispute'. Dunoff, above fn 86, at 1088, 1101.

[116] C Wold, 'Multilateral Environmental Agreements and the GATT: Conflict and Resolution?' 1996 *Environmental Law* (26) 841. Similarly, the TRIPS Agreement could be amended to accommodate some central elements of the CBD by requiring an applicant for a patent on biological materials to disclose the source and country of origin of biological materials used in the invention, give evidence of prior informed consent, and provide proof of equitable benefit sharing among the patent-holder and groups that assisted the patent-holder in obtaining the requisite knowledge and/or biological materials. WTO Secretariat, see fn 9, at 42.

[117] Charnovitz, above fn 68, at 355.   [118] WTO Secretariat, above fn 9, at 39.

[119] Ibid.

Negotiations could also address the permissibility of PPM standards, such as a carbon tax on electricity or eco-labelling requirements, as well as the permissibility of precautionary measures to address potential harms about which there exists little scientific evidence. Likewise, negotiations could tackle the permissibility of levying eco-duties on products from Members whose domestic laws fail to internalize the environmental costs associated with the production process.

More generally, the WTO framework could be expanded through the adoption of an agreement on Trade-Related Aspects of Environmental Protection, analogous to the TRIPS Agreement. Such an agreement might include any number of environment-related provisions that would work to standardize environmental protection across national borders. For example, it might begin by recognizing certain environmental prerequisites for WTO membership. It could also require importing countries to impose an environmental tariff on commodities to ensure the internalization of environmental costs.[120] Or the agreement might forbid imports of goods that are produced in contravention of certain multilateral environmental standards (for example, goods produced with materials derived from internationally recognized endangered species). Additionally, the agreement could be structured to accommodate environment-related dispute settlement, and the enforcement mechanism of the WTO could then be used to ensure compliance with these multilaterally agreed environmental standards.

2.   *Development of Common Environmental Standards through a Global Environmental Organization*

A host of scholars and policymakers have proposed that some type of Global Environmental Organization (GEO) or World Environmental Organization (WEO) be established to counterbalance the WTO and address international market failures that result in environmental harms.[121] The exact scope and powers of the proposed organization are contested among GEO advocates. But in broad strokes, the GEO might, *inter alia*, work to centralize the environmental regime under one institutional umbrella, coordinate the current mass of MEAs, discipline violators, create new policy, disseminate information and conduct research, and fulfil environmental support and advocacy functions at the WTO. Moreover, the GEO could develop common international environmental standards to replace national standards that

---

[120]   See, eg, British House of Commons, Environment Committee, *World Trade and the Environment*, (17 June 1996) at paras 134–38, discussed in S Charnovitz, 'A Critical Guide,' see above fn 68, at 344.

[121]   Esty, above fn 3; S Charnovitz, 'A World Environment Organization' 2002 *Columbia Journal of Environmental Law* 27(2) 323; GF Kennan, 'To Prevent A World Wasteland: A Proposal' 1970 *Foreign Affairs* (48) 401, at 411–2; F Biermann, 'The Case for a World Environment Organization' 2000 *Environment* (Nov) 28–29.

hinder trade, in much the same way that the federal government establishes uniform environmental rules within the US federal system.[122]

Many environmentalists have lent support to this idea in the hope that centralization might empower the international environmental regime and allow it to stand up to the WTO, or at least better moderate the trade-environment debate. Some free trade advocates have also come out as pro-GEO, betting that the creation of a strong environmental organization would help bridge the gap between trade and environment and might steer countries away from the 'inappropriate' use of trade measures.[123]

Other environmentalists have rejected a GEO as impractical, and point out that in many ways the fragmentation of the environmental regime has been of great benefit, allowing for rapid growth and development in disparate areas. Establishing a GEO, they argue, would 'overload the carrying capacity of the international organizational landscape', doing little more than adding 'layers of non-productive bureaucracies, detracting from the necessary focus at the national and regional level'.[124]

VI. CONCLUSION

The trade and environmental regimes are two of the most dynamic in all of international law. That they have bumped up against one another from time to time, as they grow in scope and depth, should not be surprising. Managing (and, when possible, avoiding) their potential conflicts, and exploiting their potential synergies, will pose a continuing challenge. Already, each regime has shown greater sensitivity to the other. The jurisprudence of the Appellate Body evidences a greater willingness to take into account environmental values, and environmental regimes have become more restrained in their use of trade measures for environmental purposes.

But despite these signs of rapprochement, an impressive number of questions remain unresolved about how far environmental regulation can go in restricting trade, and how far the trade regime can go in restricting environmental measures.

---

[122] RB Stewart, 'International Trade and Environment: Lessons from the Federal Experience' 1992 *Washington & Lee Law Review* 49(4) 1329, at 1337.

[123] R Ruggiero, *Opening Remarks to the High Level Symposium on Trade and the Environment*, Speech (15 March 1999), at <http://www.wto.org/english/tratop_e/devel_e/hlstat_e.htm> (last visited 26 May 2008).

[124] Ambassador KG Anthony Hill, 'It's time to make the global debate local' in Najam, above fn 91, 9, at 12.

In general, the same States are involved in both regimes. Ultimately, they could themselves decide what balance they wish to strike between trade and environmental values. Thus far, however, they have declined to do so. Rather than making these politically difficult decisions, they have preferred to allow trade and environment issues to be addressed in a piecemeal way, through case-by-case review. This approach creates uncertainty and requires adjudicative bodies to make what are essentially policy choices. But given the contextual nature of the inquiry and the multiplicity of relevant factors—the purpose of a measure, whether it is unilateral or multilateral, territorial or extraterritorial, scientifically, or morally based—this is perhaps the best of an imperfect set of alternatives.

Selected Bibliography

N Barnasconi-Osterwalder et al., *Environment and Trade: A Guide to WTO Jurisprudence* (London: Earthscan, 2006)

J Cameron, P Demaret, and D Geradin (eds), *Trade and Environment: The Search for Balance* (London: Cameron & May, 1994)

S Charnovitz, *Trade Law and Global Governance* (London: Cameron & May, 2002)

BR Copeland and MS Taylor, *Trade and the Environment: Theory and Evidence* (Princeton: Princeton University Press, 2005)

DC Esty, *Greening the GATT: Trade, Environment, and the Future* (Washington, DC: Institute for International Economics, 1994)

A Najam, M Halle, and R Melendez-Ortiz (eds), *Trade and Environment: A Resource Book* (Geneva: International Institute for Sustainable Development, 2007)

G Sampson, *The WTO and Sustainable Development* (Tokyo: UNU Press, 2005)

G Shaffer, 'The World Trade Organization under Challenge: Democracy and the Law and Politics of the WTO's Treatment of Trade and Environment Matters' 2001 *Harvard Environmental Law Review* 25(1) 1

R Steinberg (ed), *The Greening of Trade Law: International Trade Organizations and Environmental Issues* (Lanham, MD: Rowman & Littlefield, 2001)

UNEP and International Institute of Sustainable Development, *Environment and Trade: A Handbook*, 2nd edn (Nairobi/Geneva: UNEP and IISD, 2005)

D Vogel, *Trading up: Consumer and Environmental Regulation in a Global Economy* (Cambridge: Harvard University Press, 1995)

E Brown Weiss and JH Jackson (eds), *Reconciling Environment and Trade* (Ardsley, NY: Transnational Publishers, 2001)

WTO Secretariat, *Trade and Environment at the WTO* (Geneva: WTO, 2004)

D Zaelke, R Housman, and P Orbuch, *Trade and the Environment: Law, Economics and Policy* (Washington, DC: Island Press, 1993)

CHAPTER 19

·····································

TRADE AND LABOUR

·····································

GABRIELLE MARCEAU*

* Views expressed in this chapter are personal to the author and do not bind the WTO Members or the WTO Secretariat. I am especially grateful to Froukje Boele and Francis Maupain for their important input on this chapter and for our rich discussions. Thank you also to Robert Anderson, Antonia Carzaniga, Steve Charnovitz, Mireille Cossy, Marie-Sophie Dibbling, Victor Do Prado, Arancha Gonzalez, Marion Jansen, and Julian Wyat for their useful comments on prior drafts.

The Members recognize that the avoidance of unemployment or underemployment, through the achievement and maintenance in each country of useful employment opportunities for those able and willing to work and of a large and steadily growing volume of production and effective demand for goods and services, is not of domestic concern alone, but is also a necessary condition for the achievement of the general purpose and the objectives set forth in Article 1, including the expansion of international trade, and thus for the well-being of all other countries.

> Article 1 of the Havana Charter for an International Trade Organization, signed at the conclusion of the United Nations Conference on Trade and Employment, Havana, Cuba, 24 March 1948

I. INTRODUCTION

JUST a short while ago the WTO Secretariat was rediscovering old wall paintings dating back to the days when the building was occupied by the International Labour Organization (ILO) Secretariat between 1927 and 1975. When the GATT took over part of the building in 1976,[1] several of those paintings glorifying the respect of work and the need for social justice were simply taken down or covered over—possibly to help forget, or maybe, even to deny, the links between trade and labour. Since then, despite their geographical proximity, the two organizations have sometimes given the impression that they were turning their back to each other.

But some things cannot be forgotten, and it seems that the WTO is destined to remember that social and labour issues are relevant to its overall goal to improve people's standards of living in a sustainable manner. If the GATT/WTO system is responsible for opening markets and favouring economic growth, trade rules alone cannot guarantee that the benefits of increasing trade will translate into tangible benefits for all people, as the WTO does not deal directly with re-distribution and other social issues necessary to ensure social justice. But today, when entering the WTO building, the new magnificent fresco you see dates back from 1931[2] and reminds us of enduring ILO principles of social justice—as if they could not remain divorced from WTO actions. The recent rediscovery of these paintings may be symbolic of the realization that trade liberalization and the improvement of labour and social conditions are not two solitudes,[3] they can find expression and operate coherently and consistently with each other.

---

[1] The UN High Commission on Refugees occupied part of the Centre William Rappard Building until 1996 when it moved to its current location.

[2] *La Paix triomphante*, by GL Jaulmes.

[3] BA Langille, 'Eight Ways to think about International Labour Standards' 1997 *Journal of World Trade* 31 (4–6) 27.

A. From the ITO to the WTO on Labour Issues

The ancestor to the WTO and GATT 1947 trade rules was the Havana Charter, a multi-lateral treaty setting up the Organization on International Trade (ITO) which was signed at the end of the UN Conference on Trade and Employment held in Havana, Cuba, from 21 November 1947 to 21 March 1948. The first chapter of the ITO Havana Charter was entitled 'Employment and Economic Activities'. Its first provision cited at the start of this chapter, remains remarkably contemporaneous and could be elo-quently argued today. But the Havana Charter was never ratified, and only part of its Chapter IV on Commercial Policies was included in the GATT 1947, initially in force on a provisional basis, and remained in place until it was absorbed into the new WTO to become the GATT 1994. The text of the GATT 1947 does not make reference to labour considerations. Today, the Preamble of the WTO Agreement proclaims that 'trade should be conducted with a view to raising standards of living, ensuring full employment . . . in accordance with the objective of sustainable development'. But for a few indirect references to labour-related considerations in trade provisions, the WTO treaty language does not refer to labour standards or to labour-related trade actions. However, initially, its source and origin—Chapter IV on Commercial Policies—was part of a broader framework that contained social and labour provisions.

B. States Must Comply With Both Their WTO and ILO Obligations

Labour standards and other labour-related issues are rather negotiated in and administered by the ILO and its Secretariat. This does not mean that WTO Members are only obliged to respect their WTO obligations and that they can ignore their ILO rights and obligations or those of other international instruments relating to labour and social considerations. On the contrary, States must comply in good faith with all their international obligations simultaneously while being able to exercise their negotiated rights. This is arguably what WTO Members wanted to confirm in the Singapore Declaration when they stated clearly '[w]e renew our commitment to the observance of internationally recognized core labour stand-ards . . . and we affirm our support for [the ILO] work in promoting them . . .'.[4] Such a ministerial political declaration does not create any WTO obligations that can be taken to a WTO dispute panel. Nonetheless, one can argue that, in making this joint declaration, WTO Members reiterated in the WTO that they will observe core labour standards, and support their promotion, while these standards are administered and monitored in another forum, the ILO. But this in turn suggests

---

[4] WTO, *Singapore Ministerial Declaration*, WT/MIN(96)/DEC (13 December 1996).

that WTO Members confirmed that they are capable of adopting and enforcing WTO trade regulations while at the same time promoting core labour standards. Otherwise why would WTO Members talk about labour standards in their trade forum? Labour and trade governmental actions can co-exist legally, consistently and harmoniously, but how (closely) can the two sets of policies be inter-linked under WTO disciplines? As discussed below, the WTO system appears to be receptive to good faith and non-protectionist labour considerations within several trade measures.

C. The Legal Relationship Between Trade and Labour

The objective of this chapter is not to pronounce on or prejudge whether there should be a more binding linkage between trade and labour protection in order to produce greater efficiency. Nor is it to assess the extent to which trade liberalization has actually made improvements in the lot of working people in the world—except to note that a recent joint study between the WTO and the ILO provides a concise and interesting summary of the state of knowledge on this subject.[5] It does not attempt to assess the space left to WTO Members to implement good faith labour and social policies, nor whether those implemented consistently with WTO are also consistent with ILO prescriptions, or effective from a labour and social perspective. The purpose of this chapter is to explore the legal relationship between WTO norms and labour norms and, in particular, whether and how labour considerations can be intertwined with the interpretation and application of the WTO rights and obligations so that WTO Members, as States, can benefit from, and comply with, both the trade and labour international regimes.

This chapter will look at the trade and labour issues from three perspectives. The first one is the extent to which some WTO multilateral and plurilateral trade disciplines refer to labour considerations or provide policy space for labour concerns. Another one is the extent to which Members can agree to make regional/plurilateral arrangements which simultaneously further trade liberalization and pursue labour objectives. The last perspective concerns unilateral trade preferential agreements, where compliance with labour standards is becoming a criterion for (increased) trade preferences.

---

[5] M Jansen and E Lee, *Trade and Employment – Challenges for Policy Research* (Geneva: WTO-ILO, 2007), at <http://www.wto.org/english/res_e/booksp_e/ilo_e.pdf> (last visited 21 May 2008).

II. The WTO and Labour Considerations – The Multilateral Dimension

A. Interpretation of the WTO

As repeatedly noted, WTO provisions cannot be read in 'clinical isolation' from the rest of international law.[6] This means that the WTO is only part of a more global system that includes several sets of rights and obligations contained *inter alia* in multiple treaties. States never agreed to give priority generally to WTO norms over other international norms, including, for example, labour norms. All international norms are *a priori* equal, except *jus cogens* and article 103 UN Charter. When reading and interpreting WTO provisions, the contexts and the general principles of law as well as other relevant international rules applicable between the parties must be taken into account, even if they originate in other fora. Whether and how this includes treaties with smaller or different membership is a matter of debate.[7]

Some terms in the WTO treaty language may indicate a possibility of referring to labour treaties or ILO instruments when interpreting them. The Preamble of the WTO Agreement itself refers to '...increasing standards of living, ensuring full employment' as goals of the WTO. Reference is also made to 'sustainable development', a concept that includes three dimensions: economic development, environmental protection, and social justice. Arguably, as it was said with respect to the relative importance of environment since the entry into force of the WTO Agreement, this specific language of the Preamble 'gives colour, texture and shading to the rights and obligations of Members under the WTO Agreement' and could lead to an evolutionary interpretation of WTO provisions that would take social or labour-related principles into account in relevant circumstances.[8] Moreover some labour norms can be considered as human rights, the protection of which may be covered by general principles of law also relevant in interpreting WTO treaty language.[9]

---

[6] Appellate Body Report, *US – Gasoline*, at 17.
[7] See chapter 12 of this Handbook.
[8] Appellate Body Report, *US – Shrimp*, at paras 153–55 and 130.
[9] On this issue see also L Bartels, 'Social Issues: Labour, Environment, and Human Rights' in S Lester and B Mercurio (eds), *Bilateral and Regional Trade Agreements: Commentary, Analysis and Case Studies* (Cambridge: Cambridge University Press, forthcoming).

B. Several Labour-Related Measures Possible in the WTO Single Undertaking

It is difficult to discuss how WTO disciplines deal with and take into account labour considerations without a basic understanding of the internal interaction between various provisions of the WTO single undertaking.[10] While the WTO Agreement and its annexes are today a single treaty, its provisions were originally negotiated through 15 different working groups. It was only towards the end of the negotiations that the creation of a 'single undertaking' was agreed and governments decided to annex the resulting text from each working group to the Marrakesh Agreement Establishing the WTO or WTO Agreement. The basic provisions of the GATT 1994 have been supplemented with new WTO agreements. For example, when assessing the WTO consistency of a domestic (technical) regulation that would contain regulatory distinctions based on labour considerations, one must not only examine Article III GATT 1994 prohibiting regulatory discrimination between imported and domestic goods, and the possibility of invoking general exceptions under the GATT 1994 to justify an otherwise inconsistent measure, but also, assess the same domestic regulation pursuant to the TBT Agreement[11] that prohibits technical regulations from being prepared, adopted, and applied more restrictively than necessary to fulfil a legitimate objective.[12] Two WTO basic principles are that all WTO provisions are simultaneously applicable and must be interpreted harmoniously so as to ensure the effectiveness of all WTO provisions.

A single trade-labour measure may be intertwined with several trade instruments simultaneously and may eventually be reviewed under several WTO agreements. For example, labour considerations can be linked to market access commitments, either in tariff or government procurement schedules and may also call for the application of the Licensing Agreement and the GATT 1994, while they could also be part of subsidies or investment programmes for which advantages are conditioned on labour considerations. Labour variables—wages, level of employment, etc—can also be invoked in trade remedies disputes, when assessing whether imports are causing injury to the domestic industry of the importing countries. In the area of trade in services, specific scheduled commitments can be made subject to certain types of conditions as well. Regional trade agreements and generalized systems of preferences contain enhanced provisions on labour standards.

---

[10] G Marceau, 'Balance and Coherence by the WTO Appellate Body: Who Could Do Better?' in G Sacerdoti, A Yanovich, and J Bohanes (eds), *The WTO at 10: The Role of the Dispute Settlement System* (Cambridge: Cambridge University Press, 2006) 326.

[11] There is no intention to make a statement here on the order of analysis. It seems more WTO-consistent to examine any such regulation first under the TBT Agreement and subsequently, if need be, under Articles XI, III, and XX GATT 1994.

[12] Arts 2.2 and 2.4 TBT Agreement.

All these situations raise a general question: whether and to what extent WTO Members' trade-related regulations and actions can be conditioned (partly) on labour considerations?[13] In that context, the first part of this chapter will examine provisions of the GATT 1994 that refer to or permit the use of labour considerations. It will then discuss the provisions of other WTO agreements that may overlap or apply simultaneously with those of the GATT 1994.

C. GATT 1994 and Labour Considerations

The GATT 1994 imposes disciplines on restrictions to trade such as tariffs, quotas, domestic regulations, and subsidies. One such rule is the prohibition against less favourable treatment of any imported 'like products'. The definition and comparison of 'like' products, and the parameters for less favourable treatment are crucial determinations.

Since its inception, the GATT 1994 has recognized that legitimate government policies may justify measures that are contrary to the basic GATT obligations in order to enforce policies other than trade such as the protection of public morals, health, or the environment.[14] The issue for us is whether the same could apply to labour policies. The new Appellate Body jurisprudence has insisted on the need to ensure that the GATT 1994 exceptions are effective and that a balance is maintained between pure trade obligations and the right of Members to give priority to policies other than trade. The GATT 1994 provisions relating to market access broadly defined (market access schedule, disciplines on regulations, and subsidies) and those providing for exceptions will thus be examined together, first. It will thereafter be easier to understand how the new TBT Agreement has transformed the GATT 1994 exceptions into WTO conditional rights and thus reinforced the right of Members to give priority to policies other than trade, so long as they are based on legitimate objectives and implemented without protectionism.

In the GATT 1994, the question of whether labour standards can condition trade-related actions is also closely linked to the issue of whether a trade regulation can make distinctions on the basis of *criteria unrelated to the products themselves*. Known as the process and production method (PPM) debate, this issue permeates the entire 'trade and . . .' debate and it is inherent to any trade-and-labour measure as its regulatory criteria are always relating to work and workers conditions and never about the product itself.

---

[13] S Charnovitz, *Addressing environmental and labour issues in the World Trade Organization* (Washington DC: Progressive Policy Institute, 1999).

[14] These matters are a selection of the exceptions listed in Art XX GATT 1994.

1. *Non-Discrimination: Most-Favoured-Nation (Article 1) and National Treatment Principles (Article III)*

Labour standards are not negotiated in the WTO, they are negotiated in other specialized fora. In the WTO, Members negotiate tariffs and subsidies reductions but do not generally negotiate the content of domestic regulations or standards *per se*. The main obligations with regard to domestic regulations or domestic standards are that they cannot maintain unjustified discrimination or be more restrictive than necessary to fulfil a legitimate objective. Some of the WTO provisions give legal value to internationally negotiated standards. For example, the SPS Agreement provides that if a Member bases its national standards on a Codex standard, such national standards are presumed to be consistent with the SPS Agreement. A similar provision exists for technical regulations under the TBT Agreement, with respect to relevant international standards that, as further discussed hereafter, may include labour standards.

Generally, the GATT 1994 prohibits 'less favourable treatment' between any two 'like' products.[15] The most-favoured nation (MFN) obligation requires WTO Members to provide any advantage, favour, privilege, or immunity that they grant to any imports to all like products imported from any WTO Member, immediately and without conditions. The mandatory respect of certain labour considerations could be viewed as such a 'condition'. In the old GATT *Family Allowance* dispute, the tariff discrimination introduced by the Belgian law against imports from countries that did not maintain a family allowance system, was condemned because this condition was not written in Belgium's Schedule and not at large.[16]

In the context of national treatment, labour considerations can affect 'likeness' or/ and the 'less favourable treatment' of the imported product.

a. *Likeness*

Traditionally, a determination of likeness would call for an assessment of criteria relating to the physical characteristics of products.[17] In the context of trade and labour, the question is whether two physically similar products can nonetheless become 'unlike' because of the manner in which they are produced—in respect or in non-respect of identified labour considerations relating to conditions of work or of workers. In the trade and environment context many developing countries argue against the consideration of the manner in which goods are produced or processed— this is the so-called 'PPM-debate'.[18] The PPM-concept is generally understood as a principle that considers that two similar products cannot become unlike on the

---

[15] With the WTO, this principle was extended to two like services and service suppliers under the GATS and to two like right-holders under the TRIPS Agreement. See also chapters 7 and 8 of this Handbook.

[16] GATT Contracting Parties, *Belgian Family Allowances*.

[17] GATT Working Party Report, *Border Tax Adjustments*.

[18] See chapter 18 of this Handbook.

basis of their method of production or process.[19] The *EC – Asbestos* dispute clarified that the determination of 'likeness' is essentially a determination of the competitive relationship between two products,[20] which is a broader criterion than physical characteristics because consumer preferences may be affected by a PPM whether it is sound or not. In determining whether this competitive relationship actually exists, the Appellate Body[21] seemed to focus largely on the physical characteristics of the products, namely their carcinogenicity or toxicity. Although it stated that these four criteria are not a closed set and may suggest conflicting evidence,[22] the Appellate Body insisted that all four criteria must be examined each time.[23] It seemed, nonetheless, to give a heavier weight to physical characteristics, or at least differences in physical characteristics, when it wrote:

In such cases [when physically similar], in order to overcome this indication that products are not 'like', a higher burden is placed on complaining Members to establish that, despite the pronounced physical differences, there is a competitive relationship between the products such that all of the evidence, taken together, demonstrates that the products are 'like' under Article III (4) GATT 1994.[24]

Accordingly, when goods are physically similar, it will be difficult to prove that they are not competing with each other.[25] While consumers may at times distinguish based on production processes, and some competitive effect is quite possible, it is difficult to envision a circumstance where the effect would be great enough to render physically similar products un-like. While it seems that non-product related distinctions would hardly make goods unlike, policy-based criteria may justify different treatments in the context of the exceptions of Article XX, discussed hereafter.[26]

b. Less Favourable Treatment

Imported products cannot be treated less favourably, but what does it mean? The *EC – Asbestos* report concluded that different treatment of like products may not

---

[19] G Marceau and JP Trachtman, 'A Map of the World Trade Organization Law of Domestic Regulation of Goods' in GA Bermann and PC Mavroidis (eds), *Trade and Human Health and Safety* (Cambridge: Cambridge University Press, 2006) 9.

[20] Appellate Body Report, *EC – Asbestos*, at paras 98–100. The four basic criteria derived from the *Border Tax Adjustment* report are: (i) the physical properties of the products in question; (ii) their end-uses; (iii) consumer tastes and habits *vis-à-vis* those products; and (iv) tariff classification. They are to be used as tools in determining this competitive relationship between products.

[21] Even more so, the dissenting member of the Appellate Body for whom the particularly different physical characteristics—toxicity—of the products at issue was irrefutable evidence against their 'likeness'. Ibid at paras 151–53.

[22] Ibid at para 120.   [23] Ibid at paras 102, 109, 111, 113, 139, and 140.

[24] Ibid at para 121.   [25] Ibid at paras 117–18.

[26] One the issue of why it is accepted that the TRIPS Agreement deals with a series of intellectual property obligations that do not affect the physical characteristics of the product to which they apply, see F Maupain, 'Is the ILO Effective in Upholding Workers' Rights?: Reflections on the Myanmar Experience' in P Alston (ed), *Labour Rights as Human Rights* (Oxford: Oxford University Press, 2005), at 133–34.

necessarily result in less favourable treatment.[27] Then, in *Dominican Republic – Import and Sale of Cigarettes*, the Appellate Body continued this line in stating that 'the existence of a detrimental effect on a given imported product resulting from a measure does not necessarily imply that this measure accords less favourable treatment to imports *if the detrimental effect is explained by factors or circumstances unrelated to the foreign origin of the product*, such as the market share of the importer in this case'.[28] The *EC – Biotech Products* report concluded that discrimination would not create less favourable treatment when the difference is justified by non-protectionist policies based on government/consumers' perceptions. The Panel concluded that there was no need to determine whether biotech and non-biotech were like products since '[i]t is not self evident that the alleged less favourable treatment of imported biotech products is explained by the foreign origin rather than, for instance, a perceived difference between biotech and non-biotech products in terms of their safety....'[29] The Panel rejected the claim of violation of national treatment. Can we extend this reasoning to measures imposing different treatment based on the respect of core labour standards by the exporting Members alleging perceived differences affecting the 'morality limits' of the importing country?

2. *Article II GATT 1994: Labour Conditions in Tariff (Goods) Schedules?*

Can Members 'negotiate' tariffs levels with conditions that would be labour-related? Recall that the report in *Belgian Family Allowances* seemed to have condemned the social condition because it was not included in Belgium's Schedule. This issue has not been addressed by the jurisprudence. Yet Article II:1(b) seems to envisage the possibility that 'terms, conditions or qualifications' may be set forth in a Member's Schedule. Do 'terms, conditions or qualifications' include labour standards?

We know that conditions cannot include limitations on the origin of a product,[30] or qualifications relating to quantitative restrictions as 'Article II permits contracting parties to incorporate into their Schedules acts yielding rights under the GATT 1994, but not acts diminishing obligations under that Agreement'.[31] The same criterion was used in *EC – Bananas III* where the Panel concluded that the footnote included in the EC's Schedule imposed what was considered to be a discriminatory tariff quota in favour of ACP countries, inconsistent with Article XIII GATT 1994. So the legal question to answer in determining whether labour conditions can be

---

[27] Appellate Body Report, *EC – Asbestos*, at para 100 (original emphasis), reads as follows: '...a Member may draw distinctions between products which have been found to be "like", without, for this reason alone, according to the group of "like" *imported* products "less favourable treatment" than that accorded to the group of "like" *domestic* products'.

[28] Appellate Body Report, *Dominican Republic – Import and Sale of Cigarettes*, at para 96 (emphasis added). For a detailed analysis of this question, see chapter 20 of this Handbook.

[29] Panel Report, *EC – Biotech Products*, at paras 7.2509–2516.

[30] GATT Panel Report, *EEC – Beef*.

[31] GATT Panel Report, *US – Sugar*, at paras 5.2–7.

negotiated in a Schedule is whether labour considerations are explicitly or implicitly prohibited by a provision of the GATT 1994?

It is difficult to conclude that labour rights considerations are explicitly prohibited by a rule of the GATT 1994, unless one argues that non-product labour related criteria (as PPM) are as such prohibited by the GATT 1994 (but as discussed later they may find application under the exceptions of Article XX), or that labour conditions constitute a *de facto* import restriction prohibited by Article XI GATT 1994—which is not clear because compliance with that condition (like a technical regulation on trade) would permit an unlimited level of imports and does not discriminate on the basis of their origin.

3. *The Exceptions of the GATT 1994: Can Labour Considerations Justify Inconsistencies with Provisions of the GATT?*

Since its inception, the GATT 1994 has always recognized that legitimate government policies may justify measures that are contrary to basic GATT disciplines. Hence, in some circumstances, non-trade values can supersede trade rules, provided that the governmental action relates to, or is necessary, to one of the non-trade policies listed in Article XX and is applied in good faith. The policies listed in Article XX can justify measures inconsistent with any of the other provisions in the GATT 1994.

There is no direct or indirect reference to labour standards in Article XX GATT 1994. However, three sub-paragraphs are sometimes invoked as allowing for some labour standards considerations: paragraph (a) for measures necessary for the protection of public morals; paragraph (b) for measures necessary for the protection of human, animal, or plant life or health; and paragraph (e) for measures relating to the products of prison labour.

The Appellate Body has articulated a two-tier test to determine whether a trade restriction may be justified under Article XX GATT 1994 (or the corresponding Article XIV GATS).[32] First, the disputed measure must contribute to the promotion of the underlying policy goal pursued (for example, protection of public morals), the assessment of which requires examination of the nature, object, and structure of the measure; noting that conditioning market access to policies unilaterally prescribed is common to each sub-paragraph of Article XX.[33] The second part of the analysis requires that the measure be applied in *good faith* and that recourse to an exception does not amount to an *abuse* or misuse of treaty rights. Specifically, the application

---

[32] Appellate Body Report, *US – Gambling*, at para 292.

[33] Appellate Body Report, *US – Shrimp*, at para 121; Appellate Body Report, *US – Shrimp (Article 21.5 – Malaysia)*, at para 137 (original emphasis): 'It appears to us, however, that *conditioning access to a Member's domestic market on whether exporting Members comply with, or adopt, a policy or policies unilaterally prescribed by the importing Member may, to some degree, be a common aspect of measures falling within the scope of one or another of the exceptions (a) to (j) of Article XX.* Paragraphs (a) to (j) comprise measures that are recognized as *exceptions to substantive obligations* established in the GATT 1994, because the domestic policies embodied in such measures have been recognized as important and legitimate in character.'

of the measure must not constitute arbitrary or unjustifiable discrimination, or amount to disguised protectionism.

In case of a dispute over the WTO consistency of a labour-related trade regulation where the general exceptions of Article XX would be involved, these questions would be asked. Is respect of (core) labour standards covered by any of the policies and non-trade values mentioned in Article XX? The second question is whether a specific labour measure complies with the exception provision and, thirdly, whether it is 'applied' in good faith under the chapeau of Article XX GATT 1994. There is no agreement among Members on this issue, nor any jurisprudence.

a. Measures Necessary for the Protection of Public Morals

In assuming that an instance of discrimination based on labour-related considerations is *prima facie* inconsistent with basic GATT obligations (Articles I, II, III, V, VIII, XI, XII, XIII, etc.) can it be justified as 'necessary for the protection of public morals'?

In *US – Gambling*, the exception for 'public morals' of GATS (similar to that of Article XX(a) GATT 1994) was defined to include standards of right and wrong conduct maintained by or on behalf of a community or nation, including measures for public order preserving the fundamental interests of a society, as reflected in public policy and law.[34] The protection of some labour standards, especially the so-called fundamental labour rights could be argued to be issues of public morals.[35] Could a Member suggest that respect of certain labour standards in the exporting country is an issue of such moral importance in its country that those goods cannot circulate in its country?[36] As noted, WTO exceptions authorize derogations based on unilateral policies, but the situation would be more straightforward if one were to speak of a determination of public morals made collectively, such as where it is supported by UN Security Council resolutions (as envisaged by Article XXI(c) GATT 1994), or as was actually the case with Myanmar,[37] for which such a determination was not only made collectively by the ILO international community in an established legal framework, but which also called for collective action on that basis.

Assuming that some labour issues are issues of public morals in the importing country (avoiding extraterritorial issues), the second question would be whether a specific labour-related measure is 'necessary'. The Appellate Body has developed a test to assess when a measure is 'necessary'. It calls for a weighing and balancing of a series of factors, including: (i) 'the relative importance of the common interests or

---

[34] Appellate Body Report, *US – Gambling*, at paras 286–96.

[35] In particular the 4 components of the 1998 ILO Declaration on Fundamental Principles and Rights at Work.

[36] If the trade action is a countermeasure, a reaction against alleged illegal actions by the exporting Member, is this measure a unilateral trade countermeasure contrary to *Mexico – Taxes on Soft Drinks* that prohibited panels from considering non-WTO disputes? This issue is further discussed below.

[37] *Measures recommended by the Governing Body under Article 33 of the Constitution – Implementation of recommendations contained in the Report of the Commission of Inquiry entitled Forced Labour in Myanmar (Burma)*, International Labour Conference, Provisional Record 6–4, 88th Session, Geneva, 2000.

values' pursued by the measure; (ii) the 'contribution of the measure to the realization of the end pursued'; and (iii) its trade impact.[38] It has been noted that '[t]he more vital or important those common interests or values are, the easier it would be to accept the measure as "necessary"'.[39] In *Brazil – Retreaded Tyres*, the Appellate Body clarified that in order to be necessary a measure needs to 'contribute' to the achievement of its objective; a contribution exists when there is a genuine relationship of ends and means between the objective and the measure.[40] This contribution needs to be material after having been weighted against its trade restrictiveness. Once the respondent has made a *prima facie* case that the challenged measure is 'necessary' along this new test, it is for the complainant to raise a WTO-consistent alternative measure that, in its view, the responding party should have taken.[41] This is a very heavy burden on the exporting Member challenging the measure, especially if the importing country's chosen level of risk is *zero*.[42] Applying this test to a national measure based, for instance, on ILO standards would call for the weighing and balancing of whether the specific measure protects fundamental values and public morals, whether it contributes to the respect of the policy goal and the importance of the trade impact.[43]

b. Measures Necessary for the Protection of Health of Persons

Does sub-paragraph XX (b) only refer to the physical health of persons and not their mental health? Is this a relative criteria?[44] Can labour considerations restricting market access be justified in measures contributing to the protection of the health of workers abroad? The latter questions point to the unresolved issue of whether Article XX can be invoked against actions taking place abroad – the

[38] Appellate Body Report, *Korea – Various Measures on Beef*, at para 162; Appellate Body Report, *Dominican Republic – Import and Sale of Cigarettes*, at para 70; Appellate Body Report, *US – Gambling*, at paras 304–11.

[39] Appellate Body Report, *Korea – Various Measures on Beef*, at para 162.

[40] Appellate Body Report, *Brazil – Retreaded Tyres*, at para 210.

[41] Appellate Body Report, *US – Gambling*, at paras 308–11.

[42] Appellate Body Report, *Australia – Salmon*, at para 125, stating that Members can fix the level of risk they want, including a level of zero.

[43] In case of a dispute where the defendant invokes ILO Conventions or standards, panels and the Appellate Body should request relevant information from the ILO (pursuant to Article 13 DSU) and discuss it with the parties, and ensure that such information is given its appropriate legal weight. In the absence of a special rule giving ILO decisions and actions specific legal value, relevant ILO instruments would be taken into account in one way or another by panel when determining whether a specific labour-related measure is consistent with the exception provisions of the GATT 1994 itself.

[44] It seems to be a relative criterion where some countries are expected to have higher and more advanced labour legislation. In *EC – Asbestos*, the Panel was concerned with technical regulations under the French labour law and said: 'We consider that the existence of a reasonably available measure must be assessed in the light of the economic and administrative realities facing the Member concerned but also by taking into account the fact that the State must provide itself with the means of implementing its policies.' Thus, the Panel considers that it is legitimate to expect a country, such as France with advanced labour legislation and specialized administrative services, to deploy administrative resources proportionate to its public health objectives and to be prepared to incur the necessary expenditure. Panel Report, *EC – Asbestos*, at paras 8.208–09.

extraterritorial application of Article XX.[45] If they cannot, it is difficult to see how an importing Member could justify restricting market access by claiming that it is contributing to protecting foreign workers from the health-related impacts of unsatisfactory working conditions, noting that the rational and effective link between the measure and the policy goal would in any case be difficult to demonstrate. Nonetheless, one of the Article XX exceptions, referring to prison labour, is inherently extraterritorial.

c. Measures Relating to the Product of Prison Labour

As opposed to the previous exceptions, prison labour clearly allows for an extraterritorial application. However, this exception is not based on any philanthropic reasoning, but purely on economic considerations to ensure fair competition. One might wonder, when taking an evolutionary interpretation,[46] whether 'forced labour' is included in the concept of 'prison labour'? To answer this question, it is of interest to refer to the ILO's standards and supervisory mechanism. Two observations can be made. First of all, ILO Convention No. 29 on Forced Labour (1930) explicitly excludes prison labour from the definition of forced labour.[47] Second, the Committee of Experts on the Application of Conventions and Recommendations (CEACR) found that this exception does not apply to privatised prison labour if it is not carried out 'under conditions which approximate a free labour relationship'.[48] The logic of the Committee seems to converge here with that of Article XX when it reasoned that 'there is the need to avoid unfair competition' between the captive workforce and the free labour market.[49]

So in order to benefit from the application of Article XX, the specific labour-related measure would have to comply with the specific provisions of one of the sub-paragraphs above mentioned. In addition, the specific labour measure would also have to comply with the consistency and good faith requirements of the chapeau of Article XX.[50]

d. Consistency with the Chapeau of Article XX GATT 1994

In addition to complying with one of the sub-paragraphs of Article XX, a challenged measure must also respect the provisions of the chapeau of Article XX which

---

[45] Appellate Body Report, *US – Shrimp*, at para 133.   [46] Ibid. at para 130.

[47] Art 2, para 2: 'Nevertheless, for the purposes of this Convention, the term *forced or compulsory labour* shall not include: (c) any work or service exacted from any person as a consequence of a conviction in a court of law, provided that the said work or service is carried out under the supervision and control of a public authority and that the said person is not hired to or placed at the disposal of private individuals, companies or associations'.

[48] ILO, *Eradication of Forced Labour*, General Survey by the Committee of Experts on the Application of Conventions and Recommendations', 96th Session, Geneva, 2007, at paras 54–61 and 98–122.

[49] Ibid. at para 122.   [50] Marceau and Trachtman, above fn 19, at 9.

has been interpreted as requiring the good faith and non-abusive application of the exceptions, in requiring *inter alia* Members to be consistent and coherent. It establishes three standards in prohibiting 'arbitrary', 'unjustifiable' discrimination between countries where the same conditions prevail, and 'disguised restriction on international trade'. Consistency and coherence in labour policies will be difficult to assess because they reflect social choices often very different among WTO Members. One relevant question is whether the obligation of good faith application of all treaties lead to the conclusion that reliance on international negotiated labour standards provides a *de facto* presumption of good faith or absence of any protectionist devise?

4. *The WTO Dispute Settlement Cannot Be Used to Enforce Non-WTO Violations*

The fact that labour is not clearly referred to in the GATT 1994 exceptions is important. In *Mexico – Taxes on Soft Drinks*, the Appellate Body decided that the WTO dispute settlement system does not have jurisdiction to determine whether a trade restriction can be justified as a countermeasure against an alleged violation of NAFTA.[51] The Appellate Body went on to say that:

[E]ven if the terms 'laws or regulations' do not go so far as to encompass the WTO agreements, as Mexico argues, Mexico's interpretation would imply that, in order to resolve the case, WTO panels and the Appellate Body would have to assume that there is a violation of the relevant international agreement (such as the NAFTA) by the complaining party, or they would have to assess whether the relevant international agreement has been violated. WTO panels and the Appellate Body would thus become adjudicators of non-WTO disputes. As we noted earlier, this is not the function of panels and the Appellate Body as intended by the [*Dispute Settlement Understanding*].[52]

In other words, as a violation of NAFTA by the US would not correspond to any of the policy justifications under Article XX, Mexico's attempt to justify its trade restriction was not accepted.

It seems, therefore, that using trade restrictions exclusively as countermeasures for violation of other treaties, such as labour treaties, would be WTO inconsistent unless the countermeasure can find application in one of the sub-paragraph of Article XX.[53]

---

[51] See G Marceau, 'Fragmentation in International law: The Relationship between WTO Law and General International Law' 2008 *Finnish Yearbook of International Law* (XVII), forthcoming.

[52] Appellate Body Report, *Mexico – Taxes on Soft Drinks*, at para 78.

[53] In the environmental context, for example, trade countermeasures against violations of an environment treaty may find justification under Articles XX (g) or XX(b) GATT 1994, especially when an environmental treaty mandates or permits a trade restriction.

D. TBT Agreement

1. *WTO Legitimate Objectives*

The TBT Agreement contains specific disciplines on 'technical regulations'.[54] The TBT Agreement seems to authorize any technical regulation so long as it is 'not…more trade-restrictive than necessary to fulfil a 'legitimate objective'.[55] But there is no definition of a (WTO) legitimate objective Norms under labour laws can be considered as technical regulation to trade.[56] But could the respect of ILO provisions, in particular core labour standards and fundamental rights,[57] be considered a 'legitimate objective', in arguing, *inter alia*, that sustainable development and its social components, is an objective of the WTO? For the Appellate Body, 'the *TBT Agreement* acknowledges the right of every WTO Member to establish for itself the objectives of its technical regulations while affording every other Member adequate opportunities to obtain information about these objectives.'[58] The Appellate Body did not exclude any such objective.[59] In the event of a challenge, it is for the Member challenging the regulation to prove that the objective is *not* legitimate and for the WTO panel/Appellate Body to determine whether an alleged objective is indeed 'legitimate'.

---

[54] This section includes excerpts from G Marceau and JP Trachtman, 'A Map of the WTO law on domestic regulations' in F Ortino and E-U Petersmann (eds), *The WTO Dispute Settlement 1995–2003* (The Hague: Kluwer, 2004), 275.

[55] Art 2.2 TBT Agreement.

[56] In *EC – Asbestos*, the Appellate Body concluded that the measure at issue—a prohibition on the use of asbestos set up pursuant to the French labour law, was a technical regulation pursuant to the TBT Agreement.

[57] In this respect the 1998 ILO Declaration on Fundamental Principles and Rights at Work is relevant. The Declaration recognizes the 'special significance' of the four categories of rights/freedoms; freedom of association and collective bargaining, elimination of forced labour, the effective abolition of child labour, and the elimination of discrimination. Additionally, the Declaration establishes that by virtue of their membership of the organization and their acceptance of the ILO Constitution, States have an obligation to 'respect, to promote and to realize' the fundamental rights whether or not they have ratified the relevant Conventions. The last paragraph states that 'labour standards should not be used for protectionist trade purposes' and the 'comparative advantage of any country should not be called into question by this Declaration', which seems to resemble greatly the text in paragraph 4 of the Singapore Declaration (1996). See the articles by BA Langille, F Maupain, and P Alston in 2005 *European Journal of International Law* 16(3) 437, 465, and 480.

[58] Appellate Body Report, *EC – Sardines*, at para 276.

[59] From the *EC – Sardines* Panel and Appellate Body Reports, one concludes that the TBT Agreement acknowledges the right of every WTO Member to establish for itself the objectives of its technical regulations while affording every other Member adequate opportunities to obtain information about these objectives (Appellate Body Report, *EC – Sardines*, at para 262); Article 2.4 TBT Agreement requires an examination and a determination whether the objectives of the measure at issue are 'legitimate' (Panel Report, *EC – Sardines*, at para 8.722).

2. *Members' Technical Regulations Based on Existing International Labour Standards?*

The WTO recognizes standards developed in other fora. The SPS agreement, for instance, provides that where a domestic standard complies with standards developed in the Codex Alimentarius Commission (FAO/WHO Food Standards) compliance with the WTO can be presumed.[60] Are ILO standards relevant international standards within the meaning of Articles 2.4. and 2.5 TBT Agreement, compliance with which would equate to presume compliance with the TBT Agreement? It is worth noting that Article 2.4 only requires that the national standards be based on existing international standards. For the Panel and the Appellate Body in *EC – Sardines*, the words 'be based on' meant that the international standard should be 'the principal constituent or fundamental principle for the purpose of enacting the technical regulation'.[61] Therefore, (if a labour policy were considered to be legitimate), a WTO-consistent technical regulation based on an ILO standard may not be fully consistent with the ILO provisions. As to how a WTO panel should interact with the ILO if its standards were invoked, one can only rely on Article 13 DSU whereby panels are authorized, but not obliged, to consult with all experts and actors relevant to a specific dispute.

3. *Does the TBT Agreement Cover Labour-PPMs?*

As mentioned, all labour standards are forms of PPMs since they operate on criteria concerned with the conditions of work and workers, not with the products themselves.[62] Many developing countries have argued that the TBT Agreement does not 'cover' regulations based on criteria not having any physical impact on the product traded. For example, PPM labelling requirements based on social considerations and on timber processes have been politically challenged in the TBT Committee.

But to remove PPM-type regulations from the coverage of the TBT Agreement would exempt them from the other requirements of the same TBT Agreement. It would be curious if non-PPM technical regulations were subject to the more stringent requirements of the TBT Agreement, while the less transparent PPM-type technical regulations were not.[63] It would be even more curious since PPM labels appear to be covered by the TBT Agreement. Moreover, the non-application of the TBT Agreement to PPM-type regulations would not make such PPM regulations

---

[60] See Art 3.2 SPS Agreement.

[61] Panel Report, *EC – Sardines*, at para 7.110; Appellate Body Report, *EC – Sardines*, at para 243. In that dispute, the international standards and the national regulation were in absolute conflict.

[62] There is an important literature on the so-called PPMs, see R Howse and D Regan, 'The Product/Process Distinction – An Illusory Basis for Disciplining "Unilateralism" in Trade Policy' 2000 *European Journal International Law* 11(2) 249; JH Jackson, 'Comments on Shrimp/Turtle and the Product/Process Distinction' 2000 *European Journal International Law* 11(2) 303.

[63] See also chapter 9 of this Handbook.

necessarily inconsistent with WTO law. If the TBT Agreement covers or applies only to product-related criteria, when challenged a labour-PPM regulation would be examined under Articles III and XI GATT 1994 and the exceptions of Article XX, and may, as discussed, be found WTO-consistent.

4. *Labels*

Under the TBT Agreement, technical regulations include 'packaging, marking, or labelling requirements as they apply to a product, process or production method'.[64] Even those who argue that PPMs are not covered generally by the TBT Agreement, agree that the TBT notification obligations cover all labels independently of the kind of information contained in the label:

In conformity with Article 2.9 of the Agreement, Members are obliged to notify all mandatory labelling requirements that are not based substantially on a relevant international standard and that may have a significant effect on the trade of other Members. That obligation is not dependent upon the kind of information which is provided on the label, whether it is in the nature of a technical specification or not.[65]

It would however seem useless for Members to notify the TBT Committee of a label regulation that the same Committee would not have the jurisdiction to examine, since the TBT substantive rules would not cover the notified PPM-label.

The TBT-compatibility of a social label has been politically tested to a certain extent in the past, principally when Belgium notified the Committee of its draft law that set up a voluntary social labelling scheme on the basis of the core ILO Conventions.[66] During the discussion in the TBT Committee of that Belgium law in question, many delegations expressed their concern about bringing labour issues into the scope of the WTO system and considered the Belgian law an unnecessary obstacle to trade. Belgium never enforced its regulation,[67] but legally the issue is still open. If we accept that labour-related labels are covered by the TBT disciplines, such labels cannot be more restrictive than necessary to fulfil their legitimate objective. There is no jurisprudence on the TBT necessity test; but, as noted, the unilateral determination of legitimate objective seems to be WTO-consistent so long as it is not protectionist.

[64] On the issue of social labelling, see C Lopez-Hurtado, 'Social Labelling and WTO Law' 2002 *Journal of International Economic Law* 5(3) 719.

[65] TBT Committee, *Decisions and Recommendations Adopted by the Committee Since 1 January 1995 – Note by the Secretariat*, G/TBT/1/Rev.7 (28 November 2000), section III:10.

[66] 1 on February 2002, the Belgian legislature enacted a government bill aiming to promote socially responsible production and notified it to the TBT Committee. TBT Committee, *Notification*, G/TBT/N/BEL/2 (16 January 2001).

[67] Discussions in the TBT Committee took place from March 2001 until March 2002 (G/TBT/M/23 (8 May 2001), at paras 9–18; G/TBT/M/24 (14 August 2001), at paras 16–26; G/TBT/M/25 (21 November 2001), at paras 49–54; G/TBT/M/26 (6 May 2002), at paras 50–53).

5. *Voluntary and Private Standards*

Calls to include labour concerns in global trade lead to a spreading phenomenon to develop voluntary and private standards. These standards have taken on a range of forms and have notably included corporate codes of conduct sponsored by NGOs or by multinational corporations themselves. The majority of such codes have included ILO standards.[68] Private standards are now raising important concerns among developing countries. They would create discriminatory advantages and constitute *de facto* restrictions. It transpires from the text of the TBT Agreement and its Code of Good Practice that some of these voluntary and private standards could fall under its remit,[69] but they have so far never been subject to litigation.

E. Agreements on Trade Remedies

The WTO contains three agreements on trade remedies: the Anti-Dumping Agreement, the SCM Agreement, and the Safeguards Agreement. These agreements contain disciplines on Members' actions taken against imports for the protection of their injured domestic industry in specific circumstances. They call for an assessment of the injury caused to the domestic industry and list criteria that must be examined by national administrations before imposing trade remedies, and by panels when assessing the WTO compatibility of national determinations. It is noteworthy that Article 3.4 Anti-Dumping Agreement and Article 15 SCM Agreement refer to 'employment, wages, utilization of capacity and productivity' among the mandatory criteria to be evaluated when assessing 'injury to the domestic industry'. The Safeguards Agreement refers in Article 3 to 'productivity, capacity utilization and employment' among the mandatory criteria to be assessed when determining whether serious injury exists.

Moreover, the reference to the possibility of extending safeguard measures to 'facilitate adjustments'[70] calls into question whether 'sustainable development' and 'full employment' principles of the Preamble could be used in interpreting such terms so as to include trade adjustments that would be defined along the ILO prescriptions. These are the only explicit references to labour considerations contained in the WTO Agreement that may call for the use of relevant international labour standards in their interpretation.

---

[68] See also *Business and Human Rights: Mapping International Standards of Responsibility and Accountability for Corporate Acts, Report of the Special Representative of the Secretary-General (SRSG) on the issue of human rights and transnational corporations and other business enterprises*, 9 February 2007, A/HRC/4/035, at paras 63–85.

[69] Arts 3, 4, and 14 TBT Agreement as well as its Code on Good Practices.

[70] The Preamble of the Safeguards Agreement states 'Recognizing the importance of structural adjustment...' and Articles 5.1 and 7.1 state that 'A Member shall apply safeguard measures only to the extent necessary... and only for such period of time as may be necessary to prevent or remedy serious injury and to "facilitate adjustment"'. Article 7.4 states 'in order to facilitate adjustment in a situation...'.

F. The GATS and Its Schedules

1. *Same Issues as With the GATT 1994*

The GATS contains general obligations applicable to all trade in services and obligations on market access and national treatment are applicable to specific services listed in Members' schedules.[71] The labour-related issues raised in the context of non-discrimination principles for trade in goods are also relevant for the GATS MFN and national treatment principles. However, the jurisprudence on like services and like producers is not very informative in terms of the criteria to be used for the determination of likeness,[72] including whether social and labour policy considerations could serve as criteria for likeness. Otherwise, GATS exceptions are largely parallel to those of the GATT 1994,[73] referring to measures necessary for the protection of public morals, for the protection of the health of people, animals and plants, but not to imports relating to prison labour. Also, Article V*bis* regulates explicitly regional trade agreements providing for full integration of labour markets. Article VI GATS was inspired by the TBT disciplines for goods. Although issues relevant to the GATT 1994 and the GATS can be similar, the very character of trade actions involving services and services suppliers brings doubt on the relevance of the GATT PPM-debate (how services are produced or delivered) into the GATS and seems rather to call for further integration of policy considerations in determining likeness.

2. *GATS Schedules*

Can WTO Members include labour considerations in their GATS schedule as a condition modifying their national treatment obligation, restricting market access, or as an additional commitment? In its footnote to Horizontal Commitment, Mode 4, the GATS Schedule of the EC refers to obligations on service suppliers to conform to '[a]ll other requirements of Community and Member States' laws and regulations regarding entry, stay, work and social security measures … including regulations concerning period of stay, minimum wages as well as collective wage agreements'.[74] So far this entry has not been challenged, but there is no time constraint for making such a challenge.[75] Since the benefits of social security programmes are usually only available to those who contributed for periods longer that the duration of the Mode

---

[71] See also chapter 7 of this Handbook.

[72] M Cossy, 'Determining "Likeness" under the GATS: Squaring the Circle?' *WTO Staff Working Paper* ERSD-2006–08 (September 2006), at <http://www.wto.org/english/res_e/reser_e/ersd200608_e.pdf> (last visited 22 May 2008); M Cossy, 'Some Thoughts On the Concept of "Likeness" in the GATS' in M Panizzon, N Pohl, and P Sauvé (eds), *GATS and the Regulation of International Trade in Services* (Cambridge: Cambridge University Press, 2008), Chapter 14.

[73] Appellate Body Report, *US – Gambling*, at para 295.

[74] See *EC's GATS Schedule*, GATS/SC/31 (15 April 1994), at 7.

[75] Panel Report, *EC – Export Subsidies on Sugar*, at para 7.69.

4 contract, some Members argue that the payment of such benefits might constitute a *de facto* national treatment discrimination. More generally, in the ongoing services negotiations, Members like Brazil and India have expressed the view that services suppliers should not be obliged to respect minimum salaries in place in the destination Member, an issue now being discussed in the Mode 4 Doha negotiations. But what they seem to challenge is the *level* of social protection, not the reference *per se* to social considerations.

G. The Agreement on Government Procurement and Its Schedules

1. *The WTO Agreement on Government Procurement (GPA)*

The GPA, signed by most of the world's industrialized countries at the conclusion of the Uruguay Round of multilateral trade negotiations in 1994, provides an international legal framework for the liberalization and governance of public procurement markets.[76] The GPA binds only those WTO Members that have become Parties to it. It imposes non-discrimination obligations on Parties' measures relating to the procurement of covered goods, services, and construction services as set out in each Party's schedules, and subject to various exceptions and exclusions; it also imposes minimum standards regarding procurement processes that are intended to ensure that the Parties' procurements are carried out in a transparent and competitive manner that does not nullify their non-discrimination commitments. The GPA also contains transparency obligations regarding procurement-related information. Currently, the Agreement, including its text and coverage (market access) commitments, is in the process of being renegotiated. The revised GPA, when it is adopted, is expected to represent a substantial improvement over the existing GPA.[77]

The scope for accommodation of labour-related concerns under the GPA has not been discussed either in the Committee on Government Procurement (GPA Committee), which administers the GPA, or in jurisprudence under the Agreement. It has, however, been argued that there are a number of ways in which such concerns might be accommodated.[78] For example, it has been suggested that in some cases it may be possible to structure labour-related conditions in ways that do not violate the basic requirements of the Agreement regarding national treatment and

---

[76] See, generally, S Arrowsmith, *Government Procurement in the WTO* (The Hague: Kluwer, 2003).

[77] RD Anderson, 'Renewing the WTO Agreement on Government Procurement: Progress to Date and Ongoing Negotiations' 2007 *Public Procurement Law Review* 16(4) 255.

[78] See C McCrudden, *Buying Social Justice, Equality, Government Procurement and Legal Change* (Oxford: Oxford University Press, 2007).

non-discrimination.[79] It has also been argued that the GPA requirements regarding tender award criteria, which permit contract awards to be based on the 'most advantageous tender', thereby also permit consideration of 'secondary criteria' such as employment considerations.[80] Certainly, the GPA Committee can, at the time that a developing country accedes to the Agreement, authorize such a country to use 'offsets'.[81] These are defined to include 'domestic content, licensing of technology, investment requirements, counter-trade and similar requirements'.[82] Training and local employment measures might be argued to fall within this definition. Also, the list of exceptions contained in Article XXIII GPA refers to measures necessary to protect public morals, order or safety and human, animal or plant life, or health; or relating to the products or services of handicapped persons, of philanthropic institutions, or of prison labour (corresponding exclusions are also set out in various Parties' schedules).

2. GPA Schedules

Apart from the above-outlined possibilities for accommodating labour-related concerns based on general provisions of the GPA, some Parties have sought to cover such concerns through flexibilities that are written into their coverage commitments under the Agreement. These include the well-known set-asides for small and minority and/or small and medium-sized enterprises which are written into the schedules of the US, Canada and Korea; the provision that is made in Japan's GPA schedules for non-application of the Agreement to contracts involving cooperatives; and exclusions that many Parties have adopted relating to procurement of agricultural products in furtherance of agricultural support or human feeding programmes. Finally, it may be noted that in many cases procurements by labour or other ministries concerned with employment or human welfare are specifically covered in the respective schedules of various GPA Parties.

H. Trade Policy Review Mechanism (TPRM)

According to the Mandate of the TPRM laid down in Annex 3 of the Marrakesh Agreement, trade and related policies are reviewed against the economic background of a Member. The TPRM reports, however, have on occasion touched upon labour issues, not only in analyzing peripheral issues relevant to the trade policy review (TPR) of the country in question, but also explicitly upon the request of Members who are free to raise concerns on 'other issues' at TPR meetings. This language implies that the mechanism is not precluded from also investigating the costs and adjustments of trade policies. There are labour implications of trade policies

[79] Arrowsmith, above fn 76, at 330.   [80] Ibid. at 342–43.
[81] Art XVI GPA.   [82] Art XVI:1 GPA, footnote.

and the Secretariat's TPR Division (TPRD) has not shied away from addressing such issues in cases where labour considerations are considered relevant for economic growth. This can be illustrated by the review of Mauritius where the TPRD noted its growing concern about the link between fiscal and social protection caused by the dual economy in the country consisting of, on the one hand, a highly-protected economy and, on the other hand, very open export zones. The TPRD noted that the tensions among labour unions originated in the differences in the labour legislation applied in the two parts of the economy.[83] In addition, in its review of China, the TPRD extensively referred to labour issues especially those relating to labour market reforms, income inequality, and labour migration.[84]

Members themselves have also on occasion insisted on the inclusion of labour standards in the TPRM. In discussions over TPRM reports, the EU and, to a lesser extent, the US have asked labour-related questions. Yet the country under review hardly ever answers such questions and the non-answers have never been challenged.

Therefore, in the context of the WTO multilateral system, Members' WTO legal framework allows Members to intertwine some labour considerations with trade measures.

III. REGIONAL TRADE AGREEMENTS AND LABOUR CONSIDERATIONS

The GATT 1947 and now the WTO explicitly authorize WTO Members to conclude regional trade agreements (RTAs) that include free-trade agreements (FTAs) and customs unions whereby they exchange reciprocal preferences subject to some conditions.[85] There has recently been significant growth both in the number of FTA negotiations and their scope. By 2010, around 400 of such agreements could be active. As noted by the WTO DG,[86] there are several reasons why Members may appear to favour FTAs. First, they seem quicker to conclude. Secondly, many of the recent FTAs contain political or geopolitical considerations. For developing countries negotiating with more powerful developed countries, there is usually the expectation of

[83] TPRD, *Trade Policy Review Mauritius – Report by the Secretariat*, WT/TPR/S/90 (5 October 2001), Part 2, Economic Environment, at paras 1–24.

[84] TPRD, *Trade Policy Review People's Republic of China – Report by the Secretariat*, WT/TPR/S/161 (28 February 2006), Part 2, Economic Environment, at paras 1–57.

[85] See also chapter 10 of this Handbook.

[86] P Lamy, 'Regional agreements: the "pepper" in the multilateral "curry"', Speech delivered at the Confederation of Indian Industries Partnership Summit 2007 – 'Emergent India: New Roles and Responsibilities' (17 January 2007), at <http://www.wto.org/english/news_e/sppl_e/sppl53_e.htm> (last visited 22 May 2008).

exclusive preferential benefits, as well as expectations of development assistance and other non-trade rewards. Thirdly, because of similarities in interests and often more common values, regional trade agreements can go into new areas such as investment, competition, technical standards, environment provisions, or labour standards where there is no consensus among WTO Members. But FTAs cannot address a series of sensitive issues such as agriculture subsidies[87] and other issues operating in world markets. In that sense, they can only complement the multilateral approach. Yet, FTAs seem to have been used as laboratories to cover new sectors and the way some of these FTAs tackle the labour standards is informative.

NAFTA was the first FTA to introduce provisions on labour standards, but only in a Side Agreement on Labour Cooperation where non-compliance is primarily subject to fines. Since 1994, the US has concluded several FTAs with references to labour standards included in the main text of the agreement. The EU is negotiating Economic Partnership Agreements (EPAs), which are essentially FTAs, the drafts of which include a commitment to the relevant ILO conventions on core labour standards. Canada has also included labour concerns in free trade agreements.

The remainder of this section recalls the main conditions for WTO-consistent RTAs and then discusses—through questions—whether and how internal labour standards may affect the WTO-consistency of FTAs.

A. Conditions for a WTO-Consistent RTA

Article XXIV GATT 1994 and Article V GATS lay down the legal framework that authorizes WTO Members to enter into RTAs. The WTO imposes three types of substantive conditions for RTAs to be WTO-consistent.[88] First, with respect to the *overall impact* of the RTA vis-à-vis other Members: there is the obligation not to raise barriers to trade with third parties (Article XXIV:5). This is quantifiable in terms of tariffs, but less easy to measure in terms of other trade regulations such as standards or rules of origin. Second, there is a so-called 'external requirement' that an FTA cannot lead to higher MFN import duties for its members, while a customs union must harmonize the external trade policies of its members and compensate affected non-members accordingly (Article XXIV:8). Third, the 'internal requirement' means that tariffs and other restrictive regulations of commerce must be

---

[87] 'There is not such a thing as a bilateral subsidy and a multilateral subsidy', P Lamy, 'Multilateral and bilateral trade agreements: friends or foes?', Annual Memorial Silver Lecture, Columbia University, New York (31 October 2006), at <http://www.wto.org/english/news_e/sppl_e/sppl46_e.htm> (last visited 22 May 2008).

[88] See G Marceau and C Reiman, 'When are Regional Trade Agreements Compatible with the WTO?' 2001 *Legal Issues of Regional Integration* 28(3) 297; N Lockhart and A Mitchell, 'Regional Trade Agreements under GATT 1994: An Exception and Its Limits' in A Mitchell (ed), *Challenges and Prospects for the WTO* (London: Cameron May, 2005) 217.

phased out on 'substantially' all trade (Article XXIV:8). Again, the tariff component can be quantified, but it is harder to determine in the case of other restrictive trade regulations as there is no agreed definition of the term. It is therefore clear that the WTO authorizes RTAs, the operation of which should not lead to situations where the non-party would 'pay the price' of internal preferences.[89] The jurisprudence has also determined that it is for the Member invoking Article XXIV as a defense to a claim of violation (for example, violation of the MFN principle)[90] to prove, first, that the RTA is WTO-consistent before arguing that the challenged measure is necessary and inherent to the RTA. This is a very heavy burden that no Member has ever succeeded in discharging.

B. An Example: The US – Peru FTA

The US–Peru FTA and its new provisions on labour provide an interesting example.[91] In that new FTA, parties reaffirm their obligations as members of the ILO and also agree to adopt and maintain in their laws and practice the core internationally-recognized labour rights, as stated in the 1998 ILO Declaration on Fundamental Principles and Rights at Work, and including a prohibition on the worst forms of child labour. The labour obligations are subject to the same dispute settlement procedures and enforcement mechanisms as the trade obligations. The FTA includes a cooperative mechanism to promote respect for the principles embodied in the 1998 ILO Declaration, and compliance with the ILO Convention 182 on the Worst Forms of Child Labour.[92] But there is no provision on any role of the ILO as an organization.

The questions to address before assessing whether labour-related regulations can take place within a WTO-consistent RTA are: (i) whether such labour requirements would be increasing trade restrictions overall, contrary to Article XXIV:5 and/or would constitute 'other restrictive regulations of commerce' that ought to be eliminated pursuant to Article XXIV(8) GATT 1994; (ii) another institutional

---

[89] See the case law on the need to maintain parallelism when applying of safeguards in the context of FTAs; for example, Appellate Body Report, *US – Steel Safeguards*, at paras 433–56.

[90] In *Turkey – Textiles*, the Appellate Body explicitly noted that Article XXIV may justify violations of provisions additional to Article I on MFN.

[91] *Final Text of the United States – Peru Trade Promotion Agreement*, signed on 12 April 2006, at <http://www.ustr.gov/Trade_Agreements/Bilateral/Peru_TPA/Final_Texts/Section_Index.html> (last visited 22 May 2008).

[92] Cooperative activities include: law and practice related to the principles and rights of the ILO Declaration; compliance with the ILO Convention 182 on the Worst Forms of Child Labour; methods to improve labour administration and enforcement of labour laws; social dialogue and alternative dispute resolution; occupational safety, and health compliance; mechanisms and best practices to protect and promote the rights of migrant workers.

question is whether an RTA party can impose WTO consistent trade restrictions against another RTA party when called upon to do so under the terms of its RTA for violations of the RTA labour provisions.

1. *Are Labour Standards Internal or External Restrictions That Would Be WTO-(In)Consistent (Art XXIV: 5 and :8)?*

There is no agreed definition or jurisprudence on the types of RTA internal restrictions which ought to be eliminated and what types of overall restrictions are prohibited,[93] nor is there any agreed criteria to assess the overall trade impact of an RTA other than those included in the GATT 1994 Understanding on Article XXIV.

Internally, the 'duties and other restrictive regulation on commerce' that should be eliminated on substantially all the trade (Article XXIV:8) should not, in all logic, be interpreted as to include WTO-consistent trade regulations. Indeed all regulation somehow *de facto* restricts trade. If a labour regulation can be WTO-consistent (under GATT 1994 or TBT), they should operate consistently within an RTA. The introduction of labour standards *only* on internal trade should not lead to restrictions with third-Members, in compliance with Article XXIV:5. If the standards are imposed against imports as well, the issue is more complex and calls for the application of the national treatment obligation where the labour-PPM issue will have to be addressed. Moreover, some have argued that WTO-consistent TBT, SPS, and competition regulations could nonetheless be viewed as raising barriers to trade with third-countries, contrary to Article XXIV:5 GATT 1994. All these questions are wide open.

2. *Can an RTA Party Impose (WTO-Consistent) Trade Restrictions Against Another RTA Party When Called Upon To Do So Under the Terms of Their RTA for Violations of the RTA Labour Provisions?*

So far the WTO has not been faced with a situation where a party to an RTA seeks to impose trade retaliation to another party pursuant to their agreement. NAFTA, for example, provides for fines if labour provisions are violated—although in case of non-payment trade countermeasures may be used. Would such a trade restriction, permitted under an RTA, be consistent with Article 23 DSU that prohibits unilateral determinations? One could argue that in allowing for RTAs, Article XXIV must provide for effective RTAs, meaning RTAs with dispute settlement provisions and operational remedies. On the other hand, it needs to be recalled that in case of conflict, the Marrakesh Agreement prevails over any other WTO provisions. But is this a conflict?

---

[93] J Mathis, 'Regional Trade Agreements and Domestic Regulation: What Reach for "Other Restrictive Regulations of Commerce"' in L Bartels and F Ortino (eds), *Regional Trade Agreements and the WTO Legal System* (Oxford: Oxford University Press, 2006) 79; WTO Negotiating Group on Rules, *Compendium of Issues Related to Regional Trade Agreements*, TN/RL/W/8/Rev.1 (1 August 2002).

Finally, in order to get a clearer picture of the situation of the RTAs by means of an exchange of factual information, the WTO GC decided to establish on a provisional basis a transparency mechanism for all RTAs that are notified.[94] It is interesting to note that on occasions the RTA Committee has discussed labour provisions where they are present.[95]

IV. CAN LABOUR CONSIDERATIONS CONDITION WTO-CONSISTENT PREFERENCE SCHEMES?

The US and the EC now include a requirement of compliance with some labour considerations as a condition for benefiting from trade preferences or from additional preferences. Pursuant to the Enabling Clause, developed country WTO Members are entitled to provide tariff preferences to imports from developing countries, so long as these preferences are 'generalized, non-discriminatory and non-reciprocal'.[96] This is the WTO legal basis for the so-called 'General System of Preferences' (GSP), instituted by UNCTAD and received in the GATT 1947 first as a waiver (1972) and then under the Enabling Clause (1979) codified in the GATT 1994. In *EC – Tariff Preferences*, the Appellate Body alluded to the possibility that preference schemes with labour standards be consistent with the Enabling Clause so long as one can argue that compliance with a labour standard is based on objective criteria favouring developing countries' development, trade, and financial needs, and that countries in similar situations are treated similarly within a fair incentive scheme.

In *EC – Tariff Preferences*, the Appellate Body had to interpret the provision of the Enabling Clause that allows for non-discriminatory preference in favour of developing countries. The Appellate Body first determined that the purpose of the Enabling Clause was to help and respond to the development, financial, and trade needs of developing countries[97] and that different developing countries may have different development needs. Thus, 'responding to the "needs of developing countries" may entail treating different developing-country beneficiaries differently'.[98] It added that the 'existence of a development, financial or trade need' must be assessed according to an objective standard; '[b]road-based recognition of a particular need, set out in

---

[94] WTO, *Transparency Mechanism for Regional Trade Agreements*, WT/L/671 (18 December 2006).
[95] WTO CRTA, *Factual Presentation: Free Trade Agreement between the United States and Australia*, WT/REG184/3 (11 June 2007), at para 71.
[96] Enabling Clause, footnote 3.
[97] Appellate Body Report, *EC – Tariff Preferences*, at paras 158–60.
[98] Ibid at para 162: authorizing preference-granting countries to 'respond positively' to 'needs' that are *not* necessarily common or shared by all developing countries.

the WTO Agreement or in multilateral instruments adopted by international organisations, could serve as such a standard'.[99] The Appellate Body added that a 'nexus' should exist between the preferential treatment and the likelihood of alleviating the relevant development, financial, or trade needs.[100] One issue is therefore whether the ILO labour standards could assist in responding to 'needs' of developing countries.

With respect to India's claim that the EC GSP was violating the non-discrimination obligation of the Enabling Clause, the Appellate Body said that 'additional preferences for developing countries with particular needs... is consistent with the object and purpose of the *WTO Agreement* and the Enabling Clause'[101] provided that identical treatment is available to all similarly-situated GSP beneficiaries.[102] It then concluded that the EC Drug Arrangement was not based on objective criteria, it was not a real incentive programme that responded to any special and objective needs of developing countries, and therefore developing countries with similar needs may not be treated similarly. This final statement of the Appellate Body contained an *obiter dictum* on labour-related preferences that is quite interesting:

Articles 10 and 25 of the Regulation, which relate specifically to the Drug Arrangements, provide no mechanism under which additional beneficiaries may be added to the list of beneficiaries under the Drug Arrangements as designated in Annex I... *This contrasts with the position under the 'special incentive arrangements for the protection of labour rights'* and the 'special incentive arrangements for the protection of the environment', which are described in Article 8 of the Regulation. The Regulation includes detailed provisions setting out the procedure and substantive criteria that apply to a request by a beneficiary under the general arrangements described in Article 7 of the Regulation (the 'General Arrangements') to become a beneficiary under either of those special incentive arrangements.[103]

Following the recommendations of the DSB, the EC adopted a revised GSP regime composed of three arrangements.[104] The third incentive provides that additional tariff preferences are granted on request to vulnerable and dependent countries that have ratified and effectively implemented the sixteen core conventions on human and labour rights and seven (out of eleven) of the conventions related to the protection of the environment and good governance.[105] Paragraph 8 of the Preamble dealing with this third programme, the so-called 'GSP plus', states that a special incentive arrangement for sustainable development and good governance is set up to promote further economic growth and thereby to respond positively to the needs of developing countries.

---

[99] Ibid at para 163.
[100] Ibid at paras 164–65: 'paragraph 3(c) suggests that tariff preferences under GSP schemes may be "non-discriminatory" when the relevant tariff preferences are addressed to a particular "development, financial [or] trade need" and are made available to all beneficiaries that share that need'.
[101] Ibid at para 169 (original emphasis).
[102] Ibid at para 173.
[103] Ibid at para 182 (original emphasis).
[104] WTO CTD, *Generalized System of Preferences – Communication from the European Communities*, WT/COMTD/57 (28 March 2006).
[105] Council Regulation No 980/2005, section 2.

This type of GSP-plus provision raises two main questions. First, can a GSP condition give an additional preference to Members for their respect of principles contained in international conventions on labour rights, a sector not covered by the WTO? Many arguments can be offered against this type of incentive.[106] If a Member challenges such a scheme in a WTO dispute, it will be for a panel to determine whether this GSP regulation addresses objective financial, trade, or development needs of developing countries, whether this is recognized as such by the recommendations of an international organization; whether it provides an objective and transparent mechanism under which GSP-plus beneficiaries may be selected; whether the scheme provides an explicit mechanism to allow countries to benefit, or lose, from the GSP-plus benefits; and whether countries in similar situations are treated similarly. Throughout this exercise the WTO objective of sustainable development is relevant. One difficult issue is whether such a scheme is really 'non-reciprocal' within the meaning of the Enabling Clause, as the grant of preferences is in return for the commitment to adhere to a set of treaties. But conditioning additional preferences to compliance with development, trade, or financial policies can be consistent with the Enabling Clause. The novelty will be to determine whether and how labour considerations address such needs. For some the answer is obvious, at least with respect to labour considerations contained in internationally negotiated conventions.

The second question relates to the determination of compliance with such international labour conventions? In the specific case of the EC scheme,[107] the ILO would be the international actor determining compliance with ILO standards. But what if a GSP scheme only refers to compliance with ILO standards without any indication of who will determine compliance? As with the situation where the TBT Agreement authorizes national measures complying with existing international standards, or where a WTO panel would need to assess the relevance of invoking compliance with any existing international standard to justify the application of a GATT 1994 or GATS exception, it would be ultimately for a panel or the Appellate Body to decide whether the national measure based on ILO standards responds to objective criteria relating to the development, financial, and trade needs of developing countries and is applied fairly. Again, an open question. A coherent approach to specialized international organizations' competence would lead a panel to request information from the ILO on this issue, pursuant to Article 13 DSU. This would not only give legitimacy to the process, but also allow for the good faith application of both the WTO and the ILO treaties.

---

[106] There is also an important economic literature against linking trade and labour. See, eg, the opposite view in S James, 'Maladjusted: The Misguided Policy of Trade Adjustment Assistance' *CATO Trade Briefing Paper* No 26, at <http://www.freetrade.org/node/794/print> (last visited 22 May 2008). On the new EC GSP–plus, see L Bartels, 'The Trade and Development Policy of the European Union' 2007 *European Journal of International Law* 18(4) 715.

[107] WTO CTD, *Generalized System of Preferences – Communication from the European Communities – Addendum*, WT/COMTD/N/4/Add.3 (29 March 2006).

V. CONCLUSIONS

Although the WTO treaty language does not make explicit reference to labour considerations, the first conclusion that emerges from the above analysis is that the 'space' that is left by the existing trade law framework for Members to promote labour and social progress objectives is far from negligible. WTO Members can indeed find ways to comply efficiently and effectively with both their trade and labour regimes.

Legally, labour standards are like any other standards: they are negotiated outside the WTO and may be intertwined with trade measures. But labour standards never relate to the physical characteristics of products but rather to the conditions of workers, and in this sense they are forms of PPMs. The legal considerations of PPMs are not clear in WTO law but, in the context of environmental measures, some non-product related criteria were accepted as WTO-consistent regulatory distinctions, in the application of the exception provisions of the GATT 1994. Arguably, some exceptions, notably the exception protecting public morals, may find application to justify some core labour related trade restrictions. Non-product labour considerations may also be consistent with the TBT Agreement, so long as they pursue legitimate objectives and are applied in good faith.

The issue of trade and labour is complex. The challenge of globalization generated by trade liberalization which constantly modifies relative situations between Members cannot be met simply by static formulas but, as pointed out in a recent report from the ILO DG,[108] calls for dynamic answers consonant with the dynamic character of the phenomenon. It is important to maintain a dynamic of progress by permanently encouraging and accompanying the efforts of all States, as Members of the WTO and ILO, to promote both economic and social progress by considering these two goals together with a view to raising people's standards of livings. The WTO DG's call for a 'Geneva consensus' seems to point exactly in that direction:

But although the opening up of markets produces benefits to many, it also creates adjustments costs which we cannot ignore. These adjustments must not be relegated to the future: they must be an integral part of the opening-up agenda. This is what I call the 'Geneva consensus': a belief that trade opening works for development but only if we address the imbalances it creates between winners and losers, imbalances that are all the more dangerous the more fragile the economies, societies or countries. This is the only way to ensure that the opening up of markets will produce real benefits to all people in their everyday lives. [...] We need to remember that trade is only a tool to elevate the human condition; the ultimate impact of our rules on human beings should always be at the centre of our consideration. We

---

[108] 'Strengthening the ILO's Capacity to Assist its Members' Efforts to Reach its Objectives in the Context of Globalization', Report V, International Labour Conference, 96th Session, Geneva, 2007, at paras 96–108.

should work first for human beings and for the well-being of our humanity. I want to believe that the new 'Geneva consensus' has the potential to succeed in contributing to the process of humanising globalization and establishing further justice and equity.[109]

Selected Bibliography

K Anderson, 'Environmental and Labor Standards: What Role for the WTO?' in AO Krueger (ed), *The WTO as an International Organization* (Chicago: University of Chicago Press, 1998) 231c

C Barry and S Reddy, 'International Trade and Labor Standards: A Proposal for Linkage' 2006 *Cornell International Law Journal* 39(3) 545

F Biermann, 'The Rising Tide of Green Unilateralism in World Trade Law: Options for Reconciling the Emerging North-South Conflict' 2001 *Journal of World Trade* 35(3) 421

C Breining-Kaufmann, *Globalization And Labour Rights: The Conflict Between Core Labour Rights and International Economic Law* (Oxford: Hart, 2006)

D Brown, 'Labor Standards: Where Do They Belong on the International Trade Agenda?' 2001 *The Journal of Economic Perspectives* 15(3) 89

S Charnovitz, 'Trade, Employment and Labour Standards: The OECD Study and Recent Developments in the Trade and Labor Standards Debate' 1997 *Temple International and Comparative Law Journal* 11(1) 131

S Charnovitz, 'The Globalization of Economic Human Rights' 1999 *Brooklyn Journal of International Law* (25) 113

S Charnovitz, SF Compa, and LA Diamond (eds), *Human Rights, Labor Rights, and International Trade* (Philadelphia: University of Pennsylvania Press, 1996)

JDR Craig and M Lynk (eds), *Globalization and the Future of Labour Law* (Cambridge: Cambridge University Press, 2006)

JA De Castro, 'Trade and Labour Standards: Using the Wrong Instruments for the Right Cause' 1995 *UNCTAD Bulletin* (34) 9, *Trade Law and Global Governance* (London: Cameron May, 2002)

R Eglin, 'Environment, Labour, and Human Rights Concerns and the International Trading System' in A. Pérez van Kappel and W. Heusel (eds), *Free world trade and the European Union: the reconciliation of interests and the revision of dispute resolution procedures in the framework of the WTO* (Köln: Bundesanzeiger, 2000) 101

R Fernandez and J Portes, 'Returns to Regionalism: An Analysis of Non-Traditional Gains from Regional Trade Agreements' 1998 *The World Bank Economic Review* 12(2) 197

R Flanagan and W IV Gould (eds), *International Labor Standards: Globalization, Trade, and Public Policy* (Stanford: Stanford Law and Politics, 2003)

F Francioni (ed), *Environment, Human Rights and International Trade* (Portland: Hart Publishing, 2001)

---

[109] P Lamy, 'Humanising Globalization', Speech, Santiago de Chile, Chile (30 January 2006), at <http://www.wto.org/english/news_e/sppl_e/sppl16_e.htm> (last visited 22 May 2008); see also P Lamy, 'Making Trade work for Development: Time for a Geneva Consensus', Emile Noel Lecture New York University Law School, New York (30 October 2006), at <http:www.wto.org/english/news_e/sppl_e/sppl45_e.htm> (last visited 22 May 2008).

B Hepple, *Labour Laws and Global Trade* (Oxford: Hart Publishing, 2005)

V Leary and D Warner (eds), *Social Issues, Globalisation and International Institutions: Labour Rights and the EU, ILO, OECD and WTO* (Leiden: Martinus Nijhoff, 2005)

F Maupain, 'La protection internationale des travailleurs et la libéralisation du commerce mondiale : un lien ou un frein ?' 1996 *Revue générale de droit international public* 45

C McCrudden and A Davies, 'A Perspective on Trade and Labor Rights' 2000 *Journal of International Economic Law* 3(1) 43

OECD, *International Trade and Core Labour Standards* (Paris: OECD, 2000)

S Polaski, *Trade and Labor Standards: A Strategy for Developing Countries*, Carnegie Endowment Report (January 2003)

R Stern and K Terell, *Labor Standards and the World Trade Organization* (Ann Arbor: University of Michigan Press, 2003)

C Summers, 'The Battle in Seattle: Free Trade, Labor Rights, and Societal Values' 2001 *University of Pennsylvania Journal of International Economic Law* 22(1) 61

C Thomas, 'Trade-Related Labor and Environment Agreements?' 2002 *Journal of International Economic Law* 5(4) 791

P van Kappel and W Heusel (eds), *Free World Trade and the European Union: The Reconciliation of Interests and the Revision of Dispute Resolution Procedures in the Framework of the WTO* (Köln: Bundesanzeiger, 2000) 101

A Vandaele, *International Labour Rights and the Social Clause: Friends or Foes* (London: Cameron May, 2004)

M Vellano, *Full employment and fair labour standards in the framework of the WTO* (Milan: Giuffré Editore, 1999) HM

H-M Wolffgang and W Feuerhake, 'Core Labour Standards in World Trade Law: The Necessity for Incorporation of Core Labour Standards in the World Trade Organization' 2002 *Journal of World Trade* 36(5) 883

CHAPTER 20

....

TRADE AND HUMAN RIGHTS

....

LORAND BARTELS*

* A number of people read and commented on this chapter, for which I am very grateful. I owe special thanks to the editors, as well as Jochen von Bernstorff, Joanna Bourke, Steve Charnovitz, Lothar Ehring, Melaku Geboye Desta, Holger Hestermeyer, Robert Howse, Sarah Joseph, Andrew Lang, and Shervin Majlessi.

I. INTRODUCTION

AT the most general level, the protection of human rights and the promotion of trade liberalization share a common objective: the betterment of the human condition. This is reflected in Article 55 of the UN Charter, which mandates the United Nations (UN) to promote both 'higher standards of living, full employment, and conditions of economic and social progress and development' and 'universal respect for, and observance of, human rights'. But despite the fact that both of these paragraphs generated significant institutions—the former was the basis for the failed International Trade Organization (ITO), from which the GATT 1947 and then the WTO emerged,[1] while the latter produced the international human rights framework—it is only in the last decade that full attention has been paid to the complex links between trade and human rights.

A. Positive Links

A creature of its time, Article 55 UN Charter focused on the individual contributions of trade and human rights to international peace. But trade and human rights are also connected directly. Proponents of trade liberalization often claim that it increases wealth, and thereby provides greater resources for the pursuit of human rights objectives.[2] And some recognition of this may be detected in Article 1(2) of the two international covenants on human rights, which states that '[a]ll peoples may, for their own ends, freely dispose of their natural wealth and resources without prejudice to any obligations arising out of international economic co-operation, based upon the principle of mutual benefit, and international law'. As this provision was drafted to prevent the despoliation of the natural resources of a 'people', especially by foreign investors,[3] it might seem odd to cite it in a trade context. But the very logic of this provision presupposes that the 'people' might want to trade their natural resources. After all, assuming that not all of these resources can be consumed

---

[1] Reflecting this lineage, the Preamble of the WTO Agreement, following Art 1 ITO Charter and the Preamble of the GATT 1947, contains most of the wording of Article 55(a) UN Charter.

[2] J Klick and F Tesón, 'Global Justice and Trade: A Puzzling Omission', Paper (2007), at <http://www.works.bepress.com/jonathan_klick/1> (last visited 26 May 2008).

[3] A Cassese, 'The Self-Determination of Peoples' in L Henkin (ed), The International Bill of Rights: The Covenant on Civil and Political Rights (New York: Columbia University Press, 1981), at 103–07; A Cassese, Self-Determination of Peoples: A Legal Reappraisal (Cambridge: Cambridge University Press, 1995), at 56; also UN Human Rights Committee (HRC), General Comment No 12, The Right to Self-Determination of Peoples, A/39/40, 13 March 1984.

domestically, how else might they dispose of natural wealth and resources 'for their own ends' and to their 'mutual benefit'?

At the aggregate level, then, trade can provide resources for the realization of human rights. But some authors have also posited that there should be an individual 'right to trade'.[4] For example, Amartya Sen has said that '[a] denial of opportunities of transaction, through arbitrary controls, can be a source of unfreedom in itself. People are then prevented from doing what can be then taken to be—in the absence of compelling reasons to the contrary—something that is within their right to do so.'[5]

Claims that there is (or should be) an individual right to trade have not gone uncontested. It has been objected that there are virtually no legal systems in which such rights are grounded in positive law.[6] There have also been disagreements at the philosophical level, provoked by the tendency of some proponents of an individual right to trade to prioritize such a right over other human rights or social interests[7] – or to have appeared to do so.[8]

Absolutist claims in favour of a right to trade are indeed problematic, because trade liberalization can have harmful effects on human rights. These negative effects are of two main types. The first is that, in the short term, trade liberalization *ipso facto* harms inefficient producers, and can also be costly at the aggregate level, especially for developing countries. In principle, these costs can be compensated by the greater earnings produced by free trade, but this does not always happen in the short term, or in some cases at all. Second, some of the rules imposed by trade regimes go beyond a simple reduction of protectionist measures, and can interfere with the ability of countries to pursue human rights objectives. These negative effects are very real, and will be discussed in more detail shortly. But even so, this does not make it impossible to assert that there is (or should be) an individual right to trade, so long as it is also acknowledged that any such right need not be absolute.[9]

---

[4] A well-known proponent of this view is E-U Petersmann. See, eg, E-U Petersmann, 'Human Rights, Markets and Economic Welfare: Constitutional Functions of the Emerging UN Human Rights Constitution' in F Abbott, C Breining-Kaufmann, and T Cottier (eds), *International Trade and Human Rights: Foundations and Conceptual Issues* (Michigan: University of Michigan Press, 2006) 29. See also R McGee, 'The Moral Case for Free Trade' 1995 *Journal of World Trade* 29(1) 69.

[5] A Sen, *Development as Freedom* (New York: Anchor, 1999), at 25, also 25–31, 112–16. A different interpretation of Sen is given by R Wai, 'Countering, Branding, Dealing: Using Economic and Social Rights in and around the International Trade Regime' 2003 *European Journal of International Law* 14(1) 35, at 42–43.

[6] P Alston, 'Resisting the Merger and Acquisition of Human Rights by Trade Law: A Reply to Petersmann' 2002 *European Journal of International Law* 13(4) 815, at 828.

[7] See McGee, above fn 4.

[8] Whether Petersmann, above fn 4, also makes such strong claims has been debated. See Alston, above fn 6, and E-U Petersmann, 'Taking Human Dignity, Poverty and Empowerment of Individuals More Seriously: Rejoinder to Alston' 2002 *European Journal of International Law* 13(4) 845.

[9] J Waldron, 'Rights in Conflict' 1999 *Ethics* (99) 503.

B. Outline of Chapter

There are two main strands in the literature on trade and human rights, one focusing on the positive and the other focusing on the negative relationship between the two fields. Having set out in introductory form the basic themes of the first strand, the remainder of this chapter is concerned with the latter. It looks at three main areas in which trade and human rights are interrelated, each time focusing on the different approaches adopted by the two subdisciplines of trade and human rights law to the issue at hand. The first of these areas concerns the negative effects of a country's trade policies on other countries, in particular protectionist trade policies. The core question addressed in this part is whether human rights obligations might be relevant in reigning in such negative effects, when these are sufficiently serious. Next, this chapter looks at the corollary problem of the losses caused by trade liberalization, in particular to the liberalizing country, and at how trade and human rights specialists have tended to understand these losses from a normative perspective. Third, this chapter considers the phenomenon of trade rules designed to promote free trade but which go beyond liberalization *per se*. Here this chapter looks at claims that such rules unduly restrict the regulatory powers of the State to pursue human rights objectives. Finally, the chapter gives an account of the ways in which the major trade and human rights institutions have reacted to these issues over the past few decades.

II. HUMAN RIGHTS IMPACTS OF TRADE POLICIES ON OTHER COUNTRIES

International law has traditionally supported the right of States to adopt whatever protectionist trade policies they choose. It was assumed that the natural state of affairs between States was autarky: the absence of trade. Accordingly, other than by way of specific trade agreements to the contrary, States were considered to be entirely free to restrict trade with each other. A classic statement to this effect is in *Nicaragua*, where the International Court of Justice (ICJ) said that '[a] State is not bound to continue particular trade relations longer than it sees fit to do so, in the absence of a treaty commitment or other specific legal obligation'.[10] But even if this might have been true once, it is increasingly doubtful that such a normative presumption in

---

[10] ICJ, *Military and Paramilitary Activities in and against Nicaragua (Nicaragua v United States of America)*, Merits, ICJ Reports (1986) 14, at para 138; also Oda J, Dissenting Opinion, at para 253.

favour of autarky can still be presumed today.[11] The devastating consequences of the trade sanctions imposed on Iraq during the 1990s have made it apparent that trade restrictions, like all state activity, can engage States' human rights obligations.[12] Arguably, the same principles should apply to the negative consequences of all trade measures, including those that are adopted for protectionist reasons.

This is no idle claim. Recent years have afforded numerous examples of the severe economic consequences of protectionist trade measures, especially on small developing (and least developed) countries. Subsidized EU rice exports have caused severe damage to uncompetitive small-scale producers in Ghana,[13] and US cotton subsidies have so depressed the world price of cotton that cotton farmers in Chad, Mali, Benin, and Burkina Faso, dependent on cotton exports, have a reduced ability to feed themselves, as well as suffering degradations of other economic and social rights.[14] The core question is whether human rights obligations apply to these situations. Before turning to this, however, it is appropriate to discuss two other normative approaches to negative external effects of countries' trade policies and other measures affecting trade.

The first of these approaches is based on normative (as opposed to descriptive) economics.[15] The idea is that distortive policies with an effect on trade, such as developed country agricultural subsidies, are 'unfair' because they interfere with the 'natural' comparative advantage of developing countries.[16] This is an attractive and popular approach, particularly within trade circles, but it suffers from a number of flaws. The first of these is its overemphasis on 'natural' as opposed to 'acquired' comparative advantage, which underemphasizes the role of education, institutions, and other 'social' factors in a country's economic makeup.[17] It is also self-defeatingly

[11] M Risse, 'Fairness in Trade I: Obligations from Trading and the Pauper-Labor Argument' 2007 *Politics, Philosophy & Economics* 6(3) 355; T Pogge, 'Recognized and Violated by International Law: The Human Rights of the Global Poor' 2005 *Leiden Journal of International Law* 18(4) 717, at 732.

[12] UN Commission on Human Rights (CHR), Sub-Commission on the Promotion and Protection of Human Rights, *The Adverse Consequences of Economic Sanctions on the Enjoyment of Human Rights – Working Paper*, E/CN.4/Sub.2/2000/33 (21 June 2000); UN Committee for Economic, Social and Cultural Rights (CESCR), General Comment No 8, *The Relationship between Economic Sanctions and Respect for Economic, Social and Cultural Rights*, E/C.12/1997/8 (5 December 1997).

[13] Oxfam, 'Kicking Down the Door: How Upcoming WTO Talks Threaten Farmers in Poor Countries', Briefing Note 72 (April 2005), at <http://www.oxfam.org.uk/resources/policy/trade/downloads/bp72_rice.pdf> (last visited 26 May 2008).

[14] J Alston, D Sumner, and H Brunke, *Impacts of Reductions in US Cotton Subsidies on West African Cotton Producers* (Boston: Oxfam America, 2007). These subsidies were ruled illegal in the Appellate Body Report, *US – Upland Cotton*. See also WTO MC, *Hong Kong Ministerial Declaration*, WT/MIN(05)/DEC (22 December 2005), at para 11.

[15] On the distinction, see A Sykes, 'Comparative Advantage and the Normative Economics of International Trade Policy' 1998 *Journal of International Economic Law* 1(1) 49.

[16] E Fox, 'Globalization and Human Rights: Looking Out for the Welfare of the Worst Off' 2002 *New York University Journal of International Law and Politics* 35(1) 201, at 211.

[17] R Unger, *Free Trade Reimagined: The World Division of Labor and the Method of Economics* (Princeton: Princeton University Press, 2007); D Tarullo, 'Logic, Myth, and the International

conservative, from a development perspective.[18] The implication is that a country with an initial advantage in basic agriculture, due to abundant land and labour, should concentrate on this sector rather than developing sectors more dependent on skills and capital. A second difficulty with this approach is that it takes a notion of economic efficiency as its normative principle, from which it follows that 'externalities' should be 'internalized' in the value of the final product.[19] However, this cannot always be done, and this approach will necessarily at some point fail to respect non-trade values.[20] There is, finally, a tactical constraint insofar as this approach is limited to 'unfair' trade: it has nothing to say about damage caused by *undistorted* competition, such as competitive rice exports from Vietnam to Ghana, or competitive banana exports from Ecuador displacing less competitive Caribbean banana exports in the EU market.

A second approach to the negative effects of trade measures is based on 'justice' or 'fairness'.[21] This approach is also attractive. It is difficult to disagree with the notion that any given legal order should be fair, and there appears to be no reason why the gains from trade cannot be considered a concrete benefit that can both be calculated and distributed fairly, though obviously there are different ways to determine fairness.[22] Furthermore, this approach is legally grounded: the Preamble to the WTO Agreement refers to the 'need for positive efforts designed to ensure that developing countries...secure a share in the growth in international trade commensurate with the needs of their economic development', and the WTO Agreement on Agriculture seeks to 'establish a fair and market-oriented agricultural trading system'. Individualizing the issue, the Universal Declaration on Human Rights claims

Economic Order' 1985 *Harvard International Law Journal* 26(2) 533, at 546–52; D Tarullo, 'Beyond Normalcy in the Regulation of International Trade' 1985–6 *Harvard Law Review* 100(3) 546.

[18] J Stiglitz and A Charlton, *Fair Trade for All: How Trade Can Promote Development* (Oxford: Oxford University Press, 2007), at 30.

[19] R Howse and D Regan, 'The Product/Process Distinction: An Illusory Basis for Disciplining "Unilateralism" in Trade Policy' 2000 *European Journal of International Law* 11(2) 249, at 280–84, argue that countries are entitled to restrict trade in order to internalize these externalities regardless of where the externalities are located. But whether this is legitimate under the ordinary rules on legislative jurisdiction is doubtful: see L Bartels, 'Article XX of GATT and the Problem of Extraterritorial Jurisdiction: The Case of Trade Measures for the Protection of Human Rights' 2002 *Journal of World Trade* 36(2) 353.

[20] On the normative underpinnings of the 'efficiency model', see F Garcia, *Trade, Inequality, and Justice: Toward a Liberal Theory of Just Trade* (Ardsley, NY: Transnational, 2003), at 14–19, and on its deficiencies in accounting for non-trade values, see J Dunoff, 'The Death of the Trade Regime' 1999 *European Journal of International Law* 10(4) 733, at 745–47.

[21] See Garcia, ibid; and Risse, above fn 11.

[22] For a focus on the natural endowments of countries: Garcia, above fn 20, at 23, 31; but see J Pauwelyn, 'Just Trade (Book Review)' 2005 *George Washington International Law Review* 37(2) 559, at 564–68. For doubts as to whether countries should be the relevant units of comparison see, eg, P Singer, *One World: The Ethics of Globalization*, 2nd edn (New Haven: Yale University Press, 2004), at 77–90.

that '[e]veryone is entitled to a social and international order in which the rights and freedoms set forth in this Declaration can be fully realized'.[23]

But there are also disadvantages to this approach. Justice is a useful principle for interpreting and reforming the world trading system. But as an approach for tackling the problem of harmful trade restrictions it is limited. For one, an approach based on justice focuses on redistribution rather than absolute harms. In addition, 'justice' tends to exist, at best, as an unenforceable principle rather than as a legally enforceable norm. This diminishes its tactical usefulness.[24] So while a justice approach can supplement a human rights approach to the damage caused by trade restrictions, it does not supersede it.

So, what about a human rights approach to this problem? In the first place, it needs to be established that human rights obligations could even be applicable to the issue at hand. One may assume that, in principle, any act by a State for which it is responsible, including its trade policies, can violate human rights obligations. But this raises two questions: do States have any obligation to respect human rights in other jurisdictions? Second, if so, are such obligations positive or negative? These questions are contested even in the context of the ICESCR, which, unlike most human rights treaties, contains no clause limiting its scope to the territory or jurisdiction of the respective State party. In its Advisory Opinion on the *Wall*, the ICJ accepted the limited proposition that the ICESCR 'applies both to territories over which a State party has sovereignty and to those over which that State exercises territorial jurisdiction',[25] but this does not really deal with the issue. Nonetheless, there is a respectable body of commentary giving affirmative answers at least to the question whether States have any obligation to respect human rights in other jurisdictions. There is more disagreement on the nature of these obligations. Some have argued that, at a minimum, the ICESCR imposes negative obligations to respect human rights in other countries.[26] Others, including the UN Committee on Social, Economic and Cultural Rights (CESCR), have gone further, stating that the ICESCR imposes positive obligations to prevent third parties from violating human rights in third countries and to facilitate the realization of these rights in third countries.[27]

---

[23] Article 28 Universal Declaration of Human Rights.

[24] See S Aaronson and J Zimmerman, 'Fair Trade?: How Oxfam Presented a Systemic Approach to Poverty, Development, Human Rights, and Trade' 2006 *Human Rights Quarterly* 28(4) 998, at 1027–28.

[25] ICJ, *Legal Consequences of the Construction of a Wall in the Occupied Palestine Territory*, Advisory Opinion, ICJ Reports (2004) 136, at para 112.

[26] W Vandenhole, 'Third State Obligations under the ICESCR: A Case Study of EU Sugar Policy' 2007 *Nordic Journal of International Law* 76(1) 73, at 83–91.

[27] CESCR, General Comment No 12, *The Right to Adequate Food*, E/C.12/1999/5 (12 May 1999), at para 36; CESCR, General Comment No 14, *The Right to the Highest Attainable Standard of Health*, E/C.12/2000/4 (11 August 2000), at paras 38–41; CESCR, General Comment No 15, *The Right to Water*, E/C.12/2002/11 (20 January 2003), at 31–6; though note that CESCR, General Comment No 8, above fn 12, at para 14, is limited to a negative obligation. See also CHR, *The Right to Food, Report of the Special Rapporteur on the Right to Food, Jean Ziegler*, E/CN.4/2006/44 (16 March 2006), at paras 28–38; and

In the case of the EU, the issue is clearer. The EU has included human rights clauses in free trade and cooperation agreements with almost all countries in the world, each of which states that human rights principles underpin the international policies of the parties.[28] These obligations are also positive.[29] Regardless of the situation under the ICESCR, it would be difficult for the EU, at least, to deny that it is under an obligation to ensure that its policies, including its trade policies, must respect, protect, and fulfil human rights in other countries.

If these considerations are valid, then there are important implications for any measures adopted by a State that have a detrimental impact on human rights extraterritorially. States bound by an applicable negative human rights obligation would not be permitted to adopt any measure with negative impacts on the enjoyment of human rights in another country. On the other hand, this would not oblige States to take positive steps to restrict or liberalized trade taking place without State involvement. If the obligations are positive, the implications are more radical. Then States would have to take positive steps to regulate (or liberalize) trade if this has a negative impact on human rights, even if the trade itself takes place without State involvement.

This result also demonstrates that a human rights approach to the issue is more fruitful than the economic efficiency approach discussed above. Not only does it bring a normative rigour to the problem which is lacking in that approach, but it is potentially of broader reach. If the human rights approach involves positive human rights obligations, States may be required to eliminate non-distortive as well as distortive economic policies.

III. Costs of Trade Liberalization

A. Costs to the Liberalizing Country

If restrictions on trade can impede the realization of human rights, the removal of trade restrictions also comes at a cost, particularly to the liberalizing country. The reason for this is simple. The removal of trade restrictions amounts to a distribution

F Coomans and M Kamminga (eds), *Extraterritorial Application of Human Rights Treaties* (Antwerp: Intersentia, 2004). For a related discussion, see R McCorquodale and P Simons, 'Responsibility Beyond Borders: State Responsibility for Extraterritorial Violations by Corporations of International Human Rights Law' 2007 *Modern Law Review* 70(4) 598.

[28] According to the EU, this clause reflects customary international law: *EU Annual Report on Human Rights*, adopted by the EU Council on 21 October 2000 (Luxembourg: EC Official Publications, 2001), at 30. On these clauses generally, see L Bartels, *Human Rights Conditionality in the EU's International Agreements* (Oxford: Oxford University Press, 2005).

[29] Bartels, above fn 28, at 145–50.

of resources from inefficient to efficient factors of production; thus, the positive effects of trade liberalization are necessarily to the detriment of those inefficient factors (which economic theory predicts will usually be those which are less abundant in any economy).[30] Nor are these costs insignificant. In addition to the temporary financial burdens of unemployment, social and, in some cases, political disruption is a common result of trade liberalization. One empirical study even claims that 'foreign economic liberalization has increased the risk of civil war in sub-Saharan Africa'.[31]

Trade liberalization also entails raw financial costs, which can be difficult in particular for developing countries to bear. The most direct of these is the loss of tariff revenue following a reduction in tariff barriers. Many developing countries derive a large part of their income from tariff revenue, on average about 25 per cent in Sub-Saharan Africa, and 15 per cent for developing countries worldwide.[32] In theory, losses in tariff revenue can be recovered via domestic taxation, and, where trade has positive effects on a country's economy, overall tax revenue will rise. However, practice does not always match the theory. One study has found that while high income countries recover all of their lost tariff revenue, middle income countries recover only 45 to 60 per cent of theirs, and low income countries (mainly least developed countries) recover as little as 30 per cent of their lost income.[33] The authors of this study note specifically that this would impact on the ability of these countries to provide funds for poverty relief and development, with 'troubling' effects on the prospects of future liberalization.[34]

It is however not just losses in tariff revenue that can be expensive for poor countries. The implementation of rules promoting trade liberalization can also be burdensome. As one author has noted, the estimated cost of trade facilitation for many small developing countries would exceed the amount they spend on education.[35]

---

[30] M Bacchetta and M Jansen, *Adjusting to Trade Liberalization: The Role of Policy Institutions and WTO Disciplines* (Geneva: WTO, 2003), at 5. The Heckscher-Ohlin theorem states that comparative advantage tends to lie with the more abundant factors; the Stolper-Samuelson theorem states that the owners of factors of production used intensively in the production of displaced goods will tend to suffer reduced real income as a result.

[31] M Bussmann, G Schneider, and N Wiesehomeier, 'Foreign Economic Liberalization and Peace: The Case of Sub-Saharan Africa' 2005 *European Journal of International Relations* 11(4) 551.

[32] T Baunsgaard and M Keen, 'Tax Revenue and (or?) Trade Liberalization', *IMF Working Paper*, WT/05/112 (June 2005), at 3; also Negotiating Group on Market Access, *Market Access for Non-Agricultural Products – Revenue Implications of Trade Liberalization – Communication from the United States – Addendum*, TN/MA/W/18/Add.2 (11 April 2003). Some regional trade agreements provide for compensation: P Walkenhorst, 'Revenue Loss Compensation Mechanisms in Regional Trade Agreements' 2006 *Journal of International Development* 18(3) 379.

[33] Ibid. at 22. There are some exceptions, such as Uganda: ibid at 23.

[34] Ibid.

[35] P Ranjan, 'International Trade and Human Rights' in T Cottier, J Pauwelyn, and E Bürgi (eds), *Human Rights and International Trade* (Oxford: Oxford University Press, 2005), at 317.

B. Costs to Third Country Consumers

It should also be noted that, while it is primarily those in the liberalizing economy that are likely to be hurt by liberalization, in some circumstances third country consumers may also suffer harm. In particular, the removal of agricultural subsidies has a negative effect on third countries (net food importing developing countries) dependent on the lower prices for agricultural products resulting from these subsidies. These losses should be factored into any calculation of the benefits of reductions in subsidies to domestic consumers and third country producers.[36]

C. Trade and Human Rights Approaches to the Costs of Liberalization

Neither the trade nor human rights communities deny these costs to liberalization. But they differ significantly on how to account for them.[37] As a rule, those in favour of trade tend to focus on the fact that, overall, liberalization tends to be welfare enhancing to the liberalizing economy, and that any losses can be compensated by the enhanced resources produced by trade liberalization. In other words, the argument is that free trade meets the economic test of Kaldor-Hicks efficiency.[38]

But whether these costs are compensated and, if so, when they are compensated is a different question.[39] As one commentator has noted, Ricardo simply assumed that 'grape growers and wine makers in England will become weavers and tailors . . . while the weavers and tailors in Portugal become grape growers and wine makers'.[40] This may well be true in the long run, but it is the short run that is relevant to human rights.[41] Where the market fails to provide an answer, governments often step in with retraining programmes and unemployment assistance. But these programmes

---

[36] Such effects were anticipated by the WTO Decision on Measures Concerning the Possible Negative Effects of the Reform Programme on Least-Developed and Net Food-Importing Developing Countries. See also K Anderson, 'Trade Liberalization, Agriculture and Poverty in Low-Income Countries' in B Guha-Khasnobis (ed), *The WTO, Developing Countries and the Doha Development Agenda* (Houndmills: Palgrave, 2004), at 57.

[37] F Garcia, 'The Global Market and Human Rights: Trading Away the Human Rights Principle' 1999 *Brooklyn Journal of International Law* 25(1) 51, at 62–76.

[38] JS Mill grudgingly settled for Kaldor-Hicks efficiency when he said that '[i]t would be better to have a repeal of the [protectionist] Corn Laws, even clogged by compensation than not to have it at all; and if this were the only alternative, no one could complain of a change, by which, though an enormous amount of evil would be prevented, no one would lose', quoted in D Irwin, *Against the Tide: An Intellectual History of Free Trade* (Princeton: Princeton University Press, 1996), at 183.

[39] LA Winters, N McCulloch, and A McKay, 'Trade Liberalization and Poverty: The Evidence so Far' 2004 *Journal of Economic Literature* 42(1) 72; also Bacchetta and Jansen, above fn 30.

[40] D Palmeter, 'A Note on the Ethics of Free Trade' 2005 *World Trade Review* 4(3) 449, at 449–50.

[41] See JM Keynes, *A Tract on Monetary Reform* (London: Macmillan, 1924), at 80.

are not always effective, particularly where unemployment is geographically concentrated and they are also often unavailable in poor countries, where the losses are most severe. In sum, trade liberalization is likely to produce costs that are both uncompensated and uncompensable, especially among the poor in developing countries. None of this means that these costs cannot be justified. But it does mean that any justification must be utilitarian in the sense of a good to the majority outweighing a detriment (even if temporary) to a minority.[42]

This all looks different from the perspective of human rights, which, at least in its most common and institutional form,[43] is predicated on a deontological philosophy in which individual rights (including economic, social, and cultural rights)[44] are inviolable, and recourse to aggregate group benefits is generally irrelevant.[45]

The difference between the two approaches is well represented by the comment by one respected trade economist and lawyer that '[h]uman rights advocates would be wise not to focus myopically on the negative aspects of open trade to the exclusion of its positive effects'.[46] A human rights advocate is likely to respond that such 'myopia' is the entire point.

There can therefore be conflicts between trade liberalization and human rights. But it is equally obvious that not all of the costs of trade liberalization will amount to human rights violations. In particular, human rights law allows for considerable flexibility in the allocation of benefits that are not necessary for the satisfaction of basic needs. As the UN Sub-Commission on the Promotion and Protection of Human Rights has put it, whereas a 'trade-off... that actually reduc[es] the level of some kind of right from the existing level in order to raise the level of some other right' is impermissible, this does not apply to 'a trade-off in terms of how much improvement we can achieve in some right relative to some other', which is 'not only compatible with the notion of indivisibility but also unavoidable'.[47]

---

[42] For a utilitarian argument that trade benefits the 'poor as a class', see Klick and Tesón, above fn 2.

[43] There are different justifications for human rights, including some that are utilitarian. See, eg, J Shestack, 'The Philosophical Foundations of Human Rights' 1998 *Human Rights Quarterly* 20(2) 200.

[44] For economic, social, and cultural rights, 'minimum essential levels' must be maintained: CESCR, General Comment No 3, *The Nature of States Parties' Obligations*, E/1991/23 (14 December 1990), at para 10.

[45] P O'Connell, 'On Reconciling Irreconcilables: Neo-Liberal Globalisation and Human Rights' 2007 *Human Rights Law Review* 7(3) 483; Wai, above fn 5, at 39–41; Garcia, above fn 37, at 71; S Leader, 'Trade and Human Rights II' in P Macrory, A Appleton, and M Plummer (eds), *The World Trade Organization: Legal, Economic and Political Analysis*, Vol II (New York: Springer, 2005), at 665, points out that Article 55(a) is silent on the human right of individuals to an adequate standard of living.

[46] A Sykes, 'International Trade and Human Rights: An Economic Perspective' in Abbott, Breining-Kaufmann, and Cottier, above fn 4, at 21.

[47] CHR, Sub-Commission on the Promotion and Protection of Human Rights, Economic, Social and Cultural Rights, *Study on Policies for Development in a Globalizing World: What Can the Human Rights Approach Contribute? – Note by the Secretariat*, E/CN.4/Sub.2/2004/18 (7 June 2004), at paras 23–24. See also OHCHR, *Principles and Guidelines for a Human Rights Approach to Poverty Reduction*

D. Trade Regimes

The fact that there are some differences in the approaches adopted by the trade and human rights communities to the costs produced by liberalization does not say much about the way in which these approaches are manifested in any given trade regime. In fact, the WTO system contains a large number of flexibilities, leaving it to its Members how far to liberalize, and containing a number of safety valves for difficult, human rights-related, situations.

As long as various conditions are satisfied, a country faced with unwanted import competition is permitted to impose trade remedies in the form of safeguards, anti-dumping, and countervailing duties[48] to raise applied rates to higher bound rates[49] and to renegotiate bound tariffs in exchange for the grant of market access in other sectors.[50] Developing countries have additional options, including import restrictions for infant industry purposes[51] and, in the case of agriculture, subsidies for low-income or resource-poor producers.[52] Finally, all WTO Members have the option of imposing trade restrictions that are necessary for the protection of human life or health, so long as there are no alternative measures reasonably available that are less trade restrictive.[53] WTO Members also have the option of restricting exports, even by way of quantitative restrictions, to prevent or relieve critical shortages of food or other essential products.[54]

In reality, however, these mechanisms are not always available to all countries. Trade remedies can only be applied following detailed investigations, which will usually exceed the capacities of very poor developing countries.[55] Renegotiations of tariff bindings will be difficult where there are few products of export interest to the affected countries with negotiating rights, and subsidies may be prohibitively expensive. Furthermore, many of these flexibilities (in particular, safeguards and

---

Strategies (Geneva: UN, 2006) 5; CESCR, General Comment No 18, *The Right to Work*, E/C.12/GC/18 (6 February 2006), at para 21.

[48] It is sometimes overlooked that these rights apply to agricultural products. See, eg, CHR, *Globalization and Its Impact on the Full Enjoyment of Human Rights, Report of the High Commissioner for Human Rights*, E/CN.4/2002/54 (15 January 2002); C Downes, 'Must the Losers of Free Trade Go Hungry? Reconciling WTO Obligations and the Right to Food' 2007 *Virginia Journal of International Law* 47(3) 619, at 639; C Gonzalez, 'Institutionalizing Inequality: the WTO Agreement on Agriculture, Food Security, and Developing Countries' 2002 *Columbia Journal of Environmental Law* 27(2) 433.

[49] There are often large discrepancies between the applied and bound rates for developing countries. For example, Ghana applies a duty rate of 20 per cent on rice but has a bound rate of 99 per cent. See WTO/ITC/UNCTAD, *World Tariff Profiles 2006* (Geneva: WTO, 2006).

[50] Art XXVIII GATT 1994.   [51] Art XVIII GATT 1994.

[52] Art 6.2 Agreement on Agriculture.   [53] Art XX GATT 1994; Art XIV GATS.

[54] Art XI:2(a) GATT 1994. 'Due consideration' must be given to the effects of such a measure on importing Members' food security: Art 12 Agreement on Agriculture.

[55] M Khor, *Globalisation, Liberalisation, and Protectionism: The Global Framework Affecting Rural Producers in Developing Countries* (TWN, 2006), at <http://www.twnside.org.sg/pos.htm> (last visited 26 May 2008).

increasing applied tariffs to the bound rate) are infrequently used by developing countries, due to a combination of IMF and WB conditionalities,[56] domestic policy, and resource constraints.[57] Conceivably, it would be worthwhile to analyze the degree to which these flexibilities meet, or, with necessary amendments, could meet human rights objectives.

IV. Trade Rules and the Regulatory Powers of the State to Pursue Human Rights Objectives

A. Introduction

The process of trade liberalization has in recent years come to be seen as posing another type of threat to the protection of human rights. This threat emerges from a set of newer trade obligations targeting covert protectionism, making the domestic regulatory environment more trade-friendly, and covering new issues with a closer relationship to domestic policy-making, namely services and intellectual property. This development has provoked concerns that trade regimes impose a deregulatory *laissez-faire* (or 'neoliberal') model on States, impairing their ability to pursue human rights objectives (among others).[58]

B. Trade Regimes

The emergence of this possible threat to regulatory autonomy must be seen in the context of ongoing changes in the ideological underpinnings of the multilateral

---

[56] WB, *Adjustment from Within: Lessons from the Structural Adjustment Participatory Review Initiative* (Washington, DC: WB, 2001); Structural Adjustment Participatory Review International Network (SAPRIN), *Economic Crisis and Poverty: A Multi-Country Participatory Assessment of Structural Adjustment* (Washington, DC: SAPRIN, 2002); R Saner and R Guilherme, 'The International Monetary Fund's Influence on Trade Policies of Low-income Countries: A Valid Undertaking?' 2007 *Journal of World Trade* 41(5) 931.

[57] FAO, *The Right to Food Guidelines: Information Papers and Case Studies* (Rome: FAO, 2006), at 63 (on the Agreement on Agriculture).

[58] O'Connell, above fn 45, at 498–501. For a liberal view, see R Sally, 'Free Trade, New Century' 2005 *Economic Affairs* 25(4) 81, at 81. In its General Comment No 3, above fn 44, at para 8, the CESCR claims to be agnostic on the issue, but this is not entirely convincing.

trading system. Originally, according to one of the most influential accounts, the GATT 1947 represented a compromise between the desire to liberalize and the need to preserve domestic regulatory autonomy.[59] The key element in this compromise was the non-discrimination rule embodied in the national treatment principle. Market access commitments had to be respected, but so long as foreign products were treated no less favourably than domestic products, the State had a free hand in its domestic regulatory policies.

This compromise began to change from the 1970s onwards,[60] and it did so in three main respects. First, the volume of domestic regulation in the post-war period, some of which had protectionist intentions, but some of which simply had unintentional trade effects, highlighted the difficulties in applying the prohibition on *de facto* discrimination. Second, beginning with the 1979 Tokyo Round Codes, and reinforced in 1995, the multilateral trading system came to adopt rules requiring that even non-discriminatory domestic regulation had to meet certain regulatory standards. Third, the 1995 TRIPS Agreement imposed positive obligations on WTO Members to enact legislation protecting the intellectual property of foreign nationals.

Each of these developments has proved controversial from a human rights perspective, as each has the potential to limit the power of the State to achieve human rights objectives. The following will discuss the extent to which, on the current state of the law, they actually do so. It begins by addressing those areas of regulatory competence, relevant to human rights, to which trade obligations do not apply.

1. *Human Rights Exceptions and Defences*

Human rights norms are relevant to a number of the exceptions found in the WTO system, which are the model for those in most regional trade agreements (RTAs).[61] The main economic exceptions have been mentioned, including those permitting countries to impose trade restrictions in cases of serious damage to their domestic industry, and shortages of food or other essential products. In addition, there are two other sets of relevant exceptions, namely the security exceptions[62] and the general exceptions for public policy reasons.[63]

---

[59] This has been described as 'embedded liberalism', meaning that trade liberalization is 'embedded' in a commitment to domestic stability: J Ruggie, 'International Regimes, Transactions, and Change: Embedded Liberalism and the Post-war Economic Order' 1982 *International Organization* 36(2) 379.

[60] R Howse, 'From Politics to Technocracy – and Back Again: The Fate of the Multilateral Trade Regime' 2002 *American Journal of International Law* 96(1) 94.

[61] L Bartels, 'Social Issues: Labour, Environment and Human Rights' in S Lester and B Mercurio (eds), *Bilateral and Regional Trade Agreements: Commentary, Analysis and Case Studies* (Cambridge: Cambridge University Press, 2008).

[62] Art XXI GATT 1994; Art XIV*bis* GATS; Art 73 TRIPS Agreement. See also chapter 25 of this Handbook.

[63] Art XX GATT 1994; Art XIV GATS; Art XIII GPA. There are no equivalent exceptions in the TBT or SPS Agreements, and the exceptions in the TRIPS Agreement are narrower.

In the category of general exceptions, in particular, there are a number of other exceptions relevant to human rights. The exception relating to 'public morals' could permit trade restrictions in a country with a public sensitive to human rights violations, so long as these are 'necessary' to protecting those morals.[64] The exceptions for measures necessary to protect 'human life' and 'human health' are sufficient to cover many domestic measures relevant to human rights protection, though it remains unclear whether this exception permits measures to protect 'humans' outside of the scope of ordinary jurisdiction of the WTO Member adopting the measure.[65] And it has been argued that the term 'products of prison labour', originally a 'social dumping' provision,[66] might be applicable to the products of forced labour,[67] though any such argument would appear to be of rather limited application.

There are also limitations on these exceptions. Measures falling under a general exception must not constitute unjustifiable or arbitrary discrimination or be a disguised restriction on trade.[68] For both the public morals and the human life and health exception, it needs to be demonstrated that such measures are both appropriate and 'necessary' to their objective, which means that there is no reasonably alternative less trade restrictive measure that achieves the same objectives. Past experience of trade sanctions to prevent child labour indicates that this may not be easy to demonstrate.[69] There is also not a perfect match between these provisions and the topics covered by human rights law. This applies particularly to affirmative action for minorities and indigenous peoples and cultural rights, a fact that has led to expanded exceptions in some RTAs.[70] Finally, these exceptions do not exist in many WTO agreements, including the SPS and TBT Agreements and the Agreement on Agriculture. As these prevail over the GATT 1994 in cases of conflict,[71] it is open to argue that a measure that, for example, violates the prohibition on discrimination in Article 2.1 TBT Agreement cannot be excused by reference to Article XX GATT 1994.

These limitations mean that it cannot be assumed that if there are conflicts between trade and human rights norms a relevant exception will be available. It may in fact be necessary to see whether human rights obligations can operate directly as a

---

[64] N Diebold, 'The Morals and Order Exceptions in WTO Law: Balancing the Toothless Tiger and the Undermining Mole' 2008 *Journal of International Economic Law* 11(1) 43.

[65] Bartels, above fn 19.

[66] E Alben, 'GATT and the Fair Wage: A Historical Perspective on the Labor-Trade Link' 2001 *Columbia Law Review* 101(6) 1410. See also chapter 19 of this Handbook.

[67] S Cleveland, 'Human Rights Sanctions and International Trade: A Theory of Compatibility' 2002 *Journal of International Economic Law* 5(1) 133, at 161–62.

[68] Chapeau of Art XX GATT 1994.

[69] The threat of the US Child Labor Deterrence Act ('Harkin Bill') in 1993 led garment manufacturers in Bangladesh to dismiss 50,000 child workers, many of whom were subsequently employed in even worse occupations: US Department of Labor, *By the Sweat and Toil of Children: A Report to Congress*, 15 July 1994, at 24, at <http://www.dol.gov/ilab/programs/ocft/> (last visited 26 May 2008)

[70] Bartels, above fn 61.   [71] General Interpretive Note to Annex 1A of the WTO Agreement.

reason for avoiding trade obligations. How this might be done depends on the norm and the forum at issue, and it is therefore impossible to say in the abstract whether a given trade or human rights obligation will prevail in case of conflict.[72] However, human rights norms have been raised as defences to violations of trade obligations in regional trade agreements,[73] and it is foreseeable that similar arguments will at some stage be made within the WTO.

2. *Rules on Discrimination*

The first issue affecting the role of the State concerns the rules disciplining (or prohibiting) discrimination against products based on their origin. These rules clearly apply to sanctions against the products (or other subjects of trade regulation) of a particular country because of human rights abuses in that country. But they also apply to measures that have a discriminatory effect, even if these do not openly discriminate on the basis of origin.[74] This could include measures disfavouring products that are produced in a manner that harms human rights, such as products manufactured by the use of child labour or groom on land expropriated from indigeneous peoples.

Rules on non-discrimination differ, but the WTO rules contain the most common principles. At least for non-preferential trade,[75] the question is whether the measures adopted discriminate against 'like' (or 'directly competitive or substitutable') products.[76] Whether products are 'like' depends on the extent to which the products share physical characteristics, end-uses, consumer preferences, and tariff classifications.[77] In cases involving process and production methods (PPMs), often the only difference will be one of consumer preference, which is an uncertain basis for determining this issue.[78]

But there is a second step: a measure will only be discriminatory if it also amounts to 'less favourable treatment'. What this means is not entirely clear. In

---

[72] HM Haugen, 'The Nature of Social Human Rights Treaties and Standard-Setting WTO Treaties: A Question of Hierarchy?' 2007 *Nordic Journal of International Law* 76(4) 435. On the law applicable in WTO proceedings, see chapter 12 of this Handbook.

[73] ECJ, Case C-265/95, *Commission v France*, [1997] ECR I-6959; ECJ, Case C-112/00, *Schmidberger* [2003] ECR I-5659; also the *ad hoc* Mercosur Tribunal (Uruguay/Argentina), 6 September 2006, available at <http://www.mercosur.int/msweb/portal%20intermediario/es/controversias/arquivos/TPR_Tribunal%20AdHoc_Laudo%20Libre%20Circulacion_ES.pdf> (last visited 26 May 2008).

[74] L Ehring, '*De Facto* Discrimination in World Trade Law National and Most-Favoured-Nation Treatment – or Equal Treatment?' 2002 *Journal of World Trade* 36(5) 921.

[75] On human rights in preferential trade see L Bartels, 'The WTO Legality of the EU's GSP+ Arrangement' 2007 *Journal of International Economic Law* 10(4) 869; Bartels, above fn 28; Bartels, above fn 61.

[76] Art III GATT 1994.   [77] Appellate Body Report *EC – Asbestos*, at paras 103 and 109.

[78] Two unadopted GATT panel reports (the *Tuna* panels) wrongly held that a measure based on production methods was not covered by the obligation to provide national treatment, see Howse and Regan, above fn 19, at 254–57. See also chapter 9 of this Handbook.

Chile – Alcoholic Beverages, the Appellate Body asked whether the *aim* of a measure indicated protectionism.[79] In *EC – Asbestos*, the Appellate Body (in an *obiter dictum*) suggested instead looking at the overall *effects* of a measure on the different 'groups' of products.[80] In *Dominican Republic – Import and Sale of Cigarettes*, the Appellate Body continued with an effects test, but added what seems to be a qualification. It said that:

... the existence of a detrimental effect on a given imported product resulting from a measure does not necessarily imply that this measure accords less favourable treatment to imports *if the detrimental effect is explained by factors or circumstances unrelated to the foreign origin of the product*, such as the market share of the importer in this case.[81]

This case concerned a requirement that all cigarette producers post a bond to ensure payment of taxes. This entailed a higher per unit cost for imported cigarettes, because the importers had a smaller market share. The reasoning of the Appellate Body seems to have been that importers do not *inherently* need to have a smaller market share; in other words, this was a factor unrelated to the foreign origin of the product.

It must be said that, read literally, the Appellate Body's test is problematic, as it would only prohibit *de jure* and not *de facto* discrimination. After all, it is the whole point of *de facto* discrimination to identify a 'relevant factor' that is seemingly 'unrelated to the foreign origin of the product'. One way of making sense of this test is to read it as a qualification of the test as stated in *EC – Asbestos,* such that even if a measure has a disproportionately detrimental impact on imported products, this does not matter if, in principle, it could have the same impact on domestic products; or if the importer is reasonably able to meet the conditions for more favourable treatment. Thus, a measure disfavouring beverages with a certain alcoholic content, or cars of a certain size, would not amount to 'less favourable treatment' even if the impact is disproportionately felt by foreign products, so long as foreign producers are reasonably able to produce these products. One could say that on the new test, existing market opportunities are exchanged for reasonably available market opportunities.

Before turning to the application of this test to human rights issues, it needs to be noted that the Appellate Body's test was misapplied by the Panel in *EC – Biotech Products*. The question in these proceedings concerned the EC's approval procedures for products containing genetically modified organisms, which had a disproportionately detrimental effect on foreign products. The Panel quoted the test

---

[79] Appellate Body Report, *Chile – Alcoholic Beverages*, at para 71.
[80] Appellate Body Report, *EC – Asbestos*, at para 100.
[81] Appellate Body Report, *Dominican Republic – Import and Sale of Cigarettes*, at para 96 (emphasis added). 'Detrimental effect' presumably means that there is a relatively greater burden on foreign than domestic products. See also chapter 21 of this Handbook.

from *Dominican Republic – Import and Sale of Cigarettes*. However, when it came to applying this test, it said this:

> . . . a mere showing that a Member has undertaken or completed a particular approval procedure in a manner which is unfavourable for a given imported product would not be sufficient to establish a 'less favourable manner' of undertaking or completing approval procedures *if the relevant Member's conduct* is explained by factors or circumstances unrelated to the foreign origin of the product.[82]

This is quite different. A factor explaining a detrimental *effect* on an imported product is not the same as a factor explaining the *conduct* of a Member, which is another way of saying the *aim* of the measure. In *EC – Biotech Products*, the Panel went to find that a relevant factor explaining the EC's procedures was the perceived greater safety risk of the imported product.[83] This factor was not origin-specific, so the measure did not violate the relevant national treatment provisions. One wonders whether the same result would have obtained had the test been correctly applied.

How then does the Appellate Body's test apply to measures adopted for human rights reasons? The specific question is whether the disproportionately detrimental impact can be explained by a factor that is not inherent to the origin of a product. This, it is suggested, will be the case if the foreign producer is not inherently disabled from meeting the more favoured conditions. Clearly, some human rights-related factors will be inherent to the origin of a product. For example, a measure favouring products produced by indigenous labour necessarily disfavours products from countries without an indigenous workforce. Other factors might have a correlation, though imperfect, with certain origins. A measure disfavouring products produced by child labour will have a disproportionately detrimental impact on products from countries with a greater prevalence of child labour. But for this factor to be considered origin-specific, it would be necessary for these countries to demonstrate that their producers are not reasonably able to meet non-child labour conditions. This may well be possible, depending on the facts. It might also be arguable that if the country has undertaken to eliminate such practices, for example by concluding a relevant ILO Convention, its producers would be deemed to be able to meet these conditions.[84]

The Appellate Body's new test, as interpreted here, does not draw a bright line. It will always be debatable whether a producer is reasonably able to take advantage of the more favoured treatment. But as a qualification to a simple test (as indicated in *EC – Asbestos*) of disproportionate impact on products of different origin, it shifts the law in the direction of regulatory autonomy, with correspondingly more tolerance of non-trade concerns, such as human rights.

---

[82] Panel Report, *EC – Biotech Products*, at paras 7.2405 and 7.2408 (emphasis added).

[83] Ibid at para 7.2412.

[84] ILO Convention No 182 Concerning the Prohibition and Immediate Action for the Elimination of the Worst Forms of Child Labour, in force 19 November 2000 (ratified by 165 countries).

3. *Rules on Domestic Regulation*

For some types of measures, there are additional requirements beyond non-discrimination. The SPS and TBT Agreements and the GATS Agreements all require that regulations must be necessary to achieve their objectives, unless (in the case of the SPS and TBT Agreements) they are based on an international standard.[85] In the SPS Agreement, a measure that is not based on an international standard must also be based on scientific evidence, where this is available.[86]

There have been concerns that these rules establish a *laissez-faire* regime.[87] To this, it must be responded that, in principle, these rules leave untouched the principle that WTO Members are entitled to set their regulatory objectives without fear of second-guessing of the legitimacy of those objectives[88] or, worse, a cost-benefit analysis 'balancing' of the value of the objective with the trade restrictiveness of the measure.[89] But this does not dispose of the issue. First, the Appellate Body has persisted in saying that the 'necessity' of a measure taken for legitimate policy reasons is to be determined by precisely that sort of cost-benefit calculation.[90] There is also scope for argument as to the standard of review applied by panels and Appellate Body to the question whether the facts (including the existence of scientific evidence) justify a given measure. The Appellate Body has been relatively deferential on this point, requiring under the SPS Agreement, for example, that the evidence should 'reasonably support' the measure at issue.[91] However, the application of this standard, in light of the difficulty of making value-neutral scientific judgments, has not always been straightforward.[92] Finally, even though overall a requirement of efficient regulation must be applauded as a contribution to good governance, it comes at a cost. Some countries might only be able to bear these costs by diverting funds otherwise available for human rights purposes.

---

[85] Art 2.2 TBT Agreement; Art 5.6 SPS Agreement; Art VI:5 GATS. The GATS rule only applies to new and unforeseen measures unless new rules are agreed, which to date has only been done in the accountancy sector. The necessity test is drawn from the jurisprudence on Article XX GATT 1994, but there it only applies to measures that have already been determined to discriminate against foreign products.

[86] Arts 5.1–5.8 SPS Agreement.

[87] See D Driesen, 'What is Free Trade?: The Real Issue Lurking Behind the Trade and Environment Debate' 2000–1 *Virginia Journal of International Law* 41(2) 279, at 300; and A Orford, 'Beyond Harmonization: Trade, Human Rights and the Economy of Sacrifice' 2005 *Leiden Journal of International Law* 18(2) 179, at 191.

[88] Appellate Body Report, *Australia – Salmon*, at para 199 (on the SPS Agreement); Appellate Body Report, *EC – Asbestos*, at para 168 (on Article XX GATT 1994).

[89] D Regan, 'The Meaning of "Necessary" in GATT Article XX and GATS Article XIV: The Myth of Cost-Benefit Balancing' 2007 *World Trade Review* 6(3) 347.

[90] Appellate Body Report, *Brazil – Retreaded Tyres*, at para 182, also paras 178 and 210.

[91] Appellate Body Report, *EC – Hormones*, at para 193. See also chapter 14 of this Handbook.

[92] M Footer, 'Post-Normal Science in the Multilateral Trading System: Social Science Expertise and the *EC–Biotech Panel*' 2007 *World Trade Review* 6(2) 281.

4. *Privatization and Deregulation*

From a human rights perspective, an additional issue of concern is the extent to which liberalization of trade in services requires the privatization (giving up government ownership) or deregulation (giving up regulatory control) of public services.[93] Privatization of the provision of services need not create human rights problems, but it may. Speaking of the right to health, one Special Rapporteur to the UN Human Rights Commission has said that while '[a]t times, the public health system can also neglect the poor and people traditionally suffering from discrimination and social injustice', these issues are highlighted in the case of higher levels of private participation in services provision.[94] The deregulation of the provision of services can have negative effects on human rights, if, for example, service suppliers are free not to supply services to sectors of the population if this is unprofitable. The following discusses the extent to which the GATS requires either the privatization or the deregulation of public services.[95]

The most important provision in the GATS in this area is Article I:3, which states that the agreement only applies to services supplied on a commercial and/or competitive basis.[96] This carve-out does not apply to all publicly supplied services. For example, it does not cover services that are provided by a mix of public and private suppliers. Having said this, even where a service is covered by the GATS, unlike the GATT 1994, not all obligations apply immediately. Those that do are the most-favoured-nation (MFN) obligation and some transparency obligations. Thus, as soon as one foreign supplier enters the domestic market, no less favourable treatment must be afforded to all other foreign suppliers. In other words, some degree of privatization is likely.

The other significant obligations in the GATS only apply once an express commitment has been made in a given services sector. The impact can be significant. Where commitments are made in a services sector, foreign services and suppliers must be permitted market access on a non-discriminatory basis (subject to any express exclusions). In principle, this means that any subsidies granted to domestic

---

[93] K de Feyter and F Gómez Isa (eds), *Privatisation and Human Rights in the Age of Globalisation* (Antwerp: Intersentia, 2005).

[94] CHR, *The Right of Everyone to the Enjoyment of the Highest Attainable Standard of Physical and Mental Health – Report of the Special Rapporteur, Paul Hunt – Addendum: Mission to the World Trade Organization*, E/CN.4/2004/49/Add.1 (1 March 2004), at para 47.

[95] See also M Krajewski, 'Services Liberalization in Regional Trade Agreements: Lessons for GATS "Unfinished Business"?' in L Bartels and F Ortino (eds), *Regional Trade Agreements and the WTO Legal System* (Oxford: Oxford University Press, 2006) 175. See also chapter 7 of this Handbook.

[96] R Adlung, 'Public Services and the GATS' 2006 *Journal of International Economic Law* 9(2) 455, at 463–7; M Krajewski, 'Public Services and Trade Liberalization: Mapping the Legal Framework' 2003 *Journal of International Economic Law* 6(2) 354; E Leroux, 'What is a "Service Supplied in the Exercise of Governmental Authority" under Article I:3(b) and (c) of the General Agreement on Trade in Services?' 2006 *Journal of World Trade* 40(3) 345.

suppliers must also be available to foreign suppliers. The resulting budgetary strain could undermine the funds available to existing public services.

What then of deregulation? Here the restrictions are similar to those discussed above, in the context of the TBT and SPS Agreements, involving transparency and 'least trade restrictive' regulation, although they only appear only apply to post-1995 measures.[97] A final constraint arises from *US – Gambling*, where the Appellate Body held that a non-discriminatory prohibition on the supply of a service was a violation of a market access obligation.[98] In theory, this could operate as a constraint on the regulatory autonomy of WTO Members,[99] though probably only by mistake (as in this case), as a WTO Member would be unlikely to make a commitment in a services sector at the same time as maintaining a domestic ban.

5. *Intellectual Property*

A special challenge to the concept of 'embedded liberalism' results from the TRIPS Agreement, which imposes positive obligations on WTO Members to protect the intellectual property of foreign nationals in their territory.[100] In turn, this has provided a platform upon which so-called TRIPs-plus obligations are becoming established in regional trade agreements.[101]

The links between intellectual property and trade are strong. Both the Universal Declaration on Human Rights and the ICESCR state that '[e]veryone has the right to the protection of the moral and material interests resulting from any scientific, literary or artistic production of which he is the author'.[102] It is difficult to contest the fact that, insofar as it operates as an instrument to this end, the TRIPS Agreement can also

---

[97] Art VI GATS.

[98] Appellate Body Report, *US – Gambling*, at para 265.

[99] J Pauwelyn, '*Rien Ne Va Plus*? Distinguishing Domestic Regulation from Market Access in GATT and GATS' 2005 *World Trade Review* 4(1) 131; F Ortino, 'Treaty Interpretation and the WTO Appellate Body Report in *US – Gambling*: A Critique' 2006 *Journal of International Economic Law* 9(1) 117; D Regan, 'A *Gambling* Paradox: Why an Origin-Neutral "Zero-Quota" is Not a Quota Under GATS Article XVI' 2007 *Journal of World Trade* 41(6) 1297; P Delimatsis, 'Don't Gamble with GATS: The Interaction between Articles VI, XVI, XVII, and XVIII GATS in the Light of the *US – Gambling* Case' 2006 *Journal of World Trade* 40(6) 1059.

[100] The GATT 1947 merely permitted a Contracting Party to protect its *domestic* market against copycat products (Art XX(d)). The TRIPS Agreement has much more extensive market access effects: by granting a potential worldwide monopoly to a rights holder, it permits a rights holder who trades products containing intellectual property to drive out competition from copycat products in all foreign markets. It also protects intellectual property that is not incorporated in traded products. In this sense, it is more an investment agreement than a trade agreement. See also chapter 7 of this Handbook.

[101] B Mercurio, 'TRIPS-Plus Provisions in Regional Trade Agreements' in Bartels and Ortino, above fn 95, 215.

[102] Art 27(2) UDHR; Art 15(1)(c) ICESCR.

be considered to promote human rights.[103] In addition, however, there are certain features of the TRIPS Agreement that have made it controversial from a human rights perspective. The first is that, in practice, the agreement amounts to a mechanism for moving royalties from developing countries to developed countries.[104] The second is that the TRIPS Agreement appears in some respect to limit the ability of WTO Members to protect human rights. For example, the TRIPS Agreement has a very broad scope for patents, requiring the patenting of genetic resources, which infringes on the freedom to engage in academic research, and of non-regenerating so-called 'terminator' seeds, which can conflict with the right to food.[105]

Even more prominent has been the debate on the extent to which these patent obligations permit WTO Members to provide access to patented essential medicines in pursuance of their obligations with respect to the right to health. This debate has involved questions concerning the scope of the TRIPS provision allowing 'limited exceptions to the exclusive rights conferred by a patent', and the scope of the power granted to a WTO Member to issue a compulsory licence for patented medicines in cases of 'national emergency or other circumstances of extreme urgency'.[106] This question has been tackled by a series of WTO declarations, decisions, and ultimately an amendment to the TRIPS Agreement (as yet unratified) reiterating that compulsory licenses may be issued for essential medicines in some circumstances and providing for a mechanism for legitimately importing such medicines from countries granting compulsory licenses for exports by countries with no manufacturing capacity.[107]

V. Institutional Responses to the Relationship between Trade and Human Rights

Until recently, neither the trade nor the human rights institutions paid any attention to the links between trade liberalization and human rights discussed in this chapter.

---

[103] R Anderson and H Wager, 'Human Rights, Development, and the WTO: the Cases of Intellectual Property and Competition Policy' 2006 *Journal of International Economic Law* 9(3) 707, at 721–27, discussing especially some statements to the contrary in CESCR, General Comment No 17, below fn 122.

[104] A Panagariya, 'TRIPs and the WTO: an Uneasy Marriage' in K Maskus (ed), *The WTO, Intellectual Property Rights, and the Knowledge Economy* (Cheltenham: Edward Elgar, 2004) 42.

[105] H Hestermeyer, *Human Rights and the WTO: The Case of Patents and Access to Medicines* (Oxford: Oxford University Press, 2006), at 181.

[106] Arts 30–31 TRIPS Agreement. For discussion, see Hestermeyer, ibid. at 234–53.

[107] See chapter 8 of this Handbook.

In almost five decades, there was barely a reference to the notion of human rights in the GATT 1947 system. In its early years, the WTO continued along this path, although this now appears to be changing. A 2002 joint study undertaken by the WTO Secretariat and the World Health Organization (WHO) did not once mention the 'right' to health; by contrast, in a 2007 joint study with the International Labour Organization (ILO) the WTO Secretariat referred to worker rights as 'a part of universally recognized Human Rights'.[108] In 2004, the WTO Secretariat also took part informally in discussions with a UN Special Rapporteur on Human Rights,[109] and in 2006 it participated as an observer at the UN Human Rights Council.[110] Some WTO Members have referred to Human Rights in negotiation proposals on agriculture[111] and intellectual property,[112] and the Preamble to the WTO Kimberley Diamonds Waiver refers to conflicts in which 'gross human rights violations ... have been perpetrated'.[113] In trade policy reviews and accession negotiations, WTO Members have also been questioned about their human rights protections, the concern being that by failing in this regard they might be undermining their market access commitments.[114] It is, of course, too early to say how much this all means. After all, other than the ILO no human rights organ has been invited to take part in a WTO meeting, even as an observer.[115] Whether a more formal acknowledgement of the links between the two fields will be made remains to be seen.

Perhaps it is understandable that an institution devoted to free trade would not have human rights as its major concern. What is surprising, however, is that, except for the topics of trade sanctions and labour standards,[116] the main human rights institutions have only recently come to focus on the potentially harmful effects of trade liberalization. As late as 1997, a UN-commissioned expert report on international inequality contrasted the 'very limited' role of the GATT 1994 with the 'transcendental importance' of the Earth Summit in Rio and the World Summit of

---

[108] WHO/WTO, *WTO Agreements and Public Health* (Geneva: WHO/WTO, 2002); ILO/WTO, *Trade and Employment: Challenges for Policy Research* (Geneva: ILO/WTO, 2007), at 66.

[109] *Report of the Special Rapporteur, Paul Hunt*, E/CN.4/2004/49/Add.1, above fn 94.

[110] UN Human Rights Council, *Report to the General Assembly on the Second Session of the Human Rights Council*, A/HRC/2/9 (22 March 2007).

[111] Discussion papers by Mauritius and Norway, reproduced in WTO Committee on Agriculture, *Note on Non-Trade Concerns*, G/AG/NG/W/36/Rev.1 (9 November 2000).

[112] *Proposal for a Ministerial Declaration on the TRIPS Agreement and Public Health*, IP/C/W/312, WT/GC/W/450 (4 October 2001).

[113] The Preamble to the WTO Decision, *Kimberley Process Certification Scheme for Rough Diamonds – Decision of 15 December 2006*, WT/L/676 (19 December 2006).

[114] S Aaronson, 'Seeping in Slowly: How Human Rights Concerns are Penetrating the WTO' 2007 *World Trade Review* 6(3) 413, at 422–27 and 434–38.

[115] The CESCR sent a statement to the third WTO MC, but this was not circulated. It is reproduced as Annex VII of CESCR, *Report*, E/2000/22 (18 May 2000).

[116] For an early academic assessment, see P Alston, 'Linking Trade and Human Rights' 1980 *German Yearbook of International Law* (23) 126.

Social Development in Copenhagen.[117] It was not much of an improvement when, two years later, a report commissioned by the same, now renamed, body described the WTO as a 'veritable nightmare'.[118] Since then, the UN human rights organs, and in particular the Office of the UN High Commissioner for Human Rights, have become more attuned both to threats potentially posed by trade liberalization (which the first report failed to see) and the reality of those threats as manifested in the WTO system (which the second misunderstood). In a series of reports, the UN High Commissioner for Human Rights[119] and Special Rapporteurs on selected rights[120] have analysed much more precisely the relationships between trade and various human rights, and have recommended that the promotion of human rights be made an objective of trade liberalization, that human rights impact assessments of trade policies should be undertaken, and that countries should develop their trade policies in conformity with their international obligations.[121] These themes have also been taken up by some of the human rights treaty monitoring bodies.[122]

---

[117] CHR, Sub-Commission on Prevention of Discrimination and Protection of Minorities, *The Relationship between the Enjoyment of Human Rights, in particular Economic, Social and Cultural Rights, and Income Distribution – Final Report*, E/CN.4/Sub.2/1997/9 (30 June 1997), at para 34.

[118] CHR, Sub-Commission on Promotion and Protection of Human Rights, *Human Rights as the Primary Objective of International Trade, Investment and Finance Policy and Practice – Preliminary Report*, E./CN.4/Sub.2/2000/13 (14 June 2000); CHR, *Final Report*, E/CN.4/Sub.2/2003/14 (25 June 2003). The report is criticized by S Dillon, 'A Farewell to "Linkage": International Trade Law and Global Sustainability Indicators' 2002–3 *Rutgers Law Review* 55(1) 87, at 102–06.

[119] CHR, *Reports of the High Commissioner for Human Rights: Globalization and Its Impact on the Full Enjoyment of Human Rights*, E/CN.4/2002/54 (15 January 2002); CHR, *Liberalization of Trade in Services and Human Rights*, E/CN.4/Sub.2/2002/9 (25 June 2002); CHR *The Impact of the Agreement on Trade-Related Aspects of Intellectual Property Rights on Human Rights*, E/CN.4/Sub.2/2001/13 (27 June 2001); CHR, *Human Rights, Trade and Investment*, E/CN.4/Sub.2/2003/9 (2 July 2003); CHR, *Analytical Study on the Fundamental Principle of Non-Discrimination in the Context of Globalization*, E/CN.4/2004/40 (15 January 2004); CHR, *Analytical Study on the Fundamental Principle of Participation and its Application in the Context of Globalization*, E/CN.4/2005/41 (23 December 2004).

[120] CHR, *The Right to Food, Report of the Special Rapporteur, Jean Ziegler*, E/CN.4/2006/44, (16 March 2006) Human Rights Council, *Report of the Special Rapporteur on the Right to Food, Jean Ziegler*, A/HRC/4/30 (19 January 2007); *Report of the Special Rapporteur, Paul Hunt*, above fn 94.

[121] W Benedek, 'The World Trade Organization and Human Rights' in W Benedek, K de Feyter, and F Marrella (eds), *Economic Globalisation and Human Rights* (Cambridge: Cambridge University Press, 2007), at 143–49.

[122] CRC, *Report*, CRC/C/121 (11 December 2002), at para 653; CESCR, *Report*, E/2001/22, E/C.12/2000/21, Supp 2 (31 December 2000), at paras 170 (Egypt), 549 (Morocco); *Observations (Costa Rica)*, E/C.12/CRI/CO/4 (23 November 2007), at para 42. For a general statement see CESCR, General Comment No 17, *The Right of Everyone to Benefit from the Protection of the Moral and Material Interests Resulting from any Scientific, Literary or Artistic Production of Which He or She is the Author*, E/C.12/GC/17 (12 January 2006), at para 56.

VI. CONCLUSION

At the most general level, there are numerous commonalities between trade and human rights. Both serve the interests of peace, the promotion of trade improves human welfare in a material sense, some human rights are important for an efficient trading system, and there are human rights arguments for reducing harmful trade barriers. But the existence of these synergies does not mean that trade and human rights imperatives can never conflict, nor is this even likely, given the social and economic disruption that is necessarily entailed by the process of trade liberalization. There are also philosophical differences between the two fields. In particular, the utilitarian ethic that continues to underpin trade liberalization contradicts the basis human rights assumption that a minimum standard of human rights protection must always be maintained. And there are legitimate concerns that trade regimes with a deregulatory model privileging the market over non-market values might limit the ability of States to pursue human rights objectives.

On the other hand, it would also be wrong to assume that, just because there are potential conflicts between the fields of trade and human rights, any given trade regime automatically privileges the interests of trade liberalization over those of human rights. Indeed, in most cases the WTO system is sufficiently flexible to permit WTO Members to pursue human rights objectives. But there are still areas of legitimate concern. From the perspective of WTO rules, the major outstanding difficulties lie in certain aspects of the TRIPS Agreement, the legality of trade measures adopted for the express purpose of protecting human rights in other countries, and ambiguities in the GATS as to whether non-discriminatory prohibitions on services may nonetheless infringe market access obligations. Furthermore, these rules are not the final word on trade liberalization. Liberalization negotiations are ongoing in multiple fora, including the multilateral level, WTO accession negotiations, and at the regional level. In all of these cases, the following would appear to be sensible: to ensure that market access commitments do not impair the ability of countries' ability to pursue human rights obligations by undertaking human rights impact assessments,[123] to commit to the appropriate flanking policies to respond to any identified problems, and to ensure that trade rules permit countries to adopt measures in favour of human rights objectives. These policies should go some way to ensuring that the process of trade liberalization serves human rights objectives instead of undermining them.

---

[123] S Walker, 'Human Rights Impact Assessments of Trade-Related Policies' in M Gehring and MC Cordonier-Segger (eds), *Sustainable Development in World Trade Law* (The Hague: Kluwer, 2005); also European Commission, *Handbook for Trade Sustainability Impact Assessment* (March, 2006) and the labour impact assessment process in section 135 of the US Trade Act of 1974 (88 Stat 1996).

SELECTED BIBLIOGRAPHY

F Abbott, C Breining-Kaufmann, and T Cottier (eds), *International Trade and Human Rights: Foundations and Conceptual Issues* (Ann Arbour: University of Michigan Press, 2006)

T Cottier, J Pauwelyn, and E Bürgi (eds), *Human Rights and International Trade* (Oxford: Oxford University Press, 2005)

K de Feyter and F Gómez Isa (eds), *Privatisation and Human Rights in the Age of Globalisation* (Antwerp: Intersentia, 2005)

F Garcia, 'The Global Market and Human Rights: Trading Away the Human Rights Principle' 1999 *Brooklyn Journal of International Law* 25(1) 51

F Garcia, *Trade, Inequality, and Justice: Toward a Liberal Theory of Just Trade* (Ardsley, NY: Transnational, 2003)

H Hestermeyer, *Human Rights and the WTO: The Case of Patents and Access to Medicines* (Oxford: Oxford University Press, 2006)

R Howse and R Teitel, 'Beyond the Divide: The Covenant on Economic, Social and Cultural Rights and the World Trade Organization', *Friedrich Ebert Stiftung Occasional Paper* No 13 (April 2007)

A Lang, 'Rethinking Trade and Human Rights' 2007 *Tulane Journal of International and Comparative Law* 15(2) 335

S Leader, 'Trade and Human Rights II' in P Macrory, A Appleton, and M Plummer (eds), *The World Trade Organization: Legal, Economic and Political Analysis*, Vol II (New York: Springer, 2005)

G Marceau, 'WTO Dispute Settlement and Human Rights' 2002 *European Journal of International Law* 13(4) 753

D Palmeter, 'A Note on the Ethics of Free Trade' 2005 *World Trade Review* 4(3) 449

E-U Petersmann, 'Trade and Human Rights I' in P Macrory, A Appleton, and M Plummer (eds), *The World Trade Organization: Legal, Economic and Political Analysis*, Vol II (New York: Springer, 2005)

CHAPTER 21

....

TRADE AND
HEALTH

....

JEFFERY ATIK

I. THE WTO AND HEALTH

SINCE the conclusion of the Uruguay Round, there has been significant alarm about the potential negative effect of the WTO system on the pursuit of public health goals by national governments. To a certain degree, the WTO-and-health debates mirror anxieties about the compatibility of environmental, labour, and human rights protections with WTO norms. The protection of public health is, traditionally, a responsibility of the State. Health measures embrace a variety of concerns. First and foremost, health policy involves the prevention and control of diseases. Furthermore, it describes a complex of initiatives undertaken by WTO Members, including the operation of health delivery systems, insurance schemes, and pharmaceutical controls.

There had been various challenges to national health measures under the GATT 1947. The onset of the WTO made avoidance of GATT norms increasingly difficult. Moreover, the WTO introduced a specific agreement dealing with certain health measures, the SPS Agreement. This agreement imposes new requirements with respect to certain categories of health measures, while expanding the scope of the presumption of regulatory correctness enjoyed by WTO Members applying those measures.

The TRIPS Agreement has also raised significant concerns about its potential effects on the pursuit of autonomous national health policies. The TRIPS Agreement mandates patent protection of pharmaceuticals (subject to transition rules) throughout the WTO membership. This in turn could lead to increases in prices or other misallocation of essential medicines in much of the least developed world, particularly in areas afflicted by AIDS, malaria, and other health emergencies.[1] The remainder of this chapter will examine the effects of the GATT 1994 and the SPS Agreement on WTO Members' health measures.

II. THE SPS AGREEMENT

A. Introduction - Relation to the GATT 1994

The SPS Agreement was a response to a series of perceived inadequacies in the GATT 1947's discipline of health measures. On the one hand, the 'necessity' requirement in Article XX was viewed as excessively difficult to meet, and hence

---

[1] See chapter 8 of this Handbook.

inadequately deferential to national discretion in health policy. As observed in the discussion of *Thailand – Cigarettes* below, consideration of alternate measures could be undisciplined in the GATT-era; a State should not be told to adopt an alternate measure that fails to achieve the level of health protection that State chooses. On the other hand, there was concern that spurious health concerns, unsupported by a scientific foundation, were being invoked to justify recourse to the Article XX(b) exception.

Whether a particular measure indeed contributes to the protection of health involves a scientific conclusion, as well as a legal conclusion. GATT panels were ill equipped, both technically and doctrinally, to evaluate scientific claims. In *Thailand–Cigarettes*, the Panel rather awkwardly consulted the WHO in order to assess scientific expertise, which it then disregarded.

Trade concerns also arose from measures qualifying under Article XX(b) GATT 1947. Health measures function as non-tariff barriers, even when justified by necessity, in the absence of harmonization. The interplay of inconsistent (though justified) health measures adopted by diverse States operates to restrict trade. Finally, the longstanding (and looming) EC – US dispute over the use of growth hormones in beef production threatened to overwhelm the existing rules structure.

The SPS Agreement creates *lex specialis* (compared to the GATT 1994) for a specific category of health measures: sanitary or phytosanitary (SPS) measures. SPS measures are defined in Annex A of the SPS Agreement as:

1. Measures to protect animals or plants from pests and diseases.
2. Measures to protect humans or animals from food risks.
3. Measures to protect humans from risks from diseases arising from animals or plants.
4. Measures to control pests.

Not all health measures fall within this definition. For example, measures controlling human exposure to carcinogens (other than food-borne carcinogens) would not be SPS measures. The SPS Agreement did not apply to the challenged measures in *US – Gasoline*, in *EC – Asbestos,* or in *Brazil – Retreaded Tyres*, and likely would not have applied (had it then been in effect) to *Thailand – Cigarettes*. These cases demonstrate the continuing role of the Article XX(b) GATT 1994 health exception in the WTO-era.

There is a common 'agricultural' character to the measures covered by the SPS Agreement: an agricultural product is either the source of risk (as in food cases) or the object of protection (as in disease and pest cases). In *EC – Hormones*, the Panel identified two elements that must be present in order to engage the SPS Agreement. First, the challenged measure must be an SPS measure as defined in Annex A.[2] Second, the challenged measure must affect international trade.[3]

---

[2] Panel Report, *EC – Hormones*, at para 8.39.   [3] Ibid at para 8.36.

Functionally, the SPS Agreement imposes new requirements on WTO Members with respect to SPS measures that are distinct from the familiar requirements of the GATT 1994. For SPS measures, compliance with the SPS Agreement is the primary normative demand imposed by WTO law. They must comply with the SPS Agreement. SPS measures that 'conform' to the SPS Agreement are presumed to be in compliance with the other WTO agreements, including the GATT 1994. Because of the mandated conformity with the SPS Agreement, and the resulting presumption of compliance with the rest of the WTO corpus, panels and the Appellate Body, when reviewing SPS measures, have focused on the SPS Agreement to the near exclusion of the GATT 1994. The SPS Agreement also makes clear that panels may consult scientific and technical experts pursuant to Article 11.2 SPS Agreement.

B.   Preference for International Standards

Like the TBT Agreement, and unlike Article III:4 GATT 1994, the SPS Agreement is concerned with both discriminatory and non-discriminatory measures. Like the TBT Agreement, the SPS Agreement displays a preference for the use of international standards. Many SPS measures meet the definition of 'technical regulations' as set out in Annex 1 to the TBT Agreement. These SPS measures are not governed by the TBT Agreement, however, as Article 1.5 TBT Agreement provides that the provisions of that agreement 'do not apply' to SPS measures as that term is defined in Annex A of the SPS Agreement. Rather, the more specific terms of the SPS Agreement apply to all SPS measures maintained by a WTO Member.

The preference for international standards is expressed several ways within the SPS Agreement. Article 3(1) provides:

To harmonize sanitary and phytosanitary measures on as wide basis as possible, [WTO] Members shall base their sanitary or phytosanitary measures on international standards, guidelines or recommendations, where they exist, except as otherwise provided for in this Agreement, and in particular in [Article 3.3].

The expectation to follow international standards thus has two avenues of escape: WTO Members may introduce idiosyncratic measures where no international standard exists; and they may impose non-standard measures when they seek a higher level of protection than would be achieved by resort to an existing international standard per Article 3.3.

While the SPS Agreement encourages the establishment of international standards (which then become the default expectation of the WTO membership), there are many areas of health concern where international SPS standards simply do not exist and where particular Members may choose to regulate. There seems little doubt that Members may take SPS measures in the absence of international standards, but in so doing they are subject to the SPS Agreement's requirement of a scientific basis. Some important SPS disputes have involved situations where no international standard was available (at times the very presence of the dispute in question may have blocked the adoption of an international standard within the appropriate body that, had it existed, might have tended to resolve the dispute). There was no international standard, for example, addressing the use of growth hormones in beef production (in *EC – Hormones*), nor with respect to the consumption of genetically modified foodstuffs (in *EC – Biotech Products*).

Article 3(4) SPS Agreement exhorts the WTO membership 'to play a full part' in the work of the central organizations involved in setting international SPS standards: the Codex Alimentarius, the International Office of Epizootics, and the institutions associated with the International Plant Protection Convention framework. Moreover, the SPS Agreement establishes a Committee on Sanitary and Phytosanitary Measures (SPS Committee) and calls on the Committee to monitor the harmonization of international SPS measures.

Where standards exist, Article 3(1) requires (subject to the exception provided in Article 3(3)) that Members 'base' their SPS measures on such standards. The requirement to 'base' national SPS measures on international standards does not mean that the international standards must be directly translated into national law. Rather, WTO Members may depart from particular provisions of the international standards and still be deemed to have 'based' their national measures on the relevant international standards and so satisfy Article 3(1) SPS Agreement.

In *EC – Hormones*, the Appellate Body distinguished the demand of Article 3(1) for measures to be 'based on' international standards from Article 3(2)'s grant of a presumption of compliance for measures that 'conform to' international standards.[4] Thus, an SPS measure may be found to be 'based on' an international standard even when it does not 'conform to' that standard. According to the Appellate Body in *EC – Hormones*, a Member may be deemed to have based its SPS measure on an international standard where it adopts 'some, not necessarily all, of the elements of the international standard'.[5]

There is, of course, an outside limit to the degree to which a national SPS measure may depart from the relevant international standard and still be deemed to be 'based on' it. In *EC – Sardines*, the Appellate Body held that a requirement of the TBT Agreement that technical regulations be 'based on' international standards is not satisfied by a technical regulation that contradicts the international standard.[6] By this reasoning, an SPS measure that contradicts an international standard likely will not be deemed to be 'based' on that standard, and will, in this case, be considered a non-conforming standard subject to the requirements of Article 3(3).

Even when international standards exist, WTO Members may depart from these in order to attain 'higher levels of sanitary or phytosanitary protection than would be achieved by measures based on the relevant international standards, guidelines or recommendations'. This facility is established by, and is circumscribed by,

---

[4] Appellate Body Report, *EC – Hormones*, at para 164.   [5] Ibid at para 171.
[6] Appellate Body Report, *EC – Sardines*, at para 258.

Article 3(3) SPS Agreement. In order for a WTO Member to sustain a non-conforming measure, there must either be (1) a scientific justification for doing so or (2) the Member must be seeking a higher 'appropriate level of protection' in accordance with the various provisions of Article 5 SPS Agreement. The non-conforming measure must be consistent with all other provisions of the SPS Agreement as well.

Article 3(2) SPS Agreement provides that SPS measures that 'conform to international standards, guidelines or recommendations shall be deemed to be necessary to protect human, animal or plant life or health' (language that reflects Article XX(b) GATT 1994) and are 'presumed to be consistent' with both the SPS Agreement and the GATT 1994. A national SPS measure that is 'based on' an international standard but does not 'conform to' the international standard so as to satisfy the express requirement of Article 3(2) does not enjoy the presumption of accordance with WTO norms provided in Article 2(4).

As a practical matter, Article 3(2) represents a bargain among the WTO membership not to use WTO norms (sourced in the GATT 1994, the SPS Agreement, or elsewhere) to attack national measures that implement international standards. Such national SPS measures enjoy substantial immunity from challenge before WTO panels and the Appellate Body.

C.   Risk Assessment and Scientific Basis

The SPS Agreement was intended to place disputes about the appropriateness of SPS measures on a firm scientific basis. Science has always been involved in disputes over health measures within the GATT system, though its role was often hidden. Challenges to the necessity of a health measure under Article XX(b) GATT 1994 always involved explicit or implicit scientific evaluation. Science is involved both in identifying the relevant health risk and then assessing a particular health measure's effectiveness (absolute and relative) in addressing that risk.

Resort to science, even in the pre-WTO era, raised some evident difficulties. The SPS Agreement was negotiated in the shadow of the long-standing dispute over growth hormones in beef production. The European production and import bans were maintained despite assertions from the US beef industry that there was no scientific basis for concern. One could easily imagine well-credentialed scientists on both sides of the debate—with an uncomfortable dispute settlement panel charged to decide which scientists were correct. The SPS Agreement was intended to place SPS disputes on a firm scientific basis—and to qualify what counts as science for resolving disputes involving SPS measures. Article 2.2 requires that SPS measures be 'based on scientific principles and ... not maintained without sufficient scientific evidence ...'.

One of the grounds provided by Article 3(3) for choosing not to follow an international standard is the presence of a 'scientific justification'. A note clarifies that a Member's determination that the international standard is not sufficient to meet its appropriate level of SPS protection must be based on 'an examination and evaluation of available scientific information in conformity with the relevant provisions of [the SPS] Agreement'.

The requirement for a scientific basis is more emphatic when a Member departs from an international standard or where there is no international standard. In these cases, Article 5.2 requires that Members conduct a risk assessment that takes 'into account available scientific evidence'.

Risk assessment is given two definitions in Annex A to the SPS Agreement. The first definition concerns disease or pest risks: 'The evaluation of the likelihood of entry, establishment or spread of a pest or diseases within the territory of an importing Member according to the sanitary or phytosanitary measures which must be applied, and of the associated potential biological and economic consequences...'. The second definition concerns food risks: '[T]he evaluation of the potential for adverse effects on human or animal health arising from the presence of additives, contaminants, toxins or disease-causing organisms in food, beverages or feedstuffs.' While the SPS Agreement invokes the term 'risk assessment' throughout, it should be remembered that the term does not refer to risk assessment generally (whatever that term might mean within the scientific community), but rather it *always* refers to one of the two specific definitions, depending on the character of the SPS measure under consideration. Thus, the dispute over the adequacy of risk assessment in *Australia – Salmon*, a disease or pest case, involves the first definition; the dispute over the adequacy of risk assessment in *EC – Hormones*, a food case, involves the second definition. Use of a single term in the SPS Agreement to invoke two distinct definitions is somewhat clumsy—and care might well be taken in transferring teaching about risk assessment from foods cases to disease/pest cases and *vice versa*.

A series of decisions of the Appellate Body have clarified what the requirement of a risk assessment entails. In *Australia – Salmon*, the Appellate Body set out three aspects for a risk assessment in a disease case. The risk assessment must: (1) identify the disease as well as its potential biological and economic consequences; (2) evaluate the likelihood of entry, establishment, or spread of the disease and associated consequences; and (3) evaluate the likelihood of entry, establishment, or spread of the disease given the implementation of the SPS measure. The Appellate Body held that a risk assessment is not a mere identification of the possibility of the entry of the disease; rather, it must assess the 'probability' of entry, establishment, or spread of the disease (though these evaluations need not be quantitative).[7]

In *EC – Hormones*, the Appellate Body made clear that in food cases (which involve the second definition of risk assessment) the ambient inability to exclude with absolute certainty any risk with respect to a food product is not a risk that may be assessed under Article 5.1.[8] Further, in *EC – Hormones*, the Appellate Body found that the Member imposing the SPS measure need not carry out the risk assessment

---

[7] Appellate Body Report, *Australia – Salmon*, at paras 121–24.
[8] Appellate Body Report, *EC – Hormones*, at para 186.

itself. With respect to the stock of SPS measures in existence at the time of the entry into force of the SPS Agreement, the Appellate Body held that these too were covered by Article 5.1's mandate for risk assessment.[9] However, the inclusion of the phrase 'as appropriate to the circumstances' in Article 5.1 may operate to prevent wholesale challenge to pre-WTO era SPS measures that continue in effect. Together, these holdings are consistent with the Appellate Body's declaration that 'no textual basis exists in Article 5 for a "minimum procedural requirement"'.[10]

Risk management is not a concept used in the SPS Agreement. Rather the national political process is viewed as setting an appropriate level of protection to be achieved and then selecting an SPS measure that achieves that level. Appropriate level of protection is defined in Annex A as '[t]he level of protection deemed appropriate by the Member establishing a sanitary or phytosanitary measure to protect human, animal or plant life of health within its territory'. While science may identify which levels of protection are achievable, the choice of such levels is a political act over which Members enjoy considerable autonomy.

D. Precautionary Principle

In *EC – Hormones*, the EC argued that the ban on the use of growth hormones in beef production could be justified by the precautionary principle, which it argued was a general principle of international law. The Appellate Body rejected this argument, and expressed doubt about the status of the precautionary principle as a general principle.[11] To the degree that the precautionary principle operates, at least with respect to SPS measures, it is through the provisions of, and limitations contained in, Article 5.7 Agreement, which provides that:

In cases where relevant scientific evidence is insufficient, a Member may provisionally adopt sanitary or phytosanitary measures on the basis of available pertinent information, including that from relevant international organizations as well as from [SPS] measures applied by other Members. In such circumstances, Members shall seek to obtain the additional information necessary for a more objective assessment of risk and review the [SPS] measure accordingly within a reasonable period of time.

In *Japan – Apples*, the Appellate Body emphasized that the facility for adopting SPS measures in instances of scientific uncertainty is provisional and is subject to the requirement that the Member resorting to the facility 'seek to obtain' additional information within a reasonable period of time.[12] Following this reasoning, Article 5.7 might not be available to justify the adoption of SPS measures where the missing 'information' is beyond reach (as in cases involving complex systems).

---

[9] Ibid at paras 188–91.   [10] Ibid at para 189.   [11] Ibid at paras 121–24.
[12] Appellate Body Report, *Japan – Apples*, at para 176.

E. Appropriate Levels of Protection

1. *Less Trade-Restrictive Means*

The concept of appropriate level of protection is utilized in a variety of tests under the SPS Agreement. The SPS Agreement embraces the 'necessity' test developed by panels and the Appellate Body under Article XX(b) GATT 1994 and improves on it by making clear that any alternate measure must meet the Member's appropriate level of protection. Article 5.6 SPS Agreement provides that:

[W]hen establishing or maintaining [SPS measures] to achieve the appropriate level of sanitary or phytosanitary protection, Members shall ensure that such measures are not more trade-restrictive than required to achieve their appropriate level of sanitary or phytosanitary protection, taking into account technical and economic feasibility.

2. *Consistency*

Article 5.5 SPS Agreement introduces a consistency test with respect to the health objectives pursued by a Member, as expressed by the concept of appropriate level of protection. It calls on WTO Members to 'avoid arbitrary or unjustifiable distinctions in the levels it considers to be appropriate in different situations, if such distinctions result in discrimination or a disguised restriction on international trade...'. A Member may not set a high level of protection with respect to a product it imports, while setting a lower level with respect to products it produces.

Australia – Salmon demonstrated that Article 5.5 could form the basis of a successful challenge to an SPS measure. Australia imposed a prohibition on fresh salmon imports from Canada in order to prevent the entry of particular pathogens that might infect Australia's salmon farms. Canada persuaded the Panel and the Appellate Body that Australia had taken inconsistent action 'in different situations', in that Australia tolerated zero risk of infection from imported salmon (as reflected in the import ban) but tolerated greater risk by permitting the importation of other fish that bore these same pathogens. Australia's inconsistency—and the fact that the object of the ban was competitive Canadian salmon—gave rise to the finding of an Article 5.5 violation.[13]

3. *Equivalency*

The SPS Agreement's equivalency norm also makes use of the concept of appropriate levels of protection. Article 4.1 provides that:

Members shall accept the [SPS] measures of other Members as equivalent, even if these measures differ from their own or from those used by other Members trading in the same product, if the exporting Member objectively demonstrates to the importing Member that

---

[13] Appellate Body Report, *Australia – Salmon*, at para 178.

its measures achieve the importing Member's appropriate level of sanitary or phytosanitary protection...

So far, there have been no disputes involving Article 4.1. An eventual dispute would involve an exporting Member establishing the appropriate level of protection of the Member resisting a finding of equivalence in order to further establish that that exporting Member's relevant SPS measures achieves that level of protection.

F.   Other Features of the SPS Agreement

In *EC – Biotech Products*, the US, Canada, and Argentina challenged the EC's failure to process marketing approval applications for certain genetically modified organisms (GMO) products during a 46-month period, asserting that Europe had been imposing a *de facto* moratorium on GMO approvals. The complainants challenged a variety of EC Member States' measures limiting GMOs as well. The Panel found the EC practice to constitute a moratorium.[14] This in turn was deemed to be inconsistent with the SPS Agreement's procedural rules (found in Article 8 and Annex C), which require avoidance of undue delay.[15] By treating the moratorium as a procedural lapse—and not as a substantive SPS measure—the Panel avoided most of the complainants' substantive objections under the SPS Agreement. By the time of the Panel's decision, it appeared that the EC moratorium had been lifted, and neither the complainants nor the EC appealed these findings. Several national measures were struck down, however, due to the absence of a risk assessment called for by Article 5.1.

III.   Health Measures and GATT 1994 Disciplines

A.   Health Measures and Article III:4 GATT 1994

National governments, in pursuit of public health policies, often seek to limit or exclude harmful products from their marketplaces. To the extent that such internal restrictions apply evenhandedly to both imported and locally-produced products, they do not raise significant international trade concerns. Where health measures are found to favour domestic products, however, they violate the national treatment

---

[14]   Panel Report, *EC – Biotech Products*, at para 7.1272.   [15]   Ibid at para 8.6.

principle in Article III:4 GATT 1994.[16] This provision applies to 'all laws, regulations and requirements affecting their internal sale, offering for sale, purchase, transportation, distribution, or use' of imported products within a WTO Member's territory. It mandates that imported products 'be accorded treatment no less favourable than that accorded to like products of national origin...'. As a non-discrimination principle, Article III:4 compares the treatment accorded to imported products and 'like products of national origin'; if there are no 'like products of national origin' there can be no actionable discrimination. The favourable treatment of 'products of national origin' is simply not relevant, for purposes of Article III:4, if those products are not 'like' the disfavoured imported products.

Absent discrimination between domestic and imported goods, States enjoy a general free hand in taking internal measures protective of health. Moreover, they are generally free to set health goals as high as they wish. International trade law will not force a State to admit harmful goods that are at odds with its health policies. Moreover, States may permit harmful goods (such as cigarettes) to be sold within their respective territories, yet may sharply limit the commercial freedom of traders in order to discourage consumption of such goods. Article III GATT 1994 is not concerned with the appropriateness of the restrictions as such; rather its concerns are with restrictions that alter or affect the competitive relationship between domestic goods, on the one hand, and imported goods, on the other hand. Article III is engaged whenever a national internal measure disproportionately affects the sale of an imported good.

EC – Asbestos illustrates the potential intrusive reach of Article III into national health regulation. It likewise represents an unusually forceful declaration of a WTO Member's ability to exclude a harmful product (imported from another WTO Member) due to its adverse health effects. This dispute involved a Canadian challenge to French laws, which banned the sale of asbestos fibres and products containing asbestos fibres. France also imposed an import prohibition on asbestos in connection with the internal prohibition on sale. The Appellate Body reversed the Panel's finding that prohibited asbestos was 'like' other domestically produced fibres that were available on the French market for purposes of Article III:4.[17] The essential carcinogenic characteristic of asbestos, which the competitive domestic products do not share, functioned to foreclose the finding of 'like products' that is a legal predicate to a successful non-discrimination claim under Article III:4. Following *EC – Asbestos*, a WTO Member may take measures against a product based on that product's associated health risks, even when other substitute products remain on the market.

In the view of the Panel in *EC – Asbestos*, to consider health risks in the Article III 'like products' inquiry would circumvent the 'necessity' requirement found in

---

[16] See also chapter 6 of this Handbook.
[17] Appellate Body Report, *EC – Asbestos*, at para 126.

Article XX(b).[18] Consideration of the carcinogenicity of asbestos would, the Panel stated, make the other *Border Tax Adjustments* likeness criteria 'totally redundant because [consideration of health risk] would become decisive when assessing the likeness of products in every case in which it was invoked, irrespective of the other criteria applied'.[19] The Panel concluded that 'it is not appropriate to apply the "risk" criterion' to resolve the like products determination.[20]

In a surprising move, the Appellate Body rejected the Panel's approach in *EC – Asbestos*, and insisted that consideration of asbestos' carcinogenic properties was not only permissible for purposes of Article III:4 like products analysis, but unavoidable.[21] In short, the Appellate Body in *EC – Asbestos* found that Canada had failed to establish that asbestos and other fibre products were like products, despite other physical similarities and similar end-uses.[22] The dominant distinguishing characteristic, preventing a finding of like products, was the unique (and extreme) risk posed by asbestos to human health.

The Appellate Body chided the Panel for not conducting a careful assessment of likeness using each of the *Border Tax Adjustments* criteria[23]—yet, as the Panel correctly anticipated, consideration of the health effects of asbestos so dominates the Appellate Body's analysis that its call to consider '*each* of those four criteria' seems like empty formalism.[24] As a practical matter, the Appellate Body's application of the *Border Tax Adjustments* factors could easily have ended after consideration of the first criterion alone: the physical properties of asbestos, on the one hand, and the other fibres, on the other hand. It is precisely the particular physical property of asbestos that leads to its carcinogenicity, as the Appellate Body observed.[25]

EC – Asbestos demonstrates that a WTO Member has two lines of defense to an Article III:4 GATT 1994 challenge: first, as to the finding of 'likeness' between a prohibited product and freely-traded domestic products due to the presence of a distinguishing health risk; and second, through the operation of the Article XX(b) health exception and the SPS Agreement.

Note the asymmetry with respect to Article XI GATT 1994 (prohibition on quantitative restrictions) challenges. Many health measures are pure import restrictions. These measures undoubtedly violate Article XI—yet are generally excepted under Article XX(b) GATT 1994 and the SPS Agreement. There is no 'first line' of defense here—the likeness of the prohibited product to freely traded domestic products does not enter into an Article XI analysis. This asymmetry may be unproblematic in many cases, given the robust protective effect of Article XX(b).

There is often controversy, as was the case in *EC – Asbestos*, as to whether an import restriction (when accompanied by domestic restrictions) is an internal measure

---

[18] Panel Report, *EC – Asbestos*, at para 8.130.   [19] Ibid at para 8.131.
[20] Ibid. at para 8.132.   [21] Appellate Body Report, *EC – Asbestos*, at para 184.
[22] Ibid. at para 141.   [23] Ibid. at para 109.
[24] Panel Report, *EC – Asbestos*, at paras 8.131–132.
[25] Appellate Body Report, *EC – Asbestos*, at para 114.

governed by Article III:4 or a pure import restriction prohibited by Article XI.[26] Had the Panel and the Appellate Body in *EC – Asbestos* (1) considered the French import ban in isolation from the French domestic prohibitions on manufacture and sale of asbestos and asbestos products; (2) proceeded to conduct an Article XI analysis (instead of an Article III:4 analysis); and (3) concluded there was an Article XI violation, the import prohibition would likely still have been upheld. Both the Panel and the Appellate Body agreed as to the availability of Article XX GATT 1994 to provide an exception in *EC – Asbestos*.

B.   Health Measures and Article XI GATT 1994

Pure import restrictions are analysed under Article XI GATT 1994. Health-motivated import restrictions are often discriminatory. It is not uncommon for a WTO Member to impose import restrictions on products originating in the territory of a particular WTO Member when there is an identifiable health risk associated with that territory. In these scenarios, it is not the risk of the generic product that triggers regulation; rather it is the incremental risk that is peculiar to a particular territory of origin. Many WTO Members imposed bans on the importation of beef from Europe during the 'mad cow' crisis, while permitting the sale of domestic beef. These bans were import restrictions and did violate Article XI GATT 1994—they were 'saved,' however, by the operation of the general exception for measures 'necessary to protect human, animal or plant life or health' found under Article XX(b) GATT 1994, as well as by operation of the SPS Agreement.

The regulatory treatment of 'like' domestic products is simply not relevant to finding a national health measure to be a prohibited import restriction under Article XI GATT 1994. It may, however, be relevant in determining whether a health measure passes the various tests contained in the chapeau to Article XX, discussed below.

There may or may not be 'like' domestic products present in instances of a health-motivated import ban. Where there is no 'like' domestic product, however, there should be some inquiry as to whether the absence is a 'natural' condition or rather a regulatory artifact. If the absence of a 'like' domestic product is 'natural' (tobacco cannot be grown in many WTO Members), the application of Article XI is appropriate; this is an instance of a stand-alone import restriction. If the absence of a 'like' domestic product is due to complementary internal prohibitions (as was the case in *EC – Asbestos*), the import restriction is properly analysed as ancillary to what is predominantly an internal measure and under Article III:4.

This result changes, however, where there is a striking difference in treatment between domestic and imported products. In these cases, the independent nature

---

[26] Panel Report, *EC – Asbestos*, at paras 8.86–99.

of an import restriction re-emerges and classification under Article XI is proper. The dispute in *Thailand – Cigarettes* provides a stark example. Thailand effectively prohibited the importation of cigarettes; formally, cigarette imports were controlled by a system of import licenses, but no licenses had been granted during the ten years preceding the dispute. During this period, Thailand continued to permit the manufacture and sale of domestic cigarettes. The GATT Panel analysed the US' complaint under Article XI GATT 1947, as a pure import restriction, without significant consideration of the restrictions on domestic cigarettes.[27] The finding of an Article XI violation in *Thailand–Cigarettes* appears fairly automatic. Mere classification of a measure as an import restriction covered by Article XI is sufficient to constitute a violation of Article XI.

Many instances of import restrictions are simply not controversial; the presence of a health risk is frequently acknowledged by the exporting WTO Member. More difficult situations arise where a certain quantum of health risk is acknowledged, but the import restriction is asserted to be disproportionate in scope or duration. Health-motivated restrictions, once in place, have a tendency to endure; and controversy often develops over the point at which an admitted risk should be deemed to have passed.

IV. JUSTIFYING NATIONAL HEALTH MEASURES UNDER ARTICLE XX GATT 1994

A. Introduction

Many national health measures are inconsistent with the prohibitions on discriminatory internal measures (found in Article III) or import restrictions (found in Article XI) in the GATT 1994. Were insistence on compliance with these norms unyielding, resulting passions surrounding the disablement of national health policy instruments might well have undone the GATT 1947. Yet from its initial 'provisional application' in 1947, the GATT 1947 has recognized a strong exception for health measures. Within Article XX, there is a specific category of measures 'necessary to protect human, animal or plant life or health'. To qualify for the 'health exception,' a measure must be shown to satisfy the Article XX(b) category description: it must be

---

[27] GATT Panel Report, *Thailand – Cigarettes*, at paras 68–71.

found to be 'necessary to protect human, animal or plant life or health'. Moreover, as is the case for all measures seeking justification under Article XX GATT 1994, the application of the measure must satisfy the demands of the Article XX chapeau.

B. Identification of Qualifying Measures Under Article XX(b) GATT 1994

1. *Measures Protecting Human, Animal or Plant Health or Life*

The determination of whether a particular measure is covered by Article XX(b) is a unitary inquiry. That said, panels typically approach the analysis in two steps. The first step examines whether the measures 'protects' human, animal, or plant health or life. A measure that does not contribute to the pursuit of a health objective cannot be exempted by Article XX(b). To some degree, the requirement that a measure contribute to a health goal insists on a rational relationship between the measure's means and that end. Specious resort to Article XX(b) can be rejected at this stage. Most controversial health measures are conceded to 'protect' human, animal, or plant health or life to some degree; the far more difficult test is found in the second step of the analysis: the inquiry into whether the health measure is 'necessary'.

2. *Measures 'Necessary' to Protect Health*

The most contentious determination under Article XX(b) is finding whether a health measure is 'necessary'. The 1990 *Thailand – Cigarettes* case was the first GATT report to examine the meaning of 'necessary' under Article XX(b). In so doing, it borrowed much of the analysis developed by the Panel in *US – Section 337* of the term 'necessary' found in Article XX(d) GATT 1947 (referring to measures 'necessary to secure compliance with laws or regulations which are not inconsistent' with the provisions of the GATT).[28] The *US –Section 337* Panel had found that:

[a contracting party] cannot justify a measure inconsistent with other GATT provisions as 'necessary' in terms of Article XX(d) if an alternative measure which it could reasonably be expected to employ and which is not inconsistent with other GATT provisions is available to it. By the same token, in cases where a measure consistent with other GATT provisions is not reasonably available, a [contracting party] is bound to use, among the measures reasonably available to it, that which entails the least degree of inconsistency with other GATT provisions.[29]

In adopting the analysis of the term 'necessary' developed in *US – Section 337*, the Panel observed that it 'could see no reason why under Article XX the meaning of the

---

[28] GATT Panel Report, *Thailand – Cigarettes*, at para 74.
[29] GATT Panel Report, *US – Section 337*, at para 5.26.

term 'necessary' under paragraph (d) should not be the same as in paragraph (b)'.[30] Perhaps the Panel can be faulted for lack of imagination. Later, the Appellate Body in *Japan – Alcoholic Beverages II* did not hesitate to observe that the term 'like products' has different meaning in the various contexts in which it appears throughout the WTO agreements.[31] The Panel's observation in *Thailand – Cigarettes* that it saw 'no reason' for according context-specific meanings to 'necessary' seems simple-minded.[32] After all, the exception in Article XX(d) is coupled to an underlying requirement that the main measure with which enforcement is 'necessary to secure compliance' be GATT-consistent; there is no comparable architecture in Article XX(b).

The 'necessity' requirement in Article XX(d) relates to the enforcement of GATT-consistent measures; it is inherently an artificial necessity. In *Thailand – Cigarettes*, the 'necessity' requirement in Article XX(b) was applied to the achievement of Thailand's 'health policy objectives'. As these objectives are set by Thailand in exercising its sovereign discretion, these too may be described as regulatory artifacts. This analysis introduced a tension that later found expression in the SPS Agreement, according to which WTO Members may freely establish their 'health policy objectives', but their health measures may be challenged with respect to their effective contribution to the achievement of those objectives. The interpretation of the term 'necessary' is the crucible of this inquiry.

Of course, what is remarkable about the report in *Thailand – Cigarettes* was its lack of concern with the general health risk posed by cigarettes; Thailand conceded that all cigarettes pose serious risks to health. In seeking to justify its import ban (which was found by the GATT Panel to violate Article XI), Thailand argued that imported cigarettes presented a heightened risk to human health that was not present in its domestic cigarettes. It was not an Article III:4 case, but rather an Article XI case, so there was no consideration of the favourable treatment accorded to the domestic like product. Consideration of domestic cigarettes became relevant, however, at the Article XX(b) stage, given the need to justify discriminatory treatment as 'necessary' by seeking to establish compelling product distinctions.

Thailand's contention in *Thailand – Cigarettes* was that permitting the importation would pose incrementally greater damage to Thai public health (by leading to increased smoking), and therefore the import ban was 'necessary'. The presence of an incremental health risk associated with imported cigarettes (beyond the risk already tolerated with respect to domestic-origin cigarettes) was a technical finding beyond the competence of the Panel. With the consent of the parties to the dispute, the Panel turned to the WHO to provide it with an expert evaluation of the risk associated with imported cigarettes.[33] While the WHO was not able to identify incremental risks associated with additives used in imported cigarettes,

[30] GATT Panel Report, *Thailand – Cigarettes*, at para 74.
[31] Appellate Body Report, *Japan – Alcoholic Beverages II*, at 114.
[32] GATT Panel Report, *Thailand – Cigarettes*, at para 74.
[33] Ibid. at paras 50–6.

it did find that countries that opened their domestic markets to cigarette imports experienced sharp increases in smoking. The Panel concluded that the import ban was not in fact 'necessary to protect human...health or life' as required by Article XX(b).[34]

In pursuing a 'less trade restrictive alternative' analysis, the Panel suggested that a combination of warning labels (including disclosure of additives) and an advertising ban were reasonably available alternatives to the import restrictions, and as such the import ban could not be held 'necessary'.[35] The Panel failed to note that these alternatives, though perhaps 'reasonably available', were likely less effective than the import ban in containing the increase in (or reducing) smoking. Consideration of alternative measures can only be appropriate if the alternatives are equally effective; an inconsistent health measure should not fail to be 'necessary' due to the presence of less-effective measures. This analytic imprecision is (somewhat) corrected in the explicit rules of the SPS Agreement, where alternatives measures must meet the WTO Member's 'appropriate level of protection' (a metric of effectiveness) to demonstrate a challenged measure's inconsistency.

In the early WTO report in *US – Gasoline*, the Panel found that the non-degradation rules were not 'necessary' to protect human, animal, or plant life or health, and thus did not qualify for the Article XX(b) exception. The Panel followed the analysis of GATT reports in *US – Section 337* and *Thailand – Cigarettes*, and inquired whether there was 'an alternative measure which [the United States] could reasonably be expected to employ and which is not inconsistent with other GATT provisions available to it'.[36] The Panel concluded that such alternatives were available, and as such the US measures were not 'necessary' as required by Article XX(b).[37] This finding was not appealed.[38]

EC – Asbestos was the first WTO report in which the Appellate Body explored the Article XX(b) exception. The Panel in *EC – Asbestos* had found that the exception applied, after having first found the French measure in violation of Article III:4.[39] The Appellate Body rejected the Panel's finding of an Article III:4 violation; the consistency of the French measure was established without resort to Article XX(b).[40] Notwithstanding an apparent violation of principles of judicial economy, the Appellate Body also reviewed the Panel's analysis under Article XX(b). It endorsed much of the reasoning and deferred to the Panel's assessment of the facts; it concluded that Article XX applied.[41]

Importantly, the Appellate Body articulated what it perceived to be France's health objective, that is, the elimination of all risks associated with exposure to asbestos. It is not clear whether the Appellate Body had any grounds for this finding beyond its

---

[34] Ibid at para 81.   [35] Ibid at paras 78–79.
[36] Panel Report, *US – Gasoline*, at para 6.24.   [37] Ibid at para 6.29.
[38] Ibid at paras 6.20–29.   [39] Panel Report, *EC – Asbestos*, at paras 8.158, 8.241.
[40] Appellate Body Report, *EC – Asbestos*, at para 148.   [41] Ibid at para 175.

consideration of the measure itself, which was quite absolute in its intolerance for the presence of asbestos in France, be it domestic-origin or imported. The Appellate Body seemingly failed to consider that the measure (in its effects on both domestic-origin asbestos and imports) might be excessive and that a less extreme measure (tolerance of some asbestos under some conditions) might be a less-trade restrictive measure that would still achieve France's 'appropriate level of protection'. The notion of 'appropriate level of protection' is found in the SPS Agreement. Although *EC – Asbestos* did not concern an SPS measure, the Appellate Body's reasoning appears informed by the SPS Agreement.

In *Brazil – Retreaded Tyres*, the EC challenged Brazil's import ban on retreaded tyres. Brazil invoked Article XX(b) to justify its import restrictions on the ground that reducing imported retreaded tyres would induce the Brazilian industry to buy used tyres in Brazil and thus effectively recycle them. The reduction in waste used tyres would lead to public health benefits, such as reducing mosquito-borne diseases. The Panel found that the import measure was provisionally justified under Article XX(b), but was applied in a manner that was inconsistent with the chapeau of Article XX.[42] In response to an adverse MERCOSUR ruling, Brazil had also exempted retreaded tyres from the MERCOSUR-area from its import prohibition. The MERCOSUR carve-out contributed to the ultimate finding of 'arbitrary or unjustifiable discrimination' that was fatal under the chapeau. But it also opened a line of attack for the EC on Brazil's 'necessary' assertion under Article XX(b). The EC and Brazil both appealed the Panel's findings on this point. The Appellate Body upheld the Panel's finding that the import restriction was indeed 'necessary to protect human…health'.[43] The Appellate Body repeated its reasoning in *Korea – Various Measures on Beef*, and found that the meaning of 'necessary' 'is not limited to that which is "indispensable"'.[44] There are several implications of the Appellate Body's interpretation of 'necessary' in *Brazil – Retreaded Tyres*. First, it held that Brazil may freely determine what its level of protection should be. This has no direct textual support in Article XX(b), rather it is a norm clearly imported from the SPS and TBT Agreements. Second, it applied the two-part 'burden-of-proof' approach to the Article XX(b) necessity analysis, which was previously developed in *US – Gambling*. Under this approach, the responding Member must establish that its measure makes a material contribution to the stated objective; and the complaining Member may rebut the presumption of necessity by identifying reasonably available alternative measures that achieve the responding Member's objectives.[45]

If anything, the Appellate Body in *Brazil – Retreaded Tyres* softened the necessity requirement by permitting the Member invoking Article XX(b) to provisionally establish necessity by demonstrating that the challenged health measure makes a

---

[42] Panel Report, *Brazil – Retreaded Tyres*, at paras 7.350–57.
[43] Appellate Body Report, *Brazil – Retreaded Tyres*, at para 183.
[44] Ibid at para 150.
[45] Ibid at para 143, relying on Appellate Body Report, *US – Gambling*, at paras 306.

'material contribution to the achievement of its [health] objectives'.[46] The onus then falls on the complaining Member to nominate reasonable alternative measures that could achieve the responding Member's objectives. The EC had suggested various alternative measures. The Panel found these were either not reasonably available or did not achieve Brazil's health objectives. The Panel thus concluded that Article XX(b) was available, and this finding was confirmed by the Appellate Body.[47]

3. *Satisfying Article XX(b) GATT 1994 by Operation of the SPS Agreement*

A health measure that meets the requirements of the SPS Agreement is 'deemed' to satisfy the GATT 1994 generally, including the provisions of Article XX(b). A note to the Preamble to the SPS Agreement clarifies that references to Article XX(b) include the Article XX chapeau. Article 2(4) SPS Agreement provides that:

Sanitary or phytosanitary measures which conform to the relevant provisions of [the SPS] Agreement shall be presumed to be in accordance with the obligations of the [WTO] Members under the provisions of GATT 1994 which relate to the use of sanitary or phytosanitary measures, in particular the provisions of Article XX(b).

Thus, an SPS measure that is inconsistent with a GATT 1994 provision can be 'saved' either by (1) resort to Article XX(b) or by (2) compliance with the Agreement. An SPS measure that 'conforms' to the SPS Agreement will enjoy the effect of Article XX(b), even if it does not strictly meet the requirements of Article XX(b) or the terms contained in the chapeau.

Many health measures fall within the scope of the SPS Agreement. As such, these measures will be analysed first under the SPS Agreement. If the measure does not conform to the SPS Agreement, a panel may decide (in exercising judicial economy) not to make a supplementary finding of inconsistency with the GATT 1994, and much will depend on what claims have been made in a particular dispute. In cases involving SPS measures, formal resort to Article XX(b) may be infrequent. Only those health measures that are not SPS measures are likely to engage Article XX(b) in the future.

C. The Chapeau of Article XX GATT 1994 and Health Measures

The chapeau of Article XX GATT 1994 requires that any qualifying health measure not be 'applied in a manner which would constitute a means of arbitrary or unjustifiable discrimination between countries where the same conditions prevail, or a

---

[46] Ibid at para 151.   [47] Ibid at para 183.

disguised restriction on international trade . . . '. In *EC – Asbestos*, the Panel found that the French ban on asbestos satisfied the requirements of the chapeau; a finding that was not appealed.[48] In *Brazil – Retreaded Tyres*, the Appellate Body rejected much of the Panel's reasoning with respect to the chapeau but it, nonetheless, found Brazil's application of the measure to constitute an arbitrary or unjustifiable discrimination and hence to fail the demands of the chapeau.[49] This finding was due to rather open discrimination (of the MFN variety) against non-MERCOSUR WTO Members. As such, Brazil's import prohibition was found to be inconsistent, notwithstanding its provisional characterization as a measure 'necessary to protect human, animal or plant life or health'.

V. CONCLUSION

The entry into effect of the SPS Agreement has marked a significant change in the coexistence of national health measures with the global trading system. The SPS Agreement applies to certain but not all health measures. If the measures at issue can be defined as SPS measures, it applies to discriminatory and non-discriminatory measures. The SPS Agreement pushes regulatory convergence, by granting significant presumptions of correctness to the adoption of national measures that conform to international standards. It also permits WTO Members to enact higher standards subject to important procedural and substantive limitations. It equally creates a special role for scientific argument in WTO dispute settlement.

For those health measures that fall outside of the scope of the SPS Agreement, the GATT 1994 principles on non-discrimination and import restrictions continue to apply. In evaluating such measures, the Appellate Body has imported an explicit provision of the SPS Agreement into the GATT 1994, namely, the principle that WTO Members may set their own appropriate levels of health protection. It has also made clear that health risks matter for purposes of 'like product' analysis, significantly curtailing the utility of Article III:4 GATT 1994 to challenge health measures. Finally, by introducing the 'material contribution' standard, the Appellate Body seems to have somewhat relaxed the 'necessary' requirement of the exception in Article XX(b) GATT 1994.

---

[48] Panel Report, *EC – Asbestos*, at para 8.240.
[49] Appellate Body Report, *Brazil – Retreaded Tyres*, at paras 233–39, 252.

SELECTED BIBLIOGRAPHY

J Atik, 'Science and International Regulatory Convergence' 1996 *Northwestern Journal of International Law & Business* 17(2–3) 736

J Atik, 'The Weakest Link: Demonstrating the Inconsistency of "Appropriate Levels of Protection" in Australia-Salmon' 2004 *Risk Analysis* 24(2) 483

J Atik and DA Wirth, 'Science and International Trade: Third Generation Scholarship' 2003 *Boston College International and Comparative Law Review* 26(2) 171

E Baris and K McLeod, 'Globalization and International Trade in the Twenty-First Century: Opportunities for and Threats to the Health Sector in the South' 2000 *International Journal of Health Services* 30(1) 187

GA Bermann and PC Mavroidis (eds), *Trade and Human Health and Safety* (New York: Cambridge University Press, 2006)

MG Bloche, 'WTO Deference to National Health Policy: Toward an Interpretive Principle' 2002 *Journal of International Economic Law* 5(4) 825

MG Bloche and ER Jungman, 'Health Policy and the WTO' 2003 *Journal of Law, Medicine & Ethics* 31(4) 529

J Bohanes, 'Risk Regulation in WTO Law: A Procedure-based Approach to the Precautionary Principle' 2002 *Columbia Journal of Transnational Law* 40(2) 323

C Button, *The Power to Protect: Trade, Health and Uncertainty in the WTO* (Portland: Hart, 2004)

S Charnovitz, 'The Supervision of Health and Biosafety Regulation by World Trade Rules' 2000 *Tulane Environmental Law Journal* 13(2) 271

T Christoforou, 'Settlement of Science-Based Trade Disputes in the WTO: A Critical Review of Developing Case Law in the Face of Scientific Uncertainty' 2000 *New York University Environmental Law Journal* 8(3) 622

D Colyer, 'The Role of Science in Trade Agreements' 2006 *Estey Centre Journal of International Law and Trade Policy* 7(1) 84

CM Correa, 'Implementing National Public Health Policies in the Framework of WTO Agreements' 2000 *Journal of World Trade* 34(5) 89

N Covelli and V Hohots, 'The Health Regulation of Biotech Foods under the WTO Agreements' 2003 *Journal of International Economic Law* 6(4) 773

AT Guzman, 'Food Fears: Health and Safety at the WTO' 2004 *Virginia Journal of International Law* 45(1) 1

C Hilson, 'Beyond Rationality? Judicial Review and Public Concern in the EU and the WTO' 2005 *Northern Ireland Legal Quarterly* 5(3) 320

RL Howse, 'Democracy, Science, and Free Trade: Risk Regulation on Trial at the World Trade Organization' 2000 *Michigan Law Review* 98(7) 2329

RL Howse, 'The WHO/WTO Study on Trade and Public Health: A Critical Assessment' 2004 *Risk Analysis* 24(2) 501

RE Hudec, 'Science and "Post-Discriminatory" WTO Law' 2003 *Boston College International and Comparative Law Review* 26(2) 185

LA Kogan, 'The Precautionary Principle and WTO Law: Divergent Views Toward the Role of Science in Assessing and Managing Risk' 2004 *Seton Hall Journal of Diplomacy and International Relations* 5(1) 77

R Labonte and M Sanger, 'Glossary on the World Trade Organization and Public Health' 2006 *Journal Epidemiology and Community Health* 60(9) 655

TH MacDonald, *Health, Trade, and Human Rights* (Seattle: Radcliffe Publishing, 2006)

G Mayeda, 'Developing Disharmony? The SPS and TBT Agreements and the Impact of Harmonization on Developing Country' 2004 *Journal of International Economic Law* 7(4) 737

TR McLean, 'International Law, Telemedicine & Health Insurance: China as a Case Study' 2006 *American Journal of Law and Medicine* 32(1) 7

ML Miller, 'NIS, WTO, SPS, WIR: Does the WTO Substantially Limit the Ability of Countries to Regulate Harmful Non-indigenous Species?' 2003 *Emory International Law Review* 17(3) 1059

J Pauwelyn, 'The WTO Agreement on Sanitary and Phytosanitary (SPS) Measures as Applied in the First Three SPS Disputes' 1999 *Journal of International Economic Law* 2(4) 641

J Peel, 'Science and Risk Assessment in International Environmental Law: Learning from the WTO SPS Experience' 2004 *American Society of International Law Proceedings* (98) 283

J Peel, 'A GMO by Any Other Name... Might be an SPS Risk! Implications of Expanding the Scope of the WTO Sanitary and Phytosanitary Measures Agreement' 2006 *European Journal of International Law* 17(5) 1009

JW Sapsin, TM Thompson, L Stone, and KE Deland, 'International Trade, Law, and Public Health Advocacy' 2003 *Journal of Law, Medicine & Ethics* 31(4) 546

J Sapsin, AM Kimball, and D Fidler, 'International Trade Agreements: Vehicle for Better Public Health?' 2005 *Journal of Law, Medicine & Ethics* 33(4) 111

J Scott, *The WTO Agreement on Sanitary and Phytosanitary Measures* (Oxford: Oxford University Press, 2007)

SK Sell, 'Trade Issues and HIV/AIDS' 2003 *Emory International Law Review* 17(2) 933

KC Shadlen, 'Patents and Pills, Power and Procedure: The North-South Politics of Public Health in the WTO' 2004 *Studies in Comparative International Development* 39(3) 76

ER Shaffer, 'Global Trade and Public Health' 2007 *Journal of Public Health Policy* 28(1) 141

ER Shaffer and JE Brenner, 'International Trade Agreements: Hazards to Health?' 2004 *International Journal of Health Services* 34(3) 467

D Victor, 'The Sanitary and Phytosanitary Agreement of the World Trade Organization: An Assessment After Five Years' 2000 *New York University Journal of International Law & Policy* 32(4) 865

JM Wagner, 'The WTO's Interpretation of the SPS Agreement has Undermined the Right of Governments to Establish Appropriate Levels of Protection Against Risk' 2000 *Law & Policy in International Business* 31(3) 855

VR Walker, 'Keeping the WTO from Becoming the "World Trans-science Organization": Scientific Uncertainty, Science Policy, and Fact-finding in the Growth Hormones Dispute' 1998 *Cornell International Law Journal* 31(2) 251

VR Walker, 'The Myth of Science as a "Neutral Arbiter" for Triggering Precautions' 2003 *Boston College International and Comparative Law Review* 26(2) 197

D Winickoff et al., 'Adjudicating the GM Food Wars: Science, Risk, and Democracy in World Trade Law' 2005 *Yale Journal of International Law* 30(1) 81

DA Wirth, 'The Role of Science in the Uruguay Round and NAFTA Trade Disciplines' 1994 *Cornell International Law Journal* 27(3) 817

DA Wirth, 'GATT – Technical Barriers to Trade Agreement – Asbestos Import Ban – National Treatment – Like Products–Health Measures – Private-party Submissions to WTO Dispute Settlement Bodies' 2002 *American Journal of International Law* 96(2) 435

CHAPTER 22

TRADE AND INVESTMENT

RODNEY NEUFELD[*]

[*] Any opinions contained herein belong to the author, not to the Government of Canada.

I. INTRODUCTION

RULES can be helpful, particularly when they apply generally. On the other hand, the selective creation, application, and enforcement of rules can lead to preferential treatment. In international investment law, there is little uniformity.

States promote investment rules in the interest of providing for stability, transparency, predictability, non-discrimination, and protection for their companies and individuals that invest abroad. The *quid pro quo* is that they offer the same standards for foreign investors wishing to invest in their State. Good investment rules make for a positive economic climate, which favours growth and jobs. This chapter does not address whether investment agreements actually achieve these goals. Rather, it proceeds from the starting point that a variety of international rules already regulate investment, while others continue to be negotiated. This has created a patchwork of bilateral and multilateral rules that apply in partial and piecemeal fashion throughout the world. Rather than creating a comprehensive international investment framework, the bilateral and regional rules result in preferential investment arrangements between certain States.

Rules on foreign investment are found in customary international law and in treaty law. Investment rules exist in thousands of bilateral investment treaties (BITs) as well as in a few multilateral treaties, including NAFTA Chapter 11 and the Energy Charter Treaty (ECT). Referring to these treaties generically as 'investment agreements', this chapter focuses on some of their common features, including their prohibition of discriminatory treatment, treatment below the minimum standard, and expropriation without compensation. While investment agreements also differ in many respects, the purpose of this chapter is to highlight some of their common ground for the purpose of comparing these agreements with the WTO's coverage of investment.

What is lacking is a universal approach to investment protection. The WTO exists as the only multilateral economic institution with near universal membership, yet it too has adopted a piecemeal approach to investment protection rules. Governmental measures are caught by WTO disciplines if they affect trade in goods or trade in services. In contrast, investment agreements have as their primary concern all governmental measures affecting investment.

A review of existing rules in the WTO and in investment agreements will show that the current patchwork of rules lacks uniformity. The provisions of investment agreements differ in many respects from WTO rules, both substantively and procedurally, with many investment agreements allowing for investor-state, in addition to state-to-state, dispute settlement.

While the number of investment agreements continues to grow, it is unclear what the future holds for investor protection at the multilateral level. The WTO may be the obvious forum for the creation of a multilateral framework. However, its current approach to investment will require a complete re-thinking if it truly aspires to cover the multi-faceted aspects of international business. The WTO will never be able to accomplish this if it continues to address investment as a secondary matter, ancillary to trade in goods or services. In the end, it must embrace rules that deal with investment as a primary matter.

II. BACKGROUND

In international law, the treaty that accords investor protection defines the meaning of 'investment'. Each treaty's coverage varies according to the intentions of the negotiators. A comparison of investment rules in the WTO with those commonly found in investment agreements, reveals a great divide in their substantive coverage, but it also shows that the way the drafters conceived of investment is different.

To 'invest' means to expend money, effort, or time into an undertaking with the intention of deriving a profit. However, 'foreign direct investment' (FDI) implies something more than the mere purchase of shares for the sake of the interest, dividends, or profits. Traditionally, States have distinguished FDI from other investment by setting a limit, usually somewhere between 10 per cent and 49 per cent, on foreign equity participation. This enables the State to vet and control investment over which a foreign domiciled person or corporation has potentially significant influence. Foreign investment not classified as FDI is known as portfolio investment.

FDI distinguishes itself from portfolio investment in that it 'consists of a transaction made by a foreigner in a host state which is intended to set up a long term relationship with a party in the host state'.[1] It is precisely this long-term relationship of dependency that differentiates FDI from other types of transactions and places the investor in a situation of vulnerability. 'The transference of assets and personnel outside frontiers of the home state, the presence of state or sovereign power in one of the parties and long duration are facets of the transaction which set them apart from other types of international business transactions'.[2] It is the vulnerability of foreign investors that has motivated States to conclude investment protection agreements as an attempt to mitigate part of the risk.

Investment agreements typically define investment very broadly, covering various forms of monetary commitments. For example, NAFTA covers all enterprises as well as their debt securities, equity securities, and loans received.[3] It also covers tangible and intangible property and interests arising from the commitment of capital or other resources. The 2004 US Model BIT seems to go further still by providing an

---

[1] M Sornorajah, *The Settlement of Foreign Investment Disputes* (The Hague: Kluwer, 2000), at 4.
[2] Ibid at 5.   [3] Art 1139 NAFTA.

open definition that includes bonds, debentures, loans, futures, options, derivatives, licenses, authorizations, and permits.[4] It is difficult to see how these commitments necessarily place the investor in a position of vulnerability. However, the Model US BIT goes on to specify that an 'investment agreement' is a written agreement that grants rights:

(a) with respect to natural resources that a national authority controls, such as for their exploration, extraction, refining, transportation, distribution, or sale;

(b) to supply services to the public on behalf of the Party, such as power generation or distribution, water treatment or distribution, or telecommunications; or

(c) to undertake infrastructure projects, such as the construction of roads, bridges, canals, dams, or pipelines, that are not for the exclusive or predominant use and benefit of the government.

The types of investments listed above are made on long-term bases, often in close cooperation with state officials as well as state enterprises, and occasionally require an important outlay of capital over a number of years before making any return. Their vulnerability explains why these investors, as opposed to mere portfolio investors, merit special protection.

In contrast to investment agreements, the primary concern of WTO rules is not to accord investor protection, but to reduce barriers to trade in goods and services. WTO agreements do not define investment. They are concerned only with investment measures that affect trade in goods and services.

III. WTO Rules Pertaining to Investment

A. GATT 1947

Arguably, the GATT 1947 was not meant to cover investment measures whatsoever. After all, this treaty, which started as the commercial policy chapter of the Havana Charter,[5] was solely concerned from its inception with goods. In contrast, the all-encompassing draft Havana Charter did contend, albeit in a very limited way, with investment. It contained best efforts provisions calling upon Members 'to

---

[4] Available at <http://www.ustr.gov/assets/Trade_Sectors/Investment/Model_BIT/asset_upload_file847_6897.pdf> (last visited 12 June 2008).

[5] *Final Act and Related Documents of the UN Conference on Trade and Employment, Havana* ('Havana Charter'), Cuba, 24 March 1948, UN Doc. ICITO/1/4 (1948).

provide reasonable opportunities for investments acceptable to them ... ' and 'to give due regard to the desirability of avoiding discrimination as between foreign investments'.[6] It would also have given the International Trade Organization (ITO) the option to 'promote the adoption of a general agreement or statement of principles regarding the conduct, practices and treatment of foreign investment'.[7]

The investment provisions of the draft Havana Charter died on paper, and the GATT 1947 was left as the sole surviving trade agreement.[8] The natural assumption may have been that the draft rules relating to investment perished along with the draft Havana Charter. Otherwise, why would the GATT Council have adopted a resolution in 1955 urging Contracting Parties to enter into negotiations directed to the conclusion of bilateral and multilateral treaties on investment?[9] Yet, twenty-five years later, within a completely altered climate, a GATT Panel brought a small degree of investor protection back to life when it decided *Canada – Foreign Investment Review Act (FIRA)*.

By the 1980s, the general mood towards foreign direct investment had begun to change. The traditional divide between capital exporting and capital importing countries was diminishing as the wave of expropriations that took place between 1945 and 1970 had come to an end.[10] For the most part, these expropriations were addressed through state-to-state and state-to-investor negotiations, culminating in compensation for the takings. A semblance of consensus between developing and developed countries was also evident in the UN General Assembly. The 1962 Resolution on Permanent Sovereignty over Natural Resources declared that '[f]oreign investment agreements freely entered into by or between sovereign States shall be observed in good faith'.[11] Within this changing climate, the US brought a complaint against Canada's Foreign Investment Review Act, arguing that it did not comply with the GATT 1947 on account of its local content, local manufacturing, and minimum export requirements.

The US asked the Panel to consider the GATT-consistency of Canada's administration of an act that encouraged foreign investment on the grounds that it would be of significant benefit to Canada. Benefits included increases in employment and exports, transfers of technology, and promotion of national industrial and economic policies. The Act did not require investors to purchase or manufacture locally made products, nor did it require them to promise to export a certain percentage of their goods. However, in administering the Act, Canadian authorities treated more favourably applications containing these types of undertakings. Once the application was

---

[6] Art 12(2) Havana Charter.   [7] Art 11.2(c) Havana Charter.

[8] See chapter 3 of this Handbook.

[9] *Resolution on Investment for Economic Development*, 4 March 1955, SR.9/42, available in G/91 (29 March 1955), at 15–16.

[10] See, generally, A Lowenfeld, *International Economic Law* (Oxford: Oxford University Press, 2002), at 405–06.

[11] UN General Assembly Resolution 1803, at para 8.

approved, the undertakings became legally enforceable. The GATT Panel ultimately concluded that the local content requirements were inconsistent with the national treatment obligation of Article III:4 GATT 1947. The export performance requirements, by contrast, were not inconsistent with GATT 1947 obligations. Despite the fact that the GATT 1947 makes no mention of investment, the *FIRA* decision confirmed that GATT 1947 obligations are applicable to government-imposed performance requirements in an investment context in so far as such requirements involve trade-distorting measures. At the same time, the Panel concluded that there is 'no provision in [GATT 1947] which forbids requirements to sell goods in foreign markets in preference to domestic markets', underscoring the limited scope of GATT 1947 obligations with respect to export requirements.[12]

B. TRIMS Agreement

In 1986, the Punta del Este Ministerial Declaration called for negotiations on investment to elaborate further provisions that may be necessary to avoid trade-restrictive and trade-distorting effects. In the end, the TRIMS Agreement proved to be less of an elaboration than a ratification of the status quo of very limited multilateral rules in manufacturing.[13] Despite the eagerness of the US and others to negotiate further coverage of investment, the TRIMS Agreement is a mere restatement of Articles III and XI GATT 1947 in a manner specific to trade-related investment measures.

Like all of the negotiating committees, the goal of the investment negotiations was to generate 'an agreement to which all nations would unanimously subscribe'.[14] However, unanimity proved difficult to achieve, resulting in the non-adoption of many of the measures originally proposed. The negotiations pitted developed countries, including the US, Canada, the EC, Japan, and Sweden against developing countries such as Argentina, Brazil, Colombia, Cuba, India, and Yugoslavia, who viewed restrictions on the use of trade-related investment measures as contrary to their development interests.[15] So, instead of elaborating on GATT 1947 provisions, the TRIMS Agreement merely confirms that Articles III:4 and XI apply to trade-related investment measures. This validated the long-standing interpretation of

---

[12] GATT Panel Report *Canada – Foreign Investment Review Act (FIRA)*, at para 5.18.

[13] T Brewer and S Young. 'Investment Issues at the WTO: The Architecture of Rules and the Settlement of Disputes' 1998 *Journal of International Economic Law* 1(3) 457, at 458.

[14] E Graham, 'Should there be Multilateral Rules on Foreign Direct Investment' in JH Dunning (ed), *Governments, Globalization, and International Business* (New York: Oxford University Press, 2001), at 486.

[15] D Price and B Christy III, 'Agreement on Trade Related Investment Measures (TRIMs): Limitations and Prospects for the Future' in TP Stewart (ed), *The World Trade Organization: The Multilateral Trade Framework for the 21st Century and U.S. Implementation Legislation* (Washington, DC: American Bar Association, 1996) 439, at 448.

the GATT held by some countries, including the USA, that trade-related investment measures that involved quantitative import measures were covered by GATT
rules on trade and that additional rules on trade-related investment measures pertaining specifically to discriminatory quantitative import restrictions were not
needed.[16]

Some argue that 'the fact that there is a separate text called an 'agreement' is a
paradox... [since] in essence, all the TRIMs agreement does is clarify the application of GATT articles'.[17] As the first WTO Panel confronted with a complaint under
the TRIMS Agreement stated:

> the TRIMs Agreement essentially interprets and clarifies the provisions of Article III (and
> also Article XI) where trade-related investment measures are concerned. Thus the TRIMs
> Agreement does not add to or subtract from those GATT obligations, although it clarifies
> that Article III:4 may cover investment-related matters.[18]

While it is true that the negotiated outcome amounts to little more than a codification
of the results of the *FIRA* decision,[19] at least the negotiations had the consequence
of endorsing the *FIRA* decision. The Contracting Parties could have undone the
FIRA decision and the Uruguay Round negotiations provided a timely opportunity
to do so. Unlike the results achieved, this would have constituted a step backwards
on investment protection within the WTO. The TRIMS Agreement is evidence that
States' comfort level with the decision, if not immediately apparent at the time, had
grown.

Had the *FIRA* decision not confirmed that GATT 1947 provisions apply in an
investment context, it remains unclear whether the Contracting Parties would have
been able to reach agreement on anything. The dispute settlement process appears to
have been instrumental in the development of investment protection in the WTO, a
trend also noticeable in the context of investor-state dispute settlement, as discussed
below.

The TRIMS Agreement provides an illustrative list of prohibited investment
measures. The list includes local content, sourcing, and some trade-balancing
requirements, as well as import and export restrictions. In *Indonesia – Autos*, the
Panel decided that the TRIMS Agreement covers local content requirements even if
they were not targeted at foreign investors, but were of general application to enterprises.[20] However, the list does not include measures that have an indirect effect on
trade such as technology transfer requirements.

---

[16] Brewer and Young, above fn 13, at 464.
[17] B Bora, 'Trade-Related Investment Measures' in B Hoekman, A Mattoo, and P English (eds),
Development, Trade and the WTO: A Handbook (Washington, DC: World Bank, 2002) at 171.
[18] Panel Report, *EC – Bananas III (Ecuador)*, at para 7.185.
[19] Graham, above fn 14, at 486; see also M Trebilcock and R Howse, *The Regulation of International
Trade*, 3rd edn (New York: Routledge, 2005), at 457.
[20] Panel Report, *Indonesia – Autos*, at para 14.73.

Although a WTO Panel has noted that the TRIMS Agreement is a 'fully fledged agreement in the WTO system' with 'an autonomous legal existence' from the GATT 1994,[21] WTO panels have largely avoided directly contending with TRIMS claims. In *India – Autos,* the Panel determined that the measure violated Article III GATT 1994, and then declined to consider the TRIMS allegations on the basis of judicial economy. In *Canada – Autos*, the Panel found that the measure did not violate Article III and therefore could not violate the TRIMS Agreement. It is difficult to reconcile this approach with the approach advocated on a number of occasions by the Appellate Body, which calls for the more specific agreement to be applied before turning to the more general agreement.[22] However, it is also difficult to disagree with the conclusion drawn by the Panel in *Canada-Autos* when it said that 'we doubt that examining the claims first under the TRIMs Agreement will enable us to resolve the dispute before us in a more efficient manner than examining these claims under Article III:4'.[23]

To date, few WTO panels have considered the TRIMS Agreement, and fewer have applied it. It is still noteworthy, however, that two of the three cases pertain to automobiles, an industry that has become truly global while at the same time relying on benefits provided by the State. The automobile manufacturers on whose behalf the cases were brought are major national enterprises, demonstrating that the TRIMS Agreement is an accessible tool for big business. It is less certain whether smaller investors also stand to benefit from the limited protections provided by it. Besides, as long as the TRIMS Agreement operates in the shadow of the GATT 1994, it will largely be ignored.

C. GATS

The limited success of the Uruguay Round negotiators to arrive at the TRIMS Agreement can be contrasted with the deal struck over services. The GATS has been hailed as a major ground-breaking achievement of the Uruguay Round,[24] and a significant step in establishing an international framework for trade in services, including FDI.[25] It seems that while the negotiators failed to reach agreement on all types of investment, they did agree to protections for services, including those provided through a commercial presence or through the presence of natural persons

---

[21] Ibid at paras 14.61–62.   [22] Appellate Body Report, *EC –Bananas III*, at para 204.

[23] Panel Report, *Canada – Autos,* at para 10.63.

[24] E Leroux, 'Eleven Years of GATS Case Law: What Have We Learned' 2007 *Journal of International Economic Law* 10(4) 749; Lowenfeld, above fn 10, at 120; P Sauvé, 'Assessing the General Agreement on Trade in Services: Half-Full or Half-Empty?' 1996 *Journal of World Trade* 29(1) 125. See also chapter 7 of this Handbook.

[25] K Kennedy, 'A WTO Agreement on Investment: A Solution in Search of a Problem?' 2003 *University of Pennsylvania Journal of International Economic Law* 24(1) 77, at 103.

of a WTO Member in the territory of another Member.[26] Commercial presence is often established through FDI, and an increasingly large percentage of FDI is thought to be in services activities. An analysis of the GATS, Annexes, and corresponding schedules shows their limited effect on liberalizing trade in services. This has led Hoekman to conclude that '[i]t is a landmark in terms of creating a multilateral disciplines [*sic*] in virgin territory; a failure in terms of generating liberalization'.[27]

With the important exception of the MFN-principle, GATS protections largely apply only where WTO Members have made specific commitments in their schedules. Market access and national treatment guarantees are conditional upon the commitments found in a Member's schedule. Commitments may apply generally across all modes of delivery, or they may be limited according to specific modes and sectors. Therefore, a Member may be open to the cross-border supply of services in a certain sector, such as telecommunications services, but not to its supply through a commercial presence. In theory, the GATS applies to all measures affecting trade in services.[28] In fact, its application is largely dictated by each Member's schedule.

The opt-out character of the GATS makes it difficult to discern the degree of services liberalization across the board. A study by Sauvé shows that virtually all commitments scheduled under the GATS represent a binding of the status quo rather than a rollback of existing restrictions to trade and investment in services.[29] Barriers to commercial presence are often not covered, because WTO Members have chosen not to include those sectors in their schedule. For those sectors where commitments have been made, restrictions on market access or national treatment for commercial presence are frequently listed as 'unbound' or exempt.[30] A study by Hardin and Holmes shows that Members have rarely made commitments for postal, educational, health, and distribution services. Where commitments have been made, such as for travel and tourism services, many restrictions exist: 'common restrictions on market access include limits on foreign ownership and authorizations based on whether certain economic, social and cultural criteria are met, particularly for sensitive sectors such as broadcasting'.[31] Moreover, a number of WTO Members list horizontal restrictions for the commercial presence mode of delivery, with investment proposals across all sectors to be notified and screened in accordance with their foreign investment legislation.

---

[26] Arts I:2 (c) and (d) GATS.

[27] B Hoekman, 'Tentative First Steps – An Assessment of the Uruguay Round Agreement on Services' 1995 *World Bank Policy Research Working Paper* No 1455, at <http://www.econ.worldbank.org/external/default/main?pagePK=64165259&theSitePK=469372&piPK=64165421&menuPK=64166093&entityID=000009265_3961019105408> (last visited 12 June 2008); see also chapter 7 of this Handbook.

[28] Art I:1 GATS.   [29] Sauvé, above fn 24, at 142.

[30] A Hardin and L Holmes, 'Service Trade and Foreign Direct Investment', *Industry Commission Staff Research Paper* (27 November 1997), at <http://www.pc.gov.au/ic/research/information/servtrad> (last visited 12 June 2008), at 250.

[31] Ibid. at 25–6.

WTO Members took the bulk of commitments with respect to commercial presence, however, rarely going beyond the regulatory status quo. The sensitivities surrounding the presence of natural persons translated into even fewer commitments being taken with respect to that mode. Where commitments exist, they likewise represent nothing more than the status quo. Restrictions on the temporary movement of persons can have an effect on FDI when, for example, an investor would like to hire experienced employees from its foreign offices. In the end, the structure of the GATS permits Members to continue to maintain significant barriers to trade in services, including with respect to foreign investment.

While the negotiators succeeded in reaching an agreement on services, they achieved only a minimal degree of liberalization, including in relation to FDI. The GATS was a promising first step to address highly sensitive areas of trade, but if not followed up by further liberalization, Members will not step far. Barriers to investment continue to be permitted where WTO Members have not scheduled commitments and where there is no violation of the MFN-principle. So, while the GATS could potentially have a significant effect on barriers to investment, in practice its impact continues to be limited.

IV. OECD

The failure to negotiate a comprehensive WTO agreement on investment has been mirrored by the failed efforts of the Organisation for Economic Co-operation and Development (OECD) to negotiate a multilateral agreement on investment (MAI). In 1995, negotiations were launched to arrive at a treaty made by the group of twenty-five OECD Members, but that would eventually be open to all States. By May 1997, negotiators had largely smoothed over any differences on the basic architecture, but cracks were surfacing on the draft agreement's would-be relationship with labour, environmental, and cultural policies.[32] Ultimately, the OECD's initiative died in 1998.

The failed OECD initiative has arguably had a negative effect on ongoing efforts at consensus-building in the WTO. Activists touting the interests of developing countries looked at the push by the OECD, often dubbed the 'club of rich nations', with a great deal of scepticism. They likely questioned why the OECD was so keen to negotiate an MAI, and why developing countries were not invited to participate in the negotiations. Any lack of transparency surrounding the negotiations and the

---

[32] Trebilcock and Howse, above fn 19, at 458.

anti-MAI clamour only added to the scepticism. The OECD's failed attempt at a multilateral framework marks an important step backwards for the creation of a global set of investment rules at a time when the historic divide between developing and developed interests had largely been bridged.

V. INVESTMENT AGREEMENTS

While global efforts towards a multilateral agreement on investment have failed to bear fruit, BITs have flourished.[33] At the same time, the provisions of the ECT and NAFTA Chapter 11 are being tested by a growing body of investor-state disputes and the workload at the International Centre for the Settlement of Investment Disputes (ICSID) has mushroomed.

NAFTA Chapter 11 and the standard BITs have much in common. They define 'investment' broadly and require State parties to accord to investors and investments protection against discrimination, whether on the basis of national treatment or MFN-treatment. They also typically oblige State parties to accord a minimum standard of treatment. They provide protection against the expropriation of an investment unless it was done for a public purpose and upon payment of full compensation.

The ECT provides similar guarantees, but is limited to investments in the energy sector. Its limitations by sector are contrasted by its broad regional coverage as it applies throughout most of Europe, east and west. However, Australia, Canada, the US, and Russia have not ratified the treaty.

The key substantive difference between investment treaties and WTO rules is in the breadth of their coverage. WTO rules ask as an initial matter whether a measure constitutes a trade-related investment measure or a measure affecting trade in services. Only if captured by any of these bodies of rules will a measure that affects an investment fall afoul of WTO obligations. For example, WTO rules prohibit discrimination on the basis of nationality, but only if such discrimination affects the investor's trade in goods or services. Given the limitations of the TRIMS Agreement and the GATS shown above, many measures affecting investment will escape the application of WTO rules, such as an export requirement or a tax on all foreign services providers where a WTO Member has opted out of GATS coverage of that particular service.

---

[33] UNCTAD estimated as of 2005 that 2,495 BITs have been concluded and 232 other agreements, many of which are bilateral, have investment provisions UNCTAD, *World Investment Report 2006: FDI from Developing and Transition Economies: Implications for Development* (New York: United Nations, 2006), at xix.

In contrast, investment treaties apply to all measures affecting investment, unless a reservation or exception applies. For example, NAFTA Chapter 11 prohibits less favourable treatment on the basis of the nationality of the investor without limitation as to whether it affects the investor's trade in goods or services. An analysis of the basic provisions will show that investment agreements provide a wider net to catch more types of measures than WTO agreements. In comparison with the WTO's service-specific coverage or coverage limited to the exchange of goods, the coverage provided by investment agreements may appear too extensive. However, it is important to keep in mind the basic rationale for investor protection, namely that foreign investors deserve special protection on account of their vulnerability.

A. Non-Discrimination

Investment agreements, like WTO agreements, typically contain two types of non-discrimination provisions: MFN and national treatment clauses. Occasionally, these two principles are lumped together in a single provision called non-discrimination or international standard of treatment. They have a long history in public international law. While they are rooted in the concepts of state sovereignty and reciprocity, they do not form part of customary international law.[34] Rather, these guarantees are offered by way of treaty.

The precise treaty language varies from provision to provision, but treaties typically require States to provide treatment no less favourable than the treatment accorded to national investors or investors from a third party. Articles 1102(1) and 1103(1) NAFTA provide:

1102(1) Each Party shall accord to investors of another Party treatment no less favorable than that it accords, in like circumstances, to its own investors with respect to the establishment, acquisition, expansion, management, conduct, operation, and sale or other disposition of investments.

1103(1) Each Party shall accord to investors of another Party treatment no less favorable than that it accords, in like circumstances, to investors of any other Party or of a non-Party with respect to the establishment, acquisition, expansion, management, conduct, operation, and sale or other disposition of investments.

The MFN comparator is the treatment accorded to investors from a third State, whereas the national treatment comparator is the treatment accorded to similarly situated domestic investors.

It is crucial to pay close attention to the text of the provision, as they vary from treaty to treaty. In the case of NAFTA, part of the assessment of whether the treatment

---

[34] R Jennings and A Watts (eds), *Oppenheim's International Law*, 9th edn (London: Longman, 1996), at 1326.

constitutes discriminatory treatment depends on whether it is accorded 'in like circumstances'. In other words, the comparator is the treatment rather than the investors or investments. This important distinction is often missed by tribunals, which are anxious to draw on findings made by other tribunals applying different treaty language.[35]

The term 'in like circumstances' in Articles 1102 (national treatment) and 1103 (MFN) NAFTA has led to much debate and a certain degree of confusion, as demonstrated by the string of NAFTA decisions to date.[36] Some interpreters have mistakenly applied a 'like products' analysis found in the GATT 1994, overly constraining the great degree of flexibility embedded in the phrase 'in like circumstances'.[37] Even decisions that do not adopt a GATT-like test improperly oversimplify the test by focusing solely or excessively on the investor's business as the comparator.[38] These decisions demonstrate a tendency to view investment matters through a trade-in-goods lens, when in fact the investment relationship is more complex and requires greater flexibility in assessing discrimination. The test for 'in like circumstances' provides the requisite amount of flexibility.

The history of the national treatment and MFN obligations dates back to well before the GATT 1947 and before the first BIT in 1959. The principle likely finds its origin in Friendship, Commerce, and Navigation Treaties used by the US in the nineteenth and twentieth centuries. These treaties employ the terms 'in like manner', 'in like cases', 'in like situations', and 'in like circumstances' with regard to various rights and obligations, relating not solely to the field of commerce. A review of a few of the treaties spanning from the mid-nineteenth to the mid-twentieth century demonstrates how the national treatment and MFN principles evolved over time.

The first thing to note is that although MFN and national treatment clauses have never been restricted to trade,[39] they have 'historically served to provide the

---

[35] See, eg, *Parkerings AS v Lithuania*, ICSID Arbitration Case No. ARB/05/8 (11 September 2007), at paras 378–80, in which the Tribunal read the requirement of 'like circumstances' into a provision that did not contain the words, then drew on a NAFTA Chapter 11 decision that incorrectly focused on whether the investors were in like circumstances, rather than whether the treatment was accorded in like circumstances.

[36] See, eg, *In the Matter of Cross-border Trucking Services (Mexico v US)*, Arbitration Panel Report (6 February 2001), at para 260; *SD Myers, Inc v Canada*, UNCITRAL Partial Award (13 November 2000), at paras 243–46; *Pope & Talbot Inc v Canada*, UNCITRAL Award on the Merits of Phase 2 (10 April 2001), at paras 73–82; *Feldman v Mexico*, ICSID Award ARB(AF)/99/1 (16 December 2002), at paras 154–80; *ADF v United States*, ICSID Award ARB(AF)/00/1 (9 January 2003), at paras 156–7; *The Loewen Group v United States*, ICSID Award ARB(AF)/98/3 (26 June 2003), at para 140; *GAMI Investments Inc. v Mexico*, UNCITRAL Final Award (15 November 2004), at paras 113–14; *Methanex Corporation v United States*, UNCITRAL Final Award (7 August 2005), at paras 17–37; *UPS v Canada*, UNCITRAL Award (24 May 2007), at paras 83–120.

[37] *Cross-border Trucking Services*, at para 260; *Pope & Talbot*, at para 79.

[38] *Loewen v United States*, at para 140; *Pope & Talbot v Canada*, at para 78.

[39] See, eg, Art III 1903 US-Spain Friendship Treaty, which applies to inheritance issues.

legal framework for the expansion of world trade by reducing discrimination'.[40] The agreements generally seek to grant equal conditions of access to each State's competitors.

Second, while the earlier treaties, such as those with Bolivia, Peru, and Spain were concerned with 'vessels in like circumstances', the later treaties extended the application of national treatment and the MFN-principle to 'nationals, companies, products, vessels and other objects, as the case may be'. The US treaties with Nicaragua (1956) and Japan (1953) defined national treatment and MFN-treatment identically, as follows:

1. The term 'national treatment' means treatment accorded within the territories of a Party upon terms no less favourable than the treatment accorded therein, in like situations, to nationals, companies, products, vessels or other objects, as the case may be, of such Party.

2. The term 'most-favoured-nation treatment' means treatment accorded within the territories of a Party upon terms no less favourable than the treatment accorded therein, in like situations, to nationals, companies, products, vessels, or other objects, as the case may be, of any third country.

The similarities between the above provisions and Articles 1102 and 1103 NAFTA are striking. Both sets of provisions assess discrimination according to whether the treatment is 'no less favourable'. Moreover, both sets of provisions focus on treatment accorded 'in like situations' or 'in like circumstances' rather than on similarly situated actors or objects.

The provisions are not concerned with the existence of like products or like investors, but with the treatment accorded, in like situations, to people, companies, or products. The emphasis is therefore on the activity of the State rather than on the product, the investor, the company, or the service provided. NAFTA negotiators adopted this formulation. It is equally found in the US model BIT, and it was also suggested by the OECD's 1976 Declaration on International and Multinational Enterprises.

The 'in like circumstances' and 'in like situations' formulations allow for a great deal of flexibility. They permit the comparison of treatment applied to two companies belonging to the same industry, but also of two companies operating in completely different sectors. Such a comparison may be appropriate where two companies, one that produces paper and the other steel, each use the same river water to cool their machinery, but the State obliges the foreign company to take more stringent environmental protection measures constituting a breach of national treatment. In short, the comparison permits the consideration of all of the relevant circumstances in which the treatment was accorded, including the policy rationale for the treatment.

---

[40] This is demonstrated by the Friendship treaties that the US entered into with Bolivia in 1863, Peru in 1870, Spain in 1903, Nicaragua in 1958, and Japan in 1953; see Jennings and Watts, above fn 34, at 1327.

The NAFTA cases show that the State's national treatment defence typically relies on the policy rationales for treating the foreign and domestic investors differently.

The analysis of whether two investors are accorded treatment in like circumstances must be completed on a case-by-case basis, taking various factors into account, including but not limited to the business sector. The analysis also includes a consideration of the actual circumstances that led to the treatment in question. It is therefore impossible to ignore the policy objectives of the government in enacting the measures at the origin of the treatment. Indeed, the US position during the OECD's MAI negotiations was that the phrase 'in like circumstances' includes built-in policy exceptions. The US delegation provided the following commentary, which was included in an explanatory footnote to the draft text:

National treatment and most favoured nation treatment are relative standards requiring a comparison between treatment of a foreign investor and on investment and treatment of domestic or third country investors and investments. The goal of both standards is to prevent discrimination in fact or in law compared with domestic investors or investments or those of a third country. At the same time, however, governments may have legitimate policy reasons to accord differential treatment to different types of investments. 'In like circumstances' ensures that comparisons are made between investors and investments on the basis of characteristics that are relevant for the purposes of the comparison. The objective is to permit the consideration of all relevant circumstances, including those relating to a foreign investor and its investment, in deciding to which domestic or third country investors and investments they should appropriately be compared, while excluding from consideration those characteristics that are not germane to such a comparison.[41]

Not all investment treaties contain MFN and national treatment provisions calling for a comparison that is as flexible as a comparison based on treatment accorded in like circumstances. Some limit the comparison to the 'same' or 'identical' circumstances.[42] Others specify that the treatment to be accorded is that which the State provides to 'any other similar investments'[43] or 'to its own like investors and investments', as in the case of the 1998 Framework Agreement on the ASEAN Investment Area.[44] By focusing on the nature and characteristics of the investor or investment rather than on the treatment, the latter provisions do not obviously

---

[41] MAI Draft Text of 1997: III. Treatment of Investors and Investments, CONFIDENTIAL DAFFE/MAI(97)1/REV2 at <http://www.citizen.org/print_article.cfm?ID=6115> (last visited 12 June 2008).

[42] See the *UN Draft Code of Conduct for Transnational Corporations*, 23 ILM 626, and Art 3(1) Agreement between the Government of the United Kingdom of Great Britain and Northern Ireland and the Government of Belize for the Promotion and Protection of Investments, 1982, 1294 UNTS 199, No 21315.

[43] Art II 1964 BIT between Germany and Kenya; see R Dolzer and M Stevens, *Bilateral Investment Treaties* (The Hague: Kluwer, 1995), at 64; see also Art IV 1992 Agreement between the Government of the Republic of Lithuania and the Government of the Kingdom of Norway on the Promotion and Mutual Protection of Investments, which does not use the word 'like' but calls for a comparison with an investor from a third state.

[44] Art 7(1)(b) Framework Agreement on the 1998 ASEAN Investment Area, at <http://www.aseansec.org/6466.htm> (last visited 12 June 2008).

call for a State's public policy considerations to be taken into account.[45] Instead of making public policy part of the likeness test, the ASEAN Framework Agreement provides for a series of public policy exceptions similar to those found in Article XX GATT 1994.

Drawing from a defined set of exceptions would presumably limit a State's ability to accord different treatment based on legitimate grounds of public policy, particularly if the exceptions are modelled on the list found in Article XX GATT 1994. Many legitimate public policies are, however, difficult to shoe-horn into Article XX GATT 1994 or Article XIV GATS. Moreover, WTO case law demonstrates that the exceptions have infrequently been invoked successfully.[46] At the same time, NAFTA case law shows that it is permissible for the State to provide different treatment on grounds of public policy or public interest. Legitimate policy objectives have been thought to include environmental protection,[47] compliance with other international agreements,[48] public safety,[49] and efforts to better control tax revenues, discourage cigarette smuggling, protect intellectual property rights, and prohibit grey market sales.[50] It has also included the distinction between courier and postal traffic on the grounds that postal administrations and expert consignment operators have different objects, mandates, and transport and deliver goods in different ways and under different circumstances.[51]

A successful non-discrimination provision is one that prevents an investor from being treated less favourably on the basis of its nationality, while allowing the State to differentiate in its treatment provided it is based on public policy. The 'in like circumstances' formulation permits this flexibility, provided it is not incorrectly limited to an analysis of 'like investors'.

B. Minimum Standard of Treatment

The minimum standard of treatment also dates back to the beginning of the twentieth century. It is found in Freedom, Commerce, and Navigation treaties, but unlike non-discrimination clauses, it is equally a principle of customary international law.[52] Article 1105 NAFTA and many BITs contain similar wording requiring each Party

---

[45]   Although note that the Tribunal did do so in *Parkerings*, above fn 35.
[46]   See chapters 6, 9, 18, 19, 20, and 21 of this Handbook.
[47]   *SD Myers v Canada*, above fn 36, at paras. 247 and 250.
[48]   *Pope & Talbot v Canada*, above fn 36, at 77 and 87; *UPS v Canada*, above fn 36, at para 117.
[49]   *Cross-border Trucking Services*, above fn 36, at paras 159, 187 and 257.
[50]   *Feldman v Mexico*, above fn 36, at para 170.
[51]   *UPS v Canada*, above fn 36, at para 117.
[52]   I Brownlie, *Principles of Public International Law*, 6th edn (Oxford: Oxford University Press, 2003), at 502–03.

to accord treatment in accordance with customary international law, including fair and equitable treatment and full protection and security.

The basic idea of the minimum standard of treatment is straightforward. It recognizes that an investor must subject himself to the laws of the host State. In return, the State promises to defend his person and secure justice for him.[53] However, determining the content of the standard has been more controversial. Some investment tribunals have used it as a catch-all for any concept linked to fairness, such as transparency or the legitimate expectations of the investor.[54] The better approach has been to recognize that the standard is informed by customary international law. NAFTA Parties have made it abundantly clear by issuing a binding interpretation stating that Article 1105(1) prescribes the customary international minimum standard, and that the concepts of fair and equitable treatment and full protection and security do not require treatment beyond what is required by customary international law.[55] Canada and the US have also added recent clarifications to their respective model BITs that full protection and security and fair and equitable treatment do not require treatment beyond what is required by the customary international law minimum standard.

Since the minimum standard takes its meaning from customary international law, a tribunal simply cannot apply its own idiosyncratic standard.[56] The terms 'fair and equitable' and 'full protection and security' cannot be interpreted in the abstract, but 'must be disciplined by being based upon State practice and judicial or arbitral case law or other sources of customary or general international law'.[57]

While it is not unusual to call on judges or arbitrators to apply an abstract concept such as fairness, one must wonder how much guidance a prospective investor can take from such an abstract provision. Legal experts regularly disagree on whether a rule of custom exists. Moreover, it is the factual record 'as a whole—not dramatic incidents in isolation—which determines whether a breach of international law has occurred'.[58] The abstract character of the principle makes it difficult to determine in advance the type of conduct that an investor can expect to avoid.

Perhaps a lack of foresight is not unreasonable in the context of investor-state protection, since an investor will resort to such a provision when its relationship with the State has completely broken down. This type of safety net undoubtedly has its

---

[53] A Bjorklund, 'Reconciling State Sovereignty and Investor Protection in Denial of Justice Claims' 2005 *Virginia Journal of International Law* 45(4) 809; M Kinnear, A Bjorklund, and J Hannaford, *Investment Disputes under NAFTA: An Annotated Guide to NAFTA Chapter 11* (Alphen an den Rijn: Kluwer, 2006), at 6–1105.

[54] See eg, *Tecmed v Mexico*, ICSID Award ARB (AF)/00/2 (29 May 2003), at para 154.

[55] NAFTA Free Trade Commission, *Notes of Interpretation of Certain Chapter 11 Provisions*, 31 July 2001, at <http://www.international.gc.ca/trade-agreements-accords-commerciaux/disp-diff/NAFTA-Interpr.aspx?lang=en> (last visited 12 June 2008).

[56] *Mondev v United States*, ICSID Award ARB(AF)/99/2 (11 October 2002), at paras 119–21.

[57] *ADF v United States*, ICSID Award ARB(AF)/00/1 (9 January 2003), at para 184.

[58] *GAMI Investments Inc v Mexico*, UNCITRAL Final Award (15 November 2004), at para 103.

purpose. However, it does not contribute much to legal certainty and predictability in the investor-state relationship if it is not clear what standard of justice an investor can expect.

The model US BIT tries to provide greater predictability by defining 'full protection and security' as 'the level of police protection required under customary international law'. The model BIT also provides examples of fair and equitable treatment, such as the obligation not to deny justice in administrative or adjudicatory proceedings in accordance with the principle of due process. In turn, a denial of justice has been defined as a '[m]anifest injustice in the sense of a lack of due process leading to an outcome which offends a sense of judicial propriety'.[59]

The definitions provided in the US model BIT confirm that the concept of minimum standard is intended to apply when the investor-state relationship is beyond repair. As such, it is a principle that is suited to investment agreements, which call for monetary damages as means of retribution. However it would be ill suited to a WTO system that permits only prospective remedies. A damages award is not forward-looking in the same way that WTO panels have called upon Members to 'withdraw' their measure or 'bring it into conformity' with WTO rules. Rather than requiring a State to bring its measure into conformity from that day forward, the purpose of a damages award is to wipe out all of the consequences of the illegal act and re-establish the situation that would, in all probability, have existed had the wrongful act not been committed. It is hard to see how such a rule could find a place within the existing WTO system whose enforcement structure is future-oriented and predicated on the ongoing relationship of the trader and the State.[60]

C. Expropriation

The prohibition against expropriation without adequate compensation exists in customary international law as well as in the majority of investment agreements. While a State's sovereignty permits the taking of private property, international law provides that it must be for a public purpose, on a non-discriminatory basis and accompanied by compensation.[61] In investment agreements, the prohibition tends to cover all forms of takings, whether direct or indirect.

Direct expropriation involves the taking of an investment by the host State through the seizure of the property or interest, or through its compulsory transfer,

---

[59] *Loewen v United States*, above fn 36, at para 132; ICJ, *Case Concerning Elettronica Sicula S.p.A. (ELSI) (US v Italy)*, Judgment, ICJ Reports (1953) 15, at para 128.

[60] See chapter 15 of this Handbook for a thorough analysis of remedies in WTO law, including the argument that it is time to revisit the mantra that the recommendation of panels to bring a measure into conformity is purely prospective.

[61] UN General Assembly Resolution 1803 (XVII); see Brownlie, above fn 52, at 514.

for example, to a state-owned enterprise or domestic investor. A State, so politically or economically motivated, can expropriate all foreign-owned property or an entire industry or sector, which is known as nationalization. Or the taking can be directed at a single investor.

While it is easy to determine whether a direct expropriation has occurred, it is not always easy to agree on the proper amount of compensation. Developing and developed States have a long history of debating the proper standard to accord compensation. While developed countries advocated for prompt, adequate, and effective compensation,[62] developing countries pushed for the lesser standard of 'just' or 'appropriate' compensation. NAFTA Chapter 11 has bridged the divide that previously existed between the US and Mexico. Compensation must be based on the fair market value of the investment, must be paid without delay, and must be fully realizable. The standard therefore looks considerably like the standard of prompt, adequate, and effective compensation.

The vast majority of modern expropriations are indirect expropriations.[63] These are government measures that result in 'the effective loss of management, use or control, or a significant depreciation of the value, of the assets of the foreign investor',[64] even if no physical taking has occurred. The case law has produced a number of factors that help determine whether an indirect expropriation has occurred. Above all is the consideration of whether the investor has been deprived of all or substantially all of its investment. Other factors that have been applied by tribunals include the intent of the State, the purpose of the measure, and the context in which the government acted. Some have also included the legitimate expectations of the investor.[65]

An indirect expropriation often consists of a series of government acts that has the effect of rendering the investor's property rights useless. One of the difficulties is to identify at which point the expropriation actually occurred. This is a matter to be determined on a case-by-case basis considering all of the relevant facts. What is clear, however, is that not every disappointment in dealing with foreign governments will be considered an expropriation: 'it is a fact of life everywhere that individuals may be disappointed in their dealings with public authorities, and disappointed yet again when national courts reject their complaints'.[66] The purpose of investment agreements is neither to eliminate the normal commercial risk undertaken by a commercial investor[67] nor to prevent governments from regulating in the public interest.

---

[62] Brownlie, above fn 52, at 509; Lowenfeld, above fn 10, at 397–403.
[63] Kinnear, Bjorklund, and Hannaford, above fn 54, at 14–1110.
[64] UNCTAD, *International Investment Agreements: Key Issues*, Vol 1, UNCTAD/ITE/IIT/2004/10, at 235.
[65] Kinnear, Bjorklund, and Hannaford, above fn 54, at 15–1110 to 17–1110.
[66] *Azinian et al v Mexico*, ICSID Award ARB(AF)/97/2 (1 November 1999), at para 83.
[67] *Feldman v Mexico*, above fn 36, at para 112.

As is the case with a breach of the minimum standard of treatment, often the only realistic form of remedy once an expropriation has occurred is compensation, or perhaps the restitution of property. Again, it is hard to imagine how such a rule could find a place within the existing WTO system, as long as its enforcement structure is future-oriented, predicated on the ongoing relationship of the trader and the State, and does not allow for direct compensation to investors by way of damages.

D. Dispute Settlement

Investment agreements do not require investors harmed by a measure to appeal to their home State to bring a case on their behalf, as entrepreneurs affected by trade measures must do in the case of the WTO. Instead, they allow investors to bring disputes on their own behalf.[68] NAFTA Chapter 11, like the US model BIT, provides for both investor-state arbitration as well as state-to-state arbitration to resolve investment disputes.[69]

NAFTA provides different options for dispute settlement depending on the substantive obligation at issue. While investment disputes may be settled through either state-to-state or investor-state arbitration, disputes relating to trade in goods and services can only be resolved through state-to-state arbitration. As a result, a corporation with a claim relating to its cross-border service must appeal to its State to take a claim on its behalf, while an investor has direct recourse to arbitration. Presumably the reason for direct access to dispute settlement goes back to the vulnerability of the investor versus the limited risks undertaken by the cross-border supplier. As the *Loewen* Tribunal noted, the purpose of Chapter 11:

is to establish 'a mechanism for the settlement of investment disputes that assures both equal treatment among investors of the Parties in accordance with the principle of international reciprocity and due process before an arbitral tribunal'. The text, context and purpose of Chapter Eleven combine to support [...] an interpretation which provides protection and security for the foreign investor and its investment.[70]

Resort to investor-state arbitration has been more common than the use of state-to-state arbitration under NAFTA. To date, over ten times as many investor-state disputes have been brought as compared to state-to-state arbitrations dealing with goods or services. The growing number of investment disputes in comparison to the three goods and services disputes serves as evidence that the traditional requirement to espouse one's claim limits access to dispute settlement.

[68] See Arts 1116 and 1117 NAFTA.   [69] Art 1115 NAFTA.
[70] *Loewen v United States*, ICSID Decision on Competence and Jurisdiction ARB(AF)/98/3 (5 January 2001), at para 53.

It is no easy task for a person or business to convince its State to bring a claim on its behalf.

The availability of monetary damages under investment agreements coupled with the ability of investors to bring cases on their own behalf has led to an explosion of cases. Successful claimants typically have no leverage to ask that the offending measure be amended or dropped, but may be awarded compensation or restitution of property.

The corollary of having experienced an explosion of cases is a greater risk of frivolous or unnecessary cases. Some cases appear to push the bounds of investment rules or are meant primarily to exert pressure on the State to change its pattern of action. Such cases are costly for the State, and therefore the taxpayer. A new ICSID procedure offers a degree of protection by allowing States to 'file an objection that a claim is manifestly without legal merit' within 30 days.[71] They arguably create negative publicity for a system of protections that has been unfairly described by critics as creating a radical expansion of corporate rights over the rights of ordinary citizens while being expensive and chilling policy making.[72] However, the attention these cases have garnered has arguably also created a better awareness of the existence of the rules and how they are meant to apply.

While frivolous claims may be the necessary cost in the operation of any dispute settlement system, it is also important to highlight the checks and balances guarding against them. An arbitration typically costs upwards of $3 million. The claimant and respondent are often asked by the tribunal to each pay a certain amount up front to set up the arbitration. These costs vary and they are usually split equally between the claimant and respondent from the outset, with each party reserving its right to request re-imbursement of costs at the end of the proceedings. The likelihood that the investor will recuperate these costs is very low, given that many tribunals ultimately decide that the costs of the arbitration should be shared equally. A number of recent cases have recognized the unfairness of having a State cover its costs, particularly where the investor has brought a frivolous claim. They have awarded costs in favour of the State, obliging the investor to pay for the entire cost of the arbitration, a greater proportion of the costs, and even part of the State's legal fees.[73]

---

[71] Art 41(5) ICSID Rules of Procedure for Arbitration Proceedings (Arbitration Rules), at <http://www.icsid.worldbank.org/ICSID/StaticFiles/basicdoc/partF.htm> (last visited 12 June 2008).

[72] See, eg, Public Citizens Global Trade Watch, 'NAFTA'S Threat to Sovereignty and Democracy: The Record of NAFTA Chapter 11 Investor-State Cases 1994–2005', at 76–82, at <http://www.citizen.org/documents/Chapter%2011%20Report%20Final.pdf> (last visited 12 June 2008).

[73] *Waste Management v Mexico I*, ICSID Arbitral Award on Jurisdiction ARB(AF)/98/2 (2 June 2000); *International Thunderbird Gaming Corp v Mexico*, UNCITRAL Award (26 January 2006), at para 220; *Nagel v Czech Republic*, Stockholm Chamber of Commerce Case 49/2002, Stockholm Arbitration Rep 2004:1; *Methanex Corp v United States*, UNICTRAL Final Award (3 August 2005), at Part VI (3) and (4); *Generation Ukraine and Link Trading v Moldovia*, ICSID Award. ARB/00/9 (16 September 2003), at para 24.8.

The growing body of investment law cases has contributed to a greater understanding of investment protection. Undoubtedly, there have been growing pains, such as the strained interpretation that a few tribunals gave to the minimum standard of treatment provision in NAFTA. The early cases showed a certain lack of comprehension of the provisions and a corresponding queasiness by the States parties.[74] These wrinkles continue to work themselves out. If there is a growing uneasiness about the blossoming investment case law it arises out of the ad hoc character of the tribunals and the risk that their decisions may diverge or may provide for double relief. The lightning rod for this debate has been the separate decisions in *CME v Czech Republic* and *Lauder v Czech Republic*.[75]

Both cases against the Czech Republic arose out of essentially the same facts relating to an investment in a Czech television station by Ronald Lauder, an American investor, who owned a Dutch company called CME, which in turn owned a Czech television station through a Czech subsidiary company. When relations soured, Lauder and CME each filed separate investment claims pursuant to the US-Czech and Netherlands-Czech BITs. The decisions of the two Tribunals could hardly have differed more, despite being based on essentially the same set of facts and on similar treaty provisions.[76] The *Lauder* Tribunal declined to find that an expropriation had taken place, but the *CME* Tribunal held that an expropriation had occurred. While the *Lauder* Tribunal awarded no damages whatsoever, the *CME* Tribunal calculated damages at $270 million. Even if the *CME* Tribunal correctly rejected the notion of *res judicata*, and correctly decided that it had no jurisdiction to consider whether Lauder and CME were essentially a 'single economic entity',[77] the two decisions demonstrate the real threat of two tribunals awarding duplicative relief.

The risks associated with ad hoc arbitration have led some to call for the creation of an appellate structure to contend with discrepancies in decisions and duplication of awards.[78] With tribunals owing their jurisdiction to differently worded bilateral treaties, it is not at all clear how such an appellate structure would work. Undoubtedly, it would be more complicated to design than the WTO Appellate Body.

---

[74] NAFTA Free Trade Commission, *Notes of Interpretation of Certain Chapter 11 Provisions* (31 July 2001), above fn 56.

[75] *CME Czech Republic B.V. v The Czech Republic*, UNCITRAL Final Award (14 March 2003); *Ronald S Lauder v Czech Republic*, UNCITRAL Award (3 September 2001).

[76] The *CME* Tribunal, which was the later tribunal, rejected the notion of *res judicata* on the basis that the parties and treaties were different, the facts might well have been different, and even those treaty claims that seemed similar on their face might be susceptible to varying interpretations, given differences in contexts, object and purpose, and the parties' subsequent practice. Ibid at paras 432–33.

[77] Ibid at para 436.

[78] See, eg, DA Gantz, 'An Appellate Mechanism for Review of Arbitral Decisions in Investor-State Disputes: Prospects and Challenges' 2006 *Vanderbilt Journal of Transnational Law* 39(1) 39.

VI. What Does the Future Hold for Investment Protection?

The number of BITs and free trade agreements (FTAs) with investment chapters continues to grow. At the same time, multilateral investment negotiations in the WTO are stalled. The WTO's half-hearted embrace of investor protection rules signals a major gap in its attempt to be a global institution dealing with all forms of trade between all nations. A number of options exist that would allow for greater coverage.[79] Nevertheless, until WTO rules substantively embrace the full coverage of all measures affecting investment, the WTO will not contain one-stop shopping for global rules required by global companies operating in global markets.[80]

As Winham points out, globalization has caused people to think differently about international trade now that trade has become integrated into a broader set of relationships that includes foreign investment, corporate alliances, and other forms of collaboration.[81] Yet, the results of the Uruguay Round did little to address rules relating to investment. By building on the GATT 1947, WTO Members kept the focus on goods and added to it a services agreement that allows carve-outs by sector. This showed Members' unwillingness to adopt a totally new thinking, something that is required if they want the WTO to remain as the source for multilateral rules for international business relations.

A WTO agreement on investment seems unlikely, at least for the foreseeable future. Still, the global economic system would benefit from a universal framework of rules on investment protection and the WTO would benefit as the keeper of these rules. The WTO Working Group on Trade and Investment continues to show signs of being plagued by the traditional divide between capital exporting and capital importing Members as negotiators struggle over the meaning of investment. Developing countries have insisted on a narrow definition of investment based on lasting economic relations and the possibility of exercising some effective control over the foreign investment.[82]

---

[79] Eg, Edwards and Lester recommend an approach to TRIMS regulation modelled on the SCM Agreement, which prohibits certain measures and exempts others; see R Edwards Jr and S Lester, 'Towards a More Comprehensive World Trade Organization Agreement on Trade Related Investment Measures' 1997 *Stanford Journal of International Law* (33) 169.

[80] See chapter 2 of this Handbook, citing G Feketekuty, 'The New Trade Agenda', *OECD Occasional Paper* No 40 (1992), at 29.

[81] See chapter 2 of this Handbook.

[82] V Motosi, 'Bilateral Investment Treaties and the Possibility of a Multilateral Framework on Investment at the World Trade Organization: Are Poor Economies Caught in Between?' 2005 *Northwestern Journal of International Law & Business* 26(1) 95, at 116.

Even if WTO Members are able to overcome the developing-developed country divide on investment rules, they will be confronted with the same problem that faced the Uruguay Round negotiators, namely that investment measures are to some extent acknowledged and covered by the GATT 1994. To complicate matters further, now they are also partly covered by the GATS.

WTO rules already intertwine. The provisions of the GATS, the GATT 1994, and the TRIMS Agreement can apply to the same measure.[83] Such overlap, while unavoidable, is confusing. It has the positive effect of ensuring that trade-distorting measures are captured. In principle, even if a WTO Agreement on investment were adopted, the GATS should continue to apply to investment. After all, foreign direct investment in services accounts for a large share of the total stock of inward investment in most host States.[84] However, maintaining the existing WTO structure based on trade in goods and trade in services, while adopting a new WTO agreement modelled on NAFTA Chapter 11 would add to the confusion. It would also risk entirely undercutting the utility of the existing WTO agreements, particularly if the new agreement permitted investor-state dispute resolution.

The NAFTA experience is telling. Disputes primarily related to the provision of cross-border services, such as *Myers v Canada*, or the provision of goods, like *Pope & Talbot v Canada*, were brought as investment disputes. The creation of a procedural right for investors to bring claims on their own behalf would drastically change WTO dispute settlement, even if an attempt were made to limit it to investment disputes, however these might be defined.

Even if WTO Members were able to bridge the existing normative gap between WTO rules and investment agreements, the WTO would not likely emerge as the primary forum to secure compliance, since the DSU does not permit investor-state claims or monetary compensation. Investor-state arbitration places the trigger for dispute resolution in the hands of the victim of the illegal treatment. Investment agreements turn to the beneficiaries of investment protections to undertake an important enforcement function.

Although WTO rules apply to investment measures, the degree to which they apply is limited. They currently do little to mitigate risk once an investment has taken place, since WTO-inconsistent measures do not give rise to damages. Adding damages to the list of available reparations would drastically change the WTO system. While the availability of damages in NAFTA's state-to-state dispute resolution has had little or no effect,[85] it is the overriding reason why investors bring disputes on their own behalves.

Without change to the type of reparations, it remains unclear how WTO dispute settlement could be used to remedy illegal expropriations or breaches of the

---

[83] Appellate Body Report, *EC – Bananas III*, at paras 221–22.

[84] See Hoekman, above fn 27, at 2.

[85] Article 2018 NAFTA provides that where a resolution cannot be achieved through the removal or non-implementation of a measure, compensation may be awarded.

minimum standard of treatment. These are obligations that, if breached, often require a payment of damages to compensate the lost investment. Occasionally the restitution of the investor's property is possible. Neither of these possibilities exists in the DSU.

The introduction of investor-state dispute settlement and the ability of panels to award damages would drastically alter the WTO system. However, WTO Members might wish to consider taking steps in this direction. They could phase in investor-state dispute settlement over a number of years after having adopted new rules on investment. This would allow Members to build up a body of case law through state-to-state dispute settlement prior to opening the door to claims brought directly by investors. Alternatively, they could provide additional checks and balances, such as the ability to provide binding interpretations, an unused power under Article IX:2 WTO Agreement. Whatever steps are taken, Members must pay careful consideration to the relationship of investment rules and rules on goods and services, particularly if they opt for investor-state dispute settlement.

Totally new thinking on investment protection in the WTO does not mean that the State will abandon its ability to make decisions in the public interest. New rules must give wide ambit to the State to implement and exercise policy. In the current WTO context, non-trade interests are carved out through specific exceptions that have been narrowly interpreted and carefully applied. In contrast, NAFTA cases dealing with national treatment show a broader consideration of measures taken for public policy reasons.

The traditional home-state/host-state divide that has also plagued WTO negotiations and committee discussions is best avoided. One avoidance tactic may be to focus on the sectors where foreign investors continue to have the greatest vulnerability. A second avoidance tactic may be to focus on the responsibility of the State to act in the public interest rather than on what its responsibilities are towards foreign investors. Along with the growing body of case law, such a discussion would contribute to the understanding that States may legitimately distinguish in their treatment of two investors without acting in a discriminatory manner or breaching the investor's right to fair and equitable treatment.

VII. Conclusion

Investor protection in the WTO differs dramatically from the protections provided by investment agreements, such as NAFTA Chapter 11, the ECT, and the thousands of existing BITs. WTO rules catch some measures that affect investment, but only on account of their effect on trade in goods or services. In contrast, the coverage of investment agreements is not limited to investment-related measures affecting trade in goods or services, but cover all government measures affecting investment.

The WTO agreements and investment agreements share some common substantive provisions, including the national treatment and MFN provisions. However, their wording differs, and consequently so does their application. For example, investment agreements often allow the State to treat two investors differently on account of public policy objectives, whereas the WTO agreements require the State to justify the different treatment through a closed list of exceptions.

Other provisions found in investment agreements do not find a home in the WTO, such as the guarantee of fair and equitable treatment and the prohibition on expropriation without compensation. These provisions would be very difficult for the WTO to embrace without re-assessing its remedial powers, since they are typically remedied through damage awards, which the DSU does not permit.

Perhaps the most important distinction between the WTO and investment agreements is that the latter permit non-state actors to bring disputes. A move away from state-to-state arbitration would be a dramatic shift for the WTO, which would likely substantially increase its caseload and lead to frivolous claims. However, investor-state arbitration has the advantage of allowing the victim of the illegal act to bring its own claim for damages obviating the need for it to convince its State to bring a claim on its behalf.

Ultimately, a rethinking of the WTO legal system is necessary before the WTO can fully embrace investment rules. Instead of focusing on sector-based trade, the rules WTO must come to recognize that trade has become integrated into a broader set of relationships that includes foreign investment. Otherwise, the WTO will continue to address investment in a secondary manner. Until the WTO agreements substantively embrace the full coverage of all measures affecting investment, they will not contain one-stop shopping for global rules required by global companies operating in global markets.

SELECTED BIBLIOGRAPHY

R Bishop, J Crawford, and M Reisman, *Foreign Investment Disputes* (The Hague: Kluwer, 2005)

R Dolzer and M Stevens, *Bilateral Investment Treaties* (The Hague: Kluwer, 1995)

R Dolzer and C Schreuer, *Principles of International Investment Law* (Oxford: Oxford University Press, 2008)

A Hardin and L Holmes, 'Service Trade and Foreign Direct Investment', *Industry Commission Staff Research Paper* (27 November 1997)

M Kinnear, A Bjorklund, and J Hannaford, *Investment Disputes under NAFTA: An Annotated Guide to NAFTA Chapter 11* (Alphen aan den Rijn: Kluwer, 2006)

A Lowenfeld, *International Economic Law* (Oxford: Oxford University Press, 2002)

G Sacerdoti, 'Bilateral Treaties and Multilateral Instruments on Investment Protection' 1997 *Receuil des Cours* (269) 251

M Sornarajah, *The Settlement of Foreign Investment Disputes* (The Hague: Kluwer, 2000)

M Sornarajah, *The International Law on Foreign Investment*, 2nd edn (Cambridge: Cambridge University Press, 2004)

M Trebilcock and R Howse, *The Regulation of International Trade*, 3rd edn (New York: Routledge, 2005)

CHAPTER 23

··

TRADE AND
COMPETITION
POLICY

··

MITSUO MATSUSHITA

I. Introduction – Philosophy Common to Competition Policy and the WTO

ALTHOUGH the WTO contains diverse principles, the basic tone of the WTO is one of free trade and the market principle in international trade. It is based on the conviction that trade unfettered by government restrictions in trade and investment contributes to the maximization of economic welfare of trading nations. For this purpose, the WTO and the GATT 1947, its predecessor, have engaged in trade negotiations with the purport of reducing and eliminating tariffs and trade barriers. Another important cornerstone of the WTO is non-discrimination, for example, between WTO Members and between domestic products and like foreign products. This is incorporated in the most-favoured nation (MFN) treatment and national treatment principles.

Competition policy, which applies both domestically and internationally, aims at promoting the freedom of business activities. For this purpose, competition policy encourages the reduction and elimination of governmental restrictions of business activities and, at the same time, prohibits and controls anti-competitive conducts of private enterprises. Competition policy, therefore, is also aimed at maximizing economic welfare of nations through the freedom of trade, and competition.

WTO law and competition policy are grounded on similar principles, that is, free trade, non-discrimination, and competition. Although the WTO is designed to deal with reducing governmental restrictions in international trade and competition policy and law primarily apply to domestic conducts of private enterprises, there is a close complementarity between them. For example, as trade liberalization progresses, it is increasingly necessary to strengthen the control of competition policy and law. These controls are necessary to eliminate anti-competitive activities of private enterprises in the form of, for example, international cartels that divide up the market. Otherwise, the effect of liberalization accomplished through international trade negotiations risks being undercut by such restrictive business activities.

The framers of the ITO Charter[1] incorporated Chapter V to deal with competition policy. The ITO Charter was aborted and the GATT 1947, its successor, did not incorporate similar principles. Today, it has become increasingly clear that the liberal international trade order is not complete without some kinds of international competition policy.

---

[1] For a general account of the ITO Charter, see C Wilcox, *A Charter for World Trade* (New York: McMillan, 1949); RR Wilson, 'Proposed ITO Charter' 1947 *American Journal of International Law* 41(4) 879–85.

II. Provisions in the WTO Agreements Relating to Competition Policy

After the late 1980s, the world witnessed a transition from the non-market economy to the market economy model. This trend was especially conspicuous after the collapse of the Soviet Union and the shift of the Chinese economy from a non-market to a market economy. More countries now operate with market economies than other economic regimes. Competition policy and law play a central role in the market economy and, as the market economy becomes dominant world-wide, competition policy has become the core of the free market. As Chief Justice Hughes puts it, competition law 'is a charter of freedom..., [which] has a generality and adaptability comparable to that found to be desirable in constitutional provisions'.[2] Reflecting this prevalence of the market economy in which competition plays a central role, the WTO covered agreements contain some provisions that pertain to competition policy and, in this sense, competition policy is already part of the WTO regime. The existence of competition policy provisions is itself noteworthy, even if they are scattered throughout different agreements and, due to the lack of a central enforcement committee or agency, are not effectively applied. Competition policy provisions exist in Article III:4 GATT 1994 as well as in the GATS, the TRIPS Agreement, the TRIMS Agreement, the Anti-Dumping Agreement, the TBT Agreement, and the Safeguards Agreement. This shows that the drafters were aware of the importance of competition policy in the WTO system.

Article III:4 GATT 1994 prohibits WTO Members from discriminating against foreign products in favour of like domestic products in the application of 'all laws, regulations and applications'. 'All laws' certainly contains competition law and, if a Member applies its competition law favouring its domestic products and disfavouring like foreign products, this would constitute a violation of Article III:4.[3] Article VIII: 2 GATS requires Members to ensure that a monopoly supplier does not abuse its monopoly position in providing services within their territories. Article 40 TRIPS Agreement specifically allows Members to enact legislation to prohibit anti-competitive conditions attached to licensing agreements in intellectual property rights such as exclusive grantback conditions, non-contest clauses, and package licenses. Article 8 TRIMS Agreement states that, when reviewing the operation of

---

[2] *Appalachian Coals, Inc v United States*, 288 US 344, 359–60 (1933).

[3] Ehlermann and Ehring maintain that the principle of national treatment enshrined in Article III:4 GATT 1994 is necessarily extended to competition laws since competition laws are part of 'all laws'. See C-D Ehlermann and L Ehring, 'WTO Dispute Settlement and Competition Law – Views from the Perspective of the Appellate Body's Experience' 2003 *Fordham International Law Journal* 12(6) 1501–61.

this Agreement, the TRIMS Council consider whether the Agreement should be complemented with provisions on competition policy. Article 3 Anti-Dumping Agreement requires that, when determining injury to a domestic industry caused by dumping, the anti-dumping authority take into account, *inter alia*, 'trade-restrictive practices of and competition between the foreign and domestic producers'.

Article 8.1 TBT Agreement provides that WTO Members shall not require or encourage private entities engaged in conformity assessment of technical standards to discriminate against foreign products.[4] Article 11.1(a) Safeguards Agreement prohibits Members from taking or seeking voluntary export restraints and, in this connection, Article 11.3 provides that Members shall not encourage or support the adoption or maintenance by public and private enterprises of non-governmental measures equivalent to voluntary export restraints (VERs). By this provision, Members are prohibited from encouraging export cartels and international cartels having the same effect as voluntary export restraint.

If the operation of these provisions were integrated into a systematic whole through a central committee or agency within the WTO, they could operate as an effective WTO competition policy, even if they were somewhat lacking comprehensiveness.

III. Transnational Business Activities and National Competition Laws

A. Extraterritorial Application of Competition Laws

About 80 countries enforce competition laws of some type. Except for the competition law of the EC, competition laws are national laws and their application is generally limited to the territories of the countries in which they are enforced. Although the application of competition law is not strictly limited to the geographical territories of States and an 'extraterritorial application' of national laws is becoming more common, the applicable area of national competition law remains basically the territory of the State in which a competition law is enforced. Although some major jurisdictions apply their laws extraterritorially, this is still exceptional.

---

[4] Therefore, if a Member encourages a private assessment entity to discriminate against foreign products, this constitutes a violation of the TBT Agreement. At the same time, in many jurisdictions, discriminatory conduct of the private assessment entity constitutes a violation of competition laws. See, eg, *National Macaroni Manufacturers Association v FTC*, 345 F. 2d 421 (7th Cir., 1965).

Business activities are becoming more and more transnational. Enterprises cross national boundaries when they export, import, invest, and engage in other business activities. They establish subsidiaries and related entities abroad and those overseas establishments act under the directives of the headquarters located in the home country. This creates a discrepancy between the transnational character of business activities, on the one hand, and the territorially bound character of the national regulatory authorities, on the other hand. National competition law authorities face a dilemma that, in order to effectively enforce their national competition laws *vis-à-vis* business activities that transcend nation-state boundaries, a measure of extraterritorial application is inevitable. However, the extraterritorial application of laws causes tensions. Even today where the global economy is predominant, States jealously safeguard their 'sovereignty' against 'legal imperialism' of other States. An extraterritorial application of competition laws began in the US and it is becoming more common practice among trading nations that have competition laws. As a result, jurisdictional conflicts arise.

B. US Antitrust Laws

Initially the US restricted the scope of application of its antitrust laws within its territory as exemplified in the Supreme Court decision in the *American Banana Company* case.[5] This decision is regarded as a classic example of the territorial principle in establishing jurisdiction not only in competition law but also in public international law. However, the US later switched to the 'effects' doctrine of jurisdiction whereby US courts exercise jurisdiction over conduct that occurs abroad if such conduct is intended to and does produce anti-competitive 'effects' within the US. The effects doctrine was first enunciated in the *Alcoa* case in 1946[6] in which Judge Learned Hand announced that a US domestic court could exercise jurisdiction over a cartel organized and carried out abroad, which restricted the quantity to produce aluminium as long as it was intended and caused the effect of limiting the supply of aluminium to the US. The effects doctrine as enunciated in this decision was confirmed by the US Supreme Court in the *Hartford Fire Insurance Company* case.[7] The Court applied US antitrust laws to an agreement entered into by US and foreign insurance companies in England which stipulated that the participants would refuse to supply reinsurance in the US on certain kinds of matters involving environmental risks.

In 1982, the US Congress enacted the Foreign Trade Antitrust Improvement Act[8] whereby the extraterritorial application of the Sherman Act was limited to situations

[5] *American Banana Company v United Fruit Company*, 213 US 347 (1909).
[6] *United States v Aluminum Company of America*, 148 F. 2d 416 (2d Cir. 1946).
[7] *Hartford Fire Insurance Co et al v California et al*, 113 S. Ct. 2891 (1993).
[8] *Foreign Trade Antitrust Improvements Act of 1982*, 96 Stat. 1233 (8 October 1982); 15 USC. 6 (a).

where conducts that occur abroad produce a direct, substantial, and reasonably foreseeable effect within the US and that effect gives rise to a claim in the US. The primary purpose of this law is to exclude activities abroad of US enterprises from the application of the Sherman Act. However, the application of US antitrust laws to conduct engaged in by foreign enterprises that produces an effect in the US remains the same. In 1995, the US Justice Department and the Federal Trade Commission jointly announced a set of guidelines on the application of US antitrust laws to conduct abroad that produces effects in the US.[9] In this set of guidelines, many examples show that US antitrust laws would apply to the conduct of foreign enterprises abroad.

However, the extraterritorial enforcement of domestic antitrust laws on conduct occurring abroad created numerous instances of tension and conflict with other nations. Such conflicts were especially intense between 1950 and 1990.[10] Without examining every case of conflict, it is helpful to highlight a few examples. In the *ICI* case,[11] a US court ordered ICI, a British company, not to assert its British patent rights against imports that would infringe such rights on the ground that the patents were used as a camouflage for a cartel agreement between ICI and du Pont, a US company. The US court also ordered ICI to assign back the patents that du Pont had owned in Britain and had been assigned to ICI. However, ICI had entered into a licensing agreement with its subsidiary, BNS, whereby the latter was given the exclusive license on the patents that the US court ordered ICI to reassign. The execution of this order would make it impossible for ICI to perform this licensing agreement with BNS. Therefore, BNS brought a suit in England against ICI and sought for an injunction prohibiting ICI from reassigning the patents to du Pont in compliance with the US court order. The English court stated that the US court order was an impermissible extraterritorial application of domestic law, which the English court could not recognize and enforce in England.[12]

The *Laker* case[13] concerned an antitrust dispute between Laker, a British airlines company, and a number of the IATA companies (British Airways, Lufthansa, Sabena, and others). Laker claimed that the IATA companies had engaged in collective dumping to drive out Laker from the air route between the US and England. Laker brought an antitrust claim in the US against the IATA companies who, in turn, sought an injunction before an English court under an English blocking statute to prohibit Laker from continuing the antitrust suit in the US.

---

[9] *Antitrust Enforcement Guidelines for International Operations*, Issued by the US Department of Justice and the Federal Trade Commission (April 1995).

[10] For a comprehensive account of extraterritorial application of US antitrust laws, see SW Waller, *Antitrust and American Business Abroad*, 3rd edn (St Paul, Minn: West Group, 1997 to date); DE Rosenthal and WM Knighton, *National Laws and International Commerce: The Problem of Extraterritoriality* (London: The Royal Institute of International Affairs, 1982).

[11] *United States v Imperial Chemical Industries, Ltd.*, 105 F Supp 215 (SDNY 1952).

[12] *British Nylon Spinners, Ltd. v Imperial Chemical Industries, Ltd.* (1953), 1 Ch. 19 (C.A. 1952).

[13] *Laker Airways v Pan American Airways*, 559 F Supp 1124 (1983); *Laker Airways v Sabena Belgium World Airways*, 731 F. 2d 909 (1984).

This injunction was affirmed by an English appellate court but eventually vacated by the House of Lords. In the US, Laker brought another suit against the IATA companies and sought an injunction to prohibit the IATA companies from continuing the lawsuits in England against Laker under the English blocking statute. The US district court granted this injunction and the Court of Appeals affirmed the decision. When affirming the lower court decision, the Court of Appeals declared that the invocation by the British court of the blocking statute and the prohibition of antitrust suit in the US amounted to an infringement of the judicial power of the US.

More recently, the application of US antitrust laws has been extended to private damages suits. In the *Empagran* case,[14] non-US private plaintiffs brought actions against the participants of an international vitamin cartel for treble damages on the basis of US antitrust laws. American, European, and Japanese companies participated in the cartel and raised prices in different countries. Non-US persons located outside the US, who had purchased vitamins at inflated prices in their home countries, brought claims under the US Foreign Trade Antitrust Improvement Act on the theory that it allows a US antitrust suit if: (a) conduct occurring abroad causes a direct, substantial, and reasonably foreseeable effect within the US, and (b) such effect is a cause of action under antitrust laws. The plaintiffs lost at the district court. The Court of Appeals reversed the decision. The Supreme Court decided that the foreign plaintiffs could recover the damage if there is proof that the effect of the illegal conduct abroad is a 'proximate cause' of the illegal effect in the US. The governments of different countries filed *amicus curiae* briefs with the Supreme Court and argued that an application of US antitrust laws to conduct abroad to rescue foreign plaintiffs, who suffered damage caused by illegal acts abroad, would amount to usurpation of the jurisdiction of those countries and would cause a hollowing out of the judicial power to provide relief to victims in those countries. Judge Breyer held that the US should shy away from 'judicial imperialism' and should respect the sovereign jurisdiction of foreign nations. However, after this decision, lower courts have been divided over how to interpret 'proximate cause'. Some courts have denied relief while others have granted it.[15] Therefore, this issue is not yet finally resolved. Those cases are but a few among many cases in which the invocation of US antitrust laws precipitated conflicts with foreign jurisdictions.[16]

---

[14] *Empagran SA v F. Hoffman La-Roche Ltd.*, 2001 WL 761360 (D.DC June 7, 2001); *Empagran SA v Hoffman-La Roche Ltd.*, 31 5F. 3d 420 (DC Cir. 2003); *F. Hoffman La-Roche Ltd v Empagran SA*, 542 US 155 (2004).

[15] *EMAG Solutions LL et al v Toda Kogyo Corporation et al*, 2005 WL 1712084 (N.D.Cal, 2005); *MM Global Services, Inc et al v The Dow Chemical Company et al*, 329 F Supp 2d 337, 2004–2 Trade Cases Pa 74,514 (11 August, 2004); *Latino Quica-Amtex SA et al v Akzo Mobel Chemicals BV et al*, 2005 WL 2207027 (SDNY), 2005–2 Trade Cases P 74,974; *In re Monosodium Glutamate Antitrust Litigation*, 2005 Trade Cases P 74, 781 (D Minn, 2 May, 2005).

[16] For other major cases, see Waller, above fn 10.

C. EC Competition Law

In EC competition law, the *Wood Pulp* case[17] established that EC competition law applies to conduct of foreign enterprises abroad. This case involved activities of American, Canadian, and other enterprises to engage in export cartels abroad in which the participants limited the supply of wood pulp to the EC. The European Commission proceeded against the export cartel ultimately holding that its activities were contrary to Article 85 (now Article 81) of the Treaty of Rome. Upon appeal, the European Court of Justice (ECJ) held that EC competition law could be applied to anticompetitive conduct of foreign enterprises abroad as long as such conduct is implemented within the EC. It is not clear whether or not this implementation doctrine is any different from the effects doctrine adopted by US courts. However, whatever difference there may be between those two doctrines regarding extraterritorial application of competition laws, there is very little difference in practice.

The *GE/Honeywell* case[18] is a recent case decided by the EC Commission in which an extraterritorial application of EC competition law was involved and a conflict arose between the EC and the US. In this case, GE, a leading US electric company, planned to acquire Honeywell, another large US electric company. Both US companies were engaged in developing and producing sophisticated avionic equipments. This corporate acquisition was to take place in the US and the US Department of Justice issued a go-sign for the reason that this acquisition would contribute to an increase of efficiency in the development and production of such equipments and to the promotion of the economic welfare of users. However, the EC Commission took a different view and prohibited the acquisition under EC competition law on the ground that this acquisition would create a market dominant enterprise and that the existence of a market dominant enterprise is a threat to the free market economy. The enforcement agencies in both jurisdictions exchanged views on this acquisition and debates ensued. However, the US and EC enforcement agencies could not come to any conciliation. Consequently, the EC Commission ordered that this acquisition should not be executed. The US Justice Department issued a statement in which it criticized the enforcement of EC competition rules against the acquisition.[19] This case can be cited as an example of a conflict arising from the enforcement of domestic competition laws to conduct of foreign enterprises abroad.

---

[17] ECJ Joined Cases C-89, 104, 114, 116, 117, 125–129/84, *Ahlstrom & Ors v EC Commission* ('Wood Pulp'), [1988] ECR 5193.

[18] EC Commission, *General Electric/Honeywell*, OJ [2004] L48/01.

[19] Antitrust Division Chief Reacts Decision to Prohibit GH/H Deal, *Antitrust & Trade Regulation Report*, 81(2015) (BNA 6 July 2001), at 15; *Daily Report for Executives*, No 128 (BNA 5 July 2001).

D. Other Jurisdictions

Article 98:2 of the Law against Restraint of Competition in Germany explicitly states that it applies to conduct that occurs outside German territory and produces an effect (Auswirkung) in Germany. It has been applied to foreign export cartels affecting the German market.[20] It has also been applied to mergers and acquisitions that occurred abroad and brought about effects in Germany, as exemplified by the *Philip Morris* case.[21]

Article 2 of the Chinese Antimonopoly Law, enacted in 2007 and scheduled to take effect in the summer of 2008, states that it applies to conduct that occurs abroad and brings about harmful results in China. In Japan, Articles 10 and 15 of the Antimonopoly Law were amended in 1998 so that its provisions on mergers and acquisitions would be applied to conduct occurring abroad.[22]

The above brief survey of 'extraterritorial application' of national laws in the major jurisdictions is intended to show that there is a wide gap between the coverage of national laws and transnational features of economic activities of enterprises.

E. Is the WTO an Appropriate Forum for Competition Policy Discussion?

A quick glance through the development of jurisdictional doctrines in major jurisdictions in competition law and tensions and conflicts among trading nations resulting from the extraterritorial application of competition laws reveals that national competition law is not necessarily an adequate instrument to deal with global and transnational business activities.

One additional problem is that the principles and the scope of application of competition laws are not the same throughout different jurisdictions. On the contrary, although many competition laws share the same or similar philosophy that the economy should be guided by free market principles and competition, there are differences in the scope of application and enforcement. For example, as stated in connection with the *GE/Honeywell* case, there is a difference between the US and the EC with regard to the control of mergers and acquisitions. There are probably

---

[20] K Markert, 'The Application of German Law to International Restraints of Trade' 1967 *Virginia Journal of International Law* 7(2) 47, at 54; K Stockmann, 'Kartellbehoerdliche Ermittlungen im Ausland' 1975 *Wettbewerb und Wirtschaft* (4) 243.

[21] Rothmanns/Philip Moris, 24 February, 1982, *WuW/E* BkartA 1943; See also Synthetischer Kaautshuk I, KG, 26 November, 1980, *WuW/E* OLG 244; Synthetischer Kautschuk II, KG, 26 November 1980/*WuW/E* OLG 2419.

[22] For details of the extraterritorial reach of the Japanese Antimonopoly Law, see M Matsushita, 'Application of the Japanese Antimonopoly Law to International Transactions' in M Bronckers and R Quick (eds), *New Directions in International Economic Law* (The Hague: Kluwer Law International, 2000) 559.

more exemptions from the application of competition law in Japan than in the US. In many developing countries, the emphasis is placed on 'development policy' or 'industrial policy' in which the government promotes certain key sectors of the economy through subsidization, consolidation of enterprises into a large unit, and sometimes allowance of cartel-like arrangements.

A review of the above situations prompts one to consider whether there can be an appropriate international framework in which competition laws of different trading nations are brought together under one umbrella, convergence of policies and laws are promoted, and coordination of enforcement policies and mechanisms among trading nations are strengthened. Indeed, this was what the framers of the ITO Charter aspired to accomplish about 60 years ago. The need for such convergence is much stronger today than then. This prompts questions, such as: what can the WTO do to deal with this situation, would the WTO not be an appropriate body in which such convergence and coordination could be accomplished? WTO law and competition policy share the common philosophy of free trade and competition and the principle of non-discrimination. So, it would serve the cause of the WTO to incorporate competition policy through an agreement. The question of the feasibility of introducing a WTO agreement on competition policy and law will be dealt with later in the chapter. It is sufficient here to state that the WTO could be an appropriate forum to discuss international competition policies, including their enforcement *vis-à-vis* transnational business activities, as well as the expansion of the reach of domestic laws in major jurisdictions and the resulting tension between trading nations.

IV. The WTO Dispute Settlement System and Competition Policy

There is no specific WTO agreement designed to cover competition policy. Some disputes have had some bearing on competition policy, as discussed in the following sections.

A. *Japan – Photographic Film*

In *Japan – Film*, the US alleged that the Japanese Government had directed Fuji, a Japanese photographic film manufacturer holding about 70 per cent of the market

share in Japan, by way of administrative measures—including informal guidance—
to build an exclusive distributorship of films in Japan and thereby excluded the sale
of films produced by Kodak, a US company, in the Japanese market. In essence, the
gist of the claim was that, when the Japanese film market was liberalized in 1970,
the Japanese government imposed 'liberalization countermeasures'; the exclusivity of the Fuji distribution system was constructed by administrative directives of
the Japanese government. The Panel found, however, that there was no ground for
the violation and non-violation complaints because the US failed to prove a linkage between alleged administrative actions including informal guidance and the
exclusive distribution system in Japan. To be covered by a WTO covered agreement,
there has to be a 'governmental measure'. In this case, the Panel found there was no
proof that there were Japanese governmental measures that restricted the entry of
US-made films into the Japanese market.[23]

The US did not appeal the Panel decision, which must therefore be treated as the
final decision. Although the US lost this case, it raised an important question of
whether the WTO covered agreements cover private restrictive activities exercised
under governmental authorization and guidance. The US attempted to show that,
though the exclusive distribution arrangement was created by Fuji, a private entity,
the Japanese government played a decisive role in building this exclusive distributorship. It could not, however, adduce pieces of direct evidence proving that it was
the government that established this exclusive distributorship. All of the evidence
produced by the US was of indirect or circumstantial character and the Panel held
that this collection of evidence was insufficient to prove that governmental measures
built this exclusive distributorship.

The US may have aimed at the wrong target. This case basically was about private restraints rather than governmental measures. Therefore, those issues should
have been considered under Japanese or US competition law. Vertical restraints are
generally dealt with under the rule of reason in US and Japanese competition law
and so it is uncertain whether such conduct constituted any violation of competition law.[24] On the other hand, issues of exclusive distributorship and difficulties in
entering the domestic market due to such exclusivity have a close relationship with
trade liberalization in the WTO regime. At the same time, this case shows that the
current WTO dispute settlement system is ineffective to challenge private restraints
on trade. Section 301 of the US Trade Act of 1974 states that tolerance towards private
restrictive conduct on the part of the government and the lack of the enforcement of competition law constitutes an unfair trade practice that could be subject
to investigation under Section 301. However, in terms of the WTO jurisprudence,
mere tolerance and non-application can hardly be said to constitute a 'measure', as
intended by WTO Members.

---

[23] Panel Report, *Japan – Film*, at paras 10.402–404.
[24] *Continental TV, Inc v GTE Sylvania Inc*, 433 US 36 (1977).

This example shows that there is a need to introduce into the WTO regime an agreement that would explicitly declare that Members are obliged to ensure the openness of the market from private restraints.

B. US – 1916 Act

US – 1916 Act dealt with issues of the US Anti-dumping Act of 1916. This law prohibited imports of a foreign product if the import price was lower than the price of such product in the home market of the exporting country and if such imports would destroy US industry or cause monopolization or restraints on trade in the US. It also provided for treble damages and criminal penalties. The EC and Japan brought a claim against the US on the ground that the Anti-dumping Act of 1916 dealt with dumping as defined in Article VI GATT 1994 and the Anti-Dumping Agreement and, if so, remedies should be limited to those authorized by those agreements, that is, the imposition of anti-dumping duties. The US, in response, argued that the Act was an antitrust statute rather than an anti-dumping statute and was not governed by Article VI GATT 1994 and the Anti-dumping Agreement. The Panel and the Appellate Body decided that, since the Act applied to dumping, it should be classified as a dumping statute. This was one of the reasons why the Panel and the Appellate Body decided that the Act was inconsistent with Article VI GATT 1994 and the Anti-Dumping Agreement.[25]

It seems, however, that the fact that the 1916 Act was an anti-dumping statute does not necessarily exclude the possibility that it also had antitrust features. The US Justice Department and the Federal Trade Commission jointly published the Guidelines for International Operations, which speak about the relationship between the 1916 Anti-dumping Act and antitrust laws. These guidelines state that although the 1916 Act is not an antitrust statute, it is closely related to predatory pricing which is a subject matter of antitrust law, suggesting that there is a close relationship between the two sets of law.[26] In an appellate decision in a treble damages case brought by a US company against a Japanese company, the US Court of Appeals in the 8th Circuit rejected the claim of the Japanese defendant that an injury to a domestic industry should be regarded as an injury to the relevant domestic industry as a whole. However, in a dissenting opinion, one of the three judges stated that an injury to a domestic industry should be considered an injury to the domestic industry as a whole. In his view, the more narrow interpretation would unduly stifle competition, one of the fundamental values of the US legal system.[27]

---

[25] Appellate Body Report, US – 1916 Act, at paras 134–38.

[26] Antitrust Enforcement Guidelines for International Operations, Issued by the US Department of Justice and the Federal Trade Commission (April 1995), at para 2.82.

[27] Tokyo Kikai Seisekusho Ltd v Goss International Corp., 2006 WL 155253 (8th Cir., Iowa, January 23, 2006).

As stated in the Guidelines on International Operations, predatory pricing exercised internationally is subject to antitrust laws (especially the Sherman Act) and situations envisaged by the 1916 Anti-dumping Act could fall under the scope of the Sherman Act.[28] It seems that the scope of antitrust law and that of the Anti-dumping Act overlap at least in part. In this sense, *US – 1916 Act* is a borderline case between those two areas of law.

C. *Canada – Dairy (Article 21.5 – New Zealand and US)*

In *Canada – Dairy (Article 21.5 – New Zealand and US)*, the issue was predatory pricing. The Canadian government was accused of having provided subsidies for exporting fresh milk. Originally the Canadian government controlled the price of fresh milk that was sold to processors of milk products for the export market. The US challenged this price control as being a direct export subsidy. The Panel and the Appellate Body held that this was an export subsidy inconsistent with the SCM Agreement. Thereupon, the Canadian government abandoned the price control of milk sold to producers of milk products to be exported. However, the US challenged the reformed system and insisted it was still inconsistent with the SCM Agreement and the Agreement on Agriculture. The Appellate Body stated that this regime could be an illegal subsidy if producers sold fresh milk at a price-below-cost of production to producers of milk products to be exported. However, the Appellate Body held that it could not determine whether the sale was below-cost due to the lack of fact-finding on the part of the Panel.

The case concerned primarily the application of the SCM Agreement. However, a below-cost sale of fresh milk by producers to producers of milk products gives the producers of milk products undue advantages. In terms of competition law, this practice could be regarded as predatory pricing and, given the extraterritorial effect of competition law in major jurisdictions, this kind of practice is subject to challenge under competition law as well as under the SCM Agreement. It provides another example of a cross-over between competition law and WTO agreements.

D. *Mexico – Telecoms*

In *Mexico – Telecoms*, the US challenged measures requiring Mexican telecommunications operators to adhere to a horizontal price-fixing agreement under the leadership of Telmex, the leading telecom company in Mexico. The Mexican regulation required Telmex to negotiate with suppliers of telecom traffics in a foreign country a single rate and then this rate applied to all other Mexican operators. The Mexican Reference Paper entitled 'Prevention of anti-competitive practices

[28]   *Matsushita Elec Inds Co v Zenith Rjadio Corp*, 475 US 574 (1986).

in telecommunications' stated that 'Appropriate measures shall be maintained for the purpose of preventing suppliers who, alone or together, are a major supplier from engaging in or continuing anticompetitive practices'. The US argued that the Mexican telecom regulation violated the Reference Paper, which is part of the GATS. The regulation directed the leading telecom company in Mexico to fix a uniform rate for telecom traffic to apply to all Mexican telecom companies dealing with telecom services between Mexico and foreign countries. The Panel held that the removal of price competition by the Mexican authorities combined with the setting of the uniform price by the major supplier had effects of a price-fixing cartel. The Mexican rule required practices by a major supplier, Telmex, that were anti-competitive within the meaning of the Mexican Reference Paper.

The case dealt with a government-sponsored cartel and its anti-competitive nature. Private cartels are covered by the competition law of major jurisdictions such as the US, the EC, Canada, Australia, and Japan. The fact that the practice was mandated by the government probably removes it from the realm of competition law as a legal matter. Still, the removal of governmental practices is a subject matter of competition policy advocacy. The GATS requires that WTO Members ensure that dominant enterprises in services areas do *not* abuse their market position; this case is a concrete application of competition policy within the framework of the GATS.

E. Trade Remedies and Competition Policy

Trade remedies in the WTO consist of anti-dumping duties, countervailing measures, and safeguards. The former two types of measures are said to deal with 'unfair' export practices on the part of exporting countries and enterprises, whereas safeguards are regarded as an emergency measure to rescue a domestic industry ailing from the lack of international competitiveness. However, regardless of whether trade remedies are measures to deal with unfair or fair export practices, their effect is to limit imports either by imposing import quota, emergency tariffs, anti-dumping duties, or countervailing duties. In fact, trade remedies are used to achieve 'protectionism' in international trade. Conduct covered by trade remedies is, at least in part, also subject to competition law. Sometimes, tension and even conflicts arise between trade remedies and competition law. The following passages review some of the major cases of such tensions.

1. *Voluntary Export Restraints*

Prior to the WTO, a serious trade issue was the relationship between VERs and competition law.[29] A VER was a device often used to resolve trade conflicts between

---

[29] See M Matsushita, 'Coordinating International Trade with Competition Policies' in E-U Petersmann and M Hilf (eds), *The New GATT Round of Multilateral Trade Negotiations–Legal and Economic Problems* (The Hague: Kluwer, 1987) 396.

exporting and importing countries. When an export of a product threatened a domestic industry of the importing country, the latter requested the exporting country to restrain exports to the importing country. The government of the exporting country invoked its export licensing powers and prohibited or restricted exports of the product in question to the importing country. Sometime the government of the exporting country directed or advised its exporters to enter into export cartels whereby exporters jointly restrained the amount of exports or fixed export prices.

VERs were often used in US/Japanese trade and EC/Japanese trade. They were employed in important areas such as steel, textiles, automobiles, machine tools, semiconductors, and some others. There are many instances in which export restraint measures exercised by the Japanese government were subjected to US antitrust scrutiny. One such case was the *US Consumers' Union* case, a case that reached the Court of Appeals, in which a US consumers group challenged a VER between the US and Japan.[30] In the face of increasing imports of steel from Japan, the US government approached the Japan Steel Export Association, a trade association composed of steel makers in Japan, and requested that the Japanese exporters restrain their exports of steel to the US. Thereupon, the Japanese exporters organized an export cartel limiting the quantity of steel to be exported to the US. The US Consumers Union challenged the US government and the Japanese exporters on the ground that the US Executive Department exceeded its authority by entering into a trade agreement with Japanese exporters without any statutory authority and sponsoring a cartel between Japanese and US industries. The District Court held that the President had a wide discretion regarding diplomacy; the power to enter into a trade agreement with foreigners was included in this discretion. With regard to the cartel issue, the US plaintiff withdrew its claim based on antitrust law. As a result, the District Court held that it would not make a ruling on this issue but, at the same time, mentioned that, had the plaintiff not withdrawn the antitrust claim, there would have been a serious issue of antitrust offense. Both the plaintiff and the defendants appealed. The Court of Appeals affirmed the decision of the District Court with regard to the power of the President to enter into a trade agreement with foreigners. Also the Court of Appeals held that, when the plaintiff withdrew the antitrust claim, it ceased to be an issue of litigation and the Court would refrain from making a judgment on this issue in one way or other. Therefore, the relationship between a VER and US antitrust law was left unresolved.

Antitrust issues were raised in other VER cases such as the Japanese VER in automobiles.[31] The Japanese government constructed an elaborate export scheme to restrain exports of automobiles to the US. The Japanese government issued a

---

[30] *Consumers Union of the US, Inc v Kissinger*, 506 F. 2d 136 (DC Cir. 1974); *Consumers Union of the US, Inc v Rogers*, 352 F Supp 1319 (USDC, D.C., 1973).

[31] See M Matsushita and L Repeta, 'Restricting the Supply of Japanese Automobiles: Sovereign Compulsion or Sovereign Collusion?' 1982 *Case Western Journal of International Law* 14(1) 47.

directive allocating the number of automobiles that each exporter could export and stated that, in case of non-compliance, the government would invoke a compulsory export licensing power and force the exporters to comply. The Japanese government requested the view of the US Attorney General as to whether this arrangement would be immunized from antitrust challenges. The Attorney General replied that 'he believe[d]' that there would be no problem.

Article 11.1(a) Safeguards Agreement, which supplements Article XIX GATT 1994, explicitly states that 'Members shall not take or seek any emergency action on imports of particular products....'. Article 11.3 states that 'Members shall not encourage or support the adoption or maintenance by public and private enterprises of non-governmental measures equivalent to those referred to in paragraph 1'. These provisions prohibit the use of VERs, whether they are exercised by governmental measures or by private enterprises at the suggestion of a government.

2. *The Relationship Between Anti-dumping and Antitrust*

The relationship between anti-dumping measures and competition policy is one of the issues discussed in the WTO Working Group on Trade and Competition, established in 1997.[32] Some WTO Members have argued that anti-dumping should be modified by the principles incorporated in competition law. Others have claimed that the constituency of anti-dumping is different from that of competition law and there exists no common ground. No consensus has been reached in the Working Group on this issue. The tension that exists between anti-dumping and competition law can also be witnessed through a number of cases.

In the *Fax Paper* case,[33] Japanese companies operating in the American market were hard pressed by competitive pressure of their US competitors and losing market share. US competitors first threatened and then ultimately filed an anti-dumping action against the Japanese companies with the US Commerce Department. To avoid a costly anti-dumping investigation and potential anti-dumping duties that would have made it impossible to continue exporting to the US, the Japanese companies entered into an agreement in Japan. The agreement fixed the price of fax paper to be exported into the US market. The US Justice Department initiated a criminal investigation and brought an indictment against the companies and their executive officers. The US District Court held that US antitrust law did not apply to the conduct of the defendants. The precedents in US jurisprudence that allowed the extraterritorial application of antitrust law all concerned civil cases and the application

---

[32] See M Matsushita, 'Interplay of Anti-dumping Remedies and Competition Laws – Tensions and Compromise between Anti-dumping and Antitrust' in M Matsushita, D Ahn, and TL Chen (eds), *The WTO Trade Remedy System – East Asian Perspectives* (London: Cameron May, 2006) 123.

[33] *US v Nippon Paper Industries Co, In., and Hironori Ichida*, 1996–2 Trade Cases, para 71, 575 (US D.C., D Mass, 1996) (district court decision); *US v Nippon Paper Industries Co, Inc, and Hironori Ichida*, 109 F. 3d 1 (1st Cir. 1999) (appellate decision); and *US v Nippon paper Industries Co, Ltd, formerly Jujo Paper Co, Ltd*, 62 F Supp 2d 173 (D.Mass 1999) (district court decision on remand).

of criminal laws needed to be more limited. The US Justice Department appealed and the Court of Appeals reversed the decision of the District Court. The Court of Appeals held that, regardless of whether the case was civil or criminal, the same provision was being interpreted (Section 1 of the Sherman Act) and the same principle of extraterritorial jurisdiction should apply. It remanded the case to the District Court. During the proceedings, some defendants pleaded guilty and settled the case. One of the defendants, Nippon Paper Company, fought the charges to the end, ultimately being held not guilty by the District Court.

There were two reasons for finding Nippon Paper Company not guilty. First, the US Justice Department did not adduce sufficient evidence to show that the alleged foreign cartel produced a direct, substantial, and reasonably foreseeable effect in US foreign commerce. Although the Japanese companies were engaged in price-fixing, they kept losing market share in the US. In fact, when they raised prices in the US market, they lost the market completely. The Court stated that this set of facts indicated that the alleged conspiracy did not produce a sufficient effect to establish the extraterritorial jurisdiction of US courts. Second, the statute of limitation had passed when the US Justice Department brought an indictment.

The *Malaysian ETR* case[34] is similar to the *Fax Paper* case, except for the fact that it arose from a private action by purchasers of the product in question. The defendants were Malaysian and other Southeast Asian companies that produced and sold ETR (rubber products) to the US and other markets. The US Commerce Department initiated an anti-dumping investigation against the Malaysian companies and determined that the highest margin of dumping was 50 per cent. The defendants decided jointly to fix the export price of ETR to the US market as a means of addressing the anti-dumping action. The US purchasers of ETR brought an anti-trust claim against the Malaysian companies and sought treble damages. The jury in the US District Court found that there was a conspiracy among the defendants but there was no direct, substantial, and reasonably foreseeable effect on US foreign commerce. It was not clear to the jury whether the price of ETR went up because of either the price-fixing agreement abroad or the imposition of anti-dumping duties. The plaintiffs did not meet the burden of proving such effect. The plaintiffs appealed to the US Court of Appeals, which stated that an anti-dumping threat cannot be used as an excuse for a price-fixing cartel because anti-dumping laws do not require cartels and uniform prices. The Court further found that the jurisdictional rule of the *Hartford Fire Insurance* case would apply. However, the Court of Appeals further decided that a direct, substantial, and foreseeable effect of this foreign cartel was not proven and that, therefore, there was no ground for applying the Sherman Act.

The *Saskatchewan Potash* case[35] also dealt with the relationship between anti-dumping and antitrust. The facts of the case are complicated, so only essential

[34] *Dee-K Enterprises, Inc et al v Haveafil Sdb Bhd et al*, 982 F Supp 1138 (US DD, EDVa, 1997); 299 F. 3d 181 (4th Cir. 2002).
[35] *Blomkest Fertilizer, Inc v Potash Corp of Saskatchewan, Inc*, 2000 Trade Cases, para 72, 812 (8th Cir. 2000).

elements will be explained. An anti-dumping investigation was initiated against Canadian potash producers. After the preliminary dumping determination, the US Commerce Department required that the respondents post bonds to meet the respective dumping margins. The respondents later entered into suspension agreements with the US Commerce Department whereby they would raise their US export prices. The major producer and exporter of potash, PCS, took the lead and decided to raise its export price by $18 per ton. All other Canadian producers quickly followed and raised their prices by that amount. US consumers of potash brought an antitrust claim and argued that this was a price-fixing cartel. The US District Court decided that, although prices were similarly raised by all Canadian producers, there was no evidence of a conspiracy. The Court reasoned that they engaged merely in 'consciously parallel but independent conduct'; it wasn't a price-fixing cartel.

A part of the US/Japan Semiconductor Agreement entered into in 1986 also deals with anti-dumping.[36] The US Commerce Department initiated an anti-dumping investigation on exports of Japanese semiconductors. The Japanese exporters entered into suspension agreements with the Commerce Department whereby the Japanese exporters promised that they would not lower their export prices below their normal value (their domestic price).

All of the US sales of Japanese semiconductors were made through the Japanese producers' affiliated companies or subsidiaries in the US. The Japanese producers stipulated the prices at which their affiliated companies and subsidiaries should sell semiconductors to US customers. If the relationship between a Japanese exporter and the US affiliated company was that of parent/wholly owned subsidiary, these two would be regarded as a single economic entity. This was not the case. Occasionally, Japanese producers owned only some portions of the outstanding stocks of the related companies. Even in this situation, the constructed export price approach in anti-dumping legislation would apply. No clear precedent currently exists to determine what constitutes a 'related company'. However, the Customs Valuation Agreement states that the test of related company should be based on five per cent or more stock ownership.[37] In antitrust law, the test of single economic entity is different. In antitrust jurisprudence, only the parent/wholly owned subsidiary is regarded as a single economic entity.[38] Therefore, a gap exists between anti-dumping law and

---

[36] See D Dallmeyer, 'The US-Japan Semiconductor Accord of 1996: The Shortcomings of High Tech Protectionism' 1989 *Maryland Journal of International Law and Trade* 13(2) 179; D Gantz, 'Symposium – Prevention and Settlement of Economic Disputes Between Japan and the United States: Part II: Application of Framework to Specific Sectors and Issues, Lessons from the US-Japan Semi-Conductor Dispute' 1999 *Arizona Journal of International and Comparative Law* 16(1) 91; CS Kaufman, 'The US-Japan Semi-Conductor Agreement: Chipping Away at Free Trade' 1994 *UCLA Pacific Basin Law Journal* 12(2) 329.

[37] Art 15:4 (d) Customs Valuation Agreement states that there is a related person relationship between two persons if 'any person directly or indirectly owns, controls or holds 5 per cent or more of the outstanding stock or shares if both of them' and if 'one of them directly or indirectly controls the other'.

[38] *Copperweld Corp v Independence Tube Corp*, 467 US 752 (1984).

antitrust law. The question was whether or not the stipulation of sales price in the US would be regarded as illegal resale price maintenance. The Japanese Vice-Minister requested the view of the US Justice Department as to whether this would be held to be illegal in US antitrust law. The Assistant Attorney General replied that such price maintenance would be regarded as an implementation of the US Anti-dumping Act and would not violate US antitrust law.

Confrontational relationships between anti-dumping and competition law are not unique to US-Japanese trade. In the *Franco-Japanese Ball Bearing* case,[39] a series of negotiations between Japanese and European ball bearing producers resulted in an agreement between the Japanese producers to restrain exports to the European market. The Japanese producers were concerned that the European producers would take steps to invoke European trade remedy laws. This arrangement, however, was challenged by the European Commission on the ground that it violated Article 85 (now 81) of the Treaty of Rome. After this agreement was scrapped as the result of the application of Article 85, the European producers brought an anti-dumping charge against the Japanese products and anti-dumping duties were imposed.

The above review of major cases in anti-dumping and competition law reveals a delicate and uneasy relationship between those two sets of law. In theory, both anti-dumping and competition law aim to maintain 'fair competition'. In reality, however, there is a wide gap between anti-dumping and competition law. In fact, there are often outright collisions between the two sets of law. The above review suggests that an agreement on competition policy and greater coordination between anti-dumping and competition principles within the framework of the WTO would ease tension between the two areas and contribute to legal stability with regard to trade remedies in relation to competition policy.

V. COMPETITION POLICY AND INTERNATIONAL COOPERATION IN THE WTO

Competition policy and the principles of the WTO have much in common. The transnational character of business activities has necessitated an application of competition law to activities abroad in some countries and there is need for international cooperation with regard to the enforcement of competition law in the face of global

---

[39] EC Commission Decision of 29 November 1974, OJ L343/19 (21 December 1974).

business activities. This calls for a consideration of whether or not, and to what extent, the WTO can play a role in promoting international competition policy.

International cooperation in competition policy has been attempted in various international organizations, such as the UNCTAD and the OECD. More recently, a new framework for international competition policy called the International Competition Network (ICN) was established. In this network, enforcement agencies, some academics, and private practitioners in the field of competition policy meet regularly, exchange views, and coordinate policy-making and enforcement activities of the agencies of the members. It functions not as a binding agreement and has no permanent secretariat. It is merely an informal framework for policy coordination.

In 1997, the Singapore WTO Ministerial Conference adopted a resolution to push forward negotiations on an agreement related to competition policy within the framework of the WTO. It established the Working Group on Trade and Competition Policy to study the matter. The Group worked actively and turned out some reports. In those reports, WTO Members expressed their views on whether an agreement on competition policy should be introduced into the WTO.[40]

There seem to be two major problems with the introduction of a competition policy agreement. One is the relationship between trade remedies, especially anti-dumping measures, and competition policy. Some Members have suggested that anti-dumping measures should be harmonized with the principles of competition policy and their trade restrictive effects should be eased. However, there has been strong opposition to this view. The opposing view, advocated by the US, suggests that anti-dumping be addressed separately from competition policy. To mix the two would cause nothing but confusion and would make it difficult for trading nations to protect legitimate interests of domestic industries against unfair trade practices. An ICPAC report,[41] submitted by a group of antitrust experts commissioned by the US Justice Department, has expressed negative views as to the desirability of introducing an agreement on competition policy into the WTO. The ICPAC report states that such an agreement may involve undue interference of the WTO into the domestic jurisdiction of its Members.

Many developing country Members have argued that an agreement on competition policy in the WTO could unduly deprive them of the freedom to engage in development or industrial policies. They have argued that it is important for developing countries to promote specific sectors of their economy by means of consolidation

---

[40] See M Matsushita, 'Competition Policy in the Framework of WTO' in AV Bogdandy, PC Mavroidis, and Y Meny (eds), *European Integration and International Co-ordination-Studies in Transnational Economic Law in Honor of Claus-Dieter Ehlermann* (The Hague: Kluwer, 2002) 305.

[41] See US Department of Justice, Antitrust Division: *Final Report, International Competition Policy Advisory Committee to the Attorney General and Assistant Attorney General for Antitrust* (2000), at <http://www.usdoj.gov/atr/icpac/finalreport.htm> (last visited 23 May 2008).

of enterprises and to allocate economic resources to the key industries. A strict enforcement of an agreement on competition policy could hamper such policies.

The question is where we should go from here. It seems clear that an introduction of a comprehensive and binding agreement on competition policy within the WTO is premature. However, there are a few scenarios that one may envisage for the future introduction of competition policy in the WTO, including: (a) a declaration in the form of a Ministerial statement that competition policy is an integral part of the WTO; (b) the adoption of a non-binding agreement whereby Members exchange information, assist each other in the enforcement of their competition law, and establish a committee on reconciliation between trade remedies and competition policy; or (c) the adoption of an agreement containing some basic binding principles (such as non-discrimination, national treatment, and transparency) while other principles are left to each Member to adopt at their choosing. There will be little room for the dispute settlement procedures in the WTO to operate in the above scheme. At this stage of development of the WTO, however, there may be no choice but to be satisfied with such a transitional approach.

VI. Conclusion

In recent times, we have witnessed a proliferation of free trade agreements (FTAs), bilaterally and regionally, partly due to the impasse of trade negotiations at the WTO. In most, if not all, of these FTAs, there are provisions for competition policy and law. Generally these provisions call, *inter alia*, for exchanging information with respect to the enforcement of domestic competition laws, regular meetings of officials in charge of competition policy, and positive and negative comity.[42] This is indeed WTO-plus.

Although, at this time, a prospect of introducing an agreement on competition policy into the WTO is not certain, time will come when the WTO will negotiate competition policy matters. When that time comes, the WTO should take an evolutionary approach and begin with an agreement that provides for mutual assistance and cooperation among the enforcement agencies of the participants and that leaves

---

[42] Positive comity means that one of the parties to an FTA applies its competition law to conduct that occurs in its territory and that adversely affects the market of the other party in order to assist enforcement of the competition law of the other party. In negative comity, one of the parties to an FTA refrains from applying its competition law to conduct that occurs in the territory of the other party and that affects the market of the former in deference of policies and interests of the other party. By applying either positive or negative comity, the parties avoid the extraterritorial application of domestic competition law in the spirit of international cooperation.

the content of competition law to each jurisdiction without imposing a set of unified norms in the hope that it will grow into a more complete agreement in the future.

SELECTED BIBLIOGRAPHY

TK Giannakopoulos, *Safeguarding Companies' Rights in Competition and Anti-dumping/ Anti-subsidies Proceedings* (The Hague: Kluwer, 2004)

T Hays, *Parallel Importation under European Union Law*, 2nd edn (Andover: Sweet & Maxwell, 2007)

CA Jones and M Matsushita (eds), *Competition Policy in the Global Trading System* (The Hague: Kluwer, 2002)

JL Kessler and S Waller, *International Trade and US Antitrust Law*, 2nd edn (St Paul, Minn: West Group, 2006)

D Knox Duvall, P McCabe, and JW Bateman, *Unfair Competition and the ITC*, 2007 edn (St Paul, Minn: West Group, 2007)

P Marsden, *A Competition Policy for the WTO* (London: Cameron May, 2006)

AK Masa'dhe, *Investment and Competition in International Prospect for WTO Law* (London: Cameron May, 2003)

WA Root, JR Liebman, and RC Thomsen II, *United States Export Controls*, 5th edn (St Paul, Minn: Thomson/West, 2006)

S Singham, *A General Theory of Trade and Competition: Trade Liberalisation and Competitive Markets* (London: Cameron May, 2007)

PART V

THE WIDER FRAMEWORK

C H A P T E R   2 4

WTO AND CIVIL SOCIETY

MARCOS A ORELLANA[*]

* The author appreciates comments by Nathalie Bernasconi and Steve Porter, and the research assistance of Melanija Radnovic, Ana Paula Ribeiro, Allison Anderson, and Sofia Plagakis.

I. INTRODUCTION

THE relationship between the governed and government has given rise to the concept of civil society as an element distinct from the State. Once the State transfers certain competences to an international organization such as the World Trade Organisation (WTO), a relationship between the international organization and the citizens of Members is established. Consequently, the demands of transparency and accountability posed by civil society upon the State are now also extended to the WTO.

The manner in which the WTO has addressed civil society's demands since its creation in 1995 has highlighted structural elements in international trade policy-making, such as the role of sovereignty in international economic law.[1] Issues concerning power relations and processes for decision-making, both of which are central elements of governance, directly relate to the legitimacy of the organization, including with respect to its acceptance by the public and its ability to deliver on its mandate.

The importance of the relations between the WTO and civil society is thus paramount in a changing world characterized by instant communications across boundaries and by global governance structures that adopt decisions affecting the public within States. However, enabling constructive forms of engagement is not an easy task. Fresh in the mind of many are the images of Seattle, where in 1999 more than 50,000 demonstrators brought the WTO Ministerial Conference (MC) to a halt.[2] Likewise, the images of the WTO MC in Cancún and Hong Kong recall thousands of people in the streets confronting armed police, tear gas, and barricades. These images also drew attention around the world to issues *relating* to trade, such as access to medicines, genetically modified organisms, and agricultural subsidies, and led to vibrant debates on the role of the WTO in these domains.

During past WTO MCs not all action involving non-governmental organizations (NGOs) took place in the streets. In Cancún, for example, a significant number of NGOs were accredited and allowed to enter the building where official talks were taking place. Many of the NGOs working inside the perimeter offered information about technical issues relating to the rules, economics, and/or social implications of policies, and many government delegations and the press welcomed this role. The fact that some NGOs were *inside* while others *outside* highlights the diversity of views in civil society, as well as different strategies that may be pursued to advance different objectives. Likewise, the fact that some governments welcomed their presence while others objected demonstrates the range of views among WTO Members

---

[1] See DC Esty, 'Linkages and Governance: NGOs at the World Trade Organization' 1998 *University of Pennsylvania Journal of International Economic Law* 19(3) 709; M Blue Jeffords, 'Turning The Protester Into A Partner For Development: The Need For Effective Consultation Between The WTO & NGOs' 2003 *Brooklyn Journal of International Law* 28(3) 937, at 938.

[2] See L Lee, 'Reading the Seattle Manifesto: In Search of a Theory' 2003 *New York University Law Review* 78(6) 2305.

on the role of NGOs. Further, the fact that the press obtained information from NGOs, in addition to official press communiqués, enhanced its reporting capabilities. All of these elements speak to the importance of the relations between civil society and the WTO, explored in this chapter.

This chapter is divided into three parts. Part I examines, in general terms, the notion of civil society and how this notion is changing in the context of globalization and global structures of governance. Part I also describes some of the NGOs actively working on trade issues, including the positions they have taken in the debate. Part II explores the challenges of legitimacy and governance in international organizations, examining developments in human rights law and international environmental law regarding access to information and transparency. Finally, Part III examines developments at the WTO regarding its relations with civil society. This section looks at issues concerning the institutional operations of the organization, as well as transparency and participation in negotiations, capacity-building, and dispute settlement.

II. CIVIL SOCIETY IN THE EARLY TWENTY-FIRST CENTURY

The vast literature on civil society has generally focused on the relationship between the State and society. In this ambit, liberal, socialist, and other political ideologies have conceptualized civil society in accordance with their views regarding the nature and functions of the State. While this analytical paradigm may have been warranted in a world where the State exercised absolute or exclusive sovereignty over its territory, in the current landscape marked by globalization and vertical transfers of sovereignty to international organizations, the emergence of a 'global public' poses interesting challenges to existing notions of civil society. In this regard, analogies between civil society at the national level and global civil society at the international level are limited by the different structures of governance, representation, and legitimacy against which they operate. The difficulties involved in conceptualizing a 'global civil society' are augmented in the absence of a global government and in the face of democracy deficits at international law.[3]

This section explores some of the issues raised by the interactions between transnational networks of non-State actors and international organizations exercising

[3] S Charnovitz, 'Non-governmental Organizations and International Law' 2006 *American Journal of International Law* 100(2) 348, at 363–68.

authority over issues that had been traditionally reserved to the policy-making processes of the State. More particularly, this section explores the notion of civil society in a globalized world, and it provides examples of some NGOs and networks active in the ambit of trade.

A. What is Civil Society in a Globalized World?

The emergence of transnational networks of non-state actors coalescing around shared values and visions regarding particular issues such as human rights, trade, and environment is a distinct feature of the international landscape in our early twenty-first century. In this light, civil society is hardly a unitary category exhausted by any one organization, view, or position, but rather a space where multiple voices debate issues, problems, and solutions.[4] Two particular developments both enable and inform the ongoing debate: first, certain problems have become global in scale and thus demand global solutions; and second, the globalization of communications has enabled the emergence of networks of NGOs that work on similar issues. Thus viewed, civil society in a globalized world enables pluralism by bringing to the arena ideas of voices from different corners of the planet with respect to issues of common concern.

The emergence of a global civil society that engages global public interest issues that lie within the mandate of international organizations presents challenges for States and international organizations. While governments retain their prerogatives as the 'representative' of society, States may also suffer from lack of capacity, capture by interest groups, or inability to pursue global public interests. At the same time, international organizations that enjoy distinct international legal personality and exercise elements of global governance are generally held to account solely to their Member States. The emergence of transnational networks of NGOs that challenge the monopolies of the State and demand transparency and accountability from international organizations gives rise to tensions that are not easily resolved within existing structures of international governance, and in fact expose the fissures and limitations of such structures.

The linkages between legitimacy, good governance, and accountability lie at the heart of emerging paradigms of global democracy, global constitutionalism, and other theories that examine the legal relations between the governed and decision-makers in a globalized world. Does the notion of global civil society subvert democratic governance by depriving democratic governments of their monopoly over the 'representation' of their people? Alternatively, does democracy at the international

---

[4] See J Keane, *Global Civil Society?* (Cambridge: Cambridge University Press, 2003), at 175. (Perhaps it is better to speak of global civil society as a dynamic space of multiple differences, some of which are tensely related or even in open conflict.)

level rest upon the availability of arenas for public debate of ideas, where tensions and trade-offs can be addressed if not reconciled? The latter approach reflects the principle of democratic inclusion, whereby everyone should have the right to a say in decision-making that affects them, including in the international arena.[5] In this sense, it does not appear that civil society purports to replace the State, but rather to enhance the international decision-making processes that produce normative outcomes affecting billions of people across countries and regions representing diverse cultures and values.

The proposition that participation by civil society enhances international decision-making is not without controversy. It has been suggested that NGO participation in the WTO, either in rule-making processes or adjudication of disputes, would not necessarily result in enhanced decision-making, given that often NGOs adopt the same positions as their governments.[6] No clear criteria exist to identify legitimate NGO voices;[7] and the interests of developing countries facing resource constraints could be further dimmed by stronger NGO presence.[8]

Overall, the strength of these arguments is limited when viewed under the light of key WTO negotiations and disputes. The argument that NGOs adopt the same position as their government assumes that NGOs 'belong to' or 'have' a government. And while NGOs are often legal entities 'incorporated' under the internal laws of a State, a distinctive feature of global civil society relates to the diminishing importance of national boundaries in determining alliances, allegiances, or articulating motives. The notion of civil society as pertaining exclusively to the relations of society and the State fails to account for globalization and the presence of international organizations exercising elements of global governance. Further illustration of this point is found in a few examples in WTO dispute settlement, particularly *Brazil – Retreaded Tyres* and *EC – Biotech Products*. In *Brazil – Retreaded Tyres*, a coalition of organizations from Europe and MERCOSUR countries presented an *amicus curiae* brief to the Appellate Body that elaborated independent analysis from the disputing governments. Similarly, in *EC – Biotech Products* a coalition of US organizations presented an *amicus curiae* brief to the Panel that challenged US assertions regarding the safety of genetically engineered organisms on the basis of scientific reports that highlighted a considerable degree of uncertainty. The conclusion that follows

---

[5] S Marks, *The Riddle of All Constitutions: International Law, Democracy, and the Critique of Ideology* (Cambridge: Cambridge University Press, 2000), at 109.

[6] A Kupfer Schneider, 'Unfriendly actions: the amicus brief battle at the WTO' 2001 *Widener Law Symposium Journal* 7(1) 93.

[7] GR Shell, 'The Trade Stakeholders Model and Participation by Nonstate Parties in the World Trade Organization' 2004 *University of Pennsylvania Journal of International Economic Law* 25(2) 703, at 718.

[8] R Nardone, 'Like oil and water: The WTO and the world's water resources' 2003 *Connecticut Journal of International Law* 19(1) 183, at 194; E Benvenisti and GW Downs, 'Distributive Politics And International Institutions: The Case Of Drugs' 2004 *Case Western Reserve Journal of International Law* 36(1) 21, at 38.

from these two examples is that NGOs will not necessarily support their government positions but will undertake independent analysis and advance independent positions.

The argument that no criteria exist to identify legitimate NGO voices assumes that some NGOs are legitimate while others are not. Variations of this argument point to a distinction between serious and 'responsible' NGOs that engage decision-making processes and 'irresponsible' groups who seek to destroy any international economic arrangement that stimulates trade and investment.[9] It would appear that any attempt at distinguishing responsible from irresponsible NGOs is unhelpful in addressing civil society's demands because it sidesteps the substantive issues and focuses on the messengers. Further, this approach fails to regard civil society as a space for open deliberation of ideas because it attempts to circumscribe the participants to the debate instead of engaging the ideas. Moreover, the experience of other international organizations shows that criteria for NGO accreditation can be established and administered. Furthermore, the fisheries subsidies negotiations, addressed further below, illustrate how NGOs can actually (and positively) influence the rule-making process.

Finally, with respect to the view that increasing NGO participation would undermine the ability of developing countries to advance their interests, the Cancún MC provides an illustrative example. In Cancún, most NGOs accredited and active *within* the perimeter rallied behind developing countries, and such informal alliances actually strengthened the bargaining position of numerous countries that had been effectively excluded from decision-making during the Uruguay Round.[10] This convergence of interests between civil society and developing countries presents somewhat of a paradox with respect to transparency and participation, an issue we will return to.

The discussion so far assumes that there is a 'global civil society'. Is this the case? Several studies that have looked at this question have examined both elements of the term: global and civil. With respect to the global characteristic, generally these studies have found that NGO participants in UN Conferences have been geographically diverse, based in multiple countries, and not just dominated in one region.[11]

The civility aspect, on the other hand, is more difficult to conceptualize. One approach is to focus on inter-relations between States and NGOs, or alternatively between international organizations and NGOs, looking at formal mechanisms for dialogue. While this methodology is interesting, it is nevertheless limited because

---

[9] P Sutherland, 'The Doha Development Agenda: Political Challenges To The World Trading System – A Cosmopolitan Perspective' 2005 *Journal of International Economic Law* 8(2) 363, at 373.

[10] S Cho, 'A Bridge Too Far: The Fall of the Fifth WTO Ministerial Conference in Cancún and the Future of Trade Constitution' 2004 *Journal of International Economic Law* 7(2) 219, at 235.

[11] E Jay Friedman, K Hochstetler, and A M Clark, *Sovereignty, Democracy, and Global Civil Society: State-Society Relations at UN World Conferences* (New York: State University of New York Press, 2005), at 158–59.

the definition of one of the actors then depends on whether the State or international organizations choose to engage formally. Another approach is to distinguish civil society from the market forces that operate in pursuit of particular economic interests.[12] This methodology focuses on the objectives of the NGOs active at the international level and their congruence with global public interests. Yet another approach to recognizing 'civility' may be to examine the ways in which NGOs choose to deliver their messages, and particularly whether groups are non-violent. This criterion distinguishes civil society from insurgents, terrorists, and other groups that resort to violence to achieve their means. There is no difficulty in recognizing, as an empirical fact, a wide and vast array of NGOs that are active in the international sphere and that seek to promote greater awareness among the world's public, to provide specialized expertise in policy-making processes, or to influence positions by decision-makers. The way in which these dynamics operate in the WTO context is explored further below.

B. Examples of NGOs Active in the Trade Arena

The sheer number of NGOs working on trade issues around the world makes it impossible to provide a comprehensive list. What may be useful, however, is to mention a couple names by way of example, if only as a way of illustrating the diversity in the field. At a general level, there are networks of NGOs as well as member-based and non-member based NGOs. The distinction influences the strategies and the views adopted by the organizations, as well as their ability to 'represent' their members. Also, some organizations actively conduct campaigns to influence public opinion, while others provide legal and technical input to policy-makers or other NGOs.

An active network of organizations, activists, and social movements worldwide is Our World Is Not For Sale (OWINFS).[13] OWINFS has two 'flagship' statements that reflect its basis of unity. The first is 'No New Round – Turn Around'; the second statement is the 'Our World is not for Sale: WTO – Shrink or Sink!'. Another active network is the Third World Network (TWN), which conducts research on economic, social, and environmental issues pertaining to the South, disseminates information, and provides a platform to represent Southern interests in international fora. Active membership organizations that have campaigned on certain trade and environment issues include the World Wildlife Fund (WWF)[14] and Friends of the Earth International (FOEI). WWF has been very active in the fisheries subsidies

---

[12] AK Lindblom, *Non-governmental Organisations in International Law* (Cambridge: Cambridge University Press, 2005), at 15.

[13] See <http://www.ourworldisnotforsale.org> (last visited 30 May 2008).

[14] See <http://www.panda.org> (last visited 30 May 2008).

negotiations, for example, and FOEI[15] has actively addressed issues such as non-agricultural market access as well as key disputes concerning hormones and genetically modified organisms. Finally, organizations conducting policy and legal analysis on trade and environment, development, and sustainability more generally include Oxfam International,[16] the International Institute for Sustainable Development (IISD),[17] the International Centre for Trade and Sustainable Development (ICTSD),[18] and the Center for International Environmental Law (CIEL).[19]

As this non-comprehensive list illustrates, civil society is not exhausted by one organization, position or perspective, but rather represents a complex space that enables a plurality of voices to enhance decision-making processes. Whether it is Oxfam with its emphasis on fair trade, ICTSD with its focus on building bridges among trade and other communities, or CIEL with its efforts at influencing the development of the jurisprudence concerning trade and environment, the existence of arenas where expert and other views may be presented will lead to more informed decisions.[20] In this regard, even those organizations that seek to dismantle the WTO have a role in shaping the international debates concerning the role of international organizations and international trade.

III. Good Governance in International Organizations

The proposition that the WTO as an international organization is embedded in the network of public international law has been somewhat controversial, especially with respect to the issue of the applicable law in the settlement of WTO disputes.[21] The implications of public international law for the WTO go beyond questions of dispute settlement, however, and concern the mandate and operations of the organization as such, including with respect to the relationship between the WTO and civil society.

---

[15] See < http://www.foei.org> (last visited 30 May 2008).
[16] See < http://www.oxfam.org> (last visited 30 May 2008).
[17] See < http://www.iisd.org> (last visited 30 May 2008).
[18] See < http://www.ictsd.org> (last visited 30 May 2008).
[19] See < http://www.ciel.org> (last visited 30 May 2008).
[20] KC Kennedy, 'Why multilateralism matters in resolving trade-environment disputes' 2001 *Widener Law Symposium Journal* 7(1) 31, at 54.
[21] See J Pauwelyn, 'The Role Of Public International Law In The WTO: How Far Can We Go?' 2001 *American Journal of International Law* 95(3) 535. See also chapter 12 of this Handbook.

The linkages between legitimacy, transparency, and participation are central to the WTO in a context of globalization. The WTO has the potential to affect people's lives in many ways, for example in connection with livelihoods, education, food, and environmental protection. Legitimacy, particularly in the face of trade-offs that result from decisions adopted by the organization, does not rest solely upon the accountability of WTO Members; rather, legitimacy also flows from the ability of the organization to conduct its operations in a transparent and participatory fashion.[22] In this regard, international human rights law illuminates the importance of access to information for good governance. Likewise, international environmental law sheds light on the significance of public participation for good governance.

A. Linkages between Legitimacy, Transparency, and Participation

With the advent of international organizations that adopt decisions on policies that traditionally have been within domestic provinces, issues regarding legitimacy and accountability arrive at the doorsteps of these new organizations. While democratic governments have built an impressive edifice of constitutional and administrative laws to address central issues of legitimacy, transparency, and participation, the new international organizations engaged in global governance appear to be in the nascent stages of developing effective mechanisms aimed at engaging the global public in their decision-making processes. This challenge of effective dialogue lies at the heart of the dilemmas posed by global governance: the need for global rules without centralized power but with political accountability.[23]

Mechanisms for dialogue between the governed and the decision-makers are central to establishing the legitimacy of international organizations. The view that accountability is due only to Member States that comprise the organization fails to account for decisions adopted by the organization that directly affect the public in the Member States. Further, decisions adopted by global institutions addressing problems shared by the international community involve matters of global public interest that thus go beyond the interests of any particular government. In addition, more open and inclusive processes of decision-making can help to overcome the democracy deficits of international governance.[24]

In this light, the vertical transfer of decision-making powers from organized polities at the domestic level to international organizations is a distinct feature of the

---

[22] Lindblom, above fn 12, at 32–36.
[23] AM Slaughter, 'A New World Order' reprinted in Zaelke et al. (eds), *Making Law Work: Environmental Compliance & Sustainable Development*, Vol 2 (London: Cameron & May, 2005) 383, at 387, 392.
[24] Charnovitz, above fn 3.

current operational landscape for international organizations such as the WTO. While engaging the public involves costs, both in time and logistics, the globalization of communication also provides opportunities for effective engagement with global civil society. In this scenario, the WTO stands to gain legitimacy from increased transparency and participation in the various dimensions of its work.

Despite the apparent weight of this proposition, WTO Members and particularly developing countries, in practice, have rejected calls for greater openness. Why? At first impression this question is puzzling, given that developing countries and NGOs that work to create better conditions for the powerless in both rich and poor countries should be natural allies.[25] It has been suggested that the explanation for the conflicts between developing countries and NGOs at the WTO can be found in their competing visions of development.[26] NGOs generally espouse a broad view of development, incorporating economic, social, cultural, political, and environmental aspects, while developing countries focus primarily on the economic aspects of development. Developing countries naturally worry about the impact of the NGO vision on their ability to implement the economic bargain achieved in the Uruguay Round.[27]

At another level, it has been noted that developing countries have rejected calls for greater openness at the WTO for fear of a diminishing role in the organization. Developing countries have raised concerns about their exclusion from the most important Uruguay Round discussions, and as a result of such exclusion the WTO covered agreements favoured industrialized nations at their expense.[28] In this vein, in a scenario where most developing countries are facing severe resource shortages to adequately participate in the workings of the WTO, admitting NGOs to the decision-making process would further threaten to exclude developing-country interests. Yet at another level, it has been argued that the WTO fails to respond to calls for greater openness because the governments of many WTO Members are themselves non-democratic, and otherwise plagued by corruption and other weaknesses.[29]

With respect to developing countries' concerns, the Cancún MC showed that developing countries and NGOs formed loose and informal alliances to challenge industrialized countries' monopoly over WTO decision-making. This example of collaboration suggests that greater openness would further strengthen developing countries' abilities to advance their interests in WTO policy-making.

[25] DD Bradlow, '"The Times They Are A-Changing": Some Preliminary Thoughts On Developing Countries, NGOs And The Reform Of The WTO' 2001 *George Washington International Law Review* 33(3–4) 503.
[26] Ibid at 505.
[27] S Ostry, 'The World Trading System: In Dire Need Of Reform' 2003 *Temple International and Comparative Law Journal* 17(1) 109, at 112. See also chapter 17 of this Handbook.
[28] JL Dunoff, 'How Should International Economic Disputes Be Resolved?' 2001 *South Texas Law Review* 42(4) 1219, at 1221.
[29] JW Head, 'Throwing Eggs at Windows: Legal and Institutional Globalization in the 21st-Century Economy' 2002 *University of Kansas Law Review* 50(4) 731, at 766.

The concern over differing visions of development can be further refined under the framework of sustainable development. Broader NGO perspectives can contribute to a global consensus over complex global issues,[30] or at least to confronting the trade-offs. In shaping these processes of dialogue between the WTO and civil society, human rights law and international environmental law provide useful insights.

B. International Human Rights Law and the Right of Access to Information

International human rights law recognizes the fundamental right to freedom of expression.[31] Recent cases, such as the *Trillium* case discussed below, have clarified the close ties between freedom of expression and access to information, in the context of democracy and good governance. The developments in this area of human rights law provide important guidance to the WTO in establishing effective channels of dialogue with civil society.

In the *Trillium* case, the Inter-American Court of Human Rights (IACtHR) ruled that every person has the right to information held by the State and that the State has a positive duty to disclose information.[32] The IACtHR observed that while the right of access to State-held information admits restrictions, these are limited and subject to stringent requirements, including that any restriction be necessary in a democratic society. It also clarified that access to information and democratic governance are inextricably linked by virtue of civil society's democratic control of the government, which fosters transparency in State activities and accountability of State officials.

While the *Trillium* case concerned States' obligations under a regional human rights convention, the reasoning of the IACtHR is not devoid of significance for the WTO and its Members. The WTO by virtue of its international legal personality is bound to observe customary international law, including applicable human rights law.[33] In determining the *content* of human rights law in relation to access to information that may be relevant for the work of international organizations, decisions

---

[30] M Leighton and E Castaneda, 'Civil Society Concerns in the Context Of Economic Globalization' 2002 *Transnational Lawyer* 15(1) 105.

[31] Art 19 ICCPR; Art 13 American Convention on Human Rights; Art 9 African Charter on Human and Peoples' Rights; Art 10 European Convention on Human Rights.

[32] IACtHR, *Claude Reyes et. al. v Chile ('Trillium')*, Judgment, 19 September 2006, at < http://www.corteidh.or.cr/docs/casos/articulos/seriec_151_esp.pdf> (last visited 30 May 2008).

[33] See ICJ, *Reparation for Injuries Suffered in the Service of the United Nations*, Advisory Opinion, 11 April 1949, ICJ Reports (1949) 174; ICJ, *Interpretation of the Agreement of 25 March 1951 between the WHO and Egypt*, Advisory Opinion, 20 December 1980, ICJ Reports (1980) 87; E Stein, 'International Integration and Democracy: No Love at First Sight' 2001 *American Journal of International Law* 95(3) 489, at 533.

by international human rights tribunals carry authority. In this light, the emphasis placed by the IACtHR on the critical role that civil society plays in holding democratic governments accountable to their citizens is relevant for the WTO by analogy, given the close linkages between democratic accountability of international organizations and transparency.

C. International Environmental Law and Public Participation

International environmental law has recognized the key role of public participation in achieving environmental protection and sustainable development.[34] This recognition flows from the contribution that civil society offers to a more informed debate and better decision-making. Developments in international environmental law concerning public participation also provide support to the WTO in its efforts at actively engaging civil society.

The Rio Declaration on Environment and Development spelled out the principle of public participation, declaring that 'environmental issues are best handled with the participation of all concerned citizens at the relevant level'.[35] This principle has also been recognized in several international treaties, such as the 1996 Convention to Combat Desertification. Also, the Aarhus Convention on Access to Information, Public Participation in Decision-making, and Access to Justice in Environmental Matters establishes the pillars of 'environmental democracy'.

Since the inception of the Aarhus Convention, the Parties recognized that the principles applicable to national authorities also needed to be applied at the international level. In Article 3.7, the Parties committed themselves to promote the application of the principles of the Convention in international environmental decision-making processes and within the framework of international organizations in matters relating to the environment. At their second meeting held in Almaty, Kazakhstan, in May 2005, the Parties adopted a set of guidelines on promoting the principles of access to information, public participation in decision-making, and access to justice in international 'forums' dealing with matters relating to the environment. Also at this second meeting, the Parties established a Task Force to consult with international forums regarding the Almaty Guidelines. In June 2006, the WTO Director-General (DG) responded to an invitation sent by the Almaty Task Force, stating that 'we share with you the important principles of transparency and participation in decision-making'.[36] The letter also noted that the WTO would welcome representatives of the

---

[34] D Hunter, J Salzman, and D Zaelke, *International Environmental Law and Policy*, 3rd edn (New York: Foundation Press, 2007).
[35] Principle 10 Rio Declaration.   [36] Letter on file with author.

UN/UNECE to convey their views on the Almaty Guidelines when attending relevant WTO meetings in which the UN/UNECE is an observer. The letter also noted, however, that the WTO Secretariat would not commit to participate in a future workshop to exchange experiences and practices relating to the Almaty Guidelines.

While it could be argued that the principle of public participation is central to emerging paradigms of global democratic governance,[37] its more modest formulations in international environmental law already provide assistance to the WTO in articulating effective dialogue with civil society. In this regard, asking whether the WTO is a trade *or* environment organization misses the mark. Not only is it distracting, it also potentially leads to the exclusion of public participation as a tool to assist the operations of the organization. International environmental law can provide guidance to the WTO in establishing constructive relationships with civil society.

The WTO stands to incorporate these advances in legal thought and articulate effective channels of dialogue with civil society. In particular, access to information and public participation may inspire the relationship between the WTO and civil society in connection with the various dimensions in the work of the organization. The three branches of the WTO, namely legislative, executive, and judicial functions, stand to benefit from increased consultation and cooperation with NGOs.[38] The next section explores how the WTO is progressing in this direction.

IV. TRANSPARENCY AND PARTICIPATION IN THE WTO

As trade decisions taken in the WTO expand their reach, they affect more varied interests and more people become interested in the forum of decision-making. In this sense, the increased demand for transparency and participation of civil society in the WTO is largely a reflection of the WTO's success.[39]

There have been many suggestions on how NGOs could contribute to WTO processes, including providing expert information and cutting edge ideas, serving as a soundboard for proposals, helping to secure political domestic support for an

[37] See C Bruch (ed), *The New 'Public': The Globalization of Public Participation* (Washington, DC: Environmental Law Institute: 2002).

[38] S Charnovitz, 'Opening the WTO to Nongovernmental Interests' 2000 *Fordham International Law Journal* 24(1) 173, at 212–16.

[39] JL Dunoff, 'Symposium 2004: Citizen Participation in the Global Trading System: Panel 1: Open Democratic Participation Scheme for the World Trade Organization: Public Participation in the Trade Regime: of Litigation, Frustration, Agitation and Legitimation' 2004 *Rutgers Law Review* 56(4) 961, at 965.

agreement, and acting as monitors of compliance with commitments.[40] Other international organizations cooperate more closely with NGOs and rely on them to perform tasks that the international organization itself may not be able to carry out.[41]

Transparency and participation in the WTO involve the institutional operation of the organization, as well as issues concerning capacity-building, negotiations, and dispute settlement. This part examines developments in these areas.

A. Institutional Operation

Article V:2 WTO Agreement states that the General Council (GC) may enter into arrangements for consultation and cooperation between the WTO and NGOs. This provision reflects the fact that NGOs had long been interested in international trade activities, during the existence of the GATT 1947. Interestingly, the provision was phrased in discretional terms, giving the GC a faculty and not an obligation to create such relationships. By contrast, Article V:1 WTO Agreement mandates the GC to make appropriate arrangements for cooperation with other international organizations having responsibilities related to the WTO.[42]

In 1996, the GC adopted guidelines on the relationship between NGOs and the WTO. The guidelines recognize the role of NGOs in fostering public awareness and agree to improve transparency and communications with NGOs.[43] The guidelines include making documents available online on the WTO website, organizing symposia, and making informal arrangements to receive the information provided by NGOs. Item VI points out that there is a consensus among Members regarding the impossibility of direct NGO participation in WTO meetings. It is understood in the guidelines that the appropriate forum for participation of civil society in the decision-making process is the domestic sphere of each WTO Member. In this regard, the guidelines reflect an attempt by the WTO to accommodate the conflicting interests of civil society that demand a greater say in trade rules, on the one hand, and Members, who want to be insulated from these complex pressures in international trade policy decisions, on the other.[44]

---

[40] S Charnovitz, 'Participation of Nongovernmental Organizations in the World Trade Organization' 1996 *University of Pennsylvania Journal of International Economic Law* 17(1) 331.

[41] JB Cawley, 'Friend of the Court: How the WTO Justifies the Acceptance of the Amicus Curiae Brief from Non-Governmental Organizations' 2004 *Penn State International Law Review* 23(1) 47, at 73. Eg, the International Atomic Energy Agency often uses NGOs to monitor the nuclear activity of countries like Iraq.

[42] Article V:2 reads: 'The General Council *may* make appropriate arrangements for consultation and cooperation with non-governmental organizations concerned with matters related to those of the WTO' (emphasis added).

[43] WTO, *Guidelines for arrangements on relations with Non-Governmental Organizations*, WT/L/162 (18 July 1996).

[44] A Reinisch and C Irgel, 'The Participation of Non-Governmental Organizations (NGOs) in the WTO Dispute Settlement System' 2001 *Non-State Actors and International Law* 1(2) 127, at 128–29.

The GC's preference for participation to occur at the national level is open to criticism. The notion that citizens' views should be channelled only through WTO Members' governments disadvantages individuals who live in countries that are not democratic. It also disenfranchises individuals in non-WTO Members, disables individuals from non-powerful countries, reinforces the tendencies of economic nationalism to dominate trade policy, reduces the competition of ideas, and reinforces status quo thinking.[45]

In developing its guidelines, the GC did not provide deeper reasons for considering the WTO different from other international organizations where public participation is admitted.[46] NGOs are routinely accredited and participate as observers in the meetings of the UN Economic and Social Council (ECOSOC), the International Labour Organization (ILO), the World Intellectual Property Organization (WIPO), the UN Commission on International Trade Law (UNCITRAL), the UN Conference on Trade and Development (UNCTAD), and other international organizations that deal with economic matters.[47] Yet, the WTO has only allowed access to plenary sessions in MC and has not allowed NGOs to observe and speak at the meetings of its subsidiary bodies.[48]

Still, the implementation of the guidelines does reveal efforts to introduce greater transparency and participation in the institutional operations of the WTO. The WTO's website provides a large number of documents for free access. It has been pointed out, however, that sometimes there are considerable delays in making them available. The WTO has attributed some delays to the time necessary for translating documents. Furthermore, certain documents have not been made public, such as submissions to the Dispute Settlement Body (unless the party in point decides to disclose it), interlocutory procedural decisions, and the panels' interim reports. The WTO website has a page especially for NGOs, a contact point for NGOs, and an e-mail address to which NGOs can direct their correspondence.[49]

Forums and symposiums are designed to improve the dialogue with the public and promote understanding of the WTO, as provided for in Article 10 of the Doha Declaration. Attendees are NGO representatives, academics, and the public at

---

[45] S Charnovitz, 'Symposium 2004: Citizen Participation in the Global Trading System: Panel 1: Open Democratic Participation Scheme for the World Trade Organization: Transparency and Participation in the World Trade Organization' 2004 *Rutgers Law Review* 56(4) 927, at 948.

[46] Ibid at 940.

[47] P Van den Bossche, 'Debating the Future of the World Trade Organization: Divergent Views on the 2005 Sutherland Report' 2005 *Journal of International Economic Law* 8(3) 759, at 766.

[48] S Charnovitz, 'WTO Cosmopolitics' 2002 *New York University Journal of International Law and Politics* 34(2) 299, at 232.

[49] The NGO page on the WTO website lists eight events as 'NGO-related activities' during the period from 2001 to 2007. Besides the annual Public Forums and Symposiums, in March 2007 there was a briefing by DG on the status of negotiations. See < http://www.wto.org/english/forums_e/ngo_e/ngo_e.htm> (last visited 30 May 2008).

large.[50] Members of civil society organize their own events during these meetings. The WTO's Public Symposium, however, is not designed to elicit any recommendations and thus stands in stark contrast with the efforts of other international institutions, such as the UN Environment Programme (UNEP), which have designed the negotiating process to benefit from civil society engagement.[51]

A clear illustration of the dialogue between the WTO and NGOs during the last decade is the debate organized in 2005 by a group of NGOs with the candidates for the WTO's Director-General (DG) position.[52] Three of the four candidates accepted the invitation to 'discuss their vision for world trade' and answered questions on their commitment to improve transparency, among other relevant issues. All candidates agreed that civil society contributed positively to the WTO. The meeting was classified as a 'major step forward' and 'a tribute to civil society's efforts' by NGO representatives.

While progress has been made in introducing transparency and participation in the WTO's institutional operations, the limits of what can be achieved appear to be determined by the idea that the WTO is an inter-governmental forum and that civil society participation ought to be channelled through Members' governments. By way of illustration, in 2006 the WTO held online chats with DG Pascal Lamy. When asked about NGO participation in the decision-making process, the DG answered that he did not believe the Members would agree to the creation of an NGO Committee that could participate in the decision-making process, and called attention to the nature of the WTO as an inter-governmental organization.

Ultimately, the conceptual boundaries of the WTO may shift to encompass a role for NGOs in its institutional operation as the WTO is further integrated in the wider corpus of public international law, as the emerging commonalities between developing countries and NGOs mature, and as the WTO gains greater awareness of the experience of other international organizations in regards to civil society engagement. Steps in this direction may include, *inter alia*, observer status for accredited NGOs in WTO meetings, greater publicity of documents in dispute settlement, and a redesign of the WTO Public Forum to feed into negotiations.

B. Capacity-Building

The WTO affirms on its website that 'helping developing countries participate more fully in the global trading system is one of the WTO's most important activities'. The

---

[50] WTO, *Summary of participation in the Public Forum*, at < http://www.wto.org/english/forums_e/public_forum_e/participation_e.doc> (last visited 30 May 2008).

[51] S Charnovitz, 'A Close Look At A Few Points' 2005 *Journal of International Economic Law* 8(2) 311, at 318.

[52] See transcripts at < http://www.tradeobservatory.org/library.cfm?refid=48511> (last visited 30 May 2008).

focus is on 'instructing developing country delegates on how their countries can gain through the trading system' through technical assistance, which is designed to improve the assimilation of WTO rules and disciplines.[53] Transparency is an important aspect of capacity-building, since the free flow of information contributes to the education of the public and officials.

The WTO has recognized that civil society participation may add to WTO efforts in capacity-building. The Institute for Training and Technical Cooperation (ITCC), created under the WTO Secretariat, is responsible for coordinating the WTO initiatives aimed at providing assistance to improve institutional and human capacity in trade issues. The ITTC started developing partnerships between the WTO Secretariat and the academic community in WTO Members.[54] On occasion, the funds for capacity-building have been used to partially cover the costs associated with the WTO's Public Forum.[55] This is an implicit recognition that improving communications and transparency is an important aspect of capacity-building.

C. WTO Negotiations

The GATT 1947 as the WTO's predecessor ascribed to the traditional diplomatic practices of secrecy and discretion. For a long period of time there was not much external scrutiny of the negotiations, and the minutes of meetings were incomplete or unclear.[56] Such secrecy in GATT 1947 negotiations has produced unwanted effects that last even today. For example, the WTO dispute settlement system would be simpler if the records of the negotiators' intent were more reliable.[57] Also, the resulting culture of confidentiality in the negotiations' remain deeply ingrained in the WTO, even though there is no legal requirement of secrecy provided for in the WTO agreements.[58]

Nevertheless, there have been developments since the GATT 1947 times with respect to transparency and participation. In 2004, the WTO started to make the draft negotiating texts public. There is no civil society committee for participatory comments from the public, but there are on-line chat forums, where issues posed by the WTO or suggested by the public may be debated. The WTO designates experts

---

[53] WTO, *Building Trade Capacity*, at < http://www.wto.org/english/tratop_e/devel_e/build_tr_capa_e.htm> (last visited 30 May 2008).

[54] WTO, *Institute for Training and Technical Cooperation (ITTC)*, at < http://www.wto.org/english/tratop_e/devel_e/teccop_e/ittc_e.htm> (last visited 30 May 2008).

[55] ICTSD, 'Trade, Civil Society Decision-Makers Convene at WTO Symposium' *Bridges Weekly Trade News Digest* 6(16) (2 May 2002), at < http://www.ictsd.org/weekly/02–05-02/story1.htm> (last visited 30 May 2008).

[56] JA Lacarte, 'Transparency, Public Debate and Participation by NGOs in the WTO: a WTO Perspective' 2004 *Journal of International Economic Law* 7(3) 683.

[57] Ibid.   [58] S Charnovitz, above fn 45, at 938.

and officials to participate in these discussions, thereby strengthening the abilities of its Secretariat to engage with civil society.

The question whether public views reach negotiators in a manner capable of influencing decision-making has, nevertheless, remained open. It may be that there is no one single answer to this question, but that it depends on issue area. In this regard, the fisheries subsidies negotiations are illustrative of successful engagement between WTO delegates and civil society, although ironically in a forum separate from the WTO.

The fisheries subsidies debate was placed in the negotiating arena by the WWF, which has prepared analysis and facilitated dialogue on the topic for a decade. After initial scoping papers and informal workshops organized by WWF and attended by WTO delegates, NGOs, and representatives of certain international organizations such as UN Environment Programme (UNEP), the topic gained much momentum as a result of its inclusion in the Doha agenda of negotiations. An interesting partnership was formed between WWF and UNEP, which jointly organized 'technical and informal' workshops before official WTO meetings.[59] In preparation of these workshops, NGOs experts conducted research on technical aspects of the negotiations.[60] This form of engagement enabled a constructive dialogue between civil society and WTO delegates that has contributed to significant progress in the fisheries subsidies negotiations. This progress has been evident in the process of consensus-building over the need for clear and strong disciplines on fisheries subsidies, as well as in the actual structure and elements of the draft produced by the chair of the negotiating group.

While staff members of the WTO Secretariat have participated in the workshops jointly organized by UNEP and WWF, the WTO as an institution has not had a formal role. In other words, no formal forum yet exists in the WTO for the type of interactions that have been facilitated by these informal and technical workshops. Yet there are many sensitive issues within the Doha agenda of negotiations, such as the relationship between the WTO and multilateral environmental agreements. Whether such a forum for civil society engagement with the WTO could lead to similar progress in negotiations remains an open question.

D. Participation in WTO Dispute Settlement

The WTO dispute settlement system exercises considerable power in the global trading regime. It has been argued that this enforcement mechanism is one of the

[59] See for all, UNEP/WWF, *Technical and Informal Workshop on WTO Disciplines on Fisheries Subsidies: Elements of the Chair's Draft Text*, Geneva (29 January 2008), at < http://www.unep.ch/etb/ events/2008FishSubWorkshop29Jan08.php> (last visited 30 May 2008).

[60] Examples of topics covered include: access agreements to the exclusive economic zone and fisheries subsidies; artisanal fisheries and sustainability; sustainability criteria for fisheries subsidies; special and differential treatment and fisheries subsidies.

reasons for the high level of compliance with WTO disciplines. Many of the cases where conflicts arise involve interests other than business and trade. For example, the Dispute Settlement Body (DSB) has heard cases involving hormones in beef for human consumption, the protection of endangered animal species, and disposal of used tyres, to name a few. Given the importance of these issues, it is understandable that civil society expects to take on a greater role in the resolution of the disputes.

Despite these expectations, public participation in the WTO dispute settlement system remains rather limited. For example, in 2004, the Appellate Body solicited comments from governments on the amendments of its Working Procedures, but did not request comments from civil society.[61] This may have been a reaction to the political backlash suffered by the Appellate Body after its experience with *amicus curiae* briefs in the *EC – Asbestos* case, discussed below.

The role of *amicus curiae* briefs has been the subject of heated controversy at the WTO. The Dispute Settlement Understanding (DSU) has no explicit provision for NGO participation, which may explain why the WTO at first did not allow NGOs any role in resolving disputes. The Appellate Body formally opened the door for *amicus curiae* briefs in *US – Shrimp*.[62] Since then there have been a number of cases where NGOs have presented written submissions to WTO panels and the Appellate Body.[63] Not only not-for-profit public interest NGOs, but also trade associations have submitted *amicus curiae* briefs in a number of cases. More often than not, panels and the Appellate Body have accepted these submissions, but have often found it unnecessary to consider them.[64]

It has been argued that this practice renders NGOs' participation illusory, since the arguments by NGOs that get any consideration are those appended to governments' submissions that echo governments' positions.[65] In addition, the fact that the contending parties' submissions are, in principle, confidential, makes it difficult for NGOs to prepare written *amicus curiae* briefs, since they do not have access to complete information regarding the case. Consequently, while panels and the Appellate Body have formally recognized their authority to consider any *amicus curiae* brief in dispute settlement, in practice they have not regarded *amicus curiae* briefs in resolving disputes.

Two reasons may explain the fate of *amicus curiae* briefs at the WTO. The first relates to the long-standing GATT effort of insulating negotiations and adjudication

---

[61] E Hernandez Lopez, 'Recent Trends and Perspectives for Non-State Actor Participation in World Trade Organization Disputes' 2001 *Journal of World Trade* 35(3) 469, at 481.

[62] Appellate Body Report, *US – Shrimp*, at paras 104–10.

[63] N Bernasconi-Osterwalder, D Magraw, J Oliva, and M Orellana, *Environment and Trade: A Guide to WTO Jurisprudence* (London: Earthscan, 2006), at 317–60.

[64] See, eg, Appellate Body Report, *US – Lead and Bismuth II*, at para 42; Appellate Body Report, *US – Countervailing Measures on Certain EC Products*, at para 76; Appellate Body Report, *US – Softwood Lumber IV*, at para 9; Appellate Body Report, *EC – Chicken Cuts*, at para 12; Appellate Body Report, *Mexico – Taxes on Soft Drinks*, at para 8; Panel Report, *EC – Biotech Products*, at paras 7.10–11.

[65] Dunoff, above fn 39, at 965.

from special interest groups that could undermine the benefits of free trade.[66] In this sense, public interest NGOs have been equated with particular industries seeking protectionist measures. For the dispute settlement mechanism to preserve the grand bargain embodied in the multilateral trading system and overcome protectionism, it should be shielded from the pressures exerted by narrow interest groups. The weakness in this argument is that it equates public interest issues with private interests, on the basis that at some point in time they may coincide in calling for a departure from certain trade disciplines. In this regard, the recognition that measures otherwise inconsistent with certain trade rules are necessary to protect human, animal or plant life and health, for example, has been part of the grand bargain since the outset of the GATT.

A second reason that explains the reluctance of WTO panels and the Appellate Body to consider *amicus curiae* briefs relates to the marked opposition by developing countries to this practice. Certain WTO Members have often objected to *amicus* participation on the grounds that non-parties should not be allowed to intervene in dispute settlement between States.[67] It has been noted that this criticism ignores the practical reality of the dispute settlement process and the significant role of non-State actors in it. So while private interests can leverage their government in dispute settlement, NGOs advocating public interest perspectives lack such leverage when their positions do not coincide with those of their government, when their government does not have adequate resources for effectively participating in dispute settlement, or when the NGO is located in a country that is not a WTO Member.[68]

EC – Asbestos provides an example of how these arguments and tensions have played out in practice. In *EC – Asbestos*, the Appellate Body *sua sponte* posted guidelines whereby prospective *amici* were required to make a request for leave to file an *amicus curiae* brief.[69] A number of developing countries called for a special meeting to discuss this issue, and the overwhelming majority of States who spoke at this meeting harshly criticized the Appellate Body's initiative.[70] The Appellate Body rejected all 17 requests that it received from those interested in filing *amicus curiae* briefs, without justification in a majority of cases, and offering a procedural justification for a few of them.[71] NGOs also made their discontent with the Appellate Body clear in public ways.[72]

---

[66] EB Bluemel, 'Substance Without Process: Analyzing TRIPS Participatory Guarantees In Light Of Protected Indigenous Rights' 2004 *Journal of the Patent and Trademark Office Society* 86(9) 671, at 690.

[67] J Keller, 'The Future Of Amicus Participation At The WTO: Implications Of The Sardines Decision And Suggestions For Further Developments' 2005 *International Journal of Legal Information* 33(3) 449, at 457.

[68] Ibid.   [69] Appellate Body Report, *EC – Asbestos*, at paras 51–52.

[70] Dunoff, above n 39, at 963; also Bernasconi-Osterwalder et al., above fn 63, at 342.

[71] Appellate Body Report, *EC – Asbestos*, at paras 55–57.

[72] Cawley, above fn 41, at 75.

E. Transparency in WTO Dispute Settlement

Transparency in dispute settlement primarily relates to access to documents and open hearings. Some steps have been taken to introduce transparency, but for the most part they have been taken by consenting disputing parties rather than by panels or the Appellate Body. While technology exists to facilitate access to pleadings and open hearings, WTO Members have generally been reluctant to open up dispute settlement to the press and the public. Among other things, this has resulted in contending parties spinning the interim decisions in their favour by giving misleading, incomplete, or ambiguous statements to the press, which is unable to verify their accuracy given that hearings, pleadings, and interim reports are not open to the public.

In general, hearings in WTO dispute settlement proceedings are closed, unless both parties agree otherwise. On three occasions, hearings before panels were open to public observation: in *US – Continued Suspension of Obligations in the EC – Hormones Dispute* and *Canada – Continued Suspension of Obligations in the EC – Hormones Dispute,* in September 2005 and September/October 2006, and in the *EC – Bananas* hearings of November 2007. In *EC – Bananas*, NGOs applauded the initiative to open the hearing and requested that the hearing be web-cast to enlarge public viewing opportunity.[73] To date, the only hearing before the Appellate Body that has been open to public viewing is the *Hormones* dispute referenced above, at the request of the disputing parties, that is, Canada, the EC, and the US. But since third parties to the dispute, including Brazil and China, did not agree to an open hearing, the live transmission was cut every time these countries intervened.[74] The Panel in *Brazil – Retreaded Tyres* also received a letter from NGOs requesting that it consult with the parties to consider the possibility of web-casting the first substantive meeting. The Panel decided that the meetings with the parties and third parties would be held in closed sessions in accordance with the procedures it had adopted at the beginning of the proceedings. This case illustrates the changing conceptual boundaries of the WTO in its relation to civil society. Before this case, Brazil had opposed NGO participation in dispute settlement and the EC had supported it. Yet, when confronted in an 'environmental' case, Brazil (the defendant) welcomed the request for open hearings and the EC (the claimant) objected to transparency. However, as noted above, in the more recent hearing before the Appellate Body in the *Hormones* dispute, Brazil as a third party opposed transparency, while the EC requested the open hearing.

---

[73] CIEL, 'CIEL and partners request web-casting of EC – Bananas hearing at the World Trade Organization', November 2007, at < http://www.ciel.org/Tae/Bananas_Webcasting_2Nov07.html> (last visited 30 May 2008).

[74] CIEL, 'CIEL attends first open WTO Appellate Body hearing in the famous Hormones dispute', July 2008, at <http://www.ciel.org>, (last visited 14 August 2008).

In relation to access to documents, the US, Canada, and the EC made their pleadings available in *EC – Biotech Products*, while Argentina did not. The interim decision was not made public, however, which allowed contending parties to represent the decision to the press in their favour. Given the confidential status of the interim report, the press was thus unable to report on it with accuracy. Still, the interim report somehow leaked a couple days after the decision was rendered, enabling academic analysis and public debate over the implications of the Panel's decision. In *Brazil – Retreaded Tyres*, Brazil made its pleadings available to the public contemporaneously to their filing, while the EC only made them available after the hearings. This practice prevented the public from having complete knowledge of the issues involved in the dispute. It also limited the contribution that prospective *amici* could make to the Panel and the Appellate Body, as they only had access to the Brazilian submissions.

In conclusion there have been certain developments in regards to transparency, such as open hearings and availability of documents in some cases, but these limited improvements are not a sufficient response to civil society's demand for a transparent and open WTO dispute settlement system.

V. CONCLUSION

Since its creation in 1995, the WTO has faced increasing demands for transparency and accountability by global civil society. These demands relate to the WTO's exercise of certain elements of global governance, including with respect to decisions that affect citizens within and beyond WTO Members. While there has been some progress in fostering dialogue between the WTO and civil society, processes for WTO decision-making remain opaque.

The WTO inherited a culture of confidentiality from the GATT 1947, which was dominated by diplomatic efforts to insulate free trade from capture by special protectionist interests. The WTO also inherited the fears of exclusion resulting from developing country experiences with the Uruguay Round. As a result, it has been slow in learning from the practice of other international organizations in regards to constructive engagement with civil society.

Globalization presents the challenge of effective dialogue between international organizations exercising elements of global governance and the global public particularly in respect of decision-making processes. In this regard, the nature and quality of such dialogue is of direct consequence to the legitimacy of the organization, particularly its acceptance by the public and its ability to deliver its mandate. While the WTO is taking initial steps to confront this challenge, the organization remains anchored in a State-centred order, where civil society can and should only engage its own government. This view denies the existence of global public interest issues and global constituencies, and ignores the challenges of global governance, in a context of globalization.

Still, recent developments present opportunities for enhanced dialogue between the WTO and civil society. The dynamics observed in the Cancún MC and beyond, where NGOs rallied in support of developing countries, may eventually influence a shift in the conceptual boundaries of the trading system. The influential role of civil society and UNEP in building consensus on the need for strong and effective disciplines on fisheries subsidies may also provide impetus for the creation of similar forums for engagement. Finally, the transparent handling of some disputes may dispel fears that open hearings and access to pleadings will unravel the multilateral trading system.

Selected Bibliography

KW Abbott, 'Economics Issues and Political Participation: The Evolving Boundaries of International Federalism' 1996 *Cardozo Law Review* 18(3) 971

CE Barfield, 'Free Trade, Sovereignty, Democracy: The Future of the World Trade Organization' 2001 *Chicago Journal of International Law* 2(2) 403

BM Bernau, 'Help for Hotspots: NGO Participation in the Preservation of Worldwide Biodiversity' 2006 *Indiana Journal of Global Legal Studies* 13(2) 617

B Bluemel, 'Overcoming NGO Accountability Concerns in International Governance' 2005 *Brooklyn Journal of International Law* 31(1) 139

DD Bradlow, 'The Times They Are A-Changing: Some Preliminary Thoughts on Developing Countries, NGOs and the Reform of the WTO' 2001 *George Washington International Law Review* 33(3–4) 503

C Carmody, 'Beyond the Proposals: Public Participation in International Economic Law' 2000 *American University International Law Review* 15(6) 1321

JB Cawley, 'Friend of the Court: How the WTO Justifies the Acceptance of the Amicus Curiae Brief from Non-Governmental Organizations' 2004 *Penn State International Law Review* 23(1) 47

S Charnovitz, 'The WTO and Cosmopolitics' 2004 *Journal of International Economic Law* 7(3) 675

S Charnovitz, 'Transparency and Participation in the World Trade Organization' 2004 *Rutgers Law Review* 56(4) 927

S Charnovitz, 'Nongovernmental Organizations and International Law' 2006 *American Journal of International Law* 100(2) 348

W Debevoise, 'Access to Documents and Panel and Appellate Body Sessions: Practice and Suggestions for Greater Transparency' 1998 *International Lawyer* 32(3) 817

JL Dunoff, 'The WTO in Transition: Of Constituents, Competence and Coherence' 2001 *George Washington International Law Review* 33(3–4) 979

JL Dunoff, 'Public Participation in the Trade Regime: Of Litigation, Frustration, Agitation and Legitimation' 2004 *Rutgers Law Review* 56(4) 961

DC Esty, 'Good Governance At The World Trade Organization: Building A Foundation Of Administrative Law' 2007 *Journal of International Economic Law* 10(3) 509

MB Jeffords, 'Turning the Protester into a Partner for Development: The Need for Effective Consultation Between the WTO & NGOs' 2003 *Brooklyn Journal International Law* 28(3) 937

JA Lacarte, 'Transparency, Public Debate and Participation by NGOs in the WTO: A WTO Perspective' 2004 *Journal of International Economic Law* 7(3) 683

VA Leary, 'Challenging Power, Civil Society at the Gates of the WTO: The View from Geneva' 1999 *American Society of International Law Proceedings* (93) 186

M Leighton and E Castaneda, 'Civil Society Concerns In The Context Of Economic Globalization' 2002 *Transnational Lawyer* 15(1) 105

J Pauwelyn, 'Report on the Future of the WTO, The Sutherland Report: A Missed Opportunity for Genuine Debate on Trade, Globalization and Reforming the WTO' 2005 *Journal of International Economic Law* 8(2) 329

J Peel, 'Giving the Public a Voice in the Protection of the Global Environment: Avenues for Participation by NGOs in Dispute Resolution at the European Court of Justice and World Trade Organization' 2001 *Colorado Journal of International Environmental Law & Policy* 12(1) 47

E-U Petersmann, 'Challenges to the Legitimacy and Efficiency of the World Trading System: Democratic Governance and Competition Culture in the WTO' 2004 *Journal of International Economic Law* 7(3) 585

A Kupner Schneider, 'Unfriendly Actions: The Amicus Brief Battle at the WTO' 2001 *Widener Law Symposium Journal* 7(1) 87

GC Shaffer, 'The World Trade Organization Under Challenge: Democracy and the Law and Politics of the WTO's Treatment of Trade and Environment Matters' 2001 *Harvard Environmental Law Review* 25(1) 1

GR Shell, 'Stakeholders Model and Participation by Nonstate Parties in the World Trade Organization' 2004 *University of Pennsylvania Journal International Economic Law* 25(2) 703

P Sutherland, 'The Doha Development Agenda: Political Challenges to the World Trading System – A Cosmopolitan Perspective' 2005 *Journal of International Economic Law* 8(2) 363

L Zhengling, 'An Analysis of the Role of NGOs in the WTO' 2004 *Chinese Journal of International Law* 3(2) 485

CHAPTER 25

....

INTERNATIONAL TRADE LAW, UNITED NATIONS LAW, AND COLLECTIVE SECURITY ISSUES

....

LAURENCE BOISSON DE CHAZOURNES
THÉO BOUTRUCHE*

* The views expressed in this chapter are personal and do not reflect the views of the Office of the United Nations High Commissioner for Human Rights.

I. INTRODUCTION

TODAY, fragmentation and unity of the international legal order has become its own topic of study[1] recognizing that a wide variety of international norms may create complex interactions and give rise to various types of conflicts.[2] It is at this time that the relationship between international trade law and United Nations (UN) law, notably in the field of collective security, seems critical. To date, however, this issue has rarely been analyzed in its full scope. In strict legal terms, this is hardly surprising as the relationship between both regimes has generally been subjected to a formalistic, hierarchical approach. Emphasis is given to the special status of the UN Charter through its Article 103, which establishes the priority of the Charter over obligations under any other international agreement in the context of maintenance of peace and security. Concerning the WTO, issues involving State national and international security are dealt with through provisions establishing relevant exceptions. Such is the case with Article XXI GATT 1994, which Members may invoke as a justification for departing from their obligations. Article XXI (c) exempts a UN Member State from its WTO obligations when it acts 'in pursuance of its obligations under the UN Charter for the maintenance of international peace and security'.[3] Such clear-cut provisions seem to leave little room for a more thoroughgoing analysis.

However, the scope of Article 103 needs further analysis before one can fully grasp the issue of the relationship between international trade law and other legal regimes. Article 103, because of its wording,[4] has mostly been interpreted from the

---

[1] International Law Commission, Fifty-eighth session, Geneva, 1 May–9 June and 3 July–11 August 2006, *Fragmentation of international law: difficulties arising from the diversification and expansion of international law*, Report of the Study Group of the International Law Commission, 13 April 2006, UN Doc. A/CN.4/L.682.

[2] J Pauwelyn, *Conflict of Norms in Public International Law – How WTO Law Relates to other Rules of International Law* (Cambridge: Cambridge University Press, 2003).

[3] Art XXI (c) GATT 1994.

[4] Article 103 reads as follows: 'In the event of a conflict between the obligations of the Members of the United Nations under the present Charter and their obligations under any other international agreement, their obligations under the present Charter shall prevail.'

perspective of a conflict of norms.[5] Such a focus has been reinforced by the specificity of Article 103, which gives the UN Charter a unique status.[6] However, one should recognize that incompatibility of norms is the exception rather than the rule within a legal system. Article 103 must also be read in terms of compatibility. This provision does not exclude the application of principles and rules of WTO law to the activities carried out by the UN Security Council under Chapter VII of the Charter in the absence of a normative conflict.[7] The legal primacy of the UN Charter is thus merely one way among several to address the manifold interactions between WTO and UN law.

Some critical changes in UN practice call for a broader approach to analyzing the relationship between WTO law and UN law. Whereas economic sanctions were for a long time the sole UN-related challenge to WTO law, the recent, surreptitiously growing economic interventionism of the UN has raised new challenges.[8] Economic sanctions mainly cover non-forcible measures adopted by the UN Security Council within the framework of its powers to maintain international peace and security under Article 41 UN Charter.[9] Those measures—be they commercial or financial embargos, aerial, naval embargoes, or the freezing of assets—pose an issue of legality under principles and rules of WTO law including the principle requiring most-favoured-nation (MFN) treatment. In such cases, the conflict rule of Article XXI (c) GATT 1994 is directly relevant. In the 1980s and the 1990s, the Security Council's increasing recourse to economic sanctions as a means of carrying out its responsibilities brought this provision to the forefront.

Article XXI (c) GATT 1994 does not address all of the complexity of the issues raised by UN sanctions. Further, and most importantly, it leaves partly unanswered questions arising from new forms of economic intervention by the UN through collective security measures. One may think of the international administration of territories such as Kosovo and East Timor or the particular case of the occupation of Iraq by the US and the UK under the unified command of the 'Authority'. Those new forms of economic intervention are developed in a fragmented and *ad hoc* way, with little attention paid to international economic law aspects. This chapter provides an overview of the UN activities in the economic field, which shows the limits of the predominant 'exception oriented' approach and the need to rethink the relationship

---

[5] See, eg, ICJ, *Questions of Interpretation and Application of the 1971 Montreal Convention arising from the Aerial Incident at Lockerbie, (Lybian Arab Jamahiriya v United Kingdom)*, Provisional Measures, Order, ICJ Reports (1992) 16, at para 39.

[6] JM Thouvenin, 'Article 103' in JP Cot and A Pellet (eds), *La Charte des Nations Unies – Commentaire article par article*, 3rd edn (Paris: Economica, 2005), at 2133.

[7] L Boisson de Chazournes, 'Collective Security and the Economic Interventionism of the UN – The Need for a Coherent and Integrated Approach' 2007 *Journal of International Economic Law* 10(1) 51, at 57–75.

[8] On this phenomenon and its implications, ibid.

[9] For an assessment of the Security Council practice, see D Cortwright and GA Lopez, *The Sanctions Decade: Assessing UN Strategies in the 1990s* (London: Lynne Rienner Publishers, 2000).

between international economic law and UN law. This rethinking appears necessary given the critical changes in the economic context of the Security Council activities, with, *inter alia*, economic threats increasingly linked to threats to international peace and security.[10] In this respect, the recently established Peacebuilding Commission represents an important change in approach, as well as the recognition of the increasing interface between collective security, maintenance of peace, and economic concerns. The parallel move in favour of strengthening and expanding the partnership between the UN and the private sector 'to promote the exercise of responsible investment in crisis areas'[11] makes this need for a new approach even more essential.

The integration of international economic law principles in post-conflict situations could contribute to the achievement of UN goals when it acts in the field of international peace and security. Peacebuilding activities, for example, require involvement in social and economic development as much as in political and institutional reform. It is crucial to address the causes of a conflict. Taking into account international trade law in carrying out such activities may help to stabilize post-conflict economies by providing the grounds for a more flexible transition once the UN is gone. A clearer reference to economic parameters in UN work may also allow for a more complete assessment of economic challenges in war-torn territories. This approach implies going beyond the mere question of the legality of UN action under WTO principles and rules and instead advocates the application of each of these bodies of norms together.

This chapter will first look at the WTO security exceptions provision, which can be invoked with regard to sanctions adopted outside the UN framework, in order to illustrate certain legal issues under WTO law. Articles XXI (a) and XXI (b) GATT 1994 have often been assessed in terms of the risk they may pose to the whole WTO system by granting States discretion to depart from their GATT obligations. However, through reference to actual practice under this article, this chapter argues that such fears were overstated and that judicial review of States' unilateral determinations under these provisions is still admissible. These developments will help to shed some light on the relationship between WTO law and UN law concerning the issue of UN economic interventionism and collective security activities. Finally, the case of small arms trade will provide an example of the complexity of the challenges WTO law faces as a result of the development of new UN instruments.

---

[10] Report of the High-level Panel on Threats, Challenges and Change, *A More Secure World: Our Shared Responsibility*, UN Doc A/59/565 (2 December 2004), at paras 17.

[11] *Report of the Secretary-General to the Security Council on the Protection of Civilians in Armed Conflict*, UN Doc S/2001/331 (30 March 2001), at para 61.

II. Economic Sanctions and Security Exceptions: An Open Door?

The WTO system provides for specific exceptions that may be invoked by Members to depart from their obligations when security is at stake. They are found in Article XXI GATT 1994 under the general heading of 'security exceptions'. However, the legal regime established under the WTO distinguishes between economic measures that a Member may adopt in accordance with the *collective* security regime of the UN Charter, and *unilateral* measures adopted by a Member for the purposes of its own security interests. Article XXI (a)-(b) GATT 1994 read as follows:

Nothing in this Agreement shall be construed

(a)   to require any contracting party to furnish any information the disclosure of which it considers contrary to its essential security interests; or

(b)   to prevent any contracting party from taking any action which it considers necessary for the protection of its essential security interests

   (i)   relating to fissionable materials or the materials from which they are derived;

   (ii)   relating to the traffic in arms, ammunition and implements of war and to such traffic in other goods and materials as is carried on directly or indirectly for the purpose of supplying a military establishment;

   (iii)   taken in time of war or other emergency in international relations.

While Article XX GATT 1994 contains explicit legal requirements in order to invoke an exception, Article XXI appears to mostly depend on a Member's own appreciation, and has been interpreted as allowing far more leeway to States in its application.[12] The fear of an abuse of this article was thus seen as a threat to the WTO system, particularly with regard to a Member's power to assess what it 'considers necessary for the protection of its essential security interests'. According to Lowenfeld, with a 'self-judging measure and no procedure created to subject assertion to international scrutiny, the provision had the potential to become a significant means for evading GATT obligations'.[13]

However, there are limits on the use of Article XXI (b). The absence of a specific legal requirement does not mean it contains no legal constraints. First, Article XXI (b) identifies in its subsections 'objective circumstances' to be considered.[14] For instance, subsection (i) limits the scope of potential action to 'fissionable

---

[12]   M Matsushita, TJ Schoenbaum, and PC Mavroidis, *The World Trade Organization – Law, Practice, and Policy* (Oxford: Oxford University Press, 2003), at 221.

[13]   See AF Lowenfeld, *International Economic Law* (New York: Oxford University Press, 2003), at 34.

[14]   Matsushita, Schoenbaum, and Mavroidis, above fn 12, at 222.

materials or the materials from which they are derived'. Second, an element of necessity must be established, what seems to open the door to international oversight.
Each State is allowed to determine what measure it considers necessary to protect
its security interests, and to determine the scope of the exception. Nevertheless,
it is still possible to assess the compatibility of the resulting measures with WTO
rules in the context of a dispute settlement procedure. Analogies can be drawn with
other fields of international law where States may take 'self-judging' decisions to
determine what is necessary. In human rights law as well as in the law on the use of
force, for instance, the condition of necessity must be met by States to invoke exceptions or derogations to justify certain acts. This self-assessment can be reviewed in
a judicial forum.[15]

Practice is scarce in terms of international oversight with regard to Article XXI (b).
A Panel was established under the GATT 1947 in *US – Trade Measures (Nicaragua)*.
The US took the position that the legal terms of Article XXI (b) such as 'security
interests' could not be the subject of examination or a decision by a Panel. The Panel
did not have the opportunity to rule on this question of principle since the terms of
its mandate prevented its review.[16] This being said, one cannot conclude that any
judicial review would be excluded in the context of another dispute.[17]

Some have considered that recourse to Article XXI (b) to justify a Member's adoption of unilateral 'sanctions' in violation of its WTO obligations is not appropriate in
the light of the specific wording and scope of this provision. First, it has been interpreted as covering mainly *export* restraints.[18] Second, the action affecting WTO
rules needs to be adopted in a particular field, at least for subsections (b) (i) and
(ii). Consequently, measures contemplated in this article seem to be more oriented
towards a State that decides on restrictive measures on the basis of what is being
traded rather than towards general measures taken against another State to 'express
disapproval of the acts of the target state or to induce that state to change some policy

---

[15] For examples of such judicial review under human rights law and *jus ad bellum*, see respectively
Human Rights Committee, *General Comment. No 27: Freedom of movement (Article 12)*, CCPR/C/21/
Rev.1/Add.9 (2 November 1999); ICJ, *Oil Platforms (Islamic Republic of Iran v United States of America)*,
Judgment, 6 November 2003, ICJ Reports (2003) 183, at paras 43, 74, and 76.
[16] GATT Panel Report, *US – Trade Measures (Nicaragua)*, at para 5.2; see also L Boisson de
Chazournes, *Les contre-mesures dans les relations internationales économiques* (Paris: IUHEI/
Pedone, 1992), at 145.
[17] With regard to the expression 'if that party considers that', in the context of retaliation under
Article 22.3 (b)-(c) DSU, the Arbitrators in the *EC – Bananas III (Ecuador) (Article 22.6 – EC)* held that
there is a certain margin of appreciation, but nonetheless some judicial review applies to whether
the Member had considered 'the necessary facts objectively'. Decision by the Arbitrators, *EC –
Bananas III (Ecuador) (Article 22.6 – EC)*, at para 52. On the unsettled nature of this debate within the
GATT/WTO Jurisprudence concerning Article XXI, see AS Alexandroff and R Sharma, 'The National
Security Provision – GATT Article XXI' in PFJ Macrory, AE Appleton, and MG Plummer (eds),
The World Trade Organization: Legal, Economic and Political Analysis, Vol I (New York: Springer/
International Law Institute, 2005), at 1573–78.
[18] See, eg, Matsushita, Schoenbaum, and Mavroidis, above fn 12, at 220.

or practice or even its governmental structure'.[19] It then appears difficult to identify measures adopted under this provision that would be of a reactionary nature. The US measures imposing an import quota for Nicaraguan sugar were adopted in retaliation for the Nicaraguan support of subversive political activities. However, the US did not rely on Article XXI as a justification.[20] This being said, one may support a broader interpretation of the expression 'protection of one's essential security interest' that goes beyond the specific reference to fissionable materials and weapons. In this respect, a State could decide to exert trade restrictions against another State, in violation of WTO principles and rules, arguing within the frame of Article XXI that unilateral economic sanctions are justified because the benefits stemming from those exports are used by the target State to support terrorist acts against that State or its citizens abroad.

While having a potential negative effect on the WTO system, the debate on the exceptions based on the protection of security interests remains marginal, in spite of the recent increase of threats to national security.

III. UN Economic Interventionism: Reconciling WTO and UN Law

Under UN law, the spectrum of measures that may be taken to confront 'any threat to the peace, breach of the peace, or act of aggression', as mentioned in Article 39 UN Charter, is very broad, ranging from the use of force to non-military measures. In practice, the Security Council has resorted to various 'economic sanctions', comprising a number of actions of an economic character under Article 41 to compel a 'troublemaking' State or, increasingly, non-State entities, in the sense of Article 39 UN Charter, to take particular steps to restore international peace and security. A careful analysis of UN practice leads to the conclusion that, although economic sanctions represent the traditional economic instrument used by the UN, it is only one aspect of growing UN economic interventionism, a phenomenon that encompasses a wide diversity of activities.[21] Activities aimed at the restoration

---

[19] See Lowenfeld, above fn 13, at 698.

[20] GATT Panel Report, *US – Sugar from Nicaragua* quoted by Matsushita, Schoenbaum, and Mavroidis, above fn 12, at 223.

[21] The mere decision to send a peacekeeping mission has some economic consequences. See M Carnahan, W Durch, and S Gilmore, *Economic Impact of Peacekeeping*, Final Report, March 2006, at <http://www.stimson.org/fopo/pdf/EIP_FINAL_Report_March2006doc.pdf> (last visited 25 January 2008).

of peace have engaged the organization in the adoption of resolutions setting up peace enforcement missions or dealing with the economic reconstruction of war-torn territories. The theatres of these operations are varied, spanning from a newly independent country to a region under international territorial administration, a State under military occupation, or a State recovering from violent internal conflict. Given the existence of the specific exception for UN Charter based actions for the maintenance of peace and security (Article XXI(c) GATT 1994) and the fact that, to date, there has been no systematic integration of economic considerations into the work of the UN Security Council, it is useful to assess the different legal issues at stake. The increasing interaction between peace and security activities and economic issues raises difficult questions in terms of the principles and rules of international law applicable in the collective security context.

A. UN Economic Sanctions Under WTO Law: The Derogations Permitted by Article XXI (c) GATT 1994

1. *Elements of UN Practice*

Within the framework of its principal responsibility to maintain international peace and security, the UN Security Council has had recourse to a wide range of measures, with those of an economic nature playing a particularly significant role. The UN Charter provides a non-exhaustive list of such measures including 'complete or partial interruption of economic relations and of rail, sea, air, postal, telegraphic, radio and other means of communication...'.[22] The Security Council has in many instances adopted these types of measures, as well as others such as the freezing of State and private assets.[23]

The cases of Sierra Leone, Liberia, and Iran offer interesting illustrations of the use of varied economic sanctions. Security Council Resolution 1132 (adopted on 8 October 1997) imposed an oil and arms embargo, as well as restrictions on the travel of members of the military junta of Sierra Leone. On 5 July 2000, the Security Council adopted Resolution 1306 requesting all States to take necessary measures to prohibit the direct or indirect imports of all rough diamonds from Sierra Leone to their

---

[22] See Article 41 UN Charter. See, for an overview, V Gowlland-Debbas, 'Sanctions Regimes under Article 41 of the UN Charter' in V Gowlland-Debbas (ed), *National Implementation of United Nations – A Comparative Study* (Geneva/Leiden/Boston: IUHEI – Nijhoff, 2004) 3.

[23] For examples of these sanctions, see on Afghanistan, Security Council Resolutions 1267 of 15 October 1999 and 1333 of 19 December 2000 adopting sanctions against the Taliban. For an account of the practice of the Security Council, see N Schrijver, 'The use of economic sanctions by the UN Security Council: an international law perspective' in HHG Post (ed), *International Economic Law and Armed Conflict* (Dordrecht/Boston: Martinus Nijhoff, 1994) 123.

territory, and also requesting that the government of Sierra Leone ensure that an effective Certificate of Origin regime for trade in diamonds be in operation in Sierra Leone. On 7 March 2001, the Security Council unanimously adopted Resolution 1343, by which it imposed sanctions on Liberia, including an arms embargo and the adoption by all States of necessary measures to prevent the direct or indirect imports of all rough diamonds. The Security Council specifically called 'upon the Government of Liberia to take urgent steps, including through the establishment of transparent and internationally verifiable audit regimes, to ensure that revenue derived by the Government of Liberia from the Liberia Shipping Registry and the Liberian timber industry is used for legitimate social, humanitarian and development purposes'.[24] Concerning Iran, the Security Council adopted a first set of sanctions to prevent Tehran from developing further its nuclear programme. Sanctions were taken in another particular field—that is, 'all items, materials, equipment, goods and technology which could contribute to Iran's enrichment-related, reprocessing or heavy water-related activities, or to the development of nuclear weapon delivery systems'.[25] When Iran failed to comply with these UN Security Council resolutions, the Security Council passed a new resolution intensifying the existing sanctions.[26]

2. *Economic Considerations Linked to the Resort to UN Sanctions*

Economic considerations linked to the resort to UN sanctions have so far been very marginal. The issue of political, humanitarian as well as economic consequences of these measures—often referred to as side effects—has led to debates within the UN on the compatibility of such sanctions with rules of international human rights law and humanitarian law. The 'side effects' issue had been raised early on with the adoption of sanctions against Southern Rhodesia, but it was with the imposition of sanctions against Iraq—over a thirteen-year period—that the issue became particularly controversial.[27] Side effects obviously affect the target State (which is the very reason for the adoption of the measures) but not necessarily in the manner in which they are intended. The most harmful consequences generally fall on the civilian population far more than on members of the government.

Third States can also be affected, as a result of the growing interdependence of domestic economic systems.[28] The UN Charter had considered the problem of the

---

[24] See also Security Council Resolutions 864 of 15 September 1993 and 1173 of 12 June 1998.

[25] Resolution 1737 of 27 December 2006, at para 3.

[26] Resolution 1747 of 24 March 2007.

[27] See, eg, D Cortright and GA Lopez, 'Sanctions Against Iraq' in D Cortright and GA Lopez (eds), *The Sanctions Decade: Assessing UN Strategies in the 1990s* (USA/London: Lynne Rienner Publishers, 2000) 37; D Malone and J Cockayne, 'The UN Security Council: 10 Lessons from Iraq on Regulation and Accountability' 2006 *Journal of International Law and International Relations* 2(2) 1, at 3.

[28] M Doxey, 'United Sanctions: Lessons of Experience' in *Second Interlaken Seminar on Targeting United Nations Financial Sanctions*, 29–31 March 1999, Swiss Federal Office for Foreign Economic Affairs, in cooperation with the UN Secretariat, 207.

effects of sanctions from the outset, but in extremely limited and ambiguous terms. Article 50 UN Charter specifies that a third State, that is, a State not targeted by sanctions, 'which finds itself confronted with special economic problems arising from the carrying out of those measures shall have the right to consult the Security Council with regard to a solution of those problems'.[29] However, the Charter gives no definition of these 'special economic problems', and offers no guarantee of compensation. It is, however, very important to concretely identify the economic impact of specific measures.[30]

Both the substance and the implementation of these measures have only rarely been considered in the light of principles and rules of international economic law, in particular those that favour free trade and non-discrimination. With regard to the growing recourse by the Security Council to measures having an economic impact, Harry Post wisely noted that 'such a series of wide-ranging, binding measures can no longer be considered limited or incidental economic curiosities (...). In terms of international economic law, it might even be said that in recent years a new "international sanctions law" is emerging with its own instruments (...), its own organs and institutions (...).'[31]

3. UN Sanctions and Article XXI (c) GATT 1994

With regard to WTO law, UN economic sanctions clearly violate the core principles that form the pillars of the international trade system. The most telling example is the decision to impose embargos or the 'complete or partial interruption of economic relations'. For instance, Security Council Resolution 757 of 30 May 1992 obliged Member States to suspend imports and exports of all commodities and products—except supplies for medical purposes—with regard to the Federal Republic of Yugoslavia.

Article XXI (c) GATT 1994 is widely invoked by States when implementing sanctions imposed by the UN Security Council.[32] In contrast to unilateral measures regarding security issues as foreseen in Article XXI (a)-(b) GATT 1994, the condition of necessity is not required for measures adopted under the UN Charter with a view

---

[29] DL Tehindrazanarivelo, *Les sanctions des Nations Unies et leurs effets secondaires: assistance aux victimes et voies juridiques de prévention* (Paris: Presses Universitaires de France, 2005).

[30] In the *Agenda for Peace*, the Secretary General recommends, with regard to the operation of Article 50 UN Charter (analyzed below) and third States affected by the application of economic sanctions, 'that the Security Council devise a set of measures involving the financial institutions and other components of the United Nations system that can be put in place to insulate States from such difficulties. Such measures would be a matter of equity and a means of encouraging States to cooperate with decisions of the Council'. Doc. A/47/277-S/24111 (17 June 1992).

[31] HHG Post, 'Introduction' in HHG Post (ed), *International Economic Law and Armed Conflict* (Dordrecht/Boston: Martinus Nijhoff, 1994) 1.

[32] Eg, consider a document from India that observes that 'while almost all of India's trading partners received most-favoured-nation treatment in the issue of import licences, import licences were not issued for imports from countries facing UN mandated sanctions, at present, Iraq, Fiji, Serbia and Montenegro', cited in *Analytical Index, Guide to GATT Law and Practice*, Vol I (WTO: Geneva, 1995), at 605.

to maintaining international peace and security. The only requirement that seems to prevail is that of a multilateral authorization given under the UN Charter. This seems to be the correct interpretation, unless one considers that a necessity requirement could be deduced from the spirit and the object of all the exception clauses, including the one referring to action pursuant to a resolution adopted by a UN body in the context of the maintenance of international peace and security. However, with practically non-existent *travaux préparatoires* and limited practice, there is very little to support this insertion of a necessity requirement.

Another issue deals with the effects of sanctions adopted under Chapter VII of the UN Charter on third States. It should be noted that the potentially disruptive effect on international trade of an abusive recourse to Article XXI GATT 1994 was invoked with regard to unilateral economic measures adopted outside of the framework of the UN Charter. The GATT Council adopted a decision in 1982 relating to Article XXI in which it asked that the interests of third States that could be injured by such actions be taken into account.[33] This decision shares the spirit of Article 50 UN Charter and it can *a fortiori* be considered to apply to actions adopted in the framework of collective security.

The case of the Kimberley Process illustrates another challenge regarding the interpretation of Article XXI (c). Considering the criteria used in Article XXI (c), one may wonder what the scope is of the expression 'obligations under the United Nations Charter for the maintenance of international peace and security' and more precisely whether this exception only applies to Security Council decisions or may also cover recommendations of the General Assembly. The issue came up in relation with the Kimberley Process, which provides for the creation of an international diamond certification programme.[34]

In 2000, the UN General Assembly adopted Resolution 55/56, calling for the adoption of measures to deal with the problem of trade in diamonds during armed conflicts.[35] This resolution was part of the extension of the 1998 Security Council decision to impose sanctions. The only diamonds permitted to be exported from Angola were those that fulfilled the criteria of a monitoring system. They must be accompanied by an official certificate of origin.[36] Subsequently, through the Interlaken Declaration of 5 November 2002, the vast majority of countries mining, trading, and cutting diamonds agreed to adopt the Kimberley Process Certification Scheme. States participating in the Kimberley Process agree to restrict trade to certified non-conflict diamonds. All diamond trade between those States and the States not participating

---

[33] GATT Council, *Decision Concerning Article XXI of the GATT*, 30 November 1982, BISD 29S/24–25. The GATT Council considered that 'in taking action in terms of the exceptions provided in Article XXI of the General Agreement, contracting parties should take into consideration the interests of third parties which may be affected', *Analytical Index*, ibid. at 605.

[34] On this process, see < http://www.kimberleyprocess.com> (last visited 25 January 2008).

[35] See also UN General Assembly Resolution 56/263, A/RES/56/263 (9 April 2002), on the role of diamonds in fuelling conflict.

[36] Resolution 1173 of 12 June 1998, at para 12(b).

in the Kimberley Process is prohibited.[37] The Security Council then gave its support to these agreements through Resolution 1459, stating that it '*strongly supports* the Kimberley Process Certification Scheme, as well as the ongoing process to refine and implement the regime, adopted at the Interlaken Conference as a valuable contribution against trafficking in conflict diamonds and looks forward to its implementation and strongly encourages the participants to further resolve outstanding issues'.[38]

On 15 May 2003, WTO Members granted a waiver of GATT provisions to allow for the above-mentioned import and export restrictions on conflict diamonds. The GC decided that 'with respect to the measures taken by a Member listed in the Annex necessary to prohibit the export of rough diamonds to non-Participants in the Kimberley Process Certification Scheme consistent with the Kimberley Process Certification Scheme, paragraphs 1 of Article I; 1 of Article XI; and 1 of Article XIII GATT 1994 are waived as of 1 January 2003 until 31 December 2006'.[39] This waiver did not cover the Kimberley Process Certification Scheme insofar as it concerned trade only in certified conflict diamonds as between the participating States. Clearly, therefore, it was believed that a waiver was not necessary for this aspect of the scheme. One may wonder why it was necessary to have a waiver for the elements related to trade in conflict diamonds with non-participating States. One cannot exclude that the waiver in this respect was a somewhat simplistic 'safety first' approach to the problem, without exploring further whether the security exception would also cover this aspect of the scheme,[40] and in particular whether the resolutions of the General Assembly would qualify as a multilateral authorization given under the UN Charter as provided for by Article XXI (c), especially in the light of the resolutions of the Security Council on the same matter.

B. Framing UN Economic Intervention: The Need to Integrate WTO and International Economic Law Principles

UN involvement in economic matters has gone far beyond sanctions. Its involvement in post-conflict activities has led the organization to deal with the management of

---

[37] Kimberley Process Certification Scheme, Section III as adopted by the Interlaken Declaration of 5 November 2002, at operative para 1. The text of the Declaration is annexed to the WTO Council for Trade in Goods, *Kimberley Process Certification Scheme for Rough Diamonds – Request for a Waiver*, G/C/W/431 (12 November 2002).

[38] Resolution 1459 of 28 January 2003, at para 1.

[39] WTO Council for Trade in Goods, *Waiver Concerning Kimberley Process Certification Scheme for Rough Diamonds: Communication*, G/C/W/432/Rev.1 (24 February 2003). The waiver was adopted by the WTO GC, *Proposed Agenda*, WT/GC/W/498 (13 May 2003), Item VI.

[40] More generally see, J Pauwelyn, 'WTO Compassion or Superiority Complex?: What to make of the WTO Waiver for "Conflict Diamonds"' 2003 *Michigan Journal of International Law* 24(4) 1177.

economies in post-conflict situations as part of a global strategy to restore peace in war-torn territories. Such interventionism does not rely on any coherent framework. It is necessary for the UN to carry out its post-conflict activities by taking into account principles of international economic law such as transparency and non-discrimination in order to achieve its objective of sustainable peace, while at the same time taking into account the peculiarities of each country. Three cases illustrate the need for a paradigm shift.

1. *Reconstruction of Economies by UN Peace-building Operations*

Some UN missions have evolved in such a way that the UN played or will play a greater role in economic management. This is illustrated by the case of Ivory Coast, even if the UN mission was only marginally involved in economic activities. In addition, several international institutions other than the UN, such as the World Bank (WB), are increasingly participating in reconstruction efforts in post-conflict situations.[41] The recently created Peacebuilding Commission may constitute a key institutional breakthrough to rationalize and coordinate UN and other agencies' economic activities.

a. *The Economic Mandate of UN Missions: The Case of Ivory Coast*

While originally established with a security-based mandate, some traditional UN peacekeeping missions became increasingly involved in economic matters, either because their mandate evolved or due to the need to coordinate with international institutions with responsibility in the economic field. Both trends derive from the key acknowledgement that economic development is a key component of the achievement of sustainable peace in a post-conflict zone. The case of Ivory Coast exemplifies these new trends.

The difficulties encountered in the peace process in Ivory Coast and the various agreements signed by the parties to the crisis caused the UN mission to evolve considerably. The UN Mission in Ivory Coast (MINUCI) was created in 2003 by Security Council Resolution 1479 following the Linas-Marcoussis Agreement concluded in January 2003. MINUCI was a political mission whose mandate was mainly to facilitate the implementation by the Ivorian parties of the 2003 agreement. On 4 April 2004, MINUCI was replaced by a UN peacekeeping operation— the UN Operation in Ivory Coast (UNOCI)—set up by Security Council Resolution 1528 (2004). Despite being 'deeply concerned by the deteriorating economic situation in Ivory Coast and its serious impact on the sub-region as a whole' and recognizing that economic development in Ivory Coast is a key element of long-term stability, the Security Council mostly limited the mandate of UNOCI to traditional

---

[41] See, on the role of international financial institutions in post-conflict situations and their relationships with the UN, KE Boon, '"Open for Business": International Financial Institutions, Post-Conflict Economic Reform and the Rule of Law' 2007 *Journal of International Law and Politics* 39(3) 514.

peacekeeping responsibility. UNOCI monitored the cease-fire of May 2003 and assisted in disarmament, demobilization, and reintegration programmes.[42] Its approach changed slightly over the next stages of the peace process, which involved economic development activities.

A Report of the Secretary-General (SG), issued in May 2007, recommended that the UNOCI be assigned responsibility for supporting the economic recovery process in Ivory Coast, in coordination with other UN agencies as well as with the International Monetary Fund (IMF) and the WB.[43] The SC endorsed this request in its Resolution 1765 of July 2007, and stressed the adaptation of the UNOCI's role to the new phase of the peace process in Ivory Coast as set out in the Ouagadougou political Agreement.[44] As implicitly suggested in the SGs latest report, this economic mandate calls for a close cooperation between the various actors that are already engaged in reconstruction and recovery activity in Ivory Coast.[45] The exact scope of UNOCI's economic role remains to be defined, but it may include 'support to the rehabilitation and re-equipment of social and economic infrastructure in the communities most affected by conflict'—one of the key objectives of the WB's recent financial grant.[46]

Ivory Coast, as well as other countries, witnessed an increasing involvement of the UN in the economic sphere after peace was restored. Economic reconstruction was used as a tool aimed at preventing hostilities from breaking out again. Carrying out such action within the narrow framework of the collective security system cannot be satisfactory. Grounding the reconstruction of Ivory Coast on economic law pillars would contribute to strengthening the autonomous and sustainable character of the economy when the UN is gone.[47] By resorting to principles of international trade law, the UN would ensure that individuals, private companies, and local entities rely on such principles,[48] rendering the transition towards UN disengagement and the integration within the international economic order easier.[49] This would also have positive consequences for third States and foreign entities. In that respect the recently established Peacebuilding Commission could be an appropriate forum for

---

[42]   Resolution 1528 of 27 February 2004, at para 6.

[43]   *Thirteenth progress report of the Secretary-General on the United Nations Operation in Ivory Coast*, S/2007/275 (14 May 2007), at para 83.

[44]   Resolution 1765 of 16 July 2007, at para 2.

[45]   The WB recently approved a US$120 million grant in support of the Ivorian government's crisis recovery programme which is being implemented within the framework of the Ouagadougou Peace Accord. See WB, Press Release, 17 July 2007, at < http://www.web.worldbank.org> (last visited 25 January 2008).

[46]   Ibid.

[47]   Noteworthy is the fact that Ivory Coast signed the GATT 1947 on 31 December 1963 and has become a WTO Member since 1 January 1995.

[48]   The protection of 'individuals and the market-place' being 'one of the principal objects and purposes of the WTO', see Panel Report, *US – Section 301 Trade Act*, at para 7.86.

[49]   If, for example, the principle of non-discrimination were applicable, specific provisions might, however, be considered to grant preference to local suppliers and contractors in order for them to help start up the local economy again and contribute to post-conflict reconstruction. There would be a need to define the adjustments, for example, in the context of procurement practices.

designing new frameworks of coordination and integration of economic parameters into the work of the UN in post-conflict situations.

b. The UN Peacebuilding Commission: A Promising Institutional Tool

Stressing 'the need for a coordinated, coherent and integrated approach to post-conflict peacebuilding and reconciliation with a view to achieving sustainable peace', States have decided to create the UN Peacebuilding Commission. It is an intergovernmental advisory body meant 'to address the special needs of countries emerging from conflict towards recovery, reintegration and reconstruction and to assist them in laying the foundation for sustainable development'.[50] This organ has promising and interesting implications with regard to the economic activities carried out under the ambit of the UN. It represents a novel opportunity to take economic considerations into account in the broader framework of reconstruction activities.

Jointly created by the Security Council and the General Assembly,[51] the Peacebuilding Commission is an advisory organ the main purpose of which is:

to bring together all relevant actors to marshal resources and to advise on and propose integrated strategies for postconflict peacebuilding and recovery. The Commission should focus attention on the reconstruction and institution building efforts necessary for recovery from conflict and support the development of integrated strategies in order to lay the foundation for sustainable development. In addition, it should provide recommendations and information to improve the coordination of all relevant actors within and outside the United Nations, develop best practices, help to ensure predictable financing for early recovery activities and extend the period of attention by the international community to post-conflict recovery.[52]

In addition to the Commission, a Peacebuilding Fund was launched on 11 October 2006 at the request of the General Assembly.[53] According to its terms of reference, the Fund 'will support interventions of direct and immediate relevance to the peacebuilding process and contribute towards addressing critical gaps in that process, in particular in areas for which no other funding mechanism is available'.[54] As the Commission is entitled to address the situation of particular countries, it initiated—between July and December 2006—its first phase of substantive consideration of two countries: Burundi and Sierra Leone.[55] Through country-specific meetings, the Commission has formulated integrated peacebuilding strategies (IPBS) as the basis

---

[50] 2005 World Summit Outcome, General Assembly, Resolution 60/1 (2005), A/RES/60/1 (24 October 2005), at para 97.

[51] See, for the Security Council, Resolution 1645 of 20 December 2005, and for the General Assembly, Resolution 60/180 of 30 December 2005.

[52] 2005 World Summit Outcome, above fn 50, at para 98.

[53] See Launch of the Peacebuilding Fund, 11 October 2006, General Assembly, PBC/4, at < http://www.un.org/News/Press/docs//2006/pbc4.doc.htm> (last visited 25 January 2008).

[54] *Terms of reference for the Peacebuilding Fund*, annexed to Report of the Secretary-General, Arrangements for establishing the Peacebuilding Fund, A/60/984 (22 August 2006), at para 2.1.

[55] Burundi has signed the GATT 1947 on 13 March 1965 and Sierra Leone on 19 May 1961. They both became WTO Members on 23 July 1995.

for its sustained support for Sierra Leone and Burundi.[56] The development of an IPBS for Burundi was endorsed by the Commission on 20 June 2007.[57] The designing of IPBS involved various UN agencies, as well as other stakeholders. To this end, a direct link was established with the UN Integrated Office in Burundi, which succeeded the UN peacekeeping operation in Burundi in 2006. This fact highlights the need to draw links between peacekeeping activities and economic reconstruction activities.

The Commission seeks to fill the 'institutional gap' in the UN system identified by the Report of the High-level Panel in 2004.[58] The approach and methodology put forward by this newly created organ will be crucial for addressing economic challenges in the rebuilding of war-torn societies. It might be worth cooperating with the WTO and relevant regional economic organizations more closely in this endeavour.

2. *International Administration of Territories by the UN*

Within its primary and traditional responsibility to maintain international peace and security, the UN Security Council has adopted new means to restore peace in war-torn territories. In the case of Kosovo and East Timor, the Council set up interim administrations responsible for fulfilling the traditional State functions, including managing the economy.[59]

These innovations inevitably led the UN to intervene in economic fields previously unexplored in terms of legal framework and economic management. This has been particularly true in the case of Kosovo, where the mission is explicitly mandated to support economic reconstruction. The UN transitional administration in East Timor is another example, although it saw less UN intervention. Moreover, there are common elements in these two experiences with regard to, *inter alia,* taxation and customs issues.[60]

Security Council Resolution 1244 created an interim administration in Kosovo.[61] The Resolution makes several references to the economic dimension of the mission, including one of the main tasks of the international civilian presence in 'supporting the reconstruction of key infrastructure and other economic reconstruction'.[62] It also

---

[56] Organizational Committee, *Provisional report on the work of the Peacebuilding Commission*, PBC/2/OC/L.1 (28 June 2007), at para 3.

[57] Ibid at para 18.

[58] Report of the High-level Panel on Threats, Challenges and Change, above fn 10, at para 261. See L Boisson de Chazournes, 'Rien ne change, tout bouge ou le dilemme des Nations Unies – Propos sur le Rapport du Groupe de personnalités de haut niveau sur les menaces, les défis et le changement' 2005 *Revue générale de droit international public* (1) 147.

[59] See, for an extensive analysis, R Caplan, *International Governance of War-Torn Territories – Rule and Reconstruction* (Oxford: Oxford University Press, 2005).

[60] See, eg, Regulation No 2000/18, UNTAET/REG/2000/18 (30 June 2000), on a Taxation System for East Timor. On the UN transitional administration in East Timor, see S Eldon, 'East Timor' in DM Malone (ed), *The UN Security Council: From the Cold War to the 21st Century* (USA/London: Lynne Rienner Publishers, 2004) 551.

[61] United Nations Interim Administration Mission in Kosovo (UNMIK).

[62] Resolution 1244 of 10 June 1999, at para 11(g).

'encourages all Member States and international organizations to contribute to economic and social reconstruction as well as to the safe return of refugees and displaced persons, and emphasizes in this context the importance of convening an international donors' conference, (. . .) at the earliest possible date'.[63] As a result, UNMIK has become involved in the creation of a viable economy and the installation of an overall programme of economic stabilization. This has been achieved through the authorization of the Special Representative of the Secretary-General (SRSG) to adopt a series of regulations, including Regulation No 1999/1 of 25 July 1999, which establishes the powers of the interim administration in Kosovo. A council responsible for economic policy has been created alongside the adoption of a legal framework through a regulation adopted by the SRSG.[64] In fact, some of these measures call into question the monetary, financial, and economic unity of the FRY.[65] The responsibility to develop and lead economic reconstruction activities to promote democracy, economic prosperity, stability, and regional cooperation in Kosovo fell to the EU in cooperation with the WB and other organizations, namely the implementation of the Stability Pact for South Eastern Europe, with considerable international support.[66]

In terms of relevant principles and norms of international law to be taken into consideration, explicit mention of principles of international human rights law is generally made in Security Council resolutions or in the instruments adopted by the authorities responsible for territorial administration and reconstruction activities.[67] However, no mention is made of principles and rules of international economic law that are relevant to these missions. No such rules are apparent from the mandate given by the UN SG to the UN Office of Legal Affairs (OLA), which was tasked with the vetting of UN regulations in East-Timor and Kosovo.[68] The then Under-Secretary General for Legal Affairs later observed that:

[63]   Ibid at para 13.

[64]   One can cite various examples of actions taken in the framework of territorial administration that concern the economic field: Regulation No 1999/16 that creates a Central Fiscal Authority of Kosovo; Regulation No 1999/9 on the Importation, Transport, Distribution, and Sale of Petroleum Products in Kosovo, as well as Regulation No 1999/20 on the Banking and Payments Authority of Kosovo.

[65]   Regulation No 1999/4 on the Currency Permitted to be Used in Kosovo. This regulation authorizes the free use of currency parallel to the Yugoslav Dinar in the payment and banking services sector, making the German Mark and, since 2000, the euro, the official currency of Kosovo. See R Bordea, *La Mission intérimaire d'administration des Nations Unies au Kosovo*, LLM. Thesis, University Paris I (September 2000), at 47.

[66]   See the Petersburg Principles on the political solution to the Kosovo crisis, Statement by the chairman at the conclusion of the G-8 Foreign Ministers held at the Petersburg Centre on 6 May 1999, statement annexed to Resolution 1244. See also the Stability Pact website, at www.stabilitypact.org (last visited 25 January 2008).

[67]   For the case of Kosovo, see, Resolution 1244, at para 11(j) as well as Regulation No 1999/1, section 2 and Regulation No 2000/38 which created the Ombudsman institution. Considering those instruments, the UN Human Rights Committee expressively stated that UNMIK is bound by human rights obligations. See *Concluding Observations of the Human Rights Committee – Kosovo (Serbia)*, CCPR/C/UNK/CO/1. (14 August 2006), 2, at para 4.

[68]   See *Report of the Secretary-General on the work of the Organization*, UN GAOR, 55th Sess, Supp No 1, UN Doc A/55/1 (2000), at para 325.

[I]t became quite an extensive activity. Not that we questioned the substantive solutions in customs, taxation, banking or whatever the subject matter was. Our task was to review the regulations from a constitutional viewpoint. That is: were they in conformity with the Charter, the pertinent Security Council resolutions, international human rights standards, etc?[69]

Human rights law may certainly be applicable with regard to some economic activities. The most significant example is the right to private property, which undoubtedly provides for legal guarantees and offers some indirect protection against abuses. Another example is the principle of non-discrimination, although its scope under human rights law[70] does not fully cover trade and investments activities. Briefly put, international human rights law does not provide full legal guarantees and might be ill suited to deal with some economic activities and ensure, for example, that these are based on principles of transparency and fair competition.

Moreover, one may well ask whether UN law is the proper yardstick to review customs, taxation or banking regulations. While the UN has set up certain rules that apply to UN personnel, such as procurement rules,[71] a wider approach that promotes and integrates general principles of international economic law would be preferable.

One might argue that the international organizations engaged in economic reconstruction activities will advocate for the application of rules that they have shaped through their normative and operational practice.[72] However, affirming as a matter of principle the importance of the international rule of law for questions related to international trade, government procurement,[73] or competition in the field of economic reconstruction still seems paramount. The procedures followed in the context of economic reconstruction would indeed benefit from explicit reference to clear legal criteria. Key standards such as openness and equity that are linked to the application of the well-established economic law principles of free competition and

[69] H Correll, 'A Challenge to the United Nations and the World: Developing the Rule of Law' 2004 *Temple International and Comparative Law Journal* 18(2) 391, at 397.

[70] On the different aspects of non-discrimination in human rights law, see S Marks and A Clapham, *International Human Rights Lexicon* (Oxford: Oxford University Press, 2005), at 265–67.

[71] See, eg, *The Financial Regulations and Rules of the United Nations*, Secretary-General's bulletin, ST/SGB/2003/7 (9 May 2003); or *United Nations Procurement Manual*, Department of Management, Office of Central Support Services, Procurement Service, August 2006, at < http://www.un.org/Depts/ptd/pdf/pm_31august2006_english.pdf> (last visited 3 August 2007).

[72] This is particularly true with regard to the principle of transparency that is gaining ground through UN practice. See Security Council Resolution 1607 of 21 June 2005 (at para 4) with respect to Liberia and Security Council Resolution 1599 of 28 April 2005. See also *Thirteenth progress report of the Secretary-General on the United Nations Operation in Ivory Coast*, above fn 43, at para 83. Concerning procurement issues, see the *Common Guidelines for Procurement by Organizations in the UN system*, at < http://www.iapso.org> (last visited 25 January 2008). For the WB practice, see *Guidelines: Procurement under IBRD Loans and IDA Credits*, May 2004, at < http://www.worldbank.org> (last visited 25 January 2008).

[73] This aspect is important if we consider the implication of many non-governmental actors, both public and private, among them non-governmental organisations (NGOs), in the management of public affairs and services, See C Stahn, 'NGO's and International Peacekeeping – Issues, prospects and Lessons Learned' 2001 *Zeitschrift für ausländisches öffentliches Recht und Völkerrecht* (61) 379, at 397.

transparency would help contribute to the reconstruction of stable domestic econo-mies in the medium and long term. It would facilitate the transition of the newly recovered economies from a system backed by UN efforts to a sustainable system interacting within the international economic order.[74]

3. *The Occupation of Iraq and the UN Resolution 1483*

The case of Iraq following the adoption of Resolution 1483 by the Security Council of 22 May 2003—albeit peculiar because of the regime of military occupation[75]— merits specific attention. The role of the UN in this context raises new questions with respect to the recourse to economic instruments, the international rule of law as well as issues of global legitimacy and coherence of the UN system in its relations with other actors, institutions, and norms.

Security Council Resolution 1483 primarily specified that the legal regime in force in Iraq at the time was that of military occupation as provided in the Hague and Geneva Conventions, and that the Coalition Provisional Authority (composed of the US and the UK) (CPA) was the occupying power. The Resolution also prescribed a role for the UN and other international organizations, but did not specify the law applicable to their activities. It was the balance of power in the international system at the time that led to the recognition that the primary responsibility for the politi-cal and economic reconstruction of Iraq was in the hands of the CPA. As such, the international community rubber-stamped a system that had been established and managed by the US and the UK. The UN was involved in the process on the basis of a very narrow mandate, breaking away from practice developed in preceding years in the area of political and economic reconstruction.[76]

In the economic field, Resolution 1483 envisioned the role of the UN and the inter-national community through a range of complex procedures, which only accorded them a right to be informed, while the decision-making power remained in the hands of the CPA. This remained true even though the UN had taken part, for the first time,

[74] This need for greater reliance on economic law is particularly true if we take into consideration the fact that institutions such as UNMIK or KFOR enjoy immunity in local courts. See Ombudsperson Institution in Kosovo, *Special Report No 1 on the Compatibility with recognized international stand-ards of UNMIK Regulation No 2000/47 on the Status, Privileges and Immunities of KFOR and UNMIK and Their Personnel in Kosovo (18 August 2000)*, 26 April 2001.
[75] The UN involvement in the Occupied Territories through the UN Relief and Works Agency can be seen—though in a very limited way—as another example of transitional administration led by the UN in a context of occupation. Discussing the categorization of powers drawn by Doyle in the context of transitional administration (MW Doyle, 'War-Making and Peace-Making: The United Nations' Post Cold War Record' in ChA Crocker, FO Hampson, and P Aall (eds), *Turbulent Peace: The Challenges of Managing International Conflict* (Washington, DC: United States Institute of Peace Press, 2001) 529), Simon Chesterman uses the case of UNRWA in Occupied Territories to reflect on the powers of administrative authorities. See S Chesterman, *You, The People: The United Nations, Transitional Administration, and State-Building* (Oxford: Oxford University Press, 2004), at 56.
[76] See L Boisson de Chazournes, 'The United Nations on Shifting Sands: About the Rebuilding of Iraq' 2003 *International Law Forum* 5(4) 254, at 257.

in the setting up of a regime where economic considerations were predominant. With regard to the delicate question of the management and exploitation of natural resources, the CPA was granted jurisdiction over export sales of petroleum, petroleum products, and natural gas from Iraq. These prerogatives were to be exercised under certain conditions and subject to oversight and audit procedures conducted by certain responsible international organizations. However, the nature and the duration of these procedures were not settled. The UN was given a coordinating role, in partnership with other international organizations, in 'promoting economic reconstruction and the conditions for sustainable development' and in 'facilitating the reconstruction of key infrastructure'.[77] The Security Council resolution basically recognized, for the most part, the system put into place by the Coalition. In exchange, it obtained the recognition of the application of the law of military occupation with the concomitant minimum rules of proper economic behaviour as will be discussed below.

The issue of the relevant legal framework to cover these economic activities and the interaction between different sets of norms such as WTO law, the law of occupation, and UN law arose in the context of two specific cases. The first one deals with the GPA—a plurilateral agreement that binds only some of the WTO Members. This Agreement also provides for an exception clause covering security aspects, albeit formulated in more restrictive terms than the above-mentioned GATT 1994 security exception provision. It does not refer to the UN Charter and specifies the types of measures that can be taken. Article XXIII specifies that:

1.   Nothing in this Agreement shall be construed to prevent any Party from taking any action or not disclosing any information which it considers necessary for the protection of its essential security interests relating to the procurement of arms, ammunition or war materials, or to procurement indispensable for national security or for national defence purposes.

2.   Subject to the requirement that such measures are not applied in a manner which would constitute a means of arbitrary or unjustifiable discrimination between countries where the same conditions prevail or a disguised restriction on international trade, nothing in this Agreement shall be construed to prevent any Party from imposing or enforcing measures: necessary to protect public morals, order or safety, human, animal or plant life or health or intellectual property; or relating to the products or services of handicapped persons, of philanthropic institutions or of prison labour.

---

[77] Resolution 1483 (2003), at para 8 (e)-(d). The recent Security Council Resolution 1770 of 10 August 2007 confirms however the trend of an increasing involvement of the UN within economic matters in Iraq. The Resolution seeks to enlarge the UN mandate in Iraq through a stronger role of the Special SRSG and the UN Assistance Mission for Iraq (UNAMI). For example, the SRSG and UNAMI, 'as circumstances permit, (. . .) shall [p]romote, support, and facilitate, in coordination with the Government of Iraq:

(iv) Economic reform, capacity-building, and the conditions for sustainable development, including through coordination with national and regional organizations and, as appropriate, civil society, donors, and international financial institutions' (at para 2).

The relevance of this provision was invoked in the context of an American decision of December 2003 in the framework of calls for tender relating to contracts for economic reconstruction in Iraq that limited the right to tender to only certain States. A memorandum titled 'Determination and Findings' sought to justify this on the basis that it was 'necessary for the protection of the essential security interests of the United States to limit competition'.[78] This raises the issue of the compatibility of such a measure with WTO rules, especially the non-discrimination principle contained in Article III GPA.[79] Could the exception of Article XXIII (1) be invoked?[80] The issue is obviously linked to the problem of the relationship between the WTO agreements, the UN Charter, and the law of military occupation. Could one consider that the US, through the CPA, was in a position to benefit from the exception clause of the GPA by arguing that the decisions were taken in the framework of a regime ratified by the Security Council in application of Chapter VII? Considering the restrictive wording of Article XXIII (1), which is limited to 'the protection of essential security interests', this argument is rather dubious. Moreover, one may question to what extent the national security exception would have been able to cover all the reconstruction contracts envisaged by Washington.

A similar legal debate, although framed in different terms, developed with regard to other decisions adopted by the CPA.[81] The Authority adopted orders and regulations, with reference to UN Security Council Resolutions, that changed the legal system in Iraq. For example, CPA Order 81, a controversial law that amends the patents and industrial design legislation, makes special reference to laws of war and UN resolutions such as Security Council Resolution 1483.[82] The Order states that 'several

[78] The Determination and Findings, 5 December 2003, at < http://www.washingtonpost.com/wp-srv/world/documents/iraqcontracts_dod20031205.pdf> (last visited 25 January 2008). Note that the US eventually extended the call for tender to all States without the previous restrictions.

[79] See G Van Calster, 'WTO Law and Contracts for Rebuilding Iraq' 2003 International Law Forum 5(4) 270.

[80] Some have considered that the US was bound by the GPA, ibid at 272. The issues of the legal profile of the CPA, as well as those relating to the specific undertakings of the US in the context of the GPA have also caught attention. In that respect, the question whether the US discriminatory practice regarding reconstruction and relief contracts in Iraq falls at all within the scope of this agreement was discussed. For an interpretation questioning the relevance of WTO GPA rules to address the US determination under the conditions of this instrument, especially with respect to which entities are covered, see J Pauwelyn, 'Iraqi Reconstruction Contracts and the WTO: "International Law? I'd Better Call My Lawyer"' Jurist Forum (19 December 2003), at < http://www.jurist.law.pitt.edu/forum/forumnew133.php#2> (last visited 25 January 2008). More generally, on the issue of responsibility for the acts of the CPA, see S Talmon, 'A Plurality of Responsible Actors: International Responsibility for Acts of the Coalition Provisional Authority in Iraq' in P Shiner and A Williams (eds), The Iraq War and International Law (Oxford: Hart Publishing, 2008, forthcoming), at < http://www.ssrn.com/abstract=1018172> (last visited 25 January 2008).

[81] See, eg, M Zwanenburg, 'Existentialism in Iraq: Security Council Resolution 1483 and the law of occupation' 2004 Revue internationale de la Croix-Rouge 86 (856) 745, at 757.

[82] Coalition Provisional Authority Order 81, 26 April 2004, Patent, Industrial Design, Undisclosed Information, Integrated Circuits and Plant Variety Law, at < http://www.iraqcoalition.org/regulations/index.html#Orders> (last visited 25 January 2008).

provisions of the current Iraqi Patent and Industrial Design Law and related legislation does [*sic*] not meet current internationally-recognized standards of protection'. It also recognizes 'the demonstrated interest of the Iraqi Governing Council for Iraq to become a full member in the international trading system, known as the World Trade Organization'. Moreover, it relies on the 'the Report of the Secretary General to the Security Council of July 17, 2003, concerning the need for the development of Iraq and its transition from a non-transparent centrally planned economy to a free market economy'. The legal basis of this Order refers to various sets of norms. It combines WTO law, law on military occupation, and UN law.

Law on military occupation strictly limits the type of changes that can be made by the occupying power and does not entail the right to modify any law.[83] However, the interaction with UN Security Council resolutions raised some complex questions to determine whether or not occupation law was fully applicable in those contexts.[84] One may nevertheless question the legality and legitimacy of those changes in Iraqi law. Although meeting WTO objectives and standards could be seen as a fair justification, there is a need to consider carefully the complex legal framework at stake, especially given the fact that WTO law is to date not binding on Iraq.[85]

Despite lingering questions, the case of Iraq offers an interesting example of emerging UN practice referring to the principle of transparency. In Iraq, the international community was granted a right of supervision through a monitoring and audit system. The International Advisory and Monitoring Board (IAMB), created in October 2003—involving, in particular, the UN, the WB, the IMF, and the Arab Fund for Economic and Social Development—had the responsibility to ensure that the funds from the sale of petroleum and natural gas were used in accordance with the principle of transparency.[86] The Iraqi government has subsequently decided to

---

[83] Article 43 of The Hague Regulations concerning the Laws and Customs of War on Land annexed to the 1907 Convention (IV) respecting the Laws and Customs of War on Land that 'the authority of the legitimate power having in fact passed into the hands of the occupant, the latter shall take all the measures in his power to restore, and ensure, as far as possible, public order and safety, while respecting, unless absolutely prevented, the laws in force in the country'. If the stabilization of an economy forms a part of the maintenance of public order and safety, questions arise as to the precise limits of this obligation.

[84] See on this issue, Boisson de Chazournes, 2007, above fn 7.70–75; A Roberts, 'Transformative Military Occupation: Applying the Laws of War and Human Rights' 2006 *American Journal of International Law* 100(3) 580.

[85] Iraq's application for accession to the WTO has been admitted by the GC on 13 December 2004, WTO News, 'Accession working parties established for Afghanistan, Iraq', 13 December 2004, at <http://www.wto.org> (last visited 25 January 2008).

[86] See Resolution 1483, at paras 14 and 20. These objectives were also used to establish the framework of the International Advisory and Monitoring Board. The *Terms of Reference for the International Advisory and Monitoring Board* state that the purpose of the IAMB is 'to promote the objectives set forth in Security Council resolution 1483 of ensuring that the Development Fund for Iraq is used in a transparent manner for the purposes set out in § 14 and that export sales of petroleum products and natural gas from Iraq are made consistent with prevailing international market best practices'. See <http://www.iamb.info/pdf/torold.pdf> (last visited 25 January 2008).

create a national oversight body to succeed the IAMB and ensure respect for transparency principle.[87] This example illustrates the positive impact that the Security Council's consideration of economic principles can have on a domestic system. However, one must also acknowledge the serious issues raised in the context of the management of Iraqi revenues. The establishment of the IAMB did not solve these issues entirely. There is therefore a crucial need to strengthen the principles of transparency and non-discrimination.

IV. WTO and the Arms Trade: The Case of Small Arms

Three international instruments cover small arms and light weapons within the framework of the UN: the Programme of Action that was adopted in July 2001;[88] the Protocol Against the Illicit Manufacturing of and Trafficking in Firearms, Their Parts and Components, and Ammunition,[89] which entered into force on 3 July 2005; and the International Instrument to Enable States to Identify and Trace, in a Timely and Reliable Manner, Illicit Small Arms, and Light Weapons, which was adopted by the General Assembly in December 2005.[90] States participating in the 2001 Conference on the Illicit Trade of Small Arms and Light Weapons in All its Aspects adopted a Programme of Action 'to put in place, where they do not exist, adequate laws, regulations, and administrative procedures to exercise effective control over the production of small arms and light weapons within their areas of jurisdiction and over the export, import, transit, or retransfer of such weapons'.[91] Restrictions imposed by

---

[87]   See the letter and annexed documents concerning the Council of Ministers of the Iraqi Republic, which adopted the decision to create the *Committee of Financial Experts*, Republic of Iraq, General Secretariat of the Council of Ministers, 22 October 2006; see also Letter from the UN Representative of Iraq to the United Nations to the Chairman of the IAMB, 31 October 2006, and Statement by the International Advisory and Monitoring Board on the Development Fund for Iraq, 6 November 2006, all those documents are available at < http://www.iamb.info> (last visited 25 January 2008).

[88]   *Programme of Action to Prevent, Combat and Eradicate the Illicit Trade in Small Arms and Light Weapons in All Its Aspects*, Report of the United Nations Conference on the Illicit Trade in Small Arms and Light Weapons in All Its Aspects, New York, 9–20 July 2001, UN Doc A/CONF.192/15.

[89]   *Protocol against the Illicit Manufacturing of and Trafficking in Firearms, Their Parts and Components and Ammunition, supplementing the United Nations Convention against Transnational Organized Crime*, General Assembly, Fifty-fifth session, Resolution 55/255 (31 May 2001).

[90]   *International Instrument to Enable States to Identify and Trace, in a Timely and Reliable Manner, Illicit Small Arms and Light Weapons*, 8 December 2005.

[91]   *Programme of Action*, above fn 88, at para II.2.

a State on the illicit trade of these weapons are one of the means for achieving the objectives of the various UN instruments on illicit trade of small arms.

In order to justify these measures with regard to WTO law, Article XXI (b)(ii) GATT 1994 specifically allows a WTO Member to take action 'it considers necessary for the protection of its essential security interests relating to the traffic in arms, ammunition, and implements of war'. Measures adopted to implement the UN Programme of Action that would otherwise contravene WTO obligations on the elimination of quantitative restrictions can be justified under this provision. Article XXI (c) might also be relied upon, in as much as the UN Programme of Action recalls the threat to the peace that illicit trade of arms represents. Adopting measures to limit arms trade would then be understood as an action taken 'in pursuance of [a State's] obligations under the United Nations Charter for the maintenance of international peace and security'. Such reading may, however, be considered too wide given the scope and nature of the 'obligations' at stake.

A WTO Member could also invoke Article XXI (b)(ii) to restrict arms exports, even if perfectly legal, to another WTO Member if there are reasonable grounds to believe that those weapons will be used against the exporting Member's territorial integrity or nationals either by the importing Member or even by non-State actors supported by the importing Member. In such a case, the notion of 'essential security interests,' as contained in Article XXI, could be read in a wide and preventive way given the increasing importance of security considerations for Members.[92] For example, the struggle against terrorist threats could lead to new restrictive measures.

The Programme of Action, which is not legally binding, calls for the development of new norms at the international level to strengthen the effort to combat illicit trade.[93] In that respect, the interaction between WTO law and other treaties and instruments in the field of arms trade could raise some very interesting questions. Mutual supportiveness between arms trade conventions and instruments and WTO principles and rules should be sought. Given the importance of ensuring cooperation and compliance by all States so to combat illicit trade of small arms, one may also envisage the resort to economic sanctions as a means to force a State to respect its commitments.

Although the debate over countermeasures is dealt with elsewhere in the Handbook,[94] it is helpful to point out here that the Protocol Against the Illicit Manufacturing of and Trafficking in Firearms, Their Parts and Components, and Ammunition is silent on reactions to non-compliance. The question is then to what extent a State party can adopt economic measures when another State does

---

[92] For a discussion of a wider definition of security interests concerning arms trade, see G Bastid Burdeau, 'Le commerce des armes: de la sécurité à la défense de l'éthique et des droits de l'homme' 2007 *Journal du droit international* 134(2) 413, at 418. In the same vein, on a similar issue of interpretation regarding whether or not a WTO Member imposing import restrictions for human rights considerations may justify its actions by invoking exceptions such as those for 'security', see G Marceau, 'WTO Dispute Settlement and Human Rights' 2002 *European Journal of International Law* 13(4) 753, at 789.

[93] *Programme of Action*, above fn 88, at para 22 (a).

[94] See chapter 15 of this Handbook.

not meet its obligations under this Protocol. The issue appears in slightly different terms when one looks at the recent Economic Community of West African States (ECOWAS) Convention on Small Arms and Light Weapons, Their Ammunition, and Other Related Materials that was signed by Member States during their 14 June 2006 Summit in Abuja. Article 27(2) of the Convention provides explicitly for the possibility of adopting collectively authorized sanctions.[95] Under that provision, the competent organ could decide upon the adoption of sanctions of an economic nature that contradict WTO rules and that could be based on Article XXI (b)(ii).

The same issue may arise in the context of future negotiations on a comprehensive international treaty establishing common international standards for the import, export, and transfer of small arms.[96]

V. Conclusions: The Need for a New Approach?

The UN is increasingly engaging in activities of an economic nature in the framework of its collective security mandate. There is therefore a need to think about the overall international legal framework for these activities in a more coherent manner. This approach should start with the recognition of the necessity to address the economic, as well as humanitarian, effects of sanctions.

Above all, while the yielding of both Article 103 UN Charter and Article XXI (c) GATT 1994 to the interests of peace and security is partly justified, it does not provide satisfying answers when it comes to the new economic role played by the UN. It is the authors' view that these provisions do not exclude taking into account WTO law and principles of international trade law within the context of collective security activities of an economic nature. An approach that takes these principles into account would improve the long term efficiency of UN action and would advance the goal of achieving sustainable peace. It would provide a coherent framework to address economic challenges arising in post-conflict situations. If economic recovery is to be a pillar of peace, UN involvement needs to be based on legal principles to secure the proper functioning of post-conflict economies. It is critical in order to ensure that post-conflict

[95] Article 27, at para 2 reads as follows: 'If the ECOWAS Mediation and Security Council considers that there is a breach of the obligations under this convention, it shall decide on the appropriate measures to be taken such as sanctions, inquiry, study or refer the matter to the ECOWAS Court of Justice.'

[96] See *Report of the United Nations Conference to Review Progress Made in the Implementation of the Programme of Action to Prevent, Combat and Eradicate the Illicit Trade in Small Arms and Light Weapons in All Its Aspects the Programme of Action*, UN Doc. A/CONF.192/2006/RC/9 (12 July 2006), at para 30; UN Press Release, 24 November 2006, DC/3053, at < http://www.un.org//News/Press/docs/2006/dc3053.doc.htm> (last visited 25 January 2008).

transition and UN disengagement do not destabilize the economy, as was identified in the Report of the Panel on UN Peace Keeping Operations.[97] This being said, careful attention should be paid to the specificities of each situation. Depending on the scale and the nature of the conflict as well as the local context, economic reconstruction may call for flexible and tailored solutions. The country-specific method at the heart of the Peacebuilding Commission's work stems from this logic.[98]

The increasing recognition of a more coordinated approach would help to go beyond the current logic of deference of WTO law towards UN law and encourage greater complementarity. This new approach is also relevant at the institutional level in terms of sharing of tasks and responsibilities. With the UN being increasingly involved in economic matters, there is a critical issue of coordination regarding the respective powers and competences of each organization involved. The existing institutional cooperation scheme between the WTO and the UN is governed by the *Arrangements for Effective Cooperation with other Intergovernmental Organizations – Relations Between the WTO and the UN* signed on 15 November 1995. The Chief Executive Board is composed of executive heads from various UN bodies, the WTO, and Bretton Woods institutions and meets twice a year under the chairmanship of the UN SG. It seeks to promote coherence both within the UN system and outside of it and serves as the main instrument to coordinate actions and policies. Such a forum could be used to further explore new approaches for the UN to take into account international economic law principles. On the other hand, the WTO as an institution should be more proactive in the promotion of international trade law principles and rules as a means to contribute to the stabilization of societies that have gone through major conflicts.

SELECTED BIBLIOGRAPHY

AS Alexandroff and R Sharma, 'The National Security Provision – GATT Art XXI' in FJP Macrory, AE Appleton, and MG Plummer (eds), *The World Trade Organization: Legal, Economic and Political Analysis*, Vol I (New York: Springer/International Law Institute, 2005) 1571

G Bastid Burdeau, 'Le commerce des armes: de la sécurité à la défense de l'éthique et des droits de l'homme' 2007 *Journal du droit international* 134(2) 413

L Boisson de Chazournes, *Les contre-mesures dans les relations internationales économiques* (Paris: IUHEI/Pedone, 1992)

---

[97]   Report of the Panel on United Nations Peace Keeping Operations, UN Doc A/55/305, S/2000/809 (Brahimi Report), at para 28.

[98]   *Provisional report on the work of the Peacebuilding Commission*, above fn 56, at para 10.

L Boisson de Chazournes, 'The United Nations on Shifting Sands: About the Rebuilding of Iraq' 2003 *International Law Forum* 5(4) 254.

L Boisson de Chazournes, 'Collective Security and the Economic Interventionism of the UN – The Need for a Coherent and Integrated Approach' 2007 *Journal of International Economic Law* 10(1) 51

KE Boon, '"Open for Business": International Financial Institutions, Post-Conflict Economic Reform and the Rule of Law' 2007 *Journal of International Law and Politics* 39(3) 513

R Bordea, *La Mission intérimaire d'administration des Nations Unies au Kosovo*, LLM Thesis, University Paris I (September 2000)

R Caplan, *International Governance of War-Torn Territories – Rule and Reconstruction* (Oxford: Oxford University Press, 2005)

S Chesterman, *You, The People: The United Nations, Transitional Administration, and State-Building* (Oxford: Oxford University Press, 2004)

H Correll, 'A Challenge to the United Nations and the World: Developing the Rule of Law' 2004 *Temple International and Comparative Law Journal* 18 (2) 391

D Cortwright and GA Lopez, *The Sanctions Decade: Assessing UN Strategies in the 1990s* (London: Lynne Rienner Publishers, 2000)

MW Doyle, 'War-Making and Peace-Making: The United Nations' Post Cold War Record' in CA Crocker, FO Hampson, and P Aall (eds), *Turbulent Peace: The Challenges of Managing International Conflict* (Washington, DC: United States Institute of Peace Press, 2001), 529

V Gowlland-Debbas, 'Sanctions Regimes under Article 41 of the UN Charter' in V Gowlland-Debbas (ed), *National Implementation of United Nations – A Comparative Study* (Geneva/Leiden/Boston: IUHEI – Nijhoff, 2004) 3

AF Lowenfeld, *International Economic Law* (New York: Oxford University Press, 2003)

D Malone and J Cockayne, 'The UN Security Council: 10 Lessons from Iraq on Regulation and Accountability' 2006 *Journal of International Law and International Relations* 2 (2) 1

G Marceau, 'WTO Dispute Settlement and Human Rights' 2002 *European Journal of International Law* 13(4) 753

S Marks and A Clapham, *International Human Rights Lexicon* (Oxford: Oxford University Press, 2005)

M Matsushita, TJ Schoenbaum, and PC Mavroidis, *The World Trade Organization – Law, Practice, and Policy* (Oxford: Oxford University Press, 2003)

J Pauwelyn, 'Iraqi Reconstruction Contracts and the WTO: "International Law? I'd Better Call My Lawyer"' *Jurist: Forum* (19 December 2003)

J Pauwelyn, 'WTO Compassion or Superiority Complex?: What to Make of the WTO Waiver for "Conflict Diamonds"' 2003 *Michigan Journal of International Law* 24(4) 1177

J Pauwelyn, *Conflict of Norms in Public International Law – How WTO Law Relates to other Rules of International Law* (Cambridge: Cambridge University Press, 2004)

A Roberts, 'Transformative Military Occupation: Applying the Laws of War and Human Rights' 2006 *American Journal of International Law* 100(3) 580

N Schrijver, 'The Use of Economic Sanctions by the UN Security Council: an International Law Perspective' in HG Post (ed), *International Economic Law and Armed Conflict* (Dordrecht/Boston: Martinus Nijhoff, 1994) 123

C Stahn, 'NGO's and International Peacekeeping – Issues, Prospects and Lessons Learned' 2001 *Zeitschrift für ausländisches öffentliches Recht und Völkerrecht* (61) 379

S Talmon, 'A Plurality of Responsible Actors: International Responsibility for Acts of the Coalition Provisional Authority in Iraq' in P Shiner and A Williams (eds), *The Iraq War and International Law* (Oxford: Hart Publishing, 2008) 41

DL Tehindrazanarivelo, *Les sanctions des Nations Unies et leurs effets secondaires: assistance aux victimes et voies juridiques de prévention* (Paris: Presses Universitaires de France, 2005)

JM Thouvenin, 'Article 103' in JP Cot and A Pellet (eds), *La Charte des Nations Unies – Commentaire article par article*, 3rd edn (Paris: Economica, 2005) 2133

C Van Calster, 'WTO Law and Contracts for Rebuilding Iraq' 2003 *International Law Forum* 5 (4) 270

C H A P T E R   2 6

....

REGULATING MULTINATIONAL CORPORATIONS AND INTERNATIONAL TRADE LAW

....

CRAIG FORCESE[*]

* My thanks to Jenn Rosen, 3rd-year LLB candidate, for her assistance on this chapter.

I. Introduction

At its most elemental, 'doing business' is the movement of goods, knowledge, and services between and within business enterprises. These exchanges are commonplace *within* States, of course. There, they are regulated by domestic laws of various sorts, albeit domestic laws sometimes informed by international instruments. When enterprises do business *across* national borders, their activities often attract designation as international trade. International trade is closely regulated by rules of international law, designed in the final instance to minimize the impediments to 'doing business' that international borders might otherwise present.

The most common business enterprise is the corporation, an amalgamation of persons and assets chartered as separate legal persons by the domestic laws of States. Since corporations are the most universal instrument of trade, trade rules affect corporations more directly than any other entity. Nevertheless, international trade law speaks in the language of States and imposes obligations at the level of State units, barely ever emphatically singling out companies as bearing obligations or rights under international trade rules. There is, in fact, no such thing as 'corporate regulation' in the international trade regime.

This situation contrasts dramatically from what exists in domestic legal systems relating to purely intra-state business activities. In the domestic laws of developed legal systems, companies are heavily regulated. Corporate and securities law describes the nature of corporate status and outlines exhaustively the relationship between companies and those who own them, their shareholders. Employment, labour, and human rights laws structure the means by which companies retain, compensate, and treat their workers. Environmental law affects the manner in which companies produce their products and consumer regulations determine, in part, the content of those goods. Few of the details in these domestic laws have close international analogues, and when they do, these international instruments only indirectly affect companies by instead imposing direct obligations on States. Moreover, these obligations are essentially unenforceable against even States, except through bodies of very limited jurisdiction like the International Court of Justice.

As a result, international trade rules lubricate corporate transactions by shackling trans-border impediments on trade and leave to the domestic domain other norms governing the probity of these transactions and the goods they produce. In a global economy where all States applied similar domestic corporate governance, consumer, environmental, labour, and related rules, this pattern would be unproblematic. In reality, however, the global economy links States with developed legal systems that curb predatory economic practices with other States that lack these checks. An international trade law system largely indifferent to trade in goods manufactured, for instance, via child labour in an environmentally deleterious manner and that may themselves be tainted with toxins, attracts many critics.

This chapter is, therefore, about something that does not truly exist: the regulation of multinational corporations by the trade law regime. Its focus must necessarily be on the implications of that gap and on the concept of corporate 'accountability' writ large; that is, the supervision and regulation of corporate activities rendering these entities responsive to a range of stakeholders, from employees to the international community. As this chapter will show, international trade law and corporate accountability occupy different solitudes, but are nevertheless connected. It is no exaggeration to say that much contemporary work in the area of corporate accountability seeks—usually inadequately—to fill legal gaps left by underdeveloped domestic legal systems. Trade law presents one potential, alternative gap-filler. This chapter suggests, however, that there may be a more harmonious means of remedying corporate accountability concerns in a globalized economy than via 'mandate creep' in the trade law regime.

First, this chapter examines the concept of 'corporate accountability', an analysis that obliges a focus on conventional understandings of corporate law and its corporate social responsibility critique. In relation to this last issue, the chapter offers a basic political economy of corporate social responsibility, juxtaposing application of the concept in underdeveloped legal systems with the situation existing in more robust legal systems. Second, the chapter examines corporate accountability from the optic of international trade law. It looks first at the relevance of conventional trade law tools—conditioned market access—as a means of inducing corporate accountability. Pointing to the shortcomings of such an approach, it then proposes a number of speculative multilateral alternatives, including retooled investor-State dispute settlement and more purely punitive mechanisms, such as smart sanctions.

II. The Concept of Corporate Accountability

The corporate form—and particularly the notion of separate legal personality and the accompanying concept of limited liability—has proved a fundamental vessel for the accumulation of capital and its application to productive enterprise. By virtue of their very success in generating wealth, corporations are now a striking, perhaps even dominant feature, of modern society.

Since its inception, however, the corporate form has raised concerns about accountability, a preoccupation enhanced by the size and prevalence of companies in the modern economy. To be 'accountable', the *Merriam-Webster Online Dictionary* indicates, is to be 'responsible' or 'answerable'. Accountability, so defined, is a key component of corporate law. The corporate form, by its nature, obliges those with capital—the shareholders—to rely on the *bona fides* of those who manage the corporate vessel in which this capital is invested, giving rise to the so-called 'agency problem'. As a direct result, the better part of corporate law is dedicated to limiting the capacity of managers to act arbitrarily and capriciously, without regard to the interests of the company's shareholders. One very straightforward, reasonably verifiable means of minimizing the prospect that managers will abuse shareholder interests is, on the one hand, to give legal primacy to these interests and, on the other hand, to define their content in very simple terms: the maximization of returns. This approach can be described as one of 'shareholder primacy'.

A. Shareholder Primacy

The doctrine of shareholder primacy dominates most thinking on the corporate form. Proponents of this shareholder primacy view urge that, in corporate law, non-shareholder considerations 'ought not to rank *pari passu* with shareholder interests'.[1] In an old saw expressed initially by economist Milton Friedman 'there is one and only one social responsibility of business—to use it [sic] resources and engage in activities designed to increase its profits so long as it stays within the rules of the game, which is to say, engages in open and free competition without deception or fraud'.[2]

Critics within the business literature have complained that this myopic, but now dominant, shareholder focus hobbles the long-term viability of companies by eroding relationships with stakeholders key to business profitability.[3] It has been fuelled, they argue, by the wrong-headed linkage of executive compensation to an inadequate measure of corporate success, namely, short-term share value.[4] As another business source notes, however, '[t]he primacy of shareholder value is one tide that isn't likely to turn in our lifetime'.[5]

In doctrinal terms, shareholder primacy is expressed most readily through the fiduciary principle extant in at least common law jurisdictions. At base, fiduciary duties comprise two key obligations: a duty of care and a duty of loyalty. Different authorities define these duties in slightly different ways. The duty of care requires directors to act with 'the care of an ordinarily prudent person in the same or similar

---

[1] WA Dimma, 'Putting Shareholders First' 1997 *Ivey Business Quarterly* 62(1), 33.

[2] M Friedman, 'The Social Responsibility of Business is to Increase its Profits' *The New York Times Magazine* (13 September 1970); M Friedman, *Capitalism and Freedom* (Chicago: University of Chicago Press, 1962), at 133.

[3] See discussion in AA Kennedy, *The End of Shareholder Value: Corporations at the Crossroads* (Cambridge, MA: Perseus Books, 2000).

[4] C Wagner, 'The Downside of Shareholder Value' 2000 *Futurist* 34(6) 10.

[5] G Colvin, 'The 1998 Don't-Get-It All-Stars' 1998 *Fortune* 137(6) 169.

circumstances'.[6] For its part, the duty of loyalty requires the director, officer, or controlling shareholder to act in the best interests of the firm. In the words of one venerable UK authority: 'A corporate body can only act by agents, and it is, of course, the duty of those agents so to act as best to promote the interests of the corporation whose affairs they are conducting'.[7] The 'best interests of the corporation' protected by fiduciary principles are commonly conflated, as a matter of law, with those of the shareholders.[8] The 'interests' of shareholders are, in turn, assumed to be the maximization of returns on their investments.[9]

B. Accountability to Other Stakeholders

Despite its prevalence, there are influential dissents to shareholder primacy. Some corporate critics, accepting shareholder primacy as the governing norm, consider companies hopelessly short-sighted in their relations with 'stakeholders' affected by their actions. These people, disenchanted with the corporate form and opposed to what they have termed 'corporate rule', combat the supposed spillover of corporate profit-maximization into the public policy arena, including in such venues as the WTO.[10] For these detractors, because corporate accountability extends only as far as shareholders, companies are, at worst, an incorrigible evil or, at best, not proper participants in the democratic policy-setting process. In part, these critics inherit a vision of the corporate form most vividly expressed in the nineteenth century, seeing in companies an unnatural combine to be carefully policed by the States that charter them.[11]

---

[6] RW Hamilton, *The Law of Corporations: In a Nutshell*, 5th edn (St Paul, Minn: West, 2000), at 447 ('A director owes a duty to the corporation to exercise proper care in managing the corporation's affairs').

[7] *Aberdeen Rail Co v Blaikie Brothers*, [1843–1860] All ER Report 249 (HL).

[8] Committee on Corporate Law, American Bar Association, 'Other Constituencies Statutes: Potential for Confusion' 1990 *The Business Lawyer* (45) 2253, at 2255 ('With few exceptions, courts have consistently avowed the legal primacy of shareholder interests when management and directors make decisions').

[9] Ibid at 2265.

[10] See, eg, R Burbach and K Danaher (eds), *Globalize This! The Battle Against the World Trade Organization and Corporate Rule* (Monroe, ME: Common Courage Press, 2000).

[11] The nineteenth-century complaint was perhaps best articulated by satirist Ambrose Bierce when he quipped, a corporation is '[a]n ingenious device for obtaining individual profit without individual responsibility'. A Bierce, *The Devil's Dictionary* (USA: Plain Label Books, 1998). In its early days in the US, the corporation was greeted by the public with a healthy dose of suspicion, not least because corporations were often viewed as devices for exploiting monopolies. AA Sommer Jr, 'Whom Should The Corporation Serve? The Berle-Dodd Debate Revisited Sixty Years Later' 1991 *Delaware Journal of Corporate Law* 16(1) 33, at 36. Some early critics went so far as to propose the abolition of the corporate form itself. D Millon, 'Frontiers of Legal Thought I: Theories of the Corporation' 1990 *Duke Law Journal* 1990(2) 201, at 207–08, citing J Willard Hurst, *The Legitimacy of the Business Corporation in the Law of the United States, 1780–1970* (Charlottesville: University Press of Virginia, 1970), at 37–41.

Other observers, more moderate in disposition but ultimately more radical in their challenge to the assumptions of corporate law, query not the propriety of corporations *per se*, but the legitimacy of the 'shareholder primacy' principle. They urge that companies have responsibilities that extend beyond maximization of return for shareholders. One variant of this thinking, associated with corporate philanthropy, urges that the company owes obligations to behave as a 'good citizen'.[12] Another, more recent view broadens the traditional ambit of 'accountability', requiring company consideration of 'stakeholder interests' as much as shareholder objectives. Put another way, while most objectors to 'corporate rule' query the legitimacy of the corporate form, supporters of the less noisy, but in many respects more far-reaching, 'corporate social responsibility' doctrine call for a kinder, gentler company. The balance of this section explores this concept of corporate social responsibility.

1. *Corporate Social Responsibility*

'Corporate social responsibility' (CSR) is an amorphous concept, one that sometimes specifies not only to whom, but also for what, companies should be accountable. For some, CSR is simply synonymous with 'ethical' behaviour by the corporation in its money-making activities. As UNCTAD puts it, '[a]t the most basic level, socially responsible business behaviour means refraining from doing harm'.[13] For others, CSR is more specifically defined. The World Business Council for Sustainable Development defines CSR as 'the commitment of business to contribute to sustainable economic development, working with employees, their families, the local community and society at large to improve their quality of life'.[14]

2. *Questions Raised by Corporate Social Responsibility*

Clearly, the term 'corporate social responsibility' is capable of encompassing a vast range of behaviour and a significant number of stakeholders, beyond shareholders. Typical 'stakeholders' listed include employees, consumers, communities, and an

---

Nineteenth century populist movements were particularly uneasy with corporations, prompting many state legislatures to restrict company size, duration, powers and purposes. Hamilton, above fn 6, at 63.

[12] In the US, corporate charitable giving was relatively uncommon prior to the mid-1930s. HW Smith, 'If Not Corporate Philanthropy, Then What?' 1997 *New York Law School Law Review* 41(3–4) 757, at 758. However, by the middle of the twentieth century corporate donations had become reasonably commonplace. Tax filings suggest that by 1997, approximately 20 per cent of companies were making charitable donations and gifts. Among the 12,000 odd companies registered with the Securities and Exchange Commission as public enterprises, over 90 per cent made charitable gifts or donations. In monetary terms, companies donated $8 billion in 1996, a figure representing 1.5 per cent of pre-tax profits. One researcher estimates companies donated a total of $103 billion between 1936 and 1997. Ibid at 766–68.

[13] See UNCTAD, *World Investment Report 2006: FDI from Developing and Transition Economies: Implications for Development* (New York: United Nations, 2006), at 232.

[14] World Business Council for Sustainable Development, *Corporate Social Responsibility: Making Good Business Sense*, at <http://www.inggroup.com.au/pdf/csr2000.pdf> (last visited 10 July 2007), at 10.

inchoate 'environment'. Exactly how and for what companies are to be account-able to these constituencies is a matter fraught with some uncertainty. As a starting point, it is sometimes observed that the scope of corporate responsibility to these constituencies may depend on that company's proximity to them; that is, whether these stakeholders lie properly within the company's 'sphere of influence'.[15] This inherently ambiguous concept only goes part way, however, in addressing the question of for what corporations are responsible.

Consider, for example, that employees are indisputably a part of every corporation's operations. In much of the world, a corporation's relations with its employees are overseen by a vast array of employment, human rights, and labour laws, many of which are designed to oblige corporations to meet minimum standards of behaviour in their workplaces. But should corporations be expected to go beyond these regulations, or to apply decent standards where they are not now required to do so? Should corporations be expected to police the workplace standards—including the rights and safety of workers—of the suppliers from whom they source?

Likewise, the efficient production of goods and services is the rationale for a market-based economy and all business corporations. There are very few companies, therefore, for whom customers are not 'stakeholders' clearly within corporate spheres of influence. Notably, numerous legal standards exist in many countries imposing a cost on corporations where they act inappropriately, producing shoddy or dangerous products or services. But should corporations meet high standards for goods and services where such legal requirements do not exist? For example, should corporations observe the privacy interests of their customers even where relevant regulations are absent? Should they avoid sending dangerous, damaged or expired products to jurisdictions that do not carefully regulate consumer safety? A related issue is whether companies producing essential medicines should price these products outside of the reach of the world's poor.

Meanwhile, all companies operate in the real, physical world. To greater or lesser degrees, the communities that surround them are within their 'sphere of influence'. Giving to local charities and other worthy causes is one form of community involvement that a socially responsible firm might consider. But should socially responsible firms also contemplate the impact of plant closure and relocation decisions on local communities? Does a company owe anything to a community it decides to leave? Should companies bribe officials to gain advantages? Another area of community relations that firms should be concerned with relates to the impact of their operations on local environments and vulnerable populations. Should companies pursue 'social impact assessments' before commencing a project, even where there is no obligation to do so? Should they conduct environmental assessments of projects in

[15] See, eg, Canada, Royal Commission on Corporate Concentration, *Report of the Royal Commission on Corporate Concentration* (Ottawa: Minister of Supply and Services Canada, 1978), at 377.

jurisdictions that do not require such studies? In addition, there are now numerous examples of acts by companies that seem to increase human rights-abusing propensities and strengthen repressive regimes. How far does a company's 'sphere of influence' extend where its presence is contributing to human rights abuses? What steps does a socially responsible company take to reduce and eliminate its negative impact? Will a responsible company withdraw from a country or project where its activities are exacerbating human rights abuses? Should a company, in all of its operations, at home and abroad, act in a way that is consistent with international human rights as found in the Universal Declaration of Human Rights? If so, then must it find some way to comply and promote all of these rights, or just those that are most material to the company's operations?

Local or national communities are not alone in being affected by company actions. Many corporations are now key players at the international level. In the words of one observer, '[a]s liberalization has expanded business opportunities and generated global corporate networks, the bargaining balance in many societies has shifted in favor of the private sector, and in developing countries particularly to TNCs [transnational corporations]'.[16] Some stress that WTO law has privileged global corporate priorities at the expense of development and other objectives. In a scathing 2002 report, for example, Oxfam urged that many of the WTO's 'rules on intellectual property, investment, and services, protect the interests of rich countries and powerful TNCs, while imposing huge costs on developing countries… [t]he WTO's bias in favour of the self-interest of rich countries and big corporations raises fundamental questions about its legitimacy'.[17] Civil society groups describe the WTO as subject to 'undue influence' from corporate lobbies: 'Big business lobbyists have privileged access to government policymakers and use it to push trade agreements that undermine the fight against poverty'.[18] Meanwhile, then UN Secretary-General Kofi Annan publicly called upon the corporate sector to promote human rights, development, and environmental values in their operations,[19] as set out in the UN 'Global Compact'. How should companies conduct themselves in relation to the international community? Is it appropriate for a responsible company to engage in

---

[16] G Kell and JG Ruggie, 'Global Markets and Social Legitimacy: The Case of the "Global Compact"', Paper presented at *Governing the Public Domain beyond the Era of the Washington Consensus? Redrawing the Line Between the State and the Market*, York University, Toronto, Canada (4–6 November 1999), at <http://www.unglobalcompact.org/NewsAndEvents/articles_and_papers/global_markets_social_legitimacy_york_university.html> (last visited 10 July 2007).

[17] Oxfam, *Rigged Rules and Double Standards: Trade, Globalisation, and the Fight Against Poverty* (2002), at <http://www.maketradefair.com/assets/english/report_english.pdf> (last visited 10 July 2007), at 6.

[18] ActionAid International, *Under the Influence: Exposing undue corporate influence over policymaking at the World Trade Organization*, at <http://www.actionaid.org.uk/_content/documents/under_the_influence_final.pdf> (last visited 10 July 2007), at 2.

[19] *UN Secretary-General Proposes Global Compact on Human Rights, Labour, Environment, in Address to World Economic Forum in Davos*, SG/SM/6881 (1 February 1999), at <http://www.un.org/News/Press/docs/1999/19990201.sgsm6881.html> (last visited 10 July 2007).

action or urge policies or promote an international system that augments profits at the risk of negative social, environmental, and human rights consequences?

As these examples suggest, the precise character of CSR is uncertain and mutable. What should be immediately apparent, however, is that at least some of these questions are in fact answered in some jurisdictions by developed regulatory regimes. In still other less robust legal systems, none of these questions are truly answered. It is to this issue that this Chapter now turns.

3. *Corporate Social Responsibility as a Regulatory Issue*

CSR is sometimes described as a 'beyond law' subject[20]—that is, a doctrine that applies in circumstances where the law prescribes no standards. It is, in other words, the arena of volunteerism. Volunteerism is not, however, the same thing as altruism. What corporations choose to do as part of a CSR policy may be (and probably often is) motivated by something other than high-mindedness. There is, for example, a literature on the 'business case' for CSR, often one that points to the importance of reputation management for business success.

From this perspective, CSR is a sensible tactic for profit-maximizing firms. It strains credulity, however, to suggest that this will always be true, or true in the same way across firms. For example, there is little reason to assume that investment in CSR by a small, junior mining company producing a raw mineral input will necessarily generate the same dividend as investment by a name-brand, image-sensitive shoe manufacturer. An apparel company trades on its reputation much more readily than a copper mining company. Moreover, the apparel firm can create a competitive market niche for an ethical product that is more difficult for a resource extraction company to develop. The drivers that might move a resource company towards CSR are likely different, and may often be tied to community relations in concession areas. In either case, CSR flows from incentives moored firmly to profit-maximization. The precise mix of these incentives will affect the firm's willingness to practice a particular form of CSR. All things being equal, a firm's behaviour in circumstances where incentives are robust will likely be different than in situations where incentives are meagre.

a. *CSR in Developed Legal Systems*

The incentive structure in a developed legal system—a jurisdiction in which the rule of law is observed and the company operates in a complicated regulatory setting created by that law—is more vigorous than in a less developed counterpart where regulations are thin and/or unenforced. For one thing, there is less space in the former sort of jurisdiction to be occupied by CSR rather than by simple legal

---

[20] See, eg, Industry Canada, *Corporate Social Responsibility: An Implementation Guide for Canadian Business*, at 5, at <http://www.strategis.ic.gc.ca/epic/site/csr-rse.nsf/en/rs00126e.html> (last visited 10 July 2007), at 5.

compliance. In a developed legal system, everything is governed by legal rules, from toxic discharges to employment relationships. Meanwhile, those areas that are not directly regulated by legal rules may still fall within the shadow of the law. A company discharging toxins in a manner compliant with environmental regulations may still cause some foreseeable harm to a particular individual cognizable in tort law, or taint the waters of a downstream riparian giving rise to an action in property law. Regulatory rules obliging full disclosure of toxic discharges may spark reporting in the media and/or recriminations from local communities that propel a company to go beyond mere legal compliance with environmental standards. Corporate law standards enabling shareholders to pose questions of management during annual meetings may drive managers to minimize the prospect of embarrassing queries. Relations with indigenous peoples in respect to a mining operation may be affected by developing doctrines of informed consent in domestic law.

Because the space for CSR is relatively meagre in developed legal systems, CSR discussions have often focused on corporate philanthropy and sometimes obscure debates on fiduciary duties and CSR. For example, while scholars repeatedly urge that shareholder primacy continues to dominate corporate law,[21] corporate law on this issue is in a state of flux in some common law jurisdictions. The UK has, in fact, legislated a 'stakeholder' approach to fiduciary duties in the recent Companies Act 2006.[22] Even in the US, 'stakeholder' rhetoric is also now common. Beginning with Pennsylvania in 1983, a majority of US jurisdictions introduced provisions in their company laws reflecting stakeholder thinking. Designed in part to allow managers to contemplate more than shareholder profit interests in assessing takeover attempts, these so-called 'other constituency statutes' generally provide that in contemplating the best interests of the corporation, directors may consider such things as the corporation's long-term interests, including in remaining independent, and the interests of shareholders, employees, customers, suppliers, and creditors, the communities in which the corporation operates, and the economy of the State and the nation. Statutes also sometimes empower directors to contemplate 'all other pertinent factors'.[23]

It is not clear that these (often controversial) changes to corporate law have affected much company behaviour. Non-shareholder stakeholder provisions have

---

[21] See, eg, Committee on Corporate Law, American Bar Association, above fn 8, at 2255; SM Bainbridge, 'Participatory Management Within a Theory of the Firm' 1996 *The Journal of Corporation Law* 21(4) 657, at 717; SM Bainbridge, 'In Defense of the Shareholder Wealth Maximization Norm: A Reply to Professor Green' 1993 *Washington and Lee Law Review* 50(4) 1423, at 1423; D Millon, 'New Directions in Corporate Law: Communitarians, Contractarians, and the Crisis in Corporate Law' 1993 *Washington and Lee Law Review* 50(4) 1373, at 1374; DG Smith, 'The Shareholder Primacy Norm' 1998 *The Journal of Corporation Law* 23(2) 277, at 280; MM Blair and LA Stout, 'A Team Production Theory of Corporate Law' 1999 *Virginia Law Review* 85(2) 247, at 253, fn 15.

[22] *Companies Act 2006*, 2006 Chapter 46, sub-s 172(1).

[23] See, eg, Pennsylvania: 15 PaCS s 1715 (2000).

been raised in only a handful of cases,[24] most of which have been cited much more thoroughly in the academic literature than by other courts. Evaluating the impact of stakeholder constituency statutes with an eye to these cases, one scholar declared that fears expressed by critics in the early 1990s have proven 'unfounded', if only because cases applying the statutes have been so uncommon and even then, peripheral to the outcome.[25]

This pattern may simply confirm the point made above: in developed legal systems, robust regulatory regimes leave relatively little to the discretion of firms and their managers. Doing the right thing is prescribed (or at least lies within the shadow of the law), even for profit-maximizing firms. In these circumstances, even an unalloyed shareholder primacy approach to fiduciary duties does not relieve a company of obligations that, absent developed legal systems, might instead fall purely within the scope of CSR.

b. CSR in Underdeveloped Legal Systems

In underdeveloped legal systems, there is often little regulation and the shadow of the law does not reach far. Emerging economies may have few environmental, consumer, employment, or other rules—or fail to enforce those rules. Civil liability concepts may be limited, or company assets may be beyond the reach of the jurisdiction. Governments may be repressive, and willing to employ scurrilous methods to supply resources to investing companies. In this environment, CSR may mean the application of standards by companies that would meet only the most basic requirements of legal compliance in their States of origin. Meanwhile, in weak States, legal underdevelopment may be compounded by economic underdevelopment. Companies may be propelled to supply needs and wants that in developed nations are supplied by the State or other economic actors—health care, education, infrastructure, and the like. UNCTAD aptly captures this notion of CSR as 'gap-filler'.[26]

In underdeveloped legal systems, CSR and volunteerism take on a different hue. The limited regulatory framework may create minimal incentives for CSR performance. Nevertheless, in response to consumer, shareholder, community, human rights, and environmental group agitation, there has been an explosion of 'voluntary' codes of corporate conduct—instruments promulgated at an international, industry, or company level that pledge companies to meet a dizzying array of standards.[27] Summarizing the key features of codes in a 2001 survey, the OECD observed as follows:

[24] See BH McDonnell, 'Corporate Governance and the Sarbanes-Oxley Act: Corporate Constituency Statues and Employee Governance' 2004 *William Mitchell Law Review* 30(4) 1227, at 1231–2.

[25] JD Springer, 'Corporate Constituency Statues: Hollow Hopes and False Fears' 1999 *Annual Survey of American Law* 85, at 121.

[26] UNCTAD, above fn 13, at 235.

[27] See R Jenkins, 'Corporate Codes of Conduct: Self-Regulation in a Global Economy' *United Nations Research Institute for Social Development: Technology, Business and Society Programme*, Paper No 2 (April 2001), at <http://www.yorku.ca/hdrnet/images/uploaded/jenkins.pdf> (last visited 10 July 2007).

The codes examined differ considerably in terms of their content and degree of detail... The codes address a variety of issues, many appearing to arise from concerns of the general public. Environmental management and labour standards dominate other issues in code texts, but consumer protection and bribery and corruption also receive extensive attention. In addition, many codes contain extensive text on fairly narrow questions of internal control and protection of shareholder value.[28]

Codes may be important tools when applied diligently by willing companies.[29] They are, however, not universally adopted (and even less often actually applied) by companies operating in underdeveloped legal systems. A 2000 UN-sponsored report cautioned, for instance, that:

Despite the considerable publicity surrounding codes of conduct, the extent to which they have been adopted so far is relatively limited. Many company codes are little more than general statements of business ethics with no indication of the way in which they are to be implemented... The reluctance of many firms to include independent monitoring as an integral part of their code of conduct gives rise to some suspicion that they may be used as a public relations exercise rather than a genuine attempt at improving conditions and performance.[30]

A World Bank (WB) study reporting on consultations with company, worker and NGO representatives raised similar concerns with the diffuse, volunteer, code of conduct approach to CSR:

Overall, the consultations, and subsequent analysis, indicate that while meaningful progress has been made in apparel, and to a lesser degree in agriculture, the existing 'system' of implementation may be reaching its limits in terms of its ability to deliver further sustainable improvements in social and environmental workplace standards.[31]

Critics of corporate activities in underdeveloped economies sometimes regard corporate codes as chaff, diverting attention from more meaningful solutions such as government regulation. They dispute the notion that companies may choose to adhere (or not) to basic standards—often standards that host States are obliged to meet by binding international human rights, labour, or environmental instruments. Instead, many actors direct their efforts at bringing corporate actions in the developing world within the shadow of the law, often that of the developed world. Some domestic drivers of CSR, such as selective, ethical investment, and shareholder

[28] OECD, 'Codes of Corporate Conduct: Expanded Review of their Contents' *Working Papers on International Investment*, No 2001/6 (May 2001), at <http://www.oecd.org/dataoecd/57/24/1922656.pdf> (last visited 10 July 2007), at 2.

[29] See, eg, Jenkins, above fn 27, at 28–9.   [30] Ibid at 26–7.

[31] WB Group, Corporate Social Responsibility Practice, *Strengthening Implementation of Corporate Social Responsibility in Global Supply Chains* (October 2003), at <http://www.siteresources.worldbank.org/INTPSD/Resources/CSR/Strengthening_Implementatio.pdf> (last visited 10 July 2007), at 2. For another critique of existing voluntary measures, see S Deva, 'Human Rights Violations by Multinational Corporations and International Law: Where From Here?' 2003–2004 *Connecticut Journal of International Law* 19(1) 1.

activism at shareholder meetings, transcend the multinational divide; activist investors are as empowered to query management about the company's activities in South Africa as in Michigan. More controversially, transnational legal liability—most notable in the form of the US *Alien Tort Claims Act*[32]—raises the spectre of damage awards in developed legal systems for actions taken in other jurisdictions.[33] In this manner, domestic legal systems are internationalized, reaching out to other States in a manner that sometimes provokes concern about extraterritorial unilateralism. Notably, these strategies presume a north-south flow of foreign direct investment; that is, northern companies from developed legal systems operating in the developing economies. Increasingly, investment is south-south,[34] thus potentially *between* underdeveloped legal systems. These sorts of operations are presumptively less susceptible to long-arm, developed legal system incentives. There is empirical reason to believe, in fact, that south-south investment is subject to fewer CSR pressures.[35]

III. Implications for the Multilateral Trade Regime

This pattern leads naturally to a discussion of corporate accountability and its relationship with the multilateral trading regime. Put simply, the multilateral trading regime presents a potentially enormous lever available to enforce standards in underdeveloped legal systems, one that is truly multilateral and not dependent on uneven extraterritorial measures. Ironically, the standards that might be linked to trade law are already prescribed by international law in the human rights, labour, or environmental context. However, trade law is distinguished from other branches of international law in one key respect: it regulates market access.

Conditioned market access is the classic blunt instrument of trade law. Intercepting problematic goods at the border and levying on them some disadvantage is what tariffs and other trade barriers are designed to accomplish. Classically, the motivations for these measures were protectionist. The same technique could, however, be

---

[32] 28 USC s 1350.

[33] See, eg, Special Representative of the Secretary-General on the issue of human rights and transnational corporations and other business enterprises, *Business and Human Rights: Mapping International Standards of Responsibility and Accountability for Corporate Acts*, UN Doc A/HRC/4/035 (19 February 2007), at <http://www.ap.ohchr.org/documents/dpage_e.aspx?s=58> (last visited 10 July 2007), at paras 26–27.

[34] UNCTAD, above fn 13, at 18.

[35] Ibid at 232 (discussing the relative prevalence of CSR among developing and developed country companies).

used for nobler purposes; that is, to induce companies who originate these suspect goods to change their ways either under pressure from admonished host governments or on their own. Conditioning market access on performance would create huge regulatory performance incentives, at least for export-dependent governments or governments amenable to lobbying by export dependent industries. Put another way, trade law conditionality has the potential to induce trading nations to enforce applicable standards and thus vitiate much of the gap-filling role CSR now plays.

The issue of conditionality and trade and environment or labour linkages has raised fierce debates.[36] This chapter only briefly reviews key questions that market conditionality would raise and queries whether trade law enforcement would remedy what ails the globalized economy. It directs more attention at alternative multilateral possibilities; ones directed not at States so much as at bringing companies themselves within the shadow of the law.

A. Conditioning Market Access

1. *Approaches to Linkage*

A number of different proposals for conditioned market access exist, among them a formal amendment to the WTO framework allowing WTO Members to discriminate against the products exported from countries not complying with relevant standards. A more modest approach hinges on the interpretation of existing WTO legal principles—most notably Article XX GATT 1994—to permit this form of discrimination.[37] Yet another, existing strategy involves selective use of preferential tariff systems currently permitted for developing countries. Since the early 1980s, developed countries have relied on Articles XXXVI and XXXVII GATT 1947/1994 to lever human rights considerations onto the agenda of their less developed trading

---

[36] See, eg, E-U Petersmann, 'Time for a United Nations "Global Compact" for Integrating Human Rights into the Law of Worldwide Organizations: Lessons from European Integration' 2002 *European Journal of International Law* 13(3) 621; P Alston, 'Resisting the Merger and Acquisition of Human Rights by Trade Law: A Reply to Petersmann' 2002 *European Journal of International Law* 13(4) 815; E-U Petersmann, 'Taking Human Dignity, Poverty and Empowerment of Individuals More Seriously: Rejoinder to Alston' 2002 *European Journal of International Law* 13(4) 845; see also the summary of positions, as of 1999, in G Tsogas, 'Labour standards in international trade agreements: an assessment of the arguments' 1999 *The International Journal of Human Resource Management* 10(2) 351. See also chapters 17–23 of this Handbook.

[37] For an overview of these ideas, see K Kolben, 'Integrative Linkage: Combining Public and Private Regulatory Approaches in the Design of Trade and Labor Regimes' 2007 *Harvard International Law Journal* 48(1) 203, at 209; see also F Emmert, 'Labor, Environmental Standards and World Trade Law' 2003 *Journal of International Law & Policy* 10(1) 75. For a specific examination of Article XX GATT 1994, see SH Cleveland, 'Human Rights Sanctions and International Trade: A Theory of Compatibility' 2002 *Journal of International Economic Law* 5(1) 133; C Thomas, 'Should the World Trade Organization Incorporate Labor and Environmental Standards' 2004 *Washington and Lee Law Review* 61(1) 347.

partners. These provisions—situated under the heading of trade and development—permit developed country Members to grant non-reciprocal tariff benefits to developing country Members. Non-reciprocal benefits under the GATT 1994 are considered non-binding on the importing country and thus can be raised again should the importing country so desire.

The US has been particularly active in tying these non-reciprocal benefits to mixed economic and geo-political concerns. For example, the US General System of Preferences (GSP) programme was created in 1974, ostensibly as a development programme favouring trade over aid.[38] In 1984, Congress revised the GSP programme to add a larger human rights dimension, tying the extension and renewal of GSP preferences to labour rights. Thus, an infringement of 'internationally recognized worker rights' may justify removal of a State from eligibility as 'a beneficiary developing country' under the system.[39] In the mid-1990s, the EU followed the US lead, introducing its own GSP labour-rights conditionalities. The EU Regulation provides extra special 'incentive' benefits to countries meeting labour standards[40] and anticipates the withdrawal of benefits where certain rights are violated.[41]

2. *Objections to Linkage*

Suffice it to say in this chapter that conditioning of this sort raises the spectre of protectionism; instruments motivated by noble purposes might be subverted as a form of disguised discrimination against foreign products. This is a fear expressed not just by developing States,[42] but also by southern civil society groups and intellectuals.[43]

This preoccupation should not be exaggerated. Careful design of these mechanisms might reduce the risk of protectionist capture.[44] Nevertheless, it is difficult to imagine that even the most intricate linkage regime could always stave off capricious use, especially when the labour, human rights, or environmental objective being

---

[38] See 19 USC ss 2461–2466. [39] 19 USC s 2462(b)(2)(G).

[40] Council Regulation (EC) No 980/2005, *Applying a Scheme of Generalized Tariff Preferences*, 2005 OJ L169/1.

[41] Ibid, Art 22.

[42] For a discussion of developing countries' objections on this ground, see K Kolben, 'The New Politics of Linkage: India's Opposition to the Workers' Rights Clause' 2006 *Indiana Journal of Global Legal Studies* 13(1) 225.

[43] See, eg, 'Third World Intellectuals and NGOs' Statement Against Linkage', 15 November 1999, at <http://www.cuts-international.org/Twin-sal.htm> (last visited 10 July 2007); K Basu, 'Compacts, Conventions and Codes: Initiatives for Higher International Labor Standards' 2001 *Cornell International Law Journal* 34(3) 487; J Bhagwati, 'The Boundaries of the WTO: Afterward: The Question of Linkage' 2002 *American Journal of International Law* 96(1) 126.

[44] For a comprehensive defence of linkage in the labour area and proposals on how best to engineer a workable system, see C Barry and SG Reddy, 'International Trade and Labor Standards: A Proposal for Linkage' 2006 *Cornell International Law Journal* 39(3) 545. For a sympathetic review of linkage proposals, see also MJ Trebilcock and R Howse, 'Trade Policy & Labor Standards' 2005 *Minnesota Journal of Global Trade* 14(2) 261.

protected is amorphous. Consider, for example, that international human rights law guarantees workers 'fair wages' and a 'decent living for themselves and their families'.[45] These standards are difficult to operationalize in a human rights context, let alone as a concept to which market access would be linked. Moreover, an aggressive approach to 'fair' wages is exactly the sort of practice that might be used for protectionist purposes to stifle the comparative advantage inexpensive labour costs provide to emerging market economies.

A second objection to conditioned market access relates to the bluntness of the instrument. Barring imports of articles produced by child labour might, for example, drive child employees out of export trades. These same children are unlikely, however, to suddenly then find themselves in schools. Instead, they may be displaced to even less salubrious occupations, like prostitution. Conditioning market access does not, in other words, cure the problems of underdevelopment that precipitate child labour. Indeed, foreclosing markets may compound economic underdevelopment, closing off avenues of trade that would otherwise bootstrap poor countries to better standards of living.

This problem may be particularly acute where trade sanctions are imposed on a country rather than on an industry or even a firm-specific basis. For example, US GSP removal plainly runs the risk of affecting economies as a whole, not simply the interests of specific elites. Notably, however, even more careful market access targeting could have undesirable impacts, an observation affirmed by informal strategies such as consumer boycotts of specific companies. Footloose brand name apparel companies, for example, may respond to such initiatives by withdrawing from problematic operations, again causing economic hardship.

A final objection to the linkage proposal also relates to targeting. Non-compliance with environmental, human rights, and labour standards may be a symptom of underdevelopment, and not always or even often the behaviour of an indifferent or malicious government. Trade linkages punish legal underdevelopment by imposing sanctions on States, and not directly on the actual economic agents responsible for the offending behaviour.[46] It may, in other words, amount to punishing the patient for the disease.

For all these reasons, the trade law regime is probably ill-equipped to remedy the lacunae produced by underdeveloped legal systems. That is not to suggest, however, a preference for the status quo, or a sanguine faith that over time, the tide of open economics will lift all ships and remedy the ills of uneven regulatory environments. There are other economic sanction-like approaches, more nuanced than conditional market access, that could be deployed to enhance corporate accountability.

---

[45] UN, *International Covenant on Economic, Social and Cultural Rights*, adopted 16 December 1966, resolution 2200A (XXI), Art 7.

[46] For a discussion on this point, see Kolben, above fn 42, at 216.

B. Beyond Conditioned Market Access

This final section imagines a number of possible multilateral mechanisms of corporate accountability; tools that extend the shadow of the law but try to minimize collateral consequences. These devices are speculative and perhaps would not survive scrutiny on grounds of political viability. In that respect, they are no different from the market conditionalities described above. On the other hand, they seem plausible from a technical design perspective and probably do not suffer to the same extent from the latter's overbreadth and undesirable second-order effects.

1. *Retooled Investor-State Dispute Settlement*

Parallel to the multilateral trading regime (and embedded in some regional trade agreements such as the NAFTA) are systems of investor-State dispute resolution.[47] These treaty rules give standing to foreign investors (usually companies) before international tribunals to challenge certain decisions of the States in which they invest. Often, the complaints concern alleged expropriation by States of company assets or opportunities or the violation of a minimum treatment standard States owe to foreign nationals.

Investment treaty systems supplement more antiquated customary international law doctrines of diplomatic protection, permitting the States of nationality to 'step into the shoes' and espouse complaints concerning the treatment of their nationals at the hands of other States. The outsourcing of diplomatic protection to wronged persons themselves aims to preserve foreign investors from the prejudices and procedural machinations—suspected or real—of national court systems. From the State's perspective, this system may be a necessary means of attracting foreign direct investment. From the investor's perspective, privatized dispute resolution is a response to investment risk. It has value, in other words.

That value should not, however, be accorded as a matter of right. Where investment risk is enhanced or induced by a company's own behaviour, investor-State dispute resolution should not immunize companies from the reaction to their behaviour. For example, if a company's poor labour practices or its close association with a prior, repressive government now replaced by a new administration intent on remedying past wrongs contributes to the reduction in the worth of its investment, it should not be compensated through dispute settlement.

a. *Conditional Access to Remedies*

Access to investor remedies might reasonably be made conditional on adequate adherence to applicable standards. By analogy to those domestic legal systems applying rules of equity, the supplicant should arrive with clean hands. A conditionality

---

[47] See also chapter 22 of this Handbook.

of this sort might be conceived as a defence to the substantive wrongs alleged by the company. Such an approach would likely require only minor tweaking in the law applied via bilateral or plurilateral investment treaties. For instance, modern customary international law and, with some variation, investment treaties permit expropriations by States if done for a public purpose, on a non-discriminatory basis and with the payment of adequate compensation.[48] The content of that public purpose and the measure of adequate compensation might reasonably be gauged with an eye to the company's own behaviour. Extracting wealth from a company to compensate for past ills, measured against international labour or human rights standards, might reasonably be considered a public purpose requiring little compensation.

In a modest way, these notions may already be emerging in the investor-State dispute settlement context. UNCTAD reported in 2006 that recent investment agreements 'tend to deal with a broader set of issues, including public concerns related, for example, to health, safety or the environment'.[49] For example, the recent US-Central America Free Trade Agreement contains language attempting to limit the likelihood that public welfare regulatory activity motivated by public health, safety, and the environment will be considered an expropriation.[50]

The model bilateral investment agreement developed by the International Institute for Sustainable Development does much the same.[51] It goes beyond current practice, however, by proposing that access to investor-State dispute settlement under investment treaties be conditioned on adherence to non-corruption obligations. Moreover, violation of other standards—including in the environmental and human rights area—is to be considered in disputes brought by investors.[52]

b. Expanded Standing

Conditionality in investor-State dispute settlement is only one possibility. More radically, the investor-State dispute settlement mechanisms might be crafted as a two-way street; that is, a system where States themselves have standing to bring claims or counterclaims against companies for violation of applicable standards. A State, for instance, whose own domestic legal system cannot reach the deep pocket assets of an investor might welcome an investor-State dispute settlement regime permitting enforcement of arbitral outcomes against the assets of firms held in foreign jurisdictions.[53] The model bilateral investment agreement

---

[48]   See, eg, JG Starke and IA Shearer, *Starke's International Law*, 11th edn (London: Butterworths, 1994), at 272.

[49]   UNCTAD, above fn 13, at xix.

[50]   CAFTA, Annex 10–C, Art 4(b), at <http://www,ustr.gov/assets/Trade_Agreements/Bilateral/CAFTA/CAFTA-DR_Final_Texts/asset_upload_file328_4718.pdf> (last visited 11 July 2007).

[51]   IISD, *Model International Agreement on Investment for Sustainable Development - Negotiators' Handbook* (Winnipeg: IISD, 2005), at <http://www.iisd.org/pdf/2005/investment_model_int_handbook.pdf> (last visited 9 February 2008), Art 25.

[52]   Ibid, Art 18.

[53]   Certainly, access to assets held by State parties to the revised investor-State dispute settlement regime could be provided in the investment treaty itself. Assuming the latter is not, however, a

developed by the International Institute for Sustainable Development proposes such a system.[54]

Opening the door to State claims would respond only to the situation where the host State has an incentive to bring a claim. In some and perhaps many circumstances, the State itself is deficient in enforcing international or domestic standards, producing the underdeveloped legal system that allows the questionable corporate behaviour in the first place. Alternatively, the State may be the agent of the wrong, and the company at best complicit.

To address these situations, an even more radical proposal would be to open investor-State dispute settlement to third party victims of corporate malfeasance. The benefits to these victims are obvious: access to an international system of adjudication removed from the perhaps corrupted national courts of host States and unencumbered by the jurisdictional concerns that arise when the courts of home or third States are deployed to adjudicate extraterritorial claims.[55]

The mechanics of such a system would, of course, be complicated. For one thing, conventional arbitral practice only imagines two sides, and is structured to allow these sides a chief role in selecting arbiters.[56] A multiparty dispute would require a more complicated selection formula and a move towards stricter rules of independence of arbitrators.[57] Further, standing rules would have to be crafted carefully to prescribe which third parties are entitled to access the international mechanism. Plain-vanilla contract disputes with suppliers, for example, seem an unlikely candidate for such a system. It would be preferable to restrict it to those with more fundamental complaints, indexed against existing international expectations.

As this observation suggests, key to expanding investor-State dispute arrangements into broader systems of justice would be the development of cogent causes of action available to the State or third parties against a company—that is, the articulation of standards against which company behaviour is measured. There are a host of plausible candidates in this exercise, drawn from the norm-creation exercises of the last decade. One possibility, for example, might be to incorporate adherence to the standards found in instruments such as the OECD Guidelines for Multinational

multilateral regime, questions might arise as to the whether arbitration outcomes could be enforced in third States. These arbitral awards may be enforceable under the widely-ratified *UN Convention on the Recognition and Enforcement of Foreign Arbitral Awards*, 330 UNTS 38, entered into force, 7 June 1959.

[54] IISD, above fn 51, Art 18.

[55] The IISD model bilateral agreement asserts that third parties should be able to bring claims in the domestic courts of the host and home State, but does not appear to endorse third party standing to initiate a dispute settlement arbitration.

[56] Article 1123, Chapter 11 NAFTA provides, for example, that 'unless the disputing parties otherwise agree, the Tribunal shall comprise three arbitrators, one arbitrator appointed by each of the disputing parties and the third, who shall be the presiding arbitrator, appointed by agreement of the disputing parties'.

[57] Even at present, rules on independence and impartiality do exist and apply to arbitrators. See UNCITRAL Arbitration Rules, adopted 28 April 1976, GA Res 31/98, Arts 9–10.

Corporations[58] into investor-State dispute settlement mechanisms. Admittedly, this is an aspirational and often vague document. It is not clear that the norms in the Guidelines are any more certain than, for example, the minimum treatment concept found in investment treaties.[59] Nevertheless, the Guidelines may not always translate easily into justiciable standards in their present form. Careful redrafting would probably be necessary.

Alternatively, a separate multilateral instrument could be concluded converting labour, environmental, human rights, and other norms already extant in international law into justiciable concepts deployable in an expanding investor-State dispute arrangement.[60]

2. Punitive Measures

Instead or in addition to a revised investor-State dispute settlement regime, it is also possible to imagine more directly punitive mechanisms.

a. Domestically-Enforceable International Corporate Obligations

First, international treaties regularly anticipate the implementation of domestic criminal (and perhaps civil) penalties for certain extraterritorial wrongdoings by private actors. Obvious examples are the recent international anti-corruption instruments,[61] treaties that authorize State parties to criminalize bribery of foreign public officials. The extension of law in this manner has an obvious impact on business corporations and their overseas operations. In the same manner, a separate international instrument might tailor existing labour, environmental, and human rights norms into individual (and not simply State) obligations and authorize domestic-level, extraterritorial enforcement mechanisms.

b. Smart Sanctions

Second, more purely multilateral punitive mechanisms might be drawn from existing international sanctions practices—that is, the tactic of imposing economic

---

[58] OECD, *The OECD Guidelines for Multinational Enterprises: Revision 2000* (France: OECD, 2000).

[59] Article 1105(1) NAFTA states that '[e]ach Party shall accord to investments of investors of another Party treatment in accordance with international law, including fair and equitable treatment and full protection and security'.

[60] The UN Sub-Commission on the Promotion and Protection of Human Rights attempted to translate international human rights obligations into the language of corporate obligations in its UN *Norms on the Responsibilities of Transnational Corporations and Other Business Enterprises with Regard to Human Rights*, UN Doc E/CN.4/Sub.2/2003/12/Rev.2 (2003). This effort was met with stiff criticism and is largely discredited. There is, however, no reason in principle why its core idea—establishing norms for companies indexed to international law—could not be pursued more comprehensively.

[61] See, eg, *OECD Convention on Combating Bribery of Foreign Public Officials in International Business Transactions*, DAFFE/IME/BR(97)20 (10 April 1998), at <http://www.oecd.org/dataoecd/4/18/38028044.pdf> (last visited 11 July 2007); *United Nations Convention against Corruption*, adopted 31 October 2003, GA Res 58/4, at <http://www.unodc.org/pdf/crime/convention_corruption/signing/Convention-e.pdf> (last visited 11 July 2007).

sanctions on States for political reasons related, for example, to human rights abuses. Economic sanctions authorized by the UN Security Council or applied in other contexts have often been blunt instruments. Critics of these sanctions have urged that comprehensive economic sanctions—measures that isolate target States entirely from the world economy—have a discernable negative impact on the most vulnerable populations, leaving the political elite untouched. Responding to these concerns, the five permanent members of the Security Council concluded in 1995 that 'further collective actions in the Security Council within the context of any future sanctions regime should be directed to minimize unintended adverse side-effects of sanctions on the most vulnerable segments of targeted countries'.[62]

These conclusions were echoed by the International Peace Academy in a 2000 study on 'smart sanctions'. As the Academy noted, comprehensive sanctions represent the bluntest form of economic coercion, one with often unpredictable and devastating humanitarian and political side effects. Conversely, '[m]ore selective, targeted sanctions resulted in fewer humanitarian difficulties'.[63] These findings led the authors to favour narrowly tailored measures and to argue 'not that targeted or selective sanctions are ineffective, but that the policy steps necessary to enhance the impact of these more limited measures have not been taken'.[64] In terms of specific economic sanctions measures, the study called financial sanctions 'the centerpiece of a targeted sanctions strategy'.[65] The effectiveness of these measures depended, in the study's words, 'on the ability to identify and target specific individuals and entities whose assets are to be frozen'.[66] This approach has since been adopted in several modern UN sanctions regimes, not least that deployed against members of Al Qaeda and the Taliban. Travel bans of sanctioned state elites are also commonplace.

There is no reason in principle why leadership-oriented financial or travel sanctions could not also be motivated by more banal concerns, including firm-level violation of internationally cognizable human rights, labour, or environmental standards. A travel ban, for example, on the chief executive officer of a mining company complicit in acts of violence against indigenous opponents of a mining concession might do as much to change corporate (and perhaps local government) behaviour as would any trade law, market access measure. At the same time, it would not cause quite the collateral damage to other players, or risk capture as protectionism.

---

[62] Letter from the Permanent Representatives of China, France, the Russian Federation, the United Kingdom of Great Britain and Northern Ireland and the United States of America to the United Nations Addressed to the President of the Security Council, UN Doc S/1995/300 (13 April 1995), at <http://www.un.org/sc/committees/sanctions/s95300.pdf> (last visited 11 July 2007). See also chapter 25 of this Handbook.
[63] D Cortright and GA Lopez, *The Sanctions Decade: Assessing UN Strategies in the 1990s* (Boulder, CO: Lynne Rienner Publishers, Inc, 2000), at 213.
[64] Ibid at 209.   [65] Ibid at 240.   [66] Ibid at 241.

Freezing assets, whether temporarily pending changes in behaviour or to facilitate direct compensation for wronged parties, could also prove potent: an apparel
manufacturer implicated in union-busting activity in an overseas operation in violation of applicable international standards could see its assets frozen elsewhere,
pending a change in its behaviour and the payment of appropriate compensation. In
addition (or alternatively), measures could come in the form of *capital* (as opposed
to material goods) market access sanctions. Penalized companies (or those affiliated
with penalized companies) could, for example, be denied listing on the capital markets pending changes in their behaviour.

None of these measures, employed sensibly, would punish economies for the
actions of recalcitrant economic actors. However, smart, focused sanctions of
this sort are utterly alien to the way the international economy operates at present. An obvious objection to their use stems from due process concerns: singling
out individuals or individual entities in an international sanctioning regime
risks miscarriages of justice unless sufficient procedural protections are provided. Indeed, in the most notable instance where a UN body singled out companies and individuals involved in dubious business practices—in this case, in
the Democratic Republic of Congo—the reaction was fierce, in part because the
initial listing was apparently made without notice to the implicated persons and
opportunity to comment.[67] Yet, a follow-up UN report employed a more satisfactory form of procedural fairness,[68] suggesting that due process standards can
be accommodated in an international process. Moreover, the due process problems in this area would be no greater than those involved in the existing terrorist
financing listing process.[69]

Smart sanctions of this sort would need to be administered. Designing the
administrative apparatus for such a system goes beyond the purview of this chapter. Suffice it to say here that the Security Council, with its peace and security
mandate, is not necessarily the best fit. There is not always a coincidence between
the basic standards companies might reasonably be expected to meet and international peace and security. An obvious, alternative *situs* for such a function in the
UN might be the Economic and Social Council (ECOSOC), or preferably some
subset of this body constituted as a quasi-judicial tribunal. The issues raised by

[67] *Final report of the Panel of Experts on the Illegal Exploitation of Natural Resources and Other
Forms of Wealth of the Democratic Republic of the Congo*, UN Doc S/2002/1146 (16 October 2002).
[68] Letter dated 15 October 2003 from the Chairman of the Panel of Experts on the Illegal
Exploitation of Natural Resources and Other Forms of Wealth of the Democratic Republic of
Congo addressed to the Secretary-General, UN Doc S/2003/1027 (23 October 2003); see also Letter
dated 17 June 2003 from the Chairman of the Panel of Experts on the Illegal Exploitation of Natural
Resources and Other Forms of Wealth of the Democratic Republic of Congo addressed to the
Secretary-General, UN Doc S/2002/1146/Add.1 (20 June 2003) (reporting reactions to the first 2002
report).
[69] See also *Security Council Adopts Measures to Ensure 'Fair and Clear' Procedures Exist for
De-Listing from Sanctions Committees*, 19 December 2006, UN Doc SC/8913 (19 December 2006).

corporate accountability do not differ tremendously from ECOSOC's existing mandate.[70] In truth, however, ECOSOC has anaemic powers in the present UN Charter. Assigning ESOSOC smart sanctioning functions could only be accomplished by (now highly unlikely) UN Charter reform, or as an outsourced function in a separate treaty regime.

IV. Conclusion

International trade law has webbed the world economy together, linking developed legal systems with their underdeveloped counterparts. It has not, however, imposed many substantive performance standards on key economic actors and the methods they employ in producing the goods that then pass along the lines of international commerce. International trade law has not, in other words, been about the regulation of multinational businesses.

And yet what passes for acceptable standards in some domestic legal jurisdictions offends greatly others. In the result, much effort has been directed at inducing companies that straddle the divide between developed and underdeveloped legal systems to comply with the most attractive standards. Much of these developments have taken place under the banner of corporate accountability and CSR, and have been characterized by frenzied standard setting and urgent efforts to bring companies within the shadow of developed legal systems' laws.

A related discussion has imagined international trade law as another and potentially more universal lever available to bootstrap underdeveloped legal systems into compliance with preferred norms. That debate has largely run aground on design concerns; that is, how to avoid the capture of a broadened trade law mandate by crass protectionist impulses.

This is not to say, however, that the international community's choices are restricted to the status quo or a hijacked trade system. This chapter has argued that there are more nuanced intermediate steps, including retooled investor-State dispute settlement systems and narrowly focused punitive measures, including smart sanctions. The day has not yet arrived when mainstream policy-makers clamour for these solutions. These approaches may, however, do less violence to an open global economic system than the current stopgap reaction; that is, the accelerating propensity to deploy domestic legal instruments in economically powerful States as tools of extraterritorial enforcement.

---

[70] B Simma et al (eds), *The Charter of the United Nations: A Commentary*, 2nd edn, Vol 2 (New York: Oxford University Press, 2002), at 988.

SELECTED BIBLIOGRAPHY

P Alston 'Resisting the Merger and Acquisition of Human Rights by Trade Law: A Reply to Petersmann' 2002 *European Journal of International Law* 13(4) 815

W Benedek, K De Feyter, and F Marrella (eds), *Economic Globalisation and Human Rights: EIUC Studies on Human Rights and Democratization* (Cambridge: Cambridge University Press, 2007)

A Clapham, *Human Rights Obligations of Non-State Actors* (Oxford: Oxford University Press, 2006)

SH Cleveland, 'Human Rights Sanctions and International Trade: A Theory of Compatibility' 2002 *Journal of International Economic Law* 5(1) 133

LA Compra and SF Diamond, *Human Rights, Labor Rights, and International Trade* (Philadelphia: University of Pennsylvania Press, 1996)

S Deva, 'Human Rights Violations by Multinational Corporations and International Law: Where From Here?' 2003–2004 *Connecticut Journal of International Law* 19(1) 1

J Dine, *Companies, International Trade and Human Rights* (Cambridge: Cambridge University Press, 2005)

F Emmert, 'Labor, Environmental Standards and World Trade Law' 2003 *Journal of International Law & Policy* 10(1) 75

AA Fatouros, *Transnational Corporations: The International Legal Framework* (London: Routledge, 1994)

J Hancock, *Investing in Corporate Social Responsibility: A Guide to Best Practice, Business Planning & the UK's Leading Companies* (London: Kogan Page, 2004)

M Hart, 'A Question of Fairness: The Global Trade Regime, Labor Standards, and the Contestability of Markets' in G Feketekuty and B Stokes (eds), *Trade Strategies for a New Era: Ensuring U.S. Leadership in a Global Economy* (New York: Council on Foreign Relations, 1998)

M Hopkins, *The Planetary Bargain: Corporate Social Responsibility Matters* (London: Earthscan, 2003)

M Hopkins, *Corporate Social Responsibility and International Development: Is Business the Solution?* (London: Earthscan, 2007)

JJ Kirton and MJ Trebilcock (eds), *Hard Choices, Soft Law: Voluntary Standards in Global Trade, Environment, and Social Governance* (Burlington, VT: Ashgate, 2004)

RL Lieberwitz, 'Linking Trade and Labor Standards: Prioritizing the Right of Association' 2006 *Cornell International Law Journal* 39(3) 641

E-U Petersmann, 'Time for a United Nations "Global Compact" for Integrating Human Rights into the Law of Worldwide Organizations: Lessons from European Integration' 2002 *European Journal of International Law* 13(3) 621

MJ Trebilcock and R Howse, 'Trade Policy & Labor Standards' 2005 *Minnesota Journal of Global Trade* 14(2) 261

JA Zerk, *Multinationals and Corporate Social Responsibility: Limitations and Opportunities in International Law* (Cambridge: Cambridge University Press, 2006)

CONCLUSION

CHAPTER 27

LAW, CULTURE, AND VALUES IN THE WTO – GAZING INTO THE CRYSTAL BALL

JOSEPH HH WEILER

I. Gazing into the Crystal Ball – Premise and Methodology

CONSIDERING the 'Future of the WTO' is a staple of the literature. From its very conception back in the 1940s as the 'would-be' International Trade Organization (ITO), through its 'doctor assisted' birth as the GATT 1947 employing the Protocol of Provisional Application (a 'provisional' application which lasted a full 47 years), through the further agonies of successive 'Rounds' culminating in the Uruguay Round and the compromises of the Marrakesh Agreement and bringing us to the present on-again-off-again trials and tribulations of Doha, the WTO/GATT has always been an incomplete project – with a reform agenda almost part of the birth certificate of each major development.

The titles of the studies comprising this literature tell the story: the excellent Warwick Commission Report of 2007 – *The Multilateral Trade Regime: Which Way Forward?*;[1] or the authoritative so-called Sutherland Report of 2004 – *The Future of the WTO: Addressing Institutional Challenges in the New Millenium*;[2] or the earlier influential Leutwiler Report of 1987 — *Trade Policies for a Better Future*;[3] and the list goes on.[4]

There is a common thread to this forward-looking literature. With differing nuances it tends to share the premises concerning the virtues of a multilateral trading system driving towards greater liberalization of the terms of trade and consolidating the associated disciplines that are designed to stamp out protectionisms and similar market-distorting State measures. The premise not withstanding, this literature is not oblivious to several of the trade-related 'discontents' of globalization – as the WTO itself is not oblivious. Addressing these is always part of the Agenda. It is a very 'reform'-oriented literature; a 'how to make the world,' or at least 'the world of trade' a better one. It tends to highlight the institutional (and political) deficiencies in the extant system and proffers recommendations that it hopes will help the Masters of the System – notably the representatives of the Members in the never-ending negotiations.

It is a successful literature – highly qualitative and to a surprising extent impactful – if not measured by change effected, at least by agenda-setting. It also has set a very strong tone to the academic and scholarly literature, including the

---

[1] The Warwick Commission, *The Multilateral Trade Regime: Which Way Forward? The Report of the First Warwick Commission* (University of Warwick, 2007).

[2] Consultative Board, *The Future of the WTO: Addressing Institutional Challenges in the New Millennium* (Geneva: WTO, 2004).

[3] *The Leutwiler Report: Trade Policies for a Better Future* (Amsterdam: Martinus Nijhoff, 1987).

[4] See, for example, E Zedillo, P Messerlin, and J Nielson, Trade for Development, *UN Millennium Project Task Force on Trade* (London: Earthscan, 2005).

legal literature. A good part of academic legal writing on the WTO, even when it is positivist and analytical, shares a systemic and normative approach, and is very commonly reform-oriented with different levels of critical distance and co-optation.

The critical literature is curious. There is, of course, the 'Rivers of Babylon' variant, that avalanche of lamentations on the woes of 'Globalization' in a never ending stream of articles and books — some more serious than others[5] — in which the WTO is to a greater or lesser degree presumptively assumed to be a principal source of all that is evil in Globalization. If you turn to the Blogosphere, the decibels just grow.[6] But if you look for serious analytical literature that actually seeks to explore and document the nexus between WTO/GATT legal disciplines and systemic social and economic injustice resulting from international trade, with the exception of fine work on TRIPS-related issues, one finds very little indeed. To my knowledge, the case for that nexus has not been made. In my view, it cannot be made: Globalization has, indeed, many discontents but they are not primarily caused by its legal disciplines – though it is difficult to prove a negative.

This is not to claim that there are no deep inequities in the current system – the most notable and justly notorious is one rooted in an inequitable distribution of tariff reductions and other barriers (including subsidies) which continue to exclude, say, agriculture to the detriment of many poorer economies (and consumers in the richer countries). There was, in my eyes, a distinct political deception in the Uruguay process whereby important systemic reform was pushed and accepted as the multilateral 'Single Undertaking' whereas the actual negotiations on terms of trade were left to multilateralized (MFN) bilateralism, where each State is on its own and which favors the rich consuming economies with plenty of trade leverage, at the expense of the poorer ones with less leverage or none at all.

From a legal perspective, however, the fact that someone struck a very bad bargain when buying a car, does not necessarily mean that there is a flaw in the law of contracts that legally embodies that bargain. It is not a change of the rules that is needed to address this very real issue, but of the content of the bargain, and of the negotiating strategy and tactics under the rules, a lesson that seems to have been learned. One might complain today of the hard line taken by, say, India or Brazil in relation to the Doha Round negotiations. Make no mistake, the hard line taken by the developing world under Doha is bred by the bitter experience of Uruguay.

---

[5] J. Stiglitz, *Globalization and its Discontents* (New York: WW Norton, 2002); L Reynolds, D Murray, and J Wilkinson (eds), *Fair Trade: The Challenges of Transforming Globalization* (Abingdon: Routledge, 2007); W Bello, *De-Globalization: Ideas for a New World Economy* (London: Zed Books, 2002).

[6] See, for example, <www.focusweb.org>.

In most of the reform literature, law is treated as instrumental, derivative and heteronomous – the medium through which the economic and political bargains are articulated and implemented and not as an independent and autonomous variable which in and of itself bestows certain qualities on the system.

There is, typically, a 'legal' chapter, focusing almost invariably on dispute settlement (and enforcement): how to make it more efficient and predictable; how to give it more teeth, how to make it more equitable in addressing differences in legal resources; how to address the problems of sanctions classically based on withdrawal of concessions and thus on consumption leverage and which penalizes individual importers and exporters arbitrarily. There are also institutional issues. In the current round of negotiations, the suspects on the agenda are, well, the usual ones, including proposals to institutionalize panels in some more fixed and permanent structure, and to give the Appellate Body the power of remand.

Perhaps I should first explain what I do not plan to do in this concluding chapter. I do not plan to replicate or summarize the abovementioned excellent reform literature. The Sutherland and Warwick Reports, to mention but two, still maintain their freshness and relevance with the militancy and occasional stridence of Sutherland being matched by the nuanced and sobriety of Warwick. Neither do I plan to summarize the critical literature. I cannot make the case that the WTO legal framework as such (outside the TRIPS Agreement) is in any direct way linked to the meaningful inequities of globalization, for the simple reason that I do not believe that to be the case. I do not think that the gnomes of Geneva stand in the dock (in any event if anyone is to stand in the dock, it would be the gnomes of Brussels, Washington, Peking, and Sydney masquerading as the gnomes of Geneva). And I certainly do not plan to engage in classical crystal ball gazing trying to predict the future – especially since in the current stage of events, any prediction may be falsified in short order.

Instead, my own brand of forward-looking will take a different stance. I will identify some areas, issues, or themes that in my view will continue, at a level below the immediate reform agenda, to underlie all future WTO discourse. These are issues that go to identity and systemic self-understanding – the Id/Ego of the WTO, its essential identikit. Even though they do not directly dictate policies, they under gird, sometimes *sub-silentio*, both the scope for and discussion of much future oriented policy discourse. I should warn that the themes selected are not the only or even most important systemic identity or self-understanding markers of the WTO. They are, however, in my view the ones where *legal* discourse as such conditions reality; ones where the lawyer or legal theorist rather than the economist or political economist are the necessary interpreters and interlocutors.

When I say that the themes chosen revolve around critical legal issues, I am employing a methodology that clearly is not limited to, or even focuses on, the meaning of law and its instrumental heteronomous features. Law – legal institutions, legal rules, and legal discourse – does not simply act as a neutral medium or transmission belt for policies determined by economic, political, and even moral considerations. Law is, additionally, both reflective and constitutive of political culture, indeed of culture in its broadest sense.[7]

Law, like literature, like sacred texts, is a cultural asset in and of itself. If, say, we want to understand in the deepest sense the political, socio-economic, and moral reality of, say, Greek and Roman antiquity or of first-century Palestine at the birth of Christianity, the historian would not only look to politics, military history, and economics. Literature, archeology, drama will tell us no less, even more perhaps, on the political and general culture of those epochs. And so will law and legal institutions. They stand as proxies for politics and economics but also for other features of culture. We can learn from them things that these other social and cultural institutions do not tell us. A simple example will illustrate this autonomous revelatory feature of law-as-culture. Consider how much we learn from the fact that in the Biblical legal system, the sanctity of life was not expressed with the legal vocabulary as the Right to Life, but as a sacred duty not to take life. Law is ubiquitous, normative, and embodies ontologically our notions of justice (and injustice.) Even for the most vile regimes, law is precisely the embodiment of their notions of (vile) justice. Law does not only reflect such cultural assets but also shapes them.

The same is true of the WTO of today. The law of the WTO is not simply a set of rules implementing policies such as most-favoured-nation (MFN) or national treatment. As we shall see, it both reflects and shapes political, social, and moral sensibilities far deeper than these specifics. If we are concerned with the inequities or moral obtuseness of the WTO system we might look to the bad bargains in the TRIPS Agreement or on terms of trade. But in these cases law will indeed be instrumental, a mere medium, and the transmission belt for political and economic bargains among unequal partners. The law itself will not be the author of the justice or injustice. And that set of sensibilities has been discussed excellently. Our focus will be, then, on the autonomous features of law, on law as autonomously reflecting and shaping the culture of the system.

I will address three issues, the first two more briefly since they are more widely discussed – that concerning the constitutional (or otherwise) architecture of the WTO system and, the other, its global (or otherwise) hegemony. The third issue, which I will treat at greater length, has received far less attention and goes to the ontological and moral self-understanding of the system.

---

[7] The most successful articulation of the law and culture nexus and its application in explaining a living legal system is, to my mind, the Israeli jurist M Mautner in his *Law and Culture* (Ramat Gan: Bar-Ilan University Press, 2008). See also, P Kahn, *The Cultural Study of Law* (Chicago: University of Chicago Press, 1999); HG Gadamar, *Truth and Method* (London: Sheed and Ward, 1979); C Geertz, *The Interpretation of Culture* (Jackson, TN: Basic Books, 1977); JG Herder, *On Social and Political Culture* (Cambridge: Cambridge University Press, 1969).

II. WTO – A Constitutional Future?

The GATT was born into an international legal system that understood itself as thoroughly intergovernmental. The State was not disaggregated both externally and internally. Externally, there was an uncritical conflation of the State (the primary unit of authority) and its government. Individuals could be the direct or indirect objects of agreements among States/governments, but were not, in and of themselves, subjects. Internally, too, fresh in the wake of World War II and following a rather short democratic tradition for most countries in the system, democracy stopped short or ground to an inefficient crawl when it came to issues of foreign policy. The government, the executive branch, was given a high degree of leeway in conducting the foreign affairs of the State – it was acting, after all, in the 'national interest' that demanded political loyalty.

Within the GATT and, more recently, the WTO the official mantra remains that it is an organization that belongs to its Members, which is taken to mean the governments of its Members. Disaggregation is on the whole anathematized.

By contrast, in the literature the sirens of disaggregation have been particularly seductive with a substantial chorus calling for one form of disaggregation – constitutionalization. Almost invariably it is the advent of the EC that represents expressly or implicitly a model. One has learned to be cautious – to repeat religiously that the WTO is not the EC and could/should not become one. But having said that, some of the principal 'constitutional' features of the WTO are pined after.

At the core of EC 'constitutionalization' was affording a growing number of its treaty articles (as well as secondary legislation) direct effect, namely endowing them with a legal quality that allows individuals to plead them before national courts in disputes with conflicting state norms, and oblige these national courts to vindicate them in such situations against such conflicting state norms. This, in and of itself, is not such a unique move and is known in many a monist system. The drama of EC 'constitutionalization' was the coupling of such an effect with the principle of supremacy (grafted from general public international law) so that provisions of the EC Treaties were not, through direct effect, merely the law of the land, but, through supremacy, the 'higher law' of the land. Through the jurisprudence of its principal judicial organ, the European Court of Justice, in collaboration with the highest courts of its Member States, the EC acquired one of the principal features of constitutional federal systems. It should be noted that we are dealing here with a self-referential autonomous legal development. The Treaties were not negotiated as such; there was even some resistance – not by the States (suddenly a meaningless concept as such) but by their governments in representations to the courts claiming that they were the Masters of the Treaties. It was driven by a certain legal logic much discussed in the famous early cases in which these developments took place.[8]

It is easy to understand the seductiveness of these developments to some or many in the WTO interpretive community.[9] Practically, there is no more efficient system of monitoring and compliance than that achieved through domestic courts giving effect, 'higher law' effect, to treaty provisions. It is the ultimate system in the 'private attorney-general' model of judicial review. Each and every trader becomes a policeman of his or her country's compliance with their obligations. And the habit of obedience of national governments to their domestic court is far higher than such habit vis-à-vis international fora. Compliance pull is enhanced by orders of magnitude in such a regime. Conceptually, it appears at least to elevate individuals to the status of subjects, who are the direct bearers of rights under the international legal regime. The rhetorical combination of 'individuals as subjects' and the conflation of direct effect with 'rights' gives constitutionalization not only a practical efficiency attractiveness, but also a normative moral patina, derived from the elevation of individuals from objects to subjects and the transformation of the system from a set of intergovernmental mutual promises to a disaggregated legal system based on rights, with 'higher law' status and in which governments are but one actor of the States and can be the authors of violations not only vis-à-vis their WTO partners but also their very own citizens. The fact that these developments in the EC emanated from legal actors based on a specific way of interpreting the legal instruments make them all the more attractive – a way of not only circumventing the difficulties of the WTO political process, but of compensating for its weaknesses.

An influential literature, even the most contemporary, continues not only to posit some form of constitutionalization as a future desideratum for a future WTO but to detect signs of steps in that direction.[10] It is not an attractive future, if it is to come. This is not because of the self-serving arguments of governments and their WTO delegates that the WTO belongs to its Members – its Members meaning them (as if a treaty is really the property of the executive branch and not a projection into the (international) public space of legislatures, citizens, and all other societal actors as well. It is also not because, a very common notion, there is some fundamental

---

[8] See, generally, JHH Weiler, *The Constitution of Europe* (Cambridge: Cambridge University Press 1998).

[9] There is a very rich literature on the issue of WTO constitutionalization. See, for example, D Cass, *The Constitutionalization of the World Trade Organization* (Oxford: Oxford University Press, 2005).

[10] See the illuminating exchange between E-U Petersmann, R Howse, and P Alston in 'Trade and Human Rights – An Exchange', *Jean Monnet Working Papers* 12/02 at <www.Jeanmonnetprogram. org/papers/02/021201.html> (last visited 3 November 2008). See also S Cho, 'Constitutional Adjudication in the World Trade Organization', *Jean Monnet Working Paper* 04/08, at <www. jeanmonnetprogram.org/paper/08/080401.html> (last visited 3 November 2008).

intrinsic difference between the EC Treaty and the WTO treaty that justifies a 'constitutional hermeneutics' for the EC but not to the WTO.[11]

The unattractiveness is rooted in many reasons but principally in the decoupling of the political and law-making process from its legal normative output.

The problem is apparent even in the EC which has far more developed political institutions than the WTO but continues, nonetheless, to suffer from a persistent democracy deficit. How does one justify according higher law status and direct effect to norms, the democratic provenance of which is suspect? Giving individuals 'rights', even rights defensible in courts, does not make them subjects if they have no appreciable participation in, or control over, the authorship of such rights. The bearers of such rights are no more subjects than the various 'subjects' of the Roman Empire who enjoyed rights granted by others. There is really no principle reason to grant slaves certain rights. Does that make them subjects? Moreover, all such 'rights' are not, of course, value-neutral or outside the political process of distributing advantages and disadvantages to competing interests of our societies. They are the outcome of two sets of flawed political processes of bargaining among unequals: the flawed process of the WTO itself, and the internally flawed process by which, say, the EU, the US, or the Canadian authorities come to craft what will be their position within the WTO negotiating game. The capture by special interests of governmental positions that are then enshrined in WTO obligations is notorious. Is there really moral advantage in constitutionalizing such? And is there pure political advantage in the judicial empowerment which results from such constitutionalization? I think only the blind fail to see that in the international legal system, sometimes the only meaningful checks and balances (to which we are accustomed as indispensable within our domestic legal systems) take place at the implementation stage. On this reading, the international system of state responsibility is a subtle mediating mechanism which assures that states/governments respect their mutual promises but allows wriggle room at the domestic implementing level. Often, the violation is the result of a special interest compromising a broader societal advantage in compliance. But again, only the wilfully blind will not accept that the right can also be the result of the influence of special interests in the first place.

This is not a plaedoyer for the status quo. The status quo must change and will change. But discourse of change in the direction of constitutionalization cannot, to be normatively credible, decouple the legal from the political, the exercise of rights from the responsibilities of power. Only if and when the WTO develops its institutional framework (and whether and how this is to take place is itself a delicate issue) will a constitutional future become normatively compelling.

---

[11] I have tried to demonstrate that the 'constitutional' outcome of the ECJ's famous decisions in the 1960s could have been achieved by using the very hermeneutic sensibilities and methods of the Appellate Body: JHH Weiler, 'Rewriting Van Gend & Loos: Towards a Normative Theory of ECJ Hermeneutics' in O Wiklund (ed.), *Judicial Discretion in European Perspective* (Stockholm/The Hague: Norstedts Juridik/Kluwer, 2003).

III. The Global v The Regional

This is an even better known story. Article XXIV GATT 1947 was considered a marginal exception and for years commanded little attention. It is only in the mid 70s that the number of RTAs began to rise and now exceeds 200, a number that is growing at a furious pace. The language of XXIV seems to regard FTAs and custom unions as positive, notwithstanding the orthodox view that at best RTAs are a transient evil to be tolerated pending a more universal and global liberalization of terms of trade. A more aggressive view[12] regards them not simply as a menace to the efficient producers in countries outside this or that FTA, but as having a chilling effect on global negotiations premised on the MFN-principle because the trade advantages within the FTA erode as the gap between RTA tariffs and general tariffs narrows.

Here the dissonance between the literature and the political praxis is reversed. Whereas the academic desideratum of constitutionalization is often met with indifference or hostility from the principal state actors, the academic critique of regionalism is met by an ever growing popularity of such. As India scuttles chunks of Doha, she gives the nod to an ASEAN FTA. Does the future look bleak?

There is no doubt that RTAs strike at the primordial norm of MFN-treatment and that RTA-induced trade diversion militates against some of the core benefits that liberalized trade is designed to produce. Additionally, the proliferation of RTAs with disparate regimes of rules of origin adds an additional distorting effect on trade patterns and the allocation of resources.

But RTAs *strictu sensu,* that is excluding bilateral FTAs, offer some distinct global systemic advantages beyond any ill-gained benefits to intra-RTA inefficient producers vis-à-vis outsiders.

RTAs continue to offer significant political benefits that spill over beyond the partners themselves. They often comprise regional States with a history of conflict, even violence. When successfully concluded and implemented, they enhance a welcome stabilizing interdependence. The experience of negotiations of RTAs and their subsequent management create habits of cooperation, compromise seeking, and even constructivist transnational communities – COREPER style – of civil servants. This has a beneficial effect that may transcend any economic benefits measured by trade volume or enhanced efficiencies. Internally, it instructs governments in the art of resisting special interests.

Likewise, powerful RTAs, especially among the less powerful, may help somewhat in redressing the classical negotiating disparities characteristic of the GATT and WTO history.

---

[12] See recently, J Bhagwati, *Termites in the Trading System: How Preferential Agreements Undermine Free Trade* (Oxford: Council of Foreign Relations/Oxford University Press, 2008).

A future of growth in RTAs is not necessarily to be regarded as a problem growing out of control and a menace to the international trading system, especially if, willy nilly, the gaps between generalized tariffs and intra-RTA tariffs continues to fall. Man shall *not* live by *bread alone* (Deuteronomy 8:3). Indeed.

IV. Aims and Deep Effects

I want to conclude by an exploration, far less part of the literature, of the nexus between legal doctrine in the WTO and its core set of moral and identitarian values.

A. Core Identity in Core Doctrine: Premise

At the core of WTO is the GATT 1994 and, it is submitted, at the core of the GATT 1994 are the provisions on national treatment. Article III (coupled with Article XX) embodies the core values of the GATT – encapsulated in the notion of abjuring affording protection to domestic production in one's own market place. It is 'constitutional' in nature since it is mandatory and applies independently of any terms of trade negotiated. It is replicated in practically all FTAs and, unlike, say, MFN, it creates a discipline requiring the most radical departure from the universally ubiquitous, and permanently politically expedient, practice of protectionism.

Significantly, the material and conceptual contours of the discipline of national treatment not only remain contested but are, *par excellence*, the creature of legal discourse and, in the thesis of this essay, the most telling examples of the law of the WTO as reflecting and constituting the deepest ontological issues of the system. The tool through which this significance will be examined is the old debate concerning the correct hermeneutic approach to Article III. Specifically, it is the debate on whether one should look merely to the effects of a State measure or also to its aims in determining a violation of the discipline of national treatment. Protagonists have been, perhaps too rapidly, keen to declare victory or, indeed, defeat. Despite many graveside eulogies, the issues remain poignant. In practically every national treatment case one can find traces of this debate and in some landmark cases, such as *EC–Asbestos*, it has taken centre stage. Like some conflicts between, say, fathers and sons, which are structural, a very part of the growing up process, and as such endemic and revelatory of the human condition, aims and effect, point to similarly endemic conflicts revelatory of the system itself. As such, it will continue to inform deep fissures well into the future.

Naturally, the purpose of my analysis will not be to rehash or argue one position or another in this classical debate. However, setting out the doctrine is indispensable for the subsequent probing of the deeper issues. Although both in the jurisprudence (case law) of panels and the Appellate Body, and in the accompanying literature, the debate seems to concern two possible methods of interpreting national treatment, I would like to suggest that articulating three possible methods will be more illuminating. First, however, the legislative matrix of national treatment. The decision in *EC–Asbestos* may serve as a useful foil on which to explicate these methods.

B. The Legislative Matrix

Article III(1) GATT 1994 – the celebrated Chapeau – applies both to taxation and regulation and provides as follows:

1. The contracting parties recognize that internal taxes and other internal charges, and laws, regulations and requirements affecting the internal sale, offering for sale, purchase, transportation, distribution or use of products, and internal quantitative regulations requiring the mixture, processing or use of products in specified amounts or proportions, should not be applied to imported or domestic products so as to afford protection to domestic production.

Article III(4) applies specifically to regulation and provides:

4. The products of the territory of any contracting party imported into the territory of any other contracting party shall be accorded treatment no less favourable than that accorded to like products of national origin in respect of all laws, regulations and requirements affecting their internal sale, offering for sale, purchase, transportation, distribution or use. The provisions of this paragraph shall not prevent the application of differential internal transportation charges which are based exclusively on the economic operation of the means of transport and not on the nationality of the product.

Article III(2) applies specifically to taxation and provides:

2. The products of the territory of any contracting party imported into the territory of any other contracting party shall not be subject, directly or indirectly, to internal taxes or other internal charges of any kind in excess of those applied, directly or indirectly, to like domestic products. Moreover, no contracting party shall otherwise apply internal taxes or other internal charges to imported or domestic products in a manner contrary to the principles set forth in paragraph 1.

Ad Article III(2) explicates:

A tax conforming to the requirements of the first sentence of paragraph 2 would be considered to be inconsistent with the provisions of the second sentence only in cases where competition was involved between, on the one hand, the taxed product and, on the other hand, a directly competitive or substitutable product which was not similarly taxed.

Finally, Article XX provides as follows:

> Subject to the requirement that such measures are not applied in a manner which would constitute a means of arbitrary or unjustifiable discrimination between countries where the same conditions prevail, or a disguised restriction on international trade, nothing in this Agreement shall be construed to prevent the adoption or enforcement by any contracting party of measures:
>
> (*a*)   necessary to protect public morals;
> (*b*)   necessary to protect human, animal or plant life or health;

C.   Methodology One – The 'Objective' Approach[13]

This is the methodology used most frequently by panels and the Appellate Body, notably in the area of taxation.

The 'objective' approach may be synthesized thus:

The regime of Article III should be read as setting a certain political legal equilibrium: Members retain fiscal and regulatory autonomy. They may impose taxation or adopt regulation as an expression of their specific socio-economic preferences. These may, and usually will, differ from country to country. Their tax or regulatory regimes should not, however, distort competition between imported and domestic products in favor of the latter.

Or, in the words of the Appellate Body in *Japan – Alcoholic Beverages II*:

Article III obliges Members of the WTO to provide equality of competitive conditions for imported products in relation to domestic products … Article III protects expectations not of any particular trade volume but rather of the equal competitive relationship between imported and domestic products.[14]

The objective method understands the problematic turn of phrase in Article III(1) – *so as* – whereby domestic taxation and regulation 'should not be applied to imported or domestic products so as to afford protection to domestic production' as indicative of an objective general prohibition: taxation and regulation may not be applied in a way that results in protection being afforded to domestic production. This prohibition applies also to taxation and regulation that, on its face, is origin-neutral. Critically, the entire phrase in Article III(1) (*should not be applied to imported or domestic products so as to afford protection to domestic production*) is understood

---

[13]   I have discussed the three methods – as a matter of analytical jurisprudence – more fully in JHH Weiler and H Horn, 'European Communities – Measures Affecting Asbestos and Asbestos-Containing Products' in H Horn and PC Mavroidis (eds), *The WTO Case Law of 2001* (Cambridge: Cambridge University Press, 2003).

[14]   Appellate Body Report, *Japan – Alcoholic Beverages II*, at 109 and 110.

on this methodology as applying to the result of the tax or regulatory regime – to its effect on the competitive relationship between domestic and imported products and not to the intention or purpose of the tax and regulatory regime. On this approach, a regulatory (or tax) regime adopted with the explicit intention of distorting competition in favour of domestic production but that, owing, say, to the stupidity of the regulator did not have that effect, would not violate Article III. The contrary, arguably more common, would be equally true: a regulatory regime adopted on an origin-neutral basis with no protectionist purpose at all, but that, nonetheless, happened to '...afford protection to domestic production' would be caught by Article III.

Under this method, a regulatory or tax measure affording protection to domestic production would, if it were to be retained, need to be justified under Article XX GATT 1994.

Generally speaking that is how the Panel proceeded in *EC–Asbestos*. It found first that the French measure violated Article III. It then found, however, that it was justified under Article XX(b). In cases such as *Japan – Alcoholic Beverages II*, the objectively determined discriminatory effect could not be justified ex Article XX and thus the tax in question stood condemned. Articles III(2) and III(4) on this reading set out the precise conditions that would trigger a violation of the general principle enunciated in the chapeau in the cases of taxation and regulation respectively, and specifically, in relation to regulation, the products of the territory of any contracting party imported into the territory of any other contracting party shall be accorded treatment no less favourable than that accorded to like products of national origin in respect of all laws, regulations and requirements affecting their internal sale, offering for sale, purchase, transportation, distribution or use. Two issues in particular require elucidation. Which and What? Which products are covered by the non-discrimination discipline? What conduct amounts to a violation of that discipline.

The first condition relates to the products – domestic and imported – to which the discipline applies. Article III(4) speaks of 'like' products. Article III(2)(i) also refers to 'like' products and Article III(2)(ii) glossed by the Ad Note includes as a second category 'directly competitive or substitutable products'. Consequently, 'likeness' in Article III(2) has been construed narrowly. The Appellate Body was emphatic in *EC–Asbestos* that the "like" products in Article III(4) may not be the same as the "like" products in Article III(2) and must be interpreted far more broadly. In fact, in order for Article III(4) successfully to give expression to the general principle enunciated in the chapeau, 'like' products in Article III(4) must be understood as covering products that are competitive and/or substitutable even if in terms of their characteristics they may not be quite so like as products under the first sentence of Article III(2). Whilst there surely will be, according to the Appellate Body, some products whose degree of substitutability is so insignificant as to exclude them from the discipline of Article III(4), under the first approach, any appreciable degree of competition would bring the products within the purview of Article III(4).

Under the objective method as reflected in the Panel Report in *EC-Asbestos*,[15] 'likeness' for the purposes of Article III(4) is thus to be determined in the market place: products are 'like' when they are in an appreciable (i.e. not *de minimis*) competitive relationship. Often times, cross price-elasticity could provide a useful indicator of such competitiveness.

Once established that two products are in such a competitive relationship and are, thus, 'like' products and subject to the discipline of Article III(4), the second trigger or legal condition relates to the conduct or content of the measure amounting to a violation. Put differently, Article III(4) gives specific expression (to use a term employed by the Appellate Body) to the general principle enunciated in Article III(1) that taxation and regulation may not be applied *so as to afford protection* to domestic production by instructing that imported products 'shall be accorded treatment no less favourable....' Compared to tax cases, it might not always be quite as easy from an economic point of view to determine in regulatory cases whether and to what extent the effect of less favourable disparate treatment actually results in distortion of the 'equality of competitive conditions' (to use the phraseology of the Appellate Body). This would be the case where the effect of the regulation would be to burden the imports more than it would burden like domestic products without actually barring the imports from the market place. A higher *ad valorem* tax rate imposed on an imported product competing with a domestic product would be understood in most circumstances as distorting the competitive relationship, usually resulting in a different price ratio between domestic and imported products before and after the tax event. One would be looking for a similar effect in relation to regulation. In *Asbestos*-type cases, the 'less favourable' is often much easier to establish since the effect of the measure is to exclude the imported product entirely from the market.

It is important at this juncture to explore further the comparison of the Which and What between Articles III(2) and III(4).

As noted above, Article III(2) provides two replies to the Which question. Like products are caught and products that are in direct competition or are substitutable are also caught by the discipline of non-discrimination. 'Like products' in the sense of Article III(2) has, according to the Appellate Body, to be interpreted narrowly and, thus, denotes products that are very substitutable, in a high degree of competition and share physical and other characteristics. Products caught by the second sentence of Article III(2) may not share as many physical and other

---

[15] There are hints in the Appellate Body Report decision that this orthodoxy is developing chinks. As we shall argue below, these cracks, if at all, are paper thin.

characteristics and the degree of substitutability and/or competition may not be quite as high.

What difference does it make? Critically, in relation to Article III(2) 'like products', the trigger for violation is any taxation on the imported product in excess of that imposed on the like domestic product. In relation to the other category, this is not the case. The other category is a broader category. Arguably, when products are 'merely' in competition with each other but not amounting to 'like' products, Article III(2) contemplates the possibility of a tax on the imported products in excess of the domestic one that does not constitute a violation. Instead it says that in relation to that category, the trigger will only be taxation inconsistent with the principles of Article III(1) – notably '... so as to afford protection to domestic production'. Whether or not this distinction makes economic sense need not be addressed here. What is important is that this distinction may seem to give some support to the hermeneutics of the objective method – since one possible way of reading it is to say that, in relation to the broader category, only a difference in taxation that is sufficient to afford protection between products only partially in competition, will trigger a violation. This reading would, it could be argued, constitute another reason not to read purpose or intent into the phrase '... so as to afford protection'; but to see it as indicating an objective state reflecting a tax or regulation that distorts competition, whether intended or otherwise.

Interestingly, in a scenario reflecting *Japan – Alcoholic Beverages II*, the US appealed the decision. It was the methodology rather than the outcome that prompted the appeal. Apparently, even in the world of pragmatic State officials typically bent on the pragmatic objective of winning cases, the methodology seemed to matter. Let us now examine the alternative methodologies through which one could reach similar results.

D. Methodology Two – Effect and Purpose ('Aims and Effect')

The second method shares one important feature with the first method. Products must be in competition with each other for Article III(4) to apply at all. And the measure in question, at least *ipso facto,* would have to give some advantage to the domestic product and so afford protection to domestic production. But these would be only necessary conditions, but not sufficient ones for a finding of an Article III violation. The effect and purpose approach maintains that any advantage given by origin-neutral regulation (or taxation) to domestic production must have been applied with that purpose in mind; that is, applied so as to afford such protection. On this reading, the mutual promise among all Members ex Article III was not to refrain from any taxation or regulation that would merely have the effect of giving protection to domestic production, but to refrain from imposing such regulation or taxation with that purpose.

A hard version of the second method would insist on detecting such purpose, almost as a *'mens rea'* test in the regulatory process. A more workable and defensible version, adopted by the US in *Japan – Alcoholic Beverages II* would be more holistic. The failure of the State to provide, at the adjudicatory stage, a plausible explanation to the measure producing the disparate impact of the second method would create a constructive presumption of bad purpose.

Applied to *EC–Asbestos*, the second method would result in a finding of no violation of Article III since on the hard version it would be difficult to impute bad purpose to the French measure. On the soft version, France could plausibly (and realistically) explain that its measure was not applied so as to afford protection to domestic production but so as to afford protection to consumers and workers. The case would not, on this reading, even reach Article XX.

It should be noted that under the first method, a State seeking to justify a measure which was factually in violation of Article III would be subjected in almost all situations to the 'least restrictive measure' test – it would not be allowed to keep the measure in place, as written, if it could be shown that the objective sanctioned by Article XX could be reasonably achieved in a manner that was less burdensome to trade. Under the effect and purpose methodology, this examination is folded into the Article III analysis. The non-choice by the State of readily available less restrictive measures would need to be justified, otherwise the presumption of bad purpose would be triggered.

E. Methodology Three – Alternative Comparators

The methodology of alternative comparators is a variation, but an important one, on the methodology of effect and purpose since in it, too, purpose is an important component. It operates, nonetheless, on a different trajectory of reasoning.

Every determination of likeness for the purpose of determining the existence of discrimination embodies, explicitly or implicitly, a comparator. In case of, say, gender or race discrimination, we may take as the comparator the essential humanity of the subjects. In the light of that comparator men and women, or whites and blacks, or Jews and Gentiles, are held to be 'like' and the norm of 'like' treatment is triggered. Differently put, one excludes as comparators colour of skin, or gender, or race and religion: as a matter of policy those are determined to be irrelevant and inadmissible comparators. If colour of skin were a legitimate comparator, then for the purposes of that comparator whites and blacks would be 'unlike' and could (and even should) be treated differently since treating the 'unlike' in a like manner is equally discriminatory to treating the 'like' in an unlike manner.

Under the first and second methodologies, the implicit comparator is market functionality of the product. It is the comparator reflective of the vocabulary of substitutability, competition, and consumer preference. Products are considered 'like' and subject to the discipline of national treatment because they meet similar needs of the consumer and hence compete with each other in the eyes of consumers on the market. Both methods share the same conception of likeness deriving from the same comparator. They differ in how they treat the plea of the State that the less favourable treatment accorded to the imported product was in pursuance of a legitimate purpose.

Under the first method, such a plea of legitimate purpose will exculpate the overall illegality of the State measure if found to fall within the parameters of Article XX. The State will have been found to discriminate since two 'like' products were treated in an unlike manner and thus Article III was violated, but the discrimination will be considered justified in pursuance of another overriding policy sanctioned under Article XX. Under the second method, there is no finding of discrimination and thus of violation of Article III. Even though like products have been treated in an unlike manner, discrimination is construed as occurring only when the less favourable treatment is imposed with the purpose of protecting domestic production.

Under the third method, the very comparator is put into question. To illustrate: in a famous tax case, Italy had a high tax on refined engine oil and a low tax on recycled engine oil. It did so for ecological reasons – to provide an economic incentive to recycle oil thus enhancing conservation and responsible disposable of used oil. From a market functional perspective, refined oil and recycled oil meet the very same needs of the consumer and are in competition with each other. Indeed, in their properties they are so similar, they are indistinguishable. The user can not, from its properties, tell the difference between refined and recycled oil. Taxing imported refined oil at a high rate and domestic recycled oil at a low rate would certainly amount to treating a like imported product in a less favourable way. Using the first method, Article III will have been held to have been violated, but the State may justify its measure under, say, Article XX(g).

Under the second method, since the purpose of the tax was not to protect domestic production (even if this was its effect) but to protect the environment, no violation of Article III will have taken place.

Under the third method, the two products are not considered like because the implicit comparator of the measure is not market functionality but an alternative comparator — ecological efficiency. Ecologically efficient products (such as recycled oil) are taxed at a low rate and ecologically inefficient products (refined oil) are taxed at a high rate. Under this methodology, by employing an alternative comparator, refined oil and recycled oil simply do not come under the discipline of national treatment and Article III – any more than diamonds and oranges would.

Applied for example to *EC–Asbestos*, the comparator implicit in the French Decree is health risk or more specifically carcinogenic potential. The Decree, on this reading, differentiates (in origin neutral fashion) between carcinogenic and cancer risk free products. By reference to the comparator of cancer risk, the two products are simply unlike products and not caught by the discipline of national treatment and non-discrimination.

F. Beyond Hermeneutics

Historically, and certainly since the advent of the WTO, panels have demonstrated a clear preference for the first method or some variant of it. The second method has been forcefully articulated in the literature and argued in some cases, but generally did not find favour and at times was explicitly rejected. Occasionally, traces of the second method can be found creeping in through the back door in the reasoning of panels and the Appellate Body (e.g. *Chile – Alcoholic Beverages*).

The third method has not featured, as such, in either literature or jurisprudence, though one can find strands of its reasoning intertwined in the articulation of the second method. Both methods are, after all, conceptually linked.

Instead of trying to argue what approach, hermeneutically or from a policy perspective, is the 'right' or 'correct' approach, I will try now to explicate the significance of the methodological dispute. It is noticeable that it was the US in *Japan – Alcoholic Beverages II* and the EC, somewhat more obliquely, in *EC-Asbestos* (arguing that there should not be a finding of violation of Article III requiring justification ex Article XX) who rejected the first method. It could be thought that they, as the two Members most commonly 'in the dock', were seeking a tactical advantage in defending measures that objectively may have a protectionist effect. One consideration could relate to the burden of proof. Under the first method, once a violation of Article III is established by reason of an imported product receiving less favourable treatment than a 'like' domestic product (likeness objectively determined), the burden of justification falls on the defending State. It is usually thought that under the second (or third) method, the burden on the complaining State would be much greater since not only would the complaining State have to prove likeness and less favourable treatment, but also bad purpose. Forensically this argument is often overstated. If one takes the US appellate submission in *Japan – Alcoholic Beverages II* as a benchmark for the actual operationability of aims and effects, it would seem that in practice once less favourable treatment of the imported like product is established, there would be a presumption of protectionist purpose unless, very much in Article XX fashion, the defending State did not justify its practice by reference to a legitimate purpose.

Another alleged practical consequence would be the range of policies available to the State. Under the first method, this range would be limited to the policies of Article XX. Under the second (and third) methods, other policies could be employed. In particular, it may be thought that given the great difficulty of amending the covered agreements, the large players would not wish to lock themselves into a list of policies that may remain static for decades. Again I would submit that here, as in the case of the burden of proof argument, from a practical point of view this difference seems more illusory than real. Article XX is broad and sufficiently open-textured to cater for most exigencies and panels and the Appellate Body have shown themselves ready to adopt such a dynamic hermeneutics in interpreting the provisions of Article XX.

In the practice of trying a case and of adopting regulations, the different methodologies do not, contrary to much heated argument, seem to make a huge difference. What is the significance behind these choices? The strongest arguments for the other methodologies are not, then, of a crude pragmatic nature – leading to tangible different results – but in the realms of concept and symbol.

It is here that we get to the crux of the analysis. In the first place, the hermeneutic debate is a proxy for fundamentally different images of the system itself. Second, though Panels and the Appellate Body have shown a clear preference for the objective 'effects' test, this attachment may be linked to contingent considerations that may evolve over time. Linking these two considerations, if a change in the contingent considerations leads to an increasing shift from the first method to the second and third methods, this will signify not merely a doctrinal shift, but a future change in the very self-understanding of the system.

G. Effects and Aims – The Ontological Dimension

One way to lead into the ontological argument is to consider the motivation (rather than the legal reasoning) of the French objection to the Panel report in *EC–Asbestos*. The objection might come under the concept of 'naming and shaming'. Discrimination, even if 'justified', has a tarring effect. To be found in violation of Article III – requiring justification – is in and of itself stigmatizing. It is wrong, it was strongly felt, to deal with the case of a State adopting an origin-neutral measure for a totally legitimate purpose even if it has the coincidental effect of giving an advantage to domestic production, as a violation of a non-discrimination provision requiring justification. Such a State should not be held to have discriminated in the first place and should not be required to justify. To be sure, successful justification under Article XX GATT 1994 liquidates the culpability of the discrimination. But, France felt that, even if the end result is the same, there is value in having cases dealt with in a correct normative context, not stigmatizing activity that should not be stigmatized and not diluting the notion of discrimination with activities that should not be so branded. It is hard to explain a certain measure of outrage at the Panel report not based on some such reasoning. But this in turn indicates that, indeed, more than pragmatic outcome is at stake, and that the WTO also represents a system of values. At stake in the hermeneutic debate between aims and effects is also an implicit contest over these values.

In part, it is a 'truth-based' argument that goes beyond the lexical hermeneutics of the text of Article III, an argument contending that there can be no discussion of discrimination that does not imply, in some way and at some level, examination of purpose and an agreed comparator. We may agree that there should be no discrimination between men and women, which means that we exclude gender as a relevant comparator for different treatment. But, assuming that we want to write our laws in a way that would, say, take account of the fact that women, not men, fall pregnant, we might want to have special provisions in our labour code concerning leave, grounds of dismissal, and the like treating men and women differently. One way to achieve this would be to say that such special dispensation for pregnant women was discriminatory (since it made provisions for women not available to men) but was exculpated by an overriding justification. Another way, perhaps with more conceptual coherence, would be to argue that for the purposes of child birth men and woman are not 'like' and therefore treating them differently is not a matter of discrimination at all. The question is not which is the advisable policy (since there is agreement on the public good of accommodating pregnancy) but an understanding of what we are doing when we wish to reconcile our outlawing of discrimination with policies that would nonetheless treat subjects differently. Aim and purpose are not, on this reasoning, added elements to the test of discrimination. They are not, in fact, an inculpating *mens rea* that is superimposed on an objective *actus reus* of discrimination. They are ontologically part of the very definition of discrimination. But even this jurisprudential consideration does not touch at the deepest significance of the debate.

At its deepest, the difference between the first method and the second and third methods stands as a proxy or signifiers of consequential considerations of moral and political identity of the WTO and its Members. The first method – even if very solicitous to diverse socio-economic choices in the construction of Article XX – establishes the WTO as a system of symbolic normative hierarchy wherein the default norm is the integrity of the market and liberalized trade. For competing norms such as public morality, ecological balance, the health of humans and animals, and even the abhorrence from slave labour, to prevail they have to be argued, justified, and limited (under the ubiquitous least restrictive method reasoning) whenever they clash with the integrity of the market. This is not a question of technical burden of proof that, as I have argued, is of no pragmatic consequence. It is a question of cultural identity, the way a society wishes to understand its internal hierarchy of values. The comparator under the effects approach is always the market functionality of products. If they are functionally similar in the market place, which means they will have a degree of substitutability and hence be in competition with each other, they are deemed to be like products that must be treated in a similar fashion by public authorities. The application of the most fundamental norm of non-discrimination attaches automatically to situations conditioned by market considerations and the material preferences of individuals *qua* consumers. The second and third methods, by contrast, are a way of thinking that does not simply allow, but also understands, that a society often manifests its most profound human values through its normative legal regimes (in this case regulation and tax) and privileges the purpose – the aim – of the regulatory regime as the factor determining the applicability of the sanction against discrimination. They do not bind the State to a single market-oriented comparator in determining the application of non-discrimination and allow the State to manifest its values through its tax and regulatory regimes with alternative comparators, such as ecological efficiency, even in relation to products that have similar market functionality. They reverse the deep-seated market default implicit in the first method. The default value becomes instead autonomy of political and moral identity requiring justification only if purposefully abused. The differences between objective effects and the market comparator and aims and alternative comparators is not in what we do – the end result is the same – but in who we are in doing what we do.

This would seem to be a matter of interpretation, Article III lends itself to any of these approaches. There is no conclusive legal argument mandating one over the others. In giving such consistent preference to the effects approach, panels and the Appellate Body have placed a very distinct moral and spiritual identity on the WTO. Many might consider this type of analysis as the epitome of the Ivory Tower, the disconnect between academic and intellectual rumination and the 'real world'. This view, I would argue, is mistaken. These considerations are very much part of the 'real world'. First, there is a utilitarian argument concerning 'image'. One notes, for example, a discrepancy between the perception of the WTO in relation to environmental concerns and the actual praxis of the organization and its adjudicatory organs. At least in part, the image of the organization with a certain autism towards the environment is a by-product of this most elemental manifestation of its basic structure of values. To be sure, it is only a subsidiary argument but it is one that is surely very much rooted in the 'real world'. Perceptions of a system have a reality transcending any essential verity. Second, and this is where we gain the insights from the studies of the relationship between law and culture, there can be no doubt that these basic hermeneutic choices, with the underlying ontological implications, help shape, at times decisively, the political culture and normative sensibility not only of the organization and its officers, but of the interpretive communities associated with it. The impact is most profound when it is subconscious, where moral and normative presumptions are not presented explicitly but are inherent in a certain type of discourse and shape indirectly the *weltanschauung* of members of an interpretive community broadly defined. This, too, is very much a 'real world' concern.

H. The Evolution of Identity and Its Future

The normative identitarian analysis is based on the doctrinal position that the legislative matrix of the covered agreements does not dictate the methodology of interpreting national treatment in any of the directions outlined. All three methods are hermeneutically plausible. Stacked in this way, one may try to explain the strong, though not uniform, attachment of panels and Appellate Body to the effects test. Also, it should be noted that Members themselves suffer from a certain schizophrenia vacillating between one approach and the other. Whence that vacillation?

One reason might be rooted in the self understanding of their own legitimacy of panels and Appellate Body. The second and third methods require a more explicit confrontation in deciding the existence of a *prima facie* violation with the good faith, or otherwise, of a Member. To reject a governmental claim using these methodologies may more frequently involve an 'I simply do not believe you' reasoning then the comfort of the objective test under the effects theory. For the decision-maker, the first method does not involve a value judgment at the level of comparator – it takes as a default presumption the competitive relationship in the market. There is a real technocratic comfort in being able to rely on market place effect. As mentioned, this method comes with quite weighty normative baggage, but it must be understandable that a new system of adjudication requires time to gain confidence and to earn confidence. It is not only an understandable trade-off, but a plausible one.

Second, the second and third methods privilege the regulatory and political autonomy of the individual State. This is matched with a reality of huge disparities of power between different actors in the system, and with a 'power entitlement' of these key players. The large consuming States are the ones who most frequently appear as defendants, are rich in legal resources, and are able to articulate public policy effectively. They also share a basic Western ideology in terms of the sensibilities of public policy. Both methods privilege this kind of power. The first method has a more 'multilateral' spirit – everyone is tied to the market logic and the functional comparator of the effects methodology, and competing public policies are those negotiated multilaterally ex Article XX GATT 1994. One can readily understand a preference for a hermeneutic approach that privileges a multilateral spirit even if it is brought not only with a overriding market ethos, but also with a skewed view of the deep meaning of discrimination. Here, too, the trade-off is understandable.

There is yet another consideration. At the end of the day, the GATT norms are addressed principally to regulators – very often the very same regulators who just yesteryear where responsible for articulating, implementing, and justifying protectionist regimes. It may be wise in such a circumstance, as a contingent matter, to aim for an 'objective' regime determining both likeness (competitive relationship in the market place) and violation (less favourable treatment leading to a protective effect) precisely for the 'naming and shaming' effect as a means of habituating the transition generation of national regulators to take the regime of non-discrimination seriously; to have their hand shake, so to speak, every time a regulation is made or defended that would treat competing imported products differently. To a cynic, the methodologies of aims and alternative comparator could appear as a 'School for Cheats'.

We are confronted here with an interesting paradox in the evolution of the normative ontology of the WTO. I argued that national treatment is at the doctrinal core of the system. Legal discourse has developed alternative ways to understand the concept as reflected in the debates between the effects approach and the aims and alternative comparator approach.

The preference for effects, I argued, represented a basic ontological choice that put the ethos of the market as the defining parameter of discrimination and that relegated all competing values to 'exceptions' with deep symbolic and cultural implications. As a matter of *substantive law*, it enshrines an ethos and sensibility mirroring the original set of GATT assumptions and immunizes them from the greater cultural diversity, which an expanded Membership would normally entail.

But paradoxically, as a matter of *process*, the adoption of the second and third methods in the current continuing asymmetries of the organization would empower the very actors who would militate against a fundamental change of those assumptions. And yet, gazing into the crystal ball, in relation to these fundamental issues, one can anticipate changing conditions that might herald a changing jurisprudence. In the first place, the confidence of and in the adjudicatory actors is growing and with it their ability to be less concerned with their own legitimacy in adjudicating individual cases. They will need to be attentive to the general climate of the organization, but less to the everyday weather of individual disputes. Second, the power asymmetries are beginning to close. New world actors are playing a greater role in the decisional games and those left out of the club of the rich and powerful have learned the lessons of empowerment through collective action. Suddenly, the greater autonomy and voice embodied in the second and third methods, might not seem as threat but as promise, as a way of shaking off the earlier assumptions of the limited club.

And with time, the safe assumption that most measures producing discriminatory effects must have been intended so to do by the habits (and internal political convenience) of protectionism may be a little less safe. Enlightened self-interest may begin to mobilize against protectionism and the WTO may be used increasingly as a tool to thwart domestic special interests militating against the collective national interest. At a certain point in this evolution, the safe harbour of the 'objective' approach may not seem so compelling and a more equilibrated attitude to political autonomy and a less crimped approach to how to define the deepest value sensibilities of the system may emerge.

INDEX

. . . .